WESTERN CIVILIZATION

A HISTORY OF EUROPEAN SOCIETY

Since 1300

Steven Hause
University of Missouri–St. Louis

William Maltby
University of Missouri–St. Louis

West/Wadsworth
I(T)P® An International Thomson Publishing Company

Belmont, CA • Albany, NY • Boston • Cincinnati • Johannesburg • London • Madrid • Melbourne
Mexico City • New York • Pacific Grove, CA • Scottsdale, AZ • Singapore • Tokyo • Toronto

History Editor: Clark Baxter
Senior Development Editor: Sharon Adams Poore
Editorial Assistant: Melissa Gleason
Marketing Manager: Jay Hu
Print Buyer: Barbara Britton
Permissions Manager: Susan Walters
Production: Greg Hubit Bookworks
Photo Research: Sarah Evertson/Image Quest
Text and Cover Design: Harry Voigt
Cover Image: National Gallery, London/A.K.G., Berlin/Superstock.Holbein, Hans the Younger, *The Ambassadors.*
Copy Editor: Colleen McGuiness
Maps: GeoSystems; Eureka Cartography
Compositor: Carlisle Communications
Printer: Von Hoffmann Press

For more information, contact Wadsworth Publishing Company, 10 Davis Drive, Belmont, CA 94002, or electronically at http://www.wadsworth.com

International Thomson Publishing Europe
Berkshire House
168-173 High Holborn
London, WC1V 7AA, Great Britain

International Thomson Editores
Seneca, 53
Col. Polanco
11560 México D.F. México

Nelson ITP, Australia
102 Dodds Street
South Melbourne
Victoria 3205, Australia

International Thomson Publishing Asia
60 Albert Street
#15-01 Albert Complex
Singapore 189969

Nelson Canada
1120 Birchmount Road
Scarborough, Ontario
Canada M1K 5G4

International Thomson Publishing Japan
Hirakawa-cho Kyowa Building, 3F
2-2-1-Hirakawa-cho Chiyoda-ku
Tokyo 102, Japan

International Thomson Publishing GmbH
Königswinterer Strasse 418
53227 Bonn, Germany

International Thomson Publishing South Africa
Building 18, Constantia Park
138 Sixteenth Road, P.O. Box 2459
Halfway House, 1685 South Africa

ISBN: 0-534-54541-6

 This book is printed on acid-free recycled paper.

ABOUT THE AUTHORS

◆ ◆

Steven C. Hause is Professor of History and Fellow in International Studies at the University of Missouri–St. Louis, where he has won the Chancellor's Award for Excellence in Teaching (1996) and the Pierre Laclede Honors College Teacher of the Year Award (1989). He is the author and co-author of three previous books on the history of the women's rights movement in modern France, which have won four research prizes: *Women's Suffrage and Social Politics in the French Third Republic,* with Anne R. Kenney (Princeton University Press, 1984); *Hubertine Auclert, the French Suffragette* (Yale University Press, 1987); and *Feminisms of the Belle Epoque,* with Jennifer Waelti-Walters (University of Nebraska Press, 1994). His essays have appeared in several journals, including *American Historical Review* and *French Historical Studies.*

William S. Maltby is Professor of History Emeritus at the University of Missouri–St. Louis, where he continues to teach on a regular basis. Among his publications are: *The Black Legend in England: The Development of Anti-Spanish Sentiment, 1558–1660.* (Duke University Press, 1971), *Alba: A Biography of Fernando Alvarez de Toledo, Third Duke of Alba, 1507–1582.* (University of California Press, 1983), and articles on various aspects of Early Modern European history. From 1977 to 1997 he also served as Executive Director of the Center for Reformation Research and as editor of several volumes and series of volumes on the history of the Reformation.

CONTENTS IN BRIEF

❖❖❖❖❖❖❖❖❖❖❖❖❖❖❖❖❖❖❖❖❖❖❖❖

CONTENTS IN DETAIL

◆◆◆◆◆◆◆◆◆◆◆◆◆◆◆◆◆◆◆

DOCUMENTS

◆◆◆◆◆◆◆◆◆◆◆◆◆◆◆◆◆◆◆◆

TABLES

◆◆◆◆◆◆◆◆◆◆◆◆◆◆◆◆◆◆◆◆◆

MAPS

◆◆◆◆◆◆◆◆◆◆◆◆◆◆◆◆◆◆◆◆◆

CHRONOLOGIES

◆◆◆◆◆◆◆◆◆◆◆◆◆◆◆◆◆◆◆◆◆

REVIEWERS

◆◆◆◆◆◆◆◆◆◆◆◆◆◆◆◆◆◆◆◆

Gerald D. Anderson
North Dakota State University

Roz L. Ashby
Yavapai College

David Bartley
Indiana Wesleyan University

Anthony Bedford
Modesto Junior College

Rodney E. Bell
South Dakota University

Richard Camp
California State University–Northridge

Elizabeth Carney
Clemson University

Sherri Cole
Arizona Western College

Jeffrey Cox
University of Iowa

Philip B. Crow

Leslie Derfler
Florida Atlantic University

Marsha L. Frey
University of Montana

Sarah Gravelle
University of Detroit

Stephen Haliczer
Northern Illinois University

Barry Hankins
Baylor University

William Hartel
Marietta College

Mack Holt
George Mason University

Frank Josserand
Southwest Texas State University

Gary Kates
Trinity University

Paul Leuschen
University of Arkansas

Eleanor Long
Hinds Community College

Olivia H. McIntyre
Eckerd College

David L. Longfellow
Baylor University

Bill Mackey
University of Alaska–Anchorage

Tom McMullen
Georgia Southern University

Paul L. Maier
Western Michigan University

Larry Marvin
St. Louis University

Carol Bresnahan Menning
University of Toledo

Jeffrey Merrick
University of Wisconsin–Milwaukee

Dennis Mihelich
Creighton University

Charles G. Nauert, Jr.
University of Missouri–Columbia

Thomas C. Owen
Louisiana State University

William E. Painter
University of North Texas

Kathleen Paul
University of Southern Florida

Nancy Rachels
Hillsborough Community College

Elsa Rapp
Montgomery County Community
College

Miriam Raub Vivian
California State University–Bakersfield

Richard R. Rivers
Macomb Community College

Kenneth W. Rock
Colorado State University

Karl A. Roider
Louisiana State University

Leonard Rosenband
Utah State University

Joyce E. Salisbury
University of Wisconsin–Green Bay

Jerry Sandvick
North Hennepin Community College

Thomas P. Schlunz
University of New Orleans

Donna Simpson
Wheeling Jesuit University

Elisabeth Sommer
Grand Valley State University

Ira Spar
Ramapo College of New Jersey

Jake W. Spidle
University of New Mexico

Roger D. Tate
Somerset Community College

Jackson Taylor, Jr.
University of Mississippi

Timothy M. Teeter
Georgia Southern University

Lee Shai Weissbach
University of Louisville

PREFACE

◆◆◆◆◆◆◆◆◆◆◆◆◆◆◆◆◆◆◆◆◆◆

"Western Civ" textbooks have been a staple of higher education for several generations. By tradition, they provide college students with a broad introduction to Western history. They must also provide an introduction to multiple aspects of the past: the political institutions and events that have traditionally defined the periods of history; the cultural, religious, and intellectual contributions of the elite; the economic conditions that have shaped everyone's life; and the military history that has so often altered the structures of Western society. These two forms of historical breadth—chronological and topical—correspond to two fundamental virtues of historical study that beginning students need to acquire: an understanding of change over time and an appreciation of historical context.

Each Western Civilization textbook also has an individual character. The special concern of this text is revealed in its subtitle, *A History of European Society*. The authors share an interest in the varieties of social history that have changed historical studies in recent years. We have tried to weave a synthesis of recent social history scholarship—broadly defined to include the history of women and the family and the history of daily life—throughout the text. We sought to locate our social history in context, in its economic and political setting and in relation to the other historical interests. War and technological development are not treated in isolation, but as phenomena that influenced, and were influenced by, social and economic structures. We have tried to give popular culture its due without sacrificing the traditional emphasis on the intellectual, scientific, and religious interests of the elite, or forgetting that popular culture and elite culture are often the same.

To combine traditional breadth and our focus on social history, we have chosen to integrate a large quantity of supporting materials and sources into the text. In addition to the maps, illustrations, and documents that usually serve this purpose for political, military, and intellectual history, we have chosen to add a large num-

ber of statistical tables, graphs, and charts needed to document social and economic history. These are closely integrated with the text, so that their basic meaning is clear, and such raw data should provide sources for many discussions. This approach is unusual in a Western Civ textbook, and it requires unusual ancillary materials to use them to best advantage in a course concerned with social history. Our collaborators at Wadsworth Publishing Company have produced a variety of these materials to assist readers.

Instructor's Manual/Test Bank   Prepared by Shan Harward, Johnson County Community College. Includes chapter outline, chapter summaries, identifications, additional resources and reading, geography and map analysis, table data analysis, publisher resources, multiple-choice questions, short essay questions, essay/critical-thought questions.

World Class Testing Tools   A fully integrated suite of test-creation, delivery, and classroom-management tools. The package includes World Class Test, Test Online, and World Class Manager software.

Study Guide   Prepared by Shan Harward. Contains chapter outlines, chapter summaries, identifications, matching questions, multiple-choice questions, fill-in-the-blank questions, chronologies, questions for critical thought, analysis of primary source documents, geography and map analysis and table data analysis.

Electronic Study Guide   This interactive study guide not only allows students to study each chapter with questions in matching, fill-in-the-blank, essay and multiple choice formats, but also allows for instant feedback when the questions are answered. If the student answers a question incorrectly, they are told why and where to go for the correct answer.

Western Civilization Map Acetates   This extensive four-color acetate package includes maps from the text and from other sources and includes map commentary prepared by James Harrison, Siena College. The acetates and commentary are packaged in a three-ring binder.

Western Civilization PowerPoint Contains all the four-color maps from the map acetate package.

Document Exercises Workbooks Prepared by Donna Van Raaphorst, Cuyahoga Community College. A two-volume collection of exercises based around primary sources, teaching students how to use documents and historiographic methods.

Map Workbooks Prepared by Cynthia Kosso, Northern Arizona University. A two-volume workbook, each featuring over 20 map exercises. The exercises are designed to help students understand the relationship between places and people through time. All map exercises incorporate three parts: an introduction, a locations section where students are asked to correctly place a city, site, or boundary, and a question section.

Encountering the Past: Through Tables, Charts, and Art Prepared by John Soares. Gives students tips on understanding data and tables in the text, as well as art. Table analysis questions are included.

Sights and Sounds of History Videodisk Short, focused video clips, photos, artwork, animations, music, and dramatic readings are used to bring life to historical topics and events which are most difficult for students to appreciate from a textbook alone. For example, students will experience the grandeur of Versailles and the defeat felt by a German soldier at Stalingrad. The video segments, averaging 4 minutes, are available on VHS, which make excellent lecture launchers.

CNN Video: Western Civilizations This great lecture launcher contains 14 video clips ranging from 1 to 5 minutes each. Topics range from an archeologist's finding of the tomb of Alexandria to a tour through the Trotsky Museum.

History Video Library

Journey of Civilization CD-ROM Takes the student on 18 interactive journeys through history. Enhanced with QuickTime movies, animations, sound clips, maps, and more, the journeys allow students to engage in history as active participants rather than as readers of past events.

Internet Guide for History Prepared by Daniel Kurland and John Soares. Section One introduces students to the Internet, including tips for searching on the Web. Section Two introduces students to how history research can be done and lists URL sites by topic.

Archer, Documents of Western Civilization, Volume I: To 1715 and Volume II: Since 1550 A broad selection of carefully selected documents.

Hammond Historical Atlas

InfoTrac College Edition This online library allows students to study and learn about history at any time of the day or night. This online database gives students access to full-length articles from more than 700 scholarly and popular periodicals, updated daily, and dating back as far as three years. Periodicals include the *Historian, Smithsonian,* and *Harper's* magazines.

Web Page Visit the *Historic Times,* the Wadsworth History Resource Center at http://history.wadsworth.com. From this full-service site, instructors and students can access many selections, such as a career center, lessons on surfing the Web, and links to great history-related Web sites. Students can also take advantage of the online Student Guide to InfoTrac, College Edition, featuring lists of article titles with discussion and critical thinking questions linked to the articles to invite deeper examination of the material. Instructors can visit the book-specific site to learn more about the text and supplements. Students can take advantage of the quizzing feature.

Acknowledgments

This effort has taken us the better part of a decade. As we have refined our thinking during that time, we have received help from dozens of people. Many colleagues at the University of Missouri–St. Louis have given us their supportive criticism: Bob Baumann, Mark Burkholder, Suzanne Hiles Burkholder, Jerry Cooper, and Kathryn A. Walterscheid have all read portions of the manuscript. A Western Civilization textbook requires the scrutiny of professors in all varieties of western history. Wadsworth Publishing obtained the assistance of dozens of reviewers, who remained anonymous to us while we worked. Their comments produced important changes in the manuscript as it matured, and we are indebted to our colleagues for the combination of correction, praise, and rebuke that helped to produce this book.

Finally, we owe our gratitude to Wadsworth Publishing, and to the specialists whom they have engaged, for producing this book. We thank Tom LaMarre, the editor who originally signed us and began to develop this book; Robert Jucha, our second editor, who oversaw the book in a transitional stage; Clark Baxter, the editor who achieved the completion of the book and carried it into production; Sharon Adams Poore, our developmental editor at Wadsworth, who has brought the whole package together; Melody Rotman, our developmental editor in the opening stages when we were groping our way; Jenny Burke, media editor; Melissa Gleason, editorial assistant at Wadsworth who helped in the hurried closing stages of the book; Greg Hubit of Bookworks for producing the finished volumes; Hal Humphrey in the production department at Wadsworth; Susan Walters of Wadsworth Publishing for her work in securing permissions; Colleen McGuiness for her careful copyediting; Joanne Rohrbach for her detailed indexing; Sarah Evertson and Sue Edelson of Image Quest for tracking down the illustrations that we requested; Kevin Kolb of Eureka Cartography for his work on the maps; Chris Feldman of Carlisle Communications, who set the book in type with exceptional accuracy; and Jay Hu in the marketing department of Wadsworth who has done much to promote our work.

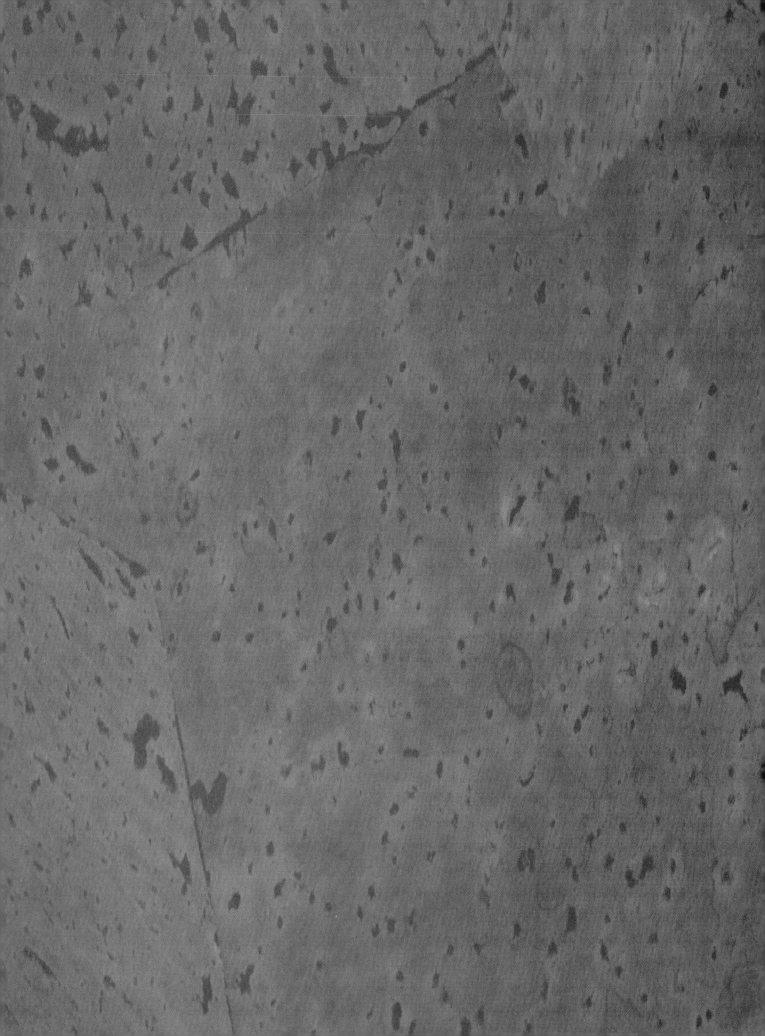

WESTERN CIVILIZATION

PART THREE

Early Modern Europe

CHAPTER 13

PLAGUE, WAR, AND SOCIAL CHANGE
IN THE "LONG" FOURTEENTH CENTURY

CHAPTER OUTLINE

The transition from medieval to early modern times is generally thought to have begun in the fourteenth century when economic decline, plague, and endemic warfare weakened the bonds of feudal society and undermined its values. Great historical transformations rarely limit themselves to the confines of a single century, and this one was no exception. Thinking, therefore, in terms of a "long" fourteenth century is helpful; that is, of an extended period of demographic, social, and political stress that in some of its manifestations lasted until well into the fifteenth century and beyond.

Chapter 13 deals with the institutional and social changes of this troubled age from the first signs of economic failure in the late thirteenth century to the demographic catastrophe of the Black Death and the social disorder that followed. It then examines the transformation of warfare: the introduction of the paid soldier, the triumph of infantry over armored cavalry, and the development of practical artillery. These changes would eventually transform the structure of society and politics by rendering feudalism obsolete, but they were also symptomatic of a world in which warfare had become almost universal. Conflict raged on Europe's eastern frontiers and was becoming institutionalized in the west, where the Hundred Years' War consumed the energies of France, England, and the Iberian kingdoms. For those who lived through these troubles, it was easy to believe that the society they had known—and perhaps the world—was nearing its end.

Famine, Economic Decline, and the Black Death (1315–50)

The fourteenth century was marked by a series of economic and demographic crises that had a profound effect on the social structure of Europe. Local crises of

◈ DOCUMENT 13.1 ◈

The Famine of 1315 in England

This dramatic account of the famine is from the English chronicler Johannes de Trokelowe. The prices may be compared with those given for the preceding century in document 12.1.

Meat and eggs began to run out, capons and fowl could hardly be found, animals died of pest, swine could not be fed because of the excessive price of fodder. A quarter of wheat or beans or peas sold for twenty shillings, barley for a mark, oats for ten shillings. A quarter of salt was commonly sold for thirty-five shillings, which in former times was quite unheard of. The land was so oppressed with want that when the king came to St. Albans on the feast of St. Lawrence [August 10] it was hardly possible to find bread on sale to supply his immediate household. . . .

The dearth began in the month of May and lasted until the nativity of the Virgin [September 8]. The summer rains were so heavy that grain could not ripen. It could hardly be gathered and used to make bread down to the said feast day unless it was first put in vessels to dry. Around the end of autumn the dearth was mitigated in part, but toward Christmas it became as bad as before. Bread did not have its usual nourishing power and strength because the grain was not nourished by the warmth of summer sunshine. Hence those who had it, even in large quantities, were hungry again after a little while. There can be no doubt that the poor wasted away when even the rich were constantly hungry. . . .

Four pennies worth of coarse bread was not enough to feed a common man for one day. The usual kinds of meat, suitable for eating, were too scarce; horse meat was precious; plump dogs were stolen. And according to many reports, men and women in many places secretly ate their own children.

vation of marginal soils could feed the ever-growing populace. A succession of bad harvests brought on by unusually cold, wet weather made these lands virtually unusable and destroyed the ecological balance between the people and their food supply. The result was widespread misery and an end to population growth. Scarcity pushed the price of bread to levels that only the rich could afford. Desperate peasants ate their seed grain, thereby destroying all hope for a harvest in the year to come. Others ate leaves, bark, and rats. Though adult deaths from malnutrition were probably rare, the demographic impact of the famine was seen in a declining rate of conception and increased infant mortality.

Predictably, trade declined. Defaults on loans increased, and the banking system was under stress. The great international banks still controlled their branches directly and had unlimited liability for their losses. If a branch failed it created a domino effect that might bring down the entire structure. This happened in 1343 when the two leading Florentine banks—the Bardi and the Peruzzi—failed, setting off a widespread financial panic. The immediate cause of their failure was the repudiation of war debts by a major borrower, Edward III of England, but both banks had been gravely weakened before the final blow.

The Black Death struck in 1347–51 upon a European population weakened by nearly two generations of hard times. Endemic in Asia since the eleventh century, the disease first entered Europe through the Mediterranean ports and spread with terrifying speed throughout the subcontinent (see map 13.1). Following the trade routes it reached Paris in the summer of 1348, Denmark and Norway in 1349, and Russia in 1351. Estimates are that within four years a third of the population of Europe died. It was the greatest demographic catastrophe in European history, and its ravages did not end with the first virulent outbreak. Subsequent epidemics occurred regularly in every decade until the beginning of the eighteenth century. Given that immunity apparently cannot be transmitted from generation to generation, the plague served as a long-term check on population growth, and most countries required more than two centuries to recover the population levels they had in 1300 (see table 13.1).

The relationship, if any, between the plague and poverty or malnutrition is unclear. In its most common form, bubonic plague is spread by fleas, which are carried by rats and other small mammals. A pneumonic form of the plague is spread by coughing. The onset of either form is rapid, and death usually comes within

subsistence became common and, for the first time in two centuries, a large-scale famine struck northern Europe in 1315–17 (see document 13.1). Southern Europe suffered a similar catastrophe in 1339–40. Overpopulation was the underlying cause. By 1300 only the culti-

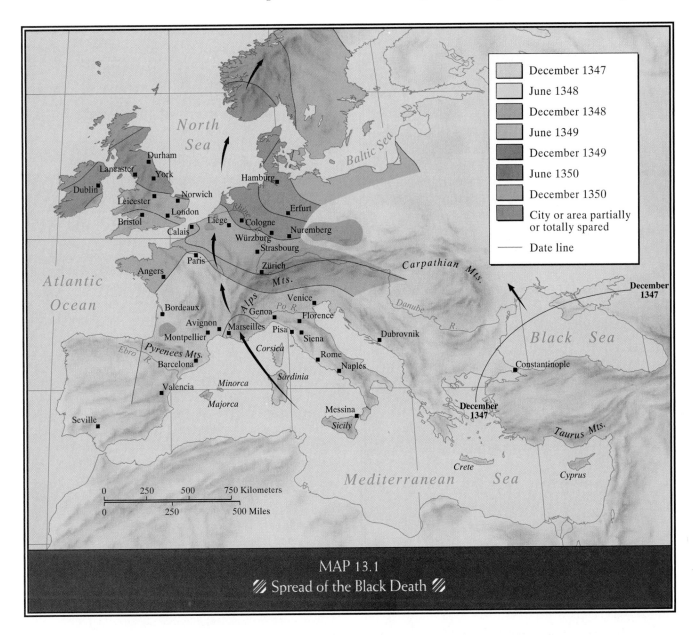

MAP 13.1
Spread of the Black Death

three days (see illustration 13.1). The mortality rate seems to have been about the same for all who contracted the disease, so that lowered resistance as a result of malnutrition likely did not play an important part in its spread. At the same time, death came most frequently to those who lived in crowded conditions. Soldiers, ship's crews, and the urban poor were at greatest risk, followed by those country folk whose poverty forced them to huddle together in their one-room cottages for warmth. The rich often escaped, either because they lived in more sanitary conditions or because, like the characters in Giovanni Boccaccio's *Decameron*, they had the means to flee from the centers of population (see document 13.2).

No one knew what caused the plague. Most probably believed that it was a visitation from God and took refuge in prayer and religious ceremonies. Flagellants paraded from town to town, beating each other with metal-tipped scourges in the hope of averting God's wrath, while preachers demanded the reform of the church on the theory that its increasing interest in secular affairs had provoked divine retribution. Some have argued that the plague created a genuine and long-lasting demand for spiritual renewal. However, other, more sinister results were evident as well. In parts of Germany whole communities of Jews were burned alive because they were thought to have spread the disease by poisoning wells (see document 13.3).

✕ TABLE 13.1 ✕

Indices of Population Increase in Europe, 1000–1950

The data presented in this table show the dramatic effects of the Black Death as well as the substantial increases in the European population between 1150 and 1250 and between 1400 and 1450. The indices are based on the figures for 100 (that is 1000 = 100). These figures are estimates only and have proved controversial.

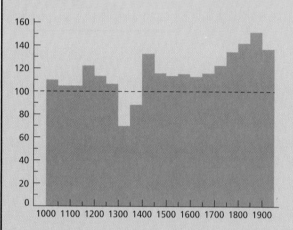

Indices per period of fifty years

Period	Index	Period	Index
1000–50	109.5	1500–50	113.0
1050–1100	104.3	1550–1600	114.1
1100–50	104.2	1600–50	112.4
1150–1200	122.0	1650–1700	115.0
1200–50	113.1	1700–50	121.7
1250–1300	105.8	1750–1800	134.3
1300–50	69.9	1800–50	141.5
1350–1400	88.2	1850–1900	150.8
1400–50	133.3	1900–50	136.7
1450–1500	115.0		

Source: B. H. Slicher van Bath, *The Agrarian History of Western Europe, A.D. 500–1800,* trans. Olive Ordish (London: Edward Arnold, 1963), p. 79.

◆ DOCUMENT 13.2 ◆

The Symptoms of the Plague

A description of the Black Death survives from one of the greatest of the late medieval writers. In 1348–53 Giovanni Boccaccio, who would later become a founder of Renaissance humanism (see chapter 14), wrote the Decameron, *a series of stories told in a villa outside Florence where a group of fashionable young people take refuge from the plague. The book begins with a description of the epidemic.*

In the year of our Lord 1348, there happened at Florence, the finest city in all Italy, a most terrible plague; which, whether owing to the influence of the planets, or that it was sent from God as a just punishment for our sins, had broken out some years before in the Levant, and after passing from place to place, and making incredible havoc all the way, had now reached the west. There, in spite of all the means that art and human foresight could suggest, such as keeping the city free from filth, the exclusion of all suspected persons, and the publication of copious instructions for the preservation of health; and not withstanding manifold humble supplications offered to God in processions and otherwise; it began to show itself in the aforesaid year, and in a sad and wonderful manner. Unlike what had been seen in the east, where bleeding from the nose is the fatal prognostic, here there appeared certain tumors in the groin or under the armpits, some as big as a small apple, others as an egg; and afterwards purple spots in most parts of the body; in some cases large and but few in number, in others smaller and more numerous—both sorts the usual messengers of death. To the cure of this malady, neither medical knowledge nor the power of drugs was of any effect; whether because the disease was in it is own nature mortal, or that the physicians (the number of whom, taking quacks and women pretenders into the account, was grown very great) could form no just idea of the cause, nor consequently devise a true method of cure; whichever was the reason, few escaped; but nearly all died the third day from the first appearance of the symptoms, some sooner, some later, without any fever or accessory symptoms.

Illustration 13.1

The Burial of Plague Victims at Tournai, 1349. Tournai is located in what is now Belgium. Similar scenes of mass burial were replayed throughout Europe during the plague years. As the death toll increased, attempts to provide coffins and individual funerals had to be abandoned. The overwhelmed survivors could only dump the bodies in mass graves.

◈ DOCUMENT 13.3 ◈

The Burning of the Jews

This passage from the Chronicle of Jacob von Königshofen *describes the destruction of the Jews at Strasbourg in 1549.*

In the matter of this plague the Jews throughout the world were reviled and accused in all lands of having caused it through the poison which they are said to have put into the water and the wells . . . and for this reason the Jews were burnt all the way from the Mediterranean into Germany, but not in Avignon, for the pope protected them there.

Nevertheless, they tortured a number of Jews in Berne and Zofingen who then admitted that they had put poison into many wells, and they also found the poison in the wells. Thereupon they burnt the Jews in many towns and wrote of this affair to Strasbourg, Freiburg, and Basel in order that they too should burn their Jews. But the leaders in these three cities . . . did not believe that anything ought to be done to the Jews. . . . Thereupon a conference was arranged to meet at Benfeld. The bishop of Strasbourg, all the feudal lords of Alsace, and the representatives of the three above-mentioned cities came there. The deputies of the city of Strasbourg were asked what they were going to do with their Jews. They answered and said that they saw no evil of them. Then they asked the Strasbourgers why they had closed the wells and put away the buckets, and there was great indignation and clamor against the deputies from Strasbourg. So finally the bishop and the lords and the Imperial Cities agreed to do away with the Jews. . . .

On Saturday—that was St. Valentine's Day—they burnt the Jews on a wooden platform in their cemetery. There were about two thousand people of them. Those who wanted to baptize themselves were spared. Many small children were taken out of the fire and baptized against the will of their fathers and mothers. And everything that was owed to the Jews was cancelled, and the Jews had to surrender all pledges and notes that they had taken for debts. The Council, however, took the cash that the Jews possessed and divided it among the working men proportionately. The money was indeed the thing that killed the Jews. If they had been poor and if the feudal lords had not been in debt to them, they would not have been burnt. After this wealth was divided among the artisans some gave their share to the cathedral or the Church on the advice of their confessors.

Thus were the Jews burnt at Strasbourg, and in the same year in all the cities of the Rhine.

◈

The Economic Consequences of the Black Death

The psychological effects of the Black Death would have a profound impact on religious belief, but its material consequences were equally dramatic (see table 13.2). Demographic collapse relieved pressure on the land. Food prices dropped immediately. Land values and rents followed close behind, declining by 30 to 40 percent in most parts of Europe between 1350 and 1400. For landholders, both lay and religious, this was a serious loss; for ordinary men and women, it was a windfall. Stunned by the horror they had experienced, the survivors found not only that food was cheaper and land more abundant, but also that most of them had inherited varying amounts of property from their dead relatives.

The delicate ecological balance of the thirteenth century no longer existed. Acreage could be diverted to pursuits that were less efficient in purely nutritional terms, but more profitable and less labor intensive. Fields were converted to pasture for grazing sheep and cattle. Marginal lands in Germany and elsewhere reverted to forest where hogs could root at will and where the next generation of peasants could presumably find cheap firewood and building material. A larger percentage of the grain crop was devoted to the brewing of beer, and in the south vineyards spread over hillsides upon which in earlier times people had sought to grow food. If the prosperity of Europeans may be measured by their consumption of meat and alcohol, these were comfortable years. Some historians have referred to the period after the Black Death as the golden age of European peasantry. It did not last long.

For most people calorie and protein consumption undoubtedly improved. Wages, too, increased, because the plague created a labor shortage of unprecedented severity. In Italy, employers tried to compensate by purchasing slaves from the Balkans or from dealers in the region of the Black Sea. This expedient was temporary and not successful. Before 1450 Turkish expansion brought an end to the trade, and although the Portuguese imported African slaves throughout the fifteenth century, they for the most part remained in Portugal. The handful of Africans who served the households of the very rich made no impact on the labor market. Wages remained high, and many people were able for the first time to leave their ancestral homes in search of better land or higher pay. Hundreds of communities were abandoned completely. Such movements cannot be accurately traced, but the cen-

---

⚜ TABLE 13.2 ⚜

Population, Prices, and Wages in England, 1300–1500

The information presented in this graph shows the relationship of agricultural prices, industrial wages and prices, and population in the century and a half following the Black Death. After dramatic rises during the crises of 1315–17 and in the decade of the 1360s, agricultural prices remained fairly steady until the 1530s. The graph is much simplified, and the index numbers are based on prices, wages, and population in 1300.

(1300 = 100)

— Index numbers of agricultural prices
— Index numbers of industrial prices and wages
— Index numbers of English population figures

Source: E. Perroy, "Les crises du XIVe siècle," *Annales,* vol. 4 (1949): pp. 167–82, as adapted in B. H. Slicher van Bath, *The Agrarian History of Western Europe, A.D. 500–1800,* trans. Olive Ordish (London: Edward Arnold, 1963), p. 139.

---

tury after 1350 appears to have been a time of extraordinary mobility in which the traditional isolation of village life diminished greatly.

These developments provoked a reaction from the propertied classes. Caught between rising wages and declining rents they faced a catastrophic reduction in their incomes. With the passage of time some eased the situation by turning to such cash crops as wool or wine. Their initial response was to seek legislation that would freeze wages and restrict the movement of peasants. Between 1349 and 1351 virtually every European government tried to fix wages and prices (see document 13.4). For the most part, their efforts produced only resistance.

The failure of such measures led to strategies based upon the selective modification of feudal agreements. New restrictions were developed and long-forgotten obligations were revived. Southwest Germany provides

◆ DOCUMENT 13.4 ◆

DOCUMENT 13.4

The Statute of Laborers

Issued by Edward III of England in 1351, this is a typical example of legislation designed to restrict the increase in labor costs created by the Black Death.

The King to the sheriff of Kent, greetings; Because a great part of the people, and especially of working men and servants, have lately died of the pestilence, many seeing the necessity of masters and great scarcity of servants, will not serve unless they may receive excessive wages, and others preferring to beg in idleness rather than by labor to get their living; we, considering the grievous incommodities which of the lack especially of ploughmen and such laborers may hereafter become, have upon deliberation and treaty with the prelates and the nobles and the learned men assisting us, with their unanimous counsel ordained:

That every man and woman of our realm of England, of what condition he be, free or bond, able in body, and within the age of sixty years, not living in merchandise, nor exercising any craft, nor having of his own whereof he may live, nor land of his own about whose tillage he may occupy himself, and not serving any other; if he be required to serve in suitable service, his estate considered, he shall be bound to serve him which shall so require him; and take only the wages, livery, meed, or salary which were accustomed to be given in the places where he oweth to serve, the twentieth year of our reign of England [that is, in 1347], or five or six other common years next before.

some instructive examples. Peasants subject to one lord were often forbidden to marry the subject of another. If they did so, their tenures would revert to the husband's lord after the couple's death. As population movements had created a situation in which few subjects of the same lord inhabited the same village, this practically guaranteed the wholesale confiscation of peasant estates. At the same time, peasants were denied access to the forests, whose game, wood, nuts, and berries were reserved for the landholders. These forest laws created enormous hardships and were similar in their effects to the enclosure of common lands by the English gentry a century later. Peasants who depended upon these re-sources for firewood and for a supplement to their diet might be driven from the land.

When such measures failed to raise enough money, landholders were often forced to sell part of their holdings to investors. If the land in question was held in fief the permission of the liege lord was usually required and could be secured by a cash payment or in return for political favors. Some of the buyers were merchants, lawyers, or servants of the crown who wanted the status provided by a country estate. Others were simply landholders who sought to consolidate their holdings at bargain rates. In either case the purchase of land tended to eliminate feudal obligations in fact and sometimes in law. The new owners had no personal ties to the peasants on their newly acquired estates and felt free to exploit their property as efficiently as possible. The net effect was to accelerate the shift toward private ownership of land that had begun with the commutation of feudal dues in the twelfth and thirteenth centuries.

Princes, too, were affected by the drop in land values. Medieval rulers drew the bulk of their ordinary revenues from exploiting their domains. Domain revenue came from a variety of dues, rights, and privileges, as well as from rents, which were an important part of the whole. Most princes were happy to make common cause with the other great landholders or to compensate for their losses by levying new taxes.

◆

Social Disorder from the Jacqueries to the Bundschuh Revolts

Attempts to reverse the economic trends set in motion by the plague created widespread discontent. In 1358 much of northern France rose in a bloody revolt called the Jacquerie (Jacques Bonhomme being more-or-less the French equivalent of John Doe). Peasants attacked the castles of their lords in one of the worst outbreaks of social violence in centuries. There was no program, no plan—only violence born of sheer desperation. In this case peasant distress was greatly aggravated by that portion of the Hundred Years' War that had ended with the French defeat at Poitiers in 1356. The countryside was devastated, and the peasants were taxed to pay the ransoms of the king and his aristocratic followers who had been captured by the English on the battlefield.

Other revolts grew less from poverty than from the frustration of rising expectations. The English revolt of 1381, known as Wat Tyler's Rebellion in memory of one of its leaders, was triggered by the imposition of a

◆ DOCUMENT 13.5 ◆

The Peasant Rebellion of 1381 in England

The following is from an account of Wat Tyler's Rebellion, written by a supporter of the king.

A justice was assigned by the king and council to go into Kent with a commission, as had been done before in Essex, and with them went a sergeant-at-arms of our lord the king, bearing with him a great number of indictments against folks of that district, to make the king rich. And they would have held session at Canterbury, but they were turned back by the commons.

And after this the commons of Kent gathered together in great numbers, day after day, without a head or chieftain. . . . But those who came from Maidstone took their way with the rest of the commons throught the countryside. And there they made chief over them Wat Teghler [Tyler] of Maidstone, to maintain them and be their councillor. And on the Monday next . . . they came to Canterbury . . . four thousand of them entering into the minster [cathedral] at the time of high mass, there made reverence and cried with one voice to the monks to prepare to choose a monk for archbishop of Canterbury, "for he who is archbishop now is a traitor [for supporting the poll tax] and shall be decapitated for his iniquity." And so he was within five days after! And when they had done this, they went into the town to their fellows, and . . . asked them if they had any traitors among them, and the townsfolk said that there were three, and named their names. These three the commons dragged out of their houses and cut off their heads. And afterwards they took five hundred men of the town with them to London. . . .

At this time, the commons had as their councillor a chaplain of evil disposition named Sir John Ball, which Sir John advised them to get rid of all the lords, and of all the archbishops and bishops, and abbotts, and priors, and most of the monks and canons . . . and that their possessions should be distributed among the laity. For which sayings he was esteemed among the commons as a prophet—and a fit reward he later got, when he was hung, drawn, and quartered, and beheaded as a traitor. After this, the said commons went to many places, and raised all the folk, some willingly and some unwillingly, till they were gathered together full sixty thousand. . . . They wrought much damage in Kent because of the hate they bore the said duke. They cast his manors to the ground and all his houses, and sold his beasts—his horses, his good cows, his sheep, and his pigs—and all his store of corn, at a cheap price. And they desired one day to have his head, and the head of Sir Thomas Orgrave, clerk of receipt and sub-treasurer of England. They . . . sent [the king] a petition, requiring that he should grant them the heads of fifteen other lords.

poll or head tax on every individual (see document 13.5). The rebels saw it as regressive, meaning it fell heavier on the poor than on the rich, and as a threat to the economic gains achieved since the plague. In Germany the exactions of princes and landholders, including the clergy, provoked a series of rebellions that flared periodically throughout the fifteenth century and culminated in the great Peasant Revolt of 1524–25. These are generally referred to as the *bundschuh* revolts after the laced boots that served as a symbol of peasant unity.

Much urban unrest also was in evidence, but its relationship to the plague and its aftermath is unclear. The overall volume of European trade declined after 1350, which was offset to some extent by continuing strength in the market for manufactured and luxury items. A more equitable distribution of wealth broadened the demand for clothing, leather goods, and various furnishings, while the rich, in an apparent effort to maintain their status in the face of economic threats, indulged in luxuries on an unprecedented scale. The trade in manufactured articles, though smaller in total than it had been in the thirteenth century, was therefore larger in proportion to the trade in bulk agricultural commodities. It was also more profitable. Towns, now considerably smaller, seem to have enjoyed a certain measure of prosperity throughout the period.

Their political balance, however, was changed by the new importance of manufacturing. Craft guilds and the artisans they represented were generally strengthened at the expense of the urban patriciate, whose rents were greatly reduced in value. The process was not entirely new. The Flemish cloth towns of Ghent, Bruges, and Ypres had been the scene of periodic revolts for a century before 1350, and outbreaks continued for years thereafter. By 1345 the guilds had triumphed, at least in

Flanders, but this in itself failed to create tranquility. The patriciate refused to accept exclusion from the government, and various factions among the guilds fought among themselves to achieve supremacy. Given the chronic discontent among the mass of laborers, most of whom were not guild members and therefore disenfranchised, riots were easy to incite almost regardless of the cause. The disturbances in the German towns of Braunschweig (1374) and Lübeck (1408) were apparently of similar origin. Political factions were able to mobilize popular discontent in the service of their own, decidedly nonpopular, interests.

The revolts of 1382 in Paris and Rouen appear to have been more spontaneous and closer in spirit to the rural uprisings of the same period, but the seizure of Rome by Cola di Rienzi in May 1347 was unique. Demanding a return to the ancient Roman form of government, he raised a great mob and held the city for seven months under the title of Tribune. The whole episode remains the subject of historical controversy. It was related to the absence of the pope at Avignon (see chapter 15). The departure of the papal court in 1305 had wrecked the Roman economy and placed the city's government in the hands of such old aristocratic families as the Orsini and the Colonna. Popular dissatisfaction kept the city in turmoil for several years even after Rienzi was forced into exile.

The revolt of the Florentine *Ciompi* in 1378 was the culmination of thirty years of civic strife. The depression of 1343 had led the *popolo grasso* (literally, fat people) to betray their city's republican traditions by introducing a despot who would, they hoped, control the population. The subsequent revolt led to a government dominated by the minor, craft-oriented guilds and to the incorporation of the semiskilled woolcarders (*ciompi*) into a guild of their own. In 1378 the Ciompi seized control of the city and introduced a popular and democratic form of government that lasted until the great merchants of the city hired a mercenary army to overthrow it in 1382.

Few of these rebellions, urban or rural, had clearly developed aims, and none of them resulted in permanent institutional changes beneficial to the rebels. For the most part the privileged classes found them easy to suppress. The wealthy still possessed a near monopoly of military force and had little difficulty in presenting a united front. Their opponents, though numerous, were poor and usually disorganized. Communication among different groups of rebels was difficult, and outbreaks of violence tended to be as isolated as they were brief. These rebellions probably did not pose a fundamental threat to the existing social order, but they inspired

fear. The chroniclers, who were by definition members of an educated elite, described appalling scenes of murder, rape, and cannibalism. They noted that women sometimes played a part in the agitation, and they regarded this as a monstrous perversion of nature. True or exaggerated, these accounts made it difficult for readers to sympathize with the rebels. The restoration of order was often followed by mass executions and sometimes by new burdens on the peasantry as a whole.

In general the social disorders of the fourteenth century weakened whatever sense of mutual obligation had been retained from the age of feudalism and probably hastened the trend toward private ownership of land. Moreover they increased the fear and insecurity of the elite, who reacted by developing an attitude of increased social exclusivity. The division between popular and elite culture became dramatic at about this time. The tendency was to ridicule and suppress customs that had once belonged to rich and poor alike but were now regarded as loutish or wicked.

Meanwhile, an impulse that must have been largely unconscious led the upper classes into new extravagance and the elaboration of an extreme form of chivalric excess. The tournaments and banquets described in the *Chronicle* of Jean Froissart (c. 1333–c. 1400) surpassed anything that an earlier age could afford and were at least partially inspired by the flowering of chivalric romance as a literary form. Ironically, this "indian summer" of chivalry occurred not only amid social and economic insecurity but at a time when the feudal aristocracy was losing the remnants of its military function.

The Transformation of Warfare: The Emergence of the Soldier

Fourteenth-century Europe suffered not only from famine and plague, but also from war. While the age was probably not more violent than others before or since, the scale and complexity of warfare was beginning to increase in highly visible ways. By 1500 the evidence was clear that the preceeding two hundred years had witnessed a military revolution.

Long before the Black Death the feudal system of warfare had begun to break down. The warrior was becoming a soldier. The term *soldier* is used here in its original meaning: a fighting man who receives a cash payment or *solde* for his efforts as opposed to one who serves in return for land or in the discharge of some nonmonetary obligation. This was an important development, not only because it changed the way in which

❖ DOCUMENT 13.6 ❖

The Changing Realities of War

Jean Froissart's account of the battle of Aljubarrota (1385) shows, perhaps unconsciously, the contrast between the rhetoric of chivalry and the harsh realities of war. The English auxiliaries refused knighthoods because they could not afford them. The battle, like many in the Hundred Years' War, was won by the side that fought on foot. Decisive contributions were made by the archers and the city militia of Lisbon, who, as commoners, massacred every knight they could capture. The action begins with an address by the king of Portugal to sixty newly created knights. It ends when the Castilians chivalrously attack the Portuguese in their carefully prepared position in a mountain pass.

"My fair sirs, the order of chivalry is more exalted and noble than imagination can suppose, and no knight ought to suffer himself to be debased by cowardice or any villainous or dirty action; but when his helmet is on his head he should be bold and fierce as a lion; and because I wish you to show your courage this day where it will be most needful, I order you to the front of the battalion, where you must exert yourselves that we may both obtain honors, otherwise your spurs will not become you." Each new knight in turn as he passed answered, "Sire we will, with God's grace, so act, that we may gain your love and approval." None of the English were knighted this day; they were invited by the King to become knights, but excused themselves for that time. . . .

The sun was now setting when the King of Castile advanced in puissant array, with banners displayed, and his men on barbed horses, shouting out, "Castile," and entered the fortified pass, where they were received with lances, battle-axes, and such a flight of arrows, that they were thrown into confusion, and many wounded or slain. The King of Portugal fought on foot in this encounter, and having placed himself at the pass with a battle-axe in his hand, performed wonders, knocking down three or four of the stoutest of the enemy, insomuch that none dared approach him. The Spaniards, as you might imagine, had a hard afternoon's work, and the fortune of war was greatly against them. All who entered the fort of the Lisboners were cut to pieces, for the Portuguese would not ransom any, whether poor or noble. The number of slain was immense.

---

wars were fought, but also because it altered the structure of western European society.

The increase in real wealth and in the circulation of money between 1000 and 1250 allowed princes to alter the basis of military service. Their own revenues, which were based in part on import-export duties and occasional levies on movable goods, were greatly augmented by the revival of trade. Beyond that the commutation of military and other services for cash helped to create substantial war revenues exclusive of taxes. Scutage, the payment of knight's fees, and similar arrangements by which even the feudal class could escape military service in return for cash payments are first noted in the mid-twelfth century. By 1250 they had become commonplace. In 1227 the emperor Frederick II demanded eight ounces of gold from every fief in his realms, but only one knight from every eight fiefs. A quarter-century later the pope declared his preference for money over personal service from his vassals. The money was used to hire mercenaries or to pay knights to extend their service, often for an indefinite period. The case of Edward I of England is typical. His attempts to subjugate the Welsh and Scots could not be abandoned every autumn when his feudal levies went home. He therefore contracted with certain knights on a long-term basis, paying their wages from the proceeds of knight's fees and from the nine great levies on moveable property that he collected between 1297 and 1302.

The need for long-service troops and the superior professionalism of those who fought year in and year out for their livelihood were decisive. By 1340 unpaid feudal service was becoming rare in western Europe, though the crown was not yet the sole paymaster of its armies. Men from the great estates were still paid by the lords who employed them. Townsmen were paid by the towns. This changed by the mid-fifteenth century in England and France and by 1480 in Spain, though towns and nobles could be called upon to provide equipment. In Italy the mercenary was dominant by 1300.

The major exceptions to this state of affairs were found in eastern Europe. In Poland a numerous class of small and middling gentry continued to perform unpaid military service throughout the fifteenth century. Those who account for this by pointing to the frontier character of Polish society would be wrong. In Hungary, Europe's most exposed frontier, even the *banderia*, a heavy cavalry unit composed of noblemen, was paid in cash at an early date, and the armies of János Hunyadi (c. 1407–56) and his son, Matthias I, were composed largely of mercenaries. Aside from such quasitribal survivals as the *szechely* of eastern Transylvania, the decision to pay or not to pay seems everywhere to have been governed by the availability of cash.

The first soldiers fought largely within the established conventions of feudal cavalry. Some were nobles, knights, or lesser folk who held land in fief but who were attempting to improve their fortunes during an age of rising prices and declining rents. Others were bastards or younger sons whose only inheritance was a sword, a horse, and a sound training in the profession of arms. They were soon joined by paid infantry, most of whom came from different social worlds. The fourteenth century also saw the evolution of infantry tactics that required either specialized skills or exceptional discipline and cohesion in battle. As those who possessed such training were rarely part of traditional feudal society, they, too, had to be paid in cash.

The skills were largely associated with the development of new or improved missile weapons. Archery had always been a factor in medieval warfare, but its effectiveness was diminished by improvements in personal armor. The introduction of the crossbow therefore marked the beginning of a major change. This weapon offered great accuracy and powers of penetration, though at a relatively slow rate of fire. It was first seen in the west during the twelfth century but was not extensively manufactured until a hundred years later. Originating in the Mediterranean, it was first used as a naval weapon and found special favor among the shipmasters of Genoa and Barcelona as a defense against pirates. When an attack was expected they lined their gunwales with crossbowmen to decimate boarding parties before the ships could engage. Men selected and trained for this purpose had become numerous in the port cities of the western Mediterranean by 1300 and were willing to transfer their skills to land when the volume of maritime trade declined. The Genoese were especially noted for their service to France during the Hundred Years' War; natives of Barcelona and Marseilles were not far behind.

The advent of the crossbowmen marked an alien intrusion into the world of feudal warfare and was resented by many knights (see document 13.6). Their world held little place for the urban poor. However, the involvement of marginal people with deviant forms of social organization was only beginning. The famous longbow was another case in point. Basically a poacher's weapon, it evolved beyond the edges of the

Illustration 13.2

The Waggenburg. This pen drawing from about 1450 shows Hussite war wagons drawn up in a circle around a tent displaying the Hussite symbol of the communion cup. The men within are firing both crossbows and the handguns first used extensively under the Taborite commanders John Žižka and Prokop the Bald.

feudal world in Wales and the English forests of Sherwood and Dean. Edward III perceived its advantages and introduced it in the Hundred Years' War with devastating effect. The longbow combined a high rate of fire with penetration and accuracy superior to that of early firearms. It required many years of training to be properly employed. As most of those who were expert in its use were marginal men in an economic and social sense they were usually happy to serve as mercenaries.

Handguns followed a similar pattern. First seen in Italy during the 1390s, they achieved importance in Bohemia during the Hussite wars when John Žižka and his Taborite followers used them against German chivalry. One of their most effective tactics was to mount gun tubes on the sides of wagons and then form the wagons into a circle, thus creating a nearly impregnable *waggenburg*, or wagon fortress (see illustration 13.2). When

Illllustration 13.3

Pikes in Action. This illustration of the opening of a battle between formations of pikemen shows the "fall" of pikes as the units come into action. It is a detail of *The Terrible Swiss War* by Albrecht Altdorfer, c. 1515.

peace returned, companies of handgun men found employment in Hungary and in the west.

Other specialists came largely from the nonfeudal world and served under long-term contracts in return for cash. Light cavalry, needed for reconnaissance and foraging, were eventually found during the fifteenth century in Hungary, Albania, and southern Spain. Miners, whose skills were increasingly valued in siegecraft, were also hired under contract, though their service was normally limited to the duration of a specific siege. Carters, muleteers, and laborers were hired as campaigns became longer and more complex and as peasants bought their way out of the service provisions of their feudal contracts.

All of these categories were overshadowed in the fifteenth century by the emergence of the pike as a primary battle weapon (see illustration 13.3). The pike was a spear, twelve to sixteen feet in length. It was used in a square formation similar to the Macedonian phalanx and could, if the pikemen stood their ground, stop a cavalry charge or clear the field of opposing infantry. Massed infantry formations of this kind had been ne-

glected during most of the Middle Ages because such tactics were incompatible with feudalism as a social system. Infantry had to be highly motivated and carefully trained to meet a cavalry charge without flinching. Neither condition applied to the majority of peasants on the great feudal estates. Their lords had every incentive to maintain this situation. In other societies, massed infantry formations were a rational adaptation to circumstances.

In medieval Europe, two main forms of social organization met this requirement: the city and the peasant league. Medieval towns were surrounded by enemies. In those areas where princely authority was weak (Italy, the Low Countries, and parts of Germany), they were forced to develop effective armies at a relatively early date. As most towns lacked either extensive territory or a large native nobility trained in the profession of arms, this meant that they had to rely on the creation of citizen militias supplemented on occasion by mercenaries. Those townsmen who could afford to bought horse and armor and tried to fight like knights. The majority served with pike or halberd (a long-handled battle axe) and drilled on Sundays and holidays until they achieved a level of effectiveness far superior to that of peasant levies. The victory of the Flemish town militias over the chivalry of France at Courtrai in 1302 was a promise of things to come.

By 1422 pike tactics had been adopted by the Swiss Confederation, one of several peasant leagues formed in the later thirteenth century to preserve their independence from feudal demands. The successful defense of their liberties earned them a formidable military reputation, and after 1444 the Swiss were regularly employed as mercenaries by the French and by the pope. Their example was taken up by other poor peasants in south Germany who emulated their system of training and hired themselves out to the emperor and other princes. Pike squares remained a feature of European armies for two hundred years, and mercenary contracting became an important element in the Swiss and south German economies.

The emergence of paid troops, new missile weapons, and massed infantry tactics changed the character of European warfare. By the end of the fourteenth century armies were larger and cavalry was declining in importance. The social consequences of these changes were profound because they tended, among other things, to monetarize the costs of war. In the simplest form of feudal warfare cash outlays were few. Men served without pay and normally provided their own food and equipment in the field. Large hidden costs existed because feudal levies consumed resources in kind, but these costs rarely involved the state. This changed dramatically with the advent of the soldier because only a sovereign state could coin money or raise taxes. As feudal nobles could rarely do either, they gradually lost their preeminent role as the organizers of war while the eclipse of cavalry reduced their presence on the battlefield. During the fifteenth century many great feudal families began to withdraw from the traditional function as protectors of society, leaving the field to men who served the sovereign for pay and privileges. In the process the state, too, was transformed. Where the feudal world had demanded little more than justice and military leadership from its kings, the new warfare demanded the collection and distribution of resources on an unprecedented scale. The monarchies of Europe were at first unprepared for such a task, and the difficulties they faced were compounded by a contemporary revolution in military technology.

The New Military Technology: Artillery, Fortifications, and Shipbuilding

The development of Western technology is often seen as a sporadic affair in which periods of innovation were interspersed with longer intervals of slow, almost imperceptible change. This is an illusion that comes from thinking of the inventions themselves instead of the complex process that created them, but periods certainly existed during which breakthroughs occurred at an accelerated rate. One of these was the later Middle Ages. Few of the changes had an immediate impact on everyday life, but their effects on war, trade, and government were great. The first is conventionally known as the introduction of gunpowder, though the technological accomplishments involved were largely in metallurgy. The second was a major revolution in the design and building of ships.

Like all technological breakthroughs, those of the later Middle Ages were made possible by earlier developments. The success of any new process or invention depends not only on its ability to utilize existing materials and techniques, but also on the presence of an effective demand. That is, technology must be affordable as well as desirable. Sufficient capital accumulation must be available to pay for its development, and customers must be willing and able to purchase the results. The increase in real wealth between the eleventh and the thirteenth centuries, and its concentration in fewer hands owing to the demographic catastrophe of the fourteenth century, provided the necessary economic base. Ideas and techniques kept pace.

The development of artillery and portable firearms is a case in point. Evolution began with the invention of gunpowder. In Europe saltpeter was first identified in the twelfth century. How or why it was combined with charcoal and sulphur is unknown, but the mixture was mentioned by Roger Bacon in 1248. A number of years passed before it was used as a propellent and its first application probably was in mining. This, however, is uncertain. Only the obstacles to its use are fully documented. Saltpeter was scarce and expensive. Years of experimentation were needed to arrive at the proper ratio of ingredients and even longer to develop grains of the proper consistency. Mistakes were often fatal, for black powder was not totally safe or dependable in use, and its chemistry has only recently been understood. Nevertheless it presented fewer problems than the

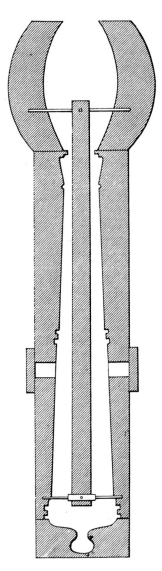

Illustration 13.4

Gun-Casting Technique (after c. 1450). The gun was cast around a core that was lowered into the mold and centered by an iron "cross" that was left in the casting. The pouring head at the top ensured that the mixture of tin and copper would not segregate during cooling and weaken the breach. The head was sawed off after the casting process was complete.

construction of the guns. Metallurgy, not powder milling, controlled the pace of artillery development.

The first guns, which appeared around the middle of the fourteenth century, were hand forged from wrought iron bars and bound with iron hoops. They were heavy, expensive, and prone to bursting when fired. In spite of these drawbacks they remained dominant until the middle of the fifteenth century when they were superseded by guns cast from bronze (see illustration 13.4). Bronze had been cast for centuries, no-

tably for church bells, but gunfounding was done on a larger scale and required more skill than the peaceful art that had preceded it. A large cannon might weigh several tons, and a number of them were required to arm a ship or besiege a town. The bronze used was approximately 80 percent copper and 20 percent tin. Large quantities of both metals were therefore required, and gun production on a large scale was prevented during the fourteenth century by the exhaustion of existing mines. Copper in particular was in short supply. In 1450 a new process was introduced that extracted copper from ores in which copper and silver were found together. Large, previously unusable deposits in Saxony, Hungary, and Slovakia thus could be exploited, and copper production increased dramatically.

The introduction of bronze cannons was further delayed by the lack of adequate furnaces and by an inability to deal with a physical property characteristic of bronze. Copper and tin tend to segregate as they cool, causing variations in the strength of the metal that might cause the guns to burst when fired. Generations of experience were needed to solve these problems. By the 1460s they were largely under control, and large numbers of bronze cannons were quickly added to European armories. Within a half-century every existing fortress was obsolete, for the high, relatively thin walls of medieval fortifications could withstand no more than a few hours of battering by the big guns. Towns and strongholds in militarily exposed areas were forced to rebuild if they were to survive. Between 1500 and 1530, Italian engineers developed a system of fortification that set the pattern for defensive works until the nineteenth century (see illustration 13.5). Walls were lowered and thickened to widths of forty feet or more. Bastions became wedge-shaped and were laid out geometrically so that every section of wall could be covered by the defender's guns. The works were then surrounded by a broad, steep-sided ditch that was usually faced with brick or stone.

The cost was enormous. The guns were expensive and required large numbers of skilled men and draft animals to maneuver. The new fortifications required less skill to construct than their medieval predecessors, but their scale was far larger and their expense proportionately high. The development of artillery had increased the already heavy burden of warfare on states and subjects alike.

The development of navies, though not taking place in earnest until the sixteenth century, was destined to have a similar effect. It rested upon changes in shipbuilding that by the fifteenth century had created

Illustration 13.5

The Bastion Trace. This aerial photo of the city of Lucca, Italy, shows fortifications erected in the sixteenth century as a response to the growing use of siege artillery. The cost of such works was immense, but no alternative existed to their construction if towns or strong points were to be protected against the new technology. Like the curtain walls of medieval times, the bastion trace held urban sprawl within strict limits. It also created a green belt around the city that could be used as a park. Once again, military necessity had transformed the European landscape.

vessels capable of crossing an ocean or using artillery in a ship-to-ship duel. The new ships were the result of a hybrid cross between two traditions of shipbuilding—the Mediterranean and the north European. The ships changed the world as few innovations have done before or since.

The dominant ship types in the medieval Mediterranean were the galley and the round ship. The galley was intended primarily for war. Long, narrow, and light, its chief virtues were speed and maneuverabilty independent of the wind. However, it was too fragile for use in the open Atlantic or for extended use in its home waters between October and May. It also lacked carrying capacity, and this, together with its high manpower requirements, limited its usefulness. Though galleys were sometimes used for commerce, especially by the Venetians, the preeminent Mediterranean cargo carrier was the round ship. As its name implies, it was double-ended and broad of beam with a high freeboard. Steered like a galley by side rudders located near the stern, it normally carried a two-masted rig with triangular lateen sails. The round ship was not fast or graceful, but it was safe, roomy, and thanks to its high freeboard, relatively easy to defend against boarders. Its carvel type construction was typically Mediterranean. The hull planking was nailed or pegged edge on edge to a skeleton frame and then caulked to create a water-tight, non-load-bearing hull.

The ships of northern Europe were different (see illustration 13.6). Most were clinker-built like the old Viking longships with overlapping planks fastened to each other by nails or rivets. Their variety was almost

infinite. By the middle of the thirteenth century the cog had emerged as the preferred choice for long voyages over open water. Of Baltic origin, the cog was as high and beamy as the roundship. A long, straight keel and sternpost rudder made it different from and more controllable than its Mediterranean counterpart. In accord with northern practice, it carried a single square sail on a mast set amidships.

In the century and a half after the Black Death these two shipbuilding traditions merged to create the full-rigged ship. The development of the cloth industry in England and the Netherlands created a North Atlantic market for alum, which was used as a fixative for dyes. This market was supplied by the Genoese, who soon found that it was economical to ship the material directly from its source on the Greek islands of Chios and Phocea to the trading center at Southampton. Cogs were well suited to this purpose, and the Genoese began to construct them in their own yards before 1350. Genoese shipbuilders were accustomed to carvel construction. As the fourteenth century progressed they were faced with dwindling timber supplies and increased prices for wood. Carvel construction was significantly lighter than clinker-built and therefore not only familiar but also cheaper. Furthermore, cogs required a smaller crew than roundships. This became important after the Black Death when the wages of seamen increased, and by 1400, carvel-built cogs on the Genoese model were used even on solely Mediterranean routes.

The addition of multiple masts was in part a response to the need for larger ships. Shipbuilders soon discovered that a divided rig offered other advantages.

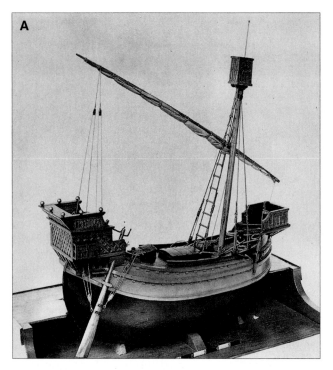

Ilustration 13.6

The Evolution of Medieval Ship Types. These three ship models represent the best current thinking on the appearance and construction of medieval ships. (A) is a medieval round ship with a lateen sail and steering oars of the type used to carry crusaders. (B) is a reconstruction of an early cog with square sail and keel carried right aft to the sternpost rudder. (C) is a model of the *Mary Rose,* Henry VIII's "great ship" that capsized in 1545. It may be regarded as an early galleon. Note the gunports.

It reduced manning requirements because smaller sails were easier to handle. It also made possible the use of different sails—combined according to need, thereby increasing speed and maneuverability under a wider variety of conditions. With Portuguese, Dutch, and Basque innovators leading the way, a recognizably modern ship had evolved by 1500.

Given the military rivalry among states, a marriage between the new shipbuilding techniques and the cast bronze cannon was inevitable. The full tactical implications of this were not immediately apparent, but by the last quarter of the fifteenth century the major states were acquiring ships capable of mounting heavy guns. A sort of arms race in which monarchs sought to outdo one another in the construction of monster warships such as the French *Cordeliere* or the English *Henry Grace à Dieu* gave way to an emphasis on the more practical

galleons of the sixteenth century. The competition to control the seas was on, and no state with maritime interests could afford to ignore it.

Centers of Conflict: The Eastern Frontiers

For much of the later Middle Ages the great north European plain, where it made a borderless transition into Asia, was in turmoil. East of the Elbe, two great movements were under way. The first was the eastward expansion of the German-speaking peoples. Population growth in the twelfth and thirteenth centuries led to the establishment of German settlements in Poland, Lithuania, and the Baltic regions as well as in Transylvania and the Ukraine. The movement was not always peaceful, bringing the Germans into conflict with the Slavs who inhabited the region. Relations improved little with time, and the German "colonies" tended to remain isolated from their neighbors by linguistic barriers and mutual resentments. In its later phases, German expansion was led by the Teutonic Knights, a military order on the crusading model. From the mid-thirteenth century the Knights attempted the large-scale conquest of Slavic as well as unclaimed land on which German peasants were then encouraged to settle.

On its eastern fringes (see document 13.7) the Slavic world was under equal pressure from the Mongols, who conquered most of Russia and the Ukraine in 1240–42 and who raided as far west as Breslau in Silesia. The center of resistance to Mongol rule became the grand duchy of Moscow, founded by the son of the Russian hero, Alexander Nevsky. Nevsky had defeated a Swedish incursion in 1238 and the Teutonic Knights in 1240. His descendants were forced to concern themselves almost exclusively with Asia. Though continuing to pay tribute to the Mongol khans, the Musovites engaged in sporadic warfare with them until 1480 when Ivan III refused payment and became, in effect, the first tsar. An early sign of the grand duchy's preeminence was the transfer of the Russian Orthodox patriarchate from Kiev to Moscow in 1299.

During the fourteenth century, Russian preoccupation with the Mongols encouraged the Teutonic Knights to step up their activities in the Baltic. Resistance was provided by the Catholic kingdom of Poland, established early in the eleventh century, and by a rapidly expanding Lithuanian state whose rulers were still pagan. In 1386 the two states merged for mutual defense. Under the leadership of the Lithuanian Jagiello, who converted to Catholicism and became king of Poland as well, the Knights were defeated at the battle of Tannenburg in 1410 (see map 13.2).

The Knights no longer existed as an aggressive force, but conflict did not end. Poland-Lithuania did not evolve into a centralized territorial state. It remained an aristocratic commonwealth with an elected king and few natural defenses. However, it was at this time a remarkably open society in which people of many faiths and languages could coexist. It even became the place of refuge for thousands of Jews. Driven from western Europe by the persecutions that followed the Black Death, they found that their capital and financial skills were welcomed by the rulers of an under-

---

◆ DOCUMENT 13.7 ◆

The Novgorod Chronicle

Novgorod was an important trading city north of Moscow. This exerpt from its city chronicle provides a vivid picture of conditions on Europe's eastern frontier in the year 1224.

A.D. 1224. Prince Vsevolod Gyurgevits came to Novgorod. The same year the Germans killed Prince Vyachko in Gyurgev and took the town. The same year, for our sins, this was not [all] the evil that happened: *Posadnik* [an elected official somewhat resembling a burgomaster or mayor] Fedor rode out with the men of Russia and fought with the Lithuanians; and they drove the men of Russia from their horses and took many horses, and killed Domazhir Torlinits and his son and of the men of Russa Boghsa and many others, and the rest they drove asunder into the forest. The same year, for our sins, unknown tribes came, whom no one exactly knows, who they are, nor whence they came out, nor what their language is, nor of what race they are, nor what their faith is, but they call them Tartars. . . . God alone knows who they are and whence they came out. Very wise men know them exactly, who understand books, but we do not know who they are, but have written of them here for the sake of the memory of the Russian princes and of the misfortune which came to them from them.

---

developed frontier state. The parallels with the Iberian kingdoms are striking. By the mid-fifteenth century Poland and Lithuania were the centers of a vigorous Jewish culture characterized by a powerful tradition of rabbinic learning and the use of Yiddish, a German dialect, as the language of everyday speech.

To the south, in the Balkan Peninsula, the fourteenth and fifteenth centuries marked the emergence of the Ottoman Empire as a threat to Christian Europe. By 1300 virtually all of the Byzantine lands in Anatolia had fallen under the control of *ghazi* principalities. The *ghazis*, of predominantly Turkish origin, were the Muslim equivalent of crusaders, pledged to the advancement of Islam. The last of their states to possess a common frontier with Byzantium was centered on the city of Bursa in northwest Anatolia. Under the

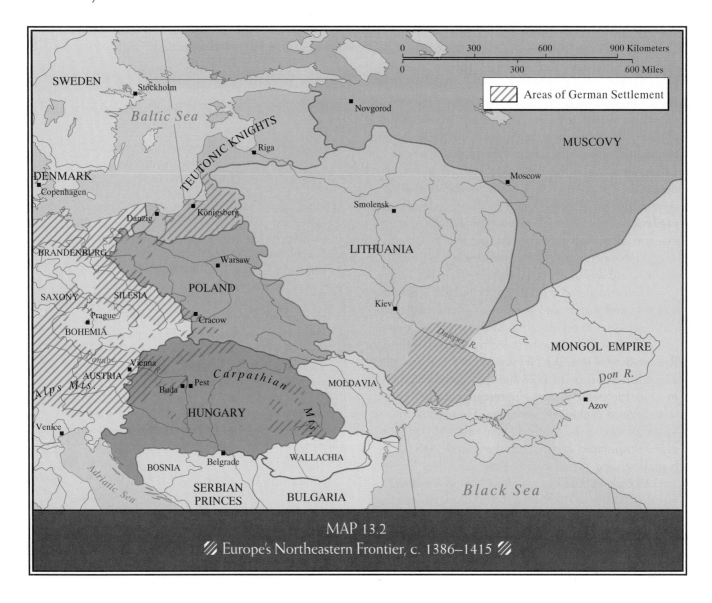

MAP 13.2

Europe's Northeastern Frontier, c. 1386–1415

aggressive leadership of Osman (1258–1324) it offered the opportunity for continued warfare to ambitious men from all over the Turkic world and a refuge to others who had fled from the Mongol advance in central Asia. With the population of the Ottoman state swelled by thousands of immigrants, the tiny emirate became the nucleus of the Ottoman Empire (see map 13.3).

From the beginning it was a serious threat to the Byzantine state revived by Michael Paleologus after the Fourth Crusade. Deprived of his Anatolian heartland and caught between the Ottomans on one side and the Serbian Empire of Stephen Dushan (d. 1355) on the other, the Greek emperor was only one of many regional princes striving for preeminence in the tangled world of Balkan politics. Taking advantage of divisions among the Christians, Osman's son, Orhan, ordered

the first Turkish invasion of Europe in 1356. The best hope of expelling him lay in an alliance between the Serbians and the Bulgarians. A history of mutual distrust inhibited their cooperation, however, and the Serbian army was defeated in 1371. By 1389 the Turks had achieved military predominance in the peninsula.

The threat to Constantinople was now imminent, and the Greeks sent missions to Rome in the hope of enlisting western support against the Turks. Negotiations broke down over theological and other issues. The pope was reluctant to compromise, and some Greeks came to believe that the Latin church was a greater threat to the survival of their religion than Islam. From the standpoint of Western intellectual development this contact between Greek and Latin scholar-diplomats would have far-reaching consequences, but politically it was a failure.

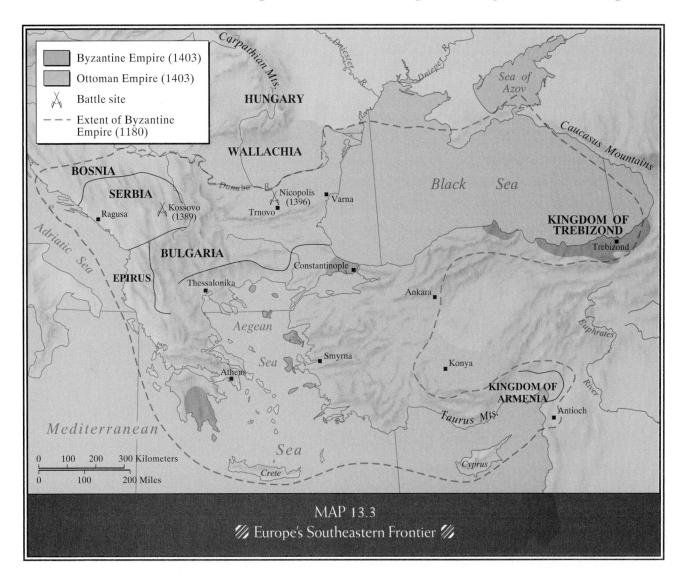

MAP 13.3
Europe's Southeastern Frontier

Meanwhile, southeastern Europe settled into a period of almost chronic warfare. The Serbs and Bulgarians were restless and unreliable tributaries of the Turks. The Byzantine emperor lacked a credible offensive force, but the Albanians remained a threat. In the northwest the Hungarians were growing uneasy. Eventually a crusade was organized by János Hunyadi, the voivod of Transylvania who would one day become king of Hungary. His defeat at Varna in 1444 and again on the plain of Kossovo in 1448 left the Turks in control of virtually everything south of the Danube. Only the Albanian mountains and Constantinople remained free.

In 1453 the great city, now seriously depopulated, fell to Mehmet "the Conqueror" after a long siege. The Byzantine Empire had ceased to exist. The church of St. Sophia became a mosque, and the Greeks, together with the other Balkan peoples, became subjects of the Ottoman sultan. Their faith and much of their culture was preserved, for the Turks did not believe in forced conversions. They would not regain political independence until the nineteenth century.

The Hundred Years' War in the West

The Hundred Years' War, though centered on France and England, was a generalized west European conflict that also involved the Low Countries and the Iberian kingdoms of Castile, Aragon, and Portugal. Because its active phases were interspersed with periods of relative peace, regarding it not as one war but as several whose underlying causes were related is probably best. The most immediate of these causes was the ongoing struggle over the status of English fiefs in France. The

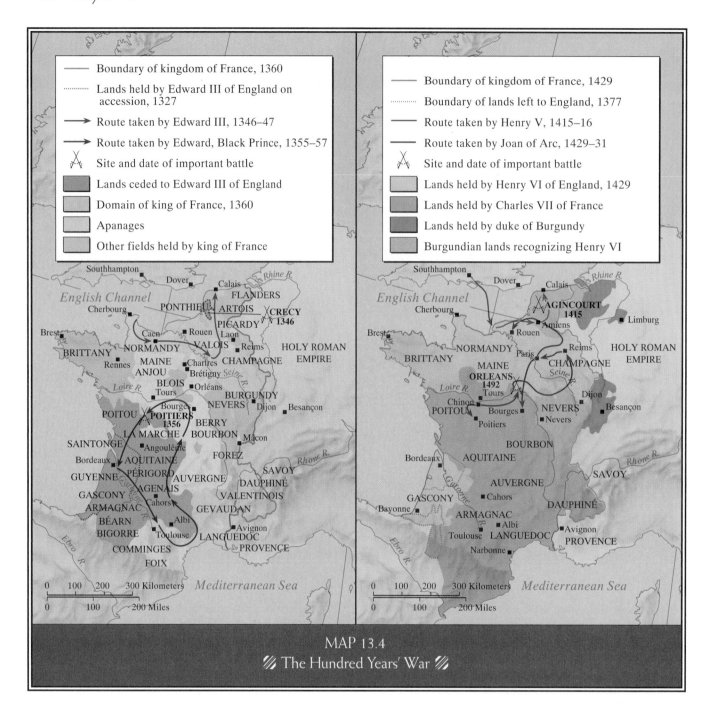

MAP 13.4
The Hundred Years' War

situation was complicated by dynastic instability and by the weakening of feudal institutions as a whole.

Of all the problems created by feudalism, none was more exasperating than the ambivalent situation of the kings of England. For two centuries they had struggled with their dual role as French vassals and as sovereign princes whose interests were frequently in conflict with those of France (see chapter 9). Every reign since that of Henry II had produced disputes over Guienne and Gascony. Another French attempt to confiscate these

fiefs led to the outbreak of the Hundred Years' War in spring 1337 (see map 13.4).

This action by Philip VI of France came at the end of a long diplomatic crisis. Nearly a decade earlier Philip had been proclaimed king when his cousin, Charles IV, died without male heirs. The claim of England's Edward III, son of Charles's sister, had been denied on the controversial premise that the Salic law forbade royal inheritance through the female line. Edward, young and beset with internal enemies, chose not to press the point. Relations gradually deteriorated when Philip began to pursue more aggressive policies on several fronts. In the year of his coronation he recaptured the county of Flanders from the urban rebels who had achieved independence from France in 1302. This represented a threat to the primary market for English wool, as Philip was now in a position to forbid its importation. Philip then changed the nature of the homage owed for Guienne from "simple" to "liege" homage, meaning that Edward was now bound to defend him "before any man." Worst of all, he supported Edward's enemies in Scotland.

By 1336 Edward was secure on his throne and began preparing for war. Papal attempts at mediation failed, and in May 1337, Philip ordered the confiscation of English fiefs in France, citing Edward's support for the Flemish rebels and other sins against feudal obligation as a pretext.

The first phase of the war went badly for France. This is at first sight surprising as England was by far the smaller and poorer of the two countries with a population only one-third that of her rival. The difference lay in superior leadership. Edward quickly proved to be not only an able commander, but also a master at extracting resources from Parliament. By defeating the French in a naval battle off Sluys in 1340 he secured control of the English Channel. Subsequent campaigns were fought on French soil, including the ones that culminated in the victories of Crécy (1346) and Poitiers (1356). In both cases, French cavalry employing traditional tactics were defeated by the imaginative use of longbows in massed formations.

The treaty of Bretigny (1360) secured a breathing space of seven years during which the locus of violence shifted to the Iberian Peninsula. Conflict there centered on the policies of Pedro of Castile, known to the Castilian aristocracy as "the Cruel" and to his other subjects as "the Just." Pedro's nicknames arose from his efforts to strengthen the crown against the landed nobility. When he became involved in a border war with Pedro "the Ceremonious" of Aragon, the latter encouraged an uprising of Castilian nobles under the leadership of Enrique of Trastámara, Pedro the Cruel's half-brother. Enrique and his Aragonese ally then sought assistance from France.

They received it in part because of a phenomenon that surfaced for the first time after the peace of Bretigny. The practice of paying troops had created a class of men whose only trade was war and who, after a generation of fighting, had no place in civilian society. For them peace was a catastrophe that forced them to become beggars or bandits. Most understandably chose the latter. Roaming the countryside, often in their original companies, they lived by systematic pillage and extortion reinforced by the threat of murder, arson, and rape. The effect of their activities on a France already weakened by war, plague, and social disorder may be readily imagined.

The new French king, Charles V, was happy to dispatch a multinational contingent of these people to Spain under the command of Bertrand Duguesclin. Pedro of Castile responded by calling in the English under Edward of Woodstock, known as the Black Prince. The eldest son of Edward III and the winning commander at Poitiers, he repeated his triumph at Nájera in 1367. The Castilian war dragged on until 1398 when Enrique was able to kill Pedro with his own hands and gain the throne. Because Enrique had won with the aid of the Castilian aristocracy, he was forced to confirm and extend their privileges, thereby guaranteeing that his successors would be faced with internal disorder. His victory was a defeat, not only for Pedro, but also for the state-building ideals he represented.

An aftereffect of the Spanish war was the pretext for reviving Anglo-French hostilities. To pay for his Castilian adventure, the Black Prince so taxed his subjects in Guienne that they appealed to Charles V for help. The war that followed was far less dramatic than the first. Charles adopted a strategy of attrition, avoiding battle whenever possible and using the tactical skills of Duguesclin to harry and outmaneuver the English. By 1380 the English presence in France had been greatly reduced, but both kingdoms were at the limit of their resources. Fighting did not end completely. The next thirty-five years may be characterized as a period of military stalemate and internal disorder in both countries.

The last stage of the war began when Henry V of England invaded the continent in 1415. Ambitious and new to the throne, he sought to take advantage of the civil war then raging in France. The French king, Charles VI, had gone mad. His brother, the duke of Orléans, was named regent, thereby arousing the envy of John the Fearless, duke of Burgundy. Burgundy was perhaps the most powerful of the king's relatives. His appanage—estates granted to members of the ruling family—included the rich duchy of Burgundy and most of what is now Belgium and the Netherlands. He was probably wealthier than the king. John arranged the assassination of Orléans in 1407 only to see another rival, Count Bertrand VII of Armagnac, installed in his place. In the struggle that followed, Burgundy tried to ally himself with England, drawing back when he perceived the extent of Henry's ambitions. The English king saw that John would do nothing to defend Charles VI or his Armagnac supporters.

The English invasion was an immediate success. Using a variant of the tactics developed at Crécy and Poitiers, Henry crushed the French at Agincourt on October 25, 1415. Alarmed by the magnitude of the French defeat, Burgundy began to rethink his position, but he, too, was assassinated in 1419 by soldiers in the pay of the Armagnacs. His son, Philip, whose nickname "the Good" belied a ferocious temper, sought revenge by allying Burgundy once again with England.

The French king was virtually isolated. In 1420 he was forced to ratify the treaty of Troyes, which disinherited his son, the future Charles VII, in favor of Henry V. When Charles VI and Henry both died in 1422, Henry's infant son, Henry VI of England, was proclaimed king of France with the English duke of Bedford as regent. The proclamation aroused great indignation in much of France where Charles of Valois was accepted as the rightful king. Charles, unfortunately, was not an inspiring figure. Inarticulate, physically unimpressive, and only nineteen years old, he retired with his supporters to Bourges where he quickly developed a reputation for lethargy and indecision. The task of galvanizing public opinion was left to an extraordinary woman, Joan of Arc.

Joan was an illiterate peasant from the remote border village of Domrémy. When she came to Charles in March 1429 she was probably no older than twenty but had already achieved local fame for her religious visions (see document 13.8). She told him that "voices" had instructed her to raise the English siege of Orleáns (see illustration 13.7), and Charles, who probably thought that he had little to lose, allowed her to go. The result was electrifying. By the time she arrived, the English had decided to give up, but the French did not know this. The apparently miraculous appearance of a young woman, dressed in armor and with her hair cut like a man's, was thought to have been the reason for the subsequent English retreat, and it created a sensation. The relief of Orleáns, which preserved the south of France for Charles, was followed by a string of victories that led to the repudiation of the treaty of Troyes and his coronation at Rheims in July. All of this was popularly attributed to Joan who was present throughout. She never commanded troops, but her inspiration gave them confidence, and even civilians, oppressed by a century of apparently pointless warfare, were roused to enthusiasm.

<hr>

◆ DOCUMENT 13.8 ◆

Joan of Arc

This is an extract from a letter written on behalf of Joan— "The Maid"—to the king of England, the duke of Bedford, and their associates in 1429. It demonstrates her sense of mission and the spirit that ultimately drove the English from French soil.

I am a chieftain of war, and whenever I meet your followers in France, I will drive them out; if they will not obey, I will put them all to death. I am sent here in God's name, the King of Hevane, to drive you body for body out of all France. If they obey, I will show them mercy. Do not think otherwise; you will not withhold the kingdom of France from God, the King of Kings, Blessed Mary's Son. The King Charles, the true inheritor, will possess it, for God wills it and has revealed it to him through *The Maid*, and he will enter Paris with a good company. If you do not believe these tidings from God and *The Maid*, wherever we find you we shall strike you and make a greater tumult than France has seen in a thousand years. Know well that the King of Heaven will send a greater force to *The Maid* and her good people than you in all your assaults can overcome: and by blows shall the favor of the God of Heaven be seen. You Duke of Bedford, *The Maid* prays that and beseeches you not to bring yourself to destruction. If you obey her you may join her company, where the French shall do the fairest deed ever done for Christendom. Answer, if you desire peace in the city of Orleáns; if not, bethink you of your great hurt soon. Written this Tuesday of Holy Week.

<hr>

Unfortunately for Joan, Charles was not quite the fool he sometimes appeared to be. When she was captured by the English in 1430 he did nothing to secure her release or to prevent her from being tried at Rouen on charges of witchcraft and heresy. He no doubt preferred to take credit for his own victories and may have regarded her popularity as an embarrassment. The verdict was a foregone conclusion. Bedford was determined to discredit her as an agent of the devil, and she was burned at the stake on May 30, 1431. Her habit of dressing as a man was taken as evidence of diabolical intent. Twenty-five years later, in a gesture of

Illustration 13.7

The Siege of Orléans, 1428–29. The English are shown at left behind their siegeworks firing across the Loire River at the city of Orléans. The siege, which involved an early large-scale use of artillery, was a turning point in the Hundred Years' War, though its outcome had little to do with the new technology. The inspirational example of Joan of Arc forced the English to abandon their siege, and they never regained the initiative.

belated gratitude, Charles VII reopened the case and had her declared innocent. The church made her a saint in 1920.

Joan's brief career offers a disquieting vision of fifteenth-century attitudes toward women, but it was a turning point for France. In 1435 Charles was reconciled with Philip the Good of Burgundy, and by 1453 the English had been driven out of France in a series of successful campaigns that left them with only the port of Calais as a continental base.

Political Turbulence and Dynastic Collapse: France, Castile, and England

Dynastic failures played a major role in continuing and intensifying the Hundred Years' War. In a system based on heredity, the failure of a ruling dynasty to produce competent heirs in a timely manner meant either a disputed succession or a regency. The effect of a disputed succession may be seen in the origins of the war itself, in which the failure of all three of Philip IV's sons to produce heirs gave Edward III of England a pretext for his quarrel with Philip of Valois, or in Castile, where a similar failure by Pedro the Cruel encouraged the pretensions of his half-brother Enrique.

Regencies occurred when the legitimate heir could not govern by reason of youth or mental incapacity. An individual regent or a regency council might be designated in the will of a dying monarch or by agreement within the royal family, but these appointments were

almost always contested. The reason lay in the structure of European elites. Each branch of the royal family and each of the great landholding clans were a center of wealth, power, and patronage to which other elements of society were drawn by interest or by hereditary obligation. Rivalries were inevitable, and the king's duty was to serve as a kind of referee, using his superior rank to ensure that no one became an "overmighty subject." Failure to perform this role in an adequate manner was often equated with bad governance.

By these standards, no regency could be good. Regents were usually either princes of the blood or connected with a particular faction of the royal family. They were partial almost by definition. Once installed they were in a position to use the wealth and power of the crown to advance their factional interests while threatening the estates and the lives of their rivals. Those excluded from a regency often felt that they had no alternative but to rebel, though their rebellions were usually directed not at the semisacred person of the king, but at his "evil counselors." This happened in the struggle between John the Fearless and the Armagnacs. The result was a civil war and renewed English intervention in France.

Other forms of dynastic failure had similar effects. In some cases, adult, presumably functional, rulers behaved so foolishly that their subjects rebelled. Castile in particular suffered from this ailment throughout much of the fifteenth century. Juan II (1405–54) left the government in the hands of Alvaro de Luna, a powerful noble whose de facto regency factionalized the grandees, the highest rank of Spanish nobles who were not princes of the blood. Juan's son, Enrique IV "the Impotent" was generally despised for his homosexuality, his tendency to promote low-born lovers over the hereditary nobility, and for his failure to maintain order. Faced with a monarchy they could neither support nor respect, the great landholding families raised private armies and kept the country in a state of near-anarchy until 1479.

In England, the regency appointed during the minority of Richard II was accepted largely because the social unrest that culminated in the revolt of 1381 forced the aristocracy to close ranks. When he came of age, the favoritism and ineptitude of the young king aroused such opposition that he was deposed and murdered in 1399. Reflecting contemporary attitudes, Richard, like Enrique IV of Castile, was accused of homosexuality. The reign of Henry VI—from 1422 to 1461 and 1470 to 1471—was even more chaotic than that of Richard II. Coming to the throne as an infant, Henry remained under the control of others throughout his life. Though respected for his piety he was wholly incapable of governing and suffered a complete mental breakdown in 1453. His incapacity led to the War of the Roses, a nine-year struggle between the Lancastrian and Yorkist branches of the royal family that ended with a Yorkist victory at Tewksbury in 1471 and the murder of yet another English king (see chapter 14).

Whether the result of royal inbreeding or sheer bad luck, these dynastic failures retarded the development of western European states. The increasing cost of and sophistication of war were a powerful impetus to the growth of royal power, but these anarchic interludes tended to interfere with bureaucratic development and to strengthen local privilege, at least temporarily. Feudal nobles whose position was threatened by economic and military change often saw them as an opportunity to recover lost ground. Above all they added to the sense of dislocation created by plague, war, and social change.

Art and Literature: The Measure of Discontent

By the end of the fourteenth century, the accumulation of disasters was having an impact on the art and literature of Europe. The bonds of society seemed to be unraveling. Lords abandoned their ostensible function as the military protectors of society and compensated for

Illustration 13.8

Nostalgia for a Past That Had Never Been. Happy peasants toil beneath the walls of a fairy tale castle in this fifteenth-century illumination, which is from the *Très riches heures du Duc du Berry*.

declining rents by preying upon their tenants. Peasants responded when they could by abandoning their tenures. The idea of mutual obligation that lay at the heart of feudalism could no longer be sustained, and many, including the fourteenth-century author of the English poem *Piers Plowman*, came to believe that greed and self-interest were everywhere triumphant. Moralists complained that the simpler manners of an earlier day had given way to extravagance and debauchery. War was endemic and all the more intolerable because it did not end for the common people when a truce was signed. They still had to pay for it through taxes while trying to defend themselves against unemployed sol-

◆ DOCUMENT 13.9 ◆

The Vision of Death

Georges Chastellain (c. 1415–75) was a Burgundian courtier best known for his Chronicle, *but he also wrote poetry. The following excerpt is from a long poem entitled* Le Pas de la Mort (The Dance of Death). *It reveals an obsession with the physical aspects of death that was typical of the age.*

There is not a limb nor a form,
Which does not smell of putrefaction.
Before the soul is outside,
The heart which wants to burst the body
Raises and lifts the chest
Which nearly touches the backbone
—The face is discolored and pale,
And the eyes veiled in the head.
Speech fails him,
For the tongue cleaves to the palate.
The pulse trembles and he pants.
The bones are disjointed on all sides;
There is not a tendon which does not stretch as to burst.

diers who often did more damage than the war itself. Plague, the conquests by the Turk, and the rule of imbecile kings were seen by many as signs of God's wrath.

The expression of these concerns varied. At one extreme was the upper-class tendency to take refuge in nostalgia for a largely fictional past. This took the form not only of chivalric fantasies, but also of the idyllic visions offered in the *Tres riches heures du Duc du Berry,* a magnificently illustrated prayer book in which happy peasants toil near palaces that seem to float on air (see illustration 13.8). At the other extreme was a fascination with the physical aspects of death (see illustration 13.9). The art of the period abounds with representations of skeletons and putrifying corpses. The Dance of Death in which corpses lead the living in a frenzied round that ends with the grave became a common motif in art and literature (see document 13.9) and was performed in costume on festive occasions. Popular sermons emphasized the brevity of life and the art of dying well, while series of popular woodcuts illustrated in horrifying detail how death would come to the knight, the scholar, the beauty, and a whole host of other human stereotypes. Not surprisingly, the word *macabre* seems to have entered the French language at about this time.

Despair became fashionable, but it was not universal. In Brabant and Flanders artists such as Roger van

Illustration 13.9

The Three Living and the Three Dead. The late medieval obsession with death is indicated by this fresco attributed to Francesco Traini (c. 1370). It illustrates the legend of the three living and the three dead and originally dominated the Campo Santo in Pisa where it served as a public reminder of the triumph of death.

Ilustration 13.10

 Detail from the Ghent Alterpiece. This panel, "The Knights of Christ," with its lovingly rendered costumes and harness is an example of fifteenth-century Flemish painter Jan van Eyck's preoccupation with the world of the senses.

der Weyden and the van Eycks developed techniques for portraying the beauties of the world with unprecedented mastery (see illustration 13.10). Their paintings, intended for display in churches and hospitals, dwelled lovingly on fine costumes, the brilliance of jewels, and the richness of everyday objects while portraying the hard, worldly faces of their owners with unflinching honesty. Regarding their work as an affirmative answer to the emphasis on death is tempting. Some certainly felt that because life was grim and short its pleasures should be enjoyed to the fullest. However, more exists to these paintings than meets the eye. Many of the beautifully rendered objects they portray are also symbols of a moral or spiritual value whose meaning would have been clear to all who saw them. The medieval fondness for allegory survived the fourteenth century and may even have grown stronger with time.

The people of the later Middle Ages still used religious language and religious imagery to express themselves. They still thought in religious, traditional, and hierarchic terms, but their faith in traditional assumptions and values had been shaken badly by events they barely understood. They looked with dismay upon what had happened, but the transformation of their world had just begun.

Conclusion

The fourteenth and fifteenth centuries are generally held to mark the end of the Middle Ages. By 1300 economic conditions had begun to deteriorate, and in 1347–50 the great epidemic known as the bubonic plague or Black Death killed nearly a third of Europe. Faced with these shocks, the bonds of feudal society began to unravel. Declining rents and the rising cost of labor impoverished the landholding classes while attempts to turn back the clock through legislation caused riot and social disorder. In the short term, peasants benefited from inheritance and high wage rates. But as the ties of feudal obligation weakened and lands were transformed from fiefs to capital investments, the face of European agriculture began to change. In many areas, stock raising began to replace row crops, and peasants were dispossessed.

Warfare, too, changed. The commutation of feudal services for cash made it possible to pay men to fight. This monetarization of warfare further undermined the position of the feudal classes because they lacked the sovereign rights to levy taxes or coin money. At the same time, the development of new weapons systems greatly increased the size and cost of armies. The Hundred Years' War, complicated by intervals of political and dynastic collapse in each of the participating countries, was fought on a scale that had no precedent in feudal times. In eastern Europe, turmoil reigned from the Balkans to the shores of the Baltic. To many, society seemed in danger of collapse, but as always, new institutions and ideas were beginning to emerge from the ruins of the old.

Suggested Readings

Attempts to understand the later Middle Ages should begin with the classic J. Huizinga, *The Waning of the Middle Ages* (1949). B. Tuchman, *A Distant Mirror: The Calamitous Fourteenth Century* (1980) is a popular, best-selling, and memorable vision of the age. For the famines, see I. Kershaw, "The Great Famine and Agricultural Crisis in England, 1315–1322," *Past and Present*, vol. 59 (May 1973). R. Gottfried, *The Black Death* (1983) is the most recent account of the plague. See also P. Ziegler, *The Black Death* (1969).

W. H. McNeill, *Plagues and Peoples* (1976) discusses the impact of epidemic disease in general. H. Miskimin, *The Economy of Early Renaissance Europe, 1300–1460* (1975) is the best study of economic matters. See J. Hatcher, *Plague, Population, and the English Economy, 1348–1550* (1977) for the economic and social consequences of the plague in England. G. Huppert, *After the Black Death: A Social History of Early Modern Europe* (1986) is a good, brief survey, while M. Meiss, *Painting in Florence and Siena after the Black Death* (1964) is a fine essay on the cultural effects of the plague. M. Mollat and P. Wolff, *The Popular Revolutions of the Late Middle Ages* (1973) surveys both peasant and urban revolts.

General works that cover military innovations in the later Middle Ages include P. Contamine, *War in the Middle Ages* (1984), which is especially good on the development of artillery, and J. Verbruggen, *The Art of War in Western Europe during the Middle Ages* (1977). On the evolution of the ship, see R. Unger, *The Ship in the Medieval Economy* (1980), F. C. Lane, *Venetian Ships and Shipbuilders of the Renaissance* (1934), and the profusely illustrated R. Gardner and others, eds., *Cogs, Caravels and Galleons* (1994).

For the tribulations of Russia, begin with D. Morgan, *The Mongols* (1986), J. Fennell, *The Crisis of Medieval Russia, 1200–1304* (1983), and C. Halperin, *Russia and the Golden Horde: The Mongol Impact on Medieval Russian History* (1985). I. Grey, *Ivan III and the Unification of Russia* (1964) is a brief biography of the founder of the Muscovite state. For Poland, see N. Davies, *Poland: God's Playground* (1981) and P. Knoll, *The Rise of the Polish Monarchy* (1971). The standard work on the Ottomans is H. Inalcik, *The Ottoman Empire: The Classical Age* (1973). S. Runciman, *The Fall of Constantinople 1435* (1965) is excellent. For late medieval Hungary, see P. Sugar and others, *A History of Hungary*, chapters 4–6 (1990).

The best accounts of the Hundred Years' War are E. Perroy, *The Hundred Years' War* (1951) and C. Allmand, *The Hundred Years' War: England and France at War, c. 1300–1450* (1988). See also D. Seward, *The Hundred Years' War: The English in France, 1337–1453* (1981). Tactics, strategy, and related matters are discussed in P. Contamine, *War in the Middle Ages* (1984) and H. Koch, *Medieval Warfare* (1978), while J. Keegan provides a compelling account of Agincourt in *The Face of Battle* (1977). M. Warner, *Joan of Arc: The Image of Female Heroism* (1981) is the best study of "The Maid." M. Postan, "The Costs of the Hundred Years' War," *Past and Present*, vol. 27 (April 1964) examines the financial impact of the war, while J. Barnie, *War in Medieval English Society: Social Values and the Hundred Years' War* (1974) looks at its social consequences. On the Hundred Years' War in Spain, see the pertinent chapters of J. O'Callaghan, *Medieval Spain* (1975), J. N. Hillgarth, *The Spanish Kingdoms, 1250–1516*, vol. 1 (1978), and C. Estow, *Pedro the Cruel* (1995).

CHAPTER 14
THE RENAISSANCE: POLITICAL RENEWAL AND INTELLECTUAL CHANGE

CHAPTER OUTLINE

Changes in the conduct of warfare and the erosion of feudal institutions after 1300 rendered the feudal monarchies of Europe obsolete. Chapter 14 begins by describing the way in which the need to pay for war created a new kind of state, administered by salaried bureaucrats and defended by paid soldiers. Though the policies of these states were governed by dynastic instead of national considerations and regional differences were accepted to a degree unimaginable today, the monarchies that emerged from this process in the later fifteenth century are the recognizable ancestors of the modern state.

At approximately the same time a new intellectual movement began in the Italian city-states and, by the end of the fifteenth century, had spread throughout Europe. Under the influence of such writers as Petrarch and Boccaccio, Italians began to reinterpret the ancient Greco-Roman past and apply the lessons of that reimagined period to their own times. In the process they transformed virtually all of the arts and sciences, gave birth to the modern study of politics and history, and created a model for liberal arts education that persisted, with some modifications, into the early twentieth century. They changed the way in which Westerners thought, not only about human affairs, but also about the physical sciences. This movement is known as the Renaissance, and the term has been used conventionally to describe the entire age in which Western learning and the state itself moved away from medieval precedents and began to lay the foundations of the modern world. The chapter will conclude by examining the origins of the Renaissance in Italy and tracing the spread and influence of the movement throughout Europe.

The Consolidation of the State (c.1350–1500)

Medieval princes had worked, with varying degrees of success, to improve administration and strengthen royal authority. Most royal governments remained modest in size and centered firmly on the royal household until the later years of the thirteenth century. Under Henry III of England (reigned 1234–72), for example, the royal budget hovered consistently in the range of £12,500 per annum. His son, Edward I, managed to spend more than £750,000 on war alone from 1297 to 1302, in part because he paid most of his fighting men in cash. Such figures indicate why the military revolution of the fourteenth and fifteenth centuries intensified the process of state building begun by such monarchs as Edward I and Philip the Fair. Faced with a massive increase in the cost of war, sovereign states had to maximize their incomes from every conceivable source to survive.

One way of achieving this was to expand the ruler's personal domain and to exploit it more efficiently. Domain revenues fell into two main categories. First, rents, fees, and other income were taken from lands held directly by the prince. The size of the domain could be increased by keeping property that reverted to the sovereign through confiscation or in default of heirs. In the feudal past such lands had often been given to other subjects almost as soon as they were received. By 1450 most states were trying to reverse this practice, and some were actively seeking new pretexts for confiscation. Second, other domain revenues came from the exercise of traditional rights that might include anything from the collection of customs duties to monopolies on such vital commodities as salt. The yield from these sources was regarded as the personal property of the crown and, like profits from the land, could be increased primarily through better administration.

Bureaucracies composed of "servants of the crown," paid in cash and serving at the pleasure of their ruler, were a legacy of the thirteenth century. They grew larger and more assertive with the passage of time. As the careers of the bureaucrats depended upon producing new revenue, they sought not only to improve efficiency but also to discover new rights for which few precedents often existed. Their efforts brought the state into conflict with privileges that had long been claimed by towns, guilds, private individuals, and the church. As such conflicts usually ended in the law courts, the state found strengthening its control over the legal system desirable. Manorial courts and other forms of private jurisdiction were therefore attacked for their independence as well as for the fines and court costs they levied that might otherwise go to the state. From the ruler's point of view, establishing courts by his or her own prerogative was far better, because a court in which the judge was a servant of the crown might de-

liver more favorable verdicts and bring in money that might otherwise be lost.

The expansion of prerogative courts, though controversial, was eased by the growing acceptance of Roman or civil law. The extensive development of canon law by the church during the eleventh and twelfth centuries had sparked a revival of interest in Justinian's code among laymen. By the thirteenth century, Roman legal principles had almost supplanted customary law in the empire and in Castile, where they formed the basis of the *Siete Partidas*, the great legal code adopted by Alfonso X (reigned 1252–84). In France and England, the principles of civil law tended instead to modify common law practice, but Roman law gained ground steadily through the fifteenth century. Everywhere, rulers—and the prerogative courts they established— preferred Roman procedures because the customary law, with its reliance on precedent and the use of juries, provided a stronger basis for resisting the claims of sovereignty. But these same virtues ensured that court proceedings would be long and therefore costly. People often asked that their cases be transferred to prerogative or civil law courts in the hope of a speedier judgment.

Though individuals might sometimes benefit from the state's activities, as a general rule, all attempts to increase domain revenue carried a high political cost. Only a strong, popular prince could overcome the entrenched resistance of powerful interests, which is why the dynastic failures of the late fourteenth and early fifteenth centuries delayed the extension of sovereignty even if they could not stop it completely.

The character of princes also affected their ability to impose taxes, the second route by which the power of the state might be increased. Taxes, unlike domain revenues, could be raised only with the consent of representative bodies. Late medieval assemblies generally voted taxes for a specified period of time, thereby forcing the princes to come back each year, hat in hand, to hear the complaints of their subjects. If the prince was popular, or if the taxes were needed to meet a genuine crisis, the sums involved might vastly exceed those generated from domain revenues, yet parliamentary bodies that held "the power of the purse" restricted the exercise of sovereignty. Most rulers no doubt preferred to "live of their own," but this was rarely possible in time of war.

The only solution to this dilemma was to convince hard-headed representatives of the landholding and merchant classes to grant at least some taxes on a perpetual basis on the theory that threats to the kingdom's integrity would never end. This was not easy, even in the interminable chaos of the Hundred Years' War, but the states that succeeded, notably France and Castile, became the great powers of the succeeding age. Not only did perpetual taxes make the revenues of these countries greater in real terms than those of their neighbors, but they also made them predictable. Budgeting for the long term became possible without the interference of elected bodies whose interests were not necessarily those of the prince. Above all, perpetual taxes made borrowing money easier because lenders could be guaranteed a return based on projected revenues.

Whether perpetual or temporary, late medieval and early modern taxes were usually levied on some form of moveable property. The governments of the day lacked the administrative technology to monitor personal incomes, and land, though it was the principle form of wealth, was usually tax exempt for a variety of political and historical reasons. The goods of merchants and artisans were fair game, as were the commodities offered for sale by peasants. Taxes on moveable property were regressive in the sense that wealthy landholders and rentiers could usually avoid them, but their impact on other social groups is hard to measure. Collection was never uniform and was rarely undertaken directly by the state. The most common practice was to negotiate the proposed yield from a tax with local authorities who would then be responsible for its collection. The rates collected were usually not those set by the legislation. Whatever their amount, late medieval taxes fell predominantly on the most economically active, if not the richest, segments of the population.

Governments knew this and attempted to encourage the transfer of resources from tax-exempt to taxable activities. This is one reason for their almost universal efforts to foster trade, mining, and manufacturing. It also helps to explain the policy, common to both England and Castile, of favoring sheepherders at the expense of those who cultivated the soil. Wool could be taxed; subsistence agriculture could not. Such policies clearly influenced economic development, but their overall impact on growth or on public well-being may have been negative. Taxes were ultimately paid by the consumer and were therefore a burden to be added to those already imposed by landholders in their efforts to compensate for falling rents.

Moreover, the maximization of tax yields often required changes in land use. Governments, through the decisions of their prerogative courts, tended to favor the extension of personal property rights over the claims of feudal privilege. An example was the English policy of encouraging landholders to enclose common lands for grazing. This practice, which reached a peak at the beginning of the sixteenth century, broke feudal precedent and sometimes forced the expulsion of peasants who needed the marginal income provided by the commons for survival. As Sir Thomas More put it, "[I]n England, sheep eat men." This was perhaps an extreme case, and enclosures may not have been as common as More thought, but everywhere the extension of personal property rights to land had the immediate effect of favoring governments and landholders at the expense of peasants. Thus, the most insistent demand of German peasant revolutionaries was for a return to the "old law" that protected their feudal status.

If one part of state building was finding new revenues, the other was developing more efficient mechanisms by which they could be spent. Most late medieval states found this more difficult than locating the money in the first place. Bureaucracies whose purpose was to supply the needs of war grew like mushrooms but remained inefficient by modern standards until after the industrial revolution. They were inhibited in part by the same sense of corporate and personal privilege that resisted other aspects of state growth, but the underlying problem was structural. Communications were poor, and no precedent had been set for many basic administrative procedures. Archives, the basic tool of record keeping, were rare before the mid-sixteenth century. Censuses were unknown outside the Italian city-states, and how they might have been conducted in such kingdoms as France with their immense distances and isolated populations is hard to imagine. To make matters worse, the costs of war continued to grow more rapidly than the sources of revenue. Neither taxation nor the development of public credit kept pace, and money was often in desperately short supply. Because soldiers and officials were often paid poorly and at irregular intervals, governments were forced to tolerate high levels of what would today be called corruption. Bribery, the sale of offices, and the misappropriation of funds were common even in those states that prided themselves on their high administrative standards. The situation would improve under the "absolutist" regimes of the eighteenth century, but the improvements were relative.

No two states were alike. Though all were confronted with the need for consolidation and new revenues, they achieved their objectives in different ways according to their circumstances and traditions. The city-states of Italy evolved along lines of their own and have been considered separately in Chapter 11. The sovereign kingdoms and principalities must be examined individually or in regional groups if their development is to be understood.

The Iberian Kingdoms: Ferdinand and Isabella

The Iberian Peninsula was in some ways an unlikely birthplace for two of the most successful early modern states. Difficult terrain and an average annual rainfall of twenty inches or less produced little surplus wealth. Ethnic, political, and religious differences were great. In 1400 no fewer than five kingdoms shared this rugged land. Portugal was probably the most homogeneous, though it possessed significant Muslim and Jewish minorities. Castile, comprising the two ancient kingdoms of León and Castile, contained not only Jews and Muslims, but also Basques and Galicians who, though devoutly Christian, possessed their own languages and cultures. The kingdom of Aragon had three separate regions: Aragon, Cataluña, and Valencia. Each of them had its own language and traditions, though the Aragonese spoke Castilian and some linguists regard Valencian as a dialect of Catalan. Finally, there was the kingdom of Granada, the last but still vigorous remnant of the Islamic Empire on European soil, and the tiny mountain kingdom of Navarre straddling the Pyrenees between Castile and France.

Portugal was the first European state to achieve consolidation, just as it would be the first to acquire an overseas empire. During most of the fourteenth century it suffered like other monarchies from intrigue, dynastic failures, and ill-advised forays into the Hundred Years' War. In 1385 the Portuguese Cortes solved a succession crisis by crowning the late king's illegitimate son as John I. In the same year, John defeated the Castilians in a decisive battle at Aljubarrotta and suppressed most of the old feudal nobility, many of whom had supported the enemy. Under his descendants, the house of Avis, Portugal avoided the revolts and dynastic failures that troubled other states and evolved virtually without interruption until 1580.

Spain was another matter. Aragon and Castile had long been troubled by civil wars. Castile established a precedent for perpetual taxes in 1367, but the usurpation of Enrique of Trastámara left the crown dependent upon the nobles who had supported him. His successors, especially Juan II and Enrique IV "the Impotent," were incapable of maintaining order, in part because their favorites aroused the jealousy of the grandees. The accession of Enrique's half-sister Isabella and her marriage to Ferdinand of Aragon brought an end to the period of anarchy and led to the eventual union of the two kingdoms (see document 14.1). Isabella and Ferdinand inherited their respective thrones in 1479, a decade after their marriage. Each ruled independently, but they cooperated on the broad outlines of policy,

◆ DOCUMENT 14.1 ◆

Isabella of Castille

Baldassare Castiglione's The Courtier *was the foremost Renaissance treatise on manners and education and was an important influence on the values of the European upper classes. Though Italian, he was well informed on Spanish affairs and believed that Isabella, far more than Ferdinand, was responsible for Spain's newfound greatness. In this passage, written perhaps a decade after the queen's death in 1504, he describes the impression that Isabella made on her contemporaries.*

[A]ll who knew her affirm that she had such a divine manner of ruling that her mere wish seemed enough to make every man do what he was supposed to do; so that men, in their own houses and secretly, scarcely dared to do anything that they thought might displease her; and this was due in large part to the admirable judgment she showed in recognizing and choosing able ministers for those offices in which she intended to use them; and so well did she know how to combine the rigor of justice with the gentleness of mercy and liberality that in her day there was no good man who complained of being too little rewarded by her nor any bad man of being too severely punished. There arose thus among the people a very great veneration for her, comprised of love and fear, and a veneration so fixed in the minds of all that it almost seems that they expect her to be watching them from heaven, and think she might praise or blame them from up there; and so those realms are still governed by her fame and by the methods instituted by her, so that, though her life is ended, her authority lives on.

and an agreement was reached that their heirs would rule a united Spain by hereditary right.

The program of the Catholic kings, as they were called, was greatly assisted by the weariness brought on by decades of civil strife. The nobles of Castile were pacified by confirming their titles to all lands acquired by them, legally or illegally, before 1466 and by the judicious granting of *mayorazgos* or entails permitting them to exclude younger children from their inheritances. This was important because, under Spanish law, property was normally divided equally among the heirs, a practice that tended to deplete a family's wealth and influence over time. In return, the grandees agreed to give up all the land they had taken illegally after 1466 and to disband their private armies.

The towns, too, had suffered in the civil wars. Clientage and kinship ties were powerful in Castilian society, and many cities had fallen under the control of factions that persecuted their rivals mercilessly. At the Cortes of Toledo in 1480 the royal towns of Castile agreed to the appointment of *corregidores*, royal officials who would reside in the city, protect the interests of the crown, and supervise elections. This ensured a high degree of royal authority over city governments and over those who were elected to represent them in the Cortes. The consequent willingness of this body to support new taxes and other royal initiatives was to become an important cornerstone of Spanish power.

None of these measures applied to Aragon. To ensure domestic peace, Ferdinand was forced to confirm a series of rights and privileges granted by his father in 1472 at the height of the civil wars. These concessions, however, were less important than they might appear. The kingdom of Aragon was far smaller than Castile and its most vital region, Cataluña, had been declining economically for more than a century. Castile was destined to be the dominant partner in this union of the crowns, and its dominance was only enhanced by its centralized institutions and higher level of taxation. In both kingdoms, administration was reformed and the crown's already extensive control over church appointments was strengthened.

With their realms at peace, the monarchs turned their attention to the kingdom of Granada. After ten years of bitter warfare, the Muslim state was conquered in 1492, the same year in which Columbus sailed for the New World. It was also the year in which the Jews were expelled from Spain, for the Catholic kings were committed to a policy of religious uniformity. Fanned by popular preachers, anti-Jewish sentiment had led to pogroms and a wave of forced conversions between 1390 and 1450. Many of these conversions were thought to be false, and the Spanish Inquisition, an organization wholly unrelated to the Papal Inquisition, was founded at the beginning of Ferdinand and Isabella's reign to root out *conversos* who had presumably returned to the faith of their ancestors. Large numbers of converts were executed or forced to do penance during the 1480s, and their property was confiscated to help finance the Granadan war. The Inquisition, as a church court, had jurisdiction over only those who had been baptized. The Jews who had escaped forced conversion were comparatively few and usually poor, but even a small minority was a threat to the faith of the

conversos. Those who still refused conversion were at last expelled. Some fled to Portugal, only to be expelled by the Portuguese as well in 1496. Others went to North Africa or found refuge within the Turkish Empire, while a few eventually settled in the growing commercial cities of the Low Countries.

The war for Granada and the supplies of money guaranteed by the perpetual taxes and cooperative legislature of Castile enabled Ferdinand to create a formidable army that was put to almost constant use in the last years of the reign. Through bluff, diplomacy, and hard fighting he restored Cerdanya and Rosseló to Cataluña and conquered the ancient kingdom of Navarre. When Charles VIII of France invaded Italy in 1495, Ferdinand used his actions as a pretext to intervene. This first phase of the Italian wars lasted until 1513. Under the command of Gonsalvo de Córdoba, "the Great Captain," Spanish armies devised a new method of combining pikes with shot that defeated the French and their Swiss mercenaries and drove them from the peninsula. Spain added the kingdoms of Sicily and Naples to its growing empire and became the dominant power in Italian affairs at the expense of Italy's independence.

Isabella died in 1504; Ferdinand in 1516. So firm were the foundations they had built that the two crowns were able to survive the unpopular regency of Cardinal Francisco Jiménez (or Ximénez) de Cisneros in Castile. The cardinal not only preserved the authority of the crown, but also made substantial progress in reforming abuses in the Spanish church and in improving the education of the clergy. When the grandson of the Catholic kings, the emperor Charles V, ascended the two thrones and unified them in 1522, he inherited a realm that stretched from Italy to Mexico, the finest army in Europe, and a regular income from taxes that rested firmly on the shoulders of Castilian taxpayers (see map 14.1).

France: Charles VII and Louis XI

France, too, emerged from the Hundred Years' War with perpetual taxes that freed its monarchs from their dependence on representative institutions. The most important of these was the *taille*, a direct tax of feudal origin that was assigned exclusively to the crown in 1439. In a series of ordinances passed between 1445 and 1459, Charles VII made it perpetual and extended it throughout his realm. The *taille* became the largest and most predictable source of crown revenue and virtually eliminated the need for the Estates General,

MAP 14.1

⚜ Europe in the Renaissance ⚜

which met only once between 1484 and 1789. The meetings of the Estates General at Tours in 1484 redoubled the royal desire to avoid future meetings by producing loud complaints about the impoverishment of the people by royal taxes (see document 14.2). Charles also laid the goundwork for a professional army, a national administration, and a diplomatic corps. That a monarch who was in many ways personally unimpressive should have accomplished so much is perhaps a tribute to his subjects' determination to drive the English from French soil. To accomplish this, they were prepared to make sacrifices that would otherwise have been unacceptable.

His son, Louis XI (ruled 1461–83), went further. Most of Louis's reign was consumed by a bitter feud with the dukes of Burgundy, who had established a formidable, multilingual state along his eastern borders.

Including Burgundy, the Franche-Comté, Artois, Picardy, the Boulonnais, and most of what is now Belgium and the Netherlands, it was almost certainly the wealthiest principality in Europe. Under Duke Philip "the Good" (d. 1467), it surpassed most kingdoms in courtly magnificence and in the richness of its musical and artistic life, but it was not a kingdom. Most of its territories were held in fief either from the Holy Roman Empire or from France. To enhance his independence, Philip had supported the English and some discontented elements of the French nobility against Louis in the League of the Common Weal, which Louis defeated in 1465. Philip's son, Charles (known to some as "the Bold" and to others as "the Rash"), hoped to weld his holdings into a single territorial state stretching from the Alps to the North Sea. His ambitions brought him into conflict with the duke of Lorraine and with

◆ DOCUMENT 14.2 ◆

Complaints of the French Estates General, 1484

When the French Estates General brought together representatives of the clergy, the nobility, and the commons (or third estate), these representatives produced pamphlets known as cahiers, describing their grievances. The following excerpt from a cahier of 1484 gives a vivid complaint of the third estate against royal taxation.

One cannot imagine the persecution, poverty, and misery that the little people have suffered, and still suffer in many ways.

First of all, no region has been safe from the continual coming and going of armies, living off the poor. . . . One should note with pity the injustice, the iniquity, suffered by the poor: the armies are hired to defend them, yet these armies oppress them the most. The poor laborer must hire the soldiers who beat him, evict him from his house, make him sleep on the ground, and consume his substance. . . . When the poor laborer has worked long, weary, sweaty days, when he has harvested those fruits of his labor from which he expects to live, they come to take a share of it from him, to pay the armed men who may come to beat him soon. . . . If God did not speak to the poor and give them patience, they would succumb in despair.

For the intolerable burden of the *taille*, and the taxes—which the poor people of this kingdom have not carried alone, to be sure, because that is impossible—the burden under which they have died from hunger and poverty, the mere description of these taxes would cause infinite sadness and woe, tears of woe and pity, great sighs and groans from sorrowful hearts. And that is not mentioning the enormous evils that followed, the injustice, the violence, and the extortion whereby these taxes were imposed and seized.

---

the Swiss, whose independence he seemed to threaten. These formidable opponents, richly subsidized by Louis, defeated and killed Charles at the battle of Nancy in 1477.

Charles died without male heirs. His daughter Mary was the wife of the Hapsburg archduke, Maximilian, who would become emperor in 1486. Under Louis's interpretation of the Salic law she could not, as a woman, inherit her father's French fiefs. Maximilian was unable to defend his wife's claims, and in 1482 Burgundy, Picardy, and the Boulonnais reverted to the French crown.

The dismemberment of the Burgundian state was the capstone of Louis's career. It was accompanied by acquisitions of equal value. Louis may have been clever and ruthless, but he was also lucky. In 1480 René of Anjou died without heirs, leaving Anjou and the French segment of Bar to the crown. Maine and the kingdom of Provence were incorporated in the following year after the death of Duke Charles II, and the rights of succession to Brittany were purchased when it became apparent that its duke, too, would die without producing male heirs. When Louis died in 1483 he left a France whose borders were recognizably similar to those of today. Luck and a consistently antifemale interpretation of the laws of inheritance played their part, but he could not have done it without a superior army, fiscal independence, and great diplomatic skill. His immense resources permitted him to take advantage of the dynastic misfortunes of others.

England: The Yorkists and Tudors

England was far smaller in land area and in population than either France or Spain. Its population was also more homogeneous, though regional differences were still important until well into the sixteenth century. Perhaps because it dominated an island whose integrity was rarely threatened by foreign enemies, it failed to develop perpetual taxes and its Parliament never lost "the power of the purse." England's development was therefore unlike that of the great continental powers, and it remained a relatively minor player in international politics until late in the early modern period.

Henry VI (reigned 1422–61, 1470–71) came to the throne as an infant and suffered from protracted bouts of mental illness as an adult. He was never competent to rule in his own right. For the first thirty years of the reign his regency council fought bitterly among themselves, brought the kingdom to the edge of bankruptcy, and lost the remaining English possessions in France with the exception of Calais. Eventually, Richard, duke of York claimed the throne with the support of a powerful segment of the nobility. Richard was descended from Edmund of Langley, the fourth surviving son of Edward III, while the king was the great grandson of Edward's third son, John of Gaunt, duke of Lancaster. The civil war that followed is called the War of the Roses because the heraldic symbol of the Yorkists was a white rose; that of the Lancastrians, a red.

In the first phase of the war (1455–61) the Lancastrians were led by Henry's formidable queen, Margaret of Anjou. She defeated the Yorkists at Wakefield and at St. Albans but failed to take London. Richard was killed at Wakefield. His son, an able commander, took advantage of her hesitation. He entered London and had himself proclaimed king as Edward IV. The struggle continued, but Edward retained the throne with one brief interruption until 1483. The last half of his reign was characterized by imaginative and energetic reforms in the administration of the royal domain. As customs duties were an important part of crown revenues, Edward used his extensive personal contacts in the London merchant community to encourage the growth of trade. He eventually became a major investor himself. The proceeds from these efforts, together with a pension extorted from Louis XI to prevent Edward from invading France, left him largely independent of Parliament. Some thought his methods unkingly, but when he died in 1483 he left behind an improved administration and an immense fortune.

He also left two young sons under the guardianship of his brother. The brother quickly had himself proclaimed king as Richard III, and the two little princes disappeared from the Tower of London, never to be seen again. This usurpation caused several of the leading Yorkists to make common cause with the Lancastrians, and in 1485, Henry Tudor, the last remaining Lancastrian claimant to the throne, defeated and killed Richard at the battle of Bosworth.

As Henry VII (reigned 1485–1509), Tudor followed the policies of Edward IV (see illustration 14.1). A subtle diplomat, he avoided war, intensified the exploitation of his domain, and encouraged the development of trade. His Welsh connections—he had been born in Pembrokeshire and was partially of Welsh descent—secured him the cooperation of the principality and laid the groundwork for its eventual union with England in 1536.

The greatest threat to Henry's regime was the belligerence of the great nobles, many of whom continued to maintain private armies. He dealt with this menace through prerogative courts, including the Court of

Illustration 14.1

Henry VII of England. This portrait by an unknown Flemish artist was painted c. 1505. Shrewd, cynical, and devoid of chivalric illusions, Henry was typical of a generation of monarchs who transformed their kingdoms into something resembling the modern state.

King's Bench and the Star Chamber, so called because it met in a room decorated with painted stars. Staffed by royal appointees, these bodies levied heavy fines for a variety of offenses against the crown that eventually destroyed the military power of the great families. Paradoxically, Henry may have been aided by several pretenders to the throne who claimed to be one or another of the missing princes and who enjoyed the support of disgruntled Yorkists or other "over-mighty" subjects. The fines, confiscations, and executions imposed after each of these episodes added to the royal domain and further reduced the number of his enemies.

When Henry died in 1509 the treasury was full and the kingdom at peace. Many of the old feudal families were either impoverished or extinct, and a new elite composed largely of servants of the crown was begin-

❖ DOCUMENT 14.3 ❖

The Golden Bull, 1356

These brief exerpts from the Golden Bull, issued by the emperor Charles IV, provide a sense of its importance as a fundamental charter for imperial governance. The oath, at least, was frequently violated.

Chapter II. [The electors are to repeat this oath after the archbishop of Mainz]: I . . . swear on the holy gospels here before me, and by the faith which I owe to God and to the holy Roman Empire, with the aid of God , and according to my best judgment and knowledge, I will cast my vote, in this election of the king of the Romans and future emperor, for a person fitted to rule the Christian people. I will give my voice and vote freely, uninfluenced by any agreement, price, bribe, promise, or anything of the sort, by whatever name it may be called. So help me God and all the saints.

Chapter VII. When any electorate falls vacant for lack of heirs, the emperor or king of the Romans shall have the power to dispose of it as if it reverted to the empire, saving the rights, privileges, and customs of the kingdom of Bohemia, according to which the inhabitants of that kingdom have the right to elect their king in case of a vacancy.

Chapter XII. It has been decided in the general diet held at Nürnberg . . . that in future, the electoral princes shall meet every year in some city of the empire four weeks after Easter.

Chapter XXV. [W]e determine and decree by this imperial edict that . . . the kingdom of Bohemia, the palatinate of the Rhine, the duchy of Saxony, and the mark of Brandenburg should never under any circumstances be separated, divided, or dismembered. In order that they be preserved in their integrity, the first-born son in each case shall succeed to them . . . unless he be incapacitated by reason of imbecility or other notorious defect. In that case . . . the succession shall go to the nearest male heir on the paternal side.

ning to develop. The authority of the crown, in other words, was great, but the state as a whole remained dependent upon domain revenues. The later Tudors would find this dependence limiting. The Stuarts would be destroyed by it.

The Holy Roman Empire

The Holy Roman Empire of the later Middle Ages should be regarded as a confederation of cities and principalities instead of as a territorial state that failed. German parallels to the growth of Spain, France, or England may be found in states such as Brandenburg, Saxony, and Bavaria, not at the imperial level. Their rulers sought, with varying degrees of success, to enhance domain revenues, control representative bodies, and impose new taxes. The imperial office was an unlikely vehicle for this type of development because it was elective and because it lacked several of the more important attributes of sovereignty.

The century before the Black Death had been one of imperial paralysis and decentralization, caused in part by papal interference. The turning point came in 1355 when Charles IV renounced his Italian claims and turned his attention to reorganizing what would soon be called the Holy Roman Empire of the German Nation. The Golden Bull of 1356 (see document 14.3) regularized imperial elections by placing them in the hands of seven permanent electors: the archbishops of Trier, Mainz, and Cologne, the duke of Saxony, the margrave of Brandenburg, the count of Palatine, and the king of Bohemia. It further declared that the territory of these princes would be indivisible and that inheritance in the secular electorates would be by primogeniture.

These measures strengthened the electors and made consolidation of their territories easier, but they did little to create a more viable imperial government. No incentive existed to increase the power of the emperor, and the lesser states feared the growing influence of the electors. Efforts to create an electoral union or *Kurfürstverein* with many of the powers of a central government were defeated in 1424, 1453, and 1500. The Common Penny, an imperial tax, was rejected by a majority of German states after it had been approved by their representatives in the Imperial Diet or *Reichstag*. The empire would remain an unstable grouping of eighty-nine free Imperial Cities together with more than two hundred independent principalities, most of which continued to divide and re-form according to the

◈ DOCUMENT 14.4 ◈

The Twelve Articles of the German Peasants

The Great Peasant War of 1524–25 was the last in a long series of revolts against the claims of lords, princes, and the church. Some of the Twelve Articles reflect the peasants' understanding of the Protestant Reformation. Most of them expressed grievances that had been accumulating for centuries. Those abridged below would have been as valid in 1424 as in 1524.

The Third Article. It has been the custom hitherto for men to hold us as their own property, which is pitiable enough considering that Christ has redeemed and purchased us without exception, by the shedding of His precious blood, the lowly as well as the great. Accordingly, it is consistent with Scripture that we should be free and wish to be so. . . .

The Fourth Article. [I]t has been the custom heretofore that no poor man was allowed to catch venison or wild fowl, or fish in flowing water, which seems to us quite unseemly and unbrotherly. . . . Accordingly, it is our desire if a man holds possession of waters that he should prove from satisfactory documents that his right has been wittingly acquired by purchase.

The Fifth Article. [W]e are aggrieved in the matter of woodcutting, for our noble folk have appropriated all the woods to themselves alone. . . . It should be free to every member of the community to help himself to such firewood as he needs in his home.

The Eighth Article. [W]e are greatly burdened by holdings that cannot support the rent exacted from them. We ask that the lords may appoint persons of honor to inspect these holdings and fix a rent in accordance with justice.

The Ninth Article. [W]e are burdened with the great evil in the constant making of new laws. In our opinion we should be judged according to the old written law, so that the case shall be decided according to its merits and not with favors.

The Eleventh Article. [W]e will entirely abolish the custom called *Todfall* [death dues], and will no longer allow it, nor allow widows and orphans to be thus shamefully robbed against God's will.

---

vagaries of partible inheritance. A few, such as Bavaria, achieved near-equality with the electoral states by introducing primogeniture. However, all sought to maximize their own power and to resist imperial and electoral encroachments.

In the process, German states—and cities—imitated the western monarchies by trying to increase revenues at the expense of traditional rights and privileges. The peasants, already squeezed by landholders trying to reverse the economic effects of a declining population, added the actions of the princes to their list of grievances and rebelled. The last and most serious of the *bundschuh* revolts was the Great Peasant War of 1524–25 that ended with the defeat of the peasant armies and the imposition of serfdom in many parts of the empire (see document 14.4). Serfs had no personal or legal rights and were usually transferred from one owner to another whenever the property on which they lived changed hands. Their status differed from that of slaves only in that they could not be sold as individuals. Serfdom was the final step in the destruction of peasant freedom.

Central and Eastern Europe

Serfdom as an institution was also established in eastern Europe. In Bohemia, Hungary, and Poland-Lithuania the growing power of aristocratic landholders deprived peasants of their traditional freedoms and blocked the development of western-style states. If western kings may be said to have tamed their nobles, in the east the nobles tamed their kings.

Bohemia and Hungary were in some ways politically similar, though Bohemia was part of the Holy Roman Empire and Hungary was not. Both were elective monarchies whose powerful Diets or representative assemblies were dominated by the landed aristocracy. Rich mineral deposits provided a source of revenues for both crowns. Once elected, a capable monarch could use this wealth as the basis for administrative and military reforms, but his achievements were unlikely to survive him. By the late fifteenth century Diets customarily demanded concessions as the price of election, and as Diets were dominated by the great magnates, their demands invariably tended to weaken the authority of the crown and threaten the rights of common people.

Bohemia, though wealthy and cultured, was convulsed throughout the fifteenth century by the Hussite wars and their aftermath. The Czechs, deeply resentful of a powerful German minority, launched what was probably the first national movement in European history. It was anti-German, anti-empire, and under the leadership of Jan Hus, increasingly associated with demands for religious reform. Hus was burned as a heretic in 1415. After many years of civil war, the Czechs succeeded in placing the Husite noble George of Podebrady (ruled 1458–71) on the throne. The king's ability and popularity were eventually seen as a threat to the great Bohemian landholders. When he died, the Diet elected Vladislav II (ruled 1471–1516), a member of the Polish Jagiello dynasty, on the promise that he would support their interests. Under Vladislav, the Bohemian nobles gained virtual control over the state, expelled the towns from the Diet, and introduced serfdom. The towns eventually achieved readmission, but the Bohemian peasantry did not recover its freedom until the eighteenth century.

The policies of Vladislav could only recommend him to the Hungarian nobility. During the long and brilliant reign of Matthias Corvinus (ruled 1458–90), the crown acquired unprecedented authority and supported a court that was admired even in Renaissance Italy. When Matthias died, the Hungarian Diet elected the more controllable Vladislav to succeed him. Vladislav and his son, Louis II, who was in turn elected king of both Hungary and Bohemia, reversed the achievements of Matthias and left the Diet free to promote repressive legislation. Driven to desperation, the peasants rebelled in 1514 only to be soundly defeated. After bloody reprisals, the Diet imposed "real and perpetual servitude" on the entire Hungarian peasant class.

By this time Hungary was on the edge of an abyss. The Turkish Empire, under the formidable Süleyman the Magnificent (reigned 1520–66), was preparing an invasion, and Louis was crippled by the aristocratic independence he had done so much to encourage. Though king of Bohemia as well as Hungary, he was unable to gain the support of the Bohemians. The Hungarians were divided not only by rivalries among the leading clans, but also by an increasingly bitter feud between the magnates and the lesser nobility. Süleyman had little difficulty in annihilating a weak, divided, and badly led Hungarian army at Mohács in 1526. Louis, along with many great nobles and churchmen, was killed, and Hungary was partitioned into three sections.

The center of the country would thereafter be ruled directly by the Turks. In the east, Transylvania became a Turkish client and tributary, while a narrow strip of territory in the west fell under Hapsburg rule.

After their union in 1386, Poland and Lithuania occupied an immense territory stretching from the borders of Baltic Prussia to the Black Sea. In spite of its ethnic and religious diversity and a substantial number of prosperous towns, it was primarily a land of great estates whose titled owners profited during this period from a rapidly expanding grain trade with the west. At the same time, the vast spaces of the north European plain and the Ukrainian steppe preserved the importance of cavalry and with it the military dominance of the knightly class.

The great magnates of both Poland and Lithuania negotiated their union after the death of Casimir the Great, and they continued to increase their power throughout the fifteenth century. The Jagiello dynasty survived mainly through capitulations. By 1500 Poland-Lithuania could be described as two aristocratic commonwealths joined by a largely ceremonial monarchy, not as a dynastic state. Serfdom was imposed in a series of edicts passed by the Polish *Sejm* or parliament between 1492 and 1501, and the crown, already elective in practice, became so in theory by 1572.

As in the case of Hungary, these aristocratic triumphs unfolded in the growing shadow of a menace to the east. Autocratic Russia, not the Polish-Lithuanian commonwealth, was destined to become the dominant power in eastern Europe, and by 1505 the borders of Lithuania were already shrinking. The process of transforming the grand duchy of Moscow into the Russian Empire began in earnest during the reign of Ivan III from 1462 to 1505. In the first thirteen years of his reign Ivan was able to annex most of the independent Russian principalities and the city-states of Vyatka and Novgorod. In 1480 he refused to pay tribute to the Mongol khans and began to style himself "tsar of all Russia." Finally, in 1492 he invaded Lithuania and, in two successive campaigns, was able to annex much of Beloruss and the Ukraine.

Ivan was not a great field general. His son-in-law claimed rather sourly that "he increased his dominions while sitting at home and sleeping." But Ivan built an effective army and introduced the first usable artillery to eastern Europe. As most of his troops were cavalry, and therefore expensive to maintain, either he or his state secretary introduced the "service land" or *pomest'e* system, which granted land directly to cavalrymen instead of paying them in cash. It was an ideal way of supporting troops in a land that was still underpopulated and cash-poor. *Pomest'e* offered other dividends as well. It created an armed class that owed its prosperity directly to the tsar and permitted him to destroy local allegiances through the massive resettlement of populations. The annexation of Novgorod, for example, was followed by the removal of more than seven thousand citizens who were located elsewhere in Russia and replaced by Muscovites, many of whom were members of this service class.

The new service class cavalry were drawn primarily from the middle ranks of society and depended for their economic survival on peasant cultivators who worked their land. To ensure the stability of the labor force, they secured an edict in 1497 that restricted peasant movement. Thereafter, peasants were allowed to change employers only during a brief period centered on the feast of St. George (April 23). It was the first step toward serfdom. True serfdom on the Hungarian or Polish model did not become general until the end of the sixteenth century. A form of short-term, limited contract slavery was introduced in the 1520s. It, too, was a precedent for serfdom because peasants sold themselves into slavery to escape debt only to discover that they had no means of survival after their contracts expired. They were forced to renew the contracts, and in time the renewals became perpetual.

The Russia of Ivan III had little in common with western states or with its immediate neighbors. The tsar was an autocrat who ruled with little regard for representative institutions. The Orthodox church was implacably hostile to Latin christendom. The *pomest'e* system, like many other Russian institutions, derived from Turkish, Persian, and Byzantine precedents, and even daily life had an oriental flavor. Men wore beards and skirtlike garments that touched the ground while women were secluded and often veiled.

In the reign of Ivan's grandson, Ivan IV "the Terrible" (1530–84), the Russian state expanded eastward, adding Kazan and Astrakhan to its dominions. An effort to annex the areas now known as Latvia and Estonia was unsuccessful. Ivan attributed this failure to dissatisfaction among the *boyars*, or great nobles, and pretended to abdicate, returning only on the condition that he be allowed to establish an *oprichnina*. A bizarre state within a state, the *oprichnina* was regarded as the tsar's private property. Land and even certain streets in Moscow were assigned to it, and the original owners were settled elsewhere. The purpose was to dismantle *boyar* estates as well as to provide income for Ivan's court and for a praetorian guard of six thousand men.

Dressed in black and mounted upon black horses, these *oprichniki* carried a broom and the severed head of a dog as symbols of their primary mission: to root out "treason" and terrorize the enemies of the tsar. They succeeded admirably. Though disbanded in 1572, the *oprichniki* represented an institutionalization of autocracy and state terror that was unique in Europe.

Russia's size and military strength made it a great power, but its autocratic system of government ensured that political effectiveness would inevitably depend upon the personal qualities of the tsar. After Ivan IV, ability was conspicuously lacking. Russia turned inward for more than a hundred years, to emerge once again under the not-too-gentle guidance of Peter the Great at the beginning of the eighteenth century.

The New Learning: Learned Culture in the Late Medieval Italian City-State

The social and political transformations of the late Middle Ages were accompanied, as great changes often are, by the development of new intellectual interests. The most important of these was the Renaissance, or, as it was sometimes called, the New Learning. The word *renaissance* means rebirth in French. It is often applied to the entire age that marked the end of the Middle Ages and the beginning of modern times, but its original meaning was more restricted. Beginning in the fourteenth century, a number of scholars became interested in the Greco-Roman past. They sought to recover the glories of classical literature because the learning of their own day seemed to them stagnant and largely irrelevant to their needs. A later generation saw the "renaissance" of classical antiquity that they created as the birth of modern times; more recent scholarship has emphasized its continuity with the medieval past. In its original form the Renaissance was a direct outgrowth of life in the medieval Italian city-state, and its first proponents were Italian.

Medieval towns were like islands in the agrarian world that surrounded them. The lives of their inhabitants differed markedly from those of the peasants, knights, and clergy who made up 90 percent of Europe's population. While much interaction occurred between town and country, not all of it was cordial. Towns meant freedom—from feudal obligation and from the rigid social hierarchies proposed by medieval theorists. The status of town dwellers was unclear. Even the richest were, by feudal standards, of humble origin, yet their wealth and literacy set them apart from the peasants. Chivalric literature affected to despise them, and ecclesiastical theorists found their activities dubious if not wicked. Trade, the lifeblood of any city, was often regarded as parasitic. The merchant bought low and sold high, profiting from the honest toil of the peasant and raising prices for everyone. The need for mechanisms of distribution was not always fully understood. Worse yet, the townsman was frequently a citizen (women, though they engaged in trade, had neither civic rights nor obligations). Under law he was compelled to vote and to hold public office if elected. Even before St. Augustine, western Christianity had been deeply suspicious of public life, regarding it as incompatible with concern for one's soul. In short, two of the most significant features of town life were either ignored by medieval writers or condemned by them outright.

A certain alienation from the norms of medieval culture was therefore to be expected among townsfolk even if it was not always fully conscious or easily articulated. This alienation was most intense in Italy. Italian town life had developed early. The acquisition of full sovereignty, rare in other parts of Europe, gave a peculiar intensity to political life in the Italian city-states while imposing heavy moral and intellectual responsibilities on their citizens. Extensive contact with the Muslim and Byzantine worlds may also have left the Italians more open to influences that came from outside the orbit of chivalric or scholastic ideas.

By the end of the thirteenth century the intellectual life of the Italian towns was beginning to acquire a distinct flavor of its own. This was evident to some extent in the works of Dante Alighieri (1265–1321). His masterwork, *The Divine Comedy*, a brilliant evocation of hell, purgatory, and paradise written in the Tuscan vernacular (the basis of modern Italian), is arguably the greatest poem ever written by a European (see document 14.5). It is filled with classical allusions and references to Florentine politics but remains essentially medieval in inspiration. The widening gap between Italian culture and that of the scholastic, chivalric north is far more striking in the city chronicles that were becoming popular with the urban elite. Unlike northern chronicles, which were often little more than a simple record of events, they increasingly sought to analyze the causes of political and economic phenomena to provide guidance for policy makers. On a less practical level, the *Decameron*, by the Florentine Giovanni Boccaccio (1313–75), was a collection of stories that portrayed the lives of city people with little reference to the conventions of chivalry. They remain a fertile source of plots for scriptwriters today.

◈ DOCUMENT 14.5 ◈

Dante: The Fate of Virtuous Pagans

In this passage from The Inferno, *Dante shows the great poets of antiquity in Limbo, a part of hell reserved for those who, though virtuous, had never been baptized. It is the home of Virgil, author of* The Aeniad, *who serves in this poem as his guide to the underworld. Dante's reverence for the ancients foreshadows that of the Renaissance, but he remains firmly tied to the traditional perspectives of medieval theology. The* Divine Comedy *is written in three sections in honor of the trinity, and Dante devised its verse form,* terza rima *(third rhyme), for the same purpose. The poet is disturbed by the fate of his ancient heroes.*

No tortured wailing rose to greet us here
but sounds of sighing rose from every side
sending a tremor through the timeless air

a grief breathed out of untormented sadness,
the passive state of those who dwelled apart,
men, women, children—a dim and endless congress.

And the Master [Virgil] said to me: "You do not question
what souls these are that suffer here before you?
I wish you to know before you travel on

That these were sinless. And still their merits fail.
for they lacked Baptism's grace, which is the door
of the true faith you were born to. Their birth fell

before the age of Christian mysteries,
and so they did not worship God's Trinity
in fullest duty. I am one of these.

For such defects we are lost, though spared the fire
and suffering of Hell in one affliction only:
that without hope we live on in desire"

That Boccaccio and another Florentine, Francesco Petrarca (or Petrarch, 1304–74), were among the first to develop a serious interest in the Roman past is no accident. Petrarch grew up in exile and spent most of his life at the papal court in Avignon, an existence that no doubt sharpened his personal sense of distance from chivalric and scholastic values. Believing, like other

Italians, that he was descended from the ancient Romans, he began to seek out classical manuscripts and to compose works in Latin that demonstrated his affinity with the antique past. Among them were letters addressed to such ancient figures as Cicero and Livy and an epic poem, *Africa*, inspired by his reading of Virgil's *The Aeniad*. His friend Boccaccio followed his lead in collecting manuscripts and compiled an encyclopedia of Greco-Roman mythology.

Petrarch is probably best known today for his sonnets written in the Tuscan vernacular, but classical studies consumed most of his working life. His efforts made an undeniably vital point. To Petrarch and to many of his readers the society of ancient Rome had more in common with that of the Italian states than did the chivalric, scholastic world of transalpine Europe. The ancients had lived in cities and had believed that good citizenship was the highest of virtues. Accordingly, they had produced a vast body of literature on rhetoric, politics, history, and the other arts needed to produce effective citizens. Many Italians would eventually find these works to be of great practical value in the conduct of their lives.

Those who did so, and who made the study of antiquity their primary task, became known as humanists. The term was coined by Leonardo Bruni (c. 1370–1444) to describe those engaged in *studia humanitatis*, the study of secular letters as opposed to theology or divine letters. The movement became popular in Florence during the political crisis of 1392–1402 when Bruni and other publicists used classical examples of civic virtue to stir up the public against Giangaleazzo Visconti, despot of Milan, and his expansionist schemes. Even more important was the enthusiasm aroused by the arrival in Italy of Greek scholars who were seeking western aid against the Turks. Petrarch had known that Roman culture had Greek roots but could find no one to teach him classical Greek. Manuel Chrysaloras, Cardinal Bessarion, and other members of the Greek delegation were able to do this for Bruni's generation and, by so doing, opened up a great literary tradition that had been lost to the west for centuries. Spurred by these developments, humanism spread from Florence and Rome to Venice and the other Italian states. By the mid-fifteenth century it was attracting followers beyond the Alps.

Humanism: Its Methods and Its Goals

Associating the early humanists with any fixed ideological or philosophical system is difficult. Most of them were either teachers of rhetoric or the editors of classical texts whose chief purpose was to study the classics and to apply ancient ideas and values to life in their own time. As such they might be found on almost any side of a given issue. But for all their variety they shared certain presuppositions that defined them as a movement. Humanists by definition believed in the superiority of ancient culture (see document 14.6). Errors, they said, were modern. Where medieval writers had seen their world as a historical extension of antiquity, the humanists saw a radical disjuncture between ancient and modern times, and they regarded the interval between the fall of Rome and their revival of antique ideals as a "middle age" of barbarity, ignorance, and above all, bad style. Immersed in the elegance of classical Latin, they were deeply concerned with form, sometimes, according to their critics, at the expense of substance.

Because they revered the classical past, they shared a preference for argument based on the authority of ancient sources and a suspicion of formal reason that bordered on contempt. The scholastics in particular were thought to be sterile and misguided, in part because of their bad Latin, but also because the nominalist rejection of reason as a support for faith had led the philosophers into pursuits that humanists regarded as trivial. Scholastics sometimes counterattacked by accusing them of irreligion. Though humanists were to be found among the critics of the church, few if any rejected conventional religious belief. The Renaissance moved Western society strongly toward secularism by reviving the ancient preoccupation with human beings and their social relationships. Writers such as Giovanni Pico della Mirandola asserted "the dignity of man" against preachers who saw humanity as wholly depraved (see document 14.7), but even Pico believed that human dignity derived largely from man's central place in a divinely established universe. Unbelief was not at issue. The humanists believed in perfecting their minds and bodies on Earth while preparing their souls for the hereafter.

Such a goal was fundamentally educational, and the humanists were predictably concerned with educational theory. Their purpose was to create *il uomo universale*, the universal man whose person combined intellectual and physical excellence and who was capable of functioning honorably in virtually any situation. It was the ancient Greco-Roman ideal, brought up-to-date and applied to life in the Italian city-state where the small size of the community forced citizens or courtiers to play many roles. Though most fully described in *The Courtier* by Baldassare Castiglione (published in 1528), it had long been present in the thinking of such educa-

❖ DOCUMENT 14.6 ❖

Machiavelli: The Virtues of Antiquity

For all of its great achievements, the Renaissance as an intellectual movement based itself on the assumption that the present was hopelessly inferior to the antique past. Niccoló Machiavelli shared the viewpoint of his age. In this passage from The Discourses *after arguing that some nations may yet retain a small measure of virtue, he concludes that Italy does not and can do no better than to imitate the virtues of its Roman ancestors. His view is both a justification of his historical method and a reminder that, while people today are inclined to see the Renaissance as a high-water mark of Western civilization, contemporaries did not agree.*

But whoever is born in Italy or Greece . . . has good reason to find fault with his own and to praise the olden times; for in their past there are many things worthy of the highest admiration, whilst the present has nothing that compensates for all the extreme misery, infamy, and degradation of a period where there is neither observance of religion, law, or military discipline, and which is stained by every species of the lowest brutality. . . .

I know not then, whether I deserve to be classed with those who deceive themselves, if in these *Discourses* I shall praise too much the times of ancient Rome and censure those of our own day. And truly if the virtues that ruled then and the vices that prevail now were not as clear as the sun, I should be more reticent in my expressions, lest I should fall into the very error for which I reproach others. But the matter being so manifest that everybody sees it, I shall boldly and openly say what I think of former times and of the present, so as to excite in the minds of the young men who read my writings the desire to avoid the evils of the latter, and prepare themselves to imitate the virtues of the former, whenever fortune presents them an occasion.

❖ DOCUMENT 14.7 ❖

Pico: The Dignity of Man

Giovanni Pico, count of Mirandola (1463–94) was something of a prodigy who, before his death at thirty-one wrote extensively on many subjects. Like many humanists he was deeply interested in magic, the occult, and Neoplatonic philosophy. In his Oration on the Dignity of Man *he produced what some regard as the classic Renaissance statement of human dignity and freedom. The argument is based largely on humanity's place in the Great Chain of Being, the hierarchical structure of the universe described by such Neoplatonic writers as Dionysius the Areopagite, but Pico's* Oration *provides a vision of human potential rarely emphasized in medieval writing.*

[God] took man as a creature of indeterminate nature and, assigning him a place in the middle of the world, addressed him thus: "Neither a fixed abode nor a form that is thine alone nor any function peculiar to thyself have We given thee, Adam, to the end that according to thy longing and according to thy judgment thou mayest have and possess what abode, what form, and what functions thou thyself shalt desire. The nature of all other beings is limited and constrained within the bounds of laws proscribed by Us. Thou, constrained by no limits, in accordance with thy own free will, in whose hand We have placed thee, shalt ordain for thyself the limits of thy nature. We have set thee at the world's center that thou mayest from thence more easily observe whatever is in the world. We have made thee neither of heaven nor of earth, neither mortal nor immortal, so that with freedom of choice and honor . . . thou mayest fashion thyself in whatever shape thou shalt prefer. Thou shalt have the power to degenerate into the lower forms of life, which are brutish. Thou shalt have the power out of they soul's judgment, to be reborn into the higher forms, which are divine.

tional theorists as Vittorino da Feltre (1386–1446) and Leon Battista Alberti (1404–72).

The heart of Renaissance education was ancient literature and history (see document 14.8). The classics were thought to provide both moral instruction and the deep understanding of human behavior without which correct action in the present is impossible. They were also a guide to style. The ability to communicate is es-

sential to political life, and good writing comes largely from immersion in good literature. Humanists taught the art of persuasion through an exhaustive study of rhetoric based on the writings of Quintilian and Cicero.

Because citizens and courtiers would almost certainly participate in war, study was thought to be

◈ DOCUMENT 14.8 ◈

The Value of the Liberal Arts

Peter Paul Vergerio (1370–1444) was a leading Renaissance educational theorist. The following is from a letter he wrote to another humanist, Ubertino of Carrara.

For no wealth, no possible security against the future, can be compared with the gift of education in grave and liberal studies. By them a man may win distinction for the most modest name, and bring honor to the city of his birth however obscure it may be. . . .

We come now to the consideration of the various subjects which may rightly be included under the name of "Liberal Studies." Among these I accord the first place to History, on grounds both of its attractiveness and its utility, qualities which appeal equally to the scholar and to the statesman. Next in importance is Moral Philosphy, which indeed is, in a peculiar sense, a "Liberal Art" in that its purpose is to teach men the secret of true freedom. History, then, gives us the concrete examples of the precepts inculcated by philosophy. The one shows what men should do, the other what men have said and done in the past, and what lessons we may draw therefrom for the present day. I would indicate as the third main branch of study, Eloquence, which indeed holds a place of distinction among the refined Arts. By philosophy we learn the essential truth of things, which by eloquence we so exhibit in orderly adornment as to bring conviction to differing minds. And history provides the light of experience.

necessary in military history and theory, the art of fortification, and ballistics. Educators regarded proficiency with weapons and physical fitness as essential for war, furthermore, like the ancients, they regarded athletic skill as as value in its own right. The Renaissance man or woman was also expected to be good company. Sports were a social skill as was dancing, the ability to play musical instruments, and the possession of a trained singing voice. Art was useful, not merely for the sake of appreciation, but also as a tool of observation. Before the camera, only drawing or sketching could preserve a record of visual impressions—or accurately portray the fortifications of one's enemies. Other useful subjects included mathematics, accounting, medicine, and the natural sciences.

The preferred means of imparting this rather daunting quantity of knowledge was in small academies or by means of a tutor. The teacher was supposed to live with his students and be a moral example and friend as well as a purveyor of knowledge. Students were not to be beaten or threatened but induced to learn by arousing their interest in the subject at hand. These humanist theories, and the classical examples from which they came, remain the basis of today's liberal arts education. They have had an enormous impact on the formation of European youth and on the development of Western culture. However, humanist education was intended only for a relatively narrow social elite: the select group that participated in public life and exercised some degree of control over its own destiny. Even women were largely excluded, though humanists such as Leonardo Bruni, Juan Luis Vives, and Thomas More argued that women should be educated in much the same way as men (see document 14.9). Such women as Vitoria Colonna and More's daughter, Margaret Roper, developed a reputation for classical learning. But for the most part, the education of upper-class women continued to emphasize the domestic and social graces as it had done for centuries.

The usefulness of the Renaissance educational ideal was in part responsible for the spread of humanism beyond the Alps. The requirements of life as a courtier or servant of the crown in England, France, or Spain were not unlike those demanded of the upper-class Italian. Such people were among the first non-Italians to develop an interest in the classics, but they were quickly followed by their princes. Isabella of Castile, for example, imported Italian humanists to raise the educational standards of her court and administration. Lawyers, too, were intrigued by humanist methods. The development of philology and of the historical analysis of texts had been among the first achievements of humanist scholarship. The legal profession in France and Germany was soon divided between those who added the new techniques to their arsenals and those who refused to do so. Above all, town councils were quick to recognize the usefulness of officials trained in the new learning. It became desirable, especially in the cities of the Holy Roman Empire, to have town clerks who could communicate with one another in classical Latin and who possessed the training to interpret and decipher old documents. Usefulness aside, the presence of learned humanists within a town or principality had become a matter of prestige.

◆ DOCUMENT 14.9 ◆

Louise Labé: The Education of Women

Though the Renaissance ideal of education extended only to a minority of women, many saw even this as a liberating step forward in the development of women as a whole. One of them was Louise Labé (c. 1524–66), an important French poet whose ideas in some ways foreshadow modern feminism. The following is from a dedicatory preface written to a friend.

Since a time has come, Mademoiselle, when the severe laws of men no longer prevent women from applying themselves to the sciences and other disciplines, it seems to me that those of us who can should use this long-craved freedom to study and to let men see how greatly they wronged us when depriving us of its honor and advantages. And if any woman becomes so proficient as to be able to write down her thoughts, let her do so and not despise the honor but rather flaunt it instead of fine clothes, necklaces, and rings. For these may be considered ours only by use, whereas the honor of being educated is ours entirely. . . . If the heavens had endowed me with sufficient wit to understand all I would have liked, I would

serve in this as an example rather than an admonishment. But having devoted part of my youth to musical exercises, and finding the time left too short for the crudeness of my understanding, I am unable in my own case, to achieve what I want for our sex, which is to see it outstrip men not only in beauty but in learning and virtue. All I can do is to beg our virtuous ladies to raise their minds somewhat above their distaffs and spindles and try to prove to the world that if we were not made to command, still we should not be disdained in domestic and public matters by those who govern and command obedience.

If there is anything to be recommended after honor and glory, anything to incite us to study, it is the pleasure which study affords. Study differs in this from all other recreations, of which all one can say, after enjoying them, is that one has passed the time. But study gives a more enduring sense of satisfaction. For the past delights us and serves more than the present.

The universities were in general more resistant to change. They remained the strongholds of Aristotelianism if for no other reason than that their traditional role had been the training of theologians. Some, however, such as John Colet at Oxford and Lefèvre d'Etaples at Paris, began to perceive the usefulness of humanism for the study of religious literature, which was another form of ancient text. Others, outside the universities, shared their concern. The most famous of those who turned humanist methods to the study of Scripture and of the Fathers of the church was Erasmus of Rotterdam (1469–1536). Believing that corrupted texts had led to false interpretations, he devoted much of his extraordinarily busy and productive life to providing authoritative editions of religious texts. Best known today for his satirical attacks on ecclesiastical ignorance and for his bitter controversy with Martin Luther over the issue of free will, he was in many ways the epitome of the humanist whose chief interests were religious (see illustration 14.2). His English friend Sir Thomas More (1477–1535) combined religious with secular interests. A lawyer who ultimately became lord chancellor to Henry VIII, he is perhaps best known for *Utopia*, his vi-

sion of a perfect society that recalls Plato's *Republic*. More also applied humanist scholarship to the law and to religious questions before being martyred for his opposition to the Reformation. He was sainted by the Catholic Church in 1935. The value of humanist studies was recognized on occasion by even the most conservative of churchmen. Cardinal Francisco Jiménez de Cisneros, archbishop of Toledo, grand inquisitor, and ultimately regent of Castile, established the University of Alcalá de Henares in 1508 to provide humanist training for the Spanish clergy. Among its first products was the Complutensian Polyglot Bible, printed in Greek, Hebrew, and Latin.

The Impact of Renaissance Humanism on the Arts and Sciences

By 1500 humanist methods and values had spread to virtually every part of Europe. Their impact on the arts and sciences was enormous, though not always what one might expect. The humanists developed classical studies as they are known today. They created the first

Illustration 14.2

⌘ **Erasmus of Rotterdam.** In this famous portrait by Hans Holbein, the greatest of the northern humanists is shown at his writing desk.

standardized editions of classical works and distributed them widely after printing with moveable type was invented, probably by Johan Gutenberg, in the mid-fifteenth century. In the process humanism gave birth to the disciplines of linguistics, philology (the study of words), and historical criticism.

In literature, however, humanist devotion to the classics retarded the development of vernacular writing for more than a century. Those with literary inclinations preferred to write in Latin, often in slavish imitation of the elaborate Roman style that had developed during the Augustan Age. When vernacular literature was revived in the sixteenth century by such figures as Tasso and Ariosto in Italy, Cervantes and Garcilaso de la Vega in Spain, Rabelais and Montaigne in France, and Marlowe and Shakespeare in England, it was transformed by classical themes and rules of composition. The fifteenth century, however, had been remarkably unproductive. Latin, in the meantime, was practically

destroyed as a living language. Because the humanists insisted on weeding out all nonclassical usages, the language ceased to evolve as it had done throughout the Middle Ages when it was the day-to-day language of diplomacy and administration in both church and state. Ironically, by the middle of the sixteenth century, Latin had largely been supplanted by the various European vernaculars in every western government outside the papal states.

The contribution of humanism to the study of history and politics was far more positive. From the beginning, humanists had regarded history as essential to a political education. At the very least it provided inspiring examples of civic virtue and cautionary tales that would help the citizen or courtier to avoid the mistakes of the past.

In the Middle Ages the dominant form of history had been the chronicle. Outside the Italian cities, chroniclers tended to record events without troubling themselves greatly over causation or the objective accuracy of their sources. The cause of historical events was after all God's will. The Greeks and Romans had taken a different view. Beginning with Thucydides, the best of them had defined their topics as questions to be answered in causal terms because they believed that human nature was consistent and that history therefore repeated itself. If history was cyclical it offered a priceless guide to action in the present, not so much because it was predictive in absolute terms, but because the process of historical causation could be understood and used by the educated to their own advantage.

The most effective exponent of this view during the Renaissance was the Florentine lawyer and sometime politician Niccolò Machiavelli (1469–1527). In works such as *The Prince* and *The Discourses on Livy* he attempted to establish rules for the conduct of political life based upon examples from the historical past (see illustration 14.3). In the process he freed political theory from the theological principles upon which it had long been based. While his name became a byword for cynicism and political manipulation, Machiavelli was in his own way an idealist. The Italian wars begun by Charles VIII of France in 1495 eventually destroyed the independence of the Italian cities with only Venice retaining full sovereignty. Machiavelli believed that this calamity could be understood and remedied only by looking with a clear eye at the way in which politics was conducted (see document 14.10).

His younger contemporary, Francesco Guicciardini (1483–1540), agreed but thought that governing one-

Illustration 14.3

Niccolò Machiavelli. This detail is from the portrait by Santi de Tito, painted when Machiavelli was still active in Florentine politics. It captures the shrewd intellect of the Renaissance political thinker who first separated politics from religion and the wit that characterized his comedies for the stage.

The Political Philosophy of Machiavelli

Niccolò Machiavelli's most famous book was The Prince *in which he appears to favor despotic rule as a means of ridding Italy of its "barbarian" invaders. However, he was an ardent republican both in theory and in his own career as secretary to the second chancery of the Florentine republic. The following passage from* The Discourses *sets out what may be taken as his real view.*

And finally to sum up this matter, I say that both governments of princes and of the people have lasted a long time, but both require to be regulated by laws. For a prince who knows no other control but his own will is like a madman, and a people that can do as it pleases will hardly be wise. If now we compare a prince who is controlled by laws, and a people who is untrammeled by them, we shall find more virtue in the people than in the prince; and if we compare them when both are freed from such control, we shall see that the people are guilty of fewer excesses than the prince, and that the errors of the people are of less importance, and may therefore be more easily remedied. For a licentious and mutinous people can be brought back to good conduct by the influence and persuasion of a good man, but an evil-minded prince is not amenable to such influences, and there is therefore no other remedy against him but cold steel.

self by the kind of rules proposed by Machiavelli was impossible. As he said in his *Ricordi,* a grim collection of musings on a variety of subjects, no two situations were the same; there were always exceptions (see document 14.11). He seems to have believed that by studying history one absorbed what he called discretion: the ability to react intelligently to unforeseen contingencies. His *History of Italy,* which examines the loss of Italian freedom in the years after 1494, is probably the first modern historical work and remains a useful source for the political and military history of the age.

By comparison with its impact on politics and history, the humanist contribution to philosophy was indirect. The Renaissance was not a great age of formal speculation, but the course of modern philosophy would be hard to imagine without the recovery of classical works that had been lost during the Middle Ages. Much of Aristotle, most of Plato and the Alexandrian Neoplatonists, the Pre-Socratics, and many of the Epicureans and Stoics were either unknown or had been studied with little regard to their historical and intellectual context. By recovering lost works and seeking a deeper understanding of the mental world that had pro-

duced them, the humanists immeasurably broadened philosophic discourse in the West. By attacking the scholastics, they opened the way for the acceptance of ideas that lay outside the Aristotelian tradition as it was then understood. They may have done little to exploit their own discoveries, but they made possible the great philosophical achievements of the seventeenth century. The impact of humanism on science was similar. Few humanists were scientists in the modern sense of the word. Many were devotees of what would now be called superstition, though the term is unhistorical. Believing that the wisdom of the ancients was superior, and aware that Greeks and Romans had believed in

◆ DOCUMENT 14.11 ◆

Guicciardini: Political Morality

These selections from the Ricordi reveal how far Renaissance political thought could stray from Christian principles. They were not intended for publication. Their tone recalls on a more personal level some of the ideas expressed by Machiavelli in The Prince. *With the exception of the first, Machiavelli would probably have agreed with all of them.*

—It is a great error to speak of things of this world absolutely and indiscriminately and to deal with them, as it were, by the book. In nearly all things one must make distinctions and exceptions because of differences in their circumstances. These circumstances are not covered by one and the same rule. Nor can these distinctions and exceptions be found written in books. They must be taught by discretion.

—Political power cannot be wielded according to the dictates of good conscience. If you consider its origin, you will always find it in violence—except in the cases of republics within their borders, but not beyond. Not even the emperor is exempt from this rule; nor are the priests, whose violence is double because they assault us with both temporal and spiritual weapons.

—Revenge does not always stem from hate or from an evil nature. Sometimes it is necessary that people will learn not to offend you. It is perfectly all right to avenge yourself even though you feel no deep rancor against the person who is the object of your revenge.

—I would praise the man who is ordinarily open and frank and who uses deception only in very rare, important matters. Thus, you will have the reputation of being open and genuine, and you will enjoy the popularity such a reputation brings. And in those very important matters you will reap even greater advantage from deception, because your reputation for not being a deceiver will make your words be easily believed.

divination, sorcery, astrology, and natural magic, some humanists deliberately encouraged a revival of these practices. Notions that would have been regarded as absurd in the days of Aquinas were taken seriously. Nevertheless, in their zeal to recover every aspect of the ancient past, they found and edited works that would eventually revolutionize Western thought. Galen in medicine, Eratosthenes and Aristarchus of Samos in cosmology, Archimedes in physics, and a host of other writers were rediscovered, edited, and popularized.

The humanists also transmitted the idea, derived ultimately from Pythagoras, that the universe was based on number. This is the basic principle of numerology, now regarded as a pseudoscience, but it inspired such figures as Leonardo da Vinci (1452–1519) to explore the mathematization of physics. Leonardo is best known today as an artist and inventor whose ideas were far in advance of their time. Though Leonardo failed in his effort regarding physics, Galileo and others would eventually learn to express physical relationships in mathematical formulae, an important step in the development of modern science (see chapter 17).

Few of these achievements had an immediate impact on the life of ordinary Europeans. The recovery of classical antiquity was an intellectual movement created

Illustration 14.4

▨ **Leon Battista Alberti's Tempio Malatesta.** The unfinished church of San Francesco at Rimini was built about 1450. Rimini was a city in the papal states whose ruler, the infamous Sigismundo Malatesta, was a great admirer of all things Roman. At his request, Alberti transformed an existing church into a Roman temple whose facade resembles a triumphal arch. Sigismundo commissioned a statue of the Virgin Mary whose features were modeled on those of his mistress, Isotta degli Atti.

Illustration 14.5

Palladio's **Villa Rotunda.** This building in Vicenza, Italy (1566–69), represents the final stage in the Renaissance adoption of Roman architectural motifs. It inspired a host of domed country houses, especially in Britain and the United States.

by and for a self-conscious elite, and many years would pass before it touched the consciousness of the general public. In one area, however, classical values intruded on material life, redefining the public spaces in which people moved and altering their visual perceptions of the world. Renaissance art, architecture, and city planning brought the aesthetic values of Greece and Rome down to street level. They eventually spread from the Italian towns to the farthest reaches of Europe and America.

Italian artists had turned to classical ruins for inspiration as early as the thirteenth century. With the emergence of humanism, ancient models became universal. The architect Filippo Brunelleschi (1377–1446) measured ancient ruins to determine their proportions. He then sketched their pediments, columns, and ornamentation with the intention of adapting Roman forms to

the purposes of his own day. Within a generation, churches were being built that resembled pagan temples (see illustration 14.4). New construction, private and public, sported columns, pilasters, and window treatments borrowed from the porticoes of Roman buildings. It was not mere antiquarianism because Brunelleschi and his successors—Alberti, Bramante, and the sixteenth-century master Palladio—knew that modern structures were different in function from those of the past. So successful were their adaptations that Roman forms and ornamentation remained a standard feature of Western architecture until the twentieth century (see illustration 14.5).

As buildings are meant to be viewed in their appropriate settings, public spaces were opened to accommodate them. Streets were widened and adorned with Roman-style loggias and colonnades. Open squares and streets laid out symmetrically like the camps of the Roman legions slowly began to replace the tangled alleys of the medieval town. The Renaissance ideal of city planning (see illustration 14.6) was fully realized only in the new cities of Spanish America, but the admirers

Illustration 14.6

⁂ **View of an Ideal City.** This rendering, attributed to Piero della Francesca (1420–92), contains many of the ideas favored by Renaissance city planners. The symmetrical design is centered on a round structure typical of early Roman temples, and the surrounding buildings bear a strong resemblance to the *insulae* of ancient Rome (see chapter 6).

Illustration 14.7

⁂ **The Anunciation, by Nicola Pisano.** This panel from the Baptistry at Pisa was completed in 1260. It demonstrates that classical models had come to influence Italian art long before the Renaissance took root as a literary movement.

of antiquity had imposed their vision of what a town should be. That vision still exists.

The revival of classical taste in painting and sculpture was equally important. Medieval artists had illustrated classical themes, and some of them, such as Nicola Pisano (c. 1220–c. 1278), had successfully imitated classical forms, though only in portraying scenes from the Bible (see illustration 14.7). In medieval practice, tales from ancient history or mythology were normally portrayed in contemporary settings because they were intended as moral or religious allegories whose message was often unlike that of their pagan originals (see illustration 14.8). To the humanists, with their archaeological view of history, this was absurd. Classical forms were appropriate to classical subjects as well as to those derived from the Bible. The imitation of classical models and the use of classical settings therefore became almost universal. Ancient ideas of beauty and proportion were adopted, especially for the portrayal of the human body.

But Renaissance art was not an exercise in antiquarianism. The technique of painting with oils, developed in the Low Countries during the fifteenth century, was soon in general use. The effort to portray the world in three dimensions, begun with the use of *chiaroscuro* or shading by Giotto (c. 1266– c. 1337), was brought to a triumphal conclusion with Brunelleschi's discovery of the mathematical laws of perspective. Their application in the paintings of Andrea Mantegna (c. 1431–1506) inspired other artists, and the viewing public soon came to accept foreshortening and perspective as the norm (see illustration 14.9).

These techniques were new. Furthermore, Renaissance artists differed from the ancients in other ways. They were not pagans, and though they admired antiquity, they retained many of the ideas and symbols of the medieval past. Their art combined classical and Christian sensibilities in a new synthesis that shaped European aesthetic values until their vision was challenged by the rise of photography and nonrepresentational art in the nineteenth century. Eventually, artists such as Michelangelo Buonarroti (1475–1564) would transcend the rules of classical composition, distorting the proportions of the human body to express dramatic

Illustration 14.8

⁄⁄ The Birth of Venus by Botticelli.
Though many Renaissance works of art
were commissioned by churchmen and
featured religious themes, some artists
felt free to explore classical themes and
motifs without a specific Christian reference. Here the Florentine painter Sandro
Botticelli (1444/5–1510) portrays the
classical myth in which Venus is born
from the sea.

Illustration 14.9

⁄⁄ St. James Led to Execution, by Andrea Mantegna. Mantegna was one of the first Renaissance painters to use the laws of
perspective discovered by the architect Filippo Brunelleschi. In
this fresco from the Ovetari Chapel, Church of the Erimitani,
Padua, painted c. 1454–57, the vanishing point is below the
bottom of the picture. Note also the classicism of the triumphal
arch.

spiritual and emotional truths (see illustration 14.10).
But even he and his Baroque followers in the seventeenth century remained well within the bounds of
classical inspiration.

Conclusion

A century ago, most historians believed that the
Renaissance marked the beginning of the modern
world. As the full implications of the industrial revolution became clear, that conviction has dimmed and the
distance between twentieth-century Westerners and the
preoccupations of the humanists has widened. Few today believe that the Renaissance was a true rebirth of
classical antiquity or as revolutionary as its more enthusiastic supporters claimed. There had been a Carolin-
gian Renaissance and a Renaissance of the Twelfth
Century. Medieval scholars knew and quoted classical
writers, but the Renaissance that began in Florence in
the generation of the Black Death was far more than
just another in a series of European infatuations with
the antique past. By rediscovering the lost masterpieces
of Greek and Roman literature, by reviving the ancient
preoccupation with history, and by reexamining scientific theories ignored during the Middle Ages, the humanists redefined learning and transformed education.
By the early fifteenth century the new learning had become the dominant movement in European intellectual

Illustration 14.10

Tombs of Giuliano de' Medici, Duke of Nemours and Lorenzo de' Medici, Duke of Urbino, by Michelangelo. Michelangelo executed this magnificent group in the New Sacristy of San Lorenzo, Florence, between 1520 and 1534. The distorted poses of the heavily muscled reclining figures as well as the dramatic arrangement of the entire piece point away from classical balance and serenity while retaining a basically antique frame of reference.

life. Directly or indirectly it remade each of the arts and sciences in its own image and changed forever the way in which Westerners looked at their world.

Selected Readings

The best survey of fifteenth-century Spain is J. Hillgarth, *The Spanish Kingdoms, 1250–1516*, vol. 2 (1978). For Ferdinand and Isabella, see F. Fernàndez-Armesto, *Ferdinand and Isabella* (1975) and P. Liss, *Isabella the Queen* (1992). Henry Kamen, *Inquisition and Society in Spain* (1985) remains the most useful survey of the Spanish Inquisition. No useful survey exists of late medieval France in

English, but J. Henneman, *Royal Taxation in Fourteenth Century France: The Development of War Financing, 1322–1356* (1971) and J. Major, *Representative Institutions in Renaissance France, 1421–1559* (1960) are outstanding monographs on the development of royal government. P. M. Kendall, *Louis XI: The Universal Spider* (1971) and R. Knecht, *Francis I* (1982) are good biographies. For Burgundy, see R. Vaughan, *Valois Burgundy* (1975) and W. Prevenier and W. Blockmans, *The Burgundian Netherlands* (1983). Surveys of England in the fifteenth century include K. B. Macfarlane, *England in the Fifteenth Century* (1981) and two studies by J. Lander, *Crown and Nobility, 1450–1509* (1976) and *Government and Community: England, 1450–1509* (1980). The best study of the War of the Roses is J. Gillingham, *The War of the Roses* (1981). *The Reign of Henry VI* (1981), *Edward IV* (1974), and *Richard III* (1982) by C. Ross are sound biographies as is S. Chrimes, *Henry VII* (1972). F. Boulay, *Germany in the Later Middle Ages* (1983) surveys the later empire. F. L. Carsten, *Princes and Parliaments in Germany: From the Fifteenth to the Eighteenth Century* (1963) is a classic study of representative institutions. The standard biography of Maximilian I is G. Benecke, *Maximilian I (1459–1519): An Analytical Biography* (1982). For eastern Europe, in addition to the sources listed in chapter 13, see the collection of essays by A. Maczak and others, *East-Central Europe in Transition from the Fourteenth to the Seventeenth Century* (1986), and on Russia, R. Crummey, *The Formation of Muscovy, 1304–1613* (1987), N. Kollmann, *Kinship and Politics: The Making of the Muscovite Political System, 1345–1547* (1987), and R. Hellie, *Enserfment and Military Change in Muscovy* (1971).

L. Martines, *Power and Imagination: City-States in Renaissance Italy* (1988) is an excellent survey of the Italian cities and their cultural preoccupations; G. Brucker, *Renaissance Florence*, 2d ed. (1983) remains the best general treatment of Florence. Two outstanding introductions to Renaissance humanism are C. Nauert, *Humanism and the Culture of Renaissance Europe* (1995) and D. Kelley, *Renaissance Humanism* (1991). See also the important essay by R. Weiss, *The Renaissance Discovery of Classical Antiquity*, 2d ed. (1988). For Petrarch, see N. Mann, *Petrarch* (1984) and K. Foster, *Petrarch: Poet and Humanist* (1987); for Boccaccio, T. Bergin, *Boccaccio* (1981). On the second generation of Florentine humanism, see H. Baron, *The Crisis of the Early Italian Renaissance* (1966) and R. Witt, *Hercules at the Crossroads: The Life, Works, and Thought of Coluccio Salutati* (1983). The western rediscovery of ancient Greece is described in D. Geanokoplos, *Greek Scholars in Venice* (1962).

Useful collections of essays on various aspects of the humanist program are found in A. Rabil, ed., *Renaissance Humanism: Foundations, Forms, and Legacy*, 3 vols. (1988) and C. Trinkhaus, *The Scope of Renaissance Humanism* (1983). Humanist ideas on rhetoric and education are explored by J. Siegel, *Rhetoric and Philosophy in Renaissance Humanism* (1968), P. Grendler, *Schooling in Renaissance Italy, 1300–1600* (1989), and A. Grafton and L. Jardine, *From Humanism to the Humanities: Education and the Liberal Arts in Fifteenth- and Sixteenth-Century Europe* (1988). Collections of essays on the role of women in the Renaissance include M. Rose, ed., *Women in the Middle Ages and Renaissance: Literary and Historical Perspectives* (1986), C. Levin and J. Watson, eds., *Ambiguous Realities: Women in the Mid-*

dle Ages and Renaissance (1987), and M. Ferguson and others, eds., *Rewriting the Renaissance: The Discourse of Sexual Differences in Early Modern Europe* (1986). See also M. King, *Women in the Renaissance* (1991), C. Jordan, *Renaissance Feminism: Literary Texts and Political Models* (1990), and L. Lawner, *Lives of the Courtesans: Portraits of the Renaissance* (1987). On the dissemination of humanism to northern Europe, see R. Weiss, *The Spread of Italian Humanism* (1964) and the collection of essays by A. Goodman and A. MacKay, *The Impact of Humanism on Western Europe* (1990). E. Eisenstein, *The Printing Press as an Agent of Change*, 2 vols. (1978) examines the impact of the printing press. Surveys of humanism in various countries are provided by F. Simone, *The French Renaissance* (1970), E. Bernstein, *German Humanism* (1983), H. Segal, *Renaissance Culture in Poland: The Rise of Humanism, 1470–1543* (1989), and M. Dowling, *Humanism in the Age of Henry VIII* (1989). On Erasmus, see R. Bainton, *Erasmus of Christendom* (1969) and J. Tracy, *Erasmus of the Low Countries* (1996).

E. Cochrane, *Historians and Historiography in the Italian Renaissance* (1981) is a good survey of an important topic. Among the immense literature on Machiavelli and Guicciardini, J. R. Hale, *Machiavelli and Renaissance Italy* (1960), F. Gilbert, *Machiavelli and Guicciardini* (1965), P. Bondanella, *Machiavelli and the Art of Renaissance History* (1973), and M. Phillips, *Francesco Guicciardini: The Historian's Craft* (1977) are especially useful. On philosophy, *The Cambridge History of Renaissance Philosophy* (1988) provides a comprehensive reference. See also P. Kristeller, *Renaissance Thought: The Classic, Scholastic, and Humanist Strains* (1961), A. Field, *The Origins of the Platonic Academy of Florence* (1988), and C. Schmitt, *Aristotle and the Renaissance* (1983). F. Hartt, *History of Italian Renaissance Art* (1979) is an introductory survey to an immense topic. K. Clark, *The Art of Humanism* (1983) is a brief but provocative essay. Among the many interesting monographs are M. Wackernagel, *The World of the Florentine Renaissance Artist: Projects and Patrons, Workshop and the Art Market* (1981), B. Cole, *The Renaissance Artist at Work: From Pisano to Titian* (1983), and L. Gildstein, *The Social and Cultural Roots of Linear Perspective* (1988). On architecture, see P. Murray, *The Architecture of the Italian Renaissance*, rev. ed. (1986), and W. Lotz, *Studies in Italian Renaissance Architecture* (1981).

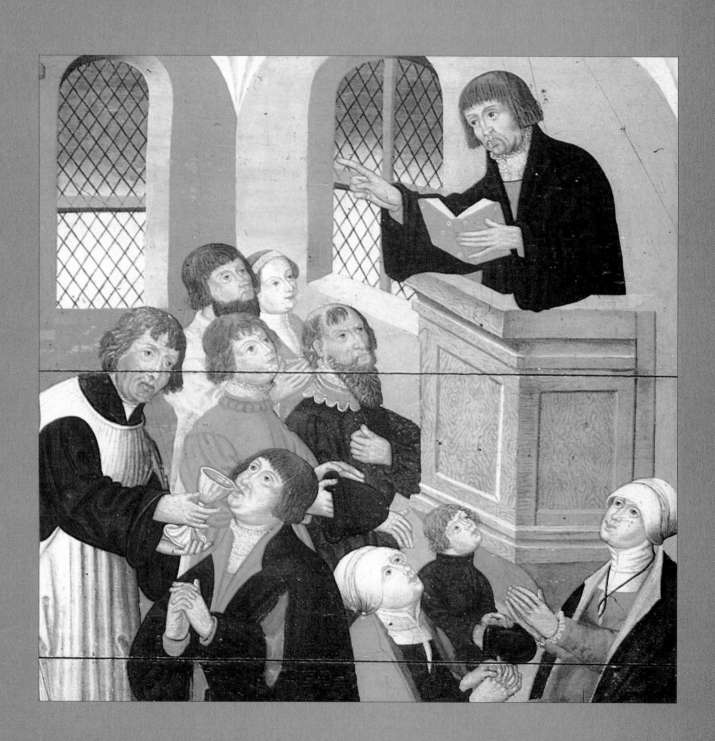

CHAPTER 15

THE RELIGIOUS REFORMATIONS
OF THE SIXTEENTH CENTURY

CHAPTER OUTLINE

M uch of Europe's religious life was transformed in the course of the sixteenth century. Scholars have called this period the Age of the Reformation, but this is somewhat misleading. There was more than one religious reformation. Several forms of piety arose that may be called Protestant, though their competing religious visions sometimes had little in common beyond opposition to the old church. Lutherans, Calvinists, Anabaptists, and a host of other groups distrusted and at times persecuted each other with un-Christian vigor. Others, such as the Antitrinitarians, were perhaps radical enough to require a classification of their own. Roman Catholicism was changed, in part by forces that had long been stirring within and in part by the church's need to defend itself against Protestantism.

All of these reformations arose from conflicts within the church and from its broader struggle with the claims of the state. Some of the issues were institutional and political. Others grew from changes in lay attitudes or from the influence of movements such as humanism and nominalism. Chapter 15 will examine the demands for church reform that arose during the later Middle Ages and describe how they grew into a series of religious movements that split western Christendom and transformed the old church even as they created new forms of religious belief.

Late Medieval Demands
for Religious Reform

The new assertiveness of the secular states brought them almost immediately into conflict with the church over rights, privileges, and revenues. That this occurred when the laity and many clergy were demanding higher standards of spirituality than ever before was the church's misfortune. Plague, war, and the perception of social collapse had raised the overall level of spiritual anxiety. At the same time, higher literacy rates, already apparent in the fourteenth century, narrowed the intellectual gap between the clergy and their flocks and led to an increased sophistication in matters religious. When the church, beset with enemies and divided internally, failed to meet this revolution of rising spiritual expectations, the call for reform became strident and ultimately irresistible.

The role of the late medieval church was broader and more closely integrated with the secular world than it is today. The pope was responsible not only for the spiritual welfare of western Christians, but also for the administration and defense of the papal states, a territory that embraced much of central Italy. At the local level, bishops, parishes, monasteries, and other ecclesiastical foundations probably controlled 20 percent of the arable land in Europe. In less-settled areas such as the north of England the total may have approached 70 percent. Many Europeans therefore lived on estates held by the church or had regular business dealings with those who managed them. Such contacts often caused resentment and may at times have encouraged the appearance of corruption.

Social services, too, were the church's responsibility. Hospitals, the care of orphans, and the distribution of charity were commonly administered by clerics as was formal education from the grammar school to the university. In an age when inns were few and wretched, monasteries often served as hotels, offering food and lodging to travelers in return for nominal donations.

Involvement with the world bred a certain worldliness. Because its practical responsibilities were great, the church was often forced to reward those in whom administrative skills were more developed than spirituality. Because the church offered one of the few available routes to upward social mobility, ambition or family interest caused many to become clerics without an adequate religious vocation. For some little choice existed. Children were often destined for the priesthood at a tender age, while unmarriageable women or those who preferred a career other than that of wife and mother had only the convent as a refuge. For women of talent and ambition, the opportunity to govern an abbey or a charitable institution was a route to self-fulfillment and public service that was otherwise unavailable in medieval society.

Not all late medieval clerics were governed by worldly motives. Alongside spiritual indifference and corruption were extreme piety and asceticism. For many people the contrast may have been too painful in an era of great spiritual need. In any case the anticlericalism that had always been present in European life ran especially high in the fourteenth and fifteenth centuries. Though by no means universal—the ties between lay people and their parish priests often remained close—it was an underlying accompaniment to the events that convulsed the church throughout this period.

Anticlericalism and the Decline of Papal Authority

Papal authority was one of the first casualties of the conflict between church and state and of the growing confusion over the temporal and spiritual roles of the clergy. A series of scandals beginning around 1300 gravely weakened the ability of the popes either to govern the church or to institute effective reforms in the face of popular demand.

In 1294 the saintly Celestine V resigned from the papacy in part because he feared that the exercise of its duties imperiled his soul. His successor, Boniface VIII, had no such concerns (see illustration 15.1). A vigorous advocate of papal authority, Boniface came into conflict with both Edward I of England and Philip IV of France over the issue of clerical taxation. The two kings were at war with one another, and each sought to tax the clergy of their respective realms to pay for it. When the pope forbade the practice in the bull *Clericis Laicos* (see document 15.1), Philip blocked the transmission of money from France to Rome. Boniface backed down, but Philip was not content with partial victories. In 1301 he convicted the papal legate, Bernard Sassier, bishop of Pamiers, of treason and demanded that Boniface ratify the decision of the French courts. This he could not do without sacrificing papal jurisdiction over the French church. When Boniface issued the decree *Unam Sanctam*, a bold assertion of papal authority over the secular state, Philip had him kidnapped at Anagni in 1303. Physically mistreated by his captors and furious over this unprecedented assault on papal dignity, Boniface died shortly thereafter.

After the brief pontificate of Benedict IX, French influence in the College of Cardinals secured the election of the bishop of Bordeaux, who became pope as Clement V (served 1305–14). The Roman populace was outraged. Riot and disorder—made worse by factional disputes between the relatives of the late Boniface and the Colonna family, which had supported Philip—convinced Clement that Rome would be an unhealthy place for a Frenchman. He decided to establish himself at Avignon, a papal territory in the south of France. The papacy would remain there for seventy-three years.

Illustration 15.1

Pope Boniface VIII. The conflict between Boniface and
Philip the Fair of France marked the beginning of a long series of
disasters for the papacy. This marble statue is attributed to
Arnolfo di Cambio.

The stay of the popes at Avignon was called the
Babylonian Captivity because the church appeared to
have been taken captive by the French as the biblical
children of Israel had been held at Babylon. It was an
international scandal for several reasons. The pope was

DOCUMENT 15.1

The Bull *Clericis Laicos* (1296)

*Here, Boniface VIII provides a clear statement of the issues at
stake in his struggle with Philip IV. The passage is followed
by the excommunication of those who would levy such taxes
and the imposition of an interdict on "all communities which
shall be culpable in such matters."*

It is said that in times past laymen practiced great
violence against the clergy, and our experience
clearly shows that they are doing so at present,
since they are not content to remain within the
limits prescribed for them, but strive to do that
which is prohibited and illegal. And they pay no
attention to the fact that they are forbidden to exercise authority over the clergy and ecclesiastical
persons and their possessions. But they are laying
heavy burdens on bishops, churches, and clergy,
both regular and secular, by taxing them, levying
contributions on them, and extorting the half, the
tenth, the twentieth, or some other part of their
income and possessions. They are striving in many
ways to reduce the clergy to servitude and to subject them to their own sway. And we grieve to say
it, but some bishops and clergy, fearing where they
should not, and seeking a temporary peace, and
fearing more to offend man than God, submit im-
providently rather than rashly to these abuses
without receiving the papal permission. Wishing
to prevent these evils, with the counsel of our
brethren and with our apostolic authority, we declare that if any bishops or clergy, regular or secular, of any grade, condition, or rank, shall pay, or
promise, or consent to pay to laymen any contributions or taxes . . . without the permission of the
pope, they shall, by the very act, incur the sentence of excommunication.

living outside his diocese, and absenteeism had long
been considered an abuse by reformers. Worse yet, the
pope seemed to be a mere agent of the French monarchy. This was not quite true. The Avignon popes were
more independent than they appeared to be at the
time, but events continued to strengthen the negative
impressions created by Clement V. Clement not only
declared that *Unam Sanctam* did not restrict the French
monarchy, but also pardoned Guillaume de Nogaret,

Illustration 15.2

The Papal Palace at Avignon. The luxury and massive size of the papal residence built during the so-called Babylonian Captivity helps to explain why the Avignon popes developed a reputation for greed and spiritual indifference.

the French minister who had kidnapped Boniface VIII. He then obliged Philip by condemning the Knights Templars, whose wealth was confiscated by the king, and by packing the College of Cardinals with French appointees who ensured that the next several popes would be French.

Clement's successor, John XXII (served 1316–34), wanted to restore papal independence but was involved in a bitter struggle with the emperor Louis IV. John had opposed the emperor's election on the grounds that Louis was the stronger of the two candidates and therefore presented a greater threat to the integrity of the papal states. The king of France agreed because Louis was equally a threat to him. When John illegally refused to accept the results of the election, the pope appeared once again to be acting in the interest of France. Subsequent popes supported France against England in the later stages of the Hundred Years' War. Their best efforts were devoted to strengthening papal finances and to the construction of a magnificent palace complex at Avignon (see illustration 15.2). Fiscal reforms backfired politically because most countries responded to it with legislation limiting papal jurisdiction and taxation within their borders. The palace was ostentatious and fostered the idea that the popes had no intention of returning to Rome. The overall impression was that the popes were subservient to France as well as greedy and luxurious.

Criticism mounted, and in 1377 Gregory XI returned the papacy to Rome. He died in the following year, and his Italian successor, Urban VI, was elected amid rioting by the Roman mob and dissension among the cardinals. Urban quickly alienated those who had elected him by his erratic behavior and by his demands for an immediate reform of the papal court. Thirteen cardinals, twelve of whom were French, left Rome. Claiming that the election had been held under duress, they elected an antipope, Clement VII. The Great Schism (1378–1417) had begun.

❖ DOCUMENT 15.2 ❖

The Decree *Sacrosancta*

By issuing the decree Sacrosancta, *the Council of Constance (1414–17) justified its deposition of three existing popes and the election of Martin V. Though repudiated by later popes, the decree helped to end the Great Schism and provided a concise statement of the conciliarist position for future generations.*

In the name of the Holy and indivisible Trinity, of the Father, Son, and Holy Ghost. Amen.

This holy synod of Constance, forming a general council for the extirpation of the present schism and the union and reformation, in head and members, of the church of God, legitimately assembled in the Holy Ghost, to the praise of Omnipotent God, in order that it may the more easily, safely, effectively, and freely bring about the union and reformation of the church of God, hereby determines, decrees, and declares what follows:

It first declares that this same council, legitimately assembled in the Holy Ghost, forming a general council and representing the Catholic Church militant, has its power immediately from Christ, and everyone, whatever his state or position, even if it be the Papal dignity itself, is bound to obey it in all those things which pertain to the faith and the healing of the said schism, and to the general reformation of the Church of God in head and members.

It further declares that anyone, whatever his condition, station or rank, even if it be the Papal, who shall contumaciously refuse to obey the mandates, decrees, ordinances or instructions which have been, or shall be issued by this holy council, or by any other general council, legitimately summoned, which concern, or in any way relate to the above mentioned subjects, shall, unless he repudiate his conduct, be subjected to condign penance and be suitably punished, having recourse, if necessary, to the other resources of the law.

The church now had two popes. England, the Holy Roman Empire, Hungary, and Poland supported Urban VI. France, Castile, Aragon, Naples, and Scotland supported Clement. International and dynastic issues were involved, and neither claimant would step down. For nearly forty years each side elected its own successors while papal administration deteriorated and the prestige of the office sank to levels not seen since before the Cluniac reforms.

The most promising solution was to convene a general council of the church. In 1409 the Council of Pisa elected Alexander V, who was generally accepted throughout Europe. However, the two prior claimants, arguing that the council had been called illegally by the cardinals instead of by a pope, refused to quit. There were now three popes. Finally, in 1413 Alexander's successor, John XXIII, called the Council of Constance, which declared itself superior to any pope (see document 15.2). John, who had in the meantime been found guilty of heresy, and the Avignon claimant Benedict XIII were deposed and Gregory XIII resigned. Martin V was elected to succeed Gregory, thereby preserving the legitimacy of the Roman line, which has since been regarded as official.

The Schism was over, but the papacy had been gravely weakened in both fact and theory. The actions of the council were supported by the work of three generations of thinkers who had come to believe that councils representing the entire body of the faithful had ultimate authority over the church and that the pope was little more than a symbol of unity. These conciliarists included such respected authorities as Jean Gerson, Henry of Langenstein, and Pierre d'Ailly. Made plausible by more than a century of papal scandals, conciliarism became a formidable obstacle to the governance of the church. Fifteenth-century popes feared with some justification that they might be deposed for any controversial act, while councils, by their nature, found making everyday administrative decisions impossible. Legally, the issue was resolved in 1460 when Pius II forbade appeals to a council without papal authorization in the bull *Execrabilis.* The memory of conciliarism nevertheless would inhibit papal efforts at reform for years to come.

Conciliarism also served as a focus for criticisms of the papacy that had been simmering since the Babylonian Captivity. Among the many sources of conciliarist thought was the *Defensor Pacis* of Marsilius of Padua. Commissioned originally by Louis IV at the height of his struggle with John XXII, it argued among other things that true *dominium* proceeded not from divine grace as administered by the church, but from the consent of the governed.

Other criticisms of the papacy, some of which were adopted by the conciliarists, grew out of the possessionist controversy. By the end of the thirteenth century, the Franciscan order had split into two main factions: the Observant or Spiritual Franciscans, who insisted on a literal interpretation of the Rule of St. Francis, which prohibited the order from owning property; and the Conventuals, who believed that the work of the order could be done only if the brothers lived an orderly life in convents and possessed the material resources with which to perform their tasks. After much argument, the Observant position was condemned by John XXII. The Observant Franciscans, who were supported by Louis IV, responded with attacks on the validity of papal authority, many of which would be used by later critics of the church.

The Struggle for the Transformation of Piety

The issue of church governance became entangled in a growing dispute over the forms of piety. This conflict, which was about two different ways of living a Christian life, had been present implicitly in the reform movements of the twelfth century. The dominant form of piety that had emerged from the early Middle Ages was forged by the monastic tradition. It saw the clergy as heroic champions whose chief function was to serve as intermediaries between the laity and a God of judgment. They did this primarily through the sacrament of communion (the Eucharist), which was considered a sacrifice, and through oral prayers of intercession. This view, with its necessary emphasis on the public repetition of formulae, was challenged in the eleventh and twelfth centuries by Bernard of Clairvaux and other monastic theorists who sought a more personal experience of God through private devotions and mental prayer. Their views were adopted by the Franciscans and eventually popularized by them, though the process was lengthy and incomplete. Personal piety was especially attractive to the Observant Franciscans, whose interpretation of the Rule of St. Francis made corporate devotions difficult.

To those who sought a transformation of their inner life through personal contact with God, the older forms of piety were unacceptable. They came to believe that excessive emphasis on the sacraments and on oral prayer encouraged complacency as well as contractualism, the habit of making deals with God in return for special favors. The point is arguable, but in their cri-

tique of popular piety they were on firmer ground. Much late medieval piety was mechanistic and involved practices that would today be regarded as abuses. The sale of indulgences, the misuse of pilgrimages, and the proliferation of masses for the dead were all symptoms of the popular obsession with death and purgatory that followed in the wake of the bubonic plague. Salvation was assured by the sacraments of the church, but every sin committed in life carried with it a sentence to be served in purgatory. As the pains of purgatory were like those of hell, without the curse of eternal separation from God, much effort was spent in avoiding them. A mass said for the soul of the dead reduced the penalty by a specified number of years. Henry VII of England, who seems to have had a bad conscience, left money in his will for ten thousand masses. Many priests survived entirely on the proceeds from such bequests and had no other duties. An indulgence was a remission of the "temporal" or purgatorial punishment for sins that could be granted by the pope out of the church's "treasury of merits." Its price, too, was related to the number of years it subtracted from the buyer's term in purgatory, and an indulgence sometimes could be purchased in advance for sins not yet committed.

These practices were offensive to an increasingly refined spirituality. Some, such as the sale of indulgences, were ultimately condemned by the Council of Trent (1545–63). Other rites, especially those concerned with the veneration of the saints and with popular festivals, were thought by some to be superstitious and even pagan in origin. Praying to St. Roche as protection against the plague and to St. Fiacre for the relief of hemorrhoids was customary. Spanish peasants believed that St. Augustine and St. Gregory could ward off locusts, because they were learned doctors of the church and locusts were by nature heretical. The origins of this notion are obscure, but locusts were tried as heretics on several occasions in the fifteenth century.

Such habits were deeply rooted in the rich and varied piety of the Middle Ages. If some religious were scandalized by them, other priests were unwilling to condemn genuine expressions of religious feeling, and still others no doubt accepted them out of ignorance. No systematic education had been established for parish priests, and thanks to absenteeism, many parishes were served by vicars or substitutes whose qualifications were minimal at best. However, the church's critics did not reject pilgrimages, indulgences, the proper use of relics, or masses for the dead. They merely wished to ground these "works" in the faith and good intentions that would make them spiritually valid.

They opposed simpleminded contractualism and "arithmetical" piety, but their concerns intensified their conflict with a church that remained immobilized by political and organizational difficulties.

Of those forms of piety that sought personal contact with God, the most ambitious was mysticism. The enormous popularity of mysticism in the later Middle Ages was in some respects a measure of the growing influence of women on religious life. Many of the great mystics were women. Others were men who became involved with the movement as confessors to convents of nuns. Mysticism may be defined as the effort to achieve spiritual union with God through ecstatic contemplation. Because the experience is highly personal it had many variants, but most of them fell into two broad categories. The first, and probably the most common, was to experience visions or infusions of the Holy Spirit in the manner of St. Catherine of Siena (1347–80) or Julian of Norwich (1342–c. 1416). The second, best typified by Meister Eckhard (c. 1260–1328) and the Rhineland mystics, was influenced by the Neoplatonic concept of ideas and aimed at a real union of the soul with God (see document 15.3). Mystics such as Eckhardt and his followers, Tauler and Suso, sought to penetrate the divine intelligence and perceive the universe as God perceives it. Both views were rooted firmly in the medieval tradition of interior piety, but Eckhart and those like him were suspected of heresy because they seemed to deny the vital distinction between the Creator and the human soul.

Neither form of experience was easy to achieve. Both involved a long process of mental and spiritual preparation that was described in an ever-growing literature. Manuals such as Walter Hilton's *Scale of Perfection* became extremely popular with lay people and were circulated in large numbers both before and after the invention of printing.

Though mysticism was essentially private, it influenced the development of a powerful corporate movement known as the *Devotio Moderna*, or modern devotion. Its founder was Gerhard Groote (1340–84) who organized a community of religious women at Deventer in the Netherlands. These Sisters of the Common Life were laywomen, not nuns. They pledged themselves to a communal life informed by contemplation but directed toward service in the world. A parallel group for men, the Brethren of the Common Life, was founded shortly thereafter by Groote's disciple Florens Radewijns. These two groups, together with the Augustinian Canons of the Windesheim Congregation, a fully monastic order also founded by Radewijns, formed the nucleus of a movement that spread rapidly through the Low Countries and western Germany. Catholic, but highly critical of the clergy, it emphasized charitable works, private devotion, and its own form of education. The goal of its adherents was the imitation of Christ. A book titled *The Imitation of Christ* by one of the Brethren, Thomas à Kempis, was a best-seller until well into the twentieth century and did much to popularize a style of piety that was the opposite of contractualism.

◈ DOCUMENT 15.3 ◈

The Mystic Experience

In this passage Jan van Ruysbroeck (1293–1381) attempts to capture the sense of unity with God that was at least one of the late medieval mystic's primary goals. In the process he demonstrates both the late medieval desire to experience God without intermediaries and the mystic's postscholastic conviction that reason is an obstacle to faith.

And after this, there follows the third way of feeling: namely, that we feel ourselves to be one *with* God; for through the transformation in God, we feel ourselves to be swallowed up in the fathomless abyss of our eternal blessedness, wherein we can nevermore find any distinction between ourselves and God. And this is our highest feeling, which we cannot experience in any other way than in the immersion in love. And therefore, so soon as we are uplifted and drawn into our highest feeling, all our powers stand idle in an essential fruition; but our powers do not pass away into nothingness, for then we should lose our created being. And as long as we stand idle, with an inclined spirit, and with open eyes, but without reflection, so long can we contemplate and have fruition. But, at the very moment in which we seek to prove and to comprehend what it is that we feel, we fall back into reason, and there we find a distinction and an otherness between ourselves and God, and find God outside ourselves in incomprehensibility.

The Heretics: Wycliffe and Hus

Other religious movements were less innocent, at least from the perspective of the church. Full-scale heresies emerged in England and Bohemia in response to the teachings of John Wycliffe (1330–84) and Jan Hus (c. 1372–1415). Wycliffe was a successful teacher of

❖ DOCUMENT 15.4 ❖

John Wycliffe: The Primacy of the Bible

During his last years, John Wycliffe became an outspoken radical. He denounced the authority of the pope, whom he called the Antichrist, insisted upon the Bible as the sole source of religious truth, and proclaimed that churchmen were trying to keep Christians from reading the Bible. He advanced these arguments in a short work entitled Antichrist's Labor to Destroy Holy Writ, *from which the following excerpt is taken.*

As our Lord Jesus Christ ordained, by the writing of the four evangelists, to make his gospel surely known, and maintained against heretics, and men out of the faith; so the devil, even Satan, devises by antichrist and his wordly false clerks, to destroy holy writ and Christian men's belief, by four accursed ways or false reasons: 1) That the church is of more authority, and more to be believed than any gospel. 2) That Augustine said he would not believe the gospel if the church had not taught him so. 3) That no man alive knows which is the gospel, but by the approv-ing of the church. 4) If men say that they believe this is the gospel of Matthew or John, they ask, 'Why believest thou that this is the gospel?' as though they would say, 'There is no cause but that the church confirmeth and teacheth it.'

These four evidences, and many more, the fiend makes, to blind men in their belief, that they should not know what is sin, or what is virtue; which is truth, which is falsehood; which is good, which is evil; which are God's commands, and which are the fiend's lies; thus to bring all men blindly to hell and their new religion. And princi-pally friars preach these evidences, and sow them among ignorant men in the country, to stop poor priests and ig-norant men, that they be not hardy to speak of the gospel, holy writ, God's commandments, joys of heaven, of sins, and of pains of hell, lest they stir men to rise out of their sins for dread of pains, and to live in virtuous life, to have the bliss of heaven.

theology at Oxford who became involved with politics during the 1370s. England was attempting to follow the French lead in restricting papal rights of appointment and taxation, and Wycliffe became the chief spokesman for the anticlerical views of Edward III's son, John of Gaunt. At first Wycliffe restricted himself to the tradi-tional arguments in favor of clerical poverty, but as his views began to attract criticism and as he came to real-ize that his personal ambitions would not be fulfilled, he drifted further into radicalism. In his last years he re-jected papal authority and declared that the Bible was the sole source of religious truth (see document 15.4). Strongly influenced by St. Augustine and committed to an extreme form of philosophical realism, he supported predestination and ended by rejecting transubstantia-tion because it involved what he saw as the annihilation of the substance of the bread and wine. In his view, sub-stance was by definition unchangeable, and the miracle of the mass was therefore an impossibility. This was heresy, as was his revival of the ancient Donatist idea that the value of the sacraments depended upon the personal virtue of the priest who administered them.

Though John of Gaunt discretely withdrew his sup-port, Wycliffe died before the church could bring him to trial. By this time his ideas and the extraordinary vio-lence of his attacks on the clergy had begun to attract popular attention. His followers, the Lollards, produced an English translation of the Bible and organized a march on London in 1413. Fearing that the egalitarian tendencies of the Lollards encouraged social disorder, Henry V suppressed the movement, but scattered com-munities preserved their traditions until the outbreak of the Protestant Reformation.

Because England and Bohemia were diplomatically aligned on the Great Schism, a number of Czech stu-dents left the University of Paris for Oxford after 1378. There they came in contact with the teachings of Wycliffe, and by 1400 his works were being openly debated at Prague. Wycliffe's ideas were popular be-cause they seemed to coincide with an already well-developed reform movement. Czech preachers had long attacked the morality of the clergy and were now demanding a Czech translation of the Bible. Great re-sentment also existed over denying the communion to the laity in both kinds. Reserving both bread and wine for the priest while giving only bread to the laity was common throughout Europe. In Bohemia the practice was seen as an expression of clerical arrogance.

Though basically religious, these issues were hopelessly intertwined with the ethnic rivalry between Czechs and Germans that had troubled Bohemia for centuries. The Kingdom of Bohemia had a large population of Germans (see chapter 13) who were often resented by their Slavic neighbors. Moreover, the church held nearly 40 percent of the land, and many of the leading churchmen were German. To many, anticlericalism was therefore an expression of Czech national feeling as well as of frustrated piety, and this association quickly drew the reform movement into the arena of imperial politics. The king, Vaclav (Wenceslas) IV, was popular with the Czechs and favored their interests. The Germans, together with the papacy, supported the schemes of his half-brother Sigismund, who would one day be emperor, but who in the meantime sought the crown of Bohemia for himself.

The University of Prague found itself at the center of these controversies. In 1409 Vaclav expelled the German students and faculty and appointed Jan Hus, a Czech professor, as rector. Hus had been attracted to Wycliffe's writings by their anticlericalism, but he also saw their extreme philosophical realism as a weapon against the German theologians, most of whom were nominalists. He did not, however, reject transubstantiation and was in general more conservative than Wycliffe on every issue save that of papal authority. Hus did not think of himself as a heretic, and in 1415 he accepted an invitation to defend his views before the Council of Constance. The invitation had been orchestrated by Sigismund who offered him a safe-conduct, but the promised guarantee was little more than a passport, and Hus was burned at the stake on July 6.

The burning of Hus provoked a national outcry in Bohemia. Taking the communion chalice as their symbol, the Czechs broke with Rome and developed a liturgy in the Czech language. When their protector, Vaclav, died in 1419, he was succeeded by Sigismund. The Hussites, as they were now called, rose in armed revolt and resoundingly defeated the papal-imperial crusades against them in 1420, 1422, and 1431. Their success resulted largely from the popularity of their cause and the military acumen of John Žižka, the leader of a radical group known as the Taborites who organized a superb army featuring the first large-scale use of handheld firearms. Finally, in 1436 the Hussites secured a treaty that guaranteed them control over the Bohemian church and confirmed their earlier expropriation of church property. Catholicism was restored to Bohemia in 1620. In spite of subsequent persecution, a Hussite church survives to this day.

The Religious Impact of Nominalism, Humanism, and the Printing Press

The religious tensions and controversies of the later Middle Ages were heightened by intellectual movements that threatened the church's authority in more subtle ways. Nominalism (see chapter 10), which grew in popularity during the fourteenth and fifteenth centuries, tended to undermine the foundations of dogma by denying that they were susceptible to rational proof. Though never the dominant school in late medieval thought, it influenced many theologians including Martin Luther.

Humanism exerted an even stronger influence on religious issues. Humanists such as Erasmus criticized the moral shortcomings of the clergy and used their mastery of rhetoric to attack the scholastic philosophers. Their belief in the superiority of ancient over modern texts contributed to the idea that scripture alone was the ultimate source of religious truth. Though many humanists, including Erasmus, remained within the old church, this concept of *sola scriptura* would be central to the teachings of the reformers. Many of them, including Zwingli, Calvin, and Melanchthon had been trained as humanists. They used humanist methodology in their analysis of sacred texts. Humanist respect for antiquity may also have influenced the growing belief that the practices of the early church most closely approximated the intentions of Christ and that subsequent developments, including the rise of the papacy, were modern corruptions.

The reform movements that destroyed the unity of western Christendom in the sixteenth century may therefore be seen as the products of a generalized dissatisfaction with the church. The development of printing, which made the writings of the reformers available to thousands of people, and the conjunction of religious reform with the political needs of certain states and cities transformed that dissatisfaction into what is usually called the Protestant Reformation.

Martin Luther and the Outbreak of the Protestant Reformation

The first and in many ways the most influential of these movements was the one created in Germany by Martin Luther (1483–1546). A monk of the Augustinian Observant order and professor of the New Testament at the University of Wittenberg in electoral Saxony,

Luther experienced a profound spiritual crisis that eventually brought him into open conflict with the church (see illustration 15.3). Like many of his contemporaries, Luther was troubled by an overwhelming sense of sin and unworthiness for which the teachings of the church provided no relief. Neither the rigors of monastic life nor the sacrament of penance could provide him with assurance of salvation. In the course of his biblical studies he gradually arrived at a solution. Based on his reading of Paul's Epistle to the Romans and on his growing admiration for the works of St. Augustine, he concluded that souls were not saved by religious ceremonies and good works but by faith alone. Human beings could never be righteous enough to merit God's forgiveness, but they could be saved if only they would believe and have faith in the righteousness of Christ.

Luther felt himself transformed by this insight. Even as he formulated it, he was confronted by the issue of indulgences. In 1517 a special indulgence was made available in the territories surrounding electoral Saxony. Its purpose was to raise money for the construction of St. Peter's basilica in Rome and to retire the debt incurred by Albrecht of Mainz in securing for himself through bribery the archbishoprics of Mainz and Magdeburg and the bishopric of Halberstadt. Albrecht had committed not only pluralism but also simony (the illegal purchase of church offices). To Luther, however, this was not the central issue. To him, as to many other clerics, the sale of indulgences was a symbol of the contractualism that beset medieval piety and blinded lay people to the true path of salvation. On October 31, 1517, he posted ninety-five theses condemning this practice to the door of Wittenberg's Castle Church.

His action was in no way unusual. It was the traditional means by which a professor offered to debate all comers on a particular issue, and the positions taken by Luther were not heretical. Furthermore, the sale of indulgences was later condemned by the Council of Trent. However, Luther's action unleashed a storm of controversy. Spread throughout Germany by the printing press, the theses were endorsed by advocates of reform and condemned by the pope, the Dominican order, the archbishop of Mainz, and the Fugger bank of Augsburg, which had loaned Albrecht the money for the elections.

In the debates that followed, Luther was forced to work out the broader implications of his teachings. At Leipzig in June 1519, he challenged the doctrinal authority of popes and councils and declared that Scripture took precedence over all other sources of religious truth. In 1520 he published three pamphlets that drew

Illustration 15.3

%% **Martin Luther.** This portrait of Luther as a young monk was painted by Lucas Cranach the Elder about a year before the Diet of Worms and shows the reformer as he must have looked when he confronted the Imperial Diet.

him at last into formal heresy. In his *Address to the Christian Nobility of the German Nation* he encouraged the princes to demand reform (see document 15.5). *On the Babylonian Captivity of the Church* abolished five of the seven sacraments and declared that the efficacy of baptism and communion were dependent on the faith of the recipient, not the ordination of the priest. He also rejected transubstantiation while arguing that Christ was nevertheless truly present in the Eucharist (see illustration 15.4). *The Freedom of a Christian* summarized Luther's doctrine of salvation by faith. Luther had not intended to break with the church, but his extraordinary skill as a writer and propagandist ignited anticlerical and antipapal feeling throughout Germany (see illustration 15.5). Compromise was now impossible, and he was excommunicated on January 31, 1521.

◈ DOCUMENT 15.5 ◈

Luther: Address to the German Nobility

Martin Luther's primary concerns were always spiritual and theological, but he knew how to appeal to other emotions as well. These extracts from his Address to the Christian Nobility of the German Nation *are a relatively modest example of the rhetoric with which he attacked the authority of the Catholic Church.*

What is the use in Christendom of those who are called "cardinals"? I will tell you. In Italy and Germany there are many rich convents, endowments, holdings, and benefices; and as the best way of getting these into the hands of Rome they created cardinals, and gave to them the bishoprics, convents, and prelacies, and thus destroyed the service of God. That is why Italy is almost a desert now. . . . Why? Because the cardinals must have the wealth. The Turk himself could not have so desolated Italy and so overthrown the worship of God.

Now that Italy is sucked dry, they come to Germany. They begin in a quiet way, but we shall soon have Germany brought into the same state as Italy. We have a few cardinals already. What the Romanists really mean to do, the "drunken" Germans are not to see until they have lost everything . . . .

Now this devilish state of things is not only open robbery and deceit and the prevailing of the gates of hell, but it is destroying the very life and soul of Christianity; therefore we are bound to use all our diligence to ward off this misery and destruction. If we want to fight Turks, let us begin here—we cannot find worse ones. If we rightly hang thieves and robbers, why do we leave the greed of Rome unpunished? for Rome is the greatest thief and robber that has ever appeared on earth, or ever will.

Illustration 15.4

The Lutheran Sacraments. This altar painting from the Lutheran church at Thorslunde, Denmark, is intended as a graphic lesson in theology. Infant baptism is shown at the left. In the center, two communicants receive the sacrament in both kinds, while the preacher at the right emphasizes the importance of God's word.

The affair might have ended with Luther's trial and execution, but political considerations intervened. His own prince, Frederick "the Wise" of Saxony, arranged for him to defend his position before the Imperial Diet at Worms in April. The new emperor Charles V was unimpressed. He placed Luther under the Imperial Ban, and Frederick was forced to protect his monk by hiding him in the Wartburg Castle for nearly a year. Luther used this enforced period of leisure to translate the New Testament into German.

Frederick's motives and those of the other princes and city magistrates who eventually supported Luther's reformation varied widely. Some were inspired by genuine religious feeling or, like Frederick, by a proprietary responsibility for "their" churches that transcended loyalty to a distant and non-German papacy. Others, especially in the towns, responded to the public enthusiasm generated by Luther's writings. Regardless of personal feelings everyone understood the practical advantages of breaking with Rome. Revenues could be

Illustration 15.5

⫸ The 'Birth' of the Pope and His Curia. This woodcut illustrates the venom and obscenity of much religious propaganda during the Reformation era. The devil is shown defecating churchmen who are then suckled by Medusa-headed demons. It accompanied a 1545 treatise by Martin Luther entitled *Against the Roman Papacy: An Institution of the Devil.*

increased by confiscating church property and by ending ecclesiastical immunity to taxation, while the control of church courts and ecclesiastical patronage were valuable prizes to those engaged in state building.

The emperor objected on both political and religious grounds. Charles V was a devout Catholic. He was also committed to the ideal of imperial unity, which was clearly threatened by anything that increased the power and revenues of the princes. Only twenty-one at the Diet of Worms, he was heir to an enormous accumulation of states including Austria, Spain, the Netherlands, and much of Italy (see chapter 16). In theory, only the Ottoman Empire could stand against him. When he abdicated and retired to a Spanish monastery in 1556, the Reformation was still intact. His power, though great, had not been equal to his responsibilities. Pressed on the Danube and in the

Mediterranean by the Turks, forced to fight seven wars with France, and beset simultaneously by Protestant princes, urban revolutionaries, and popes who feared the extension of his influence in Italy, Charles failed utterly in his attempts to impose orthodoxy. The empire remained open to religious turmoil.

Other Forms of Protestantism: The Radicals, Zwingli, and Calvin

Some of that turmoil began while Luther was still hidden in the Wartburg. The reformer had believed that, once the gospel was freely preached, congregations would follow it without the direction of an institutional church. He discovered that not all of the pope's enemies shared his interpretation of the Bible. Movements arose that rejected what he saw as the basic insight of the reformation: salvation by faith alone. To many ordinary men and women, this doctrine weakened the ethical imperatives that lay at the heart of Christianity. They wanted a restoration of the primitive, apostolic church—a "gathered" community of Christians who lived by the letter of Scripture. Luther had not gone far enough. Luther in turn thought that they were *schwärmer*, or enthusiasts who wanted to return to the works righteousness of the medieval church. Faced with what he saw as a fundamental threat to reform, Luther turned to the state. In 1527 a system of visitations was instituted throughout Saxony that for all practical purposes placed temporal control of the church in the hands of the prince. It was to be the model for Lutheran Church discipline throughout Germany and Scandinavia, but it did not at first halt the spread of radicalism.

Because these radical movements were often popular in origin or had coalesced around the teachings of an individual preacher, they varied widely in character. Perhaps the most radical were the Antitrinitarians, who rejected the doctrine of the Trinity and argued for a piety based wholly upon good works. Under the leadership of two Italian brothers, Laelio and Fausto Sozzini, they found converts among the Polish nobility but had little influence on western Europe. The most numerous were the Anabaptists, a loosely affiliated group who were the spiritual ancestors of the modern Mennonites and Amish. Their name derives from the practice of adult baptism, which they saw not only as a sacrament, but also as the heart of the redemptive process. Baptism was the deliberate decision to follow

◈ DOCUMENT 15.6 ◈

The Anabaptists Reject Civic Life

In 1527 a group of Anabaptists met at Schleitheim on the Swiss-German border to clarify issues connected with their teachings. The result was the Schleitheim Confession, *a document widely accepted by later Anabaptists. In this excerpt, demands are made for separation from the world.*

Fourth. We are agreed as follows on separation: A separation shall be made from the evil and the wickedness which the devil planted in the world; in this manner, simply that we should not have fellowship with them, the wicked, and not run with them in the multitude of their abominations. This is the way it is: Since all who do not walk in the obedience of faith and have not united themselves with God so that they wish to do his will, are a great abomination before God, it is not possible for anything to grow or issue from them except abominable things. For truly all creatures are in but two classes, good and bad, believing and unbelieving, darkness and light, the world and those who have come out of the world, God's temple and idols, Christ and Belial; and none can have part with the other.

To us then the command of the Lord is clear when He calls us to separate from the evil and thus He will be our God and we shall be his sons and daughters.

He further admonishes us to withdraw from Babylon and the earthly Egypt that we may not be partakers of the pain and suffering which the Lord will bring upon them.

From all this we should learn that everything which is not united with our God and Christ cannot be other than an abomination which we should shun and flee from. By this is meant all popish and anti-popish works and church services, meetings and church attendance, drinking houses, civic affairs, the commitments made in unbelief [oaths] and other things of that kind, which are highly regarded by the world and yet carried on in flat contradiction to the command of God.

Therefore there will also unquestionably fall from us the un-Christian, devilish weapons of force—such as sword, armor and the like, and all their use for friends or against one's enemies.

Christ and could therefore be made only by a responsible adult acting in complete freedom of will. It signified entrance into a visible church of the saints that must, by definition, be separate from the world around it. Most Anabaptists were therefore pacifists who would accept no civic responsibilities, refusing even to take an oath in court (see document 15.6).

This rejection of civic responsibility was seen as a threat to the political order. Hatred of the Anabaptists was one issue on which Lutherans and Catholics could agree, and in 1529 an imperial edict made belief in adult baptism a capital offense. Hatred became something like panic when an atypically violent group of Anabaptists gained control of the city of Münster and proclaimed it the New Jerusalem, complete with polygamy and communal sharing of property. They were eventually dislodged and their leaders executed, but the episode, though unparalleled elsewhere, convinced political and ecclesiastical leaders that their suspicions had been correct. They executed tens of thousands of Anabaptists throughout Germany and the Low Countries, and by 1550 the movement had dwindled to a remnant. A group of survivors, afterwards

known as Mennonites, were reorganized under the leadership of Menno Simons. Their moderation and emphasis on high ethical standards became a model for other dissenting groups.

Meanwhile, another kind of reform had emerged in Switzerland. Zürich, like other Swiss cantons, was a center of the mercenary industry. By 1518 a growing party of citizens had come to oppose what they called the exchange of blood for money. The innovations of Gonsalvo de Córdoba had cost the Swiss their tactical advantage on the battlefield, and their casualties during the latter part of the Italian wars had been very heavy. Moreover, the trade had enriched a few contractors who were now thought to exert undue influence on local politics while compromising the city's neutrality through their relations with France and the papacy. One of the leading spokesmen for the antimercenary forces was a priest, Huldrych Zwingli (1484–1531), who had been a chaplain to the troops in Italy. He had received a good humanist education and, like Luther, was known for attacking indulgences and for sermons that relied heavily on the Scriptures. In 1519 the antimercenary party gained control of the Zürich city council and named Zwingli people's priest of the city's main church, a post from which he was able to guide the process of reform.

Zwingli's concept of reformation grew out of the democratic traditions of his native land. Believing that each congregation should determine its own policies under the guidance of the gospel, he saw no real distinction between the government of the church and that of the state. Both elected representatives to determine policy. Both should be guided by the law of God. He therefore proceeded to reform the city step by step, providing guidance and advice but leaving the implementation of reforms to the city council.

Like Luther, Zwingli was challenged at an early date by those who felt that his reforms were insufficiently thorough. In responding to such Anabaptist critics as Conrad Grebel and Georg Blaurock, Zwingli developed teachings that were at variance with Luther's as well. When the Anabaptists asked how a child could be baptized if the efficacy of the sacrament depended upon the faith of the recipient, Zwingli responded that the faith was that of the parent or guardian and that the sacrament was in effect a covenant to raise the child as a Christian. The rite was analogous to circumcision among the Jews. He also rejected Luther's doctrine of the Real Presence in communion and argued, after some hesitation, that for those with faith Christ was present in spirit though not in body.

Zwingli's ideas were theologically original and appealed strongly to other reformers, but Luther rejected them at the Marburg Colloquy in 1529. The failure of this meeting marked the beginning of a separation between the Lutheran and Reformed traditions that persists to this day. It also coincided with a vote by the Imperial Diet to enforce the Edict of Worms against all non-Catholics. Those who protested against this measure, Lutheran and Reformed, became known as Protestants. In the meantime, the efforts of Zürich to export its reformation to other parts of Switzerland led to conflict, and Zwingli was killed, sword in hand, at the battle of Kappel.

Among those influenced by Zwingli's teachings was John Calvin (1509–64). Calvin was born at Noyon in France, the son of a wealthy lawyer who for most of his career had been secretary to the local bishop (see illustration 15.6). A brilliant student, Calvin was educated at Paris and at Orléans where he earned a law degree. His interests eventually turned to humanism and then to theology. In 1534 he adopted the reformed faith. His conversion bore immediate fruit in *The Institutes of the Christian Religion*, a more-or-less systematic explanation of reformed teachings. The first edition appeared in

Illustration 15.6

John Calvin. The reformer is shown here as he must have looked during his early years at Geneva.

March 1536, and though Calvin continued to revise and expand it throughout his lifetime, this early effort contained the basic elements of his mature thought.

Calvin is best known for his uncompromising position on predestination, holding, like Zwingli, that God divides the elect from the reprobate by His own "dread decree" (see document 15.7). Luther, like St. Augustine, believed that God predestines certain individuals to salvation, but he had stopped short of declaring that some are predestined to hell. To Calvin, this seemed illogical. To select some is by definition to reject others. This doctrine of "double predestination," like many of his formulations on the sacraments and other issues, may be seen as refinements of ideas originally suggested by others, but Calvin was far more than a mere compiler. He made reformed doctrines more intelligible, educated a corps of pastors who spread his teachings to the farthest corners of Europe, and provided a model for the governance of Christian communities that would be influential for generations to come.

The unlikely vehicle for these achievements was the small city of Geneva. When Calvin arrived there in

❖ DOCUMENT 15.7 ❖

John Calvin: Predestination

The importance of John Calvin's doctrine of predestination has probably been overstated. It was neither unique to him nor the center of his own theology, which emphasized what he called the knowledge of God. Nevertheless, the power of this summary statement from the Institutes of the Christian Religion *indicates why Calvin's teachings on predestination made an indelible impression.*

As Scripture, then, clearly shows, we say that God once established by his eternal and unchangeable plan those whom he long before determined once for all to receive into salvation and those whom, on the other hand, he would devote to destruction. We assert that, with respect to the elect, this plan was founded upon his freely given mercy, without regard to human worth; but by his just and irreprehensible judgment he has barred the door of life to those whom he has given over to damnation. Now among the elect we regard the call as a testimony of election. Then we hold justification [that is, acceptance by God] another sign of its manifestation, until they come into the glory in which the fulfillment of that election lies. But as the Lord seals his elect by call and justification, so, by shutting off the reprobate from knowledge of his name or from the sanctification of his Spirit, he, as it were, reveals by these marks what sort of judgment awaits them.

July 1536, the city was emerging from a period of political and religious turmoil. It had long been governed by a bishop whose appointment was controlled by the neighboring dukes of Savoy. The belated development of civic institutions and dissatisfaction with Savoyard influence led to an alliance with the Swiss cantons of Bern and Fribourg and to the overthrow of the bishop. The Bernese, who had accepted the Reformation while remaining nominally Catholic for diplomatic reasons, then dispatched a French refugee, Guillaume Farel, to convert the French-speaking Genevans. Farel was a fine preacher, but he realized that he was not the man to organize a church. When Calvin stopped at Geneva on his way from Ferrara to Strasburg, he prevailed upon the young scholar to stay and assist him in the task of reformation.

Calvin's first years in Geneva were full of turmoil. Though they had no love for the pope, the Genevans resisted Calvin's attempts to reform their morals. He established the kind of godly commonwealth he sought only with great difficulty. His opponents finally discredited themselves by supporting Miguel Servetus, an antitrinitarian executed by the Genevan city council as a heretic in 1553. This act, now regarded as an example of gross intolerance, was universally applauded by Catholics and Protestants and secured Calvin's position in the city until his death.

Calvin's Geneva has been called a theocracy, but Calvin believed in the separation of church and state. Neither he nor any other Genevan pastor could hold public office, and the temporal affairs of the Genevan church were guided by an elected committee or presbytery of laymen. The city continued to be governed by its two elected councils. These bodies were empowered, as in Zürich, to enforce conformity in faith and morals. A Consistory, composed of church elders and certain municipal officials, was responsible for defining both. Geneva soon became known as a center of the Reformed movement and as a refuge for those who were persecuted elsewhere. An academy was established to train pastors who were then dispatched to create missionary congregations in other parts of Europe. They were most successful in France, the Netherlands, and in those countries such as Hungary, Bohemia, and Poland where resistance to German culture inhibited the spread of Lutheranism. When the reformer died in 1564 Calvinism was already a major international movement.

The English Reformation

England's revolt against the papacy was an example of reformation from the top. Henry VIII (reigned 1509–47; see illustration 15.7) and his chief minister, Cardinal Thomas Wolsey (c. 1475–1530), had little use for reformed doctrines. Henry had even earned the papal title "Defender of the Faith" for publishing an attack on Luther's view of the sacraments and would probably have been content to remain in the church had he not decided to divorce his queen, Catherine of Aragon.

Catherine had suffered a series of miscarriages and stillbirths. One child, Mary, survived, but Henry feared that without a male heir the succession would be endangered. He resolved to ask for a papal annulment and to marry Anne Boleyn, a court lady with whom he had fallen in love. His request posed serious difficulties for

Illustration 15.7

✍ Henry VIII of England. This portrait by Hans Holbein shows the king as he looked at the time of the Reformation.

pope Clement VII. The emperor Charles V was Catherine's nephew. Charles vehemently opposed the divorce, and as his troops had recently sacked Rome (1527), albeit in the course of a mutiny, the pope was intimidated. Moreover, the basis of the request struck many canon lawyers as dubious. Catherine had originally been married to Henry's brother Arthur, who died before he could ascend the throne. To preserve the vital alliance with Catherine's father, Ferdinand of Aragon, Henry VII had quickly married her to his second son, but this had required a papal dispensation because marriage to the wife of one's brother is prohibited by Leviticus 18:16 and 20:21. Another biblical passage, Deuteronomy 25:5, specifically commands such marriages, but an annulment would involve repudiation of the earlier dispensation. Moreover, the fact that the marriage had endured for eighteen years raised what canon lawyers called "the impediment of public honesty."

Clement temporized. He appointed Cardinals Wolsey and Campeggio as legates to resolve the matter on the theory that their opinions would cancel each other out. Henry could not wait. In 1529 he deprived Wolsey of his secular offices and took Thomas Cromwell (1485–1540) and Thomas Cranmer (1489–1556) as his advisers. These two, a lawyer and a churchman, respectively, were sympathetic to reformed ideas and firm supporters of a strategy that would put pressure on the pope by attacking the privileges and immunities of the church in England.

This strategy was implemented primarily through the Reformation Parliament that sat from 1529 to 1536. Though its proceedings were managed to some extent by Cromwell, a consistent majority supported the crown throughout. Parliament passed a series of acts that restricted the dispatch of church revenues to Rome and placed the legal affairs of the clergy under royal jurisdiction. Finally, in 1532, Anne Boleyn became pregnant. To ensure the child's legitimacy, Cranmer married the couple in January 1533, and two months later he granted the king his divorce from Catherine. He was able to do so because William Warham, the archbishop of Canterbury and a wily opponent of the divorce, had died at last (he was at least ninety-eight), permitting Henry to appoint Cranmer in his place. In September Anne Boleyn gave birth to a daughter, Elizabeth, and in 1534 Parliament passed the Act of Supremacy, which declared that Henry was "the only supreme head of the Church in England."

Opposition was minimal. John Fisher, bishop of Rochester and Sir Thomas More, the great humanist who had been Henry's lord chancellor, were executed for their misgivings, but most of political England either supported the king or remained indifferent. The Lincolnshire rebellion and the northern revolt known as the Pilgrimage of Grace were localized reactions to Henry's proposed closing of the monasteries in 1536 and he suppressed them easily. The dissolution of the monasteries proceeded apace. Unfortunately for his successors, Henry chose to sell off the monastic properties at bargain basement prices. By doing so he enriched those who had supported him in the Reformation Parliament and satisfied his need for ready cash. His failure to incorporate these lands into the royal domain deprived the crown of renewable income.

Henry now ruled the English church. He closed the monasteries and convents and adopted Coverdale's English Bible, but other changes were minimal. The clergy remained celibate (with the exception of Cranmer, who had been secretly married before his appointment as archbishop of Canterbury), and the principles of Catholic theology were reaffirmed in the Six Articles of 1539. A visibly Protestant English church began to emerge only after Henry's death in 1547.

In 1536 Henry arranged the execution of Anne Boleyn on charges of adultery and had their marriage annulled. His third wife, Jane Seymour, gave him a male heir in 1537 but died in childbirth, and three subsequent wives failed to produce further children. Both Mary and Elizabeth were officially illegitimate. Jane Seymour's son, aged ten, ascended the throne as Edward VI under the regency of his uncle, Edward Seymour, duke of Somerset. Somerset was a convinced Protestant with close ties to Cranmer and to the continental reformers. He and the young king, "that right godly imp," lost little time in abolishing the Six Articles, encouraging clerical marriage, and imposing Cranmer's *Book of Common Prayer* as the standard liturgy for English churches. An Order in Council abolished images in an act of official iconoclasm that destroyed centuries of English art.

In 1550 Somerset was succeeded by the equally Protestant duke of Northumberland who imposed a revised edition of the new liturgy and adopted the Forty-Two Articles, also written by Cranmer, as an official confession of faith. The articles proclaimed salvation by faith, reduced the sacraments to two, and denied transubstantiation, though not the Real Presence. Though many lay people remained loyal to the old church, they found no effective way to express their views. Aside from a brief and unsuccessful rebellion in the west of England, little resistance emerged. In 1553 Edward died at the age of sixteen. His sister Mary assumed the crown and immediately restored Catholicism with the assent of Parliament, which demanded only that she not return the lands taken from the church.

Mary's reign was a failure. Her marriage to Philip II of Spain aroused fears of Spanish-papal domination even among those English who were still unfavorably disposed to Protestantism. Her persecution of the reformers, though hardly the bloodbath portrayed in John Foxe's *Acts and Monuments,* the great martyrology of the English reformation, deeply offended others and earned her the historical nickname "Bloody Mary." When her sister, Elizabeth, succeeded her in 1558 she was able to restore a moderate Protestantism leavened by virtual tolerance for all who would acknowledge the royal supremacy. The Elizabethan Settlement, as it is called, was the foundation on which modern Anglicanism would be built after years of effort and struggle.

The Catholic Reformation

Not all reformations of the sixteenth century were anti-Catholic. The church transformed itself as well in a movement that is sometimes called the Counter Reformation, but not all reforms undertaken by Catholics in the sixteenth century were a response to the challenge of the reformers. Cardinal Francisco Jiménez de Cisneros had begun to reform the church in Spain long before Luther nailed his Ninety-Five Theses to the church door, and similar changes were introduced in France by Cardinal Georges d'Amboise between 1501 and his death in 1510. Even Wolsey had attempted to reform the English monasteries during the 1520s. The impetus behind these reforms arguably came from the secular authorities and were largely directed toward the revival of monastic life. However, each of these cardinals received broad legatine authority from several popes, and monastic reform was a central issue in the late medieval church.

Moreover, the reform of existing orders and the creation of new ones was often undertaken without secular involvement. The Theatines, confirmed by the pope in 1524, were an outgrowth of the Oratory of Divine Love whose origins date to 1494. The Barnabites (1533–35), Somaschi (1540), and the Capuchins, an order of reformed Franciscans, were all voluntary associations of churchmen pledged to the ideal of monastic reform. The female counterpart of the Capuchins was founded by Maria Laurentia Longo (d. 1542), and in 1535 Angela Merici (c. 1473–1540) founded the Ursulines, an order that would play a decisive role in the education of Catholic women for centuries. None of these foundations was related in any way to the Protestant threat. Most popes regarded the proliferation of religious orders with suspicion. Their rivalries had long been a fruitful source of trouble, and most reform-minded clerics believed in consolidation rather than in new confirmations.

Of all the religious orders founded or reformed during the sixteenth century the Society of Jesus, or Jesuits, played the largest part in the struggle against Protestantism, but they had been created for other purposes. Their founder, Ignatius of Loyola (1491–1556), was originally inspired by the idea of converting the Muslims. After a long period of educational and religious development that produced *The Spiritual Exercises,* a manual of meditation that remains the foundation of Jesuit discipline, he and nine companions formed their order in 1534. Their asceticism, vigor, and vow of

◆ DOCUMENT 15.8 ◆

Jesuit Obedience

This passage is taken from the Prima Summa, *a document drawn up by Ignatius of Loyola and his followers in 1539 for submission to Pope Paul III. It captures, in brief form, the spirit of the new order and describes the character of the Jesuits' obedience to the pope.*

All the companions should know and daily bear in mind, not only when they make their first profession but as long as they live, that this entire Society and each one individually are soldiers of God under faithful obedience to our most holy lord Paul III and his successors, and are thus under the command of the Vicar of Christ and his divine powers not only as having an obligation to him which is common to all clerics, but also as being so bound by the bond of a vow that whatever His Holiness commands pertaining to the advancement of souls and the propagation of the faith we must immediately carry out, without any evasion or excuse, as far as in us lies, whether to the Turks or to the New World or to the Lutherans or to others, be they infidel or faithful. For this reason those who would join us, and before they put their shoulders to this burden, should meditate long and hard whether they possess the spiritual riches to enable them to complete this tower in keeping with the counsel of the Lord.

unconditional obedience to the pope led to their confirmation in 1540 (see document 15.8).

Though the order did little to convert the Muslims, it achieved moderate success in Asia under the leadership of St. Francis Xavier (1506–52). In Europe the Jesuits became the intellectual shock troops of the Counter Reformation. Their high standards in recruitment and education made them natural leaders to reconvert areas of Europe that had deserted to Protestantism. Jesuit missions helped to restore a Catholic majority in regions as diverse as Bavaria and Poland. An important means of achieving this was through education. Jesuit academies combining humanist educational principles with religious instruction spread through the subcontinent after 1555 and served much the same purpose for men that the Ursuline academies served for women.

Efforts of this sort were essentially spontaneous, arising from reform-minded elements within the church, but the papacy itself was not idle. Reform was difficult if not impossible until the ghost of conciliarism was laid to rest, and for this reason the popes proceeded with great caution. Clement VII, besieged by the mutinous troops of Charles V and the demands of Henry VIII, accomplished little. Paul III (reigned 1534–49) at first sought reconciliation by appointing a commission to investigate abuses within the church. Its report, a detailed analysis with recommendations for change, caused great embarrassment when the contents leaked to the public. Then an attempt to negotiate a settlement with the Lutherans broke down at the Regensburg Colloquy in 1541. These failures encouraged a policy of repression, and in 1542 the Roman Inquisition was revived under the direction of Gian Pietro Caraffa, an implacable conservative and one of the founders of the Theatine order. Later, as Pope Paul IV (served 1555–59), Caraffa would conduct a veritable reign of terror against those whom he regarded as corrupt or heretical. To protect the faithful from intellectual contamination, he also established the celebrated *Index Librorum Prohibitorum,* an ever-expanding list of books that Catholics were forbidden to read.

Repression alone could not solve the problems of the church. In spite of the obvious danger to papal authority, Paul III decided to convene a general council at Trent in 1542. Sessions were held from 1543 to 1549, in 1551–52, and in 1562–63 (see illustration 15.8). Much disagreement arose over goals and the meetings were often sparsely attended, but the Council of Trent was a conspicuous success.

Theologically, Trent marked the triumph of Thomism. Luther's ideas on justification, the sacraments, and the priesthood of all believers were specifically rejected. The medieval concept of the priestly office and the value of good works was reasserted, and at the organizational level efforts were made to correct most of the abuses that had been attacked by the reformers. These included not only the clerical sins of pluralism, absenteeism, nepotism, and simony, but also such distortions of popular piety as the sale of indulgences and the misuse of images. The strengthening of ecclesiastical discipline was one of the council's greatest achievements.

Knowing that many of the church's problems arose from ignorance, the delegates mandated the use of catechisms in instructing the laity and the establishment of diocesan seminaries for the education of priests. The Council of Trent, in short, marked the beginning of the

Illustration 15.8

The Final Session of the Council of Trent, 1563. Attributed to Titian, this painting shows the conclusion of the great council whose decrees inspired the Catholic Church until the 1960s.

modern Catholic Church (see document 15.9). Its institutional principles and the forms of piety that it established were not substantially modified until Vatican II (1962–65).

The Political, Economic, and Social Consequences of Reform

The impact of the sixteenth-century reformations has been the subject of much scholarly debate. The religious unity of western Christendom was clearly shattered (see map 15.1), but this had always been more an ideal than a practical reality. Politically, cities and territorial states were the chief beneficiaries of reform, for Protestantism tended to increase their control over church patronage and revenues. Even Catholic states exhibited more independence because the papacy became more cautious in its claims than it had been in the Middle Ages. Though hardly decisive, reform was therefore an important influence on the development of the modern state.

The economic consequences of the Reformation are far less clear. The idea that Protestantism somehow liberated acquisitive instincts and paved the way for the development of capitalism is highly suspect if for no

other reason than that capitalism existed long before the Reformation and that the economic growth of such Protestant states as England and the Netherlands can be explained adequately in other ways. In some areas, notably England, the alienation of church property may have accelerated the capitalization of land that had begun in the years after the Black Death, but in others it served primarily to increase the domain revenues of the crown. In Denmark, for example, 40 percent of the arable land was under direct royal control by 1620, primarily because the crown retained church lands confiscated during the Reformation.

The reformers also sought to change the status of European women. Beginning with Luther and Zwingli, they rejected the ideal of clerical celibacy and declared that a Christian marriage was the ideal basis for a godly life. They specifically attacked medieval writings that either condemned women as temptresses or extolled virginity as the highest of female callings and drew attractive and sentimental portraits of the virtuous wife. A chief virtue of that ideal women was her willingness to submit to male authority, but the attachment of the reformers to traditional social hierarchies should not be misinterpreted. The companionate marriage in which wife and husband offered each other mutual support was the Reformation ideal (see document 15.10). If women were subordinate it was, as Calvin said, because

◈ DOCUMENT 15.9 ◈

The Council of Trent: Purgatory

The following decree, from the twenty-fifth session of the Council of Trent (December 3–4, 1563), illustrates something of the council's approach. It reaffirms the doctrine of purgatory, specifically rejected by Protestants, in which the faithful are punished for their sins before being allowed the full benefits of salvation, but it tries to avoid misinterpretation and abuses. The last section deals with masses for the dead, another practice that had sometimes led to scandal and was universally condemned by Protestants.

Since the Catholic Church, instructed by the Holy Ghost, has, following the sacred writings and the ancient traditions of the Fathers, taught in sacred councils and very recently this ecumenical council that there is a purgatory and that the souls there detained are aided by the suffrages of the faithful and chiefly by the acceptable sacrifice of the altar, the holy council commands the bishops that they strive diligently to that end that the sound doctrine of purgatory, transmitted by the Fathers and the sacred councils be believed and maintained by the faithful of Christ, and be everywhere taught and preached. The more difficult and subtle questions, however, and those that do not make for edification and from which there is for the most part no increase of piety, are to be excluded from popular instructions to uneducated people. Likewise, things that are uncertain or that have the appearance of falsehood they shall not permit to be made known publicly and discussed. But those things that tend to a certain kind of curiosity or superstition, or that savor of filthy lucre, they shall prohibit as scandals and stumbling blocks to the faithful. The bishops shall see to it that the suffrages of the living, that is the sacrifice of the mass, prayers, alms and other works of piety which they have been accustomed to perform for the faithful departed, be piously and devoutly discharged in accordance with the laws of the Church, and whatever is due on their behalf from testamentary bequests or other ways, be discharged by the priests and ministers of the Church and others who are bound to render this service not in a perfunctory manner, but diligently and accurately.

◈ DOCUMENT 15.10 ◈

A Protestant View of Marriage

The reformer of Strasbourg, Martin Bucer (1491–1551), was more generous than most in his attitude toward women. Here, he argues that under certain circumstances a woman may leave her adulterous or abusive spouse and be free to remarry.

For the Holy Spirit says that there is neither male nor female in Christ. In all things that pertain to salvation one should have as much regard for woman as for man. For though she is bound to keep her place, to put herself under the authority of her husband, just as the church does in relation to Christ, yet her subjection does not cancel the right of an honest woman, in accordance with the laws of God, to have recourse to and demand, by legitimate means, deliverance from a husband who hates her. For the Lord has certainly not made married woman subvervient to have her polluted and tormented by the extortions and injuries of her husband, but rather so that she may receive discipline from him, as if from her master and savior, like the church from Christ. A wife is not so subject to her husband that she is bound to suffer anything he may impose upon her. Being free, she is joined to him in holy marriage that she may be loved, nourished, and maintained by him, as if she were his own flesh, just as the church is maintained by Christ. . . . Again, though a wife may be something less than her husband and subject to him, in order that they be rightly joined, the Holy Spirit has declared, through its apostle, that man and woman are equal before God in things pertaining to the alliance and mutual confederation of marriage. This is the meaning of the apostle's saying that a wife has power over the body of her husband, just as a husband has power over the body of his wife (1 Corinthians 7). . . . Hence, if wives feel that their association and cohabitation with their husbands is injurious to salvation as well of one as of the other, owing to the hardening and hatred on the part of their husbands, let them have recourse to the civil authority, which is enjoined by the Lord to help the afflicted.

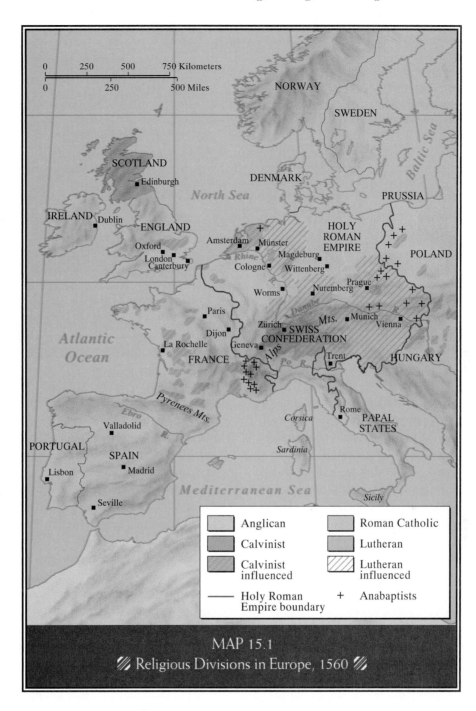

MAP 15.1
Religious Divisions in Europe, 1560

women "by the very order of nature are bound to obey." To him, other reformers, and Catholic theologians, the traditionally ordered family was both part and symbol of a divinely established hierarchy. To disrupt that hierarchy risked chaos.

The Reformation endorsement of women was qualified, but it increased the status of wife and mother and placed new demands upon men, who were encouraged to treat their wives with consideration. As early as the 1520s some German towns permitted women to divorce husbands who were guilty of gross abuse. The reformers also encouraged female literacy, at least in the vernacular, because they wanted women to have access to the Scriptures. The impact of these prescriptions on the lives of real women may be questioned. On the negative side, the Protestant emphasis on marriage narrowed a woman's career choices to one. Catholic Europe continued to offer productive lives to women who chose not to marry, but Protestant women could rarely escape the dominance of men. If they did, it was through widowhood or divorce, and Protestant societies offered no institutional support for the unmarried. St. Teresa de

Illustration 15.9

A Village Wedding. In this painting, Pieter Bruegel the Younger illustrates the sort of peasant behavior that political and ecclesiastical authorities hoped to restrict in the later sixteenth century.

Avila, Angelique Arnauld, Madame Acarie, Jeanne de Chantal, and the other great female figures of post-Tridentine Catholicism had few Protestant counterparts.

From the standpoint of the reformers, whether Catholic or Protestant, such issues were of secondary importance. Their primary concern was the salvation of souls and the transformation of popular piety. The modern historian Jean Delumeau has suggested that the reformations of the sixteenth century christianized Europe for the first time in that they sought to impose orthodoxy upon a popular religion hitherto characterized by pagan survivals and other folk beliefs of dubious origin. Heroic efforts were made to catechize or otherwise educate the laity in most parts of Europe, and after about 1570 an increasing tendency was seen toward clerical interference in lay morals. Catholic church courts and Protestant consistories sought to eliminate such evils as brawling, public drunkenness, and sexual misbehavior. Inevitably the churchmen were forced to condemn the occasions on which such activity arose. The celebration of holidays and popular festivals came under scrutiny as did public performances of every kind from street jugglers to those of Shakespeare and his troop of actors. Dancing aroused special concern. No one worried about the stately measures trod by courtiers, but the rowdy and often sexually explicit dances of the peasants seemed, after years of familiarity, to induce shock (see illustration 15.9).

Civil authorities supported this attack on popular culture for practical reasons. The celebration of holidays and popular festivals encouraged disorder. When accompanied as they usually were by heavy drinking, public amusements could lead to violence and even riots. Moreover, like street theater, most celebrations contained seditious skits or pageants. They mocked the privileged classes, satirized the great, and delighted in the reversal of social and gender roles. The triumph of a Lord of Misrule, even for a day, made magistrates nervous, and prudence demanded that such activities be regulated or prohibited outright. Popular beliefs and practices were attacked with equal vigor. The authorities rarely took action against academic magic, astrology, or alchemy—sciences that, though dubious, were widely accepted by the wealthy and educated—but they no longer tolerated folk magic. In some cases official suspicion extended even to the traditional remedies used by midwives and village "wise women."

The epidemic of witch hunting that convulsed Europe in the late sixteenth and early seventeenth centuries may have been related to these concerns. In the century after 1550 Protestant and Catholic governments in virtually every part of Europe executed more than sixty thousand people for being witches or satanists. Medieval thinkers such as Thomas Aquinas had denied the power of witches, but a later age thought differently. Magistrates and learned men built theories of a vast satanic plot around their imperfect knowledge of folk beliefs. Their ideas crystallized in manuals for witch hunters, the most famous of which, the *Malleus Maleficarum* (Hammer of Witches) went through

◈ DOCUMENT 15.11 ◈

Why Women Are More Likely to Be Witches

The Malleus Maleficarum (Hammer of Witches) was published in 1486 by two Dominicans, Heinrich Krämer and Jakob Sprenger. Here, the authors explain why women were more likely to be witches than men. Their arguments lend credibility to the charge that the witch craze was fueled in part by misogyny.

As for the question, why a greater number of witches is found in the fragile sex than among men . . . a fact that it were idle to contradict, since it is accredited by actual experience, apart from the verbal testimony of credible witnesses. . . . The first [reason] is that they are more credulous. . . . The second reason is that women are naturally more impressionable, and more ready to receive the influence of a disembodied spirit; and that when they use this quality well they are very good, but when they use it ill they are very evil. The third reason is that they have slippery tongues, and are unable to conceal from their fellow-women those things which by evil arts they know.

But the natural reason is that she is more carnal than a man, as is clear from her many carnal abominations. And it should be noted that there was a defect in the formation of the first woman, since she was formed from a bent rib, that is a rib of the breast, which is bent as it were in a contrary direction to a man. And since through this defect she is an imperfect animal, she always deceives.

And indeed, just as through the first defect in their intelligence they are more prone to abjure the faith; so through their second defect of inordinate affections and passions they search for, brood over, and inflict various vengeances, either by witchcraft or by some other means. Wherefore it is no wonder that a great many witches exist in this sex . . . .

To conclude. All witchcraft comes from carnal lust, which is in women insatiable.

---

twenty-nine editions between 1495 and 1669 (see document 15.11). Its authors, like most people in early modern Europe, believed that in a providential world there could be no accidents; evil required an explanation. Otherwise unexplained disasters were caused by witches who gained extraordinary powers through worshipping the devil and used those powers to injure their neighbors. The community could be protected only by burning witches alive.

In this case, ordinary people shared the concerns of the intellectual elite. Accusations of witchcraft tended to multiply in waves of hysteria that convulsed entire regions. Many of those denounced were no doubt guilty of trying to cast spells or some other unsavory act, but the victims fit a profile that suggests a generalized hostility toward women and perhaps that the persecutions were in part a means of exerting social control (see illustration 15.10). The great majority of those burned were single women, old and poor, who lived at the margins of their communities. The rest, whether male or female, tended to be people whose assertive or uncooperative behavior had aroused hostility.

The trials subsided after 1650, but not before other traditional beliefs had been discredited by their association with witchcraft. Some of these involved "white"

magic, the normally harmless spells and preparations used to endure good harvests or to cure disease. Others were "errors," or what the Spanish Inquisition called "propositions." This was a broad category that included everything from the popular notion that premarital sex was no sin to alternative cosmologies devised by imaginative peasants. Post-Tridentine Catholicism, no less than its Protestant rivals, discouraged uncontrolled speculation and was deeply suspicious of those forms of piety that lacked ecclesiastical sanction. Popular beliefs about the Virgin Mary, the saints, and miracles were scrutinized, while lay people claiming to have religious visions were ridiculed and sometimes prosecuted.

The efforts of the reformers, in other words, bore modest fruit. Drunkenness proved ineradicable, but some evidence is available that interpersonal violence decreased and that behavior in general became somewhat more sedate. Though lay morals and religious knowledge improved slowly if at all, the forms of piety were transformed in some cases beyond recognition. Many ideas and practices vanished so completely that historians of popular culture can recover their memory only with great difficulty. Devotion based upon personal contact with God through mental prayer became common in virtually all communions. Catholics

Illustration 15.10

The Witch's Sabbath. In this woodcut by Hans Baldung Grien (1484–1545) witches concoct a potion while another engages in night flight on the back of a goat. The artist, like many of his contemporaries, clearly associates satanism with female sexuality.

abandoned the sale of indulgences and consciously sought to limit such abuses as the misuse of pilgrimages and relics. Protestants abandoned all three, together with Latin, vigils, the cult of the saints, masses for the dead, and mandatory fasts. By 1600 the religious landscape of Europe was transformed, and much of the richness, vitality, and cohesion of peasant life had been lost beyond all hope of recovery.

Conclusion

Unlike the Renaissance, the Protestant Reformation arose from specific, well-articulated grievances that had been festering since before the Black Death. With the

support of princely and city governments that hoped to benefit from attacking the church, it destroyed the ancient unity of Christendom and allowed the emergence of long-suppressed forms of piety. The Catholic Church, in response to the Protestant threat as well as to internal demands for reform, renewed itself. Both sides worked for the suppression of popular beliefs and practices that seemed un-Christian to the learned elite of the day, but on other matters the lines of conflict had been firmly drawn. Protestants and Catholics began to diverge, not only on matters of faith and ritual, but also in their intellectual formation and social attitudes. In the aftermath of the Reformation crisis, Europe found itself divided along religious and political lines, with a newly militant Catholicism confronting its Protestant rivals on the battlefield as well as in the schools and pulpits.

Suggested Readings

The problems of the late medieval church are best summarized in F. Oakley, *The Western Church in the Later Middle Ages* (1979). S. Ozment, *The Age of Reform, 1250–1550: An Intellectual and Religious History of the Late Medieval and Reformation Europe* (1980) carries its analysis through the early Protestant Reformation. The best studies of the papacy at Avignon are G. Mollat, *The Popes at Avignon, 1305–1378* (1963) and Y. Renouard, *The Avignon Papacy, 1305–1403* (1970). On the Great Schism, see W. Ullmann, *Origins of the Great Schism* (1949) and R. Swanson, *Universities, Academics, and the Great Schism* (1979). The conciliar movement is analyzed in F. Oakley, *Natural Law, Conciliarism, and Consent in the Late Middle Ages* (1984), B. Tierney, *Foundations of the Conciliar Theory* (1955), and A. Black, *Council and Commune: The Conciliar Movement* (1979). A good survey of the papacy is J. A. F. Thompson, *Popes and Princes, 1417–1517: Politics and Polity in the Late Medieval Church* (1980). For the clergy, see D. Hay, *The Church in Italy in the Fifteenth Century* (1977) and D. Knowles, *The Religious Orders in England*, 3 vols. (1950–59). Various aspects of late medieval mysticism are covered in J. Clark, *The Great German Mystics: Eckhart, Tauler, and Suso* (1949) and D. Knowles, *The English Mystical Tradition* (1961). A. Kenny, *Wyclif* (1985) is a good introduction to the English heretic. For Hus and the Hussites, see M. Spinka, *John Hus: A Biography* (1979) and H. Kaminsky, *A History of the Hussite Revolution* (1967).

Good biographies of Luther include R. Bainton, *Here I Stand: A Life of Martin Luther* (1950), the more modern J. Kittelson, *Luther the Reformer* (1986), and the revisionist work by H. Oberman, *Luther: Man between God and Devil* (1992). M. Edwards, *Luther's Last Battles* (1983) deals with the reformer's later years. The substantial literature on the Reformation in the cities includes B. Moeller, *Imperial Cities and the Reformation* (1982), S. Ozment, *The Reformation in the Cities* (1975), G. Strauss, *Nuremburg in the Sixteenth Century* (1978), and T. A. Brady, *Ruling Class, Regime, and Reformation at Strassburg* (1978).

G. H. Williams, *The Radical Reformation* (1962, 1991) is a comprehensive account that covers Anabaptists, Spiritualists, and Antitrinitarians. See also the shorter M. Mullett, *Radical Religious Movements in Early Modern Europe* (1980). For the Anabaptists, see C. Krahn, *Dutch Anabaptism: Origins, Spread, Life, and Thought, 1450–1600* (1981) and C.-P. Clasen, *Anabaptism: A Social History, 1525–1618* (1972). For the aftermath of the Münster episode, see R. Po-Chia Hsia, *Society and Reformation in Münster, 1535–1618* (1984). The most accessible biography of Zwingli is probably G. Potter, *Zwingli* (1976). A. McGrath, *A Life of John Calvin* (1990) is a good introduction. See also the brilliant, if somewhat difficult, study by W. Bousma, *John Calvin* (1988) and W. Monter, *Calvin's Geneva* (1967). On the English Reformation, the interpretation of G. Dickens, *The English Reformation* (1964) has been challenged, among others, by J. J. Scarisbricke, *The Reformation and the English People* (1984) and C. Haigh, *The English Reformation Revised* (1987). The best biography of Henry VIII remains J. J. Scarisbricke, *Henry VIII* (1968); for Cranmer, see D. MacCulloch, *Thomas Cranmer* (1996). The standard accounts of Edward VI and his reign are by W. K. Jordan, *Edward VI, the Young King: The Protectorship of the Duke of Somerset* (1970) and *Edward VI, the Threshold of Power: The Dominance of the Duke of Northumberland* (1970). The most reliable studies on Mary are by D. Loades, *The Reign of Mary Tudor* (1979) and *Mary Tudor: A Life* (1989).

Good surveys of the Catholic Reformation include G. Dickens, *The Counter Reformation* (1969), M. O'Connell, *The Counter Reformation, 1559–1610* (1974), and L. Chatellier, *The Europe of the Devout: The Catholic Reformation and the Formation of a New Society* (1989). See also the important revisionist interpretation of J. Delumeau, *Catholicism from Luther to Voltaire* (1977). For the origins of the Jesuits, see J. O'Malley, *The First Jesuits* (1993). The standard history of the Council of Trent remains H. Jedin, *History of the Council of Trent*, 2 vols. (1957–61).

On the consequences of reform, G. Strauss, *Luther's House of Learning* (1978) has proved as controversial as the views of Delumeau. For the effect of the Reformation on women and the family, see S. Ozment, *When Father's Ruled: Family Life in Reformation Europe* (1983), M. Wiesner, *Working Women in Renaissance Germany* (1986), L. Roper, *Work, Marriage, and Sexuality: Women in Reformation Augsburg* (1985), and J. Irwin, *Womanhood in Radical Protestantism, 1525–1675* (1989). For popular culture and its struggles, see P. Burke, *Popular Culture in Early Modern Europe* (1978), R. Muchembled, *Popular Culture and Elite Culture in France, 1400–1750* (1985), D. Sabean, *Popular Culture and Village Discourse in Early Modern Germany* (1985), and M. Mullett, *Popular Culture and Popular Protest in Late Medieval and Early Modern Europe* (1986). B. Levack, *The Witch-Hunt in Early Modern Europe* (1987) is a broad survey of the witch persecutions. Among the many good regional studies are H. C. E. Midelfort, *Witchhunting in Southwestern Germany, 1562–1684* (1972) and E. W. Monter, *Witchcraft in France and Switzerland* (1976).

CHAPTER 16

OVERSEAS CONQUEST AND RELIGIOUS WAR TO 1648

CHAPTER OUTLINE

◆◆◆◆◆◆◆◆◆◆◆◆◆◆◆◆◆◆◆◆◆

The age of the Renaissance and Reformation marked the beginning of European conquests overseas. The great European voyages of the fifteenth and sixteenth centuries and the conquests that resulted from them have few historical parallels. The Phoenicians, Arabs, and Polynesians performed extraordinary feats of navigation, but only the Europeans made a systematic effort to explore the entire planet and to impose their ideas of government and religion upon a significant portion of it. Their purpose in the first instance was to expand the resources available to the emerging monarchies of western Europe. The conquests were therefore an extension of the state-building process, but a religious motive was evident, too, which at times recalled the Christian triumphalism of the Crusades. To say that European expansion overseas changed the world forever is an understatement. Though it laid the foundations of a world market and added much to Europe's store of wealth and knowledge, it did so at a terrible cost in human misery.

Chapter 16 describes how and why Europeans attempted to impose their rule on far-off peoples whom they scarcely knew, and what effect these early efforts had on European politics and society. It then examines the imperial rivalries of the early sixteenth century and the so-called Religious Wars of 1559–1648, which virtually destroyed the European state system. These conflicts were largely an outgrowth of the rivalry between developing states. The wars of the sixteenth century stretched the resources of princes to the breaking point. This led to massive unrest as subjects sought to recover rights and privileges lost to rulers who were desperate to pay for war. Both the subsequent revolts and the international rivalry that helped to sustain them were complicated by religious issues that made them extremely difficult to resolve. In the end, the wars of what has been called the Iron Age brought much of Europe to the brink of political and economic disintegration.

The Portuguese Voyages to Africa, India, and Brazil

The process of overseas exploration began appropriately enough in Portugal, the first modern monarchy and the center of the fourteenth-century revolution in shipbuilding. The Portuguese state had been effectively consolidated by John I in 1385. Like other medieval rulers, he and his descendants hoped to maximize domain revenue by increasing taxable commerce. The gold and ivory of Africa were a tempting goal, but that trade was dominated by Moroccan intermediaries who shipped products from the African heartland by camel caravan and sold them to Europeans through such ports as Ceuta and Tangier. The Portuguese knew that enormous profits could be realized by sailing directly to the source of these commodities and bypassing the middlemen, who were in any case Muslims and their traditional enemies. Additional benefits could be derived from safe access to the rich fisheries off the coast of Mauretania.

These considerations, and others of a more spiritual nature, inspired Prince Henry "the Navigator" (1394–1460) to establish a center for navigational development on the windswept bluffs of Sagres at the far southwestern tip of Europe. A son of John I, Henry also hoped to make contact with the legendary Christian ruler Prester John, who was said to live somewhere in central Africa. Failing that, the Portuguese could attempt the conversion of Africans to Christianity on their own.

While Henry's cosmographers and mathematicians worked steadily to improve the quality of charts and navigational techniques, his captains sailed ever further along the African coast, returning with growing quantities of gold, ivory, pepper, and slaves, for the enslavement of Africans was part of the expansionist enterprise from the start. In the process they colonized four groups of islands, the Azores, Madeira, the Cape Verdes, and the Canaries, though they lost the latter to Spain after 1475. Their ships were fast, handy caravels that combined the best features of northern and Mediterranean construction (see illustration 16.1). Their instruments were improved versions of the compass, the quadrant, and the astrolabe (see illustration 16.2). The compass had been introduced to the Mediterranean in the twelfth or thirteenth century, probably by the Arabs. The quadrant and the astrolabe permitted the sailor to find his latitude based on the elevation of the sun above the horizon. Because no accurate way existed to measure either the passage of time or the ship's speed, navigators relied upon dead reckoning to calculate longitude. This was little more than inspired guesswork, but by the fifteenth century skilled seamen could locate their positions with surprising accuracy.

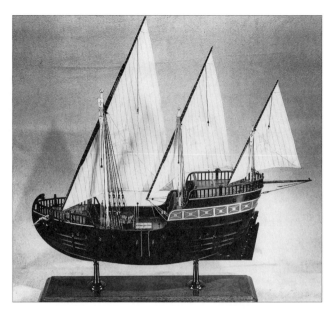

Illustration 16.1

🌊 **A Portuguese Caravel of the Fifteenth Century.** Though rarely more than seventy or eighty feet in length, these vessels were extremely seaworthy and formed the mainstay of Portugal's explorations along the coasts of Africa and in the Atlantic. This one is lateen rigged for better performance to windward, but some of them carried square sails as well, usually on the foremast.

Before the death of Prince Henry, the Portuguese adopted the idea of sailing around the tip of Africa to India as their primary goal. By so doing they hoped to bypass the Italian-Arab monopoly and gain direct access to the spice trade. In 1487 Bartolomeu Dias reached the Cape of Good Hope, then returned to Lisbon without proceeding further. The Portuguese had learned that the currents along the African coast flowed northward and that the winds in the latitudes below the equator were shifting and contrary. Reaching India was theoretically possible by hugging the African coast, but it would take so long that crews might die of starvation or disease before arriving at their destination.

All major voyages were suspended for nine years. Portuguese navigators were secretive and the nature of their research or deliberations is unknown, but when Vasco da Gama set forth in 1496 he followed an entirely different route. Using full-rigged ships with greater storage capacity than the light and maneuverable caravels, he sailed southwest across the Atlantic

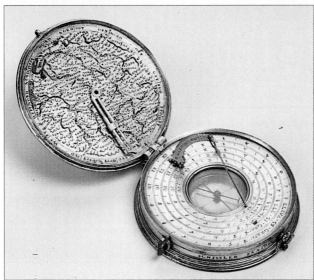

Illustration 16.2

///// **Navigational Instruments.** A brass equatorium (top) was used for calculating planetary longitudes. The astronomical *compendium* (bottom) was made at Augsburg in 1588. It contains an astrolabe/quadrant, a compass, a sundial, a table of latitudes, and several other instruments. Gadgets of this kind, though works of art, were far too expensive and delicate for use by ordinary mariners.

almost to the coast of Brazil. Though he apparently did not suspect the existence of the South American continent, his successor, Pedro Alvares Cabral, landed there in 1500 while following a similar course. From Brazil, the Portuguese caught the westerly tradewinds for a rapid voyage back across the Atlantic to the southern

tip of Africa. Like Dias, da Gama found passing the capes difficult. He finally reached Calicut on the coast of India, the heart of the spice trade, in May 1498.

His arrival disturbed political and commercial relationships that had endured for centuries. Indian and Arab merchants found the newcomers rude and barbaric and their trade goods of little interest. Though the voyages of da Gama and Cabral made a profit, only the judicious use of force could secure a major Portuguese share in the trade. After 1508 Afonso de Albuquerque (1453–1515) tried to gain control of the Indian Ocean by seizing its major ports. Aden and Ormuz eluded him, but Goa became the chief Portuguese base in India and the capture of Malacca (1511) opened the way to China. A Portuguese settlement was established there at Macao in 1556. Trade with Japan was initiated in 1543, and for seventy-five years thereafter ships from Macao brought luxury goods to Nagasaki in return for silver.

These achievements earned Portugal a modest place in Asian commerce. The Portuguese may have been the first people of any race to trade on a truly worldwide basis, but the total volume of spices exported to Europe did not immediately increase as a result of their activities. Furthermore, the Arab and Gujerati merchants of the Indian Ocean remained formidable competitors for more than a century. To the east, trade between China and the Coromandel Coast of India increased in response to a sustained period of Indian demographic growth, but Europeans failed to achieve a dominant position in these waters until after 1650. When they did, it was the Dutch and then the English who benefited, for the Portuguese Empire was by this time in decline (see map 16.1).

◆

Columbus and the Opening of America

Meanwhile, the Spanish, by sailing west, had reached America. Isabella of Castile and Ferdinand of Aragon regarded the expansion of their Portuguese rivals with dismay and believed, as Prince Henry had done, that they were obligated by morality and the requirements of dynastic prestige to spread the Catholic faith. When a Genoese mariner named Christopher Columbus proposed to reach Asia by sailing across the Atlantic, they were prepared to listen.

Columbus had offered the same project to the Portuguese in 1484 and was turned down. They apparently found him both demanding and ignorant. A self-educated man, Columbus accepted only those

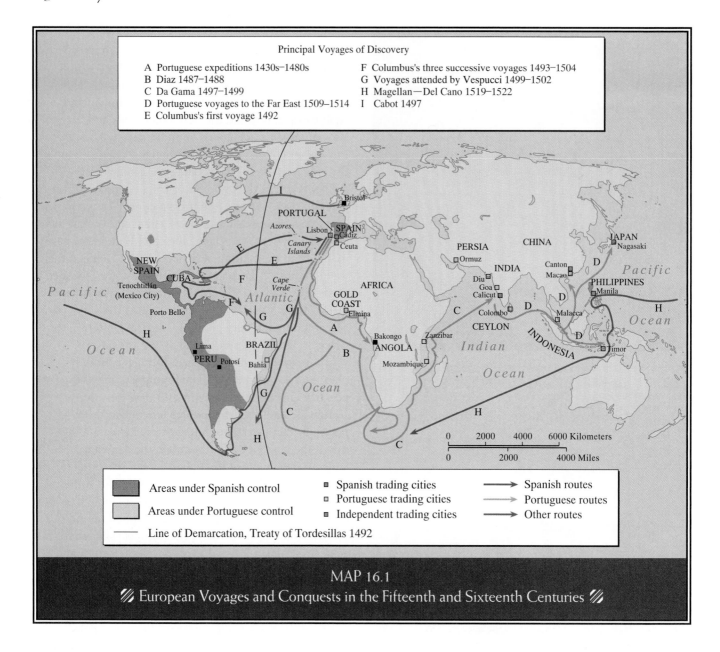

Principal Voyages of Discovery

A Portuguese expeditions 1430s–1480s
B Diaz 1487–1488
C Da Gama 1497–1499
D Portuguese voyages to the Far East 1509–1514
E Columbus's first voyage 1492

F Columbus's three successive voyages 1493–1504
G Voyages attended by Vespucci 1499–1502
H Magellan—Del Cano 1519–1522
I Cabot 1497

Areas under Spanish control
Areas under Portuguese control
Line of Demarcation, Treaty of Tordesillas 1492

Spanish trading cities
Portuguese trading cities
Independent trading cities

Spanish routes
Portuguese routes
Other routes

MAP 16.1
Ⓐ European Voyages and Conquests in the Fifteenth and Sixteenth Centuries Ⓐ

theories that supported his own and underestimated the circumference of the globe by nearly seven thousand miles (see illustration 16.3). His first reception in Spain was no better, but Columbus persisted. He eventually gained the support of the queen and of Ferdinand's treasurer, who found ways to finance the voyage with little risk to the crown. In August 1492, Columbus set sail in the ship *Santa Maria* accompanied by two small caravels, the *Pinta* and the *Niña*. Their combined crews totaled about ninety men. Columbus sailed southwest to the Canary Islands and then westward across the Atlantic, taking advantage of winds and currents that he could not fully have understood. In spite of the season he encountered no hurricanes and, on

October 12, sighted what he believed to be an island off the coast of Japan. It was one of the Bahamas.

Columbus made three more voyages before his death in 1506, insisting until the end that he had found the western passage to Asia. The realization that it was a continent whose existence had only been suspected by Europeans was left to others. One of them, a Florentine navigator named Amerigo Vespucci (1454–1512), gave it his name. The true dimensions of the "New World" became clearer in 1513 when Vasco Núñez de Balboa crossed the Isthmus of Panama on foot and became the first European to look upon the Pacific.

The achievement of Columbus has been somewhat diminished by his own failure to grasp its significance

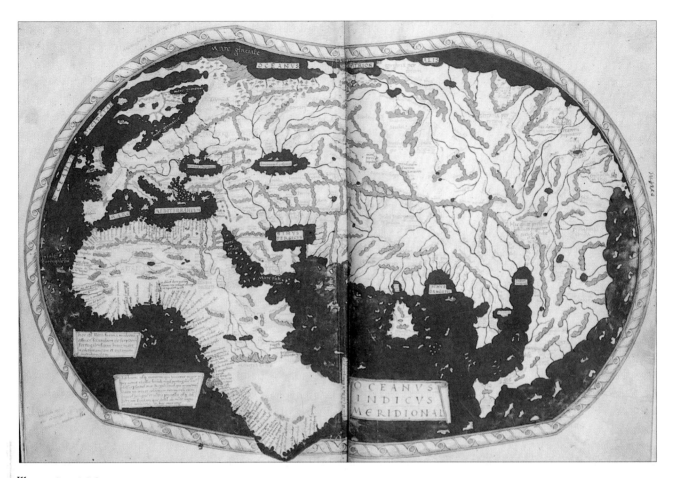

Illustration 16.3

⁄⁄ **The World before Columbus.** This map of the world was published by Henricius Martellus about 1489. It shows Asia as described by Ptolemy and Marco Polo, and Africa as described by Dias before the voyage of Vasco da Gama. Note that the Americas are missing.

and by the fact that others had no doubt preceded him. The Vikings visited Newfoundland and may have explored the North American coast as far south as Cape Cod. Portuguese and Basque fishermen had almost certainly landed there in the course of their annual expeditions to the Grand Banks, but being fishermen, they kept their discoveries secret and these early contacts came to nothing.

The voyage of Columbus, however, set off a frenzy of exploration and conquest. By the Treaty of Tordesillas (1494), the Spanish and Portuguese agreed to a line of demarcation established in mid-Atlantic by the pope. Lands "discovered" to the east of that line belonged to Portugal; those to the west belonged to Spain. The inhabitants of those lands were not consulted. This left Brazil, Africa, and the route to India in Portuguese hands, but a line of demarcation in the Pacific was not defined. Much of Asia remained in dispute.

To establish a Spanish presence there, an expedition was dispatched in 1515 to reach the Moluccas by sailing west around the southern tip of South America. Its leader was Fernando Magellan, a Portuguese sailor in Spanish pay. Magellan crossed the Pacific only to be killed in the Moluccas by natives unimpressed with the benefits of Spanish sovereignty (see document 16.1). His navigator, Sebastian del Cano, became the first captain to circumnavigate the globe when he brought the expedition's only remaining ship back to Spain with fifteen survivors in 1522 (see illustration 16.4). The broad outlines of the world were now apparent. Two more centuries of exploration would be required before the complete map as known today took shape. By the time Luther confronted the Diet of Worms, Europeans were active on every continent except Australia and Antarctica (see map 16.1).

The First Colonial Empire: Portugal

Conquest and the imposition of European government accompanied exploration from the beginning. The Portuguese made no effort to impose their direct rule on

◆ DOCUMENT 16.1 ◆

The Hazards of a Long Voyage

This extract is taken from a firsthand account of Fernando Magellan's voyage around the world by Antonio Pigafetta, but similar conditions might be expected on any sea journey if it lasted long enough. The disease described is scurvy, which results from a deficiency of vitamin C. It was a serious problem even on transatlantic voyages. The cause was not understood until the eighteenth century, but captains could usually predict the first date of its appearance in a ship's company with some accuracy.

Wednesday, November 28, we debauched from that strait [since named after Magellan], engulfing ourselves in the Pacific Sea. We were three months and twenty days without getting any kind of fresh food. We ate biscuit, which was no longer biscuit, but powder of biscuits swarming with worms, for they had eaten the good. It stank strongly of the urine of rats. We drank yellow water that had been putrid for many days. We also ate some ox hides that covered the top of the mainyard to prevent the yard from chafing the shrouds, and which had become exceedingly hard because of the sun, rain, and wind. We left them in the sea for four or five days, and then placed them on top of the embers and so ate them; and we often ate sawdust from boards. Rats were sold for one-half ducat a piece, and even then we could not get them. But above all the other misfortunes the following was the worst. The gums of both the lower and upper teeth of some of our men swelled so that they could not eat under any circumstances and therefore died. Nineteen men died from that sickness. . . . Twenty-five or thirty men fell sick.

large native populations, in part because they lacked the manpower to do so and in part because the primary purpose of Portuguese expansion was trade. Instead they established a series of merchant colonies to collect goods from the African, Indian, or Asian interior for transshipment to Portugal in return for cash or European commodities. These colonies were rarely more than towns protected by a Portuguese garrison and governed by Portuguese law. They were not for the

most part self-sustaining. To prosper they had to maintain diplomatic and commercial relations with their neighbors while retaining the option of force, either for self-protection or to obtain a favorable market share in regional trade. Because Portugal's population was small, there was no question of large-scale immigration. Governors from Albuquerque onward sought to maintain colonial populations and to solidify Portuguese control by encouraging intermarriage with native peoples.

As a handful of interlopers on the fringes of a great continent, the Portuguese could not hope to impose their faith on the mass of its inhabitants. Within the colonies Roman Catholicism was the official religion and orthodoxy was protected by the Inquisition, but little effort was made to proselytize the surrounding countryside. The best they could do was to support the efforts of the newly founded Society of Jesus. The Portuguese helped introduce Jesuit missionaries to China where they were generally welcomed, and in 1549 a Portuguese ship brought St. Francis Xavier (1506–52) to Japan. Japan had been convulsed by civil wars since 1467, and the resulting sense of disintegration may have helped the Jesuits to gain large numbers of converts. So great was their success that they aroused the jealousy of traditionalists. The reformer Toyotami Hideyoshi expelled the fathers in 1587 and actively persecuted their converts.

Communication between these far-flung stations and the mother country was maintained by the largest ships of the age, the thousand-ton carracks of the *Carreira da India*. The voyage around the tip of Africa took months and the mortality among crews was dreadful, but profit to the crown made it all seem worthwhile. To discourage smuggling, everything had to be shipped to and from a central point—the Guinea Mines House at Lagos, near Sagres—where royal officials could inspect the cargoes of spice and silks and assess the one-third share owed to the king. In return, the monarchy provided military and naval protection for the colonies and for the convoys that served them. Colonial governors, though appointed by the crown, enjoyed the freedom that comes from being far from home. Corruption flourished, but Portuguese rule was rarely harsh.

Where controlling large tracts of land became necessary, as in Brazil, the Portuguese established captaincies that were in fact proprietary colonies. Captains-general would be appointed in return for their promise to settle and develop their grants. The model was the settlement of Madeira. However, Brazil evolved into a society based upon African slavery. Its most valu-

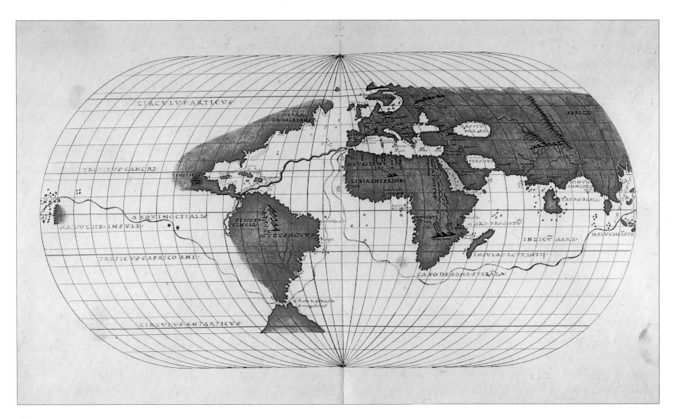

Illustration 16.4

⧅ **The World after Magellan's Circumnavigation.** This map of the world is taken from an atlas published by Batista Agnese at Venice in 1536. It shows the course taken by Magellan and his crew in 1519–22. The dimensions of Africa are far better under- stood than they were in 1489, and South America is portrayed with reasonable accuracy, though much of North America remains *terra incognita.*

able resources were dye woods and a climate ideal for growing sugar, a commodity for which Europeans had already begun to develop an insatiable craving.

Both industries were labor intensive and involved a high mortality among workers. Europeans would not endure the harsh conditions, while the Native American population of Brazil was relatively small and semi-nomadic. Those Indians who were not killed by disease or violence took refuge in the interior, and their place was taken by large numbers of Africans imported from Portuguese trading stations along the west coast of Africa. Slaves were generally sold to the Portuguese by other Africans who had captured them in warfare or for profit (see document 16.2). Once sold, they were held in vast pens or barracoons until they could be packed into the holds of ships for the journey to America (see illustration 16.5). The horrors of this trade cannot be exaggerated, but its morality was not seriously questioned for three hundred years. All of the colonial powers participated, and all believed that it was essential to the economic well-being of their empires.

◈

The Spanish Empire in Mexico and Peru

The first Spanish attempts at colonization resembled the Portuguese experience in Brazil. Columbus had set a bad example by trying to enslave the native population of Hispaniola. Similar unsuccessful efforts were made at Cuba and elsewhere in the Caribbean. The Indians died of disease and overwork, fled to the mainland, or were killed while trying to resist. African slaves were then imported to work in the mines and sugar-cane fields. Royal efforts eventually were able to bring the situation under control, but in the meantime, the conquest of Mexico and Peru had changed the basic nature of Spanish colonial enterprise. For the first time, Europeans sought to impose their rule on societies as complex and populous as their own.

The various nations of central Mexico were grouped into political units that resembled city-states. Their combined population almost certainly exceeded that of Spain. By the fifteenth century, most of these

❖ DOCUMENT 16.2 ❖

A Slave's Voyage to the West Indies

Olaudah Equiano was an Ibo from what is now Nigeria. He was sold to slave traders at the age of eleven and shipped to Bridgetown, Barbados, on an English ship. In later years he purchased his freedom, traveled widely, and became one of the founders of the first free black colony in Africa at Freetown, Sierra Leone. Here he describes the passage to the New World as experienced by millions of Africans.

When I recovered a little, I found some black people about me, who I believed were some of those who brought me on board, and had been receiving their pay; they talked to me in order to cheer me, but all in vain. I asked them if we were not to be eaten by those white men with horrible looks, red faces, and long hair. They told me I was not. . . .

Soon after this, the blacks who brought me on board went off and left me abandoned to despair. I now wished for the last friend, death, to relieve me, but soon to my grief, two of the white men offered me eatables; and, on my refusing to eat, one of them held me fast by the hands and laid me across, I think, the windlass, and tied my feet while the other flogged me severely. I had never experi-

enced anything of this kind before; and although not being used to the water, I naturally feared that element the first time I saw it; yet, nevertheless, could I have got over the nettings, I would have jumped over the side; but I could not. . . .

At last, when the ship we were in had got in all her cargo . . . we were all put under deck. . . . The closeness of the place, and the heat of the climate, added to the number in the ship, which was so crowded that each had scarcely room to turn himself, almost suffocated us. This produced copious perspirations so that the air soon become unfit for respiration, from a variety of loathsome smells, and brought on a sickness amongst the slaves, of which many died, thus falling victim to the improvident avarice, as I may call it, of their purchasers. The wretched situation was again aggravated by the galling of the chains, now become insupportable; and the filth of the necessary tubs, into which the children often fell, and were almost suffocated. The shrieks of the women and the groans of the dying rendered the whole a scene of horror almost inconceivable.

---

peoples had become either subjects or tributaries of the warlike Aztecs whose capital, Tenochtitlán, was a vast city built in the midst of a lake where Mexico City now stands. With a force that originally numbered only six hundred men, Hernán Cortés seized control of this great empire in only two years (1519–21). He could not have done it without the assistance of the Aztecs' many native enemies, but his success left Spain with the problem of governing millions whose culture was wholly unlike that of Europeans.

The problem was compounded in Peru a decade later. In 1530 Francisco Pizarro landed at Tumbez on the Pacific coast with 180 men and set about the destruction of the Inca Empire. The Incas were the ruling dynasty of the Quechua people. From their capital at Cuzco they controlled a region nearly two thousand miles in length by means of an elaborate system of roads and military supply depots. More tightly organized than the Mexicans, Quechua society was based on communal landholding and a system of forced labor that supported both the rulers and a complex religious establishment that did not, unlike that of the Aztecs,

demand human sacrifice. Pizarro had the good fortune to arrive in the midst of a dynastic dispute that divided the Indians and virtually paralyzed resistance. By 1533 the Spanish, numbering about six hundred, had seized the capital and a vast golden treasure, but they soon began to fight among themselves. Pizarro was murdered in one of a series of civil wars that ended only in 1548.

The rapid conquest of two great empires forced the Spanish crown to confront basic issues of morality and governance. The monarchy conceived of itself as the legitimate extension of God's rule on Earth. It was therefore obligated to provide for the spiritual welfare of its subjects and to govern according to the Christian principles of natural law. The unrestrained exploitation of Americans by the *conquistadores* was therefore doubly intolerable. Theoretically it undermined the prestige and authority of the crown and dissolved the bonds that tied its subjects to their ruler. In practical terms, it made effective government impossible.

Tension between conquerors and the crown had begun with Columbus. His enslavement of the Indians and high-handed treatment of his own men led to his

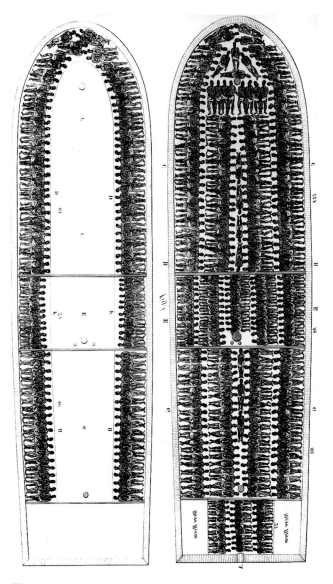

Illustration 16.5

⧉ **Packing a Slave Ship.** This diagram comes from an antislavery tract published in 1791, but the method of loading a ship to maximize the number of slaves carried had been used from the beginning of the trade. Many of the people who were packed like this below decks for weeks or perhaps months would not survive the voyage.

replacement as governor of Hispaniola. Balboa was executed for his misbehavior in Darien by officials sent from Spain. To regularize the situation, the *encomienda* system, an institution with deep medieval roots, was introduced after the conquests of Mexico and Peru. Conquistadores were to provide protection and religious instruction for a fixed number of Indians in return for a portion of their labor. The system failed. The conquistadores were for the most part desperadoes, members of a large class of otherwise unemployable military adven-

TABLE 16.1

Population Decline in Central Mexico

Little agreement exists on the size of Mexico's pre-Columbian population. These figures are more conservative than most but reflect a stunning rate of mortality.

Region	Population in 1530–35	Population in 1568
Basin of Mexico (excluding Mexico City)	589,070–743,337	294,535–297,335
Mexico City	218,546–273,183	109, 273
Morelos	460,797–614,396	153,599
Southern Hidalgo	257,442–321,802	128,721
Tlaxcala	140,000–165,000	140,000–165,000
West Puebla		
Above 2000 meters	160,664–200,830	80,332
Below 2000 meters	152,412–190,515	38,103
Total	1,978,931–2,509,063	944,563–972,363

Source: Adapted from William T. Sanders, "The Population of the Central Mexican Symbiotic Region, the Basin of Mexico, and the Teotihuacán Valley in the Sixteenth Century," in *The Native Population of the Americas in 1492*, 2d ed., William M. Denevan (Madison, Wis.: University of Wisconsin Press, 1992), p. 128.

turers that had survived the wars of Granada or of Italy. They had braved great dangers to win what they thought of as a New World and had no intention of allowing priests and bureaucrats to deprive them of their rewards.

In the meantime, the Indians of the mainland had begun to die in enormous numbers like those of the islands before them. Though many were killed while trying to defend themselves, most fell victim to European diseases for which they had developed no immunities. Smallpox was probably the worst. Estimates of mortality by the end of the sixteenth century range as high as 90 percent, and though all figures from this period are open to question, the conquest clearly was responsible for the greatest demographic catastrophe in historical times (see table 16.1).

Given the state of medical knowledge, little could be done to control the epidemics, but church and state alike were determined to do something about the conquistadores. The Dominican friar Bartolomé de Las Casas (1474–1566) launched a vigorous propaganda

◈ DOCUMENT 16.3 ◈

The Plea of Las Casas

The views of reformer Bartolomé de Las Casas, as expressed in this brief passage, may have influenced the emperor Charles V, but they were not accepted by most Europeans for centuries to come.

Therefore all mankind is one, and all people are alike in that which concerns their creation and all natural things, and no one is born enlightened. From this it follows that we must all be guided and aided at first by those who were born before us. And the savage peoples of the earth may be compared to uncultivated soil that brings forth weeds and useless thorns, but that has within it such natural virtue that by labor and cultivation it can be made to yield sound and useful fruits.

◈ DOCUMENT 16.4 ◈

Proclamation of the New Laws in Peru

In 1544 a new viceroy, Blasco Nuñez Vela, introduced the New Laws to Peru. The popular outrage recounted here by Francisco López de Gómara led to a serious but unsuccessful revolt under the leadership of Gonzalo Pizarro, the conqueror's brother.

Blasco Nuñez entered Trujillo amid great gloom on the part of the Spaniards; he publicly proclaimed the New Laws, regulating Indian tributes, freeing the Indians, and forbidding their use as carriers against their will and without pay. He told them, however, that if they had reason to complain of the ordinances they should take their case to the emperor; and that he would write to the king that he had been badly informed to order those laws.

When the citizens perceived the severity behind his soft words, they began to curse. [Some] said that they were ill-requited for their labor and services if in their declining years they were to have no one to serve them; these showed their teeth, decayed from eating roasted corn in the conquest of Peru; others displayed many wounds, bruises, and great lizard bites; the conquerors complained that after wasting their estates and shedding their blood in gaining Peru for the emperor, he was depriving them of the few vassals he had given them.

The priests and friars also declared that they could not support themselves nor serve their churches if they were deprived of their Indian towns; the one who spoke most shamelessly against the viceroy and even against the king was Fray Pedro Muñoz of the Mercedarian Order, saying . . . that the New Laws smelled of calculation rather than of saintliness, for the king was taking away the slaves that he had sold without returning the money received from them. . . . There was bad blood between this friar and the viceroy because the latter had stabbed the friar one evening in Málaga when the viceroy was *corregidor* there.

campaign on behalf of the Indians that ended in a series of debates at the University of Salamanca (see document 16.3). The issue at stake was whether or not the Indians were rational beings. If they were, according to Aristotle and the teachings of the church, they could not be enslaved. Las Casas won his point. Between 1542 and 1543, the emperor Charles V (1500–58) issued the so-called New Laws, forbidding Indian slavery and abolishing the encomienda system.

These debates and the policies that arose from them represent the only sustained, systematic effort by an early modern European government to develop an ethical basis for colonial rule. They inspired a school of political thought that flourished in Spain until the middle of the seventeenth century. If Indians continued to be treated abominably, at least they were accepted as legitimate members of Spanish society. Africans were not so fortunate. Even Las Casas accepted the morality of the slave trade because he knew nothing of African society and culture. He had seen only its sick, demoralized victims as they emerged from the filthy holds of the slave ships and decided that they were not rational creatures.

The edicts for the protection of the Indians met with powerful resistance (see document 16.4), and not until the reign of Philip II from 1556 to 1598 did a system of governance become fully implemented that would last throughout the colonial era. The basis of that system was the establishment of Mexico and Peru as kingdoms to be ruled by viceroys who were the personal representatives of the king. The viceroys were assisted by the *audiencia,* a committee of lawyers that served both administrative and judicial functions. All colonial appointments were made directly by the king on the advice of the Council of the Indies. The council, which met in Spain, also heard judicial appeals from the colonies, recommended legislation, and appointed committees of inquiry to investigate official conduct during and after each term of office.

Though Spanish colonial government was centralized and authoritarian, individual subjects—including Indians—had the right to appeal to any official body, and not a few took their complaints directly to the king. It was for its time an effective system, though requests might take a year or more to reach Spain, and even longer for an answer to return. This was in part because trade and communications were also centralized. Like the Portuguese, Spain tried to limit access to its colonial trade. Foreigners were excluded, and all goods were to be shipped and received through the Casa de Contratación, a vast government establishment in Sevilla. From the middle of the sixteenth century, French and English adventurers sought to break this monopoly and eventually became a threat to Spanish shipping in both Caribbean and European waters. By this time, massive silver deposits had been discovered at Potosí in what is now Bolivia (1545) and at Zacatecas in Mexico (1548). Bullion shipments from the New World soon accounted for more than 20 percent of the empire's revenues, and a system of convoys or *flotas* was established for their protection.

The Biological and Economic Legacy of the Conquests

None of these measures prevented the European conquests from having a disastrous effect on native Americans. The extermination of millions of people was unintentional, but the effort to destroy traditional American cultures was deliberate. The Spanish in particular believed that the conversion of the Indians depended in large part upon forcing them to live as Europeans. Wherever possible they leveled their temples and built churches upon the ruins. They destroyed cities and rebuilt them along Spanish lines, while extensive intermarriage between Spaniards and Americans tended to weaken the cultural identity of the latter. Religious instruction sought not only to instill Catholi-

cism but also to obliterate traditional beliefs. This campaign against memory was remarkably successful though many of the old ways survived as folklore or as superficially Christianized myths. The introduction of horses, cattle, hogs, and sheep to a society with few sources of power or animal protein was by comparison a modest benefit, though its value has been questioned by modern ecologists and vegetarians.

Asians and Africans had their own rich heritage of disease, and the European incursion did little to worsen it. Demographically, Asia appears to have been unaffected while the world population of Africans and African Americans increased in spite of the terrible mortality of the slave trade. The descendants of those who survived the slave ships became more numerous in the Americas, though the wretched conditions imposed by slavery kept their rate of growth far below that of whites. Meanwhile, the cassava, a starchy South American root, became the potato of West Africa and permitted a substantial increase among the populations that had eluded the slavers. Economically, individuals in both Asia and Africa may have prospered from trading with the Europeans, but native economies as a whole were harmed by what amounted to a foreign appropriation of surplus wealth. Everywhere the European exploitation and mistreatment of native peoples left an enduring legacy of resentment.

The effect of the conquests on Europe was also great, though long delayed. European population levels remained almost static until after about 1730 when the potato, a tuber first cultivated in the Peruvian Andes, was gradually accepted as a cheap food source. It could be grown with a minimum of labor in cool, damp climates and became a famine-proof staple for the poor until the appearance of the potato blight, another American import, in the 1840s. Without potatoes, feeding the tens of thousands of workers who migrated to town during the industrial revolution or supporting the huge conscript armies of the nineteenth century would have been difficult.

Other American species such as tomatoes, bell peppers, and chilies did little more than promote dietary variety in both Europe and Africa, while maize, the staple food of Mexico, was used primarily as animal fodder in Europe. In the early stages of colonization, luxury items had a greater impact. American chocolate and tobacco became popular in the seventeenth century. Sugar, a Middle Eastern plant formerly cultivated in small quantities, became available for mass consumption when huge sugar plantations were established in Brazil and the Caribbean. Coffee, another Middle Eastern product, established a similar rise in popularity when its introduction to the New World in the eighteenth century allowed for growth for the first time on a large scale.

Economically and politically, America's entry into the world market increased the overall volume of world trade, while its massive exports of gold and silver increased the European money supply. Early modern rulers began to think that it was better to increase revenues by seizing new territory and by expanding trade than by exploiting their existing subjects more efficiently. The idea, though popular with their subjects, was based in part upon an illusion. Trade and colonies provided additional pretexts for war. Their protection demanded the establishment of fortresses and the maintenance of expensive deep-sea navies. During the sixteenth and early seventeenth centuries the cost and intensity of European warfare reached new heights. As was obvious well before 1600, even if the primary cause of these conflicts was rarely colonial rivalry, their scope was becoming global.

A Clash of Empires: The Ottoman Challenge and the Emperor Charles V

The wars that plagued sixteenth- and early seventeenth-century Europe were for the most part a continuation of old dynastic rivalries, complicated after 1560 by rebellion and civil war in nearly all of the major states. These struggles were pursued with unparalleled vigor even though most Europeans believed, or claimed to believe, that the survival of Christendom was threatened by Ottoman expansion.

The structure of the Ottoman state forced the sultans to maintain a program of conquest even after the fall of Constantinople. Their personal survival often depended upon its success. Because the sultans practiced polygyny on a grand scale, inheritance was by a form of natural selection. Each of the sultan's legitimate sons was given a provincial governorship at the age of fourteen. Those who showed promise acquired more offices and more military support until, when the sultan died, one of them was in a position to seize power and murder his surviving brothers. The role of the military in securing and maintaining the succession meant that its loyalty had to be ensured at all times. The most important component of the army was the Janissaries, an infantry composed of men who were technically slaves of the sultan. Male children were taken as tribute from conquered areas, converted to Islam, and raised as soldiers. Originally, the Janissaries were forbidden to marry, but they were not immune to the attractions of wealth and power. Like the Praetorian Guard of ancient Rome, they were capable of overthrowing a sultan if their ambitions were not achieved. War gave them booty, governorships, and new recruits. Keeping them as busy as possible was a wise course of action.

The Turks first became a serious threat to western Europe in the reign of Süleyman I (the Magnificent, reigned 1520–66). In 1522 his fleet drove the Knights of St. John from their stronghold at Rhodes, thereby permitting unimpeded communications between Constantinople and Egypt. After defeating the Hungarians at Mohács in 1526, Süleyman established control of the central Hungarian plain. The Austrian Hapsburgs were able to claim a narrow strip of northwestern Hungary, but Transylvania under the voivod János Zapolya (d. 1540) became a Turkish tributary, Calvinist in religion, and bitterly hostile to the Catholic west. Then, in 1529 and again in 1532, Süleyman besieged Vienna. He failed on both occasions, largely because Vienna was beyond the effective limits of Ottoman logistics. But the effort made a profound impression. The Turk was at the gates.

In retrospect, the attacks on Vienna probably were intended only to prevent a Hapsburg reconquest of Hungary. They were not repeated until 1689. In 1533 a new Turkish offensive was launched at sea. Fleets under the command of Khair-ed-Din, a Christian convert to Islam known as "Barbarossa" for his flaming red beard, ravaged the coasts of Italy, Sicily, and Spain and threatened Christian commerce throughout the Mediterranean.

The brunt of these struggles ultimately fell upon the Spanish Empire. In 1517 Charles of Hapsburg (1500–58) ascended the thrones of Castile and Aragon to become Charles I, first king of a united Spain. He was the son of Juana "la Loca" (the Crazy), daughter of Ferdinand and Isabella, and Philip "the Handsome" (d. 1506), son of the emperor Maximilian I and Mary of Burgundy. His mother lived until 1555, but she was thought to be insane and had been excluded from the succession. From her, Charles inherited Spain, its possessions in the New World, and much of Italy, including Naples, Sicily, and Sardinia. On the death of his grandfather Maximilian in 1519, he gained the Hapsburg lands in Austria and Germany and the remaining inheritance of the dukes of Burgundy including the seventeen provinces of the Netherlands. In 1521 he was elected Holy Roman emperor as Charles V (see illustration 16.6).

Illustration 16.6

Charles V. This portrait was painted by Titian after the battle of Mühlberg (1547) in which Charles defeated the Protestant princes of the Schmalkaldic League. It shows the emperor as he often was—on horseback and at war.

The massive accumulation of states and resources embroiled the young emperor in endless conflict. Though he had placed the Austrian lands under the rule of his brother Ferdinand, king of the Romans, Charles was forced to defend Vienna in person against the Turks. Because Turkish naval efforts were directed primarily against his possessions in Spain and Italy, he thought it necessary to invade Tunis in 1535 and Algiers in 1541. The Valois kings of France, seeing themselves surrounded by Charles's territories, fought seven wars with him in thirty years. This Hapsburg-Valois rivalry was in some ways a continuation of the Italian wars at the beginning of the century, but it was fought on three fronts: northern Italy, the Netherlands, and the Pyrenees. As a devout Catholic, the emperor also tried in 1546–47 and again in 1552–55 to bring the German Protestants to heel but received no help from the papacy. Paul III, fearing imperial domination of Italy, allied himself with the Most Christian King of France, who was in turn the ally of the major Protestant princes and of the Turks.

The empire of Charles V was multinational, but in time its center of gravity shifted toward Spain. Charles, born in the Low Countries and whose native tongue was French, became dependent upon the revenues of Castile, the only one of his realms in which permanent taxation had been established. Spanish soldiers, trained in the Italian wars, became the core of his army. Castilian administrators produced results, not endless complaints about the violation of traditional rights or procedures, and by 1545 his secretary, his chief military adviser, and his confessor were Spanish. Charles in 1556 retired, sick and exhausted, to the remote mona-stery of Yuste in the heart of Spanish Extremadura. His son, Philip II (reigned 1556–98), was Spanish to his fingertips. His father's abdication left him Italy, the Netherlands, and the Spanish Empire while the Hapsburg lands in central Europe were given to Charles's brother Ferdinand, who was elected emperor in 1558.

The war between France and Spain came to an end in 1559 with the treaty of Cateau-Cambrésis, but the underlying rivalry remained. Both sides were simply exhausted. Though Philip was forced to repudiate his father's debts, the predictability of Castilian revenues and a dramatic increase in wealth from the American mines soon restored Spanish credit. The policies of the new king would be those of the late emperor: the containment of Islam and of Protestantism, and the neutralization of France.

The Crisis of the Early Modern State

The wars and rebellions of the later sixteenth century must be understood in this context. Moreover, the cost of war had continued to grow, forcing the state to increase its claims upon the resources of its subjects. By midcentury, nobles, cities, and their elected representatives had begun to resist those claims with unprecedented vigor. Reassertions of ancient privilege were brought forth to counter demands for more money or for greater royal authority. This heightened resistance was based in part upon economics. A series of bad harvests, partially attributed to the Little Ice Age that lasted from the 1550s to well after 1650, worked together with monetary inflation to keep trade and land revenues stagnant. Real wealth was not increasing in proportion to the demands made upon it, and though European elites continued to prosper by comparison with the poor, they grew ever more jealous of their prerogatives.

The controversies that arose in the wake of the Reformation made matters worse. Outside the Iberian Peninsula, the populations of most states were now bitterly divided along confessional as well as economic lines. Because nearly everyone believed that religious tolerance was incompatible with political order, each group sought to impose its views upon the others. This attitude was shared by many who were not fanatics. In a society that had always expressed political and economic grievances in religious language, the absence of a common faith made demonizing opponents easy and reaching compromise difficult if not impossible.

In the light of these struggles, the evolution of dynastic states, for all its success, apparently had not resolved certain basic issues of sovereignty. The relationship of the crown to other elements of the governing elites was still open to question in France, England, and the Netherlands. In the Holy Roman Empire the role of the emperor was imperfectly defined, and many of the empire's constituent principalities were engaged in internal disputes. Underlying everything was the problem of dynastic continuity. The success of the early modern state still depended to an extraordinary degree upon the character and abilities of its ruler. Could its basic institutions continue to function if the prince were a child or an incompetent? Some even doubted that they could survive the accession of a woman.

The French Wars of Religion and the Revolt of the Netherlands

The peace of Cateau-Cambrésis was sealed by the marriage of Isabel of Valois, daughter of Henry II of France, to Philip II of Spain. The celebrations included a tournament in which the athletic, if middle-aged, Henry died when a splinter from his opponent's lance entered the eye socket of his helmet. The new king, Francis II, was a sickly child of fifteen. The establishment of a regency under the leadership of the Guise family marked the beginning of a series of conflicts known as the Wars of Religion that lasted until 1598. The Guise were from Lorraine and unrelated to the royal family. Their ascendancy threatened the Bourbons, a clan descended from Louis IX and headed by the brothers Antoine, king of Navarre, and Louis, prince of Condé. It was also a threat to Henry's widow, Catherine de Médicis (1519–89), who hoped to retain power on behalf of her son Francis and his three brothers. Yet another faction, headed by Anne de Montmorency, constable of France, sought, like Catherine, to play the Guise against the Bourbons for their own advantage.

At one level the Wars of Religion were an old-fashioned struggle between court factions for control of the crown, but the Guise were also devout Catholics who intensified Henry II's policy of persecuting Protestants. Most French Protestants, or Huguenots, were followers of John Calvin. In 1559 they numbered no more than 5 or 10 percent of the population, but their geographic and social distribution made them a formidable minority. Heavily concentrated in the south and west, Calvinism appealed most to rural nobles and to the artisans of the towns, two groups with a long history of political, regional, and economic grievances (see document 16.5). The nobles were for the most part trained in the profession of arms; unhappy artisans could easily disrupt trade and city governments.

Searching for allies, the Bourbons found the Huguenots and converted to Protestantism. The conflict was now both religious and to a degree regional, as the Catholics of Paris and the northeast rallied to the house of Guise, who were secretly allied with Philip II of Spain. Francis II died in 1560, shortly after Condé and the Huguenots tried unsuccessfully to kidnap him at Amboise. He was succeeded by his brother, Charles IX (reigned 1560–74), who was closely controlled by Catherine de Médicis, but the wars went on. Though the Huguenots were not at first successful on the battlefield, they gained limited religious toleration in 1570.

◆ **DOCUMENT 16.5** ◆

The Defense of Liberty Against Tyrants

In both France and the Netherlands, the Protestants had to justify their revolt against the monarchy. One of the most important theorists to do so was Philippe du Plessis-Mornay, a councillor to Henry of Navarre, the leader of the Bourbon faction who later became Henry IV. Plessis-Mornay based his argument on an early version of the social contract theory, which argued that all rulers received their power from the people. His ideas would have a powerful impact on the political thinkers of the Enlightenment and on the framers of the United States Constitution. This is an exerpt from his treatise, Vindiciae contra tyrannos.

Thus, at the beginning all kings were elected. And even those who seem today to come to the throne by succession must first be inaugurated by the people. Furthermore, even if a people has customarily chosen its kings from a particular family because of its outstanding merits, that decision is not so unconditional that if the established line degenerates, the people may not select another.

We have shown . . . that kings receive their royal status from the people; that the whole people is greater than the king and is above him; that the king in his kingdom, the emperor in his empire, are supreme only as ministers and agents, while the people is the true proprietor. It follows, therefore, that a tyrant who commits felony against the people who is, as it were, the owner of his fief; that he commits *lèse majesté* [treason] against the kingdom or the empire; and that he is no better than any other rebel since he violates the same laws, although as king, he merits even graver punishment. And so . . . he may be either deposed by his superior or punished under the *lex Julia* [the Roman law on treason] for acts against the public majesty. But the superior here is the whole people or those who represent it. . . . And if things have gone so far that the tyrant cannot be expelled without resort to force, they may call the people to arms, recruit an army, and use force, strategy, and all the engines of war against him who is the declared enemy of the country and the commonwealth.

Illustration 16.7

The Massacre of the Innocents. In this work of art by Pieter Breughel the Younger, which is also a powerful propaganda piece, Spanish soldiers terrorize a Flemish village. The figure at the head of the troops bears a strong resemblence to the duke of Alba as he looked in 1567. To make a political point, Breughel the Younger may have repainted an earlier version of this work that had been done by his father.

Meanwhile, the Netherlands had begun their long rebellion against the king of Spain. The seventeen provinces of the Low Countries were now the richest part of Europe, an urbanized region devoted to trade and intensive agriculture. Though divided by language (Dutch or Flemish was spoken in the north and west, French or Walloon in the south and east), they shared a common artistic and intellectual tradition and an easygoing tolerance for foreigners and heretics. Though a majority of the population remained Catholic, Lutherans and Calvinists flourished in the major cities. Government was decentralized and, from the Spanish point of view, woefully inefficient. Philip II was represented by a regent, his half-sister Margaret of Parma (1522–86), who presided over the privy council and the councils of finance and state. Seventeen provincial estates, all of which were represented in the States General, controlled taxes and legislation. A virulent localism based on the defense of historical privilege made agreement possible only on rare occasions. Taxes were usually defeated by squabbles over who should pay the largest share—nobles or townspeople. No common legal code existed, and a host of independent legal jurisdictions were controlled by nobles whose administration of justice was often corrupt.

None of this was acceptable to Philip II. He was determined to reorganize the government, reform the legal system, and root out heresy by reforming the church along the lines suggested by the Council of Trent. All of these proposals struck directly at the wealth and power of the Netherlandish nobles. Philip's plan to reorganize

the governing councils weakened their authority, while legal reform would have eliminated the feudal courts from which many of the nobles drew large revenues. Though his reform of the church sought to increase the number of bishops, the king was determined to end the purchase of ecclesiastical offices and to appoint only clerics whose education and spirituality met the high standards imposed by the Council of Trent. The ancient custom by which nobles invested in church offices for the support of their younger sons was at an end.

Four years of accelerating protest by leading members of the aristocracy accomplished nothing. Finally, in 1566, a wave of iconoclasm brought matters to a head. The Protestants, acting in opposition to Philip's plan for ecclesiastical reform and encouraged by members of the higher nobility, removed the images from churches across the country. In some areas, iconoclasm was accompanied by rioting and violence. Though the regent's government was able to restore order, Philip responded in shock and anger. In 1567 he dispatched his leading general, the duke of Alba (1507–82), to put down what he saw as rebellion (see illustration 16.7). Though Alba was at first successful, the harshness of his government alienated virtually every segment of opinion. When he attempted to introduce a perpetual tax in 1572, most of the major cities declared their allegiance to William "the Silent," Prince of Orange (1533–84), the man who had emerged as leader of the revolt (see document 16.6).

Though William was not yet a convert to Protestantism, he attempted to form an alliance with the

❖ DOCUMENT 16.6 ❖

William of Orange: Call for Revolt

In 1572 the Sea Beggars, a group of refugees from the Netherlands, were expelled from England by Elizabeth I and seized the little town of Brille not far from Rotterdam. William of Orange, who had taken refuge in Germany, used this opportunity to issue the following call for revolt. It gives vigorous expression to the grievances of the Netherlands against Alba's regime and marks the true beginning of the revolt against Spain. Note, however, that Granvelle had been out of the country for eight years and that William still maintains the fiction that he is doing this for the sake of Philip II, who has been misled by his counselors.

We, William, by the grace of God, prince of Orange, count of Nassau . . . [and so on] seek for each and every estate . . . and for all the good inhabitants of the Netherlands of every station, freedom and deliverance from the present enslavement by cruel, foreign and bloodthirsty oppressors.

We suffer with all our heart over the multidinous and excessively cruel violences, the excessive burdens, taxes of ten, twenty, and thirty percent, and other imposts, exactions, burdens, seizures, slayings, expulsions, confiscations, executions, and innumerable other unparalleled and intolerable inflictions, intimidations, and oppressions which the common enemy, with his Spaniards, bishops, inquisitors and other dependents, continues daily with un-

precedented novelty and violence to inflict upon you, your wives and your daughters, and your souls, bodies, and goods. After so many years this now grows steadily worse under the name of His Royal Majesty, but without his knowledge, in violation of his oath, and contrary to the liberties and privileges of the country, although in fact at the instigation of Cardinal Granvelle and the Spanish Inquisitors, whose purpose it is to put into effect the decisions of the Council of Trent and the Inquisition of Spain. These events are so public and well known, especially to you who see, fear, and suffer them yourselves that I do not need to give any broader account of them. . . .

Now various lords and friends are ready to offer us renewed help and assistance on sea and on land. Indeed, the enemy has already suffered notable damage from ourselves and our collaborators, who have entered this country and taken over various harbors, cities, places, and districts which have placed themselves in our hands for their deliverance on behalf of his Royal Majesty. They have shown what each and every one of you should do if you do not wish to draw perpetual harm upon yourselves, through your own guilt, bringing yourselves and your descendants into perpetual slavery and peril of soul, body, and property.

French Huguenots, who, under the leadership of Gaspard de Coligny, had gained new influence with Charles IX. The situation was doubly perilous for Spain because Philip II, while maintaining Alba in the Netherlands, had renewed his father's struggles with the Turk. The Mediterranean war culminated in the great naval victory of Lepanto (October 7, 1571), but Philip's treasury was once again exhausted. French intervention in the Netherlands was averted only by the Massacre of St. Bartholomew (August 23–24, 1572) in which more than five thousand Protestants, Coligny included, were killed by Catholic mobs (see illustration 16.8). The massacre revived the French civil wars and permitted Alba to retake many of the rebellious towns, but the duke was recalled in 1573 and his successors were unable to bring the revolt under control. Margaret's son, Alessandro Farnese, duke of Parma (1545–92), finally was able to reimpose Spanish rule on the ten southern provinces in 1585.

By this time, the seven northern provinces had organized into an independent state with William of Orange as stadtholder or chief executive. The United Netherlands was Dutch in language and culture. Enriched by trade, secure in its control of the sea, and defended by the heavily fortified "water line" of three broad rivers—the Rhine, the Maas, and the Waal—the new republic was almost invulnerable to Spanish attack. It was also Protestant. The government was dominated by Calvinists, and William converted to Protestantism before he was assassinated by a Spanish agent in 1584. Refugees from Spanish rule, most of them French–speaking Calvinists, poured into the north, while a number of Dutch Catholics headed south into what is now Belgium.

These developments critically altered the balance of power in northern Europe. Philip II was still determined to recover his lost provinces and to assist the Catholics of France in their battle against the

Illustration 16.8

▨ **The Saint Bartholomew's Day Massacre.** On August 24, 1572, several thousand Huguenots, including their leader, Gaspard de Coligny, were massacred at Paris by Catholics. This engraving shows the murder of Coligny in sequence against a background of other atrocities. At right, Coligny is shot. At right, the wounded man is killed in his bed and dropped naked from his window.

Illustration 16.9

▨ **Elizabeth I of England.** This portrait from the workshop of Nicholas Hilliard dates from c. 1599, a time of great political difficulty for the queen. It is a propaganda piece intended to convey the wealth, majesty, and vigor of a ruler who was already in her sixty-sixth year.

Huguenots. The English, restored to Protestantism by Elizabeth I (ruled 1558–1603; see illustration 16.9), were equally determined to prevent a concentration of Spanish power on the coasts of the North Sea (see map 16.2). When Parma took Antwerp, the largest and richest city in the Netherlands in 1584, they sent an expeditionary force to support the Dutch.

Though a prosperous land of about three-and-a-half million people, Elizabethan England was no match for the Spanish Empire. It had the core of a fine navy but no army worthy of the name. Perpetual taxes were unknown, and the improvidence of Henry VIII had left his daughter with meager revenues from the royal domain. In the event of war, funds had to be sought from Parliament, and Parliament continually tried to interfere with the queen's policies. It was especially incensed at her refusal to marry, in part because it thought a woman incapable of governing on her own, and in part because it feared disorder if she died without an heir.

Parliament need not have worried about Elizabeth's ability (see document 16.7), but this last concern, at least, was real. Catholics everywhere had rejected Henry VIII's divorce. To them, Elizabeth was illegitimate, and Mary Stuart, queen of Scots (1542–87), was the true queen of England. A devout Catholic, descended from Henry VII and connected on her mother's side to the house of Guise, Mary had been driven from Scotland in 1568 by a coalition of

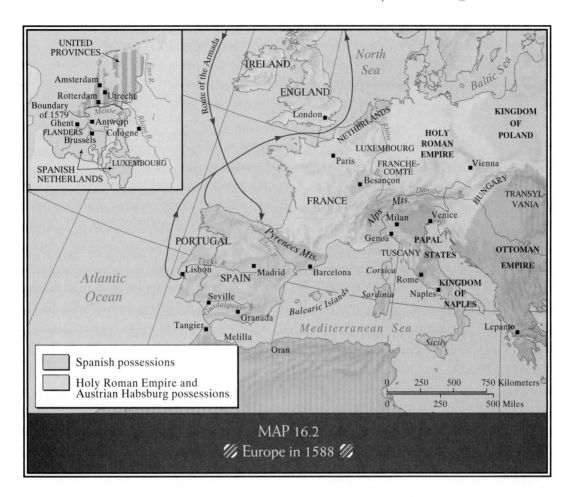

MAP 16.2
Europe in 1588

Protestants inspired by the reformer John Knox and led by her kinsman the earl of Moray. Elizabeth offered her refuge but held her under house arrest for nineteen years before ordering her execution in 1587.

Mary was killed not only because she had plotted against Elizabeth, but also because the English queen was convinced that war with Spain was inevitable. Elizabeth wanted no rival to encourage the hopes of Philip II or of her own Catholic subjects. These fears, too, were realistic, because for more than twenty years Elizabeth had pursued a course of intermittent hostility toward Spain. She had encouraged her subjects, notably Sir John Hawkins and Sir Francis Drake, to raid Spanish colonies in the Caribbean and in 1586 sent an English force to assist the Dutch. From the Spanish point of view, the execution of Mary was the last straw. Philip responded by sending a fleet to invade England. The great Spanish Armada of 1588 failed (see illustration 16.10), but the disaster did not end the war. Philip rebuilt his navy and tried again without success in 1595, while Drake and the aged Hawkins made another vain

attempt on Havana and Cartagena de Indias in the same year.

By this time the Spanish were at war in France as well. In 1589 the Bourbon leader, Henry of Navarre, emerged from the "War of the Three Henrys" as the only surviving candidate for the throne. Henry of Guise and Henry III, the last surviving son of Catherine de Médicis, had been assassinated by each others' supporters. Philip thought that, if France were controlled by Huguenots, the Spanish Netherlands would be crushed between two Protestant enemies, and he sent Parma and his army into France. This expedition, too, was a costly failure, but Henry's interests turned out to be more political than religious. He converted to Catholicism in the interest of peace and ascended the throne as Henry IV (reigned 1589–1610). To protect the Huguenots he issued the Edict of Nantes (1598), which granted them freedom of worship and special judicial rights in a limited number of towns, most in the southwest. In some respects, a state within a state was created, but the ordeal of France was over.

◆ DOCUMENT 16.7 ◆

The "Golden Speech" of Elizabeth I

The political skills of Elizabeth I are revealed in a speech delivered to a disgruntled Parliament in 1601. Parliament had protested her granting of monopolies to various courtiers, and the queen was forced to give way. The speech was intended to smooth over the dispute and to restore some of her waning popularity, but it was a masterpiece of public relations that helps to explain her success as ruler. A brief extract is given below.

Since I was queen, yet did I never put my pen unto any grant, but that, upon pretext and semblance made unto me, it was both good and beneficial to the subject in general; though a private profit to some of my ancient servants, who had deserved well at my hands. . . .

That my grants should be grievous to my people and oppressions privileged under color of our patents, our kingly dignity shall not suffer it; yea, when I heard it, I could give no rest to my thoughts until I had reformed it. . . .

To be a king and wear a crown is a thing more glorious to them that see it than it is pleasing to them that bear it; for myself, I was never so enticed with the glorious name of king, or royal authority of a queen, as delighted that God had made me his instrument to maintain his truth and glory and to defend this kingdom (as I said) from peril, dishonor, tyranny, and oppression.

There will never be a queen sit in my seat with more zeal for my country, and care for my subjects, and that sooner with willingness will venture her life for your good and safety, than myself. For it is not my desire to live nor reign longer than my life and reign shall be for your good. And though you have had, and may have many princes, more mighty and wise, sitting in this state; yet you never had, or shall have, any that were more careful and loving.

The Thirty Years' War

The resolution of the French wars and the death of Philip II in 1598 marked the end of a political cycle. The Netherlands continued to struggle under the leadership of William's son, Maurice of Nassau (1567–1625), until a ten years' truce was concluded in 1608, but it was a truce, not a treaty. Though Spain was financially exhausted, it still refused to recognize the Dutch state. War was expected to break out again when the truce expired in 1618. The war, when it came, was much more than a resumption of the Dutch Revolt. It involved all of the European states and turned central Europe into a battleground from 1618 to 1648.

The first phase of the Thirty Years' War began with a struggle for the crown of Bohemia. In 1555 the Peace of Augsburg had established the principle *cuius regio, eius religio;* that is, princes within the empire had the right to determine the religious beliefs of their subjects. Calvinists, however, were excluded from its provisions, and issues regarding the disposition of church properties and the conversion of bishops were left in dispute. Since then, two electoral principalities, the Palatinate and Brandenburg, had turned Calvinist, and several bishops had converted to Protestantism while retaining possession of their endowed lands. Violent quarrels arose over these issues and by 1610 the empire was divided into two armed camps: the Protestant Union and the Catholic League.

The Bohemian controversy arose because Matthias, king of Bohemia in 1618, was also Holy Roman emperor, a Catholic Hapsburg, and uncle of the future emperor Ferdinand II of Austria (1578–1637). Matthias was determined to preserve Bohemia for the faith and for his family, and in 1617 he secured the election of Ferdinand as his successor to the throne of Bohemia. This election was opposed by many of the Bohemian gentry and lesser nobility. They were for the most part Calvinists or Hussites and feared persecution from the devout Ferdinand and his Jesuit advisers. On May 23, 1618, an assembly of Bohemians threw three of the Hapsburg's regents from a window of the Hradschin palace, appointed a provisional government, and began to raise an army.

The "Defenestration of Prague" was an act of war. Revolt spread to the hereditary lands, threatening not only Bohemia but also the basic integrity of the Hapsburg state. Worse yet, the king of Bohemia was an elector of the empire. If the Bohemians elected a Protestant, the Protestants would have a majority of electors just as a new imperial election appeared imminent. Matthias was in poor health and Ferdinand hoped to succeed him as king of Bohemia as well as emperor. Ferdinand needed time to muster support, but in June 1619 he invaded Bohemia with the army of the Catholic League, drawn largely from his ally, Bavaria. The Bohemians responded by offering the crown to a Calvinist prince, Frederick V (1596–1632), elector palatine and son-in-law of James I of England.

Illustration 16.10

The Spanish Armada, 1588. This painting by an unknown artist shows a critical moment in the defeat of the Spanish Armada. The Spanish fleet had anchored off Gravelines on the

Flemish coast to support an invasion of England by the duke of Parma. The English sent fireships into the anchorage, forcing them to scatter and to abandon the invasion.

Frederick accepted after the death of Matthias and the election of Ferdinand as emperor on August 28. It was a tragic mistake. He was supported by only a part of the Protestant Union. James I refused to help, and a diversionary attack on Hungary by Bethlen Gabor (1580–1629), the Calvinist prince of Transylvania, was eventually contained by the Hapsburgs. Finally, on November 8, 1620, Frederick and his Protestant allies were soundly defeated at the White Mountain near Prague. Frederick's cause was now hopeless. The Spanish truce with the Netherlands had expired, and the palatinate lay squarely across the route by which Spanish troops and supplies were sent to the Low Countries. While Frederick's forces fought to preserve his claim to Bohemia, a Spanish army invaded his ancestral lands.

A second phase of the war began in 1625 when Christian IV of Denmark (1577–1648) emerged briefly as the champion of Protestantism. Christian's Lutheranism was reinforced by his territorial ambitions in north Germany, but he was no match for the imperial generals. By 1629 he was out of the war. His place was taken by the formidable Gustav Adolph of Sweden

(1594–1632). Since the reign of Erik XIV, from 1560 to 1568, Swedish policy had aimed at control of the Baltic. Wars with Russia and Poland had taught Gustav the art of war and given him all of Livonia, a territory roughly equal to present-day Estonia, Latvia, and Lithuania. He now sought to defend his fellow Protestants and to establish Swedish control over Mecklenburg and Pomerania on the north German coast. His brilliant campaigns, financed in part by France, came to an end when he died victorious on the battlefield at Lützen on November 16, 1632.

The last phase of the war (1535–1648) continued the Franco-Swedish alliance, but with France acting openly as the leader of the anti-imperial forces. Henry IV had died at the hands of an assassin in 1610, leaving the queen, Marie de Médicis, as regent for the nine-year-old Louis XIII (1601–43). Her regency was unpopular, but the disasters of 1560 were not repeated. Louis seized power from his mother in 1617 and, after 1624, entrusted much of his government to Armand de Plessis, cardinal duke of Richelieu (1585–1642). One of the ablest statesmen of the age, Richelieu was alarmed

MAP 16.3
The Thirty Years' War

by the Spanish-Imperial alliance and returned to the anti-Hapsburg policies of Francis I. He pursued the war through surrogates until the death of Gustav Adolph forced him into the open. The Spanish were by this time in irreversible decline, and their defeat by the French at Rocroi (1643) marked the end of their military power. Bavaria was ravaged by a Franco-Swedish force in 1648, and peace was at last concluded on October 24 of that year.

The Treaties of Westphalia brought the Thirty Years' War to an end, leaving France the dominant power in Europe (see map 16.3). The Netherlands, which had fought Spain in a series of bitter actions on land and sea, was at last recognized as an independent state, while the German principalities, many of which had been devastated, were restored to the boundaries of 1618. Bohemia reverted to the Hapsburgs, but imperial authority as a whole was weakened except in the Hapsburg lands of southeastern Europe. It was a meager return for three decades of unparalleled violence.

The English Civil War

England did not participate in the Thirty Years' War because the early Stuart monarchs, James I (reigned

1603–25) and Charles I (reigned 1625–49), were caught in a political dilemma from which they could not escape. Like Denmark and Sweden, England was a "domain" state: the regular revenues of the crown came not from taxes, which could be levied only by Parliament, but from the royal domain. This was not necessarily a disadvantage. The Danish monarch held more than 40 percent of the arable land in Denmark and derived vast revenues from the Sound Tolls levied on every ship passing from the North Sea into the Baltic. The Swedish royal estate derived great wealth from export duties on copper and iron, the country's major exports. Both countries were therefore able to exert a political and military influence wholly disproportionate to their size.

England had no comparable sources of revenue. The failure of Henry VIII to retain monastic lands taken at the time of the Reformation left the crown without sufficient property to "live of its own." Even import and export duties, though technically part of the domain, had to be authorized by Parliament. The resulting poverty, already evident under Elizabeth, restricted the crown's ability to reward its supporters. Worse, it forced her Stuart successors to seek wealth in ways that profoundly offended their subjects (see document 16.8). Knights' fines, ship money, *quo warranto* proceedings, and the abuse of wardships struck directly at property rights and aroused a firestorm of opposition.

Much of this opposition was at first centered in the legal profession where such jurists as Sir Edward Coke (1552–1634) revived the common law as a protection against royal prerogatives, but in the end Parliament proved to be the crown's most formidable adversary. Between 1540 and 1640 the wealth and numbers of the landholding gentry, the professions, and the merchant community had increased enormously. These elements of the English elite dominated the House of Commons, which took the lead in opposing royal policies. The Stuarts feared their disaffection and would have preferred to rule without calling Parliament. Except for relatively short periods, this was impossible. Even the smallest of crises forced the crown to seek relief through parliamentary taxation.

The growing resentment in Parliament might have been better managed had it not been for the personalities of the Stuart kings. Neither James nor Charles was capable of inspiring great loyalty. James was awkward, personally dirty, and a homosexual at a time when homosexuality was universally condemned. His son was arrogant and generally distrusted, while the court as a whole was thought to be morally and financially corrupt. Though James, who annoyed his subjects with

---

◈ DOCUMENT 16.8 ◈

The English Petition of Right, 1628

The 1628 Petition of Right summarized Parliament's grievances against Charles I, who was trying to solve his financial problems through illegal and arbitrary means. The objections are based largely upon perceived violations of the Magna Carta, also known as the Great Charter. The following are exerpts from a much longer document.

And where also, by the statute called the Great Charter of the Liberties of England, it is declared and enacted that no freeman may be taken or imprisoned, or be disseised of his freehold or liberties or his free customs, or be outlawed or exiled or in any manner destroyed, but by the lawful judgment of his peers or by the law of the land. . . .

They do therefore humbly pray your most excellent majesty that no man hereafter be compelled to make or yield any gift, loan, benevolence, tax, or such like charge without common consent by act of parliament; and that none be called to make answer, or take such oath, or to give attendance, or be confined, or otherwise molested or disquieted concerning the same, or for refusal thereof; and that no freeman, in any such manner as is before mentioned, be imprisoned or detained; and that your majesty would be pleased to remove the said soldiers and mariners [who had been quartered in the counties to enforce the king's measures]; and that the foresaid commissions for proceeding by martial law may be revoked and annulled; and that hereafter no commissions of like nature may issue forth . . . lest by colour of them any of your majesty's subjects be destroyed or put to death, contrary to the laws and franchise of the land.

---

treatises on everything from the evils of tobacco to witchcraft, wrote eloquently in support of the divine right of kings, the legitimacy of his family's rule was continually undermined by his own behavior and by the devious policies of his son.

The religious question was more serious. Elizabeth, not wishing "to make windows into men's souls," had established a church that was Protestant but relatively tolerant. Some of her subjects had retained a fondness for the ideas and liturgical practices of the old church, while others, known as Puritans, followed Calvin with varying degrees of rigor. James was a Calvinist who commissioned the King James Bible in 1611 and established Protestant colonists in northern Ireland in the same year. He quarreled with the Puritans over church governance and other matters, but he managed to avoid an open breach as they grew more powerful over the course of his reign. Charles, however, supported the anti-Puritan reforms of Archbishop William Laud (1573–1645). Though Laud was no Catholic, Queen Henriette Marie (1609–1669) heard Mass regularly. She was the sister of Louis XIII and a strong personality who exerted great influence over her husband. The Puritans suspected that Charles meant to restore Catholicism. Faith, as well as liberty and property, was thought to be at risk.

Twenty years of increasingly bitter conflict between Parliament and the crown led to civil war in 1642. The Scots rebelled in 1638 when Charles tried to introduce the English *Book of Common Prayer* at Edinburgh. To pay for the Scottish war, he summoned what is called the Long Parliament because it met from 1640 to 1660. In response to his call for money, the Commons impeached Archbishop Laud and Charles's chief minister, Thomas Wentworth, earl of Strafford. They then abolished the prerogative courts of Star Chamber and High Commission. When Charles failed to impeach the parliamentary leaders he fled from London, and Parliament decided to raise an army in its own defense.

After three years of hard fighting the royalists were defeated at Naseby (June 14, 1645), but serious divisions had appeared in the parliamentary ranks. The army was now dominated by Independents, who favored a congregational form of church government, while the Parliament they served was controlled by Presbyterians. The Independents refused to disband without guaranteed freedom of conscience and the removal of certain Presbyterians from Parliament. The Scots, fearing a threat to their own Presbyterian church order, were alarmed. Charles sought to capitalize on these strains by abolishing the Scottish episcopate in return for Presbyterian support, but the Scots and their English allies were defeated by the army at Preston (August 17–20, 1548). The victors now felt that compromise was impossible. In December the army captured Charles and purged the Commons of its Presbyterian members. A court appointed by the Rump, as the remnant of Parliament was now called, sentenced the king to death. He was beheaded at Whitehall on January 30, 1649.

For all practical purposes England was governed by the army. A republican constitution had been established, but real power lay in the hands of Oliver Cromwell (1599–1658), the most successful of the parliamentary generals. In 1653 he was named lord protector of the Commonwealth of England, Scotland, and Ireland. A radical Protestant, Cromwell attempted to reform English society along Puritan lines while following a vigorous policy abroad. After subduing the Scots he fought a naval war with the Dutch (1552–54) and started another with Spain in 1656. The Irish Catholics, who had massacred thousands of Protestants in 1641, were ruthlessly suppressed.

Cromwell had refused to accept the crown when it was offered to him in 1657, but when he died in the following year he left the Protectorate to his son Richard. Richard's rule was brief and troubled. He was forced to resign after only nine months, and a Convention Parliament restored Charles II (1630–85), son of Charles I, on May 8, 1660. The English had tired of Puritanism and military rule.

The Price of Conflict: Fiscal Crisis and Administrative Devolution

Surprisingly, this age of troubles was in many places a time of intellectual, literary, and artistic achievement. A distinction must be made between those regions that were combat zones, those that remained peaceful but were forced to assume heavy financial burdens, and those that were virtually untouched by the fighting. Even the most devastated regions experienced peace for at least a portion of the century between 1560 and 1660; their recovery was sometimes rapid.

In some cases the experience of war produced literary masterpieces. The age of the religious wars was not a golden one for France, but it produced the elegant and skeptical essays of Michel de Montaigne (1533–92), an antidote to sectarian madness. In Germany, the wreckage of the Thirty Years' War was nearly complete, but it was wryly chronicled in Grimmelshausen's *Simplicissimus*. *Don Quixote*, one of the greatest of all literary classics, was written by Miguel de Cervantes (1547–1616), who had lost an arm at Lepanto. It is, at least in part, a satire on his countrymen's fantastic dreams of glory.

Political turmoil gave birth to political theory. The English Civil War convinced Thomas Hobbes (1588–1679) that political salvation lay in *Leviathan*, an autocratic superstate, while *Oceana*, by James Harrington (1611–77) reflected the republican ideals of the Commonwealth. In *Paradise Lost*, Cromwell's Latin secretary, John Milton (1608–74), created a Puritan epic to rival the vision of Dante. Drama, too, flourished in the England of William Shakespeare (1564–1616) and in the Spain of Lope de Vega (1562–1635) and Calderón de la Barca (1600–81). The Netherlands, which after the 1590s enjoyed prosperity and internal peace in the midst of war, surpassed its own earlier achievements in the visual arts and became the center of a school of painting that influenced artists throughout northern Europe.

But if learning and the arts flourished, at least in some places, the struggles of the age were often highly destructive of political and economic life. This resulted primarily from the ways in which war was organized and fought. Armies had become vastly larger and more expensive in the course of the sixteenth century, and the wars were almost interminable. Given their political objectives, it could not have been otherwise. The French Wars of Religion were a struggle between two, and at times three, irreconcilable segments of the country's elite. Most of the battles were classic cavalry actions that resulted in a clear victory for one side or the other, but which could not end the war. Only the destruction of a major segment of the population could have prevented the losers from trying again.

In the Netherlands, the primary goal of both sides was to take and hold land or, conversely, to deny it to the enemy. After 1572 the war became a series of sieges that, thanks to the defensive value of the bastion trace, lasted months if not years. Both sides tended to avoid battles because their troops were, in the short term at least, irreplaceable. Sixteenth-century tactics demanded professional soldiers. The recruitment, training, and movement of replacements to the war zone took months, and positions under constant enemy pressure could not be left even partially defenseless.

If the war in the Netherlands was virtually static, the situation in Germany during the Thirty Years' War was too fluid. Central Europe had become a kind of power vacuum into which unpredictable forces were drawn. Bloody battles were fought only to see the victor confronted with yet another set of enemies. It is hard to imagine what, other than sheer exhaustion, might have ended the struggle. War, as Michael Roberts has said, "eternalized itself."

No early modern state could afford this. Even the wealthiest European monarchies lacked the ability to recruit and maintain full-scale standing armies. They re-

lied instead on a core of subject troops (or, as in the French Wars of Religion, troops personally and ideologically committed to a cause), supplemented by a far larger number of mercenaries. The latter were usually recruited by contractors who commanded them in the field. If the mercenaries were not paid, they left; if they stayed, they had little incentive to risk their lives unnecessarily. Their employers had little control over their actions, and even subject troops were capable of mutiny if they were left too long unpaid.

War, in other words, was a chaotic business. Rank in the modern sense meant little because officers sometimes refused to obey the orders of those who might have been their inferiors in civilian life. There were no uniforms, and weapons were not for the most part standardized. Logistics were a nightmare. An army might number anywhere from 30,000 to 100,000 combatants. The troops were housed either in makeshift field shelters or quartered on the civilian populations of the war zones, which meant that civilians might be forced to provide food and housing for months on end. The close contact between soldiers and civilians bred hostility and led to chronic breakdowns in military discipline. To complicate matters further, camp followers numbered at least three and often six for each combatant. These women and children were the support troops who made shelter, foraged for food, and nursed the sick and wounded. No army could function without them, but together with the men they made up a society that lived by its own rules with little concern for civilian norms.

The system reached a peak of absurdity during the Thirty Years' War when contractors such as the imperial general Albrecht von Wallenstein (1583–1634) offered recruits a month's pay—which they had to give back to pay for their arms and equipment—and then marched them so far from their homes that they could not easily return. From that point onward they were expected to live off the land. Such practices account for much of the dislocation caused by the German wars. It was safer to join an army with one's family than to remain at home to be robbed, raped, or killed by marauding soldiers (see document 16.9). Whole villages were depopulated only to reconstitute themselves wherever they found themselves when the war ended.

When a state tried to provide adequately for its troops, the costs were prohibitive and could lead to social breakdown. The fate of Spain is an example (see document 16.10). In the 1570s Philip II was spending 140 percent of his annual revenues on warfare. The uncovered balance was provided by loans, often at high

❖ DOCUMENT 16.9 ❖

Soldiers Loot a German Farm

The novel Simplicissimus *by Hans von Grimmelshausen
(c. 1622–74) was based in part on the author's own experiences in the
Thirty Years' War. In these passages from the beginning of the book,
the title character Simplicissimus, who is not as simple as he appears,
describes the sack of his parent's farm. Like the hero, people took to the
roads or joined the armies to avoid such horrors.*

The first thing these troopers did in the blackened room
of my Dad was to stable their mounts. Thereafter, each
fell to his appointed task, fraught in every case with ruin
and destruction. For although some began to slaughter,
cook, and roast, as if for a merry banquet, others stormed
through the house from top to bottom, ransacking even
the privy, as though they thought the Golden Fleece
might be hidden there. Some packed great bundles of
cloth, apparel, and household goods, as if to set up a stall
for a jumble sale, but what they had no use for they
smashed and destroyed. Some thrust their swords into the
hay and straw as if they had not enough sheep and pigs to
slaughter. Others emptied the feather-beds and pillows of
their down, filling them instead with meat and other
provender, as if that would make them more comfortable
to sleep on. Others again smashed stoves and windows as

if to herald an everlasting summer. They flattened copper
and pewter utensils and packed up the bent and useless
pieces; chests, tables, chairs, and benches they burnt,
though in the yard they could have found many cords of
firewood. Finally, they broke every dish and saucepan, either because they preferred their food roasted or because
they intended to have no more than a single meal there.

And now they began to unscrew the flints from their
pistols and to jam the peasant's thumbs into them, and to
torture the poor lads as if they had been witches. Indeed,
one of the captives had already been pushed into the
bread oven and a fire lit under him, although he had confessed nothing. They put a sling around the head of another, twisting it tight with a piece of wood until the
blood spurted from his mouth, nose, and ears. In short,
each had his own device for torturing peasants, and each
peasant received his individual torture. . . . Of the captured women, girls, and maidservants I have nothing in
particular to tell, for the warriors would not let me see
what they did with them. But this I do know: that from
time to time one could hear pitiful screams coming from
different parts of the house, and I don't suppose my Mum
and Ursula fared any better than the others.

rates, from Italian or Dutch bankers. Not even American silver could long sustain this kind of expenditure,
and in time the economy of Castile was badly damaged
(see table 16.2). The other Spanish kingdoms were exempt from most forms of taxation, but in Castile taxes
increased to the point that peasants were forced from
the land and took refuge in the cities where the church
periodically distributed grain and oil to the poor. Commerce and industry were virtually destroyed. Declining
production increased the country's dependence on imports, which lowered the value of Spanish money and
worsened an inflation that had been fueled for years by
silver from the Indies. When Philip II died in 1598, the
population of Castile had been shrinking for nearly a
decade.

Economic decline provoked a chain reaction that
raised the costs of war by increasing the interest on
government loans, while unfavorable exchange rates
raised the cost of goods and services that Spain had to
purchase in Germany or the Netherlands. Troops were
often poorly supplied or left without pay for as much as

three years at a time. This caused mutinies, which prolonged the wars and raised costs even higher. Similar
problems arose in other countries, but they were far
more serious in Spain because the military effort lasted
for more than a century and a half. From the wars of
Granada to the Peace of Westphalia, little opportunity
existed for recovery.

Philip III (ruled 1598–1621) and his minister, the
shrewd but lethargic duke of Lerma, tried to provide
Spain with a much-needed respite from war but were
unable to restrain the aggressive tendencies of their
viceroys. When Philip IV's chief minister, the energetic
count-duke of Olivares (1587–1645), tried to spread
the burdens of taxation and recruitment to other Spanish realms, he faced rebellion. Portugal, which had
been annexed by Philip II in 1580 after its king died
without heirs, declared independence in 1640.
Cataluña, on the other side of the peninsula, rebelled in
the same year. The government of Olivares lacked the
resources to stop them, and Portugal remains free to
this day. Cataluña returned to the fold in 1652 after

◆ DOCUMENT 16.10 ◆

Economic Conditions in Spain

This letter, written in the mid-seventeenth century by an unnamed Spanish bureaucrat to his queen, describes the effects of generations of war on the Spanish economy.

Señora, every day the occupation of my office brings me to many places in which I see and recognize miseries that until these times were never seen or heard of: towns that only a few years ago had one thousand heads of families do not have five hundred today, and in those that had five hundred there are scarcely signs of one hundred. In all these places there are innumerable persons and families that pass one or two days without eating, and others who merely eat herbs that they have gathered in the countryside as well as other types of sustenance never heard of or used before. . . . And therefore, it is certain, Señora, that there have been many deaths and illnesses everywhere

this year, and everyone has assured me that these have been caused by mere want. La Mancha, Señora, has been depopulated and many families have emigrated to Madrid, where there have now gathered more poor people than have ever been seen. La Alcarria is deserted, prostrate, and poor; parents cannot help their children, nor brothers their brothers, even though they are watching them die. And in places where poor people were never seen, today they roam about in great gangs. The rest of the province of Toledo is in the same condition, and if were not for that pastor and prelate (the Cardinal) who gives so many lavish and repeated alms and helps with so many necessities, it is certain that one would see misfortunes never imagined, but since it is not possible to help everyone, many are experiencing those misfortunes already.

◆ TABLE 16.2 ◆

Crown Income and Debt in Castile

These figures (in millions of ducats) provide an idea of the financial burdens imposed on the Castilian economy by war. During most of this period, nonmilitary costs rarely rose above 10 percent of the annual budget.

Year	Revenue	Debt	Interest on debt
1515	1.5	12	0.8
1560	5.3	35	2.0
1575	6.0	50	3.8
1598	9.7	85	4.6
1623	15.0	112	5.6
1667	36.0	130	9.1

Source: C. Wilson and G. Parker, eds., *An Introduction to the Sources of European Economic History* (Ithaca, N.Y.: Cornell University Press, 1977), p. 49.

minished outside his hereditary lands. Russia was still emerging from its "Time of Troubles," the period of anarchy that followed the death of Ivan the Terrible. The Romanov dynasty, established in 1613, had difficulty dealing with a series of Cossack rebellions and with the heresy of the Old Believers, a movement that rejected all innovation in the Russian church. Though Cromwellian England had briefly tapped the country's wealth in the service of the state, the restoration of Charles II revived many of the old conflicts between crown and Parliament and the king's wealth was once again severely limited. France with its enormous wealth was more resilient, but when the four-year-old Louis XIV ascended the throne under a regency, a series of aristocratic rebellions known as the Fronde (1648–52) revealed that the foundations of the monarchy were by no means fully secure. At midcentury only the Dutch Republic appeared strong and stable, and for Europe's monarchies the years of turmoil clearly had done little to resolve the problem of sovereignty.

France emerged as a greater threat to its liberties than Castile.

Spain was in some respects a special case, but the condition of Europe as a whole after a century of war and rebellion was grim. Most of the German states were a shambles, while the emperor's role was much di-

Conclusion

The intellectual and spiritual changes of the sixteenth century were achieved amidst a climate of escalating violence. The terrible logic of military rivalry forced the

new monarchies to expand as a condition of survival, but neither their resources nor their administrative technology could support indefinite growth. The age of the Renaissance saw the discovery of the New World and the first unprecedented efforts by Europeans to impose political control on overseas populations. The Reformation was in a sense made possible by a titanic struggle between France and the Holy Roman Empire that was greatly complicated by the expansionist designs of the Turks. By 1560 these conflicts had pushed the major European states beyond the limits of their resources, but the dynamic of competition allowed them no respite. They demanded yet more of their subjects and, because they feared that religious diversity was incompatible with public order, insisted ever more stridently on uniformity in religion.

A reaction was probably inevitable. The French Wars of Religion, the Revolt of the Netherlands, and the English Civil War marked the growth of powerful resistance against the claims of the state. The Thirty Years' War saw the near-breakdown of the state system. In each case religion served as an additional grievance and helped to render the conflicts interminable by encouraging people to dehumanize their opponents. War, fueled by religion and by the inability of states to control their own armies, fed upon itself. By 1648 the governments of Europe clearly could not survive without fundamental reform.

Suggested Readings

The standard introductions to the history of European expansion overseas remain J. H. Parry, *The Age of Reconnaissance: Discovery, Exploration, and Settlement, 1450–1650* (1963, 1981) and B. Penrose, *Travel and Discovery in the Age of the Renaissance, 1420–1620* (1952, 1962). See also G. Scammell, *The World Encompassed: The First European Maritime Empires, c. 800–1650* (1981). In addition to the sources on shipbuilding and navigation mentioned in chapter 13, see C. Cipolla, *Guns, Sails, and Empires: Technological Innovation and the Early Phases of European Expansion, 1400–1700* (1975). Portuguese expansion is described in B. Diffie and G. Winius, *Foundations of the Portuguese Empire, 1415–1580* (1979) and C. .R. Boxer, *The Portuguese Seaborne Empire, 1415–1825* (1969). Among the best biographies of Columbus are S. Morison, *Admiral of the Ocean Sea: A Life of Christopher Columbus* (1942) and F. Fernández-Armesto, *Columbus* (1991). The best book on the conquest of Mexico remains the eyewitness account of B. Díaz del Castillo, *The True History of the Conquest of New Spain*, trans. A. Maudsley (1966), and the best overall descriptions of the Spanish imperial system are still C. H. Haring, *The Spanish Empire in America* (1947), J. H. Parry, *The Spanish Seaborne Empire* (1966), and C. Gibson, *Spain in America* (1966). For Las Casas and the debate over the In-

dians, see L. Hanke, *Bartolomé de Las Casas: An Interpretation of His Life and Thought* (1951) and *The Spanish Struggle for Justice in the Conquest of America* (1965); for the treatment of Indians, see L. B. Simpson, *The Encomienda in New Spain* (1966), C. Gibson, *The Aztecs under Spanish Rule* (1964), and J. Lockhart, *Spanish Peru, 1532–1560: A Colonial Society* (1968). Two fundamental essays on the impact of the conquests are A. Crosby, *The Columbian Exchange: Biological and Cultural Consequences of 1492* (1972) and J. H. Elliott, *The Old World and the New, 1492–1650* (1970).

H. Inalcik, *The Ottoman Empire: The Classical Age, 1300–1600*, 2d ed. (1985) remains the best English source on the Ottomans. The standard biographies of Charles V are K. Brandi, *The Emperor Charles V* (1939) and M. Fernández Alvarez, *Charles V: Elected Emperor and Hereditary Ruler* (1975). M. Rady, *The Emperor Charles V* (1988) is a brief, but useful, handbook. For good general histories of Spain in the sixteenth century, see J. H. Elliott, *Imperial Spain* (1963) and J. Lynch, *Spain under the Habsburgs*, vol. 1, 2d ed. (1981). Good studies of Philip II and his reign include H. Kamen, *Philip of Spain* (1997), P. Pierson, *Philip II of Spain* (1975), and G. Parker, *Philip II* (1978).

The best surveys of the French Wars of Religion are probably M. Holt, *The French Wars of Religion* (1993), J. H. M. Salmon, *Society in Crisis: France in the Sixteenth Century* (1975), and R. Mandrou, *Introduction to Modern France, 1500–1640: An Essay in Historical Psychology* (1975). Important local studies include P. Benedict, *Rouen During the Wars of Religion* (1981) and B. Diefendorf, *Beneath the Cross: Catholics and Huguenots in Sixteenth Century Paris* (1991). The best account of the revolt of the Netherlands is G. Parker, *The Dutch Revolt* (1977). See also P. Geyl, *The Revolt of the Netherlands*, 2d ed. (1966) and A. Duke, *Reformation and Revolt in the Low Countries* (1990). For Alba, see W. Maltby, *Alba: A Biography of Fernando Alvarez de Toledo, 3rd. Duke of Alba* (1983). There is no reliable modern biography of William of Orange. English foreign policy in this era is described by R. B. Wernham, *Before the Armada* (1966). A vast literature exists on the Spanish Armada of 1588. The classic G. Mattingly, *The Armada* (1959) and C. Martin and G. Parker, *The Spanish Armada* (1988) are excellent. On Elizabeth I, see W. MacCaffrey, *Elizabeth I* (1993), J. Ridley, *Elizabeth I: The Virtues of Shrewdness* (1987), and S. Bassnett, *Elizabeth I: A Feminist Perspective* (1988). The most reliable treatment of the Thirty Years' War is G. Parker, *The Thirty Years' War* (1984). For Gustav Adolph, see M. Roberts, *Gustavus Adolphus and the Rise of Sweden* (1975); for Wallenstein, G. Mann, *Wallenstein: His Life Narrated* (1976). The literature on the English civil wars is enormous. Begin with L. Stone, *The Causes of the English Revolution* (1972) and C. Russell, *The Causes of the English Civil War* (1990), then see R. Ashton, *The English Civil War: Conservatism and Revolution, 1604–1649* (1976), J. Morrill, *The Revolt of the Provinces: Conservatives and Radicals in the English Civil War, 1630–1650* (1976), and two books by M. Kishlansky: *The Rise of the New Model Army* (1979) and *Parliamentary Selection: Social and Political Choice in Early Modern England* (1986). Among the better works on Cromwell are C. Hill, *God's Englishman: Oliver Cromwell and the English Revolution* (1976), and R. Howell, *Cromwell* (1977).

To understand the military history of the sixteenth and seventeenth centuries, begin with J. R. Hale, *War and Society in Renaissance Europe, 1450–1620* (1985) and two enlightening special studies, G. Parker, *The Army of Flanders and the Spanish Road, 1567–1659* (1972) and J. Guilmartin, *Gunpowder and Galleys: Changing Technology and Mediterranean Warfare at Sea in the Sixteenth Century* (1975). G. Parker, *The Military Revolution: Military Innovation and the Rise of the West, 1500–1800* (1988) provides a global perspective.

For the development of fortification, see C. Duffy, *Siege Warfare: The Fortress in the Early Modern World* (1979). The later chapters of J. H. Elliott, *Imperial Spain* (1963) and the same author's monumental *The Count-Duke of Olivares: Statesman in an Age of Decline* (1986) deal with seventeenth-century Spain. See also R. Stradling, *Europe and the Decline of Spain, 1580–1720* (1981) and H. Kamen, *Spain in the Later Seventeenth Century* (1980).

CHAPTER 17

PREINDUSTRIAL EUROPE: SCIENCE, THE ECONOMY, AND POLITICAL REORGANIZATION

CHAPTER OUTLINE

The political troubles of the late sixteenth and early seventeenth centuries did not preclude extraordinary developments in other areas. A new Europe, and perhaps a new world, seemingly began to emerge from the ashes of the old. The scientific revolution changed the way Europeans thought about the physical universe. England, France, and above all the Netherlands challenged the Iberian powers and created substantial empires of their own. In the process they greatly expanded Europe's presence in world markets and accumulated capital in unprecedented amounts. The Netherlands emerged, however briefly, as a major power and a center of high culture. Eventually, states that had been nearly shattered by a century of war and revolution began to reconstruct themselves, reforming their governmental institutions, curbing the power of local elites, and gaining control over the armies and navies whose independence had threatened to engulf them. The model for many of these changes was the France of Louis XIV.

When Louis died in 1715, the major governments had achieved a measure of internal stability, and Europe as a whole was on the threshold of the greatest transformation in its history. The industrial revolution that began in the later eighteenth century would eventually bring an end to the biological old regime and its characteristic social structures. This, far more than the Renaissance and Reformation, marked the dawn of the modern age. Science inspired the industrial revolution; the accumulation of great wealth in the hands of a relative few provided the capital. Chapter 17 will therefore conclude with a brief description of the preindustrial economy and of the social changes it created.

Medieval Science and the Scientific Revolution

The scientific revolution of the late sixteenth and seventeenth centuries has no parallel among modern intellectual movements. Its impact was comparable to that made by the thinkers of ancient Greece because, like them, it changed not only ideas but also the process by which ideas are formulated. The Renaissance and the Reformation, for all their importance, were rooted in traditional patterns of thought. They could be understood without reordering the concepts that had permeated Western thinking for more than two thousand years. The development of modern science, though in some ways an outgrowth of these earlier movements, asked questions that were different from those that had been asked before and by so doing created a whole new way of looking at the universe. Modern science and the scientific method with which it is associated may be the one body of European ideas that has had a transforming effect on virtually every non-Western culture.

To appreciate the radicalism of the new views, examining what they replaced is useful. In 1500 the basic assumptions of science had changed little since the days of Pliny. The universe was thought to be organized according to rational principles. It was therefore open to human observation and deduction, but the principles of scientific inquiry were limited to those activities alone. As in other fields of thought, the logic of Aristotle, rooted firmly in language and in the meaning of words, was accepted as the most powerful tool of analysis. Scientific description therefore tended to be qualitative rather than quantitative. Accurate observation provided clues to the nature or essential quality of the object being observed. Reason could then determine the relationship of that object to other objects in the natural world.

This was important because ancient science believed that all parts of the universe were interrelated and that nothing could be studied in isolation. Today this idea is called holistic, or perhaps organic. It was stated expressly in Aristotle and, metaphorically, in the popular image of the individual human being as a microcosm of the universe as a whole. It formed the basis not only of academic science but also of the applied sciences of the day: medicine, natural magic, astrology, and alchemy. The last three were partially inspired by the Hermetic tradition, a body of occult literature that was supposedly derived from ancient Egypt. It was regarded with suspicion by the church because its practitioners were thought in various ways to interfere with Providence, but its theoretical assumptions did not conflict with those of the Aristotelians. Many, if not most, of the early scientists were as interested in astrology or alchemy as they were in physics and made no real

distinction between the occult and what would today be regarded as more legitimate disciplines.

Whatever their interests, the learned agreed that the world was composed of the four elements—earth, air, fire, and water—and that the elements corresponded to the four humors that governed the body as well as the signs of the zodiac. Magic, "the chief power of all the sciences," sought to understand these and other relationships between natural objects and to manipulate them to achieve useful results (see illustration 17.1). The causes of natural phenomena were of academic but little practical interest and were generally explained teleologically. That is, they were understood in terms of the result they were intended to produce. Virtually everyone believed that the world had been created for a purpose and that the behavior of natural objects would necessarily be directed to that end. This preconception, together with the tendency to describe objects in qualitative terms, ensured that causation, too, would usually be explained in terms of the nature or qualities of the objects involved. It was a view that

Illustration 17.1

An Alchemist at Work. This painting by Giovanni Stradano is dated 1570 and shows that the occult tradition in medieval science remained alive and well into the early modern era. The alchemist (in spectacles) is supervising the work of his assistants.

comported well with a providential understanding of the world.

Ideas of this kind are now found largely in the pages of supermarket tabloids, but they were once universally accepted by learned people. They provided a rational, comprehensive, and comforting vision of what might otherwise have been a terrifying universe. They have little in common with the principles of modern science, which substitutes measurement for qualitative description and attempts to express physical relationships in quantitative, mathematical terms. Because its vision of the world is mechanical instead of organic and providential, modern science concentrates heavily on the causes of physical and biological reactions and tries to reject teleological and qualitative explanations. It is more likely to ask "why?" than "what?" and has few compunctions about isolating a given problem to study it. Correspondences based upon qualitative or symbolic relationships are ignored.

The Origins of Modern Scientific Thought: Physics from Copernicus to Newton

Methodologically, modern science seeks to create a hypothesis by reasoning logically from accurate observations. If possible, the hypothesis is then tested by experiment and a mathematical model is constructed that will be both explanatory and predictive. The scientist can then formulate general laws of physical behavior without becoming entangled in the emotional overtones of language. The scientific model of the universe tends to be mechanistic rather than organic, mythological, or poetic. It is not necessarily godless, but its predictability does away with the need for divine intervention on a regular basis.

An intellectual shift of this magnitude did not occur quickly. Its roots are found in several traditions that coexisted uneasily in late medieval and Renaissance thought: the Aristotelian, the experimentalist, and the humanistic. During the sixteenth century a process of fusion began as thinkers adopted elements of each in their attempts to solve an ever-growing list of problems. The problems arose mainly from the perception that old, accepted answers, however logical and comforting they may have been, did not square with observed reality. The answers, and the accumulation of methods by which they were achieved, laid the groundwork of modern science.

The Aristotelian tradition contributed a rigorous concern for accurate observation and a logical method for the construction of hypotheses. In the wake of Ock-

hamist criticism, many Aristotelians, especially in the Italian universities, had turned their attention to the physical sciences, often with impressive results. Their tradition remained vital in some places until the eighteenth century. Experimentalism, once the province of medieval Franciscans and Joachimites, was revived and popularized by Sir Francis Bacon (1561–1626), the lord chancellor of England. Like his predecessors, he accomplished little because his hypotheses were faulty, but the elegance of his prose inspired a host of followers. His contemporary Galileo Galilei (1564–1642) used experiment to greater effect, though many of his best demonstrations were designed but never performed. The humanist tradition contributed classical texts that reintroduced half-forgotten ideas, including the physics of Archimedes and the heliocentric theories of Eratosthenes and Aristarchus of Samos. It also encouraged quantification by reviving the numerological theories of Pythagoras.

The thinkers of the sixteenth and seventeenth centuries were interested in nearly everything, but they achieved their greatest breakthroughs in astronomy and physics. The Copernican theory, though by no means universally accepted, became their starting point. Copernicus had brought the traditional cosmology into question, but his system with its epicycles and circular orbits remained mathematically complex and virtually incomprehensible as a description of physical reality (see illustration 17.2).

A more plausible model of the cosmos was devised by Johannes Kepler (1571–1630), court astrologer to the emperor Rudolph II. Kepler's views were a fusion of organic and mechanistic ideas. He believed that the Earth had a soul, but as a follower of Pythagoras he thought that the universe was organized on geometrical principles. The Copernican epicycles offended his notions of mathematical harmony. He wanted to believe in circular orbits, but when he posited eccentric circles that did not center on the Sun he was left with a minute discrepancy in his formulae. It was a terrible dilemma: The circle may have been the perfect geometric figure, but he could not accept a universe founded on imperfect mathematics. In the end, he decided that planetary orbits had to be elliptical. This solution, which proved to be correct, was not generally accepted until long after his death, but Kepler did not mind. Like the number-mystic he was, he went on searching for other, more elusive cosmic harmonies that could be described in musical as well as mathematical terms.

Meanwhile, Galileo rejected the theory of elliptical orbits but provided important evidence that the planets

(a)

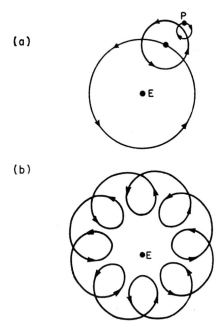

(b)

Illustration 17.2

/// **The System of Epicycles as Used in Ptolemaic Cosmology.**
Epicycles were needed to predict the position of the planets, especially in the case of eccentrics and retrograde motions. These diagrams illustrate that the results were almost unimaginable. Drawing (a) shows an epicycle (P) on an epicycle, on a circular planetary orbit around the Earth (E). Drawing (b) shows the path a planet would have to take through space if this system of compound circles were taken literally. Copernicus and many of his contemporaries were dissatisfied with the Ptolemaic theory.

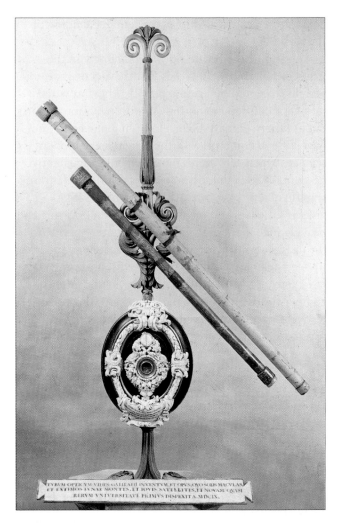

Illustration 17.3

/// **Galileo's Telescopes (c. 1610)** With instruments like these Galileo discovered the moons of Jupiter and launched a new era in observational astronomy. He also gained support for his work by donating them to wealthy patrons.

rotated around the Sun. A professor at the University of Padua, Galileo was perhaps the first thinker to use something like the modern scientific method. He quarreled with the Aristotelians over their indifference to mathematical proofs and denounced their teleological obsession with final causes, but like them he was a careful observer. Unlike them, he tried to verify his hypotheses through experiment. From the Platonists and Pythagoreans he adopted the view that the universe followed mathematical laws and expressed his theories in mathematical formulae that were intended to be predictive. His vision, however, was mechanistic, not mystical or organic.

Galileo's exploration of the planets was inspired by the invention of the telescope. The basic principles of optics had been discovered by the Aristotelians, and eyeglasses were introduced early in the sixteenth century. By 1608 Dutch and Flemish lens grinders were combining two lenses at fixed distances from one another to create the first telescopes. Using a perfected

version of the telescope that he had built himself, Galileo turned it upon the heavens (see illustration 17.3). The results created a sensation. His discovery of the moons of Jupiter and the phases of Venus seemed to support the Copernican theory, while his study of sunspots raised the unsettling possibility that the Sun rotated on its axis like the planets.

Perhaps because he was not interested in astrology, Galileo ignored the problems of planetary motion that obsessed Kepler. Instead he concentrated on the mechanics of motion. Kepler had established the position of the planets with his *Rudolphine Tables* of 1627 but had been unable to explain either the causes of their motion or what kept them in their orbits. The issue had perplexed the ancients because they believed that rest was the normal state of any object. The Aristotelians had argued that an object remains at rest unless a force is applied against it and that the velocity of that object is proportionate to the force exerted in moving it. As a result, finding an explanation for why a projectile continued to move after the impetus behind it had ceased was difficult. Galileo turned the problem on its head by proving that a body in motion will move forever unless it is slowed or deflected by an external force and that the application of uniform force results in acceleration instead of motion at a constant rate. Movement is therefore as natural a state as rest. Once it had been set in motion by its Creator, the universe could in theory go on forever without further intervention.

It was a profoundly disturbing vision. To Galileo, God was the Great Craftsman who created the world as a self-sustaining and predictable machine. To those who saw the universe as an organic entity upon which God still imposed His will, such a view was not only frightening but also blasphemous. It brought Galileo before the Papal Inquisition. He was tried because he defended the Copernican system and because his ideas undermined a worldview that had prevailed for nearly two thousand years. Yet the importance of this celebrated trial should not be exaggerated. Galileo's condemnation forced him to retire to his country villa; it did not prevent him or any other Italian from proceeding with research along the lines he had suggested. Galileo was arrogant and bad-tempered with patrons and opponents alike. He was also a brilliant writer and publicist (see document 17.1). Had his ability to attract enemies not equaled his genius, the episode might never have occurred.

The mechanistic view of the universe was destined to triumph over its predecessor and the church would not again mount a frontal attack against it. René Descartes (1596–1650), the most influential philosopher of his day, developed a mechanistic vision that attempted to integrate philosophy, mathematics, and the sciences into a coherent, unified theory. He failed, but his efforts inspired others such as Pierre Gassendi (1592–1655), who attempted to revive the atomic theories of the Epicureans. To do so, he was forced to posit the existence of a vacuum. The possibility of nothingness had been denied by virtually everyone from Aristotle to Descartes, but the results of barometric experiments by Toricelli and by Blaise Pascal (1623–62) could be explained in no other way. In 1650 Otto von Guericke ended the debate by constructing an air pump with which a vacuum could be created. These efforts in

◆ DOCUMENT 17.1 ◆

Galileo: Scientific Proof

In this exerpt from The Assayer, *Galileo attacks an opponent for arguing in the traditional manner by compiling lists of authorities who support his position. It shows not only the gulf that separated scientific thinking from that of the traditionalists, but also provides some indication of how Galileo made enemies with his pen.*

Sarsi goes on to say that since this experiment of Aristotle's has failed to convince us, many other great men have also written things of the same sort. But it is news to me that any man would actually put the testimony of writers ahead of what experience shows him. To adduce more witnesses serves no purposes, Sarsi, for we have never denied that such things have been written and believed. We did say they are false, but so far as authority is concerned yours alone is as effective as an army's in rendering the events true or false. You take your stand on the authority of many poets against our experiments. I reply that if those poets could be present at our experiments they would change their views, and without disgrace they could say they had been writing hyperbolically—or even admit they had been wrong. . . .

I cannot but be astonished that Sarsi would persist in trying to prove by means of witnesses something that I may see for myself at any time by means of experiment.

turn inspired Robert Boyle (1627–91) to formulate his laws about the behavior of gases.

Interest in scientific inquiry was assuming the proportions of a fad. All over Europe, men of leisure and education were examining the physical world and developing theories about it. Many, including Boyle and Pascal, were also gifted writers whose work inspired others to emulate them. Science was becoming a movement, and in only a matter of time that movement was institutionalized. The English Royal Society and the French Academie des Sciences were founded in the 1660s, the latter under the patronage of Louis XIV's minister, Jean-Baptiste Colbert (1619–83). Colbert, like England's King Charles II, was quick to perceive the possible connection between the new science and improved technologies for war, agriculture, and manufacturing. Not all of the work performed was useful, and much of it remained tied to the earlier vision of an organic, providential universe, but mechanistic and mathematical views gained ground steadily throughout the century.

In physics, the movement culminated in the work of Isaac Newton (1642–1727). A professor at Cambridge and a member of the Royal Society, Newton was in some respects an odd character who spent at least as much time on alchemy and other occult speculations as he did on mathematics and physics. In spite of this, he formulated the laws of planetary motion and of gravity, thereby completing the work begun by Kepler and Galileo and establishing a cosmology that dominated Western thought until the publication of Einstein's theories in 1904.

In his *Principia*, or *Mathematical Principles of Natural Philosophy*, presented to the Royal Society in 1686, Newton formulated three laws of motion: (1) Every object remains either at rest or in motion along a straight line until it is deflected or resisted by another force (the law of inertia); (2) The rate of change in the motion of an object is proportionate to the force acting upon it; and (3) To every action there is an equal and opposite reaction. These formulations accounted not only for the behavior of moving objects on Earth, but also for the continuing movement of the planets. He then perfected Kepler's theories by demonstrating how the planets move through a vacuum in elliptical orbits under the influence of a force centered upon the Sun. That force was gravity, which he defined as the attractive force between two objects (see document 17.2). It is directly proportionate to the product of their masses and inversely proportionate to the square of the distances between them. To many, these theories explained the mysteries of a universe that acted like clockwork—smooth, mechanical, and eternal. Newton, who was a deeply religious man, would not have been pleased at the use to which his ideas would soon be put by the philosophers of the eighteenth-century Enlightenment.

Medicine: From Galen to Harvey

Mechanistic views would also triumph in medicine, but the process by which they did so was more convoluted than it had been in physics. Physicians moved from mechanism to magic and back again in the course of the sixteenth century. The works of the ancient Greek anatomist Galen had long been known through Arabic

◈ DOCUMENT 17.2 ◈

Newton: Gravity

In The Mathematical Principles of Natural Philosophy *Sir Isaac Newton describes his revolutionary concept of gravity and, in the process, sets forth some of his thoughts on scientific method.*

Hitherto, we have explained the phenomena of the heavens and of our sea by the power of gravity, but have not yet assigned the cause of this power. This is certain, that it must proceed from a cause that penetrates to the very centers of the sun and planets, without suffering the least diminution of its force; that operates not according to the quantity of the surfaces of the particles upon which it acts (as mechanical causes used to do) but according to the quantity of solid matter which they contain, and propagates its virtue on all sides to immense distances, decreasing always in the duplicate portion of the distances. . . .

Hitherto I have not been able to discover the cause of those properties of gravity from the phenomena, and I frame no hypothesis; for whatever is not deduced from phenomena is to be called an hypothesis; and hypothesis, whether metaphysical or physical, whether of occult qualities or mechanical, have no place in experimental philosophy. In this philosophy particular propositions are inferred from the phenomena, and afterward rendered general by induction. Thus it was the impenetrability, the mobility, and the impulsive force of bodies, and the laws of motion and gravitation were discovered. And to us it is enough that gravity does really exist, and acts according to the laws that which we have explained, and abundantly serves to account for all the motions of the celestial bodies, and of our sea.

commentaries and translations. Galen's views were mechanistic in the sense that he was careful to relate the form of organs to their function and had little use for magic or for alchemical cures. The recovery and translation of original Galenic texts by the humanists popularized his teachings, and by the early sixteenth century his influence dominated academic medicine.

In response, a Swiss physician and alchemist who called himself Paracelsus (1493–1541) launched a frontal attack on the entire medical establishment. Declaring that "wise women" and barbers cured more patients than all of the Galenists put together, he proposed a medical philosophy based upon natural magic and alchemy. All natural phenomena were chemical interactions between the four elements and what he called the three principles: sulphur, mercury, and salt—the combustible, gaseous, and solid components of matter. Because the human body was a microcosm of the universe and because diseases were produced by chemical forces acting upon particular organs of the body, sickness could be cured by chemical antidotes.

This chemical philosophy was widely accepted. Its hermetic and neoplatonic overtones recommended it to many scholars, while those who practiced it may have killed fewer patients than their Galenist opponents. Paracelsus believed in administering drugs in small, carefully measured doses. He rejected bleeding, purges, and the treatment of wounds with poultices whose vile ingredients almost guaranteed the onset of infection. As a result, the bodies of his patients had a fighting chance to heal themselves and he was credited with miraculous cures.

The war between the Galenists and the Paracelsians raged throughout the mid-sixteenth century. In the end, the Galenists won. Their theories, though virtually useless for the treatment of disease, produced new insights while those of Paracelsus did not. Andreas Vesalius (1514–64) was shocked to discover that Galen's dissections had been carried out primarily on animals. Using Galenic principles, he retraced the master's steps using human cadavers and in 1543 published his *De humani corporis fabrica* (On the Structure of the Human Body). Though not without error, it was a vast improvement over earlier anatomy texts and a work of art in its own right that inspired others to correct and improve his work (see illustration 17.4). The long debate over the circulation of the blood, culminating in William Harvey's explanation of 1628 (see document 17.3), was also a Galenist enterprise that owed little or nothing to the chemical tradition.

By the time microscopes were invented in Holland at the beginning of the seventeenth century, the anatomists had seized the initiative. The new device strengthened their position by allowing for the examination of small structures such as capillaries. Blood corpuscles were described for the first time and bacteria were identified, though a full-fledged germ theory would not be verified until the nineteenth century. These discoveries made sustaining the ancient metaphor of the human body as a microcosm of the universe even more difficult. The body was beginning to look more like a machine within a machine.

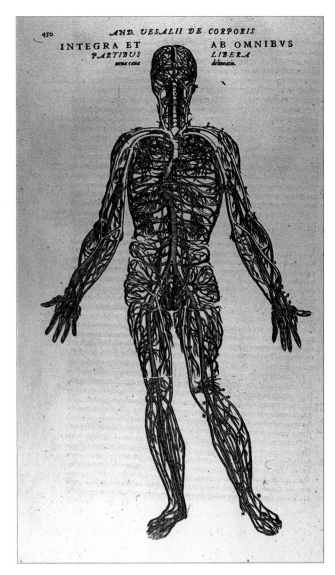

Illustration 17.4

A Diagram of the Veins. This diagram is from Andreas Vesalius (1514–64), *De humani corporis fabrica.* The venous system was especially important to physicians because drawing blood was the primary treatment for many ailments. As impressive as these drawings are, they contain anatomical errors. Vesalius did not understand the circulation of the blood and based some of his ideas on the dissection of animals (see the arrangement of veins at the base of the neck). However, his work, with its magnificent illustrations, is still a remarkable monument to the anatomical revolution.

The Expansion of the Northern Powers: France, England, and the Netherlands

In the years when Galileo and others were transforming European thought, seafarers from France, England, and the Netherlands continued the work of mapping the

◆ DOCUMENT 17.3 ◆

William Harvey: Conception

William Harvey (1578–1657) is best known as the physician who first described the circulation of the blood, but as this selection indicates, he was no more consistent in his application of scientific method than most of his contemporaries. Old modes of thinking had survived along with the new. In this description of conception he reverts to inadequate observation, metaphorical language, philosophical idealism, and sheer male vanity.

[As] the substance of the uterus, when ready to conceive, is very like the structure of the brain, why should we not suppose that the function of both is similar, and that there is excited by coitus within the uterus something identical with, or at least analogous to, an "imagination" or a "desire" in the brain, whence comes the generation or procreation of the ovum? For the functions of both are termed "conceptions" and both, although the primary sources of every action throughout the body, are immaterial, the one of natural or organic, the other of animal actions; the one

(viz., the uterus) the first cause and beginning of every action which conduces to the generation of the animal, the other (viz., the brain) of every action done for its preservation. And just as a "desire" arises from a conception of the brain, and this conception springs from some external object of desire, so also from the male, as being the more perfect animal, and as it were, the most natural object of desire, does the natural (organic) conception arise in the uterus, even as the animal conception does in the brain.

From this desire, or conception, it results that the female produces an offspring like its father. For just saw we, from the conception of the "form" or "idea" in the brain, fashion in our works a form resembling it, so, in like manner, the "idea" or "form" of the father existing in the uterus generates an offspring like himself with the help of the formative faculty, impressing, however, on its work its own immaterial form.

globe and exploiting its economic resources. The centralized, closely controlled empires created by the Iberian powers had been resented from the first by northern Europeans who wished to engage in the American trade. French pirates and privateers were active in the Caribbean after the 1530s and sacked Havana in 1556. A colony of French Protestants was massacred by the Spanish near the present site of St. Augustine, Florida, in 1565. However, neither of these failures inhibited French, English, and Dutch captains from trying to enter the Caribbean market. The Englishman John Hawkins (1532–95) tried to break the Spanish-Portuguese monopoly by introducing cargoes of slaves in 1562 and again in 1567 but was caught by the incoming *flota* in 1567 and barely escaped with his life. One of his surviving captains, Francis Drake (c. 1543–96), raided Panama in 1572–73 and attacked Spanish shipping in the Pacific when he circumnavigated the globe in 1577–79.

To many in England these efforts, however inspiring, were no substitute for the establishment of permanent English colonies. Commercial interests and the growing political and religious rivalry with Spain demanded nothing less. The first English settlement in North America was planted on Roanoke Island, North

Carolina, in 1585 but disappeared before it could be reinforced. Subsequent efforts at Jamestown (1603) and Plymouth (1620) were more successful. The Spanish claimed sovereignty over North America but lacked the resources to settle it or to protect it against interlopers. The native American population was, by comparison with that of Mexico or Peru, small, scattered, and politically disunited. The obstacles to settlement were therefore easy to overcome, and by 1650 the English were established at various locations along the entire Atlantic seaboard from Newfoundland to the Carolinas.

From the standpoint of global politics and immediate gain, these North American colonies were something of a disappointment. They produced no precious metals and offered England few strategic advantages. With the notable exception of tobacco from Virginia and Maryland, they had little of value to export and quickly became self-sufficient in everything but luxury items. In the meantime, the French had established themselves in the St. Lawrence valley and were developing an important trade in furs from the North American interior. English competition in the form of the Hudson's Bay Company did not emerge until 1670.

Expansion in the Caribbean remained a primary goal. An English colony was established on the uninhabited island of Barbados in 1624, and sugar was introduced in 1640. By 1660 its sugar exports made Barbados the most valuable of English colonies while its position to windward of the Spanish Main made it virtually invulnerable to Spanish attacks. Sugar colonies of equal wealth were established by the French on the nearby islands of Guadeloupe and Martinique. By this time, Spanish power was in decline. In 1656 an English fleet seized Jamaica. Eight years later the French West India Company took possession of some settlements that had been established years before by French buccaneers in the western part of Hispaniola and laid the foundations of St. Domingue, the rich slave colony that would one day become Haiti.

The French and English, like the Spanish and Portuguese, wanted their colonial systems to be self-contained and closed to outsiders, but in practice, this was as difficult to achieve as it had been for their rivals. Both France and England governed their possessions on the proprietary model, and neither developed anything like the elaborate colonial bureaucracy of Spain. Royal authority tended to be correspondingly weak. Distance, the limitations of sailing ship technology, and the perishability of certain cargos, notably slaves, encouraged smuggling and made it difficult to suppress. Planters and merchants had nothing to gain from dealing exclusively with their own countrymen when others might offer better prices or more rapid delivery. Cargos could always be landed secretly in remote coves, but much illegal activity was conducted in the open, for governors were under enormous pressure to look the other way.

Almost from the beginning, the chief beneficiaries of this illegal trade were the Dutch, whose maritime activities increased during their revolt against Spain. The Dutch had some ninety-eight thousand ships registered by 1598, but ships and skill were not enough. They needed bases from which to conduct their operations. Between 1621 and 1640 the newly formed Dutch West India Company seized Curaçao, St. Eustatius, St. Maarten, and Saba in the Caribbean and established a colony called New Amsterdam on the present site of New York. From 1624 to 1654 the Dutch controlled much of the Brazilian coast, and in 1637 they captured the African fortress and slave-trading station of Elmina from the Portuguese. Brazil and New Amsterdam were expensive ventures. The Dutch, like the Portuguese, lacked the manpower to impose their rule on large geographic areas, and when the English seized New Amsterdam in 1664 the West India Company settled down to a more modest, and in the end more profitable, career as a trading company based on Curaçao and St. Eustatius.

Only in the East did the Dutch manage to establish something like regional hegemony. Dutch traders first appeared in East Indian waters in 1595. Bypassing India, they sailed directly to the Spice Islands (Indonesia), rounding the Cape of Good Hope and running due east in the so-called roaring forties before turning north to Java or Sumatra. The fast but dangerous trip brought them directly to the sources of the Portuguese and Indian spice trade. To improve efficiency and minimize competition, the Dutch traders organized in 1602 into the East India Company.

Under the governor-generalship of Jan Pieterszoon Coen (1587–1629), the company's forces destroyed the Javan town of Djakarta and rebuilt it as Batavia, center of Dutch enterprise in the East. Local rulers were forced to restrict their trading activities to rice and other local necessities while European competition was violently discouraged. English traders especially had been active in Asian waters since 1591. They formed their own East India Company on Christmas Day in 1600 but lacked the ships and capital to match the Dutch. Coen expelled most of them from the region by 1620. His successors attacked the Portuguese colonies, seizing Malacca in 1641 and the Indian bases shortly thereafter, but Goa survived a Dutch blockade and remained in Portuguese hands until 1961. The Japanese trade fell into Dutch hands when the Portuguese were expelled in 1637, and for two centuries a Dutch trading station in Nagasaki harbor provided that country's only contact with the West.

By 1650 the Dutch had become the dominant force in Europe's Asian trade. More than one hundred Dutch ships sailed regularly to the East, exchanging German arms, armor, linens, and glass for spices and finished silks. Even the surviving Portuguese colonies were forced to deal largely through Dutch intermediaries. The major exception was Macao, which continued to export Chinese silks to Spain via Manila. This monopoly was successfully challenged in the eighteenth century by the revived British East India Company and to a lesser degree by the French, but the Dutch remained in control of Indonesia until the outbreak of World War II.

❖

The Golden Age in the Netherlands

Long-distance trade made the Netherlands an island of wealth and culture amidst the turmoil of the early seventeenth century (see illustration 17.5). A century before, the economy of the region had been dominated by Antwerp. Its merchants traded in wool from Spain

Illustration 17.5

The Amsterdam Bourse, or Stock Exchange. This painting by Job Berckheyde shows the Bourse as it was in the seventeenth century. Though not the first such exchange in Europe, it was by far the largest and most important of the early modern period. Small shareholders and great capitalists traded shares in the East India Company and many smaller enterprises.

and England, finished cloth from the towns of Brabant and Flanders, wine from the Iberian Peninsula, and a variety of products exported from Germany to England and Scandinavia. The city's prosperity, however, did not survive the Revolt of the Netherlands. Antwerp is located at the head of navigation on the Scheldt, a broad estuary whose western approaches are controlled by the Zeeland towns of Vlissingen (Flushing) and Middelburg. When the Zeelanders joined the Dutch revolt, they cut off Antwerp from the sea and destroyed its prosperity.

Amsterdam took its place. Set in the marshes where the Amstel River meets the IJ, an inlet of the Zuider Zee, the city was virtually impregnable to attack by sea or land. Already the center of the Baltic trade, it grew

enormously after 1585 when southern refugees poured in, bringing their capital with them. When Maurits of Nassau took the lands east of the Ijssel from Spain between 1591 and 1597, contact with Germany improved and Amsterdam replaced Antwerp as the conduit through which goods flowed from the German interior to the Atlantic and North Sea. The repeated failure of Spanish and Sicilian harvests in the same years made Amsterdam a dominant force in the Mediterranean trade as well. Dutch merchants had established themselves in the Baltic ports of Riga and Gdansk (Danzig) at an early date. The Amsterdam exchange determined the price of wheat, and vast quantities were shipped southward in Dutch ships, together with timber, Swedish iron, and other northern products.

Shipbuilding, always a major industry in the ports of Holland and Zeeland, expanded with the growth of the carrying trade. Economies of scale, better access to Baltic naval stores, and the presence of a skilled maritime population enabled the Dutch to charge lower shipping rates than their competitors. With the founding of the East and West India companies, this advantage became global. The axis of the spice trade shifted from Lisbon to Amsterdam while Dutch skippers took advantage of the delays occasioned by the *flota* system and by a general shortage of Iberian shipping to intrude upon the commerce of the Americas. The profits from these sources generated investment capital, and Amsterdam soon became Europe's banking center as well as its commercial hub.

In these years, the modern city with its canals and high, narrow townhouses took shape. For all its wealth and beauty, however, Amsterdam was never more than the largest of several towns that supported and at times competed with each other in a variety of markets. The Dutch republic was overwhelmingly urban. A network of canals linked its cities and provided cheap, efficient transportation. Agriculturally, though a few large estates remained, most of the land was divided into relatively small plots and cultivated intensively to grow produce and dairy products for the nearby towns. Most peasants were independent farmers and relatively prosperous. Pockets of urban misery existed, but no real industrial proletariat was evident outside the cloth towns of Haarlem and Leiden. Dutch society was therefore resolutely bourgeois. Hard work, thrift, and cleanliness were valued; ostentation was suspect.

A series of extraordinary painters provide a vivid picture of Dutch life in the seventeenth century. Jan Vermeer (1632–75) portrayed bright, spotless interiors and virtuous housewives at work in an idealized vision of domesticity that was central to Dutch notions of the good life (see illustration 17.6). Rembrandt van Rijn (1606–69), Frans Hals (c. 1581–1666), and a host of others left brilliant portraits of city magistrates, corporate directors, and everyday drunks as well as grand illustrations of historical events. The brooding skies and placid landscapes of the Netherlands were painted by such masters as Ruisdael and van Goyen, while dozens of still lifes dwell lovingly on food, flowers, and other everyday objects.

The political and the social structure of the republic rested on the values of the late medieval city, preserved tenaciously through the long struggle against Spanish regalism. Each town elected a council, which in turn elected representatives to the Provincial Estates. The States General was elected by the provinces. The

Illustration 17.6

Woman with a Water-Jug (c. 1663). This painting by Jan Vermeer is of a Dutch interior of the golden age. The leaded window, the map on the wall, and the oriental carpet covering the table indicate modest luxury and refer to Holland's contacts with a wider world. Much of Vermeer's work celebrates Dutch domesticity, cleanliness, and a love of light appropriate to Holland's dark and rainy climate.

stadtholder, when there was one, was not a king, but a kind of "first citizen" with special responsibilities for the conduct of war on land. Five admiralties, each of which was nominally independent and each of which supplemented its own warships with vessels leased from the chartered companies, conducted war at sea.

Local privilege was built into the system at every level, and conflict among the various components of the body politic was normally intense. Fortunately, the leadership of the councils, states, directorships, and committees formed a kind of interlocking directorship. A great merchant, banker, or rentier might hold several elected offices in the course of a lifetime, as well as directorships in one or more of the chartered companies. The Dutch republic was an oligarchy, not a democracy, but the existence of a well-defined group of prominent citizens facilitated communication, dampened local rivalries, and helped to ensure a measure of continuity in what might otherwise have been a fragmented and overly decentralized system.

National policies were remarkably consistent. Trade, even with the enemy, was encouraged and the states supported freedom of the seas long before Hugo Grotius (1583–1645), attorney general of Holland, publicized the modern concept of international law. Though aggressive in its pursuit of new markets and the protection of old ones, Dutch foreign policy was otherwise defensive.

Tension between the governing elite and the stadtholders of the House of Orange dominated internal politics. At times the struggle took the form of religious antagonism between extreme Calvinists, who tended to be Orangists supported by the artisan class, and the more relaxed Arminians, who rejected predestination and were supported by the great merchants. Class feeling played a major part in these struggles, but by comparison with other countries, both sides remained committed to religious toleration. Jewish settlement was actively encouraged and Catholics were generally protected from harassment. Holland became a refuge for the persecuted, many of whom, such as Descartes and the philosopher Baruch Spinoza (1632–77), a Sephardic Jew, added luster to its intellectual life. The Dutch republic was an oasis of tolerance as well as prosperity.

The Reorganization of War and Government: France under Louis XIV

Most seventeenth-century states were not as fortunate as the Dutch. Between 1560 and 1648 France, Spain, England, and the German principalities all suffered in varying degrees from military stalemate and political disintegration. Public order, perhaps even dynastic survival, depended upon the reorganization of war and government. The restructuring of virtually every European state after 1660 has been called the triumph of absolutism (see document 17.4), but the term is in some ways misleading. No government before the industrial revolution could exert absolute control over the lives of its subjects. To do so even approximately requires modern transport and communications, but if by absolutism one means the theoretical subordination of all other elements of a country's power structure to the crown, the word is at least partially descriptive. The Spain of Philip II met this definition in the sixteenth century; after 1660 the model for all other states was the France of Louis XIV.

Louis XIV (ruled 1643–1715) came to the throne as a child of four. To the end of his life he harbored childhood memories of the Frondes and was determined to

◆ **DOCUMENT 17.4** ◆

Absolutism in Theory

Jacques-Bénigne Bossuet, bishop of Meaux (1627–1704) was court preacher to Louis XIV and tutor to his son. In this passage, which reveals something of his power as a preacher, he describes the divine basis of royal absolutism in unmistakable terms.

The royal power is absolute. . . . The prince need render account of his acts to no one. . . . Without this absolute authority the king could neither do good nor repress evil. It is necessary that his power be such that no one can escape him, and finally, the only protection of individuals against the public authority should be their innocence. This confirms the teaching of St. Paul: "Wilt thou not be afraid of the power? Do that which is good" [Rom. 13:3].

God is infinite, God is all. The prince, as prince, is not regarded as a private person: he is a public personage, all the state is in him. As all perfection and all strength are united in God, so all power of individuals is united in the person of the prince. What grandeur that a single man should embody so much!

Behold an immense people united in a single person; behold this holy power, paternal and absolute; behold the secret cause which governs the whole body of the state, contained in a single head: you see the image of God in the king, and you have the idea of royal majesty. God is holiness itself, goodness itself, and power itself. In these things lies the majesty of God. In the image of these things lies the majesty of the prince.

avoid further challenges from the French aristocracy at all costs. He knew that their influence derived from the networks of patronage that had long dominated rural life and used the fact that such networks are ultimately dependent upon favors to destroy them as independent bases of power. As king of a country in which perpetual taxation had long been established, Louis had more favors to hand out than anyone else. He developed the tactic of forcing aristocrats to remain at court as a condition of receiving the titles, grants, monopolies, offices, and commissions upon which their influence was based. By doing so he bound them to himself while cutting them off from their influence in the countryside.

Illustration 17.7

Versailles. This view of the west front of Louis XIV's palace shows only a portion of the whole, but it provides a sense of the grandeur that Louis and his architects, Louis Le Vau and Jules Hardouin-Mansart, were attempting to convey as they created a magnificent stage set for the politics of the Sun King.

This was the real purpose behind the construction of Versailles, a palace large enough to house the entire court while separating it from the mobs of Paris, twelve miles away (see illustration 17.7). To occupy his new courtiers, Louis developed an elaborate ritual centered around his own person. Every royal action was accompanied by great ceremony, and proud aristocrats contended for the honor of emptying the king's chamberpot or handing him his shirt (see illustration 17.8). The world of Versailles was cramped, artificial, and riddled with intrigue, but it was a world controlled in every particular by a king who knew what was happening under his own roof (see document 17.5). To stay was to sacrifice one's independence; to leave was to lose all hope of honor or profit. By 1670 the French nobility had been domesticated.

The centralization implied by Versailles was extended to the royal administration, though in this case Louis followed precedents established by Henry IV and Richelieu. Richelieu in particular had worked to replace the old system of governing through councils with ministries, in which one man was responsible to the crown for each of the major functions of government. He had also brought royal authority to the provinces by introducing intendants, commissioners who supervised the collection of taxes and served as a constant check on local authorities. Louis expanded and perfected this system. Intendancies transcended provincial borders, further weakening the ties of local privilege. The ministers of war, finance, foreign affairs, and even of roads and bridges reported directly to the king who, unlike his father, served as his own prime minister. Louis may have been the Sun King, surrounded by ritual and devoted to

the pleasures of the bed, the table, and the hunt, but he was a hard worker. At least six hours a day, seven days a week, were devoted to public business. Significantly, he usually drew his ministers from the *nobles de la robe,* the great legal dynasties of the French towns, not from the old nobility.

Because war was the primary function of the early modern state and accounted for the vast majority of its expenditures, every effort was made to bring the military under control. Louis instituted a series of reforms under the guidance of the war ministers Michel Le Tellier (1603–85) and his son, the Marquis de Louvois (1639–91). A tableau of ranks, comparable to that used by most modern armies, established a hierarchy of command that in theory superseded civilian titles. The cost of quartering troops was allocated to entire provinces instead of to specific towns, and, like military justice, financial arrangements were placed under the control of the intendants.

On the battlefield, the French army abandoned the old combination of pike and shot in favor of volleys of musket fire from ranks that were rarely more than three deep. Based on the innovations of Gustav Adolph, this tactic required regular drill and marching in step, practices that had first been introduced by Maurice of Nassau but generally ignored by other armies. To improve discipline and unit cohesion, barracks, uniforms, and standardized muskets were all adopted by 1691. Combined with the scientific principles of siege warfare perfected by Sebastian le Prestre de Vauban (1633–1707), the reforms of Le Tellier and Louvois created what might be called the first modern army. It was given ample opportunity to prove itself.

Illustration 17.8

🎐 **Louis XIV.** This 1701 painting by Hyacinthe Rigaud is an example of art as political propaganda. This vision of the king's magnificence was painted on the eve of the War of the Spanish Succession. Even at sixty-three, Louis was proud of his legs and sensitive about his height, hence the elevator shoes.

In the early years of his reign, Louis's foreign policy was aggressive and, in the best French tradition, anti-Hapsburg. His invasion of the Spanish Netherlands in 1667–68 brought him into conflict with the Dutch republic, which he tried to destroy in a bitter war that lasted from 1672 to 1679. Faced with almost certain destruction, the Dutch overthrew their government and made William III of Orange (1650–1702) stadtholder. Holland saved itself by flooding the countryside, and William's diplomacy brought Spain, Sweden, Brandenburg, and the Holy Roman Empire into the war. France

fought them all to a standstill, but the alliance was a precursor of things to come.

Emboldened by the favorable terms he had negotiated at the Peace of Nijmegen (1679), Louis then tried to annex all territories that had ever belonged to France, whether in the Netherlands, Italy, the Pyrenees, or the Rhineland. Hostility to the Holy Roman Empire made him the only Christian prince to oppose the liberation of Hungary from the Turks (1682–99), though it was at last achieved with the assistance of Eugene of Savoy (1663–1736), a prince who had been raised at

◆ DOCUMENT 17.5 ◆

Louis XIV at Versailles

The memoirs of Louis de Rouvroy, Duc de Saint-Simon (1675–1755) provide a detailed, if often venomous, picture of life at the court of Louis XIV. Here Saint-Simon, an aristocrat, describes the king's method of controlling the French aristocracy.

The frequent fêtes, the private promenades at Versailles, the journeys, were means on which the King seized in order to distinguish or mortify the courtiers, and thus render them more assiduous in pleasing him. He felt that of real favors he had not enough to bestow; in order to keep up the spirit of devotion, he therefore unceasingly invented all sorts of ideal ones, little preferences and petty distinctions, which answered his purpose as well.

He was exceedingly jealous of the attention paid him. Not only did he notice the presence of the most distinguished courtiers, but those of inferior degree also. He looked to the right and the left, not only upon rising but upon going to bed, at his meals, in passing through his apartments, or his gardens of Versailles, where alone the courtiers were allowed to follow him; he saw and noticed everybody; not one escaped him, not even those who hoped to remain unnoticed. He marked well all the absentees from the court, found out the reason of their absence, and never lost an opportunity of acting towards them as the occasion might seem to justify. With some of the courtiers (the most distinguished), it was a demerit not to make the court their ordinary abode; with others, 'twas a fault to come but rarely; for those who never or scarcely ever came it was certain disgrace. When their names were in any way mentioned, "I do not know them," the King would reply haughtily. Those who presented themselves but seldom were thus characterized: "They are people I never see;" these decrees were irrevocable.

For the rest of his life he followed a basically defensive policy, but it was too late. In the War of the League of Augsburg (1689–97), Louis fought a powerful Anglo-Dutch coalition while France suffered through one of the worst economic depressions in its history. In the War of the Spanish Succession (1701–14), his armies were consistently defeated by an allied army commanded by John Churchill, duke of Marlborough (1650–1722). Not even France could sustain such burdens indefinitely, and when the Sun King died in 1715, the country was in a severe, if temporary, decline.

French Absolutism: A Model for Reform

The power of Louis XIV was not unlimited. Within France, his intentions were subject to modification by local privilege and by the rulings of the *parlements*, superior courts that could determine the validity of royal edicts under law. Moreover, neither he nor his successors were able to solve basic problems of credit and finance. Until the revolution of 1789, the kings of France were forced to borrow against tax revenues, which were then farmed out to the creditors. Tax farming by private individuals was not only inefficient but also woefully corrupt and left no room for the sophisticated financial practices being devised by Louis's Dutch and English rivals.

In spite of these shortcomings and of the uneven success of Louis's foreign policy, the France of Louis XIV became a model for other princes. From Spain to the Urals, they copied his court etiquette, his system of military and administrative organization, and even the architectural style of Versailles, which became the pattern for dozens of palaces and country estates. The last Hapsburg king of Spain, Charles II "the Bewitched" died childless in 1700, and the final war of Louis's reign was waged to place a Bourbon on the Spanish throne. The new ruler, Philip V (reigned 1700–46), began a process of reform that by 1788 had created a near replica of French administration. Austrian archduke Charles (1685–1740), though he failed to gain the allegiance of the Spanish in the War of the Spanish Succession, received the Spanish Netherlands as a consolation prize at the Peace of Utrecht in 1713. This territory, the present-day Belgium, was incorporated into the Austrian Empire as Hungary had been in 1699. After his election as Charles VI in 1711, he began to reform the far-flung Austrian administration on French lines.

Most of the German princes followed suit, though it could be argued that Frederick Wilhelm I of Prussia

his court and who became one of his most formidable enemies. At the same time, Louis's revocation of the Edict of Nantes and expulsion of the Huguenots in 1685 alienated Europe's Protestants. Many believed that he aimed at nothing less than French hegemony, and by 1689 nearly all of Europe had turned against him.

Illustration 17.9

🖎 **Peter the Great.** The tsar is shown by a Dutch painter during his visit to the Netherlands in 1697.

(1688–1740) had already carried reform beyond anything achieved by Louis XIV. Set without geographic defenses in the midst of the North German plain, Brandenburg-Prussia had been devastated in the Thirty Years' War and remained vulnerable to the shifts of central European politics. A veteran of the war of the Spanish Succession, Frederick Wilhelm resolved to turn his kingdom into a military power of the first rank and ended by making its administration subservient to the army. After 1723 his government was little more than a branch of the *kriegskommisariat* or war ministry, but his reforms laid the groundwork for Prussia's emergence as a major power.

Perhaps the most spectacular efforts at reform were undertaken by Peter I "the Great" of Russia (1672–1725). Like Louis XIV he had survived a turbulent regency in his youth and came to the throne determined to place his monarchy on a firmer basis (see illustration 17.9). Peter realized that to do so he would have to copy Western models, and he spent 1697–98 traveling incognito to France, England, and the Netherlands as part of what he called the Grand Embassy. When he returned, he immediately began

to institute reforms that, though Western in inspiration, were carefully adapted to Russian conditions (see document 17.6).

Using knowledge acquired firsthand in the shipyards of Holland and England, Peter supervised the building of a navy that could control the Baltic. The *streltsy*, or palace guard that formed the core of the Russian army and had long been a fruitful source of plots against the tsars, was destroyed and replaced by an army organized on the French model. Peter, however, raised his troops through conscription for life, a method suggested by Louvois that could not be implemented in the less autocratic atmosphere of France. The new forces served him well. In the Great Northern War (1700–20), he broke the power of Sweden and established Russian control over Estonia, Karelia, and Livonia. To consolidate his gains and to provide Russia with an all-weather port, he built the modern city of St. Petersburg near the mouth of the Neva River and made it his capital.

Internally, Peter established a series of colleges or boards to supervise the work of thirteen new governmental departments and divided the country into fifty provinces, each with its own governor appointed by himself. He created a table of ranks for civilian officials and opened state service for the first time to men of middle-class origin. To compensate the hereditary nobility for its loss of state positions, Peter abandoned the distinction between *pomest'e* and hereditary lands, and he introduced primogeniture. In some cases he resorted to large-scale distributions of land and serfs. The condition of the latter predictably worsened, and peasant rebellions were put down with memorable savagery.

The Emergence of England as a World Power

The system created by Peter the Great was more autocratic than its Western models—and more permanent. It lasted without major modifications into the nineteenth century. The situation in England was very different. Though Charles II reclaimed his father's throne in 1660, the fundamental issue of sovereignty had not been resolved. Like his predecessors, Charles was reluctant to call Parliament into session, and the taxpaying gentry were as unwilling as ever to provide adequate support for the crown. Shrewd, affable, and personally popular, the new king avoided open confrontations with his subjects, but his freedom of action was limited by poverty. For a time he even accepted a pension from Louis XIV, who hoped for English support against the Dutch. For this reason, England did not for some time

◆ DOCUMENT 17.6 ◆

The New Dress Code of Peter the Great

In his desire to modernize Russia, Peter the Great was alert to the symbolic importance of dress. In the following decrees, he sought to change the appearance of the Russian people.

1701—Western Dress shall be worn by all the boyars[,] . . . members of our councils and of our court[,] . . . gentry of Moscow, secretaries[,] . . . provincial gentry, . . . government officials, strel'tsy, members of the guilds purveying for our household, citizens of Moscow of all ranks, and residents of provincial cities . . . excepting the clergy . . . and peasant tillers of the soil. The upper dress shall be of French or Saxon cut, and the lower dress and underwear—waistcoat, trousers, boots, shoes, and hats—shall be of the German type. They shall also ride German saddles. The womenfolk of all ranks, including the priests', deacons' and church attendants' wives, the wives of the

dragoons, the soldiers, and the strel'tsy, and their children shall wear Western dresses, hats, jackets, and underwear—undervests and petticoats and shoes. From now on no one is to wear Russian dress or Circassian coats, sheepskin coats, or Russian peasant coats, trousers, boots, and shoes. It is also forbidden to ride Russian saddles, and the craftsmen shall not manufacture them or sell them at the marketplace.

1705—Henceforth, in accordance with this, His Majesty's decree, all court attendants[,] . . . provincial service men, government officials of all ranks, military men, . . . members of the wholesale merchant's guild, and members of guilds purveying for our household must shave their beards and moustaches. But if it happens that some do not wish to shave their beards and moustaches, let a year tax be collected from such persons.

develop the administrative structures that were being adopted on the continent.

Only in the creation of a modern navy could the English keep pace. Before 1660 England, like other countries, had possessed a handful of fighting ships that were supplemented in time of war by contracting with private owners who provided both ships and crews for the duration. No permanent officer corps existed, and fleets were typically commanded by men who owed their positions to civilian rank or to military experience on land. Administration was minimal, often temporary, and usually corrupt. The success of 1588 and the remarkable performance of the Commonwealth navies showed that such fleets could do well if they were properly motivated. But the system as a whole was analagous to military contracting on land: It was at best inefficient and at worst uncontrollable.

Both Charles II and his brother James, duke of York (1633–1701) were deeply interested in naval affairs, and their unswerving support of secretary of the Admiralty Samuel Pepys (1633–1703) enabled him to introduce reforms that, in effect, created the English navy. Pepys, who is probably best known today for his famous diary, created a permanent corps of naval officers who attained their rank by the passage of formal examinations. To ensure their availability when needed, they were kept on half-pay when not at sea. Provisioning

and repair facilities were improved, and the number of royal ships increased under the command of a reformed Admiralty. By the end of the century, even tactics had been changed to permit better control of battle fleets.

But a reformed fleet was in itself no guarantor of world-power status. Colbert had introduced similar measures in France, only to have his plans abandoned during the fiscal crisis of the 1690s. Great ships, like great armies, need a consistent supply of money. Ironically, England achieved this only by overthrowing the men who had made the naval reforms possible. When Charles II died in 1685, his brother ascended the throne as James II. A convert to Roman Catholicism, James instituted policies that alienated virtually every segment of the English elite, and in the fall of 1688 he was deposed in favor of his daughter Mary and her husband, William of Orange. As stadtholder of the Netherlands and king of England, William III brought the island nation into the Grand Alliance against Louis XIV. The Glorious Revolution changed the basis of English politics. By overthrowing one king and effectively appointing another, Parliament and those it represented had at last resolved the issue of sovereignty. Parliament and not the king would rule England. Under William and again under his sister-in-law Anne (reigned 1702–14), Parliament showed an unprecedented willingness to open its purse and support massive outlays

❖ DOCUMENT 17.7 ❖

Dutch Trade in Decline

The problem of maintaining Dutch trade reached a crisis during the War of the Spanish Succession (1702–13), when the conflict closed many traditional markets. The following memo was presented to the States General in 1706 by Adrianus Engelhard Helvetius, who points out that Holland's English allies were quick to take advantage of his countrymen's misfortunes.

The commerce of the United Provinces in Europe has never been in worse condition than it is today. During the course of earlier wars, although Dutch vessels were also open to the attacks of privateers, at least they could take refuge in the Atlantic and in the Mediterranean ports under Spanish rule, which are now closed to them. Furthermore, even when they were completely barred from the trade of France, they still continued to ply both the Baltic trades, which they continue to enjoy, and the trades of Spain, the kingdoms of Naples and Sicily, and Spanish Flanders, which now they have good reason to miss. Not only is the market greatly reduced for their cloth, both of their own manufacture as well as that made in India and the Baltic, and for their other wares, spices, salt fish, etc., but they are also deprived of the profitable return trade in wool, wine, and necessary commodities. . . .

As a result, there are frequent bankruptcies, word of which scares people and discourages them from entrusting money to the merchants, whose own funds are limited, as they are in the habit of doing in peacetime. This decline even affects the domestic commerce of the country, which is suffering badly, especially thanks to the cunning manipulations of the English, who take advantage of the opportunity to raise themselves upon the ruins of their allies.

The English, a people as fierce as they are capable, being convinced that the States General need their help so badly that they would not dare dispute anything with them, follow the maxim of making the Dutch pay their auxiliary troops, even when they are engaged in battle. They supply them with goods of every kind, sending cloth and Indian fabrics which are forbidden in England, butter, tallow, even manufactured candles, grain, etc., and in this they manage to make a profit on the support of troops for which they ought to be paying themselves.

for war, knowing that a weakened monarchy could not use the money to subvert the freedoms of its subjects.

The wealth that underwrote England's command of the sea and financed the campaigns of Marlborough on land came from nearly a century of unparalleled economic growth. England's growing commercial strength was based in part on geographic advantage. Faced with the implacable hostility of Louis XIV, the Dutch were forced to spend much of their wealth defending their borders on land. England, an island, was spared this expense. Moreover, with their deep water ports and location to windward of the continent, the English could disrupt Dutch trade by blocking access via the English Channel. The Anglo-Dutch wars of 1652–53, 1665–66, and 1672–73 were fought over this issue. As George Monk, the English general-at-sea in the Second Dutch War said: "[W]hat we want is more of the trade the Dutch now have." Dutch seamen acquitted themselves well, but the cost of battles in which more than a hundred ships might be engaged on each side, together with the need to provide convoys for trading vessels

even in peacetime, gradually eroded their competitive advantage (see document 17.7).

Even favorable geography probably could not have given England a decisive lead had it not been for a system of credit and finance that became the envy of Europe. The revolution of 1688 paved the way for the land tax of 1692 and the extension of excise taxes to a wide range of consumer goods. England acquired the benefits of permanent taxation for the first time in its history. The Bank of England, established in 1694, then stabilized English finances by underwriting government war loans. In the eighteenth century it became the first of Europe's central banks, allowing private bankers to draw upon its gold reserves in periods of financial crisis.

Credit, backed by reliable taxation, paid for the fleet, Marlborough's armies, and the large subsidies that England paid to its continental allies. England, which became Great Britain when it merged with Scotland in 1707, was therefore able to expand its empire and protect its markets more easily than the Dutch, whose war fleet declined after 1673 and whose decentralized institutions blocked the formation of more effective credit mechanisms. English trade, which had been expanding steadily throughout the seventeenth century, became a flood during the War of the Spanish Succession when the British navy swept the seas of all rivals (see Table 17.1). In time the enormous wealth derived largely from overseas markets would provide the capital for the industrial revolution and further strengthen English claims to great power status.

Preindustrial Economy and Society

The economic policy that underlay these developments is called mercantilism. Mercantilism was not really a theory, but a set of assumptions that had long been implicit in the rivalries among states and in the beginnings of European expansion overseas. Accepted by nearly everyone, these assumptions were applied with unusual consistency by Colbert, as Louis XIV's minister of finance. Mercantilists defined wealth as a nation's store of gold and silver instead of as the total value of its goods and services. This was in part because cash paid for war and therefore could be translated directly into power and prestige. Because wealth was defined in monetary terms and because economic growth rates are typically slow in preindustrial societies, the world's wealth was regarded for practical purposes as a fixed quantity. Economic and military policy was therefore a zero-sum game, the purpose of which was to acquire a surplus of gold and silver at the expense of one's neighbors. This was done by ensuring that exports exceeded imports. A country should become as self-sufficient as possible while encouraging the development of trades that might find an external market for their products (see document 17.8).

To Colbert (see illustration 17.10) and his contemporaries in other lands, this meant protection of the home market through tariffs and the development of an overseas empire that could produce commodities unavailable in the mother country. Ideally, the empire should have varied components: tropical colonies to produce dye woods, sugar, cotton, indigo, and chocolate; northern colonies to produce timber, furs, and naval stores. The colonies would produce these raw materials in return for manufactured goods from home, and every effort was made to subsidize the manufacture of luxury items that could be shipped to the colonists or sold to unwary foreigners for cash.

TABLE 17.1

English Trade Balances

The most active phase of the War of the Spanish Succession lasted from 1701 to 1711. During that period the English lost 1,061 merchant ships to enemy raiders, while the English balance of trade (surplus of exports over imports) increased enormously, owing primarily to increased exports of cloth and grain to Portugal, Holland, Germany, and Russia and to decreased imports from France and Spain. Because the increase in trade more than compensated for the subsidies sent to the continent for war, the British were, in mercantilist terms, net beneficiaries of the war.

Year	Extra-European trade balance	Overall trade balance
1699–1701	£ 489,000	£ 974,000
1702	233,000	971,000
1703	515,000	1,745,000
1704	968,000	1,519,000
1706	836,000	2,705,000
1707	672,000	2,024,000
1708	630,000	2,022,000
1709	271,000	2,111,000
1710	825,000	2,486,000
1711	969,000	2,731,000

Source: Adapted from D. W. Jones, *War and Economy in the Age of William III and Marlborough* (Oxford: Basil Blackwell, 1988), p. 220.

To protect trade and colonies, a fighting navy was essential, for the line between war and commerce was necessarily blurred. The goal of both was wealth and power, and trade was "war by other means." War, in the mercantilist view, was the normal state of things while peace was an aberration, a temporary lull between periods of hostility. The European game of annexations and sieges was therefore extended to every corner of the globe. Conflicts with parochial names such as the War of the League of Augsburg and the War of the Spanish Succession were the first world wars in history.

Expanded trade did not, however, create universal prosperity. It increased the number of professionals and created job opportunities for a growing middle class of bookkeepers, accountants, and small tradesmen, but it also concentrated immense wealth in the hands of a few. In England, some of these investors were

◈ DOCUMENT 17.8 ◈

Mercantilist Principles

The following prescription for a country's prosperity was written in 1684 by Philipp Wilhelm von Hornick, an Austrian lawyer and government official.

If the might and eminence of a country consist in its surplus of gold, silver, and all other things necessary or convenient for its *subsistence*, derived so far as possible, from its own resources, without *dependence* upon other countries . . . the following nine rules are especially serviceable.

First, to inspect the country's soil with the greatest care, and not to leave the agricultural possibilities of a single corner or clod of earth unconsidered. Above all, no trouble or expense should be spared to discover gold and silver.

Second, all commodities found in a country, which cannot be used in their natural state, should be worked up within the country; since the payment for *manufacturing* generally exceeds the value of the raw material by two, three, ten, twenty, or even a hundred fold. . . .

Third, for carrying out the above rules, there will be need of people, both for producing and cultivating the raw materials and for working them up. Therefore, attention should be given to the population, that it may be as large as the country can support.

Fourth, gold and silver once in the country . . . are under no circumstances to be taken away for any purpose, so far as possible, or allowed to be buried in chests and coffers, but must always remain in *circulation*.

Fifth, the inhabitants of a country should make every effort to get along with their domestic products, to confine their luxury to these alone . . . (except where great need leaves no alternative, or if not need, widespread, unavoidable abuse, of which Indian spices are an example).

Sixth, in case the said purchases were indispensable . . . they should be obtained from these foreigners at first hand, so far as possible, and not for gold and silver, but in exchange for other domestic wares.

Seventh, such foreign commodities should in this case be imported in unfinished form, and worked up within the country, thus earning the wages of *manufacture* there.

Eighth, opportunities should be sought night and day for selling the country's superfluous goods to these foreigners in manufactured form . . . and for gold and silver.

Ninth . . . no importation should be allowed under any circumstances of commodities of which there is sufficient supply of suitable quality at home, and in this matter neither sympathy nor compassion should be shown foreigners . . . For all friendship ceases when it involves my own weakness and ruin.

---

merchants and bankers while others were great landholders who invested in trade. The aristocratic prejudice against commerce largely vanished in the seventeenth century, in part because the composition of the titled nobility had changed. Families remained who could trace their ancestry to the remote feudal past, but many more had been ennobled for their services to the monarchy in recent times. Their immediate ancestors had been lawyers or servants of the crown, and they continued to maintain close ties with the urban world from which they had come. This was as true in France or Germany as it was in England. It had always been the case in Italy, and even in Spain the fabled prohibition against *hidalgos* (literally, sons of somebody), engaging in trade, was largely ignored.

Those who turned their back on new sources of wealth eventually lost both power and status. Commerce, even if conducted at one remove by investing with urban bankers and merchants, had become for many the primary source of new capital. Much of this new wealth was committed to ostentation in an effort to bolster the investor's social position and ensure access to the royal court, but much of it was also reinvested.

Economic and Social Stratification

Capital accumulated by trade would later provide the massive sums needed for the industrial revolution, but it did nothing to halt the growth of rural poverty and may have increased it by accelerating the capitalization of land, a process that had been under way since the fourteenth century. One effect of increased trade was therefore to intensify social polarization. In the seven-

Illustration 17.10

⊘ **Jean-Baptiste Colbert.** The minister of Louis XIV and greatest exponent of mercantilist policies is shown here in a contemporary engraving by Jacques Lubin.

teenth and eighteenth centuries the rich grew richer while the poor grew poorer (see Table 17.2).

The degradation of peasant life was most obvious in those regions that provided agricultural produce for the world market. The growing European demand for grain encouraged Russian, Polish, and Prussian landholders to impose or extend the institution of serfdom. Production for export was best achieved on huge estates whose labor force could be minutely controlled. Left to their own devices, peasants would diversify crops and develop other economic strategies to enhance security. To landholders this was a diversion of effort that prevented them from maximizing their profits. Serfdom, like New World slavery, was therefore a way to industrialize agriculture. But by limiting peasant survival strategies, it dramatically reduced rural standards of living while enriching those who were already wealthy.

Social polarization was almost as great in England, the center of commercial growth (see Table 17.3). The condition of English peasants may have improved for a time after the Black Death, but it declined steadily after the mid-fifteenth century. The rich were better able than the poor to invest in land, develop it, and profit from the cultivation of cash crops. Smallholders found it increasingly difficult to compete. Royal policy compounded the problem by supporting the retention of feudal ties while permitting the enclosure of common lands; that is, when landholders appropriated land previously shared by the inhabitants of an entire village. Deprived of the marginal income that enabled them to survive, thousands of peasants were forced to surrender their copyholds and leave their homes with little more than the clothes on their backs.

Most found obtaining work difficult if not impossible. The shift toward grazing reduced the demand for agricultural labor, while population growth after the mid-fifteenth century depressed wages. The situation worsened throughout the sixteenth and seventeenth centuries. Increased criminal activity and a growing population of sturdy beggars alarmed the authorities. Poor Laws based on the assumption that poverty and homelessness were the results of deliberate choice accomplished nothing. Neither migration to America nor the expansion of urban employment fully relieved the pressure. Eighteenth-century London may have been the commercial center of the world, but its slums were as enormous as its wealth. Unable to find work, England's dispossessed became a vast urban proletariat whose squalid, gin-soaked existence was immortalized in the drawings of William Hogarth (1697–1764) and in the novels of Henry Fielding (1707–54).

In some regions, capitalization of the land encouraged social polarization without a major increase in trade. Spanish peasants, faced from the 1580s with heavy taxation and declining yields, borrowed money from urban investors to improve their land. When they found themselves unable to redeem their *censos* (a form of bond), the holders foreclosed and seized their property. By 1650 the population of Madrid had swelled to more than 100,000 as displaced peasants sought charity from the city's many religious houses and from an increasingly hard-pressed government. Lawyers, speculators, and officials amassed large estates but could provide only inefficient absentee ownership.

Though the consolidation of properties, common to virtually every other part of Europe, was resisted successfully by the French crown, prosperity in the countryside remained elusive. Since the fifteenth century, French courts had generally supported peasant rights

⫶ TABLE 17.2 ⫶

English Wages and Prices, 1541–1702

While wages doubled between 1541 and 1702, the price of ordinary food items tripled. The result was a severe decline in the living standards of laboring families. However, most contemporaries thought that English workers were far more prosperous than their counterparts in France or the Netherlands and richer still than the peasants of central and eastern Europe.

Wages or prices	1541–82	1583–1642	1643–1702
Weekly wages			
Carpenter	5s.	6s. 2 3/4d.	10s. 2 3/4d.
Farm laborer	3s.3d.	4s. 10d.	6s. 4 3/4d.
Mason	4s. 10d.	6s. 5 3/4d.	9s. 10 1/2d.
Prices			
Barley (quarter)	8s. 5 3/4d.	19s. 9 3/4d.	22s. 2 1/2d.
Beer (barrel)	2s.		10s.
Chicken (1)	1d.	3d.	1s. 4d.
Goose (1)	4d.	1s. 4d.	3s.
Oatmeal (quarter)	20s. 4 3/4d.	37s. 9 1/4d.	52s. 11d.
Wheat (quarter)	13s. 10 1/2d.	36s. 9d.	41s. 11 1/2d.

Source: Figures adapted from John Burnett, *A History of the Cost of Living* (Harmondsworth: Pelican Books, 1969), pp. 71, 80–81.

⫶ TABLE 17.3 ⫶

English Incomes, 1688

The following figures are contemporary estimates. If accurate, they reveal a disparity in wealth that is far greater than that found in most modern industrialized countries. The income figures are in millions of pounds sterling.

Class	Number of families	Income	Percentage of families	Percentage of income
Nobility, gentry, officials	53,000	9.816	4	23
Merchants and traders	10,000	2.400	1	5
Freeholders and farmers	330,000	16.960	24	39
Shopkeepers and artisans	100,000	4.200	7	10
Military officers and clergy	19,000	1.120	2	2
Laborers, servants, paupers, seamen, common soldiers, and so on	849,000	9.010	62	21
Total	1,361,000	43.506	100	100

Source: Gregory King, *Natural and Political Observations*, in *Two Tracts by Gregory King*, ed. G. E. Barnett (Baltimore, Md.: Johns Hopkins University, 1936), p. 31.

against those of the landowning nobility. The reasons were largely political—supporting the claims of peasants tended to break up concentrations of aristocratic power in the countryside—but by 1700 French peasants were the freest in Europe. Unfortunately, the wars of Louis XIV made them among the most heavily taxed. In terms of surplus extraction, they had exchanged their oppressive landholders for a no less demanding king. At the same time, the increase of private ownership in an age of demographic growth led inevitably to the subdivision of properties. Partible inheritance was still the norm in France, and though more than half of the rural population owned a plot of land at century's end, it was rarely big enough to support a family. Thousands of peasants were forced into the labor market to pay their taxes at a time when wages were in decline. The terrible famines of the 1690s showed that freedom offered little protection against hunger.

The growth of poverty did not go unnoticed by the more fortunate. Though in retrospect it obviously was caused by changes in economic relationships that had been aggravated by endemic warfare and the meager harvests of the Little Ice Age, contemporaries drew other conclusions. The attitude toward the poor began to change.

In medieval theory, if not always in practice, the poor were specially favored by God and entitled to charity. Begging symbolized the apostolic poverty of the friars, and the giving of alms, whether to the church or to the poor, was a good work and a mark of piety. In the more conservative, Catholic regions of southern Europe this view persisted into modern times. In the north it was replaced by fear and apprehension well before the Reformation. Augsburg adopted punitive measures against beggars and the homeless in 1459. Paris followed in 1473. In 1495 an ordinance of Henry VII of England condemned vagrants to three days in the stocks, following which they were to be whipped and returned to their place of origin. It would be a model for later English Poor Laws. Charles VIII of France in the following year decreed that beggars be sent to row in the galleys. In the decades to come, such humanists as Erasmus, More, and Juan Luis Vives would write against begging, while religious reformers such as Luther, Calvin, and Zwingli agreed that no virtue existed in poverty.

To the Protestant theologians, work performed in a Christian spirit was sanctifying. One of the more enlightened approaches to poverty was the establishment of workhouses in which vagrants and petty criminals could rehabilitate themselves through labor. The Amsterdam *rasphuis*, founded at the beginning of the seventeenth century, was a model institution. Inmates worked twelve to fourteen hours a day turning logs of Brazil wood into sawdust so that the powder could be incorporated into dyes. The monotony of their day was enlivened by sermons and floggings. A similar institution was established for women, who spun endless yards of thread to be sold by the city government. The idea behind all of these measures was that the poor were willfully lazy and that they could be reformed only if they were subjected to rigorous discipline.

The Rise of Gentility

Hostility to the poor was encouraged by their frightening numbers and by the popular revolts that had occurred between the Black Death and the Great Peasants' War of 1524–25. Virtually everyone understood that economic polarization was a danger to the social order. What they did not understand was that the effects of polarization were being augmented by a redefinition of elite values that, consciously or not, dehumanized the poor in the eyes of their "betters."

European elites had always justified their privilege by claiming some form of superiority. The knights of the first feudal age had taken pride in their strength and courage. In the absence of an immediate threat to society, their descendants had declared that such qualities were hereditary and enhanced them by cultivating chivalric courtesy. Early modern elites retained a self-proclaimed monopoly of these virtues and merged them with others that reflected the values of Renaissance humanism and of the late medieval urban life from which it had emerged. Refinement of taste and intellect became the new hallmarks of status (see document 17.9).

Much of this gentility derived from a common education. Minimal acquaintance with the classics and an appreciation for classic aesthetics were essential. The gentleman or gentlewoman valued harmony, symmetry, and balance. Classical standards were reflected not only in the high-minded dramas of Racine or Calderón, but also in the architecture of Andrea Palladio (1508–80). Baroque art and architecture with its rich decoration and extravagant visual harmonies gradually gave way to a more restrained style based on what was thought to have been the taste of ancient Rome. This Palladian interpretation of Roman aesthetics became the model for hundreds of palaces, country houses, and churches and persisted well into the nineteenth century. Its influence may be seen in the reconstruction of London by Sir Christopher Wren (1632–1723) after the great fire of 1666.

As the seventeenth century wore on, "reason," too, became important in the sense that superstition and extreme religiosity were rejected in favor of a more detached, "scientific" view of the world. The new science encouraged people to believe that the divine order was

A Gentlewoman's Day

In this letter Dorothy Osborne, a young English woman of good family, describes her day to the man she would one day marry, the diplomat Sir William Temple. It reflects both the seventeenth-century ideal of gentility and contemporary attitudes toward the working poor.

I rise in the morning reasonably early, and before I am ready I go round the house until I weary of that, and then into the garden until it grows too hot for me. About ten o'clock I think of making me ready, and when that's done I go into my father's chamber, from whence to dinner, where my cousin Molle and I sit in great state in a room, and at a table that would hold a great many more. . . . The heat of the day is spent in reading or working [presumably needlework], and about six or seven o'clock I walk out into a common that lies hard by the house, where a great many young wenches keep sheep and cows, and sit in the shade singing ballads. I go to them and compare their voices and beautie to some ancient shepherdesses that I have read of, and find a great difference there, but trust me, I think these are as innocent as those could be. I talk to them, and find they want nothing to make them the happiest people in the world but the knowledge that they are so. Most commonly when we are in the midst of our discourse, one looks about her, and spies her cows going into the corn, and then they all run as if they had wings at their heels. . . . When I have supped, I go into the garden, and so to the side of a small river that runs by it, when I sit down and wish you were with me.

rational instead of providential or based upon frequent interventions by a wrathful diety. A growing faith in the possibility of a rationally ordered society accompanied the growth of absolutism, while holistic, magical, or apocalyptic visions—and sometimes the display of emotion—became the province of the poor and ignorant.

Manners and deportment were an even more important mark of status. Those who wished to be taken seriously adopted models of carriage, speech, and gesture based equally upon courtly models and the precepts of the classical rhetoricians. The stage, with its abundance of noble characters, provided instruction for those who lacked access to polite society. Table manners improved with the introduction of the fork, and books were written as guides to correct behavior. In time the natural movements of ordinary people came to seem crude and loutish.

Clothing, too, mirrored the growing separation between the classes as the fashions of the rich became more elaborate and expensive. Men in particular cultivated the art of magnificence with lace collars, massive wigs, and brocaded waistcoats that were sometimes trimmed in gold. To be seen in one's own hair was unacceptable even on the battlefield. Attempts to imitate the dress and bearing of the upper classes were common, but education, good manners, and a suit that cost as much as a middle-class family's annual income were hard to counterfeit. Presumption of this sort was met with ridicule and often with violence, for upper-class men still carried swords or weighted canes. Another mark of gentility, the idea of comfort, adapted more easily to the lives of ordinary people.

Magnificence in domestic architecture was a legacy of the sixteenth century. The Louvre, the chateaux built along the Loire in the time of Francis I, and the country houses of Tudor England were the legitimate ancestors of Versailles. Like Versailles, they had subordinated comfort to grandeur. Their furniture, like that of the medieval castle, remained minimal. The great houses of the seventeenth century were no less ostentatious, but their owners packed them with furnishings in the modern manner. Chairs, tables, carpets, and what-nots proliferated. Though rooms were still set aside for ceremonial and social functions, they were supplemented by sitting rooms and other cozy spaces for the private enjoyment of the owner's family. The sheer luxury of these interiors could not be matched by ordinary households, and tens of thousands of Europeans continued to huddle in wretched cottages. The general level of domestic comfort, however, rose steadily after about 1650. Chimneys and glazed windows became common in the homes of town dwellers and in those of the more secure peasants, while inventories of household goods begin to show a steady increase in chairs, tables, and linens.

◆

Conclusion

Through all of this, the basic human ecology that had remained in effect since Neolithic times changed little. Though European populations had shifted geographically, they were in aggregate not much bigger in 1700 than they had been in 1200. This was a triumph in itself, for the terrible losses of the fourteenth and fifteenth centuries had at last been made good. It demonstrates that the ancient balance between births and deaths was being maintained. The major change was a shift toward urbanization. The flight from rural poverty had made Paris, London, and Constantinople enormous cities with more than half a million people each. Naples, Amsterdam, Lisbon, and Madrid had also grown. However, many famous towns had progressed little in size or aspect since the Middle Ages, and at least 85 percent of all Europeans still earned their primary living through agriculture. For most of them, the conditions of material life remained medieval.

All of this would change dramatically with the coming of the industrial revolution. The development of mass production technology and its attendant advances in nutrition, medicine, and public health is a watershed in human history. The year 1715 marked more than the death of Louis XIV. Since then, only one real crisis of subsistence occurred in western Europe: the Irish potato famine of 1846–48. Furthermore, no outbreaks of the plague were seen. By 1900 the biological old regime would be largely a memory in the West, and the basic structures of human society would be changed almost beyond recognition.

Suggested Readings

Good surveys of the scientific revolution include A. R. Hall, *The Revolution in Science, 1500–1700* (1983), A. Debus, *Man and Nature in the Renaissance* (1978), A. G. R. Smith, *Science and Society in the Sixteenth and Seventeenth Centuries* (1972), and M. Boas, *The Scientific Renaissance: 1450–1630* (1962). For the occult and hermetic traditions, see B. Vickers, *Occult and Scientific Mentalities in the Renaissance* (1986), W. Shumaker, *The Occult Sciences in the Renaissance: A Study in Intellectual Patterns* (1985), and F. Yates, *Giordano Bruno and the Hermetic Tradition* (1964). Mathematics is covered by P. Rose, *The Italian Renaissance of Mathematics: Studies on Humanists and Mathematics from Petrarch to Galileo* (1975). Medieval ideas on cosmology may be found in P. Duhem, *Medieval Cosmology: Theories of Infinity, Place, Time, Void, and the Plurality of Worlds* (1985), a condensation of the ten-volume original. For astrology, see E. Garin, *Astrology in the Renaissance: The Zodiac of Life* (1983).

Copernicus stands at the beginning of modern cosmology. See E. Rosen, *Copernicus and the Scientific Revolution* (1984) and T. Kuhn, *The Copernican Revolution: Planetary Astronomy in the Development of Western Thought* (1971). A. Koestler, *The Sleepwalkers: A History of Man's Changing Vision of the Universe* (1959) is a broad, often ironic, survey. The standard biography of Kepler is M. Casper, *Johannes Kepler* (1959). A vast literature exists on Galileo; the

works of S. Drake, *Galileo at Work: His Scientific Biography* (1978), *Galileo* (1980), and *Galileo: Pioneer Scientist* (1990) are standards. On Newton, see R. Westfall, *The Life of Isaac Newton* (1993) and B. Dobbs, *The Foundations of Newton's Alchemy* (1973). The development of medicine is surveyed by W. Wightman, *The Emergence of Scientific Medicine* (1971). Specialized studies include A. Debus, *The Chemical Philosophy: Paracelsian Science and Medicine in the Sixteenth and Seventeenth Centuries*, 2 vols. (1977), C. O'Malley, *Andreas Vesalius of Brussels, 1514–1564* (1964), and G. Whitteridge, *William Harvey and the Circulation of the Blood* (1971). The founding of the academies is described in R. Hahn, *The Anatomy of a Scientific Revolution: The Paris Academy of Sciences, 1666–1803* (1971) and M. Purver, *The Royal Society, Concept and Creation* (1967). M. Jacobs, *The Cultural Meaning of the Scientific Revolution* (1988) and L. Schiebinger, *The Mind Has No Sex? Women in the Origins of Modern Science* (1989) are useful essays on science as an intellectual movement.

On the expansion of the northern powers, see C. R. Boxer, *The Dutch Seaborne Empire, 1600–1800* (1965) and R. Davis, *English Overseas Trade, 1500–1700* (1973). J. Israel, *The Dutch Republic: Its Rise, Greatness, and Fall, 1477–1806* (1995) is a monumental survey, and S. Schama, *The Embarrassment of Riches: An Intepretation of Dutch Culture in the Golden Age* (1987) is an ambitious study of Dutch culture. K. Haley, *The Dutch in the Seventeenth Century* (1972) remains useful. For Dutch politics, see two studies by H. Rowen, *Jan de Witt: Grand Pensionary of Holland, 1625–1672* (1978) and *The Princes of Orange: The Stadholders of the Dutch Republic* (1985).

J. Black describes military changes in *European Warfare, 1660–1815* (1994) and *A Military Revolution? Military Change and European Society, 1550–1800* (1991). See also A. Corvisier, *Armies and Societies in Europe, 1494–1789* (1979) and M. Anderson, *War and Society in the Old Regime, 1618–1789* (1988). On the reorganization of the state in France, see M. Greengrass, *France in the Age of Henri IV: The Struggle for Stability* (1984), D. Parker, *The Making of French Absolutism* (1983), and H. Rowen, *The King's State: Proprietary Dynasticism in Early Modern France* (1980). Two good studies of Richelieu are by J. Bergin, *The Rise of Richelieu* (1991) and *Cardinal Richelieu: Power and the Pursuit of Wealth* (1985). See also A. Knecht, *Richelieu* (1991), the insightful essay by J. H. Elliott, *Richelieu and Olivares* (1984), and R. Bonney, *Society and Government in France under Richelieu and Mazarin, 1624–61* (1988). J. Collum, *The State in Early Modern France* (1995) is a recent overview. J. B. Wolf, *Louis XIV* (1968) and O. Bernier, *Louis XIV* (1988) are good studies of the Sun King. See also P. Goubert, *Louis XIV and Twenty Million Frenchmen* (1970). Sources on seventeenth-century Spain are listed in chapter 16. For surveys covering the German-speaking states, see H. Holborn, *A History of Modern Germany, 1648–1840* (1965) and M. Hughes, *Early Modern Germany, 1477–1806* (1992). The standard work on the Austrian Empire is R. J. W. Evans, *The Making of the Habsburg Monarchy, 1550–1700* (1979); on Prussia, see F. Carsten, *The Origins of Prussia* (1954) and H. Rosenberg, *Bureaucracy, Aristocracy, and Autocracy: The Prussian Experience, 1660–1815* (1966). Good studies of Peter the Great include B. Sumner, *Peter the Great and the Emergence of Russia* (1962), M. Anderson, *Peter the Great* (1978), and the popular R. Massie, *Peter the Great* (1980). For the

English Restoration, see R. Hulton, *The Restoration: A Political and Religious History of England and Wales, 1658–1667* (1985). English politics after the Restoration are described by J. R. Jones, *Country and Court: England, 1658–1714* (1978) and *The Glorious Revolution of 1688 in England* (1972). R. Hutton, *Charles II* (1989) is a good biography.

The theory of mercantilism is described in E. Hecksher, *Mercantilism*, 2 vols. (1935). On the preindustrial economy, see F. Braudel, *Civilization and Capitalism in the Fifteenth to Eighteenth Century*, 3 vols. (1981–84), J. de Vries, *The Economy of Europe in an Age of Crisis* (1976), and H. Kellenbenz, *The Rise of the European Economy: An Economic History of Europe from the Fifteenth to the Eighteenth Century* (1976). D. W. Jones, *War and Economy in the Age of William III and Marlborough* (1988) analyzes the impact of the wars on British trade. On finance, see P. Dickson, *The Financial Revolution in England, 1688–1756* (1967).

PART FOUR

Modern Europe in the Age of Agricultural Society, 1715–1815

CHAPTER 18

THE SOCIAL AND ECONOMIC STRUCTURE OF THE OLD REGIME

CHAPTER OUTLINE

◆◆◆◆◆◆◆◆◆◆◆◆◆◆◆◆◆◆◆◆◆◆

European society before the political and industrial revolutions of the late eighteenth century is known as the Old Regime. The eighteenth century, with its passion for measurement, provided a statistical picture of the Old Regime that completes an understanding of this vanished world and throws the changes wrought by modern times into stark relief. For most people in the eighteenth century, life was little changed from the Middle Ages and closer in its essentials to that of ancient Rome than to the late twentieth century. Though global commerce was growing and signs were seen of increased capital accumulation and preindustrial development, the vast majority of Europeans were still engaged in agriculture. Society reflected this by remaining hierarchical. A majority of the population worked the land but owned little or none of it, while most of the wealth continued to be held by a small landowning elite. If anything, the gap between rich and poor had widened since 1500.

Chapter 18 examines the social and economic structure of the Old Regime. The chapter starts by looking at the population of Europe, then considers the social categories, called estates, into which people were divided. (The term *social class* is a product of nineteenth-century analysis.) The majority of Europeans lived in rural villages, so the chapter next surveys the rural economy, including preindustrial manufacturing. This leads to a detailed examination of three major social categories: the aristocracy, the peasantry of rural Europe, and town dwellers. The urban economy leads to a discussion of national economies. This section covers mercantilism, the dominant economic philosophy of the Old Regime, and the global economy.

N TABLE 18.1 N

Estimated Population of Europe in 1700

Country	Population (in millions)
France	19.3
European Russia	17.0
German states	13.5
Bavaria	2.4
Saxony	2.0
Prussia	1.6
Italian states	13.0
Two Sicilies	3.0
Papal States	2.0
Venice	1.8
Piedmont	1.7
Austrian Empire	11.0
Poland	9.0
Spain	7.5
Great Britain	6.4
Turkish Empire	6.4
Ireland	2.5
Portugal	2.0
Holland	1.9
Sweden and Finland	1.5

Source: B. R. Mitchell, ed., *European Historical Statistics, 1750–1970* (London: Macmillan, 1975), pp. 17ff; and Jack Babuscio and Richard M. Dunn, eds., *European Political Facts, 1648–1789* (London: Macmillan, 1984), pp. 335ff.

The Population of Europe in the Old Regime

Historians do not know with certainty how many people lived in Europe in 1680, or even in 1780. Governments did not yet record births and deaths (churches usually documented them), and they did not conduct a regular census of the population. The first modern census in England, for example, was held in 1801. Isolated census data exist for the eighteenth century, such as a Swedish census of 1750 and the Spanish census of 1768–69, but most population figures are estimates based on fragmentary records, local case studies, and demographic analysis.

The best estimate is that Europe in the middle of the eighteenth century (c. 1750–70) had a total population of 150 million people (see table 18.1)—less than one-seventh of the count at the end of the twentieth

century. Spain, the richest world power of the sixteenth century, had a population of 9.2 million in 1769. A good estimate of the population of Great Britain (England, Scotland, and Wales) at the beginning of the eighteenth century is 6.4 million—less than the population of London in 1998. The strength of France during the Old Regime can be seen in its estimated population of 19.3 million in 1700. In all countries, most people lived in small villages and on isolated farms. Even in a city-state such as the republic of Venice, more than 80 percent of the population was rural. In France, one of the most developed countries of the Old Regime, the figure was more than 75 percent.

The Economic Structures of the Rural World

Most of Europe lived, as their ancestors had, in small villages surrounded by open fields. The land was parceled for farming in many ways, but the general pattern was consistent: Peasants and small farmers inhabited and worked land that belonged to aristocrats, the state, or the church (see map 18.1). A typical village left some woodland standing (for gathering food and fuel), set aside some of the worst soil as wasteland (for grazing livestock), maintained some land as commonly owned, and left most of the land unfenced in open fields. Enclosed, or fenced in, fields were rare, but in some regions of western Europe—such as southwestern England, Brittany in western France, and the Netherlands—the land was already subdivided by fences, stone walls, or hedgerows. Enclosure had occurred in some places to assist livestock farming and in others where peasants had been fortunate enough to acquire their own land. In most of Europe, however, the arable land was still farmed in the open field system. From the midlands of England to eastern Europe (especially the German states and Russia), open fields were divided into long rectangular strips of approximately one acre each, defined by grass pathways between them. A peasant family usually worked several strips scattered around the community, plus a kitchen garden near home. This was an inefficient system, but one that allowed the bad and good fields to be shared more equitably. In other regions of Europe (such as Spain, southern France, and Italy) the open fields were divided into small, irregular plots of land that peasant families farmed year after year.

Whatever system of land tenure was used, most plowland was planted with the grains on which the

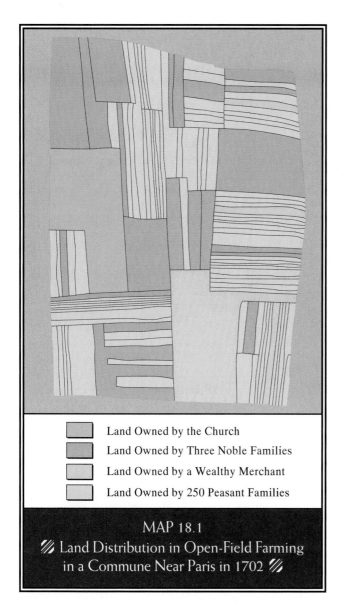

Land Owned by the Church

Land Owned by Three Noble Families

Land Owned by a Wealthy Merchant

Land Owned by 250 Peasant Families

MAP 18.1
Land Distribution in Open-Field Farming in a Commune Near Paris in 1702

◈ DOCUMENT 18.1 ◈

An Eighteenth-Century Sharecropping Contract

This list summarizes the chief points of a contract negotiated in southern France in 1779 on behalf of a great landowner. It was an agreement "at half fruits"—a 50/50 sharing of the crop between a marquis and the father and son who farmed his land. A study of this contract has estimated that this land would yield a harvest of 100 setiers of wheat. Thus, the peasant sharecroppers paid (1) 20 setiers off the top to the marquis; then (2) 10 setiers of wheat as the price of cutting and flailing the wheat, leaving a harvest of 70 setiers. They then paid (3) 35 setiers as "half fruits" and (4) 20 setiers for seed. The result was 55 setiers to the marquis, 15 setiers for the peasant family. A family of five ate 20 setiers of wheat per year.

1. The lease shall be for one year, at "half fruits" and under the following conditions.
2. The lessees will furnish the seed.
3. Before the division of the harvest, the marquis will receive twenty setiers of wheat off the top.
4. The lessees will deliver the wheat already cut and flailed, at no cost to the marquis.
5. The lessees must use the "three field" system of planting—1/3 of the land planted to wheat, 1/3 to some other grain, and 1/3 left unplanted.
6. If the lessees do not leave 1/3 of the land fallow, they forfeit the entire harvest.
7. All livestock will be held in common with profits and losses equally shared.
8. If there is a shortage of hay and straw for the livestock, the lessees must pay half of the cost of buying forage.
9. The lessees must maintain the land, including making drains for water, cutting brush, pruning vines. . . etc.
10. In addition to sharing the crop, the lessees must pay a rent of 72 chickens, 36 capons, and 600 eggs.
11. The lessees must raise pigs, geese, ducks, and turkeys, to be divided evenly; they must purchase the young animals to raise at their own expense.
12. The lessees must make their own ploughs and pay for the blacksmith work themselves.

---

world lived—wheat, rye, barley, and oats. These crops were usually rotated annually, and each field laid fallow on a regular basis, normally every third year (see document 18.1). Leaving a field unplanted was needed for the replacement of nitrates in the soil because chemical fertilizers were unknown and animal manure was scarce. Fallow fields had the secondary advantage of providing additional pasture land for grazing.

Scientific agronomy—the study of field-crop production and soil management—was in its infancy in the Old Regime, but noteworthy changes were appearing. In Britain, the improvements suggested by the studies of Jethro Tull and the Viscount Charles Townshend significantly increased eighteenth-century harvests. Tull, a gentleman farmer and scientist in Berkshire, wrote *Horse-Hoeing Husbandry* (1731) based upon his observations of cultivating field crops. This work introduced a

Illustration 18.1

An Alsatian Market Town. Such market towns stood at the center of the rural economy. They provided small rural communities with goods and services while allowing peasants to sell their produce at weekly outdoor markets. Many such markets remain little changed to the present.

new system of plowing and hoeing to pulverize the soil, which produced higher yields on unfertilized soil. English farmers listened to Tull because in 1701 he had invented a seed drill that had increased yields and decreased labor. Townshend advocated a planting system that eliminated the need for summer fallowing of plowland. His Norfolk, or four-course, system rotated plantings of a root crop, barley, clover, and wheat. Townshend championed the choice of turnips as the root crop so vigorously (because they provided both nitrogen fixation and fodder for livestock) that he became known as "Turnip Townshend." Ideas such as these, circulated by a growing periodical press, raised crop yields to the extent that England fed an increasing population and still exported grain in the early eighteenth century.

Most European agriculture was not so successful, and peasant families faced a struggle to survive. Their primary concern was a harvest large enough to pay their obligations to the landowning aristocracy, to the royal tax collector, and to the church in the form of a compulsory tithe as well as to provide seed grain for the next year, with food leftover to sustain life for another year. The yield per acre was higher in western Europe than in eastern Europe, which explains much of the comparative prosperity and strength of the west. Each grain sown in Russia and Poland yielded an average harvest of four grains, while Spanish and Italian peasants harvested six grains, and English and Dutch farmers averaged more than ten grains. Peasants typically supplemented their meager stock of grains with

the produce of a small garden and the luxury of some livestock such as a few pigs or chickens. Surplus of grain would be sold or bartered—a money economy was not yet the rule throughout the rural world—at the nearest market town (see illustration 18.1) to acquire necessities that could not be produced at home. Even when livestock was slaughtered, peasants rarely ate the entire animal; they generally sold the choicer cuts of pork and kept the fatty remnants for soups, stews, or crude bacon.

Home production was an essential feature of this rural economy and meant more than churning butter or making cheese at home. Domestic manufacturing often included making all of a family's clothing, so many peasants learned to spin yarn, weave cloth, or sew clothing. This part-time textile production sometimes led to the sale of excess household products, and in some textile regions domestic manufacturing evolved into a system of production known as cottage industry (see illustration 18.2) in which a peasant family purposely made goods for sale instead of for use in the home. Cottage industry sometimes grew into a handcraft form of industrial manufacture (often called protoindustrialization), when entrepreneurs negotiated contracts with peasant spinners and weavers. An entrepreneur might provide raw materials and pay peasant spinners to produce homespun threads; the yarn could then be delivered to a peasant weaver who also worked at home. This "putting out" system of textile manufacture stimulated later industrialization by developing manufacturing skills, marketing networks, and a class of

Illustration 18.2

⧸⧸ **Cottage Industry.** The textile industry began in rural cottages, not great factories. This scene depicts a family textile shop for making knitwear. Note the sexual division of labor: Women spin and wind yarn while a man operates a knitting frame, making stockings.

prosperous provincial entrepreneurs. By some estimates 10 percent of the rural population of Old Regime Europe was engaged in cottage industry.

Domestic manufacturing, like farming, depended upon a family economy; that is, everyone worked. Peasant society generally followed a sexual division of labor in which, for example, men did most of the plowing and women played an important role in the harvest. In the production of textiles, women did most of the spinning and men were more likely to be weavers. However, the labor of every family member, including children, was needed if the family were to survive. As an old poem recalls:

> Man, to the Plow
> Wife, to the Cow
> Girl, to the Yarn
> Boy, to the Barn
> And your Rent will be netted.

Working women were thus essential to the family economy long before industrialization and urbanization transformed families and work. A study of peasant women in eighteenth-century Belgium, for example, has found that 45 percent of all married women were listed in government records as farmers and 27 percent were recorded as spinners; only 6 percent were listed without an occupation. Unmarried adults, men and women alike, were at a disadvantage in this rural economy, but the burdens fell hardest on spinsters (an archaic term suggesting the occupation of many

unmarried women) and widows who were often the poorest members of a rural community.

The rural community of peasant families was typically a village of fifty to a few hundred people (see table 18.2). In parts of Europe, these villages had corporate structures with inherited rules and regulations. These might regulate weights and measures, or they might regulate morality and behavior such as the control of stray dogs or mandatory church attendance. Village assemblies, led by elders or by the heads of the households controlling most of the land, often held powers such as assigning land use (as they did in most German states and in Russia), dictating farming methods and crop rotation, settling disputes, collecting taxes, and even arranging marriages. Women were usually excluded from participation, though widows were sometimes accepted. Recent research has identified some exceptionally democratic villages in which women participated with full rights.

Corporative Society and the *Ständestaat*

Europeans of the Old Regime lived in highly stratified societies and generally accepted their fixed place in the hierarchy. In two-thirds of Europe (France, Savoy, part of Switzerland, Denmark, the German states, Austria, Bohemia, Hungary, the Danubian provinces, Poland, and Russia) law and custom divided people into estates. The division of the population into such bodies, with separate rights, duties, and laws, is known as corporative society, or by its German name, the *Ständestaat*.

Corporative society was a legacy of the Middle Ages. In much of western Europe, the legal basis for it had disappeared, whereas eastern Europe remained caste-ridden. Everywhere, hierarchical ideas provided the foundations of society. The structure of corporative society resembled a pyramid. Most of the population (peasants and laborers) formed the base of the pyramid while a few privileged people (aristocrats and wealthy town dwellers) sat at the top, with a monarch at the pinnacle. Everyone was born to a position in the hierarchy, a position that, according to most churches, was divinely ordained, and little social mobility was evident from one order to another. Each estate possessed a corporative identity with reciprocal rights and duties. In theory, peasants and workers provided the economic foundation of the state and supported it with their taxes and labor while the monarch and the aristocracy reciprocated by protecting them and their rights.

⚑ TABLE 18.2 ⚑

The Social Structure of Three French Villages

This table presents the social composition of three villages in eastern France in the late eighteenth century. It classifies rural families by their occupation and by their income level within each occupation. The income is calculated on the basis of the amount of taxes paid. The only noble family (a count whose domain included all three villages) had an annual income over 100,000 livres; no one else in these villages had an income above 5,000 livres.

Social classification	Income level in percent			
	Rich	Well-to-do	Middling	Poor
Nobility and gentry (2 households)	50.0	50.0	0.0	0.0
Farmers (77 households)	0.0	23.4	75.3	1.3
Winegrowers (29 households)	0.0	0.0	79.3	20.7
Shepherds, forest keeper and so on (9 households)	0.0	0.0	33.3	66.7
Millers (3 households)	0.0	33.3	66.7	0.0
"Bourgeois" town dwellers (8 households)	0.0	37.5	62.5	0.0
Legal officials (2 households)	0.0	100.0	0.0	0.0
Artisans such as smiths and weavers (85 households)	0.0	0.0	78.8	21.2
Tavern keepers (11 households)	0.0	9.1	81.8	9.1
Day laborers (94 households)	0.0	0.0	39.4	60.6
Widows and unmarried women (43 households)	0.0	0.0	34.9	65.1
Entire community (363 households)	0.3	6.6	57.1	36.0

Source: Robert Forster, *The House of Saulx-Tavannes: Versailles and Burgundy, 1700–1830* (Baltimore, Md.: Johns Hopkins University Press, 1971), pp. 252–53.

Historians have mostly studied corporative society in France, where the population was divided into three estates. The clergy, approximately 1 percent to 2 percent of the nation, comprised the first estate. The aristocracy, also less than 2 percent of the population, formed the second estate. The remaining 97 percent of France, from bankers to vagabonds, collectively made up the third estate. In central Europe, the *Ständestaat* often contained four orders (*Stände*) because Scandinavian and German law divided what the French called the third estate into two parts, an order of town dwellers and another of peasants. The Swedish constitution of 1720, one of the first constitutions of the Old Regime, was an advanced document that weakened the monarchy, but it retained the ideal of corporative society. German jurisprudence perpetuated this division of the population throughout the eighteenth century. Johann Moser, a scholar who summarized Germanic law in a fifty-volume compendium published in the 1740s, reiterated the principles of the *Ständestaat*, and they were embodied in the legal reforms of the era, such as the Frederician Code in Prussia.

The society of the Old Regime was more complicated than simple legal categories suggest. Many variations of corporative society could be found across Europe. In England, the legal distinctions among social groups were mostly abolished during the seventeenth century. The English aristocracy remained a privileged and dominant elite, but a new stratification based upon nonlanded wealth was also emerging (see table 18.3). In contrast, Russian fundamental laws perpetuated a rigid corporative society, and eighteenth-century reforms only tightened the system. In central Europe, yet another pattern developed where reformers known as cameralists refined the definitions of social categories. Austrian tax laws adopted in 1763, for example, divided the population into twenty-four distinct categories.

The composition and condition of each estate varied across Europe. The Polish aristocracy included 10 percent of the population compared with 1 percent in France; this meant that the Polish aristocracy included barefoot farmers who lived in simple homes with earthen floors. Only 1 percent of Poles lived in towns of ten thousand, compared with more than 15 percent of England and Wales. Sometimes, as in Spain, peasants lived in farming towns, but they were not part of an urban estate. But everywhere, peasants were the majority. In England, 65 percent of the population lived by

⚜ TABLE 18.3 ⚜

The Social Structure of England in the Old Regime

The data in this table are based upon statistical calculations made by Gregory King in the last years of the seventeenth century. The original calculations were based upon a study of the tax rolls, to determine the relative size and wealth of various social groups.

Social group	Individuals on tax rolls	Population (with families)	Percentage of England
Aristocracy	4,560	57,000	1.0
Nobility (peers)	160	6,400	0.1
Landowning gentry	172,000	1,036,000	18.8
Small farmers	550,000	2,050,000	37.2
Rural poor	400,000	1,300,000	23.6
Rural total	726,560	3,143,000	57.0
Merchants	10,000	64,000	1.2
Educated professions	25,000	145,000	2.7
Law	10,000	70,000	1.3
Clergy	10,020	52,520	0.9
Government service	10,000	70,000	1.3
Urban trades	110,000	465,000	8.5
Skilled artisans	60,000	240,000	4.4
Shopkeepers	50,000	225,000	4.1
Laborers	360,000	1,275,000	23.2
Vagrants and others	0	30,000	0.5
Urban total	525,020	2,101,520	38.3
Military officers	9,000	36,000	0.7
Soldiers and sailors	85,000	220,000	4.0
Military total	94,000	256,000	4.7

farming; in France and Sweden, 75 percent of the population were peasants; in Poland, the peasantry included 85 percent of the nation—95 percent in some regions.

The rights and duties of people in each estate also varied from country to country, with the most striking differences evident between eastern and western Europe. Historians frequently express this division of Europe by an imaginary line called the Elbe-Trieste line, running from the mouth of the Elbe River on the North Sea to the Adriatic Sea at the city of Trieste (see map 20.1). West of the Elbe-Trieste line (including Scandinavia), peasants could own farm land. French peasants, for example, owned between 30 percent and 40 percent of the arable land, although it was frequently of the poorest quality. East of the Elbe River, peasants lived in a form of legal servitude called serfdom. Millions of serfs were deprived of legal and civil rights, including the right to own land. Even those states that permitted peasant land ownership, however, saw little of it. Swedish peasants accounted for 75 percent of the population but owned only 31 percent of the land; the king and the aristocracy, less than 5 percent of the population, owned 69 percent of the land in 1700. Sweden, however, was far ahead of most of Europe in peasant land ownership. In Bohemia, one of the richest provinces of the Hapsburg Empire, the monarch owned

Illustration 18.3

✎ Aristocratic Life. Although the aristocracy was a diverse social group ranging from the immensely rich to impoverished families who lived much like peasants, a common image that aristocrats presented was the idleness of fortunate people who need not work to survive. No image better captures the enjoyment of aristocratic frivolity than J. H. Fragonard's *The Swing,* shown here.

5 percent of the land and the nobility owned 68.5 percent, while peasants owned less than 1 percent.

The Aristocracy: Varieties of the Privileged Elite

The pinnacle of the social structure in rural communities was the aristocracy, who enjoyed a life of comparative ease (see illustration 18.3). In most countries, aristocrats formed a separate legal caste, bound by different laws and traditions that gave them special privileges, such as tax exemptions and the right to unpaid labor by the peasantry. Nobility was considered a hereditary condition, which originated when a monarch granted noble status to a family through a document called a patent of nobility. In each generation, the eldest son would bear the title of nobility (such as duke or count) and other males in the family might bear lesser titles. Lesser aristocratic status was

typically shown by the aristocratic particule within a family name; this was usually the word *of* (*de* in French, *di* in Italian, *von* in German). Pretenders sometimes tried to copy this habit, but the nobility zealously guarded its privileged status. In Venice, a Golden Book recorded the names of the nobility; in the German states, an annual publication (the *Almanac of Gotha*) kept watch on aristocratic pedigrees.

The aristocracy was a small class, but it was not homogeneous. Gradations of status depended upon the length of time that a family had been noble, the means by which it had acquired its title, and the wealth and political influence that the family held. One of the distinctions frequently made in western Europe separated a "nobility of the sword" composed of families ennobled for centuries as a result of military service to the monarch from a "nobility of the robe" composed of families more recently ennobled through service to the government. In central and eastern Europe, important distinctions rested upon the number of serfs an aristocrat owned. The aristocracy might include an elite of less land and wealth, known as the gentry, although in some countries, such as Britain, the landowning gentry did not possess aristocratic titles. While the gentry enjoyed a comfortable existence, it was far removed from the wealth of great nobles (see table 18.4).

The highest nobles often emphasized the length of time their family had been noble. Most aristocratic families of the Old Regime had received their titles within the previous century or two, but an "ancient nobility" of families titled for five to ten centuries considered themselves the peers (or superiors) of the royal family. The high aristocracy stressed its historic nobility by numbering its titles. British history provides a good example. The leading figure in early eighteenth-century English politics, Sir Robert Walpole, was not born to a noble title. Walpole's adroit political career made him the first British prime minister and the architect of the preeminence of the House of Commons over the House of Lords. For such accomplishments (and for his support of the Hanoverian monarchy), he was ennobled as the first earl of Orford in 1742. One of Walpole's leading opponents, however, could stress the importance of ancient lineage: He was the fourth duke and eighth earl of Bedford, heir to a pedigree nearly three hundred years old and a title that originated with the third son of King Henry IV, born in 1389. Thus, the earl of Bedford was unlikely to consider the earl of Orford his equal. And both of them yielded precedence to the earl of Norfolk, whose title dated back to the year 1070, shortly after the Norman conquest of England.

▶ TABLE 18.4 ◀

The Finances of a Great Noble in the Eighteenth Century

This table has excerpts from the financial records of a French noble family, the counts and countesses of Tavannes. The unit of measure is the livre, which had approximately the same value as an English shilling (one-twentieth of the pound sterling). Figures are given for mixed years because only partial records have survived.

Income or expenses	Amount
Income from land owned by the count	
Rent for lands in region #1 (annual average, 1696–1730)	5,000+
Rent for lands in region #2 (annual average, 1699–1726)	3,500+
Rent for lands in region #3 (annual average, 1698–1723)	8,700+
Income from sale of wood from forest in region #3 (1788)	40,000+
Gross revenue from all land (after paying upkeep and wages) in 1788	86,269
Income from pensions given by the king	
Total pensions for 1754	46,900
Pension as commander of royal forces in Burgundy	26,250
Income from seigneurial dues (obligations paid by peasants)	
Total dues paid in 1788	26,986
Income from the inheritance of the countess (1725)	
Income from four houses in Paris (value = 200,000)	10,000
Income from investments (value = 367,938)	8,698
Total capital inherited in 1725	803,924
Wages paid to the count,s staff (1780–86)	
Annual wages for the count's agent in Paris	800
Annual wages for a forest warden in Burgundy	200
Annual wages for a gardener or a maid in Burgundy	70
Annual wages for a chef in Paris	945
Annual wages for a coachman in Paris	720
Personal expenses	
Total personal expenses in 1788	62,000
Expenses for clothing, jewelry, and gifts in 1788	20,000
Expenses for the theater in 1788	2,000
Monthly expenses for Roquefort cheese (January 1784)	32
Monthly expenses for cognac (January 1784)	30
Monthly expenses for cayenne coffee (January 1784)	30

Source: Data from Robert Forster, *The House of Saulx-Tavannes: Versailles and Burgundy, 1700–1830* (Baltimore, Md.: Johns Hopkins University Press, 1971), passim.

The Old Regime also stressed the route by which nobility had been achieved. The highest status (and usually the greatest wealth) belonged to nobles who had earned their titles as military and political honors. Many forms of service to the state earned ennoblement, however. Some offices, such as presiding over a provincial parlement (law court) in France, automatically car-

ried a title. Thus, each generation produced new nobles from families previously headed by lawyers or bankers. This new nobility of the robe was often vigorous and ambitious, and it earned great royal preferment. Another route to ennoblement was economic. Monarchs faced financial problems during the Old Regime, and they often thanked the bankers who saved them with a

Illustration 18.4

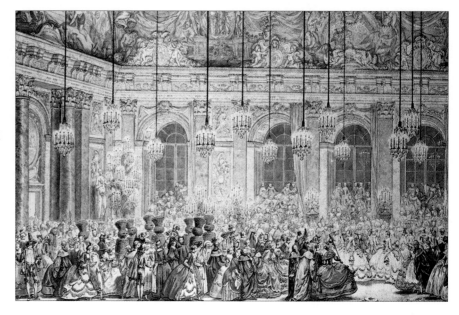

An Aristocratic Ball. Gala events, such as this "Ball of the Clipped Yew Trees," were a common feature of daily life for the court aristocracy of mid-eighteenth-century France. This contemporary engraving manages to depict both the pleasures of that social class and the opulence of building, ornament, and dress that others might notice.

title. Thus, a family of English cloth merchants, the Barings, set up a bank in the eighteenth century and soon acquired a minor peerage. The founder's son became a baron, and two of his grandsons became earls, but the earls of Bedford and Norfolk did not consider the banking earls to be their peers. Worse yet (in the eyes of the old aristocracy) were venal titles: Desperate monarchs might sell a title of nobility to a merchant or financier. Because ennoblement was a royal decision, the route to a title could be companionship in the gaming room or the bedchamber, and more than one noble family owed its title to great-grandmother's affectionate nature.

Many of the fine distinctions within the aristocracy were simply matters of pride within a caste that paid excruciating attention to comparative status. The aristocratic competition for precedence, however, involved real issues of power and wealth. Only the top 5 percent (perhaps less) of the aristocracy could hope to be presented at court and meet the royal family; fewer still were invited to live at the royal court, hunting with King Louis XV of France in the royal forests, sharing the evening tabagerie (a smoking and drinking session) with King Frederick William I of Prussia, or enjoying the life of lavish dinners and balls (see illustration 18.4). Yet a position at court was often the route to political office, military command, or perhaps a pension providing a lifetime income. Most provincial nobles lacked the opportunities for such advancement.

The provincial aristocracy, living on inherited lands in the rural world, encompassed a great range of social and economic conditions. The Spanish, for example,

distinguished between grandees (a term for the greatest nobles, such as the dukes of Alba) who possessed immense estates and national influence, locally important aristocrats (called *caballeros*) who owned enough land to live as a privileged elite, and a comparatively poor gentry (called *hidalgos*) who were said to have more titles than shirts. Such distinctions existed across Europe. In the east, a few families of grand seigneurs owned most of the land (and the serfs on it) while thousands of aristocrats owned little or nothing. The Polish aristocracy, known collectively as the *szlachta,* included 700,000 to one million people, but only thirty to forty magnate families possessed the wealth and power normally associated with the nobility. Part of the *szlachta* worked on the estates of great nobles as bailiffs, stewards, or tenant farmers; most of this caste lived as small farmers on rented land, and many were so poor that they were known as the *golota,* a barefoot aristocracy. Similarly, the landowning aristocracy of Russia (the *dvoriane*) included noble lords owning more than a thousand souls (as serfs were often called) and a comfortable gentry owning hundreds of serfs, but the majority were relatively poor and owned few serfs (see table 18.5).

Landownership further illustrates the complexity of generalizing about the aristocracy as if it were a homogeneous group. Ownership of significant amounts of land usually identified an aristocrat, and in many countries, only an aristocrat could own land. In some countries, the purchase of a noble's land included the privileges attached to it or even the title. However, some countries (particularly in western Europe) already had a class of successful landowning farmers without

⬧ TABLE 18.5 ⬧

Variations within the Russian Aristocracy in 1774

Category	Serfs owned	Percentage of aristocracy
Grand seigneur	More than 1,000	a
Gentry	101–1,000	
Impoverished	21–100	25
Poor aristocracy	Fewer than 20	59

aCombined total for grand seigneur and gentry = 16.

Source: Data from Richard Pipes, *Russia under the Old Regime* (New York, N.Y.: Penguin, 1974), p. 178.

aristocratic titles. In England, the landowning gentry were technically not aristocrats, but in other countries they held the same social, economic, and political position as the lesser nobility did. In France, wealthy landowning peasants exercised great influence in their communities and were considered local notables, although they did not share the legal privileges of the aristocracy.

The Privileged Status of the Aristocracy

The wealth and power of the high nobility present one of the most vivid images of the corporative society of the Old Regime. Some aristocrats enjoyed dizzying wealth and a life of luxury. In the Austrian Netherlands (now Belgium), the duke of Arenberg had an annual income eighteen times the income of the richest merchant. In Poland, Prince Radziwill kept ten thousand retainers in his service. In England, the top four hundred noble families each owned estates of ten thousand to fifty thousand acres. In Russia, Empress Catherine the Great gave one of her discarded lovers a gift of thirty-seven thousand serfs, and Prince Menshikov owned 100,000 serfs. In Bohemia, one hundred noble families owned one-third of the entire province, and the poorer members of this group owned land encompassing thirty villages. In Spain, the count of Altamira owned the commercial city of Valencia.

Such wealth produced breathtaking inequality. The count of Tavannes in France paid a gardener or a maid on his provincial estates seventy livres per year, and the valued chef at his Paris residence earned 945 livres per year; yet the count lavished twenty thousand livres on clothing and jewelry (see table 18.4). The count's

monthly expenditure on coffee and cognac totaled nearly a year's wages for a servant, and his budget for theater tickets would have cost the total yearly earnings of twenty-eight servants. Sustaining a life of such extreme luxury led many lesser nobles into ruinous debt. Extravagance and debt became so typical of the nobility (including royalty) in the eighteenth century that some countries, such as Spain, made arresting aristocrats for their debts illegal.

In addition to enormous wealth, nobles held great power. They dominated offices of the state, both in the government and in the military. In some countries, notably Sweden, Prussia, and Russia, the concept of aristocratic service to the throne had led to an arrangement in which the aristocracy accepted compulsory state service and received in return a legal monopoly over certain positions. The eighteenth-century Russian Charter of the Nobility, for example, stated: "The title and privileges of the nobility . . . are acquired by service and work useful to the Empire." Therefore, it continued, whenever the emperor "needs the service of the nobility for the general well being, every nobleman is then obligated . . . to perform fully his duty." In return for this compulsory service, the Charter of the Nobility recognized the right of nobles to buy and sell villages, excluded nobles from some taxes that fell on commoners, gave nobles a monopoly of some positions, and spared nobles some of the punishments (such as flogging) specified in Russian law. Even in countries where state service was not compulsory, the aristocracy monopolized many positions. In much of Europe, only aristocrats could become army officers. Nobles universally dominated the highest positions in government. At the beginning of the eighteenth century, the chief minister of the king of France was a marquis, the prime minister of the king of Prussia was a count, the head of the state council of the Hapsburg Empire was a count, the chief minister of the tsar of Russia was a prince, and the chief adviser to the king of Spain was a cardinal. For the century before the French Revolution of 1789, the chief ministers of the kings of France were (in order): a marquis, a cardinal, a duke, a duke, a cardinal, a marquis, a count, a minor aristocrat, a duke, a duke, and a count. Every chancellor of the Hapsburg Empire during that same period was a count. Commoners in such offices were rare, and they were usually ennobled for their service; they might enter office a commoner and leave an earl.

In addition to personal wealth and powerful offices, aristocrats of the Old Regime usually held a privileged position in the law, exceptional rights on their landed

Illustration 18.5

The Corvée. The highway system of eighteenth-century Europe required a great deal of labor to maintain it. In most of central and eastern Europe, where serfdom survived, monarchs expected great landowners to require roadwork as part of the ro-

bot owed by serfs. In France, where serfdom had largely disappeared, peasants were required to pay a tax, called the *corvée*, by their labor, like the roadwork shown here.

estates, and great power over the people who lived on their land. In most countries, nobles were governed by substantially different laws than the rest of the population. Some countries had a separate legal code for aristocrats, some had legal charters detailing noble privileges, some simply adopted laws granting special treatment. Legal privileges took many forms. Exemption from the laws that applied to commoners was one of the most cherished. Aristocrats were often exempted from most taxes that fell on peasants or town dwellers, and they tenaciously defended their exemptions even as the monarchy faced bankruptcy. In Hungary, the Magyar nobles were free from all direct taxes such as those on land or income; they guarded this privilege by giving regular contributions to the throne, but nobles controlled the process and the amount themselves. Legal exemptions took many forms, such as the exclusion of Spanish nobles from arrest for indebtedness. Aristocrats were exempt from the *corvée*, a labor tax by which peasants were obliged to maintain roads and bridges (see illustration 18.5). Penal codes usually exempted

nobles from the corporal punishment common in eighteenth-century justice, such as flogging and branding.

Aristocratic privilege varied significantly from country to country. In Britain and the Netherlands, most exemptions were abolished by revolutions in the seventeenth century. Both countries made aristocrats and commoners equal before the law and allowed neither tax exemptions nor a monopoly on offices. Yet important privileges persisted there, too. English nobles held hereditary control of the upper house of Parliament, the House of Lords, and the right to be tried only by a jury of their peers.

The core of aristocratic privilege was found on their provincial estates. An aristocrat, as lord of the manor, held traditional manorial rights over the land and its inhabitants. These rights are also known as feudal rights, because many had survived from the feudal system of the Middle Ages, or seigneurial rights, because the lord of the manor was known as the seigneur. Manorial rights increased significantly as one passed from western Europe to eastern Europe, where peasants remained in the virtual slavery of serfdom. But even in regions where serfdom no longer existed, aristocratic landowners were often entitled to feudal dues (payments in money or in kind), to unpaid labor by peasants in the seigneurial fields, or to both. Thus, peasants might be expected to harvest an aristocrat's crops before they could harvest their own and then to pay a percentage of their own crops to the same aristocrat. The aristocracy enjoyed many other privileges at the expense of the peasantry. Many nobles were entitled to hunt through any fields, whatever the damage to peasant crops. Some still enjoyed a medieval right called the *jus prima noctae;* it permitted a noble to spend the wedding night with a peasant's bride.

Seigneurial rights in many countries (particularly in central and eastern Europe) also included the powers of local governance. The seigneur provided, or oversaw, the functions of the police, the judiciary, and civil government on his lands; a noble might thereby preside over the arrest, trial, and punishment of a peasant. Many aristocrats thus governed their provincial estates as self-sufficient, miniature kingdoms. A study of the Old Regime manors of Bohemia shows this vividly. Only the noble landowner was legally a citizen of the larger state (the Austrian Empire). The residents of the noble's villages and farmlands were completely under his jurisdiction. Peasants farmed their fields for him. He conscripted them for the *corvée,* selected them for service in the Austrian army, and collected their taxes for the Hapsburg government. The same lord arrested draft evaders or tax delinquents and punished them, and peasants could not appeal his justice. Peasant revolts typically resulted in laws that strengthened aristocratic control.

Variations within the Peasantry: Serfdom

The majority of Europeans during the Old Regime were peasant farmers, but this peasantry, like the aristocracy, was not a homogeneous class. The foremost difference distinguished free peasants from those legally bound by virtual slavery. Outright slavery no longer existed in most of Europe by 1700, although European governments allowed slavery in their overseas colonies. Portugal (the only country to import African slaves into Europe), the Ottoman Empire, and the Danubian provinces of Moldavia and Wallachia (where 200,000 gypsies were enslaved) were exceptions.

Multitudes of European peasants still lived in the virtual slavery known as serfdom, a medieval institution that had survived into the Old Regime (and would last

into the nineteenth century in parts of Europe). Serfdom was not slavery, but it resembled slavery in several ways. Serfs could not own land. They were bound to the soil, meaning that they could not choose to migrate from the land they farmed. In addition, serfs might be sold or given away, or gambled away. Entire villages could be abolished and relocated. Serfs might be subjected to corporal punishment such as flogging. One Russian count ordered the whipping of all serfs who did not attend church, and the penalty for missing Easter Communion was five thousand lashes. A Russian decree of 1767 summarized this situation simply: Serfs "owe their landlords proper submission and absolute obedience in all matters."

The distinction between serfdom and slavery was noteworthy. Unlike slaves, serfs were not chattel property (property other than real estate). Serfs were rarely sold without including the land that they farmed or without their families. Serfs enjoyed a few traditional legal rights. They could make a legal appeal to a village council or a seigneurial court. They could not press charges or give evidence against nobles or their bailiffs, so their legal rights protected them within the peasant community but not against their lords.

Serfdom survived in some portions of western Europe and became more common as one traveled east. East of the Elbe River, serfdom was the dominant social institution. In parts of France and the western German states, vestigial serfdom still restricted hundreds of thousands of people. In Prussia and Poland, approximately 20 percent of the peasants were free and 80 percent serfs. In Hungary, only 2 percent of the peasants were free; in Denmark and in the Slavic provinces of the Austrian Empire (Bohemia and Silesia), perhaps 1 percent; in Russia, less than 1 percent.

Variations did exist within serfdom. In Russia, a peasant family typically belonged to a noble landowner, but 40 percent of the serfs were state serfs farming the imperial domains. These state serfs had been created by Peter the Great when he seized lands belonging to the Russian Orthodox Church. Those who labored for the nobility experienced conditions as diverse as did their seigneurs; more than 30 percent of landowners held small farms with fewer than ten serfs, while 16 percent of the Russian nobility owned estates large enough to encompass an entire village of one hundred or more serfs. The great nobility possessed so many souls that many served as house serfs, domestic servants whose life differed significantly from their counterparts who labored in the fields.

◆ DOCUMENT 18.2 ◆

A Traveler Observes the Life of Russian Serfs

One of the difficulties facing social historians is that the surviving records of the past were (by definition) written by literate, educated people. The illiterate masses could not record the conditions of their lives for posterity. Historians must therefore rely on the indirect evidence provided by observers (and their deductions from other sources). Alexander Radishchev (1749–1802) was a Russian writer who opposed serfdom and wrote about it, resulting in his exile to Siberia. The following excerpt is Radishchev's description of his meeting with a serf, as published in his A Voyage from St. Petersburg to Moscow (1790).

The corduroy road tortured my body; I climbed out of the carriage and (walked). A few steps from the road I saw a peasant ploughing a field. The weather was hot. . . . It was now Sunday. . . . The peasant was ploughing very carefully. The field, of course, was not part of his master's land. He turned the plow with astonishing ease.

"God help you," I said, walking up to the ploughman. . . .

"Thank you sir," the ploughman said to me, shaking the earth off the ploughshare. . . .

"You must be a Dissenter, since you plough on a Sunday."

"No, sir, I make the true sign of the cross," he said, showing me the three fingers together. "And God is merciful and does not bid us starve to death, so long as we have strength and a family."

"Have you no time to work during the week, then, and can you not have any rest on Sundays, in the hottest part of the day, at that?"

"In a week, sir, there are six days, and we go six times a week to work on the master's fields; in the evening, if the weather is good, we haul to the master's house the hay that is left in the woods. . . . God grant that it rains this evening. If you have peasants of your own, sir, they are praying to God for the same thing."

". . . But how do you manage to get food enough, if you have only the holidays free?"

"Not only the holidays: the nights are ours, too. If a fellow isn't lazy, he won't starve to death."

The basic legal obligation of serfs was compulsory, unpaid labor in the fields of landowners. This obligatory labor, called *robot* in much of central and eastern Europe, was defined by law but varied significantly from region to region. In Prussia, for example, serfs owed the Junker aristocrats two or three days of unpaid labor every week and more during the harvest. Junkers, however, needed more labor than their serfs provided and therefore hired some free peasants. The feudal labor laws of Bohemia specified three days per week of *robot*, plus harvest labor "at the will" of a noble. A law of 1775 defined a day of labor as eight hours during the winter, twelve hours during the spring and summer, and fourteen hours during the harvest. Russian serfs commonly worked six days per week for a landowner (see document 18.2). In some regions, however, a different system applied: Serfs farmed an allotment of land and gave the landowners a large percentage of the harvest.

A study of the serfs in the Baltic provinces of Russia reveals how these obligations added up. A family of eight able-bodied peasants (including women) owed their master the following: two field workers for three days per week, every week of the year; ten to twelve days of miscellaneous labor such as livestock herding; four trips, totaling about fifty-six days of labor, carting goods for the seigneur; forty-two days of postal-relay services; and twenty-four days of spinning flax. In addition to such labor, European peasant families owed feudal payments in kind, such as grain, sheep, wool, chickens, and eggs. Even then they could not keep their remaining production. They had to guard 20 percent to 25 percent of a harvest as seed for the following year. Peasants also usually owed a compulsory tithe to an established church—approximately 10 percent of a harvest—and taxes to the government, which frequently took between 30 percent and 40 percent of the crop. Consequently, a family of serfs was fortunate if it could retain much more than 25 percent of their harvest. Studies have found that serfs owed 73 percent of their produce in Bohemia, 75 percent in eastern France, 83 percent in Silesia, and 86 percent in parts of Galicia. Such figures changed from year to year, but the burden remained crushing. The trend during the Old Regime saw such burdens decline in western Europe but become more severe in the east. Serfdom became harsher in Prussia and Russia when the monarch required state

Illustration 18.6

The Home of a Successful Peasant Family. Eighteenth-century peasant homes often had only one room, which was used for all purposes, including housing animals. This Breton family from a village near Morbihan possessed considerable wealth in its horses, cattle, and pigs. Note the limited furnishings and the absence of windows.

service by the aristocracy and granted the nobles reciprocal claims upon their serfs.

Serfdom was not unchallenged. Peasant rebellions occurred during the Old Regime (see chapter 20). Another type of protest came from the educated classes. One Russian author, Alexander Radishchev, opposed serfdom so vigorously that he was exiled to Siberia. Johann Justi (1702–71), a lawyer and professor in Austria, gave one of the best articulated arguments against serfdom in *Foundations of the Power and Happiness of States* (1760). Justi argued that serfdom "could only have arisen in the most barbarous times" and that "sensible times cannot perpetuate it without disgrace." Many countries considered the abolition of serfdom. King Frederick IV of Denmark attempted to abolish it in 1702, but his efforts were ineffective because he had to compromise with the nobility, as would other reformist rulers. Denmark did not abolish serfdom until 1787, when the king received the support of the Reventlow Commission for this decision. Savoy ended serfdom in 1771 and Baden did so in 1783. The revolutionary age led to the end of serfdom in many other regions, but parts of eastern Europe saw serfdom survive into the second half of the nineteenth century. Russia abolished it in 1861, and the last state to have legal serfdom was Romania (the Danubian provinces), where it lasted until 1864.

Variations within the Peasantry: Free Peasants

The free peasants of western and central Europe had been escaping from the burdens of serfdom since the

fourteenth century. The evolution of a money economy reduced the importance of feudal services by enabling some peasants to commute *robot* or *corvée* with cash. Princes had strengthened their governments by challenging aristocratic prerogatives, and royal courts had, at times, favored peasants when they sued their lords over the collection of additional rents and taxes. To increase revenues from import and export tariffs, some governments had also encouraged a shift to livestock production by allowing aristocrats to enclose their own, and sometimes their tenants', lands. As a result, the capitalization of land was far advanced in the west by 1700, though most families still owed at least some feudal obligations to the landowning aristocracy. Whereas eastern serfs were fortunate to keep 25 percent of their harvest, free peasants could expect to keep more than half. Two different studies of Old Regime France have found that peasants owed between 33 percent and 40 percent of their total production in feudal dues, taxes, and tithes.

The condition of free peasants varied greatly according to the forms of land tenure. The most prosperous peasants were landowners themselves. The studies of the French free peasantry found that nearly four million peasants owned some land and their own home (see illustration 18.6) in the eighteenth century, though most families owned so little land that they could not afford to market any of their harvest. Although most free peasants were landless, one group of them found relatively comfortable lives. The most successful of the landless French peasants were usually tenant farmers, about 10 percent to 20 percent of the landless population. Tenant farmers rented land, typically for a long term—such as nine years—for a fixed money payment, and they then made the best profit that they could after paying the rent. Such long-term contracts protected peasant families from eviction after a single bad harvest, and many aristocrats discovered the advantages of short-term contracts, which were typical in Spain. Other tenant farmers managed the rented lands but did not labor in the fields themselves, or they became wealthy by trading in grain or other commodities.

The other 80 percent to 90 percent of landless peasants were not as fortunate as the tenant farmers. The most secure group were usually sharecroppers, often called *métayers*. They produced most of the grain marketed in France by farming the estates of great landowners under contracts negotiated as free peasants. The sharecropping contract (see document 18.1) typically provided leased land in return for a large share of its yield. Sharecropping contracts provided these peasant families with the means of survival, but little more. Below the sharecroppers was a lower class of agricultural laborers. Some worked for wages, others, called cotters in many countries, worked for the use of a cottage. Some found only seasonal employment (working to harvest grapes in the autumn, for example), in some cases living as migrant laborers, traveling with the changing harvests. Thus, the peasantry included a range of conditions that saw some peasants employed as laborers (or even domestic servants) by other peasants. Most villages held one or two rich peasant families and several who were well-to-do. The percentage of the landless and cotters varied greatly from region to region. In Saxony, it was 38 percent; in Baden, 45 percent. Although emancipated from most feudal obligations, the free peasantry was subject to other financial burdens. The landless poor suffered the most. Military conscription—known colloquially as the blood tax—often took young men for extremely long periods of time. Forced service of ten or twenty years was not unusual in the eighteenth century.

The Urban Population of the Old Regime

Urban Europe in the eighteenth century ranged from rural market towns of two thousand people to great administrative and commercial capital cities of 500,000. Important regional towns—such as Heidelberg, Helsinki, and Liverpool—often had populations below ten thousand. A population of 100,000 constituted a great city, and only a few capital cities reached that level in the early eighteenth century (see table 18.6 and

◣ TABLE 18.6 ◢
The Great Cities of Europe in 1700

Table shows all European cities with a population of 70,000 or more in 1700

City	Population
Constantinople	700,000
London	575,000
Paris	500,000
Naples	300,000
Amsterdam	200,000
Lisbon	180,000
Madrid	140,000
Venice	138,000
Rome	135,000
Moscow	130,000
Milan	125,000
Vienna	114,000
Palermo	100,000
Lyons	97,000
Marseilles	90,000
Brussels	80,000
Florence	72,000
Seville	72,000
Granada	70,000
Hamburg	70,000

map 18.2). Berlin had fifty-five thousand people in 1700. St. Petersburg reached sixty-eight thousand in 1730. Buda and Pest were then separate towns with a combined total of seventeen thousand people. Many cities, such as Geneva, with a population of twenty-eight thousand in 1750, were so small that residents could easily walk their full width for an evening stroll.

The largest city in Europe sat on its southeastern edge: Constantinople (now Istanbul), the ancient capital of the Ottoman Empire, had an estimated 700,000 persons. The two dominant cities in the development of modern European civilization, London and Paris, both exceeded 500,000 people, but no other cities rivaled them. Rome was smaller than it had been under the Caesars, with a population of 135,000 in 1700. Such large cities were the centers of western civilization, but they did not yet make it an urban civilization. If one defines *urban* as beginning at a population of ten thousand people, Europe was only 9.4 percent urban at the end of the eighteenth century; if the definition goes

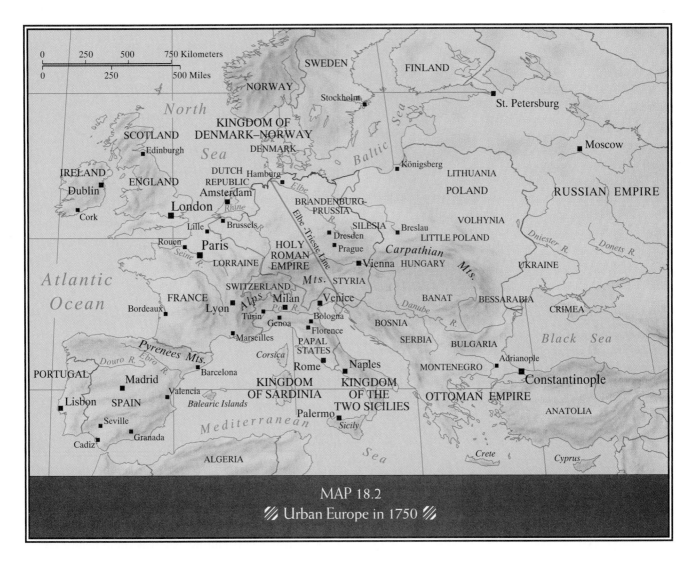

MAP 18.2

Urban Europe in 1750

down to towns of five thousand people, Europe was 12.1 percent urban. Even if one counts small farming towns of two thousand people (which were different from manufacturing and commercial towns), Europe was still less than one-fourth urban, although some regions were one-third urban.

In legal terms, cities and towns of the Old Regime were corporate entities (hence the terms *incorporated* and *unincorporated* for towns). Towns held legal charters, often centuries old, from the government. Charters specified the rights of town dwellers—collectively called the bourgeoisie (from the French term *bourg*, for town) or burghers (from the similar German term)—rights that the rural population did not enjoy. As in the Middle Ages, the old German saying held true: "City air makes one free." The urban population thus formed a clearly defined estate, lacking many of the privileges of the aristocracy but freed from the obligations upon the peasantry. Hence, they came to be seen as a "middle" class. As a group, they possessed significant nonlanded

wealth although they did not rival the wealth of landed nobles. Studies of wills probated during the Old Regime have shown that nobles possessed more than two-thirds of the wealth. A study of England in the 1740s has shown that the landowning aristocracy and upper gentry (a total of less than 3 percent of population) owned 95 percent of the national wealth.

Many countries, particularly those east of the Elbe-Trieste line, prohibited peasants from migrating to the towns and obtaining urban freedoms. Bavarian law, Austrian law, and the Prussian legal code, for example, all bound German peasants to stay on the soil. Even in western Europe, some town charters restricted residence and citizenship, usually to people who showed a means of support. Cities needed migration, however. Conditions were generally so unhealthy that the death rate exceeded the birthrate. Cities could only maintain their size or grow by attracting rural immigrants. Thus, restrictions on population mobility began to disappear during the Old Regime. London grew rapidly in the

Illustration 18.7

⧚ **Feeding a Great City.** Cities such as London and Paris, with populations of more than 500,000, were dependent upon food transported from the countryside. To handle the difficult logistics of food distribution, cities created large food markets in the center of town, such as Les Halles in Paris or Covent Garden in London, depicted in this eighteenth-century painting by Balthasar Nebot, *Covent Garden with Saint Paul's Church.*

TABLE 18.7

Manufacturing in Eighteenth-Century England

These figures indicate the range and relative importance of English manufactures in 1770. They are expressed as a percentage of the total manufacturing output.

Product	Percentage
Textiles	28
Wool	15
Linen	8
Silk	4
Cotton	1
Leather	19
Building	12
Clothing	11
Food and drink	8
Metal	5
Mining	5
Paper and printing	1

Source: Data from Myron P. Gutman, *Toward the Modern Economy: Early Industry in Europe, 1500–1800* (New York, N.Y.: Knopf, 1988), pp. 120–21.

eighteenth century, yet recorded more deaths than births in every year of the century until 1790; in 1741, burials outnumbered baptisms by two to one.

The Social and Economic Structure of Urban Europe

The towns of the eighteenth century varied in their function as well as their size. Capital cities formed a special category of large cities where government and finance were centered, and the population was so huge that it was a challenge just to feed them (see illustration 18.7). The next range of major cities were usually manufacturing centers (such as Lyons and Granada) or great port-cities (such as Marseilles, Hamburg, and Liverpool). Important regional towns similarly varied, as centers of administration (both governmental and religious) and manufacturing. European towns were not yet characterized by the heavy industry or mass production associated with modern urban life (see table 18.7). Economic historians have estimated that in 1750 Britain had attained only 10 percent of the industrialization that it would reach by 1900; France, the Italian states, and the German states were only at 7 percent to

9 percent. Manufacturing in the eighteenth century chiefly meant textiles. Combined textile manufacturing (wool, cotton, linen, and silk) accounted for 28 percent of all British manufacturing, whereas combined heavy industries (mining, metalworking, and construction) accounted for only 22 percent. Textiles similarly provided the traditional basis of urban prosperity in many regions of continental Europe, such as northeastern France, Flanders, and the city-states of northern Italy.

The occupational structure of towns varied with the town's function. A study of Bayeux, a provincial administrative town in Normandy, found a working adult male population of twelve hundred. Their employment shows how an administrative town was different from the image of towns as manufacturing centers. Slightly more than 10 percent of the men of Bayeux were in the educated professions, mostly lawyers and officials or people trained in medical arts—physicians, surgeons, and apothecaries. An additional 1 percent were tax collectors (an independent occupation) for the monarch or the regional nobility. The prosperous great merchants (not shopkeepers) who traded in regional agricultural or manufactured goods constituted nearly 3 percent of the male population. At the opposite end of Bayeux's social spectrum, 10 percent of the population were urban laborers—a low number that shows that this was not a manufacturing town. Between the two extremes, approximately 75 percent of the male population were engaged in trades. Most of them worked in the production or distribution of food (grocers, butchers, and bakers), clothing (tailors, cobblers, and wig makers), and housing (hoteliers and innkeepers or the building trades). The remainder of the population practiced other trades characteristic of urban life: coopers, goldsmiths, clock makers, saddlers, cabinetmakers, drapers, dozens of other crafts whose practitioners were called artisans.

At the pinnacle of the urban social structure sat the wealthy patrician class of the big cities and great manufacturing towns—a bourgeoisie of banking and finance, of manufacturing and commerce (see illustration 18.8). This urban oligarchy lacked the hereditary titles and privileges of the aristocracy. They were not yet as wealthy as nobles, and they held much less political power. But many families possessed enough wealth to live nobly and aspired to aristocratic status. A few members of this urban elite might enter the aristocracy through state service, and some families married into the aristocracy by providing lavish dowries to daughters who married nobles in debt. This wealthy class lived handsomely, but they represented only a small percentage of urban population, just as aristocrats did in the rural world.

The typical town dweller in the Old Regime was an artisan, and the dominant feature of an artisan's life was the guild—yet another corporation (see illustration 18.9). Guilds had developed in Europe in the late Middle Ages (between the twelfth and fifteenth centuries) for the purpose of organizing craft production. They received statutes or charters specifying their rights from the monarch, making them corporations like the towns

themselves. Guild charters were still being reaffirmed by monarchs in the late eighteenth century, as the king of Saxony did in 1780. These corporate charters gave the guilds monopolistic control of manufacturing in

Illustration 18.8

▨ **The Rising Middle Class.** The wealthy middle class of businessmen, merchants, manufacturers, and bankers became increasingly influential in the eighteenth century despite being largely excluded from aristocratic circles and institutions. In this painting a prosperous British merchant flaunts his wealth: his docks and warehouses outside the window, his country estate in the painting, his gold on the table, and his richly dressed family.

Illustration 18.9

▨ **Guild Labor in the Towns.** The larger towns of Europe were centers of skilled artisanal labor such as the German metalworkers depicted in this engraving. The master of such a shop would typically employ one or more journeymen; train children as apprentices in the trade; and entrust the business side of the shop to his wife, who oversaw sales and kept the records.

their respective trades. Thus, only a member of the coopers' guild could make barrels. Such monopolies extended to all manufacturing for sale or for exchange, but not for home use, and this naturally caused some tension between urban guilds and rural domestic manufacturing. The men of an urban tailors' guild, for example, could fight against the sale of any goods produced by women who worked as seamstresses in the surrounding countryside. Guilds used their charters and elaborate sets of rules to regulate all aspects of a trade. They restricted access to, or training in, each occupation; defined the standards of acceptable quality in goods offered for sale; and regulated the right to sell goods. Limiting the number of guild members in a town checked competition. Such practices were stoutly defended by guild members as guarantees of high quality and the ready availability of goods; others saw them as impediments to competition and innovation.

Membership in a guild involved three stages of development: apprenticeship, when one learned the basic skills of a trade; journeyman, when one developed these skills as a paid employee; and master of a craft, when one obtained the full privilege of practicing it, including the right to train apprentices and hire journeymen. Children became apprentices, learning a trade from a master, at an early age (see document 18.3). A study of the guilds of Venice, for example, shows that apprentice goldsmiths began at age seven, weavers at twelve; by age eighteen, one was too old to apprentice in most crafts. A child had to meet many requirements of the guild (such as proof of legitimate birth or practice of Christianity) and pay fees to both the guild and the master before becoming an apprentice. Many people were thus automatically excluded from becoming guild members—perhaps because they were too poor, perhaps because they were Jewish. The children of masters had additional advantages. Guild regulations usually required masters to accept the children of other guild members as apprentices, to house them in their homes, and to provide them with adequate training and experience in a trade. Apprentices, in turn, were obliged to serve their masters for a fixed period of years (typically three or four, but often more) without pay. Upon the completion of their training, apprentices became journeymen and were expected to leave the town of their training and journey to work for wages with masters in other towns. The journeyman carried papers identifying him and his experience, signed by each of the masters for whom he had worked. Only after several years of such travels could a craftsman hope for acceptance as the master of a trade.

◆ DOCUMENT 18.3 ◆

A Contract of Apprenticeship in the Gunsmithing Trade, 1704

Contracts of apprenticeship could be negotiated through the appropriate guild or with a master craftsman. The following contract, from a small town in south central France, was negotiated by the widow of a craftsman (a master glove maker) to apprentice her son to a master in another craft (gunsmithing).

Were present Antoinette Faugeyron, widow of Jean Haste, master glovemaker, who of her own free will has apprenticed her son, Jean Haste, present here, to Claude Serre, gunsmith of this town, also present here, who accepts him in order to teach him well and conscientiously, as much as is in his power, the art of gunsmithing, which consists in the filing and forging of gunplates. (Serre) promises to teach him the secrets necessary to that effect. The said apprenticeship has been contracted for two years, beginning today and to be finished on the same day at the end of the said two years, during which time the said Serre shall feed and lodge the said apprentice and furnish him all the tools necessary to the said trade, and the said Faugeyron shall furnish his clothes and do his laundry, and all the work done by the said apprentice during the said time shall belong to the said Serre. The said apprentice shall not leave without a legitimate excuse, in which case the said Serre can take another (apprentice) at the expense of the said Faugeyron; conversely, the said Serre cannot dismiss the said apprentice without a legitimate excuse, and in this case the latter can learn another trade at the expense of the said Serre. Also, the present apprenticeship has been contracted at the price of thirty livres, half to be paid in cash now and half after the end of one year (by the widow Haste).

Master craftsmen were important figures in a town. They controlled the guilds and therefore most of the occupations. They determined the quality and the supply of manufactured goods, and they regulated job training and employment in the trades. The shops of these master craftsmen, however, operated in a manner similar to the family economy of peasants. Masters

Illustration 18.10

/// **Domestic Servants.** Most of the aristocracy and much of the middle class enjoyed comfortable daily lives through the work of domestic servants. Elaborate clothing and luxurious homes were impossible without servants. The kitchens of the well-to-do were filled with servants such as "The Kitchen Maid" in Jean-Baptiste Chardin's painting here. However, many urban and rural workers eagerly sought the greater comforts of life in service.

domestic service was already becoming one of the largest sources of employment for the unskilled. Studies have found that 7 percent of the population of Ypres (Belgium), 15 percent of Münster (western Germany), and 20 percent of London were working as domestic servants. They lacked the independence and economic prospects of artisans, but they escaped from the poverty of unskilled labor while finding some comfort and security in the homes of their employers. For unmarried women, domestic service was often the only respectable employment available.

National Economies: The Doctrine of Mercantilism

Economics is an ancient word whose derivation goes back to Aristotle's *Oikonomia*, but economics as a field of study and theory is a recent development. In the eighteenth century, the word was used in a limited sense—it essentially meant household management. Economics dealt with the value of commodities used in the home (their "use-value") rather than in commerce ("exchange-value"). Thus, economics was not studied by scholars or government experts. Economics in the modern sense formed a small part of the study called moral philosophy. The first university professorship in political economy was created at the University of Naples in 1754, and the field of political economy (the precursor of modern economics) chiefly prospered in Scotland under the leadership of theorists such as Adam Smith, the most important founder of modern capitalism.

Despite the limited study of political economics in the Old Regime, governments followed a well-developed economic philosophy known as the mercantile system. The doctrine of mercantilism did not stress the predominant feature of the economy of the Old Regime (agriculture) or the greatest form of wealth of that world (land). Instead, the mercantile system chiefly concerned manufactures, trade, wealth in gold and silver, and the role of the state in encouraging these. The basic principle of mercantilism was a concept called autarky—the idea that a state should be self-sufficient in producing manufactured goods and should import as few foreign goods as possible. Simultaneously, the state sought export markets for its own goods. A favorable balance of trade occurred when the value of exports exceeded that of imports. To achieve a favorable balance of trade and the consequent accumulation of wealth in gold required government regulation of the economy.

were expected to marry and to lead respectable lives. They usually maintained their workroom, shop, and residence in the same building. Women were generally excluded from an independent role in a guild, but they were an integral part of the craftsman's family economy. The wife of a master usually handled sales in the shop, kept the accounts for her husband's business, and managed the household. If a master died, his widow had the right to keep their shop, to hire the journeymen to work in it, and to manage the business. The children of a guild family were normally apprenticed to another master, and they were replaced in the family economy by the unpaid apprentices being trained by the master.

The lower rungs of the urban social structure were domestic servants (see illustration 18.10) and the laboring poor. At the beginning of the eighteenth century,

An important aspect of the mercantilist regulation of the economy was state support for manufactures and commerce. This government intervention took many forms, such as absolute monopolies, especially in foreign trade. Many governments of the Old Regime chartered monopolies on the models of the British East India Company and the Dutch East India Company. During the 1720s alone, the Austrians chartered the Ostend Company to control trade with the Indies, the French merged several trading monopolies as the French Indies Company, and the Spanish gave the Chartered Company of Guipuzcoa (Caracas) a monopoly of the American trade. The shareholders in these mercantilist monopolies usually became rich. The Ostend Company, for example, paid its investors 137 percent interest in its first seven years (nearly 20 percent per annum) while serving the emperor's interests by reviving the port of Ostend, stimulating Belgian business, and bringing Austria closer to self-sufficiency.

The mercantilist practice of creating chartered companies with protected privileges applied to much manufacturing in Europe. The French monarchy, for example, held a state monopoly in tapestries and porcelain, high-quality manufactures that could be profitably traded abroad. Prussia created a state tobacco monopoly and Russia held a state salt monopoly. Many countries followed the Dutch example by chartering a national bank similar to the Bank of Amsterdam (1609). These banks served many important functions, such as supplying the mint with metals for coinage or providing the trading monopolies with credit. Parliament chartered the Bank of England in 1694 and gave it the privilege of printing paper money in 1718. The French created a Banque royale in 1717; the Prussians, a Bank of Prussia in 1765.

Mercantilism encouraged manufacturing through direct aid and state regulation of business. Direct aid might include subsidies, interest-free loans, or bonuses to manufacturers. Regulation took the form of explicit legislation. The French monarchy, for example, regulated mines, iron works, glass factories, and paper mills. French law specified what type and quality of raw materials could be used, which equipment and manufacturing processes must be employed, and standards of quality for the finished product. The French then sent factory inspectors to visit manufacturing sites and guarantee compliance with the law. A decree of 1740 explained that this procedure would maintain the quality of French manufactures and protect French trade from

"the negligence and bad faith of the manufacturers and merchants." Such regulations were partially successful, but they also discouraged experimentation, innovation, and expansion. The zenith of mercantilist regulation came in Portugal in 1756 when the government created the Junta do Comércio with powers to regulate all businesses.

The most common mercantilist laws were tariffs and Navigation Acts. Tariffs placed taxes on goods entering a country to discourage imports (which produced an unfavorable balance of trade and drained gold from a country) and to protect domestic manufactures from foreign competition (see document 18.4). Peter the Great of Russia, for example, levied heavy taxes on imported goods in 1724, even though Russians relied upon European manufactures and luxury goods. In 1767 Charles Townshend, the British chancellor of the exchequer (minister of finance), drafted one of the most famous tariffs of the Old Regime: a high tax on glass, lead, paints, paper, and tea imported into Britain's American colonies, which led to the Boston Tea Party. While governments imposed such restrictions upon imports, they simultaneously controlled trade through Navigation Acts requiring that goods shipped into (or out of) a country be carried only on ships of that country, or that goods shipped into a country's colonies must depart from a port in the mother country. The model for this legislation was English navigation laws of 1651 and 1660, and by the eighteenth century most maritime countries had adopted similar Navigation Acts.

Mercantilism was not unchallenged. Governments in the early eighteenth century remained generally pleased with the successes of mercantilism (Britain and France both had very favorable balances of trade), but by midcentury mercantilist policies were drawing increasing criticism. A group of theorists called the Physiocrats began to suggest major changes in economic policy, and their ideas supplanted the mercantile system with the basic doctrines of capitalism. The Physiocrats, led by French theorist François Quesnay, believed in limiting the powers of government, especially the power to intervene in economic activities. Quesnay and others proposed the abolition of monopolies and special privileges, the replacement of these policies by open competition in an unregulated marketplace, and the substitution of free trade for tariffs. The physiocratic school did not win great influence with the monarchical governments of the eighteenth century,

❖ DOCUMENT 18.4 ❖

Mercantilist Business Regulation: The British Hat Act of 1732

In accordance with the doctrine of mercantilism, governments of the Old Regime adopted legislation to regulate imports and exports. Adhering to this policy Britain adopted the following law in 1732. Its purpose was to prevent American competition with hatmakers in Britain.

Whereas the art and mystery of making hats in Great Britain hath arrived to great perfection, and considerable quantities of hats manufactured in this kingdom have heretofore been exported to his Majesty's plantations or colonies in America, who have been wholly supplied with hats from Great Britain;

and whereas great quantities of hats have of late years been made, and the said manufacture is daily increasing in the British plantations in America, and is from thence exported to foreign markets, which were heretofore supplied from Great Britain,

and the hat-makers in the said plantations take many apprentices for very small terms, to the discouragement of the said trade, and debasing the said manufacture:

Wherefore, for preventing the said ill practices for the future, and for promoting and encouraging the trade of making hats in Great Britain, be it enacted. . . :

That . . . no hats or felts whatsoever, dyed or undyed, finished or unfinished, shall be shipt, loaden or put on board any ship or vessel in any place or parts within any of the British plantations. . . .

and also that no hats or felts, either dyed or undyed, finished or unfinished, shall be loaden upon any horse, cart, or other carriage, to the intent or purpose to be exported, transported, shipped off, carried or conveyed out of any of the said British plantations to any other of the British plantations, or to any other place whatsoever, by any person or persons whatsoever.

And it is hereby further enacted by the authority aforesaid, that no person residing in any of his Majesty's plantations in America shall . . . make or cause to be made, any felt or hat of or with any wool or stuff whatsoever, unless he shall have first served as an apprentice in the trade or art of felt-making during the space of seven years at the least;

neither shall any felt-maker or hat-maker in any of the said plantations imploy, retain or set to work, in the said art or trade, any person as a journeyman or hired servant, other than such as shall have lawfully served an apprenticeship in the said trade for space of seven years;

nor shall any felt-maker or hat-maker in any of the said plantations have, take or keep above the number of two apprentices at one time, or take any apprentice for any less term than seven years,

And be it further enacted by the authority aforesaid, That no person or persons inhabiting in the said plantations . . . shall retain or set on work, in the said art of felt making, any black or negro.

---

but it opened the debate that ended mercantilism. Adam Smith employed many of the ideas of the physiocrats in writing his *Inquiry into the Nature and Causes of the Wealth of Nations* (1776), the cornerstone of the new political economy.

❖
Global Economies: Slavery and the Triangular Trade

European world trade grew and changed significantly during the Old Regime. In the seventeenth century, global trade chiefly linked Europe to India and the Far

East, as the chartering of the great east Indies companies indicates. This trade had originally concentrated upon the spice islands because great fortunes could be made by bringing pepper and other aromatic spices back to Europe, but the largest Asian trade evolved into competition for mainland markets such as India. During the seventeenth century, trade with the Indies might reward shareholders with more than 100 percent profits on their investment. The rewards were so rich that merchants were tempted into illegal competition with the state-chartered monopolies. One of the dominant families of eighteenth-century Britain, the Pitts (for one of whom Pittsburgh is named), owed its position to an ancestor whose brazen defiance of the East India

Illustration 18.11

▨ **Slave Labor on a Caribbean Sugar Plantation.** The European craving for sugar created a growing slave economy in the West Indies. In this engraving, an armed white overseer (lower right) watches sugar making from harvesting sugarcane (center left edge) to milling it (upper right) and compressing it in molds.

Company produced the fortune that bought later Pitts marriages into the aristocracy and the corrupt seat in Parliament from which William Pitt rose to fame. By the eighteenth century, however, the focus of European global trade had turned to Africa and the Americas, where the profits had become larger.

The profits of eighteenth-century trade, and much of Europe's prosperity, depended upon slavery. The most profitable exploitation of slavery was a system called triangular trade, which began in the 1690s. The corners of this triangle were in Europe, Africa, and the Americas. British merchants were the most adept at the triangular trade, but it was practiced by slave traders from many countries. These slavers began their commerce by taking European manufactured goods (particularly textiles) to the western coast of Africa. These goods were sold or bartered for African slaves who were offered for sale by local African rulers, by rivals who had taken them prisoner, or by Moslem slave traders. In the second leg of the triangular trade, a ship filled with slaves made the Atlantic crossing to European colonies in the Americas. The British, for example, brought slaves to Caribbean colonies (where 85 percent of the population lived in slavery) such as Jamaica and Barbados or to the mainland colonies in North America (where 20 percent of the population lived in slavery). African slaves were then sold to plantation owners, and the revenue was used to buy the agricultural goods (chiefly tobacco in North America and sugar in the Caribbean), which slave labor had produced. On the third leg of the triangle, these goods were returned to England, where they were sold at

huge profits. In this triangular pattern of trade, few ships covered all three legs of the triangle.

All European states with American colonies (including Holland and Denmark), and a few states without colonies (notably Prussia), participated in the slave trade. The French triangular trade sent textiles, jewelry, and hardware to west Africa; then shipped slaves to Saint Domingue (Haiti), Guadeloupe, and Martinique in the Caribbean; and finally brought sugar and coffee back to France. The French amplified the British system by reexporting sugar to the rest of continental Europe. That sugar was the commodity upon which the Caribbean slave economy rested (see illustration 18.11). Sugarcane was not cultivated in Europe, and sugar was not yet extracted from beets. Slave-produced sugar from America sustained a growing European love of sweets. The European addiction to sugar cost humanity dearly: During the century 1690–1790, one African died for every ton of sugar shipped to Europe. When the consumption of Caribbean sugar reached its peak in 1801, the cost had become one dead slave to provide the sugar for every 250 consumers in Britain.

The scale of the slave trade was immense (see table 18.8). The British Board of Trade estimated in 1709 that British colonies needed twenty-five thousand additional slaves each year—four thousand for Barbados, five thousand for North America, and twelve thousand for Jamaica. When Britain obtained the *Asiento*, the contract for supplying slaves to Spanish America, in 1713, English slave traders brought an additional five thousand slaves for Spanish colonies. The French delivered only four thousand slaves per year in the early eigh-

❦ TABLE 18.8 ❦

Estimated Slave Population of European Colonies in the Americas, 1770

Region	Total population	Slave population	Percentage in slavery
Spanish colonies	12,144,000	290,000	2.4
Mainland	12,000,000	240,000	2.0
Caribbean	144,000	50,000	34.7
British colonies	2,600,000	878,000	33.8
Mainland	2,100,000	450,000	21.4
Caribbean	500,000	428,000	85.6
Portuguese Brazil	2,000,000	700,000	35.0
French Caribbean	430,000	379,000	88.1
Dutch Caribbean	90,000	75,000	83.3
Danish Caribbean	25,000	18,000	35.0
Total, Mainland colonies	16,100,000	1,390,000	8.6
Total, Caribbean islands	1,189,000	950,000	79.9

Source: Adapted from data in Robin Blackburn, *The Overthrow of Colonial Slavery, 1776–1848* (London: Verso, 1988), p. 5.

teenth century, but that figure rose to an average of thirty-seven thousand slaves per year by the 1780s. Britain and France alone sold approximately 3.5 million African slaves in the Americas during the eighteenth century. An average of 10 percent to 20 percent of the slaves died during an Atlantic crossing (50 percent to 75 percent on voyages when scurvy or amoebic dysentery broke out on the ship), so the number of African slaves initially taken was closer to four million. Adding the Portuguese, Dutch, Danish, and Prussian slave trade, the grand total probably surpasses five million Africans. The demand for slaves was so high because the average life expectancy of a Caribbean slave was seven years after arrival.

During the eighteenth century, signs were evident that this economy would also change. Moral revulsion with slavery began to create antislavery opinion, both in Europe and the Americas. An American, Samuel Sewall, published an antislavery tract, *The Selling of Joseph,* as early as 1700. Two Portuguese Jesuits who served in Brazil, Jorge Benci and Giovanni Andreoni, published works in Europe attacking slavery. By 1727 the Society of Friends (widely known as the Quakers) had begun an abolitionist crusade. The moral arguments against slavery made slow progress because they faced powerful

economic arguments that slavery was essential for both the colonial and the home economies. The Portuguese example illustrates both the progress and its slowness. Royal decrees abolished the slavery of American Indians (1755) and Asians (1758), then freed any African slave brought into Portugal (1761), and finally emancipated all African slaves held in Portugal (1773). But these decrees permitted the continuance of the slave trade and the perpetuation of African slavery in the Portuguese colony of Brazil, where it continued until 1888.

◈

Conclusion

The social and economic structures of eighteenth-century Europe were rooted in the soil, much as they had been for centuries. Agriculture dominated the economy, and ownership of the land consequently shaped the social structure. Strong, old institutions such as the monarchy and the church held much of the land, but the largest share of the wealth of Europe was held by a small elite of hereditary nobles who owned the land. The majority of the population (90 percent in some regions) worked the land without owning it. These realities can obscure great variations: The general term *peasant* applied to a vast social category, whose members ranged from comfortable landowners who hired others to farm their lands, to serfs whose feudal obligations bound them to the soil in a condition comparable to slavery. Similarly the general term *aristocrat* applied to a small percentage of society (about 2 percent on average), but it covered a range of conditions, from barefoot farmers to the most powerful families in Europe. Peasants and aristocrats characterized the socioeconomic structure of the Old Regime, but corporative society held another important estate—a middle class of town dwellers that included a range of landless occupations such as laborers, domestic servants, skilled artisans, educated professionals, and merchants.

This description could also be applied to earlier centuries in Europe, but it would be a mistake to conclude that the Old Regime was a static, unchanging society. The population of Europe was growing, putting great pressure on the long-standing system of land tenure and agricultural production. Towns and cities were increasing in both size and importance, stimulated by population pressures and improved manufacturing. Global trade, especially across the Atlantic, was producing great wealth outside of the agricultural world, stimulating further change. The prevalent economic philosophy of the age, mercantilism, focused government attention upon manufacturing more than farming, accelerating the pace of change in the late eighteenth century.

Suggested Readings

For broad overviews of the eighteenth-century economy, see J. H. Clapham and others, eds., *The Cambridge Economic History of Europe*, 10 vols. (1941–89) and C. Cipolla, ed., *The Fontana Economic History of Europe*, 6 vols. (1972–76). Compare these with the more recent R. Floud and D. McCloskey, eds., *The Economic History of Britain since 1700*, 2 vols. (1993), which is highly statistical, and C. H. Lee, *The British Economy since 1700* (1986), which gives a broader view. R. Forster, ed., *European Society in the Eighteenth Century* (1967) is an exceptional collection of contemporary readings on both social and economic topics.

For European agriculture and the peasantry in the Old Regime, see J. Blum, *The End of the Old Order in Rural Europe* (1978), an exceptionally valuable work; B. H. Slicher van Bath, *The Agrarian History of Western Europe, A.D. 500–1850* (1963); T. H. Ashton and C. Philpin, eds., *The Brenner Debate: Agrarian Class Structure and Economic Development in Pre-Industrial Europe* (1987), a good introduction to controversy on this subject; J. Thirsk, ed., *The*

Agrarian History of England and Wales, vol. 5: 1640–1750 (1984); A. R. H. Baker and R. A. Butlin, eds., *Studies of Field Systems in the British Isles* (1973); M. Turner, *English Parliamentary Enclosure* (1980); G. E. Fussell, *Jethro Tull: His Influence on Mechanized Agriculture* (1973); T. Devine, *Farm Servants and Labour in Lowland Scotland, 1770–1914* (1984); J. G. Gagliardo, *From Pariah to Patriot: The Changing Image of the German Peasant, 1770–1840* (1969); R. Evans, *The German Peasantry* (1986); D. W. Sabean, *Property, Production and Family in Neckerhausen, 1700–1870* (1990) on life in a small German village; and P. Kolchin, *Unfree Labor: American Slavery and Russian Serfdom* (1987), a provocative comparison.

For the aristocracy, see M. L. Bush, *Noble Privilege* (1983), an overview; A. Goodwin, ed., *European Nobility in the Eighteenth Century* (1953); J. V. Beckett, *The Aristocracy in England, 1660–1914* (1986); J. Cannon, *Aristocratic Century: The Peerage of Eighteenth-Century England* (1984); G. E. Mingay, *The Gentry* (1976); F. L. Ford, *Robe and Sword: The Regrouping of the French Aristocracy after Louis XIV* (1953); G. Chaussinand-Nogaret, *The French Nobility in the Eighteenth Century* (1985); R. Forster, *The Nobility of Toulouse in the Eighteenth Century* (1960); R. Forster, *The House of Saulx-Tavannes* (1971); J. Blum, *Lord and Peasant in Russia from the Ninth to the Nineteenth Century* (1961); B. Meehan-Waters, *Autocracy and Aristocracy: The Russian Service Elite of 1730* (1982) and R. E. Jones, *The Emancipation of the Russian Nobility, 1762–1785* (1973).

For eighteenth-century industry, see L. A. Clarkson, *Proto-Industrialization: The First Phase of Industrialization* (1985) and M. Berg, P. Hudson, and M. Sonenscher, eds., *Manufacture in Town and Country before the Factory* (1983). For mercantilism, the Physiocrats, and eighteenth-century economic thought, see E. Fox-Genovese, *The Origins of Physiocracy* (1976), J. Keay, *The Honourable Company: A History of the English East India Company* (1991), and H. Furber, *Rival Empires of Trade in the Orient, 1720–1750* (1976).

For urban history and social classes, see P. Hohenberg and L. Lees, *The Making of Urban Europe, 1000–1950* (1985), a broad overview; J. de Vries, *European Urbanization, 1500–1800* (1984), important but heavily statistical; J. Ward, *Metropolitan Communities: Trade Guilds, Identity, and Change in Early Modern London* (1997); P. Corfield, *The Impact of English Towns, 1700–1800* (1982); P. Benedict, ed., *Cities and Social Change in Early Modern France* (1989); M. Walker, *German Home Towns: Community, State, and General Estate, 1648–1871* (1971); J. M. Hittle, *The Service City: State and Townspeople in Russia, 1600–1800* (1979); and G. Rozman, *Urban Networks in Russia, 1750–1800* (1976). For the urban social classes, see J. Hecht, *The Domestic Servant Class in Eighteenth-Century England* (1981), B. Hill, *Servants: English Domestics in the Eighteenth Century* (1996), C. C. Fairchilds, *Domestic Enemies: Servants and Their Masters in Old Regime France* (1984), S. Maza, *Servants and Masters in Eighteenth-Century France* (1983), R. Forster, *Merchants, Landlords, and Magistrates* (1980), A. J. LaVopa, *Grace, Talent, and Merit: Poor Students, Clerical Careers, and Professional Ideology in Eighteenth-Century Germany* (1988), and A. Black, *Guilds and Civil Society in European Political Thought from the Twelfth Century to the Present* (1984).

For economic theory and history, see E. Heckscher, *Mercantilism*, 2 vols. (1955), the standard work; I. Wallerstein, *Mercantilism and the Consolidation of the European World-Economy* (1980); J. Blow, *British Commercial Policy and Trade Expansion, 1750–1850* (1972); J. G. Clark, *La Rochelle and the Atlantic Economy during the Eighteenth Century* (1981); E. Fox-Genovese, *The Origins of Physiocracy* (1976); and R. Meek, ed., *The Economics of Physiocracy* (1962).

For the slave trade economy, see especially P. D. Curtin, *The Atlantic Slave Trade* (1969); P. D. Curtin, *The Rise and Fall of the Plantation Complex* (1990); J. Rawley, *The Transatlantic Slave Trade* (1981), which offers a good general history; R. L. Stein, *The French Slave Trade in the Eighteenth Century* (1979); and J. Walvin, *Black Ivory: A History of British Slavery* (1994).

CHAPTER 19

DAILY LIFE IN THE OLD REGIME

CHAPTER OUTLINE

For most Europeans the basic conditions of life in the eighteenth century had changed little since the agricultural revolution of Neolithic times. Chapter 19 describes those conditions and shows in dramatic terms how life at the end of the Old Regime differed from that of the present day. It begins by exploring the basic relationships between people and their environment, including the density of population in Europe and the barriers to speedy travel and communication. The chapter then examines the life of ordinary people, beginning with its most striking feature: low life expectancy. The factors that help to explain that high level of mortality, especially inadequate diet and the prevalence of epidemic disease, are then discussed. Finally, the life cycle of those who survived infancy is considered, including such topics as the dangers of childbirth; the Old Regime's understanding of childhood; and its attitudes toward marriage, the family, sexuality, and reproduction.

People and Space: Population Density, Travel, and Communication

The majority of the people who lived in Europe during the Old Regime never saw a great city or even a town of twenty-five thousand people. Most stayed within a few miles of their home village and the neighboring market town. Studies of birth and death records show that more than 90 percent of the population of the eighteenth century died in the same region where they were born, passing their lives amid relatively few people. Powerful countries and great cities of the eighteenth century were small by twentieth-century standards (see population tables in chapter 18). Great Britain numbered an estimated 6.4 million people in 1700 (less than the state of Georgia today) and Vienna held 114,000 (roughly the size of Fullerton, California, or Tallahassee, Florida). People of the late twentieth century are also accustomed to life in densely concen-trated populations. New York City has a population density of more than fifty-five thousand people per square mile, and Maryland has a population density of nearly five hundred people per square mile. Most peo-ple of the eighteenth century did not know such crowding: Great Britain had a population density of fifty-five people per square mile; Sweden, six (see table 19.1).

Life in a rural world of sparse population density was also shaped by the difficulty of travel and commu-nication. The upper classes enjoyed a life of relative mobility that included such pleasures as owning homes in both town and country or taking a "grand tour" of historic cities in Europe. Journeymen who sought expe-rience in their trade, agricultural laborers who were obliged to migrate with seasonal harvests, and peasants who were conscripted into the army were all excep-tions in a world of limited mobility. Geographic obsta-cles, poor roads, weather, and bandits made travel both slow and risky. For most people, the pace of travel was walking beside a mule or ox-drawn cart. Only well-to-do people traveled on horseback, fewer still in horse-drawn carriages (see illustration 19.1). In 1705 the twenty-year-old Johann Sebastian Bach wished to hear the greatest organist of that era perform; Bach left his work for two weeks and walked two hundred miles to hear good music. After Napoleon Bonaparte graduated from a French military school in 1784, he walked 125 miles to Paris.

TABLE 19.1
European Population Density

Population density is measured by the number of people per square mile.

Country	Population density in 1700	Population density in the 1990s
Austrian Netherlands (Belgium)	153	853
Dutch republic (Netherlands)	119	959
Italian states (Italy)	112	499
German states (Germany)	98	588
France	92	275
Great Britain	55	616
Spain	38	201
Sweden	6	50

Source: Jack Babuscio and Richard M. Dunn, eds., *European Political Facts, 1648–1789* (London: Macmillian, 1984), pp. 335–53; and *The World Almanac and Book of Facts 1995* (Mahwah, N.J.: World Almanac Books, 1994), pp. 740–839.

Travelers were at the mercy of the weather, which often rendered roads impassable because of flooding, mud, or snow. The upkeep of roads and bridges varied greatly. Governments maintained a few post roads, but other roads depended for their upkeep upon the conscription of local labor such as the *corvée* (see

Illustration 19.1

⁄⁄ **Coach Travel.** Horse-drawn car-riages and coaches remained the primary form of public transportation in Europe before the railroad age of the nineteenth century. Postal service, business, and government all relied upon a network of highways, stables, and coaching inns. In this illustration, travelers in the Pyrenees wait at a coaching station and hotel while a wheel is repaired.

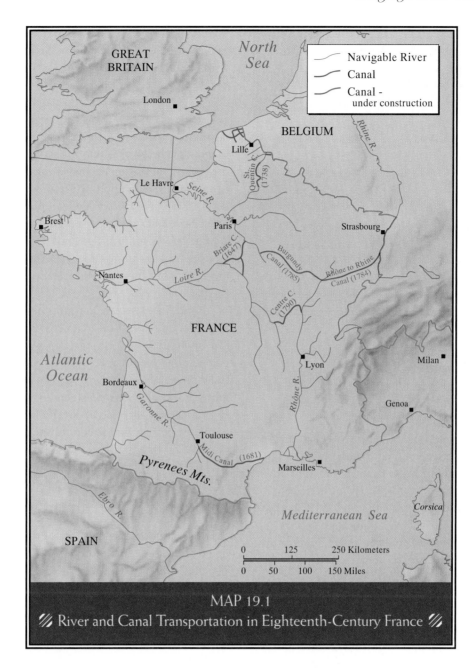

MAP 19.1

%/ River and Canal Transportation in Eighteenth-Century France %/

chapter 18). An English law of 1691, for example, simply required each parish to maintain the local roads and bridges; if upkeep were poor, the government fined the parish. Brigands also hindered travel. These bandits might become heroes to the peasants who protected them as rebels against authority and as benefactors of the poor, much as Robin Hood is regarded in English folklore. In southern Italy, Gaetano Vardarelli is remembered for sharing his plunder with the poor and forcing landowners to distribute free bread to them. Oleksa Dovbush became a similar bandit-hero in Austria. Whatever their popularity with the homebound poor, such highway robbers made travel risky for the few who could afford it.

The fastest travel, for both people and goods, was often by water. Most cities had grown along rivers and coasts. Paris received the grain that sustained it by barges on the Seine; the timber that heated the city was floated down the river. The great transportation projects of the Old Regime were canals connecting these rivers. The French built canals linking the Seine and the Loire in the early seventeenth century, connecting the ports of the English Channel to inland waterways in the 1680s, and joining the Seine and the waterways of eastern France in the 1740s (see map 19.1). Travel on the open seas was normally the fastest form of travel, but it depended on fair weather. A voyager might be in England four hours after leaving France or trapped in port

TABLE 19.2

Average Speed of Mailing a Letter from Venice in 1700

Destination	Time
Genoa or Rome	3–4 days
Munich or Vienna	5–6 days
Paris or Antwerp	7–8 days
London, Lisbon, Copenhagen, or Warsaw	10–11 days
Constantinople	17–21 days
Moscow	24–28 days

Source: Calculated from maps in Fernand Braudel, *The Mediterranean and the Mediterranean World in the Age of Philip II* (New York, N.Y.: Harper, 1972), 1:366.

for days. If oceanic travel were involved, delays could reach remarkable lengths. In 1747 the electors of Portsmouth, England, selected Captain Edward Legge of the Royal Navy to represent them in Parliament; Legge, whose command had taken him to the Americas, had died eighty-seven days before his election but the news had not yet arrived in Portsmouth.

Travel and communication were agonizingly slow by twentieth-century standards. In 1734 the regular coach trip between Edinburgh and London (372 miles) took twelve days; the royal mail along that route required forty-eight hours of constant travel by relay riders. The commercial leaders of Venice could send correspondence to Rome (more than 250 miles) in three to four days, if conditions were favorable; messages to Moscow (more than twelve hundred miles) required about four weeks (see table 19.2). When the French philosopher Voltaire went from Geneva to Paris (fewer than 350 miles) in 1788, his carriage made seventy-two changes of horses at relay stations and still took four days to arrive. When King Louis XV of France died in 1774, this urgent news was rushed to the capitals of Europe via the fastest couriers: It arrived in Vienna and Rome three days later; Berlin, four days; and St. Petersburg, six days.

Life Expectancy in the Old Regime

The living conditions of the average person during the Old Regime holds little appeal for people accustomed to twentieth-century conveniences. A famous writer of the mid-eighteenth century, Samuel Johnson, described the life of the masses as "little to be enjoyed and much to be endured." The most dramatic illustration of Johnson's point is life expectancy data. Although the figures vary by social class or region, their message is grim. For everyone born during the Old Regime, the average age at death was close to thirty. Demographic studies of northern France at the end of the seventeenth century found that the average age at death was twenty; a century later, that life expectancy at birth ranged between twenty-eight years and thirty-two years. Data for Sweden in 1755 give an average life of thirty-three. A comprehensive study of villages in southern England found a range between thirty-five and forty-five. These numbers are misleading in some ways (because of infant mortality), but they contain many truths about life in the past.

Short life expectancy meant that few people knew their grandparents. Research on a village in central England found that a population of four hundred included only one instance of three generations alive in the same family. A study of Russian demography found more shocking results: Between 20 and 30 percent of all serfs under age fifteen had already lost both parents. Similarly, people who lived into their forties and fifties often found that they had few childhood friends left alive. When the French philosopher Denis Diderot in 1759 returned to the village of his birth at age forty-six, he found that not a single person whom he knew from childhood had survived. Life expectancy was significantly higher for the rich than for the poor. Those who could afford fuel for winter fires, warm clothing, a superior diet, or multiple residences reduced many risks. The rich lived an estimated ten years longer than the average in most regions and seventeen years longer than the poor.

Disease and the Biological Old Regime

Life expectancy averages were low because infant mortality was high, and death rates remained high throughout childhood. The study of northern France found that one-third of all children died each year and only 58 percent reached age fifteen. However, for those who survived infancy, life expectancy rose significantly. In a few healthier regions, especially where agriculture was strong, the people who lived through the terrors of childhood disease could expect to live nearly fifty more years.

The explanation for the shocking death rates and life expectancy figures of the Old Regime has been

TABLE 19.3
The Causes of Death in the Eighteenth Century

	Deaths in Edinburgh in 1740		Deaths in the United States in the 1990s	
Rank	Cause	Percentage	Cause	Percentage
1	Consumption (tuberculosis)	22.4	Heart disease	32.6
2	Smallpox	22.1	Cancer	23.4
3	Fevers (including typhus and typhoid)	13.0	Stroke	6.6
4	Old age	8.2	Pulmonary condition	4.5
5	Measles	8.1	Accident	3.9

Source: Data for 1740 from John D. Post, *Food Shortage, Climatic Variability, and Epidemic Disease in Preindustrial Europe* (Ithaca, N.Y.: Cornell University Press, 1988), p. 241; data for the United States from *The World Almanac and Book of Facts 1995* (Mahwah, N.J.: World Almanac Books, 1994), p. 959.

called the biological old regime, which suggests the natural restrictions created by chronic undernourishment, periodic famine, and unchecked disease. The first fact of existence in the eighteenth century was the probability of death from an infectious disease. Natural catastrophes (such as the Lisbon earthquake of 1755, which killed thirty thousand people) or the human violence of wartime (such as the battle of Blenheim in 1704, which took more than fifty thousand casualties in a single day) were terrible, but more people died from diseases. People who had the good fortune to survive natural and human catastrophe rarely died from heart disease or cancer, the great killers of the late twentieth century. An examination of the 1740 death records for Edinburgh, for example, finds that the leading causes of death that year were tuberculosis and smallpox, which accounted for nearly half of all deaths (see table 19.3).

Some diseases were pandemic: The germs that spread them circulated throughout Europe at all times. The bacteria that attacked the lungs and caused tuberculosis (called consumption in the eighteenth century) were one such universal risk. Other diseases were endemic: They were a constant threat, but only in certain regions. Malaria, a febrile disease transmitted by mosquitoes, was endemic to warmer regions, especially where swamps or marshes were found. Rome and Venice were still in malarial regions in 1750, and Rome remained malarial until the 1930s when Benito Mussolini's government finally drained the Pontine Marshes, a project attempted for centuries. When Napoleon's army marched into Italy in 1796, his soldiers began to die from malaria before a single shot had been fired.

The most frightening diseases have always been epidemic diseases—waves of infection that periodically passed through a region. The worst epidemic disease of the Old Regime was smallpox. An epidemic of 1707 killed 36 percent of the population of Iceland. London lost three thousand people to smallpox in 1710, then experienced five more epidemics between 1719 and 1746. An epidemic decimated Berlin in 1740; another killed 6 percent of the population of Rome in 1746. Social historians have estimated that 95 percent of the population contracted smallpox, and 15 percent of all deaths in the eighteenth century can be attributed to it. Those who survived smallpox were immune thereafter, so it chiefly killed the young, accounting for one-third of all childhood deaths. But it did not spare those adults who had avoided childhood infection, not even the rich and powerful. In the eighty years between 1695 and 1775, smallpox killed a queen of England, a king of Austria, a king of Spain, a tsar of Russia, a queen of Sweden, and a king of France. In 1700 it killed the eleven-year-old heir to the throne of England, the duke of Gloucester, thereby ending the Stuart dynasty. Smallpox ravaged the Hapsburgs, the royal family of Austria, and completely changed the history of their dynasty. Between 1654 and 1763, the disease killed nine immediate members of the royal family, causing the succession to the throne to shift four times (see genealogy 19.1). The death of Joseph I in 1711 cost the Hapsburgs their claim to the throne of Spain, which would have gone to his younger brother Charles. When Charles accepted the Austrian throne, the Spanish crown (which he could not hold simultaneously) passed to a branch of the French royal family. The accession of Charles to the

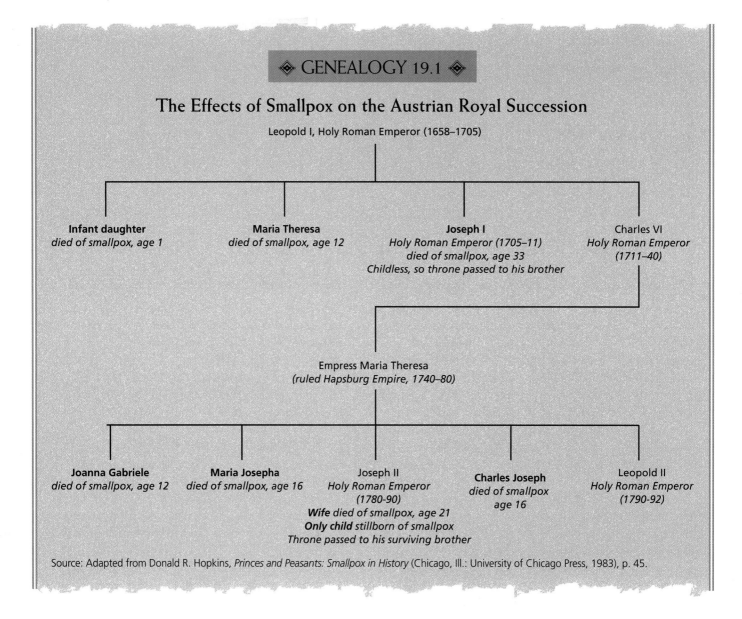

◆ GENEALOGY 19.1 ◆

The Effects of Smallpox on the Austrian Royal Succession

Leopold I, Holy Roman Emperor (1658–1705)

Infant daughter
died of smallpox, age 1

Maria Theresa
died of smallpox, age 12

Joseph I
Holy Roman Emperor (1705–11)
died of smallpox, age 33
Childless, so throne passed to his brother

Charles VI
Holy Roman Emperor
(1711–40)

Empress Maria Theresa
(ruled Hapsburg Empire, 1740–80)

Joanna Gabriele
died of smallpox, age 12

Maria Josepha
died of smallpox, age 16

Joseph II
Holy Roman Emperor
(1780-90)
Wife *died of smallpox, age 21*
Only child *stillborn of smallpox*
Throne passed to his surviving brother

Charles Joseph
died of smallpox
age 16

Leopold II
Holy Roman Emperor
(1790–92)

Source: Adapted from Donald R. Hopkins, *Princes and Peasants: Smallpox in History* (Chicago, Ill.: University of Chicago Press, 1983), p. 45.

Austrian throne also meant that his daughter, Maria Theresa, would ultimately inherit it—an event that led to years of war (see chapter 20).

Although smallpox was the greatest scourge of the eighteenth century, signs of a healthier future were evident. The Chinese and the Turks had already learned the benefits of intentionally infecting children with a mild case of smallpox to make them immune to the disease. A prominent English woman, Lady Mary Wortley Montagu, learned of the Turkish method of inoculating the young in 1718, and after it succeeded on her son, she became the first European champion of the procedure (see document 19.1). Inoculation (performed by opening a vein and introducing the disease) won acceptance slowly, often through royal patronage. Empress Maria Theresa had her family inoculated after she saw

four of her children die of smallpox. Catherine the Great followed suit in 1768. But inoculation killed some people, and many feared it. The French outlawed the procedure in 1762, and the Vatican taught acceptance of the disease as a "visitation of divine will." Nonetheless, the death of Louis XV led to the inoculation of his three sons.

While smallpox devastated all levels of society, some epidemic diseases chiefly killed the poor. Typhus, spread by the bite of body lice, was common in squalid urban housing, jails, and army camps. Typhoid fever, transmitted by contaminated food or water, was equally at home in the unsanitary homes that peasants shared with their animals.

The most famous epidemic disease in European history was the bubonic plague, the Black Death that

❖ DOCUMENT 19.1 ❖

Mary Montagu: The Turkish Smallpox Inoculation

Lady Mary Wortley Montagu (1689–1762) was the wife of the British ambassador to the Ottoman Empire. While living in Constantinople, she observed the Turkish practice of inoculating children with small amounts of smallpox and was amazed at the Turkish ability to prevent the disease. The following excerpts are from a letter to a friend in which Montagu explains her discovery.

Mary Montagu to Sarah Chiswell, 1 April 1717:

I am going to tell you a thing that I am sure will make you wish yourself here. The smallpox, so fatal and so general amonst us, is here entirely harmless [because of] the invention of "engrafting" (which is the term they give it). There is a set of old women who make it their business to perform the operation. Every autumn in the month of September, when the great heat is abated, people send to one another to know if any of their family has a mind to have the smallpox. They make parties for this purpose, and when they are met (commonly 15 or 16 together), the old woman comes with a nutshell full of the matter of the best sort of smallpox [the fluid from a smallpox infection] and asks what veins you please to have opened. She immediately rips open that which you offer to her with a large needle (which gives no more pain than a common

scratch) and puts into the vein as much venom as can lie upon the head of her needle, and after binds up the little wound with a hollow bit of shell, and in this manner opens four or five veins. . . .

The children, or young patients, play together all the rest of the day and are in perfect health till the eighth day. Then the fever begins to seize them and they keep to their beds for two days, very seldom three days. They have very rarely above 20 or 30 [smallpox sores] on their faces, which never leave marks, and in eight days time they are as well as before their illness. . . .

Every year thousands undergo this operation . . . [and] there is no example of any one that has died of it. You may believe I am very well satisfied of the safety of the experiment since I intend to try it on my dear little son. I am a patriot enough to take pains to bring this useful invention into fashion in England, and I should not fail to write to some of our doctors very particularly about it if I knew any one of them that I thought had virtue enough to destroy such a considerable branch of their revenue for the good of mankind, but [the smallpox] is too beneficial to them. . . . I may, however, have the courage to war with them.

---

killed millions of people in the fourteenth century. The plague, introduced by fleas borne on rodents, no longer ravaged Europe, but it killed tens of thousands in the eighteenth century and evoked a special cultural terror. Between 1708 and 1713, the plague spread from Poland across central and northern Europe. Half the city of Danzig died, and the death rate was only slightly lower in Prague, Copenhagen, and Stockholm. Another epidemic spread from Russia in 1719. It reached the port of Marseilles in 1720, and forty thousand people perished; the plague moved along the Mediterranean during the following year, killing thousands more at other ports. Russia experienced another epidemic in 1771, killing fifty-seven thousand people in Moscow alone.

Public Health before the Germ Theory

Ignorance and poverty compounded the dangers of the biological old regime. The germ theory of disease transmission—that invisible microorganisms such as

bacteria and viruses spread diseases—had been suggested centuries earlier, but governments, scientists, and churches dismissed this theory until the late nineteenth century (see chapter 24). Instead, the dominant theory was the miasma theory of contagion, holding that diseases spring from rotting matter in the earth. Although the miasma theory delayed the conquest of epidemic disease, it did support some wise public health measures, such as Pope Pius VI's 1779 order that another attempt be made to drain the Pontine Marshes. And even without the germ theory, people realized that they could contract smallpox or the plague from people who had the disease, so they fled epidemics whenever they could. Acceptance of the miasma theory perpetuated dangerous conditions. Europeans did not understand the dangers of unsanitary housing, including royal palaces. Louis XIV's palace at Versailles was perhaps the greatest architectural ornament of an epoch that produced the breathtaking beauty of baroque art, and it became the model for an age of glorious palaces symbolizing the power of absolute monarchy, but human excrement accumulated in the corners and corridors of Versailles, just as it accumulated in dung-heaps alongside peasant cottages. One of the keenest observers of that age, the duke de Saint-Simon, noted that even the royal apartments at Versailles opened out "over the privies and other dark and evil smelling places."

The great cities of Europe were filthy. Few had more than rudimentary sewer systems. Gradually, enlightened monarchs realized that they must clean their capitals, as King Charles III (Don Carlos) ordered for Madrid in 1761. This Spanish decree required all households to install piping on their property to carry solid waste to a sewage pit, ordered the construction of tiled channels in the streets to carry liquid wastes, and committed the state to clean public places. Such public policies significantly improved urban sanitation, but they were partial steps, as the Spanish decree recognized, "until such time as it be possible to construct the underground sewage system." The worst sanitation was often found in public institutions. The standard French army barracks of the eighteenth century had rooms measuring sixteen feet by eighteen feet; each room accommodated thirteen to fifteen soldiers, sharing four or five beds and innumerable diseases. Prisons were worse yet.

Another dangerous characteristic of Old Regime housing was a lack of sufficient heat. During the eighteenth century the climatic condition known as the Little Ice Age persisted, with average temperatures a few degrees lower than the twentieth century experienced. Winters were longer and harder, summers and growing seasons were shorter. Glaciers advanced in the north, and timberlines receded on mountains. In European homes, the heat provided by open fires was so inadequate that even nobles saw their inkwells and wine freeze in severe weather. Among the urban poor, where many families occupied unheated rooms in the basement or attic, the chief source of warmth was body heat generated by the entire family sleeping together. Some town dwellers tried heating their garrets by burning coal, charcoal, or peat in open braziers, without chimneys or ventilation, creating a grim duel between freezing cold and poisonous air. Peasants found warmth by bringing their livestock indoors and sleeping with the animals, exacerbating the spread of disease. Their hovels needed animal warmth. Arthur Young, a traveler who published accounts of conditions in rural France in the 1780s, reported that the houses of most peasants had no glass windows; openings in the walls might be covered with shutters or waxed paper. Their homes also lacked chimneys. Smoke from cooking or heating escaped through a hole in the roof or hung in the air.

In a world lacking a scientific explanation of epidemic disease, religious teaching exercised great influence over public health standards. Churches offered solace to the afflicted, but they also offered another explanation of disease: It was the scourge of God. This theory of disease, like the miasma theory, contributed to the inattention to public health. Many churches organized religious processions and ceremonies of expiation in hopes of divine cures. Unfortunately, such public assemblies often spread disease by bringing healthy people into contact with the infected. Processions and ceremonies also prevented effective measures because they persuaded churches to oppose quarantines. Churches were not alone; merchants in most towns joined them in fighting quarantines. This did not mean that diseased people were welcomed. In Scandinavia, for example, the law required lepers walking in public to ring bells to warn citizens to flee.

Medicine and the Biological Old Regime

Most Europeans during the Old Regime never received medical attention from trained physicians. Few doctors were found in rural areas. Peasants relied on folk medicine, consulted unlicensed healers, or allowed illness to run its course. Many town dwellers received their medical advice from apothecaries (druggists). The propertied classes could consult trained physicians, although this was often a mixed blessing. Many medical doctors were quacks, and even the educated often had minimal training. The best medical training in Europe was found at the University of Leiden in Holland, where Hermann Boerhaave pioneered clinical instruction at bedsides, and similar programs were created at the College of Physicians in Edinburgh in 1681 and in Vienna in 1745. Yet Jean-Paul Marat, one of the leaders of the French Revolution, received a medical degree at Edinburgh after staying there for a few weeks during the summer of 1774.

Medical science practiced curative medicine, following traditions that seem barbaric to later centuries. The pharmacopeia of medicinal preparations still favored ingredients such as unicorn's horn (ivory was usually used), crushed lice, incinerated toad, or ground shoe leather. One cherished medication, highly praised in the first edition of the *Encyclopaedia Britannica* (1771), was usnea, the moss scraped from the scalp of prisoners

A Novelist Satirizes the Medical Practice of Bleeding

Alain-René Lesage (1668–1747) was a Breton writer who showed his finest skills in his satires. He depicted human shortcomings and sufferings with a remarkable good humor, which suggests how people of the Old Regime coped with the difficulties of life. Lesage's masterpiece is the picaresque romance Gil Blas *(1715). The protagonist (Blas) holds many different jobs that enable him to observe life. The following excerpt describes how a doctor bleeds a priest (one of Blas's employers) to death.*

I served the priest Sédillo for three months. He fell ill; a fever came on, and this aggravated his gout. For the first time in his life, he called in a physician. . . . I went for Doctor Sangrado and brought him to the house. He was a tall, withered, wan man, who for forty years at least kept Clotho [the mythological figure who cut the thread of life] busy with her shears. This learned physician had a grave appearance . . . , but his jargon sounded great to the ears of the uninformed . . .

After having studied my master's symptoms, he said to him solemnly: "Common practitioners in this case would doubtless prescribe the traditional routine of salts, diuretics, purgatives . . . pernicious drugs invented by quacks. All chemical preparations seem made only to injure. I use simpler and more efficacious means. What is your usual diet?"

"I generally live on soups," replied the Canon, "and eat my meat with rich gravy."

"Soups and rich meats!" cried the doctor in surprise. "I am no longer surprised to find you ill. Luxurious living is like poisoned bait: it is a trap set by sensuality, a trap to cut short the days of wretched man. You must renounce pampering your appetite; the most boring food is the best for health. . . ."

"And do you drink wine?" he added.

"Yes," said the canon, "but diluted with water."

"Oh! It doesn't matter how you dilute it," replied the physician. "This is licentiousness with a vengeance! A frightful diet! You ought to have been dead years ago! How old are you?"

"I am entering my 69th year," replied the canon.

"Just as I said," responded the physician, "a premature old age is always the result of intemperance. If you had only drunk pure water all your life, and had been content with simple food . . . you would not now be tormented."

The licentiate promised to obey the doctor in all things. . . .

Doctor Sangrado then sent me for a surgeon whom he named, and ordered him to take from my master about 18 ounces of blood by way of a beginning. He then said to the surgeon, "Come back in three hours and do the same thing again; start over again tomorrow. It is a mistake to think that blood is necessary to preserve life. You can never bleed a patient too much."

The good canon, imagining that so great a doctor could not argue wrongly, allowed himself to be bled without resistance. When the doctor had ordered these frequent and copious bleedings, he said that we must also make the canon continually drink warm water. We heated the kettles in a hurry and . . . we began with pouring down two or three pints in as many swallows. An hour later we set upon him again; then, returning to the attack time after time, we fairly poured a deluge of water into his poor stomach. The surgeon, on the other hand, seconding our efforts by the quantity of blood he drew off, reduced the old canon to death's door in less than two days. . . .

[After learning of a possible inheritance], I promised to pray for his soul after his death. This event happened anon, for the surgeon having bled him once more, the poor old man, already much weakened, expired almost immediately. As he was breathing his last, the physician appeared and looked rather foolish in spite of the habit he had of dispatching his patients. . . . He coolly observed as he left that the patient had not been bled enough and had not drunk enough water. The medical executioner—I mean the surgeon—seeing that his job was done, followed the doctor, both remarking that they had said he would not recover, the very first day they saw him.

hung in irons. The medical profession also favored treatments such as bleeding (the intentional drawing of blood from a sick person) or purging the ill with emetics and enemas. The argument for bleeding was derived from the observation that if blood were drawn, the body temperature dropped. Because fevers accompa-

nied most diseases, bleeding was employed to reduce the fever. This treatment often hastened death (see document 19.2). King Louis XV of France was virtually bled to death by his physicians in 1774, although officially he succumbed to smallpox. As Baron von Leibnitz, a distinguished German philosopher and scientist,

Illustration 19.2

An Eighteenth-Century Hospital. This scene of a German hospital ward in Hamburg depicts many aspects of premodern medicine. Note the mixture of patients with all afflictions, the nonsterile conditions, the amputation of a leg on a conscious patient, the arrival of a daily ration of bread, and the administration of the last rites to a patient.

observed, "[A] great doctor kills more people than a great general."

The treatment given to King Charles II of England in 1685, as he died of an apparent embolism (a clot in an artery), shows the state of learned medicine. A team of a dozen physicians first drew a pint of blood from his right arm. They then cut open his right shoulder and cupped it with a vacuum jar to draw more blood. Charles then received an emetic to induce vomiting, followed by a purgative, then a second purgative. Next came an enema of antimony and herbs, followed by a second enema and a third purgative. Physicians then shaved the king's head, blistered it with heated glass, intentionally broke the blisters, and smeared a powder into the wounds (to "strengthen his brain"). Next came a plaster of pitch and pigeon excrement. Death was probably a relief to the tortured patient.

Hospitals were also scarce in the Old Regime. Nearly half of the counties of England contained no hospital in 1710; by 1800, there were still only four thousand hospital beds in the entire country, half of them in London. Avoiding hospitals was generally safer in any case (see illustration 19.2). These institutions had typically been founded by monastic orders as refuges for the destitute sick, and most of them were still operated by churches in the eighteenth century. There were a few specialized hospitals (the first children's clinic was founded at London in 1779), and most hospitals typically mixed together poor patients with a variety of diseases that then spread inside the hospital. Patients received a minimal diet and rudimentary care but little medical treatment. The history of surgery

is even more frightening to people accustomed to twentieth-century standards. In many regions, surgeons were still members of the barbers' guild. Because eighteenth-century physicians did not believe in the germ theory of disease transmission, surgeons often cut people in squalid surroundings with no thought for basic cleanliness of their hands or their instruments. Without antisepsis, gangrene (then called hospital putrefaction) was a common result of surgery. No general anesthetics were available, so surgeons operated upon a fully conscious patient.

In these circumstances, opium became a favorite medication of well-to-do patients. It was typically taken as a tincture with alcohol known as laudanum, and it was available from apothecaries without a prescription. Laudanum drugged the patient, and it often addicted survivors to opium, but it reduced suffering. Many famous figures of the eighteenth and nineteenth centuries died, as did the artist Sir Joshua Reynolds in 1792, "all but speechless from laudanum." Others died as Voltaire did, while suffering from painful kidney problems in 1778, partly as a result of massive overdoses of laudanum.

Subsistence Diet and the Biological Old Regime

The second critical feature of the biological old regime was a dangerously inadequate food supply. In all regions of Europe, much of the population lived with chronic undernourishment, dreading the possibility of

Illustration 19.3

🏭 **Bread: The Staff of Life.** Most Europeans obtained more than 50 percent of their total calories from eating bread, and for large groups of people the figure reached 75 percent of all calories. Life in Europe (and public tranquility for governments) depended upon a reliable chain of grain production, the milling and transportation of flour, and the baking of bread. The greatest reference book of the century, the *Encyclopédie,* included several illustrations on this chain of life, such as the public bakery depicted here, where dough is kneaded (right), shaped into loaves (center), and baked (left).

famine. A subsistence diet (one that barely met the minimum needed to sustain life) produced chronic malnutrition. Subsistence diets weaken the immune system, making people more vulnerable to contracting diseases and less able to withstand their ravages. Diet was thus a major factor in the Old Regime's high mortality rates and short life expectancies.

Most of Europe lived on vegetable foods, chiefly starches. The biblical description of bread as "the staff of life" was true (see illustration 19.3). Bread consumption varied by region and social class, but most people obtained 50 percent to 75 percent of their total calories from bread, so interruptions of the grain supply meant suffering and death. In good times, a peasant family ate several pounds of bread a day; in lean times, they might share one pound of bread (see table 19.4). A study of the food supply in Belgium has shown that the nation consumed a per capita average of one-and-a-quarter pounds of cereal grains per day. In poorer regions (or harder times), the reliance upon grains could go higher. A study of eastern Prussia has shown that the adult population lived on nearly three pounds of grain per day. Peasant labors there received their entire annual wages in starches; the quantity ranged from thirty-two bushels of grain (1694) to twenty-five bushels of grain and one of peas (1760).

Bread made from wheat was costly because wheat yielded few grains harvested per grain sown (see chapter 18). As a result, peasants lived on coarser, but bountiful, grains. Their heavy, dark bread normally came from rye and barley. In some poor areas, such as Scotland, oats were the staple grain. To save valuable fuel, many villages baked bread in large loaves once a month, or even once a season. This created a hard bread that had to be broken with a hammer and soaked in liquid before it could be eaten. For variety, cereals could be mixed with liquid (usually water) without baking to create a porridge or gruel.

Supplements to the monotonous diet of cereal starches varied from region to region, but meat was a rarity. In a world without canning or refrigeration, meat was consumed only when livestock were slaughtered, in a salted or smoked form of preservation, or in a rancid condition. A study of the food supply in Rome in the 1750s has shown that the average daily consumption of meat amounted to slightly more than two ounces. For the lower classes, that meant a few ounces of sausage or dried meat per week. In that same decade, Romans con-

◣ TABLE 19.4 ◢

Grain Consumption in the Eighteenth Century

The highest rate of grain consumption during the Old Regime was usually associated with the lowest standards of living. High rates indicate severely unbalanced diets; low rates are found in prosperous regions where other foods were more available.

Region	Period	Per capita daily grain consumption
Holland	1798	0.7 pounds
France	c. 1700	1.3–1.4 pounds
England	18th century	1.4 pounds
Hanover	c. 1750	1.4 pounds
France	1775–1780	1.4–1.7 pounds
East Prussia	1750–1800	2.8 pounds[a]
Burgundy	18th century	3.1 pounds
Flanders	1710	3.2 pounds[b]

Source: Condensed from data in B. H. Slicher van Bach, "Agriculture and the Vital Revolution," in *The Cambridge Economic History of Europe*, edited by M. M. Postan and others (Cambridge: Cambridge University Press, 1977), 5:84.

[a]For people over 12 years old.

[b]Includes grain for beer.

◣ TABLE 19.5 ◢

Food in the Budget of a Berlin Worker's Family, c. 1800

Expense	Percentage
Food	
Bread	45
Other vegetable products	12
Animal products (meat and dairy)	15
Beverages	2
Total food	74
Nonfood	
Housing	14
Heating, lighting	7
Clothing, other expenses	6
Total Nonfood	27

Note: Figures exceed 100 percent because of rounding.

Source: From data in Fernand Braudel, *The Structures of Everyday Life* (New York, N.Y.: Harper and Row, 1981), p. 132.

sumed bread at an average varying between one and two pounds per day. Fruits and fresh vegetables were seasonal and typically limited to those regions where they were cultivated. A fresh orange was thus a luxury to most Europeans, and a fresh pineapple was rare and expensive. Occasional dairy products plus some cooking fats and oils (chiefly lard in northern Europe and olive oil in the south) brought urban diets close to twenty-five hundred calories per day in good times. A study of Parisian workers in 1780 found that adult males engaged in physical labor averaged two thousand calories per day, mostly from bread. (Figures of thirty-five hundred to four thousand are common today among males doing physical labor.) Urban workers often spent more than half of their wages for food, even when they just ate bread. A study of Berlin at the end of the eighteenth century showed that a working-class family might spend more than 70 percent of its income on food (see table 19.5). Peasants ate only the few vegetables grown in kitchen gardens that they could afford to keep out of grain production.

Beverages varied regionally. In many places, the water was unhealthy to drink and peasants avoided it without knowing the scientific explanation of their fears. Southern Europe produced and consumed large quantities of wine, and beer could be made anywhere that grain was grown. In 1777 King Frederick the Great of Prussia urged his people to drink beer, stating that he had been raised on it and believed that a nation "nourished on beer" could be "depended on to endure hardships." Such beers were often dark, thick, and heavy. When Benjamin Franklin arrived in England, he called the beer "as black as bull's blood and as thick as mustard."

Wine and beer were consumed as staples of the diet, and peasants and urban workers alike derived much of their calories and carbohydrates from them, partly because few nonalcoholic choices were available. The consumption of milk depended upon the local economy. Beverages infused in water (coffee, tea, cocoa) became popular in European cities when global trading made them affordable. The Spanish introduced the drinking of chocolate (which was only a beverage until the nineteenth century) from America, but it long remained a state secret and a costly drink. Coffee drinking was brought to Europe from the Middle East, and it became a great vogue after 1650, producing numerous urban coffeehouses. But infused beverages never re-

Illustration 19.4

Alcohol. Alcohol consumption rates during the eighteenth century were significantly higher than they are today. Drinking to excess was one behavior pattern that cut across social classes, from the taverns in poor districts advertising "dead drunk for a penny" to the falling down drunks of the upper class depicted in Hogarth's "A Midnight Modern Conversation" here. Note that smoking pipes is nearly universal and that women are excluded from this event. See also the chamber pot in the lower right corner.

placed wine and beer in the diet. Some governments feared that coffeehouses were centers of subversion and restricted them more than the taverns. Others worried about the mercantilist implications of coffee and tea imports. English coffee imports, for example, sextupled between 1700 and 1785, leading the government to tax tea and coffee. The king of Sweden issued an edict denouncing coffee in 1746, and when that failed to control the national addiction, he decreed total prohibition in 1756. Coffee smuggling produced such criminal problems, however, that the king legalized the drink again in 1766 and collected a heavy excise tax on it. Even with such popularity, infused beverages did not curtail the remarkable rate of alcohol consumption (see illustration 19.4). In addition to wines and beer, eighteenth-century England drank an enormous amount of gin. In 1733 the nation consumed a gallon of gin per capita. Only a steep gin tax in 1736 and vigorous enforcement of a Tippling Act of 1751 reduced consumption from 8.5 million gallons of gin per year to 2.1 million gallons during the 1750s.

Typical diets varied greatly according to social status (see illustration 19.5). The best historical records showing the range of diets are those describing the lavish meals of monarchs and those listing the meagre fare in institutions. At the bottom of the social scale, adult male inmates sentenced to labor in a Dutch prison in the 1780s received fifteen meals per week, and they chiefly lived on bread, dried peas, and a gruel of oats; they received meat once a week (see table 19.6). In contrast, the privileged seminarians of the Cistercian order in southern France consumed a varied diet of nearly five thousand calories per day in the 1750s. This included 2.3 pounds of bread, 6 ounces of red meat, 9.7 ounces of poultry, an egg, and a pint and a half of wine every day, plus frequent additions. At the top of the social hierarchy food was even more abundant and varied. Ostentatious quantities of food were prepared, with leftovers consumed by courtiers and servants or given to the poor. The contrast between the lavish diet at the top of society and the chronic undernourishment at the bottom can be seen at the table of Louis XIV of France. His sister-in-law, a German princess, wrote: "I have often seen the king eating four full plates of soup, a whole pheasant, a partridge, a big dish of salad, two big slices of ham, some mutton with juice and garlic, a plate of pastry, and then fruit and some hard-boiled eggs."

The Columbian Exchange and the European Diet

The most important changes in the European diet of the Old Regime resulted from the gradual adoption of foods found in the Americas. In a reciprocal Columbian exchange of plants and animals unknown on the other continent, Europe and America both acquired new foods (see map 19.2). No Italian tomato sauce or French fried potato existed before the Columbian exchange because the tomato and potato were plants native to the Americas and unknown in Europe. Similarly, the Columbian exchange introduced maize (American corn), peanuts, many peppers and beans, and cacao to Europe. The Americas had no wheat fields, grapevines,

A

B

C

Illustration 19.5

 Diet and Social Class.   Much of the population of eighteenth century Europe lived on little more than bread. If the harvest were too bad, the lower classes faced famine. In this illustration, troops try to maintain order when bread is distributed during a famine.

Three exotic beverages that had been introduced into the European diet—coffee, tea, and chocolate—were fashionable among the limited population of eighteenth-century Europeans who could afford them. A British middle-class family (illustration B) enjoys the habit of a late afternoon tea. Note how the high status (and cost) of tea is marked with a silver service and fine china cups, which the woman proudly displays.

For rich aristocrats, a single individual's dinner at a feast could cost enough to feed a peasant family for a year. The great dinner illustrated in C was a celebration hosted in Paris in 1707 by the duke of Alba in honor of the birth of a Spanish prince.

☙ TABLE 19.6 ☙

The Diet in an Amsterdam Prison, 1781

John Howard was an English reformer who toured European prisons in the 1770s and 1780s to compare the conditions in them. He praised Dutch prisons for having the best conditions, and he reported that adult male prisoners who worked a full shift received two meals per day and a third meal on Wednesday, following the menu below.

Time	Meal
Daily breakfast	One and one-half pounds of bread, with butter
Daily beverage ration	Four pints of weak beer
Monday noon	Peas with salt and vinegar
Tuesday noon	Boiled peas
Wednesday noon	Gruel of oats or barley boiled in milk
Wednesday evening	Gruel of oats or barley boiled in milk
Thursday noon	Fish with milk or butter
Friday noon	Boiled peas
Saturday noon	Gruel of oats or barley boiled in milk
Sunday dinner	One-half pound of beef or pork with beans

or melon patches; no horses, sheep, cattle, pigs, goats, or burros. In the second stage of this exchange, European plants established in the Americas began to flourish and yield exportation to Europe. The most historic example of this was the establishment of the sugarcane plantations in the Caribbean, where slave labor made sugar commonly available in Europe for the first time, but at a horrific human price.

Europe's first benefit from the Columbian exchange came from the potato, which changed diets in the eighteenth century. The Spanish imported the potato in the sixteenth century after finding the Incas cultivating it in Peru, but Europeans initially refused to eat it because folk wisdom considered all tubers dangerous. Churches opposed the potato because the Bible did not mention it. Potatoes, however, offer the tremendous advantage of yielding more calories per acre than grains do. In much of northern Europe, especially in western Ireland and northern Germany, short and rainy summer seasons severely limited the crops that could be grown and the population that could be supported. Irish peasants discovered that just one acre of potatoes, planted in soil

that was poor for grains, could support a full family. German peasants learned that they could grow potatoes in their fallow fields during crop rotation, then discovered an acre of potatoes could feed as many people as four acres of the rye that they traditionally planted. Peasants soon found another of the advantages of the potato: It could be left in the ground all winter without harvesting it. Ripe grain must be harvested and stored, becoming an easy target for civilian tax collectors or military requisitioners. Potatoes could be left in the ground until the day they were eaten, thereby providing peasants with much greater security. The steady growth of German population compared with France during the eighteenth and nineteenth centuries (with tremendous historic implications) is partly the result of this peasant decision and the educational work of agronomists such as Antoine Parmentier, who showed its merits in his *Treatise on the Uses of the Potato.* Just as the potato changed the history of Germany and Ireland, the introduction of maize changed other regions. Historians of the Balkans credit the nutritional advantages of maize with the population increase and better health that facilitated the Serbian and Greek struggles for independence.

The European diet included little sugar and few sweets until before the arrival of American cane sugar. Until the late seventeenth century few Europeans had even tasted sugar. A German chemist, A. S. Marggraf, discovered the sugar in beetroots in 1747, but this did not change European diets significantly until the nineteenth century. By 1750 sugar had become readily available to the propertied classes, and Europeans began to develop the modern addiction to sugar. The growing demand for sugar thereby helped to perpetuate slavery in European colonies.

Famine in the Old Regime

Even after the introduction of the potato and maize, much of Europe lived on a subsistence diet. In bad times, the result was catastrophic. Famines, usually the result of two consecutive bad harvests, produced starvation. In such times, peasants ate their seed grain or harvested unripe grain and roasted it, prolonging both life and famine. They turned to making bread from ground chestnuts or acorns. They ate grass and weeds, cats and dogs, rodents, even human flesh. Such disasters were not rare. The records of Tuscany show that the three-hundred-year period between 1450 and 1750 included one hundred years of famine and sixteen years of bountiful harvests. Agriculture was more successful in

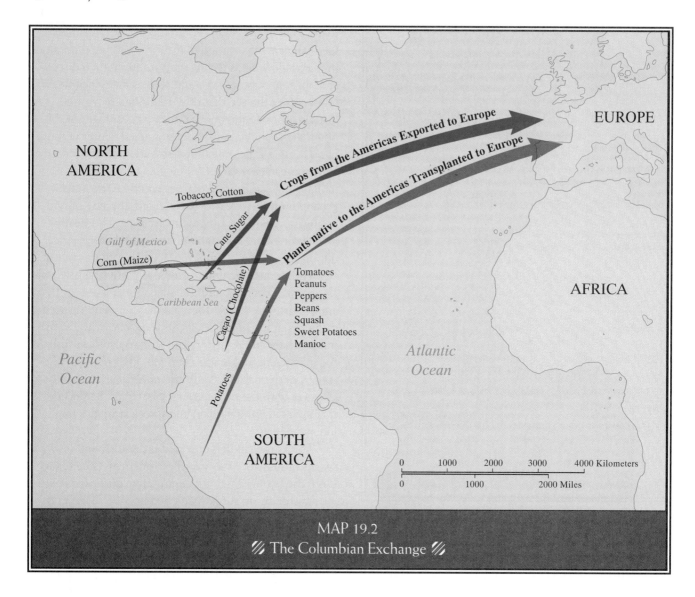

NORTH
AMERICA

Gulf of Mexico

Caribbean Sea

Pacific
Ocean

SOUTH
AMERICA

Tobacco, Cotton

Cane Sugar

Corn (Maize)

Cacao (Chocolate)

Potatoes

Crops from the Americas Exported to Europe

Plants native to the Americas Transplanted to Europe

Tomatoes
Peanuts
Peppers
Beans
Squash
Sweet Potatoes
Manioc

Atlantic
Ocean

EUROPE

AFRICA

0   1000   2000   3000   4000 Kilometers

0   1000   2000 Miles

MAP 19.2
The Columbian Exchange

England, but the period between 1660 and 1740 saw one bad harvest in every four years. France, an agriculturally fortunate country, experienced sixteen years of national famine during the eighteenth century, plus local famines.

The worst famine of the Old Regime, and one of the most deadly events in European history, occurred in Finland in 1696–97. The extreme cold weather of the Little Ice Age produced in Finland a summer too short for grain to ripen. Between one-fourth and one-third of the entire nation died before that famine passed—a death rate that equaled the horrors of the bubonic plague. The weather produced other famines in that decade. In northern Europe, excess rain caused crops to rot in the field before ripening. In Mediterranean Europe, especially in central Spain, a drought followed by an onslaught of grasshoppers produced a similar catastrophe. Hunger also followed seasonal fluctuations. In

lean years, the previous year's grain might be consumed before July, when the new grain could be harvested. Late spring and early summer were consequently dangerous times when the food supply had political significance. Winter posed special threats for city dwellers. If the rivers and canals froze, the barges that supplied the cities could not move, and the water-powered mills could not grind flour.

Food supplies were such a concern in the Old Regime that marriage contracts and wills commonly provided food pensions. These pensions were intended to protect a wife or aged relatives by guaranteeing an annual supply of food. An examination of these pensions in southern France has shown that most of the food to be provided was in cereal grains. The typical form was a lifetime annuity intended to provide a supplement; the average grain given in wills provided fewer than fourteen hundred calories per day.

Diet, Disease, and Appearance

Malnutrition, famine, and disease were manifested in human appearance. A diet so reliant on starches meant that people were short compared with later standards. For example, the average adult male of the eighteenth century stood slightly above five feet tall. Napoleon, ridiculed today for being so short, was as tall as most of his soldiers. Meticulous records kept for Napoleon's Army of Italy in the late 1790s (a victorious army) reveal that conscripts averaged 5′2″ in height. Many famous figures of the era had similar heights: the notorious Marquis de Sade stood 5′3″. Conversely, people known for their height were not tall by later standards. A French diplomat, Prince Talleyrand, appears in letters and memoirs to have had an advantage in negotiations because he "loomed over" other statesmen. Talleyrand stood 5′8″. The kings of Prussia recruited peasants considered to be "giants" to serve in the royal guards at Potsdam; a height of 6′0″ defined a giant. Extreme height did occur in some families. The Russian royal family, the Romanovs, produced some monarchs nearly seven feet tall. For the masses, diet limited their height. The superior diet of the aristocracy made them taller than peasants, just as it gave them a greater life expectancy; aristocrats explained such differences by their natural superiority as a caste.

Just as diet shaped appearance, so did disease. Vitamin and mineral deficiencies led to a variety of afflictions, such as rickets and scrofula. Rickets marked people with bone deformities; scrofula produced hard tumors on the body, especially under the chin. The most widespread effect of disease came from smallpox. As its name indicates, the disease often left pockmarks on its victims, the result of scratching the sores, which itched terribly. Because 95 percent of the population contracted smallpox, pockmarked faces were common. The noted Anglo-Irish dramatist Oliver Goldsmith described this in 1760:

> Lo, the smallpox with horrid glare
> Levelled its terrors at the fair;
> And, rifling every youthful grace,
> Left but the remnant of a face.

Smallpox and diseases that discolored the skin such as jaundice, which left a yellow complexion, explain the eighteenth-century popularity of heavy makeup and artificial "beauty marks" (which could cover a pockmark) in the fashions of the wealthy. Other fashion trends of the age originated in poor public health. The vogue for wigs and powdered hair for men and women alike derived in part from infestation by lice. Head lice could be controlled by shaving the head and wearing a wig.

Dental disease marked people with missing or dark, rotting teeth. The absence of sugar in the diet delayed tooth decay, but oral hygiene scarcely existed because people did not know that bacteria caused their intense toothaches. Medical wisdom held that the pain came from a worm that bored into teeth. Anton van Leeuwenhoek, the Dutch naturalist who invented the microscope, had seen bacteria in dental tartar in the late seventeenth century, and Pierre Fauchard, a French physician considered the founder of modern dentistry, had denounced the worm theory, but their science did not persuade their colleagues. For brave urban dwellers, barber-surgeons offered the painful process of extraction. A simple, but excruciating, method involved inserting a whole peppercorn into a large cavity; the pepper expanded until the tooth shattered, facilitating extraction. More often, dental surgeons gripped the unanesthetized patient's head with their knees and used tongs to shake the tooth loose. Whether or not one faced such dreadful pain, dental disease left most people with only a partial set of teeth by their forties.

The Life Cycle: Birth

Consideration of the basic conditions of life provides a fundamental perspective on any period of the past. Social historians also use another set of perspectives to examine the history of daily life: an examination of the life cycle from birth to old age (see table 19.7). Few experiences better illustrate the perils of the Old Regime than the process of entering it. Pregnancy and birth were extremely dangerous for both mother and child. Malnutrition and poor prenatal care caused a high rate of miscarriages, stillbirths, and deformities. Childbirth was still an experience without anesthesia or antisepsis. The greatest menace to the mother was puerperal fever (child-bed fever), an acute infection of the genital tract resulting from the absence of aseptic methods. This disease swept Europe, particularly the few "laying-in" hospitals for women. An epidemic of puerperal fever in 1773 was so severe that folk memories in northern Italy recalled that not a single pregnant woman survived. Common diseases, such as rickets (from vitamin deficiency), made deliveries difficult and caused bone deformities in babies. No adequate treatment was available for hemorrhaging, which could cause death

⋈ TABLE 19.7 ⋈

A Comparison of Life Cycles

Life cycle characteristic	Sweden, 1778–82	United States (1990 census)
Annual birthrate	34.5 per 1,000 population	15.6 per 1,000 population
Fertility rate	145.2 births per 1,000 women	69.2 births per 1,000 women
Infant mortality (age 0-1)	211.6 deaths per 1,000 live births	9.2 deaths per 1,000 live births
Life expectancy at birth		
Male	36 years	71.8 years
Female	39 years	78.8 years
Life expectancy at age 1		
Male	44 years longer (45 total years)	72.3 years longer (73.3 total)
Female	46 years longer (47 total years)	78.9 years longer (79.9 total)
Life expectancy at age 50		
Male	19 years longer (69 total years)	26.7 years longer (76.7 total)
Female	20 years longer (70 total years)	31.6 years longer (81.6 total)
Population distribution	ages 0–14 = 31.9%	ages 0–19 = 28.9%
	ages 15–64 = 63.2%	ages 20–64 = 58.7%
	ages 65+ = 4.9%	ages 65+ = 12.5%
Annual death rate	25.9 deaths per 1,000 population	8.5 deaths per 1,000 population

Source: Swedish data from Carlo M. Cipolla, *Before the Industrial Revolution* (New York, N.Y.: Norton, 1976), pp. 286–87; U.S. data from *The World Almanac and Book of Fact, 1995* (Mahwah, N.J.: World Almanac Book, 1994), p. 957; and *Information Please Almanac, Atlas, and Yearbook 1994* (Boston, Mass.: Houghton Mifflin Co., 1993), pp. 829, 848, 850–52.

by bleeding or slower death by gangrene. Few ways existed to lower the risks of difficult deliveries. Surgical birth by a cesarean section gave the mother one chance in a thousand of surviving. Attempts to deliver a baby by using large forceps saved many lives but often produced horrifying injuries to the newborn or hemorrhaging in the mother. A delicate balance thus existed between the deep pride in bearing children and a deep fear of doing so. One of the most noted women of letters in early modern Europe, Madame de Sévigné, advised her daughter of two rules for survival: "Don't get pregnant and don't catch smallpox."

The established churches, backed by the medical profession, preached acceptance of the pain of childbirth by teaching that it represented the divine will. The explanation lay in the Bible. For "the sin of Eve" in succumbing to Satan and being "the devil's gateway" to Adam, God punished all women with the words: "I will greatly multiply thy sorrow and thy conception; in sorrow thou shalt bring forth children" (Gen. 3:16). Even when the means to diminish the pain of childbirth became available, this argument sustained opposition to it.

The Life Cycle: Infancy and Childhood

Statistics show that surviving the first year of infancy was more difficult than surviving birth. All across Europe, between 20 percent and 30 percent of the babies born died before their first birthday (see table 19.8). An additional one-fourth of all children did not live to be eight, meaning that approximately half of the population died in infancy or early childhood. A noted scientist of the 1760s, Michael Lomonosev, calculated that half of the infants born in Russia died before the age of three. So frightful was this toll that many families did not name a child until its first birthday; others gave a cherished family name to more than one child in the hope that one of them would carry it to adulthood. Johann Sebastian Bach fathered twenty children in two marriages and reckoned himself fortunate that ten lived into adulthood. The greatest historian of the century, Edward Gibbon, was the only child of seven in his family to survive infancy.

The newborn were acutely vulnerable to the biological old regime. Intestinal infections killed many in the first months. Unheated housing claimed more. Epidemic diseases killed more infants and young children

◀ TABLE 19.8 ▶

Infant Mortality in the Eighteenth Century

Percentages represent deaths before the first birthday; they do not include stillbirths.

Country	Period	Percentage of deaths before age 1
England	pre-1750	18.7
	1740–90	16.1
	1780–1820	12.2
France	pre-1750	25.2
	1740–90	21.3
	1780–1820	19.5
German states	pre-1750	15.4
	1740–90	38.8
	1780–1820	23.6
Spain	pre-1750	28.1
	1740–90	27.3
	1780–1820	22.0
Sweden	pre-1750	n.a.
	1740–90	22.5
	1780–1820	18.7
United States	1995	0.8

Source: European data from Michael W. Flinn, *The European Demographic System, 1500–1820* (Baltimore, Md.: Johns Hopkins University Press, 1971), p.92; U.S. data from *The World Almanac and Book of Facts, 1997* (Mahwah, N.J.: World Almanac Books, 1996), p. 962.
n.a. = Not available.

than adults because some diseases, such as measles and smallpox, left surviving adults immune to them. The dangers touched all social classes. Madame de Montespan, the mistress of King Louis XIV of France, had seven children with him; three were born crippled or deformed, three others died in childhood, and one reached adulthood in good health.

Eighteenth-century parents commonly killed unwanted infants (daughters more often than sons) before diseases did. Infanticide—frequently by smothering the baby, usually by abandoning an infant to the elements—has a long history in Western culture (see illustration 19.6). The mythical founders of Rome depicted on many emblems of that city, Romulus and Remus, were abandoned infants who were raised by a wolf; the newborn Moses was abandoned to his fate on the Nile. Infanticide did not constitute murder in eighteenth-century British law (it was manslaughter) if done by the mother before the baby reached age one. In France, however, where infanticide was more common, Louis XIV ordered capital punishment for it, although few mothers were ever executed. The frequency of infanticide provoked instructions that all priests read the law in church in 1707 and again in 1731. A study of police records has found that more than 10 percent of all women arrested in Paris in the eighteenth century were nonetheless charged with infanticide. In central and eastern Europe, many midwives were also "killing nurses" who murdered babies for their parents.

Illustration 19.6

◢ Infanticide. The murder of newborn children was shockingly common in the age before effective birth control. Laws punishing infanticide existed in most countries, but treatment was usually more lenient than for the murder of an adult. This eighteenth-century German print teaches strict application of the law: A smothered baby is found hidden under its mother's bed (upper left), the mother is condemned (lower left), and she is led off to a public execution (right).

TABLE 19.9
Famine and Abandoned Children in France, 1692–1710

In the table below, years of famine are shown in bold type.

Children Abandoned

Year	At Paris	At Lyon
1692	1,971	567
1693	**2,894**	**906**
1694	**3,788**	**1,545**
1695	1,767	404
1708	1,759	454
1709	**2,525**	**1,884**
1710	1,698	589

Source: Compiled from data in Jean Sandrin, *Enfants trouvés, enfants ouvriers: 17ᵉ–19ᵉ siècle* (Paris: Aubier, 1982), p. 18.

Illustration 19.7

Abandoned Children. One of the most common forms of population control in the eighteenth century (and continuing through the nineteenth century) was the abandonment of newborn children. Because so many babies were left at churches and public buildings, and a shocking number were left to die outdoors, governments created foundling homes where babies could be abandoned. To encourage mothers to use foundling homes, many of them (such as this one in Italy) built revolving doors to the outside, allowing women to leave a baby without being seen or speaking to anyone.

A slightly more humane reaction to unwanted babies was to abandon them in public places in the hope that someone else would care for them. That happened so often that cities established hospitals for foundlings. The practice had begun at Rome in the late Middle Ages when Pope Innocent III found that he could seldom cross the Tiber River without seeing babies thrown into it. Paris established its foundling hospital in 1670. Thomas Coram opened the foundling hospital at London in 1739 because he could not endure the frequency with which he saw dying babies lying in the gutters and dead ones thrown onto dung-heaps. The London Foundling Hospital could scarcely handle all of the city's abandoned babies: In 1758, twenty-three hundred foundlings (under age one) were found abandoned in the streets of London. Abandonment increased in periods of famine and when the illegitimate birthrate rose (as it did during the eighteenth century). French data show that the famine of 1693–94 doubled the abandonment of children at Paris and tripled it at Lyon (see table 19.9). Abandonments at Paris grew to an annual average of five thousand in the late eighteenth century, with a peak of 7,676 in 1772, which is a rate of twenty-one babies abandoned every day. Studies of foundlings in Italy have shown that 11 percent to 15 percent of all babies born at Milan between 1700 and 1729 were abandoned each year; at Venice, the figures ranged between 8 percent and 9 percent in 1756–87 (see illustration 19.7).

The abandonment of children at this rate overwhelmed the ability of church or state to help. With 390,000 abandonments at the Foundling Hospital of Paris between 1640 and 1789—with thirty abandonments on the single night of April 20, 1720—the prospects for these children were bleak. Finances were inadequate, partly because churches feared that fine facilities might encourage illicit sexuality, so the conditions in foundling homes stayed grim. Whereas 50 percent of the general population survived childhood, only 10 percent of abandoned children reached age ten. The infant (before age one) death rates for foundling homes in the late eighteenth century were 90 percent in Dublin, 80 percent in Paris, and only 52 percent in London (where infants were farmed out to wet nurses). Of 37,600 children admitted to the Foundling Hospital of Moscow between 1766 and 1786, more than thirty thousand died. The prospects of the survivors were poor, but one noteworthy exception was Jean d'Alembert, a mathematician and coeditor of the *Encyclopédie*, who was discovered in a pine box at a Parisian church in 1717.

Young children were often separated from their parents for long periods of time. Immediately after birth, many were sent to wet nurses, foster mothers whose occupation was the breast feeding of infants. The studies of France show that more than 95 percent of the babies born in Paris in 1780 were nursed commercially, 75 percent going to wet nurses in the provinces. As breast feeding normally lasted twelve to eighteen months, only wealthy parents (who could hire a live-in wet nurse) or the poorest might see their infant children with any frequency. The great French novelist Honoré de Balzac was born in 1799 and immediately dispatched to a wet nurse; he bitterly remembered his infancy as being "neglected by my family for three years."

Infant care by rural wet nurses was not universal. It was most common in towns and cities, especially in social classes that could afford the service. The poor usually fed infants gruel—flour mixed in milk, or bread crumbs in water—by dipping a finger into it and letting the baby suck the finger. Upper-class families in England, France, and northern Italy chose wet-nursing; fewer did so in Central Europe. Every king of France, starting with Louis IX (Saint Louis), was nurtured by a succession of royal nurses; but mothers in the Hapsburg royal family, including the empress Maria Theresa, were expected to nurse their own children. Wet-nursing increased in the eighteenth century in imitation of the habits of the aristocracy. For some mothers, exhausted by the delivery or in poor health, it was a physical necessity. Others, particularly women working in shops and factories, found returning to work an economic necessity.

Separation from parents remained a feature of life for young children after their weaning. Both Catholicism, which perceived early childhood as an age of innocence, and Protestantism, which held children to be marked by original sin, advocated the separation of the child from the corrupt world of adults. This meant the segregation of children from many parental activities as well as the segregation of boys and girls. Many extreme cases existed among the aristocracy. The Marquis de Lafayette, the hero of the American revolution, lost his father in infancy; his mother left the infant at the family's provincial estate while she resided in Paris and visited him during a brief vacation once a year. Balzac went straight from his wet nurse to a Catholic boarding school where the Oratorian Brothers allowed him no vacations and his mother visited him twice in six years.

Family structures were changing in early modern times, but most children grew up in patriarchal families. Modern parent-child relationships, with more emphasis upon affection than upon discipline, were beginning to appear. However, most children still lived with the emotional detachment of both parents and the stern discipline of a father whose authority had the sanction of law. The Russian novelist Sergei Aksakov recalled that, when his mother had rocked her infant daughter to sleep in the 1780s, relatives rebuked her for showing "such exaggerated love," which they considered contrary to good parenting and "a crime against God." Children in many countries heard the words of Martin Luther repeated: "I would rather have a dead son than a disobedient one." In several countries, fathers possessed the legal right to request the imprisonment of disobedient children; in France, fathers did so by obtaining a *lettre de cachet* from the government.

Childhood had not yet become the distinct and separate phase of life that it later became. In many ways, children passed directly from a few years of infancy into treatment as virtual adults. Middle- and upper-class boys of the eighteenth century made a direct transition from wearing the gowns and frocks of infancy into wearing the pants and panoply (such as swords) of adulthood. This rite of passage, when boys went from the care of women to the care of men, normally happened at approximately age seven. European traditions and laws varied, but in most economic, legal, and religious ways, boys became adults between seven and fourteen. Peasant children became members of the household economy almost immediately, assuming such duties as tending to chickens or hoeing the kitchen garden. In the towns, a child seeking to learn a craft and enter a guild might begin with an apprenticeship (with another family) as early as age seven. Children of the elite were typically sent away to receive their education at boarding schools. Children of all classes began to become adults by law at age seven. In English law seven was the adult age at which a child could be flogged or executed; the Spanish Inquisition

◈ DOCUMENT 19.3 ◈

Arranged Marriages in the Eighteenth Century

Richard Brinsley Sheridan (1751–1816) was an Irish dramatist who wrote comedies of manners for the London stage. One of his greatest plays, The Rivals (1775), made fun of the tradition of arranged marriages. In it, a wealthy aristocratic father, Sir Anthony Absolute, arranges a suitable marriage for his son, Captain Jack Absolute (who is in love with a beautiful young woman), without consulting him. In the following scene, Captain Absolute tries to refuse the marriage and Sir Anthony tries first to bribe him and then to coerce him.

Absolute: Now, Jack, I am sensible that the income of your commission, and what I have hitherto allowed you, is but a small pittance for a lad of your spirit.

Captain Jack: Sir, you are very good.

Absolute: And it is my wish, while yet I live, to have my boy make some figure in the world. I have resolved, therefore, to fix you at once in a noble independence.

Captain Jack: Sir, your kindness overpowers me—such generosity makes the gratitude of reason more lively than the sensations even of filial affection.

Absolute: I am glad you are so sensible of my attention—and you shall be master of a large estate in a few weeks.

Captain Jack: Let my future life, sir, speak my gratitude; I cannot express the sense I have of your munificence. —Yet, sir, I presume you would not wish me to quit the army?

Absolute: Oh, that shall be as your wife chooses.

Captain Jack: My wife, sir!

Absolute: Ay, ay, settle that between you—settle that between you.

Captain Jack: A wife, sir, did you say?

Absolute: Ay, a wife—why, did I not mention her before?

Captain Jack: Not a word of her sir.

Absolute: Odd, so! I mus'n't forget her though. —Yes, Jack, the independence I was talking of is by marriage—the fortune is saddled with a wife—but I suppose that makes no difference.

Captain Jack: Sir! Sir! You amaze me!

Absolute: Why, what the devil's the matter with you, fool? Just now you were all gratitude and duty.

Captain Jack: I was, sir—you talked of independence and a fortune, but not a word of a wife!

Absolute: Why—what difference does that make? Odds life, sir! If you had an estate, you must take it with the live stock on it, as it stands!

Captain Jack: If my happiness is to be the price, I must beg leave to decline the purchase. Pray, sir, who is the lady?

Absolute: What's that to you, sir? Come, give me your promise to love, and to marry her directly.

Captain Jack: Sure, sir, this is not very reasonable. . . . You must excuse me, sir, if I tell you, once for all, that in this point I cannot obey you. . . .

Absolute: Sir, I won't hear a word—not one word! . . .

Captain Jack: What, sir, promise to link myself to some mass of ugliness!

Absolute: Zounds! Sirrah! The lady shall be as ugly as I choose: she shall have a hump on each shoulder; she shall be as crooked as the crescent; her one eye shall roll like the bull's in Cox's Museum; she shall have a skin like a mummy, and the beard of a Jew—she shall be all this, sirrah! Yet I will make you ogle her all day, and sit up all night to write sonnets on her beauty.

---

withheld adult interrogation until age thirteen. Twelve was the most common adult age at which children could consent to marriage or to sexual relations.

Tradition and law treated girls differently from boys. In the Roman law tradition, prevalent across southern Europe and influential in most countries, girls never became adults in the legal sense of obtaining rights in their own name. Instead, a patriarchal social order expected fathers to exercise the rights of their daughters until they married; women's legal rights then passed to their husbands. Most legal systems contained other double standards for young men and women. The earliest age for sexual consent was typically younger for

a girl than for a boy, although standards of respectable behavior were much stricter for young women than for young men. Economic considerations also created double standards: A family might send a daughter to the convent, for example, instead of providing her with a dowry.

The Life Cycle: Marriage and the Family

Despite the early ages at which children entered the adult world, marriage was normally postponed until later in life. The image perpetuated in popular culture by sources such as *Romeo and Juliet* does not apply to the

Illustration 19.8

⬛ **Marriage Contracts.** For the propertied classes of the eighteenth century, marriage remained an economic negotiation conducted by parents, lawyers, notaries, and unemotional experts. Love was often a secondary consideration that might accompany marriage. William Hogarth satirized the marital practices of the prosperous in a series of paintings entitled "Marriage à la Mode." In the painting here, "The Contract," the negotiators discuss family trees, deeds, and investments without a word from the betrothed.

eighteenth century. Royal or noble children might sometimes be married in childhood for political or economic reasons, but most of the population married at significantly older ages than those common in the twentieth century.

A study of seventeenth-century marriages at Canterbury (southern England) has found that the average age of men at a first marriage was nearly twenty-seven; their brides averaged 23.6 years of age. Research on England in the eighteenth century shows that the age at marriage rose further. In rural Europe, men married at twenty-seven to twenty-eight years, women at twenty-five to twenty-six. Many variations were hidden within such averages. The most notable is the unique situation of firstborn sons. They would inherit the property, which would make marriage economically feasible and earlier marriage to perpetuate the family line desirable.

Most people had to postpone marriage until they could afford it. This typically meant waiting until they could acquire the property or position that would support a family. Younger sons often could not marry before age thirty. The average age at first marriage of all males among the nobility of Milan was 33.4 years in the period 1700–49; their wives averaged 21.2 years. Daughters might not marry until they had accumulated a dowry—land or money for the well-to-do, household goods in the lower classes—which would favor the economic circumstances of a family. Given the constraints of a limited life expectancy and a meager in-

come, many people experienced marriage for only a few years, and others never married. A study of marriage patterns in eighteenth-century England suggests that 25 percent of the younger sons in well-to-do families never married. Another historian has estimated that fully 10 percent of the population of Europe was comprised of unmarried adult women. For the middle class of Geneva in 1700, 26 percent of the women who died at over age fifty had never married; the study of the Milanese nobility found that 35 percent of the women never married.

The pattern of selecting a mate changed somewhat during the eighteenth century. Earlier habits in which parents arranged marriages for children (especially if property was involved) were changing, and a prospective couple frequently claimed the right to veto their parents' arrangement. Although propertied families often insisted upon arranged marriages (see document 19.3), it became more common during the eighteenth century for men and women to select their own partners, contingent upon parental vetoes. Marriages based upon the interests of the entire family line, and marriages based upon an economic alliance, yielded with increasing frequency to marriages based upon romantic attachment. However, marriage contracts remained common in those cases (see illustration 19.8).

After a long scholarly debate, historians now agree that Western civilization had no single pattern of family structure, but a variety of arrangements. The most

DOCUMENT 19.4

The Husband in the Law: The Frederician Code of 1750

The Frederician Code, adopted in Prussia under Frederick the Great, was one of the greatest efforts to reorganize a legal system during the eighteenth century. It was chiefly the work of the minister of justice, Samuel von Cocceji. He relied on the principles of Roman law but also drew ideas from Germanic customary law and from the "enlightened" philosophy of the eighteenth century. The following excerpt states the legal rights of a husband; a similar section specified the rights and privileges of the wife, without curtailing the authority of husband.

1. As the domestic society, or family, is formed by the union of the husband and wife, we are to begin with enumerating the advantages and rights which result from this union.

2. The husband is by nature the head of his family. To be convinced of this, it is sufficient to consider, that the wife leaves her family to join herself to that of her husband; that she enters into his household, and into the habitation of which he is the master, with intention to have children by him to perpetuate the family.

3. Hence it follows, judging by the sole light of reason, that the husband is master of his own household, and head of his family. And as the wife enters into it of her own accord, she is in some measure subject to his power; whence flow several rights and privileges, which belong to the husband with regard to his wife.

For, (1) the husband has the liberty of prescribing laws and rules in his household, which the wife is to observe.

(2) If the wife be defective in her duty to her husband, and refuse to be subject, he is authorized to reduce her to her duty in a reasonable manner.

(3) The wife is bound, according to her quality, to assist her husband, to take upon her the care of the household affairs, according to his condition.

(4) The husband has the power over the wife's body, and she cannot refuse him the conjugal duty.

(5) As the husband and wife have promised not to leave each other during their lives, but to share the good and evil which may happen to them; the wife cannot, under pretext, for example, that her husband has lost his reason, leave him, without obtaining permission from the judge.

(6) For the same reason, the wife is obliged to follow her husband when he changes his habitation; unless, (a) it has been stipulated by the contract of marriage, or otherwise, that she shall not be bound to follow him if he should incline to settle elsewhere; or (b) unless it were for a crime that the husband changed his habitation, as if he had been banished from his country.

common pattern was not a large family, across more than two generations, living together; instead, the most frequent arrangement was the nuclear family in which parents and their children lived together. Extended families, characterized by coresidence with grandparents or other kin—known by many names, such as the *Ganze Hauz* in German tradition or the zadruga in eastern Europe—were atypical. A study of British families has found that 70 percent were comprised of two generations, 24 percent were single-generation families, and only 6 percent fit the extended family pattern. Studies of southern and eastern Europe have found more complex, extended families. In Russia, 60 percent of peasant families fit this multigenerational pattern; in parts of Italy, 74 percent.

Family size also varied widely. Everywhere except France (where smaller families first became the norm), the average number of children born per family usually ranged between five and seven. Yet such averages hide

many large families. For example, Brissot de Warville, a leader of the French Revolution, was born to a family of innkeepers who had seventeen children, seven of whom survived infancy; Mayer and Gutele Rothschild, whose sons created the House of Rothschild banks, had twenty children, ten of whom survived. The founder of Methodism, John Wesley, was the fifteenth of nineteen children. Households might also contain other people, such as servants, apprentices, and lodgers. Studies of eighteenth-century families in different regions have found a range between 13 percent and 50 percent of them containing servants. A survey of London in the 1690s estimated that 20 percent of the population lodged with nonrelatives.

One of the foremost characteristics of the early modern family was patriarchal authority. This trait was diminishing somewhat in western Europe in the eighteenth century, but it remained strong. A father exercised authority over the children; a husband exercised

Illustration 19.9

The Family. Attitudes toward the family were beginning to change in the eighteenth century, as indicated by the increasing habit of the wealthy to commission paintings of the entire family. Note the subtle symbolism of this painting: The wife sits at the center of the family, with the husband somewhat in the background of family matters. The father relates to his eldest son and heir, but he is turned slightly away from his other children.

authority over his wife. A woman vowed to obey her husband in the wedding ceremony, following the Christian tradition based on the words of Saint Paul: "Wives, submit yourself unto your own husbands, as unto the Lord." The idea of masculine authority in marriage was deeply imbedded in popular culture. As a character in a play by Henry Fielding says to his wife, "Your person is mine. I bought it lawfully in church." The civil law in most countries enforced such patriarchy. In the greatest summary of English law, Sir William Blackstone's *Commentaries on the Law of England* (1765–69), this was stated bluntly: "The husband and wife are one, and the husband is that one." A compilation of Prussian law under Frederick the Great, the Frederician Code of 1750, was similar: "The husband is master of his own household, and head of his family. And as the wife enters into it of her own accord, she is in some measure subject to his power" (see document 19.4). On these matters too, families were beginning to change in the eighteenth century (see illustration 19.9).

Few ways of dissolving a marriage existed in the eighteenth century. In Catholic countries, the church considered marriage a sacrament and neither civil marriage by the state nor legal divorce existed. The church permitted a few annulments, exclusively for the upper classes. Protestant countries accepted the principle of divorce on the grounds of adultery or desertion, but divorces remained rare, even when legalized (see illustration 19.10). Geneva, the home of Calvinism, recorded an average of one divorce per year during the eighteenth century. Divorce became possible in Britain in the late seventeenth century, but it required an individual act of parliament for each divorce. Between 1670 and 1750, a total of 17 parliamentary divorces were

granted in Britain, although the number rose to 114 between 1750 and 1799. Almost all divorces were granted to men of prominent social position who wished to marry again, normally to produce heirs.

Where arranged marriages were still common, the alternative to divorce was separation. The civil laws in many countries provided for contracts of separation, by which the maintenance of both partners was guaranteed. Simpler alternatives to divorce evolved in the lower classes, such as desertion or bigamy. The most extraordinary method, practiced in parts of England well into the nineteenth century, was the custom of wife sale. Such sales were generally by mutual consent, but they nonetheless resembled cattle sales. They were sufficiently common that Thomas Hardy could make such a sale central to the plot of *The Mayor of Casterbridge*, one hundred years later (1886). Though the Old Regime was fundamentally an era of indissoluble, lifelong marriage, this did not mean a couple lived together for long periods of time. Given the average age at marriage in the mid-twenties and the average age at death (for people who reached the mid-twenties) in the mid-forties, the typical marriage lasted for approximately twenty years.

The Life Cycle: Sexuality and Reproduction

Ignorance about human sexuality was widespread during the Old Regime, and remarkable theories still circulated about human reproduction, many of them restatements of sex manuals inherited from the ancient world. Medical science held that the loss of one ounce of semen debilitated a man's body the same way that the

Illustration 19.10

💧 Divorce. Although the law varied greatly from state to state, the legal dissolution of marriages remained rare in eighteenth-century Europe. When divorce was legalized in France at the end of the century, few were granted. In this French watercolor, the judge who was to divorce a young couple urges them to forget their lovers and reunite for their child's sake.

LE DIVORCE.

loss of forty ounces of blood would and that a woman's menstruation could turn meat rancid. Consequently, physicians advised people to avoid all sex during the summer because a man's body would become dried out. Similarly, people were taught to avoid sex during menstruation because a child conceived then would be born diseased. (Ignorance of the ovarian cycle meant they did not realize that conception was impossible then.)

There were other disincentives to sexual activity. The strongest came from Christian moral injunctions. A Christian tradition regarding sex as unclean and chastity as a spiritual ideal, dated from St. Paul and St. Jerome. Only marital intercourse was permissible, and then only for procreation; other sexual activity was understood to be a violation of the Seventh Commandment forbidding adultery. Good Christians were expected to practice chastity during pregnancy (when conception was impossible), on Sundays, and during the forty days of Lent.

In addition to the disincentives of medical advice and Christian teaching, poor health, uncleanliness, fears of pregnancy or venereal disease, and repressive laws also restricted behavior. Laws varied regionally, but most sexual practices were against the law. Ecclesiastical courts in Catholic countries tried priests and laity alike for sexual offenses; secular courts acted in a similar manner in Protestant countries. A study of the archdiocesan tribunal at Cambrai (annexed to France in the late seventeenth century) has found that 38 percent of the moral offenses involved unmarried sex, 32 per-

cent adultery, and 11 percent incest. Punishments ranged from death (for incest between father and daughter) to providing a dowry (for seducing a virgin). Bestiality merited burning to death, for both the human and the animal. Pornography (broadly defined) often led to imprisonment, as it did for Denis Diderot. Sentences to a public pillory, a flogging, or being paraded through the streets with a shaved head were also common.

Homosexuality was universally illegal before the French Revolution (which legalized consenting adult relationships in 1791). Assessing its frequency is difficult. It had been a crime in England for centuries, normally punished by the pillory, and a public execution for homosexuality took place as late as 1772. Yet homosexuality was relatively open in England in the eighteenth century and gentlemen's clubs of homosexuals existed with impunity in London, though periodic arrests of sodomites (the term *homosexual* was not coined until the late nineteenth century) occurred, such as the police campaign of 1707. King Frederick William I of Prussia was horrified to discover that both of his sons—the future Frederick the Great and Prince Henry, whom the Continental Congress briefly considered as a constitutional king for the United States—were homosexuals. Frederick William considered executing Frederick and made him watch the execution of his lover, Hans von Katte. This did not deter Frederick from taking his military tutor, Count von Keyserling, as a lifelong lover. Similar laws and family reactions did not restrain the homosexual (and transvestite) brother of Louis XIV, the duke d'Orléans. The double standard obscures the extent of lesbianism in the eighteenth century even more, but high society enjoyed widespread rumors about many prominent figures such as Queen Anne of England. Contemporary works such as Mary Wollstonecraft's *Mary: A Fiction*, Diderot's *La Religieuse*, and Fielding's *The Female Husband* indicate that the subject was much discussed.

As the partial tolerance of homosexuality suggests, the eighteenth century was a period of comparatively relaxed sexual restrictions, especially compared with the more repressive sixteenth and seventeenth centuries. Some historians even describe the Old Regime as a period of sexual revolution. In Protestant countries, strict moral Puritanism weakened, and Catholicism repudiated its own version of Puritanism—Jansenism. In all countries, the ruling classes set an example of permissiveness. Most monarchs (who married for reasons of state, not for love) kept lovers, gently called favorites. Louis XV kept a small personal brothel, called Deer Park, near the royal palace at Versailles; Catherine the Great had an equally long list of favorites. Augustus the Strong, king of Poland and elector of Saxony, fathered at least 365 children, only one of them legitimate. Unmarried liaisons were typical of life at royal courts, and the habit spread until many men of rank kept mistresses. By the late eighteenth century, the sexuality of the elite had become so open that fashionable women in London and Paris wore diaphanous veils in public, exposing their breasts.

The double standard remained a feature of the relaxed sexual standards. Tribunals assessing sex crimes typically gave harsher sentences to women, particularly for adultery. Women at the highest levels of society might act with some freedom if the legitimacy of heirs were certain. But European culture attached a value to female virginity and chastity and still associated a man's honor with the chastity of his female relations.

One of the foremost disincentives associated with eighteenth-century sexuality was the circulation of the venereal diseases (VD) syphilis and gonorrhea. These diseases, commonly called the pox, were rampant in the ruling classes and found in most of the royal families of Europe. Louis XIV, Louis XV, and Napoleon all had VD. Syphilis was not as fatal as when epidemics of it swept Europe in the fifteenth and sixteenth centuries, but it remained a debilitating disease. Gonorrhea was pandemic in urban Europe. The famous Venetian lover Giovanni Casanova contracted eleven cases of VD during his life although he survived until age seventy-three. James Boswell, the distinguished British writer,

caught gonorrhea seventeen times. An examination of advertising in English periodicals of the eighteenth century has found that the commodity most frequently offered for sale was quack cures for VD. Physicians could provide only limited help; their favored cure was treatment with mercury, a dangerous poison.

Prostitution was one of the chief sources of the spread of venereal diseases. It was illegal but generally tolerated in public brothels. The open prostitution of the Middle Ages, with municipally operated (and even church-operated) brothels, no longer existed. Yet large numbers of prostitutes were found in all cities. King Frederick I of Prussia tried to end prostitution in Berlin by closing all brothels in 1690, causing an increase of prostitution practiced in taverns. When the Prussian government decided to tolerate brothels again, a survey of 1765 found that Berlin contained nearly nine thousand prostitutes in a population of approximately 120,000 people. The Parisian police estimated an even higher number of prostitutes there—between twenty thousand and thirty thousand, or one of every eight women of marriageable age. Even in the shadow of the Vatican, 2 percent of all adult women were officially registered prostitutes.

Draconian measures did not eliminate prostitution. The Austrian government sought to end it in Vienna in the 1720s with harsh treatment of prostitutes. After the failure of such punishments as the pillory or being made to sweep the streets with shaved heads, the government staged a public decapitation of a prostitute in 1723. Yet the empress Maria Theresa soon created a Chastity Commission to study the subject anew. Governments chose to control prostitution by limiting it to certain districts and keeping it off the streets or by registering prostitutes, thereby permitting some public health control and taxation. Governments were mostly concerned about the spread of disease (particularly to military garrisons) more than the condition of the women (frequently domestic servants who had been seduced or girls from the country who could not find employment) driven by economic necessity to prostitute themselves.

Another subject of social concern about eighteenth-century sexuality was the general increase in illegitimate births (see table 19.10). Illegitimacy had been relatively uncommon, particularly in rural areas, in the seventeenth century. The rate for rural France had been only 1 percent of all births. During the eighteenth century, and particularly after 1760, both illegitimate births and premarital conceptions increased significantly. The illegitimacy rate remained high because the practice of birth control was limited both by Christian moral

N TABLE 19.10 N

Premarital Conception and Illegitimate Birth in the Old Regime

Country	Period	Percentage of premarital conceptions	Percentage of illegitimate births
England	pre–1750	19.7	2.6
	1740–90	37.3	4.3
	1780–1820	34.5	5.9
France	pre–1750	6.2	2.9
	1740–90	10.1	4.1
	1780–1820	13.7	4.7
German states	pre–1750	13.8	2.5
	1740–90	18.5	3.9
	1780–1820	23.8	11.9
Spain	pre–1750	n.a.	5.4
	1740–90	n.a.	5.1
	1780–1820	n.a.	6.5
United States	1940	n.a.	3.5
	1960	n.a.	5.3
	1980	n.a.	18.4

Sources: Data for the Old Regime from Michael W. Flinn, *The European Demographic System, 1500–1820* (Baltimore, Md.: Johns Hopkins University Press, 1971), p. 82; data for the United States from *Information Please Almanac Atlas and Yearbook 1989* (Boston, Mass.: Houghton Mifflin Co., 1989), p. 788.

injunctions and by slight knowledge of effective procedures. Tertullian had established the theological view of birth control in the third century, asserting that "to prevent a child being born is to commit homicide in advance." Religious opposition to birth control continued in the eighteenth century, even in Protestant Europe: It was the divine will that people "be fruitful and multiply." Despite Christian teaching, a significant percentage of the English upper classes and the general population of France practiced some forms of birth control in the eighteenth century, and both populations experienced a decline in their fertility rate compared with the rest of Europe. France had a birthrate of forty per one thousand population in the mid-eighteenth century, falling to thirty-three per one thousand at the end of the century, thirty per one thousand in some areas. Many people clearly had found economic advantages in smaller families and had chosen to put economic factors above religious ones.

Judging the extent to which knowledge about birth control circulated is difficult. Christianity offered one traditional method: abstinence. *Coitus interruptus* was practiced, but its extent is unknown. The French

philosopher Jean-Jacques Rousseau discussed (with disapproval) that method of birth control ("cheating nature") in his *Discourse* of 1753 as well as many forms of nonreproductive sex, such as oral and manual sex. (Rousseau also fathered five illegitimate children and abandoned them to foundling homes.) Those who practiced birth control employed such methods. Condoms (made from animal membranes) had been virtually unknown in the seventeenth century but were available in late eighteenth-century London and Paris, although they were chiefly employed against VD, not for family planning. Knowledge about female means of control, such as douching, also began to circulate in that period.

Abortion was also used to terminate unwanted pregnancies during the Old Regime. A Christian tradition received from Aristotle and passed onward by Roman law held that a soul was implanted in the fetus at the time of "animation" or "the quickening." Though all abortions were illegal, both moral law and criminal law distinguished between those before and after "ensoulment." The means of attempting abortions were crude and dangerous. Folk knowledge circulated about supposed abortifacient drugs and vegetal or mineral poisons, however, and the learned reference work of the century, the French *Encyclopédie*, discussed them in detail.

The Life Cycle: Old Age

Statistical averages showing the low life expectancies of the Old Regime should not produce the mistaken conclusion that older people were rare in the eighteenth century. Twenty percent of all newborns reached the age of fifty, and 10 percent lived until seventy. French demographic studies have found that, in the 1740s, 17 percent of men and 19 percent of women would reach age sixty; by the 1770s, this had risen to 24 percent for men and 25 percent for women. The aged clearly represented a significant group in society. The Swedish data on the life cycle reveal that nearly 5 percent of the population in 1778 was sixty-five or older. This represents more than 100,000 elderly citizens in the population of a small country. Once someone had survived to the age of fifty, his life expectancy was not greatly different than it would be in the twentieth century.

Thus, a large proportion of the powerful and famous individuals who are remembered from the eighteenth century had life spans typical of twentieth-century leaders. King Louis XIV of France lived to be seventy-seven (1638–1715); his successor, Louis XV, died at sixty-four (1710–74). The three Hanoverian kings of eighteenth-century England (George I, George II, and George III) died at an average age of seventy-five (sixty-seven, seventy-seven, and eighty-two, respectively). Empress Catherine II of Russia and King Frederick II of Prussia earned their appellation, "the Great," partly because they lived long enough to achieve greatness—Catherine died at sixty-seven, Frederick at seventy-four. And the eight popes of the eighteenth century, who were typically elected at an advanced age, died at an average age of nearly seventy-eight; four lived into their eighties. Similar life spans characterized many of the famous cultural figures of the Old Regime. Christopher Wren and Anton van Leeuwenhoek both lived into their nineties; Goethe, Goya, Kant, and Newton all lived into their eighties.

The ancient world had considered that old age, a separate stage of life, began between the ages of fifty and sixty—the great physician Hippocrates had considered fifty-six the onset of old age, and Aristotle argued that it began at fifty. The medieval Christian view may have pushed the frontiers of old age back a slight amount (St. Augustine held it began at sixty), but it differed little from the ancient views that old age at its best was a time for spiritual retreat from worldly concerns and preparation for death, at its worst a derisory phase of decrepitude and incompetence. The elderly might be consulted for their wisdom, but they were often derided. From the plays of Aristophanes, where old men were twice as foolish as children, to the plays of Shakespeare, where King Lear is made to realize that he is "a very foolish old man . . . not in my perfect mind," European culture often portrayed the elderly as more pitiful than wise. As with other attitudes, such as the nature of marriage and the family, that image began to change in the eighteenth century and a more modern, respectful mentality began to establish itself. Changing attitudes were especially important in the lives of old women who had long suffered the worst mistreatment, such as being accused of witchcraft.

Conclusion

By focusing on the most basic issues of daily life (such as health and diet) and the most universal experiences of living (such as birth, marriage, and aging) social historians are able to portray historical continuity and change especially well. Life in eighteenth-century Europe was in many ways like it had been for centuries. The biological old regime closely resembled the conditions of life in ancient Greece and Rome; the dreaded horsemen of plague and famine defined life in much the same ways. Yet there were signs of historic change, too. The slow acceptance of inoculation against smallpox or the foods of the Columbian exchange pointed toward a modern Europe with vastly lower levels of disease and higher standards of nutrition. The name attached to the era, the Old Regime, is from political history, which links the eighteenth century to a vanished old order of monarchy and aristocracy. Just as two centuries were required for the political evolution of modern Europe, the evolution of daily life and the conquest of the biological Old Regime would take time. But life in the eighteenth century was far from static, as the shifting attitudes toward arranged marriages or large families show.

Suggested Readings

Useful reference books for the social history of this period include P. Stearns, *Encyclopedia of Social History* (1994), J. Trager, ed., *The Food Chronology* (1995), and G. C. Kohn, ed., *Encyclopedia of Plague and Pestilence* (1995).

For a general social history of the Old Regime, the master-work is F. Braudel, *Civilization and Capitalism, 15th–18th Century*, 3 vols., especially vol. 1, *The Structures of Everyday Life* (1985). For demographic studies and population, see M. W. Flinn, *The European Demographic System, 1500–1820* (1981), the standard work on western Europe; M. Anderson, *Population Change in Northwestern Europe, 1750–1850* (1988); T. McKeown, *The Modern Rise of Population* (1976); J. Knodel, *Demographic Behavior in the Past* (1988); R. Rotberg and T. Rabb, eds., *Marriage and Fertility* (1981) and their *Population and Economy: Population and History from the Traditional to the Modern World* (1986); E. A. Wrigley and R. S. Schofield, *The Population History of England* (1989); and L. Moch, *Moving Europeans: Migration in Western Europe since 1650* (1992).

For sickness and disease, see the pertinent chapters in W. McNeill, *Plagues and Peoples* (1976), the pioneering work in this field; R. Porter and D. Porter, *In Sickness and in Health: The British Experience, 1650–1850* (1988); J. C. Riley, *The Eighteenth-Century Campaign to Avoid Disease* (1987); D. Hopkins, *Princes and Peasants: Smallpox in History* (1983); and G. Miller, *The Adoption of Inoculation for Smallpox in England and France* (1957). For public health and medical history, see C. Cipolla, *Miasmas and Disease: Public Health and the Environment in the Pre-Industrial Age* (1992); L. S. King, *The Medical World of the Eighteenth Century* (1958); G. B. Risse, *Hospital Life in Enlightenment Scotland* (1986); W. F. Bynum and R. Porter, eds., *Medical Fringe and Medical Orthodoxy, 1750–1850* (1987); and M. Ramsey, *Professional and Popular Medicine in France, 1770–1830* (1988).

For diet, nutrition, and famine, see R. Rotberg and R. Rabb, eds., *Hunger and History* (1985); L. Newman, *Hunger in History* (1990); J. Walter and R. Schofield, eds., *Famine, Disease, and the Social Order in Early Modern Society* (1989); E. Forster and R. Forster, eds., *European Diet from Pre-Industrial to Modern Times* (1975); R. B. Outhwaite, *Dearth, Public Policy, and Social Disturbance in England 1550–1880* (1991); W. J. Shelton, *English Hunger and Industrial Disorder* (1973); R. Wells, *Wretched Faces: Famine in Wartime England, 1763–1803* (1988); W. Monahan, *Year of Sorrows: The Great Famine of 1709 in Lyons* (1993); S. Kaplan, *Provisioning Paris: Merchants and Millers in the Grain and Flour Trade during the Eighteenth Century* (1984); J. Komlos, *Nutrition and Economic Development in the Eighteenth-Century Hapsburg Monarchy* (1989); R. Salaman, *The History and Social Influence of the Potato* (1949); S. W. Mintz, *Sweetness and Power* (1985); J. Walvin, *Fruits of Empire* (1997); and T. Brennan, *Public Drinking and Popular Culture in Eighteenth-Century Paris* (1988).

For sexuality, see T. Hitchcock, *English Sexualities, 1700–1800* (1997); R. Mitchison and L. Leneman, *Sexuality and Social Control: Scotland, 1660–1780* (1990); R. Wheaton and T. Hareven, eds., *Family and Sexuality in French History* (1980); G. S. Rousseau and R. Porter, eds., *Sexual Underworlds of the Enlightenment* (1987); K. Gerard and G. Hekma, eds., *The Pursuit of Sodomy: Male Homosexuality in Renaissance and Enlightenment Europe* (1988); R. P. Maccubbin, ed., *'Tis Nature's Fault: Unauthorized Sexuality during the Enlightenment* (1987), and L. Faderman, *Surpassing the Love of Men* (1994), on the history of lesbianism. For birth and population control, see A. McLaren, *A History of Contraception* (1992), P. Hoffer and N. Hull, *Murdering Mothers: Infanticide in England and New England, 1558–1803* (1884), M. Jackson, *New-Born Child Murder: Women, Illegitimacy, and the Courts in Eighteenth-Century England* (1996), and O. Ranum, *Popular Attitudes toward Birth Control in Pre-Industrial France and England* (1972).

For the history of the family, see M. Anderson, *Approaches to the History of the Western Family* (1980), an excellent introduction; A. Plakans and T. Hareven, eds., *Family History at the Crossroads* (1988), articles from the *Journal of Family History*; T. Rabb and R. Rotberg, eds., *The Family in History* (1973); M. Mitterauer and R. Sieder, *The European Family* (1982); R. O'Day, *The Family and Family Relationships, 1500–1900* (1994); the works L. Stone, especially *The Family, Sex, and Marriage in England, 1500–1800* (1977) and *Uncertain Unions: Marriage in England, 1660–1753* (1992); P. Laslett and R. Wall, eds., *Household and Family in Past Time* (1972); R. Wall, J. Robin, and P. Laslett, eds., *Family Forms in Historic Europe* (1983); A. Plakans, *Kinship in the Past: An Anthropology of European Family Life, 1500–1900* (1987); S. Woolf, ed., *Domestic Strategies: Work and Family in France and Italy, 1600–1800* (1991); J. Goody, *The Development of Family and Marriage in Europe* (1983); J. O'Barr, D. Pope, and M. Wyer, eds., *Ties That Bind: Essays on Mothering and Patriarchy* (1990); J. Dupaquier and others, eds., *Marriage and Remarriage in Populations in the Past* (1981); J. Gillis, *For Better, For Worse: British Marriages, 1600 to the Present* (1988); J. Flandrin, *Families in Former Times* (1979), on early modern France; J. F. Traer, *Marriage and Family in Eighteenth Century France* (1980); M. Darrow, *Revolution in the House* (1989) on changing families in France at the end of the eighteenth century; H. Medick and D. W. Sabean, eds., *Interest and Emotion: Essays on the Study of Family and Kinship* (1984), a collection focusing on the German states; D. Kertzer and R. Saller, eds., *The Family in Italy* (1991); R. Phillips, *Putting Asunder: A History of Divorce in Western Society* (1991); and L. Stone, *The Road to Divorce: England, 1530–1987* (1993).

The most helpful general works for the history of women included an excellent anthology by S. G. Bell and K. M. Offen, eds., *Women, the Family, and Freedom*, 2 vols. (1983), B. Anderson and J. Zinsser, *A History of Their Own: Women in Europe from Prehistory to the Present*, 2 vols. (1988); M. Boxer and J. Quataert, eds., *Connecting Spheres: Women in the Western World, 1500 to the Present* (1987); and R. Bridenthal, C. Koonz, and S. Stuard, eds., *Becoming Visible: Women in European History* (1987). See also B. Hill, ed., *Eighteenth Century Women* (1984), an anthology of primary sources; L. Tilly and J. Scott, *Women, Work, and Family* (1978), a classic introduction; B. Hanawalt, ed., *Women and Work in Pre-Industrial Europe* (1986), which covers many occupations; and U. Frevert, *Women in German History* (1988).

For stages of the life cycle, see the pioneering work of P. Ariès, *Centuries of Childhood* (1962) and *Western Attitudes toward Death* (1976); H. Cunningham, *Children and Childhood in Western Society since 1500* (1995); the work of L. Pollock, *Forgotten Children: Parent-Child Relations from 1500 to 1900* (1984) and *A Lasting Relationship: Parents and Children over Three Centuries* (1990); M. Mitterauer, *A History of Youth* (1992); J. Gillis, *Youth and History* (1981); L. de Mause, ed., *The History of Childhood* (1974); I. Ben-Amos, *Adolescence and Youth in Early Modern England* (1994); D. Hunt, *Parents and Children in History* (1972), on early modern France; J. Gelis, *His-*

tory of Childbirth* (1991); J. Towler and J. Bramall, *Midwives in History and Society* (1986); H. Marland, ed., *The Art of Midwifery* (1993); A. Wilson, *The Making of Man-Midwifery: Childbirth in England, 1660–1770* (1995); J. Lewis, *In the Family Way: Childbearing in the British Aristocracy, 1760–1860* (1986); V. Fildes, *Wet-Nursing: A History from Antiquity to the Present* (1988); G. Sussman, *Selling Moth-ers' Milk* (1982), on French wet-nursing; R. O'Day, *Education and Society, 1500–1800* (1982), on British schools; J. Melton, *Abolutism and the Eighteenth-Century Origins of Compulsory Schooling in Prussia and Austria* (1988); J. McManners, *Death and the Enlightenment* (1981); and D. G. Troyansky, *Old Age in the Old Regime* (1989).

CHAPTER 20

THE POLITICAL EVOLUTION OF THE OLD REGIME, 1715–89

CHAPTER OUTLINE

T his chapter examines European politics during the last age of monarchical domination (see map 20.1). Several varieties of monarchy emerged during the late seventeenth century—from limited monarchies, restricted by constitutions, parliaments, or aristocracies, to autocratic monarchies, with few restraints on despotic powers. In most of them, royal advisers began to evolve during the eighteenth century into cabinets of ministers led by a prime minister; in some, parliaments eventually gained control over the cabinet system.

A prominent example of the latter was England under the Hanoverian kings, a monarchy severely limited by the strength of Parliament and the restrictions of the unwritten constitution. Under the first prime minister, Sir Robert Walpole, a cabinet system controlled by Parliament had emerged by the 1730s. In France, the weakness of the Bourbon monarchy was revealed after the death of Louis XIV, whose successor permitted a resurgence of aristocratic power based upon control of the high courts or *parlements*. The costs of war and an inadequate system of taxation produced a financial crisis that helped precipitate the French Revolution.

Autocratic Prussia, meanwhile, emerged as a great power in the eighteenth century owing to the strength of its army. Frederick the Great tried to balance despotism and militarism with ideas of enlightened reform. Austria, however, is a better illustration of enlightened despotism, partly in the reign of Maria Theresa, but chiefly under Joseph II, the most advanced of eighteenth-century autocrats. Chapter 20 concludes with a discussion of Russia, where the monarch had despotic power and few restraints. Catherine II preserved autocracy in Russia by enlisting the support of powerful aristocrats.

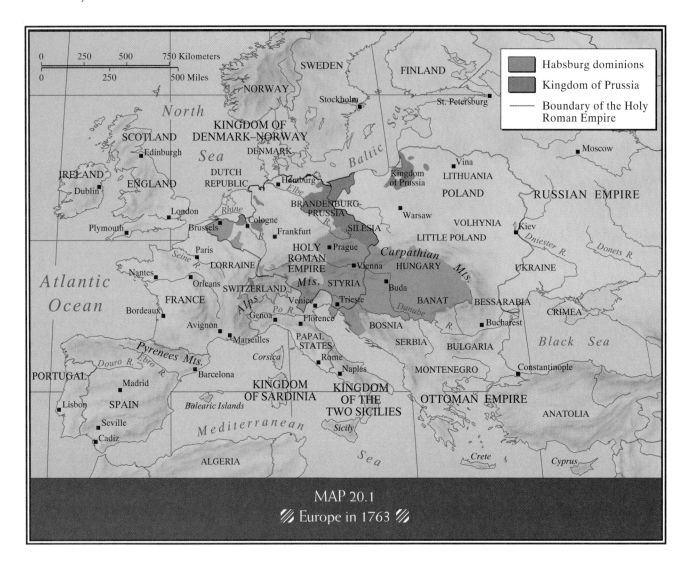

MAP 20.1
Europe in 1763

The Structures of Government: Monarchy

The basic political characteristic of the Old Regime was—as it had been for more than one thousand years—monarchical government. In the strictest sense, monarchy meant the rule of a single person who held sovereignty (supreme power) over a state and its inhabitants. Some monarchs, such as the Romanov emperors and empresses of Russia, held exalted titles and sovereignty over vast territories; others, such as the dukes of Modena in northern Italy, merely held noble titles and sovereignty over small, vulnerable states. The power of monarchs was frequently challenged by the nobility, disputed by provinces, or attacked in open rebellions. But the concept of monarchy was almost universally accepted at the beginning of the eighteenth century. Even the skeptical intellectuals of that era still supported it, and only a few small states, such as the city-state of

Genoa in northern Italy, sustained governments without monarchs, usually called republics.

The forms of monarchy varied significantly: from absolute monarchy (in which the monarch claimed unrestricted powers) to limited monarchy (in which clear legal limits were placed on royal sovereignty, to the benefit of the propertied classes). Absolutism remained the predominant form of European monarchy. The English poet William Cowper summarized it simply: "I am monarch of all I survey/My right there is none to dispute." Most monarchs wanted such power and aspired to emulate the absolute monarchs of the seventeenth century, King Gustavus Adolphus of Sweden and especially King Louis XIV of France, the exemplars of the era called the age of absolutism. The theory of absolute monarchy held that rulers received sovereignty directly from God. They governed by divine right, representing within their realm the sovereignty of God over all things. This idea rested on the exegesis of such biblical statements as "No authority exists unless it comes from God." Churches taught obedience to the monarch as a religious duty: God had given sovereignty, and "No one but God can judge the king." Resisting a monarch was to attack God's order. An anonymous poem of the eighteenth century entitled "The Vicar of Bray" summarized the alliance of throne and altar in a succinct rhyme:

> Unto my flock I daily preached
> Kings were by God appointed,
> And damned was he that durst resist
> Or touch the Lord's anointed.

Despite such ideas, true autocratic monarchy—most often called despotism—was rare, but parts of central and eastern Europe still lived under despotic rulers who were unrestrained by laws and acted as they wished. A despot might strangle an opponent with his bare hands, have another torn apart by dogs, or have his own son and heir flogged to death, as Tsar Peter the Great of Russia did.

Most monarchs could not exercise such unrestrained powers. Their governments were limited monarchies, or mixed monarchies, a contradiction in terms. The powers of monarchs were limited by traditional privileges that earlier rulers had granted, a strong legal system enforced by independent courts, a strong nobility, the powers of an established state religion, rights delegated to a representative assembly, or financial dependency on others. The Braganza kings of Portugal were limited by the power of the Catholic Church; the Bourbon kings of the Two Sicilies (southern Italy), by having to ask an assembly for the money to rule. The Bourbon kings of France faced a resurgent aristocracy that used the law courts (*parlements*) to thwart the royal will.

The most formal restrictions upon royal sovereignty were constitutional laws. Few states possessed a constitution in the modern sense of a single written document, and few peoples even had any expectation that they might obtain one. Sweden, where a century of absolutism had culminated in the disastrous Great Northern War (1700–21) ending Sweden's claims to be one of the great powers, adopted the strictest constitution of the era in 1720. The Sweden nobility accepted the rule of a queen on the condition that she accept a document limiting her power and benefiting the upper classes. Most constitutions were less formal, usually a set of customary privileges claimed by the aristocracy as the ancient constitution of their national traditions. In Hungary, the Magyar aristocracy (the magnate class) held virtual autonomy. When the Hapsburgs incorpo-

rated Hungary into the Austrian Empire, the Hungarians insisted upon the prerogatives of their ancient constitution and rebelled when they believed it to be violated. The English constitution is the most studied model of limiting monarchical power, but it, too, did not exist in a single document stating these limits. It was a body of constitutional law dating back to the Magna Carta of 1215 in which King John had acknowledged limits to his power. The English revolutions in the seventeenth century had extended this process by breaking the power of the Stuart royal family and establishing the dominance of parliamentary government. An unusual form of limited monarchy existed in Poland, where succession to the throne occurred by election. A representative body (the *Sejm*) of the Polish landowning gentry (the *szlachta*) chose each new king and claimed traditional rights, called "the five eternal principles," including the right to renounce allegiance to the king. This so weakened Poland that a Polish state fell prey to its stronger neighbors, losing vast territories to Austria, Prussia, and Russia in "the partition of Poland" (1772) and then ceasing to exist after two more partitions in the 1790s (see chapter 22).

Republican governments held that sovereignty belonged to the citizens, usually to some privileged portion of them. Both the idea and the word had been inherited from ancient Rome. Republicanism slowly evolved into the modern sense of republic—in which sovereignty is held by citizens who elect a government and delegate limited powers to it—but this form did not apply during the Old Regime. In the eighteenth century, a republic meant a state in which the leaders (possibly a monarch) held power by the choice of their subjects (usually a small minority). The elective monarchy of Poland and the mixed government of Holland could be seen as republican. Most of the republics of 1715 were oligarchies—the rule of the few instead of the rule of one—typically small city-states in Italy. The only great power to attempt republican government during the eighteenth century was revolutionary France during the 1790s.

The Evolution of Government: Parliaments, Ministers, and Cabinets

Most countries of the Old Regime, except autocratic states such as Russia, possessed a representative assembly, typically called a parliament today but more often called a diet (from the Latin *diaeta*, a place of assembly). Diets had existed in Europe for centuries. The oldest was the Icelandic *Althing*, founded in A.D. 930, a century before the country converted to Christianity. In some strong monarchies, such as France and Spain, assemblies existed in theory but not in practice. The French Estates General had once been a powerful body, elected by all classes of the population and able to limit taxation. However, it met only when convoked by the king, and between 1614 and 1789 French kings never called a meeting. The Spanish *Cortes*, a unicameral assembly of noble and clerical representatives, typically met only at the beginning of a reign to swear homage to the new king. In Württemberg, Duke Eberhard Ludwig ruled for forty years, from 1693 to 1733, and permitted only one meeting of the Diet during his entire reign. That meeting opposed a standing army and the levying of taxes, but the duke proceeded to raise an army, collect taxes, and prevent further meetings of the Diet. Most diets were equally impotent; only the British Parliament and the Swedish *Rikstag* had genuine legislative power. One of the most important trends in modern European political history has been the evolution of greater powers exercised by parliaments, but this trend was slow during the eighteenth century, when it was largely confined to Britain and France.

The most powerful political figures of the eighteenth century were usually the advisers chosen by the monarch to manage the government. Another important trend in political history was the slow evolution of these royal advisers into a modern government. Advisers gradually became ministers of state, charged with the direction of a bureaucracy, such as the Ministry of Finance or the Ministry of War. In efficient governments, the advisers worked together as a cabinet of ministers, pursuing a common policy. During the eighteenth century this evolved into the cabinet system of government in Britain, culminating in the recognition of one minister as the head of the government, or the prime minister. Only the most energetic and able of monarchs, such as Frederick the Great of Prussia, served as their own prime minister, directing the bureaucracy. Instead, such strong leaders as Sir Robert Walpole in Britain (served 1721–42), Cardinal Fleury in France (served 1726–43), Count Kaunitz in Austria (served 1753–92), and Count Arvid Horn in Sweden (served 1718–39) laid the bases of modern ministerial government. The final stage of this evolution is known as ministerial responsibility, when the prime minister and the cabinet no longer served at the king's pleasure but were responsible to parliament and held office only as long as a majority supported them. Signs of ministerial responsibility were evident in eighteenth-century Britain, but the idea developed in the nineteenth century and was not widely accepted until the twentieth century.

Many ministers were selected by royal whim. The most powerful adviser might be the king's private secretary, as was Alexandrea de Gusmao, the strongest statesman in midcentury Portugal. Or power might be hidden behind a minor office. For example, the title of Adam Moltke, who dominated the government of Denmark for a generation, was master of the royal household. The two most influential advisers to King Louis XV of France were the man who had been his childhood tutor and one of the king's mistresses.

The Rise of Parliamentary Government in Hanoverian England

The strength of parliamentary government in England was the result of seventeenth-century revolutions that limited the royal power of the Stuart kings. When it became clear that the royal line was dying out, Parliament asserted its supremacy and selected a German princess from the House of Hanover (a relative of the Stuarts) as the heir to the throne. Thus, in 1714 the throne of England passed to a German, the elector of Hanover. He took the title of King George I, beginning the House of Hanover. His heirs took the names George II and George III, so eighteenth-century England is known as Georgian England as well as Hanoverian England.

King George I did not speak English, and he never bothered to learn the language of his new kingdom, although he had already learned Latin, French, and Italian. He preferred life in Germany and made long trips to Hanover, where he kept a series of plump mistresses whom the English press loved to satirize. The king married his own cousin, then accused her of adultery, divorced her, and imprisoned her for thirty years. This monarch did not win the affection of the English people who generally considered him indolent and ignorant. One of the sharpest tongued Englishmen, Samuel Johnson, summarized him simply: "George I knew nothing and desired to know nothing; did nothing and desired to do nothing." Yet George founded a dynasty that outlasted the French Bourbons, the Austrian Hapsburgs, the Prussian Hohenzollerns, and the Russian Romanovs; his family was renamed the House of Windsor during World War I and it continues to reign nearly three hundred years later.

The character of King George I contributed to the supremacy of Parliament. He showed little interest in government, and because of the language barrier, even his addresses to Parliament had to be read by someone else. Parliament further asserted itself with a new coronation oath, requiring each monarch to swear to obey parliamentary statutes. It established a mandatory term of office for itself, gained tighter control over the budget and the army, and produced a Bill of Rights that guaranteed citizens many liberties. But the most important effect of George I's disinterest in governing was that it allowed the development of the cabinet system of government.

George I's adviser Sir Robert Walpole became the first prime minister in British history and the architect of the cabinet system (see illustration 20.1). Walpole did not come from the titled nobility but was the son of large landowners with nearly a dozen manors in eastern England. Because he was not the eldest son, Walpole studied for the church and only assumed management of the family estates after the death of his brother. His marriage to a rich merchant's daughter brought him a dowry of £20,000 and the independence for a parliamentary career. He championed the Hanoverian succession and won the confidence of the royal family. George I and George II allowed him independence to shape the government, and Walpole accepted with enthusiasm. Given the preeminence of Parliament in Britain, Walpole also had to win the confidence of that body, and he did so through remarkable managerial skills. He won the backing of the gentry in Parliament by cutting the land tax from 20 percent to 5 percent. He gained the faith of others by restoring order to British finances after a crisis caused by stock speculation—known as the South Seas Bubble—destroyed public confidence. He got the support of manufacturing interests with a policy favorable to foreign trade. The key to Walpole's success, however, was probably his patronage system in which he tried to find a job or an income for everyone who would support him. "There is enough pasture for all the sheep," Walpole said, and he delighted in spreading patronage to bishops and dukes. His opponents thought this scandalous. Jonathan Swift put it bluntly: "The whole system of his ministry was corruption; and he never gave bribe or pension without frankly telling the receivers what he expected from them." But in this way, Sir Robert Walpole held power for twenty-one years and laid the foundations of modern parliamentary government.

The British Parliament of the eighteenth century (see illustration 20.2) was far from a modern, democratic legislature. The upper house, the House of Lords,

Illustration 20.1

Walpole and Cabinet Government. Sir Robert Walpole is considered the first prime minister of Britain and one of the most important founders of the European cabinet system of government. In this painting by Joseph Coopy, Walpole is seen speaking to cabinet ministers seated around the table.

remained a bastion of the aristocracy where membership was inherited by the eldest son along with the family title. The lower house, the House of Commons, was elective, but voting was limited to adult males who paid forty shillings a year in property taxes, on the theory that men of property had a vested interest in orderly government. This meant that fewer than 250,000 voted—approximately 3 percent of the nation. In addition to the poor, women, criminals, Catholics, Jews, some Protestants (notably Quakers), and nonbelievers were barred from voting. A Qualification Act required that to become a member of parliament (M.P.) a candidate must own land worth £300, leaving a tiny fraction of the nation eligible for office. Walpole, however, encouraged the dominance of the House of Commons and accepted that his cabinet stood collectively responsible to that body.

British voters typically deferred to the leadership of a small elite of great landowners. According to a study

Illustration 20.2

The House of Commons. Parliamentary government was the institution that most distinguished the English monarchy from the other great powers. The lower house of Parliament, the elective House of Commons, effectively limited the power of the Hanoverian kings in contrast to the absolute monarchies of continental Europe. The House of Commons, shown here listening to a speech by William Pitt, was far from modern democracy, however, and was still dominated by the landowning aristocracy. Note how the physical arrangement divides parliament into two sides (the government and the opposition), encouraging a two-party system.

of British politics at the accession of King George III, this pattern of deference meant that only one voter in twenty acted independently and that a few prominent families controlled the House of Commons. The constituency of Wenlock in western England, for example, had a few hundred electors. Throughout the eighteenth century, they deferred to the leadership of the Forester family, choosing eight members of that family to represent them in the House of Commons. Constituencies were drawn on unequal lines: Some constituencies, called pocket boroughs, were owned by a single family, which had the seat in its pocket and chose the M.P.; others, called rotten boroughs, had so few votes that the seat could be bought. In 1761 the borough of Sudbury openly advertised that its seat in the House of Commons was for sale. The vast lands owned by the duke of Newcastle included seven boroughs for which he personally selected the M.P. In such ways, 111 wealthy landowners controlled more than two hundred seats in Parliament.

Eighteenth-century England also witnessed the origins of a political party system. Members of Parliament generally split into two large factions, not yet political parties in the modern sense, called the Tory and Whig parties. The Tories were somewhat more conservative (in the sense of supporting royal authority) than the Whigs (who were monarchists and defenders of the Hanoverian settlement, but who spoke for parliamentary supremacy). The leaders of both factions typically came from the aristocracy. Political parties did not yet dominate elections. A famous study of politics in the

Georgian age concluded that party did not determine the outcome of a single election in the voting of 1761. Nonetheless, the Whigs—including Walpole—won a majority in the first elections under King George I and generally dominated British politics for the next two generations.

The strongest of Walpole's successors, William Pitt the Elder, strengthened the position of prime minister and the cabinet system of government. Like Walpole, Pitt was not born to the aristocracy, but he managed to die holding both the nickname "the great commoner" and the noble title the earl of Chatham. He was the grandson of a merchant who had made a fortune trading in India in illegal competition with the East India Company. That wealth had bought Pitt's marriage into high society and his seat in Parliament representing the most famous of all rotten boroughs, Old Sarum. Pitt was polished and Oxford educated; his rise in Parliament was largely the result of exceptional oratorical skills. As prime minister during the Seven Years' War of 1756–63, Pitt's vigorous leadership helped to secure global victories over France, demonstrated the strength of cabinet government even in times of crisis, and made the government popular.

The evolution of parliamentary government in England was an important stage in the growth of European civilization, but noteworthy criticisms were made of government by a cozy, aristocratic elite. The loudest voice came from the son of a distiller, John Wilkes. Wilkes had an Oxford education and a helpful marriage to a wealthy older woman. Gibbon found him

❖ DOCUMENT 20.1 ❖

Wilkes: Reform of Parliament, 1776

All wise governments, and well-regulated states, have been careful to mark and correct the various abuses, which a considerable length of time almost necessarily creates. Among these, one of the most striking and important in our country is the present unfair and inadequate representation of the people of England in Parliament. . . .

[N]o less than 22 towns sent members to the Parliament of Edward I [in the 13th century], which have long ceased to be represented. The names of some of them are scarcely known to us. . . . What a happy fate has attended the boroughs of Gatton and Old Sarum, of which, although [they are now deserted ruins] the names are familiar to us: the clerk regularly calls them over, and four respectable gentlemen represent their departed greatness. . . . Great abuses, it must be owned, contrary to the primary ideas of the English constitution, were committed by our former princes, in giving the right of representation to several paltry boroughs. . . . The marked partiality for Cornwall, which single county still sends, within one, as many members as the whole kingdom of Scotland, is striking. . . .

[I]t has been demonstrated that this number of 254 members [of parliament] are elected by no more than 5,723 persons. . . . [T]he mean, and insignificant [constituencies], so emphatically stiled *the rotten part of our constitution*, should be lopped off, and the electors of them thrown into the counties; and the rich, populous, trading towns, Birmingham, Manchester, Sheffield, Leeds, and others, be permitted to send deputies to the great council of the nation.

---

a delightful friend, filled with "inexhaustible spirits, infinite wit and humor, and a great deal of knowledge" but added that "his life is stained with every vice." Wilkes spent much of his wife's dowry to win election to Parliament in 1757, and he earned notoriety by publishing a barbed weekly journal named the *North Briton*, where he offended many people by discussing rumors of M.P.s sleeping with the king's mother. As the leader of British radicalism, Wilkes called for the reform of Parliament, abolishing rotten boroughs and redistributing seats in a fairer representation of population (see document 20.1).

George III was the most complex and important of the Hanoverian kings. He was the first Hanoverian to be born and educated in England. Although some British historians have described him as "an unbalanced man of low intelligence," George began his long reign—from 1760 to 1820—as a popular, hard-working king, considered a decent man of domestic virtues (in contrast to his predecessors and many of his ministers) and high patriotism. George III was also the first Hanoverian to intervene deeply in politics, the first to try to rule. He was stubborn and arbitrary, and he fought with Pitt and other ministers, dismissing them from office; he tried to abolish the emerging system of political parties; and for approximately a dozen years, he effectively ran the government through the choice of weak ministers and lavish application of Walpole's patronage system. George III is often best remembered for the mental imbalance that began to afflict him in 1765—now thought to have been caused by the metabolic disease porphyria—and led to his being stripped of royal powers in 1811. But for many years he was a formidable political figure, strong enough to order the arrest of Wilkes, who was expelled from parliament.

By 1780 the House of Commons had begun serious consideration of reforming itself. The house regularly received petitions from around the land, such as the Yorkshire Petition of 1780, demanding changes in representation. Reform won an important ally in 1783 when William Pitt the Younger (the son of Pitt the Elder) adopted the cause and introduced a bill to disenfranchise thirty-six rotten boroughs and to give seventy-two more seats to London and the counties. Pitt won the support of many Whigs but could not persuade the prime minister of his own Tory party to accept reform. His last attempt, in 1785, failed by a vote of 248–174, and fairer electoral laws waited for half a century. The House of Commons also voted to preserve the position of the privileged elite in 1787, when reformers tried to repeal the Test Acts that gave members of the Church of England a monopoly of positions in universities, military commands, and the government. Pitt led the opposition to that bill.

The political process did not stop with kings, parliaments, and radical reformers: The eighteenth century was an age of turbulent protest. One study has identified

275 urban disturbances in Britain between 1735 and 1800. The most common problem that drew crowds into the streets was hunger. Scarce or expensive bread caused food riots because many people lived on the margins of survival. Labor riots were also common during periods of high unemployment. Such protests in England frequently became anti-Irish demonstrations, such as the 1736 riots of London construction workers fearful that Irish immigrants were taking their jobs and driving down the price of labor. Sometimes crowds protested specific bills in Parliament, as the people of Glasgow did in 1725 (against a tax on beer) and London workers did in 1736 (against a tax on gin).

Religious hatred was a common cause of riots in the eighteenth century, and English crowds regularly expressed their anti-Catholicism with "pope-burnings." When the House of Commons in 1778 voted to abolish legal restrictions upon the seventy-eight thousand Catholics living in England, the public uproar grew into one of the largest riots of the century. A vehement defender of Protestant dominance, an M.P. named Lord George Gordon founded the Protestant Association in 1779 to lead a protest campaign. In June 1780 Gordon led sixty thousand militant Protestants in a march on Parliament that precipitated three days of anti-Catholic riots, known as the Gordon Riots or the "No Popery Riots" (see illustration 20.3). Mobs assaulted Catholic chapels, major prisons, and the Bank of England. George III used the army to quell the riots, killing 285 members of the crowd. Gordon was tried for treason and acquitted; his campaign delayed Catholic emancipation for fifty years.

Illustration 20.3

🖾 **The Gordon Riots.** Urban riots were a recurring feature of eighteenth-century Europe, even in the prosperous states of the west. London suffered severe riots, of which the worst were the Gordon Riots of 1780. The Gordon Riots, in which crowds attacked churches and church property under the banner of "No Popery," drew on deep anti-Catholicism in Protestant England. The illustration here shows the rioters setting fire to Newgate Prison in London.

Britain and the Struggles of Empire

The eighteenth century was an age of nearly constant warfare for Britain; wars were fought in Europe, in North America, in India, and on the high seas. The British contested both French and Spanish power in Europe—fearing the hegemony of either Catholic power—and battled the French for global empire. And British military policy was successful in both objectives. The War of the Spanish Succession (1701–14) checked the French pursuit of continental hegemony, and a simultaneous war in North America (Queen Anne's War) resulted in a significant growth in English power. The War of the Quadruple Alliance (1718–20) seriously curtailed Spanish power.

War was one of the few political questions that deeply interested the Hanoverian kings. George I and George II gladly left English domestic politics in the hands of Walpole, but they resisted his policy of peace and international commerce. Both kings felt that the English army and navy represented the best defense of their Hanoverian homeland, and they accepted costly warfare to defend it. George II was the last king of England to take personal command of an army in the field, fighting in the War of the Austrian Succession in 1743. George III thus inherited a huge national debt (£138 million) along with the throne, the result of military profligacy. He, too, fought constant wars, however, and quintupled the English national debt to £800 million (see table 20.1).

The immense war debt that King George III inherited was the cost of participation in the first true world war—the Seven Years' War in Europe (1756–63), and

❧ TABLE 20.1 ❧

British War Finances, 1702–83

War	War expenditure (in millions)	Government income (in millions)	Deficit in loans (in millions)	Percentage borrowed
War of the Spanish Succession, 1702–13	£93.6	£64.2	£29.4	31.4
War of the Austrian Succession, 1739–48	£95.6	£65.9	£29.7	31.1
Seven Years' War, 1756–63	£160.6	£100.6	£60.0	37.4
American Revolution, 1776–83	£236.5	£141.9	£94.6	39.9
Total	£586.3	£372.6	£213.7	36.4

Source: Adapted from data in Paul Kennedy, *The Rise and Fall of the Great Powers* (New York, N.Y.: Random House, 1987); p. 81.

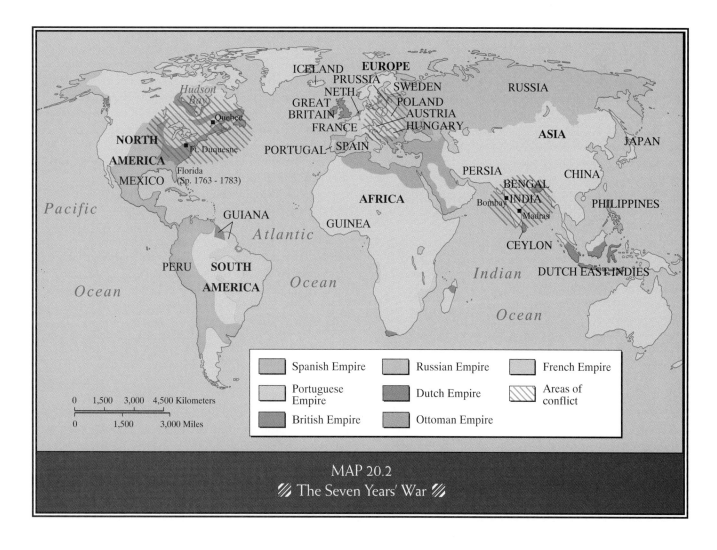

MAP 20.2

❧ The Seven Years' War ❧

its simultaneous theaters known as the French and Indian Wars in North America and the Bengal Wars in India (see map 20.2). This global war produced a mixed blessing: The British Empire won but wound up deeper in debt; Britain became the dominant colonial power in the world, but she thereby acquired even greater administrative costs. The British nation—like many others during the Old Regime—was loathe to pay the taxes needed to repay war debts, support military expansion, and meet the expenses of empire. In 1764 the Tory

◆ DOCUMENT 20.2 ◆

The Stamp Act and the Stamp Act Congress, 1765

The British Stamp Act, 1765

An act for granting and applying certain stamp duties, and other duties, in the British colonies and plantations in America, towards further defraying the expenses of defending, protecting, and securing the same. . . .

Be it enacted . . . that from and after [November 1, 1765] there shall be raised, levied, collected, and paid unto his Majesty, his heirs, and successors, throughout the colonies and plantations in America. . . .

For every skin or piece of vellum or parchment or sheet or piece of paper, on which shall be ingrossed, written or printed, any declaration, pleas, replication, rejoinder, demurrer, or other pleading, or any copy thereof, in any court of law . . . a stamp duty of three pence.

For every skin [etc.] . . . for any certificate of any degree taken in any university, academy, college, or seminary of learning . . . a stamp duty of two pounds.

For every skin [etc.] . . . for any note . . . for any kind of goods, wares, or merchandize, to be exported from . . . the said colonies and plantations, a stamp duty of four pence.

For every skin [etc.] . . . for any grant, appointment, or admission of or to any publick beneficial office or employment . . . a stamp duty of ten shillings.

For every skin [etc.] . . . for any license for retailing of spirituous liquors . . . a stamp duty of twenty shillings.

For every skin [etc.] . . . for any probate of a will . . . a stamp duty of five shillings.

Resolutions of the American Stamp Act Congress, 1765

The members of this Congress, sincerely devoted with the warmest sentiments of affection and duty to His Majesty's person and Government . . . with minds deeply impressed by a sense of the present misfortunes of the British colonies on this continent; having considered as maturely as time will permit the circumstances of the said colonies, esteem it our indispensable duty to make the following declarations. . . .

I. That His Majesty's subjects in these colonies owe the same allegiance to the Crown of Great Britain that is owing from his subjects born within the realm. . . .

II. That His Majesty's liege subjects in these colonies are intitled to all the inherent rights and liberties of his natural born subjects within the kingdom of Great Britain.

III. That it is inseparably essential to the freedom of the people, and the undoubted rights of Englishmen, that no taxes be imposed on them but with their own consent, given personally or by their representatives.

IV. That the people of these colonies are not . . . represented in the House of Commons in Great Britain.

V. That the only representatives of the people of these colonies are persons chosen therein by themselves, and that no taxes ever have been, or can be constitutionally imposed on them, but by their respective legislatures. . . .

VIII. That the late Act of Parliament, entitled *An Act for granting and applying certain stamp duties . . .* , by imposing taxes on the inhabitants of these colonies . . . (has) a manifest tenancy to subvert the rights and liberties of the colonists.

---

government chose a compromise it thought safe: New taxes would be imposed in the colonies, which were the source of many imperial costs, but not in the British isles. The issue of this policy was the Stamp Act of 1765, a tax on the American colonies, requiring that a tax stamp be attached to official documents such as a will, a liquor license, or a college degree. The furious reaction in many colonies, especially Massachusetts and Virginia, held that such taxes could not be imposed under British law without the consent of those being taxed. Representatives of nine American colonies (Britain possessed more than thirty colonies in the Americas) assembled in a Stamp Tax Congress and

adopted an angry resolution challenging the decision of Parliament as subverting "the rights and liberties of the colonists" (see document 20.2).

The confrontation over taxation simmered for a decade and led to the American Revolution of 1776–83. Parliament initially backed down in the face of American protests and rescinded the Stamp Tax in 1766. It adopted, however, a Declaratory Act asserting the right to adopt laws or taxes for the colonies "in all cases whatsoever." Consequently, new taxes were voted in 1767: The Townshend Duties—named for the Tory chancellor of the exchequer, Charles Townshend, who proposed the tax—imposed import duties on basic goods such as glass, paint, paper, and tea entering the colonies. Renewed protests led to the repeal of these duties in 1770, except for the import tax on tea. The escalating battle over taxes led in 1773 to the Boston Tea Party, a protest in which colonists dumped tea overboard from ships in Boston harbor. Parliament responded with the Coercive Acts of 1774, closing the harbor and quartering troops in Boston. A few months later, in April 1775, the battles of Lexington and Concord began the military phase of the revolution.

Although the British had won a global war in 1763, they were in a weaker position in 1775. They were deprived of the help that Americans had given them during the Seven Years' War. There was now no continental war to preoccupy and divide the European powers. One by one, the European powers exploited Britain's vulnerable position and declared war upon her. France entered the war in 1778, Spain in 1779, and Holland in 1780. The financial and military assistance of these states—especially the French—plus the division of British opinion over the war, helped to decide the war. France, for example, secretly sent supplies and money to the American revolutionaries in the early phase of the fighting, then sent increasingly larger armies, such as the force of six thousand men that arrived with Count Jean de Rochambeau in 1780. By the later phases of the war, French forces were decisive. In the battle fought at Yorktown, Virginia, in 1781, the largest army was neither British nor American but French. Facing such growing forces, the British accepted the independence of thirteen of her American colonies in 1783.

The American Revolution obliged the British to reconsider the situation in other territories. Both nearby (in Ireland) and around the world (in India), Britain faced problems. The Anglo-Protestant domination of Ireland had grown steadily during English battles with Catholicism at home and abroad in the seventeenth and eighteenth centuries, especially after the Protestant victory in the battle of the Boyne in 1690. One striking consequence of these struggles could be seen in land tenure. In 1603 Catholics had owned 90 percent of the land in Ireland; in 1778, they owned 5 percent (see table 20.2). Land tenure was at the center of British difficulties in governing Ireland. In the 1760s Catholic secret societies had protested the pattern of evicting Irish Catholics from the soil and leaving them at the mercy of absentee landlords who collected extortionate rents. When Parliament considered improving conditions in Ireland, such as the Relief Act of 1778, the result was a Protestant backlash. Protestants in the northern counties of Ulster founded the Protestant Volunteers, a paramilitary force of forty thousand armed men to defend

N TABLE 20.2 N
Land Ownership in Ireland, 1603–1778

The English, under King Henry II, conquered the eastern coast of Ireland in the twelfth century and kept control there for the next five centuries. An Irish rebellion in the mid-seventeenth century led to the English conquest, under Oliver Cromwell, of all of Ireland and to the English policy of colonizing the island. One consequence was the transfer of land ownership from the Irish Catholic population to the implanted population of Scots, Welsh, and English Protestants. The following table summarizes the effects of this colonization on land tenure.

Year	Catholic ownership (in percent)	Protestant ownership (in percent)
1603	90	10
1641	59	41
1688	21	79
1703	15	85
1778	5	95

Source: Ruth D. Edwards, *An Atlas of Irish History*, 2d ed. (London: Methuen, 1973); p. 178.

their privileged position. The House of Commons capitulated to the chief demand of the Protestants by creating a Protestant-dominated parliament in Ireland known as Grattan's Parliament, which survived until Ireland was merged into the United Kingdom in 1801.

The British also had to reconsider their government of India. The Seven Years' War had solidified their control of the Indian subcontinent, but that control was exercised by the British East India Company, an anachronistic monopoly created in the age of mercantilism. Lord North, the Tory prime minister whose policies helped to precipitate the American Revolution, adopted a reforming policy for India. In 1771 he entrusted the government of India to a reformist governor-general, Warren Hastings, and in 1773 he secured the adoption of a Regulating Act that required audits of the East India Company's books. Hastings soon fought with the royal council appointed for India. With the loss of thirteen colonies in America, the House of Commons paid careful attention to the possibility of misgovernment in India. Thus, William Pitt the Younger secured the adoption of an India Act in 1784, putting the region under the direct control of the government instead of a corporation. The following year, Hastings was ordered home to stand trial for corruption.

Illustration 20.4

Cardinal Fleury. André-Hercule de Fleury (1653–1743) observed politics at the court of Louis XIV as the queen's almoner. This earned him a bishopric and the job of tutoring Louis XV, who came to the throne at age five. This, in turn, earned him appointment to the College of Cardinals and virtual control of the government of France for two decades.

The Vulnerable Monarchy of Bourbon France

In contrast to the situation in England, the French monarchy carried the powers of absolutism into the eighteenth century: Louis XIV, *le Roi Soleil* (the Sun King), the most powerful of the seventeenth-century monarchs, died in 1715 after the longest reign in the history of European monarchy, nearly seventy-three years. Advocates of limiting absolutism had placed their hopes in the heirs of Louis XIV, but within a single year (1711–12), Louis's son, grandson, and eldest great-grandson all died. The death of Louis XIV consequently brought to the throne his five-year-old great-grandson, Louis XV, who would reign for most of the eighteenth century (from 1715 to 1774).

Louis XIV had practiced the distrustful but shrewd administrative principle of fragmenting power near to the throne, and he extended this policy after death by a will dividing the powers of the regency to rule France until Louis XV came of age. The regent of France during the childhood of Louis XV was his cousin, Philippe II, the duke d'Orléans, a liberal and tolerant man, although profligate enough to be considered dissipated even in the context of royal families. The duke skillfully obtained full power by making a deal with the chief judicial body in France, the *parlement* of Paris: The parlement invalidated the will of Louis XIV, and in return, Philippe d'Orléans allowed the fifteen parlements of France greater powers to review (and block) royal decrees. Thus, when Louis XV reached age thirteen and began to rule without a regent in 1723, he inherited a streamlined government, but he faced well-entrenched opposition from the aristocratic parlements.

Louis XV was an intelligent and capable young man, amiable enough to be called Louis "the Well-Beloved." He was not interested in controlling the government as his great-grandfather had; he liked the idea of absolutism but lacked enthusiasm for the daily chores of governing. Consequently, at age sixteen Louis XV entrusted the government of France to his tutor,

Cardinal Fleury (see illustration 20.4), who served as the virtual prime minister of France (without the title) between 1726 and 1743. Louis, who had been married at age fifteen for reasons of state, amused himself with a variety of women while Fleury used his long tenure, as Walpole did in Britain, to stabilize and organize the government.

When Fleury died, Louis XV tried to restore the system of Louis XIV—ruling personally instead of trusting a minister to govern. Like George II of England, he took command of his army and led it into battle in 1744. Ministers who wanted too much power were reduced to the shadows, as was a finance minister of 1759 who left behind his name for that condition: Etienne de Silhouette. Instead of trusting a prime minister and a cabinet, Louis chiefly took advice from his official mistress, the Marquise de Pompadour (see illustration 20.5), whom he established at Versailles in 1745. For twenty years, until her death in 1764, Madame de Pompadour exercised the greatest control over French domestic affairs. She exerted a generally liberal and enlightened influence on French policy, but she was not able to master the king's greatest problem: Like George III of England, he found that he had inherited a government deep in debt, with disordered finances and no ready solutions.

The French Financial Crisis and the Resurgent Aristocracy

The foremost problem facing Louis XV was the disastrous state of French finances created by high military expenses and low taxation. The wars of Louis XIV left France in debt and near bankruptcy. The debt amounted to 36 percent of the government's budget in 1739. Royal opulence compounded the problem: The cost of maintaining the royal family, splendid palaces such as Versailles, and the life of the royal court exceeded 10 percent of the national budget, whereas all expenditures on social welfare, including royal pensions, got only 8 percent of the budget. The extravagant spending on luxuries could reach absurd levels. A single piece of furniture for a royal palace, gilded and bejewelled, cost more than the servant who dusted it could earn in two thousand years (see table 20.3).

Cardinal Fleury established financial order in France, but he could not resolve the underlying problems of inadequate taxation and therefore could not eliminate the debt. The principal direct tax, the *taille*, was collected on land and property, but it was inadequate because the aristocracy, the church, and some

Illustration 20.5

Madame de Pompadour. Jeanne Antoinette Poisson (1721–64) was the daughter of a commoner, but she married wealth and hosted a salon in the 1740s, which included both Voltaire and Montesquieu. She met King Louis XV in 1744, and within a year he had moved her to Versailles and ennobled her as the marquise de Pompadour. As the king's official mistress and later as his confidant, she exercised significant power (especially as an opponent of clerical influence and a defender of the philosophes) in an age when women had few routes to political influence. This portrait is by François Boucher.

towns had exemptions from it. Attempts to create an income tax without exemptions, such as the *dixième* (10 percent) of 1710, had been blocked by the aristocracy, the church, and the parlements. The right to collect indirect taxes, such as tax stamps on documents, had been sold to "tax farmers" for a fixed sum, while they collected whatever excess they could. Many traditional taxes, such as the salt tax (*gabelle*), had been cut for some regions and could not be increased.

The Seven Years' War converted an intractable financial problem into a national crisis. France was a populous, rich, and powerful land, but the government was facing bankruptcy. The war cost most of the French colonial empire and 50 percent of French world

☒ TABLE 20.3 ☒
The Cost of Royal Extravagance, 1760

The following bill was presented by a Parisian jeweller in 1760 for a single piece of furniture, a jewelled, lacquered writing desk called an *escritoire*. To understand this level of royal spending, compare it with the annual incomes and prices in livres shown in Table 18.4.

Component of a lacquer desk with flower vase, powder box, and sponge case	Cost in livres
Gold	3,464
Lacquer	528
Labor (cabinet maker, joiner, and lock maker)	360
Labor (sublet jewellery work)	6,148
Miniature portrait of the empress	600
Packaging box with copper mounts	30
Labor (packaging)	28
Jewels	66,000
Total	77,158

Source: Condensed from data in Nancy Mitford, *Madame de Pompadour* (New York, N.Y.: E. P. Dutton, 1968); p. 276.

☒ TABLE 20.4 ☒
French National Budget, 1774

Note that this simplified version of the budget shows some success in lowering the cost of the national debt, but the figure remains frighteningly high. To meet these expenses, the government had to borrow 5 percent of the total, thereby sending the debts back upward.

Expenses	Percentage
Army	33
Service on debt	30
Royal court	10
Royal pensions	6
All other	21

trade. The national debt rose to 62 percent of the national budget in 1763, and it was growing because of huge interest obligations and a rigid tax structure; new loans to restructure the debt could reduce the percentage of the budget consumed but perpetuate the problem. So finances became the dominant issue in France during the twilight years of the Old Regime: What reforms could be adopted to avoid bankruptcy? The battle over that issue created one of the century's most important political battles: Would the solution be dictated by the king and his advisers or would the aristocracy, using institutions such as the parlements, determine the outcome? Ultimately, neither side won. The financial crisis led France to one of the greatest revolutions of modern history (see table 20.4).

King Louis XV, once beloved, was unable to handle these problems. His indebted and ineffective government, his life of luxury and debauchery, even his implication in a grain price-fixing scandal produced unpopularity and stately torpor. He had relied for years upon the advice of Madame de Pompadour, and her death in 1764 left the king in despair. He slowly became an eighteenth-century stereotype, the aging

voluptuary. After a few years of entertaining himself with a royal brothel at Versailles known as Deer Park, Louis selected another official mistress in 1769. Unfortunately, Madame du Barry lacked the insights and education of Madame de Pompadour. Her plebeian origins did not prepare her for court intrigue, but she still tried to influence politics.

The dominant figure in the French government after the Seven Years' War was Duke Etienne de Choiseul, a capable soldier-statesman who had been sponsored by Madame de Pompadour. Choiseul effectively rebuilt French military strength after 1763 but not French finances. To his credit, Louis XV attempted a solution. He ordered that a wartime tax, the *vingtième*—"the twentieth," a 5 percent income tax that fell on all classes—remain in force. This provoked a virtual rebellion of aristocrats who believed themselves exempt from such taxes. The aristocratic lawyers and magistrates of the *noblesse de robe*, who controlled the parlements of the higher court system, formed the center of the resistance (see illustration 20.6). The Parlement of Paris ruled that the king's decree was illegal. In the south of France, the Parlement of Toulouse even arrested the royal governor who tried to enforce the tax law.

Louis XV capitulated to the parlements in 1764, rescinding the *vingtième* and changing his government. This did not end his battles with the parlements. When he tried to introduce a road building program in Brittany, relying upon a royal *corvée* to provide labor, Breton nobles and the Parlement of Rennes protested. The frustrated king ordered the arrest of the president of the

Illustration 20.6

The French *Parlements*. The French *parlements*, which were high courts of appeal, were a different institution from the English parliament, which was a legislative body. There was a parlement in each of thirteen provinces in eighteenth-century France, and the magistrates in each court were nobles (the nobility of the robe) who owned their office. The parlements resembled parliament in their mutual resistance to royal power. In this illustration, however, a parlement is seen deliberating an issue involving the church, as the proud princes of the church parade in the foreground.

Parlement of Rennes, but this provoked a united protest from all fifteen parlements, claiming that they represented the nation whenever the Estates General (which had last met in 1614) was not in session. As the Parlement of Rouen stated, they considered themselves "the custodian and the depository" of the French constitution, and the king must bend before the law.

This time the king stood firm. In 1766 he sent royal troops to occupy the seat of the Parlement of Paris, then personally appeared before the parlement to express his anger. "I will not allow," Louis told the magistrates, this usurpation of power. "The magistrates are my officers, charged with the truly royal duty of rendering justice to my subjects." Louis insisted that the duties of the parlements did not restrict his sovereignty: "In my person only does the sovereign power rest. . . . To me alone belongs legislative power, unconditionally and indivisibly." To underscore his claim to absolute power, Louis XV named a new government, headed by René de Maupeou, to fight the parlements. In 1771 Maupeou abolished the parlements and created a simpler court system in which the magistrates were salaried state employees instead of owners of their office. He hoped to create a new tax system, both fairer and sufficient for the fiscal crisis, without facing an aristocratic veto. The aristocracy, backed by many philosophes who detested royal absolutism, naturally raised vociferous opposition. But much opinion also supported the king. Voltaire stood with Maupeou's dismissal of the parlements, saying that he would rather be governed by a fine lion than by two hundred rats.

The aristocracy won the day in 1774, when Louis XV died. His nineteen-year-old grandson, Louis XVI, possessed generally good intentions, but he was too timid, inexperienced, and weak-willed to stand up to the nobility. His first acts were to dismiss Maupeou and to restore the parlements. Consequently, he faced a strengthened aristocracy throughout his reign. In 1777, when Joseph II of Austria visited his sister, Queen Marie Antoinette, in Paris, he concluded that the government of France was "an aristocratic despotism."

Louis XVI also inherited the desperate financial situation. In the year of his coronation, the state's revenues were 5 percent below its expenditures, increasing a debt that consumed a third of the budget just in interest payments. Those problems soon worsened. Beginning in 1778, France was again at war, supporting—and financing—the American Revolution. Other problems were beginning. The foremost source of French wealth was agriculture, and in 1774 an agricultural recession began. Farm profits, which translated into tax revenue, plummeted in 1775, and they never again during the Old Regime reached the levels of 1772–74. The decade between 1777 and 1786 saw five harvests in which the average farmer lost money, plus two other poor harvests (see chart 20.1).

The reign of Louis XVI did show signs of hope, as a result of a reforming ministry led by the minister of finance, Robert Turgot, and the interior, Chrétien Malesherbes. Malesherbes was a liberal who had defended the publication of the *Encyclopédie*. Turgot was a minor aristocrat who had reached high office in a

◆ CHART 20.1 ◆

The Recession in French Agriculture, 1774–86

This chart plots the average annual profits in livres of French lease-hold farmers. For comparative data on the value of the livre, see table 18.4 and table 20.3. Note the comparative prosperity of the 1770s (in which five of six years produced profits of more than 100 livres) and the comparative hardships of the 1780s (in which only one year of seven produced a profit of 100 livres and four of seven years produced losses).

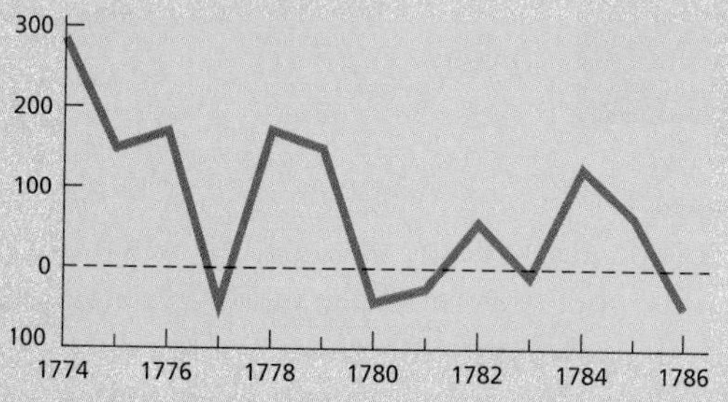

Source: Data in Michel Vovelle, *The Fall of the French Monarchy, 1787–1792* (Cambridge: Cambridge University Press, 1984); p. 84.

typical way for a venal society: He bought his position for 100,000 livres. He was also a free-thinker and a leader of the enlightened economic school of the Physiocrats, whose doctrines he explained in the *Encyclopédie*. In a series of decrees known as the Six Edicts (1776), Turgot and Malesherbes laid the basis for economic recovery. The edicts abolished the monopoly of the guilds to stimulate economic competition. They abolished the burden of the *corvée* on peasants and replaced it with a tax on all landowners. And they eliminated most internal tariffs on the grain trade to bring down the price of bread. At the same time, Turgot cut government spending, especially in the portion of the budget devoted to royal pensions and the royal court.

The reforms of 1774–76 made many enemies. The opposition of the parlements, pressure from powerful guilds, and intrigues at court brought down Turgot in 1776 and Malesherbes followed him. The Parlement of Paris, for example, claimed that the Six Edicts "imperil the constitution" (see document 20.3). The magistrates carried the day: Guild monopolies, the *corvée*, and inter-

nal tariffs were all restored. Another capable minister of finance, a Swiss-born, Protestant financier named Jacques Necker, succeeded Turgot. Necker had made a fortune as a banker during the Seven Years' War. His home was one of the most influential centers of the Enlightenment, where his wife, Suzanne (a prominent writer and the daughter of a Swiss pastor), and their daughter, Germaine (later famous as the Baroness de Staël, also a distinguished writer), directed a brilliant salon. Necker lived at the center of a network of financial, political, and intellectual leaders, and they shaped a series of enlightened reforms during his ministry from 1778 to 1781. He drafted a royal decree for Louis XVI, abolishing the limited form of serfdom that survived in France, but the decree applied only to royal lands. It condemned serfdom in principle and urged aristocrats to follow the king's lead; it did not force abolition in respect for the principle of private property. Few aristocrats followed the king, so serfdom lingered in France. It was mostly concentrated in eastern France, in a recently annexed region known as the Franche-Comté. There, the parlement—most of whose members owned serfs—refused to register the royal decree.

In financial matters Necker similarly followed a cautious route to avoid another open battle with the aristocracy. He attempted further royal economies and minor tax adjustment. Unfortunately, Necker's ministry coincided with the French entry into the American Revolution. He had no choice except financing the war effort by further borrowing, thereby worsening the government's plight. Louis XVI, who had sworn a coronation oath to exterminate Protestantism and who chaffed under Necker's economies for the royal household, used Necker's failure to solve the crisis as grounds for his dismissal in 1781. Necker thereupon published a book, *Compte rendu* (Accounts Given, 1781), which showed a shocked world the extent of the French deficit.

The successors of Turgot and Necker as ministers of finance during the 1780s were utterly unable to break the logjam by which the aristocracy blocked meaningful tax reform. Charles de Calonne, a courtier and less able financier, skirted the edges of bankruptcy by continually increasing the debt. He, too, concluded that a new tax was essential and proposed a land tax, to be paid by aristocrats and the church as well as commoners. To win aristocratic support, an Assembly of Notables (a body of uncertain constitutional basis) was called in 1787; the assembly failed to agree upon anything except opposition to Calonne's tax. This led to Calonne's ouster and yet another minister of finance,

◆ DOCUMENT 20.3 ◆

The Parlement of Paris Protests a Royal Edict, 1776

The desire to relieve the burdens of the people is too worthy of praise in a sovereign and conforms too much to the wishes of your parlement for the latter ever to conceive the thought of dissuading Your Majesty from such a noble and legitimate goal.

But when projects that hold out this pleasing prospect lead to real and aggravated injustices, and even imperil the constitution and tranquility of the state, it is our faithful duty, without seeking to place obstacles in the way of your beneficence, to set the barrier of the law against the imprudent efforts being made to pledge Your Majesty to a course of action the dangers and stumbling-blocks of which have been concealed from you. . . .

This is not, Sire, a struggle between rich and poor, as some have tried to convince you. It is a question of Estate, and a most important one, since it is a matter of knowing whether all your subjects can and must be treated indiscriminately, whether differences in conditions, ranks, titles and preeminence must cease to be acknowledged among them. To subject nobles to a tax to redeem the *corvée* . . . is to declare nobles subject to the *corvée* like commoners. . . . [N]oblemen, the descendants of those ancient knights who placed or preserved the crown on the head of Your Majesty's forefathers . . . could be exposed to the humiliation of seeing themselves dragged off to the *corvée*!

---

who sought even bigger loans, asked the parlements to approve new taxes, and met yet another rejection.

The consequence of the aristocratic rejection of new taxes was that the French national debt reached 100 percent of the budget in 1789. A second consequence was that the aristocracy forced Louis XVI to call elections for the Estates General. The Parlement of Besançon had proposed that solution in 1783 and others had adopted the idea. Louis resisted, trying instead his grandfather's idea of abolishing the parlements in 1788. He finally conceded defeat, however, and agreed to a meeting of the Estates General in May 1789—which led directly to the French Revolution.

◆

The Hapsburg Empire in the Age of Maria Theresa

In contrast to Britain, where Parliament had broken the power of the king, or to France, where the resurgent aristocracy was restricting the power of the king, in Austria the Hapsburg family still held nearly absolute power during the eighteenth century. The political evolution in Austria—known as enlightened despotism—showed how monarchy could respond to new problems.

The Hapsburg Empire dominated Germanic central Europe at the start of the eighteenth century, dwarfing

its rivals in size, population, and military might. Prussia numbered only 1.6 million persons and Bavaria 2.0 million; the Hapsburg lands held 11.0 million. In the first decades of the century, Hapsburg armies under the skillful command of Prince Eugene of Savoy had fought well in the War of the Spanish Succession, and the peace treaties of 1714 gave the Hapsburgs the Austrian Netherlands (Belgium) and Lombardy. Wars with the Ottoman Empire at the end of the seventeenth century had acquired the Kingdom of Hungary, including vast territories in eastern Europe. Thus, in 1714 Vienna controlled lands from Brussels in the west to Milan in the south, Belgrade in the east, and Prague in the north—plus the crown of the Holy Roman Empire. This gave the Hapsburg emperor Charles VI, who reigned from 1711 to 1740, daunting political problems. The heterogeneous, polyglot realm was united only by the person of the Hapsburg monarch.

Hungary gave Charles the most difficulty. The magnate class had been largely autonomous under the Turkish sultan, and their diet expected no less from the Hapsburgs. Some Hungarian nobles even claimed a remarkable right, the *jus resistandi*, which legalized resistance to central authority. Charles VI realized that "[I]t is very important that quiet should prevail in this country," and he made numerous concessions to the Hungarians, such as promises to continue their Diet, to tolerate religious minorities (many nobles were Protestants), and not to tax the magnates. Such concessions to regional rights, however, meant that Austria lagged behind rivals such as Prussia in the development of a centralized authority and bureaucracy.

The second formidable political problem confronting Charles VI was the issue of his successor. Charles had come to the throne in 1711 upon the death of his brother, the emperor Joseph I, because Joseph had no sons to succeed him, and the Salic Law prevented the election of Joseph's daughters as Holy Roman Empress. Charles, however, faced the same problem: His only son died in infancy, and all Hapsburg lands thus probably would pass to his daughter, Maria Theresa, who would not become Holy Roman Empress but who could, under Austrian law, inherit the family dominions. Charles knew that powerful men, both at home and abroad, might challenge his succession, particularly if the throne passed to a woman; he therefore devoted much of his reign to guaranteeing Maria Theresa's succession and preventing a war of Austrian succession. For Charles, the issue was not protecting his daughter or defending the rights of women, it was the perpetuation of the dynasty and the territorial integrity of the far-flung Hapsburg lands. For his subject peoples, however, his death would open the prospect of independence or enhanced autonomy. For the European powers, it suggested the dismemberment of the Hapsburg Empire or annexation of choice parts of it.

The solution Charles VI proposed was a document called the Pragmatic Sanction. It proclaimed that the Hapsburg lands were indivisible, and it outlined the Austrian succession through Maria Theresa or other female relatives. Charles obtained the agreement of his family and published the Pragmatic Sanction in 1719. For the next twenty years he bargained within the empire and abroad, buying acceptance of the Pragmatic Sanction. Negotiations with the Hungarian Diet produced its acceptance in 1723, at the price of further weakening Viennese central authority over Hungary. A lifetime of diplomatic bribery bought the consent (sometimes recanted and bought again) of the European powers. Britain, for example, accepted the Pragmatic Sanction by a treaty of 1731; Charles paid Britain by closing the Austrian trading company (the Ostend Company) that competed with the British in global commerce. The king of Spain signed in return for the duchy of Parma.

Maria Theresa inherited the Hapsburg dominions in 1740 at the age of twenty-three, and she stayed on the throne until her death in 1780. She possessed energy and determination but an empty treasury and a weakened army. She began to reorganize the government and entrust many decisions to two powerful ministers, a chancellor for domestic affairs and a chancellor for foreign affairs, but the Pragmatic Sanction failed almost immediately. Her realm accepted her, and the Hungarians were chivalrous in her defense, but the duke of Bavaria, the king of Spain, and the elector of Saxony each claimed the Hapsburg crown for himself. The Holy Roman Empire sided with Bavaria, choosing the duke to be emperor. The king of Prussia demanded the province of Silesia as his price for honoring the Pragmatic Sanction. When Maria Theresa refused to surrender Silesia, the Prussians invaded it, beginning a series of wars known collectively as the War of the Austrian Succession (1740–48).

The war went poorly for Maria Theresa at first. The Prussians occupied Silesia. France, Spain, and Bavaria joined an alliance against her. The support of Britain and Holland, however, prevented the partitioning of the Hapsburg Empire. When the duke of Bavaria died in 1745, the electors of the Holy Roman Empire acknowledged the stability of Maria Theresa's position by choosing her husband, the duke of Lorraine, as Emperor Francis I. The belligerents reached the same conclusion about Maria Theresa in 1748, ending the War of the Austrian Succession in a treaty that sustained the Pragmatic Sanction except for permitting Prussia to retain Silesia.

The Hapsburg Empire had survived the coronation of a woman and the political problems that she inherited, but it had not overcome them. Maria Theresa's empire remained internally divided and less efficient than her rivals, although conditions improved when she entrusted the government to a strong chancellor, Count Kaunitz. Perhaps the worst problem confronting the Hapsburg Empire was that a hungry rival for leadership in central Europe, Prussia, had risen on the northern frontier. Within a few years, Austrian armies again found themselves engaged with the Prussians. The Seven Years' War devastated both countries, leaving no true victors. When peace came again in 1763, the Austrian Empire remained firmly in the grip of Maria Theresa, but even larger financial and administrative problems now plagued her. She faced the problems of recovery and reorganization, even establishing a national budget for the first time in her reign. The death of her husband in 1765, however, plunged her into grief: In a world of arranged, loveless marriages Maria Theresa had been deeply attached to Francis (see illustration 20.7). The young, exuberant empress who had loved theatricals and dances became a solemn, with-

Illustration 20.7

🖉 **Two Views of Enlightened Despotism in Austria.** The empress Maria Theresa (1717–80) came to the throne at age twenty-three and immediately faced a Prussian invasion intended to seize land from a weak young woman. She reigned for forty years, however, and withstood two great wars in central Europe. She typically chose to present herself not as the strong leader but as the good mother to both family and nation. In this family portrait, Maria poses with her husband and her eleven children, including the future emperor Joseph II (standing in right center).

Joseph II, the eldest son of Maria Theresa, was the Holy Roman Emperor for twenty-five years and shared power with his mother (women could not be emperor) in Austria from 1765 to 1780 before ruling in his own right until 1790. Joseph was a stubborn and impatient young man who repeatedly argued with his mother about creating more far-reaching reforms. His typical self-image was significantly different from hers: In this illustration (one of many versions of this theme) Joseph teaches modern agricultural techniques to peasants.

drawn, and increasingly religious figure who gave more and more of the government to trusted nobles such as Count Kaunitz.

The Hapsburg Monarchy and the Enlightened Despotism of Joseph II

Solving the postwar financial problems of the 1760s led Maria Theresa into direct conflict with the aristocracy. In 1764 she tried to force the Hungarians to carry a fairer share of imperial taxes, but the Magyar magnates blocked her plans in the Hungarian Diet. The Hungar-ian resistance to tax reform led Maria Theresa in a surprising direction—toward the emancipation of the peasantry from the bondage of serfdom. Maria Theresa's most influential adviser in the emancipation of the serfs was her son, Joseph, whose reign in Austria would later provide the best illustration of enlightened despotism in eighteenth-century European monarchism (see illustration 20.7).

Joseph was Maria Theresa's first son, born most inconveniently in 1741 when his mother was confronted with the War of the Austrian Succession. His mother ordered that he not be given a rigorous, military education, and Joseph consequently acquired many of his ideas from his independent reading of the philosophes, not from strict tutors. Joseph came to see himself as the embodiment of the Enlightenment, the person who could link reason with absolute powers. When his father died in 1765, Joseph became the Holy Roman Emperor and coregent with his mother in Austria. Maria Theresa shared some of her son's reformist ideas but tried to keep tight control of him and his friends, whom she called the *Aufklärungs* (Enlightenment) Party. After her death in 1780, Joseph could enthusiastically write, "I have made philosophy the legislator of my empire," but the same was not true of Maria Theresa. She had learned to rule in tough circumstances, and her policies often showed this. She believed in the use of torture, she was a brutal anti-Semite who launched a pogrom to drive all Jews out of Bohemia, and she often betrayed a startling insensitivity to the life of a peasant nation. But her stern, and sometimes cruel, policies created the stable, centralized government with a well-regulated army and well-balanced treasury that would make the enlightened policies of her son possible.

The mixed personalities of mother and son launched enlightened despotism in Austria with a compromise version of emancipation of the serfs. Years of famine and periodic peasant rebellion had shown that the serfs needed some relief. Joseph urged his mother to act, and Maria Theresa accepted his arguments. As she later wrote to her son, "The lords fleece the peasants dreadfully. . . . We know, and we have proof of the tyrannical oppression under which the poor people suffer." Maria Theresa hesitated to act against the interests of the great landowners, but the tax-resistance of the Hungarian nobles angered her enough to proceed. The emancipation of the peasantry in the Hapsburg Empire began with an imperial decree of 1767 named the *Urbarium*. This gave Hungarian peasants a leasehold on the soil that they worked and the legal freedom to leave the land without the permission of the local lord. It did not, however, abolish the *robot*, the compulsory labor tax that peasants owed to lords. During the 1770s, mother and son slowly extended this emancipation. Peasant obligations were separately reduced in each part of the Hapsburg lands: first in Austrian Silesia (1771), then in lower Austria (1772), Bohemia and Moravia (1775), and Styria (1778). After a rebellion by Bohemian peasants in 1775, another imperial decree converted the detested *robot* into a money tax on serfs in all royal lands.

Joseph II carried this work to its logical conclusion—the complete emancipation of the serfs—after the death of his mother in 1780. His decree of 1781 (the *Untertanspatent*) gave peasants in Austria, Bohemia, and Galicia the right to appeal to the state in any disputes with their lords. That same year he abolished serfdom in Austria. Peasants there obtained the right to marry, to move to the city, and to learn a trade without permission. Then, between 1781 and 1785, Joseph extended this emancipation to his other domains. Joseph II had practical reasons for his policy, such as asserting royal power against the aristocracy and creating a more efficient economy, but the ideas of the Enlightenment were an important factor. As the Patent to Abolish Serfdom of 1781 stated in its preface, "reason and humanity alike require this change." That did not mean, however, that Joseph was simply a gentle philosopher: He was both despot and enlightened. He had autocratic instincts, and those around him often commented on his domineering, uncompromising, irritable character.

Maria Theresa's financial needs and Joseph II's reforming zeal led to similar policies regarding the Catholic Church. The financial crisis of 1763 convinced the devout empress that she should challenge some of the tax exemptions and privileges of the church. She began by asking the church to make a greater "voluntary contribution" to the treasury and to limit future property donations to the church (which became tax-exempt land), but the Vatican refused. This led to imperial decrees restricting the church's acquisition of land, beginning with a patent that applied to the duchy of Milan in 1767. Thus, the financial crisis brought the monarchy into conflict with the church just as it had with the nobility, and this led to a variety of reforms. In 1768 the first tax on the clergy was created. In 1771 a decree established the maximum amount of property that an individual could bring to the church when joining a monastic order. In this struggle, Joseph pressed his mother even harder than he did against the aristocracy, and after her death, he acted vigorously. Between 1781 and 1789, Joseph closed more than seven hundred monasteries with thirty-six thousand members, leaving twenty-seven thousand monks and nuns in the empire. He seized the lands of the dispersed orders, thereby raising revenues for the state and converting church properties into schools. In all matters, he tried to break the power of Rome over the Catholic Church in Austria, a national religious policy known as Josephinism.

Joseph II's reputation for enlightened despotism went beyond the battles that he and his mother fought against the aristocracy and the church. Many of his reforms, however, still sprang essentially from the need for governmental efficiency and greater revenue (see document 20.4). He reformed the provincial administration, for example, replacing fifty-four bureaucrats in

◈ DOCUMENT 20.4 ◈

Letters of Emperor Joseph II on His Reforms

To the Vice-Chancellor of Austria, March 1785:

The present system of taxation in my dominions, and the inequality of the taxes which are imposed on the nation, form a subject too important to escape my attention. I have discovered that the principles on which it is founded are unsound, and have become injurious to the industry of the peasant; that there is neither equality, nor equity . . . it can no longer continue. . . .

I give you the necessary orders to introduce a new system of taxation, by which the contribution, requisite for the wants of the state, may be effected without augmenting the present taxes, and the industry of the peasant, at the same time, be freed from impediments. Make these arrangements the principal object of your care, and let them be made conformably to the plan which I have proposed.

To an Austrian Noble, December 1787:

Till now the Protestant religion has been opposed in my states; its adherents have been treated like foreigners; civil rights, possession of estates, titles, and appointments, all were refused them.

I determined from the very commencement of my reign to adorn my diadem with the love of my people, to act in the administration of affairs according to just, impartial, and liberal principles; consequently, I granted toleration, and removed the yoke which had oppressed the Protestants for centuries.

Fanaticism shall in the future be known in my states only by the contempt I have for it; nobody shall any longer be exposed to hardships on account of his creed; no man shall be compelled in the future to profess the religion of the state. . . . [M]y Empire shall not be the scene of abominable intolerance.

one district with eight. Between 1785 and 1789 he established a new tax law, based on physiocratic principles such as equal assessment of property. To make such laws effective, Joseph II ordered a census and survey of his empire, enforced by the army. His new tax law marked the end of feudalism in another way: It abolished both the ancient peasant labor obligation, the *robot*, and the compulsory tithe, which peasants paid to the church. Peasants still owed high taxes, typically amounting to 30 percent of their production (12.2 percent to the state and 17.8 percent to nobles), but this was far less than the confiscatory 70 percent many had previously paid.

Joseph II also earned recognition for enlightenment by responding to two great concerns of the philosophes: the toleration of religious minorities and the Beccarian modernization of law codes. In 1781 he issued the Edict of Toleration that extended the rights of full citizenship to Protestants and Jews. Such minorities were allowed to enter businesses and professions or to hold previously closed offices. They obtained the right to hold religious services, although regulations still restricted such details as the right to have churches with steeples or bells. Joseph's policy was again a mixture of enlightened ideals and practical politics. Emancipating the minorities brought people of talent into state ser-

vice and promoted economic growth. Joseph admitted this in the Edict of Toleration, saying that he granted it because he was "convinced on the one hand of the perniciousness of all restraints on conscience and, on the other, of the great benefits to religion and the state from true Christian tolerance."

Joseph II's legal reforms came in a series of decrees in the 1780s, chiefly 1787–88. He introduced both a new Civil Code and a new Penal Code. Together they abolished torture and the death penalty (except in military courts martial), introduced civil marriage and burial, ended class distinctions in the law, permitted religious intermarriage, eliminated several categories of crime (such as witchcraft and religious apostasy), and even forbade the ancient aristocratic tradition of primogeniture, which concentrated inheritance in the hands of the eldest son.

These reforms did not make Joseph II universally popular. To achieve them, he enhanced and centralized the powers of the state, and this included unwelcome autocracy such as a strong police. He was hated in many provinces, where he sought to enforce the rule of Vienna over local traditions, including the mandatory use of the German language in business and government. He infuriated both the aristocracy and the Catholic Church by attacking their traditional rights.

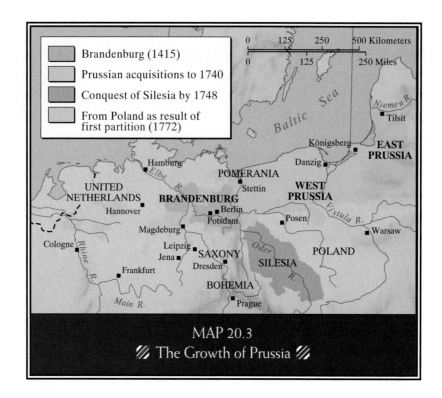

MAP 20.3
The Growth of Prussia

The Army, the Bureaucracy, and the Rise of Hohenzollern Prussia

One of the most important political facts of the eighteenth century was the rise of Prussia (see map 20.3). The elector of Brandenburg had acquired the province of Prussia in the seventeenth century, making the combined state of Brandenburg-Prussia an important, but still secondary, German state. The Holy Roman Empire recognized this state as the Kingdom of Prussia in 1701. It was an absolute monarchy with an impotent Diet and obedient aristocracy, known as the Junker class. It was one of the most autocratic states in Europe, but strict, able administration by the House of Hohenzollern provided a solid basis for development.

The ruler at the beginning of the century, Frederick I, did little to advance Prussia into the ranks of the great powers. He admired the sophisticated life of the French royal court at Versailles and devoted his reign to making Berlin glitter with the same elegance. The generation gap between Frederick and his son, King Frederick William I, who reigned from 1713 to 1740, could not have been larger. Frederick William was a cruel, semiliterate man who detested his father's world as effeminate; he favored drunken nights with his advisers and soldiers. In the words of their successor Frederick II, Frederick I sought to turn Berlin into the Athens of Germany, then Frederick William I tried to make it Sparta.

Although contemporary observers found King Frederick William personally loathsome, they acknowledged that he was the person who converted Prussia into one of the great powers. His son, Frederick II—whose love of books, music, French, and men so horrified his father that he beat him violently, imprisoned him, and considered executing him—became Frederick "the Great" partly because he inherited the strong state that his father built. The rise of the Prussian state under Frederick William derived from several factors: the unchallenged authority of the monarchy, the subservience of the aristocracy to a duty called state service, an emphasis upon building a strong bureaucracy and the army officer corps, and the hoarding of resources through niggardly expenditure and the avoidance of war. Frederick William I, in short, neither admired nor copied western models of government. He took the concept of compulsory state service by the aristocracy from despotic Russia. Prussian nobles were expected to serve as army officers or as civil servants; in return they obtained a monopoly of many posts and great control over the peasants on their estates.

Frederick William's administration of Prussia rested on more than the domestication of the aristocracy and the conscription of bureaucrats. He made Prussia a center of the study of cameralism (state administration) and founded university positions in cameral studies. This set standards of professionalism for civil servants and bred a bureaucracy admired for its efficiency. What began as a duty for conscripted aristocrats grew into an honor that brought distinction. The best indication of Prussian administrative efficiency came in state finances. Monarchs in France, Spain, and Austria faced bankruptcy; Frederick William had inherited nearly empty coffers himself. But his Ministry of Finance, created in 1713, and its tax-collecting bureaucracy soon became the envy of Europe. A study of Frederick William's finances has shown that he doubled his revenue while reducing expenditures—chiefly by cutting the extravagant royal court that his father had maintained.

King Frederick William I became known as a miser, but he did not economize on military expenditures. European armies were changing in the early eighteenth century; larger armies, maintained in peacetime, were becoming common. Württemberg had a standing army of six thousand men in 1700; Poland, an army of twelve thousand. Saxony and Spain kept peacetime armies of approximately thirty thousand men. Frederick William inherited a standing army set at twenty-seven thousand men in the late seventeenth century; by 1740 he had tripled its size to eighty-three thousand. To do this, Frederick William divided Prussia into military districts in 1730, assigning an enrollment quota of new soldiers to each; when recruitment fell short in 1733, he added conscription. This meant that Prussia kept 4 percent of its population in uniform, a number previously unthinkable. An important element of this policy, however, was that soldiers be taken from the lowest levels of society, so that the large army not disrupt the productive classes of peasants and workers. Criminals and debtors were released from prison to serve in the army. As Frederick II later explained this policy, "useful, hardworking people should be guarded as the apple of one's eye" because they paid the taxes that supported the army. The doctrine of state service gave sons of the aristocracy a monopoly of the ranks in the officer corps, and this meant that nearly 15 percent of the aristocracy was serving as army officers. Prussia, as Voltaire wryly commented, was not so much a country with an army to defend it, as it was an army with a country to support it.

Frederick William built the Prussian army upon such rigid discipline that he became known as "the sergeant-king" (see illustration 20.8). The Prussian ideal was an army that gave cadaver obedience—even the dead would still obey orders. Creating this obedience went far beyond the famous goose-step drilling of Prussian soldiers: Flogging and even mutilation were common punishments. The penalty for desertion was to have one's nose and an ear cut off, followed by a life sentence to slave labor. Nonetheless, desertion remained so common that Prussian army regulations re-

quired the cavalry to surround the infantry during any march through a wooded area. Capital punishment was also common, and it could be administered for merely raising a hand against an officer. This did not mean that Frederick William I frequently risked the lives of his soldiers. Prussia remained neutral in three major wars during his reign. When he did choose to fight, against troubled Sweden, he continued the expansion of Prussia with the acquisition of West Pomerania.

The Prussian Monarchy of Frederick the Great

Frederick William I's kingdom was inherited by his third son, the twenty-eight-year-old Frederick II, in 1740. The new king got absolute power, an enlarged kingdom, an efficient administration, a full treasury, and a feared army—the material opportunity to become Frederick the Great. His life did not begin that way. As a third son, he had not been expected to reach the throne. As a son of Frederick William, he had been expected to accept a rigid education and rigorous military training. Instead, Frederick had rebelled against his father at eighteen; formed an intimate relationship with his tutor, Lt. Katte; and tried to run off with him. Frederick William sentenced both men to death for desertion, forced Frederick to witness the beheading of his lover, and then imprisoned him with a suspended death sentence. Frederick William pardoned his son, then married him off. Frederick accepted military training and learned his lessons well but infuriated his father again in his twenties by deciding that French literature and music were more interesting (see illustration 20.8). Frederick became an excellent flute player and wrote flute compositions throughout his life. When he came to power and built Sans Souci ("Carefree")—an ornate palace with French gardens—in Potsdam, outside Berlin, he delighted in the visits of Johann Sebastian Bach, with whom he played duets, and Voltaire, with whom he debated philosophy. Frederick became such a voluminous writer that his collected works run for thirty volumes.

Frederick II did not become known as Frederick the Great for writing poetry and incidental pieces for the flute. When he came to the throne in 1740, he turned to the task of government with enthusiasm, and he worked to extend his father's accomplishments. To the bureaucracy he added a system of competitive examinations for promotions and his own tireless labor as "the first servant of the state." He insisted upon daily written reports from his ministries and poured over them in a bureaucratic toil that would have been unthinkable for most monarchs. And when Frederick II decided upon

Illustration 20.8

Two Views of Enlightened Despotism in Prussia. The rise of the Prussian state rested on an unusually large army for a small state, a thoroughly trained army that was maintained with brutal discipline. Frederick the Great, who spent more time in warfare than music, approved of the flogging of his soldiers because he expected cadaver obedience from them—the will to follow his orders even after death. He preferred, however, to present a cultivated and intellectual side to his monarchy. He corresponded with the philosophes and invited Voltaire to stay with him at his palace in Potsdam, "Sans Souci" (Carefree). Frederick was a fine musician and spent many hours composing his own music. In this illustration he plays the flute at Sans Souci.

ways to improve his kingdom, he did not hesitate to act. When he learned of the benefits of the potato, for example, he forced the nation to adopt it. He distributed free seed potatoes to the peasants in 1744, then issued an edict demanding that they grow potatoes or have their ears and nose cut off, and sent the army to check on crops being grown.

But the rebellious and artistic Frederick became Frederick the Great as a soldier. Unlike his father, he was not reluctant to use the Prussian army. He came to the throne of Prussia in May 1740, five months before Maria Theresa inherited the Austrian throne; by December 1740 they were at war. Of his first twenty-three years on the throne of Prussia, Frederick was at war with Austria for fifteen years. He began by ignoring the Prussian promise of 1726 to honor the Pragmatic Sanction and invading Silesia in the first of three wars he would fight with Maria Theresa, sometimes called the Silesian Wars. Frederick II was neither a brilliant innovator nor a great battlefield strategist, but he was a superb tactician who found ways to defeat larger, or better placed, armies by concentrating his forces against a portion of his enemies. His success as a general was linked to a strategy of exhaustion in which he fought in indirect ways (such as occupying territory and destroying crops or commerce) rather than engaging in grand battles until one side or the other was annihilated. This won Silesia, Frederick's reputation as a genius, and international recognition of Prussia as a great power (see document 20.5).

Another part of Frederick II's reputation rests on his claim to enlightened despotism alongside Joseph II of Austria. At the beginning of his reign, Frederick showed promise of becoming one of the most enlightened statesmen of the century. Within a few months, he abolished torture in criminal procedures, established freedom of religion, granted limited freedom of the press, and founded the Berlin Academy of Science. That early promise was poorly fulfilled, however. Frederick remained attached to the ideals of the Enlightenment, in theory, but seldom enacted them. He remained a philosopher king, especially in contrast to his martinet father. His later years saw few reforms, however, and they were chiefly to improve Prussian finances, curing the problems he had created himself with long wars.

Frederick II did continue to build the Prussian army. The standing army of twenty-seven thousand that Frederick William I had expanded to eighty-three thousand approached two hundred thousand near the end of Frederick II's reign. He did this by subordinating all government activity to the military. During a peacetime army buildup in 1752, Frederick gave the army 90 percent of the Prussian budget. This extended to far-reaching arms of the Prussian army, such as the Splitberger arms factory at Potsdam, which manufactured fifteen thousand muskets per year, and the military warehouses at Berlin and Breslau, which stored enough grain to feed sixty thousand soldiers for two years. Frederick also expanded the army by implementing the plan of a Prussian civil servant, Justus Moser, for army reserves. Moser conceived the idea of universal military training with most citizens remaining active in a militia in case they were needed. Frederick the Great was proud of his army and intolerant of criticism of it. He did not hesitate, for example, to execute Jesuit

◆ DOCUMENT 20.5 ◆

Frederick the Great: The Nature of Monarchy, 1787

Essay on the Forms of Government

With respect to the true monarchical government, it is the best or the worst of all others, according to how it is administered.

We have remarked that men granted preeminence to one of their equals, expecting that he should do them certain services. These services consisted in the maintenance of the laws; a strict execution of justice; and employment of his whole powers to prevent any corruption of manners; and defending the state against its enemies. . . .

Princes and monarchs, therefore, are not invested with supreme authority that they may, with impunity, riot in debauchery and voluptuousness. They are not raised by their fellow citizens in order that their pride may pompously display itself, and contemptuously insult simplicity of manners, poverty and wretchedness. . . .

If the prince, through debility, should abandon the helm of the state to mercenary hands, I mean to ministers, in that case, each having different views, no one proceeds on general plans; the new minister fritters away what he finds already established, however excellent that may be. . . .

There is but one general good, which is that of the state. . . . [T]he sovereign represents the state; he and his people form but one body, which can only be happy as far as united by concord. The prince is to the nation he governs what the head is to the man; it is his duty to see, to think, and act for the whole community, so that he may procure it every advantage of which it is capable.

priests who taught that deserting the army was not a mortal sin.

Frederick's militarism nearly destroyed Prussia. During the 1750s, Count Kaunitz of Austria engineered a brilliant diplomatic revolution that allied the Hapsburgs with Russia and England and included promises of the return of Silesia to Austria. Frederick chose war on his own terms and kept Silesia, but following the Seven Years' War, Prussia was, in the words of one historian, "a bleeding stump, drained of vitality." The war killed more than 10 percent of the population (500,000 of 4.5 million), and by 1763 boys of fourteen were being conscripted to fight. More than one hundred towns and villages had been burnt to the ground, and thirteen thousand families had lost their homes. The devastated towns of Prussia included Berlin, which the Russian army put to the torch in 1760. The overflowing treasury that Frederick II had inherited had been squandered on war, forcing Frederick to face the critical question of eighteenth-century government: taxation. "No government can exist without taxation," he wrote. "This money must necessarily be levied on the people; the grand art consists of levying so as not to oppress." He, like his peers, failed at the "grand art." Taxes were levied in inverse proportion to the ability to pay them: The rich and powerful had exemptions from taxation, so the poor and the middling were expected to carry the burden. That system worked in comfortable times, but the Seven Years' War broke it. Far from paying taxes, much of the population was near starvation in 1763. The monarch himself, although only fifty-one years old, seemed broken by age: His back was stooped, his face gaunt, his teeth missing, and he was plagued with both diarrhea and hemorrhoids. He returned to Berlin in military triumph known as *der alte Fritz* (Old Fritz)—partly an affectionate compliment, partly a sad comment. "It is a poor man who is coming home," the king acknowledged in 1763.

Frederick the Great's postwar policies necessarily focused on economic recovery, which was the same issue that threatened to consume George III and Louis XV. To achieve recovery, he ruled with the iron fist of the absolute monarch. Frederick placated the Prussian aristocracy, which kept its dominance of the bureaucracy and its monopoly of army rank. He did not intervene in the relationship between lords and peasants; there was no Josephine emancipation of the serfs or equalization of taxes in Prussia. In return, Frederick avoided the restrictions that British monarchs faced in Parliament or French monarchs encountered in the parlements. The aristocratic bureaucracy, which could slow down or circumvent his policies, was his greatest obstacle. As one professor of cameralism put it, "Far from being an unlimited monarchy, [Prussia] is a thinly veiled aristocracy [that] rules the country in undisguised form as a bureaucracy."

Little room existed for enlightenment in the despotism of Frederick the Great's later years. He was still remembered as the king who had insisted that "[A]ll religions must be tolerated," but he extended few freedoms. When the German dramatist Gotthold Lessing followed Voltaire's footsteps to Berlin with high hopes,

he left protesting against a stifling environment: "Don't talk to me about your Berlinese freedom of thought and writing. It only consists of the freedom to make as much fun as you like of religion. . . . Let someone in Berlin stand up for the rights of the peasants, or protest against despotism and exploitation as they do now even in France and Denmark, and you will soon know by experience which country is to this day the most slavish in Europe." Some modern scholars, however, have concluded that Frederick was the greatest of the enlightened despots. One French historian, impressed by a king of intellect and culture, concluded that he possessed "the most complete character of the eighteenth century, being the only one to unite idea with power."

Catherine the Great and Despotism in Romanov Russia

The eighteenth century began in Russia, as it did in France, with one of the most powerful autocrats of the seventeenth century still holding the throne. When Peter the Great of Russia died in 1725, he left behind a royal succession even more troubled than Louis XIV's legacy to France. The French got a five-year-old king and a resurgent aristocracy; the Russians got a generation of chaotic government. In 1718 Peter's son and heir to the throne, Alexis, became involved in political intrigues at court. As a result, Peter had Alexis, his only child, tortured to death. When Peter died a few years later, he left behind a large royal family, but no clear heir. The palace guards consequently chose Peter's wife, Catherine (a former Livonian serf), as the next monarch, and the great nobles at court accepted a woman on the throne for the first time because they believed that they could control her. A Supreme Privy Council of nobles thus came to exercise central power in Russia, led by Prince Alexander Menshikov, Peter's former minister and Catherine's former lover. Catherine died two years later, but the privy council retained power in Russia for thirty-seven years; their intrigues selected two women and three children to sit on the throne. The nobility sought to shackle the monarch, as the English, the Poles, and the Swedes had done, and French aristocrats were seeking to do. They won many rights in the turbulent years between 1725 and 1762, but they failed to break monarchical autocracy. The Empress Anna (a niece of Peter the Great), for example, was offered the throne in 1730 on the condition that she accept a list of restrictions: She must have the approval of the council to marry, name an heir, impose taxes, declare war, name new nobles, or issue a royal decree (*ukase*). Anna accepted, then defied the agreement. In such ways, absolute powers survived in 1762, when a strong monarch, Catherine II, arrived on the throne.

Catherine was the daughter of an impoverished German duke who had married her off at age sixteen to a feeble-minded grandson of Peter the Great, the grand-duke Peter. After childhood worries that a spinal deformity would make Catherine an ugly, unmarriageable drain on her family, she grew into an attractive woman with deep black hair contrasting with a pale complexion. Before she had matured into such physical attractiveness, however, the future empress had built her identity around her education and her strong, probing mind. Her intelligence won the attention of the Russian royal family when hunting for a wife for the uneducated heir to the throne, Grand-Duke Peter. When Peter was unable to consummate the marriage, members of the royal family who were desperate to perpetuate the dynasty advised Catherine to find a lover who could produce children. She cheerfully complied and began a series of affairs that were among the most notorious features of her reign—although they hardly distinguished her from the behavior of male monarchs such as George I of England or Louis XV of France.

Catherine's lovers have historical importance because one of them, Grigori Orlov, an officer in the royal guards, helped her to usurp the throne. When her husband was crowned Czar Peter III in 1762, the army began to conspire against him because he favored an alliance with a recent Russian enemy, Frederick the Great of Prussia. Orlov became a leader of this conspiracy. When Peter threatened the arrest of his estranged wife, a military coup overthrew him and named Catherine empress. Her husband soon died in prison, apparently killed by one of Orlov's brothers and possibly with the connivance of Catherine, who ascended the throne at age thirty-two.

Catherine II of Russia reigned from 1762 until 1796. She initially faced significant opposition because she was a foreigner, Lutheran-born in an Orthodox land, and sexually scandalous. She obtained (and used) great power largely because she was able to strike a bargain with the aristocracy—the *dvorianstvo* class. Like Frederick II of Prussia, the basis of her reign became this compromise: She would enhance the position of the aristocracy and make no reforms at their expense. Catherine settled the deal by seducing the foremost leader of the old nobility, Nikita Panin, who then endorsed her claim. Thereafter, she exercised autocratic

powers with a skill that rivaled Peter the Great, earning a reputation for enlightened despotism, although the evidence is greater for her despotism than for her enlightenment. She initially accepted, but later opposed, an imperial *ukase* drafted by Panin that would have delegated legislative power to a council of nobles. She did restore to the nobility freedoms it had lost under Peter the Great. She abolished compulsory state service by all aristocrats but kept nobles in high diplomatic and military posts, winning the gratitude of many. She granted a monopoly on vodka production to nobles, winning others.

Catherine II best placated the aristocracy by her policy on serfdom. She had read enough of the philosophes to be an enlightened enemy of serfdom in principle, and one of her first decrees upon coming to the throne had been to alleviate the conditions of serfs on the royal estates. As European Russia contained fifty million peasants—55 percent of them serfs on the royal estates—this was no small matter. And Catherine talked of abolishing serfdom. Her actions, however, were different: She consistently extended the power of aristocrats over their serfs. A decree of 1765, for example, gave them the right to send troublesome peasants to Siberia.

Catherine's shrewd politics solidified her despotic authority by raising the Russian aristocracy to a level of power that they had not previously known. The culmination of this trend occurred in 1785 when Catherine issued the Charter of the Nobility, which codified the collective rights of the *dvorianstvo*, such as freedom from state service. It gave aristocrats the sole right to acquire serfs, which town dwellers and even free peasants had sought. It excluded the aristocracy from taxation and from corporal punishment.

Partly for consolidating imperial power for thirty years, and partly for her enlightened reforms, Catherine II became known as Catherine the Great. The enlightened side of her record, however, is ambiguous. She read many of the philosophes before ascending to the throne, and she was apparently much influenced by Blackstone, Beccaria, and Montesquieu. She corresponded with Voltaire and hosted Diderot on a visit to Russia. Her devotion to the ideals of the Enlightenment, however, remained stronger in theory than in action. She found it difficult to enact the ideas she liked. Diderot was dazzled to find "the soul of Brutus in the body of Cleopatra," but Catherine thought the philosopher's schemes were "sheer prattle." She wrote to him in 1770, rejecting many reforms for Russia, "All your work is done on paper, which does not mind how you treat

❖ DOCUMENT 20.6 ❖

Catherine the Great's Instructions for a New Law Code, 1768

Of the situation of the people in general

33. The laws ought to be so framed as to secure the safety of every citizen as much as possible.

34. The equality of the citizens consists in this: that they should all be subject to the same laws.

35. This equality requires institutions so well adapted as to prevent the rich from oppressing those who are not so wealthy as themselves. . . .

36. General or political liberty does not consist in that licentious notion, that man may do whatever he pleases.

37. In a state or assemblage of people that live together in a community where there are laws, liberty can only consist in doing that which every one ought to do, and not to be constrained to do that which one ought not to do.

38. A man ought to form in his own mind an exact and clear idea of what liberty is. Liberty is the right of doing whatsoever the laws allow: And if any one citizen could do what the laws forbid, there would be no more liberty, because others would have an equal power of doing the same.

39. The political liberty of a citizen is the peace of mind arising from the consciousness that every individual enjoys his peculiar safety; and in order that the people might attain this liberty, the laws ought to be so framed that no one citizen should stand in fear of another; but that all of them should stand in fear of the same laws.

---

it. . . . But I, poor empress, must work upon human skin, which is much more ticklish and irritable."

Catherine's greatest effort at enlightened government produced almost no result. In 1767 she summoned a Legislative Commission of 564 delegates, representing all classes except the serfs. Only twenty-eight members were named to the commission, and the rest were elected. Catherine charged the commission with the task of considering the complete reform of the laws of Russia. To guide the commission, Catherine prepared one of the most famous documents of her reign, the Grand Instructions (*Nakaz*) of 1767 (see document 20.6). These instructions contained both halves of enlightened despotism. They opened by asserting that "[T]he sovereign is absolute, for there is no other authority but that which centers in his single person." That statement of despotic power was followed by many enlightened principles: Catherine opposed torture and capital punishment, called for a government based on the division of powers, and indicated her hostility to serfdom. The potential for change was enormous. As Panin reacted to the *Nakaz*, "[T]hese principles are strong enough to shatter walls!"

Despite the great promise of its beginning, the Legislative Commission of 1767–68 did not reform Russia. It received more than fourteen hundred petitions (more than one thousand of them from free peasants), held more than two hundred meetings, and quibbled over details. The commission agreed to vote Catherine a new title ("the Great and All-Wise Mother of the Fatherland"), but it could not agree upon a legal code. At best, it gave Catherine ideas for later years.

The need for reform in Russia was dramatized by a rebellion of serfs and the Cossacks of southern Russia in 1773–75, known as Pugachev's Rebellion. Emilian Pugachev was a Cossack—a people who had lost their autonomy in 1772—and a deserter from the Russian army. He organized discontented serfs, Cossacks, and religious minorities into a rebel army in 1773. Pugachev announced that he was Czar Peter III, claiming he had been dethroned by Catherine and the great nobles. He formed a "royal court" among the rebels and proclaimed the emancipation of the serfs, giving them the incentive to fight for his victory (see document 20.7). Pugachev's rebels withstood the Imperial army for nearly two years, capturing the town of Kazan, and stimulating serf rebellions throughout the region. The government took Pugachev so seriously that new defenses were built around Moscow to prepare for his attack. The rebellion collapsed in 1775 when Pugachev's own forces betrayed him. He was taken to St. Petersburg, exhibited in an iron cage, and then beheaded. Catherine ordered that Pugachev not be tortured but agreed that his questioning could include the artful extraction of his teeth. Her

◈ DOCUMENT 20.7 ◈

Pugachev: Emancipation of the Serfs, 1774

We, Peter III, by the Grace of God Emperor and Autocrat of All Russia, etc.

This is given for nationwide information.

By this personal decree, with our monarchical and fatherly love, we grant [freedom] to everyone who formerly was in serfdom or in any other obligation to the nobility; . . . while to the Cossacks [we restore] for eternity their freedoms and liberties; we terminate the [military] recruiting system, cancel personal and other monetary taxes, abolish without compensation the ownership of land, forest, pastures, fisheries, and salt deposits; and we free everyone from all taxes and obligations which the thievish nobles and extortionist city judges have imposed on the peasantry and the rest of the population. We pray for the salvation of your souls and wish you a happy and peaceful life here [on earth] where we have suffered and experienced much from the above-mentioned thievish nobles. Now since our name, thanks to the hand of providence, flourishes throughout Russia, we make hereby known by this personal decree the following: all nobles who have owned [estates granted by the state] or [inherited estates], who have opposed our rule, who have rebelled against the empire, and who have ruined the peasantry should be seized, arrested, and hanged; that is, treated in the same manner as these unchristians have treated you, the peasantry. After the extermination of these opponents and thievish nobles everyone will live in a peace and happiness that shall continue to eternity.

principles against torture did not protect Pugachev's followers. Special troops scoured the countryside, tracking down rebellious serfs. Most were executed "according to Christian canon"—cutting off their hands and feet before beheading them, then leaving the bodies to rot at roadside while heads were displayed on pikes in town.

Catherine II achieved her most important reforms in the aftermath of Pugachev's rebellion, but they did little to improve the conditions of serfdom. First, she reorganized the government of Russian provinces in 1775, hoping that more efficient government could solve local problems. Catherine divided Russia into fifty administrative provinces, each of which was then subdivided into districts. She then allowed greater self-government at both the district and province level. Local nobles were named to head district governments. Councils, elected by town dwellers as well as nobles, shared in the government. Separate courts were established for nobles, burghers, and free peasants. Catherine carried this administrative reform further in 1785 when she issued the Charter of Towns. Like the reorganization of provincial government in 1775, this charter mixed the Old Regime's corporative society with ideas of the Enlightenment. Following the strict hierarchy of corporative society, the charter divided the urban population into six legal categories, ranging from the great merchants and leaders of the wealthiest guilds down to manual laborers. It allowed all six categories of town dwellers, including the unskilled working class, to participate in elections for the town council. Catherine the Great thus gave signs of enlightened aspiration, and she achieved a few noteworthy changes. But the foremost characteristic of her reign was still despotism, and the condition of the serfs worsened significantly under her rule.

◈

Conclusion

As the eighteenth century drew toward a close, Europe remained a civilization dominated by the institutions of monarchy and aristocracy. This was true in all five of the great powers, although the nature of monarchy and the balance of power between monarchy and aristocracy varied sharply from state to state. In western Europe, the absolute powers of the throne had been broken in England and were being severely tested in France; in central and eastern Europe, the monarchs of Austria, Prussia, and Russia retained more despotic powers, although this typically rested upon some compromise with the nobility. Historians often ask whether the greatest royal leaders of the era—the enlightened despots, Maria Theresa and Joseph II of Austria, Frederick II of Prussia, and Catherine II of Russia—are best understood as despots or as enlightened rulers. This question could equally be extended to the aristocracy: Were the British Parliament, the French *parlements*, the Junkers, and the *dvoriano* wiser rulers? In many countries, the collision between monarchy and aristocracy would contribute to political upheaval within the next generation (see chapter 22).

Whatever the balance of political power, all governments of the Old Regime faced a similar set of problems. Warfare was near the top of the list; the eighteenth century was among the more bellicose in European history. The century began with two wars in progress involving great powers, and between 1701 and the beginning of the French Revolution in 1789 only twenty-two years passed when none of the great powers was at war. Perhaps the foremost problem created by the War of the Austrian Succession, the Seven Years' War, and the American Revolution was economic: The monarchies of Europe became debtor states, and governments searched for new taxes to pay for war debts. This cycle of problems became intertwined with the struggle over monarchical power. Although the outcome remained unclear during the Old Regime, these problems threatened the end of the age of royal power.

Suggested Readings

Useful reference books for basic information about eighteenth-century political, diplomatic, and military history are J. Babuscio and R. M. Dunn, *European Political Facts, 1648–1789* (1984) and C. Cook and J. Stevenson, eds., *British Historical Facts, 1760–1830* (1980).

Good survey histories of the Old Regime can be found in W. Doyle, *The Old Order, 1660–1800* (1978), M. S. Anderson, *Europe in the Eighteenth Century,* 2d ed. (1976), I. Woloch, *Eighteenth-Century Europe* (1982), and O. Hufton, *Europe: Privilege and Protest, 1730–1789* (1980). The volumes in *The Rise of Modern Europe* series edited by W. Langer are now dated but remain helpful on many subjects; see W. L. Dorn, *Competition for Empire, 1740–1763* (1940) and L. Gershoy, *From Despotism to Revolution, 1763–1789* (1944). G. Rudé has written both a good general survey in *Europe in the Eighteenth Century: Aristocracy and the Bourgeois Challenge* (1972) and the noteworthy *The Crowd in History: A Study of Popular Disturbances in England and France, 1730–1848* (1964), which is an extremely influential book in changing interpretations about the century.

For a focus on Britain, see the dated but still valuable introduction by J. H. Plumb, *England in the Eighteenth Century, 1714–1815* (1950) and J. C. D. Clark, *English Society, 1688–1832* (1985). For the huge literature on eighteenth-century politics, the starting point is the works of L. B. Namier, *England in the Age of the American Revolution* (1961) and *The Structure of Politics at the Accession of George III* (1957) and F. O'Gorman, *Voters, Patrons, and Parties: The Unreformed Electorate of Hanoverian England, 1734–1832* (1989). See also R. Hatton, *George I: Elector and King* (1978); J. M. Black, *Robert Walpole and the Nature of Politics in Early Eighteenth-Century Britain* (1990); J. Brooke, *King George III* (1972); J. Brewer, *Party Ideology and Popular Politics at the Accession of George III* (1976); C. Hibbert, *King Mob* (1958); which is helpful for the Gordon riots; E. M. Johnston, *Ireland in the Eighteenth Century* (1974); T. Bartlett, *The Fall and Rise of*

the Irish Nation: The Catholic Question, 1690–1830 (1992); J. Black, *Pitt the Elder* (1992); J. Ehrman, *The Younger Pitt,* 2 vols. (1969–83); J. W. Derry, *Charles James Fox* (1972); and A. Williamson, *Wilkes* (1974).

For France, see R. E. Mousnier, *The Institutions of France under Absolute Monarchy, 1598–1789,* 2 vols. (1984); C. B. A. Behrens, *The Ancien Regime* (1967); J. H. Shennan, *Philippe, Duke of Orléans, Regent of France, 1715–1723* (1979); A. M. Wilson, *French Foreign Policy during the Administration of Cardinal Fleury, 1726–1743* (1936); B. Stone, *The French Parlements and the Crisis of the Old Regime* (1986); J. H. Shennan, *The Parlement of Paris* (1968); O. Hufton, *The Poor in Eighteenth Century France, 1750–1789* (1974); J. Ruff, *Crime, Justice and Public Order in Old Regime France* (1984); J. W. Merrick, *The Desacralization of the French Monarchy in the Eighteenth Century* (1990); J. C. Riley, *The Seven Years' War and the Old Regime in France* (1986); J. F. Bosher, *French Finances, 1770–1795* (1970); and D. Dakin, *Turgot and the Ancien Regime in France* (1965).

For the Austrian Empire, see E. Wangermann, *The Austrian Achievement, 1700–1800* (1973); C. A. Macartney, *Maria Theresa and the House of Austria* (1969); P. G. M. Dickson, *Finance and Government under Maria Theresa, 1740–1780* (1987); T. C. W. Blanning, *Joseph II and Enlightened Absolutism* (1970); D. Beales, *Joseph II* (1987); P. P. Bernard, *The Limits of Enlightenment: Joseph II and the Law* (1979); W. E. Wright, *Serf, Seigneur, and Sovereign: Agrarian Reform in Eighteenth-Century Bohemia* (1966); P. Bernard, *Jesuits and Jacobins: Enlightenment and Enlightened Despotism in Austria* (1971); and K. A. Roider, Jr., *Austria's Eastern Question, 1700–1790* (1982).

For Prussia, see S. B. Fay, *The Rise of Brandenburg-Prussia to 1786* (1981); a short but clear introduction; H. W. Koch, *A History of Prussia* (1978); J. Sheehan, *German History, 1770–1866* (1989); M. Hughes, *Law and Politics in Eighteenth-Century Germany* (1988); J. Gagliardo, *Germany under the Old Regime, 1600–1790* (1991); H. Brunschwig, *Enlightenment and Romanticism in Eighteenth-Century Prussia* (1974); H. Rosenberg, *Bureaucracy, Aristocracy, and Autocracy* (1958); R. A. Dorwart, *The Administration Reforms of Frederick William I of Prussia* (1953); L. Frey and M. Frey, *Frederick I: The Man and His Times* (1984); G. Ritter, *Frederick the Great: A Historical Profile* (1968); C. Duffy, *Frederick the Great: A Military Life* (1988); and W. Hubatsch, *Frederick the Great of Prussia* (1975).

For Russia, see P. Dukes, *The Making of Russian Absolutism, 1613–1801,* 2d ed. (1990); M. Raeff, *Understanding Imperial Russia: State and Society in the Old Regime* (1984); J. Alexander, *Catherine the Great: Life and Legend* (1989); I. de Madariaga, *Russia in the Age of Catherine the Great* (1981); J. P. LeDonne, *Ruling Russia: Politics and Administration in the Age of Absolutism, 1762–1796* (1984); P. Longworth, *The Three Empresses: Catherine I, Anne, and Elizabeth of Russia* (1972); M. Curtiss, *A Forgotten Empress: Anna Ivanova and Her Era* (1974); J. Brennan, *Enlightened Absolutism in Russia: The Reign of Elisabeth, 1741–1762* (1987); J. T. Alexander, *Emperor of the Cossacks: Pugachev and the Fronter Jacquerie of 1773–1775* (1973); and D. C. B. Lieven, *Russia's Rulers under the Old Regime* (1989); which looks at the bureaucracy.

For enlightened despotism, see the general discussion in F. Hartung, *Enlightened Despotism* (1957) and L. Krieger, *Kings and Philosophers, 1689–1789* (1970). See also M. Raeff, *The Well Ordered Police State: Social and Institutional Change through the Law in the Germa-*

nies and Russia, *1600–1800* (1983); H. M. Scott, ed., *Enlightened Absolutism: Reform and Reformers in Later Eighteenth-Century Europe* (1990); and A. Lentin, ed., *Enlightened Absolutism, 1760–1790* (1985).

For regions not covered in this chapter, see D. Carpanetto and G. Ricuperati, *Italy in the Age of Reason, 1685–1789* (1987); S. J. Woolf, *A History of Italy, 1700–1860* (1979); E. Cochrane, *Florence in the Forgotten Centuries, 1527–1800* (1973); J. T. Lukowski, *Liberty's Folly: The Polish-Lithuanian Commonwealth in the Eighteenth Century* (1991); D. Kirby, *Northern Europe in the Early Modern Period: The Baltic World, 1492–1792* (1990); H. A. Barton, *Scandinavia in the Revolutionary Era, 1760–1815* (1986); B. Jelavich, *History of the Balkans,* vol. 1: *Eighteenth and Nineteenth Centuries* (1990); J. Lynch, *Bourbon Spain, 1700–1808* (1989); R. Herr, *The Eighteenth-Century Revolution in Spain* (1958); R. M. Hatton, *Charles XII of Sweden* (1968); J. Gagliardo, *Reich and Nation: The Holy Roman Empire as Idea and Reality, 1763–1806* (1980); U. Dann, *Hanover and Great Britain* (1991); H. Liebel, *Enlightened Bureaucracy versus Enlightened Despotism in Baden, 1750–1792* (1965); J. A. Vann, *The Making of a State: Württemberg, 1593–1793* (1984); T. C. W. Blanning, *Reform and Revolution in Mainz, 1743–1803* (1974); and D. Kosary, *Culture and Society in Eighteenth-Century Hungary* (1987).

For European overseas empires, see J. H. Parry, *Trade and Dominion: The European Overseas Empires in the Eighteenth Century* (1971); D. K. Fieldhouse, *The Colonial Empires: A Comparative Study from the Eighteenth Century* (1966); C. R. Boxer, *The Dutch Seaborne Empire, 1600–1800* (1965); and C. R. Boxer, *The Portugese Seaborne Empire, 1415–1825* (1969).

For military history, see A. Corvisier, *Armies and Societies in Europe, 1494–1789* (1979); especially interesting for conditions in the military; M. S. Anderson, *War and Society in Europe of the Old Regime, 1618–1789* (1988); G. Parker, *The Military Revolution* (1988); J. M. Black, *A Military Revolution? Military Change and European Society, 1550–1800* (1990); and J. Childs, *Armies and Warfare in Europe, 1648–1789* (1982).

CHAPTER 21

THE CULTURE OF OLD REGIME EUROPE

CHAPTER OUTLINE

This chapter looks at the culture of eighteenth-century Europe from several perspectives. It begins by looking at traditional "high culture"—the art and architecture, the music and drama of the educated classes. A transition occurred from the baroque style to a revival of classicism, which became the dominant style in the arts of the eighteenth century. The discussion then focuses on "popular culture" in the lives of ordinary people. It compares a basic institution of high culture, the salon, with the equivalent institution of popular culture, the coffeehouse.

Although other themes seemed to dominate the culture of the eighteenth century, Christianity remained central to European civilization. Chapter 22 explains the religious division of Europe into Protestant, Catholic, and Orthodox regions and examines the position of Jewish, Islamic, and dissenting Christian minorities. Most of the chapter is devoted to the dominant intellectual phenomenon of the eighteenth century, the Enlightenment. Described are the origins of the Enlightenment in seventeenth-century skepticism, the rationalism of the scientific revolution, and the cultural revival of classicism. The basic concepts that connected enlightened thought—natural law, reason, and progress—are then explained. This leads to a discussion of the French Enlightenment, French philosophes, and the most typical work of the Enlightenment, the *Encyclopédie*. After describing the Enlightenment in other parts of Europe, the chapter ends with an examination of its impact on religion and government.

High Culture: From the Baroque to the Classical

The predominant cultural style of the seventeenth century, known as the baroque, still dominated many of the arts—including architecture, painting, sculpture, furniture making, and music—in the early eighteenth century.

llustration 21.1

Secular Rococo Architecture. As the monarchs of Europe emulated the French Bourbons in building lavish new palaces, they did not make precise copies of Versailles. Instead they built luxurious homes in the newest architectural style. The Wittelsbach family, who ruled the south German state of Bavaria, were among the most active builders, and their palaces included Schloss Nymphenburg at Munich, whose gilded rococo "Hall of Mirrors" is shown here.

The baroque appealed to the emotions and spirituality through the grandiose, the ornately decorated, the extravagantly expressed. Whether looking at the energetic statues of Bernini, paintings of suffering martyrs by Caravaggio, or the voluptuous pastel nudes of Rubens, the viewer was overwhelmed by the lavish baroque style. Architects brought baroque emotions to palaces and churches, composers brought them to oratorios and fugues, artisans even sought the baroque style in gilded chairs and writing tables. From Chippendale furniture in English homes, to the ornate gates of Place Stanislas in Nancy, the Spanish steps and piazza in Rome, the curved columns of the Karlskirche in Vienna, and Frederick the Great's Sans Souci in Potsdam, the rich and powerful made Europe look baroque. This style culminated in an extravagant artistic style, characterized by fanciful curved forms and elaborate ornamentation, known as rococo (see illustration 21.1). Sans Souci Palace was rococo—there a warrior king could write French poetry, compose flute music, and dispute philosophers in a home he helped to design, with the gaudy yellow walls and the plump cherubs a soldier wanted.

Historians chiefly remember the high culture of the eighteenth century for the reaction against the baroque style. A revival of the styles and aesthetics of the classi-cal Graeco-Roman world rapidly supplanted the baroque during the middle decades of the century. Neoclassical style, like earlier periods of classicism in European civilization, drew upon the widespread admiration of ancient civilization. The elegant simplicity of classical architecture—characterized by symmetry, mathematical proportions, the harmony of forms, and severe rules—contrasted sharply with the ornate baroque and the rococo. This contrast became a vogue in the 1740s after archaeologists began to excavate the Roman cities of Pompeii and Herculaneum, which had been buried (and preserved) by volcanic ash in A.D. 79. A classical revival swept European architecture, producing such masterpieces as the Romanov Winter Palace in St. Petersburg (now the Hermitage Museum), La Scala opera house in Milan, and the Royal Crescent in Bath, England. In some cases, neoclassical buildings closely resembled classical structures built eighteen hundred years earlier (see illustration 21.2). All across Europe, great landowners had ancient "ruins" constructed as part of their landscaping.

Classicism soon came to dominate the arts of the eighteenth century. Histories of the ancient world, such as Edward Gibbon's *The Decline and Fall of the Roman Empire*, became popular reading together with the ancients

The Parisian church of St. Mary Magdalen, known as la Madeleine, was begun in 1764 and redesigned several times. The final version, a neoclassical temple with imposing Corinthian columns, bears a striking resemblance to the Maison Carrée, built eighteen hundred years earlier.

Illlustration 21.2

⑦ **The Classical and the Neoclassical.** One of the finest surviving works of Roman architecture is the Maison Carrée, a Corinthian temple constructed in 16 B.C. in Nîmes, France, where large numbers of Roman army veterans were given land in their retirement.

Illustration 21.3

⑦ **Neoclassical Painting.** Jacques-Louis David (1748–1825) was perhaps the greatest of the neoclassical painters. He rejected the rococo in favor of simple, balanced, realistic drawing. Many of his works dramatize classical legends such as "The Oath of the Horatii" (1785), in which three brothers vow to save Rome. One survived, victorious for Rome, to face a classical tragedy; his sister wept, not for her brothers, but for her fiancé, slain by her brothers. The last brother proved his devotion to Rome by killing her, and the people acquitted him of murder. This painting thus became a forceful piece of patriotic (and republican) propaganda.

themselves. Universities required Latin and Greek of their students, and in some countries an honors degree in classics became the best route to a high-paying job or a government post. Painters, sculptors, dramatists, poets, and composers all mined classical literature for inspiration. The French painter Jacques-Louis David, for example, inspired a generation of politicians with his dramatic canvases—such as "The Oath of the Horatii"—depicting stirring moments in Roman history (see illustration 21.3). Music was perhaps most shaped by eighteenth-century classicism. The strict attention to form, the mathematical precision, the symmetry

Illustration 21.4

// **Popular Festivals.** One of the centers of popular culture was the festival. These were often religious holidays, although many of the activities were decidedly secular. This oil painting by Francesco Guardi entitled "The Feast of Maundy Thursday in Venice" shows "equilibrists" entertaining a festival crowd.

learned from architecture became the basis of a new music: The development of the sonata, the symphony, the string quartet, and the concerto so changed musical composition that the name *classical music* remained long after the classical era.

Popular Culture in the Eighteenth Century

In recent decades, cultural historians have paid closer attention to the culture of the lower classes, as distinct from the high culture of the elite. The distinction is not absolute, because high culture and popular culture are often remarkably similar. In the eighteenth century, the plays of Shakespeare were popular with the agricultural classes of rural England, who welcomed the touring troops of actors who brought drama to the countryside. In London, David Garrick's famous theater on Drury Lane was as popular with the artisans and laborers who flocked to the cheap seats as it was with the wealthy who bought the boxes. In the capitals of opera such as Milan and Vienna, few shopkeepers could afford to attend the lavish productions. But Mozart had a popular following, too, and versions of his operas were produced in lower-class music halls.

Popular culture and high culture also intersected for the converse reason: The well-bred, well-educated, and well-off also frequented the robust entertainments of ordinary folk. The world of popular culture—a world of rope-walkers, jugglers, and acrobats (see illustration 21.4); of village bands and workers' music halls; of folktales and folksong; of races, fights, animal sports, and gambling (see illustration 21.5); of marionettes, pantomimes, and magic lantern shows projected on smoke; of inns, taverns, public houses ("pubs"), cafes, and coffeehouses; of broadsheets and limericks; of carnivals and fairs; of entertainment in public parks and on the village commons—was not the exclusive province of the laboring classes who gave these their meanings and values. High culture honored this intersection by regularly borrowing from popular culture, from the folk theme that reappeared as a leitmotif in a symphony or the tales of oral culture that reappeared in learned anthologies.

A good illustration of the parallels in high culture and popular culture can be seen in two of their centers: the salon (high culture) and the coffeehouse (popular culture). The salon, a social gathering held in a private home where notable literary, artistic, and political fig-

Illustration 21.5

🎇 **Cock Fighting.** Blood sports were a widely shared feature of eighteenth-century popular culture. Many other animals were used in such recreations, which included bearbaiting, bullfights, and dog-and-rat fights. Upper-class concerns about the brutality of the lower classes, antigambling morality, and crusades for the protection of animals slowly eliminated some, but not all, of these sports.

ures discussed the issues of the day, characterized the educated world of high culture in the eighteenth century (see document 21.1). Salons were typically organized and directed by women of grace and style who shaped European culture by sponsoring rising young talents, protecting unpopular opinions, finding financial support for impoverished writers, and sometimes fostering political intrigues (see illustration 21.6). The salons glorified conversation—about the life of the mind and the republic of letters, the arts, politics and policies, scandal and gossip, and wit and flirtation. Salon hostesses were sometimes the wives, daughters, or the

◆ DOCUMENT 21.1 ◆

The Salon of Madame Geoffrin

Marie-Thérèse Geoffrin (1699–1777) was the hostess of one of the most influential salons because she had an exceptional ability to encourage artists, writers, and philosophers. Her skills as a hostess raised the daughter of a valet to correspond with kings. The following sketch was written after her death but provides a vivid portrait.

Madame Geoffrin . . . was born in 1699 and her mother died a year later in giving birth to a son. She lost her father in 1706, when she was only seven. The two children were confided to the care of their maternal grandmother, Mme Chemineau. The father of the little girl who will one day become Mme Geoffrin . . . had been a valet of the wardrobe at Court. His wife, Mlle Chemineau, was of higher social position for she was the daughter of a small banker. . . .

Mme Chemineau decided that [Thérèse's] education must be religious. She recommended pious reading, and the little girl fulfilled all her religious duties in her parish church. . . . The Church had a great influence on the youthful Thérèse, for it was in St. Roch's that she attracted the attention of François Geoffrin. She was fourteen and he was forty-eight. An idyll. Geoffrin had worked all his life in the mirror trade. . . . [H]e became head cashier [of] the most considerable glass manufactory of France. . . . He bore so good a reputation that one cannot suspect him of perversity: Thérèse had won his heart (as he had won his wife's heart) by her piety. . . . She brought him 185,000 livres to add to the 250,000 livres that he possessed. You will protest that with her dowry Thérèse could have found a younger husband. But François Geoffrin was greatly respected in the parish. . . . The couple lived a quiet life in the Rue Saint Honoré. . . .

At this juncture Mme de Tencin [a famed salon hostess and the mistress of the regent of France] came to live in Rue Saint Honoré. . . Everyone knew the manner of Mme de Tencin's life. . . . [W]e dare not describe these orgies. . . . One would have supposed that Mme Geoffrin could never set foot in the house of such a woman as Mme de Tencin, [but] against all that could be anticipated, Mme Geoffrin went to Mme de Tencin's and struck up a friendship with her. . . . There she met Montesquieu [and] Fontenelle. When she came to know Fontenelle and the rest of Mme de Tencin's friends, Mme de Geoffrin was about thirty. . . . Mme de Tencin was aging and she was not rich: men of mind were not indifferent to little presents. . . . Mme de Geoffrin offered the possibility of better things and all aspired to be received in her house. . . . [She] was not slow to learn that to attract writers, philosophers and scholars it is well to offer succulent repasts. . . .

Mme de Geoffrin lived prudently. . . . She did not spend her income. Most of her fortune was invested in the glass manufactory. At one time the business was in a bad way, and Mme Geoffrin, who was a director, pointed out which member of the staff would have the ability to pull the business round. Her surmise was correct: prosperity was restored.

The originality of her salon was that she received painters, sculptors, and engravers as well as men of letters, an innovation. . . . By thus enlarging her circle, she outran Mme de Tencin. The Wednesday night suppers were supplemented by Monday dinners. . . . [At them] Mme de Geoffrin always imposed on her guests the tone of the best society. She knew how to stop conversations that wandered on dangerous ground. She distrusted politics too. . . . [S]he would not allow political discussions in her house.

mistresses of powerful men, such as the duchess de Maine, the mistress of Philippe d'Orleans, the regent of France; some were prominent intellectuals in their own right. Their ranks included women such as Madame de Lambert, the author of *Advice of a Mother to Her Daughter* (1734), which advocated university education for women. Another salon hostess, Louise d'Epinay, won the French academy's prize for 1774 for her *Conversations with Emile.*

The habit of organizing salons originated in the French aristocracy, but it was adopted by other elements of the educated classes and spread across Europe. By the middle of the century, salons were flourishing in London, Berlin, Vienna, Rome, and Copenhagen, usually assuming a national character somewhat different from Parisian salons. In England, they ranged from the formal salon of Elizabeth Montagu, the granddaughter of Lady Mary Wortley Montagu, who forbade such

Illustration 21.6

⧓ **The Salon of Madame Geoffrin.** Marie-Thérèse Geoffrin (1699–1777) was the hostess of one of the most influential salons of eighteenth-century France (see document 21.1). In presiding over such private meetings of writers, philosophers, artists, and politicians, women played a central role in the shaping and transmission of the ideas of the Enlightenment.

frivolity as playing cards, to the less formal salon of Mary Monckton, the countess of Cork, which included such prominent figures as Samuel Johnson. Salons in the German states provided an opportunity for Jewish families to win social acceptance previously denied them. Moses Mendelssohn began the habit of holding open houses for intellectuals, and his daughter, Dorothea von Schlegel, built on this habit to emulate the French salons. Most German salons, however—such as those of Henrietta Herz and Rachel Levin at Berlin, or Fanny Arnstein at Vienna—insisted upon a stricter sexual respectability than characterized Parisian salons.

The coffeehouse served a similar cultural role for other social strata (see chapter 19). Coffeehouses—and sometimes taverns, which were less expensive and less formal—served as meeting houses, reading rooms, and debating halls. The daily newspaper was at the center of this phenomenon (see chronology 21.1). Dailies were born and began to flourish in the eighteenth century, starting with the *Daily Courant* in London in 1702. Moscow had a newspaper later that same year, Berlin a daily paper from 1704, and Rome from 1716. Paris even had a women's newspaper, advocating the equality of the sexes—*Le Journal des dames,* founded in 1759—before it had a daily newspaper. Larger Sunday newspapers appeared in London in 1780. Until the technological innovations of the mid-nineteenth century, however, these newspapers remained expensive and their circulation low. Institutions compensated for the high cost of newspapers. Subscription libraries and "reading societies" appeared in the German states as early as 1704. But the coffeehouse provided the most popular solution by subscribing to multiple newspapers, holding public readings of newspaper stories for the benefit of the illiterate majority, and providing the sociable setting. The towns and cities of eighteenth-century Europe were filled with coffeehouses. The first coffeehouse opened

◈ CHRONOLOGY 21.1 ◈

The Development of the Eighteenth-Century Newspaper Press

1702   The first daily newspaper, the *Daily Courant* (London)

1702   First Russian newspaper, *Moskovskaya Viedomosti* (Moscow Gazette)

1704   *Vossische Zeitung*, Berlin

1717   *Diario di Roma*, Rome

1749   *Berlingske Tidende*, Copenhagen

1759   *Le Journal des dames* founded at Paris

1777   First French daily newspaper, *Le Journal de Paris*

1780   First Sunday newspapers in London: the *British Gazette* and the *Sunday Monitor*

1783   First daily in America, the *Pennsylvania Evening Post*

1785   The *Times* of London founded as the *Daily Universal Register*

central Europe opened in Vienna in 1683, after a few sacks of coffee were taken from a retreating Turkish army. After the eighteenth-century boom, the Viennese all but lived in fifteen thousand coffeehouses. Coffeehouses became so popular in Berlin that Frederick the Great blocked the importation of coffee as a drain on the national wealth—a hint at how expensive coffee was initially.

◈

Religion and Eighteenth-Century Culture

Christianity stood at the center of European culture in the eighteenth century, as it had for more than a thousand years. Although European civilization was almost exclusively a Christian civilization, it was split into many conflicting sects. The religious map of the Old Regime followed lines drawn by the Peace of Westphalia in 1648, which had ended a period of ferocious religious warfare (see map 21.1). At the simplest level, most of northern Europe was Protestant, most of southern Europe was Roman Catholic, and much of eastern Europe was Orthodox. Protestant Europe included Great Britain, the Dutch republic, the northern German states (notably Hanover, Saxony, and Prussia), all of Scandinavia, part of divided Switzerland, and pockets in eastern Europe (notably in Hungary). Catholic Eu-

in Paris in 1672 and soon failed; in 1754, however, fifty-six were flourishing. There were none in London in 1650, but more than two thousand had opened by 1725 (see illustration 21.7). The first coffeehouse in

Illustration 21.7

◢◢ A London Coffeehouse. Coffeehouses were frequently centers of intellectual, political, or economic activity alongside the drinking of the new beverage. This London coffeehouse of 1705 is frequented by well-to-do gentlemen who are bidding for the exchange of commodities. Note the candles: Pins were stuck into candles and bidding continued until you could "hear a pin drop." One such coffeehouse, opened by Edward Lloyd at the end of the seventeenth century, sold maritime insurance and evolved into Lloyd's of London.

Catholic majority

Orthodox majority

Orthodox minority

Muslim majority

Protestant majority

Protestant minority

(1865) Date of Jewish Emancipation

Arctic Ocean

SWEDEN
99% Lutheran
(1865)

NORWAY
(1851)

North Sea

RUSSIA
Orthodox
3% Jewish
1% Lutheran
(1917)

SCOTLAND
Presbyterian (Calvinist)
Catholic
Episcopal (Anglican)

DENMARK
99% Lutheran
(1848)

PRUSSIA
Lutheran
Calvinist
Catholic
Jewish
(1850)

IRELAND
70% Catholic
20% Presbyterian
10% Anglican

ENGLAND
& WALES
90% Anglican
8% Dissenter
2% Catholic
Methodist
Jewish
(1890)

NETHERLANDS
65% Calvinist
35% Catholic
(1796)

HANOVER
99% Lutheran
(1871)

SAXONY
99% Lutheran
(1868)

POLAND
49% Catholic
40% Orthodox
7% Jewish
4% Lutheran

BAVARIA
99% Catholic

HUNGARY
48% Catholic
27% Orthodox
15% Calvinist
8% Lutheran
2% Jewish
(1867)

FRANCE
98% Catholic
2% Calvinist
Jewish
(1791)

SWITZERLAND
60% Calvinist
40% Catholic
(1874)

Atlantic Ocean

PIEDMONT
2% Protestant
(1848)

Corsica

ITALIAN
STATES
99% Catholic
(1848-1870)

Black Sea

PORTUGAL
99% Catholic
(1910)

SPAIN
99% Catholic

Sardinia

Balearic Islands

Mediterranean

Sicily

OTTOMAN EMPIRE
(1908)

Sea

0   300   600   900 Kilometers

0   300   600 Miles

MAP 21.1

Religious Population of Eighteenth-Century Europe

rope included Portugal, Spain, France, all of the Italian states, the southern German states (notably Bavaria), and the Austrian Empire, plus most of the population in religiously divided Ireland and Poland. Orthodox Europe included Russia plus large portions of Poland and the Ottoman Empire (such as Greece and Serbia).

This religious division of Europe left many minority populations inside hostile countries. Important Catholic minorities existed in Britain (only 2 percent of the population, but including many powerful families), Holland (35 percent), Switzerland (40 percent), and Prussia (especially after the annexation of Silesia). Similar Protestant minorities were found in Ireland (30 per-

cent), France (2 percent, but disproportionately important, like Catholics in Britain), Piedmont (2 percent), Poland (4 percent), and Hungary (23 percent). In addition to Christian minorities, Europe contained small Jewish and Moslem populations. Jews were forbidden to live in some countries (notably Spain) but formed a small minority (less than 1 percent) in many states, especially Britain, France, Holland, and Prussia; they constituted larger minorities in eastern Europe, chiefly in Poland (7 percent), Hungary (2 percent), Russia, and the Ottoman territories. Moslems were almost entirely confined to the Ottoman Empire, in the provinces of modern Bosnia and Albania, with only traces of the once flourishing Islamic culture of Iberia and the Mediterranean to be found.

Protestant Europe included three predominant faiths: Anglicanism, Calvinism, and Lutheranism. Virtually all of the membership of the Anglican Church (the Church of England) was found in England, Wales, Scotland, and Ireland. Lutheranism was the dominant form of Protestantism in the German states and Scandinavia, and Lutheran minorities were scattered in many east European states. A variety of Calvinist churches—usually called the Reformed Church—existed in western Europe. Their traditional center was Geneva, where Calvin had established his church. Calvinist churches were predominant in Switzerland, Holland (the Dutch Reformed Church), and Scotland (the Presbyterian Church); Calvinist minorities existed in many states, notably France—where the Reformed Church was illegal though 500,000 followed it in secret—Prussia, and Hungary.

In addition to these primary Protestant churches, many smaller Christian sects existed in 1700, and more were founded during the eighteenth century. Small populations of diverse Protestants—such as Quakers (the Society of Friends) in England and the Baptists in central Europe—lived even within Protestant states. In England, approximately 8 percent of the population, collectively called Dissenters or Nonconformists, belonged to Protestant sects outside of the Church of England.

The Roman Catholic Church was more unified and centralized than Protestantism, but it, too, encompassed diversity. Catholicism remained united by the authority of the pope and by the hierarchical administrative structure directed by the Vatican. However, the eighteenth-century papacy was weaker than it had been in earlier centuries. Rome lacked the strength to resist the absolute monarchs of Catholic lands. Louis XIV of France had created a virtually autonomous French Catholic Church, often called the Gallican Church. (Gallicanism meant that the king named French cardinals and bishops himself and decided whether papal decrees would apply in France.) Other Catholic monarchs copied the French administrative independence from Rome, as the kings of Piedmont did in the early eighteenth century and Joseph II of Austria did later. When the anti-Catholic Frederick the Great of Prussia wrote in 1750 that the pope is "an old neglected idol" who survived by the charity of kings, it was not a total exaggeration. Variations of Catholicism also depended upon the local strength of individual orders (such as the Jesuits) or doctrines (such as Jansenism). The Jesuits began the eighteenth century as the most important of all Catholic orders. They were rigorously trained men who had acquired global influence through their educational and missionary efforts, and they had increasingly turned their attention to politics. Their role in statecraft made the Jesuits controversial, however, and they were expelled from Portugal in 1759, from France in 1762, from Spain and many Italian states in 1767, and finally dissolved by Pope Clement XIV in 1773. Jansenism, named for a Dutch theologian, was equally controversial for teaching an austere, puritanical—almost Calvinistic—form of Catholicism, particularly in Belgium and France, and the doctrine was condemned by a papal bull (the traditional name for a papal edict sealed with a "bulla").

Important differences existed between Catholicism and Protestantism, shaping cultural differences in Europe. These extended far beyond matters of faith—beyond the fine points of theological doctrines, such as the nature of Christian sacraments or the route to salvation. Protestant pastors, unlike Catholic priests, married and raised families, frequently producing dynasties of preachers when their sons also entered the church and their wives and daughters took leading roles in Protestant organizations. Protestant states abolished the monastic orders that existed in Catholic countries and seized church lands; thus, the church had a greater physical presence in Catholic countries through landownership and especially the far greater size of the clerical population. The Catholic Church owned 10 percent of the land in France and 30 percent in some regions, 10 percent to 15 percent of the land in Bohemia and northern Italy, 15 percent of Castile and central Spain, and 40 percent of Naples and southern Italy. The ecclesiastical population of Portugal has been estimated at 80,000 to 300,000—at least 4 percent of the population, and perhaps as much as 15 percent, wore the garb of holy orders. A study of the island of Corsica has found that a population of 220,000 people sustained sixty-five monasteries. The town of Valladolid, Spain, with a population of twenty-one thousand supported forty-six monasteries with an ecclesiastical population of 1,258—6 percent of the population. This physical presence of this church was dramatically different in England, where a population of 5.8 million people, 90 percent of whom were nominally Anglican, sustained eleven thousand clergymen in the Church of England—less than 0.2 percent of the population. The culture of Tuscany, which was one-tenth the size of England yet supported more than twice the ecclesiastical population of England, was more strongly shaped by religion (see table 21.1).

✖ TABLE 21.1 ✖

Ecclesiastical Populations in Catholic Europe

This table combines the data from three studies of Catholic Europe in the eighteenth century: a town in eastern France (Besançon), a region in north central Italy (Tuscany), and a town in northwestern Spain (Valladolid). Although the data are incomplete, each of these studies found that the people supported an ecclesiastical population of at least 3 percent of the total population. If Valladolid supported as many priests as the other communities did, then it had an ecclesiastical population of approximately 7.5 percent of the total population.

Region	Date	Population	Priests	Percentage priests	Orders	Percentage in orders	Church total	Percentage of ecclesiastic population
Besançon	1709	17,000	275	1.6	571	3.4	846	5.0
Tuscany	1745	891,000	12,050	1.4	15,388	1.7	27,438	3.1
Valladolid	1759	21,000	n.a.	n.a.	1,258	6.0	n.a.	n.a.

Source: Calculated from data in Carlo M. Cipolla, *Before the Industrial Revolution* (New York, N.Y.: Norton, 1976), pp. 79–80.
n.a. = Not available.

Within these variations, all of Europe—whatever their beliefs or, increasingly, their disbelief—lived in a deeply Christian culture. Churches provided most of the social services that existed for the poor, crippled, aged, orphaned, released prisoners, and reformed prostitutes. Such fundamental institutions as hospitals and schools were run by the church, not by the state. Schools provide perhaps the best illustration of the Christian character of European civilization. Few people received a formal education in the eighteenth century—most of the population in all countries remained illiterate—but the majority of the schools that existed were run by churches. The Presbyterian Church ran most of the schools in Scotland, the Anglican Church the majority of the schools in England, the Lutheran Church dominated Scandinavian education, and the Orthodox Church conducted most of the schools in Russia. In many Catholic countries—including Spain, Portugal, Poland, and most of the Italian states—the church totally controlled teaching; in all Catholic countries, Catholic teaching orders such as the Jesuits and the Piarists supplied teachers. Religion formed a large part of the educational curriculum. The need to be literate to read the Bible was frequently the decisive reason in creating new schools, especially in Protestant faiths that stressed Bible reading.

Religion remained central to both high culture and popular culture. However, the great epoch of cathedral building had passed, Christian themes no longer dominated painting and sculpture, and literature had entered a thoroughly secular age; European culture reflected an "age of reason" more than an "age of faith." Still, the arts of the eighteenth century relied heavily upon religion. Goethe's *Faust* (1773), one of the masterpieces of German literature, is a Christian tragedy of lost faith and damnation. The dominant buildings of the age were royal palaces and stately homes, yet many of the structures that characterized baroque and rococo architecture were churches, such as the lavish Karlskirche in Vienna and the Cádiz Cathedral (see illustration 21.8). Even at the peak of the neoclassical boom in architecture, some of the most representative buildings of the age were churches, such as St. Geneviève in Paris, now known as the Pantheon. Composers may have favored secular subjects for the flourishing opera of the eighteenth century, but many of the masterpieces of baroque music originated in Christianity, such as Marc-Antoine Charpentier's powerful *Te Deum*. Johann Sebastian Bach long earned his living as cantor and organist at the Thomaskirche in Leipzig, where he composed a huge array of music on Christian themes, such as his *Mass in B minor*. Haydn began his career in the choir at the court chapel in Vienna and went on to compose music for the mass as well as court music. Telemann spent most of his career as director of church music in Hamburg. And perhaps no music composed in the eighteenth century is more famous than Handel's *Messiah*.

Christianity similarly remained central to popular culture and the rhythms of daily life. The sound of church bells marked the time of day for most Europeans, and a church clock was often the only timekeeping that the poor knew until late in the eighteenth century. Sunday remained the day of rest—often the

Illustration 21.8

Ecclesiastical Rococo Architechure. Much of the finest rococo architecture is found in the eighteenth-century churches of
Germanic central Europe. The Abbey Church at Ottobeuren,
shown here, uses colored stucco, marble, frescoes, and gilded
frames to achieve a spectacular image.

only day of rest—for shopkeepers, laborers, and peasants alike. The only vacation most people knew came
from religious holidays and festivals, and the calendar
of the Old Regime was filled with such days. In addition to the universal holidays of the Christian calendar,
such as Christmas and Easter, every region, village, and
occupation added the celebration of patron saints.

When governments tried to curtail the dozens of
church holidays, workers in many regions responded
by inventing "Saint Monday" in whose honor they
might rest on that day.

Most governments maintained a state religion, re-
warding its members and limiting the rights of non-
members. In Denmark and Sweden, non-Lutherans

could not teach, hold public office, or conduct religious services. In Britain, a series of laws called the Test Acts excluded non-Anglicans from military command, sitting in parliament, or attending Oxford or Cambridge universities. Catholics could not live in London, nor Protestants in Paris, in 1750. Restrictions were stricter in regions where the Inquisition retained power. More than seven hundred Spaniards condemned by the Inquisition were burnt at the stake between 1700 and 1746; the last burning for heresy in Spain came in 1781. The Inquisition exerted a greater force on European culture by regulating behavior. A trial before the Inquisition in 1777 listed some of the behavior that true Christians must cease: (1) eating meat on Friday; (2) crossing one's legs during a church service; (3) believing that the Earth revolved around the Sun; (4) not believing in acts of the faith, such as ringing church bells during a storm to beg God to stop it; (5) owning prohibited books, listed on the church's Index of forbidden books; (6) corresponding with non-Catholics; and (7) disputing the idea that only Catholics could go to Heaven. No Protestant equivalent of the Inquisition existed, but that did not make Protestant lands models of toleration. Denmark forbade Catholic priests from entering the country under threat of the death penalty; Danish law exiled anyone who professed belief in Catholicism and confiscated their property.

The Enlightenment and Its Origins

The eighteenth century is one of the most famous periods in the history of European thought. Historians often call that century the Age of Enlightenment (or the Age of Reason) because eighteenth-century writers smugly considered their epoch more enlightened than earlier eras. It was an age that cherished universities, learned academies, scientific laboratories and observatories, libraries, philosophic journals, books (especially great reference works), and talking about all of them (see map 21.2). Although the term *the Enlightenment* was not used during the eighteenth century, synonymous terms—particularly the German term, *Aufklärung*—were used.

The history of the Enlightenment focuses on the influential thinkers and writers of the age. They are usually identified by a French name, the *philosophes*, which is a broader term than *philosophers* in English. The importance of the Enlightenment rests in the circulation of the ideas of the philosophes among a small literate population and the influence of these ideas in

changing the Old Regime. The Enlightenment was thus an experience shared by a tiny fraction of the population, an educated elite. The central ideas of the Enlightenment are frequently simplified to a few basic concepts. The philosophes often did disagree with each other. They differed by temperament, beliefs, and the perspectives of different times and places. Nonetheless, a few concepts were nearly universal: (1) *skepticism*—questioning the validity of assumptions about society and the physical world without regard for traditional authority; (2) belief in the existence of *natural laws*—such as the law of gravity—that govern both the social and physical worlds; (3) confidence that *human reason*, rigorously applied, can discover these natural laws and establish them as the basis of human activity; and (4) optimism that the application of reason and obedience to natural laws will produce *progress*, leading to the perfection of human institutions.

One of the most eminent German philosophes, Immanuel Kant, summarized many of these attitudes in an essay of 1784 entitled "What Is Enlightenment?" His definition of Enlightenment was the liberation of individuals from direction by others (see document 21.2). Kant held that people achieved this liberation when they resolved to use their reason and to follow its dictates. Thus, he suggested a Latin motto for the Enlightenment: *Sapere aude!* (literally, "Dare to know!"), which he translated as "Have the courage to use your own reason!" Put differently, Kant saw "a revolt against superstition." Most philosophes shared this attitude (see illustration 21.9). As one of them, Denis Diderot, wrote to another, Voltaire, in 1762: "Our motto is, 'No quarter for superstitions.'"

The Enlightenment developed from several trends in European thought (see chapter 17). Skepticism had been one of the dominant themes of seventeenth-century philosophy, chiefly associated with the French philosopher René Descartes. In works such as the *Discourse on Method* (1637), he had advocated universal doubt; that is, the doubting of everything until it can be proven. Cartesian skepticism included doubting one's own existence, or the existence of God, until such existence was demonstrated. In one of the most famous aphorisms of European civilization, Descartes concluded "Cogito, ergo sum" ("I think, therefore I am")—the ability to reason proved the thinker's existence. Philosophic skepticism was thus well established before the Enlightenment, and precursors such as Pierre Bayle had even taken the dramatic step of applying skeptical philosophy to the Bible. Bayle, a Frenchman whose advanced ideas forced him to live in the greater freedom of Holland, proposed "a detailed refutation of the

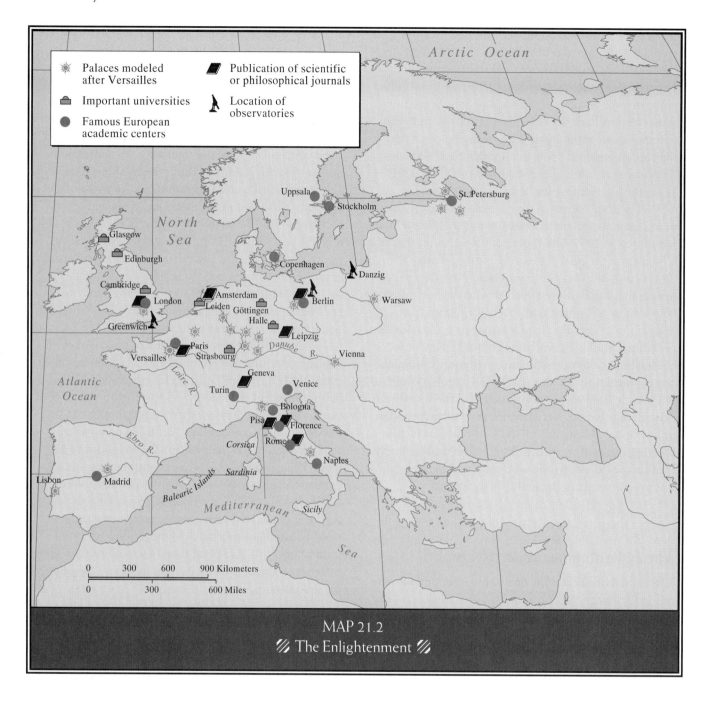

MAP 21.2

The Enlightenment

unreasonable deference given to tradition," and he included Christianity within that tradition. All religious questions, including the reading of the Bible, "require the use of reason." Not only did Bayle help to found the field of biblical criticism, but he also conveyed to the eighteenth century the belief that Cartesian universal doubt applied to everything.

A second fundamental source of the Enlightenment thought was the scientific revolution of the seventeenth century, especially Sir Isaac Newton's synthesis of the accomplishments of many scientists. The Newtonian synthesis seemed so brilliant to the educated classes

that many agreed with the judgment of the astronomer Edmond Halley: "It is not lawful for mortals to approach divinity nearer than this." Newton had built upon a period of dramatic increase in human understanding of the physical and natural world, especially in the field of astronomy. The scientific revolution had destroyed the geocentric theory of the universe, instead placing the Sun at the center in a heliocentric theory. This required sweeping, counterintuitive adjustments in European thought. For the heliocentric theory to be true, the Earth must move, at tremendously high speeds, around the Sun and rotate constantly on its

◆ DOCUMENT 21.2 ◆

Immanuel Kant: Enlightenment

Immanuel Kant (1724–1804) was a distinguished German philosopher and a professor of logic and metaphysics at the University of Königsberg in eastern Prussia. He was already famous for his greatest work—The Critique of Pure Reason (1781)—when he published the essay "What Is Enlightenment?" (1784), from which the following excerpt is taken.

Enlightenment is man's leaving his self-caused immaturity. Immaturity is the incapacity to use one's intelligence without the guidance of another. Such immaturity is self-caused if it is not caused by lack of intelligence, but by lack of determination and courage to use one's intelligence without being guided by another. *Sapere Aude!* Have the courage to use your own reason! is therefore the motto of the enlightenment.

Through laziness and cowardice, a large part of mankind, even after nature has freed them from alien guidance, gladly remain immature. It is because of laziness and cowardice that it is so easy to usurp the role of guardians. It is so comfortable to be a minor! If I have a book which provides meaning for me, a pastor who has conscience for me, a doctor who will judge my diet for me, and so on, then I do not need to exert myself. I do not have any need to think; if I can pay, others will take over the tedious job for me. . . .

But it is more nearly possible for a public to enlighten itself: this is even inescapable if only the public is given its freedom. . . . All that is required for this enlightenment is *freedom;* and particularly the least harmful of all that may be called freedom, namely the freedom for man to make public use of his reason in all matters.

Illustration 21.9

The Philosophes. In this engraving by Jean Huber, several of the most famous philosophes take dinner together. Voltaire sits in the center with his arm raised. Both editors of the *Encyclopédie* are present: d'Alembert sits in profile at the left end of the table and Diderot sits beside Voltaire's raised arm. Condorcet, who suffered the saddest fate of the philosophes, sits with his back to the painter.

axis. The Sun did not rise or set, it merely appeared to do so because the rotation of the Earth turned a viewer toward or away from the Sun. Christian theologians fought such conclusions for more than a century. The Catholic Church placed the writings of astronomers on the Index of prohibited books; and Martin Luther denounced astronomers as fools. The legacy of the scientific revolution to the Enlightenment thus included a willingness to challenge authority with reasoned evidence. The Catholic Church fought this reasoning with the argument that "it is the Holy Spirit's intention to teach us how to go to heaven, not how the heavens go."

The Enlightenment canonized Newton because he convinced the intelligentsia that the new astronomy was correct and the churches were wrong. Newton was a professor of mathematics at Cambridge University. His accomplishments included the invention of differential and integral calculus—simultaneously with the German mathematician Georg von Leibnitz—and advanced studies of mechanics, dynamics, and motion. His greatest fame resulted from stating the Principle of Universal Gravitation (the law of gravity) in his masterwork, *Principia mathematica* (1687). The "universal" element of the law of gravity fascinated the philosophes of the eighteenth century. Newton proved to them that human reason could discover "the universal qualities of all bodies whatsoever." Voltaire, who popularized Newton's work in *Elements of the Philosophy of Newton* (1738), proclaimed him "the greatest and rarest genius that ever rose for the ornamentation and instruction of the species." The English poet Alexander Pope was equally lavish in praising the Newtonian synthesis in his *Essay on Man* (1734): "Nature and nature's law lay hid in night/God said, 'Let Newton be,' and all was light." And around the Western world, philosophes placed a bust of Newton in their study—as Thomas Jefferson did at Monticello—as a reminder that human reason could find universal natural laws.

A third source of Enlightenment thought, alongside philosophic skepticism and scientific rationalism, was the revival of classicism (see chronology 21.2). Like the humanists of the Renaissance, the philosophes revered the Graeco-Roman past, but with a different emphasis. To them, antiquity represented the historical model of a society that had revered scientific observation and reasoned objectively from these observations. This admiration of antiquity implied the rejection of knowledge supported only by authority, dogma, or superstition—the traits that the philosophes often associated with the history of Europe after the fall of Rome. As Diderot wrote to Catherine the Great, "The Greeks were the teachers of the Romans; the Greeks and Romans together have been ours."

Natural Law, Reason, and Progress

When the scientific revolution convinced the European intelligentsia that natural laws existed, the philosophes concluded that laws governing human activity—the organization of governments, economic relations, the efficient operation of prisons, and the writing of history—similarly "lay hid in night." Such laws merely awaited the Newton of economics or penology. The belief in natural law was not new; ancient authors had asserted its existence, too. The scientific revolution merely allowed thinkers to embrace this old idea with a new self-confidence.

One of the leading figures of the French Enlightenment, the Baron Charles-Louis de Montesquieu, illustrates this interest in natural law in his writings on political theory. Montesquieu was a wealthy provincial noble, educated in law, who inherited a position in the Parlement of Bordeaux. Although he was elected the chief justice of the parlement, he was more interested in theories of government than in the day-to-day drudgery of his highly political job. He sold his office—such positions were often the property of nobles in the eighteenth century—and turned to writing. His *The Spirit of the Laws* (1748) became one of the most widely influential books of the century, joining the seventeenth-century works of John Locke, who had attacked the divine right of royalty and asserted the divine royalty of right, in laying the foundations of modern political theory (see chapter 17).

Montesquieu began *The Spirit of the Laws* by asserting that people, like the physical world, are "governed by invariable laws." This did not mean laws promulgated by the government and enforced by the courts; Montesquieu called that type of law "positive laws." Instead, Montesquieu meant laws in a scientific sense—laws that exist in nature, laws that state "fixed and invariable relationships" just as much as the law of gravity did. For example, Montesquieu believed that natural law proclaimed the need for food and the attraction of the sexes. Other natural laws governing human relations were less certain. Montesquieu, for example, asserted that people were, by nature, peaceful rather than warlike. One consequence of asserting the existence of natural laws and trying to define them was that they might be different from the positive laws enforced by the government or the moral laws of the established church. Philosophes such as Montesquieu insisted that positive law must therefore be changed to agree with natural law. "The intelligent world," he wrote, "is far from being so well governed as the physical."

References to "nature" and "nature's law" are found in a great variety of eighteenth-century works in addition to Newton's physics, Pope's poetry, and Montesquieu's political theory. The most typical work of the Enlightenment, the French *Encyclopedia of the Arts and Sciences* (the *Encyclopédie*), devoted three full articles to natural law. Jean-Jacques Rousseau wrote one of the famous books in the history of education, *Emile, or Concerning Education* (1762), stressing natural education. "Nature," he wrote, "never deceives us; it is always we who deceive ourselves." The first draft of the American Declaration of Independence proclaimed that people were entitled to independence and self-government by "the Laws of Nature." Not all philosophes used the theory of natural law, however. But even those who rejected it—as did the Scottish philosopher David Hume, who called it a "fallacious and sophistical" theory—discussed the idea at length.

To discover natural laws, the philosophes relied on skepticism and rationalism. Skepticism meant questioning and criticizing everything. "A thing is not proved when no has ever questioned it," wrote one of the editors of the *Encyclopédie*. "Skepticism is the first step toward the truth." Kant insisted upon the skeptical evaluation of everything, including church and state, in *The Critique of Pure Reason* (1781):

> Our age is the age of criticism, to which everything must be subjected. The sacredness of religion, and the authority of legislation, are by many regarded as grounds for exemption from the examination by this tribunal. But, if they are exempted, they become the subjects of just suspicion, and cannot lay claim to sincere respect, which reason accords only to that which has stood the test of a free and public examination.

◆ CHRONOLOGY 21.2 ◆

Landmark Works of the Enlightenment

1702 Daniel Defoe's *The Shortest Way with Dissenters* satirizes intolerance

1710 Gottfried Leibnitz's *Théodicée* proclaims this "the best of all possible worlds"

1721 Baron Montesquieu's *Persian Letters* derides French institutions

1725 Madame de Sévigné's posthumous *Letters* reveal life of the aristocracy

1725 Giambatista Vico's *Principles of a New Science* proposes a science of society

1729 Sir Isaac Newton's *Principia mathematica* translated into English from Latin

1733 Voltaire's *Letters Concerning the English* popularizes Newtonian science and representative government

1734 Madame de Lambert's *Advice of a Mother* advocates university education for women

1736 Bishop Joseph Butler's *Analogy of Religion* defends Christianity against Deism

1737 Lady Mary Wortley Montagu's *The Nonsense of Common Sense* questions accepted ideas

1739 David Hume's *A Treatise of Human Nature* states utilitarian principles

1739 Sophia's *Woman Not Inferior to Man* asserts the equality of women

1741 Johann Süssmilch's *The Divine Order* pioneers the field of statistics

1748 David Hume's *Essays Concerning Human Understanding* states case for complete skepticism

1749 Baron de Montesquieu's *The Spirit of the Laws* establishes study of comparative government

1751 Denis Diderot and Jean d'Alembert publish the first volume of the *Encyclopédie*

1755 Jean-Jacques Rousseau's *Discourse on the Origin of Inequality* attacks the social order of Europe

1755 Samuel Johnson publishes first comprehensive dictionary of the English language

1758 Claude Helvétius's *De l'esprit* asserts the principle of enlightened self-interest

1759 Voltaire's *Candide* satirizes ideas and institutions of the eighteenth century

1762 Jean-Jacques Rousseau's *The Social Contract* propounds radical ideas about rights and liberties

1762 Jean-Jacques Rousseau's *Emile* urges "natural" education

1763 Voltaire's *Essay on Toleration* denounces religious intolerance

1764 Cesare Beccaria's *Treatise on Crimes and Punishments* urges penal reforms

1764 Voltaire's *Philosophical Dictionary* criticizes both church and state

1768 Joseph Priestley's *Essay on the First Principles of Government* stresses the happiness of citizens

1770 Baron d'Holbach's *The System of Nature* attacks organized religion

1771 First edition of the *Encyclopedia Britannica* appears

1776 Edward Gibbon's *The Decline and Fall of the Roman Empire* published

1776 Adam Smith's *The Wealth of Nations* outlines principles of capitalist economics

1777 John Howard's *The State of the Prisons* exposes horrible prison conditions

1779 Gotthold Lessing's *Nathan the Wise*, a dramatic poem on toleration published

1781 Immanuel Kant's *Critique of Pure Reason* published

1781 Moses Mendelssohn's *On the Civil Amelioration of the Condition of the Jews* published

1781 Johann Pestalozzi's *Leonard and Gertrude* advocates the reform of education

1782 Joseph Priestley's *A History of the Corruptions of Christianity* criticizes the church

1784 Immanuel Kant's "What Is Enlightenment?" urges people to dare to use their reason

1788 Immanuel Kant's *Critique of Practical Reason* states "the categorical imperative" for behavior

1789 Jeremy Bentham's *Introduction to the Principles of Morals and Legislation* published

1792 Mary Wollstonecraft's *A Vindication of the Rights of Woman* calls for equal education

1795 Marquis de Condorcet's *Progress of the Human Spirit* proclaims the doctrine of progress

1798 Thomas Malthus's *Essay on the Principle of Population* foresees world overpopulation

Most philosophes shared this glorification of reason. Montesquieu stressed that reason must be the basis of law. An American philosophe, Thomas Jefferson, advised: "Fix reason firmly in her seat, and call on her tribunal for every fact, every opinion." Denis Diderot, the coeditor of the *Encyclopédie*, wrote that the philosophe must be "actuated in everything by reason." The use of reason was as important to a thinker, he insisted, as grace was to a Christian.

The insistence upon rationalism caused collisions between the philosophes and the established authorities. This was especially true of the Christian churches, which insisted upon the primacy of faith as a standard of knowledge rather than, or in addition to, reason. One of the first popes directly rejected reason as the standard of the church, arguing that "[i]f the word of God could be comprehended by reason, it would no longer be wonderful." The conflict between reason and faith had interested many thinkers across the centuries, but faith had remained the Christian standard even after the Protestant Reformation, when Martin Luther had condemned reason as "the Devil's Harlot." The philosophes recognized the conflict between reason and faith, and they typically insisted upon the primacy of reason. Diderot, one of the most adamant rationalists, said that reason and faith are "not only incompatible, but in direct contradiction to each other. . . . [W]e are compelled to say either that faith is a chimera or that reason is useless." He, and most of the philosophes, preferred to break "the fetters that faith laid upon reason."

Despite such conflicts, the philosophes were generally confident that the use of human reason to discover natural laws would produce a better world. Thus, the glorification of reason led to an optimistic cult of progress. The French mathematician Jean d'Alembert, Diderot's coeditor of the *Encyclopédie*, thought "it is impossible to deny that philosophy has shown progress among us. Day by day natural science accumulates new riches." The greatest champion of the doctrine of progress was another French mathematician, the marquis Antoine de Condorcet, whose *Progress of the Human Spirit* (1795) foresaw nothing less than "the indefinite perfectibility of the human race"—a passage written shortly before Condorcet died in a prison of the French Revolution (see document 21.3). Other leaders of the Enlightenment were not so optimistic, but most shared the premise of the cult of progress: Emphasis should be shifted from thoughts of eternal salvation to those of earthly happiness.

◆ DOCUMENT 21.3 ◆

Condorcet: Progress

[T]here will remain one last picture for us to sketch: that of our hopes, and of the progress reserved for future generations, which the constancy of the laws of nature seems to assure them. . . . In spite of the transitory successes of prejudice and the support it receives from the corruption of governments or peoples, truth alone will obtain a lasting victory. We shall demonstrate how nature has joined together indissolubly the progress of knowledge and that of liberty, virtue, and respect for the natural rights of man; and how these, the only real goods that we possess, though so often separated that they have even been held to be incompatible, must on the contrary become inseparable from the moment when enlightenment has attained a certain level in a number of nations. . . . Once such a close accord has been established between all enlightened men, from then onwards all will be the friends of humanity, all will work together for its perfection and its happiness.

The French Enlightenment and the Encyclopédie

Although skepticism and rationalism attracted the educated classes of many regions, the home of the Enlightenment was in France, where the authority of church and throne were already weakened and the political duel between the aristocracy and the monarchy (see chapter 20) created an environment more favorable to radical thought than existed in most of Europe. The most famous and internationally read philosophes were French, as the universal use of a French word for them suggests (see illustration 21.9). Voltaire's famous satiric novel *Candide* (1759), filled with witty criticism of the Old Regime, went through eight editions in the year of its publication alone. Rousseau's radical political tract *The Social Contract* (1762) had thirteen French editions in 1762–63. Montesquieu's *The Spirit of the Laws* (1748) saw twenty-two French editions by 1751 and ten editions in its English translation by 1773; it had appeared in Dutch, Polish, Italian, and German editions by the 1780s and was so widely read that it was translated into Latin for the benefit of well-educated people in regions with less common languages, such as Hungary.

Nothing characterizes the French leadership of the Enlightenment better than the publication of the twenty-eight volumes of the *Encyclopédie* by Diderot and d'Alembert between 1751 and 1772. Many of the most famous writers of the eighteenth century contributed to what was perhaps the greatest intellectual accomplishment of the Enlightenment. The idea of compiling an encyclopedia was not new. The word itself came from the classical Greek *encyclios*—meaning instruction in the whole circle of learning—in both the arts and the sciences. Many famous efforts had been made to encompass the entire circle of learning, from Pliny's *Natural History* in the first century A.D. through a number of encyclopedic works in the seventeenth century. Diderot and d'Alembert did not produce the first encyclopedia of the Enlightenment, which saw a passion for comprehensive reference works. Johann Jablonski of Danzig, the secretary of the Prussian Academy, produced a short encyclopedia, the *Allgemeines Lexikon* ("The General Dictionary") in 1721. Johann Zedler, a Leipzig bookseller, had already completed a sixty-four volume *Grosses, vollständiges Universal Lexikon Aller Wissenschaften und Künste* ("The Great, Complete Universal Dictionary of All the Sciences and Arts") before the first volume of the *Encyclopédie* appeared. A London clergyman, John Harris, published the first English-language encyclopedia of the Enlightenment in 1704, and Gianfrancesco Pivati produced the first Italian encyclopedia in 1746–51.

Denis Diderot was an unlikely figure to supersede these massive works (see document 21.4). He was the son of a lower-middle class family—his father was a cutlery maker—in provincial France. Diderot received his formal education from the Jesuits, then prepared for two years for a career in the church; he was so devout that he fasted, slept on straw, and wore a hair shirt. Further study in Paris, however, changed Diderot into a Bohemian writer who broke with church and family alike, angering the former with his writing and the latter with his behavior. Like many philosophes, Diderot's writings earned him poverty and time in a royal prison. Thus, he eagerly accepted the opportunity to edit an encyclopedia, which was originally intended to be merely a translation of an English work.

The resultant *Encyclopédie* was a work of uneven quality and numerous inaccuracies, but it nonetheless became *the* encyclopedia. It owed its fame and influence to two characteristics. First, it was a collaborative enterprise, not simply the work of its editors. The contributors included many of the most influential writers of the Enlightenment; Condorcet, Montesquieu, Rousseau, and Voltaire all wrote for the *Encyclopédie*, with Voltaire

◆ DOCUMENT 21.4 ◆

Diderot: Prospectus for the *Encyclopédie*

Diderot published a prospectus for the Encyclopédie *in 1750, hoping to get enough subscribers to finance the beginning of the project. More than one thousand people subscribed after reading this document.*

It cannot be denied that, since the revival of letters among us, we owe partly to dictionaries the general enlightenment that has spread in society and the germ of science that is gradually preparing men's minds for more profound knowledge. How valuable would it not be, then, to have a book of this kind that one could consult on all subjects and that would serve as much to guide those who have the courage to work at the instruction of others as to enlighten those who only instruct themselves! . . .

The majority of these (older encyclopedias) appeared during the last century and were not completely scorned. It was found that if they did not show much talent, they at least bore the marks of labor and knowledge. But what would these encyclopedias mean to us? What progress have we not made since then in the arts and sciences? How many truths discovered today, which were not foreseen then? True philosophy was in its cradle; the geometry of infinity did not yet exist; experimental physics was just appearing; there was no dialectic at all; the laws of sound criticism were entirely unknown. . . . The spirit of research and competition did not motivate the scholars; another spirit, less fecund perhaps, but rarer, that of precision and method, had not yet conquered the various divisions of literature; and the academies, whose efforts have advanced the arts and sciences to such an extent, were not yet established.

alone contributing more than forty articles. Baron Paul d'Holbach wrote on the history of religion, including daring essays on priests and theocracy that made him one of the most controversial philosophes. Two leading Physiocrats, François Quesnay and Jacques Turgot, summarized the economic ideas that dominated contemporary thought and would be adopted by many governments. Such contributors guaranteed the

◈ DOCUMENT 21.5 ◈

Excerpts from the *Encyclopédie*

Each of the subjects in bold type are entries in the Encyclopédie, *from which brief excerpts are taken.*

Censors of Books: Name given to men of learning who are in charge of the examination of books to be printed. . . . These censors have been created in various states in order to examine literary works and pass judgment on books which are to be printed, so that nothing would become public that could seduce minds with false doctrines or corrupt morals with dangerous maxims.

Humanity: Is a feeling of good will toward all men. . . . This noble and sublime enthusiasm is tortured by the sufferings of others and tormented by the need to relieve such suffering; it fills men with the desire to traverse the world in order to do away with slavery, superstition, vice, and misfortune.

Intolerance: The word intolerance is generally understood to designate the savage passion that prompts us to hate and persecute those who are in error. . . . Ecclesiastic intolerance consists in considering as false all religions other than one's own. Teaching, persuasion, and prayer—these are the only legitimate means of spreading the faith. Whatever means provoke hate, indignation, and scorn are blasphemous. . . . Whatever means would tend to incite men to rebellion, bring the nations under arms, and drench the earth with blood are blasphemous.

Natural Law: The term is taken to designate certain principles which nature alone inspires and which all animals as well as men have in common. On this law are based the union of male and female, the begetting of children as well as their education, love of liberty, self-preservation, concern for self-defense. . . .

We understand by natural law certain laws of justice and equity which only natural reason has established among men, or better, God has engraved in our hearts. The fundamental principles of law and all justice are: to live honestly, not to give offense to anyone, and to render unto each whatever is his. . . . Since this natural law is based on such fundamental principles, it is perpetual and unchangeable: no agreement can debase it, no law can alter it or exempt anyone from the obligation it imposes.

Negroes: For the last few centuries the Europeans have carried on a trade in Negroes whom they obtain from Guinea and other coasts of Africa and whom they use to maintain the colonies established in various parts of America and in the West Indies. To justify this loathsome commerce, which is contrary to natural law, it is argued that ordinarily these slaves find the salvation of their souls in the loss of their liberty, and that the Christian teaching they receive, together with their indispensable role in the cultivation of sugar cane, tobacco, indigo, etc., softens the apparent inhumanity of a commerce where men buy and sell their fellow men as they would animals used in the cultivation of the land.

Encyclopédie a large readership and extended the influence of the French Enlightenment across Europe.

The second reason for the importance of the *Encyclopédie* was that the ideas and opinions that it contained made it notorious. The *Encyclopédie* did not merely record information, it became a forum for the philosophes. They began in the first volumes by criticizing despotic government and the established church; subsequent volumes contained direct attacks. As early as 1752, with only two volumes in print, King Louis XV of France ordered the *Encyclopédie* "to be and to remain suppressed." The support of friends in high places—especially the king's mistress, Madame de Pompadour—allowed publication to proceed, but it did so amidst controversy. In 1759 French courts turned the

work over to a panel of churchmen and scholars to censor. The government again denounced it, this time for causing "irreparable damage to morality and religion." Pope Clement XIII condemned it for "false, pernicious, and scandalous doctrines and propositions, inducing unbelief and scorn for religion." None of these threats, including excommunication for mere possession of it, stopped the publication (see document 21.5).

The Enlightenment beyond France

French leadership may have been unquestioned, but the Enlightenment was a widespread experience (see chronology 21.3). The German Enlightenment (the

❖ CHRONOLOGY 21.3 ❖

Landmarks of the Enlightenment Outside of France

1701 University of Venice founded

1702 First daily newspaper, the *Daily Courant*, published in London

1702 First subscription library founded in Berlin

1704 First Prussian newspaper published in Berlin: *Vossische Zeitung*

1711 Berlin Academy of Sciences founded, with Gottfried von Leibnitz as president

1712 Spanish Bibliotheca nacional founded at Madrid

1713 First Italian newspaper published, *Diario de Roma*

1714 Academia Española founded at Madrid

1718 Accademia dei Scienze, Lettere, ed Arti founded at Palermo (Sicily)

1721 University of Caracas founded (Venezuela: Spanish Vice-Royalty of New Spain)

1725 St. Petersburg Academy of Sciences founded

1726 First Scottish lending library founded at Edinburgh

1727 American Philosophic Society founded at Philadelphia

1728 University of Habana founded (Cuba: Spanish Vice-Royalty of New Spain)

1729 Academia de buenas letras founded at Barcelona (Spain)

1731 The Royal Dublin Society founded

1731 The Philosophical Society founded at Edinburgh

1734 University of Göttingen (Prussia) founded

1738 Excavation of Roman town of Herculaneum (destroyed by volcano, A.D. 79) begun

1739 Royal Society of Edinburgh founded

1741 Swedish Royal Academy of Sciences founded at Stockholm

1741 Linnaeus founds the Botanical Gardens of Uppsala (Sweden)

1742 Danish Royal Academy of Sciences and Letters founded at Copenhagen

1743 University of Santiago founded (Chile: Spanish Vice-Royalty of Peru)

1746 Princeton University founded (British colony of New Jersey)

1747 Tuscan Bibliotheca nazionale founded at Florence

1747 National library of Poland founded at Warsaw

1749 Giacobbo Pereire invented a sign language for deaf mutes

1753 Royal charter granted to found the British Museum

1754 Danish Academy of Arts founded at Copenhagen

1755 First Russian university founded at Moscow

1759 Bavarian Academy of Sciences founded at Munich

1760 Kew Botanical Gardens opened outside London

1760 Norwegian Royal Society of Sciences founded

1761 Johann Süssmilch launched the study of statistics

1764 University of Cagliari (Sardinia) founded

1773 Societas Scientiarium Bohemica founded at Prague

1775 Spanish Royal Economic Society founded at Madrid

1776 University of Zagreb founded (Croatia: Venetian Republic)

1779 Royal Academy of Sciences founded at Lisbon

1782 Royal Irish Academy founded at Dublin

1784 Ukrainian University of Lvov founded (Poland, later Russia)

1786 Swedish Academy founded at Stockholm

Aufklärung) drew on the excellence of German education, from compulsory education laws to superior universities. Rulers even encouraged the process in some regions. Frederick the Great of Prussia considered himself a philosophe and corresponded with Voltaire. He wrote dozens of books and composed more than one hundred symphonies, sonatas, and concertos. And he typically bought five copies of each book by the philosophes, to have one at each of his palaces. Frederick kept Prussian intellectuals on a short leash, however, and once said that the way to punish a region was to have it governed by philosophers. But he allowed sufficient tolerance that letters flourished, as they had begun to do under his grandfather (Frederick I), whose Berlin had boasted the first subscription library (1702), one of the first newspapers (the *Vossische Zeitung*, 1704), and an Academy of Sciences (1711). Hapsburg Austria, in contrast, was largely closed to the Enlightenment by strict censorship, intolerance of minorities, and the hostility to science of the Austrian Catholic Church. Alchemists outnumbered chemists in Vienna in the early eighteenth century. When Mary Wortley Montagu visited, she concluded, "I don't find that learned men abound there."

The German Enlightenment produced a number of notable figures. The century began with Gottfried von Leibnitz, Newton's equal as a mathematician and superior as a philosopher, presiding over the Berlin Academy. Leibnitz's reputation suffered somewhat when Voltaire's *Candide* ridiculed a sentence taken out of context from his *Théodicée* (1710): "God created the best of all possible worlds." His philosophy, however, did much to establish the scientific concept of natural law in eighteenth-century thought. And Leibnitz came closer than Voltaire to being the intellectual who mastered all fields of thought, from the scientific to the philosophic.

At the end of the century, the *Aufklärung* produced Germany's greatest poet, Wolfgang von Goethe. Goethe was at the center of a remarkable intellectual circle in Weimar that marks the beginnings of modern German literature; it included the poet and dramatist Friedrich von Schiller and the philosopher Gottfried von Herder. The dramatist Gotthold Lessing in Leipzig and Berlin, the philosopher Moses Mendelssohn in Dessau and Berlin, Immanuel Kant in Königsberg, Johann Süssmilch (one of the founders of the science of statistics) at Berlin, and the Bavarian Academy of Sciences in Munich show that the German Enlightenment spread widely across central Europe.

Other parts of Europe were centers of the Enlightenment. A Swedish Enlightenment, evident in northern Europe, was known as the Gustavian Enlightenment because it was encouraged by King Gustavus III of Sweden. It centered upon the Swedish Royal Academy of Sciences (1741), Linnaeus's Botanical Gardens at Uppsala (1741), and the Swedish Academy at Stockholm (1786). There was also a noteworthy Neapolitan Enlightenment and a Scottish Enlightenment, which included Adam Smith (one of the founders of capitalist economics), David Hume (one of the greatest skeptics of the age), and James Hutton (one of the founders of

modern geology). The prestige of the Enlightenment was so great that historians in every country have labored to show their national role in it, but for some regions—such as Spain, Portugal, and eastern Europe—the local Enlightenment was limited. In Spain, the hostility of the church limited the movement to a minority of the governing class. The largest periodical in Spain had a circulation of 630 copies, and a daring aristocrat who spoke publicly of the importance of reason was brought before the Inquisition on charges of heresy. Only a total of 280 books were published in Polish (including translations) in 1740. In Rumania, precisely two people were permitted to travel to western Europe during the entire second half of the eighteenth century. In Hungary, the first periodical introducing French thought attracted 140 subscribers. Yet even in such circumstances pockets of the Enlightenment could be found; for example, one aristocratic family, the Czakys, assembled a personal library of more than five thousand volumes, four thousand of them in French. And scientific societies were founded at Warsaw, Cracow, Danzig (Gdansk today), and Breslau (Wroclaw today).

The Enlightenment and Christianity

Wherever the Enlightenment stirred the educated classes, it had important implications for European civilization. This becomes especially clear when one views the relationship between the Enlightenment and Christianity. Many of the philosophes bluntly attacked Christian beliefs and institutions, challenging the churches in ways that might have led them to the stake in other eras. Hume, for example, applied skepticism to Christianity: "[T]he Christian religion not only was at first attended by miracles, but even at this day cannot be believed by any reasonable person without one." Diderot called Christianity "the most prejudicial of all the superstitions of the earth" (see document 21.6). Privately, he denounced the Judeo-Christian deity as "a partial God who chooses or rejects, who loves or hates, according to his caprice; in short, a tyrant who plays with his creatures."

Such ideas were not limited to one or two radical, dechristianized writers. Tom Paine attacked the concept of the Trinity ("The notion of a Trinity of Gods has enfeebled the belief in one God.") and the Bible ("Whenever we read the obscene stories, the voluptuous debaucheries, the cruel and tortuous executions, the unrelenting vindictiveness with which more than

DOCUMENT 21.6

Diderot: The Church

Denis Diderot studied to become a priest but instead became one of the church's sharpest critics. The following excerpt is taken from a short work that he published in 1775, "Discourse of a Philosopher to a King."

Sire, if you want priests you do not need philosophers, and if you want philosophers you do not need priests; for the ones being by their calling the friends of reason and the promoters of science, the others the enemies of reason and the favorers of ignorance, if the first do good, the others do evil.

You have both philosophers and priests; philosophers who are poor and not very formidable, priests who are rich and very dangerous. You should not much concern yourself with enriching your philosophers, because riches are harmful to philosophy, but your design should be to keep them; and you should strongly desire to impoverish your priests and to rid yourself of them. . . .

But, you will say to me, I shall no longer have any religion.

You are deceived, Sire, you will always have one; for religion is a climbing and lively plant which never perishes; it only changes form. That religion which will result from the poverty and degradation of its members will be the least troublesome. . . .

And if you deign to listen to me, I shall be the most dangerous of all philosophers for the priests. For the most dangerous is he who brings to the monarch's attention the immense sums which these arrogant and useless loafers cost his state; he who tells him, as I tell you, that you have a hundred and fifty thousand men to whom you and your subjects pay about a hundred and fifty thousand crowns a day to bawl in a building and deafen us with their bells. . . .

Since you have the secret of making a philosopher hold his tongue, why not employ it to silence the priest?

who consort with prostitutes, and priests who spread venereal disease; other churchmen committed robbery, torture, and murder. Edward Gibbon ended his monumental, six-volume *The Decline and Fall of the Roman Empire* with the conclusion that Christianity was one of the primary causes of the fall of Rome. He portrayed a church filled with "the inevitable mixture of error and corruption" contained in all human institutions.

The most famous critic of Christianity during the Enlightenment was Voltaire, the pen name of a Frenchman named François-Marie Arouet. Voltaire, the frail child of a Parisian legal official, received the finest classical education from the church, at the Jesuit *collège* Louis-le-Grand. A priest who admired Voltaire's intelligence led him into a freethinking group whose members did not hesitate to criticize or deride any institution. Voltaire threw himself into this sport and wrote a poem satirizing the regent, the duke of Orleans. Under the arbitrary legal system of the Old Regime, this poem was sufficient grounds for Voltaire's imprisonment without a trial. Thus, at age twenty-three, Voltaire was thrown into the Bastille for eleven months. Shortly after his release, Voltaire insulted another powerful noble who arranged to have the young poet beaten by a gang of thugs and imprisoned in the Bastille a second time. Voltaire wisely chose exile in England after his second release, which led to his admiration of Newton. His collisions with authority had already made him one of the sharpest critics of the Old Regime.

Voltaire's principal criticism of Christianity was the intolerance that he found among Christians. He was not the first philosophe to adopt this theme. Daniel Defoe had already written a stinging satire in 1702 entitled *The Shortest Way with Dissenters*, a book that persuaded too few people because Defoe was pilloried in public stocks and sent to prison. Voltaire returned to the theme so often that he made tolerance one of the highest principles of the Enlightenment. In a *Treatise on Tolerance* (1763), he denounced the Catholic Church for the mentality that led to the cruel murder of Jean Calas, a Protestant merchant who was tortured to death in 1761 on the fallacious charge that he had murdered his son to prevent him from converting to Catholicism. Voltaire demanded that Christians learn complete tolerance: "It does not require any great art of studied elocution to prove that Christians ought to tolerate one another. I will go even further and say that we ought to look upon all men as our brothers. What! call a Turk, a Jew, a Siamese, my brother? Yes, of course; for are we not all children of the same father, and the creatures of

half the Bible is filled, it would be more consistent that we call it the word of a demon than the word of God. It is a history of wickedness that has served to corrupt and brutalize mankind."). Voltaire's *Candide* ridiculed churchmen by depicting a friar who seduces women, monks

the same God?" Voltaire returned to this theme in his *Philosophical Dictionary* (1764): "Of all religions, Christians ought doubtless to inspire the most tolerance, although hitherto the Christians have been the most intolerant of men." By the end of the eighteenth century, many other philosophes adopted Voltaire's theme. Moses Mendelssohn, the great Jewish philosopher of the Enlightenment, published a powerful plea for the freedom of conscience, the toleration of minorities, and the separation of church and state—*Jerusalem* (1783). Mendelssohn also served as the model for the title character in Lessing's passionate call for toleration, *Nathan the Wise* (1779).

The criticism that the philosophes leveled upon Christianity became so widespread that some historians have called the eighteenth century an age of modern paganism. However, the Enlightenment was not simply an atheist campaign. Some of the most distinguished philosophes were churchmen, such as the Anglo-Irish philosopher George Berkeley, an Anglican bishop. The institutional hostility of the Catholic Church to the Enlightenment did not stop many individual Catholic churchmen from being enthusiastic participants. One study of the *Encyclopédie* has shown that, in some regions of France, priests bought the majority of copies. Pope Benedict XV was an intellectual himself, a friend of Montesquieu and Voltaire. In 1744 he permitted the publication of Galileo's condemned works; in 1757 he stopped enforcing the decrees against books teaching the heliocentric theory of the universe. Many philosophes sought to reconcile Christianity and science, theology and reason, as Leibnitz did in *Théodicée* (1710). Some stressed the limits of human reason: Pope's "Essay on Man" exalted Newton but also said it was "presumptuous" to believe that reason could explain everything.

Most of the Enlightenment skeptics retained some form of belief in God, if only as an "Omniscient Architect" or "Designing Deity," terms favored by Montesquieu in *The Spirit of the Laws*. The most widespread form of belief balancing rationalism and skepticism with a belief in a supreme being is known as Deism (sometimes Theism, the term Voltaire preferred). Deism was neither a structured religion nor a coherent body of religious beliefs. Instead it was an individualistic blend of reason, skepticism, and moral virtue combined with a rejection of religious intolerance, dogmatic belief, and powerful ecclesiastical institutions. A large percentage of the eighteenth-century elite favored deism over organized religion, including not only

French intellectuals such as Voltaire, Rousseau, and Montesquieu, but also such prominent colonial figures as Benjamin Franklin, George Washington, and Thomas Jefferson.

The Enlightenment and Government

The Enlightenment had equally grave implications for the monarchical governments of the Old Regime. The same application of skepticism and rationalism, the same search for natural laws, meant criticism of monarchy and aristocratic privilege. Rousseau, for example, bluntly styled himself "Jean-Jacques Rousseau, enemy of kings" and did not hesitate to sign letters to Frederick the Great that way. Diderot was more dramatic with his hostility: "Let us strangle the last king with the guts of the last priest!" Voltaire, who had good reasons to despise the powerful, treated them to the same acidic ridicule in *Candide* as churchmen received. When Candide and a companion arrived in a new kingdom, for example, they "asked one of the lords-in-waiting how he should behave in saluting His Majesty; should he fall on his knees or should he grovel, should he put his hands on his head or his behind, or should he just lick the dust off the floor . . . ?"

The criticism of a monarch who could imprison authors without a trial was a risky business. Voltaire's stay in the Bastille and Diderot's in the dungeon at Vincennes are only two of the most famous examples of the attempts to control troublesome writers. A study of French records has shown that the police kept thorough files on French authors; fully 10 percent of all writers in 1750 had spent some time in prison, usually the Bastille. The police used royal *lettres de cachet* to pursue such critics of the government, especially pamphleteers. Authors risked public whippings or even life sentences to the galleys for publishing their ideas. And the works of even the most famous writers were regularly censored by many authorities. Rousseau's *Emile*, for example, was not only condemned by the Catholic Church and placed on the Index of prohibited books, but it was also condemned by the Sorbonne (University of Paris), the General Assembly of the Clergy, and the Parlement of Paris. Fortunately for Rousseau, only his book was burnt in a public ceremony.

Consequently, early eighteenth-century writers sought indirect ways, such as Voltaire's satires, to make their point. When Archbishop François Fénelon wanted to criticize the king, he hid his satire in the form of an ancient epic. Fénelon's *Télémaque* reports the travels of the son of the Homeric hero, Ulysses; by describing Telemachus's visits to strange lands, Fénelon could comment on many forms of government and hide his comments on France. The book was banned and consigned to public fires anyway. Montesquieu similarly disguised his first critical comments in an epistolary novel (a novel in the form of letters), *The Persian Letters* (1721). These fictional letters were purportedly written by Persian visitors to Europe, whose naive comments hid barbs. One letter, for example, explains that the king of Spain owns many gold mines, but the king of France (who owns none) is richer because he has found a way to make unlimited money from the vanity of his subjects: He sells them offices, titles, and honors.

One strong criticism of government occurred naturally to writers—attacking censorship. Claude Helvétius, a rich government official under Louis XV, made one of the most vigorous attacks in 1758. His *De l'esprit* ("Essays on the Mind") was blunt: "To limit the press is to insult the nation; to prohibit the reading of certain books is to declare the people to be either fools or slaves." His book was condemned by the parlement and burnt by the public executioner in 1759. In England, where the tolerance of ideas was slightly greater—but censorship was practiced nonetheless—even jurists gave the philosophes some support. William Blackstone, a judge, a member of parliament, and one of the founders of modern university training in law, published four volumes of the extremely influential *Commentaries on the Laws of England* (1765–69). He cautiously concluded: "The liberty of the press is indeed essential to the nature of a free state, but this consists in laying no previous restraints upon publication, not in the freedom from censure for criminal matter when published."

As with the parallel battle against religious intolerance, not everyone agreed with the attack upon censorship. Conservatives rallied to the defense of the government, just as they stood by the church. Samuel Johnson, a journalist and lexicographer, is a good example. Johnson was a deeply conservative man who despised writers such as Voltaire and Rousseau; his famous *Dictionary* (1755) defined "Conservative" as "Having the power of opposing diminution or injury" (see document 21.7). He thought it a splendid idea that writers of their sort should be sent to penal colonies. And he stoutly defended censorship: "No member of society has a right to teach any doctrine contrary to what society holds to be true."

As the Enlightenment progressed, political writers became bolder in their criticism. The opposition of

---

◈ DOCUMENT 21.7 ◈

Excerpts from Samuel Johnson's *Dictionary*

Samuel Johnson (1709–84) was a journalist, lexicographer, teacher, and essayist—a "man of letters." His Dictionary *(1755) was the first comprehensive dictionary of the English language. It filled two huge volumes, the equivalent of ten modern volumes. The dictionary was a prodigious work for one person. Its definitions are often idiosyncratic, showing Johnson's wit and irascibility, but they also give an insight into the mind of the eighteenth century.*

Army: A collection of armed men, obliged to obey one man.

Astrology: The practice of foretelling things of the knowledge of the stars; an art now generally exploded, as without reason.

Atom: Such a small particle as cannot be physically divided.

Conservative: Having the power of opposing diminution or injury.

Crack-hemp: A wretch fated to the gallows.

Dormitory: A burial place.

Electricity: A property in some bodies whereby, when rubbed so as to grow warm, they draw little bits of papers, or such like substances to them.

Ethnick: Heathen; pagan; not Jewish or Christian.

Freethinker: A libertine; a contumner of religion: "Atheist is an old-fashioned word: I'm a freethinker."

To Lecture: To instruct insolently and dogmatically.

Mother (#5): Hysterical passion; so called, as being imagined peculiar to women.

Papistry: Popery: "A great number of parishes in England consist of rude and ignorant men, drowned in papistry."

Proletarian: Mean; wretched; vile; vulgar.

Louis XV, the French courts, and the Catholic Church did not stop the publication of the *Encyclopédie*. Its essay on "Government" shows how radical the criticism had become. It stated that society exists under a civil constitution that invests rulers with their power, but those rulers are "bound therein by the laws of nature and by the law of reason." Nature and reason both dictated that the "purpose in any form of government [is] the welfare" of civil society. Thus, the bold argument continued, society should expect "to abrogate laws that are flaws in a state" and even to change governments if needed.

> Some political writers claim that all men who have been born under one government do not have the liberty to institute another one. Each person, they say, is born the subject of his father or of his prince, and consequently each person is under a perpetual obligation of subjection or fidelity. This reasoning is more specious than solid. Men have never regarded any natural subjection in which they are born, in regard to their father or to their prince, as a bond that obliges them without their own consent to submit to such authority. Sacred and profane history furnish us with frequent examples of a multitude of people who have revoked the allegiance and the jurisdiction in which they are born.

Such ideas were not new to the Enlightenment. The English political theorist John Locke had made eloquent statements of them in the late seventeenth century, especially in his *Second Treatise on Civil Government* (1690). Locke, however, had written in comparative freedom and in a state where royal absolutism had already been broken by two revolutions.

Voltaire returned to France from his exile in England (1726–29) filled with similar willingness to write of his opposition to absolutism. His *Philosophical Letters* (1734) praised the English for their form of government and suggested it as a model for the rest of Europe. "The English nation," he wrote, "is the only one of earth that has successfully regulated the power of its kings by resisting them; and which, after repeated efforts, has established that beneficial government under which the Prince . . . is restrained from doing ill."

Baron Montesquieu, however, produced the most widely studied political analysis of the era (see document 21.8). His *Spirit of the Laws* stands as the founding work of modern comparative government. Montesquieu adopted the ancient political observation—used by both Aristotle and Cicero—that three basic forms of government exist: a republic, in which the people or their representatives govern; a mixed monarchy, in which a king reigns with constitutional limits and aristocratic checks upon his power; and a despotism, in which the monarch holds unchecked, absolute power. Montesquieu contended that none of these was a perfect, universal form of government because governments should be appropriate to local conditions. He proposed features of the ideal government, however.

◆ DOCUMENT 21.8 ◆

Montesquieu: Law, Liberty, and Government

The Spirit of the Laws

Law in general is human reason inasmuch as it governs all the inhabitants of the earth: the political and civil laws of each nation ought to be only the particular cases in which human reason is applied. . . .

There are three species of government: republican, monarchical, and despotic. . . . A republican government is that in which the body, or only a part of the people, is possessed of the supreme power; monarchy, that in which a single person governs by fixed and established laws; a despotic government, that in which a single person directs everything by his own will and caprice. . . .

There is no word that admits of more various significations, and has made more varied impressions on the human mind, than that of Liberty. . . . Political liberty does not consist in an unlimited freedom. . . . Liberty is a right of doing whatever the laws permit. . . .

It is necessary from the very nature of things that power should be a check to power. A government may be so constituted, as no man shall be compelled to do things which the law does not oblige him, nor forced to abstain from things which the law permits. . . .

In every government there are three sorts of power: the legislative, the executive in respect to things dependent on the law of nations; and the executive in regard to matters that depend on the civil law. . . . When the legislative and executive powers are united in the same person, or in the same body of magistrates, there can be no liberty.

He championed "liberty," which he carefully defined: "Liberty does not consist in an unlimited freedom. . . . Liberty is a right of doing whatever the laws permit." This careful definition of liberty shifted the focus to the laws; Montesquieu said, "Law in general is human reason." This made the question of liberty and the laws one of how reason shaped the government that made the laws that defined liberty.

This line of reasoning led Montesquieu to state two of the most famous political theories of the eighteenth century: (1) the theory of the separation of powers and (2) the theory of checks and balances. Montesquieu first argued that the centers of power within the state— the executive, the legislative, and the judicial powers— should not be held by the same person or institution. "When the legislative and executive powers are united in the same person . . . there can be no liberty." He then added that these separated centers of power should check and balance each other: "Power should be a check to power." Such ideas had many dramatic implications for the eighteenth century. They meant, for example, that powerful institutions controlled by the aristocracy, such as the French parlements, must check the potential despotism of a king.

By the late eighteenth century, the Enlightenment produced even more radical political arguments. Tom Paine, the son of a quiet English Quaker family who became an active participant in both the American and the French revolutions, wrote passionate pamphlets and carefully reasoned multivolume works of political theory. One of his pamphlets, *Common Sense* (1776), attacked monarchical government and advocated a republic—arguments aimed at the British colonies in America. His *Rights of Man* (1791–92) defended the legislation of the French Revolution, attacked monarchical government, and called on the English to overthrow George III. The government of Britain indicted him for treason.

Jeremy Bentham took Enlightenment political and social thought in yet another direction. Bentham was a lawyer with a comfortable inherited income that allowed him to pursue his writing, which he deeply imbued with Enlightenment attitudes. He saw his writings as "an attempt to extend the experimental method of reasoning from the physical branch (sciences) to the moral." His *Principles of Morals and Legislation* (1789) called for rationalist legislation, favoring the least possible legislation and the least possible government. "Every law," Bentham believed, "is an evil, for every law is an infraction of liberty." This reasoning contained the germ of one of the dominant political gospels of the nineteenth century, classical liberalism.

Perhaps the most radical political theorist of the Enlightenment was Jean-Jacques Rousseau, a Franco-Swiss philosophe who never experienced the comfortable life that Montesquieu, Voltaire, and Bentham knew. Rousseau was the son of a watchmaker and a pastor's daughter. He was born in austere, Calvinist Geneva where stern laws regulated behavior. His

mother died in the week of his birth, and his father deserted him as a child, fleeing imprisonment for dueling. Rousseau was raised by his mother's strict religious family and apprenticed to an engraver, but he ran away from Geneva at sixteen. During the remainder of his youth, Rousseau wandered as a vagabond. He survived as a beggar, domestic servant, tutor, music teacher, and the kept lover of an older woman. When he settled in Paris in 1744, he had a hatred of the rich but gave no signs of converting this into literary fame. Some of Rousseau's revolutionary anger showed in an early essay, the *Discourse on the Origin of Inequality* (1755). His concern was not "natural" inequality among individuals, but "moral or political inequality, because it depends on . . . the consent of mankind." The discourse went on to demand nothing less than the complete reorganization of society to eliminate inequalities based upon factors such as rank or race. Before the *Discourse* was finished, Rousseau attacked the concept of private property, which he considered "the worst of our institutions."

> The first man who, after fencing in a piece of ground, took it into his head to say: *This is mine*, and found people simple enough to believe him, was the true founder of civil society. How many crimes, wars, murders, how many miseries and horrors would not have been spared the human race by him who, pulling up the stakes or filling in the ditch, had cried out to his fellow men: Take care not to listen to this impostor; you are lost if you forget that the fruits belong to all and the earth to none.

The same passion characterized Rousseau's more complex masterpiece, *The Social Contract* (1762). It opened with one of the most famous sentences of the Enlightenment: "Man is born free, but is everywhere in chains." The great human emancipation that Rousseau desired led him to propose an ideal government that mixed democracy and authoritarianism. Rousseau, the enemy of kings, admired democracy and stimulated its growth in Europe with sentences such as: "No man has a natural authority over his fellow men." This reasoning led Rousseau to state the right of people to use force to resist forced obedience to authority: "As soon as [a people] can throw off its yoke, and does throw it off, it does better; for a people may certainly use, for the recovery of their liberty, the same right that was employed to deprive them of it." Rousseau also believed, however, that democracy would only work with "a people who were Gods." He criticized democracy because "it is contrary to the natural order" that a minority should always be governed by a majority. Thus, he introduced the concept of an abstract force, called "the general will," which would compel all members of society to desire the common good. Paradoxically, Rousseau's ideas thus encouraged both a democratic-egalitarian attack upon the Old Regime and a form of absolutism, the very concept of which had led to the initial Enlightened critiques of government.

The Spread of Rationalism

The Enlightenment had a tremendous impact on Western civilization because it spread skepticism and rationalism to many fields of human activity. Even the study of history felt the influence of these doctrines. Gibbon's *The Decline and Fall of the Roman Empire,* for example, showed the advantages of a reasoned study of the sources. The Neapolitan Enlightenment offered similar lessons in history. Giambattista Vico's *Principles of a New Science* (1725) urged scientific standards: Scholars should seek "the universal and eternal principles (such as every science must have)." Another Neapolitan historian, Pietro Giannone, suggested that this meant historians must write "histories of the kingdom" that contained more than the "lives of the kings." So Giannone began his masterwork with the words, "The history of the Kingdom of Naples which I am undertaking will not deafen readers' ears with the clash of arms and the din of battle. . . . This is to be a civic history."

Another leader of the Enlightenment in Italy, Cesare Beccaria, applied the scientific standards of careful observation and reasoning to another human activity, the punishment of crimes. Beccaria, a wealthy Milanese noble, studied prison conditions in Milan, and he was horrified by the conditions he discovered: Criminal charges were brought in secret, the accused had few opportunities to offer a defense and produce evidence, trials held before a jury were rare, torture was used both to determine guilt and to punish it, barbarous physical punishments such as branding and mutilation were commonplace, and people were executed for minor crimes. Beccaria's *Treatise on Crimes and Punishment* (1764) marked the beginning of modern criminology, and it led to more humane standards in European civilization. His argument was simple: "It is better to prevent crimes than to punish them" (see document 21.9). Therefore, he said, "Every punishment that does not arise from absolute necessity is tyrannical." Beccaria accepted preventive punishments—to stop a criminal from committing the same act again or to inhibit someone else from committing that crime—but he argued force-

---

◆ DOCUMENT 21.9 ◆

Beccaria: Penal Reform

Cesare Beccaria (1738–1794) was a Milanese nobleman who became one of the leaders of the Italian Enlightenment. He was an economist, a government official, a jurist, a professor at the University of Milan, and a pioneer of criminology and penology. His Tratto dei Delitti e delle Pene *(Treatise on Crime and Punishment, 1764), from which the following excerpt is taken, advocated many fundamental reforms such as the abolition of both torture and capital punishment.*

Of the Right to Punish: Every punishment which does not arise from absolute necessity, says the great Montesquieu, is tyrannical. A proposition which can be made more general thus: Every act of authority of one man over another, for which there is not an absolute necessity, is tyrannical. It is upon this that the sovereign's right to punish crimes is founded; that is, upon the necessity of defending the public liberty, entrusted to his care, from the usurpation of individuals. . . .

Of the Intent of Punishments: . . . [I]t is evident that the intent of punishments is not to torment a sensible being, nor to undo a crime already committed. Is it possible that torments and useless cruelty, the instrument of furious fanaticism or the impotency of tyrants, can be authorized by a political body? Can the groans of a tortured wretch recall the time past or reverse the crime he has committed?

The end of punishment, therefore, is no other than to prevent the criminal from doing further injury to society and to prevent others from committing the same offense. . . .

Of Torture: The torture of a criminal during his trial is a cruelty consecrated by custom in most nations. It is used with the intent of either making him confess his crime, or explaining some contradictions, or discovering his accomplices, or for some kind of metaphysical and incomprehensive purgation of infamy. . . . The very means employed to distinguish the innocent from the guilty will most effectually destroy all difference between them. It would be superfluous to confirm these reflections by examples of innocent persons who from the agony of torture have confessed themselves guilty.

fully against any form of torture. However, he found it "a cruelty consecrated by custom in most nations."

A leader of the German Enlightenment, Johann Süssmilch, applied rationalism differently; he studied records about ordinary people. Süssmilch, a Lutheran pastor in Prussia, studied demographic data—birth, marriage, and death records—with such systematic thoroughness that he pioneered the field of statistics. Süssmilch's *The Divine Order* (1741) proved basic demographic patterns, such as more boys are born than girls, but boys and men have a higher mortality rate. His calculations enabled Süssmilch to compile the first life expectancy tables, and his work was so accurate that it was used for more than a century, until the vital revolution of modern history changed mortality rates.

One of the most far-reaching Enlightenment criticisms of the human condition focused on the inequality of women. The word *feminism* did not yet exist—it was a nineteenth-century coinage—and no organized campaigns for women's rights had been established. But several philosophes shaped these later developments by challenging accepted attitudes about the inferiority of women. A few prominent philosophes, such as Condorcet and Holbach, championed the equality of women, but most leaders of the Enlightenment did not. Instead, a few educated women, despite lacking the advantages of their famous colleagues, began to publish their own reasoned arguments about the condition of the sexes. It is indicative of the status of women that one of the most forceful works, an English pamphlet entitled *Woman Not Inferior to Man*, was published anonymously in 1739 by an author known only as "Sophia, A Person of Quality" (see document 21.10). "Everyone who has but a degree of understanding above the idiot," Sophia wrote, can "observe the universal prevalence of prejudice and custom in the minds of Men." Sophia did not mince words: Men exercised a "tyrannical usurpation of authority" over women.

The most influential advocate of the equality of the sexes, and one of the most important founders of feminist thought, was another Englishwoman—Mary Wollstonecraft. Wollstonecraft, the daughter of an alcoholic and abusive father, learned to support herself despite having only a limited education. She and her sister directed a school near London, and this led Wollstonecraft to begin writing texts and tracts on education. Success introduced her to literary circles in London, where she met radical writers who encouraged her to continue her writing. She practiced some of her radical ideas in her own life, living with a man and having a child outside marriage. Wollstonecraft found only

◈ DOCUMENT 21.10 ◈

Sophia's *Woman Not Inferior to Man*

"Sophia, A Person of Quality" was the pseudonym of an unknown author who anonymously published a forceful pamphlet on the equality of women in 1739. This work, Woman Not Inferior to Man, or A Short and Modest Vindication of the Natural Right of the Fair Sex to a Perfect Equality of Power, Dignity, and Esteem with Men, *employed many of the basic concepts of the Enlightenment, as the following excerpt shows.*

If a celebrated Author had not already told, that *there is nothing in nature so much to be wonder'd at as THAT WE WONDER AT ALL;* it must appear to every one, who has but a degree of understanding above the idiot, a matter of the greatest surprize, to observe the universal prevalence of prejudice and custom in the minds of the *Men.* One might naturally expect to see those lordly creatures, as they modestly stile themselves, everywhere jealous of superiority, and watchful to maintain it. Instead of which, if we except the tyrannical usurpation of authority they exert over us *Women,* we shall find them industrious in nothing but courting the meanest servitude. Was their ambition laudable and just, it would be consistent in itself, and this consistency would render them alike imperious in every circumstance, where authority is requisite and justifiable: And if their brutal strength of body entitled them to lord it over our nicer frame, the superiority of reason to passion, might suffice to make them blush to submit that reason to passion, prejudice, and groundless custom. If this haughty sex would have us believe they have a natural right of superiority over us, why do not they prove their charter from nature, by making use of reason. . . .

What I have hitherto said, has not been with an intention to stir up any of my own sex to revolt against the *Men,* or to invert the present order of things, with regard to *government* and *authority.* No, let them stand as they are: I only mean to show my sex, that they are not so despicable as the *Men* would have them believe themselves.

limited happiness, however, and once attempted to drown herself in the Thames River.

From these poignant experiences, Mary Wollstonecraft found the materials for her masterwork, *A Vindication of the Rights of Woman* (1792). She, too, constructed her argument for women in the language of the Enlightenment. "In what," she asked, does human "pre-eminence over the brute creation consist? The answer is clear . . . in Reason." Because women possessed reason as well as men, they were equally preeminent and should be treated that way: "[I]f they be really capable of acting like rational creatures, let them not be treated like slaves." And she proclaimed her own, unequivocal stand, unwilling to submit to domination by men: "I love man as my fellow; but his scepter, real or usurped, extends not to me, unless the reason of an individual demands my homage; and even then the submission is to reason, and to not to man."

◆

Conclusion

The culture during the eighteenth century has been one of the most widely admired and praised ornaments of European civilization. Traditionalists have been drawn to the last great age of the European aristocracy, the last period of strong monarchy, and the last epoch in which established churches directed most of the population. They have been fascinated by the glittering opulence of the baroque culture. It was an age of spectacular palaces and stately homes and an age of dazzling, opulent rococo churches. This was the last flowering of the hierarchical world of the old elites, and its richness will long be admired.

But the eighteenth century is more often remembered as the age of a new elite, of the educated and articulate philosophes. The members of this new elite of the mind often came from the old centers of privilege and position (Montesquieu was a baron and Condorcet a marquis), but many influential voices had modest origins (Rousseau was a runaway apprentice and Wollstonecraft a self-supporting teacher). They were an elite, however; they may have spoken on behalf of the many, but they were usually speaking to a relatively small percentage of a largely illiterate population. Historians have consequently argued about the true influence of the new elite. How much influence did their rationalism and skepticism have? Their progressive ideas challenged the Old Regime in the most fundamental ways, questioning every power and privilege of the old elites of land, altar, and throne. The eighteenth

century would end with the vast upheaval of the French Revolution, in which aristocracy, clergy, and royalty all lost their historic roles in European society. But historians have never agreed whether the old elites had failed so badly that they precipitated the revolution, or whether the new ones had stimulated revolution with their thorough criticisms.

Suggested Readings

Reference works helpful for eighteenth-century cultural history include J. Babuscio and R. M. Dunn, *European Political Facts, 1648–1789* (1984), which has chapters on the Enlightenment and the church as well as those on politics; J. Black and R. Porter, *A Dictionary of Eighteenth-Century World History* (1994), whose entries include bibliographic suggestions; and P. H. Reill and E. J. Wilson, *Encyclopedia of the Enlightenment* (1996), which is the most helpful for topics covered in this chapter.

European high culture during the eighteenth century has drawn a good deal of attention. For a general introduction to art in its social context, see A. Hauser, *The Social History of Art*, 4 vols. (1951). For the baroque period, see J. R. Martin, *Baroque* (1977), E. Hempel, *Baroque Art and Architecture in Central Europe* (1965), G. Bazin, *Baroque and Rococo* (1964), and A. Blunt, ed., *Baroque and Rococo* (1978); for comparison to the neoclassical, see H. Honour, *Neo-classicism* (1968). For art history, see M. Levey, *Rococo to Revolution: Major Trends in Eighteenth Century Painting* (1966), N. Pevsner, *Academies of Art Past and Present* (1973), and A. Brookner, *Jacques-Louis David* (1980). For architectural history, see J. Rykwert, *The First Moderns: The Architects of the Eighteenth Century* (1980), and J. Summerson, *The Architecture of the Eighteenth Century* (1986). For music, see W. Weber, *The Rise of Musical Classics in Eighteenth-Century England* (1992), and G. Abraham, ed., *Concert Music, 1630–1750* (1986). For other fields mentioned in the text, see C. Gilbert, *The Life and Work of Thomas Chippendale* (1978), J. D. Hunt and P. Willis, *The Genius of the Place: The English Landscape Gardens, 1620–1820* (1975), R. Porter, *Edward Gibbon: Making History* (1988), N. Boyle, *Goethe: The Poet and the Age*, 2 vols. (1991), and F. J. Lamport, *Lessing and the Drama* (1989).

The best introductions to popular culture in the eighteenth century are P. Burke, *Popular Culture in Early Modern Europe* (1978); D. Roche, *The People of Paris: An Essay in Popular Culture in the Eighteenth Century* (1987); and R. Darnton, *The Great Cat Massacre* (1984), which contains several provocative essays. For the new cultural history of the eighteenth century, a good starting point is L. Hunt, ed., *The French Revolution in Culture* (1989). For topics in popular culture, see R. A. Houston, *Literacy in Early Modern Europe: Culture and Education, 1500–1800* (1988), P. Curry, *Prophecy and Power: Astrology in Early Modern England* (1989), R. Allen, *The Clubs of Augustan London* (1933), and B. Levack, *The Witch-Hunt Craze in Early Modern Europe* (1987).

For religion in the eighteenth century, see W. J. Callahan and D. Higgs, eds., *Church and Society in Catholic Europe in the Eighteenth Century* (1979); F. Heyer, *The Catholic Church from 1648 to 1870* (1969); G. R. Cragg, *The Church and the Age of Reason, 1648–1789*

(1960); G. Henningsen and others, *The Inquisition in Early Modern Europe* (1986); N. Sykes, *Church and State in England in the Eighteenth Century* (1934), which is not outdated despite its age; M. R. Watts, *The Dissenters: From the Reformation to the French Revolution* (1978); B. Hilton, *The Age of Atonement: The Influence of Evangelicalism on Social and Economic Thought, 1750–1865* (1988); E. G. Rupp, *Religion in England, 1688–1791* (1986); J. Redwood, *Reason, Ridicule, and Religion: The Age of Enlightenment in England, 1660–1750*; D. Van Kley, *The Jansenists and the Expulsion of the Jesuits from France, 1757–1765* (1975); T. Tackett, *Priest and Parish in Eighteenth-Century France* (1977); P. T. Hoffman, *Church and Community in the Diocese of Lyon, 1500–1789* (1984); and J. McManners, *French Ecclesiastical Society under the Ancien Regime* (1960). For the Orthodox church in eighteenth-century Russia, see J. Cracraft, *The Church Reform of Peter the Great* (1971). For disbelief, see A. Kors, *Atheism in France, 1650–1729* (1990). For the Jewish minority, see J. I. Israel, *European Jewry in the Age of Mercantilism, 1550–1750* (1985). For smaller churches, see H. Rack, *Reasonable Enthusiast: John Wesley and the Rise of Methodism* (1989), and F. E. Stoeffler, *German Pietism during the Eighteenth Century* (1973).

For overviews of the Enlightenment, see the works of P. Gay, especially his *The Enlightenment: An Interpretation*, 2 vols. (1966–69) and *The Party of Humanity: Essays in the French Enlightenment* (1964); N. Hampson, *The Enlightenment* (1968); E. Cassirer, *The Philosophy of the Enlightenment* (1951); and P. Hazard, *European Thought in the Eighteenth Century from Montesquieu to Lessing* (1963). See also the essays in R. Porter and M. Teich, eds., *The Enlightenment in National Context* (1981); R. Anchor, *The Enlightenment Tradition* (1967); J. Cottingham, *The Rationalists* (1988); and D. Goodman, *The Republic of Letters* (1994), which explores the sociology of the Enlightenment.

For important topics during the Enlightenment, see J. Censer, *The French Press in the Age of Enlightenment* (1994), R. Darnton, *The Business of the Enlightenment: A Publishing History of the 'Encyclopédie,' 1775–1800* (1979), M. Hunt and others, eds., *Women and the Enlightenment* (1984), N. Gelbart, *Feminine and Opposition Journalism in Old Regime France* (1987), S. Spencer, ed., *French Women and the Age of the Enlightenment* (1984), D. Bien, *The Calas Affair: Persecution, Toleration, and Heresy in Eighteenth-Century Toulouse* (1960), R. Darnton, *The Literary Underground of the Old Regime* (1982), R. Darnton, *Mesmerism and the End of the Enlightenment in France* (1968), T. Schlereth, *The Cosmopolitan Ideal in Enlightenment Thought* (1977), M. Jacob, *The Radical Enlightenment: Pantheists, Freemasons, and Republicans* (1981), and R. Hahn, *The Anatomy of a Scientific Institution: The Paris Academy of Sciences, 1666–1803* (1971).

For prominent figures of the Enlightenment and their ideas, see H. Mason, *Voltaire* (1981), R. Shackleton, *Montesquieu: A Critical Biography* (1961), M. H. Waddicor, *Montesquieu and the Philosophy of Natural Law* (1970), C. Blum, *Rousseau and the Republic of Virtue* (1986), A. M. Wilson, *Diderot* (1972), M. Cranston, *The Noble Savage: Jean-Jacques Rousseau (1754–1762)* (1991), J. Shklar, *Men and Citizens: A Study of Rousseau's Social Theory* (1965), K. Baker, *Condorcet: From Natural Philosophy to Social Mathematics* (1975), T. Hankins, *Jean D'Alembert: Science and the Enlightenment* (1970), I. L. Horowitz, *Claude Helvétius: Philosopher of Democracy and Enlightenment* (1954), A. C. Kors, *D'Holbach's Circle: An Enlightenment in Paris* (1977), H. E. Allison, *Lessing and the Enlightenment* (1966), N. Boyle, *Goethe: The Poet and His Age* (1991), and C. Tomalin, *The Life and Death of Mary Wollstonecraft* (1974).

CHAPTER 22

THE FRENCH REVOLUTION AND NAPOLEON, 1789–1815

CHAPTER OUTLINE

◆━◆━◆━◆━◆━◆━◆━◆━◆━◆━◆━◆━◆━◆━◆

The end of the eighteenth century brought extraordinary upheaval. The French Revolution (1789–99) challenged the institutions of the Old Regime and provoked bitter struggles in which millions of people died. The turmoil in France gave way to a general European conflict (1792–1815) as great coalitions formed to halt the spread of revolution. The revolutionary government survived these attacks until 1799 when one of its own military heroes, Napoleon Bonaparte, seized power and created an authoritarian government. In a series of brilliant campaigns he extended French rule over much of Europe until, in 1815, he was defeated by the combined armies of a European coalition.

Chapter 22 surveys this upheaval, starting with its origins in the economic and social problems of the Old Regime. The French attempt to address those problems led to a series of revolutionary governments that abolished the monarchy, the aristocracy, and the established church. A revolutionary bill of rights and an idealistic constitution promised an age of liberty and equality, and the revolutionary government fulfilled much of this promise by abolishing slavery and by emancipating religious minorities. The French Revolution, however, is a complex, paradoxical subject. The story of great accomplishment is also a story of great violence. The revolution produced dictatorial governments and public executions, so many people remember the revolution only as a "reign of terror." One of the best known passages in English literature, the opening of Charles Dickens's *A Tale of Two Cities* (1859), summarizes this revolutionary duality: "It was the best of times, it was the worst of times . . . it was the spring of hope, it was the winter of despair."

◈

The Origins of the French Revolution

The French Revolution grew from the combination of an intractable economic crisis and the inability of the

Illustration 22.1

▨ **Poor Harvests and the Monarchy.** Many problems confronted Louis XVI in the late 1780s. One of the most urgent was a succession of poor harvests and the danger of starvation. In this sympathetic image, the King is shown dispensing charity to the poor in the winter of 1788–89.

Bienfaisance de LOUIS XVI, au Grand Hiver de 1788

government to govern. King Louis XVI could neither raise taxes nor pay his bills. A recession and falling prices hurt small farmers and urban workers. French manufacturing suffered in competition with the English, especially in the textile industry. Unemployment reached dangerous levels, passing eighty thousand in Paris in December 1788 (approximately one-third of the adult workforce), while poor harvests in 1787–88 produced shortages of wheat, which rose in price to record levels by mid–1789 (see illustration 22.1). The price of bread in Paris, normally eight or nine sous for a four-pound loaf, hit 14.5 sous. Such circumstances often caused rioting in preindustrial Europe.

Ominous signs were evident in 1788–89 that France was a volatile society. Bread riots occurred in many districts. Some villages refused to ship their grain. In towns, crowds, often led by women, attacked granaries, mills, and bakeries. The crowds typically forced sales at "the just price" (an old Christian idea); in Rouen, for example, they cut the price of bread in half. Another example of urban unrest, the Réveillon riots, occurred at Paris in April 1789. Workers at the Réveillon wallpaper factory protested a pay cut by burning the owner in effigy and pillaging his home and factory. Before the riots ended, workers fought a twelve-hour battle with royal troops, resulting in the deaths of a dozen soldiers and more than two hundred workers.

Historians generally agree that such troubles became a revolution when four overlapping movements converged: (1) An aristocratic revolution had been building for many years, as aristocrats used institutions such as the parlements to thwart the king, especially on tax reform. This revolution forced Louis XVI to hold elections for the Estates General in 1789. (2) A bourgeois revolution challenged the aristocratic leadership of the reform movement and sought to limit aristocratic control of high government offices. (3) A peasant revolution went beyond disturbances over grain and became an armed uprising against the remnants of feudalism. This rebellion connected the common people to the reformers and made it extremely difficult for Louis XVI to act against them. (4) An urban working-class revolution turned the fury of the crowd from small targets, such as the Réveillon factory, to large political targets. The revolution of the crowd pressed reformers to extend the revolution.

The Estates General and the Beginning of the Revolution

Faced with bankruptcy, Louis XVI promised his critics in November 1787 that he would hold elections for the Estates General (the first since 1614) within five years.

Illustration 22.2

The Three Estates. Cartoons were often the most effective political tracts of the eighteenth century. The message of this one is both clear and revolutionary: The two privileged estates, the clergy and the aristocracy, are crushing the common man who must bear their weight and the boulder of taxation.

Under continuing pressure, Louis finally agreed that representatives from each of the three estates (the clergy, the aristocracy, and all others) that comprised the population of France (see chapter 18) could assemble in May 1789. His decision launched the first modern political debate in French history. Should the third estate (97 percent of the population) have more deputies than the others? Should the three estates meet together or separately? If the estates voted separately, the third estate would remain dominated by the clergy and the aristocracy (see illustration 22.2). Such issues produced a flood of political pamphlets. The most famous of these was written by a provincial priest, the abbé Emmanuel Sieyès (1748–1836), who defended the third estate in a work entitled *What Is the Third Estate?* (1789, see document 22.1). Sieyès's answer was "Everything!" The aristocracy, he added, was like "some horrible disease eating the living flesh of some unfortunate man."

Louis XVI agreed to double the representation of the third estate, but he insisted upon preserving traditions—the estates would meet separately. He permitted freedom of the press for the elections and asked that each district submit statements of their grievances (*cahiers des doléances*). Most cahiers condemned absolutism and praised constitutional monarchy; many

pledged loyalty to Louis XVI, but none acknowledged his "divine right." They called for a French parliament to control taxation and legislation. The cahiers attacked hated aspects of the Old Regime (such as the arbitrary royal power of arrest by *lettres de cachet*) and demanded new freedoms (such as freedom of the press). Each cahier also expressed the interests of the estate that produced it. The first estate, for example, wanted clerical control of education, denounced immorality in the press, and objected to the toleration of Protestantism.

The Estates General met in Versailles, a short walk from the royal palace. It opened with a royal speech asking for new taxes. The deputies of the third estate, chiefly lawyers, rejected holding such discussions in separate meetings, and they asked other deputies to join them in legislating reforms. Nine priests agreed, and the combined group proclaimed itself the French National Assembly. A political revolution had begun. The deputies were locked out of their meeting hall, so they assembled at a nearby indoor tennis court and swore not to adjourn without preparing a constitution. Within a few days, 612 of 621 deputies of the third estate had signed the Tennis Court Oath; 149 priests and a few nobles joined them.

The king naturally resisted these events. He did not panic because he had learned from dealing with the parlements that he could suspend their business, transfer the meeting to a distant province, or even arrest troublesome leaders. Thus, he simply declared the decisions of the third estate illegal. He offered the hope of a constitution, with important reservations. "The King wills," he said, "that the traditional distinctions between the three orders of the state should be preserved in its entirety." Deputies of the defiant third estate chose to continue the National Assembly. As one liberal deputy, the Count de Mirabeau (1749–91), said, "We shall not leave our places except by the power of bayonet." Louis considered using the army but concluded, "Oh, well, the devil with it, let them stay." In fact, the king's ability to use French troops against the National Assembly was uncertain. Few were stationed in Versailles, and their loyalty was dubious. One regiment had refused to fire on demonstrators and another had vowed not to act against the third estate. So Louis called in German and Swiss reinforcements from the provinces (foreigners constituted 25 percent of his army). He still felt confident enough to do nothing when the National Assembly discussed a constitution. The revolution, however, quickly passed beyond his ability to control it.

◆ DOCUMENT 22.1 ◆

The Abbé Sieyès's *What Is the Third Estate?* (1789)

Emmanuel Joseph Sieyès (1748–1836), remembered as the abbé Sieyès, was a Catholic priest who became a prominent leader of the French Revolution. On the eve of the revolution he was a vicar in the cathedral town of Chartres, where he sympathized with the reform movement. He was a little known figure in 1789 when he published What Is the Third Estate? *The pamphlet was so impressive that he was soon offered the post of archbishop of Paris. He served several regimes during the revolutionary era, including Napoleon, who made him a count.*

The plan of this essay is fairly simple. We have three questions to ask:

1. What is the Third Estate? Everything.
2. What has it been thus far in the political order? Nothing.
3. What does it demand? To become something. . . .

It is enough at this point to have made it plain that the pretended usefulness of a privileged order for public service is only vain imagination; that without it, all that is tiresome in such service is done by the Third; that without it, the higher positions would be infinitely better filled; that they should naturally be the prize and reward for talent and recognizable services; and that if the privileged have succeeded in usurping all the lucrative and honorific posts, it is both an injustice shocking to the majority of citizens and a betrayal of the public interest.

Who, then, would dare to say that the Third Estate does not contain everything needed to form a complete nation? It is like a strong, robust man, one of whose arms is still enchained. If the privileged order were removed, the nation would not be something less, but something more. What would it be without the privileged order? Everything, but an everything free and flourishing. Nothing can function without it; everything would function infinitely better without the others. . . .

What is a nation? A body of associates living under a *common* law and represented by the same legislature. . . . Is it not certain that the noble order has privileges, exemptions, even rights distinct from the rights of the great body of citizens? Thereby it is apart from the common order. . . . The Third therefore includes everything that belongs to the nation; and everything not of the Third cannot be regarded as being of the nation. What is the Third? Everything.

◆

The Revolutionary Crowd: The Bastille and the Great Fear

The political revolution begun by the aristocracy and expanded by the deputies of the third estate changed in July 1789, driven by crowds of commoners in both town and country. The revolutionary crowd ("the mob" to hostile observers) has been the subject of historical controversy. Some authors depict the crowds as purely destructive and conclude that they were comprised of criminals, vagabonds, and the unemployed. Edmund Burke, the most eloquent enemy of the revolution, called the crowd "a band of cruel ruffians and assassins." Recent study, however, has shown that the revolutionary crowds were comprised of wage earners, journeymen, artisans, and shopkeepers (see table 22.1). Of the people arrested during the Réveillon riots, for example, 19 percent came from the building trades (chiefly masons), 13 percent from transportation (chiefly dockworkers), and 12 percent from clothing trades (chiefly cobblers).

The Parisian crowd changed the revolution in July 1789. The price of bread, fear of foreign troops, concern that the National Assembly would be closed, and the agitation of revolutionary orators (notably Camille Desmoulins, a twenty-nine-year-old radical lawyer) created a volatile situation. On July 11, Parisians burned the customs gates to the city, as a protest against the tariffs collected there that they blamed for the high price of bread and wine. The next day, German soldiers fired on a crowd, and a riot followed. On the morning of July 14, eight thousand people attacked a royal barracks and took thirty-two thousand muskets and twelve artillery pieces. They used those arms later that day in the most famous act of the revolutionary crowd—the attack on the Bastille. The Bastille was a formidable fortress, towering nearly one hundred feet over eastern Paris, with thirty-foot-thick walls (see illustration 22.3). It was less important for the seven prisoners it held than as a symbol of despotism, in which such famous prisoners as Voltaire had been confined. (Studies have found that 10 percent of all French writers of the eighteenth

TABLE 22.1

The Social Composition of Revolutionary Groups

Arrests at the Bastille (1789)		Emigrés (1789–99)	
Trade category	Percentage	Class category	Percentage
Furniture trades	17.1	Third estate	58.0
Building trades	14.2	(Peasantry	19.4)
Clothing trades	10.1	(Workers	14.3)
Metal workers	10.1	Clergy	25.2
Transport trades	6.8	Nobility	16.8
Food Trades	5.3		
Other	36.4		

Deputies in the convention (1792–95)		Jacobin clubs (1793–95)	
Profession	Percentage	Profession	Percentage
Lawyers	47.7	Shopkeepers	45.0
Businessmen	8.9	Farmers	9.6
Clergy	7.3	Businessmen	8.2
Civil servants	6.8	Lawyers	6.8
Medicine	6.1	Other professions	6.9
Farmers	5.1	Civil servants	6.7
Other	18.1	Other	16.8

Victims of the terror (1793–94)		Vendéen counterrevolutionaries (1793)	
Class category	Percentage	Class category	Percentage
Working class	31.2	Peasantry	46.1
Peasantry	28.1	Artisans and workers	37.5
Upper middle class	14.0	Bourgeois	11.8
Lower middle class	10.6	Clergy	2.9
Nobility	8.2	Nobility	1.8
(Old nobility	6.2)		
(Robe nobility	2.0)		
Clergy	6.5		
Other	1.4		

Note: Total percentage may exceed 100 because of rounding.

Source: Colin Jones, ed., *The Longman Companion to the French Revolution* (London: Longman, 1988), pp. 120, 168, 186, 199; Charles Tilly, *The Vendée* (Cambridge, Mass.: Harvard University Press, 1976), p. 328; and George Rudé, *The Crowd in the French Revolution* (Oxford: Oxford University Press, 1959), pp. 246–48.

century were locked up in the Bastille at least once.) Perhaps more important, it held five tons of gunpowder, defended by only eighty-two French soldiers and thirty-two Swiss. During a four-hour battle on July 14 (which became a French national holiday), one soldier and ninety-eight civilians were killed. The victorious crowd, which included many cabinetmakers and cobblers but no lawyers (see table 22.1), finished the day with an act that led to their image as a blood-thirsty mob; the brutal murder of the governor of the Bastille. Louis XVI spent the day hunting; his remarkable diary entry for July 14 read: "Nothing." The next day,

Illustration 22.3

⫸ **Storming the Bastille.** On July 14, 1789, a popular uprising succeeded in capturing a one-hundred-foot-tall fortress-prison in Paris, known as the Bastille. This event, celebrated each year as a French national holiday, had many emotional overtones about attacking tyranny and liberating prisoners, but the chief aim of the crowd was to seize the supply of gunpowder stored in the Bastille. The governor of the prison was brutally murdered and his head paraded around on a pike.

stunned by the news from Paris, he went to the National Assembly and promised to withdraw the provincial troops.

Neither the king nor the National Assembly had adjusted to the insurrection in Paris when similar events occurred in rural France. The rural disturbances of July and August 1789, known as "the great fear," were a response to rumors. Some rumors held that the king wished to liberate the peasantry but expected them to take the lead. Worse rumors held that aristocrats, frustrated by events in Versailles, were preparing some terrible revenge or that armies of vagrants (whose numbers were high) were to be set loose on the peasantry. Peasants armed themselves in self-defense. When brigands did not appear, the frightened population turned their anxiety on the chateaux of their seigneurs. Some aristocrats were forced to renounce their feudal rights. In other places, peasants burned the records of the feudal dues that they owed, and sometimes the chateau as well.

◆

The Legislative Revolution of the National Assembly, 1789–91

The actions of the Parisian crowd and the peasantry had two important effects on the National Assembly

(also called the Constituent Assembly because it was writing a constitution). First, they strengthened the assembly because the king could not suppress it without fear of violence. Second, the rebellions encouraged the deputies to extend the revolution (see chronology 22.1).

A legislative revolution began on "the night of August 4th" (see illustration 22.4). Debates on the great fear led to a remarkable scene: Some aristocrats proposed ending their own privileges. Without preparation or committee studies, the deputies voted a series of decrees that began with: "The National Assembly completely abolishes the feudal regime." The night of August 4 marked the end of feudal servitude (such as the *corvée*) and taxes, the feudal rights of the aristocracy (such as hunting on peasant farmland), the manorial courts of aristocratic justice, "tithes of every description" owed to the Catholic Church, and the sale of public offices, which were opened to all citizens.

Three weeks later, the National Assembly adopted another historic document, a French bill of rights named the Declaration of the Rights of Man (see document 22.2). A draft of this declaration had been proposed by a famous veteran of the American Revolution who now commanded the French National Guard, Marquis Marie de Lafayette. Many individuals shaped this great document, including Maximilien Robespierre (later the leader of the Reign of Terror),

◈ CHRONOLOGY 22.1 ◈

The French Revolution, 1789–92

May 1789	Opening of the Estates General

The National Assembly (1789–91)

June 1789	Third estate proclaims the National Assembly
June 1789	Tennis Court Oath not to disperse
July 1789	Fall of the Bastille
July 1789	Beginning of "the great fear" in rural France
August 1789	Abolition of feudalism, tithes, venal offices
August 1789	Declaration of the Rights of Man
October 1789	Women's march on Versailles
November 1789	Nationalization of church property
December 1789	Civil equality of Protestants
February 1790	Suppression of monasteries
March 1790	Abolition of the *lettres de cachet*
May 1790	Nationalization of royal land
June 1790	Nobility abolished
July 1790	Civil Constitution of the Clergy
October 1790	Abolition of internal tariffs
April 1791	Pope Pius VI denounces the revolution
June 1791	Chapelier Law outlaws unions and strikes
June 1791	Louis XVI's flight to Varennes and arrest
July 1791	Massacre on the Champ de Mars
July 1791	Law against seditious meetings
September 1791	Emancipation of Jews
September 1791	Constitution of 1791 adopted
September 1791	Declaration of the Rights of Woman

The Legislative Assembly (1791–92)

November 1791	Decree against émigrés
November 1791	Decree against nonjuring priests
June 1792	Crowds invade the Tuileries Palace
July 1792	Brunswick Manifesto against the revolution
August 1792	King's powers suspended
August 1792	Prussia invades France
September 1792	Legalization of divorce
September 1792	September massacres
September 1792	Battle of Valmy forces Prussians to retreat
September 1792	French monarchy abolished

Illustration 22.4

⧈ **The Legislative Revolution.** On the night of August 4, 1789, depicted here, the National Assembly began a legislative revolution that fundamentally changed France. They abolished the feudal regime, including servitude such as the *corvée*, privileges of the aristocracy, tithes owed to the church, privileges of cities, and the ownership of state offices.

◈ DOCUMENT 22.2 ◈

The Declaration of the Rights of Man, 1789

1. Men are born and remain free and equal in rights. Social distinctions can be based only upon public utility.

2. The aim of every political association is the preservation of the natural and imprescriptable rights of man. These rights are liberty, property, security, and resistance to oppression.

3. The source of all sovereignty is essentially in the nation; no body, no individual can exercise authority that does not proceed from it in plain terms.

4. Liberty consists in the power to do anything that does not injure others; accordingly, the exercise of the natural rights of man has no limits except those that secure to the other members of society the enjoyment of these same rights. These limits can be determined only by law.

5. The law has the right to forbid only such actions as are injurious to society. . . .

6. Law is the expression of the general will. All citizens have the right to take part personally, or by their representatives, in its formation. It must be the same for all, whether it protects or punishes. . . .

7. No man can be accused, arrested, or detained except in the cases determined by the law and according to the forms that it has prescribed. . . .

8. The law ought to establish only penalties that are strictly and obviously necessary, and no one can be punished except in virtue of a law established and promulgated prior to the offence. . . .

9. Every man being presumed innocent until he has been pronounced guilty. . . .

10. No one should be disturbed on account of his opinions, even religious. . . .

11. The free communication of ideas and opinions is one of the most precious rights of man; every citizen then can freely speak, write, and print, subject to responsibility for the abuse of this freedom in the cases determined by the law. . . .

14. All the citizens have the right to ascertain, by themselves or by their representatives, the necessity of the public tax, to consent to it freely. . . .

15. Society has the right to call for an account of his administration from every public agent.

17. Property being a sacred and inviolable right, no one can be deprived of it, unless a legally established public necessity evidently demands it, under the condition of a just and prior indemnity.

Thomas Jefferson (the American diplomatic representative in Paris), and Rabaut Saint-Etienne (a Protestant pastor who demanded religious freedom). The bill of rights that they wrote promised freedom of religion, freedom of speech, freedom of the press, due process of law, and the prohibition of cruel and unusual punishment. It did not grant equal rights to religious minorities (Protestants received this in December 1789; Jews had to wait until September 1791), freedom for the black slaves in French colonies (adopted in February 1794, see illustration 22.5), or equal rights for women (which the revolution never accepted)—see documents 22.3 and 22.4)—but in 1789 it was the greatest statement of human rights in Europe.

Louis XVI rejected the August reforms. A risky strategy, his action defended tradition, but it angered the National Assembly and the people of Paris. The people forced the issue. Their fears of a royal counter-revolution were exacerbated by the food crisis. The harvest of 1789 was good, but a late season drought had slowed the work of the water-powered mills that ground grain into flour. Thus, August and September 1789 again witnessed bread riots led by the women of Paris.

Historians call those days on which the action of the crowd changed the course of events "revolutionary *journées*" ("revolutionary days"). The angry housewives and working women of Paris led such a journée on October 5, 1789. Their target was the king. When Louis blocked the August reforms, talk circulated in Paris about a march to Versailles to bring him to Paris. On the rainy Monday morning of October 5, the women of Paris did just that. A procession of several thousand set out for Versailles, chanting "Let's fetch the baker!" A few hours later, a reluctant Lafayette led twenty thousand members of the National Guard to support them. After a small clash on the grounds of the royal palace, Louis XVI agreed to accept the August decrees and to move into his Tuileries Palace (today the Louvre

Le mme Garakterise par une femme ayant sur la tete le foi sacre
De l'amour de la patrie, que le autres l'homme uni et l'homme
De college Berretre dans de une Corne d'abondance un banancer
de des Campagnes fondu, il s'appuye sur les droits de l'homme a
dont de l'ordre non le libere clairs, mes garantist, les gens
Le Calcet la raison le pousse par la nature qui et l'ournesse

Les Mortels Sont Cgaux Ce n'est pas La Naissance
Cet La Seule Vertu qui fait La Difference

De fruits ayant de l'on mulle. Che le montie sur un Cadre de peu. Dia
qui fortes. Le Demon de l'andremant s'apparte qui par Son manie
sont deux Cuzes l'egualite. Le Demon de la Jusstice et du par.
L'inournales prit a travenser La mer qui fait Le Julics

Illustration 22.5

◻ **Two Views of the French Revolution.** At its most idealist stage, the French Revolution emancipated Protestants, Jews, and slaves. In this illustration, the revolution is glorified for proclaiming "all mortals are equal." The scales of justice find a white man and a black man to be precisely equal. The emancipated slave holds a copy of the *Declaration of the Rights of Man*, while the devils of inequality are driven away.

Although women played important roles at many stages of the revolution—from leading the early bread riots to leading the march on Versailles to bring back Louis XVI, from the early *cahier* campaigns to the passionate political rhetoric of Olympe de Gouges—the revolution did not give women equality before the law. There were several women's political clubs in the early stages of the revolution, such as the one depicted here, but a revolutionary decree closed them.

Museum) in Paris. He also brought a caravan of flour from the royal supplies.

The National Assembly moved to Paris, too, confident that it now controlled France. The deputies deprived the king of the right to dismiss them or to veto the constitution they were writing. Their effort to shackle royal power included one mistake: They excluded royal ministers from the assembly. This blocked the evolution of a cabinet system of government and the principle of ministerial responsibility to parliament.

The move to Paris stimulated the growth of political clubs (the precursors of political parties), which became one of the distinguishing features of the revolution. These clubs had roots in the salons of the Old Regime, organizations such as Masonic lodges, and the excited political meetings of 1788–89. They became the voice of Parisian radicalism and then the center of revolutionary power. One of the most influential clubs was the Cordeliers, named for a Catholic order whose monastery it rented. The Cordeliers included three of

❖ DOCUMENT 22.3 ❖

Olympe De Gouges's *Declaration of the Rights of Woman,* 1791

Olympe de Gouges (1748–93) is the pseudonym adopted by the illegitimate daughter of a provincial butcher. She claimed aristocratic parentage (hence the "de"), ran off with an army officer at age sixteen, and wound up alone in Paris, where she became celebrated for both her writing (chiefly comedies) and beauty in the 1780s. She supported the revolution and founded one of the clubs of women that Robespierre closed. Her opposition to Robespierre, especially her protest at the execution of Louis XVI, led to her being sent to the guillotine in 1793.

Man, are you capable of being just? It is a woman who poses the question; you will not deprive her of that right at least. Tell me, what gives you sovereign empire to oppress my sex?

1. Woman is born free and lives equal to man in her rights. . . .

4. Liberty and justice consist of restoring all that belongs to others; thus, the only limits on the exercise of the natural rights of woman are perpetual male tyranny; these limits are to be reformed by the laws of nature and reason. . . .

10. No one is to be disquieted for his very basic opinions; woman has the right to mount the scaffold; she must equally have the right to mount the rostum.

❖ DOCUMENT 22.4 ❖

The Committee of General Security Rejects Women's Rights, 1793

Should women exercise political rights and meddle in affairs of government? To govern is to rule the commonwealth by laws, the preparation of which demands extensive knowledge, unlimited attention and devotion, a strict immovability, and self-abnegation . . . . Are women capable of these cares and of the quality they call for? In General, we can answer no. . . .

[W]omen's associations seem dangerous. If we consider that the political education of men is at its beginning, that all its principles are not developed, and that we are still stammering the word liberty, then how much more reasonable is it for women, whose moral education is almost nil, to be less enlightened concerning principles?

the most prominent radicals of the city: Camille Desmoulins (the orator who helped to precipitate the attack on the Bastille), Jean-Paul Marat (a physician whose radical newspaper, the *Friend of the People,* had shaped the journée of October 5), and Georges Danton (a radical lawyer who had married into middle-class wealth and purchased a venal office in the royal courts). The most important club, the Jacobins, drew their name from a rented Jacobin convent and their membership from Parisian small businessmen (see table 22.1). The Jacobins were especially influential because their membership included more than two hundred deputies. Jacobins ranged from moderates such as Lafayette to radicals such as Robespierre, but the latter soon predominated. In the first year, the club grew to more than twelve hundred members and 150 affiliated provincial clubs. The term *Jacobinism* soon entered political discourse to identify their militant ideas and actions.

Pushed by these radical clubs, the National Assembly continued its revolutionary legislation. Its attention soon fell on the Catholic Church, which seemed to hold an answer to the economic crisis. In November 1789 the revolutionary, and nonreligious, bishop of Autun, Charles Talleyrand, convinced the assembly to "put at the disposal of the nation" all lands belonging to the church. This confiscated a huge amount of land—typically 20 percent of the farm land in a region, although it reached 40 percent in some areas. The assembly then sold interest-bearing bonds, called *assignats,* secured by this land. The assignats gradually circulated as revolutionary paper money. The notes could be redeemed for land and the value of the land was sufficient to cover them, but the public had little confidence in paper money, so assignats depreciated in value. By late 1791 they had lost 25 percent; a year later, 40 percent.

The National Assembly followed the nationalization of church lands with other legislation on the church. The loss of its lands and the abolition of the mandatory tithe left the church with limited income. This led the assembly to break the concordat with the Vatican and proclaim a new relationship between the church and the state, known as the Civil Constitution of the Clergy of July 1790. The Civil Constitution converted priests into state employees and doubled their salaries, but it cut the number, income, and powers of the aristocratic bishops by changing their posts into elective state offices, no longer filled by the pope. The law required clerics to swear loyalty to the constitution or be removed from office. By mid-1791, 60 percent of French priests (the "juring," or constitutional, clergy) had accepted this arrangement; more than 95 percent of the bishops refused.

The legislative revolution proceeded rapidly. The assembly addressed the economic crisis by abolishing internal tariffs (October 1790), nationalizing royal land (May 1790), and creating a land tax (November 1790). It sought governmental efficiency by reorganizing local government (December 1789) and the judiciary by abolishing the parlements (September 1790). It decreed the civil equality of Protestants (December 1789) and ex-slaves (May 1791). And it continued to attack the elites of the Old Regime: The assembly abolished monasteries and most religious orders (February 1790) and then the nobility (June 1790). One of its most far-reaching reforms, however, restricted the rights of workers. The Chapelier Law of June 1791 abolished the guilds and outlawed trade unions, shaping French labor history for nearly a century.

One omission in this torrent of reform was women's rights, despite the active role of women in the revolution (see illustration 22.5). The pamphlet campaign of early 1789 had included women's grievances; one petition to the king, for example, had called for educational and economic opportunities. A few women in religious orders had voted for representatives of the first estate. More than a dozen women had been among the conquerors of the Bastille. Women had led demonstrations over bread and the march on Versailles. They had formed political clubs, such as Théroigne de Méricourt's Friends of the Law, which was denied affiliation by the Cordeliers. And when the Declaration of the Rights of Man failed to mention women, Olympe de Gouges responded with a brilliant manifesto entitled *Declaration of the Rights of Women* (1791). "Man, are you capable of being just?" she asked (see document 22.3). Although a few men, such as Condorcet, responded

supportively, the answer remained no. Traditional attitudes about the role of women in society persisted, fears about the subservience of women to the church abounded, and a multitude of arguments (such as the lesser education of women) were advanced to perpetuate male dominance. Soon, the revolutionaries even closed women's clubs (see document 22.4).

The greatest accomplishment of the National Assembly came in September 1791 when it produced the first written constitution in French history. This document incorporated many of the decrees of the previous months. The Declaration of the Rights of Man formed the preamble. Louis XVI retained power as a constitutional monarch, but most power was vested in a unicameral parliament called the Legislative Assembly, which he could not dissolve. Elections were complicated. Adult male citizens were divided into "active" citizens (who got to vote, based on how much tax they paid) and "passive" citizens (who had full civil rights, but no vote). Elections were indirect: Active citizens chose representatives who met to elect deputies. This allowed 4.3 million people to vote, excluding women, men under age twenty-five, criminals, servants, nonjuring priests, and men who paid less than three days' wages in taxes. Fewer people voted for the Legislative Assembly than had voted for the Estates General. The percentage who voted, however, was higher than the electorate for the House of Commons in Britain.

Before the Constitution of 1791 took effect, another dramatic event changed the course of the French Revolution. On June 20, 1791, Louis XVI fled for the eastern frontier. He had long resisted this idea, so his flight was hastily planned and poorly executed. A postmaster recognized the king, and at the village of Varennes the National Guard arrested him. Louis XVI returned to Paris as a prisoner. "There is no longer a king in France," he said. His flight to Varennes led to talk of abolishing the monarchy and creating a republic. For more than a year after the king's arrest, however, the revolutionary government allowed an aristocrat to continue publishing a royalist newspaper on his behalf.

Europe and the Revolution

The arrest of Louis XVI accelerated the growth of counterrevolutionary opinion. The most dramatic expression of this in France had been emigration from the country. The émigrés (those who fled) had been led by the king's younger brother and future successor, the count of Artois, who left in July 1789. Each major event of the revolution increased the number of émigrés. The total ultimately reached 104,000. Adding twenty-five thousand people who were deported (chiefly nonjuring priests), 2 percent to 3 percent of the population left France. Most émigrés came from the third estate, but priests and aristocrats fled at higher rates (see table 22.1). In contrast, counterrevolutionary emigration to Canada during the American Revolution took 3 to 5 percent of the population. The émigrés concentrated in Koblenz and other towns near the border where they tried to organize the enemies of the revolution. They created counterrevolutionary councils and armies, and they sought assistance from the crowned heads of Europe. They aided a rebellion in southern France, where Catholics blamed the Protestant population for the revolution. They built ties to nonjuring priests, especially in western France where a bitter civil war in the region of the Vendée would soon be fought.

The émigrés got little help at first. European opinion was divided, but it was generally more favorable to the revolution than to émigré nobles. The English poet William Wordsworth summarized the enthusiasm of the educated classes in a few lines of poetry: "Bliss was it in that dawn to be alive, But to be young was very heaven!" Such opinions were not limited to intellectuals. Charles James Fox, a leader of the Whig Party in Britain, called the revolution "much the greatest event that ever happened, and much the best."

The earliest opponent of the French Revolution was King Charles IV of Spain who was horrified by the treatment of the Catholic Church, but Spain was too weak to intervene. Catherine the Great of Russia dreaded the menace of French revolutionary ideas, but she was too far away to act, except against her own intelligentsia. The Hapsburg emperors Joseph II and Leopold II carefully watched events in France because their sister, Marie Antoinette, was the queen and a target of popular abuse, but they initially accepted French reforms.

The most thoughtful critic of the revolution was Fox's rival in the House of Commons, Edmund Burke. Burke became one of the founders of modern conservatism with his attack on the revolution, *Reflections on the Revolution in France* (1790). "France," he wrote, "by the perfidy of her leaders, has utterly disgraced the tone of lenient council." The revolution was an "undignified calamity." The most influential early enemy of the revolution was Pope Pius VI. Pius had fought for years against the Josephine reforms in Austria. The French Revolution presented a greater threat by abolishing the

tithe, seizing church lands, and abolishing monastic orders. Pius chiefly directed his anger, however, at the Civil Constitution because it flatly removed the church from papal control. In April 1791 he sent the encyclical letter *Caritas* to French bishops, forbidding the oath to the constitution. That oath, Pius insisted, was "the poisoned fountainhead and source of all errors." The French assembly answered by annexing the papal territory of Avignon (once the seat of the medieval papacy). Avignon was an enclave in southern France whose citizens were culturally French and had petitioned for annexation. Soon the French ambassador at Rome had been murdered, Parisian crowds had burnt the pope in effigy, and Pius VI had become a leader of the European counterrevolution.

The arrest of the French royal family at Varennes persuaded Leopold II to help his sister and her family. In July 1791 he sent a circular letter to the monarchs of England, Spain, Prussia, Naples, Sardinia, and Russia, urging them to join him in a protest to the French. He wanted "to vindicate the liberty and honor of the most Christian King and his family and to limit the dangerous extremes of the French revolution." Most rulers were unwilling to act. King George III of Britain abstained because the revolution weakened France, and he felt it was divine retribution for the French intervention in the American Revolution. The only ruler who joined Leopold II was King Frederick William II of Prussia. Together they issued the Brunswick Manifesto (1792) denouncing "the anarchy in the interior of France." Soon they would invade France.

European opinion gradually became polarized. As a Dutch conservative wrote in 1791, two parties were forming in all nations. One, a party of popular sovereignty and democratization, attacked all governments "except those arising from the free consent of those who submit to it." The other party held traditional values and, therefore, counterrevolutionary sentiments. It accepted government "by one or several persons over the mass of the people, a government of divine origin and supported by the church." The French Revolution was only the largest part of a democratic revolution that included liberal Polish nobles struggling against Russian influence; English dissenters campaigning for parliamentary reform; Rhineland Jews seeking emancipation; Irish peasants dreaming of French aid against the English; and Dutch, Belgian, and Swiss "patriots" who revived earlier rebellions.

In Ireland, for example, the French Revolution stimulated rebellion against English rule. Lord Edward Fitzgerald and Wolfe Tone led the United Irishmen in seeking independence. Fitzgerald, a veteran of the American Revolution, a member of the Irish parliament, and a twenty-first-generation member of the Catholic nobility, and Tone, a Protestant radical pamphleteer, visited France to observe the revolution and seek aid. Fitzgerald was so moved that he renounced his ancient title. Their efforts coincided with a revolt of the Irish peasantry. The ironic result of this reveals the complexity of the debate over the French Revolution: Devout Irish Catholic peasants ignored the attitude of the papacy and lit candles in prayer for the success of the French, who had attacked the church but who might also attack the English.

The Legislative Assembly and the Wars of the Revolution

Elections for the Legislative Assembly took place in the aftermath of the flight to Varennes and the promulgation of *Caritas* and the Brunswick Manifesto. The new assembly of 745 deputies left a permanent mark on political discourse as a coincidence of its seating arrangement in a semicircular amphitheatre. As a speaker faced the assembled deputies, conservative members who defended the king sat on the right side. This group, led by members of the Feuillant Club, became the Right. On the left wing sat the radical members from the Jacobin and Cordeliers clubs. Less militant revolutionaries, who later became known as the Girondins (because many came from the region of the Gironde), sat in the middle. Thus was born the political vocabulary of "left," "right," and "center."

International tension distracted the Legislative Assembly from further reform. Instead, the assembly adopted legislation against the émigrés, branding those who did not return as conspirators. In February 1792 the state seized their property. Similar decrees against nonjuring priests followed in November 1792. Such legislation worsened French relations with the Austro-Prussian alliance. In March 1792 a belligerent, counter-revolutionary Francis II had succeeded to the Hapsburg throne. By this time, the Girondins, whose foreign policy was more radical than their revolutionary aims, dominated the French assembly. They argued that war with the counterrevolutionaries would rally the French to defend the revolution, test the sympathies of Louis XVI, and export the revolution to other peoples. The leading Girondist, Jacques Brissot, said simply: "War is a

blessing to the nation." Francis II and Brissot had led their countries to war by April 1792.

A Prussian army invaded eastern France in August 1792 and won several victories, but the course of the war shifted in September when a French army under General Charles Dumouriez met the Prussians near the town of Valmy and forced the invaders to withdraw. In the words of the German poet Johann von Goethe, the battle of Valmy meant that "here and today begins a new age in the history of the world." This was poetic exaggeration, but it made a point: The allies would not quickly crush the French Revolution. A few weeks later, Dumouriez and an army of forty-five thousand underscored that point by marching into Hapsburg lands on France's northern border (today's Belgium) and winning a decisive victory at the town of Jemappes.

The War of 1792 grew into the War of the First Coalition (1793–95) when Britain, Spain, and Russia joined the alliance against the revolution, which had become passionately antimonarchical. Though this seemed like one of the most unevenly matched wars in history, the French not only survived it, but they also occupied the lowlands, the German Rhineland, and Northern Italy. They were able to do so because the revolution, among its other accomplishments, transformed the nature of modern warfare.

France had a larger population than most of her rivals, and in the early years of the revolution high unemployment made recruitment easy. The army grew from 180,000 men in 1789 to 650,000 in 1793. Then in August 1793 the assembly decreed universal military conscription (the *levée en masse*), placing the entire nation "in permanent requisition for army service." France soon had an unprecedented one million men in uniform. A conscript army of this size could not function according to the time-honored rules of European warfare. Though armed with the proceeds of revolutionary confiscations, it could feed itself only by living off the lands it conquered. Moreover, tactics had to be revised because intensive training had become impossible. Under reforms adopted by "the organizer of victory," Lazare Carnot, the French infantry advanced in deep columns instead of the traditional line, taking advantage of its superior numbers and revolutionary enthusiasm to overwhelm more disciplined enemies.

The new tactics proved successful, but France's European enemies faced other problems as well. For example, the Austrian and Prussian armies had long supply lines, whereas the French were fighting closer to home. Then there was the Polish question. Though

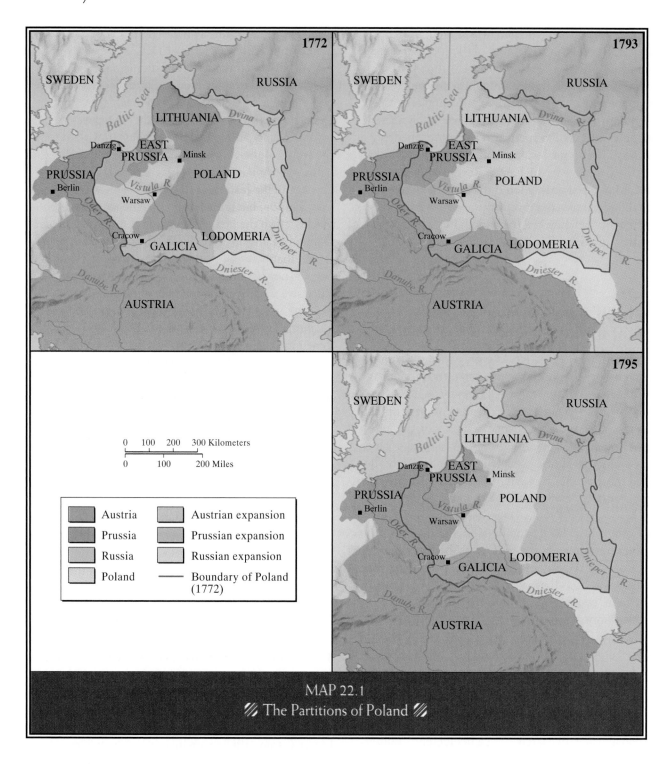

MAP 22.1
The Partitions of Poland

Catherine the Great opposed the French Revolution, she was more interested in annexing parts of neighboring Poland. This forced the Austrians and the Prussians to hold large forces on their own Polish borders, and it soon led to the second and third partitions of Poland in 1793 and 1795, respectively (see map 22.1). By the time the eastern powers had seized the last fragments of Poland, the armies of the French Revolution had won much of western Europe.

The First Republic: The Convention

The War of 1792 changed the revolution and led to the abolition of the monarchy and the creation of a republic. Once again, the Parisian crowd took the initiative. Austro-Prussian threats on Louis XVI's behalf inspired demonstrations against the king, including an attack on the Tuileries Palace. The Legislative Assembly then suspended Louis's remaining powers and reenacted all legislation he had vetoed. Then, in "the revolution of August 10th" the assembly decided to create a new legislature. It would be called the Convention in honor of the Constitutional Convention recently held in America. Representatives to the Convention would be elected by universal manhood suffrage, and they would write a more democratic constitution. Among its final acts, the Legislative Assembly moved Louis XVI to a royal prison and urged the Convention to abolish the monarchy.

The late summer of 1792 also saw ominous hints of revolutionary authoritarianism. The assembly sent commissioners into provincial France hoping to rally support, but their powers often created opposition. Then the assembly required a loyalty oath of all government employees, and it gave those who refused two weeks to leave the country. Other laws permitted searches of homes for arms and counterrevolutionary suspects. The attack on the Catholic Church also continued. All surviving Catholic associations (such as teaching orders) were abolished, religious processions and public ceremonies were prohibited, and divorce was legalized.

This same period witnessed one of the worst atrocities of mob violence, known as the September Massacres. The allied invasion, the implications of the Brunswick Manifesto, and the defection of people such as Lafayette (seen as proof of widespread treason) created fears of a conspiracy linking the internal and external enemies of the revolution. In the resultant panic, mobs stormed the prisons, apparently hunting for counterrevolutionaries. It was like the great fear of 1789, but this time the target was suspected enemies rather than châteaux. There were sixty-five lynchings around France. In Paris, the result was a massacre. During the first week the government did nothing for five days while the mobs slaughtered eleven hundred inmates, three-fourths of whom were nonpolitical prisoners such as common criminals and prostitutes.

Elections for the Convention thus took place in volatile circumstances. The 749 new deputies were chiefly lawyers (47.7 percent); fifty-five were priests and several others were former aristocrats, including Louis's revolutionary cousin, the former duke of Orléans, now called Philippe Egalité (see table 22.1). The deputies were young—two-thirds were under age forty-four. No faction held a majority, but universal suffrage and the war produced a radical body. Jacobins and their allies, called *Montagnards* (mountain dwellers) because they sat in the upper levels, accounted for 40 percent of the seats; their ranks included a Parisian delegation led

by such radicals as Danton, Marat, and Robespierre. The Girondins and their allies, led by Brissot and Roland, fell to less than 25 percent. The first year of the Convention was a struggle for predominance between these two factions, and the Jacobins won.

The Convention proclaimed a new order during its first week. Deputies voted unanimously to abolish the monarchy and create a republic. A committee began work on a new constitution, to be submitted to the people for ratification. When the Convention later invented a new calendar, this week in September would begin the new year, and September 1792 started Year I of the republican era.

The success of republican armies in 1792–93 meant that the greatest issue before the Convention became the fate of Louis XVI. A committee recommended that he be tried for treason, based upon his secret contacts with the governments that had invaded France. The trial of the king before the Convention began in December. Few doubted his guilt, revealed by his secret correspondence, and the deputies convicted him by a vote of 683–0. The debate over his sentence, however, caused bitter divisions. Jacobins advocated the normal death penalty. Passionate speakers insisted that "[k]ings are in the moral order what monsters are in the natural." Many leaders of the revolution, such as the abbé Sieyès, favored execution; even the king's cousin voted with the regicides. Louis XVI was condemned by a vote of 387–334 and beheaded on the guillotine in January 1793 (see illustration 22.6). The break with the Old Regime, the war with monarchical Europe, and the battle against internal counterrevolution no longer allowed compromises.

War consequently dominated the life of the Convention (1792–95). The deputies still aspired to reform society. Their noteworthy laws promised primary education (May 1793) and secondary education (February 1795), envisioning schools open to all citizens. Robespierre, who had long championed the rights of minorities, scored his greatest triumph with the abolition of slavery in French colonies (February 1794), pushing the republic far ahead of Britain or the United States (see document 22.5). The Convention's constitution, adopted in June 1793 and known as the Constitution of the Year I, summarized much of this egalitarian idealism. It began with an expanded version of the Declaration of the Rights of Man; it stated, "The aim of society is the common welfare." That led to a constitutional assertion (Article Twenty-one) of the welfare state: "Every French citizen has a right to existence. . . . Public assistance is a sacred debt . . . Society owes subsistence to its unfortunate citizens, either in providing work for

Illustration 22.6

///// **The Execution of Louis XVI.** The French republic, proclaimed in 1792, convicted the former Louis XVI of treason for the crime of plotting with the foreign powers that had invaded France. He was executed in January 1793 in a large public square, located at the end of the former royal gardens. In this illustration the crowd is shown the head of the king. The square where the guillotine stood, previously known as "Place Louis XV" and renamed "Place de la Revolution," is today known by the peacemaking name of "Place de la Concorde."

them, or in assuring the means of existence for those who are unable to work." Other articles were similarly innovative. One provided for easy amendment of the constitution ("One generation cannot subject future generations to its law."), and another ended tax exemptions for the rich ("No citizen is exempt from the honorable obligation to contribute to the public expenses.").

◆

Civil War and the Reign of Terror

Whatever the intentions and accomplishments of the Convention, it is chiefly remembered for one of the most horrifying periods of modern history, the Reign of Terror (1793–94), when thousands of people were publicly executed. At the same time, a bloody civil war took tens of thousands of lives. The central issue in both tragedies was whether the revolution or the counterrevolution would prevail.

The crisis began with the war against the European coalition. In early 1793 the Austrians defeated the

armies of General Dumouriez in the Austrian Netherlands and moved toward the French frontier. While the French braced themselves for an invasion, Dumouriez stunned them by defecting to the allies, making military catastrophe seem imminent. In addition to the Austrians on the northern frontier, Prussians were besieging French forts in the east, Italian troops were invading from the southeast, the Spanish army had crossed the southern border, and the English navy was threatening several ports. In Paris, many reasonable people agreed that the war effort required desperate measures.

The Convention's efforts to defend France, however, enlarged the problem. Plans to draft 300,000 men produced antidraft riots across France, chiefly in the west. This, plus continuing food shortages, the execution of the king, and the dechristianization of France, created opposition to the republic. By March 1793 peasant rebels in the Atlantic region of the Vendée (see table 22.1) had won several battles against the government. The Convention soon had to take units of the regular army from the frontier to combat the Vendéens,

◆ DOCUMENT 22.5 ◆

Robespierre: Equality for Minorities

The Rights of Jews (1791)

How could one . . . accuse the Jews of persecutions of which they themselves have been the victims in different countries? On the contrary, those are national crimes which we should expiate by restoring to them the imprescriptible rights of man of which no human power could deprive them. . . . Restore them to happiness, to the *Patrie*, to virtue by giving back to them the dignity of men and of citizens. Let us remember that it can never be politic, whatever one may say, to condemn a large group of men living in our midst to degradation and oppression. How could the interests of society be grounded upon the violation of the eternal principles of justice and reason which are the very basis of all human society?

The Rights of African Blacks in the Colonies (1791)

But what then, especially in the colonies, are the civil rights left to [African blacks] without political rights? What is a man deprived of the rights of an active citizen in colonies under the domination of whites? He is a man who cannot take part in any way in political deliberations, who cannot influence, either directly or indirectly, the most moving, the most sacred interests of the society of which he is a member. He is a man who is governed by magistrates whose selection he cannot determine in any way. . . . He is a degraded being whose fate is left to caprice, to passions, to the interests of a higher caste.

Illustration 22.7

Toussaint Louverture. Pierre Toussaint Louverture (c. 1743–1803), the son of African slaves, led the greatest slave rebellion in modern history. His insurrection (1791–93) won freedom for Haitian slaves and led to the creation of the first black republic. Although Toussaint joined with French revolutionary forces in fighting the British, Napoleon sought to restore slavery in Haiti. A French army captured Toussaint and brought him to France, where he died in prison.

who now called themselves the Royal Catholic Army. Resistance to the Convention spread quickly, particularly to cities that resented the centralized control of Paris. In May 1793 moderates in Lyons overthrew the Jacobin municipal government. Their federalist revolt soon reached Marseilles and Toulon, and by the summer of 1793 the federalists were as great a problem as the Royal Catholic Army. When the new government of Lyons executed the deposed Jacobin mayor, the Convention sent an army to besiege the city. In August the counterrevolutionaries at Toulon turned their port over to the British.

Ironically, the republic also faced an uprising from people who felt that the revolution had not yet gone far enough. The French colony of Saint Domingue (today Haiti) faced a slave rebellion supported by the English and the Spanish. This uprising produced one of the greatest black heroes of the resistance to slavery, François Toussaint, known as Pierre Toussaint Louverture (see illustration 22.7). Toussaint was an educated ex-slave who had risen to the powerful position of steward on a large plantation before joining the rebellion. His abilities were so highly regarded that when the Convention abolished slavery (February 1794), the deputies offered Toussaint the rank of general to join them; he accepted because the British and the Spanish kept slavery.

The context of the Reign of Terror, therefore, was a desperate fight to save the republic and the revolution. The men of the Convention, who had executed Louis XVI, were also fighting for their lives, and they chose harsh measures. The revolution had already turned toward authoritarianism under the Legislative Assembly. The Convention went much further, reducing newly won liberties to a Jacobin dictatorship. Enactment of the constitution was postponed and severe laws adopted (see document 22.6). Advocacy of a monarchical restoration and economic crimes such as hoarding were made capital crimes, to be tried before a special Revolutionary Tribunal. The freedom of the press to criticize the revolution was curtailed. A Law of Suspects expanded police powers, allowing the arrest of anyone "who by their conduct, their connections, their remarks, or their writings show themselves the partisans of tyranny or . . . the enemies of liberty." And a twelve-person executive committee with ill-defined powers, called the Committee of Public Safety, was created.

The Committee of Public Safety defended the revolution ferociously. In June 1793 the Convention was purged of moderate deputies, chiefly Girondins. A Reign of Terror, directed against spies, traitors, counter-revolutionaries, profiteers, hoarders, and corrupt officials had begun. Leaders of the Convention spoke with extraordinary candor. Danton called for them to "drink the blood of the enemies of humanity." Louis Saint-Just, an uncompromising twenty-six-year-old terrorist, was even more chilling: "Punish not only traitors, but even the indifferent." Maximilien Robespierre soon dominated the Committee of Public Safety (see document 22.7). The puritanical provincial lawyer who had built his career as an opponent of capital punishment and a defender of human rights led a terror that he defined as "nothing but prompt, severe, inflexible justice." The instrument of this severe justice was the guillotine, a machine for human decapitation previously used in other countries. The guillotine became a gruesome symbol of the terror, crudely called "the republican razor" or "the widow" (because it made so many). It had been introduced, however, by a physician, Dr. Joseph Guillotin, as a humanitarian form of swift execution, in contrast to the horrible tortures employed by the Old Regime such as being broken on the wheel, drawn and quartered, or torn with pincers.

The Reign of Terror lasted for thirteen months, from June 1793 until July 1794. During those months,

◈ DOCUMENT 22.6 ◈

Legislating a Reign of Terror, 1793

Press Law (March 1793)

1. Whoever shall be convicted of having composed or printed works or writings which incite to the dissolution of the national representation, the reestablishment of monarchy, or any other power which constitutes an attack upon the sovereignty of the people shall be . . . punished with death.

2. The vendors, distributors, and hawkers of these works or writings shall be condemned to an imprisonment which shall not exceed three months, if they declare the authors, printers, or other persons from whom they have obtained them; if they refuse[,] . . . two years in prison.

The Law of Suspects (September 1793)

1. Immediately after the publication of the present decree, all the suspect persons who are in the territory of the republic and who are still at liberty shall be placed under arrest.

2. These are accounted suspect persons: (i) those who by their conduct, their connections, their remarks, or their writings show themselves the partisans of tyranny or federalism and the enemies of liberty; (ii) those who cannot . . . justify their means of existence. . . . (iv) Public functionaries suspended or removed from their functions by the National Convention. . . . (v) Those of the former nobles . . . who have not constantly manifested their attachment to the revolution; (vi) those who have emigrated from France.

Law on Dangerous Priests (October 1793)

1. Priests subject to deportation and taken with arms in their hands[,] . . . [t]hose discovered in possession of permits or passports delivered by French émigré leaders[,] . . . [a]nd those provided with any counter-revolutionary symbols, shall be delivered within twenty-four hours to the executioner of condemned criminals and put to death.

. . .

12. Ecclesiastics who have taken the oath [of the Civil Constitution], as well as that of liberty and equality, . . . and shall be denounced [for violating the oath] shall be embarked without delay and transferred to the east coast of Africa. . . .

18. Every citizen is required to denounce the ecclesiastic whom he shall know to be subject to deportation.

◆ DOCUMENT 22.7 ◆

Robespierre: The Revolution and Its Ideals, 1794

It is time to define clearly the goal of the Revolution and the end which we wish to reach. . . . What is the goal toward which we strive? The peaceful enjoyment of liberty and equality . . .

We wish an order of things where all the base and cruel passions are chained, all generous and beneficent passions aroused by the laws . . . where distinctions are born only of equality itself; where the citizen is obedient to the magistrate, the magistrate to the people, and the people to justice; where the country assures the well-being of each individual . . . [and] commerce [is] the source of public wealth and not just of the monstrous opulence of a few families. . . .

What kind of government can realize these wonders? Only a democratic or republican government: these two words are synonymous, in spite of the abuses of popular usage. . . . Democracy is not a state where the people, in a continual assembly, settles by itself all public affairs. . . . Democracy is a state where the sovereign people, guided by laws which are its work, does itself all which it can do well, and through delegates all which it cannot do itself. . . .

[W]hat is the fundamental principle of democratic or popular government. . . ? It is virtue; I speak of the public virtue which produced so many marvels in Greece and Rome, and which ought to produce even more astonishing ones in republican France; of that virtue which is nothing else but love of the country and its laws. . . .

If the force of popular government in peace is virtue, that of popular government in revolution is both *virtue and terror*; virtue, without which terror is deadly; terror, without which virtue is powerless. Terror is nothing but prompt, severe, inflexible justice; it is then an emanation of virtue.

---

tribunals around France ordered an estimated fourteen thousand to seventeen thousand executions; the most famous, the Revolutionary Tribunal of Paris, accounted for more than twenty-seven hundred (see table 22.2). The overwhelming majority of the executions (71 percent) were in regions of civil war, especially the Vendée; of those, 75 percent were rebels caught with weapons in their hands. Despite stereotypes in popular literature, most of the people executed were workers (31 percent) and peasants (28 percent), not aristocrats (8 percent) or priests (7 percent). The revolutionary tribunals acquitted many people. The tribunal at Marseilles, for example, acquitted more than 50 percent of the accused and sentenced 31 percent to death. Four tribunals in southeastern France had total executions of five people. The Parisian tribunal sent many famous figures to the guillotine: Members of the royal family (such as the duke of Orléans), leaders of the Old Regime (Malesherbes), noted scholars (the distinguished chemist Antoine Lavoisier), leading Girondins (Brissot), and feminists (Olympe de Gouges) all died there. Some, such as Condorcet, escaped that fate only by committing suicide.

The civil war was especially bloody. Lyons was conquered, with ruthless reprisals, in October 1793; more than sixteen hundred people were executed. The Vendéen counterrevolution dragged on for years with enormous casualties and mass executions of rebels. One ferocious representative of the revolution in the Vendée—Jean-Baptiste Carrier—drowned prisoners in the Loire River by the hundreds, proclaiming, "We shall turn France into a cemetery rather than fail in her regeneration." A minimum of eighty thousand Vendéens died; some estimates for the civil war put the dead at more than 200,000. (By contrast, total war-related deaths during the American Revolution were fewer than ten thousand; in the American Civil War, more than 600,000.)

◆

The Thermidorean Reaction and the Directory, 1794–99

The Reign of Terror reached its peak in December 1793–January 1794, when 49 percent of the executions (mostly in the west) occurred (see illustration 22.8). In Paris, however, the Jacobin dictatorship accelerated the terror in June and July 1794, accounting for 57 percent of the executions there. Like the god Saturn in classical mythology, the revolution consumed its own children; even Danton was executed. Revulsion and fear then

◆ TABLE 22.2 ◆
The Reign of Terror, 1793–94

Executions by the Paris Revolutionary Tribunal

Total executions in France

Class category	Number	Percentage	Class category	Number	Percentage
Nobles	533	19.4	Nobles	1,156	8.2
Clergy	240	8.7	(Old	878	6.2)
Middle class	1,443	52.6	(Robe	278	2.0)
(Upper	903	32.9)	Clergy	920	6.5
(Lower	540	19.7)	Middle class	3,452	24.6
Workers	478	17.4	(Upper	1,964	14.0)
Unknown	53	1.9	(Lower	1,488	10.6)
Total	2,747		Workers	4,389	31.2
			Peasants	3,961	28.1
			Unknown	200	1.4
			Total	14,078	

Crimes leading to capital sentences, 1793–74

Sentences of the Marseilles Tribunal, 1794

Crime	Number	Percentage	Sentence	Number	Percentage
Sedition	10,456	72.1	Acquitted and freed	461	50.4
Counterrevolutionary opinion	1,302	9.0	Held for further investigation	97	10.6
Conspiracy	703	4.8	Held for precaution until peace	44	4.8
Espionage	457	3.2			
Federalism	427	2.9			
Refractory clergy	293	2.0	Sentenced to death	282	30.9
Emigration	212	1.5	Sentenced to prison	28	3.1
Corruption	104	0.7	Sentenced to deportation	1	0.1
Treason	96	0.7			
Counterfeiting	58	0.4	Held as prisoner of war	1	0.1
Other	397	2.7			
Total	14,505		Total	914	

Source: Donald Greer, *The Incidence of the Terror during the French Revolution: A Statistical Interpretation* (Cambridge, Mass.: Harvard University Press, 1935), p. 164; Colin Jones, ed., *The Longman Companion to the French Revolution* (London: Longman, 1988), p. 120; and William Scott, *Terror and Repression in Revolutionary Marseilles* (New York, N.Y.: Macmillan, 1973), p. 147.

produced a conspiracy against Robespierre. The Convention ended the terror by arresting him in what is called the Thermidorean reaction (named for the date in the republican calendar). Robespierre attempted suicide, but he, Saint-Just, and other leading Jacobins went to the guillotine.

During 1794–95, the Convention labored to remove the more extreme aspects of the Jacobin dictatorship, starting with the abolition of the Jacobin clubs.

The tribunals were closed and prisoners were released. The Law of Suspects was repealed and new judicial guarantees instituted. The Convention recalled deputies who had been purged. To placate federalists, the powers of the central government were reduced. An amnesty was offered to all rebels who laid down their arms. Freedom of religion was gradually restored, with churches separated from state control. Following these efforts to restore order, the Convention wrote a new

Illustration 22.8

🖎 **The Reign of Terror.** During 1793–94, the Revolutionary Tribunal at Paris ordered the execution of 2,747 people, mostly from the middle class (not the aristocracy and the clergy). At its peak, this Reign of Terror took fourteen hundred lives in the summer of 1794. The cartoon speculates that guillotines would spring up everywhere, a monument would mark the burial of "all of France," and then Robespierre would execute the last Frenchman, the executioner.

constitution to keep it. The Constitution of the Year III (1795) was the third in the short history of the revolution. It, too, began with a declaration of rights, which was significantly renamed the Declaration of the Rights and Duties. Article One stated a right of security alongside liberty and equality.

France remained a republic with a broad suffrage including most (male) citizens, but it was now constituted with many safeguards, such as the separation of powers. A bicameral legislature, for example, included a lower house that introduced all legislation and an upper house with the power to block it. As a further safeguard, the upper house was a Council of Ancients, whose 250 members had to be at least forty years old—a reaction to the fact that in 1793 Robespierre had been thirty-five years old, Danton thirty-four, and Saint-Just twenty-six. The new government was called the Directory because the constitution also created an executive branch with that name. The Directory had five members, chosen by the legislature from among its own members and prohibited from succeeding themselves in office. The Convention bequeathed great difficulties to the Directory. It had won many victories in the war against monarchical Europe, signing peace treaties with Prussia, Holland, and Spain. It had beaten the Vendéen counterrevolutionaries, and it had ended the terror. Economic problems, however, remained; government ministers were given salaries measured in wheat because the currency was so unstable. Royalism was resurgent, and in some regions this had produced a "white (the symbol of royalism) terror" against former Jacobins. Simultaneously, however, new militants demanded further revolution. Gracchus Babeuf, a radical journalist, founded the Conspiracy of Equals in 1795, to restore the Constitution of the Year I and to create greater egalitarianism. Babeuf's manifesto, which later generations have seen as an important precursor of Communism, bluntly proclaimed, "In a true society, there should be neither rich nor poor."

The Directory preserved the moderate republic by using the army against royalists, executing extremists such as Babeuf, and repudiating much of the national debt. It became increasingly conservative when elections in 1797 returned only thirteen of the surviving 216 members of the Convention. The Directory was soon characterized by the return of individuals who had gone into hiding or fled the country. Talleyrand became foreign minister in July 1797; Sieyès became a director in 1799. The Directory thus attempted to stand in the political center, dreading both Jacobinism and royalism. It was a republic that distrusted republicanism, reflecting French exhaustion and apathy. This made it vulnerable to conspiracies, as Talleyrand realized when he attended a meeting of the directors and guards confiscated his cane as a potential weapon. "It appears to me," he said, "that your government is terribly afraid of being poked with a stick." He was not surprised when the Directory fell in a military coup d'état in 1799.

The Revolutionary Wars and the Rise of Napoleon

Napoleon Bonaparte was born the second son of a minor Italian noble on the island of Corsica. The family became French when Louis XV bought Corsica from the republic of Genoa, whose government had become exasperated with Corsican rebellion. Napoleon's father had accepted the French occupation, a French patent of nobility, and a position in the government of Corsica. This enabled him to send the nine-year-old Napoleon to the Royal Military Academy for sons of the aristocracy in 1778. The poor, skinny, provincial Bonaparte was unpopular, but he was a good student. His mathematic skills determined his future: The artillery needed officers who could calculate trajectories. He graduated two years early, in 1785, and became a lieutenant in the royal artillery.

Napoleon harnessed his high intelligence to hard work. "Work is my element," he later wrote in a diary. He proved this as a young officer by working eighteen hours per day, typically eating only one meal and sleeping four or five hours. He kept these habits as emperor; on the two nights before his victory at Austerlitz (1805), Bonaparte slept a total of three hours. This trait enabled him to issue more than eighty thousand written orders in his fifteen-year reign, an average of fifteen documents per day. Even "the love of a woman," he noted at age twenty-two, "is incompatible with one's life work."

Lieutenant Bonaparte was a political radical. He had read the philosophes and admired Rousseau. He had contempt for the church and hatred for kings: "There are few of them who have not merited dethronement," he wrote. When the revolution began, he joined the Jacobin club. His revolutionary politics and the emigration of royalist officers led to Napoleon's rapid promotion. Then, in 1793, Napoleon found himself in the right place at the right time. Returning from Corsica to the south of France shortly after the people of Toulon had turned their port over to the British, Napoleon was placed in command of the artillery. In three months, Napoleon had forced the British to withdraw. Toulon capitulated to the army of the republic, and Napoleon became a general at age twenty-five. The fall of Robespierre resulted in Napoleon's imprisonment for Jacobinism, but the republic needed successful generals and soon restored his rank. When royalist demonstrations in Paris threatened the Directory, General Bonaparte used his artillery, loaded with small balls (the size of grapes), on the crowd. By killing demonstrators with "a whiff of grapeshot," he preserved the government, won powerful friends, and received his choice of commands.

French armies were in a strong position in 1795. The lowland provinces of modern Belgium had been taken from the Austrians and annexed to France. The coalition had collapsed over the Polish question. A peace treaty with Prussia had given France the left bank of the Rhine River and recognized a French claim to Holland. The Dutch had been given their own republic, the first of several "sister republics" in western Europe created by French armies (see map 22.2). Spain had left the war against France, Britain had no troops on the continent, and Austria had been stalemated. Victory in the Vendée had freed French armies.

Napoleon decided to force the Austrians to accept peace by driving them from northern Italy. His victory at the battle of Arcola (November 1796), where the Austrians lost more than 40 percent of their army, did just that (see table 22.3). Within a few months, Napoleon had created two sister republics in Italy—the Ligurian republic (formerly Genoa) and the Cisalpine republic (Lombardy, Modena, and part of Venetia). He had also demonstrated the exceptional skills of leadership that made soldiers willing to fight for him (see document 22.8). Italian nationalists began to dream that Bonaparte was the hero who would liberate Italy and unify the small Italian states into a strong modern state. In October 1797 Francis I signed the Treaty of Campo-Formio, accepting French expansion and the sister republics. Other sister republics soon followed, in Switzerland (the Helvetian republic), central Italy (the Roman republic), and southern Italy (the Neapolitan, or Parthenopean republic).

Napoleon next sought a strategy to use against the British. He chose to challenge their global position by invading Egypt—a threat to British control of the Mediterranean and to British India. He arrived there in 1798 with an army of thirty-eight thousand and a corps of archeologists who helped found the study of Egyptology. A sweeping victory in the battle of the Pyramids gave him Cairo, but a British fleet commanded by Horatio Nelson destroyed the French fleet at the battle of Aboukir Bay. This cut Napoleon's supply lines and forced him to return to France.

When Napoleon Bonaparte returned to France in 1799, he was a national hero (see illustration), and he was dangerous. He combined aristocratic birth with a Jacobin youth. He had won great battles against foreign enemies and had saved the Directory from its roy-

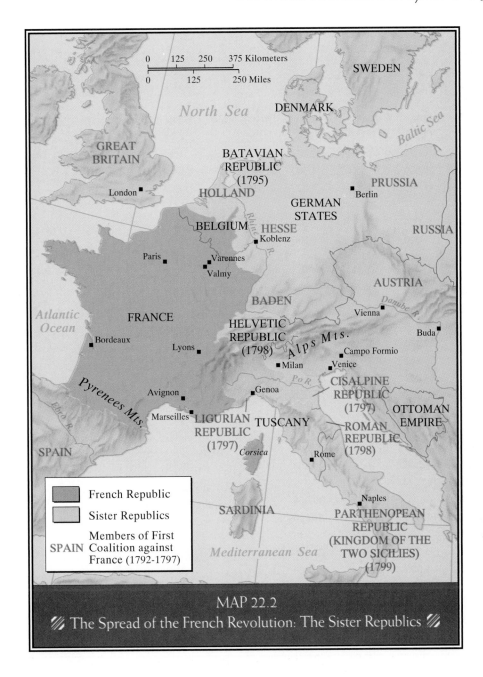

MAP 22.2
✎ The Spread of the French Revolution: The Sister Republics ✎

alist enemies. Now he delivered learned lectures on ancient Egypt and met with prominent scholars. Politicians soon had visions of the "man on horseback" saving France from the Directory, and Napoleon seized that opportunity. He overthrew the Directory in a military coup d'état in Brumaire (November) 1799. The coup had the support of several leaders of the Directory, notably Sieyès (the dominant director), Napoleon's brother Lucien (president of the legislature), and the unscrupulous minister of police, Joseph Fouché (a mathematics teacher who had been a Jacobin during the Reign of Terror and a leader of the Thermidorean reaction). Napoleon blithely announced that "the Revo-

lution is at an end," and within one month he had produced the Constitution of the Year VIII (1799), dissolving the republic.

France under Napoleon

The Constitution of 1799 created the Consulate, an authoritarian regime with some democratic elements. It put executive power in the hands of three consuls but added that "the decision of the First Consul (Napoleon) shall suffice." Legislative power was fragmented among

✠ TABLE 22.3 ✠
The Military Campaigns of Napoleon, 1796–1815

Decisive battle	States at war	Army size	Ratio of advantage	Losses	Percentage of army lost	Peace treaty resulting
Italian campaign						
Arcola	France	20,000	1.2:1	4,500	22.5	Campo Formio
(1796)	Austria	17,000		7,000	41.2	(1797)
Egyptian campaign						
Pyramids	France	25,000	1.2:1	300	1.2	
(1798)	Turks	21,000		5,000	23.8	
Italian campaign						
Marengo	France	28,000		7,000	25.0	Lunéville
(1800)	Austria	31,000	1.1:1	14,000	45.2	(1801)
War of Third Coalition						
Austerlitz	France	73,200		9,000	12.3	Pressburg
(1805)	Austria	85,400	1.2:1	27,000	31.6	(1805)
Jena	France	96,000	1.8:1	5,000	5.2	
(1806)	Prussia	53,000		25,000	47.2	
Friedland	France	80,000	1.3:1	8,000	10.0	Tilsit
(1807)	Russia	60,000		20,000	33.3	(1807)
Austrian campaign						
Wagram	France	170,000	1.2:1	32,000	18.8	Schönbrunn
(1809)	Austria	146,000		40,000	27.4	(1809)
Russian campaign						
Borodino	France	133,000	1.1:1	30,000	22.6	
(1812)	Russia	120,000		44,000	36.7	
Battle of the Nations						
Leipzig	France	195,000		73,000	37.4	Paris
(1813)	Allies	365,000	1.9:1	54,000	14.8	(1814)
The 100 days						
Waterloo	France	72,000		32,000	44.4	Second Paris
(1815)	Allies	120,000	1.7:1	22,000	18.3	(1815)

many bodies: one to draft bills, a separate body to debate them, another to vote on them, and a fourth to rule on the constitutionality of these acts. All were elected by universal manhood suffrage, but it was diluted by three stages of indirect voting: voters chose representatives, who chose representatives, who chose a list of representatives from which the first consul named the legislators. Even with such restrictions, Napoleon permitted only "a single party and a single will."

The nearest approach to popular sovereignty in Napoleonic government was the plebiscite. Some legislation, such as the constitution itself, was submitted to a direct vote of adult men. A plebiscite of February 1800 ratified the Constitution of 1799 by a reported vote of three million to fifteen hundred. Electoral fraud, directed by Lucien Bonaparte as minister of the interior, doubled the favorable vote and the actual vote fell far below the turnout in 1793; in Paris only 23 percent voted. It is also noteworthy that Napoleon enforced the constitution before holding the plebiscite.

Napoleon's reign, from 1799 to 1814, mixed such techniques with a refined Old Regime despotism and revolutionary reformism. The trend of his regime, however, was unmistakably toward dictatorship. "Liberty," he said, "is a need felt by a small class of people. . . .

◈ DOCUMENT 22.8 ◈

Napoleon: Proclamations to His Soliders, 1796

Proclamation to the Army of Italy, March 1796

Soldiers, you are naked, ill fed! The government owes you much; it can give you nothing. Your patience, and the courage you show in the midst of these rocky mountains, are admirable; but they win you no glory. You bask in no fame. I seek to lead you into the most fertile plains in the world. Rich provinces, great cities will be in your power. There you will find honor, glory, and riches. Soldiers of Italy, are you lacking in courage. . . ?

Proclamation to the Army of Italy, April 1796

Soldiers! In the last two weeks you have won six victories, you have captured the banners of twenty-one enemy armies, fifty pieces of artillery, several fortifications, you have conquered the richest part of Piedmont, and you have taken 15,000 prisoners while killing or wounding more than 10,000 men.

Until now you have fought for sterile rocks, made famous by your efforts but worth little to your *Patrie* [homeland]. . . . Lacking everything, you have supplied everything. You won battles without cannon, you crossed rivers without bridges, you made forced marches without shoes, you made camp without brandy and sometimes without bread. Soldiers of liberty! Only republican phalanxes could have endured what you have endured. Soldiers, we owe you our thanks! The *Patrie* will owe its prosperity to your efforts. . . .

The two armies which recently boldly attacked you are now fleeing from you in terror: wicked men who laughed at your misery . . . are now confounded and trembling.

But, soldiers you have done nothing compared to what remains to be done. . . . You still have great battles to fight, cities to capture, rivers to cross. Is there anyone among you whose courage is flagging? . . . No? All of you wish to return to your villages, filled with pride, able to say, "I was with the victorious Army of Italy."

. . . [M]y friends, I promise you victory. But there is one condition which you must swear to honor: to respect the people whom you liberate. . . . Otherwise you would not be the liberators of the people; you would be their scourge. . . .

People of Italy! The French army comes to break your chains. The French people is the friend of all peoples. . . . [Y]our property, your religion, your customs will be respected. We are fighting as generous enemies, and we only want to crush the tyrants who enslave you.

[T]herefore, it may be repressed with impunity." He produced his second constitution in 1802, awarding himself the consulate for life. Two years later, his third constitution (France's sixth of the revolutionary era) created an hereditary empire and reduced the legislative bodies to mere ornaments. He celebrated with an elaborate coronation, crowning himself at Notre Dame Cathedral in December 1804.

Napoleon was not a simple counterrevolutionary, but he used his autocratic powers to undo some of the works of the French Revolution. He abolished divorce to preserve the traditional family. He legalized slavery again, hoping to boost the economy of Caribbean colonies. Denouncing the "pretensions of gilded Africans," he imprisoned Toussaint Louverture, who died in a French jail in 1803, shortly before Haiti became the first black republic. And Bonaparte reestablished nobility as an honor for his generals and civil servants. Whereas Louis XVI had named approximately ten nobles per year, Napoleon averaged one a day.

Despotism was evident from the beginning of Napoleon's rule. In January 1800 he closed sixty of the seventy-three newspapers in France, and he soon shut others. "Three hostile newspapers," Napoleon told his staff, "are more to be feared than a thousand bayonets." Next he added censorship of the theatres. Then he took control of all printing, requiring the submission of all manuscripts to the government for prior censorship. Bonapartist thought control even reached into the mails. He instructed postmasters to open letters and take notes for him. Fouché's police enforced such regulations. Although he could sometimes be lenient, Napoleon usually dealt harshly with his opponents. He ended Vendéen resistance by ordering an army "to burn down two or three large villages as a salutary example." He jailed political prisoners, including many former Jacobin colleagues, without a trial. A plot against him in 1804 led him to execute a dozen people, including a member of the royal family, the duke d'Enghien, whom Napoleon seized by invading a neutral country.

Napoleon never silenced all of his critics. A remarkable example of defiance was given by Germaine de Staël, Necker's brilliant daughter, who called Napoleon "Robespierre on horseback." She organized a Parisian salon, with participants ranging from royalists to Jacobins, as a center of criticism. Napoleon was a misogynist who referred to women as "machines for making babies," but Madame de Staël fascinated him, and he merely banished her from Paris. She continued to insist that defending freedom in France was more important than winning foreign wars.

A balanced portrait of Napoleon must also see an enlightened side to his despotism. He tried to reunite France by welcoming home émigrés willing to accept his regime, and many aristocrats accepted the amnesty of 1802 to serve Napoleon. A similar compromise reestablished the Catholic Church. Napoleon had no religious faith himself, and his motive was purely pragmatic. He deposed one pope in 1798 and imprisoned another in 1809. He felt, however, that "[r]eligion is excellent stuff for keeping the common people quiet." This led him to negotiate the Concordat of 1801 with Pope Pius VII, recognizing Catholicism as "the religion of the vast majority of French citizens" and permitting it to be "freely practised." This treaty cost the Vatican many concessions. Pius VII accepted the confiscation of church lands, agreed that priests would be salaried employees of the state, permitted Napoleon to name French bishops, and even allowed a clerical "oath of fidelity" to the government.

In reestablishing Catholicism, Napoleon preserved the revolutionary protection of religious minorities. Protestants received their own state charter in 1802. Jews obtained new guarantees of their emancipation, although this did not prevent outbreaks of anti-Semitism in eastern France. Napoleon's attitudes toward Jews were sometimes suspect, but his defense of Jewish emancipation made France a center of nineteenth-century toleration. The Jewish population of Paris, which had been fewer than five hundred in 1789, reached three thousand in 1806, a tribute to his comparative toleration. And Napoleon carried Jewish emancipation into regions that his armies conquered, especially in western Germany.

Napoleon even enhanced some ideas of the revolutionary era. He completed a Jacobin project for the codification of French laws, producing the Civil Code (known as the Napoleonic Code) of 1804, then codes of commercial law (1807) and penal law (1810). The codes eliminated scores of antiquated laws, perpetuated much revolutionary legislation, and standardized the laws. Among the most far-reaching elements of the codes were detailed laws of private property, which protected people who had acquired property during the revolution. The Napoleonic Code was also bluntly paternalistic, explicitly treating women as subordinates of men and blocking their emancipation throughout the nineteenth century.

The Napoleonic Code, carried abroad by French armies, became the most influential modern legal system (see map 22.3). Poland, Belgium, and some of the west German states kept it after the fall of Napoleon. Romania, Italy, and Spain later adopted substantial parts of it; in the Netherlands, Portugal, and Egypt, reformers were greatly influenced by it. The Napoleonic Code shaped legal systems as far away as Louisiana, Haiti, and Quebec, and it served as the legal model throughout South America.

Napoleon also revived the revolutionary effort to expand education. A national school system existed, but only on paper. Napoleon considered the schools, like the churches and the law, to be instruments of social stability. "My principle aim," he said, "is to secure the means for directing political and moral opinion." Thus he provided the widest educational opportunity in the world, but his schools operated with "military discipline."

Napoleon's greatest accomplishment as the heir of the French Revolution was to sustain and expand a democratic meritocracy, often called "the career open to talent." In a world still characterized by corporate society, the Napoleonic Empire offered great opportunities for the able, whatever their social origin or religion. Bright students from poor backgrounds could rise to the top. No institution provided greater opportunities than his army, where soldiers could rise rapidly through the ranks despite humble origins. In one of Napoleon's favorite clichés, every soldier had a field marshal's baton in his napsack, and it was up to him to find it. His closest marshal, Joachim Murat, was the son of an innkeeper. In an act that would have been unthinkable under the monarchy, Murat married Napoleon's sister Caroline and became king of Naples. Other marshals were born the sons of a cooper, a miller, a mason, and a stableboy; they considered Napoleon the personification of revolutionary ideals.

The Napoleonic Wars

Napoleon devoted most of his time to war; he stayed in France for only one-third of the days in his reign. When he became First Consul in 1799, France was at

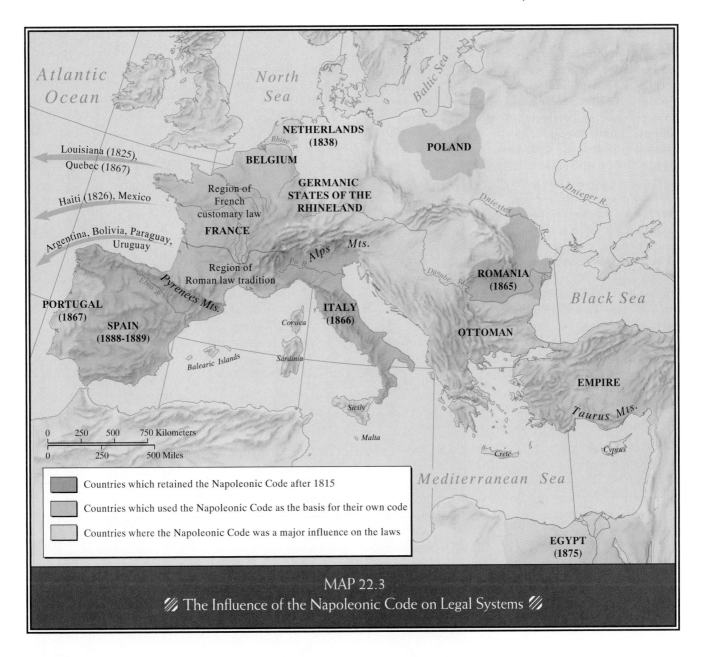

MAP 22.3

※ The Influence of the Napoleonic Code on Legal Systems ※

war with the remnants of the Second Coalition. France still relied on the numerical strength provided by the levée en masse, but battles were comparatively small. Napoleon's victory at Arcola, for example, had matched twenty thousand French soldiers against seventeen thousand Austrians. During the next fifteen years, Napoleon fought nearly permanent war against Europe. His armies occupied Madrid, Rome, Vienna, Berlin, and Moscow. This required the standing conscription of young Frenchmen, usually for five years. By 1814 he had drafted 2.6 million men and led more than one million of them to their death (see illustration 22.9).

These huge numbers help to explain Napoleon's victories (see table 22.3). He had won his early battles

with armies of twenty thousand to thirty thousand; even the revolutionary army at Valmy had numbered only fifty-nine thousand. By the time of the Third Coalition (1805–07), Napoleon often sent 100,000 men into a battle, and that number soon seemed small. Much of his success came from having the largest army, or from maneuvering until he obtained numerical superiority. When he had the advantage, Napoleon was ruthless. The Prussians learned this at the battle of Jena (1806): A French army of ninety-six thousand crushed a Prussian force of fifty-three thousand, then pursued them relentlessly. Napoleon lost 5.2 percent of his army while the Prussians lost 47.2 percent. When Napoleon lost such advantages, he began to lose bat-

Illustration 22.9

🟦 **The Napoleonic Wars.** The great neoclassical painter Jacques-Louis David (see illustration 21.3) became court painter to Napoleon and created several immense canvases glorifying his regime. None was greater propaganda than his "Napoleon Crossing the Alps" en route to his victory in Italy, following the path of earlier conquerers whose names are immortalized in Alpine stone. The heroic rider astride a fiery charger is far from the truth, however. Napoleon chose a cautious crossing of the Alps on the back of a sure-footed burro.

The white stallion remains, but little of the romantic heroism of Napoleon seen in Jacques-Louis David's painting survives in Ernest Meissonier's "The French Campaign, 1814." Here, a somber emperor leads an exhausted army that had been beaten repeatedly for two years.

tles. Numbers alone do not account for Napoleon's military reputation, however. His skillful use of artillery, especially concentrated artillery firing rapidly (versus the accepted wisdom of conserving ammunition), won some battles. His use of elite cavalry units as shock troops to attack infantry won others. But his military greatness was less a matter of brilliant strategies than inspired opportunism.

As warfare changed from formal engagements of small professional armies to the ruthlessness of mass armies (see table 22.3), other changes followed. In 1793 the Austrian army in the Netherlands had paid rent to Dutch farmers for permission to camp in their fields. Later, the retreating Austrians found themselves pushed against the Rhine River without sufficient money to pay for ferry service across the river; instead of seizing the ferries, the Austrians awaited the French and surrendered. In contrast, Napoleon encountered a different psychology of war when he invaded Russia in 1812. The Russians used a "scorched earth" strategy: They burnt the farms and fields of the Russian peasantry instead of leaving food supplies for the French.

By 1805 Napoleon faced a Third Coalition of Britain, Austria, and Russia. Concluding that an invasion of England was impractical, Napoleon marched his army from Boulogne into central Europe and won major victories over the Austrians at Ulm (October 1805) and combined Austro-Russian forces at Austerlitz (December 1805). Napoleon was so proud of his great victory at Austerlitz that he adopted all children of the French soldiers killed in that battle, promising that the government would support them, educate them, and find husbands for the daughters and jobs for the sons. He then pressed his troops on, and they defeated the Prussians, who had belatedly joined the coalition, at Jena (October 1806) and the retreating Russians at Friedland (June 1807). In less than two years of fighting, Napoleon had gained control of central Europe. The only setback to his plans had come at sea: In October 1805 Admiral Horatio Nelson had destroyed the French fleet near the Spanish coast off Cape Trafalgar, making an invasion of England impossible.

Napoleon exploited his victories to redraw the map of Europe (see map 22.4). He abolished the Holy Roman Empire, reducing Francis I to emperor of Austria. In 1806 he amalgamated sixteen states of western Germany into a puppet state called the Confederation of the Rhine. Others were merged to create the Kingdom of Westphalia, where Napoleon's brother Jerome became king. Holland was also made a kingdom and given to another brother, Louis Bonaparte. The terri-

tory that Prussia had seized in the second and third partitions of Poland was taken from her to form another client state, the grand duchy of Warsaw. Italy was divided into three regions: Northern Italy became the Kingdom of Italy, with Napoleon as the nominal king; central Italy was directly annexed to France; and southern Italy became the Kingdom of Naples, with Napoleon's brother-in-law, Murat, named king. Territory along the Adriatic Coast (previously governed by Venice) and the northern coast of Germany were also directly annexed to France. Spain was given to a third brother, Joseph Bonaparte.

By 1810 most of Europe was under Napoleon's control, with Portugal, Britain, Scandinavia, Russia, and most of the Balkans remaining free. Prussia and Austria retained their independence, but they faced numerous controls. Prussia, for example, was limited to an army of forty-two thousand men and was made to host a French garrison. Austria, after attempting a Fourth Coalition and suffering another defeat at Wagram in 1809, was bound to France by a marriage in 1810 between Napoleon and Francis's teenaged daughter, Maria Louisa. As an angry Russian aristocrat said in the opening sentence of Leo Tolstoy's *War and Peace*, the great cities of Europe such as "Genoa and Lucca are now just family estates of the Buonapartes."

Napoleon tried to fight Britain with economic warfare. His Berlin Decrees of 1806 ordered the cessation of all commerce and communication with Britain. This plan, known as the Continental System, failed because it required more cooperation than Napoleon could compel. The loss of easy access to inexpensive English manufactures caused some Europeans to defy the Continental System. When Czar Alexander I of Russia refused to cooperate, Napoleon decided to invade Russia. He did so despite unresolved difficulties in western Europe, where the Spanish resistance to Joseph Bonaparte had already created an independent Cortes (1810) and produced a liberal constitution (1812). The Spanish had received the support of a British army commanded by Sir Arthur Wellesley. Spanish and British armies were already pushing back the French in Wellesley's brilliant Peninsular Campaign, which would earn him the title of the duke of Wellington.

Napoleon's Grande Armée of 600,000 men nonetheless invaded Russia in June 1812 and won several initial battles. This included the bloodiest battle of the nineteenth century, at Borodino where forty-four thousand Russians were killed in a single day. (In contrast, fifty-five thousand Americans were killed in the decade of the Vietnam War.) Russian armies, however,

revolutionary National Assembly of 1789; J. Godechot, *The Taking of the Bastile, 14 July 1789* (1970); G. Rudé, *The Crowd in the French Revolution* (1959); D. Greer, *The Incidence of Emigration during the French Revolution* (1951); M. Sydenham, *The Girondins* (1960); M. Kennedy, *The Jacobin Clubs in the French Revolution*, 2 vols. (1982–88); C. J. Mitchell, *The French Legislative Assembly of 1791* (1988); D. Jordan, *The King's Trial* (1979); A. Patrick, *The Men of the First French Republic* (1972), which looks at the Convention; R. R. Palmer, *Twelve Who Ruled* (1941), which covers the Committee of Public Safety; J. Godechot, *The Counter-Revolution: Doctrine and Action, 1789–1804* (1972); and M. Lyons, *France under the Directory* (1975).

For women and the revolution, see J. Landes, *Women and the Public Sphere in the Age of the French Revolution* (1988); S. Melzer and L. Rabine, eds., *Rebel Daughters: Women and the French Revolution* (1992); O. Hufton, *Women and the Limits of Citizenship in the French Revolution* (1992); for religion and the revolution, see J. McManners, *The French Revolution and the Church* (1969) and T. Tackett, *Religion, Revolution, and Regional Culture in Eighteenth-Century France: The Ecclesiastical Oath of 1791* (1986). For the peasantry, see P. Jones, *The Peasantry in the French Revolution* (1988); C. Tilly, *The Vendée* (1967), covering the civil war in western France; and J. Markoff, *The Abolition of Feudalism* (1996). For urban workers, see A. Soboul,

The Sans-Culottes (1964) and R. Cobb, *The Police and the People* (1970). For prominent individuals, see N. Hampson, *The Life and Opinions of Maximilien Robespierre* (1974), N. Hampson, *Danton* (1978), R. B. Rose, *Gracchus Babeuf: The First Revolutionary Communist* (1978), and C. L. R. James, *The Black Jacobins: Toussaint L'Ouverture and the San Domingo Revolutoin* (1980). For the spread of the revolution, see T. C. W. Blanning, *Origins of the French Revolutionary Wars* (1986); R. R. Palmer, *The World of the French Revolution* (1971), for the "sister republics"; and M. Elliott, *Partners in Revolution: The United Irishmen and France* (1982)

For the Napoleonic era, see G. Lefebvre, *Napoleon* (1969), L. Bergeron, *France Under Napoleon* (1981), and M. Lyons, *Napoleon Bonaparte and the Legacy of the French Revolution* (1994). For the Napoleonic wars, see J. R. Elting, *Swords around a Throne: Napoleon's Grand Armée* (1988), O. Connelly, *Blundering to Glory: Napoleon's Military Campaigns* (1987), D. Chandler, *Napoleon's Marshals* (1987), and D. Chandler, *Waterloo and the Hundred Days* (1987). For Napoleonic Europe, see O. Connelly, *Napoleon's Satellite Kingdoms* (1965), G. H. Lovett, *Napoleon and the Birth of Modern Spain* (1965), and S. J. Woolf, *Napoleon and the Integration of Europe* (1991). For prominent individuals, see E. Longford, *Wellington*, 2 vols. (1969–72) and M. Gutwirth, *Madame de Staël, Novelist* (1978).

Europe in the Age of Industrialization, 1815–1914

CHAPTER 23

INDUSTRIALIZATION AND THE SOCIAL AND ECONOMIC STRUCTURE OF EUROPE

CHAPTER OUTLINE

Industrialization began in the late eighteenth century and by 1900 had dramatically transformed the economy and social structure of Europe. Chapter 23 looks at this process of industrialization. It begins with two demographic changes associated with industrialization: a population explosion and urbanization. This "vital revolution" was in turn the product of changes in European agriculture that allowed a larger population to be fed. After analyzing these changes, the chapter then focuses on the industrialization of Great Britain, often called the industrial revolution. It starts with handcraft manufacture and cottage industry, then explains the impact of the steam engine. This leads to a discussion of the most important elements of early industrialization: the iron and coal industries, textile manufacturing, and the railroads.

Economic changes of this magnitude transformed society, but their immediate impact has been the subject of controversy. After examining the positive and negative sides of life in the new urban world, the chapter focuses on the changing class structure of Europe with special attention to the new middle class and the urban working class. It then discusses the impact of industrialization on women, children, and the family. Analysis of these questions permits an introduction to what has been called the standard of living debate: Did the conditions of daily life improve or deteriorate during industrialization?

The chapter ends by tracing the spread of industrialization across Europe, stressing the "take-off period" of industrial growth during the mid-nineteenth century, followed by the "second industrial revolution" in which German industrial output began to match and even outstrip that of Great Britain.

The Population Explosion

One of the most important developments in modern European history was a dramatic increase in population during the eighteenth and nineteenth centuries. The population of Europe had been slowly rising for centuries, but severe checks, caused by poor diet and nutrition, epidemic disease, primitive medical care, warfare, and repressive government, had limited that growth. Great Britain offers a vivid illustration. After William the Conqueror won control of England in 1066, he ordered a survey of his new realm; the resultant Domesday Survey (1086) determined that England had a population of 3.5 million. A good estimate of England in 1750—no official census took place until 1801—is a population of 6.5 million, which meant an increase of three million people in seven hundred years, an average growth rate of less than 1 percent per decade.

In contrast to that history of slow population growth, what happened during the late eighteenth century and the nineteenth century must be called a population explosion. A continent inhabited by perhaps 110 million people in 1700 became a continent of 423 million people in 1900. This near quadrupling of Europe meant a growth rate of nearly 10 percent per decade, compared with the historic pattern of less than 1 percent. Britain, where the European population explosion began, provides the best illustration of this growth. Beginning in 1750, the British isles experienced three consecutive decades of 6 percent population growth, followed by stunning decennial increases of 9 percent, 11 percent, 14 percent, and 18 percent. The astonishing population boom meant that a country that had grown by three million people over seven hundred years then grew by eleven million people in one hundred years.

The British population explosion continued into the nineteenth century and became a widespread (although not universal) European phenomenon (see table 23.1). During the eighteenth century, population growth in most of the major states of Europe was approximately 35 percent to 40 percent—36 percent in the Austrian Empire, 37 percent across the Germanic states of central Europe, 39 percent in the Italian states, and 40 percent in Spain. France, the most populous and most powerful state of western Europe, experienced a slightly faster rate of growth (55 percent) but did not approach the remarkable 82 percent growth in Britain. In the nineteenth century, the rate of growth in Austria, Italy, and Spain increased to 70–85 percent, but the British rate of growth had soared to more than 150 percent, causing the population density to surpass one hundred inhabitants per square mile in large portions of Europe (see map 23.1). Only Germany and Russia—

where population growth was more than 200 percent—kept up with Britain. France, which pioneered modern birth control practices, did not experience such a dramatic population explosion, and the nineteenth-century growth rate there (45 percent) was lower than that of the eighteenth century (55 percent).

The beginning of this population explosion so shocked one English economist, the Reverend Thomas Malthus, that he wrote the most famous book about population ever published, *An Essay on the Principle of Population* (1798), warning about the dangers of this trend. Malthus argued that unchecked population growth tended to increase at a geometric rate (one, two, four, eight, sixteen, thirty-two), while the means of subsistence to support those people increased only at an arithmetic rate (one, two, three, four, five, six). The contrast between these two rates, known as the Malthusian principle, prompted the pessimistic conclusion that, without some preventive restraints on population increase, the future of humankind would be a story of catastrophic checks on population.

The Vital Revolution

Life under the biological old regime had limited population growth (see chapter 19). The conquest of the biological old regime, through the improvement of diet and the conquering of disease, amounts to a great vital revolution. The vital revolution that began in the late eighteenth century and extended through the twentieth century is arguably the most important revolution in modern history, even when compared with famous political and economic revolutions. Demographers measure the vital revolution with a variety of statistics, but the most important are straightforward: the birthrate (usually stated in terms of the annual number of births per one thousand or ten thousand people in the population) and the death rate. The population of Europe had grown very slowly for centuries for the simple reason that the birthrate and the death rate remained similar. If one studies the birth and death data for early eighteenth-century Britain, the balance of the biological old regime becomes clear (see chart 23.1). In 1710 British births exceeded deaths by 316 to 286 (per ten thousand); if that excess of births could be sustained, there would be a significant growth of population. By 1720, however, the birthrate (314) and the death rate (311) were almost identical. Then in 1730, the death rate (349) exceeded the birthrate (339) and that pattern continued in 1740. For the generation between 1710

✴ TABLE 23.1 ✴

The European Population Explosion, 1700–1900

The data in this table reflect historical boundaries at the date shown and therefore are not perfectly comparable. For example, the population of Alsace-Lorraine is included in France in 1800 and in Germany in 1900.

State	1700 Population (in millions)	1800 Population (in millions)	Growth, 1700–1800 (in percent)	1900 Population (in millions)	Growth, 1800–1900 (in percent)
The Great Powers					
Austria-Hungary	11.0	15.0	36.4	25.9	72.7
European Russia	17.0	29.0	70.6	106.2	266.2
France	17.3	26.9	55.5	39.0	45.0
Germany	13.5	18.5	37.0	56.4	204.9
Italy	13.0	18.1	39.2	33.4	84.5
United Kingdom	8.9	16.2	82.0	41.5	156.2
Western Europe					
Spain	7.5	10.5	40.0	18.1	72.4
Portugal	2.0	2.8	40.0	5.4	92.9
Belgium	a	a		6.7	
Netherlands	1.9	2.1	10.5	5.1	142.9
Denmark	1.3	1.9	46.2	2.6	36.8
Sweden	2.0	2.3	15.0	5.1	121.7
Switzerland	1.2	1.7	41.7	3.3	94.1
Eastern Europe					
Greece	b	b		2.4	
Serbia	b	b		2.5	
Montenegro	b	b		.2	
Bulgaria	b	b		4.0	
Romania	b	b		5.8	
Ottoman Empire in Europe	6.4	11.5	79.7	4.8	

Source: Calculated from data in Jack Barbuscio and Richard M. Dunn, *European Political Facts, 1648–1789* (London: Macmillan, 1984), pp. 335–53; Chris Cook and John Paxton, *European Political Facts, 1848-1918* (London: Macmillan, 1978), pp. 213–32; A. Goodwin, ed., *The New Cambridge Modern History* (Cambridge: Cambridge University Press, 1965), 8:714–15; B. R. Mitchell, *European Historical Statistics, 1750-1970* (London: Macmillan, 1975), pp. 19–24.

a. Part of the Austrian Empire. No separate data available.

b. Part of the Ottoman Empire. No separate data available.

and 1740, the biological old regime kept a virtually even balance between births and deaths. Beginning in 1750, however, British birthrates remained steady at a high level (between 366 and 377 per ten thousand) for decades, while the death rate plummeted, hitting 300 in 1770, then falling to 211 by 1820. The huge gap between 366 births and 211 deaths per ten thousand population is the demographer's measure of the vital revolution, the source of the population explosion, and the pattern that frightened Malthus.

The European death rate, especially the infant mortality rate, remained frightfully high during the eighteenth century, and in many years the death rate surpassed the birthrate (see chapter 19). Studies of regions of Europe that had higher birthrates than Britain did—such as the region of Lombardy in northern Italy—have shown that great increases in the number of births did not necessarily produce a significant population increase. If the twin guardians of the biological old regime, diet and disease, were not beaten, the death rate simply consumed the higher birthrate. The vital revolution of the late eighteenth century owed more to the improvement of diet than to the conquest of disease: The benefits of the Columbian exchange, such as the potato (see chapter 19) and the agricultural revolution meant that Europe could feed a larger population. The great medical advances of the vital revolution mostly came in the nineteenth and twentieth centuries (see chapters 24 and 31), although the slow conquest of smallpox had begun with Mary Wortley Montagu and Edward Jenner in the eighteenth century.

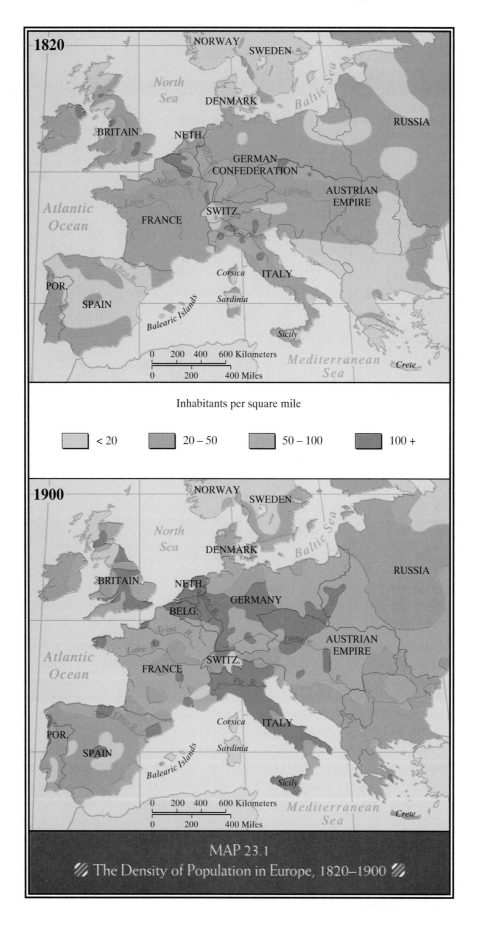

1820

Inhabitants per square mile

< 20   20 – 50   50 – 100   100 +

1900

MAP 23.1

The Density of Population in Europe, 1820–1900

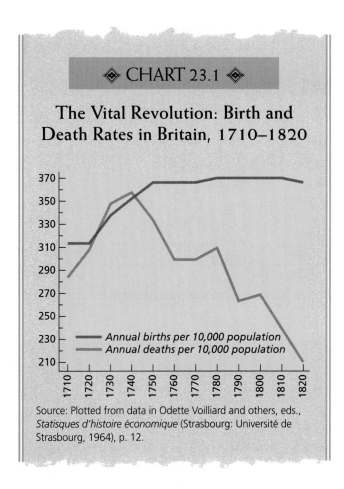

◆ CHART 23.1 ◆

The Vital Revolution: Birth and Death Rates in Britain, 1710–1820

— Annual births per 10,000 population
— Annual deaths per 10,000 population

Source: Plotted from data in Odette Voilliard and others, eds., *Statisques d'histoire économique* (Strasbourg: Université de Strasbourg, 1964), p. 12.

The Urbanization of Europe

The vital revolution led to the urbanization of European civilization. For more than two thousand years, the greatest centers of European civilization—from ancient Athens and Rome through the Italian city-states of the Renaissance to London and Paris in the Old Regime—had been its cities. By 1750 European cities had been growing in size and numbers for centuries. But the eighteenth century was not yet an urban society; the European economy remained predominantly agricultural (see chapter 18). The study of Europe's population also reveals a rural society: In every country, the majority of the population lived on farms and in small villages.

The population explosion that began in Britain in the late eighteenth century and continued during the nineteenth century transformed Europe into an urban society. In 1750 more than 65 percent of the population of Britain was employed in agriculture; the census of 1850 found that more than 50 percent of the population lived in towns and cities, making Britain the first predominantly urban society in history. The early nine-

teenth century was consequently a period of remarkable urban growth. The population explosion not only created an urban society (including towns of ten thousand or more), but it also created huge cities. Between 1750 and 1800, nineteen towns in Europe doubled in size, and fifteen of them were located in Britain. No town in France, none in the Italian states, nor any in Russia grew so rapidly, but in northern England—from Lancashire in the west, across the midlands to Yorkshire in the east—seven towns doubled in size. And the impact of the population explosion was just beginning. During the next half-century, 1800–50, seven British cities (five of them in northern England) tripled in size, some nearly quintupling (see table 23.2).

British cities were not huge by late twentieth-century standards, but they were astonishing by contemporary standards because the population explosion had not yet transformed the continent. Britain was strikingly different from the rest of Europe. The port of Liverpool on the northwestern coast of England, a town that had become prosperous during the slave trade, grew so fast in the early nineteenth century that it surpassed such capital cities as Moscow and Madrid in size (see table 23.3). In 1850 the British isles contained seven cities larger than Rome, the historic center of Europe. Nearly a quarter of the British population lived in metropolitan areas of 100,000 or more, while only 4.6 percent of France and 2.3 percent of Spain lived in such urban regions. The great Swiss cities of Geneva (31,000) and Zürich (17,000) were suddenly smaller than British towns such as Bradford (104,000). In 1800, two of the ten largest cities in Europe (London and Dublin) were in the United Kingdom (U.K.); by 1850, four of the ten largest (London, Liverpool, Glasgow, and Manchester) were in the U.K. and three more (Dublin, Birmingham, and Edinburgh) were in the second ten.

When the effects of the population explosion reached continental Europe, so did urbanization. Just as the English cities of Manchester, Birmingham, Leeds, and Sheffield had exploded from regional towns into major urban centers, new cities grew in Europe. Essen, in the Ruhr valley of western Germany, changed from a small town of 4,000 people in 1800 into a sprawling city of 295,000 in the early twentieth century. The transformation of Łodz (Poland) was even more dramatic: A village of 200 people in 1800 became a city of 315,000 in 1900. By 1900 only three of the largest cities in Europe (London, Liverpool, and Manchester) were in Britain.

⚜ TABLE 23.2 ⚜

The Growth of British Cities, 1801–51

Population was determined through a decennial census.

City	1801	1811	1821	1831	1841	1851
Liverpool	82,000	104,000	138,000	202,000	286,000	376,000
Glasgow	77,000	101,000	147,000	202,000	275,000	345,000
Manchester	75,000	89,000	126,000	182,000	235,000	303,000
Birmingham	71,000	83,000	102,000	144,000	183,000	233,000
Leeds	53,000	63,000	84,000	123,000	152,000	172,000
Sheffield	46,000	53,000	65,000	92,000	111,000	135,000

Source: B. R. Mitchell, *European Historical Statistics, 1750–1970* (London: Macmillan, 1975), pp. 76–78.

⚜ TABLE 23.3 ⚜

The Major Cities of Europe, 1800–1900

This table provides lists of the largest cities in Europe from 1800 to 1900. Changes in these lists illustrate the relationship between industrialization and urbanization. British cities are highlighted in bold-faced type. Note the importance of British cities in the data for 1850, a date often chosen as the point at which Britain had become a predominantly industrial society.

Europe in 1800 City	Population	Europe in 1850 City	Population	Europe in 1900 City	Population
London	1,117,000	**London**	2,685,000	**London**	6,586,000
Paris	547,000	Paris	1,053,000	Paris	2,714,000
Naples	427,000	St. Petersburg	489,000	Berlin	1,889,000
Moscow	250,000	Naples	449,000	Vienna	1,675,000
Vienna	247,000	Vienna	444,000	St. Petersburg	1,267,000
St. Petersburg	220,000	Berlin	419,000	Moscow	989,000
Amsterdam	201,000	**Liverpool**	376,000	Hamburg	931,000
Lisbon	180,000	Moscow	365,000	Budapest	732,000
Berlin	172,000	**Glasgow**	357,000	**Liverpool**	704,000
Dublin	165,000	**Manchester**	303,000	**Manchester**	645,000
Rome	163,000	Madrid	281,000	Warsaw	638,000
Madrid	160,000	**Dublin**	272,000	Brussels	599,000
Palermo	139,000	Brussels	251,000	Naples	564,000
Milan	135,000	Milan	242,000	Madrid	540,000
Venice	134,000	Lisbon	240,000	Barcelona	533,000
Hamburg	130,000	**Birmingham**	233,000	Amsterdam	511,000
Barcelona	115,000	Amsterdam	224,000	Munich	500,000
		Edinburgh	202,000	Milan	493,000

Source: B. R. Mitchell, *European Historical Statistics, 1750–1970* (London: Macmillan, 1975), pp. 76–78; Chris Cook and John Paxton, *European Political Facts, 1848–1918* (London: Macmillan, 1978), pp. 213–32.

The Agricultural Revolution

The first explanation of the vital revolution, and therefore of the population explosion and its corollary urbanization, was an improved food supply. Although the nineteenth century still experienced famines in some regions (especially Russia) and occasional disasters such as the potato famine of the 1840s, the pattern of regular subsistence crises that characterized early modern history ended by the middle of the nineteenth century. The average European diet remained poor by late twentieth-century standards, but it had significantly improved since the eighteenth century, producing better general health, greater resistance to disease, and higher rates of healthy reproduction.

The improved food supply is best seen in late eighteenth-century Britain, where the population explosion began. The improvement had many sources. Despite restrictive tariffs on grain imports known as the Corn Laws, Britain imported an increasing amount of food after 1780, and this provided partial support for a larger, healthier population. British grain imports stood at 200,000 tons in 1780, rising steadily to 3.7 million tons in 1800, and then to 7.5 million tons in 1840. At the same time, the improvements in British internal transportation—particularly canals, toll roads, and railroads—reduced food prices in urban areas. Food shipment improved rapidly during the nineteenth century as new technology allowed the preservation of food for transportation, beginning with the adoption of a sterile canning process that a Parisian chef, François Appert, had invented for Napoleon's armies in 1804.

The greatest source of an improved food supply in Britain, however, was an increase in British harvests so significant that historians have called it an agricultural revolution. The agricultural revolution involved both extensive use of land (more acres planted) and intensive use of the land (higher yields per acre). The stimulus to both developments was simple: Grain prices rose with the population, previous bad harvests had left few grain reserves, and a generation of war with France sometimes interrupted the importation of grain (which fell from 4.6 million tons to 2.9 million tons in the years following 1810).

Extensive use of the soil provides obvious, although often difficult, possibilities. Valuable land could be reclaimed by draining marshes and wetlands, such as the fens of eastern England or the marshes of central Italy. In other regions of Europe, especially Scandinavia and eastern Europe, sparsely populated woodlands and wildernesses could be cleared and planted. Wherever the science of agronomy established modern crop rotation, the tradition of leaving fields lie fallow every third year could be abandoned. This alone produced a 10 percent increase in arable land in some regions.

The most impressive side of the agricultural revolution—more intensive use of the land—achieved an unprecedented rise in European productivity. Scientific farming, such as improved understanding of fertilizers, significantly improved the harvest per acre. The beginnings of modern farm mechanization—from Jethro Tull's development of seed drills to replace the manual broadcasting of seeds to Andrew Meikle's invention of the threshing machine in 1784—produced more efficient harvests. Such developments increased the ratio of grain harvested to grain sown. In Britain, the wheat harvest went from a yield of 7-to-1 to a ratio of 10.6 to 1; at that rate, the British harvest was nearly twice as productive per acre as the rest of Europe and three times as successful as farming in eastern Europe.

New crops were also an important part of the agricultural revolution. The introduction of winter crops in some regions, the continuing arrival of new American crops from the Columbian exchange (see chapter 19), and the steady acceptance of root crops (such as the potato and the sugar beet) greatly changed European diets. The potato grew in more northerly climates and poorer soils than most grains; it had a three-to-four-month cycle to harvest, compared with ten months for many grains; and a single crop yielded twice as much nutrition per acre as grains did. Consequently, by the early 1840s, one-third of the population of England and one-half of Scotland lived on the potato. Even higher rates of potato consumption were found in Ireland and parts of Germany.

The Controversy over Enclosure

Clearing forests or swamps and harvesting more crops per acre were not the only changes by which the agricultural revolution fed the growing population of the British isles. The greatest source of new acreage being farmed resulted from a controversial political decision known as enclosure. This term simply means the enclosing of farm land within fences (see illustration 23.1). The laws of enclosure, however, had more profound results than that description suggests, leading some historians to argue that it was a necessary condition for industrialization. By ancient tradition, most villages in Britain reserved a portion of local land

Illustration 23.1

///// **Enclosure of Open Fields.** During the eighteenth century, the countryside began to look different in many regions. Laws required that farm fields be enclosed within walls, fences, or planted hedgerows, which cut the countryside into parcels of arable ploughland or pasturage, as seen in this photograph of the English countryside. Enclosure led to higher productivity at the price of dislocating poor farmers.

called the commons for the use of all residents. No one could plant crops on the commons, but anyone could graze animals, forage for food (such as berries or acorns), and gather firewood there. Enclosure of the commons within fences meant that the land could be plowed to increase the national grain production, but the traditional rights of citizens ended, forcing many of them off the land. Enclosure in a larger sense ended the open field system of agriculture, in which the land was divided into numerous small strips. In 1700, 50 percent of English farmland, and most of continental farmland, was in open field strips. By 1850 virtually all of rural Britain was enclosed (see document 23.1).

Enclosure produced more farmland and more efficient farms. Each enclosure required an act of Parliament, and four thousand such acts of enclosure were voted between 1750 and 1850, although a General Enclosure Act of 1801 served as a model for most others. By these acts, the commons lands were sold in some villages and distributed among the landowners in others. This led to the consolidation of individual strips into single farms and the failure of small farms where the owners had depended upon the commons. The resulting farms were larger than the sum of the strips because they incorporated the paths that had separated the strips, and they became larger yet as uncompetitive small farms were absorbed. By the early nineteenth century, two-thirds of British farmland was in large estates. Enclosure raised agricultural production as well as con-

troversy. The benefits were larger than simply that more land was put under the plow and therefore more food was produced. Enclosure of the commons meant the segregation of herds of livestock, reducing disease transmission and permitting selective breeding. The selective breeding experiments conducted with sheep by Robert Bakewell, for example, saw the average weight of sheep brought to market rise from twenty-eight pounds in 1710 to eighty pounds in 1795. Larger farms encouraged crop rotation because the entire acreage did not have to be planted in the same subsistence grain for the farm family. Consolidation of the open field strips meant that farm equipment did not have to be moved great distances.

Enclosure provoked opposition because of the human effects on the rural population. Marginal farmers suffered worst. Without strips of common farmland, many families could not survive by agriculture. Others faced failure because they had depended upon the commons to graze a pig or a few geese. As one angry poet put it, "The law locks up the man or woman who steals the goose from off the Common; But leaves the greater villain loose who steals the common from the goose." Historians have debated the amount of suffering caused by enclosure, and they have generally agreed that it is a question of long-term gains for most of society versus short-term suffering for much of society. The people driven from agriculture were often those who populated the growing cities, and life in those new cities was often extremely unpleasant.

❖ DOCUMENT 23.1 ❖

Two Views of the Enclosure of the Commons

Oliver Goldsmith in "The Deserted Village" (1770) fostered the anti-enclosure view.

Sweet smiling village, loveliest of the lawn,
Thy sports are fled, and all thy charms withdrawn;
Amidst thy bowers the tyrant's hand is seen,
And desolation saddens all thy green:
One only master grasps the whole domain. . . .
Far, far away, thy children leave the land.

Ill fares the land, to hastening ills a prey,
Where wealth accumulates, and men decay;
Princes and lords may flourish, or may fade . . .
But a bold peasantry, their country's pride,
When once destroy'd, can never be supplied.

Frederic Eden in The State of the Poor *(1797) argued in favor of enclosure.*

[T]he allegation has been so often repeated, that the laboring classes of the nation have been injured by the consolidation . . . [that] the author trusts it will not be deemed foreign to his purpose to remark that, if large farms do, in fact . . . lessen labor, and thence enable the cultivators of the earth to bring its various produce to market at a cheaper rate, it seems decidedly to prove that they are of great national utility. . . .

If the consolidation of several small farms into one should be found . . . to bear hard on the owners of small farms, and perhaps on cottagers and laborers, this is an evil to be lamented indeed, but not of such a magnitude as that it should be suffered to counteract the greater good which may be expected to result from the improvement. At any rate, the inconveniences and the distresses thus provided can be but temporary; whilst the advantages to be expected from a contrary system are such as promise to be permanent.

❖ Handcraft, Cottage Industry, and the Steam Engine

The agricultural revolution, the vital revolution, and the population explosion of late eighteenth- and nineteenth-century Europe were all important factors in making possible a dramatic transformation of the European economy known as industrialization, in which manufactured goods began to replace agriculture as the dominant sector of the economy. Large-scale factory production began to replace handcraft manufacture; machinery and inanimate power sources began to replace human labor. Such large-scale industrialization did not happen suddenly or universally—factories, traditional production, and agriculture coexisted within a country, and usually within a region. Nonetheless, industrialization was such a dramatic change that contemporaries and historians (especially in Britain) have sometimes called it the industrial revolution.

The pressure of growing population demanded (and rewarded) great increases in the production of essential goods, such as the woolen and cotton textiles needed for clothing. Such goods had long been made by traditional handwork methods of spinning thread and weaving cloth (see chapter 18). This handwork production of textiles had spawned a form of manufacturing known as cottage industry, in which entrepreneurial middlemen engaged people to produce textiles in their homes (hence "cottage industry"), provided them with raw materials, paid them for finished work, then transported the goods to town for sale. This form of employment in home spinning and weaving lasted throughout the nineteenth century in some regions, but beginning in the mid-eighteenth century, technological innovations replaced human skills and power with machines. Industrialization was the broad process by which machines, operated by hundreds of people in urban factories, replaced the production of handcraft workers in small shops and cottages.

Illustration 23.2

A Coal Mine during Early Industrialization. Coal was the primary new power source of industrialization. Pumps driven by steam engines, such as the Newcomen Engine, made it possible to tunnel below the water table. Note the use of child and female labor in much of this mine to cart coal in narrow spaces: It was usually cheaper to use children than pit-ponies. A lamp is located where a miner works at the coal face; the open flame risked explosions if the miner encountered underground gases.

The age of industrialization was opened by a single new technology—the steam engine, which provided the power source for the innovations that followed. The principle of steam power was not new. It had been known in the ancient world and had long been the subject of study and experimentation. No single person invented the steam engine, although popular culture in English-speaking countries credits James Watt, while the French credit Denis Papin. In reality, the steam engine was the culmination of the work of many people. The first effective machines were developed in the 1770s by Watt, a maker of precision instruments for scientists at the University of Glasgow.

The initial use of the steam engine was in mining. Steam-powered pumps such as the Newcomen Engine could remove water from mine shafts that passed below the water table. This permitted much deeper mining, which in turn facilitated vastly greater coal extraction; the coal then could be burned to operate more steam engines. As coal became more plentiful and less expensive, and as steam engine technology proved successful,

TABLE 23.4

European Coal Production, 1820–40

The data in this table are national outputs of coal in millions of tons.

Country	1820	1830	1840
Austria	.1	.2	.5
Belgium	a	2.3	3.9
Britain	17.7	22.8	34.2
France	1.1	1.8	3.0
German states	1.3	1.8	3.9

Source: B. R. Mitchell, *European Historical Statistics, 1750–1970* (London: Macmillan, 1975), pp. 360–61.

a. Belgium did not exist in 1820.

the engine found other applications. Steam-powered bellows at forges changed metallurgy, producing more and finer steel. Steam-powered mills for grinding grains or sugar freed millers from dependence upon rivers. Experiments applied steam power to transportation, including the first steam automobile (1769), steamboat (1783), and railroad locomotive (1804). The locomotive was the perfect symbol of the steam revolution because it was merely a giant steam engine with wheels attached.

The Age of Iron and Coal

Industrialization quickly came to depend upon plentiful resources of iron, from which the machinery of steam technology was made, and coal, with which it was powered. Both iron and coal had been mined in Europe for centuries, but the scale of this mining was small. The total European output of pig iron in 1788 was approximately 200,000 metric tons, of which the British mined 69,000 tons. Most countries produced so little iron that they kept no national records of it. Coal mining was a similarly small-scale industry.

Great Britain had the good fortune to possess exceptionally rich deposits of both natural resources. When the steam engine permitted—then demanded—greater coal mining, Britain exploited those resources (see illustration 23.2) to become the world's first industrial power and to establish an enormous lead in industrial might (see table 23.4). During the French Revolution and the Napoleonic Wars, the British output of pig iron tripled to 248 metric tons; with peace, the output tripled again by the early 1830s. In 1850 Britain smelted 2.3 million met-

Illustration 23.3

⧄ **The Coalbrookdale Ironworks at Night.** Nothing better symbolized the powerful changes of early industrialization than a large ironworks with its great coke furnaces stoked. Such ironworks were typically located on a country river, where wood, coal, and water were plentiful. This painting depicts the most important early ironworks, Abraham Darby's works in central England.

ric tons of iron, more than one-half of the total supply of iron in the world (see illustration 23.3). British coal mining similarly overwhelmed the rest of the world. In 1820 the Austrian Empire mined 100,000 tons of coal, France and the German states each mined slightly more than 1 million tons, and Britain mined 17.7 million tons. Twenty years later, Austria, France, and the German states had all tripled their output; combined, they produced 3.8 million tons of coal, but that was barely one-tenth of Britain's 34.2 million tons of coal. By midcentury, Britain mined more than two-thirds of the world's coal. Consequently, the British also generated more steam power than all of continental Europe combined and four times as much power as their nearest industrial rival. The British dominance in coal, iron, and steam production—and their application to manufacturing—built an industrial leadership so great that Britons naturally spoke of their "industrial revolution" (see map 23.2).

The Machine Age and the Textile Factory

The availability of inexpensive steam power and iron for machinery led to an age of remarkable inventiveness. In the century between 1660 and 1760, the British government had registered an average of six new patents per year; applications of steam technology drove that average to more than two hundred patents per year in the 1770s, more than five hundred per year in the 1790s, more than one thousand per year by the 1820s, and nearly five thousand per year by the 1840s. The British inventions of the early industrial age were not the result of excellent technical schools; continen-

tal schools such as the Schemnitz Academy in Hungary or the École des Ponts et Chaussées (the first engineering school) in France were far superior. Most British inventions were the inspiration of tinkerers and artisans. One of the most important inventors of the early industrial age, Richard Arkwright, was a semiliterate barber with an exceptional mechanical aptitude.

The earliest beneficiary of the new technology was the textile industry. Woolen goods had been a basic British export for centuries; in the early eighteenth century woolens accounted for 25 percent to 33 percent of export revenue. Cotton goods were a newer export, produced from raw cotton imported from Britain's American colonies. In 1700 these textile industries had not changed much from medieval industry. Fibers were spun into thread by hand, perhaps with a spinning wheel, perhaps with simpler tools such as the distaff. The threads were then woven into cloth on handlooms. Spinning was usually done by women (hence the terms *spinster* or *distaff side*); weaving, by men. The entire handcraft process fitted comfortably into a rural cottage.

The new technology of the steam age soon threatened cottage industry. Machines first changed the spinning of thread: James Hargreaves's spinning jenny allowed one person to spin thread onto multiple spindles, producing ten times as much thread—soon one hundred times as much thread—as a good manual spinner. Richard Arkwright's water frame mechanized the spinning of threads to produce stronger thread with less labor. The spinning mule of 1779 combined the spinning jenny, the water frame, and the steam engine to produce forty-eight spindles of high-quality thread

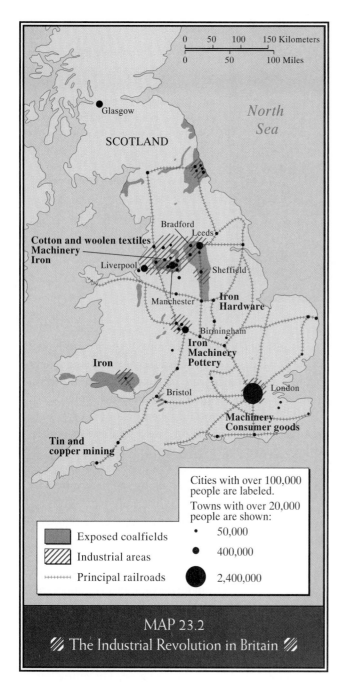

MAP 23.2

/// The Industrial Revolution in Britain ///

Cities with over 100,000 people are labeled.

Towns with over 20,000 people are shown:

- 50,000
- 400,000
- 2,400,000

- Exposed coalfields
- Industrial areas
- Principal railroads

The consequence of this new technology was the textile factory (see illustration 23.4). There, the steam engine could be linked to the spinning mule, to the power loom, or to banks of dozens of each. All goods, from raw cotton to coal, could be delivered to a single, convenient site, chosen for inexpensive transportation costs such as proximity to mines, location on a river, or nearness to a great harbor. Instead of having the looms of cottage industry scattered around the countryside, they were now grouped together in a single building or factory complex, where an overseer could control the pace and quality of work. Steam-powered textile machinery produced high-quality, uniform cloth, at high speeds, and in vast quantities.

The first steam loom factory opened at Manchester, in northern England, in 1806. By 1813 there were 2,400 power looms operating in Britain, concentrated in Lancashire, the Midlands, and Yorkshire. A decade later, there were more than 10,000 textile factories using power looms in Britain. At midcentury, there were 250,000 power looms in the country. The resultant change in the scale of textile manufacturing was even greater than those numbers suggest. Whereas a master weaver with thirty years of experience could produce two bolts of cotton cloth a week on a handloom, a fifteen-year-old boy at a power loom could produce seven bolts. Britain dominated global commerce in textiles, especially in the British Empire and Latin America, and British merchants began to dream of the day they could sell a shirt to everyone in China.

The woolen industry, which had older traditions, resisted the innovations that transformed the cotton industry and mechanized more slowly. Most wool remained handloomed in 1840. Cotton, however, was a new industry without such resistance to change. It even attracted innovation, such as patents to make cotton velvet, to create ribbed cloth for stockings, or to print patterns on cotton cloth. Consequently, cottons surpassed woolens as Britain's foremost export in 1803; by 1830 cotton—a plant not native to the British isles—accounted for more than 50 percent of Britain's foreign trade income. The British, who had a well-developed global commerce already in place, became textile merchants to the world. More than half of the world's cotton cloth came from Britain (see chart 23.2).

The Railroad Age

The new economy required improved transportation. Food had to be transported to factory towns in far greater quantities than before. Iron, coal, machinery,

simultaneously. Looms were also mechanized: The mechanical improvement of John Kay's flying shuttle loom allowed one person to do the work of two, and Edmund Cartwright patented the first steam-powered loom in 1785. Power spinning and weaving demanded greatly increased supplies, and technology again accelerated textile production when machines such as Eli Whitney's cotton engine (colloquially known as the cotton gin) enabled a single worker to extract the same quantity of raw cotton that previously required fifty workers.

Illustration 23.4

The Factory System. The development of steam-powered machines to spin thread or to weave cloth led to the creation of vast factories where many machines could be linked to a single power source. Hand manufacture in cottage industry survived into the twentieth century, but most textiles were soon produced in factories such as this German mill of the 1840s. Note that the workers are women and the overseers are men.

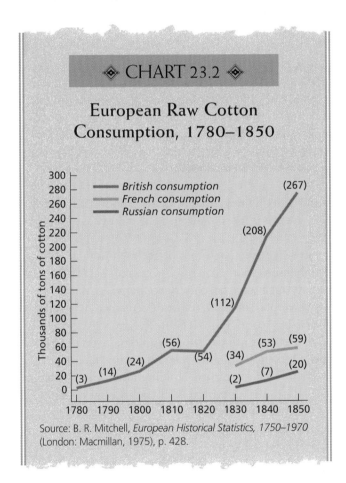

❖ CHART 23.2 ❖

European Raw Cotton Consumption, 1780–1850

Source: B. R. Mitchell, *European Historical Statistics, 1750–1970* (London: Macmillan, 1975), p. 428.

illustration 23.5). Railroads were the culmination of industrialization in Britain, not a cause of it.

Transportation in Britain had improved significantly in the century before 1825. The trip between London and Edinburgh that took twelve days in 1734 required four days in 1762 and forty hours on the eve of the railroad age. The chief developments in eighteenth-century transportation involved canal, road, and bridge building. Britain had two thousand kilometers of canals in 1700 and sixty-five hundred kilometers in 1830. Transportation on rivers and these canals was the most efficient means of moving great weights, such as shipments of iron and coal. The development of canals serving Manchester cut the cost of coal to factory owners by 50 percent in the late eighteenth century, so the textile boom there owed more to waterways than to railways. Canals and rivers, however, had one major drawback: They sometimes froze in the winter, ending the distribution of goods.

Road building and maintenance improved tremendously during the eighteenth century. In 1700 Britain relied upon a system of compulsory labor (similar to the French *corvée*), under local supervision, to do roadwork. Consequently, many roads in England were in worse condition than when the Romans evacuated in the fourth century A.D. Then, in 1706, Parliament legalized turnpike trusts—associations allowed to build and operate toll roads. By 1750 there were 143 of these trusts in Britain, and they had opened fifty-five hundred kilometers of toll roads. As industrial development demanded better transportation, the turnpike trusts grew rapidly; in 1790, 519 trusts operated 24,100 kilometers of roads.

Many technical advances made the British transportation system the best in Europe. An ironmaster

raw wool, and cotton had to be brought together. Manufactured goods had to be distributed. People had to be moved in large numbers. The railroad solved these problems, but the first steam locomotive was not built until 1804, and the first public railway—the Stockton-to-Darlington Railway—did not open until 1825 (see

Illustration 23.5

// The Stockton-Darlington Railway. The railroad locomotive was the apotheosis of the steam engine. Little more than a steam engine with wheels, it dramatically changed societies and economies. The first passenger railroad line, whose grand opening in 1825 is depicted in this engraving, ran twenty-seven miles in northern England between the towns of Stockton and Darlington. Chiefly the work of engineer George Stephenson, the line initially carried six freight cars, six passenger cars, fourteen wagons for workers, and a special coach for the director.

named Abraham Darby III, whose family had built the world's largest blast furnaces and foundry, constructed the world's first iron bridge, a 295-foot-long "wonder of the age" that amazed gawking tourists and changed transportation. Similarly, a Scottish engineer named John MacAdam improved roads—subsequently called macadamized roads—by cambering them for drainage and paving them with crushed stones. (The black-topped road treatment known as macadam was named in his honor, but it was not yet in use.) The improvement in highway transportation was so dramatic the coach companies began to remove the qualification "God Willing" from their time schedules.

The railroad was the culmination of these trends and was so successful that it ended the age of canals and coaching. Railroads began with an old idea borrowed from the coal mines. Since the seventeenth century, collieries had used wooden rails to guide horse-drawn coal wagons; by the 1760s many mines were switching to cast iron rails. Richard Trevithick, an English mining engineer, won the race to develop the first practical vehicle to carry passengers and goods, by designing a high-pressure steam engine in 1800. In early 1804 Trevithick's locomotive, riding on colliery iron rails, pulled five wagons containing seventy passengers and ten tons of iron ore, for a distance of 9.5 miles at a speed of nearly five miles per hour.

George Stephenson, an inventor who had devised the miner's safety lamp, built on Trevithick's work to start the age of railroad service. Stephenson built the forty-three kilometer Stockton-to-Darlington Railroad

in the early 1820s to serve the heavy industries of the midlands—so the first train became known as Stephenson's Rocket. He then turned to a more important line, a railroad linking the mills of Manchester with the port of Liverpool. Many people opposed this development, and dire predictions were made of the impact of railroads: The smoke and sparks from coal-burning locomotives would kill flora and fauna, start wildfires, and destroy foxhunting. When the Liverpool-Manchester line opened in 1830, however, the railway age had unmistakably begun. It carried 445,000 passengers and ninety-eight thousand tons of goods in its first full year. Stephenson's railroad was so successful that, of the twenty-nine stage coach services between Manchester and Liverpool in 1830, only one remained in business in 1832.

On the continent, where rapid industrialization did not begin until after the end of the Napoleonic Wars in 1815, a railroad-building boom that started in the late 1830s supported industrialization. For much of the mid-nineteenth century, Britain kept a huge lead in railroad lines, as it did in iron, coal, steam, and textiles. Ten years after the Stockton-Darlington line opened, no railroads had been built in Austria, the Italian states, Russia, or Spain; all of the German states combined contained only six kilometers of railroad track. Fifteen years after the railroad age began, 63 percent of all European track was in Britain (see table 23.5). Railroads were already changing the continental economy, however. A railway connecting the Belgian seaport of Antwerp with the Rhine River port of

┌───┐

✕ TABLE 23.5 ✕

The Beginning of the Railroad Age in Europe, 1825–50

	Railway lines open, in kilometers					
Country	1825	1830	1835	1840	1845	1850
Great Britain	43	157	544	2,390	3,931	9,797
Ireland	n.a.	n.a.	n.a.	21	150	865
Total United Kingdom	43	157	544	2,411	4,081	10,662
Austrian Empire	n.a.	n.a.	n.a.	144	728	1,357
Belgium	n.a.	n.a.	20	334	577	854
Denmark	n.a.	n.a.	n.a.	n.a.	n.a.	30
France	n.a.	31	141	410	875	2,915
German States	n.a.	n.a.	6	469	2,143	5,856
Italian States	n.a.	n.a.	n.a.	20	152	620
Netherlands	n.a.	n.a.	n.a.	17	153	176
Russia	n.a.	n.a.	n.a.	27	144	501
Spain	n.a.	n.a.	n.a.	n.a.	n.a.	28
Switzerland	n.a.	n.a.	n.a.	n.a.	n.a.	25
Total continent	n.a.	31	167	1,421	4,772	12,362
Total Europe	43	188	711	3,832	8,853	23,024
Percent in United Kingdom	100	84	77	63	46	46

Source: B. R. Mitchell, *European Historical Statistics 1750–1970* (London: Macmillan, 1975), pp. 581–82.
n.a. = Not available.

└───┘

Cologne was inaugurated in 1843; this Iron Rhine became one of the world's industrial arteries and made Antwerp the third largest port in the world (after London and New York). In the second half of the nineteenth century, gigantic railroad stations became a dominant feature of the urban landscape and a central nexus of the economy.

The Urban World

The impact of industrialization upon European society was most vivid in the growing cities. The population explosion, the decline in agricultural employment, the rise of the factory system, and the improvements in transportation combined to uproot thousands of people. Young adults, and sometimes whole families, found themselves so desperate for employment that they chose migration to the growing factory towns.

Unprecedented growth changed the nature of cities and urban life, but there was a range of types of towns and cities (see illustration 23.6). Older towns often still stood within their medieval defensive walls. The urban and the rural were intertwined in such towns, sometimes with farmland within the walls and usually with important farming surrounding the town. Urban families often still had gardens or even orchards. Livestock lived inside the towns, and it was not unusual to see a pig wandering the streets. A 1786 census of Hanover—an important German capital and the home of the English royal family—found 365 head of cattle living within the town walls, but no sidewalks, paved streets, or sewer system. This remained true of the new industrial towns: Transplanted animals lived alongside uprooted workers in the shadow of the factory.

The modern city emerged painfully during the late eighteenth and nineteenth centuries. London began the habit of numbering street addresses and invented sidewalks in the 1760s. Watt developed steam heating for his office, and his steam pipes were the first central heating. Experiments with the newly plentiful supply of coal led William Murdock to the invention of indoor

Illustration 23.6

/// **The Nineteenth-Century Urban World** The rapid urbanization of nineteenth-century Europe encompassed a variety of towns and cities rather than a homogeneous urban world. One of the most typical towns remained the centuries-old regional town that provided marketing, specialized craftsmen, professional services, higher education, or an administrative center for the church or government. The town of Bayeux in Normandy, which had been a bishopric since the fourth century, illustrates this type of established regional town.

A more typical town to represent the new urbanization is Le Creusot in central France. It began to emerge as an important metallurgical center in the late eighteenth century and prospered as the home of Schneider, one of the most important ironworks in Europe. Le Creusot never grew to be a large city, remaining an industrial town, as the prominent smokestacks of this sketch show. (Compare this view to the close association of Bayeux with the countryside.)

Paris was the second-largest city in Europe in 1800 with a population of 547,000. During the nineteenth century, Paris more than quintupled to 2,714,000 by receiving an enormous migrant population and by annexing its suburbs. This growth required significant investment in such infrastructure as sewer and water systems, streets and wide boulevards, and new housing. The rebuilding of Paris directed by Georges Haussmann during the Second Empire, shown here, became a model of urban renewal.

❖ DOCUMENT 23.2 ❖

Two Visitors Describe Conditions in Manchester

Observers were often startled by living conditions in the early industrial revolution, and many of them wrote vivid descriptions of what they had seen. The most famous include an unattractive portrait of Manchester in Charles Dickens's novel Hard Times *(1854) and a blunt denunciation of conditions there in Friedrich Engels's* The Condition of the English Working Class in 1844 *(1845). Many others can be compared with these. Alexis de Tocqueville, chiefly remembered for his description of America in* Democracy in America *(1835), also visited Britain and wrote about life in Manchester. Elizabeth Gaskell, a novelist whose pictures of industrial conditions rivals Dickens's, was especially vivid in* Mary Barton *(1848). Other startling descriptions can be found in the report of a parliamentary investigation known as the Ashley Report (1851). The following excerpts, one from de Tocqueville and one from Dickens, give a hint of contemporary shock.*

Alexis de Tocqueville, *Journeys to England and Ireland* (1835)

Thirty or forty factories rise on the tops of the hills I have just described. Their six stories tower up; their huge enclosures give notice from afar of the centralization of industry. The wretched dwellings of the poor are scattered haphazard around them. Round them stretches land uncultivated but without the charm of rustic nature, and still without the amenities of a town. The soil has been taken away, scratched and torn up in a thousand places, but it is not yet covered with the habitations of men. The land is given over to industry's use. The roads which connect the still disjointed limbs of the great city show, like the rest, every sign of hurried and unfinished work; the incidental activity of a population bent on gain, which seeks to amass gold so as to have everything at once, and, in the interval, mistrusts all the niceties of life. Some of the roads are paved, but most of them are full of ruts and puddles into which foot or carriage wheel sinks deep. Heaps of dung, rubble from buildings, putrid stagnant pools are found here and there among the houses over the bumpy, pitted surfaces of the public places.

Charles Dickens, *Hard Times* (1854)

Coketown [Manchester] . . . was a town of red brick, or of brick that would have been red if the smoke and ashes had allowed it; but as matters stood it was a town of unnatural red and black, like the painted face of a savage. It was a town of machinery and tall chimneys, out of which interminable serpents of smoke trailed themselves forever and ever, and never got uncoiled. It had a black canal in it, and a river that ran purple with ill-smelling dye, and vast piles of buildings full of windows where there was a rattling and a trembling all day long, and where the piston of the steam engine worked monotonously up and down like the head of an elephant in a state of melancholy madness. It contained several large streets all very like one another, and many small streets still more like one another, inhabited by people equally like one another, who all went in and out at the same hours, with the same sound upon the same pavements, to do the same work, and to whom every day was the same as yesterday and tomorrow, and every year the counterpart of the last and the next.

lighting—the burning of coal gas to provide better illumination than candles did. By 1807 the city of London was installing Murdock's gaslights on the streets; by 1820 gaslights were common in the homes of the well-to-do. The 1820s also saw London and Paris invent new public transportation systems: the horse-drawn omnibus, soon supplemented by urban railroads. The French Revolution led to a big change in city life—the invention of the restaurant, a result of the emigration of aristocrats who left behind many unemployed chefs. In 1789 Paris had only one restaurant (as distinct from inns or cafes); in 1804 there were more than five hundred and the institution was spreading. By the middle of the nineteenth century, the manufacturing economy had created vast department stores (such as the Bon Marché in Paris) and even arcade-shopping centers (such as the Galleria in Milan).

Urban life during industrialization was not entirely rosy. The industrial and manufacturing towns such as Manchester, Essen, and Łodz initially grew too fast for amenities to keep pace with the population (see document 23.2). Housing, fresh water, sewers, and sanitation were dangerously inadequate. An attractive environment (such as trees or clean air) or convenient services (such as shops or schools) were rarer. Many contemporaries recorded their horror at the sight of factory towns. Charles Dickens depicted Manchester as a dreadful place blackened by the soot of ubiquitous coal burning. Elisabeth Gaskell, who rivaled Dickens for vivid details, described the nightmare of life in such conditions. In *Mary Barton* (1848), Gaskell described the squalid conditions of life in a slum cellar, where starvation and typhus competed for the lives of a family sleeping on beds of damp straw.

Even the old cities could not keep up with their growth. In the Westminster district of London, residents living within one block of Parliament complained to the government in 1799 about the stinking odor of their street, which had not been cleaned of horse and human waste in six months. In that same district of the richest city on Earth, air pollution was so terrible during hot weather that Parliament usually voted for an early summer recess. But those who went north for the summer, as the poet laureate Robert Southey did, might not escape deplorable conditions. The air in Edinburgh was so bad, Southey claimed, that "you might smoke bacon by hanging it out of the window." Much of nineteenth-century urban history thus became the story of urban renewal. Paris became a much more pleasant city with the construction of the comprehensive sewer system that Victor Hugo described as a central setting of *Les Misérables*. In 1800 Paris had a total of twenty kilometers of sewers; by the late nineteenth century, more than two thousand kilometers. Paris was also a model of urban renewal above ground. In the 1850s and 1860s a government plan devised by Baron Georges Haussmann tore down many of the dark buildings and narrow streets surviving from medieval Paris and replaced them with the broad boulevards and graceful residences of a "city of light" (see illustration 23.6). The Austrian government chose to modernize Vienna by tearing down the fortifications that screened the city and replacing them with a broad, circular boulevard known as the Ringstrasse, aside which the city built its public buildings, beginning with an opera house and soon including a new city hall (*Rathaus*), university, stock exchange, National Theatre, Parliament, and Palace of Justice.

Changing Class Structures

The beginning of the industrial age changed the social order of the city as much as its physical appearance. Industrialization created a new elite, based upon the wealth created by the mines, the factories, the rails, the markets, and the financial institutions connecting them. This was a wealth based on capital, not land; a wealth

of merchants, manufacturers, industrialists, and financiers. The British social critic Thomas Carlyle called them "Captains of Industry"; others referred to "Lords of the Loom," "Railroad Kings," and a dozen similar titles. Heavily industrialized regions, such as Alsace, created a wealthy new aristocracy of families—such as the Koechlins, the Japys, and the Peugeots—who had taken the lead in introducing power looms, new textile printing processes, or the manufacture of heavy machinery. The Koechlin family of Mulhouse went from the comfortable life provided by a successful weaver in a cottage industry to the immense wealth of factory owners within a single generation. The leading families of this industrial bourgeoisie formed an elite different from the landed aristocracy. During the nineteenth century, this small social group, together with older elites of middle-class wealth (such as mercantile and banking wealth) and members of the educated professions (such as physicians, lawyers, teachers, and journalists) would challenge the political dominance of the Old Regime alliance of monarchy, aristocracy, and established churches. For the members of the prosperous middle class, the age of industrialization was an exciting and comfortable epoch (see illustration 23.7).

The new bourgeoisie may have been the most influential class in the changing society of the industrial age, but it was relatively small. A larger change in the social structure was the rapid growth of a class of urban workers who operated the steam engines, power forges, spinning mules, power looms, and trains. These men and women of the working class—or the proletariat, as this social class was frequently called—often formed the majority of a town's population. A study of the social structure in Belgium textile towns found that approximately half of the population was employed as spinners or weavers in the new factories. But a textile town might still have a quarter of its population employed in agriculture, including both farmers who lived in the town and agricultural laborers, or a quarter engaged in the traditional artisanal trades and crafts of the guilds. The educated professions, the industrial middle class, and the traditional upper classes of wealth remained small—less than 5 percent of the population.

Age, Gender, and the Family

The new industries initially favored the employment of men in all jobs, but the textile mills adopted the sexual division of labor that had typified cottage industry: Women did most of the spinning and men did most of

Illustration 23.7

▨ **Middle-Class Comfort.** Views of European life during industrialization vary sharply depending upon the social class perspective of the observer. The middle class grew significantly in size and prosperity during the nineteenth century, and middle-class views such as this sentimental English print of a holiday dinner recall that progress. The life of the servants (the largest form of employment for women) depicted here was not so rosy, but it was markedly more comfortable than industrial work.

⋈ TABLE 23.6 ⋈

Employment in British Cotton Factories, by Gender, 1835

The data presented in this table clearly demonstrate the importance of women's labor during the industrial revolution; in every region of the United Kingdom, women represented the majority of the workforce in the cotton mills. Long before the late twentieth century discussion of women working outside the home, they were essential to the economy. To see the breadth of women's labor, see table 23.7.

Region	Number of men	Percentage of men	Number of women	Percentage of women
England	88,266	48.2	94,861	51.8
Ireland	1,639	38.0	2,672	62.0
Scotland	10,529	32.3	22,051	67.7
Wales	452	39.3	699	60.7
Total United Kingdom	100,886	45.6	120,283	54.4

Source: A. Aspinall and E. Anthony Smith, eds., *English Historical Documents* (London: Eyre and Spottiswoode, 1959), 11:512.

the weaving. Many employment traditions quickly broke down, however. Machines often required few skills or little strength to make superior textiles; factory owners often favored women and children for wage labor because they worked for less than men. Women soon held the majority of the jobs in textile mills (see table 23.6), and some occupations became feminized jobs, held only by women (see illustration 23.8). Some factory owners spoke of a woman's dexterity and many thought (often erroneously) of women as a less truculent labor force. However, low wages remained the de-

cisive factor. A study of women workers in London in 1848, for example, found that women earned 34 percent of men's wages. When Parliament investigated working conditions, factory owners candidly admitted that they preferred women because they could pay them less and because women would work hard to provide for their children. As one mill owner testified, women "are attentive, docile . . . and are compelled to use their utmost exertions to procure the necessities of life." Early in industrialization, therefore, women became the majority of textile factory workers. A study of

Illustration 23.8

/// **Women Workers.** Women worked in many occupations before industrialization—in the rural family economy, in cottage industry, in family-run shops, in domestic service—but the factory system put a sharp new focus on the role of women in the economy. Many occupations were entirely feminized, often be-

cause employers felt justified in paying women less than half of a man's wage. In the contemporary illustration here, women in an English pen-grinding factory appear to constitute 100 percent of the workforce.

Scottish cotton mills in 1835, for example, found that women held two-thirds of all jobs. Textiles remained one of the foremost employers of women throughout the nineteenth century. But this low-paid existence was so precarious that thousands of women were forced into prostitution to survive, a plight dramatized by the character of Fantine in Victor Hugo's *Les Misérables* (1832) but visible to any contemporary on the streets (see chapter 24).

Whether the factory hired men, women, or children, factory employment changed the family economy. Instead of a husband, wife, and children working together—at different tasks on a farm, in domestic production, or in a shop—factory employment split the family apart in individual employment for individual wages. As factory wages remained low, such employment led all family members to take full-time employment, and it encouraged large families in which children went to work at an early age. Economic historians label the new arrangement a "family wage economy" in which family members pool their earnings from different jobs.

Not all towns became centers of textile manufacturing or heavy industry. Older towns, such as York, England, still prospered on traditional handcraft manufacturing and as commercial and marketing centers. The social structure in such towns was different, especially when considering gender. Women constituted nearly one-third of the labor force in York in 1851 (a typical figure for the nineteenth-century economy), but barely 1 percent of working women held jobs in factory manufacturing (see table 23.7). Far more women—30 percent of working women—worked in traditional handcraft manufacturing and small shops. But the majority of the working women of York labored in the century's chief occupation for women, domestic service. The middle-class prosperity of industrialization, and the low wages paid to women of the working class, created a market in which all members of the middle class were expected to keep household servants and even members of the lower middle class, such as shopkeepers, could afford a cook or a maid. Across Europe, the unmarried daughters of the lower classes filled these posts; they often did so ea-

TABLE 23.7

The Labor Force in York, England, 1851

Labor category	Percentage of men	Percentage of women
Agriculture	9.9	2.1
Building trades	11.9	0.1
Craft manufacturing/shops	42.7	29.9
Domestic service	3.5	58.9
Factory manufacturing	8.9	1.1
Public service/professions	9.4	5.8
Transportation	7.6	1.6
Other	6.1	0.4
Number in labor force	11,225	5,129
Percentage of labor force	68.6	31.4

Source: Louise A. Tilly and Joan W. Scott, *Women, Work, and Family* (New York, N.Y.: Routledge, 1978), p. 86.

gerly because a servant's post meant a more comfortable life than factory work did.

Although working women faced terrible exploitation during industrialization, the treatment of working children was even worse. In the agricultural society of the Old Regime, children had worked as part of the family economy, and they had begun farm work at an early age. Urban children had traditionally left home to become apprentices in their early teens, and some trades took children at an earlier age. But none of these experiences prepared observers for the exploitation of children in the early industrial age.

Children were employed in mining as young as five to seven years old. Mine owners argued that children were needed because their size enabled them to fit into tight places. Often, however, they were used for tasks such as sorting coal or even to replace the ponies that pulled ore carts (see illustration 23.2). Furthermore, small wages were as important as small size. Studies of child labor during industrialization have found that these practices accounted for 15 percent to 20 percent of mining labor. It was unhealthy, dangerous work, and hundreds of children died in the mines each year (see table 23.8). In 1838, for example, 122 British mine workers under the age of eighteen died in the mines; fourteen were preteenage children who died by falling down mineshafts, fifteen died in mine collapses, thir-

teen died in gas explosions, three drowned, and four were crushed by trams.

The factory age expanded this use of child labor. Factories such as Josiah Wedgwood's famous pottery typically employed as much as 30 percent of their labor force in workers under the age of eighteen. The textile mills pushed that policy to new extremes. Studies have found that the early British cotton mills averaged 40–50 percent of their labor force under the age of eighteen; the worst offenders relied upon children for 70–80 percent of their labor. Some mills had 20 percent of their employees below the age of ten. Less than half of the mills used corporal punishment to discipline the child labor force, but all relied on strict discipline to keep the children docile. The use of child labor in the textile mills continued for most of the nineteenth century, but it declined from such high rates. A study of child labor in France in the 1840s (see table 23.9) found that textile mills employed more than 72 percent of all child labor in France, and both the cotton and woolen industries still relied upon children for nearly 20 percent of their labor force. European society initially permitted this treatment of children because the prevalent political philosophy (classical liberalism) and economic theory (laissez-faire capitalism) both insisted that governments not intervene in the economic process or regulate industries (see chapter 25). As society learned of the conditions of child labor, however, many governments chose to adopt protective child labor laws (sometimes restricting women's work, too) rather than insist upon pure economic principles.

The Standard of Living Debate

The subject of the exploitation of women and children in the industrial economy raises one of the most heated debates in modern historical scholarship, a controversy known as the standard of living debate. On one side of this debate, social historians depict the ghastly living and working conditions of workers in the early industrial age; on the other side, economic historians show a steady improvement in the cost of living and the standards of living for the working class. The optimists look back at the new industrial towns and see affordable workers' cafes in the bright illumination of Murdock's gaslights. When the pessimists look back, they smell the stench of uncollected refuse in the streets and the

✳ TABLE 23.8 ✳

Death of Children Mineworkers in Britain in 1838

Cause of death	Under age 13	Age 13–18	Age 18–21	Total
Mine collapses and rock slides	15	14	72	101
Gas explosions	13	18	49	80
Falling down shaft	14	16	36	66
Drowning in mines	3	4	15	22
Crushed by tram	4	5	12	21
Gas suffocation	0	2	6	8
Drawn over pulley	3	0	3	6
Other	6	5	36	47
Total	58	64	229	351

Source: Compiled from data in Elizabeth Longmate, *Children at Work, 1830–1885* (London: Longman, 1981), p. 35.

✳ TABLE 23.9 ✳

Child Labor in the French Textile Industry, 1845

Industry	Children employed	Children as a percentage of that industry's labor force	Percentage of all child labor employed in that industry
Cotton	44,828	18.3	31.2
Woolen	26,800	18.6	18.7
Cotton blend	11,038	23.9	7.7
Silk	9,326	5.6	6.5
Hemp and flax	7,232	12.8	5.0
Wool and silk	4,765	12.5	3.3
Textile total	103,989	——	72.4

Source: Lee S. Weissbach, *Child Labor Reform in Nineteenth Century France* (Baton Rouge, La.: Louisiana State University Press, 1989), p. 19. Reprinted by permission of the publisher.

foul dampness in typhus-infected cellar bedrooms. Both viewpoints contain an important historical truth, and the debate is not resolved. The optimistic version rests chiefly on tables of economic data, and the pessimistic version stresses the testimony of people who lived through industrialization (see document 23.3).

The early critics of industrialization were numerous. They ranged from England's greatest romantic poet, William Wordsworth, who wrote in 1814, "I grieve, when on the darker side of this great change I look," to the cofounder of Marxist socialism, Friedrich Engels. Engels, the son of a rich German industrialist,

lived in Manchester and studied manufacturing there in 1844. His conclusion was brutal: "I charge the English middle class with mass murder." The contemporary British historian who coined the name *industrial revolution* also reached a shocking conclusion; he called industrialization "a period as terrible as any through which a nation ever passed."

The anger of such critics has derived chiefly from the conditions in the new factories and factory towns. Life in that world had an undeniably grim side. Conditions in textile factories were so bad that another poet, William Blake, named them "dark Satanic mills." These

◈ DOCUMENT 23.3 ◈

The Daily Life of English Factory Workers in 1833

These details of the daily life of factory workers are drawn from an account published in 1833 by Peter Gaskell, entitled The Manufacturing Population of England. *Although Gaskell sometimes used a tone of moralistic superiority (note the section on smoking and drinking), he was also motivated by genuine sympathy (note word choice such as "immured" or "deprived").*

Personal Appearance: . . . Their complexion is sallow and pallid—with a peculiar flatness of feature. . . . Their stature is low—the average height of 400 men, measured at different times, and at different places, being 5′6″. Their limbs slender, and playing badly and ungracefully. A very general bowing of the legs. Great numbers of girls and women walking lamely or awkwardly. . . .

The Daily Round: . . . Rising at or before day-break, between four and five o'clock the year round, scarcely refreshed by his night's repose, he swallows a hasty meal, or hurries to the mill without taking any food whatever. At eight o'clock half an hour, and in some instances forty minutes, are allowed for breakfast. In many cases, the engine continues at work during the mealtime, obliging the laborer to eat and still overlook his work. . . . This meal is brought to the mill, and generally consists of weak tea, of course nearly cold, with a little bread; in other instances, of milk-and-meal porridge. Teas, however, may be called the universal breakfast, flavored of late years too often with gin. . . .

At 12:00 the engine stops, and an hour is given for dinner. The hands leave the mill, and seek their homes, where this meal is usually taken. It consists of potatoes boiled, very often eaten alone; sometimes with a little bacon. . . .

Again they are closely immured from 1:00 till eight or nine, with the exception of 20 minutes, this being allowed for tea. . . .

It must be remembered that father, mother, son, and daughter are alike engaged; no one capable of working is spared to make home . . . comfortable and desirable. . . .

Food and Drink: The staple diet of the manufacturing population is potatoes and wheaten bread, washed down by tea or coffee. Milk is but little used. Meal is consumed to some extent, either baked into cakes or boiled up with water, making a porridge. . . . Animal food forms a very small part of their diet, and that which is eaten is often of an inferior quality. . . .

House Furnishings: The houses of great numbers of the laboring community in the manufacturing districts present many of the traces of savage life. Filthy, unfurnished, deprived of all the accessories to decency and comfort. . . . [O]ne or two rush-bottomed chairs, a deal table, a few stools, broken earthenware, such dishes, one or more tin kettles and cans, a few knives and forks, a piece of broken iron serving as a poker[,] . . . a bedstead made up of sacking, a heap of flocks, or a bundle of straw . . . and all these cooped in a single room. . . .

Housing Arrangements: . . . [T]he houses are of the most flimsy and imperfect structure. . . . One of the circumstances in which they are especially defective, is that of drainage and water-closets. Whole ranges of these houses are either totally undrained, or only very partially. . . . The whole of the washings and filth from these consequently are thrown into the front or back street, which being often unpaved and cut up into deep ruts, allows them to collect into stinking and stagnant pools; while fifty, or even more than that number, having only a single convenience common to them all, it is in a very short time completely choked up with excrementitious matter. . . .

It very frequently happens that one tenement is held by several families, one room, or at most two, being generally looked upon as affording sufficient convenience for all household purposes of four or five individuals. . . . [M]odesty is annihilated—the father and the mother, the brother and the sister, the male and female lodger, do not scruple to commit acts in the presence of each other, which even the savage hides. . . .

Smoking and Drinking: Tobacco is very largely consumed by the male and female laborers indiscriminately; hundreds of men and women may be daily seen inhaling the fumes of this extraordinary plant, by means of short and blackened pipes. Smoking too is an almost universal accompaniment to drinking—a pernicious habit, prevailing to a frightful extent in this portion of the population. . . . In Manchester alone there are very near if not quite one thousand inns, beer-houses, and gin-vaults. Of these, more than nine-tenths are kept open exclusively for the supply of the laboring population. . . . They are open at the earliest hour, when the shivering artisan is proceeding to his work, holding out to him a temptation utterly irresistible—and remain open during a considerable portion of the night ministering their poisons.

◈ DOCUMENT 23.4 ◈

Work Rules in a Prussian Factory, 1844

Good order and harmony must be looked upon as the fundamentals of success, and therefore the following rules shall be strictly observed. . . :

(1) The normal working day begins at all seasons at 6 AM precisely and ends, after the usual break of half an hour for breakfast, an hour for dinner and half an hour for tea, at 7 PM. . . . Workers arriving two minutes late shall lose half an hour's wages; whoever is more than two minutes late may not start work until after the next break. . . .

(2) When the bell is rung to denote the end of the working day, every workman . . . shall leave his workshop and the yard, but is not allowed to make preparations for his departure before the bell rings. Every breach of this rule shall lead to a fine of five silver groschen. . . .

(3) No workman . . . may leave before the end of the working day without having first received permission from the overseer. . . .

(4) Repeated irregular arrival at work shall lead to dismissal. . . .

(6) No worker may leave his place of work otherwise than for reasons connected with his work.

(7) All conversation with fellow-workers is prohibited. . . .

(9) Every worker is responsible for cleaning up his space in the workshop. . . .

(12) It goes without saying that all overseers and officials of the firm shall be obeyed without question and shall be treated with due deference. Disobedience will be punished by dismissal. . . .

(15) Every workman is obliged to report to his superiors any acts of dishonesty or embezzlement on the part of his fellow workmen. If he omits to do so, and it is shown after the subsequent discovery of a misdemeanor that he knew about it at the time, he shall be liable to be taken to court as an accessory after the fact.

the waist. But the environment was hardly erotic: Machines filled the air with a deafening roar, the nose with overheating grease, and the eyes and lungs with cotton dust. This combination gave Manchester the world's highest rate of bronchial ailments, a life expectancy sharply below the national average, and a horrifying infant mortality rate of 50 percent.

Jobs in these dreadful conditions also required workers to adapt to a new discipline (see document 23.4). Most workers came from the countryside, where they were accustomed to agricultural work defined by the rhythms of nature—the seasons, daylight, weather—or to such self-disciplined labor as spinning or weaving at home. Factory work was a regime of rules enforced by an overseer, regimentation by the clock or the pace of a machine. Typical industrial work rules forbade talking or singing. Fines for misbehavior were deducted from wages. The first large spinning factory in England fired an average of twenty workers per week and averaged a 100-percent turnover within one year. One of the most famous novels of the nineteenth century, Gustave Flaubert's *Madame Bovary*, ends with the thought that life in the dark, Satanic mills was appropriate punishment for sin. The protagonist of the novel, Emma Bovary, commits adultery and then suicide. Her relatives refuse to accept the care of Emma's orphaned daughter; the child is punished for the shame of Emma's behavior by being sent to earn her living in a cotton mill.

Other contemporaries defended the conditions of industrialization. Frederick Eden began the optimistic tradition with his defense of agricultural enclosures in *The State of the Poor* (1797). Eden acknowledged that the consolidation of farms might hurt small farmers and farm laborers, but he argued that the difficult straits that they faced were "but temporary" and they must be balanced against "the greater good which may be expected from the improvement." Early champions of industry went further in their defense of the factory system. Andrew Ure, a Scottish scientist angered at the criticism of industrialization, wrote a thoroughly optimistic book in 1835, entitled *The Philosophy of Manufactures* (see document 23.5). To Ure, the factory system was nothing less than "the great minister of civilization." He found workers to be "willing menials" who were "earning abundant food, raiment, and domestic accommodation without perspiring at a single pore."

Economic historians have shown much data to support the optimistic view that industrialization improved life for most people. The most obvious argument is that of the conquest of the biological old regime and the

unregulated workplaces had terrible safety standards; with no guards on the new machinery, mutilating accidents were common. Factories were unbearably hot, so men, women, and children often worked stripped to

◆ DOCUMENT 23.5 ◆

Andrew Ure: The Factory System, 1835

Andrew Ure (1778–1857) was a Scottish chemist and the author of several reference books about chemistry, mining, and manufacturing. He wrote The Philosophy of Manufactures *(1835) to respond to the criticism of factory conditions.*

In my recent tour, continued during several months, through the manufacturing districts, I have seen tens of thousands of old, young, and middle-aged of both sexes—many of them too feeble to get their daily bread by any of the former modes of industry—earning abundant food, raiment, and domestic accommodation without perspiring at a single pore, screened meanwhile from the summer's sun and the winter's frost, in an apartment more airy and salubrious than those of the metropolis, in which our legislative and fashionable aristocracies assemble. In those spacious halls, the benign power of steam summons around him his myriads of willing menials, and assigns to each the regulated task, substituting for painful muscular effort on their part the energies of his own gigantic arm and demanding in return only attention and dexterity to correct such little aberrations as casually occur in his workmanship. The gentle docility of this moving force qualifies it for impelling the tiny bobbins of the lace machine with a precision and speed inimitable by the most dexterous hands, directed by the sharpest eyes. Hence, under its auspices . . . magnificent edifices, surpassing far in number, value, usefulness, and ingenuity of construction the boasted monuments of Asiatic, Egyptian, and Roman despotism, have within the short period of fifty years risen up in this kingdom to show to what extent capital, industry, and science may augment the resources of the state while they meliorate the condition of its citizens. Such is the factory system, replete with prodigies in mechanics and political economy, which promises in its future growth to become the great minister of civilization.

significantly increased life expectancy (see chapter 24). Newborn infants in 1700 had an average life expectancy of less than forty years; by 1824 it had reached fifty years. Witnesses might describe terrible living conditions during industrialization, but increased life expectancy must prove that conditions had improved in some substantial ways.

Industrialization not only coincided with a longer life expectancy; evidence exists that it improved the quality of daily life for most people. Economic historians substantiate this assertion with evidence about wages paid to workers and prices charged for goods. If wages increase more than prices over a long period of time, economists conclude that the quality of life has improved. Such data are difficult to obtain and to interpret, but they can show the long-term benefits of industrialization. Not surprisingly, data for the early nineteenth century show that the price of essential textile goods (such as a suit of clothes) decreased. Improvements in agriculture and transportation lowered the price of some food and drink, such as a barrel of beer that had to be shipped from a brewery to a town. Wages of workers did not improve greatly, and in some preindustrial occupations—such as a handloom weaver—they declined severely. But the data show a general pattern of improvement. Whereas a carpenter working in the London region had to work thirteen or fourteen days in 1800 to earn enough money to buy a suit, the same carpenter's wages in 1830 bought a suit in seven or eight days.

Industrialization also provided luxuries that workers previously could not afford. By the 1840s railway expansion led to inexpensive excursion tickets. Railroads reinforced the rigid social structure of nineteenth-century Europe by segregating passengers according to the class of tickets they bought, but the existence of cheap second- or third-class tickets led to the birth of the working-class holiday. For the first time, most of the population of London could afford a day trip to the seashore. Workers had little leisure time to enjoy this benefit, but inexpensive travel allowed more than one-third of the total population of Great Britain to visit the world exposition in London in 1851.

◆

From the British Industrial Revolution to Continental European Industrialization

British industrialization dwarfed the manufactures of any other country in the late eighteenth and early nineteenth century, but Britain was not unique in experiencing industrial development. In the textile industry, for example, Belgium had been an important manufacturer of cloth for centuries and rapidly industrialized following the British example. Textile towns such as

Manchester developed across Europe, from Mulhouse in Alsace to Łodz in Poland. Many regions experienced their own industrial revolutions. Industrialization in the Rhône valley of southeastern France, for example, assured predominance in the manufacture of silk. Mechanical and chain-driven looms came into use there in the 1770s, although they had been known in China for centuries. In 1801 Joseph Jacquard of Lyons invented a silk loom that used punch cards to direct a mechanical loom to weave elaborate patterns in silk—a brilliant system that provided the inspiration for computer cards in the twentieth century. By the 1780s, more than 23 percent of the population of Lyons worked in the silk industry. The delicacy of silk work delayed the development of a power silk loom, but when one was developed in the mid-nineteenth century, Lyons remained the center of silk manufacturing because it was located near the rich coal fields of St. Etienne.

The industrialization of continental Europe was slowed by the French Revolution and the Napoleonic Wars. Postwar economic problems were severe, and Europe remained in a depression until 1820. Governments hurried to demobilize their expensive armies, and this left hundreds of thousands of veterans unemployed. Jobs were scarce because governments also canceled wartime contracts for food, uniforms, and equipment, leading to the dismissal of agricultural, textile, and metallurgical workers. Most governments were deep in war debt; Prussia, for example, could barely pay the interest on war loans. Governments promised to cancel the war taxes needed for big armies, but that created the combination of high debt and reduced revenue when governments needed huge sums of money to rebuild the regions devastated by war. Roads and bridges required immediate attention to support the recovery of commerce. Some governments, such as Bourbon France, tried to raise revenue with protective tariffs, but this led to the further contraction of foreign trade. Bad weather and poor harvests compounded all of these problems. Consequently, Britain enjoyed a long lead in industrialization.

Nevertheless, Europe experienced steady industrialization in the early nineteenth century. Traditional textile regions, such as Alsace and Normandy in France, rapidly adapted to the age of the spinning mule and the power loom. A study of the Alsatian textile industry has shown its expansion from a total of 48,000 spindles in 1812 to 466,000 spindles in 1828. There were only 426 power looms in Alsace in 1827, but there were 6,000 a decade later and more than 18,000 power looms in 1856. The strength of conti-

nental textiles in the nineteenth century is shown by the English language, which borrowed European words for textiles: Elegant Jacquard silks came from Lyons, and sturdy cotton denim came "from Nîmes" (*de Nîmes* in French).

Another sign of continental industrialization was the beginning of the railroad age in the 1830s and 1840s. Here, too, Britain long retained the pioneer's advantage, but Europe slowly caught up (see table 23.5). The French opened a small line in 1828 to connect the coal fields of St. Etienne with the national canal and river system, but they were slow to build a large railroad network. No passenger service was established between Paris and Lyons until the 1850s. In most countries, the first tracks were laid in the 1830s or 1840s. Progressive statesmen such as Count Camilio Cavour of Piedmont-Sardinia made their reputations as early champions of the railroad. Cavour was convinced that "their economic importance will be from the outset magnificent," and by 1850 the Italian states had more miles of track than Russia and Spain combined.

The country that most profited from the beginning of continental industrialization was Prussia. This was partly the result of Prussian military success, which led to the annexation of rich mineral deposits. The wars of Frederick the Great had acquired the coal fields of Silesia and the defeat of Napoleon brought Prussia the iron and coal deposits of the Rhineland. The Prussian government also encouraged industrialization. Karl Freiherr vom Stein reorganized the government after the catastrophic loss to Napoleon in 1806. Stein secured the abolition of serfdom in 1807, and the emancipation edict had far-reaching economic provisions that opened landownership and granted the aristocracy freedom to choose any occupation. Friedrich von Motz, the Prussian minister of finance in the 1820s, presided over a similar modernization that included the abolition of internal tariffs; free trade treaties with neighboring German states; and finally the formation of the *Zollverein*, a customs union that propelled Prussia toward the economic leadership of central Europe. King Frederick William IV encouraged industrialization by his love of trains: The king supported railroad construction at a time when the emperor of Austria detested railroads and impeded their construction. The Prussian Railway Fund of 1842 provided government assistance to private companies investing in railroad expansion. And Prussia sponsored the Union of German Railways in 1847 to guarantee that compatible rail systems were built throughout the German states.

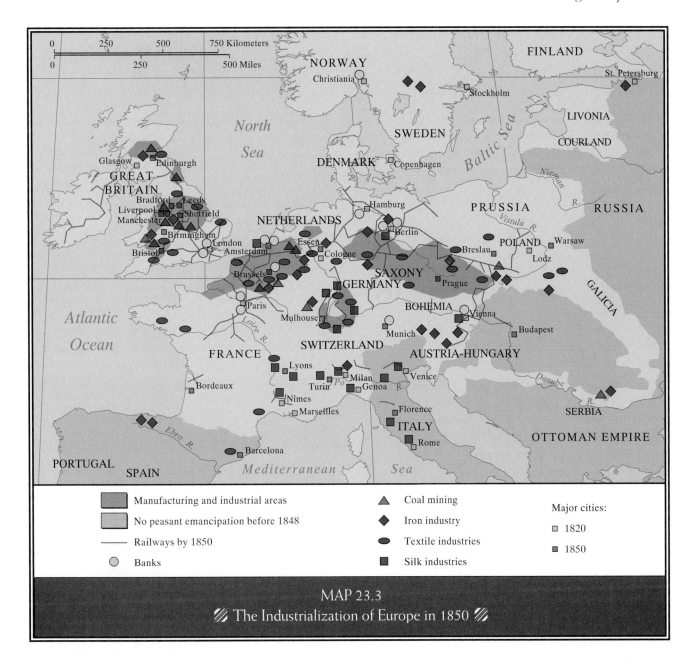

Manufacturing and industrial areas

No peasant emancipation before 1848

Railways by 1850

Banks

Coal mining

Iron industry

Textile industries

Silk industries

Major cities:
1820
1850

MAP 23.3
The Industrialization of Europe in 1850

The European Industrial "Take-Off"

Economic historians use the term *take-off phase* to describe the period when a nascent industrial economy begins to expand rapidly. For much of western and central Europe, the take-off of industrialization occurred in the middle of the nineteenth century (see map 23.3). The word *capitalism* was coined during this mid-century generation, and Karl Marx published his famous critique of industrial capitalism, *Das Kapital.* The British celebrated their new society in a spectacular world's fair in London, known as the Crystal Palace Exhibition

(1851), which showed the world the latest technical and mechanical wonders. Not surprisingly, some historians call this period the "age of capital."

Industrialization did not spread evenly across Europe, and the great powers did not industrialize in the same ways. Nor did the take-off phase mean that continental production caught up to Britain in a single generation. Between 1851 and 1869, British heavy industry continued to grow at a steady rate; iron production increased by 20 percent and coal production by 119 percent (see table 23.10). The French growth rate in iron production tripled British growth and nearly doubled it

---

✻ TABLE 23.10 ✻

The Take-Off of Heavy Industry in Europe, 1851–69

The data in this table show that Britain was already heavily industrialized in 1851, but none of the other great powers was. The data summarize output in millions of metric tons and show growth in percent. Note that the huge growth in iron and coal output in France and the Germanic states of central Europe—their industrial take-off—still left them far behind British production. Note also the comparison between French industrialization and German industrialization, which is much more rapid; this contrast had great implications for the balance of power on the continent.

Country	Output in 1851		Output in 1860		Output in 1869		Growth 1851–69	
	Iron	Coal	Iron	Coal	Iron	Coal	Iron	Coal
Austria	.5	1.0	n.a.	3.2	.7	6.6	40.0	560.0
Britain	9.7	50.2	8.2	81.3	11.7	109.2	20.6	118.9
France	1.8	4.4	3.0	8.3	3.1	13.5	72.2	202.3
Zollverein	.8	7.8	1.3	16.7	3.1	34.3	287.5	339.7

Source: Compiled from data in B. R. Mitchell, *European Historical Statistics, 1750–1970* (London: Macmillan, 1975), pp. 360–61, 387.

---

in coal. However, in 1869 French iron production remained barely one-fourth of the British rate and coal production one-eighth. Prussia and the smaller German states of the Zollverein increased iron and coal production at rates that suggest the terms *industrial revolution* and *take-off phase.* Both iron and coal production nearly quadrupled within a generation. German rates did not yet threaten British leadership, but the Zollverein had passed French production and the rate of production portended a future Anglo-German rivalry.

The continental industrial take-off can also be seen in the expansion of railroad networks (see table 23.11). The midcentury was an age of railway construction across the continent. Austria, Belgium, Italy, and Spain all built large national systems. Russia remained backward; in 1850 tiny Belgium had a larger railroad network. By 1870 a Russian building program had added more than ten thousand kilometers of track, but that meant that a country of more than twenty-two million square kilometers was served by half as much railroad as Great Britain, a country of 300,000 square kilometers. France and Germany both neared the size of the British network in 1870, but they, too, were much larger.

Such data show that France industrialized at a significant pace but never experienced the exponential rate of change that characterized the British industrial revolution or German industrialization. No population explosion occurred in France, and the government never completely abandoned the mercantilist tradition of a centrally directed economy. The mid-century government of Napoleon III encouraged the industrial take-off with institutions such as the Crédit Foncier, which provided low-interest business loans. A Railroad Law of 1857 guaranteed the interest payments of private railroad bonds, so investors could not lose. This law so stimulated railroad building that a system with 2,915 kilometers of track in 1850 grew to 16,465 kilometers before 1870.

German industrial development varied regionally, with the greatest strength concentrated in Prussia and

---

✻ TABLE 23.11 ✻

European Railroad Expansion, 1850–70

Data are kilometers of railroad track in use.

Country	1850	1860	1870
Austria	1,357	2,927	6,112
Belgium	854	1,729	2,897
Britain	9,798	14,603	19,987
France	2,915	9,167	16,465
Germany/Zollverein	5,856	11,089	17,211
Italy	620	2,404	6,429
Russia	501	1,626	10,731
Spain	28	1,649	5,295

Source: Compiled from data in B. R. Mitchell, *European Historical Statistics, 1750–1970* (London: Macmillan, 1975), pp. 581–84.

Illustration 23.9

The Krupp Works at Essen. The Krupp family have been armaments makers at Essen, in the Ruhr River valley of western Germany, since the sixteenth century. The Krupp Works pioneered modern steel manufacturing. Under Alfred Krupp (1812–87), "the cannon king," the firm contributed significantly to German unification; under his son Fritz (1854–1902), the Krupp Works became the largest steel works in the world.

the Rhineland. The German take-off was rapid. Between 1851 and 1857, the number of Prussian joint-stock companies, and their total capitalization, tripled. Prussian legislation encouraged British-style laissez-faire capitalism. New mining laws, for example, ended state control of coal mines, broke the powers of the miners' guild, and cut the taxes on mines by 50 percent. Prussian coal production sharply increased. The Krupp Works of Essen showed the similar growth of the metallurgical industry. Krupp had been a small, and nearly bankrupt, iron foundry with seven employees when it began to manufacture ordnance in 1847. Alfred Krupp won the firm's first government contract in 1859, and within a decade the Krupp Works became the largest arms manufacturer in central Europe, with iron and steel mills that made it one of the largest industrial combines in the world (see illustration 23.9).

Conclusion

The industrial revolution and the spread of urban industrial society are among the most profound changes that humanity has experienced. If one focuses on economic structures and the society associated with them, industrialization was the biggest change since the shift from hunting-and-gathering civilizations to agricultural societies. If one focuses on modern history, the industrial revolution and the vital revolution must stand alongside the French Revolution as the strongest features of modernity.

The industrialization of Europe began with a population explosion in the late eighteenth century. After centuries of limited growth, Europe grew from a continent of 110 million people in 1700 to 423 million in 1900. The source of this population explosion was a vital revolution in which the restraints of the biological old regime were overcome. The initial key to the vital revolution was the improvement of diet through an agricultural revolution that increased the food supply. The consequence of rapid population growth was the urbanization of Europe because neither land nor agricultural employment were sufficient to support the larger population.

While the population was growing rapidly, technological innovations led to new employment in the cities. The steam engine, originally devised to drain water from mines, provided a source of power for a variety of new machines. The textile industry best exploited this power source, using steam engines for power spinning and weaving. This led to the birth of the textile factory where steam-powered machinery such as Cartwright's power loom employed thousands of laborers.

The economic success of industrialization created a powerful class in society, an industrial and manufacturing middle class that possessed great wealth in capital from the profits of coal and iron mining, metallurgy, factory manufacturing, and large-scale commerce. At the other end of the social scale, industrialization produced a large urban working class who labored in the mills and the mines. They often endured dreadful working and living conditions, and they suffered severe economic exploitation; women and children constituted a large percentage of the new industrial labor force and received especially bad treatment. Such issues have led to a long-standing debate between social historians (who depict the wretched conditions of life in the early industrial age) and economic historians (who present data to show that the standard of living improved during industrialization).

The industrial revolution chiefly took place in Great Britain at first, although important pockets of industrialization were evident on the continent. After the Napoleonic Wars, industrialization spread in Europe, reaching the take-off stage of rapid growth during the mid-nineteenth century. Great Britain became a predominantly urban and industrial society in the census of 1850, and several decades passed before other nations matched that standard, but the gap was closing.

Suggested Readings

In addition to the works cited here, see the suggested readings for chapter 18.

The indispensable reference book for modern European economic history is B. R. Mitchell, ed., *European Historical Statistics, 1750–1970* (1975); B. Bunch and A. Hellemans, eds., *The Timetables of Technology* (1993) is helpful for industrial technology.

For additional demographic studies, see C. Corsini and P. Viazzo, eds., *The Decline of Infant and Child Mortality: The European Experience, 1750–1990* (1997), A. Bideau and B. Desjardins, eds., *Infant and Child Mortality in the Past* (1997); M. Flinn, *British Population Growth, 1700–1850* (1970); J. Saville, *Rural Depopulation in England and Wales, 1851–1951* (1957); R. Mitchison, *British Population Change since 1860* (1977); L. Moch, *Paths to the City: Regional Migration in Nineteenth Century France* (1983); K. Bade, ed., *Population, Labour, and Migration in Nineteenth- and Twentieth-Century Germany* (1987); M. Walker, *Germany and the Emigrations, 1816–1865* (1964); and D. Baines, *Emigration from Europe, 1815–1930* (1995).

For the industrial revolution, see the older, but still classical, work by P. Mantoux, *The Industrial Revolution in the Eighteenth Century* (1961); T. S. Ashton, *The Industrial Revolution* (1948), a brief introduction, stressing the human side; D. Landes, *The Unbound Prometheus: Technological Change and Industrial Development in Western Europe from 1750 to the Present Day* (1969); P. Dean, *The First Industrial Revolution* (1965); E. A. Wrigley, *Continuity, Chance, and Change: The Character of the Industrial Revolution in England* (1988); and R. M. Hartwell, ed., *The Causes of the Industrial Revolution* (1967), an anthology presenting several conflicting perspectives. For industrialized Britain, see J. H. Clapham, *An Economic History of Modern Britain*, 3 vols. (1926–39), and F. Crouzet, *The Victorian Economy* (1982).

For continental and comparative industrialization, see A. Milward and S. Saul, *The Economic Development of Continental Europe,*

2 vols. (1977–79); T. Kemp, *Industrialization in Nineteenth-Century Europe* (1985); C. Trebilcock, *The Industrialization of the Continental Powers, 1780–1914* (1981); W. O. Henderson, *The Industrial Revolution in Europe* (1961) and *The Industrialization of Europe, 1780–1914* (1969); F. Crouzet, *Britain Ascendant* (1990), on the continental effort to catch up; P. O'Brien and C. Keyder, *Economic Growth in Britain and France, 1780–1914* (1978); J. H. Clapham, *The Economic Development of France and Germany, 1815–1914* (1936); C. Kindleberger, *Economic Growth in France and Britain* (1964); and A. L. Dunham, *The Industrial Revolution in France, 1815–1848* (1955).

For steam power, see R. L. Hills, *Power from Steam: A History of the Stationary Steam Engine* (1989), and H. W. Dickinson, *James Watt, Craftsman and Engineer* (1936). For heavy industrialization, see M. Flinn and others, *The History of the British Coal Industry,* 4 vols. (1984–87); D. Reid, *The Miners of Decazeville* (1985); and C. K. Hyde, *Technological Change and the British Iron Industry, 1700–1870* (1977). For the textile industries, see N. B. Harte and K. G. Ponting, eds., *Textile History and Economic History* (1973); S. D. Chapman and S. Chassagne, *European Textile Printers in the Eighteenth Century* (1981); A. P. Wadsworth and J. de Lacy Mann, *The Cotton Trade and Industrial Lancashire, 1600–1780* (1931); D. A. Farnie, *The English Cotton Industry and the World Market* (1979); and R. S. Fitton, *The Arkwrights: Spinners of Fortune* (1989), which focuses on Sir Richard Arkwright. For transportation and the railroad age, see H. J. Dyos and D. Aldcroft, *British Transport: An Economic Survey from the Seventeenth Century to the Twentieth* (1969); and G. W. Hawke, *Railways and Economic Growth in England and Wales* (1970).

For urbanization, see R. Rotberg and T. Rabb, eds., *Industrialization and Urbanization* (1982); M. D. George, *London Life in the Eighteenth Century* (1984); A. Briggs, *Victorian Cities* (1965), noteworthy essays on several industrial cities; L. D. Schwarz, *London in the Age of Industrialization* (1992), which stresses living conditions; F. Sheppard, *London, 1808–1870* (1971); D. Olsen, *The Growth of Victorian London* (1976); the works of J. Merriman on French urban history, especially *The Margins of City Life* (1991) and *French Cities in the Nineteenth Century* (1981), with essays by many scholars; and D. Jordan, *Transforming Paris* (1995), on Haussmann.

For social classes and industrialization, see S. G. Checkland, *The Rise of Industrial Society in England, 1815–1885* (1964); R. J. Morris, *Class and Class Consciousness in the Industrial Revolution, 1780–1850* (1979); R. S. Neale, *Class in English History, 1680–1850* (1981); H. Perkin, *The Origins of Modern English Society, 1780–1880* (1991); P. Joyce, *Visions of the People: Industrial England and the Question of Class, 1848–1914* (1991); P. Pilbeam, *The Middle Classes in Europe, 1789–1914* (1990); G. Crossick and H.-G. Haupt, eds., *Shopkeepers and Master Artisans in Nineteenth-Century Europe* (1984); C. Emsley and J. Walvin, eds., *Artisans, Peasants, and Proletarians, 1760–1860* (1985); L. Davidoff and C. Hall, *Family Fortunes: Men and Women of the English Middle Class* (1987); T. Koditschek, *Class Formation and Urban Industrial Society* (1990); J. Rule, *The Labouring Classes in Early Industrial England, 1750–1850* (1986); E. P. Thomson, *The Making of the English Working Class* (1963), a classic study of social class; A. J. Rieber, *Merchants and Entrepreneurs in Imperial Russia*

(1982); J. A. Ruckman, *The Moscow Business Elite* (1984); T. Mac-Bride, *The Domestic Revolution: The Modernization of Household Service in England and France, 1820–1920* (1976); P. Horn, *The Rise and Fall of the Victorian Servant* (1989); and M. Ebery, *Domestic Service in Late Victorian and Edwardian England, 1871–1914* (1976).

For women and industrialization, see the suggested readings for chapter 19 and the many helpful essays in L. Frader and S. Rose, eds., *Gender and Class in Modern Europe* (1996) and in D. Hafter, ed., *European Women and Preindustrial Craft* (1995); J. Lown, *Women and Industrialization: Gender at Work in Nineteenth-Century England* (1990); I. Pinchbeck, *Women Workers and the Industrial Revolution, 1750–1850* (1981); M. Vicinus, ed., *Suffer and Be Still: Women in the Victorian Age* (1972); S. Burman, ed., *Fit Work for Women* (1979);

J. Lewis, *Women in England, 1870–1950* (1984); A. John, *Unequal Opportunities: Women's Employment in England, 1800–1918* (1986); J. Coffin, *The Politics of Women's Work* (1996), a case study of the garment trades in France; and R. E. Glickman, *Russian Factory Women* (1984).

For the standard of living debate, see A. Taylor, ed., *The Standard of Living in Britain in the Industrial Revolution* (1975); J. Williamson, *Did British Capitalism Breed Inequality?* (1985); F. Engels, *The Condition of the Working Class in England* (1844), the original passionate Marxist indictment; G. Himmelfarb, *The Idea of Poverty: England in the Early Industrial Age* (1985), a response to the Marxist view; and H. Kaelble, *Industrialization and Social Inequality in Nineteenth Century Europe* (1986).

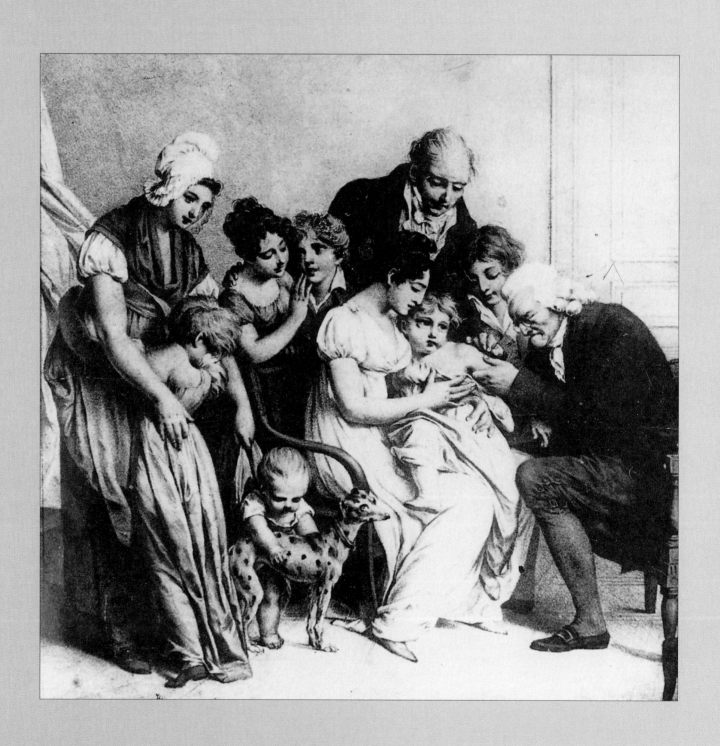

CHAPTER 24

DAILY LIFE IN THE NINETEENTH CENTURY

CHAPTER OUTLINE

◆ ◆

This chapter examines the dramatic changes in the daily life of Europeans during industrialization. The biggest changes were so dramatic that they constitute a vital revolution. In 1800 the average European male had a life expectancy at birth of about thirty-five years, but a boy born in 1900 could expect fifty years and his sister fifty-two years. Chapter 24 discusses the medical and scientific explanations of this great change. Historians attribute 15 percent of all European deaths during the eighteenth century to smallpox; in a typical year, smallpox, typhus, and typhoid together accounted for 35 percent of all deaths. By the early twentieth century, these diseases caused less than 1 percent of deaths in the most advanced regions of Europe. Similarly, the typical adult man of 1800 stood about 5'1" tall, but in the early twentieth century the average reached 5'6". The history of this vital revolution often receives less attention than the actions of princes, popes, and presidents, but no leader affected daily life as much as the conquest of disease and the improvement of diet did. This chapter sets the vital revolution of the nineteenth century alongside the French Revolution and industrial revolution as the formative forces of modern history.

Chapter 24 also looks at other aspects of daily life—the stages of the life cycle. It begins with birth and shows the falling birthrate caused by growing acceptance of birth control. For youth, the nineteenth century meant the beginning of compulsory education. The next great stage in life, marriage, increasingly began at a later age and produced a smaller family than the Old Regime had experienced. Even as basic an aspect of daily life as human sexuality changed during the nineteenth century, and the chapter considers such attitudes as the double standard and new laws regarding sexuality, such as legal prostitution and the banning of homosexuality.

European Demography and the Increase in Life Expectancy

Nineteenth-century demography is a good illustration of historical perspective: The subject looks very different if viewed from the perspective of the mid-eighteenth century or the late twentieth century. The life expectancy of a European male born in 1998 is seventy-two to seventy-four years; females average seventy-eight to eighty-one years. (The figures for the United States are seventy-two and seventy-nine years, respectively.) Typical rates for 1750 ranged between twenty-eight and thirty-three years. Thus, a mean life expectancy of fifty years seems short or long, depending upon one's perspective. The tripling of the average human life was a gradual development over a long duration, but the chief changes occurred in the nineteenth century (see table 24.1). The benefits arrived unequally, and many regions did not experience them until the twentieth century. Scandinavians already expected fifty-five to sixty years of life for a child born in 1900, while Russians still lived in a biological old regime with life expectancies of thirty to thirty-five years, with Spaniards and Italians (forty to forty-five years) in between. Life expectancy also varied by social class; the wealthy usually lived longer than laborers did. A study conducted for the British parliament in 1842 found that in Manchester the average age at death was thirty-eight for professionals, twenty for shopkeepers, and seventeen for the working class.

Many ways are available to study improving life expectancy, but an obvious place to start is the decreasing death rate. The annual mortality rate in the eighteenth century was usually above thirty deaths per one thousand population; it reached thirty-five to thirty-six deaths per one thousand in England in the 1740s. This means that 3 percent of the population died each year. That rate plummeted during the nineteenth century. The lowest mortality rate in Europe on the eve of World War I was a Danish rate of 13.2 per thousand. (Late twentieth-century rates are near to twelve per thousand.) The worst rates were in southern and eastern Europe: Spain had a death rate of 22.8 per thousand and Russia, 29.0, and both represented significant improvements over eighteenth-century rates. The unhealthy environment of cities meant that rates there resembled rural eighteenth-century rates; mortality in Moscow and St. Petersburg was 30–35 per one thousand in the 1880s. Paris (24.4), Berlin (26.5), and Vienna (28.2) also had high death rates.

TABLE 24.1
Life Expectancy in the Nineteenth Century

Country	Period	Male life expectancy at birth (in years)	Female life expectancy at birth (in years)
England and Wales	1838–54	39.9	41.8
	1901–10	48.5	52.3
	1989	72.0	78.0
Denmark	1835–44	42.6	44.7
	1911–15	56.2	59.2
	1989	72.0	79.0
France	1817–31	38.3	40.8
	1908–13	48.4	52.4
	1989	72.0	80.0
Germany	1871–81	35.5	38.4
	1910–11	37.4	50.6
	1989	71.5	78.1
Italy	1876–87	35.1	35.4
	1901–11	44.2	44.8
	1989	73.0	80.0
Russia	1896–97	31.4	33.3
	1989	64.0	74.0
Spain	1900	33.8	35.7
	1910	40.9	42.5
	1989	74.0	80.0
Sweden	1816–40	39.5	43.5
	1901–10	54.5	56.9
	1989	74.0	81.0
United States	1989	72.0	79.0

Source: André Armengaud, "Population in Europe, 1700–1914," in *The Industrial Revolution*, edited by C. Cipolla (London: Collins, 1973), p. 36; *The World Almanac and Book of Facts 1991* (Mahwah, N.J.: World Almanac Books, 1990). pp. 684–770.

The falling mortality rate of the nineteenth century chiefly resulted from declining infant and childhood mortality. A study of Dutch demography has found more than 23 percent of all deaths in Holland in 1811 were infants below the age of one; 41 percent of the dead were children younger than ten. Such figures fell sharply. French rates fell from 16.2 percent of all infants dying in the year of their birth (1840) to 11.1 percent (1910); British rates fell from 15.4 percent (1840) to 10.5 percent (1910). These rates, too, were worse in southern and eastern Europe. Russian infant mortality was especially horrifying—51.9 percent between 1864 and 1879, 36.3 percent for the period 1883–97, and 30.5 percent on the eve of World War I. (The U.S. rate is poor for 1990, but it barely surpasses 1 percent for the total population and just under 2 percent for the

African American population.) As the general death rates imply, infant mortality rates remained high in cities. Madrid and Bucharest both had rates of 21 percent in 1909; Moscow, nearly 32 percent. In the prosperous west, rates were high in manufacturing towns. Roubaix, a French textile center, had an infant mortality rate nearly twice the national average. Death rates remained terrible throughout the years of childhood. In 1897 nearly 50 percent of the children born in rural Russia died before age five, and 68.7 percent did not reach ten. As terrible as such numbers seem in the perspective of the 1990s, they nevertheless represented significant improvement by comparison to the eighteenth century. In 1750 the death rate in London for children before age five had been more than 75 percent; in 1914 only 15 percent of English children died before their fifth birthday. The important facts, therefore, are the decline of infant mortality and the consequent increase in life expectancy.

Disease in Nineteenth-Century Europe

The foremost explanation of these falling death rates lies in the history of contagious disease. One study has suggested that diseases explain 94 percent of all European deaths in the year 1850. The dominion of disease included wars; typhus killed more of Napoleon's soldiers than Wellington's army or the Russian army did (see illustration 24.1). That pattern remained true across the century: Typhus, typhoid, cholera, and smallpox killed more soldiers than enemy fire did. As late as the Boer War (1899–1902), the British army lost 6,425 soldiers in combat and 11,327 soldiers to disease. Contagious diseases killed more people than heart attacks or cancer did, because fewer people lived long enough to experience degenerative problems. At midcentury, even measles killed more people than cancer did. Such death rates contrast sharply with late twentieth-century experience. In 1848 the British deaths from diseases carried by microorganisms stood at 1,296 per 100,000 population (see table 24.2); in late twentieth-century America, the death rate for acquired immune deficiency syndrome (AIDS, 8.6), cancer (199.2), and heart disease (311.9) combined do not reach half of that 1848 rate for contagious diseases.

In the late eighteenth century, Edward Jenner had pointed European civilization toward the conquest of contagious diseases (see chapter 19), but the lesson of smallpox vaccination was learned very slowly. In Jenner's homeland, less than 1 percent of the population

Illustration 24.1

🔲 **Typhus and Warfare.** Dreadful military hygiene meant that eighteenth- and nineteenth-century armies regularly lost more soldiers to typhus than they did on the battlefield. Typhus was a febrile disease, spread by the bite of a body louse that thrives in poor sanitary conditions. It was commonly found in armies, jails, and slums. In this illustration, Napoleon's army in Spain during the Peninsular War (1808–14) is stricken with typhus.

was vaccinated in 1801. Bavaria adopted compulsory vaccination in 1807, and the British government required it in 1835, but many states were slower (see illustration 24.2). Vaccination of all Germans became mandatory in 1874, during the smallpox epidemic of 1870–75, which killed more than 500,000 people in Europe. The Vatican outlawed vaccination, and Catholic states suffered higher death rates. Spain did not require vaccination until 1902, but the new policy did not come in time to prevent thirty-seven thousand Spanish smallpox deaths between 1901 and 1910. Even these numbers seem small compared with the horrors of public health in Russia. Four hundred thousand Russians died of smallpox in 1901–10, and one Orthodox sect still fought against vaccination, calling the resultant smallpox scar "the mark of the Anti-Christ." In contrast, Denmark recorded only thirteen smallpox deaths during that decade, and Sweden became the first country ever to go through an entire year (1895) with no smallpox deaths.

Tragedies such as the smallpox epidemic of 1870–75, or the Spanish and Russian crises of 1901–10, are noteworthy facts, but the virtual disappearance of smallpox in Denmark and Sweden is more important in understanding the nineteenth century as an age both of disease and the conquest of it. Childhood diseases—such as measles, whooping cough, and scarlet fever—account for less than 0.1 percent of deaths in the

⚜ TABLE 24.2 ⚜

The Death Rate in England from Infectious Diseases, 1848–1901

Disease	1848 deaths per million population	1901 deaths per million population	Percentage change
Airborne diseases	7,259	5,122	−29.4
Tuberculosis (respiratory)	2,901	1,268	−56.3
Bronchitis, pneumonia, influenza	2,239	2,747	+22.7
Scarlet fever and diphtheria	1,016	407	−59.9
Whooping cough	423	312	−26.2
Measles	342	278	−18.7
Smallpox	263	10	−96.2
Ear, pharynx, larynx infections	75	100	+33.3
Water- and food-borne diseases	3,562	1,931	−45.8
Cholera, diarrhea, dysentery	1,819	1,232	−32.3
Typhoid and typhus	990	155	−84.3
Tuberculosis (nonrespiratory)	753	544	−27.8
Sexually transmitted diseases	50	164	+228.0
Syphilis	50	164	+228.0
Other diseases attributable to microorganisms			
Convulsions and teething	1,322	643	−52.4
Appendicitis and peritonitis	75	86	+14.7
Puerperal fever	62	64	+3.2
All others	635	458	−27.9
Total attributable to microorganisms	12,965	8,468	−34.7
Other death rates	8,891	8,490	−4.5
Heart diseases	698	1,673	+139.7
Cancer	307	844	+174.9
Violence	761	640	−15.9

Note: Data for 1848 are an average for the period 1848–54.

Source: Calculated from data in Thomas McKeown, *The Modern Rise of Population* (London: Academic Press, 1976), pp. 54–55, 58, 60, 62.

Illustration 24.2

⚜ **Smallpox Vaccination.** If historians periodized the past on the basis of daily life instead of war and revolution, modern history would not start with dates such as the French Revolution (1789) or the defeat of Napoleon (1815). A more important date would be 1796, when Edward Jenner successfully vaccinated a young boy against smallpox. The gradual acceptance of vaccination during the nineteenth century—such as in this French scene of 1820—led to the total elimination of smallpox, a scourge that had killed more people than wars and revolutions combined.

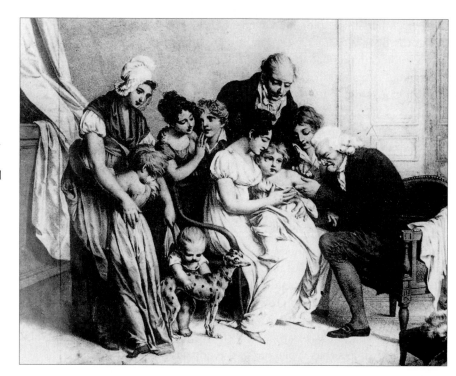

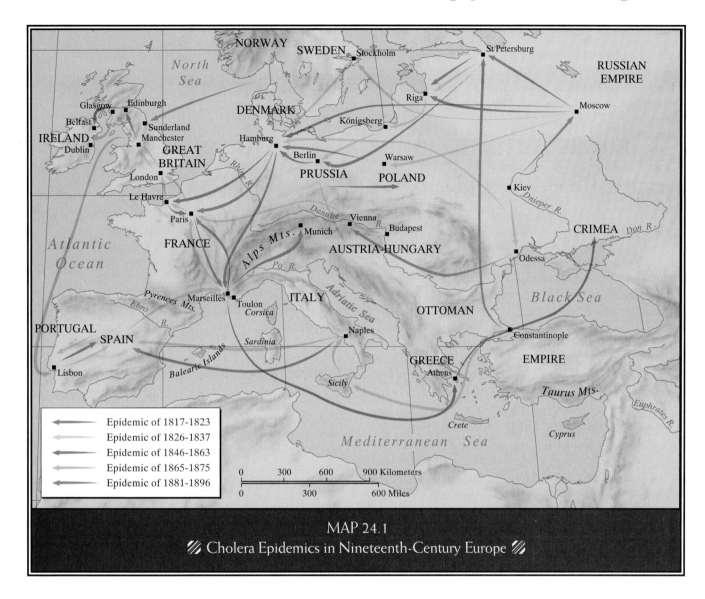

MAP 24.1
Cholera Epidemics in Nineteenth-Century Europe

Western world in the late twentieth century, but they remained virulent killers during the nineteenth century. An outbreak of scarlet fever killed nearly twenty-thousand children in Britain in 1840. The inhabitants of Denmark's Faeroe Islands suffered badly in 1846 because they had experienced sixty-five years without a case of the measles. No one had acquired immunity to the disease in childhood, and when a worker brought measles to the islands, 78 percent of the population (6,100 people) caught the disease and 106 adults died.

The most persistent epidemic disease of nineteenth-century Europe was cholera, an acute diarrheal disease usually transmitted through contaminated drinking water. Major epidemics swept Europe repeatedly—in 1817–23, 1826–37, 1846–63, 1865–75, and 1881–96 (see map 24.1). They typically arrived from India, where cholera was endemic along the Ganges River. That path of infection, combined with poor pub-

lic health standards, meant that Russia suffered terribly from cholera. One study has found that Russia endured fifty-eight years of cholera epidemic between 1823 and 1926. In that century, 5.5 million Russians contracted cholera and 2.1 million of them died.

A cholera epidemic of 1831–33 was especially severe. It initially moved from India to Persia to Russia. The Russian army sent to suppress the Polish revolution of 1830–31 carried cholera into central Europe. This biological tax on military action took 1,835 lives in Berlin (nearly 1 percent of the population) before moving westward. The epidemic reached Glasgow (population 202,000) in February 1832, and before it left, 1.6 percent of the city had died. When the epidemic struck Paris, it killed 2.5 percent of the population (19,000 people). If a catastrophe had that impact on New York City in 1990, it would kill 183,000 people in ten months.

Illustration 24.3

✍ Sewer Systems. Between 1854, when John Snow demonstrated a connection between sewage-contaminated drinking water and cholera, and 1884, when Robert Koch identified the organism that transmitted cholera, progressive city governments launched sewer construction and clean water programs. British and French programs contributed to a significant reduction in cholera there by the 1890s, while other societies, such as Germany and Russia, suffered terribly. In Paris, the huge network of sewers so fascinated people that they figured as a prominent setting in Victor Hugo's *Les Misérables* and became a tourist attraction, as seen here.

Such numbers were basic facts of life in the nineteenth century. London had 20,000 cholera deaths in 1849–53, chiefly because the city dumped untreated sewage into the Thames River and collected drinking water nearby. Between 1853 and 1856, cholera killed 52,000 people in Britain and 140,000 in France, not counting 18,000 Anglo-French soldiers who died of cholera during the Crimean War. After an English doctor, John Snow, proved that cholera was spread by contaminated water, sewer systems and water filtration plants spared Britain and France the worst ravages of later epidemics (see illustration 24.3). This lesson, like smallpox vaccination, was only accepted slowly, however. Snow's message might have prevented the epidemic of 1884–85, which killed more than 120,000 people in Spain, or the epidemic of 1892–93, which ravaged the German port of Hamburg, killing 8,600 people in a few months (see table 24.3). A study of the Hamburg epidemic has highlighted the correlation between social class and disease: The higher a person's annual income, the lower the chance of catching cholera or of dying from it. The poor died at a rate twelve to thirteen times higher than the rich did. Both Hamburg and its more affluent suburb of Altona took their water from the same source, but Altona had a filtration system. Hamburg had a death rate of 13.4 per thousand; Altona, 2.1. The rich and famous did die—the composer Peter Tchaikovsky died later in that same epidemic—but the public health standards for their neighborhoods spared them much of the suffering found in cities.

Medicine, Public Health, and the Conquest of Disease

In 1800 the medical profession was virtually powerless to prevent diseases, the foremost exception being Jenner's smallpox vaccine, announced in 1798. Physicians had no power over infectious diseases because they did not know what caused them. They also had limited ability to control pain or to perform surgery because they lacked anesthetic drugs. During the vital revolution of the nineteenth century, those facts changed: Scientists proved the germ theory of disease transmission (which led to antiseptic surgery and to the conquest of many infectious diseases) and they discovered effective anesthetics. Nothing in all of modern history is more important than these facts for the improved quality of daily life.

The germ theory of disease transmission held that organisms invisible to the naked eye caused contagious diseases. These microorganisms (a term coined in 1880) might be spread by air (as was smallpox), by water or food (as was cholera), or by sexual intercourse (as was syphilis). The germ theory had been proposed by a Roman physician in the first century B.C., but physicians repeatedly rejected it in favor of other theories, such as the humoral theory (humors in the body were unbalanced) of the ancient world. The microscope revealed the existence of microorganisms in the seventeenth century, but scientists still favored the miasmal theory of diseases, which stressed vapors arising from the ground. The medical establishment remained so reluctant to accept the germ theory that in 1892 a German

TABLE 24.3

The Hamburg Cholera Epidemic of 1892

Annual income in marks (1 mark = 25¢)	Number of people	Percentage who caught cholera	Percentage who died
800–1,000	28,647	11.4	6.2
1,000–2,000	32,848	10.0	5.5
2,000–3,500	14,544	4.7	2.7
3,500–5,000	6,125	4.0	2.2
5,000–10,000	5,649	3.1	1.6
10,000–25,000	3,328	1.8	1.0
25,000–50,000	1,182	1.7	1.1
50,000+	834	0.6	0.5

Source: Richard J. Evans, *Death in Hamburg* (Oxford: Oxford University Press, 1987), p. 408. Used by permission of the publisher.

physician drank a beaker full of cholera bacteria to prove that microorganisms did not cause the disease. He did not die, but his theories did.

The germ theory was important for several reasons. First, it led to greater cleanliness, thereby reducing disease transmission. Without the knowledge that invisible organisms transmitted disease, no need existed for antiseptic conditions. Without antisepsis, doctors' offices, hospitals, and surgeries were deadly places. Hospitals packed fifty or sixty people into shared wards, where they also shared diseases. Surgeries had walls and floors impregnated with the waste of recent operations, the floors typically sprinkled with sawdust to soak up the mess. Surgeons wore frock coats, spattered with the blood of their patients; they tied whipcord, used to sew incisions shut, to their buttonholes, where it dangled in the blood of other patients. Doctors treated one patient after another often without washing their hands, and surgeons operated without washing their implements. Not surprisingly, survival rates were low. Even maternity wards were deadly, often having a 25 to 30 percent death rate for new mothers from puerperal fever, spread by physicians who performed examinations with unwashed fingers. General infections were so common that they were simply called "hospital disease." As Florence Nightingale later lamented, "The very first requirement in a hospital is that it should do the sick no harm."

The research of French chemist Louis Pasteur and German physician Robert Koch convinced the medical world to accept the germ theory of disease transmis-

sion. Pasteur's early work proved that microorganisms in the environment caused fermentation in beverages and the decay of organic matter. This knowledge led Pasteur, Koch, and others to the identification of the bacilli causing various diseases and then to the creation of vaccines against them (see document 24.1). Pasteur's research showed how to keep dairy products and beer fresh by eliminating microorganisms (through "pasteurization") and led to a vaccination against rabies. Koch conducted similar work on tuberculosis, and in 1882 he isolated the bacillus of the disease that had killed an encyclopedia full of the creative artists of the nineteenth century, including the English romantic poet John Keats (at twenty-five), the Polish pianist Frederic Chopin, the French painter Paul Gaugin, and the Italian violinist Nicolo Paganini.

Even before Pasteur's final proof of the germ theory a few physicians had called for antiseptic medicine without being able to prove their case. The greatest early champion of antisepsis was Dr. Ignaz Semmelweiss, whose ideas earned him the nickname "the savior of mothers" and the scorn of his colleagues. Semmelweiss was an assistant in Vienna's maternity clinic in the 1840s. He observed high rates of puerperal fever among women whose doctors treated patients in other parts of the hospital, and this convinced him that simple cleanliness could reduce the death rate. Semmelweiss asked that doctors wash their hands in a chloride of lime solution before delivering a baby. He required such antisepsis in the Viennese delivery ward in 1847, and within a few weeks the death rate from puerperal

Illustration 24.5

Canned Food. Methods of preserving food in sealed metal cans—by boiling them—were developed for the military in the first years of the nineteenth century, but the cost of canned food was high when it first reached the stores in the 1830s. The first cans were handcrafted, and a worker produced approximately one can per hour, so a single can of meat or fish cost nearly as much as a working-class family paid for a week's rent. Factory methods, shown in this scene from 1870, increased production until prices fell and the average family's diet improved.

vided, with more variety and more protein. The people of Antwerp received 10 percent of their calories from meat and nearly a quarter from animal products in 1850—a big change from eighteenth-century averages. Similar studies of the German diet in the mid-nineteenth century found an average of 1.3 ounces of meat per day, an amount that seems paltry if compared with late twentieth-century Europe but an amount that would have indicated prosperity in the eighteenth century. An increased consumption of fruits and vegetables came more slowly; they typically remained expensive, or seasonal, food for most people. The introduction of canned foods for Napoleon's army did not yield widespread improvements until the 1850s and 1860s (see illustration 24.5). It also did not initially offer great availability of canned fruit or vegetables, because demand was highest for canned meats and canning was expensive.

Most studies of food consumption show steady improvement across the nineteenth century. The study of workhouse diets in Britain, for example, found that men received 2,350 calories in the 1880s–1890s, an improvement of nearly 20 percent from the 1830s; the diet of women in workhouses rose to 2,070 calories, an increase of slightly more than 10 percent. Thus, the poorest level of British society, whom the government treated with intentional stringency, ate better, too. Similarly, a study of German diets found that by 1910 per capita meat consumption had reached 4.5 ounces per day. Even if much of this came in tin cans, or much of it were horse meat (a habit promoted in European armies), this average would have seemed utopian in the eighteenth century.

The chief explanation for this improvement is that food prices declined significantly. The age of free trade ended tariffs on food and permitted the importation of cheaper food from around the world. In London, for example, the Napoleonic Wars had kept the price of a loaf of bread—then a four-pound loaf—artificially high at eleven to seventeen pence (approximately twenty-three to thirty-five cents), and it had fallen to a range of eight to twelve pence (seventeen to twenty-five cents) in peacetime under the Corn Laws. The repeal of the Corn Laws in 1846 produced a price of seven to eight pence (fifteen to seventeen cents) per loaf. That price fluctuated, but it dropped to an average of five to six pence (ten to twelve cents) for the years 1895–1914. Thus, even if a worker's wages remained unchanged during the entire century, in 1900 they bought nearly three times as much bread as they had in lean years at the start of the century and nearly twice as much bread as they had under the Corn Laws.

Technology also drove down food prices. Vacuum canning, refrigeration, and steam ships enabled Europeans to exploit the agricultural wealth of Argentina, Australia, Canada, and the United States. The cost of shipping goods fell sharply. A study of French costs has shown that shipping goods by sea in 1825 added six centimes to the price for every kilometer that a ton of food was shipped, and once these goods reached France, highway transportation added thirty-three centimes for every kilometer a ton was carted. In 1905, when steamships had replaced sails, sea transportation had fallen to 2.4 centimes (a decrease of 58 percent); railroads had similarly replaced horse-drawn carts, and land transportation had fallen to 5.4 centimes (a decrease of 84 percent). Thus, foreign food fell in price simply because bringing it to market cost less. This competition drove down the price of locally produced food.

The European dietary changes begun by the Columbian Exchange (see chapter 19) accelerated during the nineteenth century. The transportation revolution enabled Europeans to sustain their growing addiction to cheap sugar even after the abolition of slavery in the Caribbean. The British consumption of sugar had tripled between 1700 and 1815, and it tripled again by the 1850s, then nearly tripled once more between 1850 and 1900, making per capita sugar consumption in 1900 twenty times as great as in 1700. Sugar had become a necessity. Furthermore, another plant from the Columbian Exchange, the potato, became an integral part of the European diet in the nineteenth century. That dependence upon the potato had catastrophic results for Ireland in the 1840s, when a disease known as the potato blight devastated the country (see chapter 25).

Data showing total consumption in a nation, or data divided to state average consumption, can be misleading. Individual consumption still varied greatly by social class. A study of the English diet in 1900 has suggested that a typical working-class family of four had a weekly food budget of fifteen shillings (about $3.75), while a middle-class family spent the same fifteen shillings for each person. Well-to-do families, who took pride in lavish entertaining, spent thirty shillings per person, sufficient to feed a worker for two weeks. Consequently, workers ate three times per day while the middle classes often consumed four meals. Working-class meals still consisted chiefly of starches, with few fruits or vegetables; meat chiefly came at a special Sunday meal, with occasional supplements such as bacon, sausage, or rabbit.

In contrast, food was a status symbol for the middle classes, the material proof of their success in reaching a standard of living previously limited to the wealthy. Overeating became a conspicuous social process; obesity, a mark of distinction. Standards of both manly and womanly appearance favored robust figures showing that a person did not live on a modest budget. One of the best-selling books of the 1890s was an advice manual for women entitled *How to Become Pleasingly Plump*. Many public figures at the turn-of-the-century cast such large shadows. The prime minister of Britain on the eve of World War I, Sir Henry Campbell-Bannerman, weighed nearly 280 pounds, and his wife was almost as obese. They ate four meals every day, such as the prime minister's regular favorite: a bowl of mutton-broth soup, a fish course of either herring or salmon, then a roast lamb, followed by a grouse, and culminating in multiple desserts, usually an apple tart with fresh strawberries, then gingerbread and butter. His predecessor at the start of the century, the marquess of Salisbury, was only slightly smaller.

The health risks of a working-class diet were different from those of middle class overeating. The foremost problem (beyond obtaining sufficient food) was the adulteration of food. As Europe changed from an agricultural society, in which people produced the food that they ate, to an urban society, in which people purchased their food in markets, unscrupulous merchants exploited the unregulated economy to sell adulterated food. A parliamentary commission found that bread often contained chalk, plaster of Paris, sand, or lime. Powdered clay was mixed with cocoa, ground nut shells with pepper. Sulfuric acid was added to gin, producing a drink with a memorable bite. Sugar was debased with a dried residue from soap boilers. Parliament concluded that 62 percent of all food sold in London was corrupted. The problem was not limited to British cities, and many countries debated pure food laws versus pure capitalism before accepting the government regulation of food, drink, and drugs. The Dutch pioneered such legislation in 1829, and regulations against adulterated food soon followed in France, Belgium, Prussia, and Spain. British merchants continued to insist upon an unregulated market until scandals forced pure food legislation in 1860 and 1872.

The adulteration of food made people initially skeptical of altered or synthetic foods, which began to appear in the nineteenth century. Only after large advertising campaigns did people begin to accept pasteurized milk in which microbes had been killed by sterilization. Two American chemists synthesized a compound in 1879 and accidentally discovered that it was extremely sweet tasting; their "saccharin" was an effective sugar substitute, but people who knew about the corruption of sugar with soap wastes were reluctant to accept a sugar containing no sugar. One of the first successful substitute foods—often called by the German term *Ersatzessen*—was a flour made from potatoes instead of grains. Margarine, the most widely used ersatz food, was invented in a French laboratory in 1869, in response to a contest sponsored by Napoleon III to discover an affordable substitute for butter. The prize-winning recipe was a mixture of beef fat and ground cow's udders. This may seem a scant improvement on the outlawed adulteration, but it was just a short step to the use of vegetable oil instead of rendered beef fat, to create the commercially successful margarines sold to the urban working class.

Drink and Drugs in the Nineteenth Century

The nineteenth century was an age of high consumption of alcohol—compared with the late twentieth century, but not with the eighteenth century—and heavy consumption of opium and cocaine, both of which were legally available. The ravages caused to the human body by excessive alcohol or drugs were poorly understood, and physicians regularly prescribed narcotics as painkillers; some even recommended heavy alcohol consumption. Governments did little to control alcohol or opium sales in 1800. Laissez-faire capitalism, which opposed government restrictions on the market, perpetuated that situation. Furthermore, alcohol taxes kept most governments in business. In 1870, for example, Britain had virtually no income tax but raised 35 percent of its total revenue on alcohol taxes. In Ireland, 54 per-

cent of all government revenue was raised by taxes on alcohol. End-of-the-century Russia raised even more income through a government monopoly on vodka.

Heavy drinking was socially acceptable. William Pitt the Younger frequently addressed Parliament while drunk; on important occasions, he stepped behind the speaker's chair and induced vomiting before making a critical speech. Even the more puritanical Gladstone drank a sherry mixture in Parliament, to ease his way through three-hour speeches. Another prime minister made himself light-headed with ether before speaking, and a fourth took a jolt of opium dissolved in alcohol. If the rich and powerful behaved that way, it is hardly surprising that people who lived in a world of epidemic disease, short life expectancy, seventy-to-eighty-hour workweeks, no welfare legislation for health or retirement, and minimal diets found solace and sociability in cafes, pubs, and beer halls. Heavy drinking was not limited to the cities. In regions where viticulture dominated the economy, peasant wine drinking was prodigious. If wretched living conditions help to explain heavy drinking, nearly universal alcoholism among the peasants of Russia and eastern Europe should be no surprise.

A variety of records reveal the extent of nineteenth-century drinking. The Antwerp study found that beer consumption in the 1820s averaged two bottles per day (twenty-three ounces) for every man, woman, and child in the population, plus approximately one bottle of wine and one bottle of gin each per month; by the 1850s nearly 10 percent of all calories consumed in the city came from alcohol. A similar survey of France in 1900 found a per capita annual consumption rate of 180 liters of wine (240 standard bottles), 27 liters of beer (more than three cases of 12-ounce bottles), and 4.7 liters of distilled spirits (more than 5 bottles of alcohol). Those averages include the entire population. If one excludes children below the age of fourteen (more than 30 percent of the population in 1900), every adult in France had to consume 325 bottles of wine per year; clearly, a significant portion of the population drank more than a bottle per day, all year long, much of it distilled to make a rough brandy. A study of Russia found that 99 percent of peasant families drank vodka. Their spending on vodka exceeded total spending for education, books, oil, gifts, priests, the poor, weddings, and funerals, which may explain why the government chose to tax vodka instead of books. Urban workers in Russia spent fully 25 percent of their total income on vodka. The home secretary (minister of the interior) of Britain offered a slightly different perspective in 1871: There was one pub for every 182 people in the kingdom, without counting refreshment rooms in railway sta-

Illustration 24.6

💫 **Drug Addiction.** Narcotic drugs were legal in nineteenth-century Europe, and many famous people used them, typically beginning for medical reasons. By the end of the century, concern about drug use was rising, as suggested by this fanciful newspaper illustration of morphine users in 1891.

tions, private clubs, and liquor stores. William Booth, the founding "general" of the Salvation Army, described British alcoholism in his book *In Darkest England*. Booth pronounced the British to be "[a] population sodden with drink, steeped in vice, eaten up by every social and physical malady." It was an age of inebriation.

Such dizzying rates of drinking led to efforts to control sales of alcoholic beverages. The first European temperance society was organized in Ireland in 1818, and such groups spread across the British Isles during industrialization. Many motives could be discerned behind the temperance campaign: Some reformers were motivated by religious morality and saw drinking as sinful; others acted from the perspective of social class—sometimes to help families in poverty, sometimes in fear of the poor and crime, sometimes angry about alcohol and absenteeism from work. Although the upper classes were notoriously heavy drinkers, most reformers agreed with employers that drink was "the curse of [the] working class." British law regulated the opening hours of alehouses in 1828 and began the licensing of pubs in 1830. Scottish clergymen won the first prohibi-

tion of alcohol—no sales on Sundays—in 1853. A variety of restrictions followed: It became illegal for workers to be paid in pubs or for publicans to collect any debts for drinking bills. By the late nineteenth century, the temperance movement was an important political force in Britain, and similar movements, such as the Blue Cross in Switzerland and France, had appeared on the continent.

By the time that temperance leagues became active in European cities, advocates of social control were also becoming concerned about opium and cocaine. Opium, which is derived from an easily cultivated flower, has been used medicinally since ancient Mediterranean civilizations; one of the oldest known Egyptian papyri praises its painkilling powers. A Swiss physician popularized medical opium in the sixteenth century in a compound he named laudanum ("highly praised"). Laudanum, a tincture of opium dissolved in alcohol, became a basic medication, and by 1800 it was widely consumed by all who could afford it. The consumption of opium for medical reasons grew during the nineteenth century, and the drug remained widely available without regulation.

Britain imported tons of opium, chiefly from the Ottoman Empire, every year. Most of this stock was reexported to the Far East, where the British were the world's pushers—they had used opium addiction as a means of opening oriental markets. The British fought two Opium Wars (1839–42 and 1856–58) to keep their drug markets open. Even subtracting the reexportation of opium, the British home market was enormous. Domestic consumption grew from 8.5 tons of opium in 1827 to 30.5 tons in 1859, spawning a network of respectable importers, auctioneers, brokers, and merchants (see table 24.6). British governments shared in this lucrative trade through an opium tariff until 1860. The abolition of the tariff cut the price of opium to approximately one shilling (twenty-five cents) per ounce, roughly an agricultural laborer's weekly wages in 1860. While the price remained high and the poor could not afford it (and while knowledge of the dangers remained low), governments did not seek to regulate or outlaw drugs.

Opium was initially a drug of the educated and upper classes, because of its cost and its circulation by physicians. In the early nineteenth century, opium abuse was far more common among famous writers than criminals or the poor. Virtually the entire literary community of romanticism used opium. Thomas de Quincey became famous for a book entitled *Confessions of an English Opium Eater* (1856), which bluntly said, "Thou hast the keys of paradise, O just, subtle, and mighty opium!" Coleridge became renowned for a

N TABLE 24.6 N

Opium Use in England, 1827–77

Year	Opium imports (in tons)	Total home consumption (in tons)	Home consumption (per 1,000 population in pounds)
1827	56.6	8.5	1.31
1837	40.3	18.5	2.48
1847	n.a.	23.0	2.67
1857	68.2	28.0	2.92
1867	136.8	n.a.	n.a.
1877	303.7	n.a.	n.a.

n.a. = Not available.

Source: Condensed from data in Virginia Berridge and Griffith Edwards, *Opium and the People: Opiate Use in Nineteenth Century England* (New Haven, Conn.: Yale University Press, 1987), tables 1–2, pp. 272–74.

poem ("Kubla Kahn") that he composed after an opium-induced fantasy. Byron took a brand of laudanum called the Black Drop and satisfied references to it appear in his writing. Shelley used opium to relieve stress. Keats consumed such large quantities that he even considered using it for suicide. Elizabeth Barrett Browning's spinal problems made her dependent on a daily dose of opium, and her husband concluded that "sleep only came to her in a red hood of poppies." Sir Walter Scott began taking huge quantities during an illness and wrote at least one of his novels under its influence. Similar lists could be drawn of political figures (the friends of George IV often found him stupefied by opium) or even famous preachers (William Wilberforce was an addict because of his ulcer medication).

Since opium addiction typically began with medicines, suppliers were druggists. Pharmacies sold pure opium without a prescription, but most sales came as lozenges, syrups, and pills. An estimated twenty-six thousand stores in Britain alone sold opium in the 1850s. This situation lasted until the Pharmacy Act of 1868 introduced the first restrictions because the government feared that workers were starting to use opium for its pleasure-giving properties. Further restrictions appeared in the 1890s when the government began to fear that immigrants, especially the Chinese, congregated in "opium dens" and plotted crimes.

As opium became less socially acceptable, the upper classes turned to cocaine. Sigmund Freud promoted the use of "this divine weed" in an essay of 1884, asserting that it "wards off hunger, sleep, and fatigue and

steels one to intellectual effort." Physicians soon offered cocaine for every imaginable complaint, including anemia, tuberculosis, syphilis, asthma, indigestion, and opium addiction. Cocaine won commercial acceptance in patent medicines, soft drinks, and fortified wines. It acquired its own roster of famous users at the end of the century, including Sir Arthur Conan Doyle (who made Sherlock Holmes a user), the French novelist Emile Zola, the French actress Sarah Bernhardt, the Norwegian dramatist Henrik Ibsen, King Edward VII of Britain, and Pope Leo XIII.

The Life Cycle: Birth and Birth Control

The subject of human reproduction led to much controversy during the nineteenth century. The century witnessed a significant decline in the birthrate, which is explained by a variety of birth control practices. Physicians, churches, and governments generally opposed the circulation of birth control information and the use of contraceptives, however; they considered them immoral and made them illegal in most places.

The search for a reliable means of birth control is as old as human records, and discussions of it are found in pre-Christian records. The early church opposed contraception and medieval canon law forbade it, but ideas about avoiding pregnancy nonetheless circulated in popular culture. The population explosion that began in the late eighteenth century (and coincided with a decline in the authority of established churches) per-

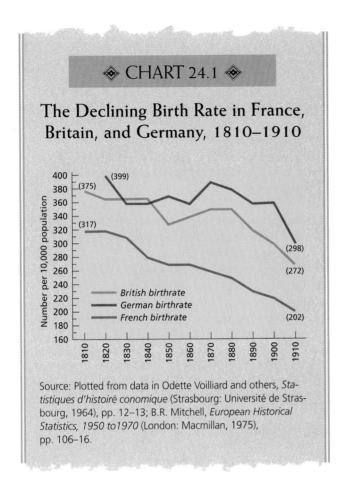

❖ CHART 24.1 ❖

The Declining Birth Rate in France, Britain, and Germany, 1810–1910

Number per 10,000 population

(375) (399)

(317)

(298)

(272)

(202)

British birthrate
German birthrate
French birthrate

1810 1820 1830 1840 1850 1860 1870 1880 1890 1900 1910

Source: Plotted from data in Odette Voilliard and others, *Statistiques d'histoiré conomique* (Strasbourg: Université de Strasbourg, 1964), pp. 12–13; B.R. Mitchell, *European Historical Statistics, 1950 to1970* (London: Macmillan, 1975), pp. 106–16.

suaded nineteenth-century reformers to circulate birth control information. These neo-Malthusians proposed a variety of (semireliable) means of contraception: the insertion of a barrier (such as a sponge) as a rudimentary form of the diaphragm; the use of simple chemical douches (such as vinegar), as a rudimentary spermicide; and the practice of male withdrawal before ejaculation, modestly described by the Latin term *coitus interruptus.* Condoms made from animal membranes had been tried for centuries, and a reusable condom of vulcanized rubber (hence its nickname) was clandestinely marketed in the 1870s, although the modern, thinner condom made of latex was not invented until after World War I.

Such methods of contraception—plus abortion, infanticide, and abandonment—were first used on a scale large enough to check population growth in France. The French birthrate in 1810 was 317 births per ten thousand population, 15 percent lower than the rate in Britain (375 per ten thousand); the rate in the German states was even higher (395 per ten thousand). The difference between the French and the Anglo-German birthrates widened during the nineteenth century, even when the British birthrate started falling in 1840 (see chart 24.1); by 1910 the French birthrate (202 per ten

thousand) was 26 percent below the British rate (272 per ten thousand) and 32 percent below the German rate (298 per ten thousand). France never experienced the population explosion that Britain and Germany did. By the early twentieth century, the French had reached zero population growth (a balance between births and deaths), despite the opposition of leaders who foresaw the depopulation of France, especially as compared with her neighbors. This trend, combined with other demographic data, leaves no doubt that the French were practicing birth control on a significant scale.

British radicals tried to spread such information. Richard Carlile, a tinsmith and printer, published a manual in 1838, entitled *Every Woman's Book,* advocating the use of a sponge barrier (see document 24.3). It and an American manual, *Fruits of Philosophy* (1832), which advocated a vinegar douche, were censored, and some booksellers were imprisoned, but their ideas circulated. In 1877 Annie Besant, a preacher's wife and campaigner for unpopular causes, and Charles Bradlaugh, a social reformer, defied the courts and sold 125,000 copies of these reprinted works. Besant summarized the various methods of birth control in *The Law of Population* (1877), which conservatives branded as "a dirty, filthy book . . . that no human would allow on his table . . . and no decently educated English husband would allow even his wife to have" (see document 24.3). Besant was sentenced to six months in prison, but the verdict was overturned on a technicality. The notoriety of these events taught the poor that methods of birth control did exist.

Similar controversies developed in many countries. Dr. Alleta Jacobs, the first woman physician in the Netherlands, opened the world's first birth control clinic in Amsterdam in 1882, despite great opposition from the medical profession. In other countries, radical feminists, such as Dr. Madeleine Pelletier in France, made the control of reproduction an essential element of women's rights. Pelletier even published one of the first works claiming the right to abortion. By the end of the century, information about both birth control and abortion circulated widely. A study of Spain has found significant use of contraception in the cities, especially in Catalonia. A study of a Berlin working-class clinic in 1913 found that 64 percent of the women used birth control.

Historical data on abortions are among the least reliable evidence confronting historians, but provocative records survive on this controversial subject. A study of abortion in France in the late nineteenth century concluded that approximately 250,000 abortions per year were performed there. It was illegal to perform or to

✦ DOCUMENT 24.3 ✦

Birth Control Advice in Victorian England

Richard Carlile Suggests a Simple Form of Contraception (1838)

The remedy for preventing conception shocks the mind of a woman at first thought; but prejudice soon flies. To weak and sickly females, to those to whom parturition is dangerous . . . [birth control] is a real blessing, as it is in all cases where children are not desired. It will become the very bulwark of love. . . . The remedy has long been known to a few in this country, and to the aristocracy in particular, who are always in search of benefits which they can peculiarly hold, and be distinct from the body of the laboring people. On the continent of Europe it has been long very generally practiced. . . .

[B]efore sexual intercourse, the female introduces into her vagina a piece of sponge as large as can be pleasantly introduced, having previously attached a bobbin or bit of narrow riband to withdraw it, it will be found a preventive to conception, while it neither lessens the pleasure of the female nor injures her health. . . . There is nothing unnatural in the circumstance, further than it is unnatural to use precautions against any other natural evil, such as a fever, a storm, or a beast of prey. . . . [P]revention is alike moral and legal, while destruction of the foetus is degrading, immoral, and illegal.

Annie Besant Surveys Birth Control Options (1877)

All thinkers have seen that since population increases more rapidly than the means of subsistence, the human brain should be called in to devise a restriction of the population, and so relieve man from the pressure of the struggle for existence. . . . Malthus proposed . . . the delay of marriage. . . . [But] the more marriage is delayed, the more prostitution spreads. . . . Later, thinkers, recognizing at once the evils of over-population and the evils of late marriage . . . have advocated early marriages and small families. . . . [Yet] how is this duty to be performed?

The check we will take first is 'natural laws'. . . . Women are far less likely to conceive midway between the menstrual periods than either immediately before or after them.

The preventive check so generally practiced in France . . . consists simply in the withdrawal of the husband previous to the emission of the semen, and is, of course absolutely certain as a preventive . . . .

The preventive check advocated by Dr. Knowlton is, on the other hand, entirely in the hands of the wife. It consists in the use of the ordinary syringe immediately after intercourse, a solution of sulphate of zinc, or of alum, being used instead of water. There is but little doubt that this check is an effective one . . . [but] there are many obvious disadvantages connected with it as a matter of taste and feeling. The same remark applies to the employment of the *baudruche*, a covering used by men of loose character as a guard against syphilitic diseases, and occasionally recommended as a preventive check.

The check which appears to us to be preferable, as at once certain, and in no sense grating on any feeling of affection or of delicacy, is that recommended by Carlile many years ago in his *Every Woman's Book*. . . . To prevent impregnation, pass to the end of the vagina a piece of fine sponge. . . .

There is a preventive check attempted by many poor women which is most detrimental to health, and should therefore never be employed, namely, the too long persistence in nursing one baby in the hope of thereby preventing the conception of another. Nursing does not prevent conception. . . .

Another class of checks is distinctly criminal, i.e., the procuring of abortion. Various drugs are taken by women with this intent, and too often their use results in death, or in dangerous sickness.

obtain an abortion throughout those years, but only one hundred to two hundred French women were convicted of the crime each year. Physicians' records from small villages show varying local rates, from 3 percent to 18 percent of all pregnancies ending in abortion. In contrast, fully 40 percent of the working-class women interviewed in Berlin in 1913 admitted that they had at

least one abortion; the entire group had terminated almost one-third of their pregnancies by abortions. The means of abortion that they reported were startling: One simply "jumped off chairs and stools." Another "sent for a [chemical] remedy that was advertised in the newspaper." And a third "poked around with a quill a little bit until blood came." Descriptions of similar

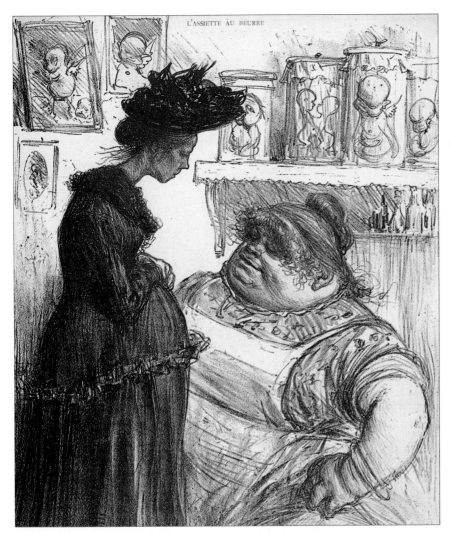

L'ASSIETTE AU BEURRE

Illustration 24.7

⟍⟍ **Abortion.** Abortion was both illegal and widely practiced in the nineteenth century. Although little reliable data exists, hundreds of thousands of abortions clearly were being performed with relatively few trials taking place. As this turn-of-the-century caricature bluntly suggests, women knew where to find a local "angel-maker."

crude and dangerous means of aborting unwanted pregnancies occur in late nineteenth-century novels, such as Zola's grim portrayal of peasant life in France, *The Land* (1887). Such sources suggest that many abortions were performed by midwives (see illustration 24.7). Despite the medical, legal, social, and religious obstacles, European women practiced birth control and abortion on a large enough scale during the nineteenth century to sharply lower European birthrates (see table 24.7). National variations in the falling birthrate were more closely associated with education and economic modernization than with religion, as the rates for Russia, Spain, and Italy show when compared with those for Britain, Germany, and France.

The increasing use of birth control did not mean that social problems associated with child birth, such as illegitimacy, abandonment, and infanticide, disappeared. Illegitimacy began to increase in the late eighteenth century and grew during the nineteenth century,

until 8 percent of all European births in the 1880s were illegitimate. This pattern varied regionally, with the highest national averages being found in Germanic central Europe. Austria, Germany, Denmark, and Scandinavia had a combined illegitimate birthrate above 10 percent, with the highest figure being in Austria (14.9 percent in 1889). Much lower rates were found in regions with early marriages (such as Serbia, which reported 1.1 percent illegitimacy) or the strictest sexual mores (such as Ireland, which reported 2.7 percent). Conversely, where late marriages were the norm, illegitimacy rose. A demographic study of rural Portugal found that, in villages where landless peasants could not marry until late in life, illegitimacy reached as high as 73 percent of all births. As the data for Ireland and Austria show, national religions were not the determining factor in illegitimate births.

Infanticide and the abandonment of newborn infants (often the same thing) remained serious social

✕ TABLE 24.7 ✕

The Declining Birthrate in Europe, 1840–1914

	Births per one thousand population						
Year	Austria	England	France	Germany	Italy	Spain	Russia
1840	38.6	32.0	27.9	36.4	a	n.a.	n.a.
1850	39.6	n.a.	26.8	37.2	a	n.a.	n.a.
1860	38.2	35.6	26.2	36.4	38.0	36.7	49.7
1870	39.8	34.6	25.9	38.5	36.8	36.6	49.2
1880	37.5	33.6	24.6	37.6	33.9	35.5	49.7
1890	36.2	30.4	21.8	35.7	35.8	34.4	50.3
1900	35.0	28.7	21.3	35.6	33.0	33.9	49.3
1910	32.5	25.1	19.6	29.8	33.3	32.7	45.1
1914	29.7	23.8	18.1	26.8	31.0	29.9	43.1
Percentage decline from 1840 to 1914	−23.1	−25.6	−35.1	−26.4	−18.4	−18.5	−13.3

Source: B. R. Mitchell, *European Historical Statistics, 1950–1970* (London: Macmillan, 1975), pp. 105–20; *The World Almanac and Book of Facts 1991* (Mahwah, N.J.: World Almanac Books, 1990), pp. 684–770.

n.a. = Not available.

a Italy did not exist as a country.

problems as they had been in the Old Regime. In Britain, the law stated that infanticide must be treated as murder, but it also said "it must be proved that the entire body of the child has actually been born into the world in a living state" before the child was legally alive and the act was legally murder. Killing an infant as it emerged from the womb thus received some legal protection, and it was a horrifying, but not uncommon, urban experience of mid-Victorian England to find dead babies in the streets, in trash heaps, or in rivers. Abandonment was sufficiently common in Victorian England that George Eliot (the pseudonym of Mary Ann Evans) could make it a central element of *Adam Bede* (1859) and make the mother who left her child to die in the woods (Hetty Sorrel) a sympathetic character.

In France, infanticide was so common that at least one thousand women were indicted for it every year from the 1840s to the 1880s; annual arrests did not fall below five hundred until 1901. One study estimates that the crime reached its nineteenth-century peak at 12 percent of all births in 1862–63. The abandonment of newborns was so widely practiced that Napoleon tried to organize it by ordering that every hospital be equipped with a turntable door, where people could deposit unwanted infants and rotate them into the hospital without being seen. In the years 1817–20, the abandonment of babies at Paris hospitals equaled one-third of the births recorded in the city, although many of these infants were undoubtedly brought to Paris from the countryside. The abandonment of babies at public institutions in France reached a recorded peak of 164,319 in 1833.

Abandonment was most common in regions where effective contraception was not well known, especially in eastern Europe. Catherine the Great had established foundling homes in Moscow and St. Petersburg, but abandoned babies soon overflowed these institutions, which then became processing centers for shipping unwanted babies to the countryside. In the 1830s the foundling home of St. Petersburg had twenty-five thousand children on its rolls with five thousand being added each year (see table 24.8); by the 1880s the home in St. Petersburg was receiving nine thousand abandoned newborns per year and the home in Moscow, seventeen thousand. A study of the province around Moscow has found that more than 10 percent of the babies born there in the late nineteenth century were abandoned by their mothers. The problem was most urgent for the large numbers of women who were domestic servants in the cities—25 percent of women in Moscow, 37 percent in St. Petersburg. Marriage was difficult for these women and economic survival virtu-

❧ TABLE 24.8 ❧

Abandoned Children in St. Petersburg, 1830–45

The range of percentages is from the possibility that none of the abandoned babies were a registered birth to the possibility that all of the abandoned babies were registered births.

These percentages do not reflect the possibility that some babies were born outside of St. Petersburg but abandoned there.

Year	New entries to St. Petersburg foundling home	Births in St. Petersburg	Percentage of newborns abandoned
1830	4,091	9,661	29.7–42.3
1835	5,226	10,313	33.6–50.7
1840	4,604	13,339	25.7–34.5
1845	5,808	19,276	23.2–30.1

Source: Calculated from data in David L. Ransel, "Abandonment and Fosterage of Unwanted Children: The Women of the Foundling System," in David L. Ransel, ed., *The Family in Imperial Russia: New Lines of Historical Research* (Urbana, Ill.: University of Illinois Press, 1978), p. 193.

ally impossible if they lost their posts, as they would if they had a child. Children who reached the foundling homes suffered terribly: Between 75 percent and 90 percent of them died each year. Similar patterns existed in western Europe, and critics were not totally wrong when they called foundling homes a system of "legalized infanticide."

The Life Cycle: Youth

No stage of the life cycle experienced a more dramatic change in daily life than the young did. The history of childhood and adolescence in nineteenth-century Europe saw the conquest of contagious ("childhood") diseases, which changed childhood from a world in which 50 percent of the population died to one where less than 10 percent did; the emergence of the idea that youth was a distinct phase of life and the consequent new attitudes and laws about different treatment of the young; and the industrial revolution, which changed the primary activities of the young, first shifting their economic roles and later requiring schooling instead of work.

The British led Europe toward a new legal treatment of the young by defining new borders between youth and adulthood. Nineteenth-century laws limited the maximum number of hours that children could work and the minimum number of years that they must attend school; laws defined the age at which the young could consent to sex or to marriage and the age at

which they could be sentenced to death. For most of the nineteenth century, the age of sexual consent for girls was twelve; a reform of British criminal law in 1875 raised this to thirteen (the French standard), and another reform in 1885 set the age of consent at sixteen. A study of French criminal justice has shown that, despite such early ages of consent, the single most common felony against persons in the late nineteenth century was the molestation of young girls. The young similarly received at least nominal protection in penal law. For most of the century, British prison populations were segregated by gender, social class, and types of crimes committed, but they were not segregated by age; a ten-year-old thief would be imprisoned with adult criminals. British penal reforms of 1854 created reformatories for youthful offenders, with fifteen being considered the age of adulthood. A Children's Act of 1908 created separate prisons (borstals) for the young and set the age of adulthood (for hanging, for example) at sixteen, to match the sexual statutes.

Industrialization and urbanization transformed the economic life of the young (see chapter 23). For many, life shifted from being farm workers in a household economy, or urban apprentices already separated from their families, to working in mines and factories and contributing to a family wage economy. By the 1840s child labor had become so common that governments began to regulate it. In France, for example, 18 percent to 24 percent of all workers in textile factories were children, and the law limited children below the age of twelve to eight hours of work per day.

Illustration 24.8

Compulsory Schooling. Few laws in modern history have changed the world as much as the universal education laws adopted in Europe in the late nineteenth and early twentieth centuries. The most immediate impact was upon the lives of children like these schoolgirls, but the consequences—such as the training of an educated class of women to be teachers or the future political and economic roles of literate citizens—were tremendously far-reaching.

TABLE 24.9

The Rise of Universal Education in Europe, 1849–1914

Country	Primary pupils		University students	
	Number (year)	Number (year)	Number (year)	Number (year)
Austria	1,450,000 (1850)	4,691,000 (1910)	11,439 (1850)	39,416 (1910)
Belgium	487,000 (1851)	964,000 (1910)	1,773 (1851)	7,910 (1910)
Britain	278,000 (1850)	6,295,000 (1910)	n.a.	n.a.
Finland	n.a.	n.a.	460 (1850)	3,238 (1910)
France	3,322,000 (1850)	5,049,000 (1910)	n.a.	41,190 (1910)
Germany	n.a.	n.a.	21,432 (1880)	70,183 (1910)
Greece	64,000 (1870)	260,000 (1910)	n.a.	n.a.
Hungary	18,000 (1850)	2,549,000 (1910)	838 (1850)	12,951 (1910)
Italy	1,025,000 (1861)	3,473,000 (1910)	6,504 (1861)	26,850 (1910)
Netherlands	n.a.	n.a.	1,082 (1850)	4,128 (1910)
Norway	n.a.	n.a.	550 (1850)	1,540 (1910)
Ottoman Empire	5,000 (1858)	2,000,000 (1895)	n.a.	n.a.
Portugal	42,000 (1849)	231,000 (1899)	898 (1850)	1,212 (1911)
Russia	n.a.	1,835,000 (1891)	n.a.	13,033 (1891)
Spain	1,005,000 (1855)	1,526,000 (1908)	7,528 (1857)	20,497 (1914)
Switzerland	n.a.	n.a.	1,966 (1887)	6,831 (1910)

Source: Data drawn from B. R. Mitchell, *European Historical Statistics, 1750–1970* (London: Macmillan, 1975), pp. 750–73; Chris Cook and John Paxton, *European Political Facts, 1848–1918* (London: Macmillan, 1978), pp. 307–15, J. Scott Keltie, ed., *Statesman's Yearbook* (London: Macmillan, 1891), pp. 855–56.
n.a. = Not available.

The Old Regime legacy of children working at an early age in agriculture, factories, mines, or apprenticeships left little room for universal education. A study of French schooling in the early nineteenth century found that more than fifteen thousand towns (40 percent of the communities in France) had no schools whatsoever. A study of Russia on the eve of emancipation (1861) found that 0.8 percent of the population was attending school. The German states had long been the leaders of European education because they had a tradition of compulsory education. In the 1850s nearly 95 percent of Prussian adults had received at least eight years of primary education; by the 1890s virtually 100 percent of German children received a primary education.

Most of Europe did not copy the German principle of compulsory education until the late nineteenth century. In 1850 the combined elementary school enrollments in Hungary, Portugal, and the Ottoman Empire amounted to fewer than 100,000 pupils—fewer than 5,000 in all of the Turkish provinces, only 18,000 in Portugal. The Ferry laws of the late 1870s and early 1880s in France gave Europe another model: mandatory, free, secular, universal education in state-run schools (see chapter 27). British education, shaped by the Forster elementary education reforms of Gladstone's "great ministry" (1868–74), provided a competing model that encouraged private, fee-paying schools. By 1914 schooling had replaced disease as the basic fact of childhood (see illustration 24.8). British primary school enrollments increased twentyfold, from 278,000 in 1850 to 6.3 million in 1910; Ottoman enrollments increased at an even higher rate, from five thousand in 1858 to nearly two million—including 924,000 girls—in 1895 (see table 24.9).

Compulsory education, like other social changes, often conflicted with traditional values and behavior. Just as conservatives opposed some of the new medical practices, such as vaccination and anesthesia, and they fought adamantly against birth control and abortion, many conservatives opposed compulsory education (see document 24.4). They argued that state-run schools gave the government too much power or that the family would be weakened. Religious leaders inveighed against the "godless school." Such arguments slowed, or blocked, universal education in some countries. The Spanish accepted only a minimum of universal education: The Moyano Education Law of 1857, which remained the basis of Spanish education until the 1960s, made schooling obligatory only until age nine and provided free schooling only for the poor. The czarist government in Russia rejected compulsory

◆ DOCUMENT 24.4 ◆

Conservative Arguments Against Compulsory Public Education

The French Ministry of Education, under the direction of a historian named Victor Duruy, did much to modernize education during the 1860s. Duruy gave libraries to primary schools, improved the salaries of teachers, sharply increased the number of schools for girls, expanded adult education, and reformed teacher training. Duruy supported the ideas of free and compulsory education, but he was a generation ahead of his time; conservative opposition to compulsory schooling was too strong, and such laws were not adopted until the 1880s. The following document was prepared in Duruy's Ministry of Education to summarize the conservative arguments.

The arguments against obligatory education can be listed under seven different headings:

1. It is a limitation upon paternal authority. The State has no right to intervene in the family to diminish the power of its head.

2. The obligation of a father to send his son to a public school cannot be reconciled with freedom of conscience, because the child is vulnerable to a religious education contrary to the faith which his father wishes to give him.

3. It is a diminution of the resources of the family: the child of the poor person performs a host of small jobs which attenuate misery for them both. Thus the government intervenes in the workplace . . . and reduces productivity.

4. Making education obligatory gives the government the sort of power which it should not have.

5. Given the present state of the schools, it is economically impossible to open them to all children.

6. The forced presence in the schools of children who refuse to learn and disrupt other students will destroy discipline.

7. Finally, compulsory education, if it is not also free education, will create a heavy new tax on peasants and workers.

education there and prevented provinces such as Finland from establishing it.

The life of schoolchildren in the nineteenth century consisted chiefly of the memorization of facts. As

Illustration 24.9

▓ **Illiteracy.** Throughout the nineteenth century, adult illiteracy remained widespread in Europe. In 1850, the majority of Europeans could not sign their names to a registry on their wedding day, as the couple in this painting by Frederick Leighton do.

Mr. Gradgrind, a teacher in Charles Dickens's *Hard Times* (1854), explained, "Now what I want is Facts. . . . Facts alone are wanted in life." There remained some variation about which facts pupils must memorize, but little doubt existed about this form of education. Girls and boys received different schooling, with boys being groomed for higher education and girls usually denied such preparation. Private (tuition paying) schools often stressed religious studies, while state schools in both the French and German models insisted upon strictly secular education. The master of a famous British school for the elite, Rugby School, stated his mission this way: "It is not necessary that this should be a school of 300 or 100, or of 50 boys, but it is necessary that it should be a school of Christian gentlemen." The French Ministry of Education, in contrast, removed Christianity from the classroom and the curriculum, teaching instead a secular moral philosophy. Most schools taught a little mathematics, more history (especially the national history), some geography (particularly as colonial empires grew), little literature, less science (sometimes omitted entirely), and a great deal of Latin and Greek, which were requirements for higher education. Classics remained the key to a university education throughout the century; although Oxford and Cambridge relaxed their Greek requirement at the turn-of-the-century, proficiency in Latin remained *sine qua non* (indispensable) at universities well into the twentieth century. This curriculum was the residue of the age when education had been reserved for people who needed little assistance with gainful employment; subjects that might lead to jobs were *infra dignitas* (beneath one's dignity).

The foremost consequence of compulsory education laws was the birth of nearly universal literacy. The vast majority of Europeans were illiterate in 1800. This varied somewhat from one region to another, differed

for men and for women, and followed the standards of social class or occupation, but the result was usually the same: Most people could neither read nor write (see illustration 24.9). Studies of marriage records—by checking the signatures on wedding certificates—reveal the scope of illiteracy (see table 24.10). In 1800, 53 percent of the women married in England signed with an "X." Twenty years later, the rates in France were 46 percent for men and 65 percent for women. As late as 1870, 58 percent of Italian men and 77 percent of Italian women still married with an "X." Census reports of 1877 show that more than 75 percent of all Spaniards could not read and write, and the Russian census of 1897 found 71 percent of men and 87 percent of women to be illiterate. Other studies have shown how illiteracy varied by a family's social position or occupation. A study of French army recruits in the 1830s found that illiteracy was rare among the sons of professionals (less than 1 percent) or civil servants (2.4 percent), but high among the sons of factory workers (58.9 percent), peasants (83.5 percent), or domestic servants (96.0

❧ TABLE 24.10 ❧

The Decline of Illiteracy in Europe, 1800–1910

The figures in this table are the percentage of newlyweds signing wedding certificates with an "X.."

	England		France		Italy		Prussia		Germany	
Date	Men	Women	Men	Women	Men	Women	Men	Women	Men	Women
1800	n.a.	53	72	n.a.	a	a	n.a.	n.a.		
1820	n.a.	n.a.	46	65	a	a	n.a.	n.a.		
1830	n.a.	n.a.	n.a.	n.a.	a	a	12	32		
1840	33	49	n.a.	n.a.	a	a	6	19		
1850	31	36	n.a.	n.a.	a	a	3	8		
1860	26	36	30	45	a	a	3	4		
1870	20	27	27	40	58	77				
1880	14	19	16	25	48	70				
1890	7	8	8	14	42	62			2	3
1900	3	3	5	6	n.a.	n.a.			0	1
1910			3	4	n.a.	n.a.			0	0

Source: *Statesman's Yearbook* (London: Macmillan, passim); Hartmut Kaelble, *Industrialization* (New York: St. Martin's, 1986), pp. 90–91.

n.a. = Not available.

[a] Italy did not yet exist as a unified country.

percent). Similar variations occurred within the regions of a country. A study of Italian illiteracy in 1911 found it low in the more prosperous north (Piedmont, 11 percent; Lombardy, 13 percent; Venetia, 25 percent) but high in the poorer south (Sicily, 58 percent; Calabria, 70 percent).

The Life Cycle: Marriage and the Family

European law in the nineteenth century still permitted marriages at an early age. British law allowed girls to marry at twelve and boys at fourteen for most of the century. Orthodox canon law accepted marriage at thirteen for girls and fifteen for boys. Literature from the era reminds readers that early marriages did occur, such as the nurse in Pushkin's *Eugene Onegin* (1832) who married at thirteen. The history of European marriage during the nineteenth century, however, is different from what the law permitted (see table 24.11). Marriage generally occurred much later—at, or after, age twenty-five—and the average age at marriage increased, reaching into the thirties in some regions. Women typically married at a younger age than men did. As social historians constantly repeat, however,

significant regional and social class variations existed to these patterns.

The average age at marriage in Britain in the early nineteenth century was approximately twenty-five for women and twenty-six for men. A study of Belgium in 1800 found a range of marital ages for men of roughly twenty-five to thirty-two, depending upon their occupation; the same data found women marrying at twenty-four to thirty. The latest averages were in Ireland, where marriage was traditionally linked to sufficient landholding to support a family. The potato famine of the 1840s taught the tragedy of having a family but no ability to feed it. One-fourth of the population of Ireland during the late nineteenth century never married, and those who did, married at an age of economic security: thirty-eight for men and thirty for women. A study of Württemberg during industrialization found that most men in agricultural and working-class occupations could not afford to marry until their early thirties. A similar pattern existed in regions of Spain.

A dramatic contrast to these marital patterns existed in eastern Europe. A study comparing Sweden and Serbia in 1900 found huge differences for people in

TABLE 24.11

Marriage Patterns in Nineteenth-Century Europe

Mean Age at Marriage in Belgium, 1800

Occupation	Men	Women
Artisans	26.8	26.6
Farmers	30.6	27.8
Servants	26.3	27.3
Shopkeepers	26.0	24.1
Spinners	29.9	29.8
Weavers	25.6	23.9
Others	32.1	27.5

Mean Age at Marriage in Württemberg, 1880–1914

Occupation	Men	Women
Agriculture	32.8	29.4
Metal worker	32.2	27.4
Textile worker	32.8	30.1

Teenage Marriage in Riazan Province, Russia, 1782–1868

Age	Proportion of females marrying as percentage of total			Proportion of males marrying as percentage of total		
	1782	1850	1868	1782	1850	1868
13	1.5	n.a.	n.a.	n.a.	n.a.	n.a.
14	6.0	n.a.	n.a.	n.a.	n.a.	n.a.
15	23.1	n.a.	1.8	7.3	n.a.	n.a.
16	21.3	14.3	19.7	22.7	n.a.	n.a.
17	16.8	24.9	35.0	18.3	n.a.	5.4
18	11.4	26.2	26.6	12.9	44.5	49.0
19	5.1	14.9	8.1	9.1	18.8	18.7
20	11.1	11.4	5.5	19.2	12.7	11.6

Source: Belgian data from Myron P. Gutman, *Toward the Modern Economy: Early Industry in Europe, 1500–1800* (New York, N.Y.: Knopf, 1988), p. 169; Russian data from Peter Czap, Jr., "Marriage and Peasant Joint Family in the Era of Serfdom," in David L. Ransel, ed., *The Family in Imperial Russia: New Lines of Historical Research* (Urbana, Ill.: University of Illinois Press, 1978), p. 111; German data from Heilwig Schomerus, "The Family Life-Cycle: A Study of Factory Workers in Nineteenth Century Württemberg," in Richard J. Evans and W. R. Lee, eds., *The German Family: Essays on the Social History of the Family in Nineteenth and Twentieth Century Germany* (Totowa, N.J.: Barnes and Noble, 1981), p. 183.

their twenties. Only 8 percent of Swedish men and 20 percent of Swedish women were married at age twenty to twenty-four, but the Serbian figures were 50 percent for men and 84 percent for women. The Serbian pattern also characterized nineteenth-century Russia, where the average age at marriage in the 1830s was eighteen for both sexes. Serfs could not postpone marriage until they possessed land of their own unless they planned never to marry. Even after emancipation, most Russian peasants in 1868 were married by age twenty. These marital patterns, like those in Ireland or Würt-

temberg, appear to have been a direct result of the economic condition of the population.

The twentieth century has seen a trend toward earlier marriage, and this trend had a harbinger in the nineteenth-century data. The French, who led many European demographic trends, had a different marital pattern. While age at marriage was increasing in the rest of Europe, it decreased in France. In 1830 French women married at an average age of twenty-five to twenty-six, much like English or Belgian women. By 1885, however, that average had fallen to just under age

❧ TABLE 24.12 ❧

Family Size in Württemberg in the 1850s and 1860s

Occupation of father	Percentage of families				
	0 children	1–3 children	4–6 children	7–9 children	10 or more children
Agricultural	31.3	33.6	22.8	7.2	4.8
Metal industry	17.1	59.9	17.1	2.9	2.9
Textile industry	21.4	32.2	25.0	14.2	7.2

Source: Heilwig Schomerus, "The Family-Life-Cycle: A Study of Factory Workers in Nineteenth Century Württemberg," in Richard J. Evans and W. R. Lee, eds., *The German Family: Essays on the Social History of the Family in Nineteenth and Twentieth Century Germany* (Totowa, N.J.: Barnes and Noble, 1981), p. 185.

twenty-three. By 1901 nearly half of French women were married in their early twenties; this has become commonplace in the late twentieth century, but it was an anomaly in the nineteenth, apparently a result of French leadership in birth control.

The institution of marriage changed during the nineteenth century. One aspect of this change was the transition from an agricultural economy to an industrial economy, which broke down the historic pattern of a household economy in which a husband and wife shared the labor of farm or shop, creating instead a family wage economy in which a husband and wife typically worked at separate jobs and pooled their wages to maintain the home (see chapters 18 and 23). Other important changes in marriage were appearing by the end of the nineteenth century, largely the result of the successes of the women's movement. The historic pattern of patriarchal marriage—of a husband's authority and a wife's obedience—a pattern sanctified by law, religion, and custom, was breaking down. Married women were winning fundamental economic rights, such as the control of their own property or wages, beginning with the British Married Women's Property Acts of 1857–82. The breakdown of the paternalistic marriage, which has continued during the twentieth century, soon touched all aspects of family life, such as control of the children.

A third fundamental change in the nature of marriage, the legal right to end the marriage, developed during the nineteenth century. The French Revolution instituted divorce, but that law was repealed by the restored monarchy. The Prussian legal code of 1794 made divorce comparatively easy there, and Bismarck imposed divorce on Catholic Germany during the *Kulturkampf* of the 1870s. Legislation of 1857 in Britain and 1884 in France permitted divorce, and Scandinavian countries adopted similar statutes. Men and women

(but significantly more women) increasingly exercised this right during the late nineteenth century. British divorces climbed from 178 per year in the late 1850s to surpass 1,000 for the first time in 1906. Divorce rates rose more rapidly in France. The first full year of divorce (1885) saw 4,000 marriages dissolved, and that number doubled by 1895, tripled by 1905. By the early twentieth century both France and Germany were seeing 15,000 divorces per year. Such figures do not compare with the "divorce revolution" of the late twentieth century, but the social trend was clear, as the Catholic Church argued in blocking divorce in Italy and Spain.

The combination of later marriage, the increased use of birth control, and the legalization of divorce meant that the average size of European families declined. The economic system no longer rewarded large families when children were obliged to attend school. The vital revolution that conquered many childhood diseases meant that parents could be confident of children surviving into adulthood without having ten or twelve of them. Whereas ten or more children had been a common family size during the Old Regime, less than 10 percent of the population now did so. By the 1850s German peasants averaged four or fewer children than they had a century earlier; even textile workers had smaller families (see table 24.12). Families continued to shrink during the nineteenth century. Completed family size for all British marriages of the 1860s included four children; for marriages in the early twentieth century, the average had fallen to two children.

A typical household of nineteenth-century Europe still retained some characteristics of the Old Regime, however. A household still meant all of the people who lived together under a common roof, and that often still included servants, apprentices, or boarders. A study of Nottingham in midcentury found that more than 20 percent of households contained a lodger, and well-to-do families had an average of two servants. Most of these domestic servants were unmarried women, and such service was the largest source of employment for women during the century. More than, 700,000 women worked as servants in mid-Victorian Britain, nearly twice as many as labored in textile industries, or twenty times as many as were engaged in all forms of education. Even middle-class families could afford at least one servant because the wages paid were shockingly low. A study of female domestic servants in London in 1895 found that a fifteen-year-old girl entering service in an upper- or middle-class family could expect an annual wage of slightly more than £7 (thirty-five dollars) per year, although the scale for girls accepted from public workhouses started below £6; a woman in her midforties, with thirty years of domestic service and important skills such as cooking, could hope to reach peak wages of slightly more than £20. The nature of the work can be judged from the Dickensian slang name for a maid-of-all-work (the only maid in a household): a *slavey*. That characteristic, both of the female work force and of middle-class households, remained common in 1914. A study of Berlin found that more women worked in service occupations than in the textile industries, and more women were residential servants than were sales clerks. Household structures, therefore, remained likely to include as many outsiders as blood relatives.

A study of Austrian household structure illustrates how nineteenth-century families became smaller, but household size remained large. Viennese census data reveal that a typical master baker and his wife had five children. But their household contained eighteen residents: six journeymen bakers, two shopgirls, and the family's three domestic servants. In another illustration, a widowed textile manufacturer in his sixties lived in a household of nine people: his two sons who had become his partners in their thirties and still lived at home, his five household servants, and his coachman.

Sexual Attitudes and Behavior in the Nineteenth Century

The nineteenth century lingers in popular memory as an age of prudery and puritanical restrictions. To describe a person or an idea as "Victorian" is to connote repressive attitudes about human sexuality commonly associated with the era. This stereotype of Victorianism

contains much truth. Respectable women who consulted a physician normally went with a chaperon; they would point out their ailments on a doll rather than touch themselves. Gynecological examinations were performed only in extreme cases, and genteel opinion held that women should endure much pain before submitting to the indignity of a pelvic exam. Prudishness governed polite conversations. The words for bodily functions (sexual or not) were unacceptable, and this ban forbade such outrages to delicate ears as *to sweat*, which was deemed much too animalistic. Decent people did not refer to *legs*—a word thought to inflame sexual passions—but to *limbs*. This taboo included the legs on furniture, and truly respectable families placed a cloth skirt around a piano, lest the sight of its limbs provoke prurient thoughts. This puritanism culminated in *Lady Gough's Book of Etiquette*, which stated the moral principle that books in a family library must be organized so that those written by men not lay next to those written by women—unless the authors were married.

This image of the nineteenth century contains much truth, but it hides truth as well. The early nineteenth century, when fashionable dress at continental balls permitted the exposure of a woman's breasts, did not correspond to the prudery of later years. Many people believed that foreign countries teemed with a sexuality unknown at home (as the British viewed France), although that may reveal more about their own behavior away from home. The upper classes, including Queen Victoria's family, did not behave by the standards of middle-class Victorianism. Victoria's predecessor on the throne, William IV, lived with a mistress for twenty years and had ten illegitimate children with her; Victoria's husband, Prince Albert, was the child of a broken marriage; and Victoria's heir, the future Edward VII, had a legion of lovers, from a famous actress to a duchess who always curtsied before climbing into the royal bed. Such exceptions to the Victorian stereotype were widespread: Nude bathing at the seashore was commonplace for most of the nineteenth century and the mid-Victorian House of Commons declined to outlaw it in 1857. Somehow bourgeois prudery coexisted with startling exceptions, such as permitting Lewis Carroll to enjoy the hobby of photographing naked young girls, including the Alice for whom *Alice in Wonderland* was written.

Historians have studied many aspects of human sexuality hidden by the stereotype of Victorianism. Subjects such as the double standard, prostitution, venereal disease, and homosexuality have all drawn the attention of social historians. The double standard behind Victorianism is clear. Sometimes it was a matter of hypocrisy: the governing and opinion-making classes said one thing in public and behaved differently in private. During Napoleon III's Second Empire, for example, the government of France stoutly defended public morality. When Gustave Flaubert published *Madame Bovary* (1857), which dared to suggest that a respectable married woman might choose to commit adultery, the government immediately indicted Flaubert for outraging public morals. The public agreed so heartily that when Edouard Manet first exhibited "Olympia," destined to become one of the most noted paintings of the century but depicting a nude woman reclining in bed, guards had to be hired to protect it from vigilante moralists. The private morality of the Bonaparte family was somewhat different from their public standard, and they welcomed the friendship of Flaubert. The emperor was as lusty as Edward VII, and his biography is filled with episodes such as the costume ball at which he found one of his mistresses, a teenaged countess who wore a transparent costume.

Another variant of the sexual double standard expected different behavior from men and women. Unmarried women were expected to remain virginal until marriage; unmarried men were assumed to be sexually active. Adultery was a serious crime for married women but less so for men. Flaubert probably would not have been arrested had his novel been *Doctor Bovary*, describing the adultery of a prominent man. The respectable double standard even taught that women did not have sexual urges. As late as 1905 an Oxford physician could seriously testify that nine out of ten women disliked sex, and the tenth was invariably a harlot.

Given the double standard of sexual behavior, the late age of marriages, and the desperate economic situation of women from the lower classes, it is not surprising that prostitution thrived during the nineteenth century. Legal and open prostitution was one of the most striking features of European cities (see illustration 24.10), and some authors have claimed that, in periods of economic distress, prostitution became the largest single form of women's employment. Women (frequently servants) who had been seduced and left with a child had little legal support (they could not even sue to prove paternity in most countries) and usually no economic support. The situation was even worse for rape victims who found many respectable jobs closed to them. Even widows could be driven to consider prostitution by their economic plight. Single factory workers, trying to live on a fraction of a man's wages,

Illustration 24.10

Legalized Prostitution. Prostitution was not only legal in nineteenth-century Europe, but it also was one of the principle occupations of women, following domestic service and work in textile factories. The police of Paris estimated that there were thirty-five thousand to forty thousand prostitutes there in 1900, although only six thousand to seven thousand were legally registered with the government. Less than 10 percent worked in fancy bordellos such as this one, painted by Toulouse-Lautrec in 1894.

faced few alternatives to supplementing their wages through prostitution.

The London police estimated that six thousand full-time prostitutes worked in the city in the 1860s and twenty-five thousand in Britain; reformers claimed that the true number was ten times higher (see document 24.5). The number of prostitutes was much higher if one includes the thousands of working women driven to supplement their wages by part-time prostitution. The data behind such assertions are notoriously variable. The number of women who registered with the Parisian police as legal prostitutes increased from 1,293 in 1812 to 6,827 in 1914, and police records show that 10,000 to 30,000 Parisian women were arrested each year for unregistered prostitution. The police estimated 34,000 prostitutes in Paris in the 1850s, 35,000 to 40,000 at the turn-of-the-century. Similar estimates for Germany range from 100,000 to 330,000 women in 1914. Munich police records, however, registered only 2,000 legal prostitutes in 1909 and 3,000 in 1911. All such numbers must be treated with caution: Some Victorian moralists counted any unmarried woman living with a man as a prostitute.

❖ DOCUMENT 24.5 ❖

A British Prostitute Describes Her Life (1849)

Henry Mayhew was a journalist in London, well known to his contemporaries as a comic writer; he was one of the founding editors of Punch. *Mayhew is better remembered by scholars today for his serious side, shown in a series of sensitive articles about the daily life of the poor. These articles were collected in several volumes under the title* London Labour and London Poor (1851–62). *The following excerpt is one of Mayhew's most moving. He originally published it in* The Morning Chronicle *in 1849, under the title "Prostitution among Needlewomen."*

She told her tale with her face hidden in her hands, and sobbing so loud that it was difficult to catch her words . . . .

I used to work at "slop work"—at the shirt [handsewing] trade—the fine full-fronted white shirts; I got 2 1/2 pence each for them [approximately 5¢]. . . . By working from five o'clock in the morning to midnight each night I might be able to do seven in the week. That would bring me in 17 1/2 pence for my whole week's labor. Out of this the cotton must be taken, and that came to 2 pence every week, and so left me 15 1/2 pence to pay rent and living and buy candles with. I was single and received some little help from my friends; still it was impossible for

me to live. I was forced to go out of a night to make my living. I had a child and it used to cry for food. So, as I could not get a living for him and myself by my needs, I went into the streets and made a living that way. . . .

My father was an independent preacher, and I pledge my word that it was the low price paid for my labor that drove me to prostitution. I often struggled against it, and many times I have taken my child into the streets to beg rather than I would bring shame on myself and it any longer. I have made pin cushions and fancy articles—such as I could manage to scrape together—and taken them into the streets to sell, so that I might get an honest living, but I couldn't. Sometime I should be out all night in the rain, and sell nothing at all, me and my child together. . . . I was so poor I couldn't have even a night's lodging on credit. One night in the depth of winter his legs froze to his side . . . .

[A]t last I left the 'house' [workhouse] to work at umbrella covering. . . . I then made from 3 shillings to 4 shillings a week [36–48 pence, 75¢–$1], and from that time I gave up prostitution. . . . Had I remained at shirt making, I must have been a prostitute to this day.

Britain, France, and Italy all enacted state-regulated prostitution. Most German states permitted municipal brothels, although after 1871 Berlin tried to eliminate them. Governments accepted regulated prostitution because it helped to control venereal diseases in naval bases and army garrisons. Prostitutes were required to have regular medical examinations and receive treatment for VD. Laws such as the British Contagious Diseases Acts of 1864 and 1866 gave the police exceptional powers to arrest any woman who was unescorted in public and to order her to have a medical examination. This abuse of women, combined with the moral opposition to prostitution and the desire to help prostitutes, led to abolitionist campaigns, such as Josephine Butler's, which won the suspension of the Contagious Diseases Acts in 1883 and their repeal in 1886. Women, typically Protestant reformers who linked moral reforms with feminism, launched abolitionist campaigns in many countries, as Avril de Sainte Croix did in France and Emilie de Morsier did in Switzerland.

Governments were right to worry about VD rates. The rate of infection and the death rate for syphilis in the 1890s were both higher than the rates for AIDS in the 1990s (see illustration 24.11). One French study found that the leading cause of death in Europe was tuberculosis (which killed 150,000 per year) but syphilis was a close second (140,000), killing three times as many people as cancer did (40,000). In Britain, where Lord Randolph Churchill demonstrated the universality of VD by slowly dying from syphilis in public, nearly 7,000 people died of VD in 1901—a death rate of 16.4 per 100,000 population (the death rate for AIDS in the United States was 8.6 per 100,000 in 1989). A German medical study of 1900 estimated even higher rates of infection there and asserted that 50 percent of German men had a venereal disease, usually gonorrhea, and 20 percent had syphilis.

European laws to regulate prostitution or to control VD were mild compared with the draconian laws against homosexuality. All sexual acts between men

Illustration 24.11

Venereal Disease. Syphilis was an incurable and often fatal disease throughout the nineteenth century, killing far more Europeans in the 1890s than AIDS killed in the 1990s. There were an estimated 43,000 AIDS deaths in the United States in 1995, compared with 140,000 syphilis deaths in Europe in 1895. European alarm in the 1890s produced the engraving entitled "The Two Faces of Love," which uses striking imagery to warn of sexual dangers.

were illegal in most countries, and sexual intercourse between men (usually called buggery or sodomy in the nineteenth century) was often a capital crime. Dutch law allowed the execution of convicted homosexuals in 1800, and twenty-two trials had taken place for the crime in 1798, but imprisonment or banishment was the usual punishment. There were seventeen convictions for homosexuality at Amsterdam in the decade 1801–10, and none resulted in an execution. Sexual intercourse between men remained a capital crime in Britain until 1861, and one or two men were hanged for it annually in the early nineteenth century. Gay men thus faced extreme dangers from blackmailers, as happened to Lord Castlereagh; the pressure led to his suicide in 1822. Others, such as the notoriously bisexual Lord Byron, fled the country.

The nineteenth-century reforms of sexual statutes typically perpetuated the criminalization of homosexuality but reduced the penalties. The penal code of the German Empire forbade "unnatural vice" between men, but sentences ranged from one day to five years. British law remained more severe. The Criminal Law Amendment Act of 1885 allowed life imprisonment for homosexuality, but it also created the lesser crime of "gross indecency," for which men could be sentenced to two years of hard labor. When that statute was reformed in 1912, it permitted the flogging of homosexuals without a jury trial. These statutes remained in force until 1967. Such statutes did not even mention lesbianism, an unthinkable subject to most Victorian legislators.

The criminalization of homosexuality led to dramatic scandals and trials at the turn of the twentieth century. The most famous trial involved a celebrated Irish writer, Oscar Wilde. Wilde was arrested for sodomy following an acrimonious and public battle with the marquess of Queensbury (a bully chiefly remembered for formulating the rules of boxing), the father of his lover. Wilde was convicted in 1895 and imprisoned until 1897, an experience that he related in *Ballad of Reading Gaol* (1898). The Wilde case led to greater recognition of the extent of homosexuality (and homosexual prostitution) but did not lead to a campaign against British homosexuals. The government could have indicted many other prominent homosexuals—such as the members of the Bloomsbury set (named for a district of London), which included the economist John Maynard Keynes, the biographer Lytton Strachey, and the novelist E. M. Forster—but the government would have been obliged to arrest several of its own members.

A larger scandal over homosexuality occurred in Germany, where the central figures were not intellectuals but the commanders of the German army, members of the imperial government, and close associates of Kaiser Wilhelm II. The policy of the German army was to court-martial homosexuals if they had been publicly identified. That policy led to two dramatic trials in 1903–1906, at which several officers were named, including the commander of the royal guard who was a member of the royal family. This led to the public admission that Prince Friedrich Heinrich of Prussia was gay. The German press then began a flamboyant investigation of homosexuality in the army and the government. The press soon focused on the kaiser's closest friend, Prince Philipp zu Eulenburg, an ambassador and a member of the House of Lords. When a police investigation began, the Berlin vice squad quickly identified several hundred prominent aristocrats, officers, and officials as known homosexuals, including General Kuno Count von Moltke, the military commandant of Berlin.

The result was another wave of courts-martial in 1907–1909. The German public soon received admissions of homosexuality from a long list of public figures, ranging from the director of the state theater to the royal equerry. As the number of homosexuals in royal and military circles became clear, one segment of the German press turned to homophobic attacks, using the affectionate nicknames that lovers revealed at trials. At the peak of this scandal, a prominent general died of a heart attack while dressed in a ballerina's tutu, to the cruel delight of political cartoonists.

The German scandals had tragic results for the individuals involved and dangerous implications for society. Kaiser Wilhelm II blamed the entire experience neither on the criminalization of homosexuality nor on the men who had broken his laws, but on the machinations of "international Jewry." He reached this bizarre and ominous conclusion because the journalist who had exposed Eulenburg was Jewish. It was equally ominous that the scandals, and the homophobic attacks, encouraged aggressive militarism, as a proof of masculinity, in Germany.

Conclusion

Historians have traditionally stressed the political history of the past. From this perspective, the great revolution that shaped the nineteenth century was the French Revolution (see chapter 22). As economic change assumed greater importance in the study of the past, historians also placed great emphasis upon the industrial revolution (see chapter 23). Many historians today place the French and industrial revolutions together as the "twin revolutions" that created modern Europe. Social historians have not yet won similar recognition for the importance of the vital revolution that significantly changed life in modern Europe, but in many ways it is more important in understanding life in the past. The sharp decline in infant mortality, the widespread fall of the death rate from infectious diseases, and the corresponding increase in life expectancy touched everyone. The medical and dietary improvements that made this improvement in everyday life possible—from the germ theory of disease transmission to cleaner standards of public health, antiseptic surgery, and the conquest of many diseases, from steadily declining food prices to great increases in the food supply—must be central to understanding the past. So, too, are the changes in Eu-

ropean social behavior, such as the use of birth control, later marriage, smaller families, compulsory education, divorce, the decline of the patriarchal family, and the growth of sexual tolerance.

Suggested Readings

See the suggested readings for chapter 19 for many works appropriate for this period. For additional social histories, see F. M. L. Tompson, ed., *The Cambridge Social History of Britain, 1750–1950*, 3 vols. (1990), especially vol. 2: *People and Their Environment*; P. McPhee, *A Social History of France, 1780–1880* (1992); R. Price, *A Social History of Nineteenth-Century France* (1987); C. Charle, *A Social History of France in the Nineteenth Century* (1994); and E. Rosenhaft, *A Social History of Germany*. Most of these works are stronger on the history of social classes than on daily life.

For food and diet, see M. Livi-Bacci, *Population and Nutrition: An Essay on European Demographic History* (1991); E. Forster and R. Forster, eds., *European Diet from Pre-Industrial to Modern Times* (1975); J. Post, *The Last Great Subsistence Crisis in the Western World* (1977), on the famines of 1816–19; J. Burnett, *Plenty and Want: A Social History of Food in England from 1815 to the Present Day* (1988); R. Floud and others, *Health, Height, and History: Nutritional Status in the United Kingdom, 1750–1980* (1990); F. Filby, *A History of Food Adulteration and Analysis* (1976); C. O'Grada, *The Great Irish Famine* (1989); C. Woodham-Smith, *The Great Hunger: Ireland, 1845–1849* (1962); D. Christian, *Living Water: Vodka and Russian Society on the Eve of Emancipation* (1990); R. Robbins, *Famine in Russia, 1891–1892* (1975); R. E. F. Smith and D. Christian, *Bread and Salt: A Social and Economic History of Food and Drink in Russia* (1984); and J. Aron, *The Art of Eating in Nineteenth-Century France* (1975).

For housing, see M. J. Daunton, ed., *Housing the Workers, 1850–1914: A Comparative Perspective* (1990), J. Burnett, *A Social History of Housing, 1815–1985* (1986), J. Tarn, *Working-Class Housing in Nineteenth-Century Britain*, (1971), L. Schwarz, *London in the Age of Industrialization* (1992), N. Morgan, *Deadly Dwellings: Housing and Health in a Lancashire Cotton Town* (1993), L. Caffyn, *Workers' Housing in West Yorkshire, 1750–1920* (1986), R. Rodger, *Housing in Urban Britain, 1780–1914* (1989), M. Daunton, *House and Home in the Victorian City* (1983), A. Wohl, *The Eternal Slum*, (1977), D. Englander, *Landlord and Tenant in Urban Britain, 1838–1918* (1983), A. Shapiro, *Housing the Poor of Paris* (1985), E. Buyst, *An Economic History of Residential Building in Belgium between 1890 and 1961* (1992), and L. Wright, *Clean and Decent: The Fascinating History of the Bathroom and the Water Closet* (1984). For homelife, see C. Davidson, *A Woman's Work Is Never Done: A History of Housework in the British Isles, 1650–1950* (1986).

For disease and public health, see D. Hopkins, *Princes and Peasants: Smallpox in History* (1983); M. Pelling, *Cholera, Fever, and English Medicine, 1825–1865* (1978); C. Kudlick, *Cholera in Post-Revolutionary Paris* (1996); R. McGrew, *Russia and the Cholera, 1823–1832* (1965); R. Evans, *Death in Hamburg: Society and Politics in the Cholera Years, 1830–1910* (1987); L. Bruce-Chwatt and J. De

Zulueta, *The Rise and Fall of Malaria in Europe* (1980); C. Quetel, *History of Syphilis* (1990); H. Zinsser, *Rats, Lice, and History* (1934), on typhus; F. B. Smith, *The Retreat of Tuberculosis, 1850–1950* (1988); D. Barnes, *The Making of Social Disease; Tuberculosis in Nineteenth Century France* (1995); K. D. Patterson, *Pandemic Influenza, 1700–1900* (1987); G. Rosen, *A History of Public Health* (1993); C. Cipolla, *Miasmas and Disease* (1992); A. Wohl, *Endangered Lives: Public Health in Victorian Britain* (1983); and W. Coleman, *Death Is a Social Disease* (1982), on public health in France.

For sexuality and population; see J. Weeks, *Sex, Politics, and Society: The Regulation of Sexuality since 1800* (1989); P. Gay, *Education of the Senses*, especially vol. 1: *The Bourgeois Experience* (1984), M. Mason, *The Making of Victorian Sexuality* (1994) and *The Making of Victorian Sexual Attitudes* (1996); K. Boyd, *Scottish Church Attitudes to Sex, Marriage, and the Family, 1850–1914* (1980); A. Copley, *Sexual Moralities in France, 1780–1980* (1989); L. Englestein, *The Keys to Happiness: Sex and the Search for Modernity in Fin-de-Siecle Russia* (1992); M. Duberman, M. Vicinus, and G. Chauncey, *Hidden from History: Reclaiming the Gay and Lesbian Past* (1989); and J. Merrick and B. Ragan, eds., *Homosexuality in Modern France* (1996).

For reproduction and population control, see the pioneering works of A. McLaren, especially *Birth Control in Nineteenth Century England* (1992) and *Sexuality and Social Order* (1983), which cover birth control and abortion in France, 1770–1920; and the exceptionally helpful work of R. Fuchs, *Poor and Pregnant in Paris* (1992); J. Banks, *Victorain Values: Secularism and the Size of Families* (1982); J. Woycke, *Birth Control in Germany, 1871–1933* (1988); J. Keown, *Abortion, Doctors, and the Law* (1988); L. Rose, *Massacre of the Innocents: Infanticide in Great Britain, 1800–1939* (1986); D. Kertzer, *Sacrificed for Honor: Italian Infant Abandonment and the Politics of Reproductive Control* (1993); and D. L. Ransel, *Mothers of Misery: Child Abandonment in Russia* (1988).

For marriage, family and children, see M. Anderson, *Family Structure in Nineteenth-Century Lancashire* (1971); R. Evans and W. Lee, eds., *The German Family* (1981); W. Camp, *Marriage and the Family in France since the Revolution* (1961); K. Lynch, *Family, Class, and Ideology in Early Industrial France* (1988); D. Kertzer, *Family, Political Economy, and Demographic Change* (1990), a study of late nineteenth-century Italy; D. L. Ransel, ed., *The Family in Imperial Russia* (1978); and A. Duben, *Istanbul Households* (1991), a valuable study of an Islamic society.

For children, see J. Walvin, *A Child's World: A Social History of English Childhood, 1800–1914* (1982), L. Rose, *The Erosion of Childhood: Childhood in Britain, 1860–1918* (1991), L. Ashby, *Saving the Waifs: Reformers and Dependent Children, 1890–1917* (1984), P. Horn, *The Victorian Town Child* (1997), E. Hopkins, *Childhood Transformed: Working Class Children in Nineteenth-Century England* (1994), C. Dyhouse, *Girls Growing Up in Late Victorian and Edwardian England* (1982), C. Heywood, *Childhood in Nineteenth-Century France* (1988), R. Fuchs, *Abandoned Children*, (1984), H. Becker, *German Youth: Bond or Free* (1976), C. Nardinelli, *Child Labor and the Industrial Revolution* (1990), P. Horn, *Children's Work and Welfare, 1780–1890* (1996), L. Weissbach, *Child Labor Reform in Nineteenth Century France* (1989), J. de S. Honey, *Tom Brown's Universe: The Development of the English Public School in the Nineteenth Century* (1977), J. Hurt, *Education in Evolution: Church, State, Society, and Popular Education, 1800–1870* (1971), L. Struminger, *What Were Little Girls and Boys Made Of?* (1983), Linda Clark, *Schooling the Daughters of Marianne* (1984), M. Lamberti, *State, Society, and the Elementary School in Imperial Germany* (1989), and J. Albisetti, *Schooling German Girls and Women* (1989).

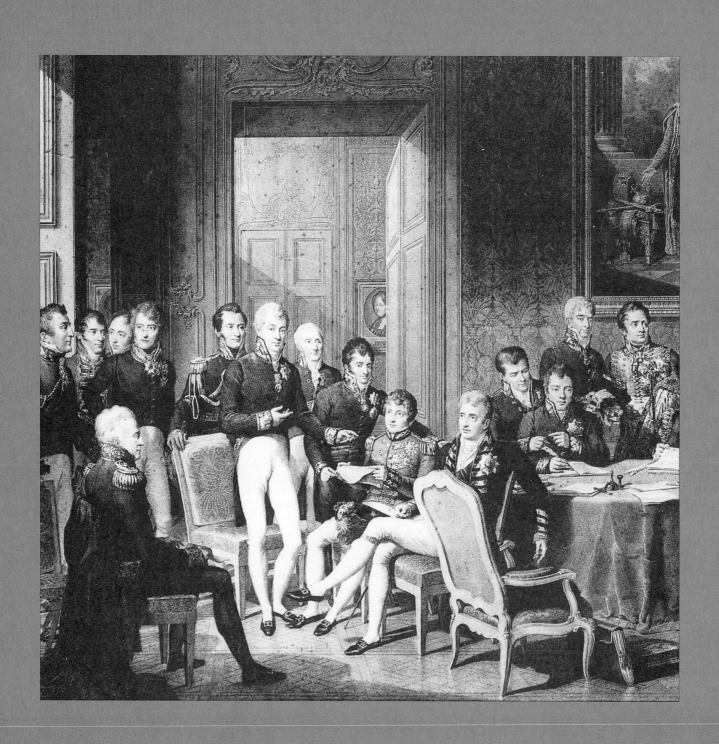

CHAPTER 25

THE DEFENSE OF THE OLD REGIME, 1815–48

CHAPTER OUTLINE

The coalition that defeated Napoleon in 1812–15 supported monarchy and the institutions of the Old Regime. During the next generation (1815–48), victorious conservatives tried to restore and defend their world. Chapter 25 examines this era, often called the age of Metternich in honor of its leading conservative statesman. It starts with monarchists reasserting the Old Regime at the peace congress of 1815 (the Congress of Vienna). Next the chapter looks at the postwar conservative alliance and its "congress system" designed to preserve that order. This leads to an examination of the conservatism seen in religious revival and in legislation to control revolutionary ideas.

The restoration of the Old Regime was widely resisted. A variety of political movements, from liberal reformism to socialist revolution, challenged the old order. These movements are discussed as well as the revolutions that they encouraged, such as the liberal-national revolutions of the 1820s and a wave of revolutions in 1830–32. The chapter goes on to examine the success of the conservative order by exploring the differing conditions of autocratic monarchy in Russia, the victories of liberalism in Britain, and the delicate compromise between monarchism and liberalism reached in France.

The Congress of Vienna and the Restoration of the Old Order

A Quadruple Alliance of Russia, Prussia, Austria, and Britain was needed to defeat Napoleon. Armies of these allies reached Paris in 1814. Within weeks, the allies reached agreements with both Napoleon and France. Napoleon received a generous settlement in return for his unconditional abdication. He kept the title of emperor (with an annual income of two million French francs) and received the Italian island of Elba to govern.

◆ DOCUMENT 25.1 ◆

Metternich: The Conservative's Faith (1820)

Prince Klemens von Metternich (1773–1859) was the Austrian for-
eign minister for nearly half a century, from 1809 to 1848. He was the
most influential statesman in post-Napoleonic Europe, and he shaped
the peace treaties of 1815, the postwar alliance system, and the antilib-
eral domestic policies of the age. The following document, which he sent
to the emperors of Austria and Russia in 1820, explains his conserva-
tive values and his reasons for his policies.

Kings have to calculate the chances of their very existence in the immediate future; passions are let loose and league together to overthrow everything which society respects as the basis of its existence: religion, public morality, laws, customs, rights, duties are all attacked, confounded, overthrown, or called in question. The great mass of people are tranquil spectators of these attacks and revolutions. . . . It is principally the middle class of society which this moral gangrene has affected, and it is only among them that the real heads of the party [of revolution] are found. . . .

We are convinced that society can no longer be saved without strong and vigorous resolutions on the part of the Governments. . . in establishing the principle of *stability,* [which] will in no wise exclude the development of what is good, for stability is not immobility. . . .

Union between the monarchs is the basis for the policy which must now be followed to save society from total ruin. . . .: Respect for all that is; liberty for every Government to watch over the well-being of its own people; a league of all Governments against all factions in all states; contempt for the meaningless words which have become the rallying cry of the factious;. . . . refusal on the part of every monarch to aid or succour partisans under any mask whatever. . . .

We are certainly not alone in questioning if society can exist with the liberty of the press. . . . Let the monarchs in these troublous times be more than usually cautious in attempting real ameliorations. . . . Let them give minute attention to the financial state of their kingdoms. . . . Let them be just, but strong; beneficent, but strict. Let them maintain religious principles in all their purity, and not allow the faith to be attacked.

Similar leniency characterized the treaty given to France, the Treaty of Paris, which restored the Bourbon monarchy. The eldest brother of Louis XVI thus returned to Paris "in the baggage of the allies." He took the title of Louis XVIII, in respect for Louis XVI's son who had died in prison. The allies considered Louis XVIII a member of the counterrevolutionary coalition, so France lost recently annexed territory (such as Belgium) but kept the borders of 1792 without losing older provinces (such as Alsace).

These treaties were secondary issues to the allies, who wanted to reconsider the entire map of Europe and restore the prerevolutionary order. Representatives from hundreds of states assembled in Vienna in 1814 for this peace congress and to celebrate the end of the revolutionary era (see illustration 25.1). The decisions of the Congress of Vienna were made by the four strongest allies. The most influential statesman was the foreign minister of Austria, Prince Klemens von Metternich. He was a native of the Rhineland, and he had been raised in the French language, which he spoke at home; Metternich only entered Austrian service after a French army drove him from his Rhenish estates in

1794. His ideas, however, won the confidence of the emperor of Austria, Francis I; they agreed that revolutionary ideas were "moral gangrene" (see document 25.1). Francis trusted Metternich to maintain a world with "no innovations." Enlightenment was so unwelcome, wrote the poet Heinrich Heine, that he should be remembered as "Prince Mitternacht" (midnight).

The allies shared variants of Metternichian conservatism. Britain was represented by the foreign secretary of a conservative government, Viscount Castlereagh. He was such a forceful spokesman for the aristocratic cause that the poor of London lined the streets to cheer his funeral procession. Prussia was represented by Prince Karl von Hardenberg who earned a reputation for liberalism for Prussian domestic reforms but who defended Prussian interests and international order with tenacity. The czar of Russia, Alexander I, the most complex and intelligent monarch of the age, often chose to represent Russia in negotiations himself. These counts, viscounts, dukes, and princes stated a guiding philosophy for the Congress of Vienna: the principle of legitimacy. Every province in Europe should be returned to its legitimate ruler, and the people of each province

Illustration 25.1

The Congress of Vienna. The peace congress following the defeat of Napoleon was also one of the most glittering assemblies in the history of the European nobility. The statesmen portrayed here redrew the map of Europe in between balls, while other aristocrats celebrated in a party that lasted for months. Prince Metternich, who dominated European affairs for the next generation, is the dandy in tight white breeches standing at left. Lord Castlereagh, whose party life would soon lead him to suicide, is seated at center with legs crossed. Prince Talleyrand sits at right with his arm on the table and his crippled foot hidden.

should be restored to their place in the legitimate (Old Regime) social order.

In theory, the doctrine of legitimacy meant the recreation of pre-1789 frontiers, monarchies, and social systems—the divinely ordained order. In reality, the decisions made at Vienna stemmed from self-interest (see map 25.1). Compensation was a truer name for the philosophy of the congress, and the four allies each annexed territory without a pretense of legitimacy. Whole regions of Europe—such as Belgium, Genoa, Lombardy, Norway, Poland, and Saxony—became the pawns of the great powers. Russia kept Finland (which it had annexed during the war) and gained most of Poland. The allies talked about the legitimacy of Polish independence, but power settled the issue: The Russian army occupied Poland and no one wanted to try to move it. The Russian concession to legitimacy was to give "Congress Poland" its own constitution. Prussia annexed half of neighboring Saxony and several small states in the Rhineland. This changed the course of Eu-

ropean history because an enlarged Prussia acquired great industrial potential and a presence in western Europe.

Britain and Austria demanded compensation to balance the gains of the Prussians and Russians. This led to a two-against-two stalemate until the four powers asked a fifth diplomat to join them—Louis XVIII's foreign minister, Prince Charles-Maurice de Talleyrand. Talleyrand had served the Old Regime as a bishop, the French Revolution as a legislator, and Napoleon as a diplomat, so he was comfortable when self-interest was more important than principle. He supported Britain and Austria, so they, too, received compensation. The British took new colonies in Africa, Asia, and the Americas plus strategic islands, such as Malta; they also insisted that a friendly state (but not a great power) control the lowlands from which an invasion of England might be launched. Consequently, the predominantly Protestant, Dutch-speaking Netherlands annexed the Catholic, predominantly French-speaking

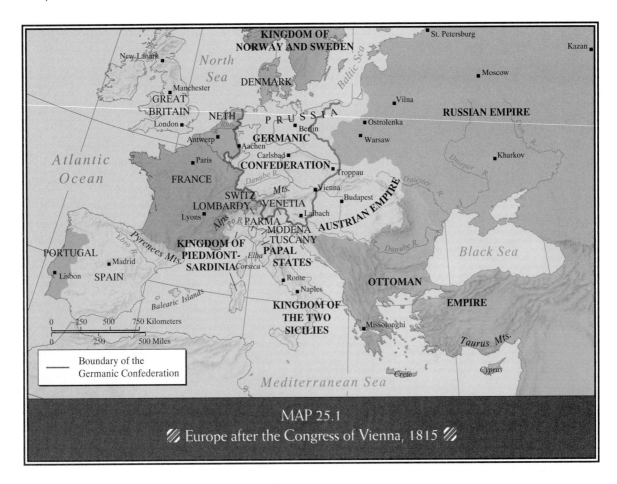

MAP 25.1

░ Europe after the Congress of Vienna, 1815 ░

region of Belgium. The Hapsburgs had previously ruled this region (then known as the Austrian Netherlands), so Austria took compensation in northern Italy: Lombardy and the Republic of Venice.

Even after their mutual aggrandizement, the great powers did not follow the principle of legitimacy. They did not resurrect the Holy Roman Empire, which had confederated two hundred German states in central Europe until Napoleon abolished it in 1806. Instead, the allies restored only thirty-nine German states, linked in a loose German Confederation with a weak Diet at Frankfurt. The dispossessed rulers kept their titles, their personal estates, and good reasons to doubt the meaning of legitimacy. Italians had their own reasons to question the validity of that principle. Lombards and Venetians discovered that they were legitimate Austrians; the Genoese learned that their historic government was not legitimate because it had been a republic; and others, such as the Tuscans, found that their legitimate rulers were members of the Hapsburg family.

Napoleon Bonaparte escaped from his lenient exile on Elba in March 1815 and returned to France during these negotiations. Louis XVIII fled and his army defected to Napoleon, but the allies rejected Napoleon's claim to the throne and assembled armies in Belgium under the duke of Wellington, who had defeated Napoleon's armies in Spain. A combination of British and Prussian armies defeated Napoleon outside Brussels at Waterloo, and his reign of one hundred days ended with harsher settlements. Napoleon became a British prisoner of war, and they held him under house arrest on the island of St. Helena until his death in 1821. A Second Peace of Paris made the French pay for accepting Napoleon's return. France lost more Rhineland territory to Prussia and more of Savoy to the Kingdom of Piedmont-Sardinia, had to pay an indemnity of 700 million francs, and endured the military occupation of northeastern France until it was paid.

The Conservative Alliance and the Congress System

After the difficult negotiations at Vienna and the shock of the Hundred Days, the allies resolved to protect their newly restored order. Alexander I, who was attracted to religious mysticism, proposed a Holy Alliance in which they would pledge to act according to the teachings of the Bible. Most statesmen agreed with Castlereagh that this was "sublime nonsense" (one called it a "holy kiss"), but they promised to act "con-

◆ **CHRONOLOGY 25.1** ◆

The Congress System, 1815–25

Date	Site	Chief participants	Accomplishments
1815	Vienna	Austria, Britain, France, Prussia, and Russia	Post-Napoleonic peace settlements
1818	Aachen	Austria, Britain, Prussia, and Russia	France readmitted to alliance
1819	Karlsbad	Austria and Prussia	Laws to control German radicals
1820	Troppau	Austria, France, Prussia, and Russia	Doctrine of military intervention
1821	Laibach	Austria, France, Prussia, and Russia	Austrian invasion of southern Italy
1822	Verona	Austria, Britain, France, and Russia	French invasion of Spain
1825	St. Petersburg	Austria and Russia	Discuss conservative alliance

formably to the words of the Holy Scriptures." In case that did not work, they also renewed the Quadruple Alliance against French armies and French ideas. Austria, Britain, Prussia, and Russia pledged "to employ all their means to prevent the general tranquility from again being disturbed."

The allies also protected the conservative order by planning regular meetings to discuss international problems. This led to a series of small congresses, also shaped by Metternich, during the next decade (see chronology 25.1). In 1818 a congress met at Aachen to recognize that the French had paid the indemnity and to welcome the government of Louis XVIII into a Quintuple Alliance to maintain the status quo. A more important congress met in 1820 at Troppau, where the three eastern powers (Austria, Prussia, and Russia) adopted the Troppau Protocol, asserting the right of the allies to intervene in smaller countries if the conservative order were threatened. A congress of 1821 used this principle to justify an Austrian invasion of the Italian states to suppress radical rebels. The congress system faced a difficult decision in 1822 when a liberal revolution occurred in Spain. The Troppau Protocol called for armed intervention to crush the revolution, but that meant a French invasion of Spain. The allies decided that they were less afraid of a French army than of a French constitution. Thus, conservatism put Metternich and Alexander I in the ironic position of cheering French military victories.

Protecting the Old Order: Religion

The conservatism of the post-1815 world is especially clear in the religious revival of that era. After an age in which philosophes satirized churches and the educated classes became skeptics, after a revolution in which churches were closed and their property seized, after an economic revolution that dechristianized many workers, and after a cynical conqueror imprisoned the pope and used religion as an instrument of political policy, many Christians were eager for their own restoration of old values and institutions.

The Vatican was a leader of the new conservatism. Pope Pius VII had slept in French jails during the revolutionary era and now retaliated against French ideas. He restored the Jesuit order, reestablished the Inquisition, and reconstituted the Index of prohibited books. Catholics were forbidden to believe that the Earth rotated around the Sun or to read Gibbon's *The Decline and Fall of the Roman Empire*. In the papal states, Pius annulled Napoleonic laws of religious toleration and reintroduced persecution of the Jews, who were returned to the ghetto and compelled to attend mass once a week. Pius ended freedom of speech and the press, outlawing statements of heresy, radicalism, or immorality. His criminal code permitted torture but outlawed vaccinations and street lighting as radical innovations.

Pope Pius VIII continued this effort to return Catholics to the Old Regime. As he explained in the encyclical *Traditi humilitati nostrae* (1829), the church must combat secularizatism in all its forms, including public schools, civil marriage, and divorce. Catholics must return to a religion based upon faith and Christian mysteries. A leading Catholic intellectual, the viscount René de Chateaubriand, had championed this attack upon rationalism in *The Genius of Christianity* (1802). Christians, Chateaubriand argued, must reject rationalism because it rejected religious mysteries: "It is a pitiful

Illustration 25.2

⚉ **Censorship of the Press.** All European governments, including those in the liberal West, adopted some form of press censorship in the early nineteenth century. In this 1834 lithograph by Honoré Daumier, a stout worker plants his feet firmly on the bedrock principle of freedom of the press. In the background, censors are restrained and kings collapse.

mode of reasoning to reject whatever we cannot comprehend."

Even political liberals embraced religious conservatism in some countries. In Spain, liberals fought an obsessively religious monarch, King Ferdinand VII, who was so devout that he personally embroidered robes for statues of the Virgin Mary in Spanish shrines. Yet Spanish liberals shared his religious beliefs. When they imposed a constitution in 1820, they rejected religious freedom. Article 12 said simply, "The religion of the Spanish nation is, and shall be perpetually, Apostolic Roman Catholic, the only true religion. The nation protects it by wise and just laws and prohibits the exercise of any other religion whatsoever." Spanish deputies in the Cortes swore an oath to "defend and preserve" the Catholic Church, "without admitting any other" religion to be practiced in Spain.

This reaction against religious toleration also characterized the Russian Orthodox Church. During the reign of Czar Nicholas I, Catholics, Protestants, and Jews all suffered restrictions. Nicholas outlawed Protestant Bible societies in 1826, believing that missionaries were leading Russians away from the Orthodox Church. Uniate Catholicism (an eastern European church in union with Rome and accepting papal authority, yet following traditional Orthodox rites) fared worse: In 1839 the czar closed their churches and forced their conversion to Orthodoxy. The Jews, as usual, suffered the worst. An 1827 edict required military service from all Jewish men, with liability to conscription starting at age twelve. A Jewish Statute of

1835 defined a limited area of the Russian Empire, known as the Pale of Settlement, in which Jews could live; those who dared to go "beyond the Pale" risked their lives.

A somewhat different conservatism characterized Protestantism. Evangelical churches (especially Pietists in Lutheran countries and Methodists elsewhere) denounced the evils of the modern world and taught obedience to established authority, as did the Vatican. Methodist governing statutes stated: "None of us shall, either in writing or in conversation, speak lightly or irreverently of the government." Prince Metternich could not have said it better. Even hymns could be counterrevolutionary: "The rich man in his castle, The poor man at the gate, God created both of them, And ordered their estate." Governments did not oppose such messages, so an evangelical "awakening" swept Britain, the north German states, and Scandinavia and even won converts in such Catholic regions as Belgium, Switzerland, and France. This development was so important that some historians have argued that the spread of Methodism in the British working class was the reason that Britain never experienced a major revolution during industrialization.

Protestants stressed another element in conservatism: Puritanical restrictions upon behavior. Evangelicals insisted upon strict sexual morality, campaigned for the prohibition of alcoholic beverages, and fought blasphemous language. One widely circulated poster, "An Evangelical Barometer," showed the stages of wickedness—from drunkenness or theatre-going, through neglect of prayer or novel-reading, to adultery or party-going on Sundays. The most famous illustration of the Protestant effort to supervise morals is the work of Dr. Thomas Bowdler and his sister Harriet Bowdler. The Bowdlers worked so avidly to censor immoral literature that they left their name behind for expurgated (*bowdlerized*) works. Harriet Bowdler began an abridgment of Shakespeare, and Thomas expanded his sister's work to produce *The Family Shakespeare* in 1818. The bowdlerized Shakespeare eliminated all passages that might "raise a blush on the cheek of modesty," such as Hamlet's famous remarks to Ophelia about sex.

Protecting the Old Order: The Law

Historians often characterize Metternichian government as an effort to curb dissent. Every state in Europe adopted such legislation as a bulwark against revolution. Freedom of the press and freedom of speech were the first targets (see illustration 25.2). Russian restrictions were so severe that writers spoke of a "censorship terror." Two of the greatest figures of Russian literature, Alexander Pushkin and Fyodor Dostoevski, were exiled—Pushkin for writing "Ode to Liberty" and Dostoevski for belonging to a radical organization. In Scandinavia, the tales of Hans Christian Andersen were banned for corrupting the youth; Dante's *The Divine Comedy* was forbidden in Prussia because the title seemed blasphemous to a censor. Two dangerous radicals were hanged during a Spanish crackdown in 1833—a man who had shouted "Hurrah for liberty!" and a woman who had embroidered the slogan "Law, Liberty, Equality."

Such counterrevolutionary legal restrictions did not stop with obvious political targets; they also had profound effects on individual families. In France, for example, the royalist government sought to rebuild the traditional family. The chief legal expression of this effort was the repeal of the divorce law adopted during the French Revolution. As Louis de Bonald, a leading philosopher of monarchism, explained the counterrevolutionary policy: "Just as political democracy allows the people, the weak part of political society, to rise against the established power, so divorce, veritable domestic democracy, allows the wife, the weak part, to rebel against marital authority. In order to keep the state out of the hands of the people, it is necessary to keep the family out of the hands of wives and children." Metternich adopted similarly motivated family legislation in Austria. A Marriage Law of 1820, for example, forbade marriage by beggars, people receiving relief, the unemployed, and migrants; it also required a "marriage permit," without which servants, journeymen, and day laborers could not marry.

<hr/>

◈ DOCUMENT 25.2 ◈

The Karlsbad Decrees, 1819

Supervision of Universities

1. The sovereign [of each German state] shall choose for each university an extraordinary commissioner. . . . The duty of this commissioner shall be . . . to observe carefully the spirit with which the professors and tutors are guided in their public and private lectures; . . . to give the instruction a salutary direction, suited to the future destiny of the students. . . .

2. The governments of the states . . . reciprocally engage to remove from their universities and other establishments of instruction, professors and other public teachers against whom it may be proved, that . . . in abusing their legitimate influence over the minds of youth . . . they shall have shown themselves incapable of executing the important functions entrusted to them. . . .

3. . . . [L]aws . . . against secret or unauthorized associations at the universities shall be maintained in all their force and vigor.

Press Censorship

1. . . . [N]o writing appearing in the form a daily paper or periodical pamphlet . . . shall be issued from the press without the previous consent of the public authority.

<hr/>

The policy of social control made schools another favorite target of conservative governments. Metternich's regulations for schools, announced at Karlsbad in 1819 (see document 25.2), put German universities under the control of the German Confederation (which he, not coincidentally, dominated). The Karlsbad Decrees put a government commissioner in charge of the universities, fired liberal professors, and closed student clubs. Francis I liked this policy; as he told a group of teachers in 1821: "I do not need scholars but obedient citizens." The arbitrary arrest and trial of teachers followed. In Prussia the harassment of liberal professors became a police recreation. This regulation of the schools reached its nadir when Friedrich Froebel opened the first kindergarten in 1837. Froebel believed that preschool children could learn through games and

❖ DOCUMENT 25.3 ❖

Instructions to the Police of Venice, 1820

Secret Orders:

Their duties include:

1. Seeking out and unmasking conspiracies, plots, plans, undertakings and enterprises that tend to endanger the safety of the sacred person of His Majesty . . . and in general all influences that might be detrimental to the internal and external public safety of the monarchy.

2. Unmasking unions, associations, corporations, secret societies and sects, whether they be ostensibly religious or not. . . .

3. Watching and directing public feeling in all classes of inhabitants, and their views on political events; surveillance over anyone who exercises a major influence on public feeling[;] . . . keeping a watch on remarks, judgments, complaints, or desires made about public dispositions and measures. . . .

4. Keeping a watch over the influence on public opinion of gazettes, newspapers, pamphlets, books, or pictures of any sort, but especially if they are of a political nature. . . .

5. The most scrupulous control, in the widest sense, over all branches of public administration, and vigilance over the official and domestic behavior of individual employees, servants, and guards. . . .

6. General control over the implementation . . . of laws in general.

7. Surveillance and control of foreign consuls, of diplomatic personnel. . . .

8. Gathering and obtaining information on the conduct of public affairs and on public opinion in foreign states bordering on Italy. . . .

10. *The Secret Service* should be ready to use salaried or voluntary *confidants* as well as *surveillance over private correspondence.*

---

activities. The Prussian government, however, deemed this a revolutionary principle that undermined the authoritarian model of education. Kindergartens were outlawed.

German education laws provided a model for other countries. Shortly after the promulgation of the Karlsbad Decrees, Alexander I adopted a similar program. His instructions for the University of Kazan (1820) eliminated free speech and freedom of inquiry: "No harmful or seductive literature or speeches in any form shall be permitted to spread through the university." Alexander, like Francis I, thought that "[t]he soul of education, and the prime virtue of the citizen, is obedience." His restrictions did not surpass the zeal of the French. In 1816 the government expelled the entire student body of their elite engineering school, the *Ecole polytechnique* (including Auguste Comte, a founder of sociology), for radicalism. Such attitudes also reached England, where one M.P denounced plans for more schools by arguing that education only taught the masses "to despise their lot in life instead of making them good servants; instead of teaching them subordination, it would render them fractious[,] . . . insolent to their superiors."

The most severe Metternichian restrictions were the political use of the police and judiciary. Modern police forces did not exist in 1815, but the revolutionary era had taught many lessons about policing (see document 25.3). Metternich had observed the methods of the French police, such as keeping files on suspects, organizations, or periodicals. He and Count Joseph Sedlnitzky founded one of the first effective police systems, using these bureaucratic techniques. Sedlnitzky's job title described his function: president of the Supreme Police and of the Censorship Office. This refinement of French policing merged the police and postal service, so letters could be read before delivery. Sedlnitzky's police also used internal passports to limit the movement of people and ideas within the empire.

In Britain, the counterrevolutionary policies of Lord Liverpool's government (1812–27) rivaled those in more despotic states. A Habeus Corpus Suspension Act denounced "a traitorous conspiracy" of radicals and authorized the arrest of "such persons as his majesty shall suspect are conspiring." A Seditious Meetings Act restricted the right of assembly by requiring prior approval for meetings of fifty or more people. A set of repressive laws, collectively called the Six Acts, forbade

Illustration 25.3

/// **The Peterloo Massacre.** Under the provisions of the Six Acts, the British government had the right to close political meetings, by force if necessary. In the most outrageous application of the law, depicted here, British cavalry use sabres to break up a meeting at Manchester in 1819. Note the crowd being attacked: Both men and women are present, and all are dressed very well.

the publication of anything the government considered seditious, authorized arbitrary searches and seizures, banned many political meetings, and taxed newspapers to make them too expensive for most of the public. The Liverpool government did not hesitate to use the British army against workers, as it did during the Spa Fields (London) Riot of 1816. This policy led to tragedy at Manchester in 1819, when sixty thousand workers assembled in St. Peter's Fields to listen to reform speakers. The Fifteenth Hussars (heroes of the battle of Waterloo) cleared the field with drawn sabers; they killed eleven people, wounded more than four hundred, and provided an ironic name for their heroism: the Peterloo massacre (see illustration 25.3).

British conservatives used the judiciary as effectively as the Austrians used the police. The British did not create a modern municipal police force until Sir Robert Peel, a reform-minded Tory, persuaded conservatives to adopt the Metropolitan Police Act of 1829. (The London police were consequently called Peelers, then Bobbies.) British conservatives had long opposed the creation of a police force. As a parliamentary report of 1818 stated, they feared that this "odious and repulsive" idea would threaten liberty and create a nation of spies. Their concerns about freedom did not prevent the political use of the courts, however. Before Peel's reforms, more than two hundred crimes were punishable by death, and these laws were often used for political effects, such as controlling workers. In 1833 the courts taught a lesson to workers by executing a nine-year-old apprentice for stealing two pence (about four cents)

worth of ink from his master's shop. British judges more often solved political problems by ordering the transportation of troublesome people to penal colonies in Australia. Irish nationalists and labor militants were especially liable to receive such sentences. One of the first efforts to organize a labor union in Britain resulted in the transportation of six farm workers (the Tolpuddle martyrs) in 1834 for taking a secret oath. The conditions of penal servitude were harsh and included corporal punishment; one Irish nationalist received one hundred lashes for singing a rebel song.

Politicized justice also typified the continent. Many governments, especially the Prussian, used the crime of *lèse majesté* (anything offensive to the dignity of the ruler) to control dissent. King Frederick William III showed the usefulness of this law in 1819. He had promised his Rhenish provinces a constitution when he annexed them in 1815, but he reneged. When a group of Rhinelanders reminded him with a petition, he ordered their arrest for *lèse majesté*. Other governments found it helpful to suspend *habeas corpus* (a writ, usually based on evidence of crime, needed in common law before a citizen can be brought before a court), the basic protection against illegal imprisonment. The British suspended *habeas corpus* in 1819, and the Spanish virtually ignored it. Ferdinand VII once had thirty-three liberals imprisoned for two years without the nuisance of a trial. French justice illustrates another method for controlling the troublesome. *Les Misérables*, Victor Hugo's novel with a criminal protagonist (Jean Valjean), describes criminals being chained to a stake in a public

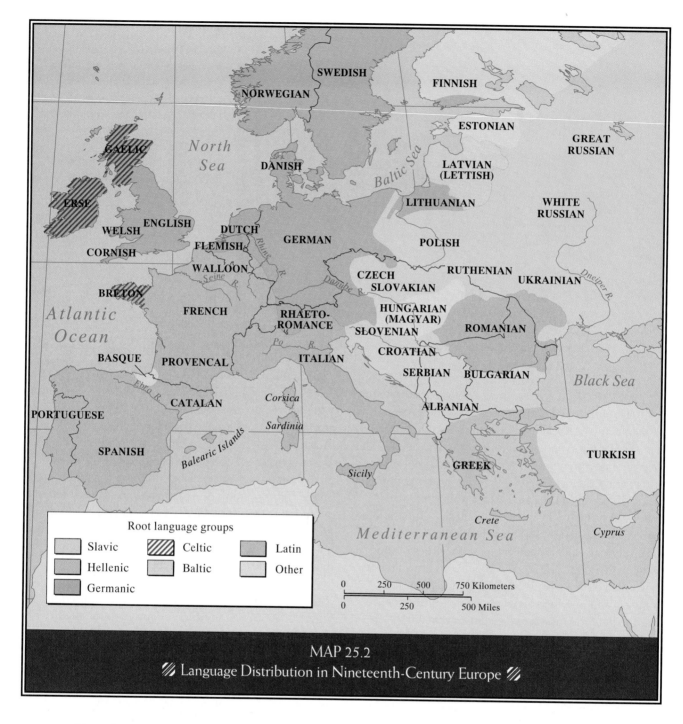

MAP 25.2

🎵 Language Distribution in Nineteenth-Century Europe 🎵

square and branded with a hot iron, so honest folk could identify and avoid them.

Challenges to the Old Order: The '-isms'

The changes that had shaken Europe in the generation before 1815—the intellectual ferment of the Enlightenment, the political upheaval of the French Revolution,

the social transformation of industrialization—had all produced pressures to reform the Old Regime. The monarchical world absorbed some change, but most ideas were resisted by conservative governments. After 1815 these ideas of change began to crystallize into political doctrines (or ideologies). These new doctrines are known as the "-isms" because they took names ending in *ism*, a linguistic vogue that began with the word *liberalism* (coined in 1820), continued with the terms *nationalism* and *socialism* in the 1830s, and soon included such doctrines as radicalism, capitalism, Marxism, and

◆ DOCUMENT 25.4 ◆

Mazzini: Instructions for Young Italy, 1831

Guiseppe Mazzini (1805–72) was one of the founders of Italian nationalism and the modern state of Italy. He greatly influenced nationalist thinking in many countries. Mazzini created a secret society, Young Italy, dedicated to the unification of all Italian states under a self-governing republic. His manifesto for Young Italy, from which the following excerpt is taken, was widely emulated.

Young Italy is a brotherhood of Italians who believe in a law of Progress and Duty, and are convinced that Italy is destined to become one nation—convinced also that she possesses sufficient strength within herself to become one. . . . They join this association in the firm intent of consecrating both thought and action to the great aim of reconstituting Italy as one independent sovereign nation of free men and equals.

By Italy we understand —(1) Continental and peninsular Italy, bounded on the north by the Alps . . . and on the east by Trieste; (2) The islands proved Italian by the language of the inhabitants, and destined . . . to form a part of the Italian political unity.

Young Italy is Republican and Unitarian.

Republican because theoretically every nation is destined, by the Law of God and humanity, to form a free and equal community as brothers; and the republic is the only form of government that ensures this future. . . . Because our Italian tradition is essentially republican; our great memories are republican; the whole history of our national progress is republican; whereas the introduction of monarchy amongst us was coeval with our decay and consummated our ruin. . . .

Young Italy is Unitarian because without unity there is no true nation. Because without unity there is no real strength.

The means by which Young Italy proposes to reach its aim are education and insurrection, to be adopted simultaneously, and made to harmonize with each other.

---

feminism. These doctrines were sometimes compatible with each other and sometimes in conflict with each other, but they all called for changes in the Metternichian order.

The first of these doctrines, liberalism, was derived from the Latin word *liber* (free) to denote a doctrine about individual freedom. Early nineteenth-century liberalism (sometimes called classical liberalism to distinguish it from later liberalism) sought individual freedoms (such as freedom of speech), laws extending such liberty to more individuals (such as minorities), and the removal of impediments to liberty (such as laws favoring members of an established national church). To achieve such aims, liberals commonly demanded two fundamental documents: (1) a constitution establishing a representative government and specifying its powers, and (2) a bill of rights guaranteeing individual liberties. Few countries possessed such constitutions or bills of rights, and most monarchs opposed them as revolutionary innovations. Liberals, therefore, were among the primary opponents of the Metternichian restoration.

A second ideology—nationalism—created additional problems for conservatives. This doctrine shifted discussion toward the collective rights of a nation. Na-tionalists asserted that it was possible to identify distinct nations, based upon shared characteristics such as language (see map 25.2). This nationalism is illustrated by a German song, Ernst Arndt's *Where Is the German's Fatherland?*: "Where is the German's Fatherland? Name me at length that mighty land! 'Where'er resounds the German tongue, Where'er its hymns to God are sung.' " Other nationalists defined their nation by a shared culture, history, or religion. All advocated the creation of nation-states independent from foreign rule, uniting members of the nation in a single, self-governing state. Nationalists considered these objectives more important than the political rights that liberals sought. As a Rumanian nationalist said in the 1840s, "The question of nationality is more important than liberty. Until a people can exist as a nation, it cannot make use of liberty." One could be both a liberal and nationalist, seeking a nation-state that granted liberty, as Giuseppe Mazzini did in his movement called Young Italy (see document 25.4), but the two objectives often conflicted with each other.

Liberalism and nationalism produced the greatest threats to the monarchical order of 1815, but other "-isms" also challenged it. Governments especially dreaded radicalism, the term they usually applied to

Illustration 25.4

⧉ Utopian Socialism at New Lanark. The most successful of the utopian ideal- ists was Robert Owen (1771–1858), an exceptionally able man who went to work in the cotton mills at age ten, was the manager of a mill by age nineteen, and was wealthy enough to buy the mills at New Lanark, Scotland, at twenty-nine. Owen devoted his wealth to creating the model community at New Lanark shown here. It provided unmatched working conditions and housing for workers, a nursery and school for their children (the separate building left of center), evening education for workers, and a co- operative store.

democratic movements. Radicals endorsed liberalism but demanded more; whereas liberals were willing to accept representative government with a limited fran- chise, radicals called for a democratic franchise and sometimes for the abolition of monarchy. In the words of Mazzini, radicals "no longer believed in the sanctity of royal races, no longer believed in aristocracy, no longer believed in privilege." Radical movements, such as the Decembrists in Russia and the Chartists in Britain, however, made conservatives think of Robe- spierre and the guillotine.

The term *socialism* was also coined in the 1830s to identify doctrines stressing social and economic equality in the industrial age. Although leading socialists came from many backgrounds, the doctrines of socialism ad- dressed the economic problems of the urban working class. Marxist socialism did not become a significant po- litical philosophy until after midcentury, but many forms of pre-Marxist socialism existed. The earliest socialism, known as utopian socialism, grew from critiques of in- dustrial society. Robert Owen, the son of a poor Welsh artisan, made a fortune as a textile manufacturer and de- voted his wealth to improving industrial conditions. He branded the factory system "outright slavery" and called for a new social order based on cooperation instead of competition. Owen applied his ideas to his own facto- ries at New Lanark, Scotland, where he limited his prof- its and invested in building a comfortable life for his workers (see illustration 25.4). This won Owen an inter- national reputation, but neither industrialists nor gov- ernments copied his ideas. Utopian socialism took different forms in France. The founder of French social- ism, Count Henri de Saint-Simon, reversed the pattern of Owen's life: He was born to the highest nobility,

squandered his fortune, and died in poverty. He was a hero of the American Revolution, a prisoner of the French Revolution, and a critic of the industrial revolu- tion. He denounced all economies in which "man has exploited man" and called for a new order based upon the principle "from each according to his capacity, to each according to his productivity."

Many other variants of socialism appeared in the generation before Karl Marx. Charles Fourier proposed utopian communities, which he called phalansteries. Fourier envisioned an idealistic, but highly structured, society whose members (including women) all shared labor and freedom. Other pioneers called for a cooper- ative socialism of workers or a Christian socialism based upon Jesus's devotion to the poor and criticism of the rich. Others envisioned a democratic socialism, on the theory that the poor would have a majority in a true democracy, and they would naturally create a so- cialist society. The champion of democratic socialism was a French journalist, Louis Blanc, who developed the idea of a strong socialist state that used the powers of government to help the poor. Blanc called for govern- ments to regulate the economy and to provide work for the unemployed in national workshops.

A final doctrine of social change, feminism, had not yet acquired that name (a late nineteenth-century coinage) but already called for reconsideration of the role of women in European society. Pioneers such as Mary Wollstonecraft, who had published *A Vindication of the Rights of Women* (1792), and Olympe de Gouges, who had been executed by the guillotine shortly after writ- ing her *Declaration of the Rights of Woman* (1791), had opened discussion of the woman question so effectively that the Metternichian reaction could not contain this

Illustration 25.5

 Women's Rights. Political clubs of women had appeared in the eighteenth century, especially during the French Revolution, when the government soon outlawed them. New clubs began to appear in the 1830s and 1840s, again to sharp criticism from men. In this caricature, Honoré Daumier delivered a sarcastic comment on them.

debate. European legal systems, especially the Napoleonic Code, but also the British common law tradition and the Germanic Frederician Code, explicitly held women in an inferior position. The rights of women were exercised for them by men (their fathers, then their husbands). Women were expected to remain confined to limited spheres of activity—*Kinder, Kirche, Küche* (children, church, cooking) in a famous German cliché. Formal education (especially higher education) and educated occupations were closed to them. The legal condition of women within marriage and the family began with an obligation to obey their husbands, who legally controlled their wives' wages, children, and bodies. Divorce was illegal in many countries and rare everywhere (it required an act of parliament in Britain) before the beginning of the modern "divorce revolution" in the second half of the nineteenth century.

Advocates of women's rights were among the critics of Metternichian conservatism because preserving the old order meant preserving the traditional place of women. Some of these early feminists found homes in the salons organized by educated women, such as Hen-

riette Herz and Rahel Levin in Berlin. Others made careers as writers, journalists, and teachers. A few political groups, chiefly radicals and utopian socialists, welcomed women members and supported women's rights. In France, women's political clubs flourished as radicalism grew in the 1830s, but they were greeted with ridicule by powerful men (see illustration 25.5).

Romanticism: European Culture in the Age of Metternich

The standards of neoclassical culture that had characterized the Old Regime did not survive into the postrevolutionary era. Even before the French Revolution, classicism had come under attack for its strict rules, formal styles, and stress upon reason. When the Congress of Vienna assembled in 1815, European high culture had become quite different. The new style, known as romanticism, reached its apogee in the age of Metternich and continued to be a force in European culture past midcentury.

Romanticism is difficult to define because it was a reaction against precise definitions and rules, and that reaction took many forms. The foremost characteristic of romanticism was the exaltation of personal feelings, emotions, or the spirit, in contrast to cold reason. The emphasis upon feelings led in many directions, from the passions of romantic love to the spirituality of religious revival. Other attitudes also characterized romanticism: a return to nature (in contrast to human works) for themes and inspiration, the admiration of the European past (especially the Middle Ages) instead of classical Greece and Rome, a fascination with the exotic and the supernatural (instead of the strictly civilized), and the canonization of the hero or genius. In addition, the politics of the age of Metternich, especially the aspirations of liberalism and nationalism, shaped romanticism.

The emphasis upon feelings, instead of (or in addition to) reason, had begun in the late eighteenth century. Rousseau, one of the central figures of Enlightenment rationalism, was a transitional figure, a precursor of romanticism who argued, "To exist is to feel!" The greatest German poet, Johann von Goethe, similarly bridged the change from the classical to the romantic. His short novel, *The Sorrows of Young Werther*, depicted feelings so strong that the protagonist's suicide began a vogue for melancholy young men killing themselves as Werther had, with moonlight falling across the last page of Goethe's book (see illustration 25.6). The name of the school of German literature that evolved around Goethe, the *Sturm und Drang* ("storm and stress") movement, suggests the intensity of this emphasis upon feelings. Romanticism was the triumph of that emphasis. At the peak of romanticism, the British poet William Wordsworth simply defined poetry as "the spontaneous overflow of powerful feelings," and the landscape painter John Constable similarly insisted that "[p]ainting is another word for feeling."

Other characteristics of romanticism were equally strong. The return to nature inspired much romantic poetry, especially Wordsworth's. It produced two generations of landscape painters, such as Constable and J. M. W. Turner, who found inspiration in natural scenery. This mood even extended to symphonic music, inspiring Beethoven's Sixth Symphony, known as the Pastoral Symphony. The romantic fascination with medieval Europe likewise had far-reaching influence. The most visible expression of it was a Gothic revival in architecture (see illustration 25.7). This produced both new construction in the flamboyant Gothic style of the late Middle Ages (such as the new Palace of Westminster, home of the British Houses of Parliament, built in

Illustration 25.6

Romanticism in Literature. Johann von Geothe's epistolary novel *The Sorrows of Young Werther* expressed many of the themes of romanticism. Werther, a troubled young man, leaves home for a secluded cottage where he finds peace in nature and reading Homer until he develops an uncontrollable passion for a beautiful young woman named Charlotte. In this illustration, a woman reading the novel is reduced to tears.

1836) and campaigns to preserve surviving Gothic masterpieces (such as Viollet-le-Duc's restoration of Notre Dame Cathedral in Paris). The same inspiration stimulated historical literature such as Hugo's *The Hunchback of Notre Dame*, Sir Walter Scott's *Ivanhoe*, and Alexandre Dumas's *The Three Musketeers;* its most lasting effect on Western literature, however, was probably the invention of the Gothic horror story, a style begun by Horace Walpole (son of the prime minister) in *The Castle of Otranto*, made famous by Mary Shelley's *Frankenstein*, and popularized in America by Edgar Allan Poe.

Many of these themes made romanticism compatible with conservative political philosophy. The focus upon nature turned high culture toward the rural world, home of aristocratic power and the bastion of conservative sentiments, instead of the industrializing world that was emerging as the new center of wealth and power. The focus upon the Middle Ages restored cultural em-

Illustration 25.7

Romanticism in Painting. This painting of the ruins of a medieval monastery in northern Germany expresses several of the themes of romanticism. The power of nature is vividly depicted (and felt?) in the stark force of winter and the weathering of the ruins. The viewer's focus is drawn, however, to the misty gothic architecture (pointed arches and portals typified late gothic churches) of a lost and moving past, which is presented with a strong dose of sentimentality.

phasis upon a world of unchallenged monarchy and universal Christianity, instead of the republicanism, constitutionalism, and liberalism. The dethronement of rationalism and the recovery of emotion encouraged the revival of religions of faith, mystery, and miracle.

But another side of romanticism found a powerful voice in the liberal and national revolutions of the early nineteenth century. The revolutionary sympathies of some romantics can be seen in Eugène Delacroix's painting "Liberty at the Barricades"; the radical poems of Percy Bysshe Shelley; the angry novels of Victor Hugo, such as *Les Misérables*; and even Giuseppe Verdi's powerful opera *Rigoletto* (which depicts the scandalous behavior of a monarch). The link between romanticism and nationalism was especially strong because many nationalists built their philosophy upon the nation's shared culture. Many peoples found part of the identity in folk tales, and their compilation (such as the work of the brothers Grimm in Germany) became a form of romantic nationalism. So did the recovery of the history of national minorities (as distinct from the history of their foreign government), as František Palacký did for the Czechs in his multivolume *History of Bohemia*. National themes were equally powerful for romantic painters, as Francisco Goya showed in a powerful canvas entitled "Execution of the Madrileños," depicting the firing squad shootings of Spanish freedom fighters. The strongest expression of romantic nationalism, however, was in music. All across Europe, nationalist composers drew inspiration from patriotic themes and folk music: Frédéric Chopin's *Polonaises* (Polish pieces),

Bedrich Smetana's tone poems about Czech scenes (*Ma Vlast*— My Country), or Franz Liszt's *Hungarian Rhapsodies*.

Challenging the Old Order: Revolutions, 1815–25

Despite their precautions, the conservative forces in power after 1815 could not prevent revolutions. More than a dozen revolutions, from Portugal to Russia, took place in the decade following the Congress of Vienna, plus historic rebellions in the British and Spanish empires. Historians normally describe these upheavals as liberal-national revolutions because most rebellions sought national independence (in Serbia, Ireland, Greece, and Spanish America) or constitutional government (in Spain) or both (several Italian states).

Conservatives believed that these revolutions were nurtured and led by radical secret societies and used this to justify restricting civil rights. Such societies did exist, the most famous being an Italian society known as the Carbonari ("the charcoal burners"). The Carbonari were founded by Filippo Buonarroti, an Italian aristocrat who had learned his sense of insurgency in France in the 1790s. By 1815 chapters of the Carbonari could be found in every Italian state; in 1820 the Neapolitan chapter claimed 100,000 members. Carbonari swore an oath to fight despotism and seek governments based on popular sovereignty, to oppose clericalism and seek secular institutions, and to challenge the foreign domination of the Italian states. Similar societies existed in most countries—in the

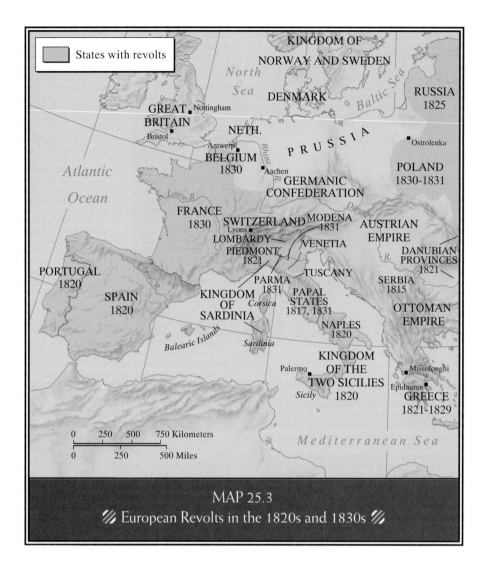

MAP 25.3

%% European Revolts in the 1820s and 1830s %%

circles of Greek businessmen (the *Hetaires*), in Polish universities (Adam Mickiewicz founded his nationalist society at the University of Vilna in 1817), in the officer corps of the Russian army (the Society of the South in Ukraine and the Society of the North at St. Petersburg), in Masonic lodges in Spain, and among Napoleonic war veterans attending German universities who founded the *Burschenschaften*.

With or without the encouragement of such societies, political uprisings were frequent occurrences in the age of Metternich (see map 25.3). While the Congress of Vienna met, a Serbian uprising against Ottoman Turkish rule began, the first in a series of Balkan revolts against the government in Constantinople. In 1816 Britain faced a slave rebellion in the Caribbean. A year later, a Carbonari-led liberal revolution was suppressed in the papal states. These uprisings provoked the conservative powers to adopt the Troppau Protocol in 1818, but barely two years later came the successful Spanish revolution (stimulated by King Ferdinand VII's

abolition of the constitution of 1812 and by the impact of wars of independence in Spanish America), which was a nagging problem for the congress system in 1820–23. In 1820 revolutions also broke out in Portugal and Naples (both seeking constitutions), then at Palermo, in Sicily. A fourth Italian state, Piedmont, experienced revolution in 1821, as did three more regions of the Ottoman Empire (Moldavia, Wallachia, and Greece) and several additional Spanish provinces in South America. Congresses of 1821 and 1822 sent Austrian armies to fight liberals in Italy and French troops into Spain. By 1823 the conservative alliance had defeated the Spanish and Italian revolutions, treating the defeated rebels with savage cruelty; for example, in Italy, captured rebels had their right hands cut off before being sent to Austrian dungeons. The British opposed the application of the Troppau Protocol elsewhere. The British navy supported the Monroe Doctrine (proclaimed by the United States to block allied intervention in America), so most of Latin America

one of the most powerful states in the world during the sixteenth and seventeenth centuries, dominating much of eastern Europe, but it had begun to collapse in the eighteenth century. The Ottoman Empire included north Africa and the Middle East, so its disintegration posed one of the thorniest problems of nineteenth-century statecraft, known as the eastern question. During the years of the congress system, revolutions broke out in Serbia, Greece, and the Rumanian provinces of Moldavia and Wallachia (on the border of Russia), but it was the Greek revolution of 1821–27 that broke the Metternichian alliance.

After the Serbs won autonomy in their revolution, a Greek congress at Epidaurus declared independence in 1822 (see document 25.5). According to the principles of the Troppau Protocol, the great powers should have supported the legitimate Turkish government. Metternich was almost alone in favoring that policy. Romantic philhellenism stimulated a pro-Greek policy in Britain and France, and for once governments agreed with the radical Shelley who wrote: "We are all Greeks. Our laws, our literature, our religion, our arts, have their roots in Greece." Russian policy was less sophisticated but more adamant: The Ottoman Empire deserved no help from the Holy Alliance because it was not a Christian state.

The Greeks won their independence in a long, brutal war that still echoes in Graeco-Turkish enmity. Greek Orthodox clergymen proclaimed a "war of extermination" against Islamic infidels, leading to the killing of twenty-five thousand civilians within six weeks; the sultan proclaimed an Islamic Holy War that produced forty thousand civilian corpses. Along the way, the patriarch of the Orthodox Church was hanged and his body thrown into the Bosphorus. This killing did not end until Britain, France, and Russia broke with Metternich and intervened in 1827. The counterrevolutionary alliance collapsed (there were no full congresses after 1822) because self-interest had prevailed over doctrine; ironically, the most conservative state in Europe had caused this.

Illustration 25.8

The Greek Revolution. The Greek revolution of 1821–1830 (or the Greek War of Independence) was one of the most successful nationalist uprisings of the Metternichian era, in part because philhellenism swept the educated classes in western countries, encouraging governments to support the Greeks. One moment of the Greek revolution became especially well-known in western Europe: the Turkish siege and assault on the Greek fortress of Missolonghi, which guarded the mouth of the Gulf of Corinth. Lord Byron, the noted English romantic poet, was devoted to the Greek cause and died at Missolonghi in 1824. Eugène Delacroix devoted one of the most famous paintings of Romanticism to the battle, "Greece in the Ruins of Missolonghi," shown here, in 1826.

won its independence from Spain. As the British foreign secretary bragged to Parliament, "I have called the New World into existence to redress the balance of the old."

The conservative alliance broke apart over the revolutions in the Balkans, where the Ottoman Empire was slowly disintegrating. This Turkish empire had been

Autocracy in Romanov Russia

The czar of Russia held enormous power in Metternichian Europe. No monarch had contributed more to the defeat of Napoleon Bonaparte: Napoleon's Grand Armée had perished in Russia in 1812, and Russian

❖ DOCUMENT 25.5 ❖

The Greek Declaration of Independence, 1822

We, descendants of the wise and noble peoples of Hellas, we who are the contemporaries of the enlightened and civilized nations of Europe, we who behold the advantages which they enjoy under the protection of the impenetrable aegis of the law, find it no longer possible to suffer without cowardice and self-contempt the cruel yoke of the Ottoman power which has weighed upon us for more than four centuries—a power which does not listen to reason and knows no other law than its own will, which orders and disposes everything despotically and according to its caprice. After this prolonged slavery we have determined to take arms to avenge ourselves and our country against a frightful tyranny, iniquitous in its very essence—an unexampled despotism to which no other rule can be compared.

The war which we are carrying on against the Turk is not that of a faction or the result of sedition. It is not aimed at the advantage of any single part of the Greek people; it is national war.

troops had occupied Paris in 1814. A lingering Russian army in Poland had changed the diplomacy at the Congress of Vienna. The czar's support had sustained the congress system, and his defection during the Greek revolution had destroyed it.

Russian internal affairs were less simple. The enigmatic Alexander I had come to the throne in 1801 at the age of twenty-four, after the assassination of his father, in which Alexander may have been involved. He was a tall and handsome youth who favored skin-tight uniforms; he had become overweight by 1815, but his vanity and his robust sexuality (which ranged from his sister to religious mystics) put him in corsets instead of loose-fitting clothes. This same Alexander was considered the most intelligent monarch of the age by both Thomas Jefferson and Napoleon Bonaparte (excepting himself). Alexander held more absolute power than anyone else in Europe and with it came the opportunity to propel Russia into the modern age by timely reforms (such as the abolition of serfdom) or to become the champion of the Old Regime. Alexander considered both.

Many historians describe Alexander I as the hope of Russian liberalism. He received a liberal education from his tutor, and he began his reign closely associated with a liberal adviser, Michael Speranski. Speranski was the son of a priest; his brilliance at school earned him a government job and caught the interest of the czar. He was a good administrator, well organized and able to write clear prose, who mixed liberal sentiments with bureaucratic caution. Speranski swayed Alexander to consider reforms. Liberals praised many of Alexander's actions. He founded four new universities (doubling the total in the empire), at Kazan, Kharkov, Warsaw, and St. Petersburg. He gave the Poles a constitution and allowed them to reopen their parliament (the *Sejm*). This led to a constitution for Finland and to discussions about a Russian constitution with Speranski. Alexander also restrained the persecution of minority religions, proclaimed religious toleration, and signed a concordat with the Vatican regularizing the status of Roman Catholics. Most important, he began to reconsider serfdom and abolished it in his Baltic provinces between 1816 and 1819 while hinting that this was a pilot project for the emancipation of all Russian serfs.

Alexander I remained, however, an autocrat unchecked by a constitution, an independent judiciary, or a parliament. He was a monarch closer to eighteenth-century enlightened despotism than to nineteenth-century liberalism, presiding over the most feudal economy in the world. He held conquered peoples against their will, no matter how generously he treated them. In his later years, Alexander preferred reactionary advisers. He yielded to their contempt for Speranski and banished his friend to Siberia (although he later made him governor-general of that province). In his place, Alexander entrusted Russian domestic policy to a leading reactionary, Alexis Arakcheyev. Arakcheyev was a cruel and arrogant man unlikely to abolish serfdom; he once ordered a young serf flogged to death because she did a poor job at her sweeping. Alexander also capitulated to religious conservatives and abandoned the policy of toleration, which they considered "a sin against the Holy Ghost." Religious repression resumed in 1821.

Alexander's death in 1825 precipitated a crisis in Russia. He had no children who could inherit the throne, so it should have passed to his eldest brother, Constantine, the governor-general of Poland; but Constantine had renounced his right to the throne in 1822. This brought to the throne Alexander's youngest brother, Nicholas, whose training (by a sadistic military tutor) had been for military command, not for government. The accession of Nicholas I in December 1825 precipitated a rebellion led by liberal army officers. These Decembrists wanted to abolish the monarchy, write a constitution, and free the serfs, but their poorly organized revolt was quickly crushed. Nicholas found that many of the Decembrists were nobles who had been his friends (including two princes and a major general), but he responded harshly nonetheless. Five were hanged and 121 others were sentenced to hard labor in Siberia. The episode left the czar bitter and even less tolerant of liberalism.

Restrictive legislation was severely tightened under Nicholas I. He created a new branch of the government, the Third Section, to centralize the police. The head of the Third Section, General Alexander Benckendorff, employed the police techniques of Metternich and Sedlnitzky, laying the basis for a more ruthless secret police in the future. Nicholas gave Benckendorff strict new laws to enforce, such as a Censorship Law forbidding all publications not "useful or at least harmless." The law even banned works considered "full of grammatical errors." In addition to Benckendorff's Third Section, the autocracy of Nicholas I relied upon the Ministry of Education to control minorities; the educational system became an instrument for the "russification" of minorities and the submission of everyone to the authority of the church and the state. This policy was summarized in a famous slogan: "Autocracy! Orthodoxy! Nationality!"

Historians sometimes contrast the repressive regime of Nicholas I with the liberal flirtations of Alexander I. Nicholas ruled for thirty years and did little to advance the emancipation of the serfs beyond banning the sale of individual serfs in 1841. More than seven hundred peasant uprisings occurred during his reign, and Nicholas repressed them with the same anger that he had shown the Decembrists. His eagerness to use the Russian army earned him the nickname "the gendarme of Europe." But contrasts are never as simple as they seem. Just as Alexander had shown an attachment to autocracy by entrusting the government to Alexis Arakcheyev, Nicholas I showed at least a mild interest in reform by recalling Speranski from Siberia and allowing him to finish his codification of Russian law.

The Liberal-Monarchical Compromise in France

In contrast to autocratic Russia, France remained the most liberal state on the continent. The Bourbon Restoration of 1814–15 required a delicate compromise between Metternichian conservatism and deeply rooted French liberalism. Allied armies could put Louis XVIII on the throne, but the Bourbons could lose it again if Napoleon were correct when he jibed that they "had learned nothing and forgotten nothing" during the revolutionary era. The Bourbon compromise rested upon Louis's acceptance of a constitution and parliament. Louis insisted that his "constitutional charter" was a royal gift to the nation (not their natural right) and that the Bourbons still had a divine right to the throne; in return, the charter also included the liberal principles of equality before the law, freedom of religion, and freedom of the press (see document 25.6). This constitution created a Chamber of Deputies, elected by eighty-eight thousand well-to-do men (0.3 percent of the population of twenty-six million), of whom fifteen thousand (0.06 percent) were eligible to be candidates. This compromise contrasted with the French republic of 1792 with its universal manhood suffrage and was less representative than Britain where 2.5 percent of adult men voted in 1815. The most democratic states in Europe were Norway and Sweden, where 10 percent voted, yet France remained decidedly more liberal than Austria, Prussia, Russia, or Spain, where there were no parliaments.

Reactionary French nobles hated this compromise and favored a Metternichian government, or even Russian government. These ultraroyalists (or "ultras") were led by Louis XVIII's younger brother, the count of Artois. The ultras had returned to France from twenty years in exile, determined to revive the Old Regime. They relied upon Louis's having no surviving sons, so Artois would inherit the throne (see genealogy 25.1). This prompted Louis to remark presciently that the fate of the Bourbon Restoration depended upon his outliving his brother. The French compromise seemed vulnerable during the first year of the Bourbon Restoration. Revenge against the supporters of previous regimes saw prominent supporters of Napoleon executed, peerages revoked, officers court-martialed, and government employees fired. The worst outrage was a vigilante bloodbath, known as "the white terror," directed against republicans and Protestants. More than two hundred people were killed in the white terror in the south of France, where Protestants were concentrated. Louis XVIII, however, prevented the ultras from gaining control of the government and from returning to former owners the lands taken during the French Revolution. The successful peasant and middle-class proprietors who had purchased this "national property" received constitutional guarantees that their land was inviolable. Louis preserved his moderate compromise until 1820,

◆ DOCUMENT 25.6 ◆

A Compromise Constitution: The French Charter of 1814

Louis, by the grace of God, King of France. . . .

Divine Providence, in recalling us to our estates after a long absence, has laid upon us great obligations. . . . A constitutional charter was called for by the actual conditions of the kingdom; we promised it . . . although all authority in France resides in the person of the king. . . . We have recognized that the wish of our subjects for a constitutional charter was the expression of a real need. . . .

Public Law of the French

1. Frenchmen are equal before the law, whatever may be their titles. . . .

2. They contribute without distinction, in proportion to their fortunes, towards the expenses of the state.

3. They are all equally admissible to civil and military employments.

4. Their personal liberty is likewise guaranteed. . . .

5. Every one may profess his religion with equal freedom, and shall obtain for his worship the same protection.

6. Nevertheless, the Catholic, Apostolic, and Roman religion is the religion of the state. . . .

8. Frenchmen have the right to publish and to have printed their opinions, while conforming with the laws which are necessary to restrain abuses of that liberty.

9. All property is inviolable. . . .

Form of the Government of the King

13. The person of the King is inviolable and sacred. His ministers are responsible [to him]. To the King alone belongs the executive power.

14. The King is the supreme head of the state, commands the land and sea forces, declares war, makes treaties.

---

when the son of Artois (and the heir to the throne) was assassinated by a Bonapartist. The king—tired, obese, sixty-five, and suffering from a bad case of the gout—then capitulated to many of the ultras' demands. French

censorship became so strict that authors could be imprisoned if their books "cast disfavor" on the government; the police received the power to make arrests based solely upon suspicion; and the Sorbonne was placed under the control of a bishop and liberal professors were fired. The electorate for the Chamber of Deputies was sharply reduced, while the rich were given a second vote.

The breakdown of Louis XVIII's compromise worsened in 1824, when Artois came to the throne as King Charles X. Historians have characterized Charles as a blind reactionary, an image that contemporary cartoonists fostered by drawing the king with his crown covering his eyes. Charles earned this image when he named the leading ultra, Count Jean-Baptiste Villèle, premier. Villèle's government adopted a Law of Indemnity (1825) to repay aristocrats who had lost land during the revolution and a Law of Sacrilege, making irreligion a capital crime.

Such extreme conservatism ended middle-class, liberal acceptance of the compromise and precipitated a revolution in 1830 that drove Charles X from the throne. When Charles tried to keep ultras as his ministers without the support of the Chamber of Deputies, elections in May 1830 showed that even rich voters opposed him. Then Charles responded in July 1830 with strict decrees known as the July Ordinances, tightening censorship further, dissolving the chamber again, and reducing electoral eligibility once more (see illustration 25.9). The July Ordinances provoked a vehement reaction in the Parisian press. Adolphe Thiers, the editor of a liberal newspaper and a future president of France, drafted a protest stating, "The government has violated legality and we are absolved from obedience." The Chamber of Deputies agreed that the king had violated the constitution, but newspapermen and politicians did not overthrow the king. Their anger became a revolution when radical insurgents took to the streets of Paris. After a few incidents of rioting (such as breaking windows in government buildings), crowds built barricades across the streets in working-class districts. Charles X was not prepared to defend his ordinances at the cost of civil war. When he sent troops into Paris, several units joined the revolution. Charles, who had learned a lesson from the execution of his eldest brother, fled into exile.

The revolution of 1830 ended the rule of the Bourbon dynasty and removed the ultras from power, but France remained a monarchy. The liberal opponents of Charles X agreed upon his cousin, Louis-Philippe, the duke of Orleans, as a new king. Louis-Philippe pos-

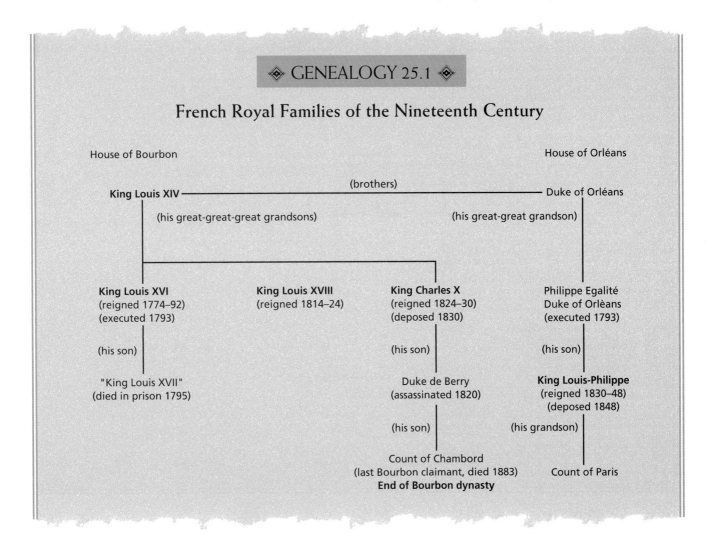

❖ GENEALOGY 25.1 ❖

French Royal Families of the Nineteenth Century

House of Bourbon

House of Orléans

(brothers)

King Louis XIV ————————————————— Duke of Orléans

(his great-great-great grandsons)

(his great-great grandson)

King Louis XVI
(reigned 1774–92)
(executed 1793)

King Louis XVIII
(reigned 1814–24)

King Charles X
(reigned 1824–30)
(deposed 1830)

Philippe Egalité
Duke of Orlèans
(executed 1793)

(his son)

(his son)

(his son)

"King Louis XVII"
(died in prison 1795)

Duke de Berry
(assassinated 1820)

King Louis-Philippe
(reigned 1830–48)
(deposed 1848)

(his son)

(his grandson)

Count of Chambord
(last Bourbon claimant, died 1883)
End of Bourbon dynasty

Count of Paris

Illustration 25.9

The Revolution of 1830. The revolution began in France with the royal proclamation of the severe "July Ordinances." In this contemporary illustration, copies of the ordinances have been posted in public (left) and crowds eagerly read them. Those who have already read them debate the situation angrily (center). Three days of demonstrations in the streets followed, and Charles X abdicated and fled into exile again.

◆ CHRONOLOGY 25.2 ◆

The Revolutions of 1830

Dates	Country	Events	Results
July 1830–August 1830	France	Paris rebels over "July Ordinances," 1830; King Charles X abdicates	Revised constitution, 1830; King Louis-Philippe, 1830
August 1830–December 1832	Belgium	Brussels rebels against Dutch rule, 1830; Belgian, 1830; declaration of independence, 1830; Belgian constitution, 1831	Dutch army shells Antwerp, French army expels Dutch army from Belgium, 1832; London Conferences recognize Belgium, 1830–32
September 1830–June 1832	German states Saxony, Hesse, Brunswick, and Hanover	Rulers dethroned, 1830; constitutions granted, 1831	Metternichian "Six Articles" restore old order, 1832
November 1830–February 1832	Poland	Revolt versus Russia, 1830; *Sejm* declares Polish independence, 1831	Russian army suppresses revolt, 1831; Polish constitution abolished, 1832
February 1831–January 1832	Italian states Modena, Parma, and papal states	Administrative concessions by pope	Austrian army suppresses revolt, 1831–33
1831	Switzerland	Demonstrations in Swiss cities, 1831	Ten cantons adopt liberal constitutions, 1831–33

sessed moderate liberal credentials. He had initially supported the French Revolution and served in its armies, then fled France during the Reign of Terror. His father had even served in the Convention and voted for the execution of Louis XVI. Louis-Philippe had courted the liberal opposition during the restoration and convinced many of them that he represented "the republic in a single individual."

The Orleanist Monarchy, also called the July Monarchy (1830–48), began with a liberalized constitution but few dramatic changes. Louis-Philippe did not have a revolutionary agenda. He expanded voting rights from 90,000 to 170,000 (0.5 percent of the nation). He relaxed censorship but still tried to control the press. He brought new social strata into the government, but that chiefly meant that an elite of wealth was joined to that of the aristocracy. Louis-Philippe did select many of his chief ministers, such as Thiers and the historian François Guizot from middle-class liberals, but they were cautious men who feared democracy. Guizot became the chief architect of the Orleanist version of the French compromise, and he achieved greater suc-

cess than Louis XVIII in creating a liberal constitutional monarchy comparable to the government in Britain.

The July Monarchy became so reknowned for supporting banking, business, and industrial interests that it was also called "the Bourgeois Monarchy." One of France's keenest political observers during the 1840s, Alexis de Tocqueville, saw this at once: "Posterity will perhaps never know to what degree the government of this time is a capitalist enterprise in which all action is taken for the purpose of profit." A major novelist of the era, Honoré de Balzac, was more acidic in *Cousin Bette* (1847), writing that the heart of French civilization was "the holy, venerable, solid, adored, gracious, beautiful, noble, ever young, almighty Franc."

Orleanist sympathies for business and industry had two important consequences. France experienced an important era of banking growth, railroad building, and industrial expansion after 1830, and the new regime deserves credit for its role in French industrialization and modernization. Simultaneously, however, the workers, shopkeepers, and students who had formed the crowds that drove Charles X into exile realized that the revolution of 1830 had made little difference in their existence. So France experienced further upheavals. The same working-class districts of Paris that had risen in July 1830 rebelled again in 1832, and Louis-Philippe used twenty-five thousand troops to suppress them. Two years later, he needed a tenth of his army to control a silk weavers' strike in Lyon. In 1835 an embittered radical built an "infernal machine" of twenty-five rifles in an iron rack and fired them with a single trigger. He killed eighteen people in a royal procession but only bruised the king. While France remained prosperous and economic development continued, such assaults remained isolated events of little consequence; in the mid-1840s, however, the French economy would suffer a severe depression, and the spectre of yet another French revolution would awaken.

The Revolutions of 1830

Metternich once observed that when Paris caught a cold, Europe sneezed. In 1830 that meant revolutions across Europe (see chronology 25.2 and map 25.3). The sneezing began in August 1830 (shortly after the fall of the Bourbon monarchy in France), with unrest in the Belgian provinces of the Kingdom of the Netherlands. The predominantly French-speaking, Catholic population of Belgium was larger than the Dutch-speaking, predominantly Calvinist population of Holland. The king was Dutch, the capital was Amsterdam, officeholders were chiefly Dutch, and national institutions predominantly Dutch. As a Belgian nationalist asked in the summer of 1830, "By what right do two million Dutchmen command four million Belgians?" The Belgian revolution of 1830 followed the French pattern: An insurrection of workers forced the issue, but the educated elite seized control of the situation. A national congress proclaimed Belgian independence in October 1830, but reluctant, middle-class Belgians supported the revolution only after the Dutch army bombarded Antwerp.

Though Louis-Philippe gave the Belgians military assistance, they won their independence at the negotiating table. The British sympathized with Belgian nationalism but feared French influence. When the Belgians accepted a German prince (who was an uncle of Queen Victoria) as their ruler instead of a French king, British support assured Belgian independence. Belgium adopted a liberal constitution, more advanced than either the British or French constitutions, in 1831.

It guaranteed freedom of the press and freedom of religion, then promised many other "inviolable" individual liberties (such as the right of association in unions), and it promoted secularization by establishing civil marriage. Such passages made the Belgian constitution a model emulated in eight countries.

Insurrection soon spread across Europe from France and Belgium, crossing the Rhine into the western German states. German antitax and food riots in 1830 revealed dissatisfaction with the Metternichian structure of Germany, but they produced no major revolution. A few smaller states, notably Saxony (1831), Brunswick (1832), and Hanover (1833), granted constitutions. Metternich considered granting a constitution in Austria, but the emperor Francis I insisted that he would tolerate "no innovation," so Metternich used the Germanic Confederation to stop the revolutions and to impose a new series of repressive laws, known as the Six Articles, to quiet protests.

The revolution of 1830 reached Poland a few weeks after crossing the Rhine. The Polish November Rising did not seek a constitution (which already existed), but an end to Russian rule. It began with a Polish army mutiny provoked when the czar prepared to send units to crush the French and Belgian revolutions. The *Sejm* declared Polish independence in January 1831. Nicholas decided that "the Poles must be made happy in spite of themselves" and sent a Russian army of 115,000 to teach them happiness. After the defeat of the Polish army at Ostrolenka and the fall of Warsaw, Poland was reunited with Russia . Nicholas I then exacerbated Polish nationalism with his retribution: Military tribunals convicted eighty thousand Poles of rebellion and the army marched them to Siberia in chains; a program of Russification ended all official use of the Polish language and closed the universities at Warsaw and Vilna; the Polish army, the Polish constitution, and the Polish Diet were all abolished.

Historians do not normally list Britain among the revolutions of 1830. Nonetheless, Britain experienced revolutionary activity in 1830–32. Rural violence, known as the Captain Swing Riots, began in Kent and covered southeastern Britain. Farm workers protested their poverty by burning hayricks and smashing the new threshing machines (the name *Captain Swing* came from the swinging flail used in hand threshing). More riots followed at Bristol, Nottingham, and Derby in 1831. The British may have avoided a revolution when Parliament conceded reforms that the liberal middle classes wanted, thus preventing the alliance of propertied classes with revolutionary workers that had

Illustration 25.10

 The House of Commons in the 1840s. Westminster Palace, the seat of the British Parliament, was a royal palace until the sixteenth century. The portion of it containing the House of Commons was destroyed by fire in 1834 and was replaced by a neo-Gothic structure, shown here. Note the distinctive physical arrangement of the seating, which divides Parliament into two parties who sit facing each other: Members of the cabinet are seated in the front row, on the left, with their supporters behind them; the opposition sits on the right. This structure was largely destroyed by a German fire bomb in 1941, but the distinct seating plan for Parliament survives.

toppled Charles X in France. Thomas Macaulay, an eloquent leader of British liberalism, warned Parliament that "great and terrible calamities" were imminent. The House of Commons, Macaulay insisted, must "reform that you may survive." Parliament (see illustration 25.10) did adopt a series of historic reforms, which perpetuated its image as a model of representative government—notably the Reform (of Parliament) Bill of 1832, the Factory Act of 1833 (regulating hours and conditions), and the Abolition of Slavery Act of 1834.

The revolutions of 1830 are important for additional reasons beyond the struggles for national independence or liberal constitutions. They showed the beginnings of important new social movements that would shape the nineteenth century. The best known of these is the rise of working class radicalism; the events of 1830 (especially in Paris) provided a preview of subsequent risings. Other movements, such as the early campaign for women's rights, also received a stimulus from the revolutions of 1830 (see document 25.7). In France, for example, the revolution led to the foundation of a feminist newspaper entitled *La Femme libre* (the Free Woman), which asked, "Shall we women remain passive spectators of this great moment for social emancipation that is taking place before our eyes?" The combination of the revolution of 1830 and the utopian socialism of men such as Charles Fourier (who promised women an equal role) encouraged the founding generation of French feminism in the 1830s and 1840s. This group included Jeanne Deroin, a self-educated teacher and journalist who later became the first French woman to run for office; Eugénie Niboyet, whose Protestant

zeal for moral reform led her to socialism and then to feminism; and Flora Tristan, whose Fourierism made her an advocate of equal rights for women.

The Advance of Liberalism in Britain

Historians usually cite Britain as the homeland of nineteenth-century liberalism and contrast it to the Metternichian reaction in central Europe. Truth exists in this contrast, but it should not obscure the strength of conservatism in post-1815 Britain. The landed aristocracy still dominated politics and society (see table 25.1). They composed less than 0.002 percent of the population but received more than 29 percent of the national income. Dukes, earls, and viscounts filled the cabinet. The House of Commons was elected by less than 3 percent of the population. If liberal reforms succeeded in that house, the House of Lords still held an aristocratic veto. The patronage system allowed this elite to perpetuate aristocratic domination of army and navy commands, the diplomatic corps, high government posts, and the leadership of the Church of England.

The Liverpool government (1812–27) pursued repressive policies. The record on minority nationalism also resembled that of Metternich and Nicholas I: The British treated the Irish much as the Austrians treated the Italians or the Russians treated Poles. The Act of Union of 1801 had absorbed Ireland completely into the United Kingdom, and the Protestant ascendancy of the eighteenth century had transferred landownership and political power in Ireland to the Protestant minor-

◆ DOCUMENT 25.7 ◆

Feminists Proclaim a Women's Revolution of 1830

An Appeal to Women

At the moment when all peoples are aroused in the name of Liberty and the proletariat calls for its own emancipation, shall we women remain passive spectators of this great moment for social emancipation that is taking place before our eyes?

Is our condition so happy that we ourselves have no demands to make? Until now woman has been exploited and tyrannized. This tyranny, this exploitation must cease. We are born free, like man, and half the human race cannot, without injustice, be in servitude to the other half. . . .

We demand equality in marriage. We prefer celibacy to slavery!

. . . Liberty, equality—that is to say, a free and equal chance to develop our faculties: this is the victory we must win, and we can succeed only if we unite in a single group. Let us no longer form two camps—that of the women of the people and that of privileged women. Let our common interests unite us.

◣ TABLE 25.1 ◣

The British Aristocracy in the Early Nineteenth Century

I. The Nobility
 A. Temporal lords: 326 families, with 8,000 members, ranked: 4 princes and princesses of royal blood
  19 dukes and duchesses
  18 marquesses and marchionesses
  103 earls and ladies
  22 viscounts and vicountesses
  160 barons and baronesses
 B. Spiritual lords: 26 archbishops and bishops
II. The Lesser Nobility
 A. Baronets: 540 families with hereditary titles "Sir" and "Lady"
 B. Knights: 350 families with nontransmittable titles "Sir" and "Lady"
 C. The gentry: 6,000 families of landowning "squires"
 D. Gentlemen: 20,000 families with inherited income and coats of arms

ity. The Catholic peasantry faced poverty and famine; suffering was so severe that some Irish nationalists have accused the British of genocide. Even British visitors to the Irish countryside were horrified by the suffering. Sir Walter Scott wrote of his 1825 visit: "Their poverty has not been exaggerated: it is on the extreme verge of human misery." Twenty years later, conditions were even worse, and during the potato famine of 1845–48, Ireland lost more than 25 percent of its population—experiencing more than 1 million deaths and losing 1.5 million refugees in a population of 8 million. Starving peasants ate their domestic pets.

Ireland needed a great defender, but the first parliamentary champion of Ireland could not take his seat in the House of Commons because British law excluded Catholics from office. Daniel O'Connell was a Jesuit-educated member of the Catholic gentry. He demanded the repeal of the Act of Union and the treatment of Ireland "not as a subordinate province, but . . . as a separate and distinct country." Lawful repeal was hardly likely. O'Connell could attract 100,000 peo-

ple to a rally, but the House of Commons stood against him by 529–34. His experiences in the French Revolution, however, had convinced O'Connell of the horror and futility of revolution, and he continued to work for a parliamentary victory and reject violence (see document 25.8).

Early nineteenth-century Britain was not yet a model of liberal democracy. The poor of London still cheered at the funeral processions of conservative leaders. And radicals, such as Percy Bysshe Shelley, denounced "leech-like" politicians who sucked the lifeblood of working people. Unlike Metternich and Nicholas I, however, Parliament accepted some important reforms between 1832 and 1846. Members did not democratize Britain, displace the governing elite, or encompass the radical agenda, but they made Britain the liberal leader of Europe. The reform of Parliament in 1832 illustrates the nature of British liberal reform (see map 25.4). It had been discussed since the 1780s, but little had been achieved except outlawing the sale of seats in the House of Commons (1809). The Reform Bill of 1832, won by the moderate liberals in a Whig government, enfranchised the new business and industrial elite, expanding the electorate from 2.1 percent of the population to 3.5 percent. The bill abolished "rotten boroughs" such as Old Sarum, the ruins of a medieval town that had no residents but still sent two members to Parliament. This eliminated fifty-six

❖ DOCUMENT 25.8 ❖

British Campaigns for the Rights of Minorities

Daniel O'Connell Demands Catholic Emancipation, 1824

In the experimental despotism which England fastened on Ireland, her mighty appetite for slavery was not gorged; and because our unfortunate country was proximate, and polite in the endurance of the burden so mercilessly imposed, it was inferred that slavery could be safely extended far and wide, and an attempt was therefore made on the American colonies. . . . [T]he Americans—the God of heaven bless them for it!—shook off the thralldom. . . . The independence of America was the first blush of dawn to the Catholic, after a long and dreary night of degradation. . . .

In Ireland, we have been blamed for being agitators. I thank God for being one. Whatever little we have gained, we have gained by agitation, while we have uniformly lost by moderation. That last word is repeated so often that I am completely sick of it. I wonder some gentlemen do not teach a parrot to repeat it.

Baron Macaulay Pleas for Jewish Emancipation, 1833

When the question was about Catholic emancipation, the cry was "See how restless, how . . . encroaching, how insinuating is the spirit of the Church of Rome. See how

her priests compass earth and sea to make one proselyte, how indefatigably they toil. . . . [W]ill you give power to the members of a church so busy, so aggressive, so insatiable?"

Well, now the question is about people who never try to seduce any stranger to join them, and who do not wish anybody to be of their faith who is not also of their blood. And now you exclaim, "Will you give power to the members of a sect which remains sullenly apart from other sects. . . ."

The honourable member [of parliament] for Oldham tells us that the Jews are naturally a mean race, a sordid race, a money-getting race; that they are averse to all honourable callings; that they neither sow nor reap; that . . . usury is the only pursuit for which they are fit; that they are destitute of all elevated and amiable sentiments. Such, Sir, has in every age been the reasoning of bigots. They never fail to plead in justification of persecution the vices which persecution has engendered. . . . We treat them as slaves. . . . We drive them to mean occupations . . . . We long forbade them to possess land. . . . We shut them out from all paths of ambition. . . . During long ages we have, in all our dealings with them, abused our immense superiority of force.

---

constituencies whose 111 seats were transferred to manufacturing towns such as Birmingham and Manchester, neither of which had representation in Parliament before 1832.

Liberal industrial reforms were modest in their range, but they pioneered European regulatory legislation. A Factory Act of 1833 established a maximum working day in textile mills for young children (nine hours) and for teenagers (twelve hours, or seventy-two hours per week) and planned for inspectors to enforce these terms. The Factory Act of 1844 extended the regulatory principle to women working in the textile mills, limiting their daily work to twelve hours and their Saturday work to nine hours (a sixty-nine-hour week) and added the requirement of protective screening around machinery. Further regulatory legislation followed: a Mines Act (1842) prohibited underground work for boys under age ten and for all women; the Ten Hours Act (1847) lowered the workday for women and teenaged boys to ten hours (a fifty-nine-hour week) without provisions for enforcement. These laws have

been controversial. Laissez-faire liberals opposed them, arguing that the state had no right to interfere with private business, while feminists have questioned the different treatment of men and women as paternalistic.

Another controversial form of liberal legislation involved the emancipation of the religious minorities— everyone who was not a member of the established Church of England. In 1815 only Anglicans could be elected to Parliament, command in the army, or enroll at Oxford; this intentional discrimination was created by a series of laws called the Test Acts. Unlike the French, who had promised religious freedom in the Constitutional Charter of 1814, or the Belgians, who provided a model of toleration in their Constitution of 1831, the British relaxed religious discrimination so slowly that it survived into the late nineteenth century. Parliament granted nonconforming Protestants ("dissenters," such as Methodists and Presbyterians) equal opportunity in 1828. In the same year, County Clare (Ireland) forced a larger reconsideration by electing O'Connell to Parliament, although Catholics were still

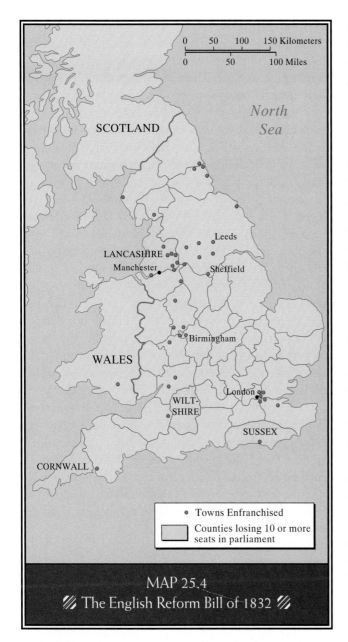

MAP 25.4

The English Reform Bill of 1832

On the map:

SCOTLAND

North Sea

Leeds

LANCASHIRE

Manchester

Sheffield

Birmingham

WALES

WILT-SHIRE

London

SUSSEX

CORNWALL

0   50   100   150 Kilometers

0   50   100 Miles

• Towns Enfranchised

Counties losing 10 or more seats in parliament

---

refused to seat him. The debate on Jewish rights showed how far Britain remained from the liberal ideal: A majority still believed in such anti-Semitic clichés as Jewish collective responsibility for the crucifixion.

Another reform debate introduced Parliament to an issue that would demand attention for more than a century—women's rights. Although Queen Victoria sat on the throne, the women of her nation had no legal identity apart from their husbands or fathers. The law treated them as minor children and in some cases lumped them together with criminals and the insane. Husbands owned and controlled their property. Husbands exercised legal control of children. A father sentenced to prison could specify that his children be raised by his mistress instead of the children's legal mother. Cultural attitudes sustained this treatment, and most women accepted it. In a best-selling book of 1842, for example, a woman tried to teach young women "to be content to be inferior to men" (see document 25.9). Queen Victoria gave scant help to the campaigns to change such attitudes and laws. She once wrote: "The Queen is most anxious to enlist everyone who can speak or write to join in checking this mad, wicked folly of 'Women's Rights' . . . *with all its attendant horrors.* . . . [I]t is a subject which makes the Queen so *furious* that she cannot contain herself." Ironically, the force of her example as a strong woman simultaneously served to advance the cause of emancipation, which she opposed.

The first changes in the legal restrictions on women resulted from the work of an outraged individual instead of a women's movement. Caroline Norton, the wife of an M.P., had an intimate friendship with a Whig prime minister, Lord Melbourne. This so enraged her husband (a confessed adulterer) that he sued the prime minister for alienation of his wife's affections. Caroline Norton then discovered she would not be allowed any role or representation in the trial because the law considered her interests to be represented by her husband. The suit failed, and the Nortons separated (she could not even divorce her husband), with the law awarding custody of their children to the father. Caroline Norton thereupon launched a pamphlet campaign that led to the Infant Custody Act of 1839, giving mothers limited rights over their infant children to age seven. Her role in the evolution of women's rights did not stop with that victory. She came from a talented family (her grandfather was the dramatist Richard Sheridan), and she supported herself comfortably by writing. In the 1850s her husband, now badly debt-ridden, legally seized all of her royalties as his property, and Caroline Norton became a central figure in the campaign to obtain a Married Woman's Property Act.

---

excluded. Many conservatives considered Catholic emancipation to be a "suicidal measure" and fought bitterly against it, but after a conservative hero, the duke of Wellington, accepted the idea, the Tories made it law in 1829. The repeal of the Test Acts and the Catholic Emancipation Act did not end religious discrimination in British laws. The new oath of office still required M.P.s to swear "on the true faith of a Christian." This excluded Quakers (who would not swear), plus Jews and Atheists (who were not Christians). Parliament debated Jewish emancipation, but four separate bills failed between 1830 and 1836. Even when a London constituency elected a Jewish M.P in 1847 (Lionel Rothschild, of the famous banking family), Parliament

◆ DOCUMENT 25.9 ◆

A Conservative Woman's View of the Role of Women, 1842

Sarah Ellis was the devout wife of an English missionary to Polynesia who later served as secretary of the London Missionary Society. She wrote extensively on women and founded a school for girls to apply the principles in her books and teach them to the lower classes. The following excerpt is taken from her book entitled The Daughters of England, *published in London in 1842.*

As women, then, the first thing of importance is to be content to be inferior to men—inferior in mental power, in the same proportion that you are inferior in bodily strength. . . .

For a man it is absolutely necessary that he should sacrifice the poetry of his nature for the realities of material and animal existence; for women there is no excuse—for women, whose whole life from the cradle to the grave is one of feeling rather than action; whose highest duty is so often to suffer and be still; whose deepest enjoyments are all relative; who has nothing, and is nothing, of herself. . . . For woman, who, in her inexhaustible sympathies can live only in the existence of another, and whose very smiles and tears are not exclusively her own. . . .

Our moral worth or dignity depends upon the exercise of good taste. . . . It is strictly in subservience to religion that I would speak of good taste as being of extreme importance to women. . . .

Love is woman's all—her wealth, her power, her very being. Man, let him love as he may, has ever an existence distinct from that of his affections. He has his wordly interests, his public character, his ambition, his competition with other men—but woman centers all that in one feelings. . . . In woman's love is mingled the trusting dependence of a child, for she ever looks up to a man as her protector, and her guide . . . would she not suffer to preserve him from harm?

Other issues received more attention than women's rights, both from contemporaries and subsequent historians. The chief interest of middle-class liberals was the repeal of the Corn Laws, the high tariffs on imported grain that kept the price of bread high, the landowning-class prosperous, and workers hungry. Repeal, however, would produce cheaper bread, healthier workers (who still relied on starches for 50 percent of their total calories), and business profits (because workers need not be paid so much if bread were not dear). To win repeal, British liberals (led by Manchester business interests) founded the Anti-Corn Law League, which became the international model of a political lobbying group. At the same time, a parallel campaign of working-class radicals known as the Chartist movement (named for the National Charter of 1838) outlined a democratic program: universal manhood suffrage, the secret ballot, the abolition of property qualifications to serve in Parliament, the payment of salaries to M.P.s (so the poor could serve), the creation of equal-sized constituencies, and annual elections (see illustration 25.11).

The fate of these two campaigns shows the cautious approach of European liberals. The leaders of the repeal campaign, John Bright (the M.P. son of a cotton-mill owner) and Richard Cobden (a wealthy Manchester textile factory owner), succeeded by courting conservatives. They convinced moderate Tories, led by Sir Robert Peel (now dubbed Re-Peel), to adopt free trade as economic orthodoxy. The same coalition, however, would not accept Chartism. The Chartists included radicals such as Feargus O'Connor, a newspaper editor whose willingness to consider violence frightened both the conservative government and the liberals who claimed to be his allies. Although Chartism summarized most elements of modern democracy, it did not come close to adoption.

◆

International Liberalism and Slavery

Nothing better illustrates the strength of conservative regimes and the weakness of liberal reformers in Metternichian Europe than the persistence of serfdom in eastern Europe and slavery in European colonies. In 1700 virtually every state in Europe had practiced one of these forms of enslavement in some part of its territory. Britain had no serfs at home but had built slave economies in America. France had both serfdom at home and slavery in its colonies. Most of Russia, Prussia, and Austria lived in serfdom, and serfs were even in Denmark and Switzerland. During the Enlightenment, three important states abolished serfdom: Savoy, Baden, and Denmark. The abolition of serfdom during the French Revolution led to the spread of this idea to Switzerland, Poland, Prussia, and Bavaria. The French abolition of colonial slavery did not, however, persuade other slave states to follow, though Denmark and

Illustration 25.11

 Chartism. This print of a Chartist rally in the 1840s is based on one of the earliest political photographs using Louis Daguerre's technique of 1839. It shows the "radicals" at a Chartist rally. Note that the vast crowd of Chartists is not quite a "mob" of "rabble": The men are well dressed, including top hats.

Britain both ended their slave trades, and the United States stopped the importation of new African slaves (see Chronology 25.3).

Abolitionists thus faced a great task in 1815. They won a few victories between 1815 and 1848, but millions of people in Western civilization remained in slavery or serfdom throughout the age of Metternich. Alexander I abolished serfdom in his Baltic provinces, and the revolutions of 1830 ended serfdom in several German states. At the beginning of 1848, however, feudal obligations still restricted peasants in the Austrian and the Hungarian portions of the Hapsburg Empire, in a dozen German states (including Saxe-Coburg-Gotha, the homeland of Queen Victoria's consort), in the Danubian provinces, and in Russia. The campaign against colonial slavery also made some progress yet left millions of people in bondage. The Congress of Vienna adopted a proclamation ending the slave trade in principle, but the same treaties accepted the existence of colonial slavery and returned lost colonies to Denmark, France, the Netherlands, and Spain knowing that these were to be slave economies. Europe then ignored the agreement ending the slave trade. The growing love of sweet foods demanded great quantities of cane sugar from Caribbean plantations, where sugar often accounted for 90 percent of the exports. Few people paused with the poet William Cowper, who wrote, "Think how many backs have smarted/For the sweets your cane affords." Thus, Bourbon France shipped more than 125,000 new slaves to the Caribbean between

1814 and 1831, and other slave states behaved similarly. In 1828 alone, 100,000 more African slaves were shipped to the Americas, despite the closing of the market in British colonies and the United States.

The Spanish revolution of 1820 led to a victory for abolitionism when the Spanish colonies won independence. The revolutionaries did not plan to end slavery at first, but Simon Bolivar realized that liberating slaves would increase his chances of victory. Bolivar adopted military manumission (freeing the slaves in areas conquered) in his campaigns after 1815, and his speech to the revolutionary congress of 1821 led to a Manumission Law. Bolivar thus doubly earned the nickname "El Libertador" (the liberator), by freeing a region from Spain and a class from slavery, but slavery persisted in those Spanish territories that did not win independence. Coffee and sugar plantations in Cuba required more than 200,000 slaves and those in Puerto Rico, 17,500.

Abolitionists won another important victory in British colonies. The British antislavery movement, led by Quakers and other Dissenters, had been gaining strength since the late eighteenth century. They found an effective leader in William Wilberforce, an M.P. and the head of an Anglican evangelical sect. Wilberforce founded the Antislavery Society with the aim of abolishing all slavery, and his movement flooded Parliament with petitions. In its first year, the Antislavery Society opened 220 local chapters and submitted 825 petitions, with hundreds of thousands of signatures.

◆ CHRONOLOGY 25.3 ◆

The Abolition of European Serfdom and Slavery

Abolition of slavery	Abolition of serfdom
1794 French colonies	1771 Savoy (Piedmont)
1821 Ex-Spanish colonies	1783 Baden
1829 Mexican republic	1788 Denmark
1834 British colonies	1789 France
1848 French colonies	1798 Switzerland
1863 Dutch colonies	1804 Schleswig-Holstein
1862–65 United States	1807 Grand duchy of Warsaw (Poland)
1870–85 (Spanish) Cuba	1807 Prussia
1878 Portugese colonies	1808 Bavaria
1888 Brazil	1816 Estonia (Russia)
	1817 Courland (Russia)
	1817 Württemberg
	1819 Livonia (Russia)
	1820 Hesse (grand duchy)
	1831 Hanover
	1831 Hesse (Electoral)
	1832 Saxony
	1832 Brunswick
	1848 Saxe-Weimar
	1848 Austria
	1849 Saxe-Coburg-Gotha
	1853 Hungary
	1861 Russia
	1864 Danubian Provinces (Rumania)

Abolitionism gained strength during the turbulent years of 1830–32, when many members of Parliament feared a revolution in Britain. At that moment, the British Caribbean experienced another slave rebellion (the third since 1815). On Christmas Day 1831, more than 20,000 Jamaican slaves revolted. The British army quelled the revolt, but 14 whites and 200 slaves were killed, while 312 more slaves were executed later. The message from Jamaica, alongside the news from Paris, Brussels, and the Kentish countryside, persuaded the Whig government to abolish slavery in the British colonies.

Conclusion

The history of the post-Napoleonic era in Europe (1815–48) can be told from two contrasting perspectives: (1) by focusing on Prince Metternich and the conservative governments of the era, who sought to preserve and protect the Old Regime society of monarchy, aristocracy, and established religion; or (2) by focusing on the reformers and revolutionaries who challenged that order and sought to change or overthrow it. It can be described as an age of general European peace (in contrast to the preceding eras), to the credit of the conservative governments, or an age of widespread domestic conflict (expressed in repressive laws and frequent rebellions), to their shame.

Expressions such as "Metternichian Europe" or "the Age of Metternich" suggest that historians have traditionally looked more at the established order. Chapter 25 has discussed both sides of this history—the conservative order created at Vienna, the Metternichian system of congresses, conservative instruments such as the Troppau Proctocol, the role of religion and the law in keeping the order, and illustrations of how this system worked in many countries; and the strong new doctrines of change known as the "-isms," the revolutions of the 1820s and especially the revolution of 1830, the successes of liberal reformers in many countries but especially in Britain and France, and a great international challenge to the old order over the issue of slavery. Instead of stressing the role of Prince Metternich, the dominant characteristic of the age was the clash between those who challenged the old order and those who defended it. The outcome of that struggle is clear today, but it remained a dramatic contest in 1848.

Suggested Readings

A valuable reference book for this period is C. Cook and J. Paxton, eds., *European Political Facts, 1789–1848* (1981), which includes military, religious, demographic, and economic information in addition to the political.

For general works on this period, the most recent surveys are R. Gildea, *Barricades and Borders* (1987), which covers the period 1800–1914; F. Ford, *Europe, 1780–1830* (1989); E. J. Hobsbawm, *The Age of Revolution* (1978); and T. Hamerow, *The Birth of a New Europe* (1983), which covers the entire nineteenth century. Valuable older studies include F. Artz, *Reaction and Revolution, 1814–1832* (1968) and W. Langer, *Political and Social Upheaval, 1832–1852* (1969), from the "Rise of Modern Europe" series.

For surveys of early nineteenth-century European diplomacy, see F. R. Bridge and R. Bullen, *The Great Powers and the European States System, 1815–1914* (1980) and N. Rich, *Great Power Diplomacy, 1814–1914* (1992); for diplomacy during the age of Metternich, see A. Sked, ed., *Europe's Balance of Power, 1815–1848* (1979); H. Kissinger, *A World Restored* (1973); P. Schroeder, *Metternich's Diplomacy at its Zenith* (1967); D. Dakin, *The Greek Struggle for Independence* (1973); and for military history, G. Best, *War and Society in Revolutionary Europe, 1770–1870* (1982).

For the "-isms," see H. Rogger and E. Weber, eds., *The European Right* (1965), for varieties of conservatism and other right-wing doctrines; G. Ruggiero, *The History of European Liberalism* (1959); L. Krieger, *The German Idea of Freedom* (1972); J. Sheehan, *German Liberalism in the Nineteenth Century* (1978); E. Halevy, *The Growth of Philosophic Radicalism* (1972), on utilitarian liberalism; S. Holmes, *Benjamin Constant and the Making of Modern Liberalism* (1984); R. Boesche, *The Strange Liberalism of Alexis de Tocqueville* (1987); G. D. H. Cole, *A History of Socialist Thought*, 5 vols. (1953–67), a classic, detailed survey; L. Kolakowski, *Main Currents of Marxism*, 3 vols. (1981), a comprehensive study; R. Hunt,

The Political Ideas of Marx and Engels, 2 vols. (1974–84); G. Lichtheim, *The Origins of Socialism* (1969), on pre-Marxians, and his *Marxism* (1964); J. Joll, *The Anarchists* (1979); G. Woodcock, *Anarchism* (1986); C. J. H. Hayes, *The Historical Evolution of Nationalism* (1931), still a valuable survey; H. Kohn, *Prophets and Peoples: Studies in Nineteenth-Century Nationalism* (1946); E. Kedourie, *Nationalism* (1985); E. Gellner, *Nations and Nationalism* (1983); and J. Barzun, *Classic, Romantic, and Modern* (1961), valuable for romanticism. For the emerging feminism of the early nineteenth-century, see J. Rendall, *The Origins of Modern Feminism* (1985); C. Moses and L. Rabine, *Feminism, Socialism, and French Romanticism* (1993); and the exceptionally valuable documents collected in E. Hellerstein and others, *Victorian Women* (1981) and in S. Bell and K. Offen, *Women, the Family, and Freedom*, 2 vols. (1983).

For the early nineteenth-century revolutions, see G. Romani, *The Neapolitan Revolution of 1820–1821* (1978), T. Anna, *Spain and the Loss of America* (1983), C. Church, *Europe in 1830* (1983), P. Pilbeam, *The 1830 Revolution in France* (1991), J. Merriman, *1830 in France* (1975), D. Pinkney, *The French Revolution of 1830* (1972), J. Betley, *Belgium and Poland in International Relations, 1830–1831* (1960), and E. Hales, *Revolution and Papacy, 1769–1846* (1966).

For the Austrian Empire in the age of Metternich, see the general overviews of A. J. P. Taylor, *The Hapsburg Monarchy, 1809–1918* (1976) and B. Jelavich, *Modern Austria* (1987). For specialized studies, see A. Palmer, *Metternich* (1972), and D. Emerson, *Metternich and the Political Police* (1968).

For Prussia and other German states, see J. Sheehan, *German History, 1770–1866* (1989), T. Hamerow, *Restoration, Revolution, and Reactions: Economics and Politics in Germany, 1815–1871* (1966), G. Craig, *The Politics of the Prussian Army, 1640–1945* (1964), and H. Schulze, *The Course of German Nationalism* (1991).

For Russia, see A. Palmer, *Alexander I* (1974); M. Raeff, *Michael Speransky, Statesman of Imperial Russia* (1979); W. B. Lincoln, *Nicholas I* (1989); N. Riasanovsky, *Nicholas I and Official Nationality in Russia* (1969); and D. Orlovsky, *The Limits of Reform* (1981), on the Ministry of Internal Affairs as the center of autocratic government.

For general studies about Britain, see E. Halévy's still impressive masterwork, *A History of the English People in the Nineteenth Century* (1961), in which the first four volumes cover the years 1815–52; and compare N. McCord, *British History, 1815–1906* (1991), for an up-to-date synthesis. For topics, see F. O'Gorman, *Voters, Patrons, and Parties: The Unreformed Electorate of Hanoverian England, 1734–1832* (1989), for the period before the reform bill; M. Brock, *The Great Reform Act* (1973), on the Reform Bill of 1832; the works of N. Gash, especially *Politics in the Age of Peel* (1977), for the period after the reform bill; compare with P. Mandler, *Aristocratic Government in the Age of Reform* (1990) and N. McCord, *The Anti-Corn Law League* (1968).

For France, see G. de Bertier de Sauvigny, *The Bourbon Restoration* (1966) and H. A. C. Collingham, *The July Monarchy* (1988), for surveys of the period 1815–48. For studies of the era, see A. Spitzer, *Old Hatreds and Young Hopes* (1971), on the revolutionary movement; V. Beach, *Charles X of France* (1971); R. Bezucha, *The Lyon Uprising of 1834* (1974); D. Johnson, *Guizot* (1975) and D. Pinkney, *Decisive Years in France, 1840–1847* (1986).

EUROPE IN AN AGE OF NATIONALISM, 1848–70

CHAPTER OUTLINE

◆◆◆◆◆◆◆◆◆◆◆◆◆◆◆◆◆◆◆◆◆◆

Chapter 26 looks at the turbulent epoch following the years of Metternichian-enforced stability. It begins with the revolutions of 1848, revolutions that convulsed two dozen countries, ended the Orleanist monarchy in France, and brought down the government of Metternich in Austria. The revolutions of 1848 achieved important reforms but did not fulfill the dreams of nationalist and republican revolutionaries. The Old Regime—and conservatism—survived. Europe in 1870 was still governed by monarchs, while aristocrats continued to dominate society though they increasingly shared power with the wealthy industrial bourgeoisie. Radical efforts to secure the rights of women and workers had achieved little, but gradual liberalization was under way in Victorian Britain and Alexander II made a dramatic attempt to modernize Russia by abolishing serfdom.

Greater change came on the battlefield. Europe experienced five wars between 1854 and 1870: the Crimean War, the War of Italian Unification, and three wars for the unification of Germany that ended in a decisive struggle between France and Prussia. This chapter describes how the modern states of Germany and Italy emerged from these conflicts, and it analyzes the internal developments that made unification possible.

◆

The Origins of the Revolutions of 1848

The event that conservatives had feared for a generation (and which Marxists predicted for the next century)—widespread revolutions—swept Europe in 1848 (see chronology 26.1). Governments fell in France, the Italian states, the German states, and the Austrian Empire; revolutionary turmoil lasted for two years. Liberals and nationalists initially won great victories. Constitutions, bills of rights, even republics sprang up. Enthusiasm for national autonomy, independence, or unification was so universal that the revolutionary period became known as "the springtime of peoples." The alliance of nationalism

❖ CHRONOLOGY 26.1 ❖

The Revolutions of 1848

Dates	Country	Revolutionary events	Outcome
January 1848–May 1848	Naples	Revolt in Sicily, short-lived constitution and independence	Revolt crushed
February 1848–June 1849	France	Revolt in Paris, abdication of king and formation of republic	Second Republic overthrown by President Louis-Napoleon
March 1848–August 1849	Piedmont-Sardinia	Constitution granted and war declared on Austria	Austrian victories force king to abdicate; constitution endures
March 1848–August 1849	Austria	Emperor abdicates and Metternich flees, constitutions in Austria and Hungary, nationalist uprisings	Austrian and Russian armies suppress all revolutions
March 1848–July 1849	Vatican states	Pope Pius IX grants constitution, but Mazzini proclaims republic	French troops crush the republic and restore the pope
March 1848–August 1849	Venice	Demonstrations drive out Austrian army, republic proclaimed	Republic capitulates to Austrian army
March 1848–December 1848	Prussia	Revolution in Berlin, king grants constitution	King dismisses assembly, keeps constitution
March 1848	Lombardy	Revolution in Milan forces Austrian evacuation	Austrian reconquest
March 1848–June 1849	Germany	National assembly in Frankfurt abolishes confederation and debates German unity	Assembly fails to create unity, dismissed by army

and liberalism drove monarchs to abdicate and sent their ministers into exile. The king of France and Guizot and the emperor of Austria and Metternich were all driven from the stage of international politics. By 1850, however, the revolutions of 1848 had collapsed in the face of military repression. Some constitutions survived, as did a few revolutionary accomplishments such as the end of serfdom in the Hapsburg Empire, but counterrevolutionary governments dominated the 1850s.

Historians have explained the revolutions of 1848 in many ways. Liberals have stressed the repressive nature of government in the Metternichian era. More conservative historians have blamed the discontent of the intelligentsia, calling 1848 a "revolt of the intellectuals." Others have noted the willingness of the newly influential middle classes (such as bankers, manufacturers, merchants, and professionals) to accept revolutionary change because they had few attachments to the aristocratic regime. Marxists have pointed to the importance of the growing urban laboring class living in poverty, while social historians have examined urbanization (many cities doubled in size between 1800 and

1848) and found an array of problems in housing, public health, and crime.

One of the more convincing explanations of the origins of the revolutions has come from economic historians. In the late 1840s Europe simultaneously experienced the last great subsistence crisis as a result of agricultural failure and the first severe depression of the industrial age. Crop failures meant expensive bread (which had also preceeded the French Revolution); the downturn in the business cycle meant high unemployment (see illustration 26.1).

The agricultural crisis began with the potato famine of 1845. Ireland suffered horribly from this catastrophe, and all regions that depended upon the potato as a staple of the diet (such as the German states) had problems. Grain famines followed in 1846 and 1847, causing hardship for many people and mortal danger for some. In the Alsatian industrial center of Mulhouse, for example, the price of bread increased 67 percent during this crisis; in some German states, the price of staple foods rose between 250 percent and 450 percent. The depression of the 1840s multiplied the

The Depression of the 1840s. Europe suffered one of the worst depressions of the industrial age during the mid- and late 1840s. Unemployment reached frightening levels in many occupations, and crops failed in several regions. This combination produced some of the last widespread food riots in European history. This German illustration depicts bread riots in Berlin in the spring of 1847; families sack a local bakery. Note the prominent role of women.

suffering and political agitation that grows when food does not. The member states of the Zollverein experienced a mild depression in textiles, but a collapse in business and banking. Between August 1847 and January 1848, 245 firms and 12 banks failed in Prussia alone. France experienced a fearful collapse of the textile industry; consumption of cotton fell by 30 percent, reducing output to the lowest level in the industrial era. The human meaning of such numbers was reduced incomes or unemployment while the price of food was skyrocketing. In Silesia, one of the hardest hit regions in Prussia, an estimated 75 percent of the population sought poor relief. In Paris, unemployment exceeded 40 percent in most trades and ranged between 50 percent and 75 percent in the worst cases. An angry Parisian radical summarized the situation: "While half of the population of Paris dies of starvation, the other half eats for two."

The revolutions of 1848 began in the homeland of revolution—France. The constitutional monarchy of Louis-Philippe had evolved into an alliance of moderate conservatives and moderate liberals that the premier, François Guizot, considered "the golden mean." Guizot's perfect balance allowed 0.7 percent of the population to vote in 1845 while preserving the status quo for the propertied classes of landlords and capitalists. By the late 1840s, the July monarchy had spawned a vocal opposition despite Guizot's restrictions on the press and political meetings. During the winter of 1847–48, those opponents tried a truly French form of protest: the banquet. Respectable middle-class critics of the regime organized large dinners and added inflam-

matory political oration to the menu. The campaign culminated in a great banquet scheduled for Paris in late February 1848, but the Guizot government prohibited that assembly. Critics of the regime met nonetheless, to march to their locked banquet hall. Workers and students swelled the parade, and by nightfall barricades were again appearing on the streets of Paris (see illustration 26.2). Louis-Philippe dismissed Guizot, and when that did not placate the demonstrators, he fled the country. Republicans, led by a radical deputy named Alexandre Ledru-Rollin, seized the Hôtel de Ville (the town hall), proclaimed the Second Republic, and named a provisional government.

The French revolution of 1848 did not immediately fall into the hands of moderates as had the revolution of 1830. Republicans kept control but were soon divided between those who favored Ledru-Rollin's democratic program (universal manhood suffrage, parliamentary government, a cabinet responsible to a majority) and social radicals who demanded help for workers and the poor. Ledru-Rollin had more support, so the provisional government concentrated on political change: It abolished "all forms of monarchy," all titles of nobility, and laws restricting political activity. In contrast, it attempted only one idea for what radicals called "the social republic," Louis Blanc's National Workshops. The workshops were a relief plan for the unemployed. (The government's first assignment for relief workers was to remove the barricades.) Democratic elections in April 1848 gave moderate republicans a large majority; shortly thereafter, it curtailed support for workers.

Illustration 26.2

Barricades in Paris. One of the characteristic features of revolutions in modern France has been the construction of barricades closing streets—mounds constructed from nearby vehicles, trees, furniture from surrounding buildings, and paving stones from the streets. Barricades such as the one shown here gave revolutionaries a strong position to confront government troops, and the neighboring buildings could hide snipers or provide objects to drop on soldiers.

The immediate consequence was an insurrection in June 1848. Workers, fearful that the counterrevolution had begun and remembering how monarchists had stolen the revolution of 1830, called for popular action. The republican government answered the demonstrations of "the June days" by giving General Louis Cavaignac dictatorial powers. Cavaignac unleashed the army on Paris and reduced unemployment with killings, arrests, and deportations. Others saw his accomplishment as ending a workers' uprising and preserving the republic. The assembly adopted a radical constitution in November 1848 and achieved a few legislative triumphs, such as the abolition of slavery in French colonies. But it had permanently alienated one of its strongest constituencies, the working class. The Second Republic managed to elect one president, but it never elected another.

The Spread of Revolution in 1848: "The Springtime of Peoples"

The February revolution in Paris encouraged March revolutions in many places (see map 26.1). It first stimulated demonstrations in the towns of the Rhineland, such as Heidelberg, where public meetings produced demands for a constitution and basic liberties. German radicals raised posters announcing that "[o]ur brothers in France have bravely led the way" and calling on Germans to follow. In many of the smaller German states, rulers quickly capitulated. Monarchs named liberal governments in Baden, Württemberg, and Saxony. The king of Bavaria abdicated. Revolution spread throughout the German Confederation in March 1848, changing central Europe so much that Germans thereafter described the "pre-March" (*Vormärz*) era as an antediluvian past.

The German revolutions of 1848 centered on three cities: Berlin, Vienna, and Frankfurt (see document 26.1). In Berlin, liberal demonstrations led to the building of barricades. King Frederick William IV sent the army into the streets and their brutality made the liberal cause more popular. The dead included several women, the "amazons of the German revolution" and harbingers of a women's rights movement. Frederick William considered all-out war on the revolution but capitulated to it instead of leading to a bloodbath.

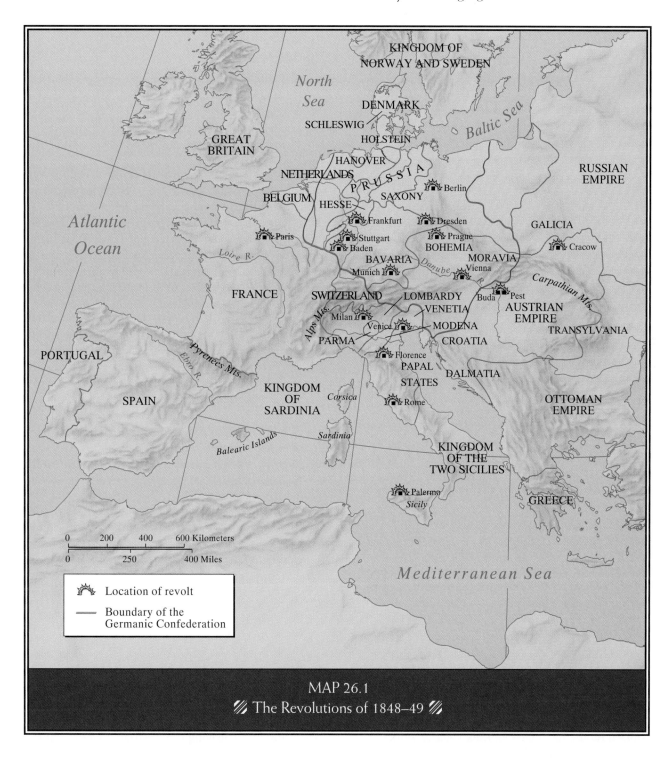

MAP 26.1

The Revolutions of 1848–49

Within a few days he abolished censorship, called elections for a new Diet (the United Landtag), and promised a liberal constitution. His "beloved Berliners," however, did not quit the barricades until he had withdrawn the army and joined them in saluting the bodies of the rebels.

In Vienna, Prince Metternich also resisted demands for liberalization and soon had more problems than he could handle. The most ominous was the awakening of nationalism throughout the empire, especially Hungarian nationalism, led by Lajos Kossuth. Kossuth was a reforming journalist who had spent four years in prison for political crimes and had been elected to the Hungarian Diet in 1847. When the news from Paris reached Buda (still a separate town from Pest), Kossuth inflamed opinion with a patriotic speech demanding Hungarian autonomy. Events soon radicalized Kossuth, who led an insurrection that declared Hungarian independence in

❖ DOCUMENT 26.1 ❖

A University Student in the Revolution of 1848

Carl Schurz (1829–1906) was a nineteen-year-old German university student in Bonn when the revolution of 1848 began. His radical politics during the revolution forced him to flee into exile, and he settled in the United States where he became a lawyer and a political ally of Abraham Lincoln. His American career included serving as a Union general during the Civil War, senator from Missouri, a cabinet member, and editor of a New York newspaper. Had he not been born in Germany, he would probably have become a serious presidential candidate. His memoirs cover his youth in Germany and the following excerpt describes the role of students in the revolution.

One morning toward the end of February 1848, I sat quietly in my attic chamber, working hard on my tragedy of *Ulrich von Hutten,* when suddenly a friend rushed breathlessly into the room, exclaiming: "What, you sitting here! Do you not know what has happened?"

"No; what?"

"The French have driven away Louis Philippe and proclaimed the republic."

I threw down my pen—and that was the end of *Ulrich von Hutten.* I never touched the manuscript again. We tore down the stairs, into the street, to the market square, the accustomed meeting place for all the student societies after their midday dinner. Although it was still forenoon, the market was already crowded with young men talking excitedly. There was no shouting, no noise, only agitated conversation. What did we want there? This probably no one knew. But since the French had driven away Louis Philippe and proclaimed the republic, something of course must happen here too. . . . We were dominated by

a vague feeling as if a great outbreak of elemental forces had begun. . . .

The next morning there were the usual lectures to be attended. But how profitless! The voice of the professor sounded like a monotonous drone coming from far away. What he had to say did not seem to concern us. The pen that should have taken notes remained idle. At last we closed our notebooks with a sigh and went away, impelled by a feeling that now we had something more important to do—to devote ourselves to the affairs of the fatherland. And this we did by seeking again as quickly as possible the company of our friends, in order to discuss what had happened and what was to come. . . . First in line, the convocation of a national parliament. Then the demands for civil rights and liberties, free speech, free press, the right of free assembly, equality before the law. . . .

Great news came from Vienna. There the students of the university were the first to assail the Emperor of Austria with the cry for liberty and citizens' rights. Blood flowed in the streets, and the downfall of Prince Metternich was the result. The students armed themselves as the armed guard of liberty. In the great cities of Prussia, there was a mighty commotion. . . . [W]e in the little university town of Bonn were also busy preparing addresses to the sovereign, to circulate them for signature, and to send them to Berlin. . . . [W]e too had our mass demonstration. A great multitude gathered for a solemn procession through the streets of the town. The most respectable citizens, not a few professors, and a great number of students and people of all grades marched.

1849 (see document 26.2). The Hungarian rebellion encouraged the other minority peoples of the Hapsburg Empire to seek freedom. In April 1848, Czech patriots led by the historian František Palacký won a separate Parliament for Bohemia. Similar claims quickly arose in Moravia (another Czech province), in Galicia (a predominantly Polish province in the north), in Dalmatia (a mixed Slavic province on the Adriatic coast), in Croatia (a southern province), and in Transylvania (a predominantly Rumanian province in the east). In the eastern half of the empire, these nationalist expectations were complicated by the claim of the Hungarians to exercise the full sovereignty previously held by the Austrians.

A liberal revolution also occurred in Vienna in March 1848. After one day of fighting between the army and demonstrators, Metternich fled to exile (see illustration 26.3), leaving the Austrian government in the hands of a feeble-minded emperor, Ferdinand I, and an intimidated group of advisers. After two more days of demonstrations, Ferdinand promised press freedom, a constitution, and an Austrian Parliament; he and the royal court then abandoned Vienna to the liberals. The liberal revolutionaries achieved two lasting successes in Austria—the abolition of serfdom and the granting of civil rights to Jews, who were allowed for the first time to live in the cities, enter the professions, and to marry freely. Several German states abolished serfdom, and

DOCUMENT 26.2

The Hungarian Declaration of Independence, 1849

We, the legally constituted representatives of the Hungarian nation, assembled in the Diet, do, by these presents, solemnly proclaim and maintain the inalienable natural rights of Hungary, with all its dependencies, to occupy the position of an independent European state—that the House of Habsburg . . . has forfeited its right to the Hungarian throne. At the same time, we feel ourselves bound in duty to make known the motives and reasons which have impelled us to this decision. . . .

Three hundred years have passed since the Hungarian nation, by free election, placed the House of Austria upon its throne. . . . These three hundred years have been a period of uninterrupted suffering for the country.

The Creator has blessed this land with all the elements of wealth and happiness. . . . If nothing had been done to impede the development of the country, Hungary would now rank amongst the most prosperous of nations. It was only necessary to refrain from curtailing the moderate share of Constitutional liberty with which the Hungarians united with rare fidelity to their Sovereigns. . . . But this dynasty cannot point to a single ruler who has based his power on the freedom of the people. . . .

Confiding in the justice of an eternal God, we in the face of the civilized world, in reliance upon the natural rights of the Hungarian nation and upon the power it has developed to maintain them, further impelled by the sense of duty which urges every nation to defend its own existence, do hereby declare and proclaim . . . a free, independent, sovereign State.

the Austrian and the Hungarian portions of the empire followed, partly as a liberal concession and partly in fear of peasant insurgency. The new Austrian Parliament (including ninety-two peasants) ended "all servile relationships together with rights and obligations coming from them," in September 1848.

The liberal victories in Prussia and Austria encouraged German nationalists to dream of a parallel triumph to unify the German states. They faced many problems, however, starting with disagreements among themselves. Many nationalists favored a comprehensive German nation-state—their "Germany" stretched "Wher'er is heard the German tongue!" This *grossdeutsch* (large German) nationalism was important to Austrians, who thought that Germany included the Hapsburg Empire. *Grossdeutsch* nationalism, however, threatened the non-German peoples of that empire, who feared their treatment as minorities in an even larger and stronger German state. Pragmatic nationalists favored a *kleindeutsch* (little German) solution that excluded Hapsburg lands or included only the German portion of them. Prussians, the rivals of Austrians for leadership of Germany, generally favored *kleindeutsch* nationalism, because it meant the exclusion or dismemberment of Austria.

The home of German nationalism during the revolutions of 1848 was the free city of Frankfurt, the seat of the German Confederation. Revolutionaries in many states called for a national Parliament to replace the confederation's Diet, and elections for the Frankfurt Parliament took place across Germany in April 1848. More than eight hundred members of this "parliament of professors" (although bureaucrats and lawyers were more numerous) met at the Paulskirche (St. Paul's Church) in Frankfurt in May (see illustration 26.4). Under the leadership of a liberal lawyer from Hesse, Heinrich von Gagern, the Frankfurt Parliament produced fervent rhetoric, but not a treasury, an army, or effective leadership of German nationalism. Liberals wrote an idealistic constitution for unified Germany. It stripped the nobility of privileges, opening the bureaucracy and the officer corps to commoners; it abolished the pillory, branding, and other forms of corporal punishment; it proclaimed "The Fundamental Rights of the German People," including civil liberties; and it promised free state education. The pressure of nonvoting women "observer-delegates," championing the program of a German feminist newspaper, the *Frauenzeitung* (the Women's Newspaper), did not persuade the men of 1848 to add women's rights.

Another dramatic chapter in the springtime of peoples began in the Italy states. Sicily rebelled against its Neapolitan monarch, King Ferdinand II, whose repressive government had produced five insurrections in eighteen years. Ferdinand's use of artillery on the civilian popularion of Messina earned him the nickname "Bomba." When revolution shook the Austrian Empire, the Hapsburg provinces in northern Italy joined in the claims of minority peoples. When news of Metternich's departure reached Milan, barricades appeared in the streets. In a battle known as "the five glorious days," the Lombards expelled the Austrian garrison from Milan.

Illustration 26.3

〽 **The Flight of Metternich.** Nothing better symbolized the initial victories of the revolutions of 1848 than the flight of Prince Metternich. In mid-March, 1848, students and professors from the University of Vienna assembled outside the provincial parliament to chant "Down with Metternich." When they were joined by large numbers of workers, the army fired on them, killing five people. A riot followed and Metternich, who found himself friendless within the government, fled the country. This contemporary Austrian cartoon ridicules the flight of the frightened statesman.

Milanese liberals told the world that the Hapsburgs had "forced on us shoals of foreigners . . . eating our substance . . . judging our rights, without knowing either our language or our customs." The news from Milan and Vienna inflamed all of northern Italy. While the fighting continued in Lombardy, rebels led by Daniele Manin proclaimed the end of Austrian rule at Venice and formed a republic. On the other side of Lombardy, King Charles Albert of Piedmont-Sardinia supported the revolution rather than face upheaval at Turin. As the Austrian army retreated from Milan, Piedmont declared war on Austria. In central Italy, rebels drove out pro-Austrian rulers and adopted constitutions. At Rome, Pius IX promised a constitution and favored the Italian cause but refused to fight Austria, a Catholic state.

The refusal of Pope Pius IX to join the Italian war led to a democratic insurrection at Rome in November 1848 in which the pope's prime minister and personal confessor were both killed. Pius fled Rome, and revolutionaries abolished his temporal powers. The Roman republic attracted two of the heroes of Italian nationalism: Giuseppe Mazzini (the theorist who had created Young Italy) and Giuseppe Garibaldi (a Genoese radical who became the most famous general of the Italian wars). Despite papal threats to excommunicate all voters, they organized the Roman republic as a "pure democracy." One of Garibaldi's first acts was to abolish the Jewish ghetto and emancipate Roman Jews. Like

the emancipation of the serfs in Germany, the emancipation of the Jews became one of the lasting accomplishments of the Italian revolution of 1848. Piedmont adopted guarantees of Jewish rights (making them freer than the Jews in Britain in 1848) and the smaller Italian states followed that example.

In mid-1848, the age of Metternich seemed over at Turin, Milan, Venice, and Rome. Austrian revolutionaries planned to grant Lombardy its independence. While constitutional governments were still being formed, however, an Austrian general dramatically changed events. Count Joseph Radetzky, the Austrian chief-of-staff during the Napoleonic Wars, commanded the garrison driven from Milan. Radetzky regrouped his forces and crushed a combined Italian army in the battle of Custozza (July 1848). The outcome at Custozza (a village in Venetia) left few doubts: Revolutionaries could not defeat determined professional armies, and they could not drive the Austrians from Italy.

The French, German, and Italian revolutions were the most significant upheavals of 1848, but important changes occurred in many countries, often when alert monarchs voluntarily introduced liberal innovations. In Denmark, a new king (Frederick VII) came to the throne in 1848 and launched a reform program culminating in the Danish constitution of 1849. Frederick accepted constitutional limits on his powers, a strengthened Parliament, widespread manhood suffrage (15 percent of the population voted in 1850 versus 4 percent in

Illustration 26.4

The Frankfurt Parliament of 1848. The high point of the German national revolution in 1848 was the election in April 1848 of a Parliament representing all German states. In this illustration, the eight hundred members of the German Parliament march into their meeting hall, St. Paul's Church in Frankfurt. A year later, soldiers dispersed the last delegates to this ineffective "parliament of professors."

Britain), guarantees of civil liberties, and the emancipation of religious minorities. In the Netherlands, King William II agreed to liberal constitutional revision. The Dutch liberals, led by a noted constitutional jurist, Johan Thorbecke, won new parliamentary authority at the expense of the throne, including the principle of ministerial responsibility to a majority in Parliament. In Belgium, King Leopold I accepted electoral reform in 1848, doubling the number of voters, though the total enfranchised remained only 2 percent of the population.

The Conservative Counterrevolution, 1849–52

Most of the changes made during the revolutions of 1848 did not survive for long. Conservatives, typically led by army commanders, went on the counteroffensive in 1849 and reasserted principles of the Old Regime. Constitutions and reforms were nullified; royal authority was reasserted. Pius IX summarized conservative sentiment in December 1848: "We . . . declare null and of no effect, and altogether illegal, every act" of the governments of 1848. The end of slavery in French colonies, the abolition of serfdom in Germany, and the emancipation of Jews in Italy remained a legacy of the revolutionary moment, but few of the governments and none of the republics of 1848 endured. The Italian republics at Venice and at Rome fell in 1849; the French Second Republic became so conservative that it helped to suppress the Roman republic and was itself overturned in 1851. The nationalist fires of 1848 turned to ashes everywhere. By 1850 a Neapolitan radical concluded, "The concept of nationality sufficed to bring about the insurrection, but it was not enough to bring victory." Alexis de Tocqueville had foreseen such problems in early 1848. "In a rebellion, as in a novel," he said, "the most difficult part to invent is the end."

Armies ended most of the revolutions. A cheery German prince summarized the situation in late 1848: "It takes soldiers to put democrats in their place." Europe had briefly been led by revolutionaries: Ledru-Rollin in Paris, Mazzini and Garibaldi in Rome, Manin in Milan, and Kossuth in Buda. At the end of the day, the true victors were generals such as Cavaignac in France and Radetzky in Austria. By 1850 Kossuth would be in prison and his radical colleagues in exile. Manin spent the rest of his life in Paris; Ledru-Rollin and Mazzini found exile in London; Garibaldi became a citizen of the United States and spent the early 1850s as a candle maker on Staten Island. Radetzky, meanwhile, ended his days as the governor-general of Lombardy and Venetia.

The military conquest of the revolution began in Prague in June 1848. The enraged army commander of Bohemia, Prince Alfred zu Windischgrätz, whose wife had been killed in riots there, ignored his orders and bombarded the city. Windischgrätz subdued Prague, then turned his armies on the Hungarians and took Buda and Pest a few weeks later. One month after the shelling of Prague, Radetzky (also resisting imperial instructions) defeated the Piedmontese at Custozza.Windisch-grätz led a polyglot imperial army againstVienna in late October 1848 and shelled his third capital into submission. The army then peremptorily executed the leaders of the government, including Robert Blum, the leader of the Saxon revolution who was visiting Vienna as the vice president of the Frankfurt Parliament. The generals entrusted the Austrian Empire to a reactionary aristocrat, Prince Felix Schwarzenberg, the owner of vast estates in Bohemia, the brother-in-law of Windischgrätz, and a member of Radetzky's staff. Schwarzenberg and the generals arranged for the mentally deficient emperor Ferdinand to abdicate and for his son to renounce the throne. This brought the emperor's eighteen-year-old grandson, Franz Joseph, to the throne. The new emperor reigned for an exceptionally long time (from 1848 to 1916) and became the sentimental symbol of the twilight of an empire. In 1848 he was simply the pawn of counterrevolutionaries who asserted that he was not bound by concessions that he had not personally made.

The military counterrevolution in Austria stiffened the will of King Frederick William IV of Prussia. A few days after the bombardment of Vienna, he again sent the army into Berlin. Under the shrewd leadership of a conservative minister of the interior, Baron Otto von Manteuffel, the Prussian counterrevolution took a more moderate form than the Austrian reaction. The revolutionary Parliament was dismissed, but Manteuffel appeased liberals by persuading the king to grant his promised constitution with a bicameral legislature. Manteuffel understood that constitutions could be conservative weapons, too. Thus, the Prussian Constitution of 1850 restated the principle of divine right and protected the Hohenzollern family by reserving crown domains that produced a huge income. The Prussian army remained an unrestricted state within the state. The government depended upon the support of the king, not the Parliament. The lower house of that Parliament (the *Landtag*) was elected by a broad manhood suffrage, but the electorate was subdivided (by taxes paid) into three classes, each of which elected one-third of the deputies. This three-class system of voting allowed 83 percent of the nation to select one-third of the deputies. The well-to-do named another third, and the richest 1 percent of the population chose the rest. If that did not guarantee moderation, the privileged orders had a veto in an upper house.

The defeat of the revolution in Vienna and Berlin doomed the national revolution at Frankfurt. In March 1849 the desperate delegates offered the crown of a unified Germany to Frederick William. Under pressure from conservatives, he rejected "a crown from the gutter," which would make him "the serf of the revolution." Austria and Prussia recalled their delegates, and the city of Frankfurt refused to host the assembly any longer. A rump Parliament briefly met in Stuttgart, but the Württemberg army disbanded it. Prince Schwarzenberg seized the opportunity to block all manifestations of nationalism. He particularly tried to kill the *kleindeutsch* vision of Germany, which elevated Prussia at the expense of Austria. He signed an alliance with the Catholic states of southern Germany (Bavaria and Württemberg) and used troops to close the Hessian as-

sembly when the *kleindeutsch* debate arose. His greatest victory came at the expense of the Prussians who were obliged in 1850 to disavow their plans for a *kleindeutsch* union and to accept the recreation of the Austrian-dominated German Confederation, in an agreement known to Austrians as the Olmütz Convention and to Prussians as the "humiliation of Olmütz."

Schwarzenberg's government also restored the conservative order in Austrian domestic affairs. His minister of the interior, Alexander von Bach, governed Austrian (in the words of one unhappy liberal) with "a standing army of soldiers, a sitting army of bureaucrats, a kneeling army of priests, and a creeping army of informers." The Austrian constitution was suspended in 1851, and the provinces were governed by a cadre of Viennese bureaucrats who attempted a vigorous "Germanification" of the minorities. Even Hungary lost its historic freedoms. Bach also negotiated a new Concordat with the Vatican in 1855, giving the church control of Austrian schools and ending a half-century of Josephinian independence from Rome. Restrictions on Austrian Jews were restored, following Pius IX's lead in Rome.

The conservative reaction swept Europe, reshaping opinion and behavior. Sören Kierkegaard, a noted Danish philosopher, concluded that "the daily press is the evil principle of the modern world" because "it will stir up all those dregs of humanity which no state or government can control." Even countries little affected by revolution experienced reaction. Nicholas I of Russia launched a new repression of intellectuals, closing discussion circles (the *kruzhki*) in the cities and sending many of their participants to Siberia. He also sent troops to defeat Kossuth. Queen Isabella of Spain demonstrated that counterrevolutionary zeal was not gender-related. She revised the Spanish constitution, eliminating restrictions on her power, and closed the Córtes in 1852. Her Concordat with the Vatican (1851) surpassed Alexander von Bach's: It gave the church control of the schools, the power of censorship, and a reaffirmed status as the sole religion permitted in Spain.

None of these counterrevolutionary victories was as startling as the events in France. General Cavaignac had demonstrated the limits of the French revolution in June 1848 by using the army against protesting workers. In December 1848 he sought the presidency of the republic against Ledru-Rollin. French voters, however, spurned both men in favor of an aspirant monarch. Prince Louis-Napoleon Bonaparte, the nephew of Napoleon Bonaparte, won more than 70 percent of the votes; he had far greater name-recognition in provincial

Illustration 26.5

The Triumph of Reaction. Few events better symbolized the defeat of the liberal-national revolutions of 1848 than one in Paris, where the revolution had begun. The barricades of 1848 had sometimes been built using nearby trees, and the French republic had converted this fact into a great symbolic act—the planting of new "Liberty Trees" along the boulevards. In 1850–51, the conservative government of Louis-Napoleon Bonaparte made its own symbolic statement by removing the Liberty Trees, shown here. This act made a philosophical statement and also denied his opponents the materials for building barricades.

France (where most voters were still illiterate), and his name stood for order after revolutionary chaos and it evoked the glorious triumphs of his uncle.

Louis-Napoleon proceeded to create an authoritarian regime. In short order, Louis-Napoleon reintroduced censorship, restricted universal suffrage, outlawed political clubs, gave the Catholic Church control of French education, and arrested radicals (see illustration 26.5). One of the founders of French feminism, Jeanne Deroin, had dared to run for office in 1849, after the assembly had laughed at her petitions; Louis-Napoleon restored order by throwing her in prison. He also demonstrated how far the republic had changed from its radical origins by sending the French army to Rome to fight on the side of counterrevolution and restore Pope Pius IX to temporal authority. In June 1849 another rising of Parisian workers provoked more severe reponses.

By December 1851 the Second Republic cast only a pale shadow of the liberal-democratic program of 1848, and President Bonaparte ended the pretense by overthrowing the republic in a military coup d'état. To replace the republic, he created a Second Empire with himself as Emperor Napoleon III (honoring Napoleon and his son as predecessors). In a proclamation to the French people, Louis-Napoleon promised to combine the merits of the republic with Metternichian order: "France regenerated by the Revolution and organized by the Emperor." The French Second Empire (1852–70) began its history as a counterrevolutionary regime well suited to the Europe of Nicholas I, Schwarzenberg, and Pius IX. Yet Napoleon III differed from them in signifi-

cant ways. He was a precursor of twentieth-century politics, and he shaped France into a unique blend of Caesarism and modern democracy. He insisted upon democratic forms, even if they were often fictions. He staged a plebiscite to approve his destruction of the republic (winning 92 percent of the votes cast) and more than once asked the people to approve the changes he made; he kept "universal" suffrage but initially allowed only one party.

The French Second Empire was an authoritarian regime—at its best a modern form of enlightened despotism, at its worst a hint of the modern police state. On one hand, Napoleon III gave a significant boost to the modernization of the French economy and a great assist to the industrialization of France, while remaining sensitive to the condition of workers, whose rights he expanded. On the other hand, a Law of Suspects (1858) allowed the government to banish or imprison anyone previously convicted of a political offense, including virtually all of the leaders of 1848; under this act, more than five hundred republicans were transported to Algeria. Although Napoleon III tried to reshape his regime into a "liberal empire" in the 1860s and allowed an opposition party, republicans never forgot that he was the "despicable assassin of the republic." No one branded him more effectively than Victor Hugo (who sat in the legislature of 1848). From exile, Hugo published a political diatribe entitled *Napoleon the Little,* taunting him as "this mummer, this dwarf, this stunted Tiberius." A fairer judgment would remember both sides of this complex man; but few understood

Illustration 26.6

Labor Unrest. The angry worker is one of the inescapable images of nineteenth-century industrialization. Here, in Honoré Daumier's oil painting entitled "The Uprising," agitated workers march past the looming presence of the factory. Trade unions gradually became legal in Europe during the mid-nineteenth century and labor unrest became more organized. During the late nineteenth century, the strike became a widespread feature of daily life although violence—both by governments and workers—was a common feature of such uprisings.

him, and many agreed with Bismarck's remark that Napoleon III was "the sphinx without a riddle."

The Labor Movement and the Rise of Socialism

Even while victorious counterrevolutionaries dreamt of restoring the old order, the social and economic transformation of industrialization created great pressures for the social changes that they resisted. One of the foremost consequences of industrialization was the rise of a labor movement expressing the needs of the industrial working class (often known as the proletariat). The dreadful working and living conditions associated with industrialization were well known by midcentury, but neither conservative governments (typically dominated by great landowners) nor their liberal opposition (typically dominated by industrialists and manufacturers) did much to address the problem. Consequently, labor unrest (see illustration 26.6) and labor movements grew. These took two different forms: (1) associations of workers in the trade unions, seeking to persuade employers to grant better wages and working conditions, and (2) political movements, usually socialist, seeking to create governments that would govern in the interest of the laboring class.

Trade union movements grew slowly because they were illegal. In some countries, the legislation abolish-

ing the monopolies of medieval guilds (such as the Chapelier Law of 1791 in France) also blocked unions. The traditional privileges of guilds survived in parts of Europe, however. German governments were still trying to legislate the principle of *Gewerbefreiheit* (the freedom to practice an occupation) in the 1850s; Denmark, Sweden, and Russia adopted such laws in the 1860s. *Gewerbefreiheit*, in turn, impeded unionism because it taught workers not to act collectively. In other countries, legislation explicitly banned trade unions, as a series of Combination Acts did in Britain. Changes in the Combination Acts in 1824–25 permitted the first legal unions, although they could neither strike nor restrain business. Other laws also restricted workers, as the "Tolpuddle martyrs" discovered in 1834 when they were convicted of the crime of taking a secret union oath. Nonetheless, British trade unionism grew during the 1840s, and the prosperity of the 1850s accelerated this growth (see document 26.3). The Amalgamated Society of Engineers, a union of mechanics founded in 1850, created a model of successful organization, based on collecting dues and offering services. Such unions of skilled labor (sometimes called "the labor aristocracy") flourished during the 1850s and 1860s, culminating in a potentially powerful alliance of unions—the Trades Union Congress—founded in 1868.

Continental Europe trailed Britain in labor organization. The revolutions of 1848 stimulated a German labor movement, but few organizations survived the political repression of the 1850s. It was the late 1860s before

◆ DOCUMENT 26.3 ◆

The Program of an Early Trade Union: The Drapers, 1845

A draper is a dealer in cloth, such as the cloth that might be used for curtains (or "drapes"). Sometimes the term also included dealers in clothing and other dry goods. As a consequence of the industrialization of textile manufacturing, there was a great expansion of the drapers' business and rapidly changing conditions of work. Drapers consequently made one of the first efforts to found a union during the industrial age. The following is the program of the drapers' union of 1845 in Britain.

The object of this association shall be to obtain an abridgment of the hours of business in the linen and woolen drapery, silk mercing, hosiery, haberdashery, lace and other trades, with a view to the physical and moral and intellectual improvement of those engaged therein:

1. by appealing to the public to abstain from shopping in the evening, by means of public meetings, sermons, lectures, tracts, and the press.

2. by representing to employers the evils arising from late hours of business and the advantage which would accrue from closing their shops at an early hour.

3. by impressing upon the minds of assistants the importance of using the time at their disposal in the improvement of their mental faculties, by the aid of literary institutions, lectures, and libraries, and by urging upon them the desirableness and advantages of industry in business, correctness of behavior, and intellectual acquirements.

4. by employing only such means as are of a peaceful and conciliatory nature, and by refusing to sanction or adopt any measure having a tendency to coerce or injure the interests of employers, however opposed they may be to the object and principles of the association.

stronger unions appeared in Germany, and these were created by the workers' political movement. Austrian labor was even more restricted and did not win the right of association until 1867. A variety of workers' societies, such as traditional journeymen's societies (*compagnon-*

nages), competed in France despite the Chapelier Law. Napoleon III felt paternalistic sympathy for French workers and approved liberal laws of 1864–68 legalizing their associations. When he died in exile years later, representatives of labor unions were the only French delegation at Napoleon III's funeral. Belgian workers similarly won the right of association in 1866. Spanish workers organized rapidly following the liberal revolution that overthrew Isabella II in 1868.

A second workers' movement, focusing on political activity, developed alongside trade unionism. This movement encompassed a wide range of political doctrines, from the radical democracy of Chartism to the anarchism of Pierre-Joseph Proudhon and Mikhail Bakunin. Socialism began to emerge as the dominant philosophy of the workers' movement in the 1860s, and Marxism slowly became the dominant form of socialism. Karl Marx was born to a comfortable middle-class Jewish family that had converted to Lutheranism because of the legal requirements for Marx's father to practice law in Trier. Marx's first effort at higher education stumbled over the student life of tavern clubs, indebtedness, and duels, but his father next sent him to the University of Berlin, an institution so rigorous that it was called "the First Guards Regiment of Learning." There Marx became an enthusiastic student of G. W. F. Hegel, the German idealist philosopher who rejected the empiricism of classical philosophy, deemphasized the individualism of liberal philosophy, and taught the preeminence of the state. Marx was deeply impressed with Hegelianism and adopted many of Hegel's concepts of the state and power, as well as his dialectic method of argument. Marx planned to become a philosophy professor, but his membership in a radical student organization during the age of Metternich closed that career to him. A brief stint as a journalist, which introduced Marx to industrial conditions, ended when censors closed his newspaper. Marx, already radicalized, began a life in exile. In France he learned revolutionary politics; in London he studied capitalist economics. By the 1850s Marx had already published several socialist works, and he had collaborated with Friedrich Engels (a factory owner's son) on *The Communist Manifesto* (1848), a concise statement of the theory of class struggle (see document 26.4). They wrote: "The history of all hitherto existing society is the history of class struggles." Only by overthrowing bourgeois society could peasants and industrial workers achieve social justice—hence their slogan, "Workers of the world, unite!" By the 1860s Marx—still in exile—was seeking to unite and direct European socialism through the International Workingman's Association, founded in

◆ DOCUMENT 26.4 ◆

The Communist Manifesto

The history of all hitherto existing society is the history of class struggles. . . . The modern bourgeois society, that has sprouted from the ruins of feudal society, has not done away with class antagonisms. It has but established new classes, new conditions of oppression, new forms of struggle in place of the old ones. . . . The epoch of the bourgeoisie possesses, however, this distinctive feature: it has simplified class antagonisms. Society as a whole is more and more splitting up into two great hostile camps, into two great classes directly facing each other: Bourgeoisie and Proletariat. . . .

All property relations in the past have continually been subject to historical change. . . . The French Revolution, for example, abolished feudal property. . . . In this sense, the theory of the Communists may be summed up in the single sentence: Abolition of private property. . . . Do you mean the property of the petty artisan and of the small peasant, a form of property that preceded the bourgeois form? There is no need to abolish that. . . . Communism deprives no man of the power to appropriate the products of society; all that it does is to deprive him of the power to subjugate the labor of others by means of such appropriation. . . .

[I]n the most advanced countries the following [program] will be pretty generally applicable:

1. Abolition of property in land and application of all rents of land to public purposes.
2. A heavy progressive or graduated income tax.
3. Abolition of all right of inheritance. . . .
5. Centralization of credit in the hands of the State, by means of a national bank with State capital and an exclusive monopoly.
6. Centralization of the means of communication and transport in the hands of the State.
7. . . . [F]actories and instruments of production owned by the State. . . .
8. Equal liability of all to labor. . . .
10. Free education for all children in public schools.

London in 1864. This association (later called the First International) assembled leaders of the workers' movement in annual congresses and kept them informed of events in other countries.

Marxist socialism was only one variant in the emerging working-class political movement of the 1860s. Although it was emerging as the strongest version of revolutionary socialism (which accepted the violent overthrow of the government as the means to power), it faced much competition from advocates of evolutionary socialism (who believed that democratic elections would lead to socialism and therefore opposed violent revolution). Marx had little influence in Britain and was virtually unknown in France. He was not even dominant in his native Germany, where Ferdinand Lassalle had more influence. Lassalle, a successful lawyer and spellbinding orator, had organized workers at Leipzig in 1862 and created a national Workers Association in 1863. His theory of state socialism, in which governments would adopt socialist programs without being overthrown by a Marxist revolution, initially appealed to German workers, but Lassalle died in a duel in 1864. A more radical workers' party appeared in 1868, organized by Wilhelm Liebknecht and August

Bebel. However, their first party congress, held at Eisenach in 1869, showed that socialism remained close to radical republicanism; the Eisenach program sought democratic reforms, not revolution (see document 26.5).

Mid-Victorian Britain

If industrial conditions were leading toward revolution, the revolution would logically be expected to come in Great Britain, the birthplace of industrial society. The British census of 1851 showed the changes associated with the industrial revolution; more than 50 percent of the population lived in towns and cities, making Britain the first urban society in history. Comparative data show how unusual Britain was: The French census of 1851 found only 25.5 percent of the population in towns; the Dutch figure (1849) was 29.0 percent; the Spanish figure (1857), 16.2 percent; the Norwegian figure (1855), 13.6 percent; and the Austrian figure (1857), 8.5 percent. Considering the percentage of the population still engaged in agriculture, the contrast becomes even more striking.

◆ DOCUMENT 26.5 ◆

The Eisenach Progam of German Socialism, 1869

1. Granting universal, equal, direct, and secret vote to all males over 20 years of age for the (national) parliament, the legislatures of the individual states . . . etc. The elected representatives should receive adequate compensation.
2. Introduction of direct legislation [i.e., initiative and veto right] by the people.
3. Elimination of all privileges based upon social rank, property ownership, birth, and religious belief.
4. Establishment of a popular militia in the place of a standing army.
5. Separation of church and state and separation of education from the church.
6. Compulsory education at the level of primary schools and free instruction in *all* public educational institutions.

7. Independence of the judiciary, introduction of the jury system and courts of trade disputes, introduction of public and oral court proceedings, and free legal aid.
8. Elimination of all indirect taxes and introduction of a single direct progressive income and inheritance tax.
9. Elimination of all laws regarding the press and the right to free association; introduction of a standard working day; limits on women's work and prohibition of child labor.
10. State support for cooperatives and state credits for independent producers' cooperatives with democratic guarantees.

Despite the pressures of urbanization and industrialization, Britain had avoided revolution in 1848. Historians have explained this British good fortune in many ways. Some have stressed the role of working-class religions (especially Methodism) that inculcated values such as the acceptance of one's social position and obedience to one's superiors. Charles Dickens put this into a prayer: "O let us love our occupations . . . and always know our proper stations." Others have extended this view to stress the importance of deference to the leadership of the upper class. As the constitutional scholar Walter Bagehot put it, "The English constitution in its palpable form is this: the mass of the people yield obedience to a select few." Economic historians have insisted that the answer is simpler: The working-class standard of living was steadily improving. A more traditional view stresses the importance of timely, but gradual, liberal reforms.

Yet mid-Victorian Britain faced problems comparable to those that enflamed Europe in 1848. The kind of nationalist rebellion that struck central Europe might have occurred in Ireland, for the Irish problem was easily as severe as the plight of Czechs or Hungarians. The potato blight of the 1840s led to terrible famine and widespread unrest. The British responded by passing repressive laws. When the moderate Daniel O'Connell died in 1847, the leadership of Irish nationalism

passed briefly to the Young Ireland movement, founded on the Mazzinian model by William Smith O'Brien. O'Brien tried to raise an insurrection at Tipperary in July 1848, but he failed and was sentenced to penal transportation to Tasmania. In the 1850s one of O'Brien's associates, James Stephens, founded the Irish Republican Brotherhood as a secret society dedicated to armed rebellion. Stephens's republican rebels became better known as the Fenians (honoring ancient Gaelic warriors, the Fianna). The Fenians planned an uprising in 1867 (for which they pioneered fund-raising among Irish immigrants in America) but were thwarted by informers. None of these groups achieved British reconsideration of the Anglo-Irish relationship.

The British showed finer statecraft in dealing with a rebellion in Canada. In 1838 the government sent the earl of Durham, one of the Whig liberals responsible for the Reform Bill of 1832, to Canada as governor-general. Lord Durham, popularly known as "radical Jack," dealt successfully with the rebellious provinces and returned to Britain to write a *Report on the Affairs of British North America* (1839), outlining his ideas for governing the region. The Durham report, recommending the union of all North American provinces into a single, self-governing state, became the Magna Carta of Canada. It took nearly thirty years before Parliament converted the Durham report into the British North

◈ DOCUMENT 26.6 ◈

Barbara Bodichon: The Status of Married Women, 1854

Matrimony is a civil and indissoluble contract between a consenting man and a woman of competent capacity. . . .

It is a punishable offense for an infant [a person under twenty-one] to marry without the consent of the father or guardians. The consent of the mother is not necessary if there be a father. . . .

A man and wife are one person in law; the wife loses all her rights as a single woman, and her existence is, as it were, absorbed in that of her husband. He is civilly responsible for her wrongful acts, and in some cases for her contracts; she lives under his protection or cover, and her condition is called coverture.

In theory, a married woman's body belongs to her husband; she is in his custody, and he can enforce his rights by a writ of habeas corpus; but in practice this is greatly modified. . . .

A man may not lend, let out, or sell his wife; such transactions are considered as being against public decency, and they are misdemeanors.

A wife's personal property before marriage [such as stock, shares, money in hand, money at bank, jewels,

household goods, clothes, etc.] becomes absolutely her husband's, unless when settled in trust for her, and he may assign or dispose of it at his pleasure, whether he and his wife live together or not. . . .

Neither the Courts of Common Law nor of Equity have any direct power to oblige a man to support his wife. . . .

Money earned by a married woman belongs absolutely to her husband. . . .

The legal custody of children belongs to the father. During the lifetime of a sane father, the mother has no rights over her children, except limited power over young infants, and the father may take them from her and dispose of them as he sees fit. . . .

A married woman cannot sue or be sued for contracts; nor can she enter into them except as the agent of her husband; that is to say neither her word nor her deed is binding in law. . . .

Neither a husband nor a wife can be witness against or for the other in criminal cases.

America Act (1867), but in so doing it provided a farsighted degree of autonomy that the Irish could only covet. Other subject peoples were less fortunate. British rule of the Indian subcontinent remained in the hands of the chartered East India Company until 1858, when an Indian rebellion (called the Sepoy Mutiny from the British perspective) of 1857–58 led to the abolition of the company and the assumption of rule by the crown.

In domestic affairs, Parliament advanced cautiously toward liberal-democratic government. This evolution extended civil rights to British Jews through the Jewish Disabilities Act of 1858, a generation after Catholic emancipation. The House of Lords had blocked Jewish (and atheist) emancipation on the argument that Britain was a Christian state and must therefore have a Christian Parliament. People unwilling to invoke the name of God in an oath had to wait another generation, until an act of 1888 emancipated them. And, in typical British gradualism, Jewish emancipation provided only equal political rights; Oxford and Cambridge remained closed to them until a further reform in 1871.

The women's rights campaign also made historic progress during the 1850s. Parliament had briefly ad-

dressed this subject after Caroline Norton's struggle to win the Infant Custody Act of 1839, but no government adopted the principle of women's rights. In the 1850s another energetic woman with high political connections, Barbara Bodichon, resumed the campaign for the rights of married women. Bodichon had been one of the first women to attend Bedford College at the University of London. She managed her own school for women and the poor and there discovered the extraordinary burden that legal restrictions placed upon a married woman. Bodichon published a pamphlet to educate the public: *A Brief Summary in Plain Language of the Most Important Laws of England Concerning Married Women* (1854). "A man and wife are one person in law," she explained. "The wife loses all her rights as a single woman, and her existence is . . . absorbed in that of her husband" (see document 26.6). That loss of legal identity was so complete that if a woman had her purse stolen, the thief could only be arrested for stealing the property of her husband. Bodichon undertook a petition campaign and gathered tens of thousands of signatures that encouraged Parliament to take a first (and naturally, partial) step toward equal rights, the Married Women's Property Act of 1857. Encouraged by this progress and by the Matrimonial Causes Act of 1857 (which created Britain's first divorce courts), Bodichon devoted her resources to financing *The Englishwoman's Journal* (1858), which became the leading voice of British feminism.

The most debated mid-Victorian reform was electoral. Radicals had been disappointed in 1832, and in the 1850s they mounted another campaign to expand the electorate. John Bright demonstrated that the Reform Bill of 1832 had not corrected the problem of rotten boroughs. He produced a list of seventy-one constituencies with a population equal to metropolitan Manchester, noting that those boroughs held 117 seats in parliament to Manchester's 3. Several bills to expand the franchise or to redistrict seats failed during the next decade, until reform won a surprising champion—Benjamin Disraeli, a leader of the Tory Party. Disraeli concluded that "change is inevitable" and decided that it would be best if a conservative government arranged this "leap in the dark."

Disraeli's Reform Bill of 1867 doubled the electorate from approximately one million (4.2 percent of the population) to two million. The new law enfranchised urban males who paid £10 per year in rent. It also adjusted the overrepresentation of England (which held 72 percent of the seats in the kingdom) and the underrepresentation of cities; it denied rural working-men the vote and explicitly excluded women by giving the vote to "every man." The debate included the first introduction of women's suffrage, however, championed by the liberal philosopher John Stuart Mill. Mill advocated women's suffrage in a speech insisting that the infringement of women's rights was "repugnant to the . . . principles of the British constitution." His motion received seventy-three votes in a house of 658 members, but that defeat led to the formation of suffrage societies in Birmingham, Manchester, and Edinburgh within the year. Two years later, Parliament accepted a partial form of women's suffrage when the Municipal Corporations Act (1869) allowed single women to vote in municipal elections.

The Crimean War, 1853–56

Between 1815 and 1853, the Metternichian balance of power had given Europe a degree of stability in international affairs and a general peace among the great powers. Then, in 1853–56, Europe witnessed the first war among the great powers since the defeat of Napoleon.

That war (see map 26.3), known as the Crimean War, was fought around the Black Sea (chiefly on the Russian peninsula of the Crimea). It demonstrated two important changes in the post-Metternichian world. First, the public discussion of international politics had changed. Ideology no longer defined relations—the politics of self-interest did. The Metternichian system had (in theory) united the great powers to defend the status quo; armies were used to defeat revolutions and to protect the conservative order. Self-interest always remained a factor, as Russia demonstrated during the Greek Revolution, but the stated principle of the age remained counterrevolutionary ideology. During the Crimean War, the great powers were candidly motivated by national interests, and they were willing to fight for them. As the nationalist foreign secretary of Britain, Lord Palmerston, told Parliament, "We have no eternal allies and we have no perpetual enemies. Our interests are eternal and perpetual, and these interests it is our duty to follow."

The second change in post-Metternichian power politics had more frightening implications: The Crimean War gave the world its first glimpse of war in the industrial age, teaching lessons that were amplified during the 1860s by the American Civil War and the wars of German unification. Metallurgical advances, the factory system using interchangeable parts, and steam-powered transportation industrialized war.

The Crimean War originated in the eastern question, the complex issue of the survival of the Ottoman Empire. The empire was "the sick man of Europe" (Nicholas I's expression), and prospective heirs clustered around the sick bed. In the late seventeenth century, the Ottoman Empire had encompassed all of southeastern Europe, almost to the gates of Vienna (see map 26.2). By the end of the Napoleonic Wars, the Ottomans had lost vast territories to the Hapsburg Empire (including both Hungary and Transylvania) and to the Russian Empire (which annexed the Crimea in 1783 and Bessarabia in 1812). In the 1850s Sultan Abdul Mejid ruled the eastern Mediterranean, the Balkans (north to the latitude of Zurich), the Middle East, and most of northern Africa. His authority was weak in many regions, and his empire was threatened by independence-minded provinces and by covetous neighbors. Egypt had won autonomy in 1811, Serbia in 1817, and the provinces of Moldavia and Wallachia (the Danubian provinces) followed in 1829; Greece won independence in 1830. The European powers disagreed on the fate of the Ottoman Empire. Russia, coveting further expansion, favored the dismemberment of

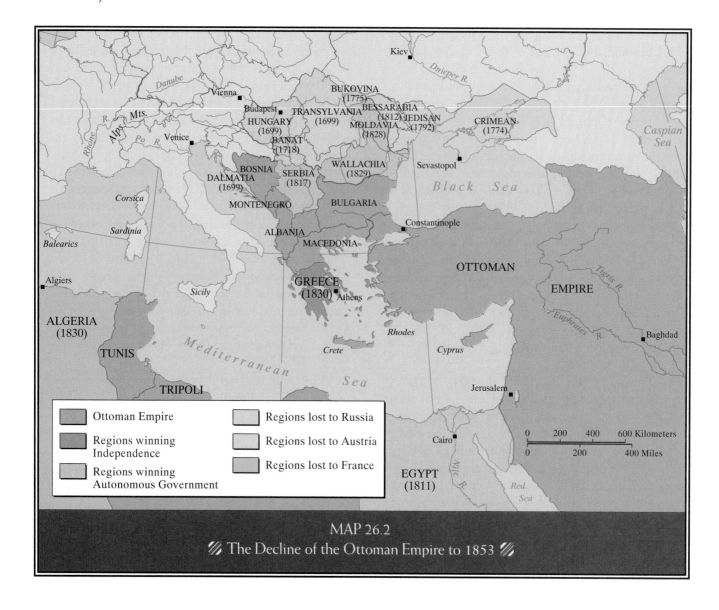

MAP 26.2

The Decline of the Ottoman Empire to 1853

the empire; the British, fearing Russian ambitions, were determined to protect their naval superiority in the Mediterranean and the land routes to India by keeping the sick man alive. These interests defined the alliances of the Crimean War: Britain and the Ottoman Empire (joined by France and later Piedmont-Sardinia) fought Russia.

The immediate origins of the war are all found in the politics of 1848. A Russo-Ottoman dispute began when the sultan accepted revolutionary refugees fleeing the Russian army. A Franco-Russian dispute followed when Napoleon III tried to build his reputation as a defender of the Catholic Church by obtaining from Abdul Mejid the right to protect Catholic interests in Jerusalem. Nicholas I wanted similar rights to protect Orthodox interests, but the British and French blocked him. Such conflicts came to a head in May 1853 when

an angry Nicholas instructed the Russian army to occupy Moldavia and Wallachia, provoking Britain and France to send a joint fleet to protect the sultan.

Fighting began when the Russian navy destroyed the Ottoman fleet off Sinope on the south shore of the Black Sea in November 1853. The Anglo-French fleet then entered the Black Sea (closed to warships by international convention) and declarations of war followed. In the autumn of 1854 the western allies landed armies on Russian soil, in the Crimean peninsula. The French and British defeated the Russian army in several battles (including the battle of Balaclava, made famous by Tennyson's description of "the charge of the light brigade") and forced them to take refuge in the besieged city of Sebastapol. More than 250,000 soldiers died in the Crimea, but both sides suffered more from disease (especially cholera) than from fighting (see table 26.1).

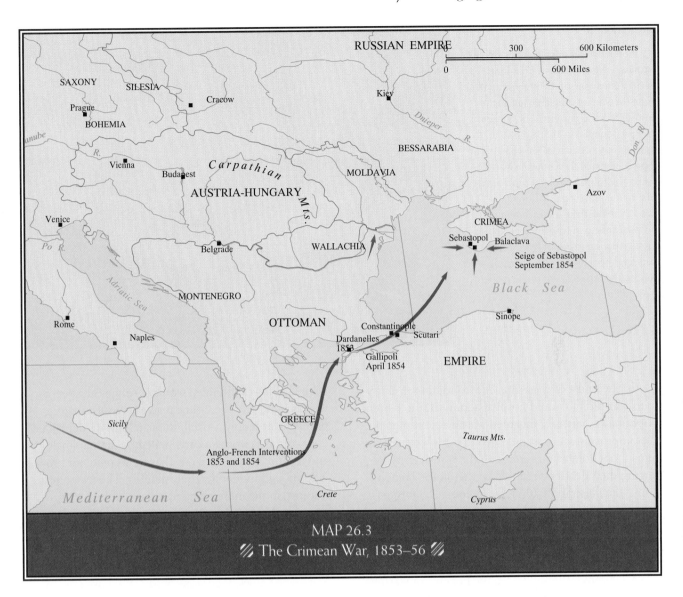

MAP 26.3

%%% The Crimean War, 1853–56 %%%

▶◀ TABLE 26.1 ▶◀

Casualties in the Crimean War, 1853–56

Country	Army	Killed by wounds	Killed by disease	Total losses	Wounded	Total casualties
Britain	98,000	4,602 (4.7%)	17,580 (17.9%)	22,182 (22.6%)	13,000 (13.3%)	35,182 (35.9%)
France	310,000	20,240 (6.5%)	73,375 (23.7%)	93,615 (30.2%)	47,000 (15.2%)	140,615 (45.4%)
Ottoman Empire	230,000	n.a.	n.a.	35,000 (15.2%)	n.a.	
Sardinia	21,000	28 (0.1%)	2,166 (10.3%)	2,194 (10.4%)		
Allied total	659.000			152,991 (23.2%)		
Russia	500,000	40,000 (8.0%)	60,000 (12.0%)	100,000 (20.0%)	120,000 (24.0%)	220,000 (44.0%)

Source: Calculated from data in Chris Cook and John Paxton, *European Political Facts, 1848–1918* (London: Macmillan, 1978), p. 177.

n.a. = Not available.

Illustration 26.7

⟆ **Florence Nightingale and Modern Nursing.** Nursing the sick has long been deemed one of the highest social duties of women, and large nursing orders such as the Society of St. Vincent de Paul (founded in 1633) and state training schools such as Kaiserswerth in Prussia predated the Crimean War. Florence Nightingale brought great attention to the profession by bringing it onto the battlefield and by running her hospital at Scutari (shown here) according to strict standards of hygiene. Her fame and her postwar efforts greatly advanced the organization of the modern nursing profession.

In the midst of these dreadful conditions, a thirty-four-year-old nurse and hospital administrator, Florence Nightingale, virtually invented wartime field-nursing. Her improvements in sanitary conditions lessened the impact of cholera and typhus on the British army, reducing their death rate far below that in the French army (see illustration 26.7). By so doing, Nightingale made nursing a respectable occupation for women, and in 1860 she founded the first modern nursing school. Through her efforts, Britain had sixty thousand trained nurses and several schools of nursing by 1900.

Governments appreciated the benefits of wartime nursing, but they were more interested in the efficient slaughter of their enemies. Britain and France won the most important battles of the Crimean War in part because their soldiers carried weapons with a range of one thousand yards while the Russian army still used smoothbore muskets with a range of two hundred yards. The large-scale use in the Crimea of rifles whose barrels were machined to close tolerances marks the beginning of industrialized warfare. It was made possible by the French invention of the Minié ball (1849), a conical bullet for rifled barrels that could be mass-produced. The next step in the industrialization of warfare came when an American, Samuel Colt, used automatic milling machines to produce interchangeable parts for the firearms themselves. His display at the Crystal Palace Exhibition of 1851 convinced the British to build an arms plant using mass-production techniques at Enfield in suburban London. The French followed the British example. The Enfield rifle and the

Minié ball revolutionized warfare. Armies must eat as well as fight, and the Crimean War revealed major problems in supply as well. Russian logistics depended upon 125,000 wooden carts pulled by draft animals, and it soon became obvious that they could not provide enough fodder for their support. The lesson was not lost on the more efficient armies of the 1860s, which learned to use railroads to transport both men and materiel.

The Crimean War was not fought to a decisive conclusion. Several events brought it to a victorious end for the allies: Piedmont-Sardinia (whose government wanted the friendship of Britain and France) joined the war against Russia; Austria (whose government feared Russian advances in the Balkans) threatened to do the same; and Nicholas I died. A peace conference at Paris in early 1856 quickly settled matters: Russia conceded some Danubian territory, promised to respect the integrity of the Ottoman Empire, and acquiesced in the neutralization of the Black Sea.

Russia in the Alexandrine Age

The thirty-seven-year-old Czar Alexander II who came to the throne of Russia in 1855 differed greatly from his father. He had spent a happier childhood, raised by humane tutors without the military discipline imposed on Nicholas. Alexander's personality was complex. He was an ascetic who sometimes slept on straw on stone floors. He had high moral aspirations and once spent a

⚜ TABLE 26.2 ⚜

Serfs and Peasants in Imperial Russia, 1858

Peasant population	1858 Census
Serfs on private-owned estates	20,173,000
Serfs on imperial lands	2,019,000
Total serfs	22,192,000
Peasants on state lands	18,308,000
Peasants from state lands working in factories and mines	616,000
Peasants from state lands allowed to work in private factories	518,000
Peasants freed by military service	1,093,000
Total peasants	20,535,000

Source: P. I. Lyashchenko, *History of the National Economy of Russia* (New York: Macmillan, 1949) and Francis Conte, ed., *Les Grands dates de la Russie et de l'URSS* (Paris: Larousse, 1990), p. 131.

Illustration 26.8

⚜ The Emancipation of the Serfs. This early Russian photograph records a historic moment of quiet drama: Czar Alexander II's emancipation edict of 1861 is read to the assembled serfs outside the palatial residence of a Russian noble.

night locked in solitary confinement in one of his prisons to understand the conditions there. As crown-prince he joined the government commission studying the "flogging gentry." He seemed well suited to be the man who freed more than twenty million people from serfdom and earned the nickname "the czar liberator." Yet his morals permitted him to take young girls as mistresses, and his reforms were insufficient to prevent six assassination attempts in four years.

Alexander II assumed the throne in 1855, determined to emancipate the serfs (see table 26.2). One of his first acts was a manifesto giving the aristocracy a pragmatic explanation: "I am convinced that . . . it is better to begin to destroy serfdom from above than to wait for that time when it begins to destroy itself from below." The thirty-year reign of Nicholas I had seen 556 serf rebellions, an average of more than one uprising per month; in the first years of Alexander's reign the rate increased to 80 peasant rebellions per year. In 1857 the new czar named a secret committee, headed by his liberal adviser Nikolai Milyutin, to prepare for emancipation. Alexander II followed the advice of the Milyutin Commission and issued an edict (*ukase*) of emancipation in March 1861 on the same day that Abraham Lincoln took the oath of office as president of the United States (see illustration 26.8). The details of emancipation were so complex that they required nearly five hundred pages. The basic provision ended serfdom, freeing more than 22,192,000 people, the majority of the Russian peasantry. Another obliged the serf-owners (most of whom opposed emancipation) to give the serfs land as a part of the emancipation. Serfs obtained "the full rights of free rural inhabitants," their homes, and arable land. Landowners, however, kept title to the land until the former serfs gradually paid for it. In the interim, the imperial government compensated landowners with bonds, and former serfs were obliged, through collective village obligations, to make the redemption payments on these bonds. Until the completion of redemption payments, peasants owed some labor to their landlords and shared their village's obligation. Emancipation began with enlightened principles but perpetuated involuntary servitude (see document 26.7).

Alexandrine liberalism went beyond the emancipation edict of 1861. Alexander II did not grant a constitution or a parliament, but his reforms made them logical expectations. In 1864 he created elective district assemblies (*zemstva*) with powers of local government. The *zemstva* were chosen by a three-class franchise similar to the voting for the Prussian *Landtag*, and legislation had to win the approval of the provincial governor, but this still left the assemblies a role in public health, education, and transportation. Educational reforms flowed from local self-government. Between the creation of the *zemstva* in 1864 and the end of Alexander's reign in 1881, 14,500 new schools opened in Russia. The tsar encouraged this trend by extending freedom to the universities. In 1864 the imperial government also reformed the judiciary and the criminal code. The new edicts, based on the principle of equality before the law, created an independent judiciary with a professional bar, abolished corporal punishment, and introduced the jury system in criminal cases. The following year produced a Press Law that relaxed censorship enough to allow the circulation of radical periodicals produced in exile, such as Alexander Herzen's *Kolokol* (the Bell), published in London.

The reforms of 1861–65 whetted the Russian appetite for further liberalization. During the remaining sixteen years of his reign, Alexander disappointed those who wanted more. He granted self-government to the cities in 1870 and reformed the army, reducing the term of service from twenty-five years to nine in 1874. But his liberalism stopped short of full westernization. He brought Russian institutions near to the level of the Austrian Empire, but not to Anglo-French standards. He began the economic modernization of his empire

◆ DOCUMENT 26.7 ◆

A Radical Prince Describes the World of Serf-owning Aristocrats

Prince Peter Kropotkin (1842–1921) was born to the highest level of the Russian nobility and spent his childhood in luxury. He turned to scholarship and became a geographer of distinction, known for his exploration of Siberia. Kropotkin slowly turned to social criticism, however, attacking the world into which he had been born. He entered radical politics in western Europe and spent several years in French prisons for his anarchism.

Wealth was measured in those times by the number of "souls" that a landed proprietor owned. So many "souls" meant so many male serfs: women did not count. My father, who owned nearly twelve hundred souls, in three different provinces, and who had, in addition to his peasants' holding, large tracts of land which were cultivated by these peasants, was accounted a rich man. He lived up to his reputation, which meant that his house was open to any number of visitors, and that he kept a very large household. We were a family of eight, occasionally ten or twelve; but fifty servants at Moscow, and half as many more in the country, were considered not one too many. Four coachmen to attend a dozen horses, three cooks for the masters and two more for the servants, a dozen men to wait upon us at dinner-time (one man, plate in hand, standing behind each person seated at the table), and girls innumerable in the maid-servants' room—how could any one do with less than this?

To maintain such numbers of servants as were kept in our house would have been simply ruinous if all provisions had to be bought at Moscow; but in those times of serfdom things were managed very simply. . . . [F]ather sat at his table and wrote the following:

"To the manager of my estate . . . Thou art ordered to send to my house, situated in the city of Moscow, twenty-five peasant sledges, drawn by two horses each, one horse from each house and one sledge and one man from each second house, and to load them with (so many) quarters of oats, (so many) of wheat, and (so many) of rye, as also with all the poultry and geese and ducks, well frozen, which have to be killed this winter.

but did not bring it into the industrial age. A tragedy of historical development is that those who begin to modernize a backward country often awaken expectations that they cannot fulfull. The czar liberator became caught in this trap of rising expectations. He ameliorated the strict rule of Poland and amnestied thousands of his father's Polish political prisoners, yet confronted a major Polish revolution in 1863. He reopened universities and granted them greater freedom, yet they became centers of intellectual discontent pressing for more reforms. The disillusionment of the educated classes became so sharp that the novelist Alexander Turgenev gave European languages a new word: *nihilists*, meaning people who respected no authorities. Alexander liberalized the press laws and harvested radical criticism. He emancipated the serfs but still faced peasant rebellions (one occurred in Kazan as early as April 1861). Terrorists set fire to St. Petersburg in 1862. Revolutionaries repeatedly tried to kill him. They ultimately succeeded, and the reign that had begun with such promise ended with his blood on the pavement.

The Unification of Italy: The *Risorgimento*

No event of the Crimean War was more surprising than the declaration of war on Russia by Piedmont-Sardinia, a distant state with no direct interests at stake. That decision was the carefully calculated work of the Piedmontese premier, Count Camillo di Cavour, the foremost architect of Italian unification. Cavour was a wealthy landowner with an advanced education in engineering and an admiration for England, which he knew much better than Sicily or Calabria. He was a short, plump, florid-faced man, a constantly cheerful hard worker who began the day at 5 A.M. His skills combined the pragmatism of the engineer and business executive with the cynical dexterity of the diplomat. Idealists detested the fact that a bourgeois liberal should succeed in unifying Italy after the Mazzinis, Manins, and Garibaldis of 1848 had failed. Cavour had long advocated the liberalization of Italy. He meant the term broadly: Scientific agriculture, modern banking, railroad building, and free trade capitalism were as important as secularized institutions, a free press, and representative government. His public career began in the political clubs of Turin, the capital of Piedmont, during the 1840s. He became prominent in 1847 when he founded a newspaper, *Il Risorgimento* (the Revival), to champion Italian independence and progressive re-

forms. The newspaper became the leading voice of liberal-nationalism, making its title a synonym for the process of unification.

The uprisings of the 1820s and the revolutions of 1848 convinced most observers that rebellion in the streets would not drive the Austrians out of Italy. The leadership of a strong state, plus foreign assistance, would be needed. Both seemed distant during the reaction of 1849. In the south, Ferdinand of Naples was arresting, imprisoning, and torturing more than twenty thousand of his citizens. In Lombardy and Venetia, Marshal Radetzky dispensed the justice of the military tribunal—a few executions, many floggings, more imprisonments, thousands of exiles. Pope Pius IX, protected by a French garrison at Rome, proscribed seven thousand people and executed priests with republican sympathies. Only in Piedmont, where King Charles Albert had abdicated in favor of his son, King Victor Emmanuel II, did the liberalism of 1848 survive. Victor Emmanuel made Piedmont the center of Italian liberalism in the 1850s. He kept the liberal constitution (the *Statuto*) that his father had granted, despite an Austrian offer to cancel Piedmont's war indemnity if he abrogated the document. In 1850, while reactionary governments held sway from Paris to St. Petersburg, Victor Emmanuel promulgated a series of secularizing laws. The Siccardi Laws, written by Cavour, limited the powers of the Catholic Church by abolishing church courts, permitting civil marriage, and restricting the number of church holidays. This version of separation of church and state, which Cavour called "a free church in a free state," persuaded nationalists such as Garibaldi and Manin to recognize the leadership of Piedmont. Cavour entered the government and soon directed the work of four separate ministries. He became premier in 1852 and kept that post for the rest of the decade, culminating in his leadership of Piedmont during a war of unification in 1859 (see map 26.4).

Cavour prepared for the war of 1859 by courting Britain and France. After sending the Piedmontese contingent to the Crimea in 1855, he raised the Italian question at the Paris Peace Conference of 1856, winning a resolution that stated: "It is necessary . . . in the interests of Europe, to apply some remedy to Italy's ills." Cavour next sought an alliance with Napoleon III. He sent his teenaged cousin (and lover), the Countess Virginie di Castiglione, to become Napoleon's mistress and an Italian secret agent. He even profited from the attempt of a disgruntled nationalist, Felice Orsini, to kill Napoleon with a series of bombs outside the Paris opera house. The emperor seemed chastened by Orsini's conspiracy, as if embarrassed that he had

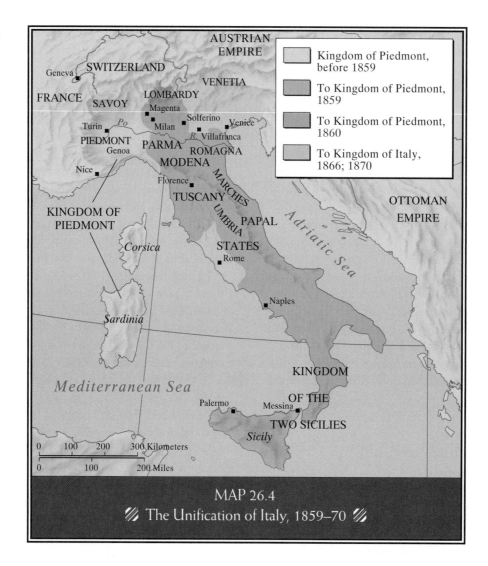

MAP 26.4

///// The Unification of Italy, 1859–70 /////

slighted the Italian cause; he allowed Orsini to make a series of patriotic pronouncements ("So long as Italy is enslaved, death is a blessing.") before sending him to the guillotine. Cavour won his French alliance in 1858. He and Napoleon III met covertly at the mineral springs resort of Plombières (eastern France) and reached a secret agreement. Napoleon pledged a French army of 200,000 men (larger than the entire Piedmontese army) "to drive the Austrians out of Italy once and for all and to leave them without an inch of territory south of the Alps." Cavour promised to return to France the province of Savoy (lost in 1815) and the coastal region of Nice, although his own mother was a Savoyard and Garibaldi had been born in Nice. In addition, Piedmont-Sardinia pledged 10 percent of its annual budget to pay the French war costs. This price did not outrage Italian opinion; Gioacchino Rossini composed a hymn of Italian gratitude that required another army of eight hundred musicians and four hundred singers to perform.

The Italian War of 1859 needed little provocation. Cavour mobilized the Piedmontese army, and the Austrians demanded that he demobilize it. When Cavour refused, the Austrians invaded Piedmont (April 1859) to teach him a lesson. This gave Napoleon III an excuse to send the French army to protect Piedmont. Bloodless revolutions soon drove pro-Austrian rulers from the small central Italian states. Allied armies entered Lombardy in June 1859 and forced the Austrians to retreat after the battle of Magenta (a village near Milan), which gave its name to a purplish-red color as a result of the quantity of blood spilled there. After another bloody but inconclusive battle, at Solferino in eastern Lombardy, the Austrian army retreated into a defensive complex of fortresses known as the Quadrilateral, and Napoleon III (who had seen battle for the first time) withdrew in nausea. More than seventy-five thousand soldiers were killed in less than two months of fighting, forty thousand of them in a single day at Solferino, and Napoleon III was not the only person horrified at the

Illustration 26.9

Garibaldi and the Unification of Italy. Giuseppe Garibaldi became the most celebrated patriot of the *Risorgimento*. He fought in the army of the Roman republic of 1848, commanded a corps in the Sardinian army during the war of 1859 against Austria, organized a volunteer army that won Sicily and southern Italy for the unified Italy in 1860, and repeatedly attacked Rome, hoping to defeat the papal army. In this romanticized Italian painting, Garibaldi leads the people forward under the banner of Italy.

spectacle of industrialized armies slaughtering each other. The Florence Nightingale of this bloody combat was another unlikely figure—J. Henri Dunant, a wealthy Swiss banker traveling in northern Italy who witnessed the battle of Solferino. The sight of the wounded, left to die in piles on the battlefield, so shocked Dunant that he devoted himself to creating an international organization to care for wounded soldiers. His efforts led to an international conference at Geneva and the (first) Geneva Convention (1864) in which twelve European states accepted Dunant's proposed relief society, the International Red Cross. In one of the final tragedies of Solferino, Dunant spent his entire fortune on this effort and lived thereafter in poverty, although he shared the first Nobel Peace Prize in 1901.

After the battle of Solferino, Napoleon III sought peace with the Austrians without consulting Victor Emmanuel II. Napoleon and Franz Joseph met privately at Villafranca (a village in Venetia) in July 1859 and agreed upon terms: Austria would keep Venetia but cede Lombardy to France, which could, in turn, give it to Piedmont. Victor Emmanuel accepted this agreement, despite the fury of Cavour, and yielded Nice and

Savoy to France after plebiscites in the central states (Parma, Modena, Romagna, and Tuscany) made it clear that they would join Lombardy in merging with Piedmont. Before this new Italian state could be organized, another uprising began in Sicily against the rule of the Neapolitan Bourbons. At that point, Garibaldi, as impetuous and idealistic as he had been in 1848, seized the initiative (see illustration 26.9). With the connivance of Cavour, he raised a volunteer army of 1,067 men, dressed them in red woolen shirts, and launched an invasion of Sicily (see document 26.8). Garibaldi's red-shirts (also known as "the 1000") evaded the Neapolitan navy, trekked overland across Sicily, and were received as liberators in Palermo after defeating the Neapolitan army and setting up a provisional government. Garibaldi next crossed to the mainland, where the Neapolitan army dissolved, allowing the red-shirts to enter Naples. Garibaldi planned to continue his march northward to take Rome, believing that "[t]he Vatican is a dagger in the heart of Italy," and an uprising to support him began in the papal states in September 1860.

DOCUMENT 26.8

Garibaldi Calls Italians to Arms, 1860

Italians! The Sicilians are fighting against the enemies of Italy, and for Italy. It is the duty of every Italian to succour them with words, money, arms, and, above all, in person.

The misfortunes of Italy arise from the indifference of one province to the fate of others.

The redemption of Italy began from the moment that men of the same land ran to help their distressed brothers.

Left to themselves, the brave Sicilians will have to fight, not only the mercenaries of the Bourbon [of the government of Naples], but also those of Austria and the Priest of Rome.

Let the inhabitants of the free provinces lift their voices in behalf of their struggling brethren, and impel their brave youth to the conflict.

Let the Marches, Umbria, Sabina, Rome, the Neapolitan, rise to divide the forces of our enemies.

Where the cities suffice not for the insurrection, let them send bands of their bravest into the country. . . .

To arms! Let me put an end, once and for all, to the miseries of so many centuries. Prove to the world that it is no lie that Roman generations inhabited this land.

Cavour seized the opportunity provided by Garibaldi's victories to unite northern and southern Italy. Using the Roman rebellion as an excuse to intervene, Cavour sent Piedmontese armies into the papal states where they won rapid victories. After plebiscites in Sicily, southern Italy, and central Italy favored union with the north, the Kingdom of Italy was proclaimed in March 1861. Victor Emmanuel became the first king of Italy, and the *Statuto* provided the basis of an Italian constitution, including a parliamentary government elected by limited suffrage (2 percent of the population). The new kingdom did not include Venetia (which was still Austrian) or Rome (where the French army remained). Garibaldi attempted another uprising in 1862 to annex Rome as the natural capital of Italy, but he was beaten in a small skirmish and retired to his farm, where he plowed fields behind a team of jackasses

he named Napoleon III, Pius IX, and Immaculate Conception. In one sense, the new Italy also included few Italians; barely 2 percent of the population spoke the Italian language, and most of the nation spoke local dialects. As one wit observed, because Italy now existed it would be necessary to invent the Italians.

Bismarck and the Unification of Germany

Following the suppression of the revolutions of 1848, Germany remained a loose confederation of thirty-nine independent states: one empire (Austria), five kingdoms (Prussia, Bavaria, Württemberg, Saxony, and Hanover), one princedom (Hesse), and an assortment of grand duchies, duchies, principalities, and free cities. Although the Hapsburgs had long dominated central European affairs, and the rough treatment of Prussia at Olmütz in 1850 showed the continuing Austrian preeminence in the confederation, the leadership of the German states was shifting to Prussia. Many reasons existed for the ascendancy of Prussia. The expansion of Prussia (and the partition of Saxony) at Vienna in 1815 had affirmed Prussia's position as the dominant state of northern Germany. The German states north of the Main River were also oriented toward Prussia in cultural and intellectual matters by the confessional division of Germany into a Protestant north and Catholic south. States such as Hanover (95.7 percent Protestant), Hesse (83.1 percent), Mecklenburg (99.3 percent), and Saxony (98.1 percent) were more comfortable with Lutheran Prussia than with Catholic Austria; many of their leaders had been educated at the Protestant universities of Jena and Berlin. Industrial leadership and command of the Zollverein also made Prussia the economic leader of central Europe. German liberals preferred Prussian to Austrian leadership. Neither could be mistaken for a radical republic, but the Prussian record of reforms, from Stein and Hardenburg in 1807 to the constitution of 1850 (with an elective Landtag), was more appealing than the oppression of Metternich or Schwarzenberg.

The Prussian domination of Germany ultimately depended upon an institution that did not thrill liberals: the army. The size of European standing armies had grown as a result of the revolutions of 1848 and the wars of the 1850s (see table 26.3). Prussia, alone among the great powers, had not gone to war since the defeat of Napoleon, so statesmen did not appreciate the importance of Prussian army reforms undertaken by Ger-

◆ TABLE 26.3 ◆

The Growth of European Standing Armies, 1830–60

Country	Army in 1830	Army in 1860	Percentage growth, 1830–60
Austria	273,000	306,000	12.1
France	259,000	608,000	134.8
Prussia	130,000	201,000	54.6
Russia	826,000	862,000	4.4

Source: Calculated from data in Paul Kennedy, *The Rise and Fall of the Great Powers* (New York, N.Y.: Vintage Books, 1987), p. 154.

◆ DOCUMENT 26.9 ◆

Bismarck's "Iron and Blood" Speech on the Military Budget, 1862

Our blood is too hot; we prefer armor too heavy for our slight body, but we should put it to use nevertheless. The eyes of Germany are not fixed on Prussia's liberalism, but upon her power. Bavaria, Württemberg, and Baden may choose the liberal path. No one for that reason will allot Prussia's role to them. Prussia must gather up her strength and hold it in readiness for the favorable moment—a moment which has already been let pass on several occasions. Prussia's borders under the Treaty of Vienna are not suitable for a healthy national life. The great questions of the day will not be decided by speeches and the decisions of a parliamentary majority—that was the mistake of 1848 and 1849—but by iron and blood.

hard von Scharnhorst and Count von Gneissenau after 1806. They had made all Prussian men liable for military service between ages twenty and thirty-nine, including a well-organized system of reserve duty that made the army potentially much larger than its apparent size. They had also adopted the revolutionary principle of commissioning and promoting officers on the basis of ability, abolishing the aristocratic monopoly of rank (yet perpetuating some exclusions, such as Jews), and had created both schools in which to train officers and the Prussian General Staff to provide the army with organization and planning. The Prussian General Staff had been quick to learn the lessons of war in the industrial age; they had, in the words of the nationalist historian Heinrich von Treitschke, "faith in the God who made iron."

The international tensions of the 1850s, especially those involving the French army, convinced the new king of Prussia, William I, that further reforms of the army were in order. In 1859 William named a new minister of war, General Albert von Roon, to supervise those reforms; Roon, in turn, selected a friend, General Helmuth von Moltke, to serve as chief of the general staff. Roon and Moltke soon saw that they would need a great deal of money for this undertaking, but their attempt to get the necessary financing precipitated a constitutional battle with the Landtag, where a liberal majority claimed the constitutional right to approve such expenditures. Roon fulminated that "in the sewer of doctrinaire liberalism, Prussia will rot without redemption," but the liberals held out against the army credits. The constitutional battle over the Prussian budget lasted for nearly three years before a desperate king selected another of Roon's friends, Otto von Bismarck,

to head the government. Bismarck was a hot-headed and mistrustful Junker (a reactionary Prussian aristocrat) who had followed a civil service career to ambassadorial posts in Frankfurt, St. Petersburg, and Paris. He was also a brilliantly pragmatic conservative who favored *Realpolitik* (a policy of realism) to defend the old order. As Bismarck put it, he "listened for the footsteps of God through history, and tried to grab hold of His coattails." Bismarck's *Realpolitik* made him at times a virtual dictator, led Prussia into three wars during the 1860s, and shoved German liberals into outer darkness; but at the end of his term as chancellor, a Prussian-dominated Germany was the strongest state in Europe.

Bismarck defeated the Landtag liberals by ignoring them and the constitution. He decided that "necessity alone is authoritative" and acted without legislative approval. To finance the army, Bismarck levied taxes, collected revenue, and spent money—all without legislation, without a budget, and without accounting. Roon and Moltke acquired breech-loading rifles (Johann von Dreyse's "needle gun") and Krupp cannons (see illustration 26.10); these weapons soon acquired substantial real estate. "Better pointed bullets than pointed speeches," Bismarck felt. He explained his unconstitutional audacity in one of the most famous speeches of the century. He told a Landtag committee

Illustration 26.10

Krupp Artillery. After the London Exhibition of 1851, the public display of the manufacturing wonders of the industrial age became the centerpiece of international fairs and expositions. The Paris Exposition of 1867 produced this ironic lithograph showing Parisians inspecting the Prussian display of cannons manufactured by the Krupp works. The same artillery was an important factor in the Prussian defeat of France three years later.

that it was the army that made Prussia great, not liberal ideals. "The great issues of the day," he said defiantly, "will not be decided by speeches and the decisions of a parliamentary majority—that was the mistake of 1848 and 1849—but by iron and blood" (see document 26.9). These words stuck. Bismarck became "the Iron Chancellor" and Germany became a land of "iron and blood" instead of liberalism.

Bismarckian diplomacy and the Prussian army created a *kleindeutsch* Germany between 1864 and 1870 (see map 26.5). Bismarck first won the friendship of Czar Alexander II of Russia by helping him during the Polish revolution of 1863. He next positioned Prussia as the defender of German nationalism by supporting the confederation in a dispute with Denmark over two duchies, Schleswig and Holstein, located at their common border. In a dispute over the inheritance of these provinces, the German Confederation endorsed the claim of a German prince and in July 1863 called for the use of force against Denmark. Within a year Bismarck had produced an anti-Danish alliance with Austria and a war with Denmark. The Danes, although no match for the combined resources of two great powers, held out for five months before surrendering Schleswig and Holstein. Bismarck did not free the duchies; instead, he negotiated the Convention of Gastein (August 1865) by which Holstein became Austrian and Schleswig, cut off by Austrian territory, became Prussian. This difficult situation soon provided the disputes that led to a war between Austria and Prussia.

Bismarck prepared Prussia for a war with Austria by the skillful diplomacy that made him the most renowned statesman of the late nineteenth century. Two months after his treaty with Austria, Bismarck held anti-Austrian negotiations with Napoleon III at Biarritz on the southwestern coast of France. Using vague assurances of fair

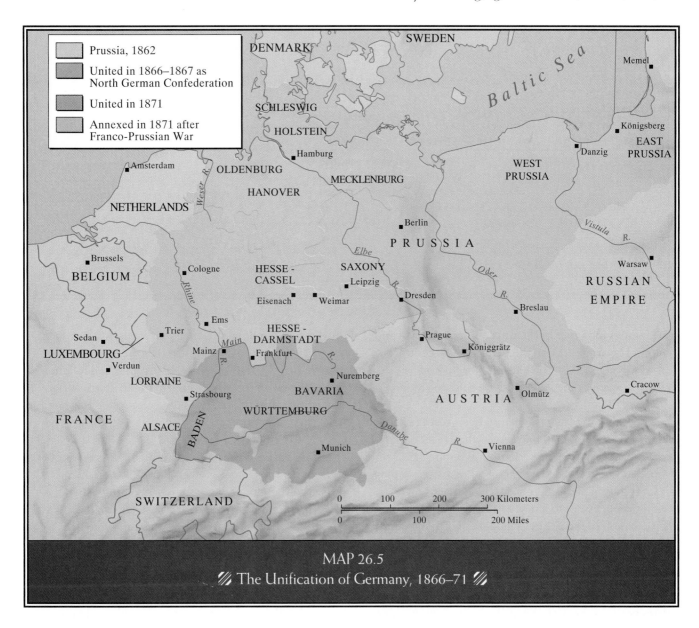

MAP 26.5

The Unification of Germany, 1866–71

compensation to France (perhaps in Belgium, perhaps in Luxembourg, perhaps on the Rhineland frontier), Bismarck won a promise of French neutrality in the event of an Austro-Prussian War plus French help in making a similar deal with Italy. The Biarritz agreement of October 1865 was followed by a Prusso-Italian alliance (April 1866); Italy would help Prussia in a war with Austria in return for Venetia. Confident that he had secured the sympathies of Russia, France, and Italy, Bismarck provoked the Austrians into war, much as Napoleon III and Cavour had done in 1859. The Austrians, confident that they remained the strongest military power in central Europe, used the Confederation to rebuke Prussia. Bismarck answered by declaring the Confederation abolished.

By June 1866 Austria and Prussia were fighting an unexpectedly lopsided Seven Weeks' War (see table

26.4). General von Moltke directed a Prussian army whose needle-guns enabled them to fire five to seven times per minute from crouching or lying positions; the Austrians used muzzle-loading guns that required soldiers to remain standing while firing two or three rounds per minute. Moltke had also learned the lessons of the American Civil War on the use of railroads to mobilize large armies. The first advantage meant that Austria suffered four times as many casualties as Prussia; the second enabled Moltke to move a fresh army into a decisive battle at the Bohemian town of Königgrätz. The Austrians, whose introduction to industrialized warfare cost them more than twelve thousand men per week, surrendered shortly after the battle of Königgrätz (also known as the battle of Sadowa, for a neighboring village). Europe had entered a new age of warfare. As

⚜ TABLE 26.4 ⚜
Human Losses in the Wars of German Unification, 1864–71

Danish War (1864)		Seven Weeks' War (1866)		Franco-Prussian War (1870–71)	
Country	Losses	Country	Losses	Country	Losses
Austria	1,100	Italy	11,197	France	580,000
Prussia	2,423	Prussia	22,376		
Allied total	3,523	Allied total	33,573	Prussia	130,000
Denmark	11,000	Austria	87,844		
		German allies	24,628		
		Allied total	*112,472*		

Source: Calculated from data in Chris Cook and John Paxton, *European Political Facts, 1848–1918* (London: Macmillan, 1978), p. 177.

Note: Losses include the category of prisoners of war.

one military observer of the wars of German unification put it, "The armies taking the field today differ from those commanded by the Duke of Wellington [in 1815] as much as the latter differed from the Roman legions."

The stunning Prussian victory over Austria changed the balance of power in Europe. By the Treaty of Prague (August 1866), the Hapsburg Empire gave Venetia to Italy and acquiesced in a Prussian reshaping of Germany. Franz Joseph had to swallow his own Olmütz and "assent to a new form of Germany without participation of the Austrian Empire." The confederation, the last remnant of centuries of Austrian hegemony in central Europe, was abolished. Several of the north German states (including Hanover) were absorbed into an enlarged Prussia. All other German states north of the Main River (including Saxony) were brought into a new confederation under Prussian domination, the North German Confederation. A few southern states (Baden, Württemberg, and Bavaria) retained their independence, although Bismarck brought them into the Zollverein and military alliances with Prussia.

Bismarck resisted the desires of army leaders and the king to annex Austrian territories, such as Galicia, because he wanted Austrian support in the future. Franz Joseph had other urgent problems—the Prussian victory gave the Hungarians the upper hand in their long-standing struggle for autonomy. Fearing that civil war could follow the humiliation of Königgrätz, the Austrian government reached a compromise (*Ausgleich*) negotiated by the Hungarian statesman Francis Deák. Deák, a moderate liberal who had resisted Kossuth's radicalism in 1848–49, sought only the restitution of the ancient Hungarian constitution granting self-

government in domestic affairs. In accepting the *Ausgleich* of 1867, the Austrians converted the empire into a dual monarchy known as the Austro-Hungarian Empire. Vienna continued to control the western half of the empire, but the Magyars now controlled the east, cheerfully accepting the task of keeping the Slavic peoples of the empire subordinated.

The Seven Weeks' War also had an important effect on central European liberalism. Austrian liberals followed the Hungarian lead in demanding many concessions. Franz Joseph agreed to a series of fundamental laws that became the Austrian Constitution of 1867. During the next three years he reduced the authority of the Catholic Church, even granting civil marriage (1868). A more important consequence of the war, however, was the defeat of liberalism in the new Germany that Bismarck was creating. The liberal majority in the Landtag capitulated in the constitutional battle; they adopted an Indemnity Bill retroactively approving the unconstitutional behavior of Bismarck and Roon. Bismarck acknowledged that he had broken the law, but he did not admit that this was wrong, he did not apologize, and he did promise to obey the constitution in the future. The German national-liberals of 1848 had decided to yield their liberalism as the price of triumphant nationalism.

The Seven Weeks' War created a crisis in Franco-Prussian relations. One month after the battle of Königgrätz, Napoleon III reminded Bismarck of their Biarritz agreement. He requested, for the promised compensation, that France receive her eastern frontiers of 1814 (before Napoleon's One Hundred Days led to the Second Peace of Paris) plus additional territory such as Luxembourg. Bismarck categorically refused such compensation as offensive to German nationalism, intentionally angering the French as he had recently provoked the Austrians. Poor relations deteriorated into a Franco-Prussian War because of a dispute over Spain. In September 1868 the Spanish army overthrew the corrupt regime of Queen Isabella and created a liberal regime based on a free press, universal suffrage, and a newly elected Córtes. The Córtes created a constitutional monarchy but had difficulty finding a member of the European royalty to accept the throne. Finally, in the summer of 1869, Prince Leopold of Hohenzollern-Sigmaringen, a relative of King William I of Prussia, accepted the Spanish throne. The candidacy of a Hohenzollern prince alarmed the French, who envisioned allied armies on their southern and eastern borders, and they demanded that Leopold withdraw. The French applied diplomatic pressure and blocked the Hohenzollern candidacy for the Spanish throne in June 1870, but this episode led to a Franco-Prussian War in July. At a meeting between William I and the French ambassador at the resort town of Bad Ems (Hesse), the ambassador pressed the king to disavow the candidacy and to promise that it would never be revived. William reported the incident to Bismarck in a telegram that became known as the Ems Dispatch. Bismarck edited the telegram to make it seem like an arrogant French insult, then released the text to the nationalist press, hoping to goad the French into war. He succeeded; France declared war two days later.

The Franco-Prussian War of 1870–71 again demonstrated the superiority of the Prussian army and the advantages of the industrial age. General von Moltke used railroads and the telegraph to mobilize his armies with remarkable efficiency. The German invasion first drove the French army out of their frontier province (Alsace). Then, after less than a month of war, Prussian armies won a crushing victory at Sedan (September 1870) and took the emperor prisoner. Incompetent leadership (which resulted in a postwar court-martial) kept a major French army inside the fortifications at Metz instead of fighting the Prussians. A citizen army known as the Army of the Loire, organized by two young republicans, Léon Gambetta and Charles de Freycinet, fought with greater distinction before being defeated than the professional army had. Despite these defeats, France did not capitulate quickly. Forcing a French surrender required a four months' siege of Paris, which held out despite Krupp artillery shelling residential districts; Parisians lived on zoo animals, domestic pets, rats, and shoe leather before accepting an armistice in January 1871.

The surprising defeat of the French army, which Europeans had considered the successor to Napoleon I's armies, had tremendous consequences for Europe. France lost Alsace and part of adjacent Lorraine, accepted a proclamation of German unification (made at the French royal palace of Versailles), and endured a German triumphal march down the Champs Elysée. Bismarck's Frankfurt Peace Treaty also cost France a huge indemnity (five billion francs) and the military occupation of northeastern France until it was paid. For France, *l'année terrible* (the terrible year) included another violent revolution and virtual civil war before the creation of the first enduring republic (the Third Republic) among the great powers. The Franco-Prussian War also led to the completion of Italian unification because the withdrawal of the French troops from Rome permitted the Kingdom of Italy to annex it. The greatest immediate effect, however, was Bismarck's merger of the North German Confederation and the south German states into the German Empire (known as the Second Reich, in recognition of the Holy Roman Empire, which Napoleon had abolished). This Germany, with its dominant army, its great industrial strength, and with royalism victorious over constitutionalism, had become the preeminent power on the continent of Europe.

Conclusion

The early nineteenth century could be interpreted as a conservative victory in reviving the Old Regime after the revolutionary age and maintaining peace among the monarchical powers. The history of Europe at midcentury shows that this balance was short-lived. The Metternichian age preserved the status quo from 1815 to 1848, but that ended in the revolutions of 1848–49. Although German, Italian, Hungarian, and Slavic revolutionaries failed in their nationalist ambitions, and armies and counterrevolutionary governments reasserted the old order in 1849–52, the revolutions of 1848 opened an era of rapid change in Europe. The subsequent political turmoil, combined with industrialization (see chapter 23), left no doubt that the forces of change were far more powerful than the forces of tradition.

The most dramatic changes in midcentury Europe came on the battlefield, not on the barricades. In 1859 French armies (still deemed the most powerful in Europe) supported Piedmont-Sardinia in a war against

Austria that culminated in the creation of the Kingdom of Italy in 1860. In a series of three wars—against Denmark in 1864, Austria in 1866, and France in 1870—Chancellor Otto von Bismarck and the Prussian army created a unified Germany (excluding Austria) in 1871. The war of 1866 also helped Magyar nationalism. In 1867 the defeated Austrian Empire became the Austro-Hungarian dual monarchy, with Hungarian autonomy in the eastern half of the empire. These midcentury conflicts showed the new face of war in an industrial age. The Crimean War (1853–56) had demonstrated the western advantage in new weaponry, and the wars of German unification saw major developments in transportation, communication, and weaponry.

While European nationalists were winning victories in the midcentury wars, European liberals were not. Few of the liberal-democratic victories in the revolutions of 1848 survived the following period of reaction. The republics of 1848, even the French Second Republic that had opened the year of revolution, all fell. A few great reforms survived, such as the abolition of slavery in French colonies and the abolition of serfdom throughout the Austrian Empire, but most constitutions and bills of rights were eliminated. The new states created in the nationalist wars, such as Bismarckian Germany, did not enshrine liberal objectives. Instead, the liberal triumphs of midcentury came in two contrasting ways: In Imperial Russia a reformer czar, Alexander II, abolished serfdom and introduced liberal reforms; in mid-Victorian England, liberals gained another partial reform of Parliament and further progress in the rights of women and minorities.

Suggested Readings

For a basic reference book, see C. Cook and J. Paxton, eds., *European Political Facts, 1848–1918* (1978). For surveys of the period, see the works listed in chapter 25 and E. J. Hobsbawm, *The Age of Capital, 1848–1875* (1979), the second volume of his history of modern Europe; the volume of the *New Cambridge Modern History* edited by J. P. T. Bury, *The Zenith of European Power, 1830–1870* (1964); R. Binkley's volume in the *Rise of Modern Europe* series, *Realism and Nationalism, 1852–1871* (1963); the classic diplomatic history for the second half of the nineteenth century, A. J. P. Taylor, *The Struggle for Mastery in Europe, 1848–1918* (1954); and G. Best, *War and Society in Revolutionary Europe, 1770–1870* (1982), for a military survey of the period.

For the revolutions of 1848, see J. Sperber, *The European Revolutions, 1848–1851* (1994), an excellent new survey; P. Robertson, *Revolutions of 1848* (1952), the standard history of the subject; F. Fetjö, ed., *The Opening of an Era, 1848* (1948), a helpful collection of essays; L. Namier, *1848: The Revolution of the Intellectuals* (1946);

and R. Lougee, *Midcentury Revolution, 1848* (1972), a brief survey of France and Germany. For local studies, see T. Hamerow, *Restoration, Revolution, Reaction* (1958), for the German revolutions; F. Eyck, *The Frankfurt Parliament, 1848–49* (1968); R. J. Rath, *The Viennese Revolution of 1848* (1957); G. Trevelyan, *Garibaldi's Defense of the Roman Republic* (1907) and P. Ginsbourg, *Daniele Manin and the Venetian Revolution of 1848–49* (1979). For the diplomacy of 1848, see J. Chastain, *The Liberation of Sovereign Peoples* (1988) and L. Jennings, *France and Europe in 1848* (1973). For the suppression of the republic in France and the Second Empire, see J. Merriman, *The Agony of the Republic* (1978) and A. Plessis, *The Rise and Fall of the Second Empire, 1852–1871* (1985). For the reaction in Austria, see A. Sked, *The Survival of the Hapsburg Empire* (1979), on Radetzky and the military suppression of the revolution.

For the labor movement, socialism, and Marxism, see G. D. H. Cole, *A History of Socialist Thought* (1953–1967), a comprehensive five-volume history. For Marx and Marxism, see S. Hook, *From Hegel to Marx* (1936), G. Lichtheim, *Marxism* (1964), L. Kolakowski, *Main Currents of Marxism*, 3 vols. (1978), R. Tucker, *The Marxian Revolutionary Idea* (1969) and *Philosophy and Myth in Karl Marx* (1972), and R. Hunt, *The Political Ideas of Marx and Engels*, 2 vols. (1974–84).

For overviews of midcentury Britain, see W. Burn, *The Age of Equipoise* (1968), an essay on mid-Victorian Britain; G. K. Clark, *The Making of Victorian England* (1972); and G. M. Young, *Portrait of an Age* (1977). For topics, see R. Davis, *Political Change and Continuity* (1972), a good local study of English politics; D. Moore, *The Politics of Deference* (1976); E. Steele, *Palmerston and Liberalism, 1855–1865* (1991); R. Blake, *Disraeli* (1967) and F. B. Smith, *The Making of the Second Reform Bill* (1966).

For the eastern question and the Crimean War, see the overview in M. S. Anderson, *The Eastern Question, 1774–1923* (1966); B. Jelavich, *Russia's Balkan Entanglements, 1806–1914* (1991); N. Rich, *Why the Crimean War?* (1985), a good synthesis; D. Wetzel, *The Crimean War* (1985), a diplomatic overview; A. Palmer, *The Crimean War* (1987), a military and diplomatic overview; P. Schroeder, *Austria, Great Britain, and the Crimean War* (1972); J. Curtiss, *Russia's Crimean War* (1979); J. B. Conacher, *Britain and the Crimea, 1855–1856* (1987); C. Woodham-Smith, *The Reason Why* (1953), a well-written account of the British campaign; A. Saab, *Origins of the Crimean Alliance* (1977), best for the Ottoman role; and W. Baumgart, *The Peace of Paris, 1856* (1981).

For the unification of Italy, see especially the works of D. M. Smith, *Victor Emanuel, Cavour, and the Risorgimento* (1971), *Cavour and Garibaldi, 1860* (1954), *Cavour* (1985), and *Garibaldi* (1956). See also F. Coppa, *Camillo di Cavour* (1973) and *The Origins of the Italian Wars of Independence* (1992); A. Blumberg, *A Carefully Planned Accident* (1990), a good study account of the war of 1859; C. Hallberg, *Franz-Joseph and Napoleon III* (1973); J. Ridley, *Garibaldi* (1974); J. Bush, *Venetia Redeemed* (1967), on the diplomacy leading to the annexation of 1866; and S. Halpein, *Italy and the Vatican at War* (1939), on the annexation of Rome.

For the unification of Germany, see T. Hamerow, *The Social Foundations of German Unification, 1858–71*, 2 vols. (1969–72); E. Anderson, *The Social and Political Conflict in Prussia, 1858–64*

(1954); G. Windell, *The Catholics and German Unity, 1866–71* (1954); and D. Showalter, *Railroads and Rifles* (1975), for the role of industrialization and technology. For Bismarck, see O. Pflanze, *Bismarck and the Development of Germany* (1990), vol. 1 covers the period of unification; and L. Gall, *Bismarck, the White Revolutionary, 1815–71* (1986). For the diplomacy of unification, see W. Carr, *The Origins of the Wars of German Unification* (1991); W. Mosse, *The European Powers and the German Question, 1848–1871* (1969); L. Steefel, *The Schleswig-Holstein Question* (1932); H. Friedjung, *The Struggle for Supremacy in Germany* (1966), for the Austro-Prussia rivalry leading to war in 1866; A. Pottinger, *Napoleon III and the German Crisis, 1865–1866* (1966); L. Steefel, *Bismarck, the Hohenzollern Candidacy, and the Origins of the Franco-German War of 1870* (1962); and R. Giesberg, *The Treaty of Frankfurt* (1966). For the wars, see G. Craig, *The Battle of Königgrätz, 1866* (1964) and M. Howard, *The Franco-Prussian War* (1961).

CHAPTER 27

EUROPE IN THE BELLE ÉPOQUE, 1871–1914

CHAPTER OUTLINE

Turn-of-the-century Europe (see map 27.1) is known as the Belle Époque (the beautiful era) because it was a period of unusual peace and prosperity compared with the preceding century or the following generation. For nearly half a century, between the Paris Commune of 1871 and the beginning of World War I in 1914, no European wars broke out among the great powers, no wave of revolutions arose. A long recession troubled people during the 1870s and 1880s, but the Belle Époque experienced nothing so severe as the great depressions of the 1840s or 1930s.

Chapter 27 examines Europe during this era of relative tranquility. It surveys the four greatest powers (the German Empire, the French Third Republic, Great Britain, and the Russian Empire) and draws some comparisons with other states. Each of the great powers made progress toward democratic societies, but the attitudes and institutions of the Old Regime still persisted. The chapter shows how reforms such as the creation of universal education in France by Jules Ferry, and the foundation of social security in Germany by Otto von Bismarck marked this democratic trend; however, it also shows a less democratic context, such as the Bismarckian attack on the Catholic Church during the *Kulturkampf*, the outbreak of the anti-Semitic Dreyfus affair in France, and the British refusal of home rule to the Irish. The final sections of the chapter discuss two of the major issues confronting European democracy during the Belle Époque: the growth of the labor movement and socialist political parties and the emergence of feminism as a mass movement. Workers, women, and other minorities all demanded a share in the emerging democracy.

The German Empire, 1871–1914

The Prussian victory in the Franco-Prussian War enabled Bismarck to bring the south German states

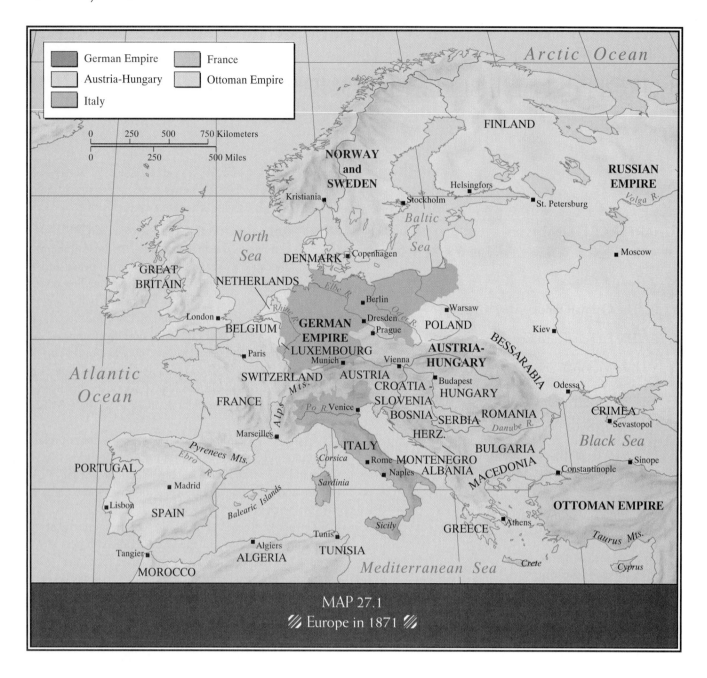

MAP 27.1
Europe in 1871

(Baden, Bavaria, and Württemberg) into a union with the Prussian-dominated North German Confederation. The result was the German Empire (called the Second Empire, or Second *Reich*, in recognition of the Holy Roman Empire). Unquestionably the most powerful state on the continent, it stretched from the newly annexed French provinces of Alsace and Lorraine in the west to the Lithuanian frontier on the Baltic Sea (nine hundred miles away); its population roughly equaled France and Spain combined or Italy and Austria-Hungary combined. The German army had proven its mastery of the battlefield; German industry was beginning to demonstrate a comparable superiority. Just as the French had been forced to swallow German military leadership, the

British increasingly lost ground to German industrial might. Germany surpassed Britain in iron consumption by the late 1890s, then in coal consumption in the early twentieth century (see chart 27.1).

Although the German army and economy were the most modern in Europe, the government and its institutions remained rooted in the eighteenth century. The Prussian army had created Germany, and the German constitution (1871) showed the dominance of Prussia. The empire was a federal government of twenty-five unequal states. Many historic states survived with their monarchies intact but subordinated to the Prussian king, who was crowned emperor (*Kaiser*) of Germany. The empire thus contained four kingdoms (Prussia,

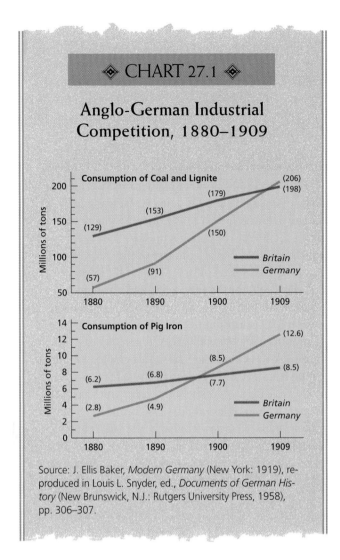

◆ CHART 27.1 ◆

Anglo-German Industrial Competition, 1880–1909

Consumption of Coal and Lignite

(Millions of tons)

- 1880: (129) Britain, (57) Germany
- 1890: (153) Britain, (91) Germany
- 1900: (179) Britain, (150) Germany
- 1909: (206) Britain, (198) Germany

Britain
Germany

Consumption of Pig Iron

(Millions of tons)

- 1880: (6.2) Britain, (2.8) Germany
- 1890: (6.8) Britain, (4.9) Germany
- 1900: (7.7) Britain, (8.5) Germany
- 1909: (8.5) Britain, (12.6) Germany

Britain
Germany

Source: J. Ellis Baker, *Modern Germany* (New York: 1919), reproduced in Louis L. Snyder, ed., *Documents of German History* (New Brunswick, N.J.: Rutgers University Press, 1958), pp. 306–307.

at any time) and could govern without the support of a legislative majority. Bismarck held office without leading any political party and without a parliamentary majority before 1887. He frankly admitted that his primary job was to preserve the monarchy: "The Prussian crown must not allow itself to be thrust into the powerless position of the English crown." The German legislature contained a lower house (the *Reichstag*), elected by universal manhood suffrage (at age twenty-five), and an upper house representing the states. The Reichstag's approval was needed for new legislation or a new budget, but the chancellor could perpetuate an old budget indefinitely and ignore the Reichstag. This constitution was a compromise between eighteenth-century absolutism and nineteenth-century popular sovereignty, a fact underscored by the absence of any German bill of rights such as the document adopted by the Frankfurt Parliament in 1848–49.

During the "founding years" of the 1870s and 1880s, Bismarck built an alliance of conservative interests to support his government and battle its enemies. By 1879 he had gained the backing of the landowning aristocracy, the growing class of wealthy industrialists, and the supporters of militarism and nationalism—an alliance that set the direction of German history. The support of this coalition enabled Bismarck to fight the *Reichsfeinde* (enemies of the empire), whom he thought threatened the new empire. His target during the 1870s was the Catholic Church (see illustration 27.1); in the 1880s he turned to socialism. The battle with the Catholic Church is known as the *Kulturkampf* (the struggle for civilization). The roots of the *Kulturkampf* lay in the confessional division of Germany and in the reinvigoration of the papacy under Pope Pius IX. The new empire held a Protestant (mostly Lutheran) majority, dominated by a Protestant state and monarch, but included a large Catholic minority. Pius IX made religion a major issue in Germany when he wrote the militant Syllabus of Errors and led the Vatican Council (1869–70) to state the doctrine of papal infallibility. The syllabus opposed cooperation with Protestantism and resisted the power of the state.

Bismarck insisted that all Germans must accept the primacy of the German state, not of the church. Between 1872 and 1875, Prussia adopted a series of "May laws" increasing state control in matters previously left to churches and expelling clerics who lacked state certification. By 1876 no Catholic bishops were left in Prussia (outside of prison) and fourteen hundred parishes were vacant. Bismarck ended the *Kulturkampf* in the late 1870s to shift his attention to socialism after Pius IX was succeeded by the more conciliatory Leo XIII and

Bavaria, Saxony, and Württemberg), six grand duchies, five duchies, seven principalities, and three free cities. All states retained some sovereignty, with separate constitutions, taxes, and laws. The Bavarians even obtained "special rights" and kept their own postal service and diplomatic corps. An enlarged Prussia, however, encompassed 65 percent of all German territory, 62 percent of the population, and the richest economic areas (the Saar, the Ruhr, and Upper Silesia). The Prussian-dominated imperial government controlled the army, decisions of war or peace, and such central economic institutions as banking and the railroads.

The emperor of Germany (the king of Prussia, William I) held genuine power under the new constitution, which was significantly less democratic than the regimes in Britain and France. The emperor named a chancellor (*Kanzler*)—the architect of unification, Prince Bismarck—to direct the government. The chancellor never needed to be elected; he remained personally responsible to the emperor (who could dismiss him

Illustration 27.1

⚡ **Church and State.** One of the most passionate European struggles of the Belle Époque involved the relationship of church and state. In Germany this grew into the *Kulturkampf* of the 1870s, in which the Catholic bishops of Prussia were jailed; in France, it led to the separation of church and state in 1905 and the closing of virtually every monastery. This German cartoon depicts the struggle as a chess match between Bismarck (on the left) and Pope Pius IX. The pope considers moving a piece inscribed "encyclical" or another marked "Syllabus" (for the Syllabus of Errors). Beside Bismarck is a box of interned Catholic pieces.

elections gave the Social Democratic Party (SPD) nearly 10 percent of the vote. An Anti-Socialist Law of 1878 showed how far Germany remained from western standards of freedom: It prohibited socialist meetings, closed socialist newspapers, restricted socialist fundraising, and permitted the harassment of the leaders of the SPD. Because the Second Reich had no bill of rights, this was all legal under German law. When trade union membership and socialist votes continued to increase, Bismarck changed his tactics. Concluding that "[s]omething positive should be done to remove the causes for socialism," he borrowed some of the legislative ideas that made socialism appealing. The deeply conservative Bismarck became one of the founders of the welfare state, telling the Reichstag that the state had "the duty of caring for its helpless fellow-citizens," adding that "[i]f someone objects that this is socialism, I do not shrink from it in the least." German health insurance began in 1883, workers' accident compensation insurance in 1884, and old age and disability pensions in 1889. These programs were kept small by granting pensions at age sixty-five when the average life expectancy at birth was forty-one. (Life expectancy did not reach sixty-five until the 1940s.) Bismarckian state socialism continued after his retirement, and German welfare programs were expanded in the 1890s and consolidated in the Imperial Insurance Code of 1911.

The death of Kaiser William I in 1888 nearly led to the liberalization of Germany, a course favored by his son, Frederick III. Frederick reigned for only a few weeks, however, before dying of throat cancer at age fifty-seven, and his son, Kaiser William II, led Germany in a different direction. William II (often known by the German form of his name, Wilhelm) came to the throne at twenty-nine. He had no links to the dreams of 1848, the constitutional crisis of the 1850s, or the wars of the 1860s. Born with a deformed arm as the consequence of a forceps delivery, he was aggressive and arrogant to hide his insecurity. Bismarck tried to restrain the impulsive young emperor: "The Kaiser is like a balloon. If you don't hold fast to the string, you never know where he'll be off to." William II, however, decided in 1890 to retire the aging old chancellor. This episode, known as "the dropping of the pilot" (see illustration 27.2) clearly reflected the young emperor's intention to rule personally. In William's words, "If Frederick the Great had had such a chancellor, he would not have been Frederick the Great."

The leaders of Wilhelmine Germany were consequently men of less ability than Bismarck. They attempted to set a new course in the 1890s but accomplished little change in domestic affairs. Their greatest task was often to restrain the undemocratic instincts of the kaiser. William summarized his political sentiments when he attended a colonial exposition and observed a crude display of an African king's hut with the skulls of his rivals posted outside: "If only I could see the Reichstag stuck up like that!"

The strongest chancellor of Wilhelmine Germany, Count Bernhard von Bülow, maintained the Bismarckian conservative coalition by giving higher agricultural tariffs to the Junkers and larger military contracts to industrialists. Bülow directed German energies to "world policy" (*Weltpolitik*). With the enthusiasm of the emperor and the energy of a strong minister of the navy, Admiral Alfred von Tirpitz, the Bülow government (1900–1909) undertook a major arms race (especially in naval construction), the extension and consolidation of a German colonial empire (reluctantly begun by Bismarck), and the assertion of German leadership in global issues.

The French Third Republic

The war of 1870–71 destroyed the French Second Empire as it created the German Second Empire. Napoleon III was taken prisoner at Sedan in September

Illustration 27.2

The End of the Bismarckian Era. Otto von Bismarck was the dominant statesman in Europe for nearly thirty years. In 1890 the thirty-one-year-old Kaiser William II ended that era by dismissing the seventy-five-year-old Bismarck; the German chancellor served at the pleasure of the monarch, not the Parliament. The cartoon shown here, from the British magazine *Punch*, summarized that event with a famous nautical metaphor, "the dropping of the pilot." During the next generation, the German ship of state lacked such a skilled hand at the helm.

Gambetta's provisional government of 1870 was replaced by an elected assembly after the capitulation of Paris in January 1871, when Bismarck allowed an armistice for the French to elect a new government to negotiate a peace treaty. Republicans and Parisians wanted to fight to the bitter end, while monarchists and the provinces favored peace. A majority of the nation would have voted against monarchy if that were the issue, but they accepted monarchist representatives as the price of peace. A French National Assembly chose Adolphe Thiers, a leader of the Orleanist monarchy and a critic of Napoleon III, as its executive. His government negotiated the Frankfurt Peace Treaty of May 1871, which cost France Alsace, much of Lorraine, and a five-billion-franc war indemnity (one billion dollars).

While the monarchist government of Thiers deliberated in suburban Versailles, Paris elected a municipal government, known as the Paris Commune of 1871, which denied the authority of the Versailles government. The Commune was a mixture of republicans, socialists, and anarchists. It did not last long enough to prepare a full program, but the Communards favored decentralized government, the separation of church and state, and a variety of social programs. Although it became a famous symbol in socialist literature, the Commune never even seized the Bank of France or the Stock Exchange. It (and smaller communes in other cities) survived only for a few weeks from March to May 1871 before falling in a bloody civil war with the monarchist Versailles government. Thiers used the French army to attack Paris (while the German army watched), and Versailles troops fought Communards street-by-street, executing anyone who was armed. The Communards responded with a similar ferocity, executing hostages (including the archbishop of Paris) and destroying monarchist monuments. The Versailles army destroyed the Commune in a week of street fighting, known as "the bloody week." Under the direction of a candidly cruel general, the Marquis de Gallifet, the army began to punish the city. Gallifet felt justified in executing anyone who had stayed in Paris during the Commune, and he set such examples as executing wounded prisoners (wounds were evidence of being involved in the fighting) or white-haired prisoners (who were thought old enough to have fought in the revolution of 1848, too). The monarchical revenge upon Paris killed ten times as many Parisians (an estimated twenty-five thousand) as the Reign of Terror had guillotined there (twenty-six hundred). An additional forty thousand military trials produced ten thousand sentences of imprisonment or deportation to a penal colony.

1870. When the news reached Paris, a bloodless revolution announced the creation of a Third Republic (honoring the predecessors of 1792 and 1848). The Third Republic became the first republic in European history to last long enough to offer a viable alternative to monarchy. Despite its rocky start, and a history filled with crises, the French Third Republic survived a generation longer than imperial Germany did.

Following this civil war, the French had great difficulty in agreeing upon a government during the 1870s.
The National Assembly held a monarchist majority,
split among supporters of three royal families: the Bourbon legitimists, who wanted to crown the grandson of
Charles X; the Orleanists, who favored the grandson of
Louis Philippe (see genealogy 25.1); and the Bona-
partists, who supported Napoleon III or his son. While
these factions squabbled, by-elections filled vacant
seats with republicans, until even Thiers admitted that
France must become a republic, "the government most
ideal in theory and most appropriate to modern societies." The constitutional laws of the Third Republic
were finally adopted in 1875. Monarchist deputies tried
to make the new regime conservative, to guard against
democracy and to provide for a future monarchical
restoration. The constitution created a strong lower
house of Parliament (the Chamber of Deputies), which
was elected by universal manhood suffrage, and balanced it with an upper house (the Senate) elected indirectly. The head of the government (the premier)
needed the support of a majority in the Chamber of
Deputies. Monarchists also insisted upon having a president (with largely ceremonial powers), hoping to
change the position to a king someday. By the end of
the 1870s, however, republicans had gained control of
both houses of Parliament and elected their own
president.

In the late 1870s and the 1880s, republicans created many of the basic laws and institutions of modern
France. Moderates led by a quiet lawyer named Jules
Ferry and radicals led by the more flamboyant Georges
Clemenceau compromised on an initial program. The
Ferry laws of the early 1880s created one of the basic
institutions of democracy—a public school system that
was free, secular, and compulsory. This legislation
opened secondary schools to women and to children of
the poorer classes. While the population of France increased by less than 8 percent between 1883 and 1913,
secondary school enrollment grew by 106 percent. The
number of girls in secondary education grew from
11,100 to 55,700. The new school system was secular
because republicans recognized that the church remained allied with the monarchy against democracy. As
Gambetta once put it, "Clericalism, there is the enemy."
Whereas 44 percent of all French children (60 percent
of all girls) were educated by the church in 1876, less
than 1 percent (0.05 percent of all boys) were in 1912.
The same sentiment also led to secular hospitals, civil
marriage and burial, and divorce, but moderate republicans stopped short of the complete separation of

◈ DOCUMENT 27.1 ◈

Clemenceau's Radical-Democratic Program, 1881

Article 1. Revision of the constitution. Abolition of the Senate and the Presidency of the Republic. Ratification of the new constitution by the
people.

Article 2. Individual freedom. Liberty of the
press, of meetings, of association, guaranteed by
the constitution. Abolition of laws against the First
International.

Article 3. Separation of church and state. Suppression of state aid for churches. . . .

Article 4. The right of children to a full education. Secular, free, obligatory education.

Article 5. Reduction of the term of military
service. Obligatory military service for all citizens.
. . . Freedom of conscience within the military.
Gradual substitution of national militias for standing armies.

Article 6. Judicial system free and equal for
all. Judges elected for short terms. Revision of the
legal codes in democratic ways. Abolition of the
death penalty.

Article 7. Sovereignty of universal suffrage. . . .
[S]horter terms of office for elected officials. . . .

Article 9. Autonomy for local governments.
Town governments to control their own administration, finances, police. . . .

Article 11. Tax reform. . . . Suppression of indirect consumption taxes. Progressive taxes on
capital or income.

Article 13. Legalization of divorce.

Article 14. Reduction in the length of the
working day. Suppression of work by children
younger than fourteen. . . . Creation of retirement
savings for the aged and the injured.

Article 15. Revision of labor laws. . . . Responsibility of employers for work-related accidents,
guaranteed by insurance.

church and state, which would have ended state aid to
the churches. Clemenceau campaigned for separation
and other radical innovations such as an income tax and
welfare legislation (see document 27.1), but most republicans still resisted such reforms.

A conservative reaction against this republicanism swept France in the late nineteenth century. A popular minister of war, General Georges Boulanger, became the symbolic leader of this reaction, and monarchists, nationalists, and Catholics rallied to "Boulangism," hoping that he would overthrow the republic. Boulangists won many seats in Parliament in the late 1880s and taught the world a lesson in electoral demagoguery, but the general, fearing conspiracy charges against him, fled the country and committed suicide. Right-wing enemies of the republic resumed the attack in the 1890s, when several republican politicians were involved in corruption surrounding a failed French attempt to build a canal across the isthmus of Panama.

The Panama Canal scandal of 1892–93 awakened one of the ugliest elements in European antidemocratic politics, anti-Semitism. Anti-Semitism remained widespread in the late nineteenth century, and newspapers and political parties blatantly called themselves anti-Semitic. Vienna elected an anti-Semite, Karl Lueger, as its mayor, and he fired Jewish officials and segregated the schools. In Germany, an Anti-Semite Party elected deputies to the Reichstag in every election from 1887 to 1912 and held eleven to sixteen seats after 1893. In Russia, the pogroms (direct attacks on Jewish communities) killed thousands and led millions to flee the country.

French anti-Semitism produced the most dramatic human rights battle of the nineteenth century—the Dreyfus affair. The French army was one of the few European armies of the 1890s to open its officer corps to Jews, and Captain Alfred Dreyfus was one of three hundred French Jewish officers in the 1890s. Dreyfus was serving as an artillery expert on the French General Staff in 1894 when French counterintelligence found evidence that artillery secrets from the General Staff were reaching the Germans. Bigoted officers convicted Dreyfus of treason and sentenced him to solitary imprisonment on Devil's Island (off the northern coast of South America), although they never possessed a shred of evidence against him (see illustration 27.3). When evidence of Dreyfus's innocence began to accumulate in the late 1890s, Dreyfusards organized to free him. An anti-Dreyfusard coalition of monarchists, Catholics, nationalists, militarists, and anti-Semites defended the army and its verdict. French anti-Semitism, especially the writings of Edouard Drumont (see document 27.2), remained a nasty element throughout the Dreyfus affair, but the battle came to focus on the issues of justice and individual rights balanced against the interests of

Illustration 27.3

The Dreyfus Affair. The 1894 court-martial of Captain Alfred Dreyfus, a Jewish officer on the French General Staff, led to the most passionate human rights debate of the nineteenth century in 1898–99, when the innocence of Captain Dreyfus was discovered but the army refused to reconsider its verdict. The debate between the defenders of Dreyfus and the defenders of the army awakened some of the most vehement anti-Semitism of the century. Here Dreyfus is stripped of his rank and watches his sword being broken before being sent to Devil's Island.

the state. The fight continued until a second court-martial reconvicted Dreyfus in 1899, and an outraged president of the republic pardoned him.

The immediate importance of the Dreyfus affair was that it led to electoral victories for the republicans, radicals, and socialists who defended Dreyfus. This made the left-wing majority feel strong enough to return to its reform agenda. In 1905 they separated church and state, ending both state financial support for, and state regulation of, the churches. In 1906 Clemenceau became premier for the first time (at age sixty-five) and created the first Ministry of Labor, which he entrusted to a socialist. In 1907 feminists won one of their foremost goals, a married women's property act known as the Schmahl Law for the woman who

◆ DOCUMENT 27.2 ◆

Edouard Drumont and Anti-Semitism: La France Juive

Edouard Drumont (1844–1917) was one of the most notorious anti-Semites of the nineteenth century. He published La France juive (Jewish France) in 1886 to show that Jewish interests ruled France. He subsequently founded an anti-Semitic league (1889) and an anti-Semitic newspaper, La Libre parole (Free Speech), which became a leading voice of the anti-Dreyfusard movement. The following excerpt is from La Libre parole.

Nothing changes for them [Jews]: they hate Christ in 1886, just as they hated Christ at the time of Tiberius Caesar, so they cover us with the same outrages. To flog a crucifix on Good Friday, to profane the Host, to soil sacred figures: these were the great joys of the Jew during the middle ages; these are his great joys today. Once upon a time, he molested children; today it is their soul that he wants with atheist education—once they drew blood, now they poison: which works better?. . .

The ghetto doesn't really worship the god of Moses, but the hideous Phoenician deity Moloch, to whom one makes human sacrifices of children and virgins. . . . It's towards him and towards Baal, whose symbol is an ass, that the Jews are endlessly drawn by racial attraction. . . .

Among the illiterate Jews, the hatred of Christianity translates into a brutal movement, an irresistible compulsion. . . . Each day brings us proof of this spirit manifesting itself in a violent. . . . Few days pass without some scandal at a church. . . . Wherever an attack against religion takes on a particularly repulsive and odious character, one finds a German Jew. . . . [T]heir hatred of God reaches a monomania.

Illustration 27.4

Hubertine Auclert. Auclert founded the women's suffrage movement in France in the 1880s and by the early twentieth century had become frustrated enough to consider using violent tactics. Her most famous demonstration—depicted here in an error-filled contemporary sketch—was to invade a Parisian polling place on election day in 1908, smash a ballot box to the ground, and trample on the exclusively masculine votes. The woman with upraised arm at left is Auclert.

Such reforms still left a large democratic agenda on the eve of World War I. Despite feminist electoral violence by Hubertine Auclert and Madeleine Pelletier in 1908 (see illustration 27.4) and the peaceful demonstrations of hundreds of thousands of suffragists, women's suffrage remained far from acceptance. Despite greater labor violence and equally large demonstrations, the forty-hour workweek remained a utopian dream. Despite their electoral successes, the Radicals were unable to win a majority for proportional representation, the right of government employees to strike, a graduated income tax, maternity leaves for new mothers, or the abolition of the death penalty. Simply debating such issues, however, made France a leader of European democratic thought.

had campaigned for it. The radicals also laid the basis of the French welfare system. Earlier governments had established state aid for neglected children (1889) and a medical assistance program (1893). Republicans now provided state support for hygienic housing (1902), needy children (1904), the aged and the infirm (1905–1906), retirement pensions (1910), and large families (1913).

Late Victorian and Edwardian Britain

Great Britain also remained a leader in the evolution of liberal-democratic institutions. Smaller states were often pioneers in adopting radical reforms—as the Scandinavian states were with women's rights—but Britain and France defined the model of parliamentary democracy for the great powers. The British model remained one of gradual evolution, but the years before 1914 witnessed two important periods of rapid change.

The first period of intensive reform came during a Liberal government of 1868–74, elected after the expansion of the franchise in 1867. The leader of this government was one the greatest figures of nineteenth-century liberalism, William E. Gladstone. Gladstone had been elected to Parliament at twenty-two, following a brilliant career at Oxford in which he had won first-class honors in two separate fields. He began his career as a cabinet minister at thirty-four and served as an M.P. for more than sixty years. Gladstone served four terms as prime minister of Britain, beginning with his "great ministry" (1868–74) and ending with a cabinet in his eighties (1892–94). He brought to government a religious scholar's moralistic temperament that made him resemble an Old Testament patriarch. One contemporary summarized him, "If he were soaked in boiling water and rinsed till he was twisted into a rope, I do not suppose a drop of fun would ooze out." Gladstone supported his moralism with an intellect that dominated Parliament. He could speak for three hours without a break or summarize an arduous debate with a long quotation in untranslated Latin, leaving few M.P.s to match him.

Gladstone's great ministry adopted nearly a dozen major reforms. He did not attempt another expansion of the franchise (although that was on his agenda) or to give women the vote (which was not in his plans). He did, however, enhance British democracy with a Secret Ballot Act of 1872. His government laid the basis for a modern educational system in Britain, making significant reforms from primary schools to universities. The Elementary Education Act of 1870 (known as the Forster Act for its author, William Forster) made primary schooling available to all children in England and Wales, from age five to thirteen. In contrast to the Ferry laws in France, the Forster Act subsidized private, tuition-paying schools and created state schools only, as Forster put it, "to complete the present voluntary system, to fill up the gaps." In Britain as in France, adult illiteracy quickly fell, from 20 percent of adult males

(1870) to 2 percent (1900). Gladstone similarly opened higher education. A University Tests Act (1871) abolished religious barriers to enrollment at Oxford and Cambridge, permitting Catholics, Jews, and nonbelievers to matriculate. At the same time, two colleges at Cambridge were opened to women, although women remained ineligible for degrees until after World War I.

Gladstone's government also tackled army reform, judicial reform, trade union rights, the civil service, and the Irish question. The sale of commissions as officers in the army was abolished, and the term of military enlistment was reduced from twelve years to six. Judicial reforms ended imprisonment for debt and created appellate courts. Workers won the complete legalization of unions and the recognition of their right to strike, but not the right to picket their employers. Civil service reforms created a modern bureaucracy by abolishing the patronage system of giving jobs to friends and supporters in favor of competitive examinations for all posts except those in the Foreign Office. Gladstone's great ministry also began to address the Irish question. An Irish Land Act gave some protection to Irish farmers who rented lands and could be evicted after poor harvests. Gladstone also disestablished the Church of Ireland (the Anglican Church in Ireland), meaning that the people of Ireland (90 percent Catholic) were no longer required to provide tax support for a Protestant state church. Such reforms built cooperation between the Liberal Party and Irish M.P.s, who pressed Gladstone to take the next logical step—grant the Irish home rule in domestic matters.

The end of Gladstone's great ministry returned to office his long-time rival, the conservative prime minister Benjamin Disraeli. In contrast to Gladstone's sober strengths, Disraeli sparkled with wit and style. He derided Gladstone's much-praised oratory as "hare-brained chatter." Disraeli had flirted with reforms in his earlier career, but in his second term as prime minister (1874–80), he steered a more traditional course, satisfying conservatives opposed to liberal reformism. As one conservative essayist, Thomas Carlyle, had summarized the attack on Gladstonian liberalism: Britain was a nation of "mostly fools" and it was dangerous to "believe in the collective wisdom of individual ignorance." Disraeli shrewdly turned the government's attention away from domestic issues and aimed for British success in foreign and colonial affairs.

Gladstone returned to his reform agenda in a second ministry (1880–85) after shocking conservatives by introducing campaigning to British politics; he toured

❧ TABLE 27.1 ❧

The Democratization of the British Electorate, 1831–86

	England and Wales		Scotland		Ireland		United Kingdom	
Year	Eligible voters	Percentage of total population	Eligible voters	Percentage of total population	Eligible voters	Percentage of total population	Eligible voters	Percentage of total population
1831	435,000	3.1	5,000	0.2	76,000	0.9	516,000	2.1
1833	656,000	3.5	64,000	2.7	92,000	1.2	812,000	3.4
1866	1,054,000	5.3	105,000	3.4	205,000	3.5	1,364,000	4.7
1868	1,960,000	9.8	236,000	7.7	222,000	3.8	2,418,000	8.4
1883	2,618,000	10.1	310,000	8.3	224,000	4.3	3,152,000	9.0
1885	4,380,000	16.9	551,000	14.7	738,000	14.3	5,669,000	16.3

Source: Compiled from data in Chris Cook and Brendan Keith, *British Historical Facts, 1830–1900* (London: MacMillan, 1975), pp. 115, 232–33.

the nation and appealed directly to the voters. This time Gladstone sought democratization and Irish home rule. His Representation of the People Bill (1884) extended the vote in rural Britain and brought the kingdom closer to the universal manhood suffrage that existed in France and Germany. The Reform Bill of 1832 had enfranchised nearly 300,000 new voters and Disraeli's Reform Bill of 1867 more than one million; Gladstone added 2.5 million people to the electorate (see table 27.1). Domestic servants were still denied the vote, as were all women. Gladstone added an act redistributing seats in Parliament, a Corrupt Practices Act limiting campaign spending, and an Affirmation Act allowing nonbelievers to serve in Parliament.

The Irish question presented greater difficulties. Home rule had become the objective of Irish politicians in the 1870s when Isaac Butt, a lawyer and the son of a Protestant clergyman, had formed a coalition of Catholics and Protestants to seek it. When Butt's movement won the support of most Irish M.P.s in 1874, it became the Irish Home Rule League. A few years later, the league found a popular successor to Butt in Charles Stewart Parnell, a Protestant landowner who had entered Parliament in 1875 at twenty-nine. Parnell managed to unite Irish nationalists, including the more militant and republican Fenians; the British increased his popularity by imprisoning him and watching while he organized a farmers' rent strike from his cell. Parnell denounced revolutionary violence in 1882, after the assassination in Dublin of the two leading cabinet members for the government of Ireland, an act known as the Phoenix Park murders. Parnell and his followers developed nonviolent tactics such as the boycott of uncooperative landlords; the name of that tactic came from a

campaign in which no servants, no farm workers, no shopkeepers, not even a postman would acknowledge the existence of a landlord in County Mayo named Charles Boycott.

Gladstone adopted the cause of home rule in 1886 and introduced the first Home Rule Bill with a three-and-one-half-hour speech at the age of seventy-seven. This issue shattered the Liberal Party. Ninety-two Liberal M.P.s, led by the prominent Liberal spokesman of the 1840s, John Bright, and Bright's protégé, a wealthy manufacturer from Birmingham, Joseph Chamberlain, left the party and formed their own faction, the Unionists. Gladstone strove to build a majority in favor of home rule but suffered another setback when Irish M.P.s were divided by a scandal over Parnell's love affair with the wife of another M.P. Gladstone defended Parnell, observing that "I have known eleven prime ministers, ten of whom were adulterers," but Parnell's career, and the chances for home rule, were ruined. Gladstone obtained the prime ministry for the fourth time in 1892. He introduced a second Home Rule Bill a few months later (1893), and his Liberal majority carried it through the House of Commons. A decade of debate, however, had entrenched conservative opposition to home rule. An aggressive Tory M.P. who had once led the progressive wing of the party, Lord Randolph Churchill, fought Gladstone under the slogan "Home Rule Means Rome Rule." This campaign encouraged resistance in the Protestant population of northern Ireland, where militants warned that "Ulster will fight." Such passions led the conservative majority in the House of Lords to crush the second Home Rule Bill, 419–41.

❖ DOCUMENT 27.3 ❖

Lloyd George: The "People's Budget"

We started [construction of] our four "Dreadnoughts" [battleships]. They cost eight millions [£] of money. . . . Somebody has to pay, and then these gentlemen [conservatives] say, "Perfectly true; somebody has to pay, but we would rather that somebody were somebody else. . . . They say, "It is not so much the Dreadnoughts we object to, it is the pensions. . . ."

The provision for the aged and deserving poor—was it not time something was done? It is rather a shame that a rich country like ours—probably the richest in the world, if not the richest the world has ever seen—should allow those who toiled all their days to end in penury and possibly starvation. It is rather hard that an old workman should have to find his way to the gates of the tomb, bleeding and footsore, through the brambles and thorns of poverty. We cut a new path for him. . . : There are many in the country blessed by Providence with great wealth, and if there are amongst them men who grudge out of their riches a fair contribution towards the less fortunate of their fellow countrymen they are very shabby rich men.

We propose to do more by means of the Budget. We are raising money to provide against the evils and sufferings that follow from unemployment. We are raising money for the purpose of assisting . . . to provide for the sick and the widows and orphans. . . .

Some of our critics say, "The taxes themselves are unjust, unfair, unequal, oppressive—notably so the land taxes. . . ." They are now protesting against paying their fair share of the taxation of the land, and they are doing so by saying, ". . . You are putting burdens upon the people which they cannot bear." Ah! they are not thinking of themselves. Noble souls! . . . [W]e were so impressed by this tearful appeal that at last we said, "We will leave [small landowners] out."

The early twentieth century witnessed a second period of radical reform in Britain, comparable to Gladstone's great ministry. The Liberal Party built a new majority in 1905, sometimes supported by the twenty-nine M.P.s of the new Labour Party, which had been organized in 1906 by a Scottish miner, Keir Hardie, and a Scottish journalist, Ramsay MacDonald. One of the first legislative actions of the new government, the Trades Disputes Act of 1906, responded to labor's greatest grievance. Gladstone's Trades Disputes Act of 1871 had given legal recognition to unions, and they had gradually gained such rights as picketing. In 1901, however, the House of Lords had rendered a dramatically antilabor ruling in a legal case known as the *Taff Vale Railway Company v. Amalgamated Society of Railway Servants*. The *Taff Vale* ruling held that a union could be sued for the actions of its members and that a union could be held liable for a company's losses during a strike. The Liberal government of 1906 repaid labor support by overturning the *Taff Vale* decision and restoring the right to strike and picket, through the Trade Disputes Act.

The Liberal coalition found its radical voice in David Lloyd George, who typified the changing nature of liberalism from a laissez-faire doctrine of noninterventionist government to an activist doctrine of governmental intervention to protect the vulnerable. A Welsh lawyer possessed of a charming yet ferocious mastery of debate, Lloyd George drafted the government's economic policies as chancellor of the exchequer (minister of finance) and led Britain into the age of welfare legislation. A Workmen's Compensation Act (1906) greatly expanded benefits; an Old Age Pensions Act (1909) replaced the workhouse system; and the National Insurance Act (1912) introduced health and unemployment insurance. The cornerstone of the liberal welfare state was the budget that Lloyd George introduced in 1909. The "people's budget" attacked the conservative tradition that the state could spend large sums for military preparations (such as large new battleships) but not for social welfare (see document 27.3). Lloyd George further angered conservatives by proposing to pay for these expenditures by taxes on the rich.

The Lloyd George budget led to the democratization of Parliament (by ending the power of the House of Lords to block legislation) and therefore to hopes for a third Home Rule Bill. The Lords, which remained an unelected body defending the interests of the landed aristocracy, traditionally held the power to veto any legislation except a budget. Lloyd George, however,

◆ DOCUMENT 27.4 ◆

Pobedonostsev: Conservative Critique of Democracy, 1898

Konstantin Pobedonostsev expressed his opposition to the liberalization of Russia in his memoirs, published after Count Sergei Witte had begun to lead Russia toward westernization.

Among the falsest of political principles is the principle of the sovereignty of the people, the principle that all power issues from the people, and is based upon the national will—a principle which has unhappily become more firmly established since the time of the French revolution. From it proceeds the principle of parliamentarianism, which, today has deluded much of the so-called "intelligentsia," and has unfortunately infatuated certain foolish Russians. It continues to maintain its hold on many minds with the obstinacy of a narrow fanaticism, although every day its falsehood is exposed more clearly to the world. . . .

What is this freedom by which so many minds are agitated, which inspires so many insensate actions, so many wild speeches, which leads the people so often to misfortune? In the democratic sense of the word, freedom is the right to political power, or, to express it otherwise, the right to participate in the government of the state. This universal aspiration for a share in government has no constant limitations, and seeks no definite issue, but incessantly extends. . . . Forever extending its base, the new democracy now aspires to universal suffrage—a fatal error, and one of the most remarkable in the history of mankind. By this means, the political power so passionately demanded by Democracy would be shattered into a number of infinitesimal bits, of which each citizen acquires one. What will he do with it, then? How will he employ it? In the result it has undoubtedly been shown that in the attainment of this aim Democracy violates its sacred formula of "Freedom indissolubly joined with Equality." It is shown that this apparently equal distribution of "freedom" among all involves the total destruction of equality. Each vote, representing an inconsiderable fragment of power, by itself signifies nothing; an aggregation of votes alone has a relative value. The result may be likened to the general meetings of shareholders in public companies. By themselves, individuals are ineffective, but he who controls a number of these fragmentary forces is master of all power, and directs all decisions and dispositions. We may well ask in what consists the superiority of Democracy. Everywhere the strongest man becomes master of the state; sometimes a fortunate and resolute general, sometimes a monarch or administrator with knowledge, dexterity, a clear plan of action, and a determined will. In a Democracy, the real rulers are the dexterous manipulators of votes. . . . [T]hey rule the people as any despot or military dictator might rule it.

Pobedonostsev's slavophilic insistence upon guarding Russia's separate historic evolution.

The Russia of the 1890s had far to go before it could compete with western Europe. The empire had a large labor supply, but restraints remained upon its mobility, because of the obligation of former serfs to help their commune repay the redemption bonds given to the landowners at the time of emancipation. Nearly 10 percent of the imperial budget depended upon these redemption payments, and rural communities kept a maximum working population in the fields. Factories consequently remained few in number and small in size before the expansion of the 1890s. A study of Ukraine has shown that factories tripled their average workforce (to forty-six hundred workers) during that decade. Russian agriculture had the potential to feed this urban population and to raise capital by exporting surpluses, but it remained too backward to fulfill the promise. At the turn-of-the-century (1898–1902), Russian farmers produced an average yield of 8.8 bushels of grain per acre, whereas British farmers supported an urban population by producing 35.4 bushels per acre. As late as 1912 the entire Russian Empire contained a total of 166 tractors.

Sergei Witte addressed Russian backwardness in several ways. Taxes on the sale of alcoholic spirits provided the largest source of revenue so Witte built a state monopoly on such sales. He put the Russian currency (the ruble) on the gold standard, to enhance credit with foreign lenders. Russia already carried a large national debt, which amounted to 5.5 billion rubles in 1891—nearly six times the annual budget of the empire (see table 27.2). Such debt had become so integral to European economics that Russia was still repaying Dutch loans of 1778 and 1815 and devoted nearly 27 percent of its budget to loan repayments. Witte believed that "[n]o country has ever developed without foreign capital" and sought new loans. He used

❧ TABLE 27.2 ❧

The Imperial Russian Budget for 1891

Anticipated revenue Amount (in rubles)		Anticipated expenses Amount (in rubles)	
Direct taxes		Military	
Land taxes	42,984,000	War Ministry	226,652,000
Trade licences	33,930,000	Navy Ministry	43,760,900
Tax on capital	11,906,000	Armaments	20,000,000
Total direct taxes	88,820,000	Total military	290,412,000
Indirect taxes		Other ministries	
Alcohol	259,481,000	Ministry of Finance	115,068,000
Sugar	20,161,000	Ministry of Interior	80,297,000
Fuel	9,529,000	Ministry of Justice	24,102,000
Matches	4,524,000	Ministry of Education	22,936,000
Stamp duties	59,075,000	Ministry of Religion	11,356,000
Tariffs	110,655,000	Foreign Ministry	4,951,000
Tobacco	28,205,000	State institutions	2,081,000
		Other	5,544,000
Total indirect taxes	491,630,000		
		Total other ministries	266,335,000
Peasant redemption payments		Transportation	
State peasants	53,432,000	Ministry	57,367,000
Liberated serfs	42,270,000	Railroad fund	42,914,000
Total peasant redemption payments	95,702,000	Total transportation	100,281,000
Extraordinary income		Monarchy	
(Bonds, loans, deposits)	65,104,000	Imperial household	10,560,000
		State domains	25,915,000
		Total monarchy	36,475,000
Other income			
State domains	88,879,000	Debt repayment and interest	
State offices	34,868,000	State bonds	191,589,000
Miscellaneous	97,300,000	Railway bonds	65,153,000
Total other income	221,047,000	Total dept repayment and interest	256,742,000
		Other	12,058,000
Total anticipated revenue	962,303,000	Total anticipated expenses	962,303,000
Imperial debt Amount (in rubles)			
State debt	3,594,731,000		
Railroad bonds	1,465,379,000		
Redemption bonds	465,130,000		
Total imperial debt	5,525,240,000		

Source: J. Scott Keltie, ed., *The Statesman's Yearbook, 1891* (London: Macmillan, 1891), pp. 861–64.

this investment to found a national bank, provide state aid in building factories, and construct the Russian railroad system. Witte created a system of state-controlled (60 percent ownership) railways. He doubled the total of working track in Russia during the 1890s, including the construction of the Trans-Siberian Railroad, a five-thousand-mile link between Moscow and the Pacific port of Vladivostok. The cost of this program, however, was a national debt so severe that state supported progress in other areas was impossible.

Industrialization increased political discontent. The living and working conditions that characterized early industrialization everywhere increased the revolutionary violence that Russia had experienced for a generation. Attempted assassinations became a regular feature of Russian politics. During the 1890s two prime ministers, an education minister, a provincial governor, and an uncle of the czar were among those killed. With no Parliament, underground radical parties flourished. Plekhanov organized the Russian Social Democratic Party in 1898, and agrarian radicals from the populist tradition created a competing organization, the Socialist Revolutionary Party, in 1901. This underground—largely led by people from educated, middle-class backgrounds—became more complex in 1903 when the Social Democrats held a party congress in London and split in two. That congress marked the emergence of Lenin in Russian revolutionary politics. Lenin (the adopted name of a lawyer born Vladimir Ulyanov) was radicalized by the execution of his older brother for plotting against the czar. Arrested in 1895 and sent to Siberia for spreading propaganda in St. Petersburg, Lenin reached Switzerland in 1900 and there published a revolutionary newspaper, *Iskra* (the Spark), to be smuggled into Russia. He joined Plekhanov (also an intellectual living in exile) in building the Social Democratic Party, but he soon rejected Plekhanov's idealistic socialism in favor of a more revolutionary doctrine. Lenin called for a small party of revolutionary leaders instead of a mass movement. In a clever propaganda stroke, Lenin named his small faction of the party the Bolsheviks (the majority), branding the more numerous supporters of Plekhanov the Mensheviks (the minority). Lenin remained in exile, however, throughout the following decade.

In addition to the underground activities of the Social Democrats and the Social Revolutionaries, open opposition existed to czarist autocracy among liberal-democratic westernizers. This movement drew its strength from the intelligentsia, the liberal professions, educated urban circles, and *zemstvo* workers who combined to organize the Union of Liberation in 1903. This group was a nascent liberal political party, critical of autocracy and calling for a constitution, a parliament, and a bill of rights.

Russia experienced a major revolution in 1905. Crushing defeat in the Russo-Japanese War of 1904–1905, a colonial war that followed the "opening of China" in 1898 (see chapter 28), led to this revolt. In mid-1904, Plehve was killed in a terrorist bombing. A few weeks later, *zemstvo* delegates assembled for a congress in St. Petersburg and asked Nicholas II to call a Russian Parliament. During the winter of 1904–1905, as the Russian army suffered reverses in the Orient, strikes and demonstrations began. A turning point came in January when an Orthodox missionary to the working-class slums of St. Petersburg, George Gapon, led a protest march to deliver a petition to Nicholas II.

Gapon (known as Father Gapon, although he had not completed his study for the priesthood) had been organizing illegal trade unions since 1903 and had recently led his followers out on strike. Their petition to the czar called for Russian democracy and help for workers and peasants. Before Father Gapon's marchers could reach the royal palace, however, the army fired upon them (see illustration 27.6). Seventy marchers were killed and 240 wounded in this "Bloody Sunday" massacre. Gapon escaped to London but was assassinated there. Strikes, demonstrations, and a naval mutiny (aboard the battleship *Potemkin* in the Black Sea) followed.

Nicholas II vacillated in response to the revolution of 1905. Count Witte was not a great champion of liberalism, but he was a pragmatist. He encouraged the czar to concede, and he drafted the documents (the August Manifesto and the October Manifesto) in which Nicholas did so. The August Manifesto promised a limited Parliament (the *Duma*) to be elected by limited suffrage. When unrest continued and a general strike was called, Nicholas II granted further concessions in the October Manifesto: a Russian constitution, a Duma with significant legislative powers, and virtually universal suffrage. The Russian Constitution of 1906 did not mark the complete surrender of autocracy. It opened with a section entitled "On the Nature of the Supreme Autocratic Power." Article Four of that section stated: "Supreme autocratic power belongs to the Emperor of All the Russias. To obey his power, not only through fear but also by conscience, is commanded by God Himself." Subsequent articles gave the czar the sole right to introduce legislation, an absolute veto over any work of the Duma, and the power to name or dismiss the government. Nicholas II nonetheless detested the constitution and soon fired Witte for leading him to it.

Four turbulent Dumas met under this constitution. The first two lasted for a few months in 1906 and 1907 before the czar prorogued them. Nicholas II decreed a new electoral law in 1907, giving greater representation to the wealthy, so the Third Duma (1907–12) obtained a conservative majority. Even middle-class liberals, organized as the Constitutional Democratic Party (known by a Russian abbreviation, the Kadets) under the leadership of Professor Paul Milyukov, opposed this government, angry that meaningful reform moved at a maddeningly slow pace. Nicholas II had promised in 1904 a program of accident and illness insurance for workers. That idea, the first piece of Russian welfare legislation, led to a draft policy in 1905, a proposal to the Duma in 1908, study by a special committee in 1910–11, and debate by the Duma in 1912.

Illustration 27.6

The Revolution of 1905. One of the decisive moments in the Revolution of 1905 came on Sunday, January 22. After three weeks of strikes and five days of a general strike, a procession of workers marched to the Winter Palace in St. Petersburg to present a petition to the czar. As the marchers neared the palace, troops opened fire on them, killing seventy and wounding 240 in what became known as "Bloody Sunday." This massacre made a quick end to labor unrest unlikely.

The dominant political figure of the Duma was the new prime minister (1906–11), Peter Stolypin, a conservative noble who had won favor for his role in suppressing the revolution in the provinces. Stolypin was not a simple antiparliamentary reactionary. He accepted the Duma and the principle of liberal modernization, but within the context of strictly enforced law and order. He met radical extremism with state extremism, and Russia saw both in large quantities. Historians have estimated that seventeen thousand terrorist assassinations (in twenty-three thousand attempts) took place between 1905 and 1914. Any official was a target. In a single day, attempts were made on every policeman walking the streets of Warsaw and Lodz; on another, one-fourth of the police force of Riga was killed. Terrorists still favored bombs and even used small children to deliver them; the youngest arrested was an eleven-year-old girl who had been paid fifty kopecks (approximately twenty-five cents) for the job.

Stolypin responded with both state violence and noteworthy reforms. He allowed instant trials in the field and the execution of sentences on the spot. Suspected terrorists were hanged in such numbers that the noose became known as a "Stolypin necktie." At the same time, however, he liberalized censorship, expanded education, and defended freedom of religion. Perhaps the most important idea of Stolypin's government was support for peasant landownership. This program created a class of nine million landowning peasants in Russia by 1914. No legislation could save

Stolypin, however. He was the most hated man in Russia, and he was shot to death (by an assassin who could have killed the czar instead) at the Kiev Opera House in 1911. This level of hatred and violence did not augur well for the solution of Russia's manifold problems, and time was running out. Stolypin's successors were increasingly consumed by foreign problems in the Balkans, problems that would soon lead to another war, another disastrous defeat, and another violent revolution.

Belle Époque Democracy around Europe

The great powers of Europe were significantly more democratic in 1914 than they had been in 1870. The French had abolished monarchy and created the first enduring republic among the great powers, with a parliamentary democracy based upon universal manhood suffrage and ministerial responsibility. The British had undertaken two periods of democratization when Gladstone more than doubled the electorate in 1884 and Lloyd George had broken the power of the House of Lords in 1911. The newly unified Germany was significantly less democratic than Britain and France—lacking such features as ministerial responsibility—but it had constitutional government that included a Parliament elected by universal manhood suffrage. Even the most autocratic state, Russia advanced toward the democratic model in the constitution of 1906 and the creation of the Duma elected by universal suffrage. Europe was clearly moving toward an age of mass participation in politics.

Many of the other states of Europe shared in this trend. Newly unified Italy shared the Piedmontese constitution and parliamentary government on the west European model. Post-Risorgimento Italy began with a limited franchise on the British model and democratized further in the 1880s under the leadership of Agostino Depretis before being led to universal suffrage by Giovanni Giolitti and the Liberal Party in 1912. A similar pattern of gradual democratization existed in many of the smaller states of western Europe. In Belgium, for example, a period of reform in the 1890s led to the direct election of the upper house of Parliament—a reform comparable to French democratization of the Senate in the 1880s and to the British restriction of the House of Lords in 1911. In 1899 Belgium became one of the European pioneers of proportional representation, an advanced form of democratic election in which smaller parties and minorities had a greater chance of being elected. Similarly, the Netherlands followed this general pattern of democratization with a major constitutional reform of 1887, which doubled the electorate; another reform of 1896 doubled it again. In Scandinavia, the trend toward democracy was even stronger. Norway, which became independent from Sweden in a peaceful agreement of 1905, adopted universal manhood suffrage and a pioneering form of women's suffrage in 1907. The Swedes also adopted universal manhood suffrage and the Finns, women's suffrage. Even Ottoman Turkey received a constitution from the Sultan, creating a bicameral legislature, in 1876; Turkish democracy, like German or Russian democracy, was limited yet a dramatic advance from the government of earlier generations.

The pattern of evolving democracy could not hide many European political problems, however. Nationalism was perhaps the most severe, troubling governments across Europe—from the Irish question in Britain to the Polish problem in Russia and Pan-Slavic nationalism in the Balkans. No government faced a more severe challenge than the dual monarchy of Austria-Hungary, which had emerged from the *Ausgleich* of 1867. This empire was an anachronism in 1900, a multinational state held together by historic obedience to the Hapsburg monarchy (see map 27.2). According to the census of 1910, the dominant German population of Austria constituted less than 24 percent of the total population, and the Magyar population of Hungary added slightly more than 20 percent; that is, the majority of the people living in the Austro-Hungarian Empire were neither Austrian nor Hungarian. More than 10 percent of the empire was Polish because the northeastern territories included the Polish province of Galicia and part of Silesia, obtained in the eighteenth-century partition of Poland. The northwest contained a large Czech population (nearly 13 percent) in the provinces of Bohemia and Moravia; adjacent regions in the Hungarian portion of the empire held large Slovak, Ruthenian, and Romanian populations (16 percent of the empire). In the south, the Hapsburgs still governed an Italian minority (2 percent) and expansion into the Balkans had acquired a larged population of southern Slavs—Slovenes, Croats, Bosnians, and Serbs—(nearly 13 percent). The ethnic mixture of the empire was further complicated by religious divisions: Slightly more than three-fourths of the population were Catholic (including splinter churches), with large minorities of Protestants and Orthodox Christians (nearly 9 percent

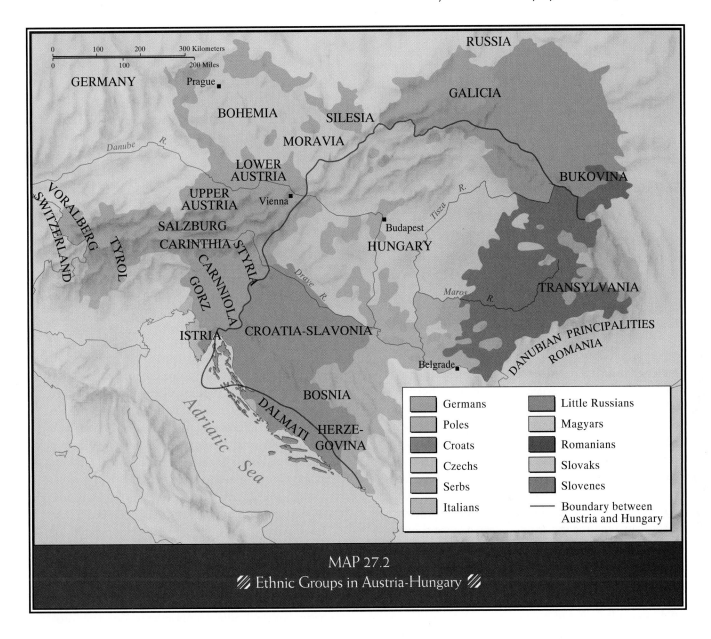

MAP 27.2

%% Ethnic Groups in Austria-Hungary %%

each) plus significant populations of Jews (4 percent) and Moslems (more than 1 percent, concentrated in the Balkans). The Jewish population of the Austro-Hungarian Empire presented more than 26 percent of the world population, second only to Russia's 37 percent; Vienna had a Jewish population of 175,000 and Budapest was the largest Jewish city on earth with 203,000 Jews (23 percent of the city). Just as the national divisions of the empire produced constant strife and nationalist revolutionary groups, the religious minorities dealt with severe anti-Semitism and anti-Islamic prejudices. The ethnic divisions of the empire made the dual monarchy a volatile society, and the consequences of this would soon be tragedy for Europe.

The Rise of Trade Unionism and Socialism

In addition to nationalism, the Belle Époque faced the second critical problem of responding to the consequences of continuing industrialization. A second industrial revolution during the later nineteenth century shared many characteristics of early industrialization. It saw rapid population growth, steady urbanization, and an agricultural revolution sufficient to feed the cities. But many changes also were evident in the new industrialization. The European economy overcame the dominance of Britain. Germany (and the United States)

Illustration 27.7

▨ **The Second Industrial Revolution.** European industrial growth in the late nineteenth century was characterized by the growth of new industries such as the chemical industry, by the increasing use of steel instead of iron, and by the arrival of new sources of power such as electricity. The era of practical electrical power began in the 1880s, but steam remained the dominant source of power into the twentieth century. This photograph of a German factory shows a moment in the transition to electrical power: Light bulbs are being mass-produced, but they are still being handmade by glass-blowers, then individually inspected.

matched British industrialization, and many countries were sufficiently industrialized to compete effectively. The foci of industrialization also changed: Steel replaced iron at the center of heavy industry, electricity began to replace steam as the source of industrial power, and new industries such as the chemical industry challenged the preeminence of textiles (see illustration 27.7).

The population boom that accompanied industrialization affected the entire continent of Europe, but it had special importance in central Europe. In 1800 the states that later formed Germany had a combined population of 18.5 million people. This was larger than the population of the Austrian Empire, the Italian states, or even Great Britain, but it provided few competitive advantages. France dwarfed the German states with a population of 26.9 million. By 1900, however, the German Empire had experienced the population explosion and grown to 56.4 million, while neighboring France had no such population boom and numbered only 39 million people. Much of the economic history, and the political history, of the nineteenth century is contained in this demographic data: France was 45 percent larger than Germany at the start of the century, but Germany was 45 percent larger than France at the end of the century.

This population trend was especially vivid in the urbanization of Germany. In 1880 Britain remained the only country in the world where a majority of the population lived in towns and cities. Belgium, which had led early industrialization on the continent, was drawing close at 43 percent urban, but both France and Ger-

many remained merely one-third urban. By the early years of the twentieth century, Germany had changed into an urban society. In 1800 Berlin's 172,000 people had made it the largest city in the German states; in 1910 unified Germany contained seventeen cities larger than Berlin had been, including the industrial cities of Essen and Duisberg in the Rhineland that had grown from sleepy villages of 4,000 people into capitals of heavy industry with populations over 200,000.

As in Britain, the continuing population explosion and urbanization in Europe were made possible by dramatic improvements in the food supply. For most of the continent, the historic epoch of subsistence and periodic famine had ended. The improvement was so dramatic that the leading economist in Germany proclaimed "emancipation from the bonds of nature." A significant part of the increased food supply was the result of the success of industrialization. The development of inorganic fertilizers greatly increased food production in countries—such as Germany—that possessed a strong chemical industry. The revolution in farm machinery also expanded European production. French farmers, for example, were conservative and slow to accept new machinery. Yet between 1888 and 1908 French agriculture changed from a national total of two hundred reaping machines and fifty harvesters to fifteen thousand reaping machines and twenty-five thousand harvesters.

The European food supply also profited greatly from importation. Vast tracts of rich virgin soil were being plowed in Argentina, Australia, Canada, Russia, and the United States. The acceptance of food in tin cans,

TABLE 27.3

European Steel Production, 1871–1911

Country	Output of steel in tons		
	1871	1891	1911
Austria-Hungary	36,000	495,000	2,174,000
Belgium	n.a.	222,000	2,028,000
Britain	334,000	3,208,000	6,566,000
France	80,000	744,000	3,837,000
Germany	143,000	2,452,000	14,303,000
Italy	n.a.	76,000	736,000
Luxembourg	n.a.	111,000	716,000
Russia	7,000	434,000	3,949,000
Spain	n.a.	90,000	323,000
Sweden	9,000	172,000	471,000

Source: Compiled from data in B. R. Mitchell, *European Historical Statistics, 1750–1970* (London: Macmillan, 1975), pp. 399–401.

the invention of ammonia-based refrigeration, and the availability of quick and inexpensive steam shipping brought the harvest of the world to the tables of Europe. Grain from the American Middle West cost 53¢ per bushel to ship from Chicago to London in 1870; by 1919 that price had fallen to 16¢ per bushel. The price of wheat in Europe consequently tumbled from $1.50 per bushel in 1870 to 85¢ per bushel in 1900.

The greatest stimulus to the second industrial revolution came from new materials, new energy, and new industries. Steel became the symbol of the new industrialization (see table 27.3). The making of steel—distinguished from iron by a higher carbon content—has been known since ancient times. It was preferred for its hardness, its strength in relation to weight, and its plasticity, but the process required to adjust the carbon content in steel had long been too expensive for widespread use. In the 1850s a British metallurgist named Henry Bessemer invented a simpler process for making steel. By sending a blast of air through molten iron, Bessemer was able to heat iron to the point where it obtained the desired carbon content. By the 1870s Bessemer's "blast furnaces" were being widely adopted in industrial countries because governments craved steel for heavy artillery, railroads, and warships. In 1871 the total European output was less than 1 million tons of steel; in 1913 tiny Luxembourg alone produced 1.3 million tons of steel. Britain had entered the steel age with the continuing advantage of plentiful iron and coal plus the pioneering role in blast furnace development. But Britain did not start with an insurmountable lead. Germany, which also possessed abundant iron and coal,

closed the production gap in the 1880s and passed Britain in steel production in the 1890s. By the start of the twentieth century, Germany produced 20 percent more steel than Britain. In 1911 Germany produced as much steel as Britain, France, and Russia combined, and on the eve of World War I, German steel production stood at eighteen times the European total of 1870. The second industrial revolution had broken the industrial dominance of Britain.

The German leadership of the second industrial revolution was even more notable in chemical industries. Chemical engineering shaped late nineteenth-century industrialization just as mechanical engineering had shaped early industrialization. The initial importance of chemistry came in the textile industry: The manufacture of cotton cloth required large quantities of alkalis, sulfuric acid, and dyes, and the expansion of textile manufactures necessitated expansion of chemical industries. Many noted chemical industries, such Friedrich Bayer's company in Germany, originated in supporting the textile industry. Bayer developed synthetic dyes from coal tar to replace the natural dyes used to color cloth; his aniline dyes permitted a vast range of new, durable colors in clothing and became a tremendous commercial success. Bayer and Company soon diversified and developed other products, such as the first aspirin, patented in 1899.

One of the consequences of this continuing industrialization and urbanization was that the largest social issue confronting governments was the question of the working class. Most workers lived arduous lives and had many valid grievances. Rapid urbanization had produced dreadful living conditions in working-class slums. The importation of cheap food improved the diet of most workers, but it also led to the depression of 1873–94 with periodic high unemployment. A study of the London working class in 1887 found that 52.3 percent of the population experienced short-term unemployment and 30.1 percent of the population was unemployed for twelve weeks or more. Governments slowly emulated the Bismarckian welfare laws of the 1880s and offered workers some measure of unemployment insurance, accident compensation, health care, or retirement benefits, but the welfare state was still in a rudimentary form and provided limited security. Working conditions were deplorable in many occupations. The coal miners and steel workers whose labor sustained heavy industry had life expectancies ten years less than other men; those who operated a Bessemer blast furnace frequently died in their thirties. Most jobs required a minimum of five-and-one-half ten-hour days per week, and many expected six twelve-hour days (see

TABLE 27.4

The Average Workweek of the 1890s

Occupation	Hours in Britain	Hours in France
Baker	70	78–96
Brickmaker	54–69	96–108
Chemical worker	53–70	64.5–72
Construction	50–55	72–48
Foundry	48–72	72–84
Metalworker	54	63–66
Miners	42.5–55	51–60
Paper worker	66–78	63
Printer	53–54	60
Railway ticket agent	56–62	90–96
Railway guard	64–70	96–108
Restaurant waiter	96	101
Textile worker	56	66–72
Tailor	54–96	66–96

Source: Gary Cross, *A Quest for Time: The Reduction of Work in Britain and France, 1840–1940* (Berkeley, Calif.: University of California Press, 1989), p. 235. Used by permission of the publisher.

table 27.4). Minimum wage legislation, overtime pay, and paid vacations did not exist.

Trade unions grew quickly under these conditions, as a new wave of unionization spread from the skilled crafts to less skilled occupations. By the early twentieth century, the leading industrial states (Britain, Germany, and the United States) each counted more than a million union members (see table 27.5). In Britain, more than 20 percent of the adult population belonged to unions in 1913. Elsewhere, lesser industrialization and restrictive legislation kept union membership smaller. Spanish unions included only 0.02 percent of the population in 1889 and 0.2 percent in 1910. Two patterns were clear: Only a minority of workers belonged to unions, but their numbers were growing significantly. As their membership grew, trade unions called strikes to win improved conditions (see table 27.6). Turn-of-the-century France experienced an average of nearly 1,000 industrial strikes per year, reaching a peak of 1,319 strikes involving 509,274 strikers in 1906. A study of these strikes has found that 56 percent sought higher wages, 15 percent sought shorter working hours, 13 percent sought the rehiring of fired workers, and 4 percent sought the abolition of certain work rules. By the eve of World War I, Britain, France, and Germany were each losing nearly five million working days to strikes every year; Europe was entering an age of mass participation more direct than the trend toward democratization.

Governments responded to trade union militancy with restrictive legislation and the use of force. In Britain, the Masters and Servants Act (1867) made any breach of contract a criminal instead of a civil offense; the Criminal Law of 1871 created a new category of crime—conspiracy—for acts committed by more than one person and included collective acts that were not crimes for individuals; and the Protection of Property Act (1875) set stiff criminal penalties for compelling a person to commit (or not commit) an act such as joining a strike. Armed with such legislation, and the pro-management sentiments that produced it, governments did not hesitate to use military force against disruptive workers in Britain or France just as in Russia. Unemployed workers demonstrated in central London in the fall of 1887. The government responded by banning labor marches. When workers persisted, they were met by armed police in the "bloody Sunday" clash of November 1887. Three of the unemployed were killed and several hundred injured. Similarly, strikes by coal miners in the Ruhr valley in 1889 led to violent clashes (known as the Herne riots) when the German government called out two battalions of infantry and a squadron of cavalry to oppose the strikers. French troops fired on strikers at the northern industrial town of Fourmies in 1891, killing nine and wounding thirty-five; the conservative government responded to the massacre by arresting Karl Marx's son-in-law, who had spoken there two days earlier, for inciting a riot. At Łodz (in Russian Poland), forty-six workers were killed in a clash in 1892; ninety-two died in a confrontation in Sicily in 1893. And Georges Clemenceau, who had risen to political prominence as a democratic radical and friend of workers, did not hesitate to call out the troops against French strikers in 1906; he even seemed to relish being called "the number one cop in France."

Workers responded with another form of mass politics—supporting political parties that promised to create governments sympathetic to them. This converted socialism from a theory into a mass movement. Socialist parties were typically led by intellectuals who combined a program of political democracy with social benefits. The Austrian Socialist Party was led by a physician, the Belgian Socialist Party by a lawyer, and the French and German parties by professors. The foremost French socialist, Jean Jaurès, began his career by writing a Latin dissertation to earn a professorship at the University of Toulouse. The clearest example of middle-class intellectuals shaping socialism was the Fabian Society founded in Britain in 1883. Its leaders were a novelist (H. G. Wells), a dramatist (George

✎ TABLE 27.5 ✎

The Growth of Union Membership in the Early Twentieth Century

Country	Union membership 1890	1900	1905	1910	1913
Britain	1,576,000	2,022,000	1,997,000	2,565,000	4,135,000
Germany	344,000	851,000	1,650,000	2,435,000	3,024,000
United States		869,000	1,959,000	2,184,000	2,753,000
France			203,000	358,000	400,000
Russia			123,000		
Austria-Hungary	47,000	135,000	482,000		
Sweden		180,000		136,000	
Belgium	13,000	43,000		116,000	
Spain	3,000			41,000	

Source: Compiled from data in Edwin R. A. Seligman, ed., *Encyclopedia of the Social Sciences* (New York, N.Y.: Macmillan, 1937), 8:9–41.

✎ TABLE 27.6 ✎

Strikes in Europe, 1896–1910

Period	Belgium Average annual strikes	Days lost	Britain Average annual strikes	Days lost	France Average annual strikes	Days lost	Germany Average annual strikes	Days lost
1896–1900	122	801,000	758	6,948,000	568	1,991,000	774	
1901–1905	94	2,451,000	427	2,744,000	691	3,132,000	1,363	2,853,000
1906–10	155	1,606,000	479	5,701,000	1,236	4,629,000	2,712	4,954,000

Source: Compiled from data in Chris Cook and John Paxton, *European Political Facts, 1848–1918* (London: Macmillan, 1978), p. 323.

Bernard Shaw), and a brilliant couple (Sidney and Beatrice Webb) who founded both a university (the London School of Economics) and several periodicals. Such leaders espoused democratic socialism and believed they would ultimately win an electoral majority. They called for radical democracy similar to the Chartist program of the 1830s or the advanced constitutions of 1848; universal suffrage (often including women's suffrage), secret ballots, salaried representatives, and proportional representation were typical political objectives. The eight-hour working day, government regulation of working conditions, and free medical care were typical social goals of democratic socialism. The German Socialist Party adopted one of the clearest statements of this agenda as its Erfurt Program of 1891 (see document 27.5). Such documents had wide influence on the European left, where they were viewed as simple humanitarianism. As a leading Austrian socialist, Alfred Adler (the pioneering psychiatrist), put it, they were "fighting for social justice."

All over Europe, however, democratic socialists contended with Marxists for control of working-class political movements (see illustration 27.8). Philosophical disputes, such as the abolition of private property, separated these two wings of the socialist movement. The greatest of these disagreements involved the seizure of power. Marxists expected the working-class victory to come through violent revolution. "Force," Marx and Engels wrote, "is the midwife of every old society pregnant with a new one." Democratic socialists rejected revolution and believed that they could achieve their objectives through elections. Moderates such as the Fabians held that socialism would arrive "bit-by-bit" as the enfranchised lower classes learned to

◆ DOCUMENT 27.5 ◆

The Erfurt Program of the German Social Democratic Party (1891)

[T]he Social Democratic Party of Germany demands, to begin with:

1. Universal, equal, and direct suffrage, with secret ballot, for all elections, of all citizens of the realm over twenty years of age, without distinction of sex. Proportional representation, and until this is introduced, legal redistribution of electoral districts after every census. Biennial legislative periods. Holding of the elections on a legal holiday. Compensation for the elected representative. Abolition of every limitation of political rights, except in the case of legal incapacity.

2. Direct legislation through the people, by means of the right of proposal and rejection. . . .

3. Education of all to bear arms. Militia in the place of the standing army. . . .

4. Abolition of all laws which limit or suppress the right of meeting and coalition.

5. Abolition of all laws which place women . . . at a disadvantage as compared with men.

6. Declaration that religion is a private affair. Abolition of all expenditure of public funds upon . . . religious objects. . . .

7. Secularization of schools. Compulsory attendance at the public national schools. Free education. . . .

8. Free administration of justice, and free legal assistance. . . . [J]udges elected by the people. Appeal in criminal cases.

9. Free medical attendance, including midwifery, and free supply of medicines. Free burial.

10. Graduated income and property tax for defraying all public expenses. . . . Abolition of all indirect taxes. . . .

For the protection of the working classes, the Social Democratic Party of Germany demands, to be begin with:

1. An effective national and international legislation for the protection of labor, on the following principles:

   a. Fixing of a normal working day, which shall not exceed eight hours.

   b. Prohibition of the employment of children under fourteen.

   c. Prohibition of night work except . . . [in necessary cases].

   d. An unbroken rest of at least thirty-six hours in every week. . . .

2. Supervision of all industrial establishments, investigation and regulation of the conditions of labor.

Illustration 27.8

▨ **The Growth of Socialist Parties.** By the early twentieth century, socialist parties such as the SFIO in France and the SPD in Germany were winning dozens of seats in Parliament and growing rapidly. These parties contained an unresolved conflict between their evolutionary, democratic wing and their revolutionary, Marxist wing—a dichotomy well symbolized in this photo of Rosa Luxemburg, a leading militant in the SPD, giving a public speech. Note that on her right is a portrait of Ferdinand Lassalle, a pioneer of moderation, and on her left is a portrait of Karl Marx, the strongest voice of revolutionary socialism.

❧ TABLE 27.7 ❧

Socialist Deputies in European Parliaments, 1880–1914

Country	Socialist deputies								Percentage of seats in 1914 Parliament
	1880	1885	1890	1895	1900	1905	1910	1914	
Austria (*Social Democrats*)	0	0	0	0	0	0	28	33	20.4
Belgium (*Workers Party*)	0	0	0	28	32	32	32	39	21.0
Britain (*Labour Party*)	0	0	0	0	2	2	29	42	6.3
France (*Socialist Party*)	0	0	0	31	57	46	78	130	22.0
Germany (*Social Democrats*)	9	24	35	44	56	81	43	110	27.7
Italy (*Socialist Party*)	0	0	0	15	33	29	41	52	10.2
Sweden (*Social Democrats*)	0	0	0	0	0	13	34	87	37.8

Source: Compiled from data in Chris Cook and John Paxton, *European Political Facts, 1848–1918* (London: Macmillan, 1978), pp. 115–43.

vote in their self-interest. Their credo was "the inevitability of gradualness." The greatest philosophic rejection of Marxism was advanced by a German socialist, Edouard Bernstein. He was driven into exile by Bismarck's harassment of socialists in the 1880s and edited a newspaper in Zürich where he developed his socialism in contact with British democratic socialists. During the 1890s he lived in London and wrote *Evolutionary Socialism* (1899) to demonstrate the errors of *The Communist Manifesto* and to advocate gradual, democratic socialism. Marx's theory of revolution, Bernstein wrote, was "a mistake in every respect."

Divisions within the socialist movement initially produced competing socialist parties in many countries, but political realism soon obliged socialists to contain their disagreements within a unified party. Thus, French evolutionary socialists (led by Jaurès) and French Marxists (led by Jules Guesde) created a unified party, known by the French initials SFIO, in 1905. British socialists, from the Fabians to the Marxist Social Democratic Federation, combined to create the Labour Party in 1906. Followers of Marx and Bernstein learned to live together within a single German party, known by its initials, SPD (see illustration 27.8). Collaboration allowed ideological debates at the congresses of the international movement known as the Second International (1889–1914), but it also led to electoral success. Bismarck's fears notwithstanding, few socialists could be found in European parliaments in the 1880s, but they were among the largest parties in 1914 (see table 27.7). The German SPD held more than 25 percent of the seats in the Reichstag, making it the second largest party; French socialists were the second largest block in the fragmented Chamber of Deputies with 22 percent

of the seats. And in the 1914 elections the Swedish Socialist Party showed that evolutionary socialists might be right: It became the largest party in Parliament with eighty-seven seats against eighty-six conservatives.

The growth of trade unions and socialist parties persuaded conservatives to reconsider working-class issues. Many still supported strict regulation and the use of troops, but others proposed, as Bismarck had, that conservative governments adopt welfare legislation to dilute the appeal of socialism and allow conservatives to define the benefits given. The Vatican gave another conservative voice to the working-class question. Pope Leo XIII urged Christians to see "that some remedy must be found, and found quickly, for the misery and wretchedness pressing so heavily and unjustly at this moment on the vast majority of the working class." In an encyclical letter named *Rerum Novarum*, Leo rejected socialism as "emphatically unjust" and suggested that the answer was in religion. This encouraged the creation of Catholic trade unions and a conservative reform campaign known as social Catholicism.

The Growth of Women's Rights Movements

Industrialization stimulated other movements. None had more far-reaching importance than the women's rights movement. Industrialization contributed to the rise of feminism by transforming the roles of women in Western societies. It broke down the traditional household economy in which women labored at home, sharing in agricultural duties or the work of a family-run shop, plus non-wage-paying work such as spinning yarn or making candles. That economic model yielded to a family wage economy in which women (and children) provided less home labor and more wage-earning labor. Families increasingly bought their yarn or ready-made clothing, candles, or vegetables; women increasingly worked outside the home to pay for them.

A study of women in the French labor force reveals these momentous changes in the lives of women. In 1872 less than 25 percent of the total female population of France worked for wages. In 1906 nearly 40 percent of the total female population (54 percent of women age twenty to sixty and 60 percent of women in their early twenties) worked for wages. Furthermore, the work women did was changing. The largest employers remained agriculture, the textile industry, and domestic service, but governments were opening white-collar positions (typically in postal and telephone services), the age of the department store was creating sales positions, the needs of businesses were opening secretarial and clerical jobs, and compulsory education laws were providing teaching jobs.

Women's employment varied across Europe—Russian law closed the civil service to women whereas a Swedish law of 1864 opened all employment to women—but the impact was similar. Educated and energetic women in increasing numbers (although still a minority of women) demanded equality with men. Conservatives, and some men who thought themselves radicals, resisted equality as staunchly as they resisted the demands of workers. *Rerum Novarum* was clear on the subject of working women: "Women are not suited for certain occupations; a woman is by nature fitted for home-work, and it is that which is best adopted at once to preserve her modesty and promote the good bringing up of children and the well-being of the family."

The women's rights movement was relatively small in the 1870s, but militants articulated comprehensive programs. The leading French militant of the 1870s, Hubertine Auclert, summarized such a program for her organization, *Droit des femmes* (Women's Rights): "The ultimate objective of *Droits des femmes* is: The perfect equality of the two sexes before the law and in morality" (see document 27.6). Feminists (a term that Auclert pioneered in the 1880s) debated priorities, but comprehensive programs soon resembled Auclert's: full political rights, open education and careers, equal civil rights, and equal pay.

Leagues with such programs existed in most of western and northern Europe by the end of the 1870s, though most pioneering feminists favored a strategy of

---

◆ DOCUMENT 27.6 ◆

Hubertine Auclert: The Equality of the Sexes, 1877

Hubertine Auclert (1848–1914) was a daughter of prosperous farmers who inherited enough money to devote her life to a political cause. She founded the women's suffrage campaign in France and organized demonstrations on behalf of women's rights. During the 1880s she edited the leading newspaper of militant feminism in France, La Citoyenne. Frustrated by the rate of progress, she considered violent protest in the early twentieth century but kept faith in democratic programs like the following.

The ultimate objective of *Droit des femmes* is: The perfect equality of the two sexes before the law and in morality.

PROGRAM: *Droit des femmes* will seek, from the beginning and by all means in its power:

1. The accession of women, married or not, to full civil and political rights, on the same legal conditions as apply to men.
2. The reestablishment of divorce.
3. A single morality for men and for women; whatever is condemned for one cannot be excusable for the other.
4. The right for women to develop their intelligence through education, with no other limitation than their ability and their desire.
5. The right to knowledge being acquired, the free accession of women to all professions and careers for which they are qualified at the same level as applies to men (and after the same examination).
6. The rigorous application, without distinction by sex, of the economic formula: Equal Pay for Equal Work.

---

starting with limited programs and postponing the issue of women's suffrage. Louise Otto-Peters, the founder of the German women's rights movement, focused on civil rights. The generation of German feminists that followed her, such as Anita Augsburg and the General Federation of German Women's Associations, also began with limited demands. Not until the turn-of-the century did women's rights advocates in most countries begin to seek political rights. Augsburg reached this

CHRONOLOGY 27.1

States Granting Women's Suffrage in Local Elections, 1861–1914

1861	Bohemia (Austria-Hungary)
1862	Sweden
1864	Russia
1865	Finland (Russian Empire)
1867	New South Wales (Australia)
1869	England (U.K.)
1869	Wales (U.K.)
1870	Utah Territory (U.S.)
1871	West Australia (Australia)
1878	New Zealand
1880	South Australia (Australia)
1881	Scotland (U.K.)
1884	Tasmania (Australia)
1890	Wyoming (U.S.)
1893	Colorado (U.S.)
1896	Idaho (U.S.)
1896	Utah (U.S.)
1907	Norway
1908	Denmark
1908	Iceland
1910	Washington (U.S.)
1911	California (U.S.)
1912	Kansas (U.S.)
1912	Arizona (U.S.)
1913	Illinois (U.S.)
1913	Alaska (U.S.)
1914	Montana (U.S.)
1914	Nevada (U.S.)

legal rights. Only a few European states gave women the right to vote, even at the local level (see chronology 27.1).

The strongest movement developed in Britain. Women in England and Wales won the vote and eligibility for office at the local level in 1869, and they pressed, with growing militancy, for full political rights for the next fifty years. Between 1870 and 1914 approximately three thousand women were elected to local boards and councils in Britain, but these offices were chiefly on school boards and social agencies dealing with infant mortality or unsanitary housing—positions considered a natural part of "women's sphere." British women, led by Lydia Becker and Millicient Garrett Fawcett, organized the first large suffrage movement and won support in the House of Commons. Though they obtained majorities—but not the support of either major party—in the House of Commons, the conservative majority in the House of Lords blocked the reform.

The women's suffrage movement in Britain became one of the most radical movements in Europe in the early twentieth century. Fawcett, the widow of a radical M.P. who shared many of his parliamentary duties because of his blindness, presided over the unification of several suffrage leagues into a National Union of Women's Suffrage Societies in 1897. It grew from sixteen founding societies to more than four hundred in 1913. Even during this period of rapid growth, militant suffragists formed new organizations to attempt more radical tactics than Fawcett used. They were dubbed "suffragettes" by a newspaper hoping to ridicule the movement, but militants accepted the label and made it famous. The most famous suffragettes, Emmeline Pankhurst and her daughters, Christabel and Sylvia, founded the Women's Social and Political Union (WSPU) in 1903 and led it to violent tactics (against property, not people) such as smashing store windows. Emmeline Pankhurst decided that they "had to do as much of this guerilla warfare as the people of England would tolerate" (see document 27.7). That decision had dreadful results: When arrested, she (and several other strong women) infuriated the government by going on a hunger strike. When hunger strikers suffered declining health, the government chose to force feed them (see illustration 27.9 and document 27.7). This sequence of events culminated in the notorious Cat-and-Mouse Act of 1913—suffragist prisoners would be released until they recovered.

Despite the remarkable example of the WSPU, moderation characterized the struggle for women's suffrage in most of Europe. Large suffrage movements had

position in 1898 but did not create her suffrage league (the German Union for Women's Suffrage) until 1902. A similar situation existed in Italy, where Maria Mozzoni fought for civil and economic rights but avoided suffragism. In France, the tireless suffrage campaigns of Auclert during the 1880s attracted only a handful of followers. The women's rights majority there, led by Léon Richer and Maria Deraismes, the founders of the French League for the Rights of Women, favored programs like Otto-Peters', concentrating upon civil and

The Pankhursts: The Life of Militant Suffragettes

Emmeline Pankhurst (1858–1928) was the daughter of a wealthy Manchester cotton magnate who married a radical lawyer and joined the first labor party. Her two daughters, Christabel (1880–1958) and Sylvia (1882–1960), joined her in a life of political activism. In the following excerpts from their memoirs, Emmeline Pankhurst explains her adoption of militant tactics and Sylvia Pankhurst talks about the consequences for suffragette prisoners.

Emmeline Pankhurst Explains Her Decision to Adopt Militant Tactics

Now we had reached a point where we had to choose between two alternatives. We had exhausted argument. Therefore either we had to give up our agitation altogether, as the suffragists of the eighties virtually had done, or else we must act, and go on acting, until the selfishness and the obstinacy of the government was broken down, or the government themselves destroyed. Until forced to do so, the government, we perceived, would never give women the vote. . . .

We had tried every other measure, . . . and our years of work and suffering and sacrifice had taught us that the government would not yield to right and justice, what the majority of the members of the House of Commons admitted was right and justice, but that the government would, as other governments invariably do, yield to expediency. Now our task was to show the government that it was expedient to yield to women's just demands. . . . We had to make English law a failure and the courts farce comedy theaters; we had to discredit the government and parliament in the eyes of the world; we had to spoil En-glish sports, hurt business, destroy valuable property, demoralize the world of society, shame the churches, upset the whole orderly conduct of life—That is, we had to do as much of this guerilla warfare as the people of England would tolerate. When they came to the point of saying to the government, "Stop this, in the only way it can be stopped, by giving the women of England representation," then we should extinguish our torch.

Sylvia Pankhurst Describes the Treatment of Suffragette Prisoners: Force-Feeding

The government was not slow to take advantage of the new tactics to inflict harsher punishments. . . . These women should not be permitted to terminate their imprisonment by the hunger strike, as thirty-seven had already done. . . . The Home Secretary ordered the medical officer to feed them forcibly by means of a rubber tube passed through the mouth or nose into the stomach. . . . Mrs. Leight had been handcuffed for upwards of thirty hours, the hands fastened behind during the day and in front with the palms outward at night. Only when the wrists had become intensely painful and swollen were the irons removed. On the fourth day of her fast, the doctor had told her that she must either abandon the hunger strike or be fed by force. She protested that forcible feeding was an operation, and as such could not be performed without a sane patient's consent; but she was seized by the wardresses and the doctor administered food by the nasal tube. This was done twice daily, from 22 September till 30 October. All her companions were forcibly fed.

developed by 1914, but they did not adopt WSPU tactics. A few militants, such as Auclert and Pelletier in France, briefly attempted violent demonstrations but found no support. Instead, the movements in France, Germany, Italy, and Russia chose campaigns of respectable moderation. Their organizations grew large by 1914 (the French Union for Women's Suffrage had twelve thousand members in seventy-five regional chapters), but none won the vote.

Feminists also concentrated on other targets. Many favored modernization of legal codes, such as the Napoleonic Code in France or the Pisanelli Code in Italy, that made wives subordinate to husbands. The most basic reform sought was a Married Woman's Property Act, such as the British had adopted in stages between 1856 and 1882, and several countries (chiefly in Scandinavia) followed. French women obtained this right with the Schmahl Law of 1907; German women did not win it before the war. Most women's rights advocates also sought the legalization of divorce. This was permissible in the German Lutheran tradition and had been established in British law in 1857. The campaign was more difficult in Catholic countries because Pope Leo XIII stongly opposed divorce and issued an encyclical in 1880 stating that "[d]ivorce is born of perverted morals." French women won a limited form of

riculum to prepare for universities in 1893 and then opening higher education to them in 1900. The Prussian Ministry of Education was more conservative and perpetuated a secondary school curriculum stressing "Household Arts" to teach "feminine precision, neatness, and patience" while denying young women the prerequisites for entering universities. The distinguished University of Berlin thus remained closed to women until 1908. In 1914 German universities enrolled a combined total of slightly more than four thousand women, who formed 6.2 percent of the student population. The situation was only slightly better for women in France, where 4,254 women students (10.1 percent of enrollment) studied in 1913.

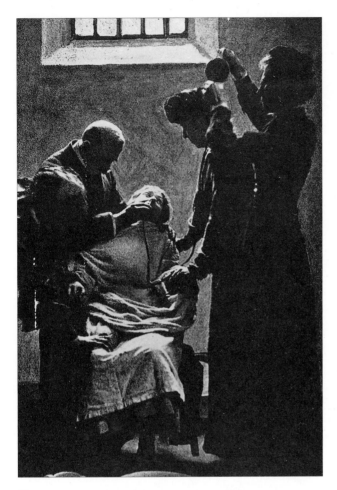

Illustration 27.9

/// **Emmeline Pankhurst.** Emmeline Pankhurst and her daughters were among the most dramatic leaders of the women's suffrage movement. In 1909 they began a campaign of violence (against property), which led to the arrest of militants dubbed "suffragettes" by the press. In prison, Pankhurst and others went on hunger strikes. The liberal government responded by force-feeding them. In this photo, Emmeline Pankhurst, then in her mid-fifties, suffers this painful procedure. Note that the prison used women to feed her.

European Culture During the Belle Époque

The Belle Époque was a period of great cultural creativity, but no single style dominated the arts and typified the era. Unlike the baroque and classical styles of the eighteenth century, or the romanticism of the early nineteenth century, no style summarizes the cultural trends of the era. Instead, the Belle Époque was an age of cultural vitality expressed in many conflicting styles. In painting, the realism of 1870 gave way to a succession of new styles, such as impressionism, fauvism, cubism, and expressionism. Realism lingered in novels and drama of social comment (such as Emile Zola's novels of ordinary life in France or Henrik Ibsen's plays of angry social criticism), a style known as naturalism, but poetry evolved into an introverted and sometimes mystical style called symbolism. Music, architecture, philosophy, sculpture, and the decorative arts produced no style that dominated the era. Yet its cultural innovations at the start of the twentieth century showed that European civilization was entering a period of fundamental change.

The best remembered cultural style of the Belle Époque was impressionism, a style of painting that originated in France in the 1860s–1880s. Impressionism produced several of the greatest artists of the century, such as Claude Monet, whose painting entitled *Impression: Sunrise* (1874) led to the name. And impressionism influenced the other arts, from music (Debussy is sometimes called an impressionist) to poetry (the symbolist poets are also called impressionists). But the Belle Époque was an era of so much change that it cannot be called the "age of impressionism."

divorce in 1884; Spanish and Italian women did not. Women's rights advocates generally had more success in seeking educational opportunities. The University of Zürich became the first to open to women (1865) and other Swiss universities followed in the 1870s. Russian women briefly won a series of university rights but they were rescinded in 1881 because of the involvement of some women in radical political groups. Germany, home of the most highly praised and emulated universities of the late nineteenth century, resisted higher education for women. The state of Baden was the most progressive, offering women a secondary school cur-

Illustration 27.10

/// **Picasso and the Revolution against Representational Art.** In the early twentieth century, Pablo Picasso and others in the Bohemian art community of Paris began a revolution in painting by attacking the "tyranny" of traditional representational art and its strict rules. His 1907 painting *Demoiselles d'Avignon* (Young Women of Avignon) used a traditional art form, the nude, to depict the body in simple geometric planes and to abolish perspective, one of the hallmarks of Western art since the Renaissance.

Belle Époque architecture illustrates both the jumble of cultural styles and the emergence of the dramatically new. Late nineteenth-century architecture first suggests an age of revivalism, because almost all past styles were exploited: Bavarians built another great castle in neorococo style, the most noted new building in central Vienna (a theater) was in neobaroque style, the Hungarian Parliament on the banks of the Danube in Budapest was neo-Gothic, the most discussed new church of the age in Paris was neoromanesque, the Dutch national museum built in Amsterdam was neo-Renaissance, and the vast Gum Department Store in Moscow was neoclassical. Despite this cacophony of styles of the past, an exciting architecture of the twentieth century began to emerge in the closing years of the nineteenth. The French built the tallest structure on earth for their world's fair of 1889 (the centennial of the revolution), and they built the Eiffel Tower in structural steel. By the 1890s this use of steel and the American-born style of building skyscrapers by attaching a masonry exterior to a metal frame had begun a profound change in the appearance of cities. Walter Gropius, a German architect who had tremendous influence on the visual arts of the new century, built the first steel frame building with glass walls in 1911.

The birth of the twentieth century seen in architecture had parallels throughout the arts. Startling innovators broke with tradition. In music, the rejection of the nineteenth-century symphonic heritage led after 1900 to efforts to compose atonal music, culminating in 1914 with Arnold Schonberg's system of composing to destroy the feeling of tonality. Other composers, such as Igor Stravinsky, boldly created dissonant harmonies. Such music so offended traditional tastes that performances were sometimes met with howls of protest from the audience; the first performance of Stravinsky's ballet *The Rite of Spring* provoked a riot in Paris in 1913. Horrified traditionalists even saw the rules of dancing begin to break down as free dance abolished the following of steps or prescribed positioning.

The breakdown of traditional styles was especially controversial in the visual arts where the popularity of photography and the cinema pressed painters to find artistic expression that these new arts could not rival. The nonrepresentational styles of painting that emerged still evoke hostility from traditionalists a century later. The most inventive artist of the twentieth century, Pablo Picasso, began his career producing works of emotional realism, but after 1904 he pioneered a style known as cubism in which shapes and structures (such as the human face) were simplified into geometric outlines (see illustration 27.10). Picasso pushed the breakdown of realism so far that a face might have two eyes on the same side of the nose. Denounced for his nonrepresentational styles, Picasso responded that his art was "a lie that tells the truth." Painting was no longer a simple depiction of the physical world; it revealed hidden truths about a two-faced world.

European thought during the Belle Époque followed a similar course. The most influential works of the era drew upon the new discipline of psychology. Novelists from Feodor Dostoevski (whose *The Brothers Karamazov* appeared in 1879–80), through Joseph Conrad (whose *Lord Jim* appeared in 1900), to Marcel Proust (whose first volume of *Remembrance of Things Past* appeared in 1913) relied upon psychological detail and insight. The inner life of characters and their subconscious motivation gained new emphasis as central features of the novel. Psychology also reshaped European philosophy. Friedrich Nietzsche, a pastor's son who reacted against the piety of his home, was such a brilliant student that he became a professor at the University of Basel at age twenty-four. Nietzsche wrote with psychological insight about the sublimation of passions and instincts, the relativity of morals, and what he called "the will to power." He had contempt for contemporary cultural and moral values and, in works such as *Thus Spoke Zarathustra* (1883), argued that "God is dead" and Christianity is based on the mentality of slaves. Such arguments did not have much immediate impact, but they grew increasingly influential in twentieth-century European thought.

Perhaps the most influential thinker of the Belle Époque was Sigmund Freud, the Austrian neurologist who founded the science of psychoanalysis. Freud's study of psychoneuroses in the 1890s led him to an analytic technique of the "free association" of thoughts, a process that he named "psychoanalysis." This, in turn, led him to the analysis of dreams. *The Interpretation of Dreams* (1900) stated his first model of the workings of the mind, a model that evolved into a description of three competing subconscious elements of the mind: the ego, the superego, and the libido (or id). Freud's attention to the libido as the seat of emotional (and especially sexual) urges led to his famous stress upon sexual explanations (especially those with origins in infantile sexuality) in *Three Contributions to the Sexual Theory* (1905). Many of Freud's theories have been controversial, and some are simply wrong, but Freud's impact upon European thought has been so enormous that he remains the most influential author of his era.

Conclusion

The name *Belle Époque* was not created during the generation before 1914; it was a nostalgic label created after the suffering of World War I made the prewar era seem immensely appealing. As with most nostalgia, the perception of a "beautiful era" is debatable. It is surely appropriate when the perspective is war and peace: Between 1871 and 1914 the European great powers experienced nearly half a century without a war among themselves. The fortunate generations of the Belle Époque lived in a much more tranquil world than those of 1848–71 or 1914–45.

Historical retrospect also suggests that the Belle Époque was a fortunate era because it was a period of significant progress toward a democratic society. Each of the great powers was more democratic in 1914 than it had been in 1870, and many other states of Europe followed this evolution of parliamentary government. This democratic spirit extended to other historic changes: The Ferry laws in France that created universal, free, secular and compulsory education and the Bismarckian reforms in Germany that launched the evolution of the welfare state both contributed to a more humane and equitable Europe.

Despite all of these positive signs, historians must not conclude that the Belle Époque was a golden age. Minority populations suffered in all of the great states of Europe. The British could not bring themselves to grant home rule to the Irish. Bismarck fought a decade-long battle against the Catholic Church. Deep anti-Semitism existed in most societies, from the pogroms in Russia to the Dreyfus affair in France. National minorities, such as the Slavic peoples of the Austro-Hungarian Empire, were no less willing to fight for self-government than the Italians and Germans had been in the mid-nineteenth century. And two huge social issues had arisen to confront European democracy: Militant workers and women were demanding a larger sense of democracy, a democracy whose promised equality they shared. The working class movement produced a trade union movement so large that it encompassed 20 percent of the adult population of Britain and produced one thousand strikes per year in France. Women's rights campaigns produced activists so dedicated that they suffered the pain and indignity of force-feeding rather than give up the fight. Clearly, many Europeans did not feel they yet lived in a "beautiful era." And European high culture, characterized by a jumble of styles all rejecting traditional culture, reflected this dissatisfaction with the past.

Suggested Readings

The most recent surveys of this period are E. J. Hobsbawm, *The Age of Empire, 1875–1914* (1987) and N. Stone, *Europe Transformed, 1878–1919* (1984); see also C. Hayes, *A Generation of Materialism, 1871–1900* (1941); O. Hale, *The Great Illusion, 1900–1914* (1971), in the *Rise of Modern Europe* series; and F. H. Hinsley, ed., *Material Progress and World-Wide Problems, 1870–1898* (1962), in the *New Cambridge Modern History* series. B. Tuchman, *The Proud Tower* (1966) is a highly readable overview of the period 1890–1914.

For surveys of imperial Germany, see V. Berghahn, *Imperial Germany, 1871–1914* (1994); H. U. Wehler, *The German Empire, 1871–1918* (1985); G. Craig, *Germany, 1866–1918* (1978); J. Sheehan, ed., *Imperial Germany* (1976); and R. Evans, ed., *Society and Politics in Wilhelmine Germany* (1978). For Bismarck, see the suggestions for chapter 26 and O. Pflanze, *Bismarck and the Development of Germany*, vols. 2–3 (1990). See also: W. O. Henderson, *The Rise of German Industrial Power, 1834–1914* (1975); R. Chickering, *We Men Who Feel Most German* (1984), for the Pan-German League; E. Evans, *The German Center Party, 1870–1933* (1981); M. Anderson, *Windhorst* (1981), a biography of Bismarck's opponent who led the Center Party; J. Retallack, *Notables of the Right* (1988), for German conservatism; D. White, *The Splintered Party* (1976), on the National Liberals; J. Röhl, *Germany without Bismarck* (1967), on the 1890s; K. Lerman, *The Chancellor as Courtier: Bernhard von Bülow and the Governance of Germany, 1900–09* (1990); L. Cecil, *Albert Ballin* (1967), a study of a wealthy businessman; L. Cecil, *Wilhelm II* (1989); K. Jaurausch, *The Enigmatic Chancellor: Bethmann Hollweg and the Hubris of Imperial Germany* (1973); and S. Suval, *Electoral Politics in Wilhelmine Germany* (1985).

For Britain, see the suggestions for chapter 26 and D. Read, *The Age of Urban Democracy: England, 1868–1914* (1994). See also H. C. G. Matthew, *Gladstone, 1809–1874* (1986), for the great ministry; P. Smith, *Disraelian Conservatism and Social Reform* (1967); A. Jones, *The Politics of Reform, 1884* (1972); A. Offer, *Property and Politics, 1870–1914* (1991); G. Bernstein, *Liberalism and Liberal Politics in Edwardian England* (1986); G. Dangerfield, *The Strange Death of Liberal England* (1961); B. Gilbert, *David Lloyd George*, 2 vols. (1987–92); F. S. L. Lyons, *Charles Stewart Parnell* (1977); P. Bew, *Conflict and Conciliation in Ireland, 1890–1910* (1987); and S. Holton, *Feminism and Democracy* (1986), for the women's suffrage campaign.

For the early Third Republic, see M. Agulhon, *The French Republic, 1879–1992* (1993) and J.-M. Mayeur and M. Rebérieux, *The Third Republic from Its Origins to the Great War* (1984), the most recent syntheses; S. Elwitt, *The Making of the Third Republic* (1975);

E. Weber, *Peasants into Frenchmen* (1976); H. Lebovics, *The Alliance of Iron and Wheat in the Third French Republic* (1988), for the conservative order; S. Edwards, *The Paris Commune, 1871* (1971); G. Gullickson, *Unruly Women* (1996), on women and the commune; J. P. T. Bury's works on Gambetta, especially *Gambetta and the Making of the Third Republic* (1973); A. Mitchell's works, especially *The German Influence in France after 1870* (1979); W. Irvine, *The Boulanger Affair Reconsidered* (1989); J.-D. Bredin, *The Affair* (1986), for a thorough account of the Dreyfus affair; M. Burns, *The Dreyfus Affair: A Family Affair* (1991); the works of B. Martin, especially *Count de Mun* (1978), for Catholic politics; R. Soucy, *Facism in France: The Case of Maurice Barrès* (1972); M. Larkin, *Church and State after the Dreyfus Affair* (1974), for the battle over the separation of church and state; J. Stone, *The Search for Social Peace* (1985), on French reform legislation; D. Watson, *Georges Clemenceau* (1974); E. Accampo and others, *Gender and the Politics of Social Reform in France, 1870–1914* (1995); and R. Nye, *Masculinity and Male Codes of Honor in Modern France* (1993), for gender.

For imperial Russia, see H. Rogger, *Russia in the Age of Modernization, 1881–1917* (1983); P. Gatrell, *The Tsarist Economy, 1850–1917* (1986); R. Robinson, *Rural Russia under the Old Regime* (1967); F. Wcislo, *Reforming Rural Russia* (1990); N. Weissman, *Reform in Tsarist Russia* (1981); D. Lieven, *Russia's Rulers under the Old Regime* (1989), on the government in 1894–1914; G. Hamburg, *The Politics of the Russian Nobility, 1881–1905* (1984); T. Von Laue, *Sergei Witte and the Industrialization of Russia* (1963); A. Verner, *The Crisis of Russian Autocracy* (1990) and A. Ascher, *Russia in Disarray* (1988), for the revolution of 1905; R. Manning, *The Crisis of the Old Order in Russia* (1982); R. Robbins, *Famine in Russia, 1891–1892* (1975); O. Crisp and L. Edmondson, eds., *Civil Rights in Imperial Russia* (1989); C. Rice, *Russian Workers and the Socialist Revolutionary Party* (1988); and V. Bonnell, *Roots of Rebellion* (1983), on workers and politics.

For Austria-Hungary, see A. May, *The Hapsburg Monarchy, 1867–1914* (1951), O. Jaxi, *The Dissolution of the Hapsburg Monarchy* (1961), and R. Kann, *The Multinational Empire*, 2 vols. (1950). For Italy, see D. M. Smith, *Italy: A Modern History* (1969); S. Saladino, *Italy from Unification to 1919* (1970); C. Seton-Watson, *Italy from Liberalism to Fascism, 1870–1925* (1967); M. Clark, *Modern Italy, 1871–1982* (1984); B. Croce, *A History of Italy, 1871–1915* (1929); and A. W. Salomone, *Italy in the Giolittian Era* (1960), for the early twentieth century. For Spain, see R. Carr, *Spain, 1808–1975* (1982); R. Herr, *An Historical Essay on Modern Spain* (1971); H. Kamen, *A Concise History of Spain* (1988); and S. Payne, *A History of Spain and Portugal*, 2 vols. (1973). For other regions, see E. H. Kossmann, *The Low Countries, 1780–1940* (1978); E. Bonjour and others, *A Short History of Switzerland* (1952); and T. Derry, *A History of Modern Norway, 1814–1972* (1973).

For the labor movement and socialism, see A. Lindemann, *A History of European Socialism* (1983), an introductory synthesis; H. Mitchell and P. Stearns, *Workers and Protest* (1982); W. Mommsen and H. Husung, eds., *The Development of Trade Unionism in Great Britain and Germany, 1880–1914* (1985); H. Clegg and A. Thompson, eds., *A History of British Trade Unions since 1889* (1964); J. Joll, *The Second International, 1889–1914* (1974), a readable introduction; J. Braunthal, *History of the International, 1864–1914* (1967), a detailed history; J. Joll, *The Anarchists* (1979); G. Woodcock, *Anarchism* (1986); A. M. McBriar, *Fabian Socialism and English Politics, 1884–1918* (1962); R. Evans, ed., *The German Working Class, 1888–1933* (1987); V. Lidtke, *The Alternative Culture* (1985), for the German socialist labor movement; V. Lidtke, *The Outlawed Party* (1966), for the German socialist party to 1890; C. Schorske, *German Social Democracy, 1905–1917* (1955); R. McGraw, *A History of the French Working Class* (1992); L. Berlanstein, ed., *Rethinking Labor History* (1993) and *The Working People of Paris* (1984); M. Perrot, *Workers on Strike* (1987); P. Hutton, *The Cult of the Revolutionary Tradition* (1981), on French socialism to 1893; H. Goldberg, *Jean Jaurès* (1962); S. Di Scala, *Dilemmas of Italian Socialism* (1980); D. Horowitz, *The Italian Labor Movement* (1963); P. Piccone, *Italian Marxism* (1983); and A. Wildman, *The Making of a Workers' Revolution: Russia Social Democracy* (1967).

For the woman question and women's rights movements, see J. C. Fout, ed., *German Women in the Nineteenth Century* (1984); B. Franzoi, *At the Very Least She Pays the Rent* (1985), on women and industrialization; R. Orthmann, *Out of Necessity* (1991), on German working women; J. Quataert, *Reluctant Feminists in German Social Democracy* (1979); J. Lewis, *Women in England, 1870–1950* (1984), on social and economic roles of women; M. Vicinus, ed., *Suffer and Be Still: Women in the Victorian Age* (1972); A. Rosen, *Rise Up Women!* (1974), for the British suffragettes; P. Bidelman, *Pariahs Stand Up!* (1982), for the early years of French feminism; S. Hause with A. Kenney, *Women's Suffrage and Social Politics in the French Third Republic* (1984) and *Hubertine Auclert* (1987); C. Sowerwine, *Sisters or Citizens?* (1982), on feminism and socialism in France; M. Stewart, *Women, Work, and the French State* (1989); J. Margadant, *Madame le Professeur* (1990), for a study of women and education; R. Stites, *The Women's Liberation Movement in Russia* (1991); and L. Edmondson, *Feminism in Russia, 1900–1917* (1984).

For European culture in the Belle Époque, see R. Shattuck, *The Banquet Years* (1968); H. S. Hughes, *Consciousness and Society* (1977); G. Hamilton, *Painting and Sculpture in Europe, 1880–1940* (1983); and H. Chipp, ed., *Theories of Modern Art* (1968), essays on the postimpressionist revolution in painting. For popular culture, see R. Sackett, *Popular Entertainment, Class and Politics in Munich, 1900–1923* (1982); L. Abrams, *Workers' Culture in Imperial Germany* (1991); and C. Schorske, *Fin de Siècle Vienna* (1961).

PART SIX

Europe in the Age of Mass Society, Since 1914

CHAPTER 28

IMPERIALISM, WAR, AND REVOLUTION, 1881–1920

CHAPTER OUTLINE

◆◆◆◆◆◆◆◆◆◆◆◆◆◆◆◆◆◆◆◆◆◆

Chapter 28 looks at three great experiences that shaped European (and global) history in the twentieth century: (1) the new imperialism (1881–1914), in which the great European powers seized control of most of Africa and much of Asia; (2) World War I (1914–18), which destroyed the last monarchical empires of the Old Regime; and (3) the Russian Revolution (1917–20), which posed a new and powerful form of mass politics to compete with democracy.

The chapter begins with the background to these great events during the Belle Époque, when the major states of Europe experienced more than two generations of peace on their home soil. It examines the Bismarckian alliance system, which divided Europe into two opposing sides, and the militarism and arms race, which made this division so dangerous. While the Belle Époque was an era of peace among the European great powers, the same powers fought dozens of imperial wars of conquest. Europeans used those years of peace to annex empires around the world. During the new imperialism they seized control of nearly 25 percent of the planet. The chapter explains how a diplomatic revolution sharpened the division of the European powers into two competing alliance systems that led to one of the bloodiest wars in history. The discussion of World War I shows how it introduced Europe to a century of "total war"—in both its destructive battles and life on the home front. The final section focuses on the Russian Revolution of 1917. This wartime revolution established Lenin's Communist government in Russia, a regime that redoubled the effort to export European politics to the rest of the world.

The Bismarckian System of Alliances, 1871–90

The German victory in the Franco-Prussian War led to the creation of a unified German Empire so strong, both militarily and economically, that it dominated Europe, yet Chancellor Otto von Bismarck still feared French revenge. After 1871 he aimed to protect Germany by negotiating treaties that would guarantee the support of the other powers and deny France potential allies. He achieved both goals through a web of alliances collectively known as the Bismarckian system, with which he dominated European diplomacy for twenty years (1871–90). Bismarck's accomplishment radically altered European statecraft. Whereas the Metternichian system had kept the peace by a delicate balance of power in which none of the great powers became too dominant and none felt too threatened, the Bismarckian system kept peace through the lopsided superiority of the German alliances and the comparative weakness of France.

French nationalists nonetheless dreamt of the day of revenge—*la revanche*—on Germany, the day when the republic would reclaim "the lost provinces" of Alsace and Lorraine, whose borders were marked on the maps of French schools in a deep black (see illustration 28.1). Realistic nationalists such as the hero of 1870, Léon Gambetta, understood that Germany had become too powerful to fight alone. The French must wait for *revanche;* in Gambetta's words, they should "[t]hink of it always, speak of it never." Despite a war scare in 1875 and a tense period during the Boulangist nationalism of the late 1880s, no French government planned a war of revenge.

The first treaty in Bismarck's alliance system was the Three Emperors' League (*Dreikaiserbund*) of 1873, an outgrowth of state visits exchanged by William I of Germany, Franz Joseph of Austria-Hungary, and Alexander II of Russia. The *Dreikaiserbund* represented an amicable understanding (an entente) among recent rivals who shared a belief in monarchical solidarity. (France remained the only republic in monarchical Europe.) The king of Italy soon embraced this counterrevolutionary league, siding with Germany despite the debt Italians owed to the French from their wars of unification. The British remained outside this league, favoring a policy of continental nonalignment that came to be called splendid isolation.

The development of the Bismarckian system accelerated as a result of warfare in the Balkans in 1875–78,

THE BOILING POINT.

Illustration 28.1

🖎 **The Eastern Question.** A British cartoon expresses European anxiety about the Balkan crisis of the 1870s. In the front row, the crowned heads of Russia, Germany, and Austria-Hungary look nervous as the Balkan caldron boils. Britain and France look on from the background.

which convinced Bismarck to seek more formal treaties. The provinces of Bosnia and Herzegovina (see map 28.1) rebelled against Turkish rule in 1875, and the Principality of Serbia intervened to support them. The Serbs had won autonomous government in their rebellion of 1817, and the principality had subsequently become the center of Pan-Slavism, an ardent nationalism dedicated to the unity of the southern Slavs. The insurrection against the Ottoman Empire next spread to Bulgaria in 1876, and the Turks responded with violent repression known in the European press as "the Bulgarian horrors." This enlarged Balkan war forced the European powers to address a problem that had come to be called the eastern question. This was the question of the survival of the Ottoman Empire—still known as "the sick man of Europe"—and the fate of territories under the control of Constantinople. The eastern question posed the danger of Austro-Russian conflict because both governments coveted Ottoman territory in the Balkans. To avoid such a confrontation, Bismarck

MAP 28.1
**The Balkans after the Congress
of Berlin, 1878**

DOCUMENT 28.1

Bismarck: The Triple Alliance

The Triple Alliance which I originally sought to conclude after the peace of Frankfurt, and about which I had already sounded Vienna and St. Petersburg . . . was an alliance of the three emperors with the further idea of bringing into it monarchical Italy. It was designed for the struggle which, as I feared, was before us; between the two European tendencies which Napoleon called Republican and Cossack, and which I, according to our present ideas, should designate on the one side as the system of order on a monarchical basis, and on the other as the social republic to the level of which the anti-monarchical development is wont to sink. . . .

I consider that the task of escaping this . . . , of sparing the present generation and their children an entrance into it, ought to be more closely incumbent on the strong existing monarchies, those monarchies which still have a vigorous life. . . . If the monarchical governments have no understanding of the necessity of holding together in the interests of political and social order . . . I fear that the international revolutionary and social struggles . . . will be all the more dangerous.

adopted the role of "the honest broker" of the eastern question and presided over the Congress of Berlin (1878) to end the fighting. The British endorsed the congress because it served their policy of preserving the Ottoman Empire rather than dismantling it. The Berlin settlement placated Turkish honor by returning some territory lost in the fighting, and it awarded Balkan territory to both the Russians (Bessarabia) and the Austrians (Bosnia-Herzegovina). Bismarck bought French backing with support for colonial expansion. The Slavic nationalist movements of the Balkans—both Serbian and Bulgarian—were not satisfied: Serbs won their independence but Pan-Slavs saw Bosnia lost to Austria; the Bulgarians won independence but lost much territory promised to them in a preliminary treaty, the Treaty of San Stefano.

The Balkan crisis of 1875–78 drove Bismarck to negotiate a close military alliance with Austria-Hungary known as the Dual Alliance (1879), which became the new cornerstone of his alliance system. The Hapsburg

prime minister and foreign minister was a Hungarian, Count Julius Andrássy, who held no grudge against Germany for the war of 1866. Secret terms of the Dual Alliance promised each country military assistance if they were attacked by Russia and guaranteed neutrality if either were attacked by any other country. Bismarck labored simultaneously to retain Russian friendship by preserving and strengthening the Three Emperors' League; he understood that "[i]n a world of five powers, one should strive to be *a trois*" (on the side with three). Italy, motivated by a growing colonial rivalry with France in north Africa, joined the Dual Alliance in 1882, converting the pact into the Triple Alliance. Germany thus acquired explicit security against France, although Bismarck publicly presented the treaty as merely a bulwark of the monarchical order (see document 28.1). To underscore his desire for Russian friendship, Bismarck later negotiated another Russo-German treaty known as the Reinsurance Treaty (1887). This

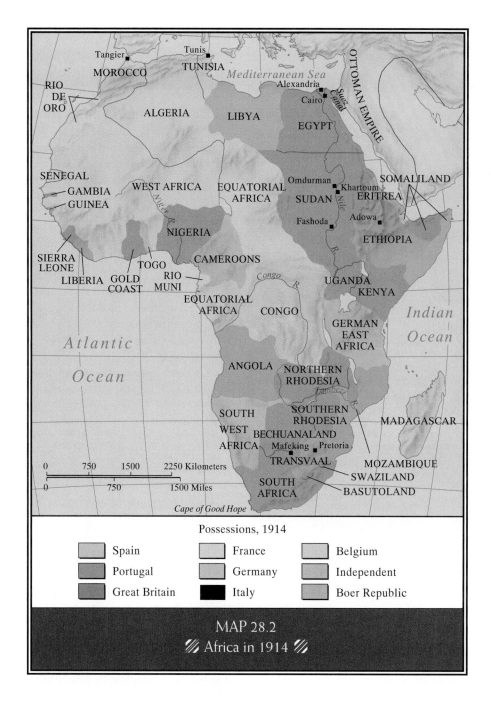

MAP 28.2

Africa in 1914

document gave a German pledge not to support Austrian aggression against Russia, and it was accompanied by significant German investment in Russian industrial development. Both governments reiterated their devotion to the status quo. Finally, Bismarck orchestrated a series of secondary treaties, such as the Mediterranean Agreements (1887), which involved other governments (including Britain and Spain) in the defense of the status quo. The network of his treaties became so complex that Bismarck enjoyed the self-bestowed image of being a juggler who could keep five balls in the air at once.

The New Imperialism, 1881–1914

The great powers exploited the European peace to annex large empires around the world. In 1871 only 10 percent of Africa had fallen under European control. Britain held the Cape Colony in South Africa and a few strips of West Africa. France had seized Algeria in 1830 and had long controlled part of West Africa including Senegal, while Portugal retained southern colonies dating back to the fifteenth and sixteenth centuries, but most of the continent remained self-governing tribal realms. By 1914 Europeans claimed virtually the entire

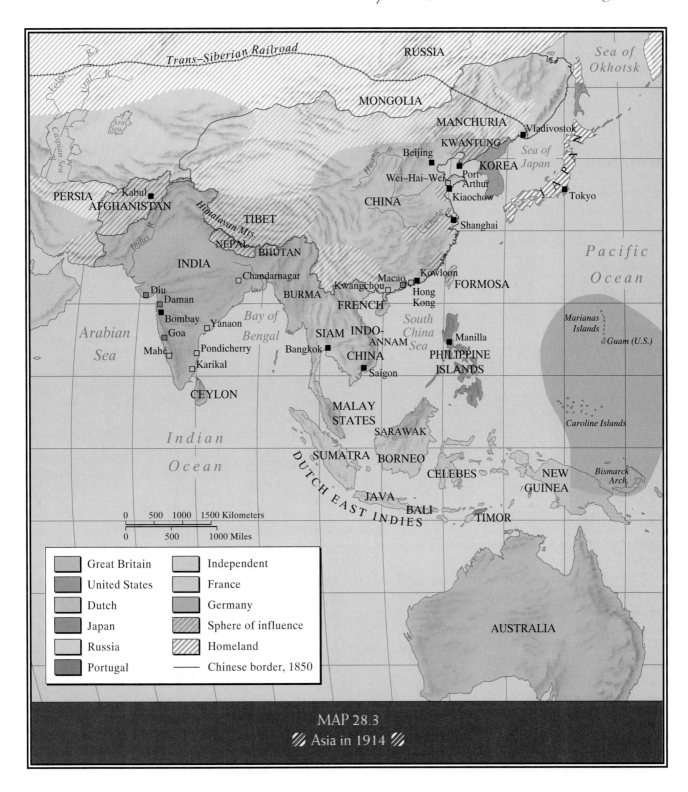

MAP 28.3

Asia in 1914

continent, leaving independent only Liberia (under American influence) and Ethiopia (claimed by Italy but unconquered) (see map 28.2). The new imperialism had also ended self-government in the Pacific by 1914. There, the Japanese, who took the Ryuku Islands in 1874 and Formosa in 1895, and Americans, who took Hawaii in 1898 and part of Samoa in 1899, joined Eu-

ropeans in building oceanic empires. Simultaneously, Britain and Russia expanded in southern Asia, Britain and France occupied most of Southeast Asia, and all of the industrial powers (including Japan and the United States) menaced China (see map 28.3). Empires were growing so fast that a leader of British imperialism, Colonial Secretary Joseph Chamberlain, gloated, "The

❖ DOCUMENT 28.2 ❖

Jules Ferry: French Imperialism (1885)

Jules Ferry (1832–1893) was a wealthy middle-class lawyer who served as premier of France for most of the early 1880s. He was a moderate republican and one of the founders of the Third Republic. His greatest accomplishments came in the creation of the French educational system (see chapter 27), but as premier he also became a leading champion of French imperialism. The following document is excerpted from one of his parliamentary speeches defending his policy.

Our colonial policy . . . rests upon our economic principles and interests, on our humanitarian visions of order, and on political considerations. . . .

[Interruptions by hecklers: "Yes, 20,000 corpses!" and "Ten thousand families in mourning!"]

Why have colonies from an economic standpoint? . . . [C]olonies are, for wealthy countries, an advantageous investment. France, which has exported a great amount of capital abroad, must consider this aspect of the colonial question. There is, however, another point, even more important: . . . For countries like France, devoted to exports by the nature of their industry, the colonial question is a question of markets. . . .

Gentlemen, there is a second point, a second set of ideas, that I must also raise: the humanitarian and civilizing side of imperialism. The honorable Camille Pelletan [another deputy] scoffs at this point. . . . He asks, "What is this civilization that one imposes with cannon shells?" . . . One must answer that superior races have rights with regard to the inferior races. They have rights because they have duties. They have the duty to civilize the inferior races. Do any of you deny, can anyone deny, that there is more justice, there is more moral and material order, more equality, more social virtues in North African society since France conquered that region? . . . Can anyone deny that it was good fortune for the people of equatorial Africa to fall under the protection of France and Britain?

. . . I add that French colonial policy . . . is inspired by another truth which you must reflect upon: a navy such as ours cannot survive with the shelters, defenses, supply bases. Just look at the map of the world. . . . No warship, no matter how perfectly organized, can carry more than a fourteen day supply of coal, and a warship short of coal is only a derelict on the high seas.

day of small nations has long passed away. The day of empires has come."

Europeans had been claiming empires around the world for centuries. Britain, France, Spain, Portugal, Denmark, and the Netherlands all held colonies taken before the nineteenth century. According to an estimate made in 1900, the frontiers of Russia had been advancing into Asia (much as the United States pushed westward) at the rate of fifty-five square miles per year since the sixteenth century. In the century between the 1770s and the 1870s, Russia fought six wars against the Ottoman Empire and four wars against Persia, in the course of which the czars annexed the Crimea, Georgia, and Armenia, then advanced into south Asia and prepared to take Afghanistan. Newly unified Italy and Germany were eager—against Bismarck's better judgment—to join this club. As Kaiser Wilhelm II said in a speech of 1901, echoing Bülow's *Weltpolitik*, Germans also expected "our place in the sun."

The empire building of the late nineteenth century, however, was different. Europeans had previously built colonial empires, sending colonists to live in distant

colonies. The new imperialism of 1881–1914 included little colonialism. Europeans sent soldiers to explore and conquer, officials to organize and administer, missionaries to teach and convert, and merchants to develop and trade, but few families of colonists. When Germany annexed African colonies in the 1880s, more Germans chose to emigrate to Paris (the capital of their national enemy) than to colonize Africa.

Earlier empires had also been based on mercantilist commerce. Colonies might provide such diverse goods as pepper, tulip bulbs, opium, or slaves, but they were expected to strengthen or to enrich the imperial state. Economic interests still drove imperialism, but the motor had changed. Imperialists now sought markets for exported manufactures, especially textiles. They dreamt, in the imagery of one British prime minister, of the fortunes to be made if every Oriental bought a woolen nightcap. The rise of trade unions inspired industrialists to covet cheaper, more manageable, colonial labor. Financiers needed to find markets for investing the capital accumulating from industrial profits. As a leading French imperialist, Jules Ferry, said, "Colonial policy is the daughter of industrial policy" (see document 28.2). The new imperialism, however, cannot be explained entirely by economics. Colonies cost imperial governments sums of money for military, administrative, and developmental expenses that far exceeded the tax revenues they produced. Many private enterprises also lost money on imperialism. In the early twentieth century, the five largest banks in Berlin appealed to the government to stop acquiring colonies because they were losing ventures. Individual investors usually lost money in colonial stocks; they frequently paid neither dividends nor interest and were sold as patriotic investments. Some businesses, and the elites who controlled them, did make great profits from captive markets; textile towns and port-cities prospered in this way and championed imperialism. A few individuals made staggering fortunes overseas, as Cecil Rhodes did in the African diamond fields. Rhodes was a struggling cotton farmer who bought a diamond claim and hired Africans to work it. When he died, he was considered the richest man on earth. His power was so enormous that a colony was named for him (Rhodesia, today Zimbabwe), and his fortune was so immense that it endowed the famous Rhodes scholarships to Oxford. Not surprisingly, Rhodes was an ardent imperialist who lamented that he could not annex the stars. Even the fantasy of striking it as rich as Rhodes, however, cannot fully explain why governments ran deficits to pay for empire.

The new imperialism must also be understood in terms of nationalism, militarism, and racism (see illustration 28.2). Imperialist politicians insisted that empire was the measure of a nation's greatness. Nationalist organizations, such as the Pan-German League, pressed their government to take more territory. It would "awaken and foster the sense of racial and cultural kinship" of Germans to know that their country occupied a city on the coast of China. Journalists, teachers, and scholars promoted similar attitudes about the greatness of empire. As a Cambridge historian wrote in 1883, "[T]here is something intrinsically glorious in an empire 'upon which the sun never sets.' " Even Cecil Rhodes insisted that his motives began with his nationalism. "I contend," he wrote, "that we [the British] are the first race in the world, and the more of the world we inhabit, the better it is for the human race. I believe it to be my duty to God, my Queen, and my Country to paint the whole map of Africa red [the color typically used to depict British colonies], red from the Cape to Cairo."

Militarism was also a significant factor in imperialism. The conquest of distant lands required larger armies and bigger budgets. Decoration, promotion, and territory were more easily won against preindustrial armies. Lord Kitchener became famous for commanding the outnumbered army that conquered the Sudan in 1896–98. Kitchener's army of twenty-five thousand defeated an army of fifty thousand because they were equipped with Maxim (machine) guns, which enabled them to kill large numbers of Sudanese with relative ease; at the decisive battle of Omdurman, Kitchener's forces suffered five hundred casualties and killed more than fifteen thousand Sudanese—"giving them a good dusting" in Kitchener's words. Thus, while the nineteenth century appears to be an age of peace for Britain when viewed in a European context, it was an epoch of constant warfare when viewed in a global context (see chronology 28.1).

In addition to economic and political explanations of imperialism, Western cultural attitudes are also important. These range from religion and humanitarianism to social Darwinism and racism. Christian missionaries formed the vanguard of imperialist intervention in Africa and Asia. They were successful in some regions: Nigeria and Madagascar, for example, are both more than 40 percent Christian today. In other regions, people resisted Christianity as an imperialist intervention; as one Indian put it, "Buddha came into our world on an elephant; Christ came into our world on a cannonball." Missionaries also taught Western attitudes and behavior, such as denouncing the depravity of seminudity in tropical climates. Textile manufacturers were not alone in concluding that "[b]usiness follows the Bible." Europeans also justified imperialism by speaking of humanitarianism. Some used crude stereotypes about abolishing cannibalism or moralistic arguments about ending polygamy; others took pride in the campaign to end the slave trade, which Europeans had done so much to develop. More educated arguments cited the abolition of practices such as *Suttee* in India (the tradition by which a widow threw herself on her husband's funeral pyre) or the benefits of Western medicine.

Humanitarian justifications for imperialism were often cloaked in terms such as the French doctrine of the *la mission civilatrice* or the title of Rudyard Kipling's poem "The White Man's Burden" (1899). Such terms suggested the social Darwinian argument that Western civilization was demonstrably superior to others, and this led to the simple corollaries that (1) in Jules Ferry's words, "superior races have rights with regard to inferior races" and (2) they had a duty to help "backwards" peoples. Kipling, for example, urged advanced states: "Fill full the mouth of Famine/And bid the sickness

So kolonisiert der Deutsche,

So kolonisiert der Engländer,

Illustration 28.2

Imperialism. The German satirical review *Simplicissimus* published this commentary in 1904: German imperialism is seen to be an extension of German militarism, whereas British imperialism is seen to be an extension of British capitalism. (The captions read, "This is the way the German colonizes.

This is the way the Englishman colonizes." The sign on the tree says, "It is forbidden to dump trash or snow here.") Other drawings in the series depicted French soldiers making love to native women and a Belgian roasting an African over an open fire and preparing to eat him.

◈ CHRONOLOGY 28.1 ◈

British Imperial Wars, 1815–1900

Date	War	Location	Result
1815	Ceylonese War	Indian Ocean	Ceylon made crown colony
1816	Barbados Rebellion	Caribbean	Slave revolt suppressed
1817–19	Assam Intervention	Southeast Asia	Assam ceded to Britain
1823	Guiana Rebellion	South America	Slave revolt suppressed
1824–26	First Burmese War	Southeast Asia	Further annexations from Burma
1831	Jamaica Rebellion	Caribbean	Slave revolt suppressed
1832	Falklands Campaign	South America	Falklands taken from Argentina
1834–35	Sixth Kaffir War	South Africa	Xhosa lands opened to settlement
1838–42	First Afghan War	South Asia	Successful British invasion
1839	Aden Campaign	Arabia	Port-town of Aden seized
1839–42	Opium War	China	Hong Kong seized
1843	Sind War	India	Baluchi lands annexed
1844–47	First Maori War	New Zealand	Maori uprising defeated
1845–46	First Sikh War	India	Sikh rebellion beaten
1846–47	Seventh Kaffir War	South Africa	Xhosa lands annexed
1848–49	Second Sikh War	India	Punjab annexed to India
1850–53	Eighth Kaffir War	South Africa	Xhosa defeated
1852–53	Second Burmese War	Southeast Asia	British merchants protected
1856–57	Persian War	South Asia	Shah forced to concede land
1856–57	Second China War	China	Trade policies defended
1857–58	Sepoy Mutiny	India	Mutineers defeated
1860–61	Second Maori War	New Zealand	Taranaki resistance beaten
1863–66	Third Maori War	New Zealand	Taranaki uprising defeated
1867–68	Abyssinian War	East Africa	Abyssinian threats ended
1868–72	Fourth Maori War	New Zealand	Maori resistance broken
1873–74	First Ashanti War	West Africa	Ashanti capital taken
1877–78	Ninth Kaffir War	South Africa	Annexation of all Kaffir lands
1878–79	Zulu War	South Africa	Natal saved from Zulus
1878–80	Second Afghan War	South Asia	Pro-British government installed
1880–81	South African War	South Africa	British withdraw from Boer lands
1882	Egyptian War	Egypt	Nationalist uprising defeated
1884–85	First Sudanese War	North Africa	Mahdist rebellion defeats English
1885–92	Third Burmese War	Southeast Asia	Burma made British colony
1896	Second Ashanti War	West Africa	Ashanti beaten
1896–99	Second Sudanese War	North Africa	Sudan reconquered
1899–1902	Boer War	South Africa	Boers defeated
1900	Third Ashanti War	West Africa	Ashanti lands annexed
1900	Boxer Uprising	China	Nationalist uprising beaten

cease." Even humanitarianism thus contained an element of the racism common in imperialism. Europeans had often viewed colonial peoples as heathens or savages. Late nineteenth-century social Darwinism worsened such stereotypes with the pseudoscientific notion that all races were locked in a struggle for survival, a struggle to be won by the fittest. Imperialists cheerfully concluded that their own nation would win this struggle. A president of the United States spoke of his desire to help his "little brown brothers" (the people of the Philippines). A czar of Russia joked about going to war with "little yellow monkeys" (the Japanese, who promptly defeated the Russians). By the early twentieth century, Western racism was so unchallenged that a major zoo exhibited an African in a cage alongside apes.

The Scramble for Africa

Historians often cite the French occupation of Tunis in 1881 as the beginning of the new imperialism. French pride had been hurt by the events of 1870–71, and it had received another blow in 1875 when the British purchased control of the Suez Canal (built by the French in the 1860s) from the khedive of Egypt. Bismarck used the distrust generated by the Suez issue to reawaken Anglo-French rivalry. At the Congress of Berlin in 1878, he encouraged the French to claim Tunis, and the congress approved. Jules Ferry, who became premier of France in 1880, used the excuse of raids by Tunisian tribes into Algeria to proclaim a French protectorate over Tunis—an act that promptly benefited Bismarck by driving the Italians into the Triple Alliance. The British responded by using nationalist riots as an excuse to extend their control of Egypt in 1882. They bombarded Alexandria, landed an army that defeated the Egyptian nationalists, occupied Cairo, and placed Egypt under the thumb of a British consul. Nationalist rebellion moved south to the Sudan in 1883. It acquired a religious fervor from an Islamic leader known as the Mahdi (messiah); the mahdists defeated several British garrisons, notably the forces of General Gordon at Khartoum (1885), and sustained an autonomous government until Kitchener's victory at Omdurman a decade later.

Anglo-French imperialism in North Africa provoked a race among European governments, known as "the scramble for Africa," to claim colonies in sub-Saharan Africa. In the five years between 1882 and 1887, Europeans claimed more than two million square miles of Africa. (The United States today totals less than 3.7 million square miles.) In 1884 alone, Germany took more than 500,000 square miles as German Southwest Africa (today Namibia), Cameroon, and Togo; two years later, they added nearly 400,000 square miles as German East Africa (today Tanzania). The largest single claim, nearly a million square miles of central Africa known as the Congo, was taken by King Leopold II of Belgium in 1885. Leopold then founded a company that brutally exploited the Congo as a gigantic rubber plantation, under the ironic name of the Congo Free State. But even land grabs that huge could

not compete with the British and French empires; by 1914 Great Britain and France each controlled approximately five million square miles of Africa.

The scramble for Africa had repercussions in European diplomacy, chiefly the reopening of the colonial rivalry between Britain and France. After General Kitchener's victory at Omdurman, his troops confronted a small French exploratory mission, the Marchand mission, which had camped on the upper Nile at the Sudanese town of Fashoda. Kitchener and Marchand both claimed Fashoda, but the size of Kitchener's forces obliged the French to leave. The Fashoda crisis showed that France remained vulnerable in 1898.

In the following months, however, the vulnerability of British diplomatic isolation was exposed by Britain's involvement in the Boer War (1899–1902). The Boers, white settlers of mixed Dutch and Huguenot descent, had created a republic, the Transvaal, in Bantu territory north of the Britain's Cape Colony in South Africa. The British annexed the Transvaal in 1877, but a revolt in 1880–81 earned the Boers autonomy under the strong leadership of President Paul Kruger. Tensions remained high, however, especially after the discovery of vast deposits of gold in the Transvaal. After a series of crises, such as the Jameson Raid into the Transvaal in 1895 (which had the backing of the prime minister of the Cape Colony, Cecil Rhodes), an Anglo-Boer war broke out in 1899. The Boers won initial victories, besieged the British at Mafeking and Ladysmith, and earned international sympathy, especially after the British placed 120,000 Boer women and children in concentration camps (the first use of this term) to limit support for Boer guerrillas and twenty thousand died, chiefly from disease. Massive British reinforcements under General Kitchener reversed the course of the war in 1900, lifting the siege of Mafeking, capturing the Boer capital of Pretoria, and again annexing the Transvaal. The Boer leaders continued resistance in two years of guerrilla fighting before accepting the British victory in the Treaty of Vereeniging in 1902.

The Boer War was the largest imperial war in Africa, but it should not distract attention from the wars of African resistance to imperialism. The British annexation of the Transvaal, for example, led them into the Zulu War of 1879, which showed that a poorly equipped African army could defeat Europeans. The Ashanti tribes of West Africa, in what is now Ghana, resisted the British in four wars during the nineteenth century, three of them fought between 1873 and 1896. The Ashanti, too, won battles against the British. The French likewise experienced defeats in fighting two Dahomeyan wars (in today's Benin); they received the added shock of having to fight Dahomeyan women soldiers who were accustomed to combat. The Mandingo tribes (in today's Ivory Coast) successfully resisted French occupation of the interior for thirteen years (1885–98) making a great hero of their chief, Samory. The Hereros (Bantu tribes of southwest Africa) and the Hottentots withstood the German army for nearly six years (1903–1908). They did not capitulate until the Germans had reduced the Herero population from eighty thousand to fifteen thousand. The Ethiopians threw out European invaders; Emperor Menelik II resisted an Italian occupation in 1896, and his forces annihilated an Italian army in the massive battle (more than 100,000 combatants) of Adowa.

Europeans eventually won most imperial wars. The advantage of modern armament is sufficient explanation, as Kitchener demonstrated in the bloody engagement on the plains of Omdurman. In the blunt words of one poet, "Whatever happens we have got/The Maxim Gun, and they have not." Europeans also held a numerical advantage whenever they chose to use it; defeats usually summoned reinforcements that Africans could not match, as the Bantus, the Zulus, and the Boers learned. The Italian army was outnumbered by eighty thousand to twenty thousand at Adowa. If Italy had wanted Ethiopia badly enough to obtain a four-to-one advantage (the Italian army and militia of the 1890s numbered nearly three million men), they, too, might have won. Europeans also succeeded in imperial conquests because of biological and medical advantages. Westerners were nourished by fairer agricultural land and more advanced agronomy. This provided an advantage in nutrition that translated into larger, healthier armies. European diseases differed from the disease pool in some parts of the world, although this was not as important in Africa as elsewhere. Invaders carrying infectious smallpox, whooping cough, or the measles (all of which could be fatal) sometimes carried a biological weapon better than gunpowder. Conversely, African diseases (especially malaria) had long blocked European penetration of the continent. When the French occupied Tunis in 1881, malaria took twenty-five times as many soldiers as combat did. Europeans knew that quinine, derived from the bark of the cinchona tree, prevented malaria, and scientists isolated the chemical in 1820, but not until the late nineteenth century did they synthesize quinine in adequate quantities to provide an inexpensive daily dose for large armies. Such scientific conquests of water- and insect-borne diseases made possible the military conquest of Africa.

Imperialism in Asia and the 'Opening of China'

Europeans began their conquests in Asia in the early sixteenth century. By the late nineteenth century (see map 28.3), Britain dominated most of south Asia (today's India, Pakistan, Sri Lanka, and Bangladesh) and Australasia (Australia and New Zealand). They had begun to expand into Southeast Asia, annexing much of Burma (now Myanmar) in 1853. This led them into competition with the French who landed troops in Annam (Vietnam) in 1858. Most of the East Indies had been claimed by the Dutch (the Dutch East Indies, today Indonesia) or the Spanish (the Philippines) for centuries. China and Japan had largely resisted Western penetration, except for toeholds such as Hong Kong, which the British leased in 1841.

The new imperialism refreshed the European appetite for Asia. Between 1882 and 1884 the French subjugated the region of modern Vietnam, and their expedition continued until Cambodia (1887) and Laos (1893) were combined with Annam to form French Indo-China (see document 28.3). This prompted the British to complete their annexation of Burma (1886) and to reach south for the Malay States (today Malaysia), which became a British-run federation in 1896. By the turn of the century, only Siam (Thailand) remained independent in the entire subcontinent, and Siamese freedom depended upon Anglo-French inability to compromise. Most of Southeast Asia had been under the loose suzerainty of the Manchu dynasty of China, and the European conquests of 1882–96 exposed the vulnerability of that regime. Japan's easy military victory in the Sino-Japanese War of 1894–95—the result of a decade of rivalry over Korea, which Japan seized in 1894—underscored that lesson. The Treaty of Shimonoseki ended that war, with China granting independence to Korea and ceding the province of Kwantung (west of Korea) and the island of Formosa (Taiwan) to Japan.

Europeans could not resist exploiting the infirmity of the Chinese Empire. Their initial intervention, however, was against the Japanese, who were obliged to return Kwantung to China. Then, in 1896, the Russians extracted a treaty allowing them to build the Trans-Siberian Railway across the Chinese province of Manchuria to the port of Vladivostok. Shortly thereafter, the Russians simply occupied Manchuria. In early 1897 the Germans followed the Japanese and Russians into China by occupying the northern port-city of Kiaochow after two German missionaries had been killed in that region. The German government also asserted that Europeans deserved concessions in return

A Chinese Governor Denounces French Imperialism (1883)

I, Vice-commandant . . . Liu Yung-fu publish this proclamation so that it be read in the four cardinal points [of the compass].

The country of Annam [modern Vietnam] . . . was a tributary of the Chinese Empire. The entire world, and even children five years old, knows that Annam is tributary of China; why does France seem to be ignorant of this fact? . . . The greed of the French is equaled only by the voracity of the shark. They wish to absorb the Empire of Annam . . . .

I have had to have brave soldiers come. They are at Hanoi. On May 13 and 14, they attacked the Catholic Mission. On the nineteenth, they fought with the French troops. The gunfire resounded like thunder. The flesh of the men has shivered from it. . . . [O]ur soldiers are courageous and are not afraid to march forward even if they have to fight one against ten. In this fight, we killed some French chiefs: a commandant with five bands [on his uniform], a captain, and two lieutenants. The number of soldiers killed is incalculable. . . . [W]e pursued them [the French] as far as the West Gate. Then the gate was closed and they have not dared to show themselves. Their conduct is condemned by the gods and by men. They merit that punishment, which is the vengeance of Heaven alone.

If France is aware of her faults and regrets them, she will withdraw her troops.

---

for their help dealing with Japan in 1895. These events launched another imperialist scramble, this time known as "the opening of China." Unlike their outright annexation of land in Africa, European governments used the genteel device of pressing the Manchu government to sign ninety-nine-year "leases" to "treaty ports" along the coast of China. During 1898 the Germans extracted a lease to Kiaochow, the Russians to the Liaodong peninsula and Port Arthur, the French to Kwangchow in the south (near to Indo-China), and the British to both Wei-Hai-Wei in the north and Kowloon (near Hong Kong) in the south. Only the Italians, who had recently

suffered the humiliation of Adowa, were denied a lease on the assumption they were unable to invade China.

While Europeans were extracting leases to Chinese territory, another war shifted imperialist attention further east, to the islands of the Pacific Ocean. The Spanish-American War of 1898—chiefly fought in the Caribbean, following a Cuban insurrection against Spanish rule in 1895—completed the collapse of the Spanish colonial empire. The victorious United States, which had won an important naval victory against the Spanish at Manila, claimed the Philippine archipelago (the largest Spanish colony) and fought a three-year war (1899–1901) to subdue Filipino nationalists led by Emilio Aguinaldo (captured in 1901). The United States chose to follow European imperialism and by the Spooner Amendment of 1901 established an American government for the islands. This stimulated a race to claim the remaining islands of the Pacific. Germany and the United States, both eager for bases to support global fleets, led this rush. Between 1899 and 1914 Germany claimed dozens of north Pacific islands (such as the Mariana Islands, the Caroline Islands, and the Marshall Islands, which would become famous battlegrounds of World War II). The United States took Hawaii (1898), Guam (1898), and Wake Island (1900), while joining Germany and Britain in dividing the Samoan Islands (1899). By 1914 no self-governing atoll survived in the Pacific.

The Asian resistance to Western imperialism, like the African resistance, was repeatedly expressed with arms. The opening of China in 1898 precipitated a turbulent period in Chinese history that included an uprising against foreigners, the Boxer Rebellion (1900–1901). The Boxers, the European name for a paramilitary organization of Chinese nationalists who hoped to expel all foreigners from China, began the uprising by attacking Christian missionaries and their converts. Violence spread to Beijing, culminating in the murder of the German ambassador and a siege of Western legations. A multinational expedition put down the Boxer Rebellion and conducted punitive missions into provincial China. The peace accords of 1901, known as the Boxer Protocol, showed the vulnerability of Manchu China, which was made to punish officials who aided the Boxers, pay a large indemnity, and yield more territory.

Japan provided the most successful opposition to European imperialism in Asia. European intervention against the Japanese in 1895, followed by provocations such as the Russian occupation of Manchuria, the lease to Port Arthur, penetration of Korea, and a refusal to recognize Japanese interests led to the Russo-Japanese War of 1904–1905. The Japanese attacked Port Arthur in February 1904, trapping the entire Russian Pacific fleet except for the ships icebound at Vladivostok. A few weeks later the Japanese army landed in Korea, advanced into Manchuria, and defeated the Russian army. In the spring of 1905 a Russian European fleet reached the Orient only to be destroyed (thirty-three of forty-five ships were sunk) in the battle of Tsushima Strait between Japan and Korea.

Resistance to European imperialism went beyond the Indo-Chinese wars of the 1880s, the Boxer uprising of 1900, and the Japanese victory of 1904–1905. Well-organized nationalist movements appeared in the early twentieth century. In 1908, for example, a group of moderate nationalists wrote a constitution for the Indian National Congress (later, the Congress Party), calmly stating their objective of winning self-government by constitutional means. The African National Congress (ANC) of South Africa originated at a similar meeting in 1912. Many of the nationalists who would lead the twentieth-century resistance to Western imperialism emigrated to Europe where they received formal and informal educations in dealing with European governments. Ho Chi Minh, the leader of Vietnamese armed resistance to French, Japanese, and American imperialism, lived in France as a young man; there he joined in the foundation of the French Communist Party. Perhaps the most impressive resistance to imperialism was begun by an Indian lawyer, Mohandas Gandhi. Gandhi began his career as a lawyer defending Indian laborers in South Africa in 1889. There he developed a policy of nonviolent resistance known by the Sanskrit word *Satyagraha*. Despite harassment, beatings, and imprisonment, Gandhi stood with the moral force of *Satyagraha* and gained a global reputation. When the frustrated British deported him to India, Gandhi brought passive resistance to Indian nationalism. When the British arrested him during World War I, Gandhi accepted imprisonment with a moving speech: "I have disregarded the order served upon me, not for want of respect for lawful authority, but in obedience of the higher law of our being—the voice of conscience."

The Diplomatic Revolution, 1890–1914

Imperial rivalries strained the Bismarckian system in Europe, but his network of alliances survived until Kaiser Wilhelm II sent Bismarck into retirement in 1890. The young emperor followed the advice of one of Bismarck's rivals, Baron Fritz von Holstein, to revise the Bismarckian system because Bismarck's promises to Russia risked losing the close alliance with Austria. Despite repeated Russian requests, the kaiser therefore decided not to renew the Reinsurance Treaty of 1887, and it lapsed three months after the dismissal of Bismarck. Instead, Wilhelm expanded the Triple Alliance in 1891, giving larger promises of support to Austria-Hungary and Italy. The consequence of the lapsing of Reinsurance Treaty was Franco-Russian friendship. The Third Republic was the most radical state in Europe—a republic in a monarchical world—and the Russian Empire the most reactionary (playing the French national anthem was a crime), but self-interest drew the two governments together. One year after Bismarck's departure, a French fleet paid a symbolic visit to the Russian port of Kronstadt (near St. Petersburg) and Franco-Russian negotiations began; French pledges of loans to help industrialize Russia quickly led to the August Convention of 1891, an informal guarantee of cooperation. Reciprocal state visits and avid French diplomacy expanded this into a military treaty, the Franco-Russian Alliance of 1894. Through this pact, the czar pledged to use the full Russian army against Germany, if Germany invaded France; the reciprocal French promise gave Russia security against Austria and Germany. To be ready for war, both sides also pledged to mobilize their armies as soon as any member of the Triple Alliance began mobilization. France was no longer isolated, and a post-Bismarckian diplomatic revolution had begun.

The 1890s witnessed a further weakening of the German position as a result of deteriorating Anglo-German relations. The rise of Germany as an industrial power caused a rivalry for markets and aroused hostile public opinion in both countries. The jingoistic press, which played an important role in fomenting the Spanish-American War of 1898, contributed significantly to the worsening relations. The trade rivalry made the British question their tradition of free trade, and newspapers were soon denouncing goods "Made in Germany." German imperialism and German sympathy for the Boers (the kaiser sent a notorious telegram of encouragement to President Kruger in 1896) worsened relations further. German colonies contributed to the emergence of a larger problem: the German decision to build a great navy. Through the efforts of Admiral von Tirpitz, Germany adopted an ambitious Naval Law in 1898 and expanded that construction program with a second Naval Law in 1900. The British, who had long counted upon "ruling the waves" as their insurance against invasion, had adopted a vigorous naval building policy in 1889 known as "the two-power standard"; that is, they would build a navy equal to the combined forces of any two rivals. This policy, in combination with the German naval laws, led Europe to a dangerous (and expensive) arms race.

When the Fashoda crisis rekindled Anglo-French colonial disputes in 1898, some British statesmen, led by Joseph Chamberlain, argued that the government must abandon splendid isolation and enter the European alliance system. Chamberlain suggested resolving Anglo-German differences and negotiating an Anglo-German alliance, but his unofficial talks with minor diplomats in 1898–1901 failed to persuade either Prime Minister Salisbury or Chancellor von Bülow, and they were flatly rejected by the kaiser. The French foreign minister who yielded to Britain in the Fashoda crisis, Théophile Delcassé, responded by seizing the opportunity to open Anglo-French negotiations over their generations of colonial differences. By skillfully expanding colonial negotiations, Delcassé became the architect of a diplomatic revolution that ended British isolation and the hegemony of the Triple Alliance. His greatest accomplishment was an Anglo-French agreement of 1904 known as the Entente Cordiale (cordial understanding). The entente was not a military treaty comparable to the Triple Alliance or the Franco-Russian Alliance. It simply resolved colonial disputes: France recognized British preeminence in Egypt, and Britain accepted the French position in Morocco. Starting with this *quid pro quo,* the two governments were able to end squabbles around the globe.

The German reaction to the Entente Cordiale was to provoke an international crisis over Morocco in 1905. Germany, which had a growing commercial interest in Morocco, had been excluded from talks on the subject and had not even received formal notification of the Anglo-French agreement, although Delcassé had conducted subsequent negotiations on Morocco to acquire the support of Spain (by giving up the Moroccan coast opposite Spain) and of Italy (by backing an Italian claim to Tripoli). The Moroccan Crisis (later called the first Moroccan Crisis) resulted from a state visit by Kaiser Wilhelm II to Tangier, Morocco, where he made a strong speech in defense of Moroccan independence and an open door in foreign trade. When Delcassé proposed that some territorial concession be made to Germany to recognize the French position in Morocco, the kaiser refused. This confrontation led, at the invitation of the sultan of Morocco, to an international confer-

ence at Algeciras (Spain) in 1906, where Delcassé's diplomacy succeeded again, although he was driven from office in France by fears that he was dangerously provoking Germany. The crisis strengthened the Entente Cordiale and prompted closer Anglo-French military conversations; and when a vote was taken at Algeciras, only Austria supported Germany. Bismarck would have been horrified to see how the diplomatic revolution had shifted the balance of power toward France. The survival of the entente cordiale convinced his successors to adopt a third Naval Law in 1906, but that in turn frightened the British enough to negotiate their territorial disputes with Russia in south Asia (Persia and Afghanistan). The French encouraged these talks and the Russians recognized the need for them in the aftermath of their defeat in 1905; the resultant Anglo-Russian Entente of 1907 divided Persia into spheres of influence and exchanged a Russian agreement to stay out of Afghanistan in return for British support for Russian naval access to the Mediterranean. This entente combined with the Entente Cordiale to create the Triple Entente. The Triple Entente did not initially include the explicit military provisions of the Triple Alliance, but Britain, France, and Russia soon entered into talks to plan military cooperation. Whereas French diplomats once worried about their isolation by Bismarck, the diplomatic revolution made Germans speak angrily of their *Einkreisung* (encirclement) by hostile competitors.

The Eastern Question and the Road to War

This division of Europe into two competing alliances meant that virtually any local crisis could precipitate a general war. Europe held several grave local problems, but the worst remained the eastern question. Bismarck's Congress of Berlin in 1878 had not settled this issue; it had merely temporized by placating the great powers; it did nothing to resolve Balkan nationalist claims or to settle the internal problems of the Ottoman Empire. Fighting resumed in the Balkans (see chronology 28.2) in the 1880s and had become severe in 1885 when Bulgarian nationalists in East Rumelia sought unity with Bulgaria and Serbia went to war to prevent the creation of a large Bulgaria on its eastern frontier. Fighting broke out twice in the 1890s, then two more times in the early twentieth century before the next major crisis,

◆ CHRONOLOGY 28.2 ◆

The Eastern Question: Balkan Conflict, 1875–1914

Date	Combatants	Cause
1875	Bosnia-Herzegovina versus Ottoman Empire	Bosnian rebellion for independence
1876	Bulgaria versus Ottoman Empire	Bulgarian rebellion for independence
1876–78	Serbia, Montenegro versus Ottoman Empire	War to support or annex Bosnia
1877–78	Russia versus Ottoman Empire	War to support or annex Balkan peoples
1878	Greece versus Ottoman Empire	War to annex Thessaly
1880	Montenegro versus Albania	Albanians resist 1878 peace settlement
1885	Eastern Rumelia versus Ottoman Empire	Rebellion for unification with Bulgaria
1885	Serbia versus Bulgaria	War over conflicting claims to Macedonia
1896–97	Crete versus Ottoman Empire	Rebellion against Turkish rule
1897	Greece versus Ottoman Empire	Greek effort to acquire Crete, Macedonia
1903	Macedonia	Civil war among ethnic groups over which state to join
1905	Crete versus Ottoman Empire	Rebellion in favor of union with Greece
1908	Balkan Crisis	Bulgarian declaration of independence
		Austrian annexation of Bosnia
		Greek annexation of Crete
1912–13	First Balkan War: Serbia, Montenegro, Bulgaria, and Greece versus Ottoman Empire	Territorial claims against Ottoman Empire
1913	Balkan War: Bulgaria versus Serbia, Greece, Romania, and Ottoman Empire	Fight over division of Macedonia
1913	Serbia versus Albania	Resistance to Serbian annexation plan

known as the Balkan crisis of 1908. The crisis began with a long-simmering rebellion of westernizers inside the Ottoman Empire, known as the Young Turk rebellion; the victorious Young Turks won numerous concessions from the Sultan and a majority in a Turkish Parliament, but they exposed the weakness of the government in Constantinople to resist changes in the Balkans.

Almost constant crises wracked the Balkans from 1908 to 1914. Austria-Hungary, which had established a claim to Bosnia and Herzegovina in 1878, took advantage of the Ottoman crisis to annex the two provinces in 1908. This act outraged Pan-Slav nationalists in Serbia who had long seen Serbia as "the Piedmont of the Balkans" and anticipated a merger with Bosnia in a union of the southern Slavs (the Yugo Slavs in the Serbian language). After the annexation, Slavic nationalists turned increasingly to revolutionary societies, such as the Black Hand, to achieve unity. The 1911 statutes of the Black Hand stated the danger

bluntly: "This organization prefers terrorist action to intellectual propaganda." The Hapsburg monarchy was soon to discover that this was not an idle threat. None of the European powers was pleased by the annexation of Bosnia, but none intervened to prevent it.

The continuing weakness of the Ottoman Empire, militancy of Balkan nationalism, and reluctance of the great powers to intervene led to a succession of crises. In 1911 a second Moroccan crisis occurred, in which Germany sent the gunboat *Panther* to Morocco to protect German interests and the French conceded territory in central Africa to resolve the dispute. In 1912 a war broke out in North Africa, in which Italy invaded Tripoli to acquire their compensation for French gains in Morocco. Later that year, open warfare began in the Balkans when Serbia, Montenegro, Bulgaria, and Greece joined to attack the Ottoman Empire and detach some the few remaining Turkish provinces in Europe; the Italians soon joined this First Balkan War (1912–13) by invading the Dodecanese Islands off the

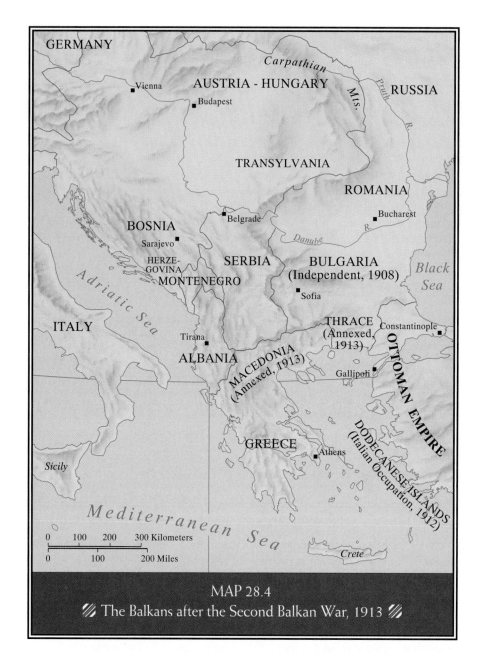

MAP 28.4

The Balkans after the Second Balkan War, 1913

coast of Turkey. After the Turks had conceded territory to all of the belligerents, they quarreled among themselves; several states fought Bulgaria, in the Second Balkan War (1913), to redivide the spoils (see map 28.4). But nationalist ambitions were still unsatisfied.

Militarism and the European Arms Race

Imperial competition, alliance system rivalries, and the Balkan crises were all happening in an age of militarism. Europe in 1900 was the scene of a heated arms race, sustained by a mentality that glorified military action. When Bismarck negotiated the Triple Alliance in 1879, the typical great power army was smaller than 500,000 men; by 1913 the average exceeded one million men, with mobilization plans for armies of three million to four million men (see table 28.1). The naval construction race between Britain and Germany was the most costly part of the arms race. The industrial age had made it possible to build enormous, steam-powered, steel battleships, equipped with long-range artillery. These dreadnoughts (from the expression "Fear God and Dread Nought") were staggeringly expensive. The construction of submarine fleets added significantly to

N TABLE 28.1 N

The European Army Buildup, 1879–1913

Country	1879		1913	
	Standing army in peacetime	Fully mobilized army for war	Standing army in peacetime	Fully mobilized army for war
Austria-Hungary	267,000	772,000	800,000	3,000,000
Britain	136,000	600,000	160,000	700,000
India	200,000		249,000	
France	503,000	1,000,000	1,200,000	3,500,000
Germany	419,000	1,300,000	2,200,000	3,800,000
Russia	766,000	1,213,000	1,400,000	4,400,000

Illustration 28.3

%/ **The Arms Race.** This 1909 photograph of British submarines in the Thames River near Westminister Palace (the seat of Parliament) conveys an eerie foreshadowing of the war. It was intended to show British naval might protecting freedom, a justification for the vast expenses of naval construction. Viewed in retrospect, it is an ironic and tragic scene because the naval competition led to German submarines, which were effective in choking British shipping.

the total (see illustration 28.3). Before the shipbuilding mania of the 1890s, Britain had an annual naval budget of £13.8 million. This took more than 15 percent of government revenues, or more than twice the amount spent on education, science, and the arts combined (£6.1 million). Then, between 1890 and 1914, annual British naval expenditures more than tripled to £47.4 million. (The total revenue raised by the British income tax in 1913 was £44 million.) The German naval budget, meanwhile, almost quintupled from £4.6 million (1871) to £22.4 million (1914).

Few people yet understood the implications of this marriage between militarism and industrialization. Cavalry troops wearing brightly colored eighteenth-century uniforms and sabres remained the image of a heroic army, although a more accurate image of an army in 1900 portrayed its machines: rapid-firing heavy artillery and machine guns such as the Maxims that had slaughtered the Sudanese. And no army could be stronger than the chemical industry that stood behind it; mass armies, and the total war that they implied, only became possible when chemists devised ways to manufacture millions of tons of explosives.

The arms race was accompanied by a popular militarism glorifying war (see document 28.4). "Eternal peace is a dream, and not even a beautiful one," held one famous general. A book entitled *Germany and the Next War* (1911) insisted that "war is a biological necessity." Writers everywhere popularized such attitudes. In the words of an Italian journalist, "We wish to glorify war—the only health-giver of the world." Or, in those of an American philosopher, "War is a school of strenuous life and heroism." Militaristic governments

◆ DOCUMENT 28.4 ◆

Heinrich von Treitschke: The Glorification of War

Heinrich von Treitschke (1834–96) was a distinguished German historian at the University of Berlin beginning in 1874. Although Treitschke was a Saxon, his passionate nationalism made him a champion of Prussian and then German nationalism. His chief work was a five-volume history of Germany in the nineteenth century, but he expressed many of his outspoken theories (including the excerpt given here) in his lectures, which were later published under the title Politics.

Brave peoples alone have an existence, an evolution or a future; the weak and the cowardly perish, and perish justly. The grandeur of history lies in the perpetual conflict of nations, and it is simply foolish to desire the suppression of their rivalry. . . .

Without war, no state could be. All those we know of arose through war, and the protection of their members by armed force remains their primary and essential task. War, therefore, will endure to the end of history, as long as there is a multiplicity of states. . . .

It is then the normal and reasonable thing for a great nation to embody and develop the essence of the state, which is power, by organizing its physical strength in the constitution of the army. We live in a warlike age; the over-sentimental philanthropic fashion of judging things has passed into the background, so that we can once more join hands . . . in calling war the forceful continuation of politics. . . . We have learned to perceive the moral majesty of war. . . . The greatness of war is just what at first sight seems to be its horror—that for the sake of their country men will overcome the natural feeling of humanity, that they will slaughter their fellow men who have done them no injury.

produced elaborate plans for possible wars. German planners, for example, were ready for an invasion of the British Isles or of Texas (supporting a Mexican invasion of the southwestern United States), although they naturally lavished their most meticulous attention, such as the creation of precise railroad timetables, on plans to invade France.

The most famous peacetime war plan was the Schlieffen Plan, named for the general who first devised it in 1892 in response to the Franco-Russian rapprochement. This plan, which was regularly revised by the German General Staff, responded to the fear that Germany might have to fight a war on two fronts at once. Schlieffen reasoned that the Russians would be slow to mobilize, but the French, able to employ modern communications and transportation, would be an immediate threat. The Schlieffen Plan therefore directed the German army to begin any war by concentrating all possible forces against the French; a rapid victory there would permit defeating the Russians afterward. To win that rapid victory over the French, the plan proposed to start any war (without regard to where it originated) by invading neutral Belgium (originally the Netherlands and Belgium). As the German strategist Karl von Clausewitz had explained a century earlier, "The heart of France lies between Brussels and Paris." The German plan for marching to Brussels and then pivoting southward was so precise that it included a timetable for each day's progress, culminating in a triumphal parade through Paris on day thirty-nine. French war planners also believed that the next war would be decided by a rapid offensive. Their 1913 regulations were straightforward: "The French army, returning to its tradition, henceforth admits no law but the offensive." This mentality, like the German notion of invading a neutral country, would cost hundreds of thousands of lives. It was expounded through a document known as Plan XVII, drafted by French generals for the reconquest of Alsace and Lorraine. Most of the French army was to be concentrated on the eastern frontier and then march into Alsace, but French planners so poorly understood what an industrial war would be like that they rejected camouflage uniforms for their great offensive and dressed soldiers in bright red trousers.

The Balkan Crisis of July 1914

Europeans little recognized the gravity of their situation in the early twentieth century; their rivalries for markets and empire, their nationalist ambitions and hatreds, their alliances and battle plans, their militarism, and their crude social Darwinian belief in "the survival of the fittest" all threatened the devastation of their civilization. Putting the matter most succinctly, Winston Churchill noted, "Europe in 1914 was a powderkeg where everybody smoked." When yet another Balkan crisis occurred in the summer of 1914, European gov-

Illustration 28.4

The Assassination of Franz-Ferdinand. The immediate cause of fighting in the summer of 1914 was the murder of the heir to the Hapsburg throne (and his wife) by a Slavic nationalist. In this photograph taken shortly before his assassination, the Archduke Franz-Ferdinand and his wife walk to the open car in which they would be shot a few minutes later.

ernments precipitated a monstrously destructive war, known to contemporaries as "the Great War" and to later generations as World War I. Some historians have called it "the suicide of the old Europe."

The Balkan crisis of 1914 began in the Bosnian city of Sarajevo. A nineteen-year-old Serbian nationalist and member of the Black Hand, Gavrilo Princip, assassinated the heir to the Hapsburg throne, the archduke Franz-Ferdinand, during a state visit to Sarajevo in late June (see illustration 28.4). The Austrian government blamed the Serbian government, which knew of the planned assassination and did not stop it, for the murder. After securing a promise that their German allies would support them in a confrontation with Serbia—a pledge known as "the blank check"—the Austrians sent a forty-eight-hour ultimatum to Serbia: The government must dissolve nationalist societies, close nationalist periodicals, end anti-Austrian propaganda, fire anti-Austrian members of the government, allow Austrian investigation of the crime inside Serbia, and arrest officials implicated. The Russian government meanwhile warned that it would not tolerate an Austrian invasion of Serbia. The Russians, too, received assurances that their allies, the French, would support them—President Poincaré of France was visiting Russia during the crisis and stood by France's staunchest ally. When Serbia accepted most, but not all, of the ultimatum, the Austrians declared war on July 28, 1914, exactly one month after the assassination in Sarajevo; they bombarded the Serbian capital, Belgrade (which sat at the border), on the next day.

The Third Balkan War quickly became a general European war. The Russians responded to it by ordering the mobilization of their army. Germany, whose war plans were predicated upon the Russians being slow to mobilize, demanded that the Russian army stand down. When the Russians did not, the German army invaded Belgium. This violation of the international treaty on Belgian neutrality ("a scrap of paper" in the phrase of the chancellor Bethmann-Hollweg of Germany) led the British to recognize that their interests were on the side of the French. For centuries, British policy had opposed the dominance of the lowlands (from where an invasion might be launched) by any strong power—by Spain, later by France, or now by Germany. European declarations of war rained down in the first days of August, until the members of the Triple Alliance and the Triple Entente were at war with each other over a crisis of Balkan nationalism. As the British foreign secretary observed, after a long cabinet meeting had chosen war and the streetlights of London were being extinguished for daybreak, "The lights are going out all over Europe." That somber statement was a good metaphor for the four years of darkness that followed; at the time, however, public opinion greeted the war with great enthusiasm (see illustration 28.5) and brisk sales were made of French (or German) dictionaries for "the stroll to Paris" (or Berlin). Only limited expressions of antiwar sentiment were heard after Jean Jaurès, the leading socialist proponent of organizing workers against war, was assassinated on July 31 (three days after the assassination of Franz-Ferdinand and the

Illustration 28.5

War Enthusiasm. The beginning of World War I was greeted with remarkable public enthusiasm. Cheering crowds volunteered to fight and hailed departing soldiers. One of the most memorable photographs of this war fever was taken in Munich on the day that war was declared, August 2, 1914. Holding his hat near the center of the happy crowd is Adolf Hitler, who soon joined a Bavarian regiment and fought in the war. The photographer, Heinrich Hoffmann, later became Hitler's court photographer.

day before mobilization of the French and German armies).

Other important belligerents entered the war slowly. The Ottoman Empire, whose continuing collapse in the Balkans had been such a factor in the coming of the war, followed its close military and economic ties with Germany and its historic territorial rivalry with Russia into the war in October 1914. Italy remained neutral, declaring that the Triple Alliance was binding only if Germany or Austria were invaded, not when they invaded small neighbors. The Italians then negotiated with both sides, and they eventually joined the entente powers in 1915, when a secret Treaty of London promised them significant territorial compensation at the expense of the Hapsburg Empire. The United States likewise remained neutral despite significant pro-British sentiment. Although a dispute over submarine warfare clouded German-American relations, President Woodrow Wilson kept the country out of war and contributed to efforts for a negotiated peace until entering the war on the side of the entente powers in 1917.

World War I: From the Invasion of Belgium to a World War

Before the war ended in November 1918, twenty-seven countries joined in the fighting. The decisive theatre of the war was the western front in France and Belgium, although the largest armies met on the eastern front

and fighting reached into the Middle East, Africa, and the Pacific Islands. More than sixty million men were mobilized to fight, including millions of Africans, Indians, Canadians, Australians, and Americans. The French, for example, conscripted 519,000 Africans to fight in Europe. By 1917 the belligerents included Japan and China (both on the side of the western Allies), Turkey (on the side of Germany and the Central Powers), and many smaller states supporting the western Allies. For example, the governments of Siam, Liberia, and Peru all found reasons to declare war on Germany.

Fighting in the west nearly resulted in a German victory in 1914. The Schlieffen Plan led to the German occupation of Brussels on the sixteenth day of the war, and a German army of 1.5 million men pushed far into France by the thirty-fifth day (see map 28.5). Simultaneously, the French invasion of Alsace and Lorraine (the battle of the Frontiers) failed and the French were driven back with heavy losses. In early September, the German army stood within a few miles of Paris. Victory seemed imminent, and the chief of staff, General Helmuth von Moltke (nephew of the Moltke of the 1860s), sent part of the army to the eastern front to protect Prussia. In a week of desperate fighting along the Marne River, in which the military governor of Paris (General Joseph Gallieni) gambled the city's garrison, which he shuttled to the front in Parisian taxicabs, the French stopped the German advance and forced the invaders to retreat to more defensible positions. Victory at the Marne saved France at a horrifying price. Of 1.3 million French field troops at the start of the war, more

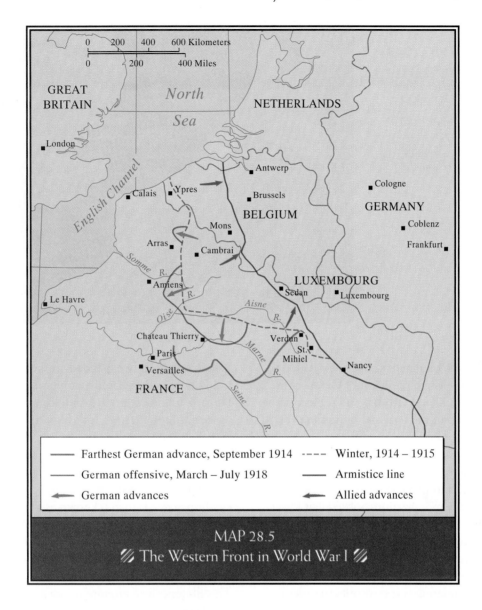

MAP 28.5

The Western Front in World War 1

than 600,000 were killed, wounded, or taken prisoner in one month of fighting. The casualty rate among French infantry officers reached two-thirds. The aftermath of the battle of the Marne was a different kind of war: After a "race to the sea" stretched the opposing armies from the English Channel to Switzerland, they fought a defensive war in which massive battles hardly budged the opposing army. By late 1914 both armies had dug into fixed positions and faced each other from a system of earthen trenches. (Trenches were typically seven to eight feet deep and six to seven feet wide, dug in a series of parallel lines with connecting lateral trenches; they were often filled with mud, standing water, vermin, or the unburied dead; and despite timbering, the walls tended to collapse (see illustration 28.6).) Despite staggering casualty rates, the line did not move more than ten miles in the next three years.

In the east, Russian armies engaged the Austrian army in Galicia and invaded East Prussia (see map 28.6), while most of the German army participated in the Schlieffen Plan in the west. They won some initial victories in Galicia, but the German and Austrian armies soon defeated the poorly equipped and commanded Russians. An outnumbered German army, led by a Prussian aristocrat and veteran of the wars of unification, General Paul von Hindenburg, and a young staff officer who had distinguished himself in the west, General Erich von Ludendorff, stopped the Russian invasion at the battle of Tannenberg in August 1914, taking more than 100,000 prisoners. Two weeks later, Hindenburg's army defeated the Russians again at the battle of the Masurian Lakes, taking another 125,000 captives and driving a demoralized enemy from Prussia. The Russian defeat was so complete that the commander

Illustration 28.6

The Western Front. This German photograph captures many features of trench warfare on the western front: the stark trench itself, in which soldiers had to stand on a ledge to see over the top; the denuded landscape, showing only rocky subsoil; and one of the devastating new weaponry of war, the machine gun.

shot himself, whereas Hindenburg became a national hero who would be elected president of Germany in 1925. Large armies and vast territory still protected the czarist government, but the first year of fighting cost nearly one million soldiers plus all of Poland and Lithuania. The Russians recovered sufficiently to stage a great offensive against the Austrians in 1916 (the Brusilov Offensive), but that campaign cost one million men and worsened demoralization. Subsequent losses were so enormous (more than 9 million Russian military casualties, including 1.7 million deaths, plus 2.2 million civilian deaths) that in early 1918 a revolutionary government negotiated a separate peace in the Treaty of Brest-Litovsk, surrendering vast territories in order to leave the war.

By 1915 secondary fronts had expanded the European conflagration into a world war. In the first weeks of the war, British and French colonial armies conquered most of the German colonies in Africa, although a German army in East Africa held out until the armistice. British and Japanese forces similarly took German positions in China and the Pacific. In southern Europe, Italy joined the western Allies in 1915, after the Treaty of London promised several Austrian provinces (such as the Tyrol and Istria). The Italian front witnessed two years of indecisive fighting, which barely shifted the lines. In late 1917 the Italians were badly defeated by forces under General Ludendorff at the battle of Caporetto, but that action came too late to change the outcome of the war. In the Balkans, the Serbians initially held out against the Austrians, but the

Balkan war quickly expanded: Turkey joined the Central Powers and declared a holy war (*Jihad*) in 1914, Bulgaria followed in 1915, and Romania joined the western Allies in 1916. Turkish participation led to bloody fighting in the Middle East. A Russo-Turkish War nearly annihilated the Armenians who were caught between them; in 1915 the Turks accused the Armenians of pro-Russian sympathies and began their forced eviction, a death march known as the Armenian Massacre. The British intervened in the Middle Eastern front (upon the advice of Winston Churchill) and in 1915 made a landing at Gallipoli, a peninsula in the Aegean Sea near the narrow passage of the Dardanelles. This ill-conceived attempt to open the straits and supply the Russians ended in 1916 with heavy British losses and a Turkish victory that established the reputation of Mustapha Kemal (later known as Attaturk), who became the first president of the postwar Turkish republic. Britain countered by aiding an Arab revolt whose success (such as the campaign led by Colonel T. E. Lawrence in Arabia) hastened the Ottoman collapse.

An important part of World War I took place at sea, but it was not the anticipated duel of dreadnoughts. Both sides were extremely cautious with their expensive super-battleships and rarely sent them to fight. Of fifty-one British, French, and German dreadnoughts afloat in 1914, only two were sunk during the entire war. The British failed to win a decisive victory against the German fleet at Jutland in May 1916, but they effectively blockaded Germany, allowing only 10 percent of prewar imports to reach shore. The German

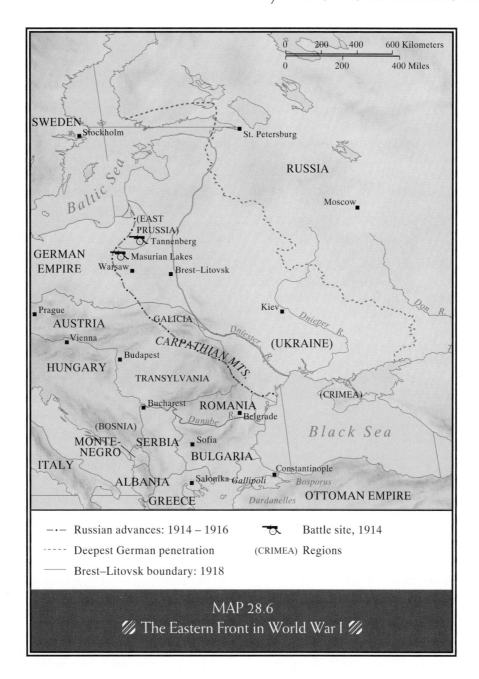

--·- Russian advances: 1914 – 1916   Battle site, 1914

----- Deepest German penetration

(CRIMEA) Regions

——— Brest–Litovsk boundary: 1918

MAP 28.6
The Eastern Front in World War I

navy scored its own dramatic successes through its mastery of the new submarine technology. Between late 1916 and late 1917, German submarines sank more than eight million tons of Atlantic shipping, threatening the British food supply but contributing to the American entry into the war on Britain's side. In 1915 German submarines sank passenger liners with Americans aboard and American ships carrying goods to Britain. Sentiment boiled over when the *Lusitania*, a passenger liner en route from New York to England with a cargo that included arms, went down with 139 Americans aboard. Germany placated American opinion with

a promise not to sink passenger liners but withdrew that promise to resume unrestricted submarine warfare in 1917; four days after that announcement, the United States broke relations with Germany and, two months later, entered the war.

Trench Warfare and the Machine Gun

World War I was ultimately decided on the western front. There, Britain, France, and Germany fought a war of attrition in which hundreds of thousands of men died in offensives that failed to break the stalemate.

◆ DOCUMENT 28.5 ◆

Robert Graves: Life in the Trenches

Robert Graves was a British poet and author who was nineteen when World War I began. He first won fame for his autobiography, published in the 1920s, that covered the war years. This excerpt is from that autobiography, entitled Goodbye to All That.

After a meal of bread, bacon, rum, and bitter stewed tea sickly with sugar, we went . . . up a long trench to battalion headquarters. The trench was cut through red clay. I had a torch [flashlight] with me which I kept flashed on the ground. Hundreds of field mice and frogs were in the trench. They had fallen in and had no way out. The light dazzled them and we could not help treading on them. . . .

The trench was wet and slippery. The guide was giving hoarse directions all the time. "Hole right." "Wire high." "Wire low." "Deep place here, sir." "Wire low." I had never been told about the field telephone wires. They were fastened by staples to the side of the trench, and when it rained the staples were always falling out and the wire falling down and tripping people. . . . The holes were

the sump-pits used for draining the trenches. We were now under rifle fire. . . . The rifle bullet gave no warning. . . . [W]e learned not to duck to a rifle bullet, because once it was heard it must have missed. . . . In a trench the bullets, going over the hollow, made a tremendous crack. Bullets often struck the barbed wire in front of the trenches, which turned them and sent them spinning in a head-over-heels motion. . . .

Our guide took us up to the front line. We passed a group of men huddled over a brazier. They were wearing waterproof capes, for it had now started to rain, and cap-comforters, because the weather was cold. They were little men, daubed with mud. . . . We overtook a fatigue-party struggling up the trench, loaded with timber lengths and sandbags, cursing plaintively as they slipped into sumpholes and entangled their burdens in the telephone wire. Fatigue parties were always encumbered by their rifles and equipment, which it was a crime ever to have out of reach. . . . [W]e had to stand aside to let a stretcher-case past.

Heavy artillery bombardment could not produce a breakthrough: Krupp guns virtually leveled the fortifications at Verdun without producing a breakthrough. The German introduction of poison gas (such as phosgene and mustard gas) at the battle of Ypres (Belgium) in 1915 and the British use of the first tanks in 1916 could not break the defensive lines. Two of the most murderous battles of human history were fought on this front in 1916—the German offensive at Verdun and an Anglo-French counterattack along the Somme River—but neither battle broke the defensive positions. The fighting around Verdun cost France 542,000 casualties and Germany 434,000, shifting the lines only slightly. The French commander at Verdun, General Henri Pétain, became famous for claiming that the Germans "shall not pass" and a national hero when they did not. (Pétain's reputation, like Hindenburg's, suffered greatly when he became a postwar head of state.)

Even while the carnage at Verdun continued, the British and French began their own offensive on the Somme River. After seven days and nights of artillery bombardment on the German trenches (see document

28.5), Allied soldiers went "over the top," walking toward the German lines, with sixty-six pounds of equipment strapped to their backs. They marched into a storm of machine gun fire, and by nightfall 40 percent of the British frontline troops and 60 percent of their officers were dead. In one day of fighting, the bloodiest day in the history of the British army, they suffered twenty thousand deaths (compared with an American death toll of fifty-eight thousand in the entire Vietnam War). When the Allies finally stopped their attack, they had pushed the German lines back a maximum of seven miles, at the combined cost of 1.2 million casualties.

The Home Front

Civilian populations suffered terribly during the war. Seven million civilians were killed, and in several countries (especially in the Balkans and eastern Europe) more civilians were killed than soldiers (see table 28.2). Civilian populations that were spared direct contact with the fighting typically endured many lesser hardships. The war brought martial law in many countries

---

✦ TABLE 28.2 ✦

Life on the Home Front in World War I

Wartime Inflation in the Prices of Consumer Goods

Prices as a percentage of 1913 prices

Country	1914	1915	1916	1917	1918	1919
France	102	140	189	262	340	357
Germany	106	142	153	179	217	415
Great Britain	100	127	160	206	227	242
Italy	96	133	201	299	409	364

Wartime Rations in Germany

Rations as a percentage of the 1913 diet

Food	July 1916–June 1917	July 1918–December 1918
Butter	22	28
Cheese	3	15
Eggs	18	13
Fish	51	5
Flour	53	48
Meat	31	12
Potatoes	71	94
Rice	4	none
Sugar	49	80

Source: *History of the World Economy in the Twentieth Century,* vol. 2: Gerd Hardach, *The First World War, 1914–1918* (Berkeley, Calif.: University of California Press, 1977), pp. 119, 172.

(starting with Germany), press censorship and the jailing of journalists (including a cabinet minister in France), harassment of foreigners and pacifists, suspension of many peacetime activities (British schools even canceled cricket), and dreadful propaganda (such as reports that the Germans were bayoneting babies in Belgium). Transportation, food, clothing, and fuel were requisitioned, regulated, or rationed by governments. The scarcity and inflated prices of daily necessities frequently left the home front as hungry as the army. The war doubled the price of consumer goods in Britain, tripled prices in France, and quadrupled those in Germany. The Allied blockade made the situation so bad in Germany that even the invention of *ersatz* foods (substitute foods, often adulterated) left the people with less than half of the nutrition in their prewar diet. During "the turnip winter" of 1916–17, much of the population survived on that humble tuber. In Russia, the scarcity of food and fuel was so severe that it was a major factor in the outbreak of revolution in 1917.

The war also led to dramatic changes on the home front. The most important change resulted from the mobilization of so many men to fight. In France, 43 percent of all adult men were conscripted, a total of 8.4 million men over five years. (All of the powers, except Britain, drafted their armies before the war; Britain was forced to end the volunteer army in 1916 when the death rate became too high to replace with volunteers.) To replace conscripted soldiers in their peacetime jobs, the French government welcomed 184,000 colonial workers into France, creating immigrant communities that would later become controversial. The principal solution for the labor shortage, however, was the recruitment of women. The war sharply increased the percentage of women in the labor force (especially in Britain and France), and it put women into jobs from which they had previously been excluded. In France, for example, women had constituted more than 35 percent of the prewar workforce. Then the French state railroads increased women workers from six thousand

Illustration 28.7

⬚ **Women War Workers.** With the largest armies in history mobilized to fight the war, the European powers found themselves critically short of labor at home. Millions of women made the war effort possible by bringing in the harvest, by serving as replacement workers in dozens of occupations, and by staffing the munitions factories that supplied armies in the field. In this British photograph, women munition workers labor in a sea of artillery shells, which women have manufactured.

to fifty-seven thousand. The Ministry of Education added thirty thousand women in secondary education. Banks, businesses, and the government all hired women to replace men on clerical and secretarial staffs. The largest opening for women, however, was in munitions factories, which employed fifteen thousand women in 1915 and 684,000 in 1917 (see illustration 28.7 and document 28.6). Without such women workers, armies could not have continued to fight. The women received less pay than the men they replaced (and typically lost their jobs at the war's end), but they contributed significantly to the long-term evolution of women's rights.

Exhaustion and Armistice, 1917–18

By 1917–18 Europe was exhausted. Combat deaths were approaching eight million; total war deaths, fifteen million. Britain also experienced rebellion at home in 1916: P. H. Pearse and the *Sinn Fein* (Gaelic for "ourselves alone") led an unsuccessful Irish nationalist uprising known as the Easter Rising. Pearse and others were executed, and many Irish nationalists were imprisoned, although only temporarily halting the Irish Revolution that produced a larger Anglo-Irish War in 1919–21 and Irish independence. The Russian Revolution of 1917, meanwhile, devastated that country. Before the war in the west ended, the revolution brought about the abolition of the Romanov monarchy, the execution of Czar Nicholas II, and a separate peace treaty with Germany. Also in 1917 fully half of the units of the French army mutinied. After a new commander in chief of French armies (General Robert Nivelle) ordered a disastrous

offensive in the Champagne region, known as the battle of the Chemin des Dames, demoralized soldiers began marching to the front, bleating like sheep going to the slaughterhouse. More than twenty thousand men deserted, more refused to fight, and discipline was not restored until some three thousand soldiers (often chosen by lot) had been executed—more than the total executed on the guillotine in Paris during the French Revolution. Similar demoralization (but not mutiny) took root in the British army after their commander, Sir Douglas Haig, ordered yet another offensive in Flanders, known as the battle of Ypres; 400,000 Britons died in that campaign. In Germany, where the civilian government was directed by the army high command (and the virtual dictatorship of General Ludendorff), the Allied blockade was bringing the nation to the brink of starvation, and discontent was so severe that defiant strikes and sabotage became widespread in early 1918. In Berlin alone, more than 250,000 workers refused to continue; their strike soon ended, but revolutionary conditions did not. Antiwar sentiment developed in many places (see illustration 28.8).

The last months of the war brought one more epic tragedy to the world. A virulent form of influenza struck in the trenches of the western front and flourished when soldiers carried it home. Before the pandemic ended in 1919, it had become the greatest public health disaster of modern history. More than two billion people worldwide contracted the disease, and somewhere between twenty-two million and thirty million people died from it—twice as many as died in the fighting. The disease spread from France to Spain,

◆ DOCUMENT 28.6 ◆

Sylvia Pankhurst: The Situation of Women War Workers

Propaganda was insistent to get women into the munition factories, and every sort of work ordinarily performed by men. The sections clamouring for the military conscription of men saw in the industrial service of women a means to their end. Feminists who were advocates of Conscription for men believed themselves adding to the importance of women by demanding that women also should be conscripts. . . .

From all over the country we cited authentic wages scales: Waring and Gillow paying 3½ d. an hour to women, 9d. to men for military tent making; the Hendon aeroplane works paying women 3d. per hour, at work for which men got 10d. per hour; women booking clerks at Victoria Station getting 15s. a week, though the men they replaced got 35s.; and so on, in district after district, trade after trade. . . .

Firms like Bryant and May's, the match makers, were now making munitions. Accustomed to employ large number of women and girls at ill-paid work, they knew by long experience that piece rates would secure them a higher production than could be induced by a bonus. Without a care for pre-war standards, in a trade new to their factory, they had fixed for munition work, often perilous and heavy, similar sweated piece rates to those paid for matches. . . .

The Munitions Act was being used to prevent workers from changing their employment in order to secure higher wages, or positions of greater responsibility, or to obtain work nearer home. . . . Leaving certificates were refused when the work was proving prejudicial to the health of the worker. . . . As the War progressed, trade after trade was put under the Munitions Act. Employers were eager to seize the powers it gave them.

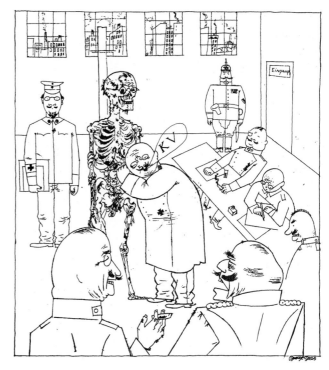

Illustration 28.8

The Rise of Antiwar Sentiment. The German artist George Grosz was one of the most caustic social critics of the early twentieth century. In this pen-and-ink drawing of 1916 entitled "The Faith Healers," he attacked the German army, whose officers are seen declaring that a decaying corpse is still "fit for active duty" (KV). Note the stereotype of smug commanders in the foreground and, through the windows, Grosz's assertion that big business and industry stood right behind the army.

flu the worst plague in American history. By comparison, AIDS killed 125,000 in its first decade.

Among the states fighting on the western front, Germany most severely felt the exhaustion of war in 1918. The Allied naval blockade and the American entry into the war left little doubt that Germany was defeated, although the fighting had not been pushed onto German soil. As the army neared collapse, the German generals called for an armistice in mid-1918. In early November, the German navy at Kiel mutinied rather than continue fighting and revolution spread to Munich (where a short-lived socialist republic of Bavaria was proclaimed) and other cities. Two days later, Kaiser Wilhelm II abdicated and fled to Holland. While militant socialists (known as the Spartacists, after an ancient Roman slave rebellion) led by Karl Liebknecht and Rosa Luxemburg sought to establish a communist regime in Berlin, a hastily formed republican government led by Matthias Erzberger met the Allied commander in chief, French Marshal Ferdinand Foch, in a

where it killed an estimated eight million Spaniards (more than 40 percent of the 1910 population) and acquired the name of the Spanish influenza. Returning British colonial troops spread the disease in India, where an estimated twelve million people perished from it. In the United States, 500,000 deaths made this

ℕ TABLE 28.3 ℕ
Losses in World War I, 1914–18

Country	Total men mobilized	Combat deaths	Percentage of forces killed	Military casualties	Percentage of forces wounded	Civilian deaths	Total war dead	Percentage population killed
Austria-Hungary	7,800,000	1,200,000	15.4	7,000,000	90.0	300,000	1,500,000	5.2
Belgium	267,000	14,000	5.2	93,000	34.8	30,000	44,000	0.6
British Empire	8,900,000	947,000	10.6	3,200,000	35.2	30,000	977,000	2.4
Bulgaria	560,000	87,000	15.5	267,000	47.7	275,000	362,000	8.3
France	8,400,000	1,400,000	16.2	6,200,000	73.2	40,000	1,440,000	3.6
Germany	11,000,000	1,800,000	16.1	7,100,000	64.9	760,000	2,500,000	3.8
Greece	230,000	5,000	2.2	27,000	11.7	132,000	137,000	2.8
Italy	5,600,000	460,000	8.2	2,200,000	39.1	n.a.	n.a	
Montenegro	50,000	3,000	6.0	20,000	40.0	n.a.	n.a.	
Portugal	100,000	7,000	7.2	33,000	33.3	n.a.	n.a.	
Rumania	750,000	336,000	44.8	536,000	71.4	275,000	611,000	8.1
Russia	12,000,000	1,700,000	14.2	9,200,000	76.3	2,000,000	3,700,000	2.4
Serbia	707,000	125,000	17.7	331,000	46.8	650,000	775,000	17.6
Ottoman Empire	2,900,000	325,000	11.4	975,000	34.2	2,200,000	2,500,000	10.1
United States	4,740,000	115,000	2.4	204,000	6.7		115,000	0.1

Source: Calculated from data in Chris Cook and John Paxton, *European Political Facts, 1848–1918* (London: Macmillan, 1978), pp. 188–89, 213–32; William L. Langer, ed., *An Encyclopedia of World History* (Boston, Mass.: Houghton-Mifflin, 1968), 976; *The World Almanac and Book of Facts, 1997* (Mahwah, N.J.: World Almanac Book, 1996), p. 184.

railroad boxcar outside Compiègne, France, and accepted strict Allied terms (which made further fighting impossible) for an armistice. The fighting stopped at a symbolic moment—the eleventh hour of November 11th.

The human cost of the war was staggering, and grim numbers only sketch its outlines (see table 28.3). More than sixty million soldiers were mobilized to fight, and nearly fifteen million people were killed (eight million military and seven million civilians), not counting the tens of millions who fell to the Spanish influenza and other war-related diseases. Most of the great powers saw between one-third to three-fourths of all military forces suffer war wounds and 10 percent to 17 percent killed. A generation of young European men was lost.

◈

The Russian Revolution: The February Revolution

The most important wartime consequence of the world war took place in Russia in 1917–20. A revolution in 1917 (the February revolution) ended the Romanov monarchy, and a second revolution a few months later (the Bolshevik, or October, revolution) brought Lenin and the Bolsheviks to power. A subsequent civil war (1918–20) led to the creation of a communist state.

The government of Nicholas II already faced extreme difficulties on the eve of World War I. The peasant majority of the nation had never achieved the economic freedom or landownership implicit in the emancipation of 1861. A growing working class, created by the beginnings of Russian industrialization, was enduring conditions as bleak as those in England in the 1840s. Minority populations such as the Poles felt the nationalist ambitions for self-rule that had swept Europe, while minority religions, especially the Jews, detested the regime that persecuted them. Much of the intelligentsia aspired to the individual rights and representative government they saw in western Europe. Such discontent had fueled the revolution of 1905, following defeat in the Russo-Japanese War. The reforms that revolution produced, however, were too few and often abrogated.

Added to these problems, World War I was a catastrophe for Russia. The Russian army's inferior preparation and equipment led to shocking defeats. In 1915

❧ TABLE 28.4 ❧
The Cost of Basic Russian Consumer Goods, 1914–17

The 1914 ruble equaled 100 kopecks or 50 cents.

Commodity	April 1914	April 1917
Sack of potatoes	1 ruble	7 rubles
Sack of wheat flour (c. 36 pounds)	2.5 rubles	16 rubles
Sack of rye flour	6.5 rubles	40 rubles
Pound of meat	10 kopecks	70 kopecks
Lard	12 kopecks	90 kopecks
One pair of shoes	5–8 rubles	40 rubles
One cubic meter of firewood	3 rubles	20 rubles

Source: Marc Ferro, *La Révolution de 1917*, vol. 1 (Paris: Flammarion, 1967), and Francis Conte, *Les Grands dates de la Russie et de l'URSS* (Paris, Larousse, 1990), p. 175.

the army suffered shortages of rifles, ammunition, and clothing; conscripts were even sent into battle without equipment. Army morale collapsed. On the home front, a shortage of skilled labor, caused by an ill-planned mobilization, led to shortages of critical supplies and chaos in their transportation and distribution. The cost of basic consumer goods rose dramatically as the government printed worthless money to pay for the war. In less than three years, the price of a pound of meat and a sack of potatoes each increased by 700 percent (see table 28.4). Food shortages became severe because peasants refused to sell grain for paper money. The government seemed mired in scandals and corruption, of which the influence of Grigori Rasputin (a religious mystic who was close to the royal family, especially the czarina), and his dramatic assassination by a group of prominent aristocrats, most aroused criticism. Russia had no stable government: Four prime ministers were dismissed in slightly more than two years, and the czar remained at the front with his army. Even moderates in the Duma expressed outrage at the incompetence and repressiveness of the government. Paul Milyukov—a historian who had been a leader of the liberal-democratic faction in 1905, a founder of the Constitutional Democratic Party ("Kadets") in the Duma, and the leading liberal critic of the war government—put it bluntly: "How did Russia get here? Stupidity or treason?" In 1916 the paper ruble reached one-half of its 1914 value and real wages fell by approximately 20 percent, prompting more than fourteen hundred strikes in Russian cities and convincing more than one million workers to walk out, despite the war. Sporadic mutinies began in the demoralized army. An imperial decree ordered conscription of 400,000 people for civilian labor, and violent resistance broke out, especially in southern portions of the empire. By winter, bread was becoming scarce in major cities.

The February Revolution of 1917 began, like many rebellions of the Old Regime, when food shortages made life intolerable for urban workers. The year began with fifty thousand workers striking in Petrograd (formerly St. Petersburg), and the number grew to eighty thousand in the next month. Demonstrations and bread riots, led by women as they had been in the French Revolution, occurred in early March 1917 (February in the old Russian calendar). By March 10th Petrograd was in the grip of nearly general strikes, and Nicholas II ordered the army to "end them tomorrow." After officers ordered soldiers to fire on the crowd on March 11, killing 150 civilians, discontented soliders of the Petrograd garrison mutinied on March 12 and joined the demonstrators. The czar tried to suspend the Duma, but parliamentary leaders refused to disband. The revolutionary tide in Petrograd was rapidly passing by the Duma, however, and the mutineers elected a competing body, a council (*soviet*) of soldiers, which joined with a soviet of labor deputies, led by Alexander Kerensky (a socialist lawyer), to set up an alternative government. On March 13 the Petrograd soviets began publishing their own newspaper, *Izvestia*, to encourage the election of workers' soviets elsewhere; on the 14th, the Petrograd Soviet issued Order #1 (*Prikaz #1*), calling on soldiers throughout the army to elect their own soviets to take control from imperial officers, and the fate of the regime was settled.

On March 15, 1917, six days after the first protest marches and four days after the army fired on the crowd, Czar Nicholas II abdicated for himself and for his son, passing the throne to his brother, the grand duke Michael, who also refused the crown. Leaders of the Duma, the Petrograd Soviet, and the Zemstva assumed power and announced a Provisional Government headed by Prince Georgi Lvov, a liberal aristocrat and Kadet who presided over the national union of Zemstva. This government included democratic centrists such as Lvov and Milyukov and democratic socialists such as Kerensky, but none of the leading Bolsheviks, who were returning from exile and attacking the government in their newspaper, *Pravda*, which circulated openly in Russia. The Provisional Government, under Lvov and soon under Kerensky, won international praise for its democratic program—an amnesty for political crimes, a constitutional assembly elected by universal suffrage, equal rights for minorities, and full civil liberties—but it remained a severely divided coalition. Lenin (who was in exile in Zurich) urged the soviets to withdraw their support from the government, and conservatives (many of whom rallied behind the Cossack commander of the Petrograd garrison, General Lavr Kornilov) considered a coup d'état to forcibly suppress the Bolsheviks.

During its brief existence, the Provisional Government faced numerous problems. It remained at war with Germany, and the governments of Britain, France, and the United States (whose help Russia desperately needed) all wanted it to remain part of the wartime coalition that could now be described as a democratic alliance against autocracy. The Provisional Government may have sealed its own fate in April 1917 when Foreign Minister Milyukov reaffirmed the Russian promise to the Allies to remain in the war, in a document known as the Milyukov Note. Nor did the government have an easy solution for the shortages of food and other critical supplies. In the spirit of a democratic revolution, the Provisional Government recognized the independence of Poland and Finland, and it accepted an autonomous government of Estonia. It also established the eight-hour workday and granted freedom of religion, but the war never allowed it to consolidate a hold on Russian public popularity. The Petrograd Soviet of Workers' and Soldiers' Deputies, meanwhile, still held the backing of those critically important groups, while the continuation of the war caused support for the Provisional Government to dwindle rapidly.

The October Revolution of 1917

The most tenacious opposition to the Provisional Government came from Lenin and his supporters in the Bolshevik faction of revolutionary socialism. Lenin had spent the war in exile in Switzerland until his clandestine return (aided by the Germans, who hoped his politics would weaken Russia) in April 1917. He expounded a simple, yet highly effective program (see illustration 28.9) known as the April Theses: (1) immediate peace, even at the cost of a harsh German treaty; (2) immediate redistribution of land to the peasants; (3) transfer of political power from the Provisional Government to the soviets; and (4) transfer of the control of factories to committees of workers. The promises of the April Theses (especially peace) contrasted vividly with the policies of the Provisional Government (especially the Milyukov Note). Lenin's

Illustration 28.9

🞇 **Lenin Exhorting the Crowd.** Among the strongest weapons that Lenin and the Bolsheviks had against Kerensky and the Provisional Government was the simple call for peace, a weapon that could be used in repeated speeches in the street. This photograph of Lenin addressing the revolutionary crowd in Moscow later became famous because of a secondary detail: The figure standing on the steps and facing the camera is Trotsky, who was edited out of most subsequent versions of this picture to hide his prominence in the revolution.

program of land and peace first won the Bolsheviks a majority on the Moscow Soviet and made Lenin's foremost lieutenant, Leon Trotsky (whose real name was Lev Bronstein), the head of the Petrograd Soviet by the early autumn of 1917. Trotsky, a Ukrainian Jewish peasant who had entered radical politics as a teenager, twice escaped from Siberian imprisonment, and was a leader of the revolution of 1905, became one of the most effective leaders of the Bolshevik revolution.

Even with the appeal of the April Theses, the Bolsheviks had the support of only a small minority of Russians. When the Petrograd Soviet of Workers' and Soldiers' Deputies held a Panrussian Congress in June and July 1917, only 105 of 822 delegates were Bolsheviks, who were far outnumbered by both Mensheviks and rural radicals just among the revolutionary parties. Lenin and Trotsky responded by forming a Military Revolutionary Committee to prepare for a second Russian revolution of 1917 and created their own military force—the Red Guards—composed of soldiers from the Petrograd garrison and armed workers, forces that were essential in open battles against Kornilov's troops. A Bolshevik party congress held in August 1917 resolved upon the conquest of power by an armed insur-

Illustration 28.10

The Bolshevik Revolution. On November 6, 1917 (October 24 in the Russian old-style calendar), Bolshevik forces staged a coup d'état in Petrograd. Forces from the Petrograd garrison, sailors from the nearby Kronstadt naval station, and workers organized as "Red Guards" seized most government offices. This photo shows the storming of the czar's Winter Palace, which was serving as the seat of the Provisional Government. Kerensky escaped, but most members of the government were arrested.

rection, though most of the party was unprepared for immediate action. Lenin and Trotsky won the backing of a majority within the party's leadership (the Central Committee) after the Russian army suffered more reverses in the war, and they orchestrated a minutely planned coup to seize power in Petrograd in early November (October in the old-style calendar). Two days of violent fighting gave the Bolsheviks control of the Winter Palace and then of Petrograd (see illustration 28.10). The Bolshevik revolution spread to Moscow on the third day, and within a week soviets of workers and soldiers held Moscow, Smolensk, Kazan, Rostov, and Tashkent (see map 28.7).

An All-Russian Congress of Soviets meeting in Moscow immediately endorsed the Bolshevik revolution and approved a new government, which Lenin organized with himself at its head. This Council of Commissars (later called the Politburo) included Trotsky as commissar (minister) of foreign affairs and his bitter rival, Joseph Dzhugashvili, known as Stalin ("the man of steel"), as commissar for the nationalities. Stalin, the son of a Georgian shoemaker, was one of the few Bolshevik leaders who could honestly claim to be a member of the working class. He had entered an Orthodox seminary at age twenty, but had been expelled for his Marxism, and before the war he had been arrested six times and twice sent to Siberia for revolutionary politics. The Council of Commisars acted quickly to consolidate the Bolshevik position by issuing Lenin's decrees on peace and land, as promised (see document 28.7). Although the decree on peace secured much support, elections for a constituent assembly nonetheless

gave the Bolsheviks only 25 percent of the vote. The council responded by creating a new secret police, known as the Cheka, to fight opponents of the revolution. The Cheka, which was not greatly different from the czarist secret police, laid the basis for the new regime to become a police state. And it showed that Lenin meant his words of 1902: "We have never rejected, and cannot reject, terror." Not surprisingly, Lenin and Trotsky closed the constituent assembly in January 1918, on the second day of its meetings.

Lenin and Trotsky fulfilled their promise to bring peace. The high command of the German army agreed to talks at Brest-Litovsk (today in Belarus) in December 1917. They presented Russia with extremely severe terms (far more severe than the treaty later given to defeated Germany) and resumed fighting when the Bolsheviks hesitated. The Russo-German Treaty of Brest-Litovsk (March 1918) showed that Lenin and Trotsky were determined to have peace. They gave up Finland, Estonia, Latvia, Lithuania, Poland, White Russia (Belarus), Ukraine, and Bessarabia. When the Germans capitulated to the Western allies in November, however, Russia repudiated the treaty.

Civil War, 1918–20

The Bolshevik seizure of power in late 1917 did not give them control of the entire Russian Empire. They had begun as a small faction in Russian politics, and they won control in Petrograd because they were well organized, had the will to act (and to act ruthlessly), and understood that land and peace were more popular

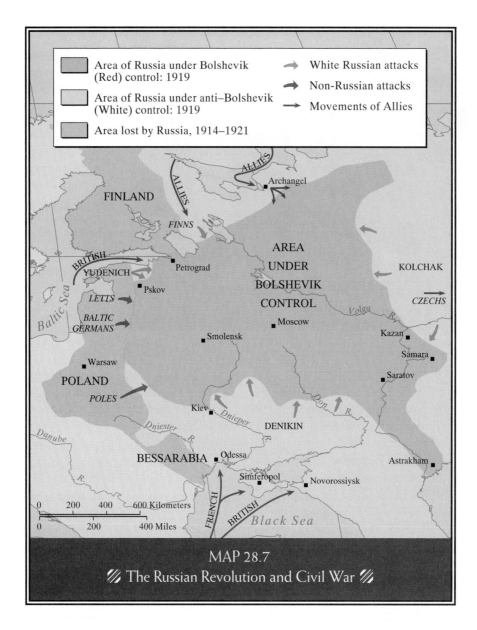

Area of Russia under Bolshevik
(Red) control: 1919

Area of Russia under anti–Bolshevik
(White) control: 1919

Area lost by Russia, 1914–1921

White Russian attacks

Non-Russian attacks

Movements of Allies

MAP 28.7
The Russian Revolution and Civil War

than parliamentary democracy. "No amount of political freedom," Lenin noted, "will satisfy the hungry." The Bolshevik government, however, faced opposition in many regions of the empire, often from larger and more popular forces. The result was a Russian civil war that continued long after the end of the world war.

When the civil war began, the Bolsheviks (renamed the Communist Party in 1918) had sufficient forces for a coup d'état but not for a war. However, they faced civil war on several fronts. They shifted the capital from Petrograd to Moscow, a city less vulnerable to foreign-supported armies, as they faced early defeats. White (anti-Bolshevik) forces soon controlled Siberia (where they installed Admiral Alexander Kolchak, formerly commander of the Baltic Fleet, as their ruler), the southern regions around Kazan, and the Ukraine,

where the Cossacks joined the anti-Bolshevik coalition. Trotsky, named commisar for war, organized a volunteer (later conscript) army known as the Red Army to fight the counterrevolutionary Whites, and brutal civil war soon stretched across the entire Russian Empire. It included a war with the Cossacks in southern Russia, wars of independence in the Ukraine and the Baltic states, intervention by several of the western Allies, campaigns in the Caucasus that led to the secession of south Asian provinces (Georgia, Armenia, and Azerbaijan), and even war in the Far East, where the Japanese invaded Russia. The intervention of the western Allies scored some brief success in Ukraine, where they supported early victories by General Anton Deniken. The Americans staged a landing at Archangel, and the British and French briefly supported a puppet govern-

❖ DOCUMENT 28.7 ❖

The Bolshevik Decree on Peace, November 1917

The workers' and peasants' government, created by the Revolution of October 24–25, and basing itself on the Soviets of Workers', Soldiers', and Peasants' Deputies, calls upon all the belligerent peoples and their governments to start immediate negotiations for a just, democratic peace.

By a just or democratic peace, which the overwhelming majority of the working class and other working people of all the belligerent countries, exhausted, tormented, and racked by the war, are craving—a peace that has been most definitely and insistently demanded by the Russian workers and peasants ever since the overthrow of the czarist monarchy—by such a peace, the government means an immediate peace without annexations (i.e., without the seizure of foreign lands, without the forcible incorporation of foreign nations) and without indemnities.

The Government of Russia proposes that this kind of peace be immediately concluded by all the belligerent nations, and expresses its readiness to take all the resolute measures now, without the least delay. . . .

The government considers it the greatest of crimes against humanity to continue this war over the issue of how to divide among the strong and rich nations the weak nationalities they have conquered. . . .

At the same time, the government declares that it does not regard the above-mentioned peace terms as an ultimatum; in other words, it is prepared to consider any other peace terms, and insists only that they be advanced by any of the belligerent countries as speedily as possible.

their plans for Russia, and heavily dependent upon the western world. The western Allies, however, were simply too exhausted by the years of fighting Germany to be interested in another prolonged battle. Shortly after they stopped supplying the Whites, the Red Army won the civil war. Ukraine (1919) and the Caucasian states (1920) were annexed again, although the Baltic states (Estonia, Latvia, and Lithuania) kept their independence. The most famous episode of the civil war did not occur on a battlefield: In the summer of 1918, the Communist government ordered the execution of Nicholas II and his family (who had been held prisoner at Ekaterinburg, on the Asian side of the Ural Mountains) when it appeared possible that White armies of Kolchak might liberate them.

During the civil war, Lenin began to consolidate Communist power. In 1918 a Congress of Soviets adopted a new constitution for Russia (the country did not become the Union of Soviet Socialist Republics (USSR), or Soviet Union, until 1922). The constitution attempted to create a "dictatorship of the proletariat," including one-party government and restrictions on freedoms of speech, press, and assembly. The government, now led by a five-man Politburo, demonstrated the police powers of this dictatorship after a socialist woman attempted to assassinate Lenin in 1918: Thousands of critics of the regime were killed in a policy called "the red terror," a grim introduction to the authoritarian violence that Europe would face during most of the twentieth century. The most far-reaching policy of the new Communist state had global implications. In the spring of 1919 Lenin created the Third International (the Comintern, 1919–43) to link Communist parties in all countries and to support revolutions around the world. Revolutionary situations existed in many war-weary countries, such as the Spartacist revolt in Berlin in early 1919. Béla Kun, a protegé of Lenin, established a short-lived Bolshevik government in Hungary later in 1919. These events alarmed anti-communist capitals around the world and led to a postwar "Red scare" in many countries.

ment of Northern Russia at Archangel, but neither the British nor the Americans were willing to accept significant involvement in the war. For a while this produced a bizarre situation in which German anti-Bolsheviks fought together with western Allies, but western forces withdrew from Russia in September 1919.

A Communist victory in the civil war was complete in most regions by 1920. The Whites were poorly coordinated among the many fronts, badly divided in

❖

Conclusion

The vast human tragedies examined in chapter 28 provide an essential context for historians who look back at the Belle Époque at the end of the nineteenth century and for those who look ahead to the larger tragedies of the twentieth century. The Belle Époque must be understood as sowing the seeds of the total war that savaged European society between 1914 and 1920. The imperial conquest that Europeans visited upon the rest of the world after 1881 might have warned imperialists of what they were capable; the glorification of war and the arms race might have been signposts on the road toward the precipice. Yet Europeans embraced war with naive enthusiasm in 1914, scarcely understanding the monstrosity of that decision. How belle could the époque be that had this denouement?

Conversely, the devastation of 1914–20 also pointed Europe toward the future. World War I was only the opening chapter in an age of total war, and the horrifying story of fifteen million war dead was only the prelude to a larger war that would claim more than fifty million lives. And the continuing story of total war would be accompanied by totalitarian government, whose roots also lay in this tragic period.

These possibilities scarcely seemed imaginable in the world of European international relations between 1871 and 1914. The dominant statesman of the age, Otto von Bismarck, perpetuated the Franco-German hostility and created the system of peacetime alliances that helped to trigger the catastrophe, but he understood his work as a conservative effort to protect the unified Germany by keeping the peace, not by causing war. The Three Emperors' League, the Dual Alliance, the Triple Alliance, and the Reinsurance Treaty were all intended to prevent another European war, yet they were a grave provocation to others and an essential cause of the diplomatic revolution (1890–1907) that encompassed the Franco-Russian Alliance, the Entente Cordiale, and the Triple Entente and left Europe divided into two armed camps whose treaties left them constantly prepared for war.

The global economic and military dominance of the European powers during the new imperialism (1881–1914) led to the conquest of vast empires in Africa, Asia, and the Pacific. Such triumphs exacerbated European rivalries. However, imperialism simultaneously created an arrogance and a sense of invincibility among the imperial states who saw how easily their weaponry could give others "a good dusting" yet who did not see a parallel danger of what would happen on the day when the Maxim gun was pointed at Europeans.

Europe would suffer the consequences for most of the twentieth century, beginning with World War I (1914–18), which brought twenty-seven countries and dozens of their colonies into a war of epic destructiveness. The war mobilized more than sixty million soldiers and killed more than fifteen million people, not counting twenty million to thirty million of added

deaths from the diseases that spread around the world from its trenches. The war also killed monarchy as the dominant system of government in Europe (see chapter 29). It finished the multinational Hapsburg and Ottoman empires, leaving nationalist battles throughout eastern Europe and the Middle East to struggle over the remains. It led to revolutions in Ireland, Arabia, Russia, and many other regions; it accelerated an anti-imperialist revolution that ranged from Gandhi in India to Ho Chi Minh in Vietnam. None of these legacies was more important than the fact that World War I left unsettled a bitter Franco-German struggle and would soon precipate a sequel, and more total, war.

World War I also stimulated revolution in Russia, bringing down another historic monarchy that teetered under the burdens of fighting the war. The Russian Revolution did not replace the Romanov dynasty with a liberal-democratic government, which the February revolution seemed to promise. Instead, the long unsolved problems of Russian modernization, when combined with the suffering of the war, produced a second revolution. The Bolshevik revolution, which created a totalitarian Communist government, hinted at an age of totalitarian government.

Suggested Readings

For the diplomatic background to the war, see the suggestions for earlier chapters and W. Langer's classic studies, *European Alliances and Alignments* (1960) and *The Diplomacy of Imperialism* (1962); R. Massie, *Dreadnought: Britain, Germany, and the Coming of the Great War* (1991), the most recent of many popular histories of the road to war; I. Geiss, *German Foreign Policy, 1871–1914* (1976); V. R. Berghahn, *Germany and the Approach of War in 1914* (1973); L. Cecil, *The German Diplomatic Service, 1871–1914* (1976); C. Andrew, *Théophile Delcassé and the Making of the Entente Cordiale* (1968); M. B. Hayne, *The French Foreign Office and the Origins of the First World War* (1993); J. F. V. Keiger, *France and the Origins of the First World War* (1983); C. J. Lowe, *The Reluctant Imperialists* (1967), on British foreign policy; Z. Steiner, *Great Britain and the Origins of the First World War* (1977); J. A. S. Grenville, *Lord Salisbury and English Foreign Policy* (1964); F. Hinsley, ed., *British Foreign Policy under Sir Edward Grey* (1977); F. Bridge, *From Sadowa to Sarajevo* (1976), for Austrian diplomacy; N. der Bagdaserian, *The Austro-German Rapprochement, 1870–1879* (1979); R. Bosworth, *Italy: The Least of the Great Powers* (1983); N. der Bagdaserian, *The Austro-German Rapprochement, 1870–1879* (1976); R. W. Seton-Watson, *Disraeli, Gladstone, and the Eastern Question* (1935) and W. Medlicott, *The Congress of Berlin and After* (1956), for the eastern question of the 1870s; P. Kennedy, *The Rise of the Anglo-German Antagonism, 1860–1914* (1980); G. Kennan, *The Fateful Alliance* (1984), on the Franco-Russian alliance; C. Howard, *Splendid Isolation* (1967); and G. Monger, *The End of Isolation* (1976), on British isolation. For public opinion, see O. Hale,

Publicity and Diplomacy (1940); and E. M. Carroll, *French Public Opinion and Foreign Affairs, 1870–1914* (1931) and *Germany and the Great Powers, 1866–1914* (1938).

For the prewar crises of 1898–1914, see earlier suggestions on the eastern question and R. Langhorne, *The Collapse of the Concert of Europe* (1981), R. Brown, *Fashoda Reconsidered* (1969), T. Pakenham, *The Boer War* (1979), I. Nish, *The Origins of the Russo-Japanese War* (1985), J. White, *The Diplomacy of the Russo-Japanese War* (1964), E. N. Anderson, *The First Moroccan Crisis* (1930), and E. C. Helmreich, *The Diplomacy of the Balkan Wars, 1912–1913* (1938).

For European imperialism, see R. Betts, *The False Dawn: European Imperialism in the Nineteenth Century* (1976), for a general introduction; L. Gann and P. Duignan, eds., *The History and Politics of Colonialism, 1870–1914* (1969), a collection of short essays; W. Baumgart, *Imperialism* (1982); W. Mommsen, *Theories of Imperialism* (1980), a good survey; V. Lenin, *Imperialism: The Highest Stage of Capitalism* (1916), the Communist indictment of imperialism; J. A. Hobson, *Imperialism: A Study* (1938), a radical critique; V. G. Kiernan, *From Conquest to Collapse* (1982), for military conquest and resistance; D. Headrick, *The Tools of Empire* (1981), for an important argument about technology and imperialism; T. Pakenham, *The Scramble for Africa, 1876–1912* (1991); J. Hargreaves, *West Africa Partitioned*, 2 vols. (1974–85); D. Gillard, *The Struggle for Asia, 1828–1914* (1977); R. Robinson and J. Gallagher, *Africa and the Victorians* (1981); W. Louis, ed., *Imperialism: The Robinson and Gallagher Controversy* (1976), essays in a major scholarly argument; H. Brunschwig, *French Colonialism, 1871–1914* (1966); J. Cooke, *The New French Imperialism, 1880–1910* (1973); W. Smith, *The German Colonial Empire* (1978); and D. Dallin, *The Rise of Russia in Asia* (1949).

For militarism and pacifism, see B. Bond, *War and Society in Europe, 1870–1970* (1984), for a survey; A. Marder, *From the Dreadnought to Scapa Flow* (1961), on the British navy; J. Steinberg, *Yesterday's Deterrent: Tirpitz and the Birth of the German Battle Fleet* (1965); P. Padfield, *The Great Naval Race* (1974); P. Kennedy, ed., *The War Plans of the Great Powers, 1880–1914* (1979); G. Ritter, *The Sword and the Scepter*, 4 vols. (1969–73), on the evolution of German militarism, and *The Schlieffen Plan* (1958); P. M. Kennedy, *The War Plans of the Great Powers, 1880–1914* (1979); S. Williamson, *The Politics of Grand Strategy* (1969), on Anglo-French preparations for war; G. Krumeich, *Armaments and Politics in France on the Eve of the First World War* (1984); and S. Miller and others, eds. *Military Strategy and the Origins of the First World War* (1991). For the peace movements, see R. Chickering, *Imperial Germany and a World without War* (1975).

For the debate over the origins of World War I, see J. Joll, *The Origins of the First World War* (1992) and L. Lafore, *The Long Fuse* (1965), both good syntheses; V. Berghahn, *Germany and the Approach of War in 1914* (1973); the controversial works of F. Fischer, especially *Germany's War Aims in the First World War* (1967); J. Keiger, *France and the Origins of the First World War* (1983); D. C. B. Lieven, *Russia and the Origins of the First World War* (1983); Z. Steiner, *Britain and the Origins of the First World War* (1977); and S. Williamson, *Austria-Hungary and the Origins of the First World War* (1991).

For World War I, see B. Tuchman, *The Guns of August* (1962), for the opening phase of the war; M. Ferro, *The Great War, 1914–1918* (1978), for a good short history; B. Schmitt and H. Vedeler, *The World in the Crucible* (1984), for a detailed overview; G. Hardach, *The First World War, 1914–1918* (1981), an economic history; E. Leed, *No Man's Land* (1979), for the soldiers' perspective; L. Haber, *The Poisonous Cloud* (1986), on chemical warfare; J. King, *Generals and Politicians* (1951), on civil-military conflict in France; and M. Kitchen, *The Silent Dictatorship* (1976), for Germany. For the home front, see J.-J. Becker, *The Great War and the French People* (1986) and J. Kocka, *Facing Total War* (1984), on German society; and R. Wall and J. Winter, eds., *The Upheaval of War* (1988). For women and the war, see G. Braybon and P. Summerfield, *Out of the Cage* (1987) and M. Higonnet and others, eds., *Behind the Lines* (1987). See also D. Smith, *The Great Departure: The United States and World War I, 1914–1920* (1965), for American entry into the war; and R. Aron, *The Century of Total War* (1954), for a thoughtful reflection on twentieth-century war.

Overviews of Soviet history are given in chapter 29. For surveys of the Russian Revolution, see R. Pipes, *The Russian Revolution* (1990), a vigorously hostile account; J. Reed, *Ten Days That Shook the World* (1935), a highly sympathetic contemporary account; E. Acton, *Rethinking the Russian Revolution* (1990), for an introduction to such interpretive debates; E. H. Carr, *The Bolshevik Revolution, 1917–1923*, 3 vols. (1950–53), for an exceptionally detailed investigation; W. H. Chamberlain, *The Russian Revolution, 1917–1921*, 2 vols. (1935); L. Lih, *Bread and Authority in Russia, 1914–1921* (1990), for the food crisis throughout the era; T. Hasegawa, *The February Revolution* (1981); W. Rosenberg, *Liberals in the Russian Revolution* (1974), for the Kadets; O. Radkey, *Russia Goes to the Polls* (1989), for the brief democracy; S. Smith, *Red Petrograd* (1985), for the revolution and workers; R. Wade, *Red Guards and Workers' Militias in the Russian Revolution* (1984); A. Rabinowitch, *The Bolsheviks Come to Power* (1976); M. Ferro, *October 1917* (1980); A. Wildman, *The End of the Russian Imperial Army*, 2 vols. (1980–87); J. Bradley, *Civil War in Russia, 1917–1920* (1975), for a brief survey of the civil war; D. Footman, *Civil War in Russia* (1975), for the military campaigns; R. Luckett, *The White Generals* (1971); P. Fleming, *The Fate of Admiral Kolchak* (1963), for the Whites; and J. F. N. Bradley, *Allied Intervention in Russia, 1917–1920* (1968).

CHAPTER 29

EUROPE IN AN AGE OF DICTATORSHIP, 1919–39

CHAPTER OUTLINE

An old Europe lay in ruins in 1919. Five years of world war had swept away four empires: the Russian, German, Hapsburg, and Ottoman. A dozen new states appeared, chiefly in central and eastern Europe, stretching from Finland in the north to Turkey in the south. The war also destroyed monarchy as the dominant form of European government, and it burdened the new democratic governments with great problems.

Chapter 29 looks at Europe in the generation after World War I. It begins by discussing the peace settlement reached at Paris in 1919 and the problems that this peace (especially the Versailles Treaty with Germany) bequeathed to the next generation. Next, it examines postwar problems (such as the reconstruction of devastated areas) and attitudes (such as conservative desires to preserve the old Europe) that derived from the war. Subsequent sections discuss the problems of postwar democracies, such as the Great Depression of the 1930s, and the controversial governments (such as the Popular Fronts in France and Spain) that tried to address them. The chapter then examines the rise of dictatorships as the typical form of European government. Separate sections focus on the forms of dictatorship in Mussolini's Fascist Italy, Hitler's Nazi Germany, and Stalin's Communist Russia.

The Peace of Paris, 1919–20

The fighting in World War I ended with the Compiègne armistice of November 1918, which disarmed Germany to the extent that further combat was impossible. Similarly, the Paris Peace Conference, which assembled in January 1919, disarmed German diplomacy; a German delegation was allowed to come to Versailles but not to negotiate. (The Allies held separate conferences for each of the defeated powers at various palaces around Paris; peace with Germany was planned at the

MAP 29.1
Europe in 1919

royal palace in suburban Versailles.) The new German republic, founded after the abdication of Kaiser Wilhelm II, could only hope that the treaty would be based on the idealistic Fourteen Points stated in early 1918, in a speech by U.S. president Woodrow Wilson (who had endorsed "peace without victory" as late as 1916). Although dozens of states sent diplomats to Paris, the basic elements of the treaties were negotiated among representatives of the "Big Four" wartime allies—chiefly by Wilson, Premier Georges Clemenceau of France,

and Prime Minister David Lloyd George of Britain, and sometimes including Premier Vittorio Orlando of Italy. This was similar to the situation at Vienna in 1815 (where France had initially been excluded from negotiations among the four victorious great powers), with an important exception: One of the great powers that had fought long for the allied cause, Russia, was an excluded pariah state in 1919, governed by Communist revolutionaries who had negotiated a separate peace with Germany.

The most important statesmen in creating the post-war world were Clemenceau and Lloyd George, neither of whom felt bound by Wilson's program. Lloyd George had run for reelection in the Khaki Election of December 1918 promising to punish German "war criminals" and saying "I'll hang the Kaiser!" Clemenceau scoffed at Wilsonian idealism with snide reminders that even God presented only ten Commandments; Europe, he added on another occasion, might consider Wilsonian moral leadership when he ended racial segregation in the United States. Unlike the situation at Vienna in 1815, the Allies were never so divided that they invited Germany to participate in negotiations. German diplomats had their first formal meeting with Allied diplomats in May 1919, when a draft treaty was presented to them; Clemenceau introduced the treaty by saying, "The time has come to settle accounts" (see illustration 29.1). The Germans, given no chance to negotiate compromises, bitterly called the treaty a *diktat* (a dictated peace) but nonetheless signed it in June 1919; the German response to the peace treaty (in contrast to the French response to the Frankfurt Treaty of 1871) became one of the most severe problems of the following generation and a major factor in the resumption of war in 1939 (see chapter 30).

The Versailles Treaty returned Alsace and Lorraine to France (as even the Fourteen Points promised) and awarded frontier territory to Belgium, restored to Denmark land lost in the war of 1864, and made major concessions to Poland (see map 29.1). The most controversial of these decisions gave part of western Prussia to the reborn state of Poland (which Prussia had played a leading role in destroying in the eighteenth century); this created a Polish Corridor to the Baltic Sea, but it isolated East Prussia as an exclave surrounded by Poland and it fostered German hatred of the treaty similar to the French reaction to the loss of Alsace in 1871. Germany was also stripped of all colonies and Russian territory annexed by the Treaty of Brest-Litovsk in 1918 (an even harsher treaty than the Versailles Treaty). The Saar River basin, a coal-rich region on the western side of the Rhine River (the Rhineland), was detached from Germany; France was given control of the Saar mines for fifteen years, after which a plebescite would determine the status of the region. The German army was limited to 100,000 men (intentionally smaller than the Polish army). Germany was denied heavy artillery, submarines, and an air force, and the entire Rhineland was demilitarized.

The most controversial section of the Versailles Treaty was Article 231, known as "the war guilt clause."

Illustration 29.1

The Versailles Peace Treaty. The peace treaty with Germany in 1919 was severe, although no worse than the treaties imperial Germany imposed on France in 1871 or Russia in 1918. From the German point of view, shown in this contemporary cartoon, the Big Three (from the left, Wilson, Clemenceau, and Lloyd George) were decapitating Germany.

This article made Germany accept responsibility for causing the war. On this basis, the German nation was to pay reparations for all civilian damage caused by the war (in contrast to the indemnity payments that France had been made to pay in 1815 and 1871)—a subject destined to become another of postwar Europe's greatest controversies. When critics asked Clemenceau if he thought that future historians would conclude that Germany had caused the war, he answered that they certainly would not conclude that Belgium had invaded Germany in 1914. As a concession to Wilson's Fourteen Points, and to ensure the enforcement of the treaty, the Allies also created a permanent international assembly known as the League of Nations—an idealistic body whose founding covenant spoke of reducing armaments and ending war but established few instruments of enforcement. The Versailles Treaty was thus an awkward compromise among the victors, and it remained controversial among them (especially in Britain), so they never did a good job of enforcing it; many historians have concluded that this adds up to an unwise treaty that led to further war.

The secondary treaties signed at Paris registered the collapse of two great empires, recognized more than a dozen new countries, and addressed territorial problems that would remain unresolved throughout the twentieth century. The Hapsburg monarchy had broken apart in mid-1918, creating separate states of Austria and Hungary. Minority populations of the empire joined the enlarged states of Poland (Upper Silesia) and Romania (Transylvania) or the newly created states of Czechoslovakia (which included the rich province of Bohemia) in the north and Yugoslavia in the south. The Treaty of St. Germain with Austria recognized these changes as a *fait accompli* and also obliged the Austrians to cede the frontier territory of the south Tyrol and the Istrian Peninsula to Italy (as promised in the Treaty of London), although Orlando walked out of the conference to protest other "unredeemed promises" of territory, such as the town of Fiume on the Adriatic. The once mighty Hapsburg Empire, which had dominated central Europe for centuries, was reduced to an Austria 12 percent of its size in 1914, left with a population of six million, and forbidden to unite with Germany. The Hungarians were made to accept the Treaty of Trianon, by which they lost 75 percent of their prewar territory and gained a long-standing enmity with their neighbors who profited from the treaty. Serbia, whose Pan-Slavic nationalism had done so much to provoke the war (and had suffered so much during the war), was rewarded with the creation of a large Yugoslavia, which also included Montenegro, part of Macedonia, Bosnia and Herzegovina, Croatia, and Slovenia.

The Treaty of Sèvres (1920), which made peace with Turkey, bequeathed the twentieth century some of its most difficult problems. Turkey received much harsher treatment than Germany had in the Versailles Treaty; the powerless sultan lost all non-Turkish portions of the former Ottoman Empire, but these territories did not become independent. Greece claimed most of European Turkey and part of the Turkish coast, Italy took Rhodes and several other Mediterranean islands, and the entire Middle East was detached from Turkey. Turkish nationalists, led by Atatürk, fought many of these losses, drove the Greeks out of Izmir and Aegean Turkey, and won a new treaty in 1923. Nonetheless, the northern part of the Middle East, territory organized as the state of Syria (including today's Lebanon), was assigned to French control as a "mandate" administered through the League of Nations. Territories formerly called Mesopotamia (today, Iraq) were made a British mandate. In the south, the center of the Arab revolt of 1916 became the independent kingdom of Hijaz (to-

day, Saudi Arabia). Other territories were organized as the states of Palestine (today, Israel) and Trans-Jordan (today, Jordan), both under British mandates. Other peoples, such as the Armenians (more than one million of whom had been killed during the war) and the Kurds of northern Mesopotamia, were denied a nation-state even as a European colony. The idea of creating a Jewish homeland in the Middle East, simmering since Theodor Herzl had witnessed the Dreyfus affair in France and organized the first Zionist Congress in 1897, was left open. The British Balfour Declaration of 1917 had stated, "His Majesty's Government view with favour the establishment in Palestine of a National Home for the Jewish People," but the treaty did not act on this declaration.

Economic Recovery and the Reconstruction of Europe in the 1920s

The cost of World War I cannot be measured precisely. More than eight million soldiers and seven million civilians had died in the fighting; counting war-related epidemics, roughly twenty million Europeans had perished. France and Germany lost approximately 10 percent of their labor force; Serbia and Montenegro lost more than 17 percent of their total population; Britain lost one-third of all men aged fifteen to twenty-four in the 1911 census and more than 40 percent of its junior officers. The casualties rate in some armies surpassed 50 percent of all personnel. The German and the Austro-Hungarian armies each reported more than five million war wounds. The French wounded included 740,000 severely crippled men, *mutilés de guerre,* who would be living reminders of the war for fifty years. The British needed forty-eight new mental hospitals just to house the sixty-five thousand cases of acute shell shock. As late as 1928, the annual total of British veterans receiving their first artificial limbs for war injuries stood at six thousand. Little wonder that a British novelist, D. H. Lawrence, wrote, "We have all lost the war. All Europe." The living and the dead alike were a "lost generation."

Economic data show similar devastation. The economic cost of World War I still cannot be counted (veterans and widows still receive benefits), and even the direct costs, such as government spending and property destroyed, can only be estimated. Postwar calculations translate into nearly 100 trillion late twentieth-century dollars. Economic historians have shown what this meant in local cases: six percent of all Belgians lost their

Illustration 29.2

⦿ Postwar Reconstruction. One of the first tasks of the 1920s was the rebuilding of devastated war zones, such as this town in northern France. In that zone, more than six thousand square miles had been laid to waste; 1,039 villages were completely destroyed and 293,000 public buildings had been demolished.

⚑ TABLE 29.1 ⚑

Industrial Recovery after World War I

Output of crude steel (*in thousands of metric tons*)

Country	1913	1919	1920	1921	1922	1923	1924	1925	1926	1927	1928
Belgium	2,467	334	1,253	789	1,565	2,297	2,875	2,549	3,339	3,680	3,905
France	4,687	1,293	2,706	3,099	4,538	5,222	6,670	7,464	8,617	8,349	9,479
Germany	17,609	8,710	9,278	9,997	11,714	6,305	9,835	12,195	12,342	16,311	14,517

Output of coal (*in thousands of metric tons*)

Country	1913	1919	1920	1921	1922	1923	1924	1925	1926	1927	1928
Belgium	24,371	18,483	22,143	21,807	21,209	22,922	23,362	23,097	25,230	27,551	27,587
France	40,844	22,441	25,261	28,960	31,913	38,556	44,982	48,091	52,453	52,875	52,440
Germany	277,342	210,355	219,416	236,962	256,353	180,474	243,189	272,533	285,240	304,447	317,136

Source: B. R. Mitchell, *European Historical Statistics, 1750–1970* (London: Macmillan, 1975), pp. 362–65, 400, 430.

homes, the nation lost 75 percent of its railroad cars, and farmers lost two-thirds of all pigs in prewar totals. The devastation in France was even worse (see illustration 29.2). The fighting had laid waste to more than six thousand square miles of northeastern and eastern France; nine thousand small factories and five thousand large factories were destroyed, as were fifteen hundred miles of railroad and thirty-three thousand miles of highway. Europe needed nearly a decade of peace merely to approach 1913 levels of production (see table 29.1). This slow recovery permitted the United States

to achieve dominance in the global economy. While France mined 7 million tons of coal in 1924, the United States mined 485 million tons; while Germany produced 9 million tons of steel that year, the United States produced 45 million tons. By 1929 the United States accounted for 34.4 percent of global industrial production, while Britain, France, and Germany combined accounted for 25.7 percent. Belgium suffered a typical, slow recovery: Belgians matched their prewar coal output in 1926, but textiles never reached prewar levels. Debt slowed the recovery. Governments had

⚅ TABLE 29.2 ⚅

Deficit Financing of World War I: National Budgets, 1914–18

The figures are in billions of 1913 dollars.

Country	Expenditure	Income	Deficit
France	32.9	5.1	27.8
Germany	37.9	5.2	32.7
Great Britain	46.7	13.3	33.4
Russia	18.3	5.0	13.3
United States	16.6	6.0	10.6

Source: Calculated from data in *History of the World Economy in the Twentieth Century*, vol. 2: Gerd Hardach, *The First World War, 1914–1918* (Berkeley, Calif.: University of California Press, 1977), pp. 155, 293.

Illustration 29.3

⚅ **The German Inflation of 1923.** One of the worst inflation crises in European history hit Germany in 1923. Prices skyrocketed and paper money lost its value overnight. Some businesses started the day with a schedule of how prices would rise during the day, and others charged people at the end of a service (such as a movie or a bus ride) instead of at the start because the price would be higher. This photo shows the nadir of a collapsing currency: A woman uses worthless paper money to light her stove.

financed the war by borrowing rather than taxing. The French government, for example, had a total wartime income of $5.1 billion but spent $32.9 billion. British and German debts were even worse. Germany had contracted loans totaling 98 billion gold marks (approximately $25 billion) and that indebtedness still left a deficit of nearly $8 billion (see table 29.2). The combined effect of such staggering debts plus the immensity of the reparations payments that Germany owed to devastated France and Belgium led many economists to conclude, as John Maynard Keynes did in *The Economic Consequences of the Peace*, that Allied economic expectations were unrealistic.

Postwar conditions worsened these problems. Fighting the war on credit had led to runaway inflation. Prices increased by 264 percent in Italy and by 302 percent in Germany during the war, and the end of fighting did not stabilize them. Germany endured another 162 percent increase in prices in 1920–21, and the worst was yet to come: In 1922–23 inflation made the German mark (valued at twenty-five cents in 1913) virtually worthless (see illustration 29.3). The price of bread went from 0.63 marks per loaf in 1918 to 250 marks in January 1923, then 3,465 marks in July, 1.5 million marks in September, and hit the absurd price of 201 billion marks for a loaf in November. This inflation devastated German society almost as badly as German arms had devastated Belgium. Unemployment posed other problems. It had stood at 3 percent before the war, but the demobilization of armies left millions of veterans jobless. Unemployment hit 15 percent in 1921

and stayed above 10 percent for years. Having seen the role of disgruntled soldiers in the Bolshevik revolution, governments were eager to remedy this situation. Many nations adopted their first unemployment compensation laws because conservatives wanted to help veterans; Italy did so in 1919, and Austria, Belgium, and Britain followed in 1920.

The Conservative Reaction of the 1920s

One widely shared postwar mood was a desire to recover the remembered tranquillity of antediluvian Europe. In an awkward American coinage, people wanted a "return to normalcy." This led to conservative elec-

❖ DOCUMENT 29.1 ❖

Pope Pius XI: Marriage, Birth Control, Abortion, and Divorce

Pius XI (served 1922–39) was a conservative pope. He condemned the Russian Revolution and the Spanish republic, and he negotiated concordats with Mussolini in 1929 and with Hitler in 1933. While condemning socialism and communism, Pius XI denounced the unfair distribution of wealth and called for fairer treatment of workers in Quadragesimo anno *(1931). He openly disagreed with Hitler's human rights record in 1937 and Mussolini's anti-Semitism in 1938. His encyclical* Casti connubi *(1930), from which the following excerpts are taken, gave the first comprehensive statement of the church's position of many issues concerning the family.*

Domestic . . . order includes both the primacy of the husband with regard to the wife and children, the ready subjection of the wife and her willing obedience, which the Apostle commends in these words: "Let women be subject to their husbands as to the Lord, because the husband is the head of the wife, as Christ is the head of the Church." This subjection, however, does not deny or take away the liberty which fully belongs to the woman . . . nor does it bid her obey her husband's every request if not in harmony with right reason or with the dignity due to a wife; nor, in fine, does it imply that the wife should be put on a level with those persons who in law are called minors. . . . But it forbids that exaggerated liberty which cares not for the good of the family. . . .

First consideration is due to the offspring, which many have the boldness to [avoid] . . . by frustrating the marriage act. . . . But no reason, however grave, may be put forward by which anything intrinsically against nature may become conformable to nature and morally good. Since, therefore, the conjugal act is destined primarily by nature for the begetting of children, those who in exercising it deliberately frustrate its natural power and purpose sin against nature and commit a deed which is shameful and intrinsically vicious. . . .

Another very grave crime is to be noted, Venerable Brethren, which regards the taking of the life of the offspring hidden in the mother's womb. Some wish it to be allowed and left to the will of the father or the mother; others . . . ask that the public authorities provide aid for these death-dealing operations. . . . Venerable Brethren, however much we may pity the mother whose health or even life is gravely imperiled in the performance of a duty allotted to her by nature, nevertheless what could ever be a sufficient reason for excusing in any way the direct murder of the innocent?

The advocates of the neo-paganism of today . . . continue by legislation to attack the indissolubility of the marriage bond, proclaiming the lawfulness of divorce. . . . Opposed to all these reckless opinions, Venerable Brethren, stands the unalterable law of God, fully confirmed by Christ, a law that can never be deprived of its force by the decrees of men, the ideas of a people, or the will of any legislator: "What God hath joined together, let no man put asunder." . . . [A]s Christ himself has explicitly confirmed: "Everyone that putteth away his wife and marrieth another, committeth adultery."

toral victories in many countries. British voters dismissed their wartime leader, Lloyd George, and gave the Tories a huge victory in 1924. The French sent Clemenceau into retirement and elected a Chamber of Deputies so full of veterans that it was called the "horizon blue" assembly (because of their uniform color). Conservative Catholic parties won landmark victories in Belgian elections of 1919 and 1921 and in Austrian elections of 1920 and 1923.

The conservative reaction typically encompassed efforts to guard morality. This led to the prohibition of alcoholic beverages in the United States and Bolshevik Russia and to lesser restrictions on drink (commonly the perpetuation of wartime regulations) around Europe. The French continued a ban on certain alcoholic beverages, and the British strictly regulated the hours when they could be sold (ending early and interrupting sales during the day). Many countries imposed higher taxes on alcohol, on the theory that people would accept "sin taxes." And most of Europe, which had allowed the consumption of narcotic drugs during the prewar Belle Époque, joined in an international convention against drugs in 1925.

More countries rewrote their laws on sexuality and reproduction, marriage and divorce. Pope Pius XI stated strict standards for Catholics in 1930, in the encyclical *Casti connubi* (see document 29.1). He opposed birth control, abortion, and divorce; birth control, for

❖ DOCUMENT 29.2 ❖

Vera Brittain: The Demobilization of Working Women

During the war, women passed rapidly into trades hitherto considered unsuitable for them, such as transport, munitions, motor manufacture and shipbuilding, and were found to be specially well-adapted to organization, supervision, and process work of all kinds. Work hitherto thought too heavy or too highly skilled was made quite feasible by means of lifting tackle (now generally considered desirable for men also) and special training, as well as by the more adequate nourishment of the worker. Numbers of women were brought back into manual labor, often the most strenuous. . . .

In industry the temporary relaxation of Trade Union regulations led to women being universally employed to replace or supplement men. . . . Statistics given by the War Cabinet Committee on Women in Industry in Great Britain and Ireland show that the 5,966,000 women who were employed in July 1914 had increased by July 1918 to 7,311,000. . . . Because of this increase in numbers, as well as owing to the efficiency shown by women in every type of occupation, the Women's Employment Committee foresaw an extension of openings for women . . . and believed that employers would gladly continue to use them after the war. . . .

These sanguine hopes were doomed to disappointment. The war had certainly given the world an object lesson in woman's achievement, but men in general showed a disturbing tendency to be appalled rather than encouraged by this demonstration of unexpected ability. . . . With the end of the necessity which had provoked war-time agreements, both sides [labor and management] were anxious to return to the old advantageous positions. . . .

The immediate result of demobilization was to add a sentimental argument to the already familiar economic and social arguments against the work of women. The Restoration of the Pre-War Practises Act, which became law in July 1918 effectually dispelled any lingering optimism as to the improvement of women's position in industry owing to the war. Women were discharged wholesale; they were not only turned out of old industries, but out of many new ones. . . . By the autumn of 1919 three quarters of a million of the women employed at the time of armistice had been dismissed. . . . By 1923, the number of [union] women was reduced to 480,000 . . . little more than half that of 1913.

---

example, was branded "criminal abuse" and "intrinsically vicious." Many governments, motivated by population losses as much as by morality, outlawed birth control or abortion. The French banned both (and information about them) in 1920. Madeleine Pelletier, the prewar feminist who had championed women's right to have abortions, was jailed in an asylum under these laws and died there. Ireland made it a felony to sell, import, or advertise any birth control device. Mussolini criminalized abortion in 1930, although Italian women still obtained 500,000 illegal abortions annually. Britain was an unusual exception where an abortion law of 1929 allowed the operation until the twenty-eighth week of pregnancy. Few European governments followed Pius's urging to outlaw divorce, which was still a relatively uncommon phenomenon. British courts, for example, granted a total of 3,747 divorces in 1920. However the details varied, the postwar mood of moral reform was larger than a Christian religious revival. At the Islamic

southeastern edge of Europe, Atatürk reformed Turkish marital law and outlawed polygamy.

Casti connubi also restated traditional views of the position of women. It instructed Catholics to accept "the primacy of the husband" and "the ready subjection of the wife" who must obey him. Many governments saw an economic benefit in this. War work by millions of women had encouraged feminists to believe that women would soon win equality in jobs and wages. They did not. Fewer Frenchwomen were working in 1921 than had been in 1906, despite the loss of 1.4 million male workers in the war. In Britain, 750,000 women lost their jobs in the first year of peace; by 1923 women were a smaller portion of labor unions than they had been in 1913, though nearly one million British workers had been lost (see document 29.2). This pattern was repeated across the continent. Although most of the major powers granted women's suffrage during or after the war, old attitudes about women remained strong.

❧ TABLE 29.3 ❧

The Decline of Infant Mortality in Europe, 1900–40

Deaths of infants under one year of age, as a percentage of live births

Year	Austria	Britain	France	Germany	Russia	Sweden
1900	23.1	15.4	16.0	22.9	25.2	9.9
1910	18.9	10.5	11.1	16.2	27.1	7.5
1920	n.a.	8.0	12.3	13.1	n.a.	6.3
1930	10.4	6.0	8.4	8.5	n.a.	5.5
1940	7.4	5.7	9.1	6.4	n.a.	3.9

n.a. = not available.

Source: B. R. Mitchell, *European Historical Statistics, 1750–1970* (London: Macmillan, 1975), pp. 130–31; data for 1991 from *The World Almanac and Book of Facts 1993* (Mahwah, N.J.: World Almanac Books, 1992), passim.

The Changing Conditions of Life in Europe

Although Europe endured tragic difficulties following World War I, seeing the era solely in terms of its problems would be misleading. Historians must keep many perspectives on the past. Cultural historians, for example, explore the mixture of vitality and decadence known in America as "the roaring twenties." The Weimar Republic is a tragic failure in the history of democracy, but its vigorous cultural history fascinates historians who look at expressionist painting, Bauhaus architecture, or the novels of Thomas Mann instead of dictatorship and depression. Historians of popular culture find an exciting interwar world by considering the impact of the automobile (private autos in use in Britain rose from 79,000 in 1919 to 2,034,000 in 1939), aircraft (British Imperial Airways began overseas passenger service in 1924 and the German Lufthansa airline started service in 1926), or the telephone (introduced in London in 1879 and still limited to an elite of 10,000 homes in Britain on the eve of the war, the two millionth phone was installed in Buckingham Palace in 1931). Historians of science treat epochal developments in physics, where scientists such as Albert Einstein, Max Planck, Enrico Fermi, and Ernest Rutherford transformed understanding of the physical world; the atom, long considered the indivisible basis of all matter, was first split in 1932.

Among the many differences from the past that are examined by social historians of the early twentieth century, the most notable may be the dramatic decline in infant mortality rates (see table 29.3). Under the biological old regime (see chapter 19), between 20 percent and 30 percent of all babies never reached their first birthday. By 1940 most of Europe had a rate below 10 percent as a result of the accelerated conquest of epidemic diseases. Between 1900 and 1940 the death rate from diphtheria for British children fell by 49 percent, measles by 76 percent, and scarlet fever by 83 percent. Hundreds of thousands of Europeans who would have died of contagious diseases in the nineteenth century now reached adulthood. In 1921, two French scientists developed a vaccine against tuberculosis, the disease that had been the greatest scourge of Belle Époque Europe. The first insulin was administered to diabetics in 1922. The most remarkable life-saving discoveries of the interwar era—the antibiotic treatment of wounds and diseases—did not have a great impact until the generation of World War II. Two of the twentieth century's most important Nobel Prizes in Medicine were awarded to men whose work contributed greatly to the conquest of disease: Scottish bacteriologist Alexander Fleming in 1945 and German chemist Gerhard Domagk in 1939. (The Nazi government made Domagk decline the prize, however.) Domagk's work led to the development of sulfa drugs, a treatment nontoxic to humans yet powerful in combating infectious diseases. Fleming discovered penicillin in 1928, though its development was left to others (Ernst Chain and Sir Howard Florey shared the 1945 Nobel Prize) and the drug was not synthesized until the war. Such "wonder drugs" were first used experimentally in 1932; penicillin saved thousands of soldiers in World War II and became widely available after the war.

European Culture after the Deluge

The Great War caused deep cultural despair in Europe. It spawned pessimism in some people, cynical frivolity in others; bitterness in many, spiritual barrenness in most. In the imagery of the Irish poet William Butler Yeats:

> Things fall apart; the centre cannot hold;
> Mere anarchy is loosed upon the world.
> The blood-dimmed tide is loosed, and everywhere
> The ceremony of innocence is drowned;
> The best lack all conviction, while the worst
> Are full of passionate intensity.

This postwar mood produced the absurdities of dadaism and surrealism, the alienated literature of modernism, and ubiquitous antiwar sentiments. Dada was the response of iconoclastic intellectuals—an intentionally meaningless art, an anarchistic "anti-art." According to the Dadaist Manifesto of the Roumanian poet Tristan Tzara, European culture should abandon everything from logic to good manners and teach spontaneous living (see illustration 29.4). The more sophisticated doctrine of surrealism also purged reason from art, replacing it with images from the subconscious, as painters such as Rene Magritte and Marcel Duchamp demonstrated.

The masterpieces of literary modernism showed similar responses to the war. The poetry of T. S. Eliot, such as *The Wasteland* (1922), stated a disillusioned lament for European civilization and asked "what branches grow out of this stony rubbish?" Another of the great works of modernism, James Joyce's *Ulysses* (1922), broke down the logical structure of the novel and fashioned a story about the commonplace events of a single day, verbalized in an inventive but sometimes incoherent form called stream of consciousness. *Ulysses* focused on the postwar mood of Leopold Bloom who, like Europe, had become bitter and dispirited.

The creative artist who best typified the postwar despair of European culture was Franz Kafka, an Austrian-Czech writer so powerful that his name became an adjective. The kafkaesque world is incomprehensible yet menacing; complex, bizarre, absurd, and ominous. Kafka wrote of people so alienated that one of them awakens to find himself transformed into a large insect; of people held in a prison where preposterous commands are tattooed onto their bodies; of a person brought to a bizarre trial in which the charges are never specified; of someone hired for a frustrating job that

Illustration 29.4

Dada. The postwar despair and cynicism of the arts produced one of its most extreme moments in June 1920 when a group of artists staged the first international dadaist art show in Berlin. At this celebration of "anti-art," Georg Grosz stood at the entry holding a banner proclaiming, "Art is dead. This is the new machine art." Among the works of dadaism intended to shock people was Marcel Duchamp's schoolboy prank, Mona Lisa with a mustache.

seems to have neither instructions nor anyone to explain it.

One of the central themes of this postwar mood was anger at war and the society that produced it or profited from it. Erich Maria Remarque, a German writer who later joined a flood of intellectual emigres to America, penned one of the most famous antiwar novels ever written, *All Quiet on the Western Front* (1929), describing the experiences of a group of schoolboys in the dehumanizing life of the trenches. Jaroslav Hasek's *Good Soldier Schweik* (1923) made fun of armies and officers (Hasek used some of his own commanders' names) by showing how easily everyone is fooled by a soldier acting stupid. Wilfred Owen's posthumously published poetry (he was killed in France one week before the armistice) described the suffering of the common soldier and burned with loathing for the war. Vera Brittain, a British volunteer nurse during the war, used her experiences to write of pacifism with such conviction that she became an officer of the Women's International League of Peace and Freedom. George Grosz, a German graphic artist (see illustration 28.8) embittered by the war, used savage caricature to attack the government, the military, and the classes that prospered while others suffered.

Ironically, the most important development in European culture in the early twentieth century was not linked to World War I and the postwar despair. A cultural revolution had begun in the early years of the century, and it triumphed dramatically in the 1920s and 1930s. The new technologies of radio and motion pictures led to the democratization of culture, the creation of mass culture. Two French chemists, Louis and Auguste Lumière, presented the first public showing of a motion picture in 1895, a one-minute film of workers leaving their factory. The first narrative film, the American-made *The Great Train Robbery,* appeared in 1903, and the silent film industry was born in the following decade. The commercial exploitation of the Lumière brothers' "cinematograph" was achieved by Charles Pathé, the first movie mogul, who made Paris the world center of the motion picture industry in the years before 1914. Although the center of the industry had shifted to Hollywood by the 1920s, booming film industries developed in interwar Europe. The British, French, and German industries each were producing more than one hundred feature films per year by the early 1930s.

An Italian inventor, Guglielmo Marconi, launched the world into the age of broadcasting in 1895, shortly before the Lumières showed the first film. Marconi's "wireless telegraphy" did not develop as rapidly as the cinema did, but individual radio transmissions in Europe and America began in the decade before the war. The first broadcast of a program of music occurred at Graz (Austria) in 1908, and the world's first station broadcasting regularly scheduled radio programs began its transmissions in Pittsburgh in 1920. That same year, the British government created a broadcasting monopoly, the BBC (British Broadcasting Company, later Corporation), and it produced the first European daily programming in 1922. Radio, like the movies, became widespread in interwar Europe. By 1930–31 radio reached most households in western and central Europe; there was a radio set for every 12 people in Britain, one per 13 in Sweden, and one per 15 in Germany. Even the slower spread of radio in Poland (one set per 104 people) or Italy (one per 172) meant that programming was reaching deeply into small towns and rural Europe.

The mass culture of radio and cinema broke the centuries-old domination of European culture by a small elite of culture-bearers. Because both industries were built by people such as Charles Pathé who sought commercial success rather than high culture, they quickly became universally available (unlike a great museum), inexpensive (unlike opera), and oriented toward the tastes and interests of the mass market (unlike cubist painting).

European Democracy after World War I

The basic political fact of the postwar era reversed a century-long trend in Europe: Most of Europe lived under parliamentary democracy in 1920 but under authoritarianism in 1939. The era had begun with popularly elected parliaments in the new states of eastern Europe, from the Finnish and Estonian assemblies of 1919 to the Turkish republic of 1922 and the Greek republic of 1924. The Hohenzollern and Hapsburg monarchies yielded to republics in Austria, Czechoslovakia, and Germany (known as the Weimar Republic for the town in which the constitution was drafted).

The enthusiasm for democracy included an expansion of its definition. Between 1915 and 1922, eighteen European countries gave women the right to vote in national elections. The trend began in Scandinavia, where Norway had led the way before the war. Denmark enfranchised women in 1915, with Finland (1917) and Sweden (1918) following. The idea then took root in the new regimes of Eastern Europe (Russia, Estonia, Latvia, Poland, Lithuania, Czechoslovakia, and Hungary) and in the Austrian and German republics. Ironically, women's suffrage found less acceptance in western Europe. Britain only allowed women to vote at the age of thirty until an equal franchise law was passed in 1928 (see illustration 29.5). In France, a conservative Senate blocked women's suffrage in 1922 and prevented women from voting until 1944. Belgium, Italy, Portugal, and Switzerland (the last state in Europe to accept women's suffrage) also rejected enfranchisement. A

Illustration 29.5

///// **Women's Suffrage.** Women won the right to vote in many European states during or immediately after the world war—including the Soviet Union (1917), Britain (1918), and Germany (1918), but not France or Italy. Women's rights campaigns still sought greater equality for women, however, including the right to vote under exactly the same conditions as for men. Here British women protest that they did not receive the right to vote until age thirty.

second expansion of democracy was proportional voting to give representation to minorities. Under traditional procedures, a group receiving 10 percent of the vote seldom won an election; advocates of proportional representation said that group deserved 10 percent of the seats in a legislature. Belgium had employed proportional representation since 1899, and varieties of that system were adopted in France, Germany, and Italy at the end of the war. Most of the new democracies followed.

Despite such trends, democracy did not flourish during the interwar years. By 1939 more than a dozen parliamentary democracies had been replaced by dictatorships. The newly independent states were especially vulnerable. General Jozef Pilsudski used the Polish army to hold dictatorial power for nearly fifteen years. An impoverished noble who had fought for Polish independence in the 1880s and 1890s, then organized a Polish army to fight Russia in the first world war, Pilsudski became the first president of Poland in 1922. However, he subsequently became disillusioned with democracy and resigned. His military coup d'état of 1926 created a limited military dictatorship, which tol-

erated a degree of opposition but did not hesitate to arrest and torture opposition leaders in 1930. Monarchies abolished political freedoms in Yugoslavia and Albania. In Hungary, Admiral Miklos Horthy governed (from 1920 to 1944) as the regent for a vacant monarchy whose restoration he prevented. Horthy, the son of a Protestant noble family, had been the last commander in chief of the Hapsburg navy and the leader of the Hungarian army that overthrew the Hungarian Communist regime of Bela Kun in 1919. Hungary retained a Parliament, but Horthy curtailed the electoral process, held a veto over legislation, and created an anachronistic upper house of Parliament controlled by nobles. Horthy collaborated with Nazi Germany and narrowly escaped trial for war crimes in 1945.

As the failed democracies of eastern Europe suggest, the era between 1919 and 1945 became an age of dictatorship. The Communist dictatorship of Joseph Stalin in the Soviet Union (ruled 1924–53); the Nazi dictatorship of Adolf Hitler in Germany (ruled 1933–45); the Fascist dictatorship of Benito Mussolini in Italy (ruled 1922–45); the military dictatorships of General Primo de Rivera (ruled 1922–30), General Francisco Franco in Spain (ruled 1936–75), and Antonio Salazar in Portugal (ruled 1926–68); and the wartime dictatorship of Marshal Henri Pétain in France (ruled 1940–45) are the characteristic regimes of the era. World War II accelerated this trend, and by 1941 only five parliamentary democracies survived in Europe: Britain, Ireland, Iceland, Sweden, and Switzerland.

German Democracy in the 1920s: The Weimar Republic

After the abdication of Kaiser Wilhelm II in 1918, a provisional government held elections for a constituent assembly to meet in the Saxon city of Weimar and create a German republic. This provisional government put down the Sparticist revolt of German Communists at Berlin in January 1919, suppressed the Soviet republic of Bavaria in April 1919, and accepted the responsibility for signing the Versailles Treaty in June 1919. Consequently, the Weimar Republic began life in the summer of 1919 detested by both the communist left and the nationalist right. The Weimar constitution contained such idealistic provisions as universal suffrage, proportional representation, popular referenda, the abolition of aristocratic privilege, and basic individual freedoms. It entrusted the government to a chancellor, who needed the support of a majority in the Reichstag, but it also created a seven-year presidency with special powers to suspend the constitution during emergencies.

Right-wing opposition to the Weimar Republic flourished immediately and dominated the early 1920s. Paramilitary leagues of war veterans, known as the *Freikorps* (Free Corps), remained a violent factor in German politics. Extremists assassinated the socialist premier of Bavaria in 1919, then Matthias Erzberger (who had bravely accepted the job of signing the Versailles Treaty) in 1921, and Walter Rathenau (an industrialist who had managed the German economy during the war and became foreign minister) in 1922. *Freikorps* troops supported monarchists in seizing control of Berlin in the Kapp *Putsch* (coup) of 1920, and the German army refused to fire on them; the *Putsch* was only blocked by a general strike of Berlin workers. Nationalists blamed republicans for a supposed civilian betrayal of the German army in 1918—the "stab-in-the-back" (or *Dolchstoss*) myth of the German defeat—even though their military hero, General Ludendorff, had been the person who admitted that military victory was impossible and called for peace. Ludendorff participated in what became the most famous right-wing conspiracy of the 1920s, the Munich Beer Hall *Putsch* of November 1923. This attempted coup introduced the world to Adolf Hitler and his small National Socialist German Workers' Party ("Nazi" as a contraction). The Beer Hall *Putsch* was easily stopped and Hitler was convicted of high treason and sentenced to prison for five years, where he dictated *Mein Kampf* (My Struggle) before his early release (see document 29.3). Hitler's book was a muddle of hatreds (of Communism, Jews, the Versailles Treaty, democracy, and the Weimar Republic), stating the right-wing agenda; initially it found few readers.

The success of parliamentary democracy in Germany depended upon winning the support of the middle classes and the peasantry away from the alternatives proposed by nationalists or communists. Many Germans were alienated, however, by the economic catastrophes of the early 1920s. The imperial government had destroyed the value of the mark by its vast borrowing and the reckless printing of money. Territorial losses and reparations payments compounded the problem. The inflation of 1922–23 destroyed the savings, pensions, and income of millions of Germans. Consequently, the German middle class, especially the lower middle class, never developed fond ties to the Weimar government.

The German republic did recover and prosper after 1924. A coalition of moderate socialists, democrats, and the Catholic Party (the *Zentrum*) brought stability to the

◈ DOCUMENT 29.3 ◈

Hitler: Anti-Semitism in *Mein Kampf* (1925)

Mein Kampf (My Struggle) originally appeared in two volumes. The first part, from which the following excerpt is taken, was written during Hitler's imprisonment and published in 1925; a second part appeared in 1928. Together they stated Hitler's political program and provided unmistakable indications of his racist thoughts and intentions. Hitler asserted that the Jews were lowest of all the races, who destroyed the civilization of other races; they were responsible for World War I and for the Bolshevik revolution. Mein Kampf did not sell well until Hitler came to power, then it sold five million copies in 1933–39 and was translated into eleven languages.

There were few Jews in Linz. In the course of the centuries their outward appearance had become Europeanized and had taken on a human look; in fact, I even took them for Germans. . . .

Then I came to Vienna. . . . Once, as I was strolling through the Inner City, I suddenly encountered an apparition in a black caftan and black hair locks. Is this a Jew? was my first thought. . . . The longer I stared . . . the more my question assumed a new form: Is this a German?

The cleanliness of this people, moral and otherwise, I must say, is a point in itself. By their very exterior you could tell that these were no lovers of water, and, to your distress, you often knew it with your eyes closed. . . .

I became acquainted with their activity in the press, art, literature, and the theater. . . . Nine-tenths of all literary filth, artistic trash, and theatrical idiocy can be set to their account. . . .

Then a flame flared up within me. . . . Hence, today I believe that I am acting with the will of the Almighty Creator: by defending myself against the Jew, I am fighting for the work of the Lord.

government. An international agreement, the Dawes Plan (1924), readjusted reparations and created a stable currency. Industrial production rose. A strong and capable foreign minister, Gustav Stresemann, risked the ire of nationalists by pursuing conciliatory policies. Stresemann, the brilliant son of an innkeeper, had risen in politics as Ludendorff's protégé and had been an ardent nationalist and imperialist, but he reconsidered his beliefs during the right-wing violence of the early 1920s, especially after the murders of Erzberger and Rathenau. His cooperation with the French foreign minister Aristide Briand restored normal peacetime conditions. Briand had risen in French politics as a socialist ally of Jean Jaurès and was the author of legislation separating church and state in 1905. Socialists expelled him from the party for accepting a cabinet post in a bourgeois government, and he began a long career as a centrist. Between 1906 and 1932 he held twenty-six cabinet appointments. As the leading voice of postwar French foreign policy, Briand twice (1924 and 1929) agreed to ease reparations payments. Briand and Stresemann negotiated the Locarno Treaty (1925), reaffirming the Franco-German frontier drawn in the Versailles Treaty. Stresemann led Germany into the League of Nations (1926) as the equal of Britain and France. In short, peace and prosperity seemed possible when Stresemann and Briand shared the 1926 Nobel Peace Prize for creating the "spirit of Locarno."

Postwar Recovery in Britain and France

The older democracies also experienced difficult times in recovering stability. Britain and France struggled with economic problems, faced social unrest, and turned to conservative governments for most of the 1920s.

At the end of the war, the British government had addressed two of its greatest prewar problems: women's rights and the government of Ireland. Lloyd George's Representation of the People Act (1918) gave women the vote at age thirty, and the Equal Franchise Act (1928) finally granted women suffrage on the same basis as men. In 1919 the American-born Lady Nancy Astor became the first woman to sit in the House of Commons; by 1929 there were 69 women candidates and 14 women M.P.s (of 615 seats). British women won other important rights in the Sex Disqualification Act of 1919 (which abolished gender barriers to universities, the professions, and public positions) and the Law of Property of 1926 (which gave all women the right to hold and dispose of property on the same terms as men). Important as this legislation was, it fell short of full equality for women, as Vera Brittain's criticism of postwar demobilization showed. Even those women who kept their jobs in the 1920s and 1930s still worked for less than half of a man's wages, and that situation was not improving. Working women's percentage of men's earnings was 48.2 percent in 1924 and 48.1 percent in 1935.

The British addressed the Irish question with mixed success. Three years after the Easter Rebellion of 1916,

Irish nationalists again rebelled against British rule. In a treaty of 1921, twenty-six (largely Catholic) counties of Ireland gained independence as the Irish Free State, although six other counties (with a large Protestant population) in the northern region of Ulster remained a part of the United Kingdom. This agreement precipitated an Irish civil war between protreaty and antitreaty forces; protreaty forces that accepted the border dividing Ireland won. (The continuing acceptance of this treaty and this border led to the reopening of the Irish question in 1969 when a militant minority of the Irish Republican Army (IRA), known as the Provos, began a terrorist campaign intended to end the union of Britain and Northern Ireland and to reunite the north with the south.)

The most severe problem that interwar Britain faced was neither the woman question nor the Irish question. It was economics. Prewar unemployment had been 3.3 percent, and it remained low until soldiers and women workers were demobilized. Unemployment hit 14.8 percent in 1921 and stayed above 10 percent for the remainder of the decade. Productivity stood at a fraction of prewar levels, many of which (such as coal production) were never reached again. The cost of living in 1921 had risen to four times the level of 1914. By 1922 marches of the unemployed and hungry had become a common feature of British daily life. And the home of capitalist free trade orthodoxy watched as its imports doubled its exports.

Britain was one of the most heavily unionized states in the world, with 30 percent of workers belonging to trade unions in 1921. The miners' unions were especially militant, and they led major strikes in 1919 and 1921. Though elections in early 1924 created a short-lived Labour Party government in which Ramsay MacDonald became Britain's first socialist prime minister, angry workers obtained little welfare legislation except the Pension Act of 1925. MacDonald, the illegitimate son of a farm laborer and a servant, had risen through self-education to become the leading theorist of British socialism. He rejected Marxist doctrines of class warfare and violent revolution and believed in an evolutionary, democratic socialism as "the hereditary heir of liberalism." After MacDonald granted diplomatic recognition to the USSR, however, the evolutionary process restored conservatives to power, and Stanley Baldwin (the son of a rich industrialist) formed his second government. Social unrest worsened under both governments. Mine owners lowered wages and lengthened the working day, leading to another wave of strikes, which culminated in the general strike (when all workers were expected to leave their jobs) of 1926.

More than 2.5 million workers in a labor force of 6 million walked out. The Baldwin government, fearful of the revolutionary potential of the general strike, made enough concessions to bring back moderate workers. With the general strike beaten, conservatives quickly passed the Trade Disputes Act of 1927 limiting the right to strike. General strikes, sympathy strikes, and strikes in many occupations (such as the police) became illegal.

The postwar government in France was a similar conservative coalition, led by Raymond Poincaré. Poincaré, educated as both an engineer and a lawyer, had held elective office since the 1880s, culminating in the wartime presidency. As premier in the early 1920s, Poincaré concentrated upon the rebuilding of France and a nationalist agenda. He expected the strict enforcement of the Versailles Treaty and ordered a military occupation of the Ruhr (permitted by the reparations agreement) when Germany defaulted on payments in 1923. French conservatives supported Poincaré in treason trials of wartime pacifists, the dissolution of the militant confederation of trade unions (the CGT), aid to big business and the peasantry, and concessions to the Catholic Church. During the mid- and late 1920s, Briand persuaded the conservative coalition to relax its anti-German nationalism, and Poincaré acquiesced in this policy to concentrate upon economic recovery. French problems were so bad that Poincaré asked and received the right to solve them by decrees without a vote of the Chamber of Deputies. He stabilized the French franc in 1926–28 by devaluing it to 20 percent of its prewar value. This meant that the government repudiated 80 percent of its foreign debt written in francs, chiefly war bonds. The conservative government also introduced heavy new taxes on inheritance and income while cutting the budget by reducing the size and income of the French bureaucracy. When Poincaré retired in 1929, his accomplishments included a stable currency, a growing economy, record industrial production, and the reconstruction of most war-damaged regions. Briand had simultaneously won guarantees of peace. Many resentments simmered below the surface, but France appeared to have made a strong recovery.

The Great Depression of the 1930s

By 1928 Europe had largely recovered from the ravages of World War I. Total productivity stood 13 percent above the 1913 level, slightly stronger in western Europe (16 percent) than central and eastern Europe (12 percent). The year 1929, however, marked the beginning of the worst economic depression of the twentieth century. This crisis began in the United States with the collapse of stock market values known as the Wall Street Crash, and it spread into a global collapse in 1929–32. Most of Europe felt the depression begin in 1930, and it soon became the deepest of the industrial age, comparable only to the depression of the 1840s, which contributed to the outbreak of the revolutions of 1848. The collapse of the American stock values, the loss of American credit, the recall of American loans to Europe, the rise of American tariffs, and the withering of exports to America caused deep declines in European production and frightening levels of unemployment. As unemployment rose, small shops went bankrupt; as world trade collapsed, big industries such as shipbuilding closed down. In 1931, when banks could not obtain repayment of outstanding loans, a wave of bank failures swept Europe. After a great Austrian bank, the Kredit-Anstalt, failed, much of the banking system of eastern and central Europe collapsed, and the wave of bank closings reached back to the United States. Most of Europe was still struggling to recover from this cycle when World War II began in 1939.

The most dramatic measure of the crisis of the 1930s is in unemployment data (see table 29.4). Despite the recovery of the late 1920s, Europe had not returned to the low levels of joblessness seen in 1913–14 (3–4 percent). Nonetheless, no one was prepared for the catastrophic unemployment of the 1930s. Most of Europe had double-digit unemployment in 1930, then rates above 20 percent in 1931–32, although predominantly agricultural economies (such as Poland) and agriculturally self-sufficient regions (such as France) suffered less. Many countries, however, experienced 30 percent jobless rates; the Dutch lived with unemployment averaging 31.7 percent for seven years (1932–38).

The Great Depression tested the Western world's belief in liberal-democratic government and capitalist economics. Many countries abandoned democracy in favor of authoritarian leadership; many surviving democracies (such as France and the United States) found that they must provide their citizens with significantly higher levels of welfare benefits. All countries (including Britain, France, and the United States) abandoned some classic precepts of market capitalism, such as free trade; many adopted the eighteenth-century economics of autarchy (self-sufficiency).

Britain illustrates the severity of the crisis. The National Insurance Act of 1911 gave Britain the largest unemployment insurance program in Europe, but it

⚜ TABLE 29.4 ⚜

Unemployment During the Great Depression, 1930–39

The data in this table are from the League of Nations.

Percentage of labor force unemployed

Year	United States	Britain	Germany	Netherlands	Norway	Poland
1930	7.8	14.6	15.3	9.7	16.6	8.8
1931	16.3	21.5	23.3	18.1	22.3	12.6
1932	24.9	22.5	30.1	29.5	30.8	11.8
1933	25.1	21.3	26.3	31.0	33.4	11.9
1934	20.2	17.7	14.9	32.1	30.7	16.3
1935	18.4	16.4	11.6	36.3	25.3	16.7
1936	14.5	14.3	8.3	36.3	18.8	15.6
1937	12.0	11.3	4.6	29.2	20.0	14.6
1938	18.8	13.3	2.1	27.2	22.0	12.7
1939	16.7	11.7	n.a.	21.8	18.3	14.1

Source: *Annuaire statistique de la Société des Nations, 1939–1940* (Geneva: League of Nations, 1940), pp. 70–71.

n.a. = not available

covered fewer than two-thirds of British workers and provided only fifteen weeks of benefits. (German unemployment legislation, by comparison, covered less than half of the labor force.) When unemployment in old industrial centers reached horrendous proportions, as it did in the Welsh coal-mining town of Merthyr Tydfil (62 percent in 1934) and the English shipbuilding town of Jarrow (68 percent in 1934), such insurance was insufficient (see illustration 29.6). A National Coalition government of all major parties (1931–35) adopted drastic measures. They abandoned the gold standard, devalued the pound by nearly 30 percent, adopted protective tariffs (including a new Corn Law in 1932), cut the wages of government employees (such as teachers and soldiers), and reduced unemployment benefits.

This produced a volatile situation in Britain. Riots in London, Liverpool, and Glasgow greeted the announced economies in 1931. Part of the royal navy mutinied. The crime rate soared. (The burglary rate for stores and shops in 1938 was 556 percent of the rate in 1900.) The unemployed marched on Parliament—one protest was known as the Jarrow Marches because much of that town marched to London in 1936 when unemployment there hit 96 percent, closing virtually every store in the town. British democracy survived, but not without enduring the birth of fascist and racist movements such as Sir Oswald Mosley's British Union of Fascists. Mosley, a former conservative M.P. who was

impressed by Mussolini, created a paramilitary fascist party under his absolute authority. He introduced Britain to black-shirted thugs, political violence, and anti-Semitic demonstrations. Parliament responded with the Public Order Act of 1936, outlawing political uniforms and strictly regulating political marches.

The French Third Republic came even closer to collapsing. French unemployment quintupled in 1932 and passed 1.3 million in early 1933. The French government, long considered unstable, became a series of short-lived cabinets: four different cabinets in 1930, three in 1931, five in 1932, four in 1933, and four in 1934. As one wit observed, tourists went to London to see the changing of the guard and to Paris to see the changing of the government. The Stavisky affair of 1933–34 showed that the French government was as corrupt as it was ineffectual. This scandal began when Alexandre Stavisky, a Ukrainian-born swindler, confessed to selling fraudulent bonds with the assistance of prominent politicians. Stavisky's death in a reported suicide and the dubious nature of investigations created a volatile antiparliamentary mood in France. Several far right-wing leagues—such as Colonel de la Rocque's *Croix de feu* (The Fiery Cross) and Pierre Taittinger's *Jeunesses Patriotes* (Young Patriots)—had flourished during the depression, and their members seized upon the Stavisky scandal as the excuse for antiparliamentary riots in the Place de Concorde in central Paris in February 1934. Thousands of right-wing demon-

Illustration 29.6

Unemployment in the Great Depression. European unemployment reached its worst levels of the twentieth century during the 1930s. Although national averages were staggering at 20 to 33 percent unemployment, some industries and communities faced even worse rates. In Jarrow, an industrial town in northern England, two-thirds of the male population was unemployed. In this photo, workers from Jarrow stage a 1936 march to London to protest insufficient government action.

strators battled with police in an attempt to attack the Chamber of Deputies. The republic survived the Stavisky riots, but fifteen people were killed and more than one thousand injured.

Léon Blum and the Popular Front in France

The depression, the Stavisky affair, and the February 1934 riots led, paradoxically, to a strengthening of the Third Republic, because they frightened political leaders into creating a powerful coalition called the Popular Front (1936–38). The parties of the French left had long fought each other, but fears of a fascist *Putsch* united them. Moderate democrats (called the Radical Party) led by Edouard Daladier, democratic socialists, trade unionists, and even Communists (frightened by the spread of fascism, which was strongly anti-Communist) supported the Popular Front under the leadership of Léon Blum, the head of the Socialist Party. Blum, a Jewish intellectual and a distinguished jurist, had entered politics at the time of the Dreyfus affair. He fought against both Poincaré's conservatism and French Communism while rebuilding the democratic socialist (SFIO) party during the 1920s. When the 1934 riots alarmed France about the strength of fascism there, Blum took the lead in creating the Popular Front and brought it to victory in the 1936 parliamentary elections, becoming the first Jewish prime minister in French history.

Léon Blum held office for only one year before the Popular Front began to crumble, but in that time he achieved Europe's most profound response to the de-

pression: a maximum workweek of forty hours, paid annual vacations of four weeks for all workers, a 12 percent raise for workers and civil servants, and acceptance of collective bargaining. Under Blum's direction, France also abandoned some aspects of capitalist economics. The Popular Front nationalized the Bank of France and parts of the armaments industry, and it undertook government regulation of basic food prices. The Blum government also restored a degree of order in France and calmed the worst fears of industrialists by ending the wave of sit-down strikes and factory occupations that had swept the country and by agreeing not to nationalize most industries. Many others were reassured by the steps taken to control far right wing groups in France. The Action française, formed by Charles Maurras during the Dreyfus affair, was closed when some of its members physically attacked Blum, and several paramilitary groups—often called the French fascist leagues—were also banned. When Blum proposed further financial reforms in 1937, however, the Radical Party deserted the Popular Front, and Blum was obliged to resign, to the cheers of many conservatives who felt "Better Hitler than Blum."

The Spanish Second Republic and the Spanish Civil War

Spain entered the twentieth century in an age of governmental instability. The nation experienced a military junta (1868–70), an elected monarch who abdicated

(1870–73), a short-lived First Republic (1873–74), and a constitutional monarchy (1874–1923) that lasted until General Primo de Rivera created a military dictatorship (1923–30). The Spanish Second Republic was created in 1931 after Primo de Rivera allowed local elections, which produced an outpouring of support for a republic.

The Spanish republic of 1931 was among the frailest of Europe's parliamentary democracies, and it faced many threats. A regional revolt broke out in 1934 when Catalonia proclaimed itself independent. The republic was also internally divided between groups of moderate, Catholic republicans led by Prime Minister Alcalá Zamora and groups of more radical, anticlerical republicans led by Manuel Azaña. Its radical constitution alarmed landowners, who feared nationalization of property; the leaders of the church, who resisted its program of secularization; and the army, whose officer corps was greatly reduced by forced retirements at half-pensions. These groups formed the nucleus of a resurgent right-wing in Spanish politics. Primo de Rivera's son launched a Spanish fascist movement known as the Falange in 1933; it later stopped using the word *fascist*, but it remained emphatically antidemocratic. The program of the Falange was clear: "Our State will be a totalitarian instrument. . . . We shall immediately abolish the system of political parties." The election of a Spanish Popular Front government in 1936, which resembled the French coalition in joining republicans, socialists, trade unions, and communists, intensified the political polarization.

The crisis of Spanish democracy culminated in the Spanish Civil War of 1936–39. War began with the revolt of army units stationed in Spanish Morocco and spread to garrison towns in Spain. The Falange joined General Francisco Franco in forming a coalition of Nationalists seeking to abolish the Second Republic and restore traditional order to Spain. A similar coalition of Loyalists, including Catalan rebels, defended the republic. The Loyalists held most of the great cities of Spain, such as Madrid and Barcelona, but the Nationalists held most of the military strength. Franco was the son of a naval paymaster, educated in a military academy, and made his reputation in colonial wars in the 1920s; his reckless bravery in combat (perhaps a compensation for his insecurity at standing only 5'3") made him the youngest general in Europe (at thirty-three) in 1926. His mixture of nationalism, military dictatorship, Falangist fascism, monarchism, and clericalism did not precisely fit the mold of fascist movements elsewhere, but it won the military support of both Mussolini, who sent Franco seventy-five thousand soldiers, and Hitler

during the civil war. The Soviet Union similarly aided the republic. General Franco, proclaimed chief of the Spanish state by the insurgents in late 1936, led the Nationalist armies in the steady destruction of the republic and Basque and Catalan separatist regimes. The civil war ended in 1939 after Barcelona fell to an assault by allied Nationalist and Italian troops and Madrid surrendered. Three years of fighting had killed more than 700,000 people in combat and at least 100,000 civilians. General Franco replaced the republic with a dictatorship that lasted until his death in 1975.

The Global Struggle for Freedom from Europe

The most ironic problem confronting the European democracies was that they opposed self-government outside of Europe. Native leaders, nationalist organizations, and armed uprisings already characterized the global resistance to imperialism before 1914. The success of Japanese arms in 1905 and Chinese revolutions in 1900 and 1911 inspired Asian nationalists, just as the Young Turk Revolution of 1908 and the Arab Revolt of 1916 stirred the Islamic world. By 1919 most regions of the world heard voices such as that of the Bengali poet Rabindranath Tagore, who won the Nobel Prize in Literature for the simple force of lines such as his prayer, "My father, let my country awake."

World War I exposed the vulnerability of European armies and eroded the moral position of Western propaganda. The Allies had proclaimed that they were fighting to make the world "safe for democracy." They had promised peace based upon principles such as "national self-determination" (in the words of Wilson's Fourteen Points), and they recruited millions of Africans and Asians to serve Europe under these banners. India alone sent 1.3 million soldiers and replacement laborers to aid Britain; Algeria, Indochina, and West Africa sent 650,000 to France. A few colonial voices had questioned the war, as John Chilembwe did in East Africa (see document 29.4). He simply asked why Africans were "invited to shed our innocent blood in this world's war." (Chilembwe wound up being shot by the police.) Most nationalists, including Ghandi, stood by their wartime governments until 1918, hoping that their loyalty would be rewarded. But World War I did not bring democracy or national self-determination to Africa and Asia. Instead, it created new colonies (especially in the Middle East) through the League of Nations mandate system. Before the ink had dried on the

◆ DOCUMENT 29.4 ◆

John Chilembwe: The European Empires in Africa (1914)

We understand that we have been invited to shed our innocent blood in this world's war. . . .

On the commencement of the war we understood that Africa had nothing to do with the civilized war. But now we find that the poor African has already been plunged into the great war.

A number of our people have already shed their blood, while others are crippled for life. And an open declaration has been issued. A number of police are marching in various villages persuading well built natives to join in the war. The masses of our people are ready to put on uniforms ignorant of what they have to face or why they have to face it.

We ask the Honorable Government of our country which is known as Nyasaland, Will there be any good prospects for the natives after the end of the war? Shall we be recognized as anybody in the best interests of civilization and Christianity after the great struggle is ended?

. . . Let the rich men, bankers, titled men, storekeepers, farmers and landlords go to war and get shot. Instead the poor Africans who have nothing to own in this present world, who in death leave only a long line of widows and orphans in utter want and dire distress are invited to die for a cause which is not theirs. . . . We hope in the Mercy of Almighty God that some day things will turn out well and that Government will recognize our indispensability, and that justice will prevail.

peace settlements, nationalists again challenged European imperialism. An Egyptian nationalist party, the *Wafd,* led an insurrection in 1919 and thereafter combined passive resistance and terrorism until the British granted them independence in 1922. A Syrian national congress proclaimed independence from France in 1920, and a similar congress at Nablus in 1922 called for the independence of Transjordan and Palestine from Britain. The French rejected Syrian independence and took Damascus by force; they then faced a decade of Druse rebellion and an all-out war in 1925–27. The British granted Transjordan autonomy in 1923 and independence in 1928, but they kept control of Palestine,

where the question of a Jewish state was already an explosive issue. The British had promised "a national home for the Jewish people" in the Balfour Declaration of 1917, but immigration led to anti-Jewish riots in 1921 and 1929. The British backed down and curbed immigration in 1930. A Pan-Arab Congress of 1937 called for Palestinian independence and condemned the projected Jewish state, but neither Palestinians nor Zionists would accept British compromises. At the other end of the Arab world, Abd el-Krim led the Riffs in a long rebellion against the Spanish and French in Morocco. He inflicted heavy losses on the Spanish in 1921 and resisted the French army for two years, 1925–26.

Anti-imperialism took a different form in India. Ghandi began his civil disobedience movement in April 1919 and the noncooperation movement in 1920. He was jailed in 1922 but still insisted upon nonviolence: "I discovered in the earliest stages that pursuit of the truth did not admit of violence being inflicted upon one's opponent, but that he must be weaned from error by sympathy and patience." The Indian nationalist movement, known as the Congress, grew increasingly radical yet accepted Ghandi's doctrines. By the 1930s Ghandi had become such a revered leader that when he announced a "fast unto death" the British capitulated to his demands in six days.

Other patterns of anti-imperialism flourished in the Far East. A scholarly Buddhist monk, U Ottama, led Burmese resistance to Britain by blending religious revival and nationalism. Islam similarly strengthened nationalism in the East Indies; on the island of Java (today, Indonesia), the Sarekat Islam had 2.5 million members opposing the Dutch in 1919. When Asian nationalist movements did not ally with such religious revivals, they often found secular support in newly formed Communist parties. The Indonesian Communist Party, organized in 1920, was typical; it drew more members by linking poverty with opposition to the Dutch than by linking poverty to Marxist-Leninist analysis. In French Indochina, Ho Chi Minh (a pseudonym meaning "He Who Enlightens") likewise found supporters for his Vietnamese Young League of Revolutionaries by uniting nationalism and communism.

Mussolini and Fascist Italy, 1919–39

The Italian constitutional monarchy survived World War I, although the king held little power. Victor Emmanuel III (reigned 1900–47), the grandson of the monarch of the *Risorgimento*, remained a figurehead monarch throughout the Fascist era. Italians had been slowly creating a parliamentary democracy, although they were accustomed to fewer civil liberties than existed in Britain or France. An electoral law of 1912 introduced universal manhood suffrage and another gave proportional representation (but not yet women's suffrage) in 1919.

Italy had candidly fought World War I for territorial compensation. It had quit the Triple Alliance and joined the Allies for the deal they offered in the Treaty of London: Italy would annex the frontier province of the Tyrol, the Istrian Peninsula at the head of the Adriatic Sea, the Dalmatian coast opposite Italy, and an African colony. When Premier Vittorio Orlando asked for this territory at the peace conference, however, President Wilson, who had not participated in the London Treaty, insisted that those regions be distributed on the basis of nationality. Consequently, Italy received only the southern Tyrol and Istria; the town of Fiume and the Adriatic coast became part of Yugoslavia. Angry Italian nationalists, the irredentists, continued to demand the unredeemed territories.

Italy paid heavily for its new territory. In addition to 500,000 combat deaths, 2.2 million military casualties, and the devastation of Venetia, the war brought a huge national debt, 400 percent inflation (see table 29.5), massive unemployment, and violent social unrest. The combination of embittered nationalism and economic hardship produced many authoritarian movements in Europe; in Italy, it led to the Fascist dictatorship. Benito Mussolini founded the Italian Fascist movement at Milan in 1919. Mussolini, the son of a radical blacksmith who had named him in honor of Benito Juárez (the Mexican anticlerical), had been an elementary school teacher, a trade union organizer, and a socialist journalist before the war. At the start of the fighting, he converted to vehement nationalism; he served as a private until being wounded and discharged. At the end of the war, he organized angry unemployed veterans at Milan into the *Fascio di Combattimento* ("Combat Group"). These black-uniformed street fighters embraced his program of strict discipline and authority. They accepted an ancient Roman symbol of such authority, the *Fasces* (a bundle of rods bound around an axe), which led to their name *Fascisti*, or Fascists; they accepted funding from large landowners and industrialists to use violence to break up trade union meetings, beat up striking workers, and terrorize peasants. During the Italian "red scare" of the *biennio rosso* (1918–20), Mussolini built Fascist popularity by a mixture of extreme nationalism and violent anti-Bolshevism. In 1919

TABLE 29.5

Inflation and the Cost of Living in Italy, 1914–21

In this table, the base 1914 cost of living = 100. Total inflation during World War I (1914–18) was 264.1 percent; during demobilization (1919–21), 55.5 percent; and during the war and demobilization (1914–21), 416.8 percent.

Year	Cost of living index	Annual inflation rate (in percent)
1914	100.0	——
1915	107.0	7.0
1916	133.9	25.1
1917	189.4	41.4
1918	264.1	39.4
1919	268.1	1.5
1920	352.3	31.4
1921	416.8	18.3

Source: Instituto centrale di statistica, *Sommario di statistiche storiche italiane, 1861–1955* (Rome: 1955), p. 172.

he backed the poet Gabriele D'Annunzio in the seizure of Fiume. Between 1919 and 1921 the Black Shirts progressed from bullies into killers. They believed, as Mussolini put it, that "a certain kind of violence is moral."

In 1921 Mussolini organized Fascism as a political party, and his doctrine (see document 29.5) and behavior provide the model for understanding the varieties of European fascism in the interwar years. The essential element of Fascism was a political program vehemently opposed to all other forms of government. It was a counterrevolutionary revolution, opposed to the revolutionary tradition of 1789 that had encouraged liberal-democratic forms of parliamentary government across Europe and equally opposed to the new revolutionary tradition of 1917 that stimulated socialist or communist forms of government—yet it was not a reactionary demand to return to monarchical authority. The Fascist alternative offered a strong authoritarian government (which became totalitarian government) buttressed with nationalism and militarism. Fascist totalitarianism, soon established with local variations in many European countries, was similar to Communist totalitarianism in creating a one-party state, headed by a single leader with dictatorial powers, maintained in power by a secret police and the use of violence, and unrestrained

◆ DOCUMENT 29.5 ◆

Mussolini's Explanation of Fascism (1932)

Fascism was not the nursling of a doctrine worked out beforehand with detailed elaboration; it was born of the need for action, and it was itself from the beginning practical rather than theoretical; it was not merely another political party but, even in the first two years, in opposition to all political parties. . . . The necessity for action did not permit research or any complete elaboration of doctrine. The battle had to be fought . . . against Liberalism, Democracy, Socialism, and the Masons. . . .

Fascism . . . believes neither in the possibility nor the utility of perpetual peace. It thus repudiates the doctrine of Pacifism—born of a renunciation of the struggle and an act of cowardice in the face of sacrifice. War alone brings up to its highest tension all human energy and puts the stamp of nobility upon the peoples who have the courage to meet it. . . .

Fascism [is] the complete opposite of . . . so-called scientific and Marxian socialism. . . . Fascism, now and always, believes in holiness and in heroism; that is to say, in actions influenced by no economic motive, direct or indirect. . . . Above all, Fascism denies that class war can be the preponderant force in the transformation of society.

. . . After Socialism, Fascism combats the whole complex system of democratic ideology, and repudiates it. . . . Fascism denies that the majority, by the simple fact that it is a majority, can direct society . . . [and] it affirms the inequality of mankind, which can never be permanently levelled. . . . Fascism denies, in democracy, the absurd conventional untruth of political equality. . . . Fascism has taken up an attitude of complete opposition to the doctrines of Liberalism, both in the political field and the field of economics [Capitalism]. . . .

The Fascist negation of Socialism, Democracy, and Liberalism must not be taken to mean that Fascism desires to lead the world back to the state of affairs before 1789. . . . Absolute monarchy has been, and it can never return. . . .

The foundation of Fascism is the conception of the State, its duty and its aim. Fascism conceives of the State as an absolute, in comparison with which individuals or groups are relative. . . . The State [is] the custodian and transmitter of the spirit of the people, as it has grown up through the centuries in language, in customs, and in faith. . . . Whoever says Fascism implies the State.

by constitutional laws, liberties, and thoughts of human rights. It differed from Communist totalitarianism by stressing nationalism instead of internationalism, by rejecting class conflict (old aristocrats and wealthy bourgeois could both flourish), and by preserving capitalist concepts such as private property.

Mussolini's variety of Fascism produced a less totalitarian dictatorship than subsequent varieties (especially Nazi Germany). He packaged his antiparliamentary, anticommunist nationalism in a rhetoric about heroism, courage, and sacrifice. He created a cult of leadership around himself in the role of *Il Duce* (the leader) and promised leadership that would change the peace treaty and the economic crisis. This attracted enough votes (chiefly veterans, small businessmen, students, and civil servants) under proportional representation to elect Mussolini and thirty-four supporters to the Chamber of Deputies in 1921. Mussolini won less than 10 percent of the vote, yet he successfully exploited Italian troubles and government weakness to gain dictatorial

powers in 1922. This began with the "march on Rome" in October 1922, when Mussolini led thousands of Fascists in a demonstration seeking his appointment as premier (see illustration 29.7). "Either they will give us the government or we shall seize it," Mussolini said. When armed Fascists seized arsenals, railroad stations, and telephone and telegraph offices, the king relented and appointed Mussolini to office. Within one month, he persuaded Parliament to give him dictatorial powers for one year, to restore economic order without the delays of the democratic process. Mussolini used his power to pack the courts, the administration, and local government with his supporters; simultaneously he browbeat the king into naming a Fascist majority in the Italian Senate. As his dictatorial powers neared their expiration, Mussolini issued a new electoral law, the Acerbo Law of 1923, that abolished proportional representation and awarded 67 percent of the Chamber of Deputies to the party with the most votes, even if it only obtained one-fourth of the votes.

Illustration 29.7

The Fascist 'March on Rome.' The culmination of Mussolini's seizure of power in postwar Italy came on October 28, 1922, when he personally led a demonstration demanding that the king name him prime minister. This photograph of the march shows Mussolini fourth from left.

Mussolini and the Fascist Party built their permanent dictatorship on the parliamentary elections of 1924. They employed mass psychology to play on popular fears, exploited their control of the courts and local government, used direct intimidation and violence as needed, and relied on outright fraud in counting the votes. This combination earned the Fascists a two-thirds majority in Parliament and a Fascist government. When a leader of the Socialist Party, Giacomo Matteotti (whose book *The Fascisti Exposed* had detailed Fascist political violence), denounced this undemocratic seizure of power, Fascist thugs kidnapped him and stabbed him to death. When socialist, liberal, and Catholic deputies walked out of Parliament in a protest known as the Aventine Secession, the Fascist majority permanently expelled them. Critical journalists were jailed.

The Fascist dictatorship in Italy quickly uprooted democratic society. All opposition parties—monarchical, democratic, Catholic, and socialist—were abolished, creating a one-party state. Universal suffrage was abolished and voting was defined by the amount of taxes paid. A Fascist Grand Council named members of Parliament and voters ratified their selections. Mussolini kept the power to govern by decree. Strict press censorship was installed. All local officials were made appointive. A secret police (the OVRA) cracked down on opponents of the regime, armed with a law permitting capital punishment for political offenses. Despite such powers, Mussolini never created a total dictatorship because he never broke the independent power of the army, the Catholic Church, or the wealthy upper classes.

The Fascist regime focused its attention on economic recovery, and it had noteworthy successes although problems remained. Mussolini abandoned capitalism in favor of state planning and state intervention, but he kept private property and profit. These steps never achieved the self-sufficient economy he sought. The Battle for Wheat increased farm acreage and production, but Italy remained dependent on imports. Unemployment was cut sharply by extending education, expanding the army, and hiring thousands for public works projects (such as draining swamps to become farmland). Labor unrest was controlled by abolishing trade unions and outlawing strikes; management was regulated and made to accept state arbitration. To keep a tranquil economy and state direction of it, Mussolini created what he called "the corporate state." All occupations were organized into "syndicates" (a syndicate even existed for intellectuals); groups of syndicates were linked as "corporations." Representatives of occupations met in a quasi-legislative body called the National Council of Corporations. The council and a Ministry of Corporations theoretically directed the economy, but the corporate state never had perfectly defined powers. It generally supported propertied interests and management, and its biggest creation was a bloated bureaucracy.

Hitler and Nazi Germany, 1928–39

Adolph Hitler and the Nazi Party similarly exploited the legacies of World War I—angry nationalism and economic crisis—in Germany. Like Mussolini and the Fascists, they mixed the legitimate political process with violence to seize power, destroy democracy, and build a dictatorship.

The Nazis remained a small and ineffective party during the Weimar recovery of the mid-1920s. In the parliamentary elections of 1928, the Nazi Party had a membership of 100,000 and received a meager 2.6 percent of the votes cast. The party attracted some support for its strident nationalism and denunciation of the Versailles Treaty, but its growth chiefly came during economic crisis. Although the full name of the party (German National Socialist Workers' Party) suggests that it was a working-class party, most urban workers voted against the Nazis; instead, the Nazis drew their electoral strength from small farmers and the lower middle class occupations known as the *Mittelstand* (chiefly small shopkeepers, artisans, and retail merchants). Such groups had suffered greatly in the nation's ordeal since 1914, were strongly nationalistic, vulnerable to economic crises, and without strong voices in the political process. When the depression hit Germany in 1930, ending American financial assistance, it brought a slump in world trade, closed banks and businesses, and produced high unemployment (30.1 percent by 1932); many people saw a solution in strong leadership.

Adolph Hitler seized power through the political crisis of the German depression. Reichstag elections in 1930 showed frightened voters seeking new solutions: Both the Communist Party and the Nazi Party registered large gains, with Hitler now leading a delegation of 107 deputies. Part of this electoral success stemmed from the effectiveness of Nazi propaganda, managed by Josef Goebbels and presented in spell-casting oratory by Hitler. Goebbels, the chief author of fulsome Nazi propaganda images of a tall, blond, Aryan race of supermen, was himself a short and dark-haired man with a withered foot from childhood polio. In addition to artful propaganda, Nazi success resulted from using the intimidation and violence that Mussolini had taught. Nazi stormtroops—at first the brown-shirted SA (short for *Sturmabteilungen*, literally "storm troopers") and later Heinrich Himmler's black-shirted SS (short for *Schutzstaffel* or "defense echelon")—fought street battles, especially against leftists. The growth in Nazi popularity persuaded Hitler to run for the presidency of Germany in 1932, but he was overwhelmingly beaten (twenty million to thirteen million votes) by the eighty-five-year-old incumbent Field Marshal von Hindenburg. In two separate Reichstag elections that year, the Nazis polled 37 percent and 33 percent of the pop-

ular vote but became the largest party in a fragmented Reichstag. Party membership stood at 849,000 in a population of 66 million.

Hitler became chancellor of Germany by gaining the support of Reichstag conservatives led by Franz von Papen, a Catholic aristocrat and former General Staff officer who had married into one of the wealthy industrial families of the Saar (see chronology 29.1). Von Papen had dedicated his political career to preserving the leadership of the Junker and industrial elites, and he believed that Hitler would do this. When Hitler became chancellor in early 1933, his lieutenant, Hermann Göring (a World War I fighter pilot and hero who had won the Iron Cross), became minister of the interior with control of the police (see illustration 29.8). Hitler immediately called Reichstag elections. The Nazis increased their electoral violence, harassing opponents, intimidating voters, and even burning the Reichstag building. The Reichstag fire was blamed on Communists and used to justify the suspension of civil liberties, including both freedom of speech and the press. Nazi violence achieved 44 percent of the votes and a parliamentary majority through the alliance with von Papen. This Reichstag voted Hitler dictatorial powers for five years in the Enabling Act of March 1933, which allowed him to change the constitution and to promulgate laws with the Reichstag's approval. (Similar Enabling Laws had been used to deal with the economic crisis and Ruhr invasion of 1923.) Hitler used these powers to begin a policy that he called *Gleichschaltung* (coordination); this simply meant the consolidation of a lasting Nazi dictatorship. In the first few months of the *Gleichschaltung*, the Nazis created a secret police force (the Gestapo), a law permitting the arrest of dissenters, secret trials in People's Courts, and the first concentration camps (Dachau, near Munich, and Buchenwald, near Weimar) for the detention of political opponents. Elective local governments, labor unions, other political parties, the upper house of Parliament, the presidency, and civil liberties were all abolished. Nazi violence also increased. On "the Night of the Long Knives" in June 1934, Himmler (a frail and sickly man with an enormous drive for power) directed the SS in the murder of approximately one thousand people—opponents of the Nazis and unreliable party members, including the leaders of the SA.

Nazi persecution of the Jews (approximately 1 percent of the German population) began almost immediately. The purge of the bureaucracy ousted Jewish civil servants, professors, and public school teachers. A government-backed boycott closed many Jewish

❖ CHRONOLOGY 29.1 ❖

The *Gleichschaltung*: Creation of the Nazi Dictatorship, 1933–34

January 1933	Adolf Hitler and Franz von Papen negotiate alliance of nationalist parties
January 1933	Hitler named chancellor with Hermann Göring as minister of interior
February 1933	The Reichstag Fire: Parliament burned and blamed on Communists
February 1933	Göring reorganizes the police and creates the Gestapo (secret police)
February 1933	Basic civil liberties (freedom of speech, press, assembly) suspended
February 1933	Law allowing for *Schutzhaft* (protective custody) for dissenters
February 1933	Political opponents sent to Dachau, the first concentration camp
March 1933	The Enabling Act gives Hitler dictatorial powers for five years
March 1933	People's Court created to try "treason" cases in secret
March 1933	Roundup arrest of German Communists, interred at Oranienburg
April 1933	Elective local governments abolished and Nazi governors appointed
April 1933	The civil service, schools, universities purged
April 1933	Government launches boycott of Jewish businesses
April 1933	Roundup arrest of leading German Socialists
May 1933	Labor unions and strikes outlawed
May 1933	Great Berlin book-burning: twenty-five thousand-volume fire
July 1933	All other political parties dissolved
July 1933	Sterilization Law for the handicapped, gypsies, blacks
January 1934	Upper House of German Parliament abolished
May 1934	Judicial system overhauled and civil liberties curtailed
June 1934	Night of the Long Knives: purge of the Nazi Party
August 1934	Office of president eliminated and its powers given to the *Führer*, Hitler

Illustration 29.8

▨ **Nazi Germany.** An aggressive foreign policy, aimed at the undoing of the Versailles Treaty, was a central element of Nazism from the start, initially giving it a paramilitary character and then putting militarism at the center of the new government's policy. The Nazi government of the 1930s often looked more like a meeting of military men than of civilian officials, as in this photo of Hitler, Göring, and Goebbels (left to right).

Illustration 29.9

Nazi Anti-Semitism. Anti-Semitism was a central element of Nazi doctrine long before the party came to power, and this led to anti-Semitic policies from the earliest days of the regime. One of the most ominous moments came on November 9, 1938, known as the *Kristallnacht* ("night of the broken glass"). Nazi hooligans attacked Jews (killing more than one hundred), burnt synagogues, and trashed more than seven thousand Jewish businesses—whose broken windows, shown here, gave *Kristallnacht* its name.

businesses. The Nuremberg Laws of 1935 (and 250 supplemental decrees) defined Jews as anyone having one Jewish grandparent (increasing the number of Jews to 2.5 million, or 4 percent of the population). These decrees stripped Jews of their citizenship, forbade intermarriage, barred them from many occupations, and restricted where they could live. Discrimination and harassment turned to violence in the late 1930s, and many Jews (such as Albert Einstein) sought to emigrate—72 percent of German Jews fled the country before emigration became impossible. On the *Kristallnacht* ("night of the broken glass," named for thousands of broken windows) in November 1938 (see illustration 29.9), the SS launched a pogrom. Rioters killed approximately one hundred Jews, trashed more than 7,000 businesses (completely destroying 815 shops), and burned 191 synagogues. More than twenty thousand Jews were arrested in the following weeks, and many of them were sent to concentration camps such as Dachau.

Nazi persecution was not limited to the Jews. Political opponents were the first to suffer under the new police state. Communists were rounded up and interred in March 1933 (barely one month after Hitler became chancellor) and the arrest of leading socialists followed in April 1933; high office was no protection, as the prime minister of Oldenburg (arrested in early March) discovered. Between July 1933 and April 1935, Nazi campaigns were launched against homosexuals, gypsies, the handicapped, and members of several religious sects, especially the Jehovah's Witnesses. A law of 1933, for example, permitted government to order the steril-

ization of the handicapped (and several other groups), starting a campaign that culminated in Operation T4, begun in 1939, to "grant mercy death" to the handicapped. The Nazi attempt to exterminate members of such groups, especially Jews, in the concentration camps (for which the word *genocide* was coined) did not begin until after World War II had started.

Nazi social policy also affected women and children, schools and churches. Nazi policy toward women, for example, sought their return to the supposed traditional "women's place": *Kinder, Kirche, Küche* (children, church, kitchen). This led to efforts to drive women out of the workplace and higher education. The first Nazi economic plan, for example, sought to cut the employment of women by 200,000 per year, while educational policy cut the enrollment of women in German universities from 18,315 in 1932 to 5,447 in 1939. The regime strongly encouraged motherhood, which had long been a central theme of the Nazi program. This led to pronatalist policies ranging from grants for large families and strict laws against abortions to punishments for remaining unmarried. World War II later changed many of these policies, bringing women back into the workplace and the universities, but Nazi ideology remained antifeminist.

The Nazi government (called the Third Reich as the successor to the Holy Roman Empire and the Bismarckian Empire) pursued tough nationalist and economic policies. Hitler, like Mussolini, kept a capitalist economy in the narrow sense that it accepted private property and individual profit; however, he quickly converted Germany to a government-planned and

-directed economy. The Nazi Four Year Plan of 1936 outlined German autarchy—a self-sufficient economy. Some industries, such as the Krupp Works and IG Farben, willingly collaborated with the Nazi plan and profited from government backing (and slave labor). Self-sufficiency made striking progress in some fields, such as gasoline production, which was 44 percent synthetic by 1938. Some industries, such as Ruhr coal, profited from Nazi help, such as forced labor, yet kept independent policies.

Nazi economic policies ended German unemployment. The unemployment rate of 30.1 percent in 1932 hit 4.6 percent in 1937, while the rest of the industrialized world remained in double digits. This was achieved through compulsory programs: conscription for military service, employment in state-funded armaments industries, drafted labor in public works projects (such as building the highway system known as the autobahn), and labor camps for young men and women. The regime financed this with other extreme measures: renouncing reparations payments, forcing involuntary loans to the government, and confiscating Jewish wealth (initially a 20 percent tax on Jewish property in 1938). Dictatorship thus achieved a form of recovery. Coal production, which stood at 110 million tons in 1933, reached 188 million tons in 1939 (a 71 percent increase); steel production rose from 7.6 million tons to 23.7 million tons (a 212 percent increase).

The Authoritarian Movements of the 1930s

Fascist Italy and Nazi Germany are the most important examples of a widespread European phenomenon in the 1930s: dictatorial regimes replaced parliamentary democracies. Governments sought order and stability, economic recovery, traditional virtues, and national pride, not "a world made safe for democracy." These authoritarian movements are often lumped together as "fascism," although many historians argue that local movements differed significantly. The fascist and authoritarian governments of the 1930s typically shared the same origins—vehement (often xenophobic) nationalism and economic hardship. They also shared the rejection of both liberal-democratic government and the communist alternative to it; instead, they called for tough new institutions. Thus, the authoritarian movement of the 1930s was counterrevolutionary (opposed to both 1789 in France and 1917 in Russia), yet it was a revolution (approving of both 1922 in Italy and 1933 in Germany).

The antidemocratic tendency of the age found advocates in all countries (including the United States, where Nazi rallies were held in Madison Square Garden). Oswald Mosley could assemble ten thousand British fascists at Albert Hall in London in 1934 to hear his plans for a Corporate State and calls for "Britain First." The French leagues that threatened the Chamber of Deputies in 1934 attracted voters with slogans such as "It is time to put rotten parliamentarianism on vacation" or "Better Hitler than Blum." A Belgian fascist movement known as the Rex, led by Léon Degrelle, won twenty-one deputies and twelve senators in the elections of 1936. In Hungary, where irredentist nationalism was strong, several parties that emulated the Nazis won a combined 38 percent of the vote and forty-eight seats in Parliament in 1939. In Norway, where one-third of the nation was jobless in 1933, the defense minister, Vidkun Quisling, left the government to lead a Norwegian fascist party; Quisling (who was shot in 1945) was a vigorous anti-Communist who campaigned to break Norwegian labor unions. Austria had a strong Nazi Party, which staged a *Putsch* and murdered the chancellor in 1934. Although this attempt to seize the government was beaten by the Austrian army, the party remained legal and strong; its leader, Arthur von Seyss-Inquart (who was later hanged as a war criminal), became minister of the interior in 1938 and chancellor of Austria after collaborating with the Nazi takeover a few months later.

In Portugal, a military junta brought a conservative economics professor (born into the peasantry and educated in a seminary), António Salazar, into the government, and he gradually acquired dictatorial powers. Salazar was an austere and reclusive man who seldom appeared in public and never traveled abroad. He cut state spending sharply, raised taxes, and achieved the political rarity of a budget surplus. In 1933 Salazar introduced a constitution to create a New State (*Estado Novo*). His authoritarian state drew on the traditional Portuguese hierarchies of the aristocracy, the military, and the clergy; it also encompassed fascist ideas borrowed from Mussolini's Italy, such as a legislature representing corporative bodies instead of individuals. However, Salazar created a depoliticized authoritarian state more than Portuguese Fascism. His antidemocratic mentality would have fit the eighteenth century as well as the twentieth century: "The people have less need of being sovereign than of being governed." By avoiding World War II, Salazar remained in power until 1968.

Stalin and Soviet Communism, 1924–39

Among the dictatorships that characterized Europe in the 1930s, none was more harshly totalitarian than the dictatorship that Joseph Stalin built in the Soviet Union. Historians cannot say with certainty how many people died as a consequence of Stalin's horrifying policies of the 1920s and 1930s, but numbers between ten million and twenty million are usually suggested.

After a decade of war, revolution, and civil war, the Russian economy lay in ruins in 1921. The output of mining and heavy industries stood at 21 percent of the prewar level, compared with figures closer to 50 percent in Belgium, France, or Germany—Russian pig iron production in 1921, for example, amounted to 100,000 tons, compared with 4.2 million tons in 1913. Exports (and the capital that they raised) had virtually ceased, standing at 1.3 percent of the 1913 total. To address this crisis, Lenin and the Politburo leadership adopted a New Economic Policy (NEP) that mixed communist theories of state ownership and planning with capitalist theories of private ownership and the free market. The NEP, Lenin explained, was a matter of taking one step backward to take two steps forward. Under the NEP, 98 percent of heavy industry, factory manufacturing, mining, and public services were state-owned; simultaneously, however, 90 percent of handicraft manufacturing, small shops, and agriculture remained privately owned. At the time of Lenin's death, 54 percent of all Soviet income still came from the private sector.

Lenin died in 1924 following his third stroke and a period of speechless incapacitation. He had favored Trotsky to succeed him, but Stalin used his leadership post in the Communist Party and maneuvering in the Politburo to isolate Trotsky. During a period of collective leadership in the mid-1920s, Trotsky was edged out of the Politburo (1925), out of the party (1927), and out of the country (1929); a Stalinist agent assassinated him in Mexico in 1940. After defeating Trotsky, Stalin then used an ideological battle to divide the Politburo and purge other leaders. The issues were the NEP and Stalin's doctrine known as "socialism in one country." Stalin asserted that the Soviet Union could create a Communist society alone; the NEP should be retained as the first step. His rivals on the left wing of the Politburo (whom he branded "left deviationists") backed Trotsky's idea of "permanent revolution"—work for revolution everywhere and continue it in Russia by ending the NEP. Stalin won this argument, and the left deviationists were ousted. In 1927, however, Stalin turned against his supporters in that fight; he purged them as "right deviationists" because they still supported the NEP. By 1928 Stalin's dictatorial power was unchallenged. He then announced his "new socialist offensive," borrowing ideas from the left deviationists and abolishing the NEP.

One of the foremost attributes of Stalin's dictatorship was the police state. The czarist secret police and the Bolshevik Cheka (reorganized as the OGPU in 1922) formed the basis of Stalin's secret police, known by a series of Russian acronyms, beginning as the NKVD (from 1926) and ending up as the KGB (from 1954). Under Feliks Dzerzhinsky and Nikolai Yezhov, the Soviet secret police became one of the most feared institutions in the world. The Bolsheviks had already established Holmogor concentration camp in Siberia for political prisoners in 1921 and had begun to use such camps (*gulags*) for forced labor in 1923. Stalin expanded this into an immense network of prison camps—named the *Gulag Archipelago* by Nobel Prize–winning novelist Alexandr Solzhenitsyn (see document 29.6). Many details about the *gulags* remain unclear, but more than ten million people were sent to such notorious camps as Kolyma or Magadan in eastern Siberia. Prisoners in the *gulag* labored at preposterous tasks such as building a railroad across the Arctic. At Pelvozh camp on the Arctic Circle, prisoners slept four men to a straw pallet, with three feet of space each; they worked fourteen-hour shifts through the Siberian winter (except when the temperature fell below minus fifty degrees Fahrenheit), dressed in light clothing and felt boots, and were fed a diet of approximately one thousand calories per day.

Stalin used these instruments of terror to build the Communist state. He ended the NEP and its privately owned shops and farms. The nationalization of this property (a process called collectivization) led to bitter fights, especially with the successful class of landowning peasants known as the *kulaks*. There were approximately twenty-five million peasant farms in the Soviet Union in 1928, with a livestock population of twenty-eight million pigs and sixty-six million cattle. By 1932 collectivization had created 250,000 large state farms (*sovkhoz*), where the government employed peasant workers to farm state land, and collective farms (*kolkhoz*), where state land was leased to a peasant community that farmed it as a collective enterprise. The kulaks resisted collectivization by burning crops,

◆ DOCUMENT 29.6 ◆

Life in the Stalinist Police State

Alexandr Solzhenitsyn Describes Being Arrested

Alexandr Solzhenitsyn is a Russian writer who won the Nobel Prize for literature in 1970. He served eight years in a concentration camp for the crime of criticizing Stalin in a letter to a friend.

For several decades political arrests were distinguished in our country precisely by the fact that people were arrested who were guilty of nothing and were therefore unprepared to put up any resistance whatsoever. There was a general feeling of being destined for destruction, a sense of having nowhere to escape from the OGPU-NKVD (which, incidentally, given our internal passport system, was quite accurate). . . . People leaving for work said farewell to their families every day, because they could not be certain they would return at night. . . .

By and large, the [police] had no profound reasons for their choice of whom to arrest and whom not to arrest. They merely had over-all assignments, quotas for a specific number of arrests. These quotas might be filled on an orderly basis or wholly arbitrarily. . . .

The majority [of those arrested] sit quietly and dare to hope. Since you aren't guilty, then how can they arrest you? . . . Others are being arrested en masse, and that's a bothersome fact, but in those cases there is always some dark area: "Maybe *he* was guilty." . . . Why, then, should you run away? After all, you'll only make your situation worse; you'll make it more difficult for them to sort out the mistake. . . . You even walk down the stairs on tiptoe, as you are ordered to do, so your neighbors won't hear. . . .

Sometimes the principal emotion of the person arrested is relief. . . . When all around they were hauling in people like yourself and still had not come for you; for some reason they were taking their time. After all, that kind of exhaustion, that kind of suffering, is worse than any kind of arrest. . . .

Once a person was arrested, he was never released; and [there was] the inevitability of a tenner, a ten-year sentence.

Nadezhda Mandelstam Describes Life in Lubianka Prison

Nadezhda Mandelstam (1899–1980) was a Russian writer and the wife of the poet Osip Mandelstam, who died in a Stalinist camp after writing a poem critical of Stalin. Nadezhda's memoirs describe his experience.

At the very first interrogation, M. [her husband] had admitted to being the author of the poem on Stalin, so the stool pigeon's task could not have been to find out something that M. was hiding. Part of the function of these people was to unnerve and wear down prisoners under interrogation, to make their life a misery. Until 1937 our secret police made much of their psychological methods, but afterwards these gave way to physical torture, with beatings of the most primitive kind. . . .

M. was put through the physical ordeal which had always been applied. It consisted mainly of not being allowed to sleep. He was called out every night and kept for hours on end. Most of the time was spent not on actual questioning, but in waiting under guard outside the interrogator's door. . . . The ordeal by deprivation of sleep and a bright light shining right in the eyes are known to everybody.

The principles and aims of mass terror have nothing in common with ordinary police work or with security. The only purpose of terror is intimidation. To plunge the whole country into a state of chronic fear . . . on every floor of every building there must always be several apartments from which the tenants have been taken away. The remaining inhabitants will be model citizens.

smashing farm implements, and slaughtering livestock. Thus, in 1934 the Soviet livestock population had plummeted to eleven million pigs and thirty-three million cattle. Stalin answered with a brutal repression aimed at nothing less than "the liquidation of the kulak class." Between five million and six million peasants (chiefly in Ukraine and the Caucasus) were executed in their villages or died in the *gulags;* another four million

died in the famine of 1933, a direct consequence of collectivization.

Stalin used the grains and profits of collectivized agriculture to feed and finance the forced industrialization of the Soviet Union. He placed the economy under a central planning office (*Gosplan*) that drafted a series of Five Year Plans directing the creation of an industrial economy. The first Five Year Plan (1928–32)

❈ TABLE 29.6 ❈

Soviet Industrialization Under the Five-Year Plan, 1928–32

Output	1928 total	Target in the plan	1932 total
Gross industrial production (in billions of 1927 rubles)	18.3	43.2	43.3
Consumer goods production (in billions of 1927 rubles)	12.3	25.1	20.2
Gross agricultural production (in billions of 1927 rubles)	13.1	25.8	16.6
Hard coal production (in millions of tons)	35.4	75.0	64.3
Iron ore production (in millions of tons)	5.7	19.0	12.1
Steel production (in millions of tons)	4.0	10.4	5.9
Electricity generated (in billions of kilowatt hours)	5.1	22.0	13.4

Source: Alec Nove, *An Economic History of the USSR* (London: Penguin, 1969, 1982), p. 192.

encompassed the collectivization of agriculture and rapid industrialization (see table 29.6). The cost of these plans in human suffering was horrifying, but they accomplished the goal of industrialization (although they did not meet their production targets in heavy industry). Russia had lagged far behind western Europe throughout the nineteenth century; by 1940, however, the Soviet Union had the third largest industrial economy in the world (behind the United States and Germany), and at Stalin's death in 1953 it stood second. The same Five Year Plans that starved the kulaks increased Soviet coal production from 36 million tons (1928) to 166 million tons (1940), steel production from 4 million tons to 18 million tons. Production often fell short of Gosplan's targets (leading to the purge of "plan wreckers"), and both efficiency and quality suffered, but Stalin made the Soviet Union into an industrial power.

Simultaneously, Stalin relied on police terror to maintain his dictatorship (see illustration 29.10). He began a new series of purges directed by Yezhov in 1936, which grew into the Great Terror (1936–39). This purge struck millions of members of the Communist Party, including virtually all surviving leaders of the Bolshevik revolution of 1917. Many of Stalin's old comrades, such as Nikolai Bukharin, the intellectual leader of the right deviationists, were convicted in public "show trials" after confessing to absurd charges such as being Nazi agents. In 1937 the purge decimated the officer corps of the Red Army, including the chief of staff and seven leading generals. By the end of the Great Terror, approximately one million people had been killed (including both Bukharin and Yezhov) and eight million to ten million sent into the *gulags*.

Illustration 29.10

 Stalin's Terror. Few regimes in history can be compared with the nightmare brutality of the Soviet Union under Stalin. Forced collectivization of agriculture and the intentional "liquidization of the kulak class" in the late 1920s and early 1930s led to the death of approximately ten million peasants, only to be followed by the Great Terror of the late 1930s in which another one million people were killed and ten million sent into the slave labor *gulag*. This photo of Stalin in the 1930s purportedly catches him in the act of signing one of those death warrants.

Conclusion

During the first half of the twentieth century Europe experienced as much suffering as it had in any epoch. War, revolution, and epidemic disease had killed more than twenty-five million people and consumed billions of dollars in 1914–21, but the following decades experienced only limited respite. Europe needed the entire decade of the 1920s to rebuild its devastated regions and to recover prewar levels of population and production. That recovery began optimistically with a widespread commitment to democracy. Old monarchies had fallen, replaced by more than a dozen new democracies such as the Weimar Republic in Germany. Women's suffrage and proportional representation characterized many European constitutions. A severe peace treaty with Germany, the Versailles Treaty, had been drawn to prevent further threats from German militarism, and a new international assembly, the League of Nations, had been created to help maintain the peace.

Many of the new democracies, however, had difficulty surviving postwar crises, especially the Great Depression of the 1930s, when unemployment exceeded 30 percent. By 1939 authoritarian government, not democracy, characterized Europe. A new, antidemocratic doctrine, Fascism, swept Europe in a variety of forms, brushing aside representative governments, constitutions, and bills of rights. Fascism's strident nationalism, militarism, and the cult of the strong leader appealed to many people who had suffered through Europe's crises. Totalitarian dictatorships arose in Fascist Italy under Mussolini and in Nazi Germany under Hitler, sharing many characteristics with totalitarianism in Communist Russia under Stalin, such as the one-party state, the police state, the dictatorial leader, and the use of political violence. However, significant differences still separated the two forms of totalitarianism, such as nationalism versus internationalism and the survival of capitalism. Other forms of authoritarianism, most of them resembling Fascism, typified Europe from Portugal to Poland.

The European crisis of the 1930s saw the loss of civil liberties in most countries and the growth of police state terror to horrifying new extremes. In the Soviet Union, ten million peasants died during Stalinization, one million party members perished in the Great Terror of the 1930s, and another ten million people were sent to the *gulags*. And worse problems were yet to come. Most of the belligerent nationalism of the 1930s—from large states such as Germany and Italy to smaller states such as Hungary—included great dissatisfaction with the peace settlements reached at Paris in 1919–20. This would soon lead Europe into World War II and into incredible new levels of human suffering.

Suggested Readings

For surveys of the interwar period, see R. Sontag, *A Broken World, 1919–1939* (1971), for political detail, and C. Kindleberger, *The World in Depression, 1929–1939* (1986), for economics.

For the Paris peace settlement, see H. Elcock, *Portrait of a Decision* (1972) and A. Sharp, *The Versailles Settlement* (1991), for overviews of the treaty with Germany; G. Schulz, *Revolutions and Peace Treaties, 1917–1920* (1972), for all of the postwar changes; I. Lederer, *Yugoslavia at the Paris Peace Conference* (1963), for a good case study; A. Mayer, *Politics and Diplomacy of Peacemaking* (1967), for the peace and the Russian Revolution considered together; M. Dockrill and J. D. Goold, *Peace without Promise: Britain and the Peace Conferences, 1919–1923* (1981); E. Goldstein, *Winning the Peace* (1991), also on Britain's role; and P. Helmreich, *From Paris to Sèvres* (1974), for peace with Turkey.

For changing social and cultural history, see A. Marwick, *War and Social Change in the Twentieth Century* (1974), J. Stevenson, *British Society, 1914–1945* (1984), W. Rubin, *Dada, Surrealism, and Their Heritage* (1968), H. Wingler, *The Bauhaus* (1969), P. Gay, *Weimar Culture* (1981), and W. Laqueur, *Weimar: A Cultural History* (1974).

For the rise of totalitarianism, see H. Arendt, *The Origins of Totalitarianism* (1973), a brilliant essay; S. Payne, *Facism* (1980); N. O'Sullivan, *Fascism* (1983); W. Lacqueur, *Fascism* (1997); and E. Nolte, *Three Faces of Fascism* (1965), which compares Germany, Italy, and France.

For Fascist Italy, see A. Cassels, *Fascist Italy* (1985), a brief introduction; F. Chabod, *History of Italian Fascism* (1963); A. De Grand, *Italian Fascism* (1989); E. Tannenbaum, *The Fascist Experience* (1972); L. Fermi, *Mussolini* (1974); M. Gallo, *Mussolini's Italy* (1974); I. Kirkpatrick, *Mussolini* (1964); D. M. Smith, *Mussolini* (1983); M. Ledeen, *The First Duce: D'Annunzio in Fiume* (1977); A. Lyttelton, *The Seizure of Power: Fascism in Italy, 1919–1929* (1987), the best source for the fascist takeover; D. Germino, *The Italian Fascist Party in Power* (1959); T. Koon, *Believe, Obey, Fight* (1985), a study of Fascist propaganda and the youth movement; R. Sarti, *Fascism and the Industrial Leadership in Italy, 1919–1940* (1971), for economics; D. Thompson, *State Control in Fascist Italy* (1991); and C. Delzell, *Mussolini's Enemies: The Italian Antifascist Resistance* (1961).

For Germany, see E. Eyck, *A History of the Weimar Republic*, 2 vols. (1962–63); E. Kolb, *The Weimar Republic* (1988); L. Hertzmann, *DNVP: Right Wing Opposition in the Weimar Republic* (1963); J. Diehl, *Paramilitary Politics in Weimar Germany* (1977); R. Waite, *Vanguard of Nazism*(1952), on the Freikorps; H. Gordon, *Hitler and the Beer Hall Putsch* (1972); J. von Kruedener, ed., *Economic Crisis and Political Collapse* (1990); H. Turner, *German Big Business and the Rise of Hitler* (1985); D. Abraham, *The Collapse of the Weimar Republic* (1986); M. Broszat, *Hitler and the Collapse of Weimar Germany* (1987); I. Kershaw, ed., *Weimar: Why Did German Democracy Fail?* (1990); W. Allen, *The Nazi Seizure of Power* (1984), a striking case study; T. Childers, *The Nazi Voter* (1983); M. Kater, *The Nazi Party* (1985); D. Orlow, *The History of the Nazi Party*, 2 vols. (1969–73); P. Aycoberry, *The Nazi Question* (1981) and I Kershaw, *The Nazi Dictatorship* (1989), essays on the various interpretations of Nazism; K. Bracher, *The German Dictatorship* (1970), perhaps the most highly regarded study of Nazism; I. Kershaw, *Hitler* (1991); R. Bessel, *Life in the Third Reich* (1987); A. Varkai, *Nazi Economics* (1990); P. Hayes, *Industry and Ideology* (1987); C. Koonz, *Mothers in the Fatherland* (1987); J. Stephenson, *Women in Nazi Society* (1975); D. Schoenbaum, *Hitler's Social Revolution* (1966); J. Conway, *The Nazi Persecution of the Churches* (1968); G. Mosse, ed., *Nazi*

Culture (1966); K. Schleunes, *The Twisted Road to Auschwitz* (1970) and A. Barkai, *From Boycott to Annihilation* (1989), for prewar anti-Semitism; R. Breitman, *Architect of Genocide* (1991), on Himmler; and R. Gellately, *The Gestapo and German Society* (1990).

For fascism and authoritarianism around Europe, see S. Payne, *Falange* (1961) and S. Ellwood, *Spanish Fascism in the Franco Era* (1987), for Spanish fascism; A. de Figuerido, *Portugal: Fifty Years of Dictatorship* (1975); H. Kay, *Salazar and Modern Portugal* (1970); J. Lewis, *Fascism and the Working Class in Austria* (1991); and B. Pauley, *Hitler and the Forgotten Nazis: A History of Austrian National Socialism* (1981).

For overviews of the history of the Soviet Union, see M. McAuley, *Soviet Politics, 1917–1991* (1992), D. MacKenzie and M. Curran, *A History of the Soviet Union* (1991), W. McClellan, *Russia: The Soviet Period* (1990), M. Malia, *The Soviet Tragedy* (1994), D. Treadgold, *Twentieth Century Russia* (1990), and A. Ulam, *A History of the Soviet Union* (1976). See also A. Ulam, *Stalin* (1989); R. Tucker, *Stalin in Power* (1990); A. Ball, *Russia's Last Capitalists* (1987), on the NEP; S. Cohen, *Bukharin and the Bolshevik Revolution* (1973); I. Deutscher, *The Prophet Outcast* (1963) and R. Day, *Leon Trotsky and the Politics of Economic Isolation* (1973), on Trotsky; R. Conquest, *The Great Terror* (1990); R. Medvedev, *All Stalin's Men* (1983) and *Let History Judge* (1989); A. Solzhenitsyn, *The Gulag Archipelago*, 3 vols. (1974–78); and J. Braunthal, *History of the International* (1967–80).

For democratic Europe, see C. Maier, *Recasting Bourgeois Europe* (1975), on postwar recovery; L. Roberts, *Civilization without Sexes* (1996), for changing mentalities about women; and K. Newman, *European Democracy between the Wars* (1970), especially for democracies that failed.

For interwar Britain, see A. J. P. Taylor, *English History, 1914–1945* (1976); C. Mowat, *Britain between the Wars, 1918–1940* (1955); T. Wilson, *The Downfall of the Liberal Party, 1914–1935* (1966); R. Lyman, *The First Labour Government, 1924* (1957); D. Marquand, *Ramsay MacDonald* (1977); M. Gilbert, *Churchill: A Life* (1991), the condensation of an eight-volume biography; E. Hopkins, *The Rise and Decline of the English Working Classes, 1918–1990* (1991); J. Lewis, *Women in England, 1870–1950* (1984); B. Gilbert, *British Social Policy, 1914–1939* (1970); D. Fitzpatrick, *Politics and Irish Life, 1913–1921* (1977); and J. Lee, *Ireland, 1912–1985* (1989).

For interwar France, see D. Watson, *Georges Clemenceau* (1974); A. Prost, *In the Wake of War* (1992), for the role of veterans in the postwar era; R. Wohl, *French Communism in the Making* (1966); J. Jackson, *The Politics of the Depression in France, 1932–1936* (1985) and *The Popular Front in France* (1988); J. Colton, *Leon Blum* (1966); W. Irvine, *French Conservatism in Crisis* (1979) and P. Larmour, *The French Radical Party in the 1930s* (1964), for a different perspective on the 1930s; the works of R. Soucy, especially *French Fascism*, 2 vols. (1986–95); Z. Sternhell, *Neither Right nor Left* (1986), a controversial analysis of fascism; and E. Weber, *Action française* (1962).

For the Spanish popular front and civil war, see G. Jackson, *The Spanish Republic and the Civil War, 1931–1939* (1965), S. Payne, *Spain's First Democracy* (1993) and *The Spanish Revolution* (1970), M. Alexander and H. Graham, eds., *The French and Spanish Popular Fronts* (1989), M. Blinkhorn, ed., *Spain in Conflict, 1931–1939* (1986), P. Preston, *The Coming of the Spanish Civil War* (1986), H. Thomas, *The Spanish Civil War* (1977), R. Carr, *The Civil War in Spain, 1936–1939* (1986), B. Bolloten, *The Spanish Civil War* (1991), V. Brome, *The International Brigades* (1966), E. H. Carr, *The Comintern and the Spanish Civil War* (1984), J. Coverdale, *Italian Intervention in the Spanish Civil War* (1975), and R. Whealey, *Hitler and Spain* (1989).

CHAPTER 30

EUROPE IN AN AGE OF TOTAL WAR: WORLD WAR II, 1939–45

CHAPTER OUTLINE

Europe had lived through a generation of enormous suffering between 1914 and 1939, but the worst was yet to come when the age of total war culminated in the largest war in history. Between 1939 and 1945, World War II killed an estimated forty million Europeans, most of them noncombatants; the global total neared sixty million. The Soviet Union, which had suffered millions of deaths in World War I, the Russian Revolution and Civil War, and then in Stalin's terror of the 1930s, now endured incredible losses; the newest estimates drawn from opened Soviet archives go as high as twenty-five million deaths. Simultaneously, in one of the most horrifying chapters in human history, Nazi Germany attempted the complete extermination of the Jews of Europe; nearly eleven million people, including six million Jews, died in German death camps. World War II ended with enormous civilian casualties as a result of the aerial bombardment of major cities. The most ominous bombing came in the events that ended the war in Asia: the detonation of atomic bombs over the Japanese cities of Hiroshima and Nagasaki.

Chapter 30 covers the events of World War II beginning with its origins in the Peace of Paris of 1919 and the European diplomatic crises of the 1930s. It concludes with the diplomatic conferences at the end of the war (no formal peace conference was held), the world's discovery of the Holocaust in Europe, and the war crimes trials (the Nuremberg Trials) of 1945–46. Most of the chapter is devoted to the events of the war in Europe, from the German invasion of Poland in September 1939 to the unconditional surrender of Nazi Germany in May 1945. World War II was a worldwide war, however, so the chapter also surveys the course of the war in Asia and the Pacific.

The Long Armistice and the Origins of World War II

The two world wars of the twentieth century were closely related to each other, with the second originating in the disputed outcome of the first. Winston Churchill, whose history of World War II won him the Nobel Prize in literature, saw the wars as a new Thirty Years' War, interrupted by a long armistice in which weary and devastated countries rebuilt their capacity to fight. The peace settlements that ended World War I, and the bitter nationalism that these treaties produced, linked the two wars. Opposition to the peace treaties was especially strong in the dictatorships that emerged during the 1920s and the 1930s, and in some cases the treaties were a significant factor in the rise of dictatorship. Defeat gave German territory to France, Belgium, Denmark, and Poland (see map 29.1); moreover, German nationalists were outraged by the war guilt clause, reparations payments, military restrictions, and the demilitarization of the Rhineland. Defeat similarly cost Russia Finland, the Baltic states, Poland, and Bessarabia; the loss of these buffers on Russia's western frontier produced anxiety in the Kremlin because neighboring states were vehemently anti-Communist. Victory failed to satisfy Italian nationalists because the treaties had denied Italy some of the territory that the Allies had promised in the Treaty of London (1915) as compensation for Italian participation in the war. Even in victorious Britain and France, many asked if World War I had been worth the cost; many British and American critics of the treaties (especially the British economist John Maynard Keynes who published a critique of the reparations provisions of the Versailles Treaty), opposed French efforts to enforce the treaty, making the campaign of German and Italian critics easier.

Battles over the peace treaties began as the ink on them dried. In 1919 alone, six armed disputes broke out over territorial settlements in Europe. The new state of Czechoslovakia and the reborn state of Poland fought over a frontier district, as did Austria and Hungary, both now small remnants of the once vast Hapsburg Empire. Italian nationalists, led by the protofascist poet Gabriele d'Annunzio, occupied the town of Fiume on the Yugoslavian border, which had been denied to Italy in the peace treaty. Thus, when the League of Nations was formally organized in January 1920, it inherited a host of problems spawned by the Peace of Paris.

The gravest issue of the early 1920s was the Versailles Treaty's provision for reparations payments by Germany to fund the reconstruction of war-torn Begium

and France. A series of Allied conferences labored to refine this question, but repeated German failures to make payments produced the first severe postwar crisis in 1923 when the Weimar government did not deliver in-kind payments of timber. The frustrated Poincaré government in France, supported by the Belgians but not by the British or the Americans, insisted upon enforcing the treaty to occupy part of western Germany and extract in-kind payments (especially coal) directly. This led to a Franco-Belgian occupation of the heavily industrialized Ruhr valley in January 1923, to a severe rupture of cooperation among the former western allies, and to a German campaign of noncooperation and passive resistance. To encourage noncooperation, the Weimar government paid striking workers by simply printing new money, therefore fueling the devastating inflation of 1923 (see chapter 29). The occupation of the Ruhr failed to provide France with reparations and cost the French hostile international opinion; Britain and America organized to save the German economy (through a restructuring of payments and massive loans known as the Dawes Plan, developed by the U.S. vice president, Charles G. Dawes), and the French retreated.

A more optimistic mood characterized Franco-German relations during the later 1920s, the result of good relations between the French foreign minister, Aristide Briand, and his German counterpart, Gustave Stresemann. This short-lived period of hope produced its most noteworthy success in the Locarno Treaty of 1925 in which France, Belgium, Germany, Britain, and Italy guaranteed the western borders of Germany (thereby granting German acceptance of the retrocession of Alsace and Lorraine to France) and established arbitration treaties to resolve future disputes. In the same spirit, Briand and Stresemann collaborated to secure German admission to the League of Nations in 1926. At its most idealistic moment, the "spirit of Locarno" stretched to create the idealistic Kellogg-Briand Pact (or the Pact of Paris) of 1928, in which the powers accepted a proposal by U.S. secretary of state Frank B. Kellogg for the renunciation of aggressive war. Although ratified by many states and embraced by the League of Nations, this toothless treaty contained no means of enforcement, not even trade sanctions. Dawes received the Nobel Peace Prize in 1925, Briand and Stresemann shared the prize for 1926, and Kellogg received it in 1929, but these awards were a measure of the world's hopes for peace in Europe, not a measure of success.

The most insistent challenge to the peace treaties of 1919 initially came from Italy. Mussolini was in power for less than a year when he attempted to annex the island of Corfu (off the coast of Albania and Greece) in mid-1923, only to be forced to back down by British pressure. He had better fortune in advancing Italian irrendentist nationalism by resolving the Fiume question in a 1924 treaty with Yugoslavia, which recognized the Italian annexation of the town. An Italo-Albanian agreement of 1926 made the small Balkan state a virtual protectorate of Fascist Italy, a preliminary step in the annexation of Albania in early 1939. In 1928 Mussolini negotiated treaties of friendship with two countries with which he envisioned future wars—Ethiopia and Greece. Ethiopia was especially important to Italian nationalists because it had been the site of the humiliating colonial defeat of 1896 (the battle of Adowa) and had been an important Italian claim denied at Paris in 1919. In 1934 Mussolini used the excuse of border clashes between Ethiopia and the Italian colony of Somaliland to resume the attempted conquest. An Italian invasion of Ethiopia in 1935 led the League of Nations to declare Italy an aggressor state and to apply economic sanctions such as an embargo on selling military goods or giving financial assistance to Italy. The League, however, could not agree upon severe sanctions (such as shutting off Mussolini's oil supplies) and thus gave little effective support to Ethiopia, which was formally annexed by Italy in 1936. The western weakness in dealing with the Ethiopian question was a major sign that the western powers lacked the resolution to stop aggression in Europe (and they showed similar timidity in responding to Japanese aggression in Asia).

Nazi Germany exploited the western irresolution. Hitler was a product of World War I, and his efforts to abrogate the Versailles Treaty led to World War II. For most of the 1930s, the victors did nothing to stop him. Hitler had made his intentions clear in *Mein Kampf* and in German political debate; within weeks of coming to power in 1933, he showed his determination to change the 1919 settlement by walking out on disarmament negotiations (leaving a clear message of German plans to rearm) and by withdrawing from the League of Nations (showing how little concern he had for western diplomacy). The most fateful western inaction came in early 1935 when Hitler bluntly renounced the disarmament provisions of the treaty and reintroduced military conscription. The disarmament clauses had permitted Germany only a small army (seven divisions in 1933) and no air force or submarines. France, and perhaps Poland, could have withstood a Germany thus fortified. Nazi conscription and construction, however, built a German army of fifty-two divisions by 1939, backed by a *Luftwaffe* (air force) of more than four thousand planes and a navy with fifty-four submarines. Hitler found bat-

tlefield training for this army by sending units to fight in the Spanish Civil War (1936–39). The *Luftwaffe*, for example, polished the dive-bombing tactics that it would use in World War II by bombing the Basque town of Guernica. Fascist cooperation in Spain led to an Italo-German alliance of 1936, which Mussolini dubbed the Axis. The Anti-Comintern Pact (1936) expanded this alliance to include Japan, and the Pact of Steel (1939) tightened the Axis.

Hitler's second great challenge to the Versailles Treaty came eleven months later, in early 1936, when he renounced the Locarno Treaty and ordered the remilitarization of the Rhineland, simply sending the German army into this frontier region. The French army could have stopped this, but the French and the British governments were irresolute and bickering over the Ethiopian question. At that time, France had a caretaker government on the eve of the most important election of the interwar era—the depression election of Léon Blum's Popular Front government; Britain had a newly elected Conservative government unwilling to send British soldiers to the continent again and even unwilling to support sanctions in the League of Nations. Consequently the World War I allies did nothing to stop the remilitarization of the Rhineland, and Hitler (whose rearmament had only just begun) won a risky gamble.

His victories in 1935–36 encouraged Hitler to overthrow the rest of the Versailles restrictions and even to plan the expansion of Germany. Hitler outlined his war plans to German military leaders in 1937. The record of that meeting, known as the Hossbach Memorandum, reveals Hitler's thinking: "The German racial community," he said, must have *Lebensraum* ("living space"), and he projected a new European war before 1943 (see document 30.1).

Hitler achieved most of his territorial goals without war (see map 30.1). A plebiscite in the Saar in 1935 restored that region to Germany by an overwhelming vote, lending some international credence to Hitler's demands for revision of the Versailles Treaty. He did not seek further territory, however, until March 1938, when he annexed Austria, an act that he preferred to call the *Anschluss* (union), which had been forbidden by the treaty. After promising to respect Austrian independence and then browbeating the chancellor of Austria, Kurt von Schuschnigg, into disbanding Austrian militias and granting an amnesty to Austrian Nazis, Hitler used the excuse of Austrian unrest (largely provoked by Austrian Nazis) to invade that country. The Austrians did not offer military resistance, and the western powers again did nothing, accepting the union as a *fait*

❖ DOCUMENT 30.1 ❖

The Hossbach Memorandum on the German Need for War, 1937

After World War II, the victorious Allies searched the German archives for documents to be used in the Nuremberg war crimes trials. The chief document used by prosecutors to prove that Hitler intended war is known as the Hossbach Memorandum, named for the colonel who took minutes at the meeting. The memorandum records a discussion at a conference between Hitler and German military leaders in November 1937.

Present: The Führer, the Reichsminister for War, the Commander-in-Chief of the Army, the Commander-in-Chief of the Navy, the Commander-in Chief of the Air Force (*Luftwaffe*), the Reichsminister for Foreign Affairs, Colonel Hossbach.

The Führer initially said that the subject matter of to-day's conference was of such high importance that further detailed discussion would probably take place in Cabinet sessions. However, he, the Führer, had decided not to discuss this matter in the larger circle of the Reich Cabinet because of its importance. . . . [H]e desired to explain to those present his fundamental ideas on the possibilities and necessities of expanding our foreign policy and in the interests of a far-sighted policy he requested that his statement be looked upon in the case of his death as his last will and testament.

The Führer then stated: The aim of German policy is the security and the preservation of the nation, and its propagation. This is, consequently, a problem of space. The German nation is composed of 85 million people, which . . . form a homogeneous European racial body which cannot be found in any other country. On the other hand, it justifies the demand for larger living space (*Lebensraum*) more than for any other nation. . . . The German future is therefore dependent exclusively on the solution of the need for *Lebensraum*. . . .

The German question can be solved only by way of force, and this is never without risk. The battles of Frederick the Great for Silesia, and Bismarck's wars against Austria and France had been a tremendous risk. . . . If we place the decision to apply force with risk at the head of the following exposition, we are only left to reply to the questions "when" and "how."

Period 1943–1945: After this date we can only expect a change for the worse. The rearming of the German Army, the Navy, and the Air Force, as well as the formation of the Officers' Corps, are practically concluded. Our material equipment and armaments are modern, with further delay the danger of their becoming out-of-date will increase. . . . In comparison with the rearmament of other nations, which will have been carried out by that time, we shall begin to decrease in relative power . . . It is certain, however, that we can wait no longer.

---

accompli. (France was again in the midst of a ministerial crisis, and the British were disposed to accept the *Anschluss.*) In a sham plebiscite, 99.75 percent of Austrians were reported to support the annexation, not counting the votes of, among others, concentration camp internees.

Shortly after the annexation of Austria, Hitler returned to his oratorical theme of "protecting the 10 million Germans living outside the Reich" and reopened the question of Czechoslovakia. He demanded that the Czechs cede to Germany the Sudetenland, a border region of western Bohemia that contained a German population (2.8 million Germans compared with 700,000 Czechs) plus Czechoslovakia's natural defenses (the Sudeten mountains and frontier fortresses) and much of its industry. When Hitler stated this claim as giving the Sudetenland "the right of self-determination," the prime minister of Britain, Neville Chamberlain, agreed to

meet with him to discuss the Czech question. Although Hitler made clear his intention to annex the Sudetenland and his willing to go to war for the Germans living there, the British and French (but not the Czech) diplomats prepared for the Munich Conference of October 1938 with Hitler. There, Chamberlain and the French premier, Edouard Daladier, agreed to the German annexation of the Sudetenland and pressured the Czech government of President Edvard Benes (who thereafter resigned) into accepting it, although the effect was to reduce Czechoslovakia to a Nazi client state. In early 1939 the rump state of Czechoslovakia was abolished, most of it (Bohemia and Moravia) becoming a German protectorate.

The western capitulation to Hitler's demands at Munich became known as a policy of appeasement—appeasing dictators by surrendering to their demands. A 1938 newsreel records the return of Prime Minister

Germany

German advances:

Reoccupied Rhineland, March 1936

Annexed Austria, March 1938

Annexed Sudetenland, October 1938

Occupied Bohemia and Moravia, March 1939

Annexed Memel, March 1939

Italy

Annexed Albania, April 1939

Poland and Hungary

Annexed Czech territory, 1938 and 1939

( ) Former independent nations: Albania, Austria, and Czechoslovakia

MAP 30.1
The Road to War, 1936–39

Chamberlain from Munich and clarifies his policy: A pleased Chamberlain waves the Munich agreement and proclaims that he has won "peace in our time," and public opinion in both Britain and France shared in the sense of relief that a war, fought over "far-off countries of which we know little" (such as Serbia in 1914), had been avoided. To many, the Munich agreement seemed like the sensible thing to do. To Chamberlain's opponents, led by Winston Churchill, Chamberlain and Daladier had made craven concessions to avoid fighting.

World War II began when Hitler sought to revise the eastern border of Germany, where the Polish Corridor and the free city of Danzig separated East Prussia from the rest of Germany. This, Hitler told the world, was his last territorial demand in Europe. Stalin neither believed this nor waited for further Anglo-French concessions. He answered western appeasement with the Nazi-Soviet Nonaggression Treaty, also known as the Molotov-Ribbentrop Pact for the foreign ministers who signed it. Germany and the Soviet Union mutually promised not to participate in an attack on each other

Illustration 30.1

⚅ The Nazi-Soviet Nonaggression Pact. On August 23, 1939, an astonished world learned that anti-Communist Germany and anti-Fascist Russia had signed a treaty pledging not to attack each other. Secret provisions planned a partition of Poland, much like those of the eighteenth century: Germany would take western Poland and Russia eastern Poland plus Estonia, Latvia, and Lithuania. When the partition took place, less than one month later, David Low, a cartoonist for the London *Evening Standard*, captured the irony and cynicism of the moment.

and to remain neutral in a war with a third party. They sealed the bargain with secret provisions of the treaty reprising the eighteenth-century partition of Poland. Germany would take the western two-thirds while the Soviet Union absorbed eastern Poland and the Baltic republics. This treaty stunned opinion worldwide—Joachim von Ribbentrop, after all, was also the author of the largest anti-Communist alliance in the world, the Anti-Commintern Pact linking Germany, Italy, and Japan (see illustration 30.1). The stunned silence did not last. A few days after concluding this treaty, Hitler used a dispute over Danzig as his excuse to send an army of 1.25 million men into Poland. Two days after the invasion began in September 1939, Britain and France declared war on Germany.

◆

The Years of Axis Conquest, 1939–42

The war in Poland showed that technology had again changed warfare. The use of tanks and airplanes to support an invading army created a powerful offensive force, in contrast to the defensive war of barbed wire and machine guns fought in 1914–18. Even the infantry had changed, with mechanized units able to move rapidly. The German army (the *Wehrmacht*) possessed another major advantage: It was more than twice as large as the Polish army, and twenty-two divisions could not stop fifty-four. The German air force (the *Luftwaffe*) destroyed most of the Polish air force on the ground in the first hours of the war, and the *Wehrmacht* swept across Poland so fast that the campaign was called a *Blitzkrieg* (lightning war). The Germans reached

Warsaw in barely one week, after a time-warp spectacle of Polish cavalry on horseback, with sword and lance, fighting in the same campaign that introduced German *Panzer* tanks. The opening days of the campaign presented one of the most hellish aspects of total war—the attack upon civilian populations. Göring ordered the "saturation bombing" of Warsaw, and the Polish capital was pounded into submission by *Luftwaffe* "dive-bombers" (*Stukas*), which dove toward the city with nerve-shattering whistles mounted in the wings. During a four-week battle, the *Luftwaffe* leveled 15 percent of all buildings (including the historic royal castle of the Polish kings) and killed forty thousand civilians. After two weeks of the German devastation of Warsaw, Stalin sent the Red Army into eastern Poland, as foreseen in the Nazi-Soviet Pact and as a precaution against German seizure of the rich oil resources of Galicia and Romania. German and Russian armies met in central Poland during the third week of the war; a few days later, independent Poland had disappeared (see map 30.2). Sixty thousand Polish dead and 200,000 Polish wounded were just the beginning of Polish suffering. Approximately six million Poles would die before the war's end, including more than three million Polish Jews. Fleeing to the Russian sector gave no safety; when a Polish army tried this, the Red Army executed forty-two hundred Polish officers in the Katyn Forest massacre.

World War II seemed to have ended before it could spread. Italy and the United States declared neutrality. Britain (sitting behind the traditional security of the English Channel) and France (sitting behind the supposed security of the elaborate Maginot Line fortifica-

MAP 30.2
World War II in Europe and North Africa

tions built across eastern France in the 1920s and 1930s) found themselves in a "phony war," sarcastically called the *Sitzkrieg* (sitting war). In Paris, donations were collected to plant roses around the Maginot Line to cheer the bored soldiers. Stalin meanwhile took advantage of this moment to annex the Baltic states and then, in November 1939, to attack Finland. The Finns held out for weeks behind exceptional fortifications devised by their commander, General Karl von Mannerheim, who made clear their refusal to concede territory to the Russians, even after Stalin copied Nazi tactics and bombed Helsinki: "We shall fight to the last old man and the last small child. We shall burn our forests and

houses . . . and what we yield will be cursed by the scourge of God." The Finns hoped for western aid that never arrived. The League of Nations expelled the USSR, and many countries sent limited supplies and sympathy, but the Finns were finally forced to surrender in March 1940 (after the Russian manpower advantage reached fifty-to-one and Russian casualties had passed 200,000) and to yield frontier territory.

The war continued in the west in 1939–40, but it was hidden from sight, on the high seas. Britain's lifeline remained, as it had been in World War I, on the Atlantic. German submarines (*Unterseeboots* or U-boats) had nearly beat the British in the first war, and an experienced U-boat commander, Admiral Karl Doenitz, now headed the German navy. However, Hitler (like Napoleon before him) had paid far less attention to naval preparation for war than he lavished on his army, leaving Doenitz a total submarine fleet of only fifty-six vessels in 1939. Doenitz launched total war on the seas (including explicit orders to attack passenger ships in convoy for Britain), and the battle of the Atlantic began shortly after the invasion of Poland. A British liner was sunk by a German U-boat on the first day of the war, and "wolf-pack" U-boat tactics sank nineteen Allied ships in two weeks, forty before the fall of Poland. In two shocking episodes for British morale, a U-boat sank a major British aircraft carrier (with the loss of 514 men) in September, and another snuck into the British base at Scapa Flow (in the Orkney Islands) and sank the battleship *Royal Oak.* The sea war soon had a major impact; by spring, Doenitz's men had sunk 688,000 tons of merchant shipping. As the German U-boat fleet increased, so did the toll in the battle of the Atlantic. By 1942 it had reached 14 million tons.

The *Sitzkrieg* ended in April 1940, when Germany attacked Denmark (with whom it had a nonaggression treaty) on the flimsy pretext that the Danes would not be able to defend themselves against an Allied attack, but in reality because it was the first step in controlling Scandinavian iron and steel. The surprised Danes could offer no resistance, and units of the Nazi army reached Copenhagen in only a few hours, forcing the king of Denmark to capitulate within twenty-four hours of the start of the war. On the same day as the Danish campaign, units of the *Luftwaffe* occupied the airports at Oslo and other major towns, and the German navy entered every major fjord on the Norwegian coast. The Norwegians—who had housed and fed thousands of German children during the starvation in the closing phase of World War I—were as astonished as the Danes had been, and they managed only slightly more resistance (although sinking a major German warship). The king of Norway and the government fled to the north, and Britain and France landed a few troops there, but the Allies (and a Norwegian government in exile) were soon forced to evacuate. In limited spring fighting German conquest had reached the Arctic Circle. In Norway, as happened in other conquered countries, a Nazi sympathizer agreed to lead a collaborationist government, and Major Vidkun Quisling thereby made his last name a synonym for traitor.

The *Blitzkrieg* came to western Europe in May 1940 with a German assault (a 4 A.M. sneak attack) on the Low Countries (as a way of flanking the fortifications of the French Maginot Line) and then on northern France.

The great cities of Amsterdam, Antwerp, and Brussels all suffered bombardment; the great port-city of Rotterdam (despite being declared an open city) was virtually flattened in withering *Stuka* attacks, which reduced two square miles of the city center (including twenty-five thousand private residences) to rubble. The destruction of Rotterdam convinced the British Royal Air Force (RAF) to bring the same sense of total war to German cities, and this strategy would devastate Germany later in the war. In addition to that devastation, the Dutch army suffered 100,000 casualties (25 percent of the army) in just five days of fighting, enough to force a surrender. The queen, and a government in exile, managed to escape to Britain, leaving the Dutch under the brutal rule of a Nazi governor, Arthur Seyss-Inquart, a meek little man who plundered the country for nearly five years and sent more than five million Dutch citizens to forced labor in Germany. (Seyss-Inquart would be executed as a war criminal in 1946.) A simultaneous *Panzer* attack on Belgium sliced between France and Belgium, and Brussels fell. The Belgians, who had endured more than four years of bloodletting without yielding in 1914–18, surrendered to the Nazis in one week.

The British had sent a large expeditionary force (the BEF) to the continent, but this army was cut off and trapped near the coast of the English Channel at Dunkirk (the northernmost port in France), with its entire left flank exposed by the fall of Belgium and the *Luftwaffe* pounding it at will. Facing almost certain catastrophe, the British chose to evacuate the BEF. In one of the most important retreats in military history, the British used every available boat (mostly civilian) from the English coast to ferry their army back across the channel. Nearly 340,000 men (including 140,000 French and Belgian soldiers) abandoned their equipment and the continental war, but thanks to the armada of nine hundred small craft (and Hitler's strange decision to halt the *Panzer* assault at Dunkirk), they survived to fight Germany on more favorable terms.

A vulnerable and demoralized France faced the Nazi *Blitzkrieg* without the allies of 1914. Although the French army of 800,000 regular forces and 5.5 million trained reserves had been considered the strongest army in Europe, it took no significant action against Germany during the *Sitzkrieg*, instead sitting in the Maginot fortications and awaiting a German attack. Many of the strongest units of the French army were lost in the debacle in Belgium, however, and much of the French air force had been destroyed on the ground in a Nazi preemptive attack. Then, two days after the Dunkirk evacuation, 120 divisions of the *Wehrmacht* poured into northern France, outflanking the Maginot

Line instead of challenging it. The German *Blitzkrieg* shattered quickly assembled French lines, as the Nazis drove past Sedan, site of the German victory of 1870, and Verdun, symbol of French resistance in 1916. By mid-June (after less than two weeks of fighting), the French army was in chaos and Paris, without significant defenses, was evacuated by the government to spare it the fate of Warsaw and Rotterdam. With the fall of France seeming imminent, Mussolini declared war on Britain and France and (in the words of U.S. President Franklin D. Roosevelt (FDR)) "stabbed her in the back" by invading the Riviera with an army of 400,000 men. France had been routed, and when the government of France turned to Marshal Henri Pétain, the hero of Verdun, he immediately surrendered. A gleeful Hitler accepted the French surrender in Compiègne, signed in exactly the same railroad boxcar where Imperial Germany had capitulated in 1918 (which Hitler ordered taken back to Berlin as a tourist attraction). And the *Wehrmacht* staged a victory parade down the Champs Elysées and hung a giant Nazi banner from the Eiffel Tower.

The fall of France led to a German peace much harsher than the Versailles Treaty. Germany reannexed Alsace and Lorraine, then occupied the northern half of France (including Paris) plus the entire Atlantic coast; all the territory was placed under a German military government. This partition of France ended the Third Republic, which had often been a troubled regime but had pioneered republican government in a monarchical world. The rump state of southern France, known as Vichy France because its capital was the spa of Vichy, was led by the eighty-four-year-old Marshal Pétain and a former conservative premier, Pierre Laval, who served as Pétain's most important deputy. They replaced French constitutional democracy with an authoritarian government that had no constitution, collaborated with the Third Reich, and launched a Fascist National Revolution (see document 30.2). Vichy France changed the national motto of "Liberty, Equality, Fraternity" to "Work, Family, Fatherland" and demonstrated the end of liberty by sending leaders of the Third Republic, such as Léon Blum, to German concentration camps. Although Pétain and Laval never produced a constitution, they did find time to emulate the Nazi *Gleichschaltung*, which was seen in restricted freedoms, the regulation of basic institutions, and institutionalized anti-Semitism.

The highest ranking leader to escape was General Charles de Gaulle, who had been an obscure brigade commander in 1939 and whose government post was undersecretary for war in June 1940. (To the dismay of

◆ DOCUMENT 30.2 ◆

Pétain: National Revolution in Vichy France

In October 1940 Marshal Pétain broadcast a radio message to the French people. It was his manifesto for a new, anti-republican France.

Frenchmen!

Four months ago, France received one of the biggest defeats in her history. . . . [T]he disaster is but the reflection of the weaknesses and blemishes of the old political regime. Yet many of you were attached to that regime. As you voted every four years, you had the impression that you were free citizens in a free State. . . .

On this mound of ruins we must now reconstruct France. The New Order must not in any sense imply a return. . . .

The new regime will be a social hierarchy. It will not rest on the false idea of the material equality of men but on the necessary idea of the equality of opportunity given to all Frenchmen to prove their ability to serve. . . . So will arise the true elites, which former regime spent years destroying. . . .

Some may fear that the new hierarchy will destroy the liberty to which they cling and for which their fathers fought at the price of their blood. They need have no fear. Authority is necessary to safeguard the liberty of the State. . . .

What does freedom, abstract freedom, mean in 1940 to the unemployed worker or the ruined small employer—except freedom to suffer helplessly in a vanquished nation? We are really only losing some deceptive illusions of freedom, in order to make sure of saving the substance. . . .

In economic policy . . . two essential principles will be our guides: the economy must be organized and controlled. Coordination of private activities by the State.

Britain and the Allies, de Gaulle became the highest ranking French official to escape when a large group of politicians trying to flee was arrested and imprisoned.) De Gaulle had favored fighting to the bitter end, but when Pétain chose to surrender de Gaulle fled to London, where he organized a government in exile known

Illustration 30.2

The Battle of Britain. The first defeat that Nazi Germany suffered, and the first turning point in the course of the war in Europe, came in an air war fought over Britain in the summer of 1940. The German *Luftwaffe*, with twenty-eight hundred aircraft, was asked to win control of the skies in preparation for an invasion of England, but the Royal Air Force (RAF), with seven hundred fighters, prevented them from doing so. In this photo, RAF pilots have just received a radar warning of approaching bombers and run to their Hurricane fighters to intercept the German planes.

as Free France. On his first day in London he addressed a famous radio appeal to the French people to continue the battle: "Has the last word been said? Has all hope disappeared? Is this defeat definitive? No! Believe me." This powerful broadcast (reproduced on clandestine posters around France) sealed de Gaulle's wartime leadership—by 1941, some forty-five thousand French troops from the Dunkirk evacuation and French colonies had rallied to him—although the British and Americans would later try to replace him.

The first German defeat came when Hitler turned his attention to Britain in the summer of 1940. To prepare for an invasion of Britain, the *Luftwaffe* contested the RAF for control of the skies over the English Channel. The future of Britain, and perhaps of Europe, rested with approximately five thousand pilots during this battle of Britain and with an untested British invention—radar—which enabled them to spot planes seventy-five miles away from the coast of England (see illustration 30.2). The *Luftwaffe* sent as many as twenty-one hundred planes over England, greatly outnumbering RAF defenses. During July 1940 the British lost nearly half of the RAF, but they shot down German planes at a higher rate and denied them control of the skies. Hitler dared not risk sending an invasion armada to sea. As the new prime minister of Britain, Winston Churchill, put it, "Never . . . was so much owed by so many to so few."

The battle of Britain entered a horrifying second phase in September 1940. Hitler decided to break British morale by obliterating London in terrorizing

bomber raids called the *Blitz*. Twenty-three consecutive days of bombing rained nearly twenty thousand tons of bombs down on the city, destroying more than 450,000 private homes and killing thirty thousand civilians but failing to break the British will. Nothing symbolized British resistance better than the leadership of Churchill, one of the greatest wartime leaders in European history. Churchill was the descendant of an eighteenth-century military hero and the son of a prominent Conservative M.P. and a wealthy American mother. He worked exceptionally hard, but he had an infuriating personality, few friends, and a record of political failure. But Winston Churchill possessed a rare eloquence that summoned up resistance to the Nazis. In his maiden speech as prime minister, he had told the nation he had nothing to offer "but blood, toil, tears, and sweat." But, he soon added, if the nation paid that price, "should the British Empire last for a thousand years, people would say 'This was their finest hour.'"

The battle of Britain drew the United States closer to the war. President Roosevelt was sympathetic, and he inched America toward intervening against the steady opposition of isolationists such as Charles A. Lindbergh and Senator Burton K. Wheeler. Since 1939 Britain had been buying 90 percent of American aircraft exports. In June 1940 (in the aftermath of the Dunkirk evacuation) Roosevelt sent $43 million worth of surplus arms (such as 600,000 rifles) to Britain. In August he struck a "destroyers for bases deal" to protect Atlantic shipping by sending fifty-one aging American destroyers to Britain. The conservative U.S. Congress limited arms sales by a strict "cash-and-carry" policy, but Roosevelt fought this short-sighted policy and called upon Congress to aid threatened democracies. The fruit of Roosevelt's efforts was the Lend-Lease Act of March 1941, which empowered the president to send arms to any nation deemed "vital to the defense of the United States." Congress initially authorized an appropriation of $7 billion for Lend-Lease arms (which grew to $50 billion during the war) and supplies began to flow from "the arsenal of democracy" to the enemies of Hitler. Then, in August 1941, FDR and Churchill met on a warship off Newfoundland and agreed upon the Atlantic Charter, a statement of war aims and postwar plans comparable to the Fourteen Points of World War I. They renounced territorial gain, called for "the destruction of Nazi tyranny," and spoke of human rights.

Despite victory in the battle of Britain and the optimism of the Atlantic Charter, 1941–42 was a dark time for opponents of the Axis (see document 30.3). Italian armies carried the war into the Balkans and North Africa in the autumn of 1940. The Italian invasion of Egypt (from their colony in Libya) threatened the Suez Canal and Middle Eastern oil supplies; both targets were so important that when British defenders drove the Italians from Egypt, Hitler reinforced the Axis effort with an elite German *Panzer* army known as the Afrika Korps, commanded by an exceptional tank commander, General Erwin Rommel, who forced the British to retreat. By June 1942 the Afrika Korps was threatening to take the Suez Canal. Simultaneously, Italian armies invaded Greece (in October 1942) and opened war in the Balkans. The *Wehrmacht* also entered this theater of the war, supporting the Italians in Greece and then invading Yugoslavia. Belgrade (severely bombed by the *Luftwaffe* in punishment for continued resistance) and Athens both fell to German occupation. The war in the Balkans continued as a guerrilla war, however, and Yugoslav partisans led by Joseph Broz (known as "Tito") never surrendered. The Balkan theater saw some of the most ferocious combat of World War II, and Yugoslavia (a nation of 14 million people in the 1930s) would lose 1.5 million to 2 million people.

But the most important theater of World War II in Europe was the eastern front. Hitler, like Napoleon before him, turned from his failure to invade England and attacked Russia. This was the logical culmination of Hitler's determination to gain *Lebensraum* in the east (outlined in the Hossbach Memorandum and before that in *Mein Kampf*), a calculation eased by his racist conviction of Slavic inferiority. In June 1941 he launched Operation Barbarosa, hitting the Soviet Union along a two-thousand-mile front in three mas-

◆ DOCUMENT 30.3 ◆

The Atlantic Charter, August 1941

A Joint Declaration by the President and the Prime Minister . . . to make known certain common principles. . . .

FIRST, Their countries seek no aggrandizement, territorial or other;

SECOND, They desire to see no territorial changes that do not accord with the freely expressed wishes of the people concerned;

THIRD, They respect the right of all peoples to choose the form of government under which they will live; and they wish to see sovereign rights and self-government restored to those who have been forcibly deprived of them;

FOURTH, They will endeavor with due respect for their existing obligations, to further the enjoyment by all states, great or small, victor or vanquished, of access, on equal terms, to the trade and to the raw materials of the world which are needed for their economic prosperity.

FIFTH, They desire to bring about the fullest collaboration between all nations in the economic field with the object of securing, for all, improved labor standards, economic adjustment, and social security.

SIXTH, After the final destruction of the Nazi tyranny, they hope to see established a peace which will afford to all nations the means of dwelling in safety within their own boundaries, and which will afford assurance that all the men in all the lands may live out their lives in freedom from fear and want;

SEVENTH, Such a peace should enable all men to traverse the high seas and oceans without hindrance;

EIGHTH, They believe that all of the nations of the world, for realistic as well as spiritual reasons, must come to the abandonment of the use of force. . . . They will aid and encourage all other practicable measures which will lighten for peace-loving peoples the crushing burden of armaments.

sive offensives—toward Leningrad (the former St. Petersburg), Moscow, and Kiev. Finland resumed its war with the Soviet Union in the north and Hungary and Romania supported Germany in the south, but the Nazi *Blitzkrieg* again won quick victories. Soviet armies were

Illustration 30.3

/// **Total War on the Eastern Front.** The German invasion of Russia in 1941 penetrated deep into Russia along three fronts; on the central front, a German army drove toward the capital of the USSR, Moscow. The photograph illustrates how total the de-fense effort became: The women of Moscow were brought out of the city in shifts to dig tank traps and antitank ditches to slow the Nazi advance.

in disarray, partly because of Stalin's purge of army commanders in the 1930s and partly because of Stalin's belief that Hitler would not attack him. (The USSR was still shipping food and military aid to Germany in the spring of 1941.) By autumn the *Wehrmacht* had pene-trated hundreds of miles into the Soviet Union. In the north they laid siege to Leningrad and subjected it to the treatment that obliterated Warsaw, Rotterdam, and Belgrade. In the center, German bombers hit Moscow in the first weeks of the war, and German armies drew within sight of the city by late fall (see illustration 30.3). In the south, the *Wehrmacht* overran the Ukraine, taking Minsk, Kiev, and Odessa and finally planting the Swastika on the banks of the Black Sea, as they had hung it from the Eiffel Tower and the Parthenon. Hitler seemed near to dominion over continental Europe. His empire stretched from the Arctic Circle in Norway to the desert of western Egypt, from the French Pyrenees to the Crimea. But he had opened Pandora's box; for the next three years, 90 percent of German deaths would happen on the eastern front.

World War II on the Home Front

Life on European home fronts during the Second World War was naturally austere. The British, who im-ported much of their food, faced strict rations of basic foods (such as meat, butter, sugar, eggs, and tea), the total loss of many foreign foods (such as oranges, ba-nanas, and chocolate), and reliance upon foods not pre-viously eaten (such as shark and whale). Rationing identity cards were issued in September 1939 (during the Polish campaign), and the first rationing began in January 1940. Britons would live with rationing for the next fourteen years—a period long past the end of the war being required to rebuild the economy. Many fami-lies dug up their lawn or flowers to plant vegetables, and towns in Britain (as in many other countries) matched that effort by ploughing public parks or ath-letic playing fields; the moat around the Tower of Lon-don, for example, was converted to such a garden. Families in the south of England also learned to live

Illustration 30.4

The Home Front. In total war there was scant respect for the distinction between a "battle front" and a "home front"—and civilian populations suffered terrible attacks in many countries. One of the most famous attacks on civilian centers was the German bombing of London, known as "the Blitz." During the German air raids, many British families took refuge in makeshift quarters, such as those shown in this photograph, set up in the tunnels of the London subway system.

without their children; 1.5 million children were moved outside German bombing range, many to refuge in Canada and the United States. The government curtailed free-market capitalism in favor of a regulated economy. Strikes were outlawed, the workweek increased to fifty-four hours, and the Ministry of Labor received the power to reassign workers to different jobs. The war effort also demanded much higher taxes. With one-third of all men between the ages of sixteen and sixty-four serving in uniform, women again entered the workforce at much higher levels, not only in factory jobs but also in a wide range of replacement positions (such as the police force, which lost much personnel to the military). Despite privations and the toll taken by the *Blitz*, British morale remained high, as the nation shared in the Churchillian determination that they would not surrender to "a monstrous tyranny, never surpassed in the dark, lamentable catalog of human crime."

Domestic conditions were much worse in the theaters of war. Russia suffered enormously from the experience of total war. Civilian populations overrun by the German army endured severe privation and frequent atrocities; these people had scarcely recovered from the suffering of forced collectivization and a subsequent famine in the 1930s. For those caught directly in the fighting, the meaning of total war was abundantly clear: The three million people of Leningrad endured a German siege lasting 890 days, and 600,000 of them died of starvation. Moscow evacuated more than one million

people and one thousand businesses toward the Ural Mountains, leaving behind "scorched earth" that supported neither the invaders nor Russians. Gosplan already regulated the Soviet economy, but regions producing 63 percent of Russian coal and 58 percent of Russian steel had fallen to the Germans, so controls became even more severe. Stalin mobilized twelve million women and children for factory work, and they constituted two-thirds of Soviet labor; they worked five or six days a week in the factory and then spent the weekend farming.

Civilian resistance in Britain and the Soviet Union contrasted with the collaboration of defeated countries such as Vichy France. The Nazi occupation of western and central Europe looted countries of their resources, both industrial and agricultural, and the Nazi puppet government of Pétain and Laval at Vichy helped in this effort. Their National Revolution sent more than one million Frenchmen to forced labor in Germany and arranged the Nazi requisition of three million tons of wheat and one million tons of meat in the unoccupied zone. Conditions in France deteriorated so far that even wine was rationed. An underground resistance movement, composed of many separate groups (chiefly Communist, but with a large Catholic element) in France, was collectively known as the *Maquis* or the French Forces of the Interior (FFI). Approximately 2 percent of the population took the risks of espionage, sabotage, or simple defiance, but the *Maquis* made a significant contribution to later stages of the war. Similar

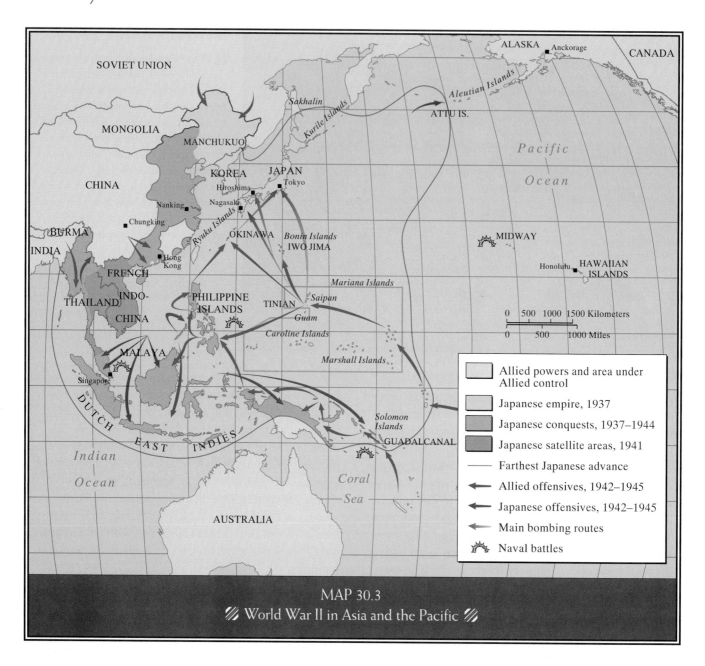

MAP 30.3

🖟 World War II in Asia and the Pacific 🖟

resistance movements existed in all occupied countries, with especially active movements in the mountain regions of Greece and Yugoslavia.

A home front could be found in Nazi Germany, too. Hitler initially strove to cushion most of the German civilian population from the impact of the war because he feared the collapse of the home front, which had been a significant factor in the German defeat in 1918. Thus military deferments remained common until 1942. Rationing was introduced in August 1939, but the level was kept unusually high (a weekly supply of one pound of meat, five pounds of bread, twelve ounces of cooking fat, twelve ounces of sugar, and one pound of ersatz coffee per person), largely through food

supplies plundered abroad. Behind such comforts, however, hid a nightmarish expression of Nazi total war at home: a euthanasia program to eliminate "useless mouths," launched at the start of the war. Between 100,000 and 200,000 of the elderly, the severely ill, the handicapped, the mentally ill, and even severely injured World War I veterans were put to death by the government with the willing cooperation of doctors, nurses, and hospital administrators. Only when Clemens von Galen, the bishop of Münster, courageously protested in 1941 did the government suspend the program (planning to resume it after victory), fearing a propaganda catastrophe if army units learned of the program of euthanasia for crippled veterans.

Illustration 30.5

Pearl Harbor. On Sunday morning, December 7, 1941, most of the United States' Pacific Fleet was at anchor at Pearl Harbor, Hawaii. Eight battleships and forty-three smaller vessels (but not three aircraft carriers, which were on duty elsewhere) were comparatively easy targets for a surprise air attack by 360 Japanese airplanes. The attack sank five battleships and killed more than two thousand men. In this photo, the USS *West Virginia* and the USS *Tennessee* are in their death throes.

The Global War

The European war had been preceded by an Asian war, which began when Japan invaded China in 1937 (see map 30.3). The Japanese had been building an Asian empire for half a century. While acquiring Formosa (won in the Sino-Japanese War of 1895), Korea (won in the Russo-Japanese War of 1904–1905), and Manchuria (occupied in 1931), Japanese nationalists developed the dream of a Greater East Asia Co-Prosperity Sphere—a slogan to cover Japanese conquest and dominance of East Asia. A second Sino-Japanese War began in 1937, and by the end of that year the Japanese Empire stretched across China as far south as Shanghai. In the course of this conquest, the Japanese army committed some of the most ruthless atrocities of the age of total war. The "rape of Nanking," which followed the conquest of that city, included the massacre of approximately 300,000 Chinese civilians, often in extremely cruel ways such as using live people for bayonet practice or nailing them to the walls of buildings. (The name of this brutality was not misplaced: The Japanese army made rape an organized aspect of warfare, victimizing perhaps eighty thousand women in Nanking.) After the fall of France in June 1940, the Japanese army landed forces in French Indochina and began the expansion of the co-prosperity sphere into Southeast Asia, where they hoped to obtain many valuable war materials. The further expansion of the Japanese meant a collision with the British Empire, which stretched across south Asia from India to Burma, Malaya, Singapore, Australia, and New Zealand. Japanese expansion similarly menaced American territories in the Pacific, stretching from Hawaii, past Guam and Samoa, to the Philippine Islands.

Britain and the United States were both drawn into the Asian war by Japanese attacks in December 1941. Japanese-American relations had deteriorated during the war in China. American sympathies for the Chinese government of Generalissimo Chiang Kai-Shek led to the prohibition of exporting war materials to Japan, although the United States had missed its opportunity to use the League of Nations (which the United States refused to join) in an effective sanctions campaign against Japan in the early 1930s. Protests, warnings, and recriminations crossed the Pacific Ocean in 1940–41, such as an American warning to Japan not to occupy Indochina. In July 1941 the military dictatorship of Japan resolved to establish the Greater East Asia Co-Prosperity Sphere "no matter what international developments take place." A few weeks later, all armed forces in the Philippine Islands were placed under the command of General Douglas MacArthur to ready them for war, and President Roosevelt froze Japanese assets in the United States. Trade between the two countries ceased. In August 1941 Roosevelt warned Japan against any further expansion in Asia saying that the United States would "take immediately any and all steps necessary" to protect its interests. Japan responded with a surprise attack on the home base of the U.S. navy at Pearl Harbor (near Honolulu, Hawaii) on December 7, 1941 (see illustration 30.5). The attack crippled the U.S. Pacific Fleet, destroying 19 warships and 150 naval aircraft and causing three thousand American casualties. Denouncing "a date which will live in in-famy," the United States declared war on Japan. As the Japanese had made simultaneous attacks upon British forces in Asia (notably in Hong Kong and Malaya), the British also declared war. Germany and Italy then de-clared war on the United States, linking the Asian and European wars into World War II.

In the six months following Pearl Harbor, the Japanese won important victories across Southeast Asia. They invaded the Philippines in late December 1941, took Manila in January 1942, drove General MacArthur to retreat, and won control of the islands in March 1942, taking a large army captive on the peninsula of Bataan. Another Japanese army drove the British out of Hong Kong in December 1941, and a third successfully invaded Burma in January 1942, cutting off British forces in Southeast Asia from those in India. The British army retreated to the stronghold of Singapore, but the Japanese took that city after a two-week siege in Febru-ary 1942, attacking from the land side (which had less fortification); sixty thousand British prisoners of war fell to the Japanese. Thereafter the British withdrew from Rangoon and the Japanese occupied most of Burma. Al-lied armies were beaten in Indonesia in March 1942, and by spring the Japanese Empire stretched from the gates of India almost to the international dateline, from Korea almost to Australia.

The turning point of the war in Asia came in a se-ries of air-sea battles in the Pacific in 1942. In the battle of the Coral Sea (May 1942), the first naval battle ever fought between ships so distant that they could not see each other, the United States stopped the Japanese ad-vance and probably saved Australia and New Zealand. In the battle of Midway (May-June 1942)—named for the U.S.-held Midway Islands, northwest of Hawaii and at the approximate midpoint of the Pacific—a U.S. fleet under Admiral Chester Nimitz fought one of the largest naval engagements in history, inflicting heavy losses on the Japanese and forcing Admiral Yamamoto to retreat. By the summer of 1942, the war in the Pa-cific had become a succession of island-hopping—amphibious invasions slowly driving toward Japan. Af-ter victories by British armies in Burma and Australian armies in New Guinea, Allied forces under Admiral Lord Louis Mountbatten slowly defeated the Japanese armies of Southeast Asia. The United States dislodged the Japanese from Guadalcanal (in the Solomon Is-lands) in early 1943 and began the reconquest of the Philippines. Bloody fighting followed on many islands, especially in the Marshall Islands and Guam in 1944 and on Okinawa in 1945, but an invasion of Japan also awaited.

◆

Allied Victory in Europe, 1942–45

The turning point of the war in Europe also came in 1942. British armies in North Africa under the command of Field Marshal Montgomery stopped the advance of the Afrika Korps in the battle of El Alamein. While the German army regrouped, an Anglo-American army of 100,000 men, under the command of General Dwight D. Eisenhower, landed in French North Africa in No-vember 1942—less than a year after Hitler had declared war on the United States. This amphibious operation re-quired 850 ships and was at that time the largest such landing in history. Caught between the armies of Eisen-hower and Montgomery, the Axis armies in North Africa suffered a series of defeats, driving them from Egypt and Algeria, then Libya, and finally from Tunisia. The last Axis troops in North Africa surrendered in May 1943.

Even before the victory in Africa, Roosevelt and Churchill had met at the Casablanca Conference of January 1943 and decided that the next stage of the war in Europe would be the invasion of Italy, "the soft under-belly of Europe" in Churchill's words. The Allies began bombing raids over Sicily and combined British, Canadian, and American armies, commanded by Eisen-hower, invaded in July. Palermo fell in two weeks and the Allies began bombing Naples, but before they could cross the Strait of Messina to the Italian penin-sula, Mussolini was deposed in a sudden coup staged by Marshal Pietro Badoglio, ending twenty-one years of Fascist rule in Italy and dissolving the Fascist Party. As the British and American armies made their first land-ings near Naples, Badoglio quickly negotiated Italy's unconditional surrender in September 1943. German armies still occupied Milan, Rome, and Naples, and German troops even liberated Mussolini to reestablish his rule. The Italian campaign therefore became a slow battle up the peninsula in 1943–45, speeded by a land-ing behind German lines at Anzio in early 1944. De-spite the rapid start to the Italian campaign, Rome did not fall until June 1944, followed by Florence in Au-gust. As the German army began to pull out of Italy, Mussolini was captured by Italian anti-Fascists while at-tempting to escape to Switzerland and was shot with-out a trial.

While the victories in North Africa and Italy were important steps in the defeat of the Axis, the decisive theater of the war was the eastern front. The German invasion of Russia had been stopped by the winter of 1941–42 and the determined defense of Moscow led by General Georgi Zhukov. Zhukov was the son of illiter-

Illustration 30.6

D-Day. The turning point of World War II on the western front came on June 6, 1944, when the Allies staged the greatest amphibious landing in history, along the shores of northern France. Landing craft such as the one shown in this photograph put an army of more than 150,000 men ashore in the first day, losing slightly more than 2,000 killed. In less than two weeks, the success of the D-Day invasion had put nearly 500,000 soldiers into the western front.

ate peasants and had a gruff and unsophisticated style, but he was one of the first commanders to master tank warfare. He so distinguished himself in saving Moscow that Stalin sent him to Leningrad, where he ordered that the city be defended street by street and that officers who retreated be shot. German assaults (which cost them 200,000 soldiers) and bombardment failed to break Leningrad. When the German siege finally ended in early 1943, half of the population of Leningrad had died.

The turning point of World War II in Europe came in southern Russia. The *Wehrmacht* had already lost nearly two million men on the eastern front before the Red Army began to counterattack in the winter of 1942–43. A campaign on the Volga River at Stalingrad was the beginning of the end for Nazi Germany, an epic battle comparable to Verdun in the First World War. The Red Army encircled a German army of 300,000 men at Stalingrad and relentlessly attacked in horrifying conditions where temperatures reached minus forty-nine degrees Fahrenheit. When the Germans gave up in February 1943, a veteran army that had sped across Belgium and Holland was reduced to ninety-one thousand starving, frostbitten prisoners of war, only six thousand of whom eventually survived Russian imprisonment. After the battle of Stalingrad, the *Wehrmacht* attempted another offensive, which led to the largest

tank battle in history—the battle of Kursk, a rail center south of Moscow. This nine-day battle involved more than two million combatants, five thousand planes, and six thousand tanks. The *Wehrmacht* lost badly, as the Red Army threw seemingly endless numbers of men and equipment into the battle. Then began a long German retreat. The Russian army recaptured Smolensk in September 1943, liberated Kiev in November, and crossed the frontier into Poland in January 1944.

The Allies had long planned to open a western front against Germany. Stalin pressed this policy to reduce the burden of the eastern front, where Russian deaths had passed the ten million mark. The western Allies responded with Operation Overlord, a plan to invade northern France with a combined army of five divisions (two British, two American, and one Canadian), commanded by General Eisenhower. They prepared elaborately, staging men and materiel in southern England and conducting bombing raids over Germany. The RAF struck Berlin with nine hundred tons of bombs in March 1943, then concentrated on the industrial Rhineland. The bombing of Essen cut the output of the Krupp armaments complex by 65 percent.

The result was the largest amphibious invasion in history, landing on the shores of Normandy on D-Day, June 6, 1944 (see illustration 30.6). An armada of five thousand ships landed 150,000 soldiers (plus thousands of vehicles and tons of supplies) on the French coast. In less than two weeks, these numbers reached nearly 500,000 soldiers and ninety thousand vehicles. The Normandy landings led to a rapid breakthrough by Allied tank forces, and by midsummer Germany clearly had lost the second battle of France, permitting armies of the British Empire, the Free French, and the United States to press into western Germany while the Russians invaded eastern Germany. This reverse precipitated an attempt to assassinate Hitler by a conspiracy within the *Wehrmacht*. The plot involved several senior officers, but the central figure was Colonial Claus von Stuaffenberg, who carried a bomb into a conference among Hitler and his military advisers. Hitler survived and the conspirators were brutally executed (Hitler filmed their deaths for evening entertainment); those implicated included General Rommel (who opposed Hitler but did not participate in the plot), who was allowed to commit suicide.

Hitler responded to the reverses of June–July 1944 with one last surprise: a wave of rocket attacks whose technology presaged the cold war and the space race. A German research program (which included many scientists who would later contribute to the space race of the 1950s and 1960s, such as Dr. Wernher von Braun) at Peenemünde, on the Baltic coast, achieved significant advances in rocketry. The results were the V-1 rockets (the *V* stands for a German word for "reprisal weapon")— flying bombs with a ton of explosives traveling 370 miles per hour—which hit London in the summer of 1944, and more sophisticated V-2 rockets, which struck London and Antwerp that autumn. V-1 and V-2 attacks delivered more than seventy thousand tons of explosives to Britain, approximately four times the amount that the *Luftwaffe* dropped in 1940; the rockets killed nearly eight thousand people but had little effect on the course of the war.

Allied armies reached Paris in August 1944 and speeded the liberation of France by making further landings in the south of France. Lyons, Brussels, and Antwerp were all liberated in September 1944, and western armies crossed into western Germany in that same month. The Allies officially recognized Charles de Gaulle's government of liberated France in October. Although the *Wehrmacht* staged a strong counteroffensive through the Ardennes forest in December 1944, the Nazi regime was crushed between western and Soviet armies. The Red Army had reached Warsaw in July 1944 and a Polish uprising joined in throwing off the Nazi occupation. The Russian army, however, waited for the Nazis to crush the Polish resistance (with

Illustration 30.7

Victory on the Eastern Front.   The turning point of the war in eastern Europe had come in 1943 when the USSR won the battle of Stalingrad. For the next two years, the Red Army under Marshal Zhukov pressed into central Europe in a campaign that culminated in the Soviet capture of Berlin in April–May 1945. In this photo, Zhukov (front, lower right) and his staff stand on the steps of the ruined Reichstag, now covered in Russian graffiti and with the Soviet flag flying above it.

245,000 Poles killed) before advancing on Warsaw (because Stalin reasoned that Polish resistance to a German occupation could easily become Polish resistance to a Russian occupation). As France was being freed in the west, Russian troops were crossing into East Prussia. The Red Army approached Berlin in early 1945 (see illustration 30.7), just as the U.S. army was crossing the Rhine River. With the war nearly over, Allied bombers delivered a horrifying final blow, a last testament to the nature of total war: The historic Saxon city of Dresden, known as "the Florence of Germany," was subjected to two days of nightmarish bombing, killing more than 130,000 civilians.

☙ TABLE 30.1 ☙

The Estimated Casualties of World War II

Country	Killed in combat	Wounded	Civilians killed	Total killed
Allied casualties				
Australia	23,000–26,000	39,000–180,000		23,000–26,000
Belgium	8,000–10,000	56,000	60,000–76,000	68,000–86,000
Britain	244,000–264,000	370,000	60,000–93,000	304,000–357,000
Canada	32,000–37,000	53,000		32,000–37,000
China	1.3 million–2.2 million	1.8 million		1.3 million–2.2 million plus
Denmark	3,000–4,000		2,000–3,000	5,000–7,000
France	200,000–400,000	400,000	200,000–350,000	400,000–750,000
Greece	17,000–74,000	47,000	325,000–391,000	342,000–465,000
India	24,000–32,000	64,000		24,000–32,000
Netherlands	7,000	3,000	200,000	207,000
New Zealand	11,000	17,000		11,000
Norway	1,000–2,000		7,000–8,000	8,000–10,000
Poland	123,000–600,000	530,000	5 million plus	about 6 million
United States	292,000	670,000	6,000	298,000
USSR	6.0 million–7.5 million		2 million–9 million plus	8 million–20 million
Yugoslavia	305,000–410,000	425,000	1.2 million	1.5 million–1.6 million
Axis casualties				
Bulgaria	7,000–10,000		10,000	17,000–20,000
Finland	79,000–82,000		2,000–11,000	81,000–93,000
Germany	3.3 million–4.4 million		780,000 plus	4.1 million–5.2 million
Hungary	140,000–180,000		280,000–290,000	420,000–470,000
Italy	78,000–162,000		146,000	224,000–308,000
Japan	1.2 million–2.0 million		280,000 plus	1.5 million–2.3 million
Romania	300,000–350,000		200,000	500,000–550,000

Source: Adapted from data in Louis L. Snyder, ed., *Louis L. Snyder's Historical Guide to World War II* (Westport, Conn.: Greenwood, 1982), p. 126.

Note: Figures show range from lowest to highest estimates. German data include Austria. Holocaust victims are counted in homeland civilians.

Mussolini and Hitler died one day apart in April 1945. While Il Duce was killed by Italian partisans, der Führer committed suicide in the ruins of Berlin a day later. Hitler's war had cost Germany more than three million combat deaths (three-fourths of them on the eastern front); more than twice that number of Russian soldiers had died, compared with a combined total of approximately one million British, French, and American troops (see table 30.1). Roosevelt also died in April, a few days before the unconditional surrender of Germany on V-E Day (Victory in Europe Day). Finishing the war in Asia thus fell to Roosevelt's vice president, Harry S. Truman.

President Truman took the painful decision to use the atomic bomb on Japan to avoid the frightful costs of invading Japan. In the late 1930s experiments with splitting the atom had begun to convince physicists around the world of the potential of a weapon based on nuclear fission. In 1939 a group of distinguished European émigré scientists (notably Enrico Fermi, Leo Szilard, and Albert Einstein) at American universities began to worry that Nazi Germany might be working on such an atomic bomb. This resulted in a historic letter from Albert Einstein to President Roosevelt explaining these possibilities (see illustration 30.8). FDR responded with top-secret (even from Congress) funding of the Manhattan Project to construct a nuclear fission bomb. An international team of scientists, many of them Jewish refugees driven from Europe by Nazi racial policies, and all of them fearful that Werner Heisenberg

Illustration 30.9

Nazi Concentration Camps. One of the first concentration camps liberated by Allied armies was Bergen-Belsen in northwestern Germany, a camp originally opened in 1941 for Allied prisoners of war but converted by Himmler into a camp for Jews from western Europe (including Anne Frank) in 1943. When the British army entered Bergen-Belsen in April 1945, they found thousands of unburied bodies (shown here) and, as the BBC reported, thousands of "scarcely human, moaning skeletons" who had been without food or water for five days.

Munich), Buchenwald (near Weimar), and Sachsenhausen (near Berlin), expanded during the war, especially in Poland, the site of such notorious camps as Auschwitz (near Cracow) and Treblinka (near Warsaw). Adolf Hitler had displayed extreme anti-Semitism to the world in *Mein Kampf* and repeated it throughout the 1930s, and his regime persecuted Jews from its earliest days. In a speech to the Reichstag in January 1939, he even warned that the Jewish race in Europe would be exterminated in the next world war. Hitler's psychotic anti-Semitism culminated in a grotesque plan to "purify Aryan blood," known as the Final Solution (*Endlösung*). The Final Solution was mass murder; approximately eleven million people were killed in the Nazi camps. Gypsies, homosexuals, Communists, the handicapped, the mentally ill, and members of sects such as the Jehovah's Witnesses were all marked for extermination, and they died in large numbers—from 5,000 German and Austrian homosexuals to 200,000 gypsies. Millions of Poles and Soviet prisoners of war (both nations were *Untermenschen*, or subhumans, in the Nazi racial cosmology) also perished in the German concentration camps. But the Final Solution was aimed first at the Jews, nearly 6 million of whom were killed (two-thirds of all European Jews), including 1.5 million children (see illustration 30.9).

Under the direction of Himmler, Reinhard Heydrich, and Adolph Eichmann, the concentration camps became a universe of slave labor and starvation, then of brutality so savage that it included medical experimentation on live people and ultimately factories for the efficient killing of people. Nazi officials had begun to discuss "a complete solution of the Jewish question" in 1941, and the concentration camps started to become death camps that year. Then in January 1942, fifteen leading Nazi officials met at Wannsee, in suburban Berlin, to plan genocide; in the Wannsee Protocol, they pledged to achieve the Final Solution. This led to grisly experimentation to find an efficient means of committing genocide: Sobibor killed 200,000–250,000 people by carbon monoxide poisoning, before the managers of the Auschwitz-Birkenau complex discovered the efficiencies of Zyclon-B (a form of Prussic acid) for gassing inmates. Poison gas was typically administered to groups of people locked into large rooms made to resemble showers; great furnaces were built to burn the bodies. More than 1.1 million people were killed in this way at Auschwitz, and meticulous Nazi bureaucrats kept detailed records of their murders. At his postwar trial, the Nazi commandant of Auschwitz, Rudolf Hoess, calmly described the entire procedure (see document 30.4).

The Holocaust witnessed heroism amid the horror. Fascist Italy joined in anti-Semitic legislation (such as a 1938 law forbidding intermarriage with Jews) and had interned foreign-born Jews, but Mussolini resisted genocide and refused to deport forty-four thousand Jews to the death camps, enabling 85 percent of Italian Jews to survive the war. Although Vichy France similarly collaborated by deporting foreign-born Jews, a heroic Protestant village in southern France, Le Chambon, led by Pastor André Tromé, saved five thousand

◆ DOCUMENT 30.4 ◆

The Commandant of Auschwitz Confesses

Rudolf Hoess (1900–47) was a decorated World War I veteran who spent much of the 1920s in prison for killing a teacher who had insulted the memory of a Nazi hero. He joined the SS and spent his career working in the concentration camps, rising from a corporal at Dachau to be the commandant of Auschwitz (1940–43). Under his supervision, 2.5 million inmates were executed, and Hoess earned an SS commendation for efficiency. At his trial he gave a remarkably calm and detailed confession of his life as a mass murderer.

In the summer of 1941—I can no longer remember the exact date—I was suddenly summoned to the Reichsführer SS [Himmler] in Berlin directly by his adjutant's office. Contrary to his normal practice, he received me without his adjutant being present and told me, in effect:

"The Führer has ordered the final solution of the Jewish question and we—the SS—have to carry out this order. The existing extermination centers in the east are not in a position to carry out the major operations which are envisaged. I have, therefore, earmarked Auschwitz for this task, both because of its favorable communications and because the area envisaged can be easily sealed off and camouflaged. . . .

"You will maintain the strictest silence concerning this order, even vis-à-vis your superiors. After your meeting with Eichmann [Himmler's SS assistant] send me the plans for the proposed installations at once. The Jews are the eternal enemies of the German people and must be exterminated. Every Jew we can lay our hands on must be exterminated. . . .

Shortly afterwards, Eichmann came to see me in Auschwitz. . . . We discussed how the extermination was to be carried out. Gas was the only feasible method, since it would be impossible to liquidate by shooting the large numbers envisaged, and shooting would place too heavy a burden on the SS men who had to carry it out, particularly in view of the women and children involved.

Eichmann informed me of the method of killing by exhaust fumes from vans, which had been implemented in the east hitherto. However, it was out of the question to use it in Auschwitz on the mass transports that were envisaged. . . . My deputy . . . [had] used gas to exterminate the Russian prisoners of war. He crammed individual cells with Russians and, protected by gas masks, hurled Zyclon-B into the cells which caused death immediately. . . . During Eichmann's next visit, I reported to him about this use of Zyclon-B and we decided to employ this gas for the future mass extermination program. . . .

Auschwitz reached its high point in the spring of 1944. . . . A triple track railway line leading to the new crematoria enabled a train to be unloaded while the next one was arriving. . . . All four crematoria operated at full blast. . . . The last body had hardly been pulled from the gas chambers and dragged across the yard behind the crematorium, which was covered in corpses, to the burning pit, when the next lot were already undressing in the hall for gassing.

Jews by hiding them, and a Capuchin monk at Marseille, Marie Benoît, saved four thousand by providing papers allowing them to escape. Danes ferried Jews to safety in Sweden so effectively that seven thousand Danish Jews escaped and only fifty-one died in the camps. A single Swedish diplomat, Raoul Wallenberg, organized a system that saved ten thousand Budapest Jews. (In a tragic irony, Wallenberg himself died in Soviet captivity.) A German businessman, Oscar Schindler, saved Jews from Auschwitz by taking them to work in his factory. Jewish self-defense also had notable moments: In April 1942 the Jewish ghetto of Warsaw fought back and killed five thousand German soldiers.

◆

Conference Diplomacy and Peace in Europe in 1945

No peace conference or treaty ended World War II in Europe. Churchill, Stalin, and Roosevelt had prepared for Germany's unconditional surrender at a series of summit conferences during the war. The Tehran Conference of 1943, for example, projected new frontiers for Poland and discussed the dismemberment of Germany. The Dumbarton Oaks Conference (in Washington, D.C.) planned an international organization—the United Nations (UN)—to keep the peace. Churchill and Stalin met in Moscow in 1944 and agreed to divide

Illustration 30.10

The Yalta Conference. The "Big Three" allied war leaders, (left to right) Prime Minister Churchill of Great Britain, President Roosevelt of the United States, and Marshal Stalin of the USSR, met at Yalta, on the Crimean Peninsula of the USSR, in February 1945 to begin the planning for peacemaking. They discussed plans for the creation of a United Nations, the dismemberment of Germany, the fate of Poland and other parts of eastern Europe, reparations, and war crimes trials.

eastern Europe into "spheres of influence"; the USSR would be preeminent in Romania and Bulgaria and have influence in Hungary and Yugoslavia.

The most important wartime conference took place in early 1945 in the Russian resort town of Yalta, on the Crimean peninsula (see illustration 30.10). Churchill, Roosevelt, and Stalin agreed to divide Germany into four zones of military occupation, with France administering the fourth. They pledged the "complete disarmament, demilitarization, and dismemberment" of Germany, including the right of occupying powers to remove German wealth, such as dismantling factories. The Potsdam Conference (in suburban Berlin in the summer of 1945) finalized the partition of Germany. The Allies agreed that Germans must "atone for the terrible crimes committed under the leadership of those whom, in the hour of their success, they openly approved and blindly obeyed." The boundary between a reduced Germany and a recreated Poland would be defined by two rivers, the Oder-Neisse Line. Much of

 DOCUMENT 30.5

The Charter of the Nuremberg Tribunal (1945)

The following acts, or any of them, are crimes coming within the jurisdiction of the Tribunal for which there shall be individual responsibility:

(a) **Crimes against peace.** Namely, planning, preparation, initiation, or waging of a war of aggression or a war in violation of international treaties, agreements, or assurances, or participation in a common plan or conspiracy for the accomplishment of any of the foregoing.

(b) **War crimes.** Namely, violations of the laws or customs of war. Such violations shall include, but not be limited to, murder, ill treatment, or deportation to slave labor or for any other purpose of civilian population of or in occupied territory, murder or ill treatment of prisoners of war or persons on the seas, killing of hostages, plunder of public or private property, wanton destruction of cities, towns, or villages, or devastation not justified by military necessity.

(c) **Crimes against humanity.** Namely, murder, extermination, enslavement, deportation, and other inhumane acts committed against any civilian population before or during the war or persecutions on political, racial, or religious grounds in execution of or in connection with any crime within the jurisdiction of the Tribunal, whether or not in violation of the domestic law of the country where perpetrated . . .

The fact that the defendant acted pursuant to order of his government or of a superior shall not free him from responsibility but may be considered in mitigation of punishment if the Tribunal determines that justice so requires.

historic Prussia thus became part of Poland. These conditions were imposed upon Germany without a formal treaty.

The Potsdam Protocol also stated the right of the victors to hold trials of war criminals. Similar trials had been planned after World War I, when the Allies had drawn up a list of 890 people to be tried, beginning with Kaiser Wilhelm II. But the trials begun at Leipzig

Illustration 30.11

The Nuremberg Trials. An international military tribunal sat at Nuremberg, Germany, between November 1945 and October 1946, to try twenty-two of the highest-ranking Nazi officials. Hitler, Himmler, and Goebbels all chose death rather than face such an experience. In this trial photograph, Göring (writing at left), Hess, and Ribbentrop (from left to center) listen to testimony against them.

in 1921 collapsed when the German high court accepted the exculpatory plea of individuals who were "just following orders." The Potsdam Protocol avoided this problem by chartering an Allied tribunal to sit at Nuremberg and by defining the crimes that would come before it (see document 30.5). This included "crimes against humanity" for acts committed against civilian populations. Twenty-two Nazi leaders were accordingly tried at the Nuremberg Trials of 1945–46, and twelve were sentenced to death. Hitler, Goebbels, and Himmler were all dead, but Göring and Ribbentrop were among the prominent Nazis at Nuremberg (see illustration 30.11). Others were tried in the east, and war crimes trials continued in the postwar era: Israel convicted and executed one of the architects of the Holocaust, Adolf Eichmann, in 1962; a French court convicted the Gestapo chief in Lyons (Klaus Barbie) as late as 1987, then tried a Vichy police official, Maurice Papon, in 1997. Similar trials (and informal revenge) covered the war zone. In France, eight hundred Vichy collaborationists were executed during the Liberation. The hero of World War I, Marshal Pétain, was convicted of treason for his collaboration with the Nazis; although de Gaulle spared Pétain's life in respect for his age and his historic role in World War I, Pierre Laval was executed. No court applied the Nuremburg precedent to other conflicts until 1996 when the United Na-

tions began war crimes trials for atrocities committed in the Bosnian War.

An international conference at San Francisco in 1945 adopted the Dumbarton Oaks plan and founded the United Nations, to replace the League of Nations (which had been so ineffectual in preventing World War II) and "to save succeeding generations from the scourge of war." Fifty-one countries (excluding the Axis powers) committed themselves to the idea of "collective security." The UN Charter created a General Assembly, to represent all countries and to debate international issues. Primary responsibility for keeping the peace, however, was given to a Security Council with five permanent members (the United States, the USSR, Britain, France, and China) and six elected members. The Security Council chose a secretary-general, the chief administrative officer of the UN who could bring issues to the council but had little power to act. Many UN bodies were subsequently created, beginning with an International Court of Justice. The charter of the UN had tried to launch the postwar era on a positive note after the epic tragedy of the war: "We, the peoples of the United Nations . . . reaffirm faith in fundamental human rights, in the dignity and worth of the human person." This led to the General Assembly's adoption in 1948 of the Universal Declaration of Rights, the first effort in history to state minimal human rights for the world (see document 30.6).

❖ DOCUMENT 30.6 ❖

The Universal Declaration of Human Rights, 1948

Preamble

Whereas recognition of the inherent dignity and of the equal and inalienable rights of all members of the human family in the foundation of freedom, justice, and peace in the world,

Whereas disregard and contempt for human rights have resulted in barbarous acts which have outraged the conscience of mankind. . . .

Now, therefore, the General Assembly *proclaims this universal declaration of human rights* as a common standard of achievement for all peoples and all nations. . . .

Article 1. All human beings are born free and equal in dignity and rights. They are endowed with reason and conscience and should act towards one another in a spirit of brotherhood.

Article 2. Everyone is entitled to all the rights and freedoms set forth in this Declaration, without distinction of any kind, such as race, color, sex, language, religion, political or other opinion, national or social origin, property, birth, or other status. . . .

Article 3. Everyone has the right to life, liberty and security of person.

Article 4. No one shall be held in slavery or servitude. . . .

Article 5. No one shall be subjected to torture or cruel, inhuman or degrading treatment or punishment.

Article 6. Everyone has the right to recognition everywhere as a person before the law.

Article 7. All are equal before the law and are entitled without discrimination to equal protection.

Conclusion

The statistics on people killed during World War II (see table 30.1), like those killed during World War I (see table 28.3), are mind-numbing. Perhaps fifty million people (the numbers will always remain estimates at best) met a violent death in the Second World War, more than half of them noncombatant civilians. Perhaps seventy-five million people perished as a result of the two parts of the combined Thirty Years' War. The history of this epic dance of death is no less mind-numbing if it is portrayed as individual suffering—of women raped and then disemboweled at Nanking, of London home-owners blown to bits at their dinner table, of children choking to death on poison gas at Auschwitz, or of teenaged conscripts freezing to death at Stalingrad. Whatever the amount of this suffering that the historian can assimilate, it should be sufficient to suggest that the twentieth century is the most violent century in all of human history. And it should suffice to raise doubts about the Enlightenment vision of the progress of the human race. The Second World War did demonstrate some forms of technical progress—from new instruments of destruction to a new capacity to engage all of mass society in total war—but that seems closer to the regression of the human race. At the most generous, agreement can easily

be reached with the historian who labeled the first half of the twentieth century, and especially the Second World War, the "age of catastrophe."

The origins of the war were deeply intertwined with the Peace of Paris of 1919, with the determination of some countries to revise treaties deemed unjust, and with the unwillingness of the victors of 1918 to enforce the peace that they had created. Controversial historical argument surrounds Hitler's determination to revise the Versailles Treaty—such as the justness of his claims and the extent to which other German statesmen might have behaved similarly—but whether historians condemn the peacemakers of 1919 or the aggressors of the 1930s, they cannot escape the conclusion that the Second World War grew directly out of the First World War.

The course of World War II in Europe divides into two contrasting phases. A period of Nazi conquest opened with the *Blitzkrieg* victory over Poland in 1939 and included a string of startling military successes for Germany in 1940–42. Denmark, Norway, Holland, Belgium, France, Yugoslavia, and Greece all fell to German arms with shocking speed. Only in the battle of Britain, in which RAF victories in the air prevented an invasion of the British Isles, and in the battle of the Atlantic, where American assistance aided Britain in keeping supply lines open, did Nazi arms fail to win in these early years. Then, in 1941, Adolf Hitler made two massive blunders that determined his defeat: He ordered the invasion of the Soviet Union in June 1941 and then declared war on the United States in December 1941. In the simplest terms, the Allies defeated Nazi Germany because the British won them time to win, the Russians sacrificed enough lives to win, and America had enough resources to win.

The closing experiences of World War II in 1945 left Western civilization with enormous new issues to face. The world learned in detail of the Holocaust, perhaps the most horrifying premeditated crime in history; it was an attempt to kill every single Jew in Europe, a crime so large that a new word—*genocide*—was needed to describe it. From the war, and from that final horror of it, however, came some signs of the humanity that might shape a better second half of the century. First, the Allies responded with the Nuremberg war crimes trials, firmly establishing in international law the principle of crimes against humanity and bringing to justice many Nazis who had grossly violated that principle. Second, the Allies created a stronger international association, the United Nations, and dedicated it to principles such as the Universal Declaration of Human Rights.

Suggested Readings

For overviews of the wartime era, see P. Calvocoressi, G. Wint, and J. Pritchard, *Total War: Causes and Courses of the Second World War*, 2 vols. (1990); and G. Wright, *The Ordeal of Total War, 1939–1945* (1968), a comprehensive survey in the Rise of Modern Europe series. For the Asian side of the war, supplement Wright with F. C. Jones, *Japan's New Order in East Asia: Its Rise and Fall, 1937–1945* (1954). For one-volume military histories, see B. H. Liddell Hart, *History of the Second World War* (1982); M. Byrd, *A World in Flames* (1970); G. Weinberg, *A World at Arms* (1994), a massive and up-to-date general history; and E. Hobsbawm, *The Age of Extremes* (1996), helpful for putting the war into context. W. Churchill, *The Second World War*, 6 vols. (1948–53) remains a remarkable accomplishment.

For the origins of the war, see C. Thorne, *The Approach of War, 1938–39* (1973) and P. Bell, *The Origins of the Second World War in Europe* (1986), for an introduction to the debate on war origins; A. J. P. Taylor, *The Origins of the Second World War* (1983), a controversial revisionist study; G. Martel, ed., *The "Origins of the Second World War" Reconsidered* (1986), for the debate on Taylor's interpretation; E. Jäckel, *Hitler's World View* (1981); W. Mommsen and L. Kettenacker, eds., *The Fascist Challenge and the Policy of Appeasement* (1983); W. Murray, *The Change in the European Balance of Power, 1938–39* (1984); G. Post, *Dilemmas of Appeasement* (1993); S. Aster, *1939* (1973); A. Adamthwaite, *France and the Coming of the Second World War, 1936–1939* (1977); R. Young, *In Command of France* (1978); G. Weinberg, *The Foreign Policy of Hitler's Germany*, 2 vols.

(1970–80); M. Cowling, *The Impact of Hitler: British Politics and British Policy* (1975); J. Haslam, *Soviet Foreign Policy*, 2 vols. (1983–84); and W. Langer and S. E. Gleason, *The World Crisis and American Foreign Policy*, 2 vols. (1953–54).

For individual crises and events, see A. Cassels, *Mussolini's Early Diplomacy* (1970), G. Baer, *The Coming of the Italian-Ethiopian War* (1967), A. Del Boca, *The Ethiopian War, 1935–1941* (1965), J. Emmerson, *The Rhineland Crisis* (1977), A. Low, *The Anschluss Movement, 1931–1938* (1985), T. Taylor, *Munich: the Price of Peace* (1979), M. Toscano, *The Origins of the Pact of Steel* (1967), E. Wiskemann, *The Rome-Berlin Axis* (1969), and A. Read and D. Fisher, *The Deadly Embrace: Hitler, Stalin and the Nazi-Soviet Pact, 1939–1941* (1988).

For prewar military readiness, see D. C. Watt, *Too Serious a Business* (1975), R. Young, *In Command of France* (1978), B. Bond, *British Military Policy between Two World Wars* (1980), E. Bennet, *German Rearmament and the West, 1932–1933* (1979), W. Deist and others, *The Build-Up of German Aggression* (1990), and B. Posen, *The Sources of Military Doctrine: France, Britain, and Germany between the World Wars* (1984).

For the early campaigns, see K. Meier and others, *Germany's Initial Conquests* (1991); and N. Rich, *Hitler's War Aims* (1974), the best study of Germany in the war. For the fall of France in 1940 and the Vichy Regime, see M. Bloch, *Strange Defeat* (1949), B. Bond, *France and Belgium, 1939–1940* (1975), R. Paxton, *Vichy France* (1982), B. Gordon, *Collaborationism in France during the Second World War* (1980), and J. Sweets, *Choices in Vichy France: The French under Nazi Occupation* (1986). For Italy during the war, see F. Deakin, *The Brutal Friendship* (1962) and M. Knox, *Mussolini Unleashed, 1939–1941* (1982). For the eastern front, see J. Erickson, *The Road to Stalingrad* (1984) and *The Road to Berlin* (1983), A. Seaton, *The Russo-German War, 1941–1945* (1990), A. Dallin, *German Rule in Russia, 1941–1945* (1981), and S. Linz, ed., *The Impact of World War II on the Soviet Union* (1985). For resistance movements, see H. Michel, *The Shadow War* (1972), H. R. Kedward, *Resistance in Vichy France* (1978), and T. Judt, ed., *Resistance and Revolution in Mediterranean Europe* (1989). For other help on the home front and economic histories of the war, see A. Milward, *War, Economy, and Society, 1939–1945* (1977), and J. Barber and M. Harrison, *The Soviet Home Front, 1941–1945* (1991).

For the Holocaust, see M. Marrus, *The Holocaust in History* (1987); R. Hilberg, *The Destruction of the European Jews* (1961); H. Friedlander and S. Milton, eds., *The Holocaust* (1980); P. Hayes, ed., *Lessons and Legacies: The Meaning of the Holocaust in a Changing World* (1991); R. Breitman, *The Architect of Genocide: Himmler and the Final Solution* (1991); and M. Gilbert, *Auschwitz and the Allies* (1981), on the west and the Holocaust.

For wartime diplomacy and the conferences, see J. Snell, *Illusion and Necessity* (1970), the best introduction to the diplomacy of 1939–45; W. Kimball, *The Juggler* (1991), on Roosevelt; D. Clemens, *Yalta* (1970); and H. Feis, *Churchill, Roosevelt, and Stalin: The War They Waged and the Peace They Sought* (1967) and *Between War and Peace* (1960), on the Potsdam conference.

For the United Nations, see R. Hilderbrand, *Dumbarton Oaks: The Origins of the United Nations and the Search for Postwar Security* (1990) and L. Goodrich, *The United Nations in a Changing World* (1974).

CHAPTER 31

THE SOCIAL AND ECONOMIC STRUCTURE OF CONTEMPORARY EUROPE

CHAPTER OUTLINE

◆◆◆◆◆◆◆◆◆◆◆◆◆◆◆◆◆◆◆◆◆◆◆

The twentieth century opened with both the economic structures and the social structures of Europe in the middle of a continuing historic change. Chapter 31 surveys these momentous changes, beginning with a study of the population of Europe—one of the most important indicators of socioeconomic change since the middle of the eighteenth century. The chapter shows how the population growth of the previous two centuries continued but slowed greatly by the end of the twentieth century. It also looks at continuing urbanization, a trend that made Europe a predominantly urban civilization but slowed in comparison to the rest of the world. The study of population also explains how Europe changed from a society that lost millions of emigrants in 1900 to a society attracting millions of immigrants in the second half of the century.

The twentieth century began with a mixed economy of agriculture and industry, in which industrialization was the dominant trend. Agriculture steadily shrank as a segment of the European economy until it employed less than 10 percent of the population of western Europe at the end of the century. The triumph of the industrial economy did not last long, however, as a third sector of the economy—the service sector—became dominant. The chapter traces some of the implications of these changes, such as the shifting role of the young, the elderly, and women in the economy.

Chapter 31 concludes with a look at social changes in twentieth-century Europe. It explains how the vital revolution of modern history accelerated, reducing the mortality rate so much that the average life expectancy of Europeans grew from forty-five years in 1900 to seventy-five years in 1990. It also examines changes in the family, such as earlier marriage, smaller family size, and divorce. To explain these changes, the chapter considers the controversial history of birth control and abortion.

TABLE 31.1
The Growth of European Population, 1700–1990

Country	Estimated population in 1700 (in millions)	Census population c. 1900 (in millions)	Census population c. 1990 (in millions)	Approximate growth 1700–1990 (in percent)
France	19.3	38.5	57.7	199
Germany	13.5	56.4	81.1	500
Italy	13.0	32.5	57.8	345
Spain	7.5	18.6	39.1	421
Britain	6.4	37.0	58.0	806
Ireland	2.5	4.5	3.6	44
Netherlands	1.9	5.1	15.2	700
Russia	16.0	126.4	149.0	
Sweden	1.5	5.1	8.7	
Europe	110	423	501	355

The Population of Twentieth-Century Europe

At the beginning of the modern era in the early eighteenth century, Europe had an estimated population of slightly more than 100 million persons. By the late twentieth century, Europe numbered more than 500 million inhabitants—approximately twice the population of the United States. Most of that population growth came during the population explosion that began in the mid-eighteenth century and continued during the nineteenth century. In 1900 the population of Europe stood at 423 million, meaning that three-fourths of Europe's modern growth had occurred before the twentieth century and the rate of growth was leveling (see table 31.1). At the end of the twentieth century, the rate of growth began to drop sharply, although the full impact of that trend will not be seen until the early twenty-first century (because demographic totals are often seen a generation after the start of a trend).

The population history of the major states of Europe underscores modern political history. In 1700 France possessed a great demographic advantage over all of its rivals in western and central Europe; France was nearly 50 percent larger than all German states added together and three times as populous as Great

Britain. By the start of the twentieth century, France had less than three-fourths of the population of unified Germany and approximately the same population as Britain. The population explosion had quadrupled Germany and quintupled Britain while not quite doubling the population of France. European population growth slowed significantly during the twentieth century, and a new balance emerged: The reunified Germany of 1990 remains the largest state in the European Union (EU) with a population of eighty-one million; Britain, France, and Italy each number approximately fifty-eight million, slightly more than 70 percent of the size of Germany. In the 1980s and 1990s, however, birthrates in Europe fell precipitously—which demographers are calling a "baby bust"—meaning that these relationships will be changed in the early twenty-first century. The birthrate in Germany dropped below a level that would sustain the same population total (demographers use a rate of 2.1 children per woman), so Germany is expected to be smaller in 2025 than in 2000, whereas France will grow slightly. Such trends raise complex questions about the balance of power within Europe and the continued preeminence of Europe as a center of world power. (Will smaller populations be an advantage or a disadvantage?)

The European population explosion of the eighteenth and nineteenth centuries shaped the important trend of urbanization. During the eighteenth century,

Illustration 31.1

⟋⟋ **Urbanization.** The concentration of population in large metropolitan regions, which had begun in late eighteenth-century Britain and had characterized many regions in the nineteenth century, continued throughout the twentieth century. At the start of the century, Europe contained half a dozen congested cities of more than one million population. This 1910 photograph of central London shows what *congested* meant before the automobile dominated cities.

all of Europe had been a predominantly rural society, with the vast majority of the population living on farms and in small villages. By 1850 Britain had become the first country in history to have the majority of its population living in cities. Although much of Europe still remained rural in 1900, nineteenth-century Europe had become an urban civilization. Population migration from agricultural communities had made London and Paris the largest cities on Earth, and it had created dozens of large cities from small towns (see illustration 31.1).

The twentieth century has seen the trend toward urbanization continue. By 1950 the majority of the population of western and central Europe lived in cities. Metropolitan Paris (the region containing the city and its suburbs) has nearly quadrupled in size during the twentieth century, growing from 2.3 million people in 1900 to 8.7 million in 1991. Yet Paris is far from the most dramatic example. Metropolitan Milan, the industrial capital of Italy, has grown nearly tenfold, from 493,000 in 1900 to 4.7 million in 1991; Moscow, center of the vast post–World War II communist empire, went from less than 1 million to more than 10 million; and the center of German industrialization, the urban conglomeration around Essen, changed from a large town of 119,000 people into the fourth largest urban area in Europe at 7.5 million people (see table 31.2).

Despite the dramatic urbanization of twentieth-century Europe seen in these figures, European growth is moderate compared with the global trend. No longer are London and Paris the largest cities on Earth; London ranked seventeenth in 1991, Paris nineteenth.

Tokyo, Mexico City, São Paulo, and Seoul are nearly twice the size of London or Paris. No European city (and only one American city, New York) ranks in the world's ten largest cities. In many ways, the European city most representative of global trends is Athens, which has exploded from a national capital of 111,000 people in 1900 to a rambling metropolitan region of 3.7 million in 1991, nearly 50 percent of the total Greek population. (By comparison, Paris contains barely 15 percent of the population of France.)

Twentieth-century European urbanization, like so many historic patterns, has not been the same in western and eastern Europe. On the eve of World War II, the population of Romania was still 82 percent rural, a figure more typical of the eighteenth century in western or central Europe (see table 27.3). As late as 1970, Yugoslavia and Albania remained less than 40 percent urban, Hungary and Romania less than 50 percent. Even in 1985 Albania, Yugoslavia, and Romania were still less than 50 percent urban (see table 31.3).

Urbanization has not been the only important trend in European population migration. The twentieth century began with Europe losing millions of people through emigration to other parts of the world. Between 1871 and 1914, Sweden lost 1.5 million emigrants—chiefly to the United States—which accounted for more than one-third of the population of Sweden in 1870. Spain and Portugal lost 1.4 million from 1901 to 1914, approximately 6 percent of their 1900 population. Over that same time period, more than 3.2 million people (chiefly Irish) left Great Britain; the richest state in the world lost nearly 8 percent of its

☙ TABLE 31.2 ☙

The Growth of European Cities, 1900–91

The data reflect the total metropolitan region.

City	1991 world ranking	1991 population (in millions)	1900 population	1991 population density per square mile
Moscow	11	10.4	989,000	27,562
London	17	9.8	6,600,000	10,429
Paris	19	8.7	2,300,000	20,185
Essen	22	7.5	119,000	10,585
Milan	38	4.7	493,000	13,806
St. Petersburg	39	4.7	1,300,000	33,614
Madrid	40	4.5	540,000	68,385
Barcelona	44	4.2	533,000	48,584
Manchester	50	3.8	645,000	11,287
Athens	59	3.5	111,000	30,237
Rome	68	3.0	463,000	43,949
Berlin	69	3.0	1,889,000	11,026
Naples	70	3.0	564,000	48,032
Kiev	79	2.8	247,000	45,095
Lisbon	87	2.4	356,000	n.a.
Vienna	91	2.3	1,700,000	n.a.
Budapest	93	2.3	732,000	16,691

Source: All 1991 data from U.S. Department of Commerce calculations, reprinted in *The World Almanac and Book of Facts 1993* (Mahwah, N.J.: World Almanac Books, 1992), p. 818; all 1900 data from B. R. Mitchell, *European Historical Statistics, 1750–1970* (London: Macmillan, 1975), pp. 76–78.

n.a. = Not available.

☙ TABLE 31.3 ☙

The Slow Urbanization of Eastern Europe

Country	Percentage of urban population in 1970	Percentage of urban population in 1985
Albania	33.8	34.4
Bulgaria	52.3	65.2
Czechoslovakia	55.5	74.1
East Germany	73.6	76.6
Hungary	46.9	58.3
Poland	52.3	60.1
Romania	40.8	49.2
USSR	56.3	65.4
Yugoslavia	38.6	46.1

Source: United Nations, *Demographic Yearbook, 1973* and *1985* (New York: 1973 and 1985), passim.

1901 population to emigration. More than 2 million people (chiefly Jews) fled Russia during the revolution of 1905 and its aftermath. Italian population loss was perhaps the most striking. In the early 1880s Italy lost a million people every five years; by the early 1890s Italy was losing a million people every three years; and in the first decade of the twentieth century, a million more people left Italy every eighteen months. By 1913 the rate of Italian exiles had reached nearly 900,000 per year. This meant that Italy was losing 2.5 percent of its total population every year, roughly the equivalent to losing the entire population of Rome (542,000), Venice (161,000), and Florence (135,000) annually.

The twentieth century thus began with Europe losing an average of 1.3 million people per year. Some fled to avoid religious persecution, others fled to avoid conscription into monarchical armies, but most of these emigrants left Europe for greater economic opportunities. Millions of Europeans lived in such hopeless poverty in 1900 that flight to the Americas, Australia,

Illustration 31.2

Immigration. The racial composition of Europe changed significantly after World War II due to immigration from colonial empires. In this illustration, three immigrants into Britain study government entry forms on their arrival at Southampton.

or the scattered corners of European empires was preferable to hunger at home. World War I nearly stopped European emigration, and in the 1920s many states (led by the United States) adopted much stricter policies on accepting immigrants. Although European emigration increased during some twentieth-century crises—especially Germans during the 1930s and many European nations in the decade following World War II—by the end of the century, Europe's migration pattern had completely reversed the pattern of 1900. Millions of non-Europeans sought to immigrate to Europe because economic opportunity was much greater there (plus smaller minorities were fleeing persecution for religious or political beliefs).

Much of the late twentieth-century immigration into Europe has its origins in the history of European colonial empires and in the age of decolonization that followed World War II. The end of empire forced imperialist governments to reintegrate European-born colonists and their descendants; the Franco-Algerian War of 1954–62, for example, led more than one million *pieds noirs* (French colonists in Algeria) to return to France in the 1960s. In many cases, the indigenous population of European colonies had the legal right to migrate to the imperial state or had legal preference in normal immigration. For example, after the islands of the Dutch East Indies won their independence as Indonesia in 1949, the Netherlands absorbed 300,000 immigrants (mostly Asian-born) from their former colony. The independence of the *maghreb* (the Arabic term for north Africa—Morocco, Algeria, and Tunisia) from France resulted in an influx of millions of north Africans

starting in the late 1960s and peaking in the 1980s. The collapse of the Portuguese African Empire in the 1970s brought another 750,000 Africans to Europe. Until strict—and often racially motivated—immigration controls were adopted by Britain in mid-1962, hundreds of thousands of south Asians (chiefly from India and Pakistan) and blacks from the West Indies migrated to Britain (see table 31.4 and illustration 31.2). These migrations of non-Europeans into Europe reversed long-standing patterns of population movement; in the case of Britain, for example, the largest group of immigrants had remained Irish through the 1950s and the 1960s.

France provides a dramatic illustration of this transformation of European population. By 1982 immigrants formed nearly 7 percent of the population of France; counting the families of immigrant workers, France was more than 8 percent immigrant. At the start of the twentieth century, less than 3 percent of the population of France was foreign-born, and nearly 90 percent of the immigrants came from Europe—nearly two-thirds of the total being Belgians and Italians who found work across the border. By the end of the century, immigration had quadrupled and most French immigrants were non-Europeans. Algerians (22 percent), Moroccans (12 percent), and nearly half of all French immigrants came from Africa; meanwhile, Italian and Belgian immigration into France fell to less than one-sixth of its early twentieth-century rate. The wars and revolutions of twentieth-century Europe also shifted millions of people across national frontiers, such as the repatriation of 1.2 million Greeks from Turkey after World War I, the migration of 200,000 Magyars from Transylvania to

TABLE 31.4
Commonwealth Immigration into Britain

Annual net commonwealth immigration

Year	West Indies	India	Pakistan and Bangladesh
1960	49,700	5,900	2,500
1961	66,300	23,750	25,100
1962	35,041	22,100	24,943
January–June	31,800	19,050	25,080
July–December	3,241	3,050	−137
1972	1,176	3,634	−3,515

Source: Adapted from data in David Butler and Anne Sloman, eds., *British Political Facts, 1900–1975,*4th ed. (London: Macmillan, 1975), p. 268.

Hungary in the 1920s, or the flight and expulsion of nearly 7.5 million Germans from Eastern Europe after World War II. But none of these migrations changed Europe as profoundly as the arrival of millions of non-Europeans as a result of decolonization.

Another important form of population migration accompanied European prosperity in the late twentieth century. The United Nations estimated in 1973 that the population of the European Common Market states plus Austria, Norway, Sweden, and Switzerland included 7.5 million foreign workers. West Germany, for example, held 2.6 million "guest workers" (*Gastarbeiter*) who constituted 12 percent of the German labor force. Nearly 20 percent of those workers came from Turkey, a figure that surpassed one-third by the late 1980s. The Turkish population of Germany passed two million in the 1990s. Although their guest-worker status (and an extremely strict German citizenship law of 1913) denied them the rights of immigrants, a study in 1977 found that one-fourth of all German guest workers had resided there for at least a decade. The foreign-born population of Germany again increased dramatically after the collapse of the Soviet bloc in 1989. Tens of thousands of ethnic Germans returned (claiming citizenship under the 1913 law), hundreds of thousands of refugees arrived (for example, 320,000 Bosnians fled the Yugoslav War), and tens of thousands of Soviet Jews were granted residence. These population trends, combined with the strict laws and a plummeting German birthrate, have combined in the late 1990s to create a situation in which more than 20 percent of the babies born in Germany are born to non-Germans.

The immigration trends of the late twentieth century have led to tense political situations in many European countries. Most European states have defined their identity in images shaped by nineteenth-century nationalism: A shared language, religion, culture, and history created a nation-state. Many states are slowly confronting a new reality of cultural diversity.

Illustration 31.3

The Persistence of Agricultural Society. Although the nineteenth century had been an age of industrialization and urbanization, at the start of the twentieth century much of Europe—such as this Russian village, photographed in 1910—remained a traditional agricultural society, little different from what it had been under the Old Regime of the eighteenth century. Nineteenth-century modernization was unevenly distributed (heavily concentrated in the west) and had significant pockets of the old society persisting in most countries.

⋈ TABLE 31.5 ⋈

The Persistence of Agricultural Society in 1900

Country	Year	Percentage employed in agriculture	Percentage employed in industry
Austria	1910	53.1	22.6
Britain	1901	9.1	51.2
France	1906	42.7	30.2
Germany	1907	37.8	43.0
European Russia	1897	74.9	9.7

Source: Combines data from Jerome Blum, *The End of the Old Order in Rural Europe* (Princeton, N.J.: Princeton University Press, 1979), p. 419, and B. R. Mitchell, *European Historical Statistics, 1750–1970* (London: Macmillan, 1975), p. 163.

Note: British data exclude Ireland.

⋈ TABLE 31.6 ⋈

The Decline of Agricultural Employment, 1920–60

	Percentage of labor force engaged in agriculture		
Country	c. 1910–11:	c. 1930–31:	c. 1960–61:
Austria	53.1	31.7	18.4
Britain	8.6	6.0	3.6
France	41.0	35.6	20.0
Germany	37.8	29.0	13.4 (West)
			17.4 (East)
Ireland	42.9	25.3 (Northern)	13.0 (Northern)
		52.1 (republic)	48.6 (republic)
Italy	55.4	35.5	29.0
Russia			23.5

Source: Calculated from tables in B. R. Mitchell, *European Historical Statistics, 1750–1970* (London: Macmillan, 1975), pp. 153–63.

Economic Structures: The Decline of Agriculture

Agriculture dominated the economy of eighteenth-century Europe but began to lose that preeminence during the industrialization and urbanization that spread rapidly after the late eighteenth century. Nineteenth-century European economic history is correctly characterized by this industrialization, which transformed western and central Europe. The vast industrial output of late nineteenth-century Europe, however, should not obscure the persistence of agricultural society. Just as the European political history of 1900 depicts the progress of democracy as well as the persistence of monarchical government and aristocratic privilege, the European economic history of 1900 must show the progress of industry alongside a surviving agricultural society. In Eastern Europe, where industrialization had not yet advanced greatly, the huge majority of the population was still engaged in agriculture (see illustration 31.3). In France, a major industrial power, less than one-third of the labor force worked in industrial occupations. Even Germany, the greatest industrial powerhouse of the continent, had less than half of its population engaged in the industrial workforce; only the British labor force showed the strong dominance of industry (see table 31.5).

Despite the noteworthy strength of agricultural society at the beginning of the twentieth century, a trend was clear: Agriculture was steadily losing its dominance of Europe's economy, employing fewer people, producing a smaller share of the gross national product (GNP). On the eve of the First World War, many major states, including Austria and Italy, still found the majority of their population on the farm (see table 31.6). By 1930 comparatively few regions—such as Ireland, eastern Europe, and the Balkans—still had such rural economies. Some of those areas remained strongly agricultural long after World War II. In Ireland, nearly 50 percent of the population was engaged in agriculture as late as 1960, but the European trend was clear: In Russia, where 75 percent of the population had been employed in agriculture at the beginning of the century, less than 25 percent were employed there by 1960; in Britain, a scant 3.6 percent of the population lived by agriculture in 1960. Not only were fewer people being employed in agriculture, but the area being cultivated was also becoming smaller. In 1913 nearly forty-five million hectares were cultivated in western Europe; that number declined during each decade of the twentieth century and by 1981 it had fallen to less than thirty-eight million hectares.

Although agriculture was no longer at the center of the European economy and employed comparatively few people, late twentieth-century European agriculture was neither weak nor unimportant. In France, where the agricultural economy was especially persistent, peasant farmers still formed 35 percent of the labor force at the end of World War II, declining to 13

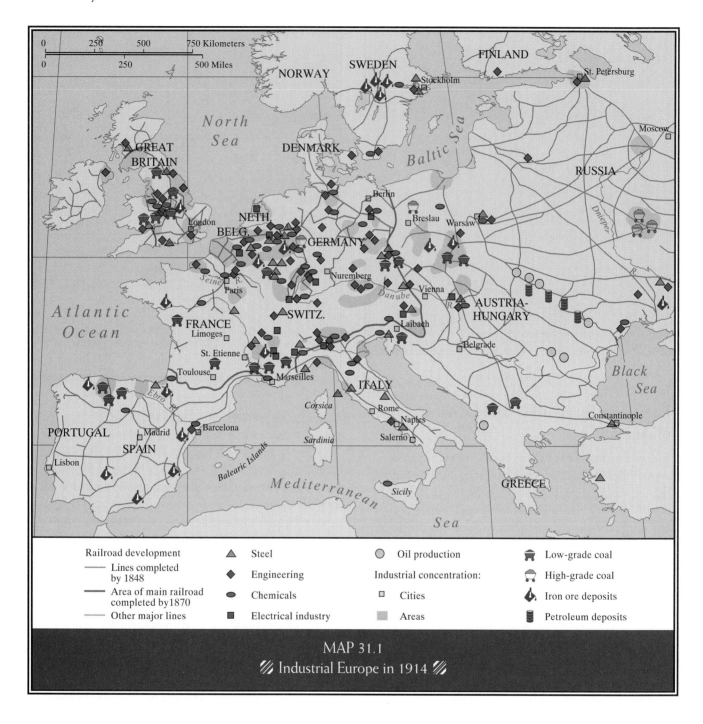

Railroad development
— Lines completed
by 1848
— Area of main railroad
completed by 1870
— Other major lines

△ Steel
◆ Engineering
⬭ Chemicals
■ Electrical industry

◯ Oil production
Industrial concentration:
▫ Cities
▨ Areas

Low-grade coal
High-grade coal
Iron ore deposits
Petroleum deposits

MAP 31.1
▨ Industrial Europe in 1914 ▨

percent in 1970 and to 8 percent in 1980. Three million people left French farming between 1945 and 1980, but French agricultural production increased during that period, because of modern machinery and farming methods. When 35 percent of the French labor force was engaged in farming, fewer than 30,000 tractors were in use; by 1967, there were more than 1.1 million. With less than 10 percent of the population engaged in agriculture in the 1980s, France was nonetheless the second largest food exporter in the world.

Continuing Industrialization

The decline of an agriculture-dominated economy in twentieth-century Europe corresponded to continuing industrialization. Most of Europe was highly industrialized by the late twentieth century, even if compared with the most advanced economies of 1900. In 1980, for example, industrial output in Czechoslovakia, Poland, or Spain far exceeded the British standard of 1900; Italian output more than tripled that standard, while West Germany and the Soviet Union vastly ex-

▶ TABLE 31.7 ◀

The Growth of European Industrial Output, 1913–80

	Percentage of British industrial output in 1900					
Country	1913	1928	1938	1953	1963	1980
Britain	127	135	181	258	330	441
France	57	82	74	98	194	362
Germany	138	158	214	224	416	747
West Germany				180	330	590
East Germany				44	86	157
Italy	23	37	46	71	150	319
Poland	a	16	19	31	66	169
Spain	11	16	14	22	43	156
Sweden	9	12	21	28	48	83
Soviet Union	n.a.	72	152	328	760	1630

Source: Adapted from data in Paul Bairoch, "International Industrialization Levels from 1750 to 1980," *Journal of European Economic History*, 11 (1982), pp. 299, 331; and Gerold Ambrosius and William H. Hubbard, *A Social and Economic History of Twentieth Century Europe* (Cambridge, Mass.: Harvard University Press, 1989), p. 187.

n.a. = Not available

ªDid not exist as an independent country.

ceeded it. Even countries with a small population base—such as Belgium, the Netherlands, or Sweden—had an industrial output in 1980 near to the German or British output of 1900.

The data on industrialization also reveal the strength of the European great powers. The British, who had the dominant economy of 1900 (see map 31.1), continued to expand their industrial output during the twentieth century despite the century's multiple catastrophes. British industrialization increased by 27 percent from 1900 to the eve of World War I; by more than one-third from 1900 to 1928, despite the consequences of World War I; by more than three-fourths from 1900 to 1938, despite the Great Depression of the 1930s; by more than double between 1900 and 1953, despite World War II; and by more than fourfold by the late twentieth century. Germany, which had been challenging British leadership in 1900, surpassed British output before World War I and remained the dominant industrial economy in Europe until World War II. Although the divided and devastated Germany fell behind in the years following World War II, by 1963 West German industrial output matched the British and within a decade far exceeded it; and the combined output of West and East Germany in the 1980s ap-

proached double British production. France, whose industrial output had never approached British levels during the nineteenth century, and whose economic strength rested on a strong combination of agriculture and industry, did not reach the Anglo-German levels of 1900 until the mid-1950s. A French industrial resurgence after 1960, however, brought France close to British levels: French industrial output had stood at 45 percent of British output at the beginning of World War I and 41 percent of British output at the beginning of World War II, but it grew to reach 82 percent of British output in 1980. Italy achieved a comparable industrial boom in the second half of the twentieth century, expanding from 18 percent of Britain's production in 1913 to 72 percent in 1980. In the same years, Spain made similar progress from 9 percent to 35 percent of the British level. Put differently, Britain had begun the nineteenth century with a dominant lead in European industrial production, and then Britain and Germany had begun the twentieth century with such dominance, but by the end of the twentieth century, many European states had industrialized to competitive levels with Britain and Germany (see table 31.7).

Industrial output data also underscore the greatest change in European political and military power during the twentieth century: the rising dominance of the Soviet Union. Imperial Russian industrialization had been meager before World War I; in the late 1920s the USSR still managed only 53 percent of British output, or 46 percent of German output. Before the death of Stalin in 1953, however, the Soviet Union had significantly surpassed the industrial production of either Britain or West Germany; by 1963 Soviet output was more than Britain and Germany combined, and by 1980 it nearly equaled Britain, Germany, France, and Italy combined.

Similar economic data provide a different perspective if historians seek to illustrate the standard of living instead of political and military power. Combining agricultural and industrial output into a figure for gross national product and then considering population to determine the GNP per capita, neither the Soviet Union nor the west European powers can match the accomplishment of Sweden. Although the Swedes had only 52 percent of the per capita GNP in Britain at the start of the twentieth century, they had surpassed the British by 1950 (partly by avoiding participation in the world wars) and had become 20 percent more prosperous than Britain and 17 percent more prosperous than West Germany in 1980.

The economic evolution of the twentieth century also requires a global perspective on European industrial might. On the eve of World War I, nearly 58 percent of the world's total industrial production came from Europe, with Britain holding a global share of 14 percent and Germany 15 percent. Europe still produced more than 50 percent of the world's industrial output on the eve of World War II. By 1980 European production had fallen to 44 percent, and Japanese production (9.1 percent) nearly equaled British (4.0 percent) and German production (5.3 percent) combined. The United States, which represented 32 percent of global production in 1913, still accounted for 31.5 percent in 1980, although that stable share is distorted by the post–World War II rise to nearly 45 percent of global production (1953) while Europe had still not recovered from wartime devastation. As the economies of East Asia grew during the 1980s and 1990s, the American and European share of global production declined.

The relative decline in European industrial output in the late twentieth century raises several related issues. The European economy came to be dominated by a new sector, neither industrial nor agricultural. In the course of this transition to a postindustrial economy, Europe (and the United States) deindustrialized their economies to a significant degree, allowing uncompeti-

tive industries to close and many forms of traditional industrial production to go overseas (especially to Asian countries) where production costs (especially labor) were much lower. By the 1990s many industrial and manufacturing sectors (including such traditional measures of economic might as steel and textiles) existed in which Western countries could import goods cheaper than manufacturing them. No image of the European economy of 2000 would have been more startling to Europeans of 1900 than the contrast between the powerful look of the smokestacks of heavy industry and the stark reality of deindustrialization (see illustration 31.4).

The Service Economy

By the end of the nineteenth century, the focus on industrial production no longer presented a complete picture of European economies and social structures. A third sector of the economy had emerged, and by the second half of the twentieth century it had grown to be as important as industrial employment. By 1980 this third sector, called the service sector, dominated the economy of Western Europe (see table 31.8). In 1910 industry employed 41 percent of the population to 30 percent for agriculture. In 1980 the service economy employed 55 percent of the labor force of Western Europe while industry had declined to 39 percent and agriculture took only 6 percent. In 1910 Europeans had expected a continually expanding industrialization; in 1980 Europe had a postindustrial economy. In Eastern Europe, however, the twentieth century witnessed industrialization, not deindustrialization: Economies that had been 75 percent to 85 percent agricultural in 1910 became 40 percent to 50 percent industrial by the 1980s. The service sector did not dominate any East European economy at the time of the revolutions of 1989, although East Germany (41 percent service to 49 percent industry) and Czechoslovakia (41 percent service to 48 percent industry) were drawing close.

The service sector, also called the tertiary sector, had always existed; it had chiefly been a relatively small, but necessary, companion to the industrial economy. The simplest distinction between industrial employment and service employment is that the former produces material goods and the latter produces customer services. Industrial employment includes most jobs in fields such as manufacturing, heavy industry, mining, construction, and energy. It is typically manual labor—blue-collar work—paid by hourly or daily wages. The service sector has long included such

Illustration 31.4

⧄ **The Industrial Economy.** At the beginning of the twentieth century, heavy industry was the source of a nation's power and wealth. This view (above) of the Krupp Works at Essen in 1912 was a fair representation of the great strength of the German economy, and the dream of the future for less developed economies.

At the end of the twentieth century, heavy industry was in sharp decline throughout the Western world, and many of the old centers of industrial and manufacturing wealth had experienced the shock of deindustrialization and unemployment. This image (left) of late twentieth-century deindustrialization shows Bristol in the 1960s.

smaller categories as banking and insurance, commerce and trade, journalism and modern communications, and a growing list of public employees. Employment in the service sector often requires more education and rarely requires physical labor; it is usually white-collar work performed in offices (see illustration 31.5). Service em-

ployees typically (but not universally) receive an annual or monthly salary, however many hours they work, frequently adding up to better total compensation.

One of the areas of most rapid growth in the service economy of the twentieth century has been government employment. This category is much larger

❈ TABLE 31.8 ❈

The Socioeconomic Structure of Twentieth-Century Europe

Country	Percentage of working population														
	1910			1930			1950			1960			1980		
	Ag.	Ind.	Ser.	Ag.	Ind.	Ser.	Ag.	Ind.	Ser.	Ag.	Ind.	Ser.	Ag.	Ind.	Ser.
Austria	32	33	35	32	33	35	33	37	30	24	46	30	9	37	54
Britain	9	52	40	6	46	48	5	49	46	4	48	48	3	42	56
France	41	33	26	36	33	31	27	36	37	22	39	39	8	39	53
Germany	37	41	22	29	40	31	23	43	38	14	48	38	4	46	50
Greece	50	16	34	54	16	30	51	21	28	56	20	24	37	28	35
Ireland	51	15	34	48	16	36	40	24	35	36	25	40	18	37	45
Italy	55	27	18	47	31	22	42	32	26	31	40	29	11	45	44
Poland	77	9	14	66	17	17	54	26	20	48	29	23	31	39	30
Spain	56	14	30	n.a.	n.a.	n.a.	50	26	25	42	31	27	14	40	46
Sweden	49	32	19	39	36	25	21	41	38	14	45	41	5	34	61
Yugoslavia	82	11	7	78	11	11	71	16	13	63	18	19	29	35	36

Note: Data for Austria, Greece, Ireland, Poland, and Yugoslavia for 1910 are post–World War I data, c. 1920. Data for Germany for 1950, 1960, and 1980 are for West Germany only.

n.a. = Not available.

Ag. = Agriculture; Ind. = Industry; Ser. = Service.

than the image of anonymous bureaucrats filling the offices of a national capital. Millions of public school teachers or postal workers are also employees of the tertiary sector. The French Ministry of Education employed 121,000 people in 1896 and more than 1 million people in 1984; in the same years, the French Ministry of Posts grew from 70,000 workers to 513,000. Thus, in a century during which the population of France increased by less than 44 percent, employees in one ministry increased by 768 percent and in another by 639 percent. Government policing, the judicial system, and—a natural consequence of taxing to finance all of the others—the Ministry of Finance also grew much faster than population did.

The service sector was already an important part of the European economy at the start of the twentieth century, but it was clearly tertiary. In 1910, for example, 41 percent of German labor was employed in industry, 37 percent in agriculture, and 22 percent in service. The service sector accounted for 26 percent of employment in France and only 18 percent of employment in Italy that year. European employment data for 1930 show that different economies coexisted in Europe: Poland remained a traditional, rural economy with 66 percent of the population employed in agriculture; Germany remained a strongly industrial economy, with 40 percent of employment there, 29 percent in agriculture, and 31 percent in service; Britain revealed the emerging pattern of the twentieth-century economy with only 6 percent of labor in agriculture and slightly more workers in the service sector (48 percent) than the industrial (46 percent).

The growth of the tertiary economy chiefly occurred after World War II. By 1980, 61 percent of all workers in Sweden were in the service sector. More than 50 percent of employment in Britain, France, and Germany were in service. Meanwhile agricultural employment had fallen to less than 10 percent of the labor force in Britain (3 percent), Germany (4 percent), Sweden (5 percent), France (8 percent), and Austria (9 percent). Thus, industrial employment still remained important in all European economies, but nowhere did it account for a majority of the labor force, as it had in Britain in 1910 (52 percent). In some economies, industrial employment was declining: In Britain it fell from 49 percent in 1950 to 42 percent in 1980; in Sweden, from 45 percent in 1960 to 34 percent in 1980.

Illustration 31.5

The Service Economy. The biggest change in Western economies during the twentieth century was the growth of a third sector of the economy, neither agricultural nor industrial, which became the dominant sector of European economies after World War II. This service economy depicted itself—as in this photograph from the early days of the computer revolution in the 1960s—as the modern and efficient sector of the economy, as compared with the smoke-stack economy of heavy industry and large factories. (Note that men work with the office computer at this date.)

In 1967 the French director Jacques Tati made a film (part of the service economy) about the cold, impersonal nature of life in the service economy. The story of *Playtime* involves visitors to Paris who see only the business and office world, encountering the beautiful, historic Paris only through pictures on post cards. In this scene, Tati makes fun of the impersonal, labyrinthine office of cubicles.

Age, Gender, and the Labor Force

Economists who study the economic vitality of a society use an index called the participation rate to measure the volume and distribution of labor in an economy. Changes in the components of the participation rate tell historians much about a changing society. The total participation rate merely counts all employed persons plus all part-time workers, expressed as a percentage of the population. As a healthy economy grows, so does the participation rate. This simple index provides economic historians with a long perspective on the twentieth century. In 1900 Europe had experienced a generation of internal peace and had a generally solid economy; the participation rate was high. Between 1910 and 1950 Europe was devastated by multiple catastrophes—World War I, the Russian Revolution, the

Great Depression, the Spanish Civil War, World War II, the Holocaust—and European economies suffered terribly. The internal peace of the cold war and the economic miracle between 1950 and the Revolutions of 1989, however, overcame the catastrophes of the first half of the century to build a stronger economy. Economists claim that the prosperity of 1990 rests on a stronger economy than the prosperity of 1910 by showing that the participation rate had grown, despite the collapse of 1910–50, and by correlating participation with productivity.

This arcane tool of economic analysis is more interesting to historians who ask "Who is participating in the economy? Who is working and who is not?" Between 1870 and 1940, for example, age became a significant factor in the changing participation rate. Compulsory education laws subtracted millions of teenagers from the labor force, thereby reducing the participation rate. The economic role of older ages has also affected the participation rate. In 1900 few programs guaranteed a paid retirement, so many people remained in the labor force beyond age sixty-five, thereby keeping the participation rate higher. Put differently, the compulsory education laws and the welfare programs of the twentieth century have sharply changed the answer to the question "Who works?"

At the same time that the economic participation rate was being reduced by new social attitudes toward age, the labor movement succeeded in its long battle to reduce the workweek. Full-time employment in 1900 typically meant a six-day, fifty-five-hour workweek; many occupations still expected sixty to seventy-two hours per week. When European countries began to regulate the workweek, standards set in the 1920s were usually close to a forty-eight-hour week; only during the massive unemployment of the Great Depression of the 1930s did countries start to adopt the century-old labor dream of a forty-hour workweek. During the European prosperity of the late twentieth century, workers in many countries of the European Union (led by Belgium and Sweden) obtained workweeks of thirty-five to forty hours.

The twentieth-century labor movement also won paid vacations. Norway introduced the first paid vacations, guaranteeing all workers two weeks by a 1919 law. Several other Western countries—including Britain and France—adopted this concept in the 1930s. It became the universal standard in postwar Europe as well as the minimum standard, because France and the Scandinavian countries increased paid vacations to three weeks. After 1970 the same prosperity that allowed workweeks of less than forty hours provided minimum paid vacations of four weeks in EU countries, while the most progressive granted five or six weeks.

The consequence of this century of transforming traditional labor was to cut both its participation rate and its productivity rate. Economic historians estimate that the annual total number of hours worked by each individual worker has been cut in half. Despite all the changes that achieved this—won by the young, the elderly, and the labor movement—other factors were so dramatic that the total participation rate and total productivity increased. One final economic trend explains this apparent paradox: the growing, and changing, employment of women.

Throughout modern history, working women have been a large and essential part of the European economy, although not always in ways that were noted in economic statistics. In the household economy of the eighteenth century, women worked alongside men in farms or shops. In the family wage economy of the industrial era, women entered the wage-earning labor force and their numbers in economic statistics grew significantly. At the start of the twentieth century, women formed 30 percent to 35 percent of the salary and wage-earning labor force in western Europe. Those percentages did not shift dramatically for most of the twentieth century, although historical circumstances sometimes caused noteworthy trends. For example, much greater employment of women was evident during both world wars and for brief postwar periods when large numbers of men were lost. (In the USSR, the death rate in World War II so reduced the postwar labor pool that women remained employed at a high rate for the entire next generation.) The employment of women sometimes fell sharply as a consequence of conservative social policy based on the theory that women belonged in the home; Mussolini, for example, managed to reduce women's share of jobs from 32 percent in 1910 to 23 percent in 1930. Despite such secondary trends, the foremost trend was that the employment of women did not significantly change between 1910 and 1970 (see table 31.9). In the first two-thirds of the century, it rose just 3 percent in Britain and 2 percent in Sweden, while falling 3 percent in France and 6 percent in Italy.

In the last third of the twentieth century, the employment of women in western Europe changed significantly. Between 1970 and 1990 women went from 32 percent of the British labor force to 44 percent; that is, the number of women employed grew by more than one-third. The growth in the employment of women

TABLE 31.9
Women in the European Labor Force, 1910–90

Country	c. 1910	c. 1930	c. 1950	c. 1970	c. 1990
	Women as a percentage of total labor force				
Britain	29.5	29.8	30.8	32.4	43.5
France	36.7	36.6	33.9	33.2	42.3
Germany	30.7	35.6	36.3	37.4	40.8
Italy	31.6	22.6	25.1	25.1	34.5
Sweden	27.8	31.0	26.4	29.8	47.8

Source: Compiled from data in B. R. Mitchell, *European Historical Statistics, 1750–1970* (London: Macmillan, 1975), pp. 153–63, and *The Information Please Almanac, Atlas, and Yearbook 1994* (Boston, Mass.: Houghton Mifflin, 1994), p. 136.

was equally dramatic in France and Italy, and it was very marked in Sweden, where women went from 30 percent of the labor force to 48 percent—meaning that the number of working women grew by more than 60 percent in one generation. This transformation of the labor market was most dramatic in regions where women previously had limited access to jobs. Women accounted for only 18 percent of the Greek labor force in 1961 and nearly doubled that share to 32 percent in a single decade. In Hungary, the employment of women nearly doubled between 1945 and 1980. Once again, the data are different for Eastern Europe. In the postwar Soviet Union, women constituted more than half of the labor force in many fields, and the figures for the employment of women declined as war deaths became less important. As late as 1960, women provided 52 percent of all labor on Soviet collective farms and produced 76 percent of all medical doctors in the USSR. A generation later, in 1987, these numbers had declined slightly to 43 percent of agricultural labor and 69 percent of physicians.

The high levels of the employment of women in the twentieth century are especially noteworthy because the two greatest job markets for women in the nineteenth century—domestic service and the textile industry—both collapsed. The role of textiles in west European industry shrank by 75 percent between 1901 and 1975. Nonetheless, the participation of women in the labor force increased, and the explanation involves several factors. The nineteenth-century and early twentieth-century economy had a limited variety of jobs available to women—typically jobs deemed similar to a

woman's role in housework, as both domestic service and textile work illustrate. Much of the explanation, therefore, is found in a new range of employment available to women. War work—demonstrating that women could effectively perform many jobs previously denied to them—was important in this trend but is insufficient to explain it, as the postwar demobilization of women suggests. The rise of the service economy was probably more important. Millions of new jobs were being created, without a tradition of being held by only one gender; so many new jobs were being created that the demand for workers virtually required the participation of women in the economy, especially in government and business offices. At the same time, demographic changes facilitated the participation of women. As the birthrate fell sharply, women spent far less of their lives in child care, thereby making them available for employment. At the same time that the service economy was booming and families were shrinking, a reinvigorated women's rights movement in the late twentieth century effectively advocated the equal treatment of women. This meant that women were not only entering new types of jobs, but they also were obtaining more jobs requiring skill or education. It did not mean, however, that women acquired economic equality in the late twentieth century; women were still typically concentrated in lower-level positions, earning lower wages than men.

The Vital Revolution of the Twentieth Century: Mortality and Life Expectancy

The twentieth century has witnessed dramatic demographic changes, continuing the vital revolution that began in the eighteenth century and flourished during the nineteenth century. None of these changes is more important for understanding life in the modern world than the falling death rate and the increase in life expectancy. In 1900 many regions of Europe—from Spain in the west to Poland in the east—had an annual death rate of twenty-five to thirty deaths per one thousand population (and some regions and subcultures had even higher rates). In the worst areas, including much of Russia, the rate was normally greater than thirty per one thousand. In the healthiest areas of western and northern Europe, mortality generally ranged between fifteen and twenty per one thousand. By the 1930s, however, the death rate had fallen below twenty per thousand in all corners of the continent; by the 1960s

TABLE 31.10

The Twentieth-Century Decline in Death Rates

Country	Death rates per 1,000 population			
	1910	1930	1960	1990
England	13.8	12.0	11.8	11.2
France	18.2	15.7	11.2	9.3
Germany	16.6	11.0	11.4	11.2
Greece	n.a.	16.8	7.8	9.3
Italy	19.2	14.1	11.7	9.4
Poland	a	14.9	7.6	10.2
Russia	28.2	17.8	7.2	n.a.
Spain	22.5	16.6	8.7	8.5
Sweden	13.9	11.6	10.0	11.0
United States	14.7	11.3	9.3	8.6

Source: B. R. Mitchell, *European Historical Statistics, 1750–1970* (London: Macmillan, 1975), pp. 127–32; B. R. Mitchell, *The Fontana Economic History of Europe: Statistical Appendix, 1920–1970* (London: Collins, 1974), pp. 28–34; *The World Almanac and Book of Facts 1995*, (Mahwah, N.J.: World Almanac Books, 1994), pp. 740–839, 959; *Information Please Almanac, Atlas, and Yearbook 1994* (Boston, Mass.: Houghton Mifflin, 1994), p. 135; U.S. Bureau of the Census, *Historical Statistics of the United States* (Washington, D.C.: Government Printing Office, 1960), p. 28.

n.a. = Not available

aDid not exist as an independent country.

tal revolution of the twentieth century also saw the population cohort aged sixty-five years or older grow steadily. The combination of better diet and nutrition (see illustration 31.6), better sanitation and public health standards, and greatly improved medical knowledge and health care delivery systems improved prospects for all. The consequence was a remarkable increase in life expectancy. In Great Britain in 1901—that is, in the most prosperous society in Europe at that time—a newborn baby boy had a life expectancy of slightly more than forty-five years. A century later, the estimated life expectancy of a newborn had grown to more than seventy-five years, an additional thirty years of life or a 67 percent increase in expectation (see table 31.12). If the twenty-first century continues similar wonders, centenarians could become commonplace, perhaps the expectancy at birth. Even without such developments, increased life expectancy has created a significantly older society. In 1910 only 6–7 percent of the population of Europe was age sixty-five or older; in the 1980s western and northern Europe had 12 percent to 17 percent of the population in that age cohort.

Illustration 31.6

Food in the Affluent Society. One of the keys to the vital revolution of the twentieth century has been a steady improvement in nutrition, especially in the period after 1945. European prosperity is typified by this French publicity photograph for a refrigerator in 1954, the year when 51 percent of the nation had acquired this appliance. For much of the world (or for much of Europe in 1854, or 1754) the regular consumption of the food on this table would have been unthinkable.

many countries were reporting mortality figures below ten per thousand. This was a dramatic revolution (see table 31.10).

The vital revolution of modern European history chiefly rested upon a decline in infant mortality, and that trend accelerated dramatically in the twentieth century (see table 31.11). In 1900 Europeans expected at least 15 percent of newborn children to die within the first year of life. In prosperous Germany, the rate for infant mortality was 23 percent; in Russia, more than 25 percent. As late as the 1920s, advanced countries such as France (12 percent) and Germany (13 percent) still had high rates. Between 1920 and 1950, the infant death rate was cut in half, then halved again between 1950 and 1970, and finally halved once more between 1970 and 1990. Thus, the century witnessed the infant mortality rate in England fall from 15.4 percent to 0.7 percent, in France from 16.0 percent to 0.7 percent, in Germany from 22.9 percent to 0.7 percent, and in Italy from 17.4 percent to 0.8 percent.

The sharp decline in infant mortality explains much, but not all, of the decline in death rates. The vi-

☙ TABLE 31.11 ☙
The Twentieth-Century Decline in Infant Mortality

Deaths of Infants under one year old, per 1,000 live births

Country	1850	1900	1920	1950	1970	1990
England	162	154	80	30	18	7
France	146	160	123	52	20	7
Germany	297	229	131	55 (West)	23 (West)	7
				72 (East)	20 (East)	
Italy	a	174	127	64	30	8
Poland	a	a	187	108	34	13
Russia	n.a.	252	n.a.	81	26	27
Sweden	146	99	63	21	12	6
Brazil						60
India						78
Nigeria						75
United States	131	141	79	23	20	9
white						8
black						18

Source: B. R. Mitchell, *European Historical Statistics, 1750–1970* (London: Macmillan, 1975), pp. 127–32; B. R. Mitchell, *The Fontana Economic History of Europe: Statistical Appendix, 1920–1970* (London: Collins, 1974), pp. 28–34; *The World Almanac and Book of Facts 1995* (Mahwah, N.J.: World Almanac Books, 1994), pp. 740–839, 959; *The World Almanac and Book of Facts 1997* (Mahwah, N.J.: World Almanac Books, 1996), p. 964; *Information Please Almanac, Atlas and Yearbook 1994* (Boston, Mass.: Houghton Mifflin, 1994), p. 135; U.S. Bureau of the Census, *Historical Statistics of the United States* (Washington, D.C.: Government Printing Office, 1960), p. 26

n.a. = Not available.

a Did not exist as an independent country.

☙ TABLE 31.12 ☙
The Growth of Life Expectancy in Twentieth-Century Britain

Government estimates of the average total life span at a given age in years

Person	1901	1931	1961	1991	2001
Male					
At birth	45.5	57.7	67.8	73.2	75.4
At age 1	54.6	62.4	69.5	73.8	75.7
At age 10	60.4	65.2	69.9	73.9	75.9
Female					
At birth	49.0	61.6	73.6	78.7	80.6
At age 1	56.8	65.3	75.1	79.2	80.9
At age 10	62.7	67.9	75.4	79.4	81.1

Source: Compiled from data in Central Statistical Office, United Kingdom, *Key Data: 1995–1996* (London: HMSO, 1995), p. 71.

The Life Cycle: Marriage and Divorce

Although many of the demographic trends of modern history find their explanation in subjects such as diet or disease, some important explanations must come from human behavior rooted in institutions such as marriage and the family. Both institutions have changed significantly during the twentieth century.

During the eighteenth and nineteenth centuries, economic restraints created a trend toward marriage at a later age. Couples did not marry without a steady job or a plot of land; many waited until they had accumulated savings or property. By the start of the twentieth century, the average age at which British men married had passed twenty-six years. For Irish men, the age was past thirty. Women in both societies married at a slightly younger age. The trend toward later marriage continued into the twentieth century, and on the eve of World War I British men were typically marrying at twenty-seven or twenty-eight. In the postwar years, however, that trend began to change, and age at marriage began to fall. By the 1960s British men were marrying a full three years younger, at twenty-four or twenty-five; British women at twenty-two or twenty-three. In eastern Europe, where earlier marriage had been common, that trend remained a dramatic contrast to western Europe. In both Denmark and France, for example, the law allows women to marry as young as age fifteen, and Irish law permits a girl to marry at age twelve, but very few marriages occur during the teenage years. In 1990, 2 percent of marriages in Denmark and 3 percent in France and Ireland involved teenaged women. In Belarus, however, 26 percent of all marriages involved teenaged girls and 3 percent involved girls fifteen or younger. Poland reported 22 percent and Bulgaria 38 percent of all marriages involved teenaged girls. Men married at an older age. Less than 0.5 percent of Danish boys married in their teens, and even in Belarus (4 percent) and Bulgaria (6 percent) the figures are significantly lower than for girls.

If the trend toward younger ages at marriage in western Europe, and very young marriages in the east, had appeared in an earlier century, it would have had a significant impact on European population because the number of childbearing years within marriage would have increased. At the start of the twentieth century, the average woman had fourteen to fifteen childbearing years within marriage. By the 1980s, however, that number had fallen below five years, despite younger marriages. Much of the explanation for this phenomenon has come from the restriction of childbearing years through the use of artificial birth control. Another part of the explanation is that the earlier marriages in the twentieth century were not necessarily longer marriages because divorce often truncated marriages during the childbearing years.

In 1900 divorce remained illegal in some countries (such as Italy and Spain), difficult to obtain in some (such as Britain), and only recently adopted in others (such as France). As twentieth-century society accepted divorce, it witnessed both the spreading legalization of divorce and the exponential growth of the rate at which marriages were dissolved (see table 31.13). Even the most devoutly Catholic states of Europe accepted divorce by the end of the century. Public support in a referendum of 1970 led to the legalization of divorce in Italy, although the law there remains cautious and requires a three-year separation before a divorce is granted. The Spanish republic introduced divorce in 1932, but it remained legal in Spain only until Franco revoked it in 1938. Divorce was not reinstituted there

	TABLE 31.13		
Country	Number of divorces in 1910	Number of divorces in 1990	Divorces as a percentage of marriages (1990)
Britain	701	165,700	41
France	15,125	106,096	31
Germany	13,008	128,729	30
Italy	0	30,778	8
Russia	n.a.	n.a.	42
Sweden	n.a.	n.a.	44

Divorce in Europe, 1910–90

Source: Priscilla Robertson, *An Experience of Women,* (Philadelphia, Pa.: Temple University Press, 1982), p. 250; Roderick Phillips, *Untying the Knot: A Short History of Divorce* (Cambridge: Cambridge University Press, 1991), pp. 185–86; *The Economist,* December 25, 1993; Martha Cronin and Julia Nasser, "Number of Marriages and Divorces in E.C. Countries," *Europe* (June 1992), p. 4; *Information Please Almanac, Atlas, and Yearbook 1994* (Boston, Mass.: Houghton Mifflin, 1994), p. 839.

n.a. = Not available

until 1981, but Spain then adopted a liberal divorce law. The last Western nation to prohibit divorce was Ireland, where the constitution expressly banned it; a referendum in 1995—the closest vote in Ireland's history—amended the constitution to permit divorce. In other countries, the divorce rate grew rapidly. By 1990, 30 percent of marriages ended in divorce in France and Germany, and more than 40 percent were dissolved in Britain, Denmark, Russia, and Sweden. The trend was vivid in post–World War II Britain: In 1950, there were 11.5 marriages and 0.4 divorces per one thousand population, a marriage to divorce ratio of 29-to-1; that ratio steadily fell to 9-to-1 in 1960 and to less than 3-to-1 in 1980. Approximately one-fourth of British divorces ended marriages before they had lasted five years, and the majority of divorces ended marriages shorter than ten years. Divorce thus significantly reduced childbearing below fourteen to fifteen years within marriage.

Childbirth, Birth Control, and Abortion

Despite the pattern of earlier marriages, the birthrate also fell sharply during the twentieth century (see table 31.14). The German birth rate of 28.2 births per thousand population in 1910 dropped to 11.4 per thousand in 1990, a remarkable 60 percent fall in the birthrate. In England, the rate fell from 28.6 per thousand in 1900 to 12.9 per thousand in 1994, a fall of 55 percent. The

♦ TABLE 31.14 ♦

The Decline in European Birthrates, 1910–90

Country	Birth rates per 1,000 population			
	1910	1930	1960	1990
England	24.2	15.3	17.9	13.9
France	18.8	17.0	18.0	13.5
Germany	28.2	16.3	18.0	11.4
Greece	n.a.	30.1	18.1	10.2
Italy	32.0	24.5	18.6	9.8
Poland	a	28.9	20.1	14.3
Russia	44.2	43.4	22.4	12.7
Spain	31.3	27.6	21.4	10.2
Sweden	23.7	14.4	14.5	14.5

Source: B. R. Mitchell, *European Historical Statistics, 1750–1970* (London: Macmillan, 1975), pp. 127–32; B. R. Mitchell, *The Fontana Economic History of Europe: Statistical Appendix, 1920–1970* (London: Collins, 1974), pp. 28–34; *The World Almanac and Book of Facts 1995* (Mahwah, N.J.: World Almanac Books, 1994), pp. 740–839, 959; *Information Please Almanac, Atlas, and Yearbook 1994* (Boston, Mass.: Houghton Mifflin, 1994), p. 135; U.S. Bureau of the Census, *Historical Statistics of the United States* (Washington, D.C.: Government Printing Office, 1960), p. 23.

n.a. = Not available

a Did not exist as an independent country.

Russian birthrate fell by more than 71 percent between 1910 and 1990.

By the late twentieth century, the birthrate in most of western Europe had fallen below the level needed to sustain population. Demographers estimate that an unchanging population requires 2.1 children born per woman in the population. (The global rate has fallen sharply, from 5.0 in the early 1950s to 2.8 in 1997.) In the late 1980s only two states (Ireland and Spain) in the European Union reached 2.1; Germany had the extraordinarily low rate of 1.3 children per woman. By the 1990s the European Union average had fallen again, to 1.4, and Catholic Italy had the lowest rate in the world for 1997, 1.2. Birthrates so low raise the strong possibility that, despite greater longevity and immigration pressures, Europe could lose population in the twenty-first century. Demographers—who have called this striking new development the "baby bust" (in contrast to the post–World War II period of high birthrates, known as the "baby boom")—have recently calculated that, if Europe could restore a rate of 2.1, the continent would still have lost 24 percent of its current population by 2060.

One natural consequence of the low birthrate was that family size became much smaller during the twentieth century. During the eighteenth and nineteenth centuries, the average family size in western and central Europe had been close to five persons. This remained true in Victorian Britain during the industrial revolution, when family size had averaged 4.75 members. Significant regional variation was evident in family size, with larger families being typical of rural communities and smaller families found in towns. The falling birthrates of the twentieth century rapidly reduced average family size. In Vienna, family size fell from 4.7 in 1890 to 4.1 in 1910, then to 3.2 in 1934, and down to 2.3 in 1961. In Germany, the national average declined from 2.9 in 1961 to 2.2 in 1993. Berlin and Hamburg both had averages of 1.9 in 1993, whereas communities of fewer than five thousand people held average families of 2.6 members. In Italy, average family size remained 4.3 members as late as 1951, when one-third of all Italian families contained five or more members. By 1980 the average Italian family had 2.8 members in the prosperous north and 3.3 members in more rural south; less than 15 percent of Italian families had five or more members. By the 1990s Italy had become the state most likely to experience a population decline in the twenty-first century.

The decline in twentieth-century birthrates and family size happened despite changing sexual attitudes that tolerated illegitimate births. In 1990 more than one-fourth of all births in Great Britain were illegitimate and 44.7 percent of births in Denmark were outside of marriage; a century earlier, Victorian Britain had low social tolerance of illegitimacy and the rate had been 5 percent. Even in Catholic countries, the stigma previously attached to having children outside of marriage has diminished. In conservative Ireland, 12 percent of 1990 births were illegitimate. In France, the number reached 26.3 percent in 1990 and passed one-third in 1995. The French showed the new social acceptability of unmarried childbirth in 1996 when the nation celebrated with President Jacques Chirac the illegitimate birth of his first grandchild. Although some parts of Europe maintained strict attitudes toward illegitimacy in the 1990s—such as Greece, where the rate was 2.1 percent—traditional sexual morality did not keep the birthrate low in Europe.

The most important explanation of falling birthrates has been the widespread practice of birth control. Information about contraception, and contraceptive devices, remained illegal in most of Europe well into the twentieth century. In the 1920s some countries (led by France) adopted stiff new prohibitions to recover population losses during World War I, but champions of women's rights in some Western countries challenged this trend. Aletta Jacobs still maintained the world's first birth control clinic, which she had opened in Amsterdam in 1878. A paleobotanist at the University of London, Marie Stopes, in 1921 opened the first British birth control clinic—the Mothers' Clinic for Constructive Birth Control. Stopes's *Contraception: Its Theory, History, and Practice* was published in 1923, and she continued to fight for easy public access to contraceptives as president of the Society for Constructive Birth Control.

Strong opposition existed to birth control clinics and contraceptives in the interwar years. Pronatalist governments, such as the conservative coalition led by Raymond Poincaré in France, the Fascist government of Benito Mussolini in Italy, and the Nazi regime in Germany, all strove to defend motherhood and to increase the population. The Vatican strongly supported this position in 1930 when Pope Pius XI issued the first encyclical opposed to birth control, *Casti connubi*. Pius XI left no doubt about the correct moral position for Catholics: "Any use whatsoever of matrimony exercised in such a way that the [sex] act is deliberately frustrated in its natural power to generate life is an offense against the law of God and of nature, and those who indulge in such are branded with the guilt of a grave sin." Some Catholic states responded to *Casti connubi*. The Irish not only outlawed birth control, but they also deemed a felony the importing, selling, or advertising of any birth control device or any birth control instructions (such as Marie Stopes's book).

European birthrates, however, show that millions of people, including Catholics, defied both church and state and practiced birth control. Birth control advocates, often led by champions of women's rights, won changes in restrictive laws after World War II. Postwar scientists also changed the nature of contraception. The principle behind oral contraceptives—changing a woman's balance of hormones—was well understood in the 1940s, and supplementary hormone pills were developed and tested in the 1950s. The first oral contraceptive, Enovid, was marketed in the United States in 1960, and "the pill" was introduced in Britain as Conovid in 1961. France legalized contraceptives in 1967; although conservative governments restricted this law in many indirect ways, the French nation voted with their bodies. An International Conference on Population held in 1994 estimated that France had the highest rate of contraception in the world. Eighty percent of all married Frenchwomen used contraceptives, while a rate of 70 percent to 80 percent was reported in

many other countries (including the United States). Spain legalized contraceptives after the death of General Franco, and 500,000 Spanish women began using the pill in the first three years that it was legal. After a long and passionate debate, Ireland legalized contraceptives in 1985 for people over the age of eighteen. And the government of Ireland even began to provide free contraceptives (although not condoms) to recipients of government-supported health care.

Conservatives, led by the Vatican, did not abandon the battle against birth control information and devices. When the birth control pill became popular in many Western countries in the late 1960s, Pope Paul VI reiterated the church's total opposition to birth control in his 1968 encyclical *Humanae vitae* (Of Human Life). Despite the clear evidence that Catholics accepted and used birth control, Pope John Paul II continued the strenuous rejection of all contraceptives in policy statements of 1987 and 1995. As late as 1995 John Paul II's encyclical, *Evangelium vitae* (The Gospel of Life), forcefully asserted that birth control was one of modern society's "crimes against life" and "a significant cause of grave moral decline."

The most controversial check on population growth, however, was not birth control but abortion. Abortion had long been illegal but had nonetheless been widely practiced in most of Europe. Pope Pius IX had denounced abortion and made it an excommunicatory sin in 1870. British laws of 1803 and 1861 had expressly outlawed abortion, providing penalties up to life imprisonment. The same statutes also criminalized many forms of assisting an abortion, such as sharing an abortifacient medication. The criminal code of newly unified Germany in 1871 made abortion a serious crime with five-year prison sentences. The French legislation of 1920 that targeted birth control also tightened the laws against abortion, establishing large new fines and longer prison sentences for performing an abortion, having an abortion, or providing information about abortion. Under those statutes, a prominent French feminist who had long championed a woman's right to control her own body, Dr. Madeleine Pelletier, was imprisoned (and died) in a mental asylum in 1939. Mussolini promulgated strict anti-abortion legislation in 1930, branding abortion a crime against "the health of the race." The foremost exception to the strict laws against abortion came in the Soviet Union, where Lenin's government legalized abortion in 1920. The decree required all physicians to perform an abortion if a pregnant woman requested it during the first two-and-one-half months of pregnancy. Stalin, however, revoked this decree and recriminalized abortion in 1936.

TABLE 31.15

Legal Abortions, 1967–90

Legal abortions in England			
Year	Married	Unmarried	Total
1967	0	0	0
1968	10,497	13,144	23,641
1969	24,403	30,416	54,829
1970	38,096	48,469	86,565
1971	55,358	71,419	126,777
1972	67,840	88,846	156,714
1973	83,001	86,361	169,362
1988	n.a.	n.a.	178,426
1989	n.a.	n.a.	180,622
1990	n.a.	n.a.	184,092

Rate of legal abortions performed per 1,000 population	
Country	1989
Bulgaria	16.1
Czechoslovakia	10.3
Hungary	8.8
Sweden	4.3
Denmark	4.1
United States	3.9
Norway	3.8
Britain	3.1
France	2.9
Italy	2.9
Poland	2.1
West Germany	1.0

Percentage of pregnancies terminated by abortion	
Country	1990
USSR	54.9
United States	29.7
Denmark	27.0
Sweden	24.9
Britain	18.6

Source: British data compiled from David Butler and Anne Sloman, eds.,*British Historical Facts, 1900–1975*, 4th ed. (London: Macmillan, 1975), p. 276; United Nations, *Demographic Yearbook, 1992* (New York, 1992), p. 291. Rates per thousand calculated using data from the *Demographic Yearbook*, reported in *Information Please Almanac, Atlas, and Yearbook 1994* (Boston, Mass.: Houghton Mifflin, 1994), pp. 130–31, 135; rates of pregnancies terminated by abortion from Michael Wolff and others., *Where We Stand* (New York: Bantam, 1992), pp. 253, 264.

n.a. = Not Available

The changing attitudes in post–World War II Europe led to the reversal of the legislation outlawing abortion (see table 31.15). Shortly after Stalin's death, the Soviet Union relegalized abortion in 1955. Abortion became legal in Britain in 1968, and nearly 24,000 legal abortions were performed that year. In the next twenty years, the number of legal abortions performed in Britain grew nearly eightfold, reaching 184,000 in 1990. At that rate, nearly 20 percent of all pregnancies in Britain ended in an abortion. By the 1970s the legalization of abortion had become a trend in Europe. Simone Veil, the minister of health, persuaded Jacques Chirac's conservative government to legalize abortion in France in 1974. A French endocrinologist, Etienne Baulieu, developed an abortifacient drug known as RU 486, and in 1980 it became widely available there. Italian voters went to the polls in the spring 1981 referendum and approved abortion by a two-to-one margin, despite papal opposition calling abortion murder. Belgium legalized abortion in 1990. Although Ireland did not legalize abortion, a controversial case in 1995 allowed Irish clinics to assist Irish women to obtain abortions abroad.

The highest rates of abortion were typically found in the Soviet Union and the states of eastern Europe. Bulgaria had an abortion rate more than four times as high (per one thousand population) as the United States did. And in 1990, 55 percent of all pregnancies in the Soviet Union were terminated by a legal abortion, in part because contraceptives remained largely unavailable. Romania, however, forbade abortions under the dictatorship of Nicolae Ceausescu and did not legalize them until he was deposed in 1989. And in Poland, where the Catholic Church played an important role in both the revolution of 1989 and the election of Lech Walesa to the presidency, abortion was again outlawed.

The Continuing Vital Revolution

The vital revolution of modern European history is chiefly explained in terms of diet and disease (see chapters 18 and 23). Twentieth-century European history—with its larger population, lower death rates, longer life expectancy, smaller families, and reduced agricultural sector of the economy—must return to these factors for explanations.

To understand the role of food in the vital revolution of the twentieth century, one must resolve a puzzle: Between 1900 and 1990 the population of Europe increased from 423 million to 501 million, while agricultural employment declined dramatically—from 32 percent of the population in Austria to 9 percent, from 41 percent of the population in France to 8 percent—and the amount of land devoted to agriculture decreased (by 15 percent in western Europe). Whereas the vital revolution of the eighteenth century had led to extensive use of the land—such as clearing forests, draining swamps, and enclosing common lands — to feed a growing population, the vital revolution of the twentieth century fed a growing (albeit more slowly) population with less land and fewer workers.

Grain has long been the key to understanding agriculture and the diet, and studies of grain production show the success of European agriculture during the twentieth century. Total European production (excluding Russia) of all grains—wheat, rye, barley, oats, and corn—stood at slightly less than 100 million tons in 1900. Good harvests preceded World War I, and production had grown by nearly 25 percent in 1913, before plummeting during the war. The European grain harvest reached prewar levels by 1929–30 but had only slightly exceeded them when World War II devastated agriculture and reduced production far below 1900 levels. In 1945, war-torn Europe produced less than 70 million tons. Between World War II and 1980, however, European agriculture experienced a miracle comparable to that of European industry. Total grain production nearly quadrupled, surpassing 250 million tons in the late 1970s. The average diet of twentieth-century Europeans is thus much healthier, and food costs are a much smaller percentage of the average person's income, in the 1990s than they were in the 1890s. The agricultural miracle and its contribution to the vital revolution are the result of a tremendous investment in the science and technology of modern agronomy. The mechanization of agriculture—the widespread use of machinery such as tractors, harvesters, and threshers—has transformed farming and required fewer people to produce more food. On the eve of World War II, fewer than 300,000 tractors were being used in all of European farming; in 1980, the total was more than 8 million. Although many environmental problems have been attributed to them, the use of chemicals—both for fertilizing the soil and as pesticides—have performed an even larger part in increasing the yield per acre. The success of biologists in developing new strains of crops or new breeds of animals has also greatly improved food production. A United Nations study of agriculture in Czechoslovakia between 1948 and 1978 shows how much these things have transformed agriculture. In the traditional Czech agriculture that persisted in 1948, the

UN calculated that the chief production factors were natural soil fertility, climatic conditions, and ground preparation; these variables explained 80 percent of the harvest size. In the modernized Czech agriculture of 1978, the UN concluded that the most important variables were fertilization, seed quality, and the use of pesticides—which accounted for 65 percent of harvest size.

While the success of European agriculture is important, the foremost factor in understanding the vital revolution of the twentieth century has been the conquest of disease. In 1901 the average life expectancy at birth stood at 49 years for British females and 45.5 years for British males, and 15 percent of British infants died before their first birthday. Almost precisely 50 percent of all deaths in Britain that year were attributable to contagious diseases. The largest cause of death was respiratory diseases, including influenza and pneumonia, which appeared on 16.8 percent of all death certificates. Tuberculosis (7.5 percent) or cholera (7.3 percent) killed almost as many people as heart disease (9.9 percent). Childhood diseases such as whooping cough, measles, scarlet fever, and smallpox were still more significant causes of death (5.9 percent) than cancer (5.0 percent). By 1990 British deaths from infectious disease had fallen from 49.9 percent to 0.4 percent. Smallpox had ceased to exist as an epidemic disease, and zero deaths were reported attributable to cholera, typhoid, diphtheria, or scarlet fever. Whooping cough and measles killed a total of eight children, compared with more than twenty thousand in 1901.

The conquest of epidemic disease had begun at the end of the eighteenth century with Jenner's smallpox vaccination. It made significant progress during the second half of the nineteenth century when Pasteur established the germ theory of disease transmission and biochemists such as Pasteur and Robert Koch began the slow process of finding vaccines that could protect people from other infectious diseases. Nonetheless, the twentieth century dawned on a world still in the grip of epidemic disease. The nineteenth century ended with yellow fever and malaria still preventing the construction of the Panama Canal, and the bubonic plague remained a rare but virulent killer that ravaged both Honolulu and San Francisco. The twentieth century began with a typhoid epidemic in New York (1903), a polio epidemic in Sweden (1905), 1.3 million deaths from bubonic plague in British India (1907), virtually annual cholera epidemics in Russia (until 1926), and a British report that the Anglo-Boer War in South Africa (1899–1902) had a British death rate from disease five times higher than the death rate from enemy fire. The

Illustration 31.7

The Vital Revolution. The conquest of disease, which had begun with Jenner's smallpox vaccination in the late eighteenth century and accelerated with the work of Pasteur and Koch in the later nineteenth century, culminated in dramatic improvements in infant mortality and the conquest of childhood diseases in the twentieth century. Here, a French scientist is culturing the serum for the diphtheria vaccine, which became a standard part of late twentieth-century inoculations.

In the second half of the twentieth century, many of the contagious diseases that had been the scourge of humanity were conquered. Heart disease and cancer had supplanted them as the foremost causes of death, and medical science turned vast resources toward combating them, as suggested by this view of open heart surgery in a French hospital in the 1970s.

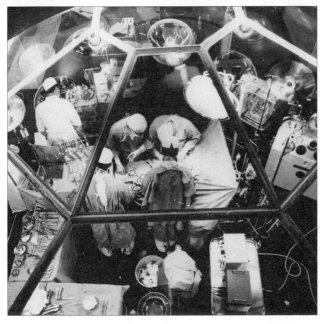

association of war and disease would persist in World War I. Tetanus spread through the trenches of the western front in 1915, a typhus epidemic took 150,000 lives in Serbia in 1915 and another killed 3 million people in Russia beginning in 1917. The Spanish influenza pandemic of 1919 became the most horrifying disease since the Black Death. Though it originated elsewhere, the disease took its name from the fact that nearly 80 percent of the Spanish population became infected. In two years, according to conservative estimates, it killed

twenty-two million people worldwide, more than twice the number of combat deaths that occurred in World War I. In short, infectious disease was still a catastrophic feature of life in the early twentieth century. Some diseases, such as malaria in Italy and cholera in Russia, remained endemic. Some, such as polio, came in frightening epidemics (such as the one that crippled Franklin Roosevelt). And some, such as influenza and venereal diseases, were universal pandemics that few could escape.

But the twentieth century also began with dramatic medical progress. The first Nobel Prizes were awarded in 1901, and the prize in physics went to Wilhelm Roentgen for the discovery of X-rays while the first prize in medicine went to a bacteriologist in Koch's Berlin laboratory for the discovery of the diphtheria antitoxin, which became a universal childhood inoculation of the twentieth century (see illustration 31.7). In 1909 another German scientist, Paul Ehrlich, opened research into a new family of drugs—antibacterial therapeutic drugs—with his development of an arsenic-based treatment for syphilis named Salvarsan. Syphilis had been one the greatest scourges of the Belle Époque, killing more Europeans per year than AIDS did at the end of the century. Salvarsan cut the syphilis infection rate in western Europe by more than 50 percent before the First World War, although its application was restricted by moralists who denounced the drug for encouraging sin.

Many of the most deadly diseases of European history gradually fell to the laboratory work of microbiologists, biochemists, and pathologists. After diphtheria and syphilis, yellow fever, typhus, tetanus, scarlet fever, bubonic plague, malaria, measles, and polio were all conquered or contained in Europe. Perhaps the most historic moment in this conquest of disease came in 1979 when the World Health Organization (WHO) announced that smallpox, the dreaded disease that had formerly killed tens of thousands of Europeans every year, had been totally eradicated. The last case of smallpox, WHO reported, had passed without transmission in 1977. Smallpox can, however, be revived because the governments of the United States and Russia have both stored samples of the smallpox virus.

The identification of the bacteria and viruses responsible for contagious diseases, and the development of vaccines, antitoxins against them, and drug therapies stand at the center of the vital revolution of the twentieth century. No element of this story is more dramatic than the discovery of the powerful drugs that became available after 1945, popularly known as the miracle drugs. Their discovery began in the late 1920s when Scottish physician and bacteriologist Alexander Fleming discovered penicillin and accelerated in 1935 when German pathologist Gerhard Domagk reported the discovery of the first antibacterial drug in a group called sulfa drugs. Many scientists contributed to the understanding and development of these miracle drugs. A French-American bacteriologist, René Dubos, developed the technique for isolating antibacterial agents in 1939. An Australian-born British pathologist, Sir Howard Florey, developed Fleming's penicillin into a powerful drug in 1940. Shortly thereafter, Selman Waksman, an American microbiologist, introduced one of the strongest miracle drugs—streptomycin—in 1944. During the late 1940s, a dozen new drugs followed from this collective effort. Thus, for much of the late twentieth century, miracle drugs such as penicillin seemed to hint at the complete conquest of disease. That optimism had faded by the 1990s, however, as viruses evolved that were resistant to many antibiotics. The fight against contagious diseases was not the only great medical contribution to the vital revolution of the twentieth century—a century that saw such remarkable procedures as open-heart surgery, a range of organ transplantation, and even successes with artificial organs (see illustration 31.7).

Conclusion

A danger confronts historians who become too realistic in their depiction of life in the past: It too easily can seem to have been a place of unrelieved suffering. The twentieth century witnessed immense, perhaps immeasurable, amounts of such suffering—during World War I, the Russian Revolution, the Great Depression, Fascist dictatorships, Stalin's terror, and the many horrors of World War II, such as the Holocaust. Similarly, social conditions and daily life revealed terrible problems during the eighteenth and nineteenth centuries—when Europeans faced widespread epidemic disease, chronic malnourishment and outright starvation, or dreadful conditions of life both at home and at work.

Among the many corrections to this portrait of the past, one of the most important is the remarkable improvements in living conditions achieved during the twentieth century, despite its many ravages. Understanding these improvements starts with population trends. The twentieth century witnessed a significant slowing of the population growth that characterized modern European history. By the end of the century, the birthrate was so low in much of western Europe that population decline appeared possible. The movement of population from rural Europe to the cities continued during the twentieth century, making most of the continent a highly urbanized society. The rate of urbanization, however, fell below the explosive growth in other parts of the world, and European cities were no longer larger than their Asian or Latin American counterparts. In addition to that form of population migration, Europe changed during the twentieth century from one that sent millions of emigrants overseas to a continent that received millions of immigrants from Africa and Asia, significantly changing the composition of Europe's population.

The economic structures of Europe also changed greatly during the twentieth century. At the start of the century, many elements of the old agricultural society still persisted, but the agricultural world was disappearing. By the end of the century, less than 10 percent of the population of western Europe was employed in agriculture. Industry, which began to supplement agriculture at the center of the European economy during the industrialization of the late eighteenth and nineteenth centuries, continued to grow in importance during the first half of the twentieth century and soon surpassed agriculture. However, during the second half of the twentieth century, a third sector—the service economy—surpassed both agriculture and industry and became the dominant element of the modern economy.

These economic trends encompassed many other changes in European society, such as the age of the labor force and the role of women in it. The mortality rate, especially the infant mortality rate, continued its historic decline. The most important explanation of these trends was the continued vital revolution, especially the conquest of many contagious diseases and the improvement of scientific agriculture. As a result, the life expectancy of Europeans changed from approximately forty-five years in 1900 to approximately seventy-five years in 1990. The institution of marriage changed in many ways as well: an earlier age at marriage, a continuation of the trend away from the patriarchal family, and a shorter duration of marriage because of the widespread acceptance of divorce. Family size shrunk steadily during the century, chiefly as a result of the widespread acceptance of birth control and abortion.

Suggested Readings

For general economic histories of the twentieth century, see C. Cipolla, ed., *The Fontana Economic History of Europe*, especially vol. 5: *The Twentieth Century* and vol. 6: *Contemporary Economies* (1976); M. M. Poston, D. C. Coleman, and P. Mathias, eds., *The Cambridge Economic History*, especially vols. 7 and 8 (1978); S. Clough, T. Moodie, and C. Moodie, eds., *Economic History of Europe: Twentieth Century* (1969); D. S. Landes, *The Unbound Prometheus* (1969), on industrial development; M. Tracy, *Agriculture in Western Europe* (1964), for the period after 1880; D. Aldcroft, *The European Economy, 1914–1990* (1993); E. A. Brett, *The World Economy since the War* (1985); A. Maddison, *Economic Policy and Performance in Europe, 1913–1970* (1973); W. Fischer, ed., *History of the World Economy in the Twentieth Century*, 6 vols. (1973–77), covering individual periods in helpful detail; and S. Pollard, *European Economic Integration, 1815–1970* (1974).

For individual countries, see D. H. Aldcroft, *The Interwar Economy* (1970), H. W. Arndt, *The Economic Lessons of the 1930s* (1963), D. H. Aldcroft and H. W. Richardson, *The British Economy, 1870–1939* (1969), I. M. Drummond, *British Economic Policy and the Empire, 1919–1939* (1972), A. S. Milward, *The Economic Effects of the World Wars on Britain* (1970), S. Pollard, *The Development of the British Economy* (1962), F. Caron, *An Economic History of Modern France* (1979), T. Kemp, *The French Economy, 1919–1939* (1972), C. P. Kindleberger, *Economic Growth in France and Britain, 1850–1950* (1964), R. Kuisel, *Capitalism and the State in Modern France* (1981), M. C. Cleary, *Peasants, Politicians, and Producers: The Organization of Agriculture in France since 1918* (1989), H.-J. Braun, *The German Econ-*

omy in the Twentieth Century (1990), K. Hardach, *The Political Economy of Germany in the Twentieth Century* (1980), G. Stolper and others, *The German Economy, 1870 to the Present* (1967), S. Clough, *The Economic History of Modern Italy* (1964), I. T. Bernd and G. Ranki, *Economic Development in East Central Europe in the 19th and 20th Centuries* (1974), A. Nove, *An Economic History of the USSR* (1966), M. Dobb, *Soviet Economic Development since 1917* (1968), and J. Taylor, *The Economic Development of Poland* (1952).

For demographic studies, see the suggestions for chapter 23 and G. Tapinos and P. Piotrow, *Six Billion People: Demographic Dilemmas and World Politics* (1978); L. Moch, *Moving Europeans: Migration in Western Europe since 1650* (1992), helpful for many twentieth-century trends; M. Marrus, *The Unwanted: European Refugees in the Twentieth Century* (1985); E. M. Kulischer, *Europe on the Move: War and Population Changes, 1917–1947* (1948); S. Castles, H. Booth, and T. Wallace, *Here for Good: Western Europe's New Ethnic Minorities* (1984); U. Herbert, *A History of Foreign Labor in Germany, 1880–1980* (1990); N. Abadan-Unat, ed., *Turkish Workers in Europe, 1960–1975* (1976); P. Ogden and P. White, eds., *Migrants in Modern France* (1989); J. Saville, *Rural Depopulation in England and Wales, 1851–1951* (1957); J. Spengler, *France Faces Depopulation* (1938); C. Dyer, *Population and Society in Twentieth Century France* (1978); K. Bade, ed., *Population, Labour, and Migration in 19th and 20th Century Germany* (1987); P. Hohenberg and L. Lees, *The Making of Urban Europe, 1000–1950* (1985); and P. Ehrlich, *The Population Bomb* (1968), for the argument on overpopulation.

For the family, gender, and the life cycle, see the suggestions for nineteenth-century social history and M. Mitterauer and R. Sieder, *The European Family: Patriarchy to Partnership from the Middle Ages to the Present* (1977); A. J. Coale and S. Watkins, eds., *The Decline of Fertility in Europe* (1986); D. Levine, *Reproducing Families: The Political Economy of English Population History* (1987); R. Evans and W. R. Lee, eds., *The German Family* (1981); J. Knodel, *The Decline of Fertility in Germany* (1974); A. McLaren, *Sexuality and Social Order* (1983), A. McLaren, *A History of Contraception* (1990); G. Bock and P. Thane, eds., *Maternity and Gender Policies* (1994); S. Pedersen, *Family, Dependence, and the Origins of the Welfare State* (1993); J. Lewis, *Women in England, 1870–1950* (1984); W. Holtby, *Women and a Changing Civilization* (1978); A. M. Anderson, *Women in the Factory* (1922); S. Burman, *Fit Work for Women* (1979); A. Marwick, *The Deluge* (1965), on Britain; D. Gittins, *Fair Sex: Family Size and Structure in Britain, 1900–1939* (1982); M. Glucksman, *Women Assemble: Women Workers and the New Industries in Inter-War Britain* (1990); H. Heclo, *Modern Social Politics in Britain and Sweden* (1974); and M. Higonnet and others, *Behind the Lines: Gender and the Two World Wars* (1987).

For disease, nutrition, and the vital revolution, see the suggestions for chapter 24 and R. Schofield, D. Reher, and A. Bideau, eds., *The Decline of Mortality in Europe* (1991), R. Stevens, *Medical Practice in Modern England* (1966), P. L. Yates, *Food Production in Western Europe* (1940), and J. Burnett, *Plenty and Want: The Social History of Food in England, From 1815 to the Present Day* (1989).

CHAPTER 32

EUROPE IN THE AGE OF THE COLD WAR, 1945–75

CHAPTER OUTLINE

◆◆◆◆◆◆◆◆◆◆◆◆◆◆◆◆◆◆◆◆◆◆◆◆

Europe was again a devastated continent in 1945 with homes, industries, transportation systems, and entire cities in ruins. Chapter 32 begins by describing the territorial changes that resulted from World War II (chiefly the division of Germany and the expansion of the USSR), the devastation in Europe caused by the war, and the years of austere living that Europeans faced to rebuild; in many areas, rationing lasted into the 1950s. The steady economic recovery of Western Europe, with aid from the U.S. Marshall Plan, produced growing prosperity in the late 1950s and the 1960s. The West German economy recovered at such a fast rate that it became know as the "economic miracle."

At the same time that Western Europe experienced this recovery, it confronted a global rivalry between the two strongest victors in World War II—the Soviet Union and the United States. This struggle never led to a shooting war between the rivals, but confrontations in the age of atomic weapons were so menacing and small regional crises so frequent that the rivalry was called the cold war. The chapter describes the European tension and crises—chiefly the creation of Communist satellite states in Eastern Europe and threats elsewhere, especially over Berlin—that led to the beginning of the cold war in the late 1940s, and it describes the confrontations of the cold war during the 1950s and 1960s.

As the great powers of Europe recovered and survived the fears of a Communist takeover, the new democracies evolved in different ways. The British, under Prime Minister Clement Attlee, developed the welfare state; the French, following the ideas of Jean Monnet, developed a new form of capitalism within a planned economy; and the Germans, under the leadership of Konrad Adenauer, created a successful democracy in contrast to the failed Weimar democracy of the 1920s. The chapter ends with an examination of how Europe changed in an age of peace and prosperity: through decolonization, the dismantling of ancient colonial empires; the beginning states of European

MAP 32.1

The European Territorial Settlement after World War II

economic unity with the creation of the European Economic Community (EEC); and the steady calming of the cold war in Europe, during a period of détente.

Postwar Europe

No peace conference was held at the end of World War II, and no treaty was drawn up with the defeated Axis powers. The map of postwar Europe was the consequence of Allied wartime conferences at Tehran, Yalta, and Potsdam and the political realities of the military

situation in 1945 (see map 32.1). Germany was significantly reduced in size from the Germany of the Versailles Treaty, and the victors then partitioned the reduced Germany into four zones of military occupation. East Prussia, the isolated exclave of prewar Germany that had been cut off by the Polish Corridor, was taken from Germany and divided by Poland and the USSR; the Soviet annexation converted the Prussian city of Königsberg into the Soviet city of Kaliningrad and the Polish annexation included the former free city of Danzig, now the Polish city of Gdansk. The eastern frontier of Germany was moved westward, to a line defined by the Oder and Neisse Rivers, giving Poland thousands of square miles of Prussia (roughly historic Silesia and Pomerania) and converting the German cities of Stettin and Breslau into the Polish cities of Szczecin and Wroclaw. In the west, France reacquired Alsace and Lorraine; in the north, Denmark recovered Schleswig. The initial division of Germany was into three zones of military occupation, under the British, American, and Russian armies. In the west, Britain and the United States shared their zones with France (which Stalin had refused to do), creating a four-power occupation. The city of Berlin, although located deep in the Soviet zone of occupation, was likewise divided into sectors administered by the great powers.

The territorial changes were less dramatic in the remainder of Europe. Austria was again detached from Germany; like Germany, it was divided into zones of occupation. Austria, Czechoslovakia, Hungary, Yugoslavia, and Romania were all restored to their approximate frontiers of 1919. The most important changes in eastern Europe involved the march of the Soviet Union westward. The Baltic states of Estonia, Latvia, and Lithuania (annexed in 1939) remained part of the USSR, as did slices of eastern Poland (much of White Russia, or Belarus), Czechoslovakia (much of Ruthenia), and Romania (the province of Bessarabia). This reversed the perspective of the Peace of Paris: The 1919 treaties had created a "cordon sanitaire" of small east European states as a barrier to the spread of Bolshevism, but eastern Europe now stood as a buffer zone protecting an expanded Soviet Union from western militarism and anticommunism.

The territorial changes of 1945, plus the memories of total war and the hard policies of new governments, led to a period of great population migration, especially of the German population now scattered in many states. More than eight million Germans left Poland and the Baltic states for Germany; they were joined by nearly three million Germans driven out of Czechoslovakia (chiefly the Sudeten Germans), by more than a million Germans fleeing the Soviet zone of occupied Germany for the west, and by nearly another million Germans from Hungary, Yugoslavia, and Romania. Approximately thirteen million Germans were uprooted in the period 1945–47. Similarly, some 3.5 million Poles moved into the territory newly acquired from Germany and 1.5 million Poles fled the territory acquired by the USSR. Hundreds of thousands of Italians (leaving the Istrian Peninsula, which was now Yugoslavian), Turks (driven from Bulgaria), and Ukrainians (leaving Poland for the Ukraine) shared this experience.

The Austerity of the 1940s and the Economic Recovery

Much of Europe lay in ruins in 1945. Great cities from London and Antwerp to Dresden and Leningrad were devastated (see illustration 32.1). Ninety-five percent of Berlin was in rubble, and forty percent of all German housing was damaged or destroyed. Much of the surviving productive capacity of Germany was dismantled and shipped to Russia. European transportation had collapsed amidst bombed out ports, rails, roads, and bridges. In Holland, 60 percent of the transportation network was destroyed, industrial output amounted to only 25 percent of the 1939 level, and thousands of acres of farmland lay flooded. As millions of war refugees spread across the continent, tuberculosis and malnutrition stalked displaced persons everywhere.

The primary characteristic of postwar Europe was the austere existence of the survivors. The European production of bread grains in 1945 stood at 50 percent of the prewar level. Food was rationed in most of Europe; bread was rationed in Britain although it had not been rationed during the war (see illustration 32.2). The wheat crop in France for 1945 totaled 4.2 million tons, compared with 9.8 million tons in the last year of peace (1938); for Italy the harvest was also 4.2 million tons, compared with 8.2 million (see table 32.1). The United Nations estimated that 100 million people were receiving fifteen hundred calories or fewer per day. Governments tried to control prices, but scarcity caused inflation. Between 1945 and 1949, prices tripled in Belgium and quintupled in France. Hungary suffered perhaps the worst inflation in world history, and the national currency was printed in 100 trillion pengo notes. Blackmarkets selling food, fuel, and clothing flourished. Simultaneously, military demobilization created widespread unemployment.

The recovery of Europe in the late 1940s and early 1950s relied upon planned economies and foreign aid. Jean Monnet, a distinguished French economist and civil servant, became the father of European mixed economics that relied upon state planning, such as his Monnet Plan of 1947. UN agencies such as the World Bank and the United Nations' International Children's Emergency Fund (UNICEF) channeled assistance to Europe, but the United States played the greatest role. In June 1947 Secretary of State George C. Marshall proposed a program of American aid to Europe. Between 1948 and 1952 the Marshall Plan sent $13 billion to Europe, with Britain ($3.2 billion),

Illustration 32.1

Reconstruction of a Devastated Europe. For the second time in thirty years, Europeans faced the task of rebuilding war-ravaged cities, industries, and infrastructure in the late 1940s.

Photographs like these could have been taken in dozens of European cities from Rotterdam to Leningrad. They show the center of Nuremburg, Germany, before and after the war.

Illustration 32.2

 Postwar Austerity. The expressions on the faces of these German women speak volumes about European austerity in the late 1940s. Consumer goods and basic commodities remained scarce and food rationing lasted well into the 1950s in many places. This 1948 photograph was taken after German currency reforms had created a new currency (the modern deutsche Mark), and its strength encouraged shopkeepers to start putting goods back into their windows. Sales were limited, but shoppers lined up for blocks.

France ($2.7 billion), and defeated Germany and Italy ($1.4 billion each) receiving the most. The USSR rejected aid. During 1948 West European industrial production reached 80 percent of its 1938 level in most countries (60 percent in Holland and West Germany). European economies showed signs of recovery but shortages, unemployment, and austerity continued in the early 1950s. By 1957, however, Prime Minister Harold MacMillan of Britain could say that "most of our people have never had it so good."

Eastern Europe and the Origins of the Cold War, 1945–49

The Red Army occupied vast regions of central and eastern Europe in 1945, by right of conquest. Russia had survived its third invasion from the west in modern times, outlasting Hitler just as it had survived Napoleon and the kaiser. The Soviet war effort had taken two or three times as many lives (as many as twenty million to twenty-five million people in the largest estimates) as British, French, German, and American deaths combined. Stalin, who ruled the USSR until his death in

TABLE 32.1
Food Production in Postwar Europe

Country	Millions of metric tons of				Millions of cattle
	Wheat	Potatoes	Sugar beets	Milk	
Belgium					
1938	0.5	3.3	1.2	3.1	1.7
1945	0.3	1.2	0.9	1.1	1.5
Czechoslovakia					
1938	1.8	7.4	3.9	4.2	4.8
1945	1.1	6.8	3.2	2.0	4.1
France					
1938	9.8	17.3	8.0	13.8	15.6
1945	4.2	6.1	4.5	7.9	14.3
Italy					
1938	8.2	2.9	3.3	n.a.	7.7
1945	4.2	1.5	0.4	n.a.	5.9
Poland					
1938	2.2	34.6	3.2	10.3	10.6
1945	0.8	21.9	3.5	2.8	3.3
Russia					
1938	40.8	42.0	16.7	29.0	50.9
1945	13.4	58.3	5.5	26.4	44.1

Source: B. R. Mitchell, *European Historical Statistics, 1750–1970* (London: Macmillan, 1975), passim.
n.a. Not available.

1953, concluded that he must exploit the vacuum in Europe to guarantee Russian security.

The summit conferences at Moscow, Yalta, and Potsdam gave the Soviet Union a strong position in Eastern Europe. Churchill had recognized Romania and Bulgaria as falling in the Soviet "sphere of influence," and the USSR had been conceded the occupation of the eastern one-third of Germany. In Yugoslavia, managed elections of 1945 (in which all opposition parties abstained) gave 90 percent of the vote and the presidency to the hero of the resistance (and prewar secretary general of the Communist Party), Marshal Tito, who held that office until his death in 1980. Multiparty democracies were announced in Poland, Czechoslovakia, and Hungary, and Communist parties formed a strong minority in each state. These democracies bore the burdens of postwar austerity during 1945–47, and each was so fragile that the Communist Party—backed by the Red Army—could seize control of the government. Poland, Czechoslovakia, and Hungary all fell to such Stalinist coups in 1947–49.

A dramatic example of the Communist takeover in Eastern Europe occurred in Czechoslovakia in 1948. Edouard Benes, the prewar president of Czechoslovakia and head of the government in exile during the war, returned to Prague to lead a provisional government in the restoration of Czech democracy, and he was again elected president of the republic. Free parliamentary elections in 1946 gave Czech Communists 38 percent of the vote, making them the largest party in the country; Communists won 114 seats and their four strongest rivals (Catholic, democratic, and socialist parties) won 178 seats, with the socialists strongest at 55. This produced a coalition government with a Communist prime minister, Klement Gottwald, plus Communist management of key ministries such as the Ministry of the Interior. The Gottwald government attempted to nationalize several Czech industries, just as socialists were doing in Britain and France; Gottwald also followed Soviet orders and refused to accept Western aid, such as the Marshall Plan, for the rebuilding of Czechoslovakia. These policies led to bitter disputes with more conservative coalition partners, conflict that Gottwald resolved in early 1948 by staging a coup d'état, naming a Communist government, and blocking elections. This coup included the mysterious death of Czechoslovakia's most prominent statesman, Foreign Minister Jan Masaryk, whose fall from a high window was labeled a suicide by the government; many other non-Communists were purged from high office. Managed elections then named Gottwald president, from

which position he solidified a Communist dictatorship. A new Czech Constitution of 1948 proclaimed a People's Democratic Republic on Soviet lines. Subsequent elections produced the anticipated results, such as the election of a new Parliament in 1954, in which Communist candidates received 99.18 percent of the vote. Gottwald's regime consolidated its power through an attack on the Catholic Church (placed under state control in 1949), a series of show trials in 1950 (similar to Stalin's trials in the 1930s), and a purge of the moderates within the party in 1951–52 (most famously, the treason trial and subsequent hanging of Rudolf Slansky, the former secretary general of the party).

Similar coups created Communist states in Hungary and Poland, where Communist-led provisional governments and the presence of the Red Army facilitated the takeover. In Hungary, free elections and a secret ballot in September 1945 gave the Communist Party only 22 percent of the vote (the third highest share) and 70 seats in parliament, far behind a Smallholders Party (an anticommunist party) which garnered 57 percent of the vote and 245 seats. Soviet interference resulted in charges of a conspiracy and "plotting against the occupying forces" being brought against many leaders of the new republic, who were rapidly purged. This led to new elections being called in 1947 and a reported 95.6 percent vote for a Communist coalition. A Soviet-inspired constitution of 1949 proclaimed Hungary a People's Republic and Hungary became a one-party state. As in Czechoslovakia, the new regime immediately combated the Catholic Church (placing Josef Cardinal Mindszenty under arrest on charges that he was conspiring to overthrow the government) and purged its own ranks.

The Communist position in Poland was strong in 1945 because many non-Communist leaders had been killed in the Warsaw uprising of 1944. Two competing governments-in-exile claimed to represent Poland, one that spent the war in Moscow, another in London. When the Red Army liberated Poland, Stalin installed the pro-Soviet government in the Polish town of Lublin, and it formed the basis of the postwar compromise government. The Communist-led provisional government did not hold elections until 1947, when its coalition received 80.1 percent of the vote and Western protests arose that the elections had not been fair. In a pattern similar to the events in Hungary and Czechoslovakia, the government nationalized land and industries, fought with the Catholic Church, punished collaborators (more than one million people were disenfranchised as a result), adopted a new constitution, and purged the party. Although other parties continued to exist, the Communist government won a reported 99.8 percent of the vote in the elections of 1952.

The creation of Communist dictatorships allied to the Soviet Union provoked a strong reaction in the West. Winston Churchill, a lifelong anti-Communist, sounded the alarm against Soviet expansionism in a speech delivered at a small college in Missouri in March 1946. Churchill said that "an iron curtain has descended across the Continent," and the term *Iron Curtain* became the Western world's cold war symbol for the border between the democratic West and the Communist East (see document 32.1).

The West first confronted Communist expansionism in the Balkans. Greece, which had remained neutral at the start of World War II but was conquered by Germany in 1941, had been a scene of intense partisan fighting throughout the war. The Greek resistance to the Nazi occupation, however, was predominantly composed of Greek Communists (similar to the situation in Yugoslavia and, to a slightly lesser degree, France), whereas the government of Greece was a monarchy (after a generation alternating among monarchy, dictatorship, and republic). The conflict between the resistance and the government produced sporadic fighting in 1944–45 and degenerated into a Greek Civil War (1946–49), widely seen as an attempted coup d'état by Greek Communists. This civil war focused western attention on the Balkans (including the vulnerability of Turkey and the strait linking the Black Sea and the Mediterranean). The geopolitical importance of this region plus growing Western anxieties about Communist expansionism led President Truman to announce aid to Greece and Turkey in 1947. This policy became the Truman Doctrine: The United States would "support free peoples who are resisting attempted subjugation by armed minorities or by outside pressures." The Truman Doctrine of aid to threatened countries blended with the Marshall Plan for aid in economic recovery; humanitarian assistance and military assistance were intertwined instruments of the cold war. American aid contributed significantly to the victory of the Greek monarchy over Communist guerrilla forces in 1949.

The most dramatic American intervention in the early days of the cold war came in the Berlin Airlift of 1948. To protest the increasing merger of the British and American zones of West Germany (dubbed "Bizonia" in 1946), the Soviet Union began to interfere with western access to Berlin and in July 1948 sealed off the city by closing all land access through the Soviet zone of East Germany. The United States considered open-

◆ DOCUMENT 32.1 ◆

Churchill: An "Iron Curtain" in Europe, 1946

A shadow has fallen upon the scenes so lately lightened, lighted by the Allied victory. Nobody knows what Soviet Russia and its communist international organization intends to do in the immediate future, or what are the limits, if any, to their expansive and proselytizing tendencies.

I have a strong admiration and regard for the valiant Russian people and for my war-time comrade, Marshal Stalin. There is deep sympathy and good-will in Britain—and I doubt not here also—toward the peoples of all the Russias. . . . We understand the Russian need to be secure on her western frontiers by the removal of all possibility of German aggression. We welcome Russia to her rightful place among the leading nations of the world. . . .

It is my duty, however . . . to place before you certain facts about the present position in Europe.

From Stettin in the Baltic to Trieste in the Adriatic, an iron curtain has descended across the Continent. Behind that line lie all the capitals of the ancient states of central and eastern Europe. Warsaw, Berlin, Prague, Vienna, Budapest, Belgrade, Bucharest, and Sofia, all these famous cities and the populations around them lie in what I might call the Soviet sphere, and all are subject, in one form or another, not only to Soviet influence but to a very high and in some cases increasing measure of control from Moscow.

Police governments are pervading from Moscow. . . . The communist parties, which were very small in all these eastern states of Europe, have been raised to preeminence and power far beyond their numbers and are seeking everywhere to obtain totalitarian control.

ing the route to Berlin by force but instead chose "Operation Vittles"—daily flights of assistance to sustain a city of two million (see illustration 32.3). The Berlin Airlift delivered more than eight thousand tons of food and supplies daily, with British and American flights landing every five minutes around the clock until the Soviet Union lifted its blockade in the spring of 1949.

Illustration 32.3

The Berlin Airlift. Berlin—located deep in the Soviet zone of occupied Germany—played an important role in the beginnings of the cold war. To protest Western arrangements for the administration of West Germany, the USSR began to interfere with traffic to Berlin and finally closed all roads and rails, claiming control of the entire city. The Western allies were determined to preserve their control of the western sector of Berlin and delivered vital supplies to the population through an airlift—chiefly the services of some three hundred U.S. C–54 cargo planes built for World War II, such as this one seen landing at Templehof Airport in Berlin.

NATO and the Warsaw Pact: Containment and Confrontation

The Truman Doctrine and the policy of the "containment" of Communism within the countries where it had been established soon prompted military alliances. Britain, France (where the government was doubly nervous because French Communists won 26.1 percent, 25.7 percent, and 28.1 percent of the votes in elections of 1945–46, making it the largest party in Parliament), and the Benelux states had signed a defensive treaty in March 1948. The blockade of Berlin and the Czech coup of 1948 led to the expansion of this alliance in 1949 into the North Atlantic Treaty Organization (NATO). Italy, Portugal, Norway, Denmark, Iceland, Canada, and the United States joined the original Allies in a twelve-member alliance that stationed American forces throughout Europe. Greece and Turkey were added to NATO in 1949. When a reunited West Germany joined the alliance in 1955, the Soviet Union countered by forming the Warsaw Pact, an alliance linking the USSR, East Germany, Poland, Czechoslovakia, Hungary, Romania, Bulgaria, and Albania. Members of the Warsaw Pact pledged to respond to aggression against any member; although such preparations never led to war between NATO and Warsaw Pact nations, this proviso was used by the USSR to send troops into member states where the Communist government was being challenged. Throughout the cold war, NATO and the Warsaw Pact kept large armed forces facing each other, with thousands of American and Soviet troops stationed in allied countries, with nuclear weapons (see map 32.2 and chronology 32.1).

The cold war, like World War II, was much larger than a European struggle. Dozens of global crises during the cold war threatened to bring the two sides to combat. The most dangerous of these crises occurred in Asia. In 1949 Mao Zedong's Chinese Communists won the war for control of China that they had begun in the 1930s. Mao took Beijing and drove his nationalist opponents, led by Chiang Kai-Shek, off the mainland to the island of Formosa (now called Taiwan). In early 1950 the U.S. Pacific Fleet patrolled the waters around Taiwan to prevent a Communist invasion. A few weeks later Mao and Stalin agreed upon a Sino-Soviet Alliance. And a few weeks after that, the armies of Communist North Korea invaded the south of that partitioned country and captured the capital city of Seoul. The United Nations adopted a resolution to send troops to Korea to block aggression—a resolution made possible because the Soviet delegate was boycotting the UN Security Council meeting and therefore not present to cast a veto. President Truman sent the U.S. army (commanded by the hero of the Pacific theatre of World War II, General Douglas MacArthur) to South Korea to join UN contingents from several countries, in the small portion of the Korean peninsula around Pusan still held by the South Koreans. After a

United States/NATO

| Missile bases: NATO |
| Troops: U.S. |
| Nuclear bombers: U.S. |
| Naval port: U.S. |
| Fleet: U.S. |
| Nuclear missile submarine: U.S. |

Soviet/Warsaw Pact

| Missile bases: Warsaw Pact |
| Troops: Soviet |
| Nuclear bombers: Soviet |
| Naval port: Soviet |
| Fleet: Soviet |
| Nuclear missile submarine: Soviet |

NATO member

NATO ally

NATO member to 1969

Warsaw Pact member

Unrest/revolt in Eastern Europe

MAP 32.2
European Cold War Alliances to 1975

UN counteroffensive, including an amphibious landing at Inchon, the North Korean army was driven back across the border (the thirty-eighth parallel) and MacArthur drove deep into North Korea, reaching the border of Manchuria. Then, in November 1951, Mao responded with Chinese "volunteers" to help the North. The Korean War (1950–53), which had begun with a near victory by North Korea and led to great danger of another world war, resulted in a stalemate and a cease-fire, perpetuating both the division of Korea at the thirty-eighth parallel and cold war anxieties.

The most frightening aspect of such cold war confrontations was the constant threat of nuclear war. The United States remained the only state with the atomic bomb for just four years (1945–49), until the Soviet Union, with significant assistance from atomic spies, detonated its first nuclear bomb. For the next quarter-century, the United States and the USSR engaged in a nuclear arms race that constantly increased the destructive power of both sides. The United States exploded the world's first hydrogen bomb, many times more destructive than the atomic bombs used on Hiroshima

◆ CHRONOLOGY 32.1 ◆

The Cold War in Europe, 1945–75

1945	Yalta meeting on postwar settlement
1945	Potsdam conference on the division of Germany
1946	Churchill's "Iron Curtain" speech on the division of Europe
1946	Civil war in Greece, Communist guerrillas against monarchist government
1947	United States announces Truman Doctrine of aid against Communist takeovers
1948	Communist coup seizes power in Czechoslovakia
1948	The Marshall Plan for American aid for European recovery
1948	Soviet blockade of Berlin circumvented by Berlin Airlift
1949	Creation of North Atlantic Treaty Organization (NATO) alliance linking United States, Canada, and Western Europe
1949	Communists seize power in Hungary
1949	Three western zones of occupation united to form Federal Republic of Germany
1951	USSR explodes its first atomic bomb
1952	Great Britain explodes its first atomic bomb
1953	Death of Stalin and rise of Khrushchev
1953	Uprising in East Germany suppressed
1955	West Germany joins NATO
1955	Soviet Union organizes Warsaw Pact of East European states
1956	Anglo-French invasion of Egypt over Suez Canal
1956	Uprisings in Poland and East Germany suppressed

1957	Soviet launching of *Sputnik* begins space race
1960	France explodes its first nuclear bomb
1961	USSR achieves first manned space flight
1961	Berlin Crisis and construction of the Berlin Wall to block emigration
1962	United States forces USSR to withdraw missiles in Cuban Missile Crisis
1962	Solzhenitsyn reveals details of the Soviet gulag
1963	Partial Test Ban Treaty signed, beginning relaxation of cold war tensions
1963	France rejects Test Ban Treaty and plans its own nuclear *force de frappe*
1966	France withdraws from NATO command
1967	Six-Day War in Middle East revives grave cold war tensions
1968	Nuclear Nonproliferation Treaty Signed
1968	USSR and Warsaw Pact nations suppress Czech liberalization
1969	United States puts astronauts on moon
1970	Rioting in Poland over austerity program
1970	Heads of West Germany and East Germany hold first official meeting
1972	President Nixon visits Moscow and signs Strategic Arms Limitation Talks Treaty
1973	West Germany and East Germany both join the UN
1975	Helsinki accords on human rights mark age of détente

and Nagasaki, in 1952 but held this lead for only a few months. The arms race then shifted to the technology of delivering nuclear bombs. The United States tested the first Intermediate Range Ballistic Missile (IRBM), capable of carrying bombs long distances, in 1953, and both sides developed Intercontinental Ballistics Missiles (ICBMs) that could reach each other's cities.

The nuclear arms race shared much of its technology with a simultaneous space race between the USSR and the United States. The space age—and an era of Soviet superiority in space—began in 1957 when a Russian rocket carried the first artificial satellite, *Sputnik,*

into orbit (see illustration 32.4). A month later, the Soviets launched a second satellite sending a dog into space and safely retrieving it. When President Eisenhower rushed an American rocket to show the world that the United States did not lag far behind, it exploded a few feet off the ground and became known as the American "Dudnik." The Soviet lead in the space race continued into the 1960s when the USSR sent the first person into outer space, the cosmonaut Yuri Gagarin. The U.S. space program of the 1960s showed that this "missile gap" was narrowing; launches of American astronauts and Soviet cosmonauts into space

Illustration 32.4

🔲 **The Space Age.** The space age began in October 1957 when the USSR successfully launched the first artificial satellite (*Sputnik*) into orbit around the Earth. A few weeks later, the Soviet Union launched the second satellite into orbit, carrying the first inhabitant of Earth to travel into space, a dog named Laika. Although the USSR also launched the first person into space, Yuri Gagarin in 1961, the United States soon overcame the Soviet lead and proclaimed victory in the space race by landing astronauts on the moon in July 1969. In this photo, visitors to the Brussels World's Fair in 1958 flock to see *Sputnik* on exhibit.

soon became commonplace. President John F. Kennedy committed the United States to win the space race by putting the first people on the moon, and by 1969 the United States succeeded in sending Apollo astronauts to the moon.

While the space race glamorized one aspect of the cold war arms race, the United States quietly took the lead in another technology capable of raining atomic bombs on the Soviet Union by building a fleet of nuclear submarines with atomic missiles aboard. By the early 1970s technology had produced the MIRV, a hydra-headed missile that could deliver separate bombs

(multiple independent reentry vehicles in the cold war lexicon) to several cities from one missile. Both sides stockpiled nuclear weapons and their delivery systems long after they attained the capacity to obliterate civilization. Simultaneously, both sides developed the philosophy of using nuclear weapons. The United States, for example, threatened the use of nuclear weapons to force negotiations to end the Korean War and again in 1962 to force the USSR to withdraw its missiles from Cuba. And both sides seriously discussed such strategies as "massive retaliation" with nuclear bombs instead of fighting traditional ground wars. One of the keenest metaphors of the cold war appeared on the cover of a scientific journal: a clock showing that the human race had reached one minute before midnight.

The nuclear arms race and the space race were enormously expensive, which would ultimately have much to do with the end of the cold war. An early sign that this was an extremely expensive burden for the USSR came in 1959, when Stalin's successor, Nikita Khrushchev, proposed the concept of "peaceful coexistence" (see document 32.2). Many in the West doubted Khrushchev's sincerity (he had recently made another speech, taunting the West with the message, "We will bury you!"), and few were yet willing to gamble on a relaxation of cold war preparedness. Many Europeans would favor peaceful coexistence by the late 1960s, when it came to be called a policy of relaxed tensions (*detente* in the French vocabulary of diplomacy).

As the nuclear balance-of-power became a balance-of-terror, the cold war became a delicate stalemate. The NATO allies restrained themselves from direct interventions in Communist countries, although discontent with Communist rule provided opportunities. A workers' revolt in East Berlin was put down by force in 1953, beginning an era of uprisings behind the Iron Curtain. A Hungarian rebellion in 1956 led to fighting in the streets of Budapest and the creation of reformist government under Imre Nagy. Nagy pledged to withdraw Hungary from the Warsaw Pact and to become neutral. A few weeks later, the Red Army invaded Hungary. The Soviet intervention led to the flight of 200,000 Hungarians to the west, 25,000 casualties in combat, and 2,000 executions (including Nagy) in reprisal. The NATO powers still chose not to go to war over Hungary. Similarly, the Soviet Union did not intervene in Western wars, such as the Anglo-French invasion of Egypt in 1956 (an attempt to keep control of the Suez Canal) known as the Suez War. When the United States later fought a second Asian war based on the

❖ DOCUMENT 32.2 ❖

Nikita Khrushchev: "Peaceful Coexistence," 1959

Nikita Khrushchev often used the annual party congress of the Communist Party to make dramatic speeches. At the congress of 1956, he opened the age of destalinization in Russia in a speech attacking "the crimes of the Stalin era." In 1959, at the Twentieth Party Congress, he declared that the basis of foreign policy should be the "peaceful coexistence" of states with differing social systems, inviting a détente in cold war tensions. Western nations did not start to trust this concept for another decade.

We all of us well know that tremendous changes have taken place in the world. Gone, indeed, are the days when it took weeks to cross the ocean from one continent to the other or when a trip from Europe to America, or from Asia to Africa, seemed a very complicated undertaking. The progress of modern technology has reduced our planet to a rather small place; it has even become, in this sense, quite congested. And if in our daily life it is a matter of considerable importance to establish normal relations with our neighbors in a densely inhabited settlement, this is so much more necessary in the relations between states, in particular states belonging to different social systems. . . . What then remains to be done? There may be two ways out: either war—and war in the rocket H-bomb age is fraught with the most dire consequences for all nations—or peaceful coexistence. . . .

The problem of peaceful coexistence betweens states with different social systems has become particularly pressing. . . . The Soviet people have stated and declare again that they do not want war. If the Soviet Union and the countries friendly to it are not attacked, we shall never use any weapons either against the United States or against any other countries. . . . Precisely because we want to rid mankind of war, we urge the Western powers to peaceful and lofty competition.

The USSR under Stalin and Khrushchev, 1945–64

No country suffered more severely from World War II than the Soviet Union. In the western quarter of the country, more than seventy thousand villages were classified as "destroyed." In a war zone of 800,000 square miles (Germany and Poland combined occupy only 210,000 square miles), 50 percent of all residences and eighty thousand schools were lost. Twenty-five million dead overshadows every other tragedy in a century of megadeath, and it explains why Stalin demanded postwar security for the USSR. The Soviet Union therefore kept the Baltic provinces plus newly conquered territories on the western frontier. The annexation of 250,000 square miles was only the first step; the creation of Communist satellites in Eastern Europe grew from the same desire for a western buffer.

Stalin began the reconstruction of the Soviet Union by plundering defeated Germany. The Yalta and Potsdam agreements recognized a Soviet right to reparations from Germany and permitted Stalin to collect them "in kind." This meant the confiscation and shipment to the USSR of billions of dollars worth of surviving German industry. Recovery was entrusted to the state planning agency, Gosplan, which drafted a Five Year Plan for 1946–50. With severe enforcement, the Soviet Union exceeded the production quotas set in this plan. Stalin promised that Soviet output would triple prewar levels, and by 1960 that standard had been met, although agricultural recovery was slower. Ironically, the speed of the Russian recovery increased cold war tensions because it underscored the enormous potential of the Soviet Union. And when the USSR launched *Sputnik* (1957) and then Yuri Gagarin (1961) into orbit, no one could doubt Soviet technical potential.

Soviet security and recovery both rested upon Stalin's dictatorship. His brutality had not diminished with age, and in 1948 he ordered another purge. The new repression was conducted by his senior lieutenant, Georgi Malenkov, and the head of his secret police, Lavrenti Beria. It did not match the Great Terror of the 1930s, but it took a terrifying toll, especially on Soviet cultural life, where writers and filmmakers were prominent victims. The purges then moved through the military, the bureaucracy, and the Communist Party. Anti-Semitism was a common feature of the purges. This culminated in the so-called Doctors' Plot of 1952 when Stalin accused Jewish physicians in the Kremlin of poisoning Soviet leaders.

policy of containing the spread of Communism, the Vietnam War (1965–75), the USSR and China gave assistance to North Vietnam and to the Communist guerrilla armies of the Viet Cong, but they both refrained from directly entering the war.

When Stalin died of a cerebral hemorrhage in early 1953, Malenkov and Beria claimed power. Despite the idealistic constitution of 1936, the USSR had no formal system for the transfer of power. Senior leaders feared that the rule of Malenkov or Beria meant continued terror. The army arrested and shot Beria on a charge of "plotting to restore Capitalism"; his secret police was reorganized as the KGB. Malenkov was dismissed from office, but to show that Stalinism had ended, he was merely sentenced to end his career as the manager of a hydroelectric plant in provincial Kazakhstan.

After a period of "collective leadership," Nikita Khrushchev emerged as Stalin's successor. Khrushchev, the son of a Ukrainian miner, had joined the Communist Party as an illiterate worker in 1918. He rose rapidly under Stalin's regime and participated in some of its crimes during the 1930s, but his dictatorship differed from Stalinist bloodletting. At the Communist Party Congress of 1956, Khrushchev announced a program of change and openly attacked Stalin. He denounced "the crimes of the Stalin era," and, as symbols of destalinizaion, Khrushchev removed Stalin's body from public display and renamed Stalingrad as Volgograd. Three years later, at another party congress, he made his famous call for relaxed economic controls and peaceful coexistence with the West. Westerners were startled by Khrushchev's crude style. For many, the enduring image of Nikita Khrushchev was a fat man in a rumpled suit, banging his shoe on a podium and shouting. Soviet dissidents still faced harassment and the *gulag* under Khrushchev, and when he fell in 1964, the Soviet Union remained a dictatorship. However, Khrushchev had taken the first steps toward the age of détente.

◆

Great Britain: Clement Attlee and the Birth of the Welfare State

In contrast to Eastern Europe and the Soviet Union, postwar Western Europe experienced the recovery of parliamentary democracy. Britain, France, the Benelux countries, Italy, the Scandinavian states, and even the reunited zones of western Germany were stable democracies by the 1950s. Spain and Portugal kept their prewar autocratic governments, but these fell after the death of Franco (1975) and Salazar (1970). The postwar Western democracies were more than mere restorations, however, and several governments expanded the European definition of democracy.

Postwar Britain led the evolution of European democracy by founding the modern welfare state. The British electorate rejected Winston Churchill's conservative government in 1945 (much as the French had rejected Clemenceau after World War I or the Russians would reject Gorbachev after the revolutions of 1989), giving the Tories only 39.9 percent of the vote in parliamentary elections. The new prime minister, Clement Attlee, received an overwhelming majority in Parliament (393–213) with which to enact socialist plans for a welfare state (see document 32.3). Attlee had been born to an upper-class family and sensitized to the needs of the poor through social work in the East End of London. After World War I he became a lecturer at the London School of Economics, a nondogmatic socialist, and a leading Labour M.P. His government planned a new British democracy based on two broad policies: (1) the adoption of welfare legislation by which the state provided all citizens with basic services "from the cradle to the grave" and (2) the "nationalization of leading elements" of the British economy, on the theory that state profits would pay for welfare services. Attlee's welfare program derived from an idealistic wartime plan, the Beveridge Report of 1942, which called for government insurance to protect the nation. The Beveridge Report laid the basis for the National Health Act (1946) and the National Insurance Act (1946), laws that promised "a national minimum standard of subsistence" to everyone. In return for a regular payroll deduction, all citizens received sick leave benefits, retirement pensions, maternity benefits, unemployment compensation, widow's and orphan's allowances, and medical care. One of the first reforms of the welfare state was a program to provide British schoolchildren (many of whom had poor nutrition from years of privation) with free milk at school, and this image did much to popularize the welfare state (see illustration 32.5). Beveridge, Attlee, and the minister for health and housing, Aneurin Bevan, gave Western Europe the model for a democratic welfare state.

The Labour government also carried out the second half of its program, the nationalization of key industries. This had been a central objective of European socialists since the late nineteenth century and a cornerstone of Labour programs since 1918. The idea had gained respectability in the 1920s when a conservative government had created the British Broadcasting Corporation as a state corporation. Nationalization gained further appeal during the depression of the 1930s when big business was widely blamed for the terrible unemployment. The Attlee government compensated the owners of private firms that were nationalized into "public corporations," and the Tory Party made only

◈ DOCUMENT 32.3 ◈

The House of Commons Debates the National Health Act (1946)

Mr. Bevan (Labour): The first reason why a health scheme of this sort is necessary at all is because it has been the firm conclusion of all parties that money ought not to be permitted to stand in the way of obtaining an efficient health service. Although it is true that the [current] national health insurance system provides a general practitioner service and caters for something like 21 million of the population, the rest of the population [24 million] have to pay whenever they desire the services of a doctor. It is cardinal to a proper health organization that a person ought not to be financially deterred from seeking medical assistance at the earliest possible stage. . . .

In the second place, the [current] national health insurance scheme does not provide for the self-employed, nor, of course, for the families of dependents. . . . Furthermore . . . in an overwhelming number of cases, the services of a specialist are not available to poor people. . . .

In the older industrial districts of Great Britain hospital facilities are inadequate. Many of the hospitals are too small—very much too small.

Furthermore—I want to be quite frank with the House—I believe it is repugnant to a civilized community for hospitals to have to rely upon private charity. . . .

Mr. Law (Conservative): . . . We accept the principle [of a national health system], and we accept the consequences that flow from it. . . . We are gladly committed to the principle of a 100% service. . . . We understand, once we accept the principle, that we are committed to a far greater degree of coordination, or planning as it is usually called, than we have ever known before . . .

[However, Conservatives] believe that [Bevan] could have established a health service equally comprehensive, better coordinated and far more efficient, if he had not been determined to sweep away the voluntary hospitals; if he had not been determined to weaken the whole structure of English local government . . ., and if he had not sought to impose upon the medical profession a form of discipline which, in our view and theirs, is totally unsuited to the practice of medicine, an art, a vocation . . . which depends above all else upon individual responsibility, individual devotion, and individual sympathy.

Illustration 32.5

🕢 **The Welfare State.** The British lived with food rationing until 1954. To improve the health of British children, the postwar Labour government in 1946 included a provision for free milk for schoolchildren in the welfare program it introduced. This photo shows boys at a grammar school in Manchester taking their daily milk break. Such programs were a dramatic success at improving the children's health, but they also became a visible symbol of the welfare state. When Margaret Thatcher set out to dismantle the welfare state, free milk was one of her first targets.

limited protests when Attlee nationalized the Bank of England in 1945 and civil aviation in 1947 (creating the parent corporation of British Air). Conservatives more vigorously contested the nationalization of the coal mines (1946) and the iron and steel industries (1950); when Churchill returned to power in 1951, his government allowed most of Labour's nationalizations to stand, denationalizing only iron and steel and road haulage. A broad conservative attack on the policies of the Attlee years did not come until the Margaret Thatcher era, beginning in 1979, when both denationalization and the dismantling of the welfare state defined her government.

Subsequent Labour governments under Harold Wilson (1964–70 and 1974–76) expanded the new sense of British democracy by legislating equal rights: The Race Relations Act (1965) outlawed racial discrimination, and the Sexual Offenses Act (1967) legalized homosexual acts by consenting adults. An Abortion Act (1967), an Equal Pay Act (1970), and the Equal Opportunities Act (1975) legislated the three chief aims of the women's rights movement. These Labour reforms of the Wilson era survived Thatcher's conservatism better than Attlee's reforms.

The French Fourth Republic: Jean Monnet and the Planned Economy

The reestablishment of a French republic also involved the rejection of a famous wartime leader and significant innovation. General de Gaulle's provisional government, which returned in the aftermath of the D-Day landings in 1944, prepared for a new constitution in France to replace both the Vichy Regime and the constitution of the defunct Third Republic. De Gaulle feared a Communist coup in France because many of the leaders of the wartime Resistance had been Communists. To block the Communists, De Gaulle chose dramatic steps: He adopted the socialist program of nationalization that Léon Blum had begun in the 1930s. The state now took control of energy and the utilities (gas, oil, and coal); most insurance companies and banking; and some prominent industrial companies, such as Renault and Air France. Twenty percent of the French economy had been nationalized by the late 1940s—a program of conservative nationalization even larger than the Labour Party's efforts in Britain.

Charles de Gaulle also gave women the vote because he believed a common stereotype (and a theory previously used against women's suffrage) holding that

◆ DOCUMENT 32.4 ◆

De Beauvoir: Emancipation of the "Second Sex"

Simone de Beauvoir (1908–86) was the daughter of a respectable bourgeois family who rebelled against the standards of her world. She became a leader of Parisian intellectual society, a novelist, and a philosopher closely associated with Jean-Paul Sartre and the school of existentialist philosophy, which held that people create their identity through acts of will throughout their existence.

French Law no longer lists obedience among the duties of a wife, and every Frenchwoman now has the right to vote; but these civil liberties remain only theoretical while they are not accompanied by economic freedom. A woman supported by a man—a wife or a mistress—is not emancipated from him because she has a ballot in her hand; if customs now constrain her less than before, this has not profoundly changed her situation; she is still bound in a state of vassalage. It is through paid employment that women have covered most of the distance separating them from men; nothing else can guarantee her freedom. Once woman ceases to be a parasite, the system based on her dependence falls apart; there is no longer any need for men to mediate between women and the universe.

women would vote conservatively, as their priests directed. While this was an important step in equal rights for women, it did not lead to a large role for women in French politics; until the socialist parliamentary victory in the spring of 1997, France remained nearly last among European states in electing women. (The French did, however, accept a woman as prime minister—Edith Cresson in the 1980s—long before Germany or the United States accepted a woman at the head of government.) De Gaulle's concession of the vote thus did not convince all French women that they had yet won equality. One prominent intellectual, Simone de Beauvoir, responded with a landmark manifesto of women's rights, *The Second Sex* (1949), showing that women were "still bound in a state of vassalage" (see document 32.4). The late twentieth-century reinvigoration of feminism throughout the Western world owed much to de Beauvoir's book, and the next generation of feminists hailed her as "the mother of us all."

The French postwar elections, which De Gaulle sought to manipulate by granting women's suffrage, divided power among three parties, each with 25 percent of the seats: a Catholic party (the MRP), the socialist party of Léon Blum (who had survived Nazi imprisonment), and the Communist Party (which was popular because of its role in the wartime resistance). When each of these parties rejected de Gaulle's ideas for a strong presidency (designed to suit his own leadership), he retired in anger to write his war memoirs. The French consequently created a new regime, a parliamentary democracy known as the Fourth Republic (1946–58), which greatly resembled the Third Republic (1871–1940). When the wars of decolonization—especially the Algerian War (1954–62)—destroyed the Fourth Republic in 1958, de Gaulle returned to politics and created his strong presidential government in the constitution of the Fifth Republic.

The greatest French contribution to postwar democracy was neither De Gaulle's concept of a presidential republic nor his specific accomplishments such as women's suffrage (which most of Europe had granted before he did). It was, instead, a democratic version of economic planning. Jean Monnet never led the government, but his Plan for Modernization and Equipment (1946), embodied in the First Plan (1947–53) and the Second Plan (1954–57), shaped the French postwar recovery. He created an "indicative plan" that set goals in important sectors (such as mining or transportation) and then provided government assistance to private businesses in reaching those goals. The plan was not compulsory, and it did not create government control over private firms. Monnet thus pioneered the "mixed economy," combining elements of capitalist and noncapitalist economics. French steel output doubled between 1950 and 1960, wheat output doubled between 1950 and 1962, and other governments soon followed Monnet.

As the French economy recovered, France became more conservative. The popularity of the Communist Party declined sharply, from 25 percent of the seats in Parliament in 1945 to 5 percent in 1988. The governments of the 1950s were so conservative that they even changed the traditional French insistence upon secular education; the Barange Law (1951) gave state aid to Catholic schools. When Charles de Gaulle founded the Fifth Republic in 1958, the conservative coalition in France—known as Gaullism—won a solid majority of electoral support and retained power throughout the

1960s and 1970s. Gaullist conservatives, however, did not try to reprivatize the nationalized sectors of the economy, to abandon the state direction of a mixed economy, or to dismantle the growing welfare state. Gaullists extended French welfare benefits several times, especially in the 1970s when they expanded a state-run system of old age pensions for the entire nation.

The Federal Republic of Germany: Konrad Adenauer and the Economic Miracle

The rebirth of German democracy followed a more difficult course. The four-power occupation of Germany created conflicting administrations. In the Soviet zone, the revived German Communist Party, led by survivors from the Weimar Republic such as Walter Ulbricht, failed to win a majority in the elections of 1946 but took control of the government with Soviet approval. By 1948 the Soviet zone was a one-party state at the center of the cold war, and millions of East Germans were emigrating to the West. The flood of refugees going west became so embarrassing that in 1961 Ulbricht closed the border. He erected a dramatic barrier in Berlin: the Berlin Wall—a brick, concrete, barbed wire, and machine gun impediment to travel—which became the most vivid symbol of the Iron Curtain (see illustration 32.6).

The Western powers slowly united their zones. Britain and the United States began the economic merger of their zones in 1946, creating Bizonia. When the French accepted the unity of western zones, the allies created the German Federal Republic (West Germany) in May 1949. The allies required that the Federal Republic's constitution (known as the *Grundgesetz*, or basic law) protect regional rights, create authority without authoritarianism, and include a liberal bill of rights.

The leading founder of the Federal Republic of Germany was Konrad Adenauer, a lawyer who had served as mayor of Cologne and a deputy during the Weimar Republic. Adenauer had survived the Nazi era in an early retirement, and he had twice been arrested by the Gestapo. He founded a conservative party, the Christian Democratic Union (CDU), which was heavily Catholic but nevertheless tried to avoid the confessional identity of the old Center Party. The CDU stood for anticommunism, free-enterprise economics, and social conservatism, but Adenauer, like many British and

Illustration 32.6

The Berlin Wall. Berlin remained at the center of the cold war in Europe and was the issue in a heated East-West dispute of 1960–61. This Berlin crisis saw renewed Soviet claims to the city and threats to close access to it. When President Kennedy and other Western leaders stood firm, the Soviet response was to close the border between East and West Germany. A wall was constructed through the center of Berlin in August 1961. In this photo, the wall curves around the historic Brandenburg Gate with winged victory riding in a chariot atop it. The gate was in the Soviet zone, where the "shoot-to-kill" area near the wall is clearly visible.

French conservatives, defended the welfare state and drew on Bismarck's example in the 1880s to advocate "socially responsible" capitalism.

The CDU mixture of conservatism and socialism won a narrow plurality of the votes for the German parliament (the *Bundestag*) in 1949 elections; the party expanded that margin to win every national election of the 1950s and the 1960s. Adenauer won the chancellorship of West Germany by a single vote by allying with a moderate third party (the Free Democrats) against a strong Social Democratic Party. Adenauer's personality was more authoritarian than democratic, but his fourteen-year chancellorship (1949–63) firmly established the Federal Republic as a Western democracy. Because of his influence, the capital of the new republic was situated in the small (100,000 population in 1939) Rhineland manufacturing town of Bonn where he had been a student, and the Federal Republic was sometimes called the Bonn republic.

The greatest accomplishment of the Bonn republic was an economic recovery called the *Wirtschaftswunder* ("economic miracle"). The *Wirtschaftswunder* owed much to American policy: Germany was included in the Marshall Plan of 1948 and was given $3.5 billion by 1961. Much of the credit for the recovery also belongs to the finance minister in Adenauer's cabinet, Ludwig Erhard. Erhard was a professor of economics at the University of Munich and the principal author of the CDU program linking free-enterprise economics with social welfare. He presided over a monetary policy that penalized savings and favored the purchase of commodities. His demand-driven economy created a huge increase in production (see table 32.2). German steel production had been 13.7 million tons in 1910. After five years of recovery, East and West Germany together produced only 13.1 million tons in 1950. By 1960 West Germany alone produced 34.1 million tons. Translated into a consumer economy, this meant that West Germany manufactured only 301,000 automobiles in 1950 but more than 3 million in 1960. This rapid growth of production virtually eliminated unemployment, which fell below 1 percent. Credit for this prosperity also belongs to the generation of workers who lived with long workweeks (typically forty-eight hours) and low wages

TABLE 32.2

The German Economic Miracle, 1945–69

Product	1949	1954	1959	1964	1969
Coal (1,000 tons)	177.0	217.6	237.3	255.0	229.8
Pig iron (1,000 tons)	7,140	12,512	21,602	27,182	33,764
Steel (1,000 tons)	9,156	17,434	29,435	37,339	45,316
Petroleum (1,000 tons)	842	2,666	5,103	7,673	7,876
Natural gas (million cubic meters)	534	87	388	1,975	8,799
Private cars (1,000s)	104	561	1,503	2,650	3,380
Electricity (million kilowatt hours)	40.7	70.5	106.2	164.8	226.1

Source: B. R. Mitchell, *European Historical Statistics, 1750–1990* (London: Macmillan, 1975), pp. 366, 372, 395, 402, 467, 481.

(twenty-five cents per hour in the 1950s—less than half of the American standard). In return for social benefits, such as four to six weeks of paid vacation per year, Germany obtained great labor peace: During the first decade of the twentieth century, Germany had lost an annual average of 6.5 million working days to strikes; during the 1960s, West Germany lost an average of 0.3 million working days.

Europe and the World: The Age of Decolonization, 1945–75

When World War II ended, Europe still held vast colonial empires. Most of Africa, the Middle East, South and Southeast Asia, the East Indies and Pacific Oceania, and the Caribbean remained under imperial rule. Movements for national independence had begun in many areas before the war. After the war, the imperial powers learned that they could not keep their empires even by fighting major wars. The resulting breakup of European colonial empires, called decolonization, is one of the most important themes of twentieth-century world history. As one non-Western nationalist put it, decolonization changed "the international structure more profoundly than did the two terrible world wars." That change happened rapidly. Most of South Asia and

the East Indies (more than 500 million people) won self-government between 1946 and 1950. Most of Africa (more than thirty countries) won independence between 1956 and 1966.

Three major patterns of decolonization emerged in the 1940s: (1) the pattern set by the British in India (granted independence in 1947) showed that Europeans could end imperialism when convinced that they must do so or pay a terrible price; (2) the pattern set by the French in the Brazzaville Conference of 1944 showed that some governments would struggle to retain empires; and (3) the pattern set by the people of the Dutch East Indies (1945–49) showed that colonial peoples could win their independence by force.

The British acceptance of decolonization began with the election of the Attlee government in 1945. Labour Party doctrine had included colonial independence since a 1926 program denounced the empire as "based on the absolute subjection of the native population." British economic weakness and war weariness also made resistance unlikely. Gandhi's continued campaign of nonviolent resistance (*Satyagraha*), massive demonstrations, and the astute political leadership of Jawaharlal Nehru won Indian independence in 1947 (see illustration 32.7). The most difficult issue facing the British was not granting independence (they realized that they had little choice), but the conditions of it: Conflicts between the Moslem and Hindu popula-

Illustration 32.7

The Age of Decolonization. For much of the world, the "age of the cold war" was a much less important image than "the age of decolonization" in which much of Africa and Asia won independence. The harbinger of decolonization was India, where resistance to British rule had grown throughout the twentieth century. In the winter of 1945–46, demonstrations swept such major cities as Bombay and Calcutta, starting an upheaval that won independence in 1947. In this photo, an explosion has taken place in the streets of Calcutta, near a crowd of demonstrators, and the British scurry to respond.

tions of India led to its partition into a largely Hindu India (with Nehru as its first prime minister) and a largely Moslem Pakistan, a bitter parting that led to much violence in 1946–48 and to brief India-Pakistan Wars in 1965, 1971, and 1984.

The British withdrawal (again with little choice) from another colonial territory created another explosive situation in the Middle East. The collapse of the Ottoman Empire and the British role in the Arab revolt of 1916 had left Britain controlling much of the Middle East after World War I as a colonial mandate (see map 32.3). The British administration of Palestine, Trans-Jordan, and the Arabian peninsula (today, Israel, Jordan, Saudi Arabia, and the Arab states of the Persian Gulf) found itself at the center of the Zionist effort to create an independent Jewish homeland in the Middle East. Zionism had grown in Europe, begun through the efforts of an Austrian journalist named Theodore Herzl, in response to turn-of-the-century anti-Semitism seen in the Dreyfus case in France, the pogroms in Russia, and the anti-Semitic mayor of Vienna. During World War I, the British foreign secretary, Arthur Balfour, had issued a statement supporting the establishment of a Jewish homeland in Palestine, and this Balfour Declaration gained great importance when a British general occupied Jerusalem and the postwar settlement put Palestine in British hands. A migration of European Jews to Palestine began during the interwar years, as did the first Arab-Jewish strife in Palestine, but British steps toward the creation of Israel were slow and Jewish

settlers formed a terrorist organization, the Irgun, to fight for independence. World War II and the Holocaust greatly accelerated both the pace of Jewish settlement and the conflict in Palestine. When the British attempted to block massive postwar immigration, the Irgun turned on the British and in 1946 blew up the King David Hotel (British headquarters), killing ninety-one. As the battle for Jewish immigration and for an independent Jewish state grew, the British found themselves in the middle of Jewish-Arab warfare. The United Nations took up the matter in 1947 and adopted a resolution in favor of the partition of Palestine, but even the UN was unwelcome at the center of this battle. In 1948 Jewish settlers proclaimed the state of Israel and were immediately confronted with an Arab attack, but the UN mediator was assassinated. An armistice in 1949 ended what was only the first Arab-Israeli War. Israel survived, but the wars to redefine Palestine continued throughout the cold war, including the Suez War of 1956 in which Britain and France still acted as colonial powers and intervened against Egypt. The most decisive war was the Six-Day War of 1967 when Israel won a sweeping military victory over Egypt, Jordan, and Syria, resulting in the annexation of territory (especially the Palestinian-populated western bank of the Jordan), which added to future disputes. Israel's neighbors regained a measure of pride, but no territory, by their greater military success in the Yom Kippur War of 1973. It, too, left the Palestinian question unresolved.

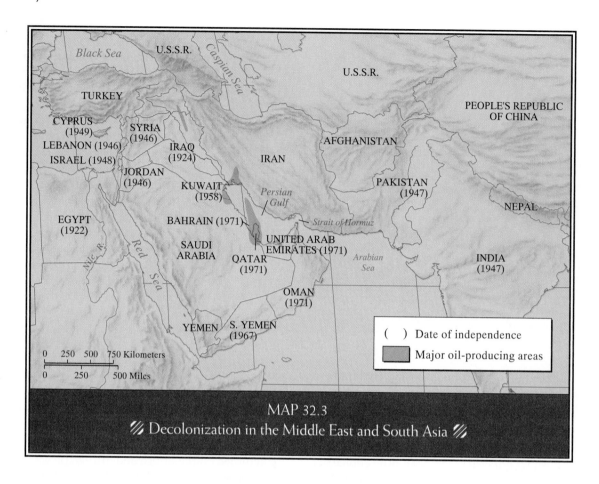

MAP 32.3
Decolonization in the Middle East and South Asia

The French began the postwar era struggling to retain their colonial empire, instead of withdrawing as the British were obliged to do in India and Palestine. A French effort to block decolonization started with the doctrine of assimilation. Advocates of assimilation believed that colonial peoples could be integrated (assimilated) into a French-speaking, French-cultured civilization in which both the metropolitan and the overseas territories were principal parts. That philosophy shaped both the Brazzaville Conference, where the French promised "the material and moral development of the natives" but not independence, and the colonial provisions in the constitution of the Fourth Republic (1946): France and her colonies formed an indissoluble French Union. So the French fought independence. While the British were granting independence to Burma (1947), the French were resisting a proclamation of independence in neighboring Vietnam. During the next generation, independent Burma produced a secretary-general of the United Nations, U Thant, while Vietnam fought nineteen years of war against France (1946–54) and the United States (1965–75).

The Indonesian pattern of guerrilla warfare became one of the predominant features of decolonization. Two days after the surrender of Japan in 1945 Indonesian leaders proclaimed a republic of Indonesia under the presidency of Achmed Sukarno, who had led resistance since 1927. When the Dutch refused independence, they had to fight an Indonesian People's Army until accepting independence four years later (see map 32.4). Variations of this pattern were repeated in all European empires. The French fought Ho Chi Minh's Vietminh forces in Vietnam until withdrawing after a shocking defeat at Dienbienphu in 1954. The British fought the Mau Mau movement of Jomo Kenyatta in Kenya from 1948 to 1957. The last country to accept decolonization, Portugal, battled guerrilla warfare in Mozambique until 1975.

Decolonization became intertwined with the cold war. The Soviet Union realized that the peoples of Africa and Asia were fighting their mutual enemies, so Moscow supported movements of national liberation. Some independence leaders were Communists, such as Ho Chi Minh, one of the founders of the French Com-

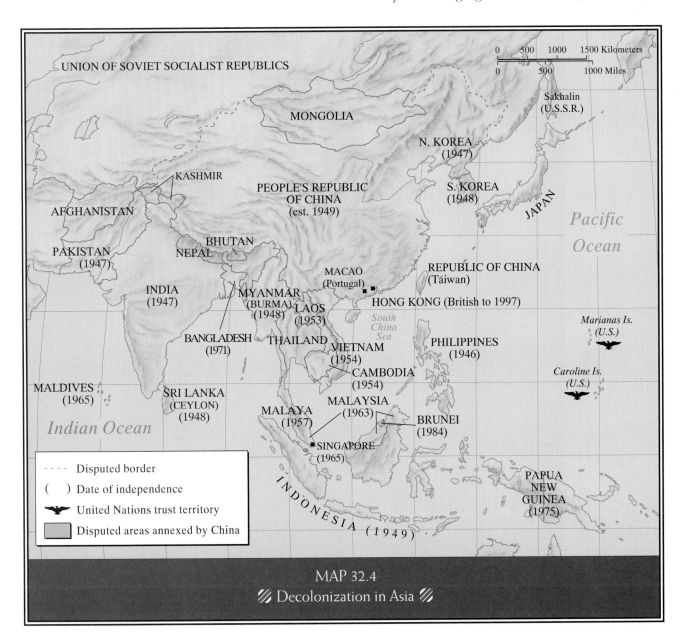

MAP 32.4
Decolonization in Asia

munist Party. Some liberation movements hid an un-
comfortable alliance between Communist elements and
nationalists; this happened in the Dutch East Indies,
where the leadership was anti-Communist and later
conducted a bloody purge of Communists. The United
States and the European imperial powers often reacted
to decolonization as if it were only a theater of the cold
war where the policy of containment applied. This led
to further Western hostility to many independence
movements and was a major factor for American involvement in Vietnam.

Leaders of newly independent states usually tried
to keep their countries out of the cold war while seeking aid from both sides. This policy of nonalignment
created a Third World between East and West. Nehru's
nonalignment, for example, committed India "to maintain friendly relations with all countries, even though
we may disagree with them in their policies or structure
of government." President Sukarno of Indonesia, President Nasser of Egypt, and Prime Minister Nkrumah of
Ghana similarly favored nonalignment. A milestone in
the growth of the Third World came in 1955 when
Sukarno hosted the Bandung Conference: Twenty-nine
independent African and Asian states met to discuss the
postimperial epoch in world history.

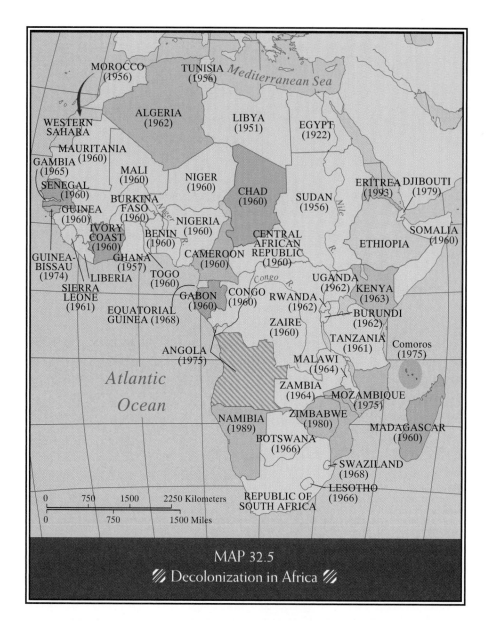

MAP 32.5

Decolonization in Africa

The turning point in decolonization came between 1957 and 1962. During those years both Britain and France acknowledged the end of their empires, and more than two dozen countries gained their independence. France had lost the disastrous war in Vietnam in 1954. Britain and France had suffered further embarrassment in the Suez War of 1956. In 1957 the British West African colony of Gold Coast had become the independent state of Ghana under the leadership of Kwame Nkrumah (see map 32.5). Nkrumah, sometimes called "the Gandhi of Africa" for his leadership of sub-Saharan independence, became the voice of the new

Africa and a revered father-figure to many anticolonialists (see document 32.5). In 1958 he led the first conference of independent African states in condemning Western colonialism and racism. Two years later, the United Nations adopted a Declaration against Colonialism stating that the ideals of the World War II Allies, embodied in the UN Charter and the UN Declaration of Human Rights, must apply to the peoples of Africa and Asia, too (see document 32.6). The remaining European empires (Belgium, Britain, France, Portugal, and Spain), plus the United States, did not support this resolution, but they could not overcome global support for it.

❖ DOCUMENT 32.5 ❖

Kwame Nkrumah: An Independent Africa (1961)

Kwame Nkrumah (1909–72) was born in the Gold Coast and educated in Britain and the United States. That education made Nkrumah a convinced anticolonialist, and he returned to Africa to found a militant political party in 1949. He became prime minister of the Gold Coast in 1951 and led the colony during its struggle for independence (1951–57), after which he became the first president of Ghana. Nkrumah was the first black head of state to win freedom.

For centuries, Europeans dominated the African continent. The white man arrogated to himself the right to rule and to be obeyed by the non-white; his mission, he claimed, was to "civilize" Africa. Under this cloak, the Europeans robbed the continent of vast riches and inflicted unimaginable suffering on the African people.

All this makes a sad story, but now we must be prepared to bury the past with its unpleasant memories and look to the future. All we ask of the former colonial powers is their goodwill and cooperation to remedy past mistakes and injustices and to grant independence to the colonies in Africa. . . .

It is clear that we must find an African solution to our problems, and that this can only be found in African unity. Divided we are weak; united, Africa could become one of the greatest forces for good in the world.

Although most Africans are poor, our continent is potentially extremely rich. Our mineral resources, which are being exploited with foreign capital only to enrich foreign investors, range from gold and diamonds to uranium and petroleum. . . . Never before have a people had within their grasp so great an opportunity for developing a continent endowed with so much wealth. Individually, the independent states of Africa, some of them potentially rich, others poor, can do little for their people. Together, by mutual help, they can achieve much. . . . Only a strong political union can bring about full and effective development of our natural resources for the benefit of our people. . . .

There is a tide in the affairs of every people when the moment strikes for political action. Such was the moment in the history of the United States of America when the Founding Fathers saw beyond the petty wranglings of the separate states and created a Union. This is our chance. We must act now.

❖ DOCUMENT 32.6 ❖

The United Nations Declaration Against Colonialism (1960)

The General Assembly, mindful of the determination proclaimed by the peoples of the world in the Charter of the United Nations to reaffirm faith in fundamental human rights, in the dignity and worth of the human person, in the equal rights of men and women and of nations large and small, and to promote social progress and better standards of life in larger freedom . . . declares that:

1. The subjection of peoples to alien subjugation, domination, and exploitation constitutes a denial of fundamental human rights, is contrary to the Charter of the United Nations and is an impediment to the promotion of world peace and cooperation.

2. All peoples have the right to self-determination; by virtue of that right they freely determine their political status and freely pursue their economic, social, and cultural development.

3. Inadequacy of political, economic, social or educational preparedness should never serve as a pretext for delaying independence.

4. All armed action or repressive measures of all kinds directed against dependent peoples shall cease in order to enable them to exercise peacefully and freely their right to complete independence.

◈ DOCUMENT 32.7 ◈

The Treaty of Rome, 1957

Preamble

[The governments of Belgium, France, Germany, Italy, Luxembourg, and the Netherlands,]

DETERMINED to establish the foundations of an ever closer union among the European peoples,

DECIDED to ensure the economic and social progress . . . by . . . eliminating the barriers which divide Europe,

DIRECTING their efforts to . . . constantly improving the living and working conditions of their peoples,

RECOGNIZING that the removal of existing obstacles calls for concerted action. . . .

ANXIOUS to strengthen the unity of their economies and to ensure their harmonious development by reducing the differences existing between the various regions and by mitigating the backwardness of the less favored,

DESIROUS of contributing by . . . common commercial policy to the . . . abolition of restrictions on international trade,

INTENDING to confirm the solidarity which binds Europe and overseas countries, and desiring to insure the development of their prosperity, in accordance with the principles of the charter of the United Nations,

RESOLVED to strengthen the safeguards of peace and liberty by establishing this combination of resources. . . .

HAVE DECIDED to create a European Economic Community. . . .

Article One

By the present treaty, the High Contracting Parties establish among themselves a European Economic Community.

Article Two

It shall be the aim of the Community, by establishing a Common Market . . . to promote throughout the Community a harmonious development of economic activities, a continuous and balanced expansion, an increased stability, an accelerated raising of the standard of living, and closer relations between its Member States.

Article Three

. . . [T]he activities of the Community shall include. . . .

(a) the elimination, as between Member States, of customs duties and of quantitative restrictions in regard to the importation and exportation of goods. . . .

(b) the establishment of a common customs tariff . . . towards third countries;

(c) the abolition . . . of the obstacles to the free movement of persons, services, and capital;

(d) the inauguration of common agricultural policy;

(e) the inauguration of a common transport policy;

Article Four

The achievement of the tasks entrusted to the Community shall be ensured by: an Assembly, a Council, a Commission, a Court of Justice.

Conservative governments in Britain and France, long the staunchest imperialists, recognized that the age of empire—or "the great western party," as one black leader termed it—was over. Prime Minister Harold MacMillan acknowledged this in a 1960 speech discussing the "wind of change" blowing across the African continent. His Tory government of 1957–64 granted Ghana, Kenya, Nigeria, and four other territories independence. President de Gaulle, who had courageously granted Algerian independence at the risk of French civil war, presided over the independence of thirteen more French African colonies between 1958 and 1962.

◈

The European Economic Community, 1945–75

The most historic trend in postwar Europe may not have been reconstruction and prosperity, the revival of democratic government, the cold war between the West and the Soviet bloc, or even the age of decolonization, but the progress toward European unity.

Postwar cooperation began with the removal of trade barriers and the negotiation of free trade agreements. A 1948 treaty linked Belgium, Luxembourg, and the Netherlands in the Benelux Customs Union. The Organization for European Economic Cooperation

Illustration 32.8

%% **The European Economic Community.** A historic step toward the economic unity of western Europe was captured in this photograph of March 1957. The six states (West Germany, France, Italy, Belgium, Netherlands, and Luxembourg) that had cooperated in the European Coal and Steel Community increased their close collaboration by signing the Treaty of Rome, which created the European Economic Community (the predecessor of the European Union), and opened a common market among them. At front and center in this picture (third from the right) is Konrad Adenauer.

(OEEC) united sixteen non-Communist states, from Iceland and Scandinavia in the north to Turkey and Iberia in the south, for the distribution of American aid from the Marshall Plan. The OEEC sparked debates about European unity, especially after the selection of Paul-Henri Spaak of Belgium as the first president of its council. Spaak called for political institutions to accompany economic unity, and a 1949 treaty founded the Council of Europe to begin such cooperation.

Meaningful economic integration began in 1950. The foreign minister of France, Robert Schuman, introduced a new plan devised by Monnet: pooling coal and steel resources under an international authority to speed recovery. Britain—in a fateful decision that long separated the British from the evolution of European unity—rejected the Schuman Plan, but France, West Germany, Italy, and the Benelux states created the European Coal and Steel Community in 1951. Monnet, a strong advocate of a United States of Europe, became the first president of the Coal and Steel Community. Despite appeals by Schuman and Monnet, British conservatives still refused to join, so the six continental states chose "to create Europe without Britain."

The Paris Treaty of 1951 that created the Coal and Steel Community also contained plans for a European Parliament to sit in Strasbourg, and the six members added other supranational institutions such as the Euro-

pean Court of Human Rights (1953), a dedication to human rights that would later become one of the hallmarks of European unity when other states sought to join. (Even if it were in Europe, the United States would be ineligible for membership because the widespread application of the death penalty in America violates the European standard of human rights.) When the Coal and Steel Community prospered, this persuaded "the Six" to begin to discuss a common market for all goods. The Rome Treaties of 1957 (see document 32.7) then created the European Economic Community (the EEC)—often called the Common Market—in which the Six accepted the gradual elimination of tariffs (1959–68) among themselves and a common tariff policy toward other countries (see illustration 32.8).

The EEC enjoyed economic advantages during the recovery of the 1950s and the prosperity of the 1960s. Its success was so clear that seven other countries (Austria, Denmark, Norway, Portugal, Sweden, Switzerland, and a reluctant Britain) formed a similar organization, the European Free Trade Association (EFTA) in 1959. The EEC, however, moved more quickly to economic and political cooperation than the EFTA did, and by the early 1960s EEC membership clearly was highly desirable. Greece obtained associate status in the EEC in 1961, with limited trade benefits, and Turkey followed in 1963. Britain, Ireland, and Norway then applied for full membership. President de Gaulle—who had never forgiven Britain and America for their treatment of him and the French government in exile during World War II and who believed that the British were unwilling to surrender any measure of sovereignty to a continental organization—vetoed British entry into the Common Market, however, leading the EEC to table all applications. Instead of expanding, the EEC chose to tighten its internal unity, and the EEC, the European Coal and Steel Community, and other organizations linking the Six were merged to form the European Community (EC) in 1967.

Charles de Gaulle remained an obstacle to expansion of the EC until his retirement in 1969, but the Six voted for expansion immediately after his departure. The EC accepted all four applications, but Norwegians rejected membership in a national referendum (53–47 percent), so the Six became the Nine. The British, whose relations with Europe had been troubled for a generation, reconsidered their membership and demanded new terms for entry into the EC. They joined in 1973, but domestic opinion still demanded concessions; after winning some agreements, the British supported membership in a national referendum in 1975. Most of non-Communist Europe then began to line up for entry into the European Community.

The Cooling Down of the Cold War: *Ostpolitik* and Détente, 1965–75

The cold war in Europe began to end in the mid-1960s, and both the Soviet and American alliance systems began to weaken. A growing rift between the USSR and China opened in the 1960s, and the USSR denounced Chinese policy as "anti-Leninist" and branded Mao a dictator. The chill worsened when the Chinese detonated their first H-bomb in 1967, and frontier incidents became common in the late 1960s. Simultaneously, American alliances were strained by the protracted Vietnam War, which was widely denounced in Europe.

The diplomatic consequences of these events were enormous, and new policies emerged during the late 1960s and early 1970s. President de Gaulle of France and Chancellor Willy Brandt of West Germany led Europe into this new era—de Gaulle by distancing France from the Western alliance in the late 1960s and Brandt by normalizing relations with Eastern Europe in the

early 1970s. These changes initially discomfitted American governments, but they helped to change American policy. President Lyndon B. Johnson and Secretary Leonid Brezhnev cautiously accepted arms control negotiations in the late 1960s, and this produced a series of important treaties in the 1970s. The next president of the United States, Richard M. Nixon, carried this policy to dramatic lengths in improving relations with the USSR and Maoist China, despite his career-long image as a dedicated anticommunist.

Charles de Gaulle opened the decade of diplomatic change in 1966 with a dramatic announcement that France was quitting its role in the NATO alliance and that NATO must leave French soil. Hostile opinion held that de Gaulle was getting even for the way that Churchill had relegated him to the background during World War II, but de Gaulle also had a vision behind his actions. He visited the USSR and Eastern Europe in 1967 to promote his vision of "Europe to the Urals." This was not his most startling idea. The French tested their first atomic bomb in 1966 and their first H-bomb in 1968, and de Gaulle then proclaimed an independent French *force de frappe* (nuclear striking force) that was aimed at *toutes azimuths* (all points of the compass).

Willy Brandt's role in the diplomatic revolution had a more pacific tone. Brandt was shaped by his wartime experience as a refugee from Nazi Germany. He became famous as the mayor of West Berlin (1957–66) at the height of the cold war, leading that isolated city during confrontations over the Berlin Wall. Brandt then became the head of the West German socialist party and led the SPD to electoral victory. As chancellor of West Germany, he introduced his own dramatic policy known as *Ostpolitik* (eastern policy). He improved relations between the two Germanys by visiting the DDR in 1970 and shaking hands with the Communist prime minister. He signed treaties with both the Soviet Union and Poland, guaranteeing Germany's postwar frontiers, especially the Oder-Neisse Line that left much of pre-war Germany inside Poland. He then negotiated a series of treaties between the two Germanys, culminating in a 1972 treaty permitting both states to enter the United Nations. *Ostpolitik* won Brandt the Nobel Peace Prize, but he resigned in 1974 when a spy scandal revealed that a member of his staff was an East German agent.

These European changes encouraged the improvement in Soviet-American relations known as *détente* (the relaxation of tension). Arms control negotiations with the USSR were controversial in the United States, and conservatives had fought against President John F. Kennedy's Test Ban Treaty (1963) in which both sides promised not to test nuclear weapons in the atmosphere, in outer space, or under the oceans. The French and Chinese nuclear explosions of 1967 persuaded Washington and Moscow to resume negotiations for the nuclear nonproliferation treaty of 1968, and this treaty encouraged the United States and the USSR to open larger Strategic Arms Limitation Talks (SALT) in 1969. Anti-Communist conservatives in America fought this policy, but it succeeded when a conservative anti-Communist adopted it. Richard Nixon, who placated anti-Communists by waging vigorous war in Asia, followed the left-wing policy of détente to new relations with the Soviet Union. Nixon and Brezhnev exchanged state visits in the early 1970s and signed a series of arms treaties, beginning with the SALT treaty of 1972. A vivid symbol of the age of détente came in the summer of 1975 when American and Russian spacecrafts docked together in outer space, but Nixon provided an even more dramatic symbol in his Chinese policy. He accepted Communist Chinese membership in the UN, flew to Beijing to meet with Chairman Mao, agreed that Taiwan was part of China, and posed for photographs atop the Great Wall of China. The cold war was ending.

An Era of Unrest and Violence, 1968–75

Although the cold war was less heated in 1970 than it had been in the 1950s, Europe faced other violence. The war in southeast Asia, which had been a battleground for thirty years—as the Vietnamese fought first to throw out Japanese conquerors, then the restored French imperial government, and finally American forces sent to fight Communism there—formed an important background for the violence of 1968–75. Fighting in Vietnam reduced the global prestige of the United States to its lowest level since World War II. Student and left-wing demonstrations in the great cities of Europe protested American militarism. Simultaneously, American military prestige suffered in 1968 when the Viet Cong's Tet (the lunar new year) Offensive overran American positions and took the fighting into the cities of South Vietnam. American moral leadership suffered when the U.S. army began a war crimes trial of American officers for killing 567 civilians in the village

of My Lai in 1969, and the evidence led to the conviction of Lt. William Calley. Such events produced great turbulence in American society, and the late 1960s and early 1970s witnessed vehement student protests on university campuses, race riots in American cities, a police riot in Chicago, an antiwar march on Washington, D.C., the assassination of two American political leaders (the Reverend Dr. Martin Luther King, Jr., and Senator Robert F. Kennedy), and the use of armed troops against protesters, resulting in the killing of four students at Kent State University.

One consequence of these events for Europe was that the United States lost much of its authority to oppose the Soviet Union when a crisis occurred in Czechoslovakia. In January 1968 the Czech Communist Party selected a liberal reformer, Alexander Dubček, for the leadership post of first secretary of the party. Dubček proposed political and economic liberties to humanize communist society. The enthusiastic Czech response to Dubček's brand of socialism led to an optimistic period known as the Prague Spring, but the reforms and the optimism were both short-lived. Brezhnev ordered an invasion of Czechoslovakia in August 1968. An occupying force of 200,000 Soviet and Warsaw Pact troops encountered Czech protests, and 650,000 soldiers were ultimately needed to end the demonstrations, oust Dubček, and install a pro-Moscow government (see illustration 32.9).

The early 1970s witnessed other changes of government by force. A military junta seized power in Greece in 1973, the Portuguese army overthrew the government there in 1974, and Turkey invaded Cyprus and partitioned it into Greek and Turkish sections in 1974. These military actions were not the most dramatic signs of European unrest, however. Militant student protests in European universities, the rise of European terrorist movements, and the rebirth of violent nationalist movements all characterized the era.

The largest European student protest occurred in Paris in the spring of 1968. Demonstrations at the University of Paris (which had an enrollment of 160,000) were part of an international youth rebellion of the late 1960s that had produced major outbreaks from the University of California to the University in Berlin a few weeks earlier. Many issues angered students, but in most protests they denounced American imperialism in Asia and the autocratic administration of their campus. The demonstrations at Paris became a global symbol of a near revolution sparked by students, as many of the revolutions of 1848 had been. They began with

Illustration 32.9

/// **Rebellion in the Soviet Bloc.** Throughout the cold war, the Soviet Union faced the problem of discontent in its satellite states in Eastern Europe. Major uprisings in East Germany in 1953, Hungary in 1956, and Czechoslovakia in 1968 were put down by force. This photo shows a scene from the Soviet-led Warsaw Pact invasion of Czechoslovakia: A Soviet tank has come under attack and crashed into a building in central Prague.

disputes on the suburban campus at Nanterre, then closed the Sorbonne, and grew into riots in central Paris. Once again, barricades closed streets in Paris. On one night, an estimated twenty-five thousand students fought the police (see illustration 32.10). The events of May 1968 assumed greater importance when industrial workers called a general strike to support the students and paralyzed much of France. The strikes and riots soon ended, but they led to the resignation of President de Gaulle a few months later.

Student protests were not the most violent legacy of the late 1960s and early 1970s. More fearsome was the rebirth of terrorism in European politics. Some terrorist movements had roots in the extreme left-wing politics of the era, including the Baader-Meinhof gang in West Germany (whose actions included setting fire to a Berlin department store) and the Red Brigades in Italy (who assassinated prominent individuals, such as the president of Fiat motors, and terrorized more by shooting people in the kneecap). International politics, particularly the Middle Eastern question, was an even greater source of terrorism. In 1972 alone, international terrorists high-jacked a German jetliner, attacked Jewish athletes at the Munich Olympic games, and sent letter bombs to businessmen in several countries.

A continuing part of the new violence in European politics was the escalation of nationalist terrorism. Basque nationalists sought independence from Spain by assassinations such as the bombing death of Spanish premier Luis Carrero Blanco in 1973. Corsican nationalists fought for independence from France by bombing public buildings. The most uncompromising terrorist

Illustration 32.10

/// **Violence in the West.** Despite the growing prosperity of Western Europe and the continuation of European peace, the late 1960s and early 1970s witnessed a range of violent forms of protest in Western Europe. Terrorist groups were active in both West Germany and Italy, and in France a rebellion of students and workers took place in May 1968. In this photo, French riot police with helmets, goggles, and shields try to hold their phalanx against demonstrators.

movement in Europe was Irish. Sectarian violence between Catholics and Protestants in Northern Ireland killed eight people in Belfast in August 1969, and the British government responded with troops to maintain order. This revived the Irish Republican Army (IRA), which hoped to drive the British out of Ulster and reunite Northern Ireland with the Republic of Ireland. The British government, however, was intransigent. In 1971 the British proclaimed emergency powers of detention and arrest and curtailed civil rights; in early 1972 Britain suspended the government of Northern Ireland and established direct rule by London. Later in 1972 British troops fired upon Catholic rioters in Londonderry, killing thirteen people in the "Bloody Sunday Massacre." By early 1973 the IRA had opened the

biggest terrorist campaign in postwar European history. A series of pub bombings in Guildford and Birmingham shocked British opinion by killing nearly thirty people in 1974, but London became the favorite IRA target. Bombs exploded there in law courts and at tourist attractions; later, the IRA would bomb a major department store during Christmas shopping, launch a mortar assault on the prime minister's residence at 10 Downing Street, attempt to assassinate the prime minister with a hotel bombing during a party conference, and set off an enormous explosion in the financial district. The first five years of public riots, sectarian assaults, vigilante justice, police and military repression, and terrorist attacks killed more than one thousand people.

Conclusion

The era following World War II is recent enough that public memory and historical analysis still wrestle with the depiction of it. The period 1945–75 began in difficult austerity for Europeans as they rebuilt their world and it ended with violence again becoming common in the political process. Throughout the epoch, the victorious Allies of World War II were divided between a Western bloc of states where democracy was restored and an Eastern bloc of states where communist dictatorships were created, and this ideological division hardened into military alliances—NATO in the west and the Warsaw Pact in the east. Although the two sides never went to war with each other, they fought a generation-long war of nerves and confrontation known as the cold war. Europeans lived with the constant threat of nuclear war, watching the arms race produce devastating weapons and knowing that they occupied the battlefield between the United States and Russia. The cold war did not produce another total war in Europe, though repeated confrontations such as the Berlin crises of 1948 and 1961 suggested that it might happen at any time. Elsewhere, the cold war encompassed many national and regional wars. The United States twice went to war in Asia—in Korea and in Vietnam—believing it necessary to contain the spread of communism. Europeans fought bitter wars, from the guerrilla wars in Indonesia and Kenya to larger wars such as France fought in Algeria, believing it would preserve European empires. Viewed in such terms, the postwar age was an age of war—perhaps, as some have suggested, it was World War III without the name.

A different sense of the age, however, suggests that Europe was witnessing the birth of a new "golden age." The Western states quickly recovered economic stability after 1945, effectively restored democratic government, and even expanded the sense of democracy by the growth of the welfare state (pioneered by the Attlee government in Britain) and the development of the mixed economy (pioneered by Jean Monnet of France). In contrast to the events of 1919–39, Europeans distinguished themselves by welcoming Germany back into the community of nations, as West Germany under Konrad Adenauer created a viable German democracy. And far-sighted governments in France, Italy, West Germany, and the Benelux states laid the basis for even greater European prosperity and longer-lasting European peace by creating the European Economic Community, which led to the rapid economic integration

and a high level of prosperity. Against the background of these successes, the historic empires of Europe accepted the loss of their former colonies—sometimes with grace, sometimes bowing before the inevitable, and sometimes through protracted force. Europeans also took the lead in ending the cold war, with Charles De Gaulle and Willy Brandt leading the United States and the USSR to the spirit of détente.

Suggested Readings

For overviews of the period, see E. Hobsbawm, *The Age of Extremes* (1994) and A. W. De Porte, *Europe between the Superpowers: The Enduring Balance* (1986).

For postwar Britain, see K. Morgan, *The People's Peace* (1992), a survey of the period 1945–90; D. Fraser, *The Evolution of the British Welfare State* (1973); J. Harris, *William Beveridge* (1977); J. Campbell, *Aneurin Bevan and the Mirage of British Socialism* (1987); J. Hinton, *Labour and Socialism* (1983); A. Horne, *Harold Macmillan* (1987); and E. Hopkins, *The Rise and Decline of the English Working Classes, 1918–1990* (1991).

For France, see J.-P. Rioux, *The Fourth Republic, 1944–1958* (1987); P. Williams, *Crisis and Compromise: Politics in the Fourth Republic* (1964); J. Charlot, *The Gaullist Phenomenon* (1971); J. Lacouture, *De Gaulle*, 2 vols. (1990–92); D. Bair, *Simone de Beauvoir* (1990); and B. Brown, *Protest in Paris: Anatomy of a Revolt* (1974), on the student uprising and labor unrest of 1968.

For West Germany, see T. G. Ash, *In Europe's Name: Germany and the Enduring Balance* (1993), J. Gimbel, *The American Occupation of Germany: Politics and the Military, 1945–1949* (1968), J. Tent, *Mission on the Rhine: Reeducation and Denazification in American Occupied Germany* (1982), A. Deighton, *The Impossible Peace: Britain, the Division of Germany, and the Origins of the Cold War* (1990), A. Grosser, *Germany in Our Time: A History of the Postwar Years* (1971), D. Bark and D. Gress, *A History of West Germany*, 2 vols. (1989), H. A. Turner, *Germany from Partition to Reunification* (1992), G. Smith, *Democracy in Western Germany: Parties and Politics in the Federal Republic* (1986), A. Shlaim, *The United States and the Berlin Blockade, 1948–1949* (1983), R. Slusser, *The Berlin Crisis of 1961* (1973), and R. McGeehan, *The German Rearmament Question* (1971).

For the Eastern bloc, see M. McCauley, ed., *Communist Power in Europe, 1944–1949* (1977), J. Rothschild, *A Return to Diversity: A Political History of East Central Europe since World War II* (1988), Z. Brzezinski, *The Soviet Bloc* (1967), G. Sandford, *From Hitler to Ulbricht: The Communist Reconstruction of East Germany, 1945–1946* (1983), D. Childs, *The GDR: Moscow's German Ally* (1988), M. Dennis, *German Democratic Republic: The Search for Identity* (1985), K. Kersten, *The Establishment of Communist Rule in Poland, 1943–1948* (1991), and M. Boll, *The Cold War in the Balkans* (1984).

For other Western states, see P. Ginsborg, *A History of Contemporary Italy* (1990), D. Sassoon, *Contemporary Italy* (1988), and P. Farneti, *The Italian Party System, 1945–1980* (1985).

For the cold war, see W. LaFeber, *America, Russia, and the Cold War, 1945–1992* (1991), A. Ulam, *The Rivals: America and Russia* since World War II (1971), J. L. Gaddis, *Strategies of Containment* (1982), J. Young, *Cold War Europe, 1945–1989: A Political History* (1991), L. Davis, *The Cold War Begins: Soviet-American Conflict over Eastern Europe* (1974), H. Feis, *From Trust to Terror: The Onset of the Cold War, 1945–1950* (1970), F. Harbutt, *The Iron Curtain: Churchill, America, and the Origins of the Cold War* (1986), W. Loth, *The Division of the World, 1941–1955* (1988), D. Yergin, *Shattered Peace: The Origins of the Cold War* (1990), S. Ashton, *In Search of Detente: The Politics of East-West Relations since 1945* (1989), A. Rubinstein, *Soviet Foreign Policy since World War II* (1992), V. Rothwell, *Britain and the Cold War, 1941–1947* (1982), M. Dockrill and J. Young, eds., *British Foreign Policy, 1945–56* (1989), H. Bull and W. R. Louis, eds., *The Special Relationship: Anglo-American Relations since 1945* (1988), A. Low, *The Sino-Soviet Dispute* (1976), H. Dinerstein, *The Making of a Missile Crisis: October 1962* (1976), T. Higgins, *The Perfect Failure: Kennedy, Eisenhower, and the CIA at the Bay of Pigs* (1987), J. Valenta, *Soviet Intervention in Czechoslovakia, 1968* (1991), A. Grosser, *The Western Alliance* (1980), R. Clawson and L. Kaplan, eds., *The Warsaw Pact* (1982), L. Kaplan, *NATO and the United States: The Enduring Alliance* (1988), F. Heller and J. Gillingham, eds., *NATO: The Founding of the Atlantic Alliance and the Integration of Europe* (1992), W. Griffith, *The Ostpolitik of the Federal Republic of Germany* (1978), and A. Pitman, *From Ostpolitik to Reunification* (1992).

For the nuclear question and the space race, see G. Herken, *The Winning Weapon: The Atomic Bomb in the Cold War, 1945–1950* (1988); L. Freedman, *The Evolution of Nuclear Strategy* (1989); M. Trachtenberg, *History and Strategy* (1991), essays on nuclear strategy, 1949–66; R. Divine, *Blowing on the Wind: The Nuclear Test Ban Debate, 1954–1960* (1978); R. Jervis, *The Meaning of the Nuclear Revolution: Statecraft and the Prospect of Armageddon* (1989); D. Gompert, *Nuclear Weapons and World Politics* (1977); D. Holloway, *The Soviet Union and the Arms Race* (1984); G. Kennan, *The Nuclear Delusion: Soviet-American Relations in the Atomic Age* (1983); R. Powaski, *March to Armageddon: The United States and the Nuclear Arms Race, 1939 to the Present* (1987); T. Rochon, *Mobilizing for Peace: The Antinuclear Movements in Western Europe* (1988); R. Taylor, *Against the Bomb: The British Peace Movement, 1958–1965* (1988); R. Divine, *The Sputnik Challenge* (1993); and P. Stares, *The Militarization of Space* (1985).

For European economic recovery and the road to economic unity, see A. Milward, *The Reconstruction of Western Europe, 1945–1951* (1984), R. Mayne, *The Recovery of Europe, 1945–1973* (1973), J. Gimbel, *The Origins of the Marshall Plan* (1976), M. Hogan, *The Marshall Plan: America, Britain, and the Reconstruction of Western Europe, 1947–1952* (1987), J. Gillingham, *Coal, Steel, and the Rebirth of Europe, 1945–1955* (1991), I. Wall, *The United States and the Making of Postwar France, 1945–1954* (1991), E. Di Nolfo, ed., *Power in Europe*, vol. 2: *Great Britain, France, Germany, Italy, and the Origins of the EEC, 1952–1957* (1992), F. R. Willis, *Italy Chooses Europe* (1971); and J. Young, *Britain, France, and the Unity of Europe, 1945–1951* (1984).

For decolonization, see R. F. Holland, *European Decolonization, 1918–1981: An Introductory Survey* (1985), P. Gifford and W. R. Louis, eds., *Decolonization and African Independence*, 2 vols. (1982–88), J. Darwin, *Britain and Decolonization: The Retreat from Empire in the Postwar World* (1988), N. Mansergh, *The Commonwealth Experience*, 2 vols. (1983), W. R. Louis and R. Owen, eds., *Suez 1956* (1989), W. R. Louis, *The British Empire in the Middle East, 1945–1951: Arab Nationalism, the United States, and Postwar Imperialism* (1987), R. Betts, *France and Decolonization* (1991), A. Horne, *A Savage War of Peace: Algeria, 1954–1962* (1987), and P. Willetts, *The Non-Aligned Movement: The Origins of a Third World Alliance* (1978).

For the era of violence, 1968–75, see D. Moss, *The Politics of Left-Wing Violence in Italy, 1969–85* (1989) and W. Laqueur, *The Age of Terrorism* (1987).

CHAPTER 33

THE NEW BELLE ÉPOQUE: DEMOCRACY AND PROSPERITY SINCE 1975

CHAPTER OUTLINE

◆◆◆◆◆◆◆◆◆◆◆◆◆◆◆◆◆◆◆◆

Chapter 33 examines contemporary Europe since the mid-1970s. The year 1975 was not an abrupt turning point in Western history, as 1914 or 1939 had been, but the events of the mid-1970s showed that the cold war was ending and a prosperous new Europe was emerging. The chapter begins by looking at this peace and prosperity, including signs of progress toward the ages-old dream of European unity. One element of European progress was the rise of women to real political power, and the chapter next looks at Great Britain under Margaret Thatcher, who introduced Europe to a firm, conservative reevaluation of that prosperity.

The most dramatic changes in Europe since the 1970s resulted from the collapse of the Communist regimes in the Soviet Union and Eastern Europe. Chapter 33 shows the background discontent, such as the rise of the Solidarity movement in Poland, that preceded this collapse. Also examined are the revolution that Mikhail Gorbachev brought to the USSR and the subsequent upheavals in Eastern Europe known as the revolutions of 1989. Two other historic events followed the collapse of Communist governments: the reunification of Germany and the Yugoslav War of 1991–95.

◆

European Peace and Prosperity

During 1975 two dramatic events gave Europe greater hope for an age of peace. The first was the end of the Vietnam War. This conflict, the last stage of thirty years of fighting to drive Japanese, then French, and finally American armies out of Southeast Asia, ended in April 1975 with the evacuation of the last American officials from South Vietnam and the fall of the Saigon government. Within a few weeks the governments of Laos and Cambodia also fell to Communist insurgents. Although this long war ended in Communist expansion, it did not greatly worsen cold war relations;

Illustration 33.1

//// **The Age of Détente.** Willy Brandt, the chancellor of West Germany, was perhaps the most influential statesman in launching the age of détente in the early 1970s. Brandt repeatedly made friendly overtures to the states of Eastern Europe, especially to East Germany and Poland—a policy known as *Ostpolitik*. He not only negotiated treaties that improved relations, but he also made a series of symbolic gestures, as seen in this photo, taken during a state visit to Poland: Brandt is silently contemplating a monument to the victims of the Warsaw ghetto, killed by Germans.

instead, it allowed them to improve, especially in Europe where the war had been widely opposed.

Despite the conflict in Southeast Asia, détente between east and west—which Chancellor Willy Brandt of West Germany had launched with his *Ostpolitik* of the early 1970s (see illustration 33.1)—had grown; the end of the war permitted even better relations among the United States, Western Europe, the USSR, and China. Détente culminated in the Helsinki Accord of 1975, in which thirty-five nations guaranteed the frontiers of 1945, renewed their support for the United Nations and the peaceful resolution of crises, swore respect for "the sovereign equality and individuality" of all states, expanded economic cooperation between the two cold war blocs, renounced the threat or use of force, and pledged respect for human rights (see document 33.1). Like most idealistic treaties—such as the UN Declaration of Human Rights of 1946, the Geneva Conventions, the Kellogg-Briand Pact of 1928, the League of Nations Charter of 1920, and the Hague Treaties of 1899 and 1906—the Helsinki Accord contained no mechanism to enforce its principles during crises, yet still promoted hope. Westerners acclaimed a treaty that obliged the USSR to honor human rights; but Soviet leader Leonid Brezhnev believed that the document still permitted actions such as the invasion of Afghanistan.

The ending of the Vietnam War and the signing of the Helsinki Accord were signs of a changing era, but the new mood was best symbolized by an event in outer space. In July 1975 American astronauts aboard an Apollo spacecraft and Soviet cosmonauts aboard a

Soyuz spacecraft docked their ships into a single orbiting craft. Russian and American commanders shook hands through open hatches, much as American and Soviet soldiers had shaken hands at the Elbe River in 1945—in an exciting moment of mutual triumph that temporarily overshadowed continuing differences.

By the late 1970s Western Europe had also developed a booming economy, which created a standard of living comparable to that in the United States. Recovery from the devastation of World War II had been largely completed by the late 1950s, and thriving European economies began to catch up with the United States during the 1960s. West Germany had become the most prosperous country in Europe, with a GNP larger than France or Britain. The economic miracle of Ludwig Erhart and Konrad Adenauer created the fastest growing economy in German history. The German model of labor relations, in which labor, management, the government, and public opinion shared a strong consensus on supporting a welfare state and promising job security in return for strike- and strife-free production, resulted in a rapidly growing economy. German unemployment fell so low that foreign guest workers (*Gastarbeiter*) from Turkey and other Mediterranean countries were needed to fill jobs. The German domestic market absorbed most of this production during the 1960s, and German foreign trade remained low at the start of the 1970s. But Germany overcame the global recession of the 1970s—which had been chiefly caused by dramatic price increases demanded by a cartel of oil producing states (OPEC)—and increased exports by 1,300 percent. The other EEC states also began export-

◆ DOCUMENT 33.1 ◆

The Helsinki Accord, 1975

The Conference on Security and Cooperation in Europe produced the most idealistic international agreement of the cold war. Thirty-five countries signed the Final Act of this conference, which became known as the Helsinki Accord.

The participating states will respect human rights and fundamental freedoms, including the freedom of thought, conscience, religion or belief, for all without distinction as to race, sex, language or religion.

They will promote and encourage the effective exercise of civil, political, economic, social, cultural, and other rights and freedoms all of which derive from the inherent dignity of the human person and are essential for his free and full development.

Within this framework the participating states will recognize and respect the freedom of the individual to profess and practice, alone or in community with others, religion or belief acting in accordance with the dictates of his own conscience.

The participating states on whose territory national minorities exist will respect the rights of persons belonging to such minorities to equality before the law, will afford them the full opportunity for the actual enjoyment of human rights and fundamental freedoms and will, in this manner, protect their legitimate interests in this sphere.

---

ing more goods, while needing fewer imports, and prospered. French agriculture prospered so well that France became the world's second largest food exporter. By the end of the 1970s the European Union had become a major economic competitor of the United States. By 1990 GNP per capita in France ($16,000) and Germany ($18,500) neared that in the United States ($19,800).

Widespread prosperity had two important consequences in Western Europe: (1) it stimulated closer economic unity, a trend that had been slowly progressing for twenty-five years, and (2) it facilitated the growth of larger commitments to the welfare state. For the first of these trends, the mid-1970s were an important turning point. The European Community (also known as the EC, the closer community that had evolved out of

the EEC in 1967)—linking France, West Germany, Italy, and the Benelux countries—was the highest degree of European economic integration ever achieved. Attempts to expand this community had failed in the 1960s when President de Gaulle of France repeatedly blocked British membership. Negotiations to expand the EC revived in the 1970s, and ambitious plans were drafted for adding Britain, Ireland, Denmark, and Norway as the first step toward the economic union of all of non-Communist Europe (see chronology 33.1). The most important (and sometimes the most troublesome) of these states, Britain, finally joined the EC in 1973. In several cases, membership treaties were submitted for public approval in a referendum. A negative vote in Norway kept that country out of the European Community, but British membership was reaffirmed in a public vote in 1975, encouraging a generation of EC growth (see map 33.1). The death of General Franco (1975) and the subsequent election of a democratic government in Spain (1977), plus free elections in Portugal (1975) that freed Iberia from the authoritarian governments of the 1930s, allowed the EC to accept both Iberian states, bringing membership to twelve. Under the leadership of Jacques Delors, who presided over the European Commission in Brussels for ten years (1985–95), and Helmut Kohl, who has strongly supported closer unity, Europe moved toward a federal unity and oversaw the transformation of the European Community (EC) into the European Union (EU) in 1991, when the Maastricht summit outlined a treaty to open European frontiers and establish a single market. By the mid-1990s, the European Union had grown to fifteen members with the addition of Sweden, Finland, and Austria. The fall of the Communist bloc led to a wave of applications from Eastern Europe, and in 1997 plans were adopted for the eventual membership of Estonia, Poland, the Czech Republic, Hungary, and Slovenia; other Eastern European applications (plus one from Turkey) have been put on a slower track.

As the European Union grew, so did its institutions. The first direct elections for the European Parliament in Strasbourg were held in 1979, and a woman, Simone Veil of France, was chosen as its first president. An agreement signed that same year created an integrated monetary system to control exchange rates, the first step toward a common European currency to be known as the Euro and tentatively set to be launched in 1999. A European summit meeting of 1985 agreed on the Single European Act, setting 1992 as the date to create a frontierless economy, allowing the free movement of workers, students, and investments. Another summit

---

◆ CHRONOLOGY 33.1 ◆

The Growth of European Union Since 1975

1973   Britain joins the European Community (EC)

1975   British referendum accepts EC membership

1975   Greece, Spain, and Portugal apply for EC membership

1979   First direct elections to the European Parliament in Strasbourg

1979   Simone Veil elected president of the European Parliament

1979   The EC creates the European Monetary System (EMS) and European Currency Unit (ECU)

1979   Britain demands reduction in its contribution to the EC budget

1981   Greece begins five-year phased entry into the EC as tenth member

1983   Governments of the ten EC members sign the Solemn Declaration on unity

1984   EC and European Free Trade Association (EFTA) sign free trade agreement

1984   European Parliament adopts treaty on creating the European Union (EU)

1985   Spain and Portugal accepted into the EC as eleventh and twelfth members

1985   Jacques Delors becomes president of the Commission of the EC

1985   Single European Act sets 1992 as date for open frontiers and single market

1986   Single European Act adopted in parliaments of all twelve member states

1987   Turkey applies for membership in the EC

1988   Delors Plan outlines closer economic unity and a common currency

1988   Margaret Thatcher denounces a growing EC "superstate"

1989   EC adopts draft Charter of Fundamental Social Rights

1989   Austria applies for membership in the EC

1990   Margaret Thatcher denounces high centralization of the EC

1990   Cyprus and Malta apply for EC membership

1991   Sweden applies for membership in the EC

1991   Maastricht Summit gives concessions to Britain on common currency and social policy

1992   Single European Act and Maastricht Treaty create open frontiers and single market: EC becomes the EU

1992   Norway and Finland apply for EC membership

1992   Twelve members of the EU agree to negotiations to expand to sixteen members

1992   Switzerland applies for EU membership

1994   Sweden, Finland, and Austria reach agreements to join the EU

1995   Norwegian national referendum again rejects EU membership

1997   EU adopts plan for Estonia, Poland, Czech Republic, Hungary, and Slovenia to join

1997   Membership plans for Latvia, Lithuania, Slovakia, Romania, Bulgaria, and Turkey postponed

---

meeting, at Maastricht (Netherlands) in 1991, drafted plans to implement this union. The European Convention on Human Rights quickly became another important part of the European Union because all potential members of the union were required to subscribe to this convention and accept the jurisdiction of the European Court of Human Rights. The strict human rights standards for membership create an obstacle to joining the EU for several countries—laws allowing capital punishment or evidence of the use of torture can exclude a country—and have been the foremost barrier to Turkish entry into the EU. (Under these human rights standards, the United States would theoretically be denied membership in the union because it allows frequent capital punishment.)

The closer federation planned at Maastricht was so controversial, however, that many governments held referenda to gain public approval of the treaty. In France, long a leader in the drive toward greater unity, a referendum of September 1992 only approved of the Maastricht Treaty by the narrow margin of 51–49 percent. Prime Minister Thatcher of Britain was the leading critic of the European Union. She attacked the Brussels bureaucracy of "Eurocrats," the plans for a common currency, the Union's common social policy (which she denounced as a backdoor route for social-

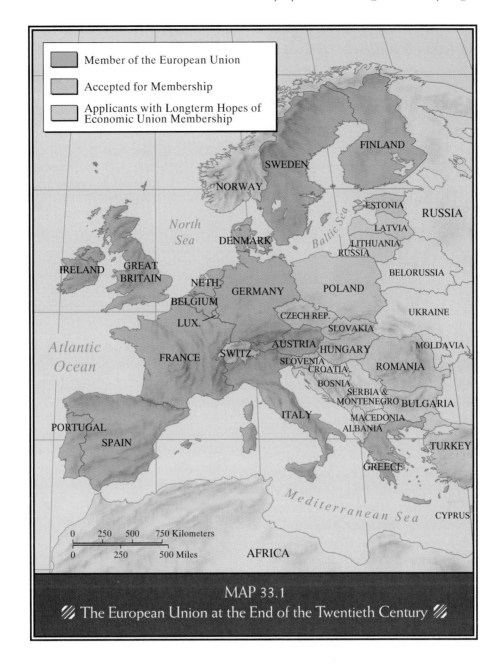

MAP 33.1
The European Union at the End of the Twentieth Century

Legend:
- Member of the European Union
- Accepted for Membership
- Applicants with Longterm Hopes of Economic Union Membership

ism into Britain), the increasing role of the European Parliament at Strasbourg (at the expense of Britain's Parliament), and the apparent birth of a European "superstate." Nonetheless, the European Union of the 1990s would have seemed impossible in the first half of the twentieth century. Historic enemies, such as France and Germany, work in friendship and close cooperation; a European Parliament meets in the Alsatian capital, directly elected in all member countries; a European executive power (the European Commission) sits in Brussels; tariffs within the union have been abolished; steps for the creation of a common European currency (the Euro) have begun.

The second trend encouraged by the new prosperity was the growth of the welfare state and social benefits. Most West European governments, following such examples as Swedish state socialism or the policies of Attlee's Britain, devoted a significant share of new wealth and production to public services and benefits. In West Germany, both the socialist governments of Willy Brandt (1969–74) and Helmut Schmidt (1974–82) and the conservative government of Helmut Kohl (1982–98) accepted high tax rates as the price of social cohesion. And the benefits of European prosperity have been great: Britain, France, and Germany all established workweeks below thirty-eight or thirty-nine hours for

TABLE 33.1 Paid Vacations in 1994	
City	Average days of paid vacation per year for all workers
Madrid	32
Frankfurt	31
Paris	28
Milan	25
London	22
New York	11
Chicago	9

TABLE 33.2
Taxation in the Late Twentieth Century

Country	Total taxation as a percentage of GNP	Percentage of taxes from income taxes
Britain	36.5	26.6
France	43.8	11.8
Germany	38.1	29.5
Italy	37.8	26.7
Sweden	56.7	37.2
United States	30.1	35.7

Source: Swedish data (1987) from *New York Review of Books*, October 24, 1991, p. 7; all other data (1989) from *New York Times*, November 29, 1992.

full pay. Britain, France, Germany, and Italy all guaranteed employees and workers a minimum of five to six weeks of paid vacation per year—compared with the two weeks standard in the United States and Japan (see table 33.1). German workers had the most exceptional treatment: a minimum of fifty-eight paid days off (eleven-and-one-half weeks) per year in combined vacation days and paid holidays. France and Italy established age sixty for retirement at full pay, with age fifty or fifty-five the standard in some occupations. In 1996 Germans were guaranteed 52 weeks of unemployment compensation, or 128 weeks after age fifty-four, at 60 percent of salary—compared with twenty-six weeks at 50 percent in the United States. All EU countries except Luxembourg granted pregnant women a minimum of three months of maternity leave, with Denmark granting six months. Many countries, led by France, have given free tuition to state universities to all students. And the entire EU is committed to free, or low cost, medical care for all; some states, led by Germany, include free nursing home care for the elderly.

The price of such benefits has been high taxation. European taxation has been so high that in the late 1980s it consumed one-third to one-half of the GNP in Britain, France, and Germany and more than 55 percent in Sweden (see table 33.2). And it has been growing: French government spending grew from 44 percent in 1987 to 52 percent in 1995. Although most of the taxation that supports this social system comes from indirect taxes—especially a Value Added Tax (VAT) hidden in the cost of goods—Europeans do notice the cost of these benefits. The unemployment of German workers, for example, is supported by a 3.25 percent payroll de-

duction from workers' gross income, matched by a 3.25 percent payment by employers; the lesser benefit in the United States is supported by a 2.3 percent tax on payroll, paid by employers. European conservatives such as Helmut Kohl of Germany have tried to reduce spending on social services during the late 1980s and the 1990s, but they have accepted both the welfare state and the taxation needed to finance it. Even the socialist president of France, François Mitterand (served 1981–95), who defended the welfare commitment, faced hard fiscal decisions and his government adopted many conservative policies. The French public, however, has been one of the staunchest constituencies for protecting the welfare state. When the conservative government proposed reduced services in 1997, French socialists under Lionel Jospin won an upset parliamentary victory.

Margaret Thatcher and the Conservative Revolution

European history was facing other great changes in the mid-1970s. The most important harbinger of the new Europe could be seen in Britain in 1975. In February 1975 Britain's Conservative Party elected Margaret Thatcher, a former minister of education, to lead the party (see illustration 33.2). That event was a landmark in European history for two reasons: (1) never in the history of parliamentary democracy had one of the great powers chosen a woman to lead them, and (2) her policies provided the first vigorous challenge to the growth of the welfare state. These dramatic changes

Illustration 33.2

※ **The Conservative Revolution.** Margaret Thatcher, the first woman to become prime minister of Britain, was one of the strongest and most successful prime ministers in British history. She was the driving force behind a conservative revolution that dismantled much of the welfare state and the nationalized economy created by the Labour government after World War II. Here, she celebrates her landslide electoral victory of 1983, which created the overwhelming majority in Parliament to adopt her program.

began in 1979 when Thatcher became the first woman prime minister in British history, a post she held and used forcefully for the longest period of any modern prime minister. Her success began an era of women reaching the top in European politics (see chronology 33.2). In 1980 Norway elected a woman prime minister, Iceland a woman president, and Portugal a woman prime minister. By the 1990s even Ireland (1990), France (1991), and Turkey (1993) had elected women as either prime minister or president. Simultaneously, European women have gained a larger share of political power at lower levels. No country, however, has a Parliament in which 50 percent of the representatives are women. Sweden, where women won 41 percent of the seats in Parliament in 1994 has the highest rate, and in the Netherlands, Denmark, and Finland women hold approximately one-third of the seats; Greece (5.3 percent) and France (6.1 percent) have the lowest percentages, with Portugal and Belgium less than 10 percent. Despite the presence of a woman at 10 Downing Street, Britain had been among the nations with a low percentage of women in Parliament during the Thatcher years; the landslide Labour victory of Tony Blair in 1997, however, included 102 women M.P.s in

the new majority—far higher than the participation of women in France, Germany, or the United States.

Thatcher was not born to the British political elite. She was the daughter of a successful small-town grocer who twice was elected mayor. Her father was also a Methodist lay preacher, and she was raised in strict family virtues drawn from religion as well as business. It was less typical of families in the 1930s that Thatcher's parents encouraged her to be ambitious and to develop her intelligence. She attended Oxford University as a scholarship student and chemistry major during the Second World War and developed her political interests in student organizations (see document 33.2). Thatcher worked briefly as a chemist after the war but was drawn to British politics in the late 1940s and soon studied law to advance that career. Elected to Parliament in 1959, she rose in Conservative Party ranks by becoming an expert on many social issues, such as education and welfare, which were often deemed the appropriate subjects for women in politics. When Edward Heath formed a Conservative government in 1970, Margaret Thatcher became minister of education and science, the only woman in the cabinet.

Thatcher built her reputation during Heath's troubled Tory government. Conservatives struggled to restrict the power of the trade unions with only limited success. Huge strikes by tens of thousands of dockworkers, miners, and industrial workers protested plans to curb wages or union powers. Simultaneously, the Heath government faced a worsening of the Irish question. Sectarian riots, police battles, and terrorist bombing became commonplace in the early 1970s. The Conservative government responded by suspending the powers of the provincial government and Parliament in Northern Ireland, establishing direct British rule of the province, escalating the number of troops sent to maintain order, and finally governing under state of emergency decrees that suspended many liberties. Amidst these crises, the British public lost confidence in the government, and Margaret Thatcher emerged as the strongest Tory leader. She had the strength to champion the conservative program of severe budget cuts even when they were immensely unpopular. As minister of education she eliminated a national program of free school milk for small children to make this point. In British popular culture she became "Thatcher, Thatcher, Milk Snatcher," but in conservative circles she became the leader of the future. She appealed to many conservatives because she embodied and defended their sense of "Victorian virtues." As Thatcher put it, "I was brought up to work jolly hard. We were taught to live within

---

◆ CHRONOLOGY 33.2 ◆

The Acceptance of Women in Political Leadership, 1974–94

1974 Simone de Beauvoir named president of French League for the Rights of Women

Barbara Castle becomes Britain's first secretary of state for social security

Simone Veil becomes France's minister for health

Eva Kolstad becomes president of Norway's Liberal Party

Françoise Giroud becomes France's first minister for women's affairs

1975 Margaret Thatcher becomes first woman to lead a major British political party

Portugal names Maria de Lourdes Pintasilgo its first woman ambassador

1976 Mairead Corrigan and Betty Williams of Northern Ireland share Nobel Peace Prize

Françoise Giroud becomes France's minister of culture

Yelena Bonner is cofounder of Helsinki Human Rights Group in the USSR

1979 Margaret Thatcher becomes first woman prime minister of Britain

Petra Kelly is cofounder of West Germany's environmentalist Green Party

Barbara Castle elected to European Parliament

Louise Weiss becomes senior member elected to the European Parliament

1980 Maria de Lourdes Pintasilgo briefly serves as Portugal's first woman prime minister

Vigdis Finnbogadottir elected first woman president of Iceland

Gro Brundtland becomes first woman prime minister of Norway

1981 Karin Ahrland becomes Sweden's minister for public health

Shirley Williams is cofounder of Britain's Social Democratic Party

1982 Gertrud Sigurdsen becomes Sweden's minister for public health

Anna-Greta Leijon becomes Sweden's minister of labor

1983 Petra Kelly is elected Green Party member of West German Parliament

Margaret Thatcher leads British conservatives to landslide reelection victory

1985 Melina Mercouri becomes Greece's minister of culture

1986 Gro Brundtland elected to second term as prime minister of Norway

Anita Gradin becomes Sweden's minister for foreign trade

1987 Anita-Greta Leijon becomes Sweden's minister of justice

Margaret Thatcher is first modern prime minister to win three consecutive terms

1990 Mary Robinson elected first woman president of Ireland

1991 Margaret Thatcher completes longest term of any modern prime minister of Britain

Edith Cresson becomes first woman prime minister of France

1992 Betty Boothroyd becomes first woman Speaker of Britain's Parliament

1993 Tansu Çiller becomes first woman prime minister of Turkey

1997 Tony Blair's Labour landslide includes 102 women as Labour M.P.s

---

our income, that cleanliness is next to godliness. We were taught self-respect. You were taught tremendous pride in your country." After Heath had lost the parliamentary elections of 1974, Thatcher challenged him for the leadership of the Conservative Party in 1975 and won. She became prime minister in 1979, following a campaign in which she promised to restore many

aspects of the nineteenth-century laissez-faire liberal economics of free enterprise. "Free choice is ultimately what life is about," she proclaimed.

The Thatcher government of 1979–90 introduced Britain (and Europe) to strict fiscal conservatism. Thatcher championed monetarist economics that called for limiting the money supply to curb inflation. She

◆ DOCUMENT 33.2 ◆

Margaret Thatcher: Her Start in Politics

Margaret Thatcher rose from modest origins as the daughter of a gro-cer in provincial England to an extraordinary political career. She be-came one of the most powerful women and dominant prime ministers in British history, the most important woman in twentieth-century Euro-pean politics. The following excerpt from her memoirs describes her en-try into politics after her graduation (as a chemistry major) from Oxford.

[As] always with me, there was politics. I immediately joined the Conservative Association and threw myself into the usual round of Party activities. In particular, I thoroughly enjoyed what was called the '39-45' discussion group, where Conservatives of the war generation met to exchange views and argue about the political topics of the day. . . . It was as a representative of the Oxford Univer-sity Graduate Conservative Association (OUGCA) that I went to the Llanddudno [Wales] Conservative Party Con-ference in October 1948.

It had originally been intended that I should speak at the Conference, seconding an OUGCA motion deploring the abolition of university seats. At that time universities had separate representatives in Parliament, and graduates had the right to vote in their universities as well as in the constituency where they lived. (I supported separate uni-versity representation, but not the principle that graduates should have more than one vote. . . .) It would have been my first Conference speech, but in the end the seconder chosen was a City man, because the City seats were also to be abolished.

My disappointment at this was, however, very quickly overcome and in a most unexpected way. After one of the debates, I found myself engaged in one of those specula-tive conversations which young people have about their future prospects. An Oxford friend, John Grant, said he supposed that one day I would like to be a Member of

Parliament. 'Well, yes,' I replied, 'but there's not much hope of that. The chances of my being selected are just nil at the moment.' I might have added that with no private income of my own there was no way I could have af-forded to be an MP on the salary then available. I had not even tried to get on the Party's list of approved candidates.

Later in the day, John Grant happened to be sitting next to the Chairman of the Dartford Conservative Asso-ciation, John Miller. The Association was in search of a candidate. I learned afterwards that the conversation went something like this: 'I understand that you're still looking for a candidate at Dartford?'

. . . 'That's right. Any suggestions?'

'Well, there's a young woman, Margaret Roberts, that you might look at. She's very good.'

'Oh, but Dartford is a real industrial stronghold. I don't think a woman would do at all.'

'Well, you know best, of course. But why not just look at her?'

And they did. I was invited to have lunch with John Miller and his wife. . . . Presumably, and in spite of any reservations about the suitability of a woman candidate for their seat, they liked what they saw. . . . ' I was asked to attend an interview, . . . with a large number of other hopefuls. . . . Very few outside the political arena know just how nerve-racking such occasions are. . . . I found myself short-listed, and was asked to go to Dartford itself for a further interview. . . . As one of five would-be candi-dates, I had to give a fifteen-minute speech and answer questions for a further ten minutes. It was the questions which were more likely to cause me trouble. There was a good deal of suspicion of women candidates. . . . I en-joyed that evening at Dartford, and the outcome justified my confidence. I was selected.'

coupled this with a promise to reduce taxes. The Con-servative government honored this promise in one sense but violated it in another: It cut income taxes, but it raised indirect taxes, especially the national sales tax known as the VAT. Thatcher cut top income tax rates from 83 percent to 60 percent in 1979 and reduced them to 40 percent in 1979; the rate paid by average

taxpayers fell from 33 percent to 30 percent and then to 25 percent. When she tried in 1990 to compensate for this huge loss of government revenue by instituting another regressive tax called the Poll Tax, antitax demonstrations drove her from office.

This conservative revolution necessitated severe reductions in government spending, especially in the budgets that Thatcher knew well—education and welfare services. Thatcher asserted that the cradle-to-grave welfare state that had evolved out of the Beveridge Plan and the Attlee reforms of the 1940s cost more than the nation could pay. The demographic portrait of the nation—greater longevity, lower employment, and lower birthrates—meant that the costs of the welfare state, which stood at 25 percent of the budget in 1979 and rose to 31 percent by 1988 (chiefly because of retirement pensions and the high cost of benefits in a period of high unemployment), would continue to rise. The Thatcher government cut some benefits directly, chiefly housing benefits, and curtailed others by taxing them or not raising them to match inflation. The results of her monetarism and budget cuts were significantly lowered inflation (5 percent), increased unemployment, reduced public services, and vehement public debate. The Tories had inherited a 5.4 percent unemployment rate in 1979 but created a 12.7 percent rate (three million people) by 1983. That problem compounded all others because it reduced productivity and increased the demand for welfare benefits.

Simultaneously, Thatcher aimed to increase the private sector of the British economy by selling off some previously nationalized enterprises. (Ten percent of the British national economy was state-run in 1979.) This policy of privatization eliminated state monopolies in some areas and sold state-run enterprises in others. This extended a cycle in British history; the Labour Party had begun nationalizations in 1945. Two of the most controversial nationalizations were privatized by Conservatives in 1951 (iron and steel, plus road haulage), and a Labour government of 1967 made a few gestures toward the party's historic commitment. (Ironically, Thatcher's privatizations happened at the same time that François Mitterand's socialist government in France was undertaking new nationalizations in 1981–82.) Thatcher now sold nationalized coal, gas, oil, steel interests such as the leading gasoline company, BP. Many internationally known firms—from Rolls Royce to British Airways—also became private, although the government often retained a large bloc of their stock.

The Thatcher government also adopted a tough policy toward labor unions and public employees. Employment Acts in 1980, 1982, and 1988, plus a Trade Union Act of 1984, changed labor relations in Britain and weakened trade unions. These laws continued a century-long battle over union powers, redefining the right to strike (by requiring a membership ballot before a strike), restricting the right to picket, making unions liable for strike damages, and curtailing union monopolies known as closed shops. These restrictions were backed by the courts and gained more force as union membership, and its willingness to strike, fell as unemployment increased.

Margaret Thatcher imposed her policies on a sometimes nervous conservative government with a forceful, intransigent style of leadership that belied generalizations about women leaders. Her tough policies and tougher style (especially in her dealings with the Soviet Union) earned her the nickname of "the Iron Lady." Thatcher also demonstrated her hard-line style during her chief foreign policy crisis. In the spring of 1982 Argentina invaded the Falkland Islands, a small British colony in the south Atlantic, claiming that they formed a historic part of the Argentine state. Against the strong opposition of the Labour Party and many members of her own party, Thatcher insisted upon taking back the Falklands by war. One month after the Argentine occupation, British troops stormed the islands and reclaimed them after a three-week land battle and several bloody encounters at sea. A year later, the Iron Lady was reelected with an overwhelming majority behind her conservative revolution.

Her success spread beyond the British Isles. The fiscal policies of Thatcherism, such as privatization, reduced taxes, and restricted welfare spending became the conservative orthodoxy in many countries. In the late 1980s conservative Gaullists in France privatized businesses that other conservative Gaullists had nationalized in the 1940s. By the winter of 1995 French conservatives led by President Jacques Chirac were so determined to cut taxes and welfare payments that they were willing to precipitate a month of strikes and labor demonstrations. In Germany, Chancellor Kohl cautiously followed a similar agenda in the mid-1990s though these polices threatened to destroy the German model of labor peace: In the largest German demonstration since World War II, 350,000 workers marched in Bonn in 1996 to protest the conservative plans.

Discontent in Eastern Europe and the Rise of Solidarity

The peoples of eastern Europe demonstrated their hostility to Communist dictatorship on many occasions after 1945. Antigovernment demonstrations in East Berlin in 1953, an anti-Soviet rebellion in Hungary in 1956, and the Prague Spring reform movement in Czechoslovakia in 1968 were the most dramatic outbursts against the Soviet system. The frustration in Eastern Europe grew from the desire for both western freedoms and

Illustration 33.3

 The Solidarity Movement in Poland. The founder and president of the workers' movement known as *Soli-darnosc* (Solidarity), which played a major role in the fall of the Communist government in Poland, was a thirty-seven-year-old electronics technician and electrical worker at the state shipyards in Gdansk named Lech Walesa. He expressed the grievances of shipbuilders so effectively that he became a national symbol of Solidarity's resistance to the government. Here, Walesa addresses dockworkers in Gdansk in 1980; three years later he won the Nobel Peace Prize.

western material conditions. The standard of living in the east was far below conditions in the west, so daily frustrations compounded the discontent.

The Soviet Union had used force to suppress East Europe protest movements, asserting a right to intervene in neighboring states. This Soviet policy was known as the Brezhnev Doctrine in analogy to the Monroe Doctrine by which the United States intervened in neighboring states of Latin America. The Helsinki Agreement of 1975, however, contained Soviet guarantees of human rights. This inspired dissidents in several of the Soviet satellites. Czech intellectuals, led by the playwright Vaclav Havel, created a civil rights movement known as Charter 77. Their manifesto charged that the Czech government violated the human rights promised at Helsinki. The campaign was short-lived. Havel, whose satirical plays had been banned since 1968, and five other civil rights activists were jailed in 1979 for the crime of subversion.

Poland witnessed the most successful challenge to Communist dictatorship in Eastern Europe. The Poles had resisted in 1956; worker protests in Poznan led to more than one hundred killings. Food riots were put down in 1970 and new strikes were suppressed in 1976, yet Poland still became the home of sustained protests in the 1980s. Rising food prices in 1980 led workers in Gdansk (formerly Danzig) to strike. The movement spread among Polish factories and industries, building a network of unions known as the Solidarity movement

(*Solidarnosc*). Solidarity was the first independent trade union in the Soviet bloc, and it grew to ten million members. Under the leadership of Lech Walesa, a Gdansk shipyard electrician who had been active in the 1976 strikes (see illustration 33.3), Solidarity strikers issued a dramatic list of demands (see document 33.3) and won changes in the government, increased wages, promises of a forty-hour workweek, a relaxation of censorship, the release of some dissidents, and the radio broadcast of Catholic Church services. Within a few months, however, a military government took power and banned the union.

The USSR warned Poland in 1981 to crack down on counterrevolution, and Poland was put under martial law with civil liberties suspended. Troops fired on strikers, killing seven. Walesa and thousands of strikers were imprisoned. Walesa won international support, however, including a Nobel Peace Prize (1983). The election of a Polish-born pope who supported Solidarity—John Paul II, the first non-Italian pope in 455 years—greatly strengthened the movement. Poland had remained strongly Catholic during the Communist regime, and Pope John Paul II's 1979 visit to Poland had strengthened the will to resist the government. In part because NATO governments warned the Soviet Union that intervention in Poland under the Brezhnev Doctrine would end détente, the movement survived in a delicate compromise with the Communist regime during the 1980s.

◈ DOCUMENT 33.3 ◈

Demands of the Solidarity Workers in Poland, 1980

Striking ship-workers at Gdansk confronted the Communist government with the following demands in August 1980.

1. Acceptance of free trade unions independent of the Communist Party and of enterprises, in accordance with Convention Number 87 of the International Labor Organization concerning the right to form free trade unions, which was ratified by the government of Poland.

2. A guarantee of the right to strike and of the security of strikes and those aiding them.

3. Compliance with the constitutional guarantee of freedom of speech, the press and publication, including freedom for independent publishers and the availability of the mass media to representatives of all faiths.

4. A halt in repression of the individual because of personal conviction.

5. Guaranteed automatic increases in pay on the basis of increases in prices and the decline of real income.

6. A full supply of food products for the domestic market, with exports limited to surpluses.

7. The selection of management personnel on the basis of qualifications not party membership.

8. Privileges of the secret police, regular police and party apparatus are to be eliminated by equalizing family subsidies, abolishing special stores, etc.

9. Reduction in the age of retirement for women to 50 and for men to 55, or after 30 years of employment in Poland for women and 35 years for men, regardless of age.

10. Conformity of old-age pensions and annuities with what has actually been paid in.

11. Improvements in the working conditions of the health service to insure full medical care for workers.

12. Assurances of a reasonable number of places in day-care centers and kindergartens for the children of working mothers.

13. Paid maternity leave for three years.

14. A decrease in the waiting period for apartments.

15. A day of rest on Saturday.

The Soviet Union of the post-Stalin era had its own dissident movement. Khrushchev's destalinization allowed enough freedom for dissident writers to risk criticism of the regime. In 1962 Alexander Solzhenitsyn was allowed to publish a novel entitled *A Day in the Life of Ivan Denisovitch,* which exposed conditions in the Soviet *gulag.* Solzhenitsyn's criticism of continuing censorship led to the banning of his subsequent books, which appeared in the West and circulated in the USSR in *samizdat* (clandestinely printed) form. His Nobel Prize in Literature (1970) gave Solzhenitsyn the stature to publish a massive history of Stalin's terror, *The Gulag Archipelago* (1973–75), which led the frustrated Soviet regime to deport him to the West. Other distinguished dissidents included the physicist considered the father of the Russian hydrogen bomb, Andrei Sakharov, who championed international arms control and Soviet civil rights so persistently that he won the Nobel Peace Prize in 1975.

Discontent in the USSR worsened after the Red Army invaded neighboring Afghanistan in 1979. The Kremlin sought to prevent the establishment of a militant Islamic government on its southern border, adjacent to Soviet republics with a large Islamic population. A minor military campaign to install a friendly government in Kabul, however, soon grew into the Soviet Union's Vietnam. Forty thousand troops were needed in the first month, as the Red Army encountered fierce resistance from Afghan rebels, the *mujahedeen.* As the war became a frustrating, no-win stalemate, the USSR met the same international hostility that the Vietnam War caused the United States. A conference of thirty-six Islamic states condemned the Soviet Union. The United Nations voted a resolution denouncing the war. A planned Soviet showcasing of Communist society, the 1980 Olympic Games, was boycotted by the United States, West Germany, and Japan. Internal dissent also increased. Sakharov and his wife, Yelena Bonner, were so troublesome to the regime that they were exiled to a Russian city closed to foreigners; Sakharov still remained a problem for the Kremlin because of his internationally publicized hunger strike.

Illustration 33.4

The Gorbachev Revolution. Mikhail Gorbachev, who became general secretary of the Communist Party of the Soviet Union in 1985, was the leading figure in the revolutions of 1989. His determined efforts to reform the USSR and Eastern Europe created the environment in which Communist governments were toppled, and this made him enormously popular across Europe, as this 1987 photo of his state visit to Prague shows. Note that Gorbachev (smiling at center) seems much happier than the man with the forced smile behind him, Gustav Husak, the president of Czechoslovakia. Gorbachev won the Nobel Peace Prize for 1990; Husak was deposed.

The Gorbachev Revolution in the USSR, 1985–89

The turning point for the USSR and Eastern Europe came in 1985 when a youthful reformist and westernizer, Mikhail Gorbachev, became the head of the Soviet Union following a succession of ineffective, elderly, doctrinaire leaders (see illustration 33.4). Gorbachev was the son of Russian peasants. He joined the Communist Party at twenty-one, rose to membership in the Supreme Soviet at thirty-nine, reached a cabinet post at forty-seven, and in 1980 became the youngest member of the Politburo at forty-nine. Gorbachev emerged as one of the energetic leaders of the Politburo during the rudderless period following the death of Leonid Brezhnev in 1982. The Soviet Union was widely considered a gerontocracy, and three aging heads of government died in quick succession between 1982 and 1985. The instability of this period encouraged the Politburo to accept the fifty-four-year-old Gorbachev as first secretary.

Gorbachev had served as minister of agriculture from 1978 and knew that Soviet farming was failing. In 1981 Brezhnev had been forced to acknowledge the regime's economic failure before the Central Committee; food production had fallen to dangerously low levels for three consecutive years and stood at an embarrassing 30 percent of the planned harvest. The Soviet Union could not feed itself and imported forty-three million tons of grain, much of it coming from the United States. Simultaneously, the war in Afghanistan was a great drain on Russian finances and morale. In 1982 the Politburo decided to seek economic stability by curtailing the enormously expensive arms race with the West. A few months later, however, President Ronald Reagan of the United States announced plans for a new weapons system, the Strategic Defense Initiative, that theoretically would provide a missile shield for the United States. This plan, soon dubbed "star wars," required vast new spending to develop antimissile technology. Reagan, who considered the USSR "the Evil Empire" and "the focus of all evil in the modern world," was willing to spend the United States deeply into debt to combat the Soviet Union. By 1985 the United States had become a debtor nation, and Mikhail Gorbachev came to power with another great concern to add to the human rights pressures, the antiwar mood, and the economic failures of the Soviet Union.

In his first weeks in power, Gorbachev launched a liberalizing revolution. He retired older leaders and hard-liners while promoting reformers and westernizers such as Eduard Schevardnadze, who replaced an old-line Communist, Andrei Gromyko, as foreign minister. Within one year, Gorbachev had changed 70 percent of all cabinet ministers and 50 percent of the higher administration. The Gorbachev revolution was characterized by two objectives: *glasnost* (openness) and *perestroika* (restructuring). *Glasnost* meant a freer political and cultural life in which criticism of the party and state were possible; Gorbachev even allowed television broadcasts depicting the quagmire in Afghanistan and its increasing casualty rate. *Perestroika* meant reforming political and economic structures to create more democracy and efficiency.

Gorbachev's two doctrines also led to a "détente offensive" to persuade the West to curtail the cold war and its costly arms race. To prove his earnestness, he announced a unilateral freeze on medium range missiles during his first month in office. In September 1985 the USSR offered a 50 percent cut in arms in return for a Western cut in the star wars program. Many Western leaders, led by Margaret Thatcher, were greatly impressed by this beginning, and European opinion soon strongly favored the curtailment of cold war military expenditures. In the fall of 1985 more than 100,000 people demonstrated in London to stop these ruinous expenses, and Gorbachev received popular greetings during visits to the West. Reagan and Gorbachev held six hours of face-to-face meetings in Geneva, but Reagan refused to back down from his star wars program, even when Gorbachev offered to eliminate all nuclear arms by the year 2000.

The Communist Party Congress of 1986 heard Gorbachev denounce the stagnation of the Brezhnev era (1964–82), much as Khrushchev had attacked Stalin thirty years earlier. The congress endorsed Gorbachev's program, and for the next four years an astonished world watched historic changes unfold. Gorbachev scored his first successes by responding to his human rights critics. During 1986 prominent dissidents such as Sakharov were gradually released from confinement. Anatoly Shcharansky was freed from his thirteen-year sentence to a prison camp for his campaign to help Russian Jews emigrate. In 1987 Gorbachev denounced Stalin's terror and praised Khrushchev's report on the crimes of the Stalin era; he most shocked devout Communists by admitting that Lenin had relied upon terror, too. A few months later, Gorbachev announced that the Soviet Union would withdraw its army of 120,000 men from Afghanistan. By early 1988 he was promising religious freedom.

Gorbachev's campaign for *perestroika* also stunned the Western world (see document 33.4). In 1987 he unveiled a startling plan to dismantle the one-party political system by allowing multiple candidates and a secret ballot. He explained that the Communist Party bore much of the blame for Russian economic stagnation and that only greater democracy could revitalize the USSR. Soviet police even tolerated a few limited demonstrations, chiefly by Baltic and south Asian peoples. More surprisingly, Gorbachev told a nation accustomed to policies defined by the tenets of Marxism-Leninism that he wanted "socialism extricated from the slag heap of dogma."

Gorbachev increased the pace of democratization in 1988. A special congress of the Communist Party voted a remarkable agenda: the enlargement of *glasnost* and *perestroika*, the reform of the judicial system, a war on bureaucratic intransigence, greater rights for minority nationalities, and the rehabilitation of Stalin's opponents purged in the 1930s. Legislation began to transfer decision making from the central government to the local level, while reducing government guarantees and financing. At this point, the speed of change began to exceed Gorbachev's control of it. A blunt-talking champion of reform, Boris Yeltsin, pushed him to go further, faster. Yeltsin's criticism of Gorbachev had led to his dismissal as Moscow party head in 1987 and then to Yeltsin's resignation of his Politburo membership. When Yeltsin called for a multiparty system of government, more than ten thousand people turned out in the streets of Moscow to support him. When Gorbachev created a new congress and held the first free elections in the history of the USSR in March 1989, Yeltsin, like Andrei Sakharov, was one of the first deputies elected to it. By early 1990 the Communist Party had lost its control of the state, multiparty politics had been legalized, and a Russian presidency created. The Gorbachev revolution had gone beyond Gorbachev. He no longer had a strong constituency of supporters inside the Soviet Union. Ardent Communists began to detest him for destroying Communism, but ardent reformers wanted leaders who would go much further. Revolutions often consume individuals who stand between the extremes, and Gorbachev was now a centrist. On May Day 1990 he was publicly booed by thousands of demonstrators, chiefly hard-line Communists and staunch Russian nationalists. Before the month was over, Yeltsin was elected to the presidency instead of Gorbachev.

◈

The Revolutions of 1989 in Eastern Europe

The Gorbachev revolution in the USSR led directly to the breakup of the Communist bloc in Eastern Europe and to the dissolution of the Soviet Union itself. The Warsaw Pact had been renewed for a term of twenty years only a few weeks before Gorbachev came to power in 1985. But four years later, the revolutions of

◈ DOCUMENT 33.4 ◈

Mikhail Gorbachev: *Perestroika* and *Glasnost* (1987)

What is perestroika? What prompted this idea of restructuring?

. . . Perestroika is no whim on the part of some ambitious individuals or a group of leaders. . . . Perestroika is an urgent necessity arising from the profound processes of development in our socialist society. This society is ripe for change. Any delay beginning perestroika could have led to an exacerbated internal situation in the near future. . . .

At some stage—this became particularly clear in the latter half of the seventies—something happened that was at first sight inexplicable. The country began to lose momentum. Economic failures became more frequent. Difficulties began to accumulate and deteriorate, and unresolved problems to multiply. . . .

The 27th Congress of the Communist Party of Soviet Union [1986] . . . was a courageous congress. We spoke openly about the short-comings, errors, and difficulties. We emphasized the untapped potential of socialism, and the Congress adopted a detailed long-term plan of action. It became a congress of strategic decisions. . . . Now we can see better and it is clear that we have to resolutely continue. . . .

The main idea . . . was the development of democracy. It is the principal guarantee of the irreversibility of perestroika. The more socialist democracy there is, the more socialism we will have. This is our firm conviction, and we will not abandon it. We will promote democracy in the economy, in politics and within the Party itself. . . .

Soviet society has been set in motion, and there's no stopping it. . . .

The greatest difficulty in our restructuring effort lies in our thinking, which has been molded over the past years. Everyone, from General Secretary [Gorbachev] to worker, has to alter this thinking. . . . We have to overcome our conservatism. . . .

The new atmosphere is, perhaps, most vividly manifest in glasnost. We want more openness about public affairs in every sphere of life. People should know what is good, and what is bad too, in order to multiply the good and to combat the bad. . . . Truth is the main thing. Lenin said: More light! Let the Party know everything. As never before, we need no dark corners where mold can reappear. . . . Glasnost is a vivid example of a normal and favorable spiritual and moral atmosphere in society, which makes it possible for people to understand better what happened to us in the past, what is taking place now . . . and, on this basis of this understanding, to participate in the restructuring effort. . . .

Every nation is entitled to choose its own way of development, to dispose of its fate, its territory, and its human and natural resources. International relations cannot be normalized if this is not understood in all countries. For ideological and social differences, and differences in political systems are the result of the choice made by the people. A national choice should not be used in international relations in such a way as to cause trends and events that can trigger conflicts.

1989 (see chronology 33.3) ended the Soviet Empire in Eastern Europe and redrew the map of Europe with few shots being fired (see map 33.2). Two years later, the USSR itself dissolved into more than a dozen separate republics (see map 33.3).

The revolutions of 1989 began in Poland and Hungary. The Solidarity movement, which had been struggling with the Communist government of Poland for nearly a decade, finally won legal recognition in January 1989. The union movement used that new status and its vast popularity to press the government to extend *perestroika* in Poland by liberalizing the political system. The government, whose only signals from Moscow were to accept restructuring, capitulated to

Solidarity in a series of April meetings and agreed to free elections for the upper house of Parliament. Lech Walesa called those meetings "the beginning of the road to democracy." That agreement guaranteed the Communist Party a large block of seats whatever the outcome of the voting, but Polish voters gave Solidarity a landslide victory (80 percent of the vote) in June 1989. In the *Sejm*, the nonelected lower house of the Polish Parliament, the agreement gave the Communist Party 38 percent of the seats and Solidarity 35 percent. The two houses would together elect the president of Poland. The Polish elections of 1989–90 ended a generation of Communist government in Poland. Solidarity candidates won 96 percent of the seats in the upper

The Revolutions of 1989 in Eastern Europe

USSR

January	Coal miners in Ukraine defy government and strike
February	Gorbachev withdraws last Soviet troops from Afghanistan
March	Elections for new Parliament give landslide victory to reformers
	Government admits that Nazi-Soviet Treaty of 1939 planned Baltic annexation
	Estonia, Latvia, Lithuania, Armenia, Azerbaijan, Georgia, and Ukraine demand autonomy
September	Azerbaijan becomes first republic of USSR to declare its independence
December	Lithuania changes constitution and abolishes Communist monopoly of power
	Presidents Gorbachev and Bush meet in Malta and declare the cold war over

Poland

January	Government legalizes Solidarity and multiple trade unions
February	Solidarity enters negotiations for reform of Polish political system
March	Government agrees to multiple party political system and calls elections
June	First free Polish elections after World War II give sweeping victory to Solidarity
August	Poland ends forty years of Communist rule
September	New Polish government launches plans for transition to market economy

Hungary

January	Reforms permit multiple political parties
March	Draft constitution ends dominance of Communist Party
September	Government violates treaties and allows massive transit of East Germans to West
October	Reformers abolish Communist Party and regroup as Socialist Party
	Parliament democratizes constitution and calls elections

East Germany

September	Hundreds of thousands of East Germans flee to West through Hungary
October	Gorbachev visits East Germany and encourages liberalization
	Mass demonstrations of New Forum in Leipzig and other cities
	President Erich Honecker forced to resign amid growing demonstrations
November	Government allows citizens to visit West without visas; thousands cross borders
	Demonstrating crowds begin to demolish the Berlin Wall
December	East German government resigns and free elections scheduled for early 1990

Czechoslovakia

October	Government troops crush student demonstrations in Prague and arrest dissidents
	Gorbachev urges Czech government to accept need for restructuring
	Civic Forum leads demonstrations in Prague, demands resignation of government
November	Entire Czech government resigns but demonstrations and strikes continue
December	Non-Communist cabinet installed in the Velvet Revolution
	Czech Parliament approves Western-style democracy and names dissident president
	Slovaks open question of cession to create separate state of Slovakia

Romania

December	Secret police shoot demonstrators seeking ethnic and religious freedom in Timisoara
	Units of army join demonstrators as National Salvation Front against Ceausescu dictatorship
	Ceausescu arrested, tried, and executed by provisional government

MAP 33.2

Europe after the Revolutions of 1989

house. In elections to the *Sejm*, many prominent Communists who were unopposed still could not win the 50 percent of the vote needed for election. Lech Walesa, the shipyard electrician and chief founder of Solidarity, won the presidency of Poland in 1990 with 75 percent of the vote. The new government immediately launched plans for the difficult transition to a market economy.

The Hungarian revolution of 1989, in contrast, began among reformers within the Communist Party. The government announced in January that Hungarian *perestroika* would allow multiple political parties, and it backed that announcement with a new constitution ending the Communist Party's monopoly of political

power. Communist reformers were so determined to end the postwar regime that they abolished their party in October 1989 and tried to reorganize themselves as a socialist party in hopes of surviving free elections. None of their decisions was more popular than the January 1990 Hungarian-Soviet agreement for the withdrawal of all Soviet troops stationed on Hungarian soil. None was a more powerful symbol than the June 1990 reopening of the Budapest Stock Exchange. But perhaps the most momentous decision of Hungarian reformers came in May 1989, when the government opened the border between Austria and Hungary, demolishing fortifications and removing barbed wire. This breech in the Iron Curtain allowed East Europeans free access to

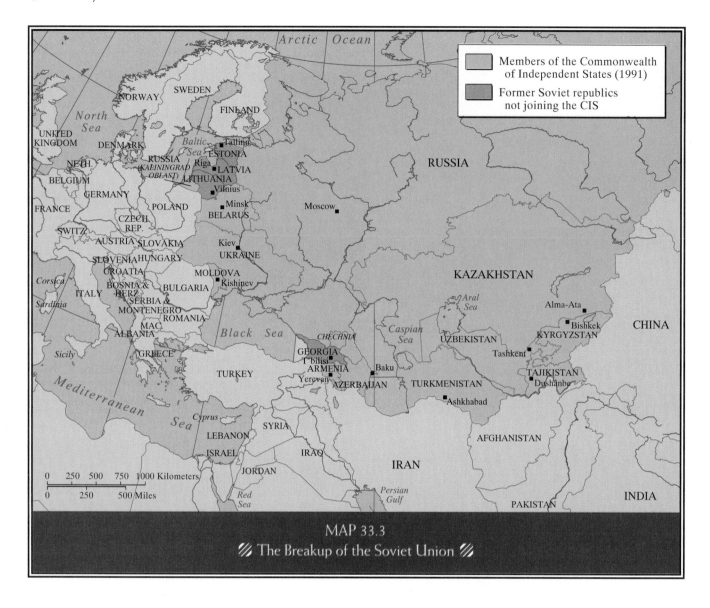

MAP 33.3

The Breakup of the Soviet Union

Western Europe. Communist states slower to embrace change now faced the prospect that thousands of their citizens might flee to the West.

The most dramatic of the revolutions of 1989 occurred in East Germany. The DDR remained a strict Communist dictatorship under Erich Honecker, the aging (seventy-seven years old) leader who had supervised the construction of the Berlin Wall a generation earlier. Honecker, the son of a militant coal miner in the Saar, had been a Communist since the Weimar Republic and had spent ten years in Nazi prisons. He had been a leading organizer of the postwar Communist Party, who rose to become the head of state security in 1958, and had served as party leader since 1971. Honecker had followed a policy of severe domestic repression and a strictly controlled economy. He was personally responsible for an order that border guards shoot to kill anyone seeking to flee to the West, and in

February 1989 he had confidently predicted that the Berlin Wall would remain standing for one hundred years.

Erich Honecker vigorously resisted reform of the Communist regime and fought against the idea of *perestroika*. The tightly bottled-up discontent of East Germans became clear in the late summer of 1989, following the Hungarian decision to open their Austrian border. By West German law, all East Germans who came to the West received automatic citizenship, but the Iron Curtain had kept that number small. Suddenly, thousands of East Germans exploited Hungarian liberalization to visit there and then cross into the West; seven thousand people fled on the first night that the border was open, and sixty thousand went to the West in the first month. The DDR was soon losing three hundred citizens—chiefly the young, the skilled, and the educated—per hour. The Honecker govern-

Illustration 33.5

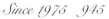 **The End of the Berlin Wall.** The Berlin wall, constructed in 1961 (see illustration 32.6), was the foremost symbol of the Iron Curtain separating East and West, the palpable image of the cold war. The opening of the Berlin Wall in November 1989—a delirious occasion to the people in this photo—quickly became the symbol of the revolutions of 1989 and the fall of Communism.

ment denounced Hungary and called for another Warsaw Pact invasion.

As East German Communists tried to close this border, they soon faced growing demonstrations in favor of reform in several cities. Leipzig became the center of the East German revolution. Leipzig became known as the *Heldenstadt* (city of heroes) as thousands of people took to the streets, marching in defiance of a heavy military presence, standing up to the threat of tanks. Honecker seriously considered turning the army loose on the crowds. At that moment, Gorbachev visited East Berlin (October 1989) and was received by crowds chanting, "Gorby, Gorby, make us free." Gorbachev, who had already publicly reversed the Brezhnev Doctrine, told Honecker that the Warsaw Pact would not act against reformers, and he urged the East Germans to choose liberalization instead of civil war. When Honecker did not unleash the army, his regime collapsed. He was forced to resign as party leader, and

he was later indicted for the crimes of the Communist era. In November the East German Politburo was replaced and plans were announced for free elections. On midnight of November 9–10, the new government opened the border between East Berlin and West Berlin at the Brandenburg Gate. A carnival atmosphere enveloped Berlin—the symbolic city of the cold war—as thousands of people walked freely into the West, and others danced atop the Berlin Wall (see illustration 33.5 and document 33.5). Berlin thus provided the most symbolic moment of the revolutions of 1989, as German crowds began to tear down sections of the hated wall. In the new spirit of the free-market economy, the Berlin Wall ended its days broken into small fragments and sold as tourist souvenirs.

The revolution of 1989 in Czechoslovakia became known as the Velvet Revolution because it, too, was a nonviolent transition, but it did not seem that way at the beginning. Encouraged by events in the Soviet

◆ DOCUMENT 33.5 ◆

The Fall of the Berlin Wall, November 1989

The following text is an eyewitness description of the opening of the Berlin Wall in November 1989. The author is Timothy G. Ash, a British journalist who was deeply involved in the transformation of Eastern Europe during the 1980s. Ash observed the momentous events of 1989, often from an inside vantage point.

Once upon a time, and a very bad time it was, there was a famous platform in West Berlin where distinguished visitors would be taken to stare at the Wall. American presidents from Kennedy to Reagan stood on that platform looking out over the no man's land beyond. They were told that this, the Potsdamer Platz, had once been Berlin's busiest square. . . . Their hosts pointed out a grassy mound on the far side: the remains of Hitler's bunker. East German border-guards watched impassively, or rode up and down the death strip on their army motorbikes.

On the morning of Sunday, 12 November I walked through the Wall and across that no man's land with a crowd of East Berliners, a watchtower to our left, Hitler's bunker to our right. Bewildered border-guards waved us through. (As recently as February their colleagues had shot dead a man trying to escape.) Vertical segments of the wall stood at ease where a crane had just dumped them, their multicolored graffiti facing east for the first

time. A crowd of West Berliners applauded as we came through, and a man handed out free city plans. . . .

Everyone has seen the pictures of joyful celebration in West Berlin, the vast crowds stopping the traffic on the Kürfurstendamm, *Sekt* corks popping, strangers tearfully embracing—the greatest street-party in the history of the world. Yes, it was like that. But it was not only that. Most of the estimated two million East Germans who flooded into West Berlin over the weekend simply walked the streets in quiet family groups, often with toddlers in pushchairs. They queued up at a bank to collect the 100 Deutschmarks 'greeting money' [about $60] offered to visiting East Germans by the West German government, and then they went, very cautiously, shopping. Generally they bought one or two small items, perhaps some fresh fruit, a Western newspaper and toys for the children. Then, clasping their carrier-bags, they walked quietly back through the Wall, through the grey, deserted streets of East Berlin, home.

It is very difficult to describe the quality of this experience because what they actually did was so stunningly ordinary. . . . And yet, what could be more fantastic? . . . Everyone looks the same as they make their way home . . . but everyone is inwardly changed, changed utterly.

Union, university students in Prague began proreform demonstrations at the start of the school year in October. The Communist government initially felt strong enough to resist change, and the first demonstrations were met with force and arrests. The Czech dissident movement had for a long time drawn its leaders from the intelligentsia who had supported the Prague Spring in 1968, drafted Charter 77 in 1977, and then grouped themselves together under the leadership of Vaclav Havel in the Civic Forum. After Gorbachev visited Prague in October 1989, the Civic Forum resumed the demonstrations, and this time they were backed by a widespread strike of workers. The Czechoslovak Communist Party initially agreed to surrender its monopoly on power and to include non-Communists in the government, but the tempest of *perestroika* could not be contained with such limited concessions. Negotiations with leaders of the Civic Forum produced an agreement

to abolish controls on the press and TV, release political prisoners, and end the Marxist control of universities. Demonstrations continued, however, and within a few weeks, the Communist government resigned. The Parliament hurriedly adopted a democratic system of government and scheduled elections; in the interim, it named Havel president of Czechoslovakia. Havel negotiated the withdrawal of the Soviet army and led Civic Forum to victory in the first free elections in June 1990. Like all of the states breaking away from their Communist past, Czechoslovakia faced great problems, including one that was especially urgent: Slovakian leaders representing the eastern portion of the country asked to separate a Czech state (the western provinces of Bohemia and Moravia) and a Slovak state.

Only in Romania did the revolution of 1989 result in a bloody conflict. The struggle began in the Transylvanian town of Timisoara, one of the centers of the

Hungarian minority population, which numbered two million. A Hungarian Protestant clergyman in Timisoara, Lazlo Tökés, had become a champion of religious and ethnic freedom there. In December 1989 the government of dictator Nicolae Ceausescu ordered Tökés deported from that region; when he refused to leave, an attempt to arrest him precipitated a demonstration of ten thousand people in Timisoara. The Romanian security police called in armed troops and tanks, then fired on the demonstrating crowds, killing several hundred people. Ceausescu had so little contact with reality that he tried to blame the bloodshed on Hungarian fascists. Romanians responded with anti-Ceausescu demonstrations in Bucharest, where fifteen thousand people demonstrated at his palace and the Romanian army refused orders to break them up. When Ceaucescu declared martial law and planned to battle protesters, some units of the army even joined the demonstrators. Two weeks of severe fighting between the army and the security police, who remained loyal to Ceausescu, killed an estimated ten thousand to eighty thousand. Ceausescu was soon caught, given a two-hour trial, and executed that same day.

The Breakup of the Soviet Union, 1989–91

The revolutions of 1989 culminated in the breakup of the Soviet Union in the early 1990s. Many of the republics that had formed the Union of Soviet Socialist Republics proclaimed their independence, and the remaining Russian republic—still one of the largest states in the world—abandoned its Communist dictatorship. The dissolution of the USSR and the end of Communist dictatorship in Russia, taken together with the impact of the revolutions of 1989 in Eastern Europe, constitute one of the most dramatic changes in modern history.

Nationalist unrest in the USSR had become open in the late 1980s. In the north, the Baltic states (Estonia, Latvia, and Lithuania) began to challenge Moscow. In 1988 the Estonians amended their constitution to permit a local veto of Soviet laws. When Gorbachev rejected this degree of autonomy, 60 percent of the entire population of Estonia (a nation of only 1.5 million) signed a petition demanding self-rule. In the south, the neighboring Asian republics of Armenia and Azerbaijan quarreled over territory and the treatment of each

other's minority population. Only an old-fashioned intervention by the Red Army in September 1988 prevented open war.

The Soviet Union began to break up in 1989. There were riots against the central government in Georgia in April, the Lithuanian legislature voted for independence in May, workers struck for local self-government in the Ukraine in July, demonstrations in all of the Baltic states called for independence in August, and Azerbaijan delivered the first formal declaration of independence in September. By the end of the year, the Estonian government had adopted a Declaration of Sovereignty, and the Lithuanian legislature had disavowed their 1940 treaty of annexation and restored their 1938 constitution, thereby abolishing the Communist monopoly of power. In early 1990 all three Baltic republics formally proclaimed their independence. Once again, revolutionary events were racing past Gorbachev's ability to manage them. He tried to block Baltic secession by reinforcing the Soviet army there and speaking tough, but a new Lithuanian president—until recently a dissident professor of music—and a Lithuanian army of fifteen hundred men refused to back down. Gorbachev made a desperate attempt to stand against the breakup of the Soviet Union by ordering an army crackdown in the Baltic states. When the Red Army fired on a protesting crowd in Lithuania, thirteen people were killed; 100,000 then turned out in Moscow to protest and Gorbachev was beaten by the openness he had fostered. Lithuania was allowed to hold a referendum in February 1991, and 91 percent of the electorate backed independence. The trend became so powerful that two months later a similar referendum was held in Georgia (Stalin's birthplace), and 90 percent voted for independence. Before the year had ended, fifteen of the Soviet republics had chosen self-rule, including the Baltic states and the European republics of Belarus (a state of predominantly White Russian population located on the eastern border of Poland), Moldova (a largely Romanian population located on the Romanian border), and Ukraine. These six newly independent states formed a solid belt stretching from the Baltic Sea to the Black Sea, separating Russia from Europe. Gorbachev kept several remaining republics and autonomous regions within the Russian Federation and persuaded the secessionist Slavic states of Belarus and Ukraine to maintain a link to the federation, collectively known as the Commonwealth of Independent States.

While the Soviet Union broke apart, the traditional Communist regime of Russia itself also collapsed. Between late 1989 and early 1991, Russia experienced constant change. Gorbachev announced a new agricultural plan to break up the collective farms and a new economic plan that introduced television advertising. Unions were given the right to strike and promptly tried it. The KGB announced that it disavowed its previous terrorism. Shevardnadze acknowledged that the Soviet invasion of Afghanistan had been illegal. The Red Army withdrew from most of Eastern Europe, slowed only by limited finances for housing them in the Soviet Union. After 100,000 public demonstrators demanded a multiparty democracy within the Russian Federation, the Communist Party agreed to end its monopoly on political power. In one of the bluntest rejections of Communism, the Russian Parliament voted in March 1990 to approve of private property, in September 1990 to allow complete religious freedom, and in May 1991 to give all Russian citizens freedom of travel, including abroad. The Soviet archives were opened and confessions poured out—from the calculation that Stalin's terror had killed twenty million people to the admission that the Soviet Union had been responsible for the Katyn Massacre of Polish officers during World War II. The city of Leningrad reverted to its historic name, St. Petersburg. Thousands of other institutions and towns simply took down the portrait, or pulled down the statue, of Lenin, or any other symbol of the regime (see illustration 33.6).

This stunning collapse of the USSR provoked conservative, anti-*perestroika* Communists to attempt a coup d'état in August 1991. Advocates of the old regime, including several leaders of the army and the KGB, held Mikhail Gorbachev under house arrest and tried to seize centers of power such as the Parliament building in Moscow. Reformers, such as Yeltsin and the mayor of St. Petersburg, resisted the coup and used the army (which did not support the conspiracy) to bombard the conspirators into submission. Boris Yeltsin, standing atop a tank and exhorting the crowd to stand up to the conspirators, became the leader of the new Russia (see illustration 33.7). As soon as Gorbachev was released, he clearly stated that he opposed the coup and believed that Russia must complete the transition to democracy (see document 33.6), but his historical moment had passed. While the ruins of the Russian Parliament still smoldered, Yeltsin shut down all offices of the Commu-

nist Party, purged hard-liners from the government, and suspended newspapers that had been sympathetic to the coup, such as *Pravda*. Crowds in Moscow vandalized the KGB building with impunity. Less than two weeks later, in September 1991, Parliament voted the dissolution of the USSR. Gorbachev remained in office until resigning in December 1991. His farewell speech did not regret his historic role. "The old system," he said, "fell apart."

One of the most important consequences of the Gorbachev revolution and the revolutions of 1989 was the end of the cold war. From Gorbachev's first days in office, he tried to find ways to reach a historic agreement with the United States—the first treaty to reduce nuclear arsenals. Gorbachev worked toward steady improvements in relations with the West, and his order for the Soviet withdrawal from Afghanistan in 1988 speeded that new trend. He further encouraged this by announcing a unilateral Soviet army reduction in Europe of 500,000 men. By late 1988 the toughest conservative in Europe, Margaret Thatcher, did not hesitate to say that she believed that the West could trust Gorbachev and deal with him when he offered to reduce Soviet military expenditures and to end the arms race.

Gorbachev won initial popularity (especially in Europe), particularly with his repeated proposals to reduce Soviet military strength, but the United States under President Reagan at first declined to join in arms and expenditure reductions. World opinion, however, gradually sensed that the cold war was ending. When Gorbachev and Reagan first met at Reykjavik, Iceland, in 1986, the United States still insisted upon building the new generation of star wars weapons. But when the two heads of state met in the Washington summit of 1987, Reagan agreed to cut nuclear arsenals and Gorbachev accepted unbalanced terms: Over the next three years, the USSR would dismantle 1,752 missiles and the United States, 859. Even conservatives now sensed that the cold war was ending, and Thatcher said so publicly in December 1988. A *New York Times* editorial of April 1989 concluded that the age of the cold war was over. During 1989–91, numerous arms reduction treaties and summit meetings underscored this conclusion. When Gorbachev met U.S. President George Bush on the island of Malta in late 1989, phrase makers concluded that the cold war had lasted "from Yalta to Malta." A few months later, Mikhail Gorbachev won the Nobel Peace Prize for 1990.

Illustration 33.6

🖎 **The Fall of the Soviet Union.** With the fall of the Soviet Union in 1991, one of the most widely repeated scenes was the destruction of the icons of the Communist regime. Hundreds of monumental statues of Lenin and Stalin were toppled, but none of these acts better symbolized the end of Communism than the one shown here: A fourteen-ton statue of Felix Dzerhinsky (the founder of the Soviet secret police) is lowered outside of the KGB headquarters in Moscow.

Illustration 33.7

🖎 **The Russian Revolution.** In a moment that solidified his leadership of the democratic revolution in Russia, Boris Yeltsin made an impromptu speech on the street in front of the Russian Parliament building. Yeltsin found the perfect symbol for his defiance of the military and the Communist regime by delivering his speech standing on top of a tank. This moment foreshadowed a darker one to follow (when Yeltsin would order tanks to fire on the defiant Parliament), but it captured the instant when the leadership of Russia passed to him.

◆ DOCUMENT 33.6 ◆

Gorbachev: Democracy in Russia, 1991

After the attempted coup of August 1991 failed to depose Mikhail Gorbachev and to restore the Soviet dictatorship, Gorbachev published a volume of his reactions entitled The August Coup *from which the following excerpt is taken.*

[E]very day since those three days in August seems at times like a week. I am finishing putting in order what I have said and thought since returning to Moscow from the south, and it is just a month since the beginning of the coup. Just a month, but how much has happened, how much has changed since then.

The attempted coup was crushed. The democrats [Boris Yeltsin and his followers] are celebrating the victory, but life demands action. It demands carefully thought through and unorthodox actions. People are discontented with the fact that their daily life is so hard and that there are no changes for the better yet. Here lies the main danger. It was precisely that which the organizers of the coup wanted to exploit. That is why there is no time to lose. We must act, push forward with the process of reform and give people economic freedom, then they will themselves realize their potential. We have a great deal to learn. We have to learn to handle the politics, the economics and the life of the state. And in that respect the democrats are still weak.

All of us have a lot to learn, so as to govern within the framework of democracy, of political and in particular economic pluralism. Otherwise, people's patience will simply be exhausted. Then there would be an uncontrolled outburst of discontent and chaos—and then just expect the worst. . . .

It was easy for me to make a decision when the plotters presented their ultimatum. I made my choice long ago. . . . However complicated the problems may be they must be resolved democratically. I see no other way but democracy.

Helmut Kohl and the Reunification of Germany, 1989–90

Two dramatic consequences quickly flowed from the collapse of the Soviet bloc: (1) in October 1990 the two Germanys reunited, when the German Democratic Republic (East Germany) joined the Federal Republic of Germany, and (2) in December 1990 Yugoslavia began to break apart and fell into an internecine civil war (1991–95), which killed hundreds of thousands and left Yugoslavia divided into six states.

The Bonn Constitution of West Germany, adopted in 1949, had encompassed the dream of a reunified Germany. Its preamble stated that "the entire German people is called upon to achieve by self-determination the unity and freedom of Germany." The cold war postponed the German dream of reunification to a distant future. The USSR uncompromisingly opposed any possibility of a strong, unified Germany near its frontiers. Many Westerners privately preferred the division of Germany; it had facilitated the postwar Franco-German rapprochement and the progress toward the European Union. Most Germans had accepted the reality of two Germanys—West Germans helped by their prosperity and East Germans by their comparative success within the Eastern bloc. Pragmatic politics had led to formal recognition of division, the repeated acceptance of the Oder-Neisse Line as the eastern frontier of Germany, the entry of two Germanys into the UN, the spirit of Willy Brandt's *Ostpolitik,* and the reassurances contained in the Helsinki Agreement of 1975. The absence of a German problem on his frontier, plus the successful arms negotiations of the age of détente, had been essential factors in facilitating the Gorbachev revolution, as important as the victory of American technology and spending to win the arms race or the unyielding pressure for human rights and freedom from within.

When the revolutions of 1989 upended the long-standing political realities in central Europe, the chancellor of West Germany was given the unexpected opportunity to become the Bismarck of the twentieth century. Helmut Kohl was an unlikely man for this comparison, but he succeeded in the role with remarkable ease. Kohl, like Adenauer before him, came from a conservative, nationalist, Catholic family from the Rhineland of western Germany. He was the first chancellor from the generation too young to have had an active role in World War II, being fifteen when the war ended. Kohl had taken a Ph.D. in political science and immediately entered local politics as a pragmatic, rather than strongly ideological, conservative. He soon won election to the Bundestag and by 1976 had become the leader of the German conservative party, the Christian Democratic Union. In 1982 he engineered the ouster of the socialist chancellor, Helmut Schmidt, by persuading a small third party, the Free Democrats, to abandon their coalition with Schmidt and form a new majority with Kohl and the CDU. Kohl promised "a government of the middle" and followed a moderate course. He embraced the German model for social peace and economic growth (requiring more concessions to labor and more support of the welfare state than British or American conservatives would accept), but he often cautiously followed Margaret Thatcher's lead, such as cutting public-sector pay or welfare expenditures. In European policy, he was one of the chief advocates of the European Union and, in foreign policy, one of the chief defenders of NATO and close ties to the United States. By 1989 he had achieved a long tenure as chancellor but had not given any signs that he would preside over one of the most important accomplishments of twentieth-century German history.

When the events of October-November 1989 reopened the German question, Helmut Kohl seized the opportunity and acted with surprising speed. On the night that the DDR opened the Berlin Wall and joyous Berliners celebrated in the streets, Kohl made a simple speech nearby: "We are, and we remain, one nation." Kohl left no doubt that he was calling for a united Germany, and he promptly produced, and the Bundestag ratified, a Ten-Point Plan for German Unity in November 1989. Point ten was clear: "We are working for a state of peace in Europe in which the German nation can recover its unity in free self-determination." The speed of Kohl's action surprised many, but he argued that something must be done to slow the torrent of East Germans migrating to the West—500,000 immigrants arrived in November alone. Confronted with the outline of German unity, world leaders could only respond as the surprised George Bush did: "We're pleased." A few weeks later, in January 1990, Mikhail Gorbachev acknowledged that German reunification was probable. Reunification had become a realistic possibility for Germans to arrange.

The East German government initially hesitated, and the prime minister of the DDR spoke of plans for a commission to study the possibilities, but the sentiment of public opinion was overwhelming. Demonstrations in East Germany denounced the old regime—especially after revelations of the activities of the *Stasi*, the former secret police—and hard-liners were forced to resign. East German elections of March 1990 settled the question. No party received an absolute majority, but 48 percent voted for a party backing immediate unification and nearly 70 percent voted for parties favoring some form of unification. The Communist Party received 16 percent of the vote. This election led directly to negotiations for unification. Helmut Kohl pressed for immediate action, and within a few weeks, the two Germanys had agreed upon a common currency and economic policy, although this typically meant that West German standards prevailed or difficult problems were postponed. More than eight thousand state-run businesses in the DDR would be privatized. Institutions in the East would be transformed; universities, for example, were given West German administrators who closed most programs in Marxism-Leninism and reduced programs in Russian language and studies.

The negotiations between the Federal Republic and the DDR were expanded into the "two-plus-four negotiations" in May 1990, bringing together the two Germanys and the four powers that had divided Germany in 1945 (Britain, France, Russia, and the United States). In these talks, the four powers accepted German reassurances about the international aspects of the new Germany. A Russo-German Treaty of July 1990 and a Treaty of Final Settlement on Germany in September 1990 stated the terms: Germany could unite and remain within NATO, but the German government must (1) reduce its standing army to fewer than 400,000 troops; (2) renounce all nuclear, chemical, and biological weaponry; and (3) provide financial assistance to Russia for the repatriation of the Soviet army. While those details were still being worked out, the two Germanys formed an economic merger based on the West German mark. Then, in October 1990, forty-five years after the postwar partition, a unified Germany of nearly eighty million population was created by the DDR joining the Federal Republic (see illustration 33.8). The first all-German elections in nearly sixty years followed in December 1990, with Helmut Kohl becoming the first chancellor of the new state. The Bundestag voted in 1991, by a narrow margin, to return the capital of Germany to Berlin in a twelve-year transition.

Illustration 33.8

German Unification. In October 1990, eleven months after the fall of the Berlin Wall, the German Democratic Republic (East Germany) ceased to exist and the two Germanys were united as the Federal Republic of Germany under the previous West German government of Helmut Kohl. Reunited Berlin, des-tined to become the capital of the new Germany in a gradual transition from Bonn, was the scene of joyous celebrations. Here, crowds assemble outside the Reichstag building in Berlin to cheer the event.

The Yugoslav War

While Germans were celebrating their union to the tune of Beethoven's "Ode to Joy," Yugoslavia was frag-menting into six states in an internecine war. Yugoslavia had been created at the Paris Peace Conference of 1919, according to the principle of "the national self-determination of peoples," by merging the independent states of Serbia and Montenegro with provinces taken from the defeated Austro-Hungarian Empire. Although Yugoslavia ("the land of the southern slavs") had been a dream of Slavic nationalists, it had always been a deli-cate federation of several different peoples (chiefly Slovenes, Croatians, Bosnians, Serbs, Albanians, and Macedonians) who practiced several different religions (chiefly Roman Catholicism in Slovenia and Croatia, Islam in Bosnia, and Orthodox Christianity in the other regions) and who spoke languages different enough to require different alphabets (see table 33.3).

Yugoslavia and the western Balkans had long been a powder keg of bitter rivalries, many of which had been exacerbated by questions of collaboration with the Nazis during World War II. The forceful personal-ity of President Tito—a Croatian who had been the leader of the predominantly Serbian resistance to Nazism—had held Yugoslavia together as a federation of equals. His refusal to follow Moscow as a satellite of the Soviet Union had earned Yugoslavia massive West-ern assistance, which helped to sustain his regime. His successors were less able to follow these policies. Re-gional nationalism increased after Tito's death in 1980,

❧ TABLE 33.3 ❧

The Ethnic Composition of Yugoslavia in 1991

Ethnic group	Percentage
Serbians	36
Croatians	20
Bosnians (Muslim)	9
Slovenes	8
Albanians	8
Macedonians	6
Montenegrins	3
Hungarians	2
Others	8

despite Yugoslavia's rotating presidency, which gave each major ethnic group a turn at leadership. The Albanian minority rioted in 1981, seeking independence. Widespread unrest was evident among the Muslim population of Bosnia in 1983. Croatian terrorists conducted a bombing campaign in 1985.

The collapse of the Yugoslav Communist Party in the revolution of 1989 worsened the federation's crisis of nationalist regionalism. Without the strong central authority that had held the federated republics together, political power passed to local authorities during 1990.

The two most westernized republics, Slovenia and Croatia, held free elections in the spring of 1990. Slovenia, the most prosperous portion of Yugoslavia, adopted a declaration of sovereignty a few weeks later, and by the end of the year a public referendum had approved secession from Yugoslavia. Croatia meanwhile prepared a new constitution that asserted the right to secede. Stimulated by these developments, the Serbian minority population in the non-Serbian republics of Croatia and Bosnia formed separatist groups that claimed the right of self-government.

The Yugoslav crisis became the Yugoslav War in 1991. Slovenia and Croatia each proclaimed their independence from Yugoslavia in July. The Serbian minority in Croatia (especially those concentrated in a region that the Serbs called Krajina) resisted this declaration and announced the secession of some districts that would join the neighboring republic of Bosnia. Serbia, the largest state of Yugoslavia, controlled the military and intervened on behalf of the Serbian minority. The Yugoslav air force bombed Zagreb, the capital of Croatia, in October 1991, and a few days later the Yugoslav army besieged and shelled the picturesque Croatian town of Dubrovnik on the Adriatic Coast. In November the Croatian city of Vukovar surrendered to Serbian forces; shortly thereafter, the first stories of war atrocities—the murder of Croatian civilians in Vukovar—began to reach the West (see illustration 33.9). By the end of 1991 the president of Yugoslavia announced that the country had ceased to exist. In early 1992 the

Illustration 33.9

❧ **War Crimes.** The Yugoslav War of 1991–95 produced evidence of terrible war crimes, which persuaded the United States to establish the first war crimes tribunal to sit since the crimes of the Holocaust were tried at Nuremberg in 1945–46. The Hague Tribunal found evidence of crimes committed by all sides in the Yugoslav War, but most of the evidence involved Serbian atrocities. This photograph shows one section of a mass grave near the town of Vukovar, where Croatian civilians were massacred by Serbs.

◆ DOCUMENT 33.7 ◆

A Child's Experiences During the Siege of Sarajevo (1992)

Zlata Filipovic began a diary at age ten. Her father was a lawyer, and Zlata enjoyed a middle-class life in Sarajevo. Zlata liked American pop music, skiing in the mountains surrounding Sarajevo, and vacations in Italy. When school began in September 1991, Zlata was in high spirits, writing about the music on MTV and her favorite pizza. War had begun in neighboring Croatia, but life in Bosnia was calm. These excerpts from Zlata's diary are from April 1992.

Serbian artillery on the ski slopes above Sarajevo began to shell Zlata's home in May, and the family moved into the inner rooms and slept on the floor. Zlata's diary became of record of death and destruction. Instead of MTV and pizza she wrote of "more blood on the streets of Sarajevo. Another massacre."

April 3, 1992: Daddy came back . . . all upset. He says there are terrible crowds at the train and bus stations. People are leaving Sarajevo.

April 4, 1992: There aren't many people in the streets. I guess it's fear of the stories about Sarajevo being bombed. But there's no bombing. . . .

April 5, 1992: I'm trying hard to concentrate so I can do my homework (reading), but I simply can't. Something is going on in town. You can hear gunfire from the hills.

April 6, 1992: Now they're shooting from the Holiday Inn, killing people in front of the parliament. . . . Maybe we'll go to the cellar. . .

April 9, 1992: I'm not going to school. All the schools in Sarajevo are closed. . . .

April 14, 1992: People are leaving Sarajevo. The airport, train and bus stations are packed. . . .

April 18, 1992: There's shooting, shells are falling. This really is WAR. Mommy and Daddy are worried, they sit up late at night, talking. They're wondering what to do, but it's hard to know. . . . Mommy can't make up her mind—she's constantly in tears. She tries to hide it from me, but I see everything.

April 21, 1992: It's horrible in Sarajevo today. Shells falling, people and children getting killed, shooting. We will probably spend the night in the cellar.

April 26, 1992: We spent Thursday night with the Bobars again. The next day we had no electricity. We had no bread, so for the first time in her life Mommy baked some.

April 28, 1992: SNIFFLE! Everybody has gone. I'm left with no friends.

April 29, 1992: I'd write to you much more about the war if only I could. But I simply don't want to remember all these horrible things.

European Union recognized the independence of Slovenia, Croatia, and Bosnia, and the United Nations accepted all three as members. Simultaneously, the republics of Serbia and Montenegro announced their merger as the new Federal Republic of Yugoslavia.

Outsiders seemed powerless to prevent an expansion of the Yugoslav War. The European Union, the United Nations, and the United States applied many forms of pressure—an embargo on arms shipments to the Balkans, a larger embargo against the new Yugoslavia and its expulsion from UN membership, repeated cease-fire negotiations, the proclamation of safe zones, and the intervention of UN peacekeeping forces to protect civilians. But a long and brutal war had begun. Serbia did not take a direct role in the fighting, but the Serbian minority in Croatia and Bosnia was so

well equipped that it conducted the war without the Yugoslav army.

In 1992 the chief theater of the Yugoslav War became Bosnia. Bosnia was an ethnically mixed region composed chiefly of Bosnian Muslims (more than 40 percent), Serbian Orthodox Christians (more than 30 percent), and Croatian Catholics (less than 20 percent). The capital of Bosnia, Sarajevo, had been considered a model city of different peoples living together harmoniously when it hosted the winter Olympic games in 1984. The Bosnian declaration of independence, however, had prompted a furious offensive—often centered on the siege and bombardment of Sarajevo (see document 33.7)—by the Bosnian Serbs, who proclaimed their own government (with a capital in nearby Pale) led by a militant Serbian nationalist, Radovan Karadzic.

Illustration 33.10

⁄⁄⁄ **The Yugoslav War.** The town of Mostar (capital of the region of Herze-govina) was once one of the symbols of the ethnic diversity of the Yugoslav re-public. It combined a largely Catholic, Croatian population with a Muslim, Bosnian population, linked by the six-teenth-century bridge (the *stari most*) that gave the town its name. During the Yu-goslav civil war, Mostar also became a symbol of ethnic hatred as the two groups killed each other. In an act sym-bolic of the destruction of the war and of the separation of populations, Croatian shelling destroyed the bridge in 1993.

For the next three years, the Bosnian Serbs, with sup-port from Yugoslavia, conquered most of Bosnia in fighting so ferocious that it shocked the rest of the world. The Bosnian Serb army, commanded by General Ratko Mladic, devastated the city of Sarajevo in con-stant bombardments. In the villages of Bosnia, Mladic imposed a policy of "ethnic cleansing"—driving all non-Serbs from an area. The war in Bosnia produced the worst atrocities in Europe since World War II. By late 1992 accusations of extreme abuses in Serbian de-tention camps, including the execution of three thou-sand people in one camp, reached the West. They were followed by a litany of horrors alleged against the Serbs—from the intentional mass rape of Bosnian women as an instrument of policy to the mass execu-tion of all Bosnian Muslim men taken captive. Interna-tional opinion became so outraged at the continuing atrocities in the Balkans that the United Nations estab-lished the first international war crimes tribunal since the Nuremberg Trials of 1945–46. The Hague Tribunal returned indictments against Croatians and Bosnian Muslims as well as Serbs, but most of the indictments and the gravest accusations were against Bosnian Serbs, whose head of state (Karadzic) and military leader (Mladic) were both indicted *in absentia.*

The fighting in the Yugoslav War had a third phase that complicated negotiations. In addition to Serbian-Croatian fighting (which started in Croatia in 1991 and expanded into parts of Bosnia) and the Serbian-Bosnian fighting (which started in Bosnia in 1992), fighting be-tween Croatian Catholics and Bosnian Moslems (over parts of Bosnia) often prevented them from forming an

effective alliance against the Serbs. This fighting was dramatized by the conflict in the town of Mostar, an-other former symbol of ethnic harmony in which a Croatian community and a Moslem community had previously lived harmoniously, linked by a centuries-old bridge. Intense fighting broke out between the two communities and the Croatians created a new symbol in 1993 by destroying the bridge (see illustration 33.10).

The first effective cease-fire of the Yugoslav War produced a delicate peace agreement in 1995. The gradual arming of Croatia had produced significant mil-itary victories against the Serbs, an international Islamic coalition had begun to support Bosnia, and the United States had even bombed Serbian positions. In Novem-ber 1995 the presidents of Serbia, Croatia, and Bosnia met in Dayton, Ohio, and signed a peace agreement brokered by the United States. Bosnian Serbs served in the Serbian delegation, but Radovan Karadzic could not negotiate alongside the other heads of government because the Bosnian Serbs were not recognized as an independent government and Karadzic remained under indictment for war crimes. The Dayton Accord dealt chiefly with Bosnia: It would remain a single state within its previous borders, but it would contain two entities—a Bosnian-Croatian federation and a Bosnian Serb republic (see map 33.4). These two would have a single central government at Sarajevo. To maintain this unusual arrangement, NATO agreed to send sixty thousand peacekeeping troops to Bosnia for one year. By 1998, fighting had shifted to Kosovo, where Albanians and Serbs fought.

MAP 33.4

The Yugoslav War, after the Dayton Accord of 1995

Legend:
- Serb Republic
- Croat-Muslim Federation
- Dayton Agreement Line

Conclusion

Europe has reached the end of the twentieth century in an age of peace and prosperity—a new "belle époque" comparable to the age before World War I. The Western economies linked in the European Union have produced a period of sustained development that has

created the highest standard of living in European history. That prosperity has sustained a comprehensive welfare state promising cradle-to-grave security and numerous benefits of daily life such as long vacations and early retirement. Europeans have learned to live with high taxation as the price of these benefits, and that model of the welfare state was vigorously challenged by Prime Minister Thatcher of Britain during the 1970s and 1980s. Thatcher's conservative revolution inspired similar restraints in Germany and France by the 1990s, but a slightly restrained welfare state has survived as the West European model of society.

The generation after 1975 witnessed even more dramatic steps toward peace. The period began in the spirit of détente, in which the conflicts of the cold war were much relaxed. The end of cold war came with the Gorbachev revolution in the Soviet Union between 1985 and 1989. That decade ended with agreements for troop withdrawals from Europe, sweeping arms reductions, and the dismantlement of many nuclear arms. European peace had not been so secure for a century.

The Gorbachev revolution had far-reaching consequences. Unrestrained reform movements in Eastern Europe grew into the revolutions of 1989, which swept away Communist dictatorships throughout the region. From the Baltic Sea to South Asia, republics proclaimed their independence. The democratic revolution that began with Gorbachev's ideas of *glasnost* (openness) and *perestroika* (restructuring) overwhelmed the USSR in 1989–91. In the 1990s Russia had a popularly elected government led by Boris Yeltsin and was struggling with the transition to democratic institutions and a free-market economy.

Two important events soon flowed from the breakup of the Soviet system. When the revolution of 1989 overturned the Communist government of East Germany and opened the Berlin Wall, the reunion of the two Germanys became possible. Helmut Kohl, the chancellor of West Germany, seized the opportunity that these events created and presided over the reunification of Germany in 1991. At the same time, the post-Communist era witnessed the dissolution of Yugoslavia in a brutal war. The Yugoslav War of 1991–95 began with the secession of four republics—Slovenia, Croatia, Bosnia, and Macedonia—from the Yugoslav republic. The large Serbian minority population in Croatia and Bosnia resisted these changes and vehemently, especially in Bosnia, fought for self-government. The 1995 Dayton Accord ratified the independence of the republics but gave the Bosnian Serbs a significant measure of autonomy.

Suggested Readings

For Britain since 1975, see K. Morgan, *The People's Peace* (1992), a survey of the period 1945–90, P. Jenkins, *Mrs. Thatcher's Revolution* (1988), and H. Young, *The Iron Lady* (1989).

For France since 1975, see M. Crozier, *Strategies for Change: The Future of French Society* (1982), J. Hollifield and G. Ross, eds., *Searching for the New France* (1991), S. Ross, S. Hoffmann, and S. Malzacher, *The Mitterand Experiment* (1987), and C. Duchen, *Feminism in France: From May '68 to Mitterand* (1986).

For West Germany since 1975, see H. A. Turner, *Germany from Partition to Reunification* (1992), D. Bark and D. Gress, *A History of West Germany*, vol. 2: *Democracy and Its Discontents, 1963–1991* (1991), P. Merkl, ed., *The Federal Republic of Germany at Forty* (1989), and E. Kolinsky, *Women in West Germany: Life, Work, and Politics* (1989).

For other states of Europe, see P. Ginsborg, *A History of Contemporary Italy: Society and Politics, 1943–1988*(1990), D. Sassoon, *Contemporary Italy: Politics, Economy, and Society since 1945* (1986), P. Farneti, *The Italian Party System, 1945–1980* (1985), C. Abel and N. Torrents, eds., *Spain: Conditional Democracy* (1984), P. Donaghy and M. Newton, *Spain: A Guide to Political and Economic Institutions* (1987), D. Gilmour, *The Transformation of Spain: From Franco to Constitutional Monarchy* (1984), and P. Preston, *The Triumph of Democracy in Spain* (1986).

For the age of détente in the cold war, see R. Garthoff, *Detente and Confrontation: American-Soviet Relations from Nixon to Reagan* (1985), A. Bromke and D. Novak, eds., *The Communist States in the Era of Detente, 1971–1977* (1978), C. Blacker, *Reluctant Warriors: The United States, the Soviet Union, and Arms Control* (1987), L. Caldwell and W. Diebold, eds., *Soviet-American Relations in the 1980s* (1981), and R. Edmonds, *Soviet Foreign Policy: The Brezhnev Years* (1983).

For the European Union, see the suggestions for chapter 32 and D. Unwin, *The Community of Europe: A History of European Integration since 1945* (1990), H. Simonian, *The Privileged Partnership: Franco-German Relations in the European Community, 1969–1984* (1985), P. Preston and D. Smyth, *Spain, the EEC, and NATO* (1984), and P. Scalingi, *The European Parliament* (1980).

For the revolutions of 1989, see S. Bialer and M. Mandelbaum, eds., *Gorbachev's Russia and American Foreign Policy* (1988), A. Braun, ed., *The Soviet-East European Relationship in the Gorbachev Era* (1990), C. Blacker, *Hostage to Revolution: Gorbachev and Soviet Security Policy, 1985–1991* (1993), J. Bornemann, *After the Wall: East Meets West in the New Berlin* (1991), J. Gedmin, *The Hidden Land: Gorbachev and the Collapse of East Germany* (1992), and J. Burgess, *The East German Church and the End of Communism* (1997).

For the Yugoslav war, see M. Glenny, *The Fall of Yugoslavia: The Third Balkan War* (1992).

DOCUMENT SOURCES

◆◆◆◆◆◆◆◆◆◆◆◆◆◆◆◆◆◆◆◆◆

Document 13.1 Trokelowe, Johannes. *"Annales,"* trans. Brian Tierney. In Brian Tierney, ed., *Sources of Medieval History,* 4th ed. New York: Knopf, 1983. **13.2** Boccaccio, Giovanni. "The Decameron." In Stories of *Boccaccio,* p. 1, trans. John Payne. London: The Bibliophilist Society, 1903. **13.3** "Chronicle of Jacob von Königshofen." In J. R. Marcus, ed., *The Jew in the Medieval World.* New York: Atheneum, 1972. **13.4** The Statute of Laborers. From *Pennsylvania Translations and Reprints,* vol. 2, no. 5, trans. Edward P. Cheyney. Philadelphia: University of Pennsylvania Press, 1897. **13.5** "The Anonimalle Chronicle," trans. C. Oman. In *The Great Revolt of 1381.* Oxford, England: Oxford University Press, 1906. **13.6** Froissart, Jean. *Chronicles of England, France, Spain, and the Adjoining Countries,* trans. Thomas Johnes. London: 1805. **13.7** *The Chronicle of Novgorod, 1016–1471,* trans. Robert Michell and Nevill Forbes. Camden Society, 3d series, vol. 25. London: Camden Society Publications, 1914. **13.8** *The Trial of Jeanne d'Arc,* pp. 165–166, trans. W. P. Barrett. London: Routledge, 1931. **13.9** Chastellain, Georges. *"Le Pas de la Mort."* In Johan Huizinga, *The Waning of the Middle Ages,* pp. 147–148. New York: Doubleday Anchor Books, 1949. Copyright © Johan Huizinga. Reprinted by permission of St. Martin's Press, Incorporated and Edward Arnold (Publishers) Limited.

14.1 Castiglione, Baldassare. *The Courtier,* pp. 237–238. trans. Charles S. Singleton. New York: Doubleday, 1959. **14.2** Bernier, A., ed. *Journal des états généraux de France tenus à Tours en 1484,* trans. Steven C. Hause. Paris: 1835. **14.3** Charles IV. "The Golden Bull." In O. J. Thatcher and E. H. McNeal, eds., *A Source Book of Medieval History,* pp. 284–305. New York: Scribner's, 1905. **14.4** "The Twelve Articles of the German Peasants." In Hans Hillerbrand, ed., *The Protestant Reformation,* pp. 65–66. New York: Harper Torchbooks, 1967. **14.5** Alighieri, Dante. *The Inferno,* Canto IV, ll. 25–42. trans. John Ciardi. New York: Mentor Books. **14.6** Macchiavelli, Niccoló. *The Discourses II* (Introduction), trans. Luigi Ricci, rev. E. R. P. Vincent. Modern Library Editions. New York: Random House, 1950. **14.7** Pico, Giovanni. "Oration on the Dignity of Man." In E. Cassirer, P. O. Kristeller, and J. H. Randall, Jr., eds., *The Renaissance Philosophy of Man.* Chicago: University of Chicago Press, 1948. **14.8** Vergirio, Peter Paul. Letter to Ubertino of Carrara. In W. H. Woodward, ed., *Vittorino da Feltre and Other Humanist Educators,* pp. 106–107. New York: Bureau of Publications, Teachers College, Columbia University, 1963. **14.9** Labé, Louise. Dedicatory preface. From J. Aynard, ed., *Les poétes lyonnais précurseurs de la Pléide.* In Julia O'Faolain and Lauro Martines, *Not in God's Image: Women in History from the Greeks to the Victorians,* pp. 184–185. London: Temple Smith, 1973. **14.10** Macchiavelli, Niccoló. *The Discourses I,* 58, trans. Luigi Ricci, rev. E. R. P. Vincent. Modern Library Editions. New York: Random House, 1950. **14.11** Guiccardini, Francisco. *Maxims and Reflections of a Renais-*

sance Statesman, trans. M. Domandi. New York: Harper Torchbooks, 1965.

15.1 Boniface VIII. *"Clericis Laicos."* In O. J. Thatcher and E. H. McNeal, eds., *A Source Book of Medieval History,* p. 310. New York: Scribner's, 1905. **15.2** Council of Constance. "Sacrosancta." In Edward P. Cheyney, ed., *Pennsylvania Translations and Reprints,* vol. 3, no. 6. Philadelphia: University of Pennsylvania Press, 1898. **15.3** Ruysbroeck, Jan van. "The Sparkling Stone," trans. C. A. Wynschenck Dom. In E. Underhill, ed., *Jan van Ruysbroeck.* London: Dent, 1916. **15.4** Wyclif, John. "Antichrist's Labor to Destroy Holy Writ." In *Writings of the Reverend and Learned John Wyclif.* Philadelphia: Presbyterian Board of Publication, 1842. **15.5** Luther, Martin. "Address to the Nobility of the German Nation," (1520), trans. Wace and Buckheim. In B. J. Kidd, *Documents Illustrative of the Continental Reformation,* No. 35. Oxford, England: Oxford University Press, 1911. **15.6** "The Schleitheim Confession." In Hans Hillerbrand, ed., *The Protestant Reformation,* pp. 132–133. New York: Harper Torchbooks, 1967. **15.7** Calvin, John. *Institutes of the Christian Religion,* vol. 2, p. 931, ed. J. T. McNeill, trans. Ford Lewis Battles. Philadelphia: Westminster Press, 1960. **15.8** Loyola, Ignatius. *"Prima Summa,"* trans. John C. Olin. In John C. Olin, *Catholic Reform,* p. 84. New York: Fordham University Press, 1990. **15.9** *Canons and Decrees of the Council of Trent,* p. 214, ed. and trans. J. J. Schroeder, O.P. St. Louis: Herder, 1950. **15.10** Bucer, Martin. *"De Regno Christi,"* book 2, chap. 34. In Julia O'Faolain and Lauro Martines, *Not in God's Image: Women in History from the Greeks to the Victorians,* pp. 200–201. New York: HarperCollins, 1973. **15.11** Kramer, Heinrich, and Sprenger, Jakob. *Malleus Maleficarum,* trans. Montague Summers. New York: Arrow Books, 1971.

16.1 Pigafetta, Antonio. *Magellan's Voyage Around the World,* ed. and trans. J. A. Robertson. Cleveland: 1902. **16.2** Equiano, Olaudah. "The Interesting Narrative of Olaudah Equiano . . ." In Philip D. Curtin, ed., *Africa Remembered,* pp. 92–94. Madison: University of Wisconsin Press, 1967. **16.3** Las Casas, Bartolomé de. *"Apologética historia de las Indias,"* trans. B. Keen. In *Latin American Civilization,* vol. 1, p. 178. Boston: Houghton Mifflin, 1974. **16.4** López de Gómara, Francisco. "Historia de las Indias," trans. B. Keen. In *Historiadores primitivos de las Indias,* vol. 1, p. 251. In *Latin American Civilization,* vol. 1, pp. 142–143. Boston: Houghton Mifflin, 1974. **16.5** du Plessis-Mornay, Philippe. *"Vindiciae contra tyrannos."* In *Constitutionalism and Resistance in the 16th Century,* trans. and ed. Julian H. Franklin. New York: Macmillan, 1969. **16.6** Gachard, L.-P. "Correspondance de Guillaume le Taciturne," vol. 6, trans. Herbert H. Rowen, *The Low Countries in Early Modern Times. A Documentary History,* pp. 40–42. New York: Harper & Row, 1972. **16.7** Townshend, H. *Historical Collections,* pp. 264–266. London: 1680. **16.8** *Journals of the House* of Lords, vol. 3. **16.9** Grimmelshausen, H. J. C. von. *Adventures of a Simpleton,* pp. 8–9, trans. W. Wallich. New York: Ungar, 1963. **16.10** Ranum, O., and Ranum, P., eds. *The Century of Louis XIV,* pp. 200–201. New York: Walker, 1972.

17.1 Galilei, Galileo. "The Assayer," trans. Stillman Drake. In Stillman Drake, *Discoveries and Opinions of Galileo,* pp. 270–271. New York: Doubleday, 1957. **17.2** Newton, Isaac. *The Mathematical Principles of Natural Philosophy,* book 3, vol. 2, p. 310, trans. Andrew Motte. London, 1803, II. **17.3** Harvey, William. "On Conception." In *The Works of William Harvey,* trans. R. Willis. London: 1847. **17.4** Bossuet, Jacques-Bénigne. "Politics Drawn from the Very Words of Holy Scripture." In J. H. Robinson, ed. *Readings in European History,* vol. 2. Boston: Ginn, 1906. **17.5** Saint-Simon [Louis de Rouvroy, Duc de Saint-Simon]. *The Memoirs of the Duke of Saint-Simon,* trans. Bayle St. John, vol. 2, p. 364, 8th ed. London: 1913. **17.6** Vernadsky, George, ed. *A Source Book of Russian History from Early Times to 1917,* vol. 2, p. 347. New Haven, CT: Yale University Press, 1972. **17.7** Helvetius. *"Mémoire sur l'état présent du Government des Provinces Unis."* In M. van der Bijl, ed., *Bijdragen en Mededeldingen van het Historisch Genootshap* 80 (1966), 226–227, trans. Herbert H. Rowen, *The Low Countries in Early Modern Times. A Documentary History.* New York: Harper & Row, 1972. **17.8** Hornick, P. W. "Austria Over All If Only She Will." In A. E. Monroe, ed., *Early Economic Thought,* pp. 223–225. Cambridge, MA: Harvard University Press, 1927. **17.9** Parry, E. A. ed. "Letters from Dorothy Osborne to Sir William Temple, 1652–1654," 3d ed. (1888). In Brian Tierney and Joan Scott, *A Documentary History of Western Societies,* vol. 2, pp. 70–71. New York: McGraw-Hill, 1984.

18.1 Forster, Robert, and Forster, Elborg, eds. *European Society in the Eighteenth Century.* New York: Harper & Row, 1969. **18.2** Radischev, Alexander. *A Journey from St. Petersburg to Moscow.* Cambridge, MA: Harvard University Press, 1958. **18.3** Hayem, J., ed. *"Mémoires et documents pour servir à l'histoire du commerce et de l'industrie en France,"* vol. 3, p. 86. Paris: 1916. In Robert Forster and Elborg Forster, eds., *European Society in the Eighteenth Century.* New York: Harper & Row, 1969. **18.4** Great Britain. *Statues at Large.* 5 George II, c. 22. London: 1733.

19.1 Montagu, Mary Wortley. *The Complete Letters of Lady Mary Wortley Montagu,* ed. Robert Halsband. 3 vols. Oxford, England: Clarendon Press, 1965. **19.2** Lesage, Alain-René. *The Adventures of Gil Blas of Santillana,* vol. 1. Edinburgh: Patterson, 1886. **19.3** Sheridan, Richard. *The Rivals.* London: 1775. **19.4** Bell, Susan G., and Offen, Karen M. eds. *Women, the Family, and Freedom: The Debate in Documents,* vol. 1. Stanford, Calif.: Stanford University Press, 1983.

20.1 Wilkes, John. *Wilkes's Speeches in Parliament.* London: 1777. **20.2** Commager, Henry S., ed. *Documents of American History,* 7th ed. New York: Appleton, Century, Crofts, 1963. **20.3** Baker, Keith M., ed. *The Old Regime and the French Revolution.* Chicago: University of Chicago Press, 1987. **20.4** "Letters of Joseph II." In Harry J. Carroll, Jr., et al., eds., *The Development of Civilization,* vol. 2. Chicago: Scott Foresman, 1969. **20.5** Frederick the Great. "Essay on Forms of Government." In Thomas Holcroft, ed., *The Posthumous Works of Frederick II.* London: 1789. **20.6** Catherine the Great. *The Grand Instructions to the Commissioners Appointed to Frame a New Code of Laws.* London: 1768. **20.7** *Pugachevshchina: Iz arkhiva Pugachva"* (Moscow, 1926). In Basil Dmytryshyn, ed., *Imperial Russia: A Source Book, 1700-1917.* New York: Holt, Rinehart and Winston, 1967.

21.1 Nozière, Fernand. "The Salon of Madame Geoffrin." In Mabel Robinson, *The Great Literary Salons.* London: Butterworth, 1930. Condensed from the version reprinted in Susan G. Bell, ed., *Women from the Greeks to the French Revolution.* Stanford, Calif.: Stanford University Press, 1973. **21.2** Kant, Immanuel. "What Is Enlightenment?" In Carl J. Friedrich, ed., *The Philosophy of Kant.* New York: Modern Library, 1949. **21.3** Condorcet, Marquis de. *Sketch for a Historical Picture of the Progress of the Human Mind.* London: J. Johnson, 1795. **21.4** Diderot, Denis. *"Prospectus à l'Encyclopédie,"* vol. 13. In Denis Diderot, *Oevres complètes.* 20 vols. Paris: 1875–1877. **21.5** Diderot, Denis, D'Alembert, Jean le Rond, et al. *The Encyclopédie: Selections,* trans. Nelly S. Hoyt and Thomas Cassirer. Indianapolis: Bobbs-Merrill, 1965. Reprinted by permission of Prentice-Hall. **21.6** Diderot, Denis. "Discourse of a Philosopher to a King." In Denis Diderot, *Interpreter of Nature,* trans. Jean Stewart and Jonathan Kemp. New York: International Publishers, 1943. **21.7** Johnson, Samuel. *Dictionary.* London: 1755. **21.8** Montesquieu, Baron de. *The Spirit of the Laws,* trans. Thomas Nugent. Cincinnati: Clarke, 1873. **21.9** Beccaria, Cesare. *An Essay on Crimes and Punishments.* London: J. Almon, 1785.

22.1 Sieyes, Emmanuel Joseph (Abbè). *"Qu'est-ce que le Tiers Etat?"* In Paul H. Beik, ed., *The French Revolution.* New York: Harper & Row, 1970. **22.2** Anderson, Frank M., ed. *The Constitutions and Other Select Documents Illustrative of the History of France, 1789–1907.* Minneapolis: 1908. **22.3** Gouges, Olympe de. *Declaration of the Rights of Woman.* 1791. **22.4** Levy, Darline G., Applewhite, Harriet B., and Johnson, Mary D., eds. *Women in Revolutionary Paris, 1789–1795.* Urbana: University of Illinois Press, 1979. **22.5** Robespierre, Maximilien. *Le Point du jour,* No. 168. In Leo Gershoy, ed. *The Era of the French Revolution, 1789–1799.* Princeton, NJ: Van Nostrand, 1957. **22.6** Anderson, Frank M., ed. *The Constitutions and Other Select Documents Illustrative of the History of France, 1789–1907.* Minneapolis: 1908. **22.7** Robespierre, Maximilien. *"Discours et rapports a la convention"* (Paris: 1965). In Wallace Adams, ed., *The Western World,* vol. 2. New York: Dodd, Mead, 1970.

23.1 Baker, Kenneth, ed. *The Faber Book of English History in Verse.* London: Faber, 1988; and Eden, Frederic. *The State of the Poor.* London: 1797. **23.2** Dickens, Charles. *Hard Times.* New York: T. L. McElrath, 1854; and Tocqueville, Alexis de. *Journeys to England and Ireland.* 1835. **23.3** Gaskell, Peter. *The Manufacturing Population of England.* London: Baldwin and Cradock, 1833. **23.4** Pollard, Sidney, and Holmes, Colin, eds. *Documents of European Economic History,* 3 vols. New York: St. Martin's, 1968. **23.5** Ure, Andrew. *The Philosophy of Manufactures.* London: C. Knight, 1835.

24.1 Pasteur, Louis. "Inoculation for Hydrophobia [Rabies]." In Raymond Stearns, *Pageant of Europe.* New York: Harcourt Brace, 1961. **24.2** Burney, Fanny. *Selected Letters and Journals,* ed. Joyce Hemlow. Oxford, England: Oxford University Press, 1986; and Simpson, James Young. "Memoirs" (London, n.d.). In Louis L. Snyder, ed., *Fifty Major Documents of the Nineteenth Century.* New York: Anvil, 1955. **24.3** Besant, Annie. *The Law of Population.* London: Freethought Publishing Company, 1877; and Carlile, Richard. *Every Woman's Book, or What Is Love?* London: 1838. **24.4** French Ministry of Education Yearbook (1863), trans. Steven C. Hause. In M. Chaulanges et al., eds., *Textes historiques, 1848–1871: le milieu du XIXe siècle.* Paris: Delagrave, 1975.

25.1 Metternich, Klemens von. *Memoirs of Prince Metternich*, 5 vols., trans. Mrs. Alexander Napier. New York: Scribner's, 1880–1882. **25.2** "Karlsbad Decrees." *The Annual Register* (1819). London: J. Dodsky, 1820. **25.3** *"Carte segrete e atti ufficiali della polizia Austriaca in Italia"* (Capolago, 1851), trans. Denis Mack Smith. In Denis Mack Smith, *The Making of Italy, 1796–1870.* New York: Harper & Row, 1968. **25.4** Mazzini, Giuseppe. *Life and Writings.* London: Smith, Elder, 1880. **25.5** Great Britain, Foreign Office. *British and Foreign State Papers, 1829.* London: His Majesty's Stationery Office, 1929. **25.6** Anderson, Frank M., ed. *The Constitutions and Other Select Documents Illustrative of the History of France, 1789–1907.* Minneapolis: 1908. **25.7** Bell, Susan G., and Offen, Karen M. eds. *Women, the Family, and Freedom: The Debate in Documents*, vol. 1. Stanford, Calif.: Stanford University Press, 1983. **25.8** Great Britain, Parliament. *Hansard's Parliamentary Debates*, April 17, 1833. London: T. C. Hansard; and Peterson, Houston, ed. *The World's Greatest Speeches.* New York: Son & Schuster, 1954. **25.9** Ellis, Sara. "The Daughters of England" (London, 1842). In Patricia Hollis, ed., *Women in Public, 1850–1900. Documents of the Victorian Women's Movement.* London: 1979.

26.1 Schurz, Carl. *Reminiscences*, vol. 1. New York: McClure, 1907. **26.2** E. O. S. [sic]. *Hungary and Its Revolutions.* London: H. G. Bohn, 1896. **26.3** "Rules of the Metropolitan Draper's Assocation" (London, 1845). In Ludwig Schaefer et al., eds., *Problems in Western Civilization.* New York: Scribner's, 1965. **26.4** Marx, Karl, and Engels, Friedrich. *The Communist Manifesto.* London: 1888. **26.5** Steenson, Gary P. *"Not One Man! Not One Penny!" German Social Democracy, 1863–1914.* Pittsburgh: University of Pittsburgh Press, 1981. **26.6** Bodichon, Barbara. "A Brief Summary in Plain Language of the Most Important Laws of England Concerning Married Women" (London, 1854). In Patricia Hollis, ed., *Women in Public, 1850–1900. Documents of the Victorian Women's Movement.* London: 1979. **26.7** Kropotkin, Peter. *Memoirs of a Revolutionist.* Boston: Houghton Mifflin, 1899. **26.8** *The Annual Register: 1860.* London: J. G. and F. Rivington, 1861. **26.9** Kohl, H., ed. *"Die politischen Reden des Fursten Bismarck"* (Stuttgart, 1892). In Ludwig Schaefer et al., eds., *Problems in Western Civilization.* New York: Scribner's, 1965.

27.1 Clemenceau, Georges. "Cahier des électeurs," trans. Steven C. Hause. *La Justice*, November 19, 1881. **27.2** Drumont, Edouard. *La France juive*, vol. 2, excerpt trans. Steven C. Hause. Paris: Marpon, 1886. **27.3** George, Lloyd. In *The Times*, July 31, 1909. **27.4** Pobedonostsev, Konstantin. *Reflections of a Russian Statesman.* London: Robert Long, 1898. **27.5** Russell, Bertrand. *German Social Democracy.* London: Longmans, 1896. **27.6** Hause, Steven C. *Hubertine Auclert: The French Suffragette.* New Haven: Yale University Press, 1987. **27.7** Pankhurst, Emmeline. *My Own Story.* London: New York: Hearst's, 1914. **27.7** Pankhurst, Sylvia. *The Suffragette Movement.* London: Longmans, 1931.

28.1 Bismarck, Otto von. *Reminiscences and Reflections*, vol. 2, trans. A. J. Butler. London: Smith, Elder, 1898. **28.2** *Journal officiel de la république française.* Debates of July 28, 1885. Trans. Steven C. Hause. Paris: Imprimerie des journaux officiels. **28.3** Liu Yung-fu. *Revue Indo-chinoise*, 40 (1932): 166. In Ludwig Schaefer et al., eds., *Problems in Western Civilization.* New York: Scribner's, 1965. **28.4** Treitschke, Heinrich von. *Politics*, vols.

1–2, trans. Blanche Dugdale and Torbenck Bille. New York: Macmillan, 1916. **28.5** Graves, Robert. *Goodbye to All That.* London: Cape, 1923. **28.6** Pankhurst, Sylvia. "The Home Front" (London: 1932). In Brian Tierney and Joan Scott, *A Documentary History of Western Societies*, vol. 2. New York: McGraw-Hill, 1984.

29.1 Pius XI. *"Casti Connubi."* In Anne Fremantle, *The Papal Encyclicals.* New York: Putnam, 1956. **29.2** Brittain, Vera. *Women's Work in Modern England.* London: Douglas, 1928. **29.3** Hitler, Adolph. *Mein Kampf.* Boston: Houghton Mifflin, 1943. **29.4** Chilembwe, John. *The Nyasaland Times*, November 26, 1914. In R. C. Bridges et al., eds., *Nation and Empires.* London: St. Martin's, 1969. **29.5** Mussolini, Benito [actually written by Giovanni Gentile]. *The Political and Social Doctrine of Fascism.* London: Hogarth Press, 1933. **29.6** Mandelstam, Nadezhda. *Hope Against Hope*, trans. Max Hayward. London: Collins & Harvill, 1971; and Solzhenitsyn, Alexandr. *The Gulag Archipelago*, trans. Thomas Whitney. New York: Harper & Row, 1973.

30.1 *Nürnburg War Crimes Trials Documents. Nazi Conspiracy and Aggression*, vol. 3. Washington, DC: U.S. Government Printing Office, 1946–1948. **30.2** Thompson, David, ed. *France: Empire and Republic, 1850–1940: Historical Documents.* New York: Harper & Row, 1968. **30.3** Snyder, Louis L. *Louis L. Snyder's Historical Guide to World War II.* Westport, CT: Greenwood Press, 1982. **30.4** Hoess, Rudolph. Nuremburg testimony. In J. Noakes and G. Pridham, eds., *Nazism, 1919–1945. A History in Documents and Eyewitness Accounts*, vol. 2. New York: Schocken, 1988. **30.5** Potsdam Protocol, Article 6. In U.S. Department of State, *Bulletin*, 13:320 (August 12, 1945):224. **30.6** Brownlie, Ian, ed. *Basic Documents of Human Rights.* Oxford: Clarendon, 1992.

32.1 Churchill, Winston. Speech at Fulton, Missouri, March 5, 1946. *Current History*, April 1946, pp. 358–361. **32.2** Khrushchev, Nikita. "On Peaceful Coexistence." In Ludwig Schaefer et al., eds., *Problems in Western Civilization.* New York: Scribner's, 1965. **32.3** Great Britain, Parliament. *Hansard's Parliamentary Debates*, April 30, 1946. London: T. C. Hansard. **32.4** Beauvoir, Simone de. *Le Deuxieme Sexe.* Vol. 2, *L'Expérience vecue.* Excerpt trans. Steven C. Hause. Paris: Gallimard, 1950. **32.5** Nkrumah, Kwame. *I Speak of Freedom: A Statement of African Ideology.* London: Heinemann, 1961. **32.6** United Nations. *Official Records of the General Assembly.* December 14, 1960. Resolution 1514. New York: United Nations. **32.7** Committee for the Common Market. *Treaty Establishing the European Economic Community.* Brussels: Secretariat of the Interim Committee, 1957.

33.1 Helsinki Accord. *New York Times*, August 2, 1975. **33.2** Thatcher, Margaret. *The Path to Power.* New York: HarperCollins, 1995. **33.3** Solidarity. "Demands of the Solidarity Workers in Poland." *New York Times*, August 28, 1980. **33.4** Gorbachev, Mikhall *Perestroika: New Thinking for Our Country and the World.* New York: Harper & Row, 1987. Copyright © Mikhail Gorbachev. Reprinted by permission of HarperCollins Publishers, Inc. **33.5** Ash, Timothy G. *The Magic Lantern: The Revolution of '89 Witnessed in Warsaw, Budapest, Berlin, and Prague.* New York: Random House, 1990. **33.6** Gorbachev, Mikhail *The August Coup.* New York: HarperCollins, 1991. **33.7** Filipovic, Zlata. *Zlata's Diary: A Child's Life in Sarajevo*, trans. Christina Pribichevich-Zovic. New York: Viking, 1994.

PHOTO CREDITS

◆◆◆◆◆◆◆◆◆◆◆◆◆◆◆◆◆◆◆◆◆◆

Nationale de France; **525** (top) Erich Lessing/Art Resource, NY; (bottom) Scala/Art Resource, NY; **530** (top) bildarchiv preussischer kulturbesitz; (bottom) Mansell/Time Inc.

Chapter 21

538 A. F. Kersting; **540** Scala/Art Resource, NY; **541**(left) Erich Lessing/Art Resource, NY; (right) A. F. Kersting; **541** (bottom), **542** Erich Lessing/Art Resource, NY; **543** Mansell/Time, Inc.; **545** Erich Lessing/Art Resource, NY; **546** Michael Holford; **550** A. F. Kersting; **553** Giraudon/Art Resource, NY

Chapter 22

570 Erich Lessing/Art Resource, NY; **572** Jean-Loup Charmet; **573** Musee de la Ville de Paris, Musee Carnavalet, Paris, France/Giraudon/Art Resource, NY; **576** J. L. Charmet/Mary Evans Picture Library; **577** Giraudon/Art Resource, NY; **579** (top and bottom) Giraudon/ Art Resource, NY; **586** Hulton Getty/ Liaison Agency; **587** Mansell/Time Inc.; **591** Giraudon/ Art Resource, NY; **598** (top and bottom) Erich Lessing/ Art Resource, NY

Chapter 23

603 Science Museum/Science & Society Picture Library; **604** Fine Art Photographic Library, London/Art Resource, NY; **612** E. T. Archive; **614** bildarchiv preussischer kulturbesitz ; **615** Science Museum/Science & Society Picture Library; **617** bildarchiv preussischer kulturbesitz; **618** Mansell/Time Inc.; **620** (top and middle) Roger Viollet/Liaison Agency; (bottom) Mansell/Time Inc.; **623** Fine Art Photographic Library, London/ Art Resource, NY; **624** Illustrated London News/Mary Evans Picture Library; **633** Mary Evans Picture Library

Chapter 24

636 Le Petit Journal/Mary Evans Picture Library; **639** Wellcome Institute Library, London; **640** Le Petit Journal/ Mary Evans Picture Library; **642** Corbis-Bettmann; **645** Jean-Loup Charmet; **648** Mary Evans Picture Library; **651, 655** Jean-Loup Charmet; **658** Hulton Getty/ Liaison Agency; **660** Frederick Leighton, "Signing the Register," The City of Bristol Museum and Art Gallery, England; **665** Erich Lessing/ Art Resource, NY; **667** Bibliotheque Nationale de France

Chapter 25

670, 673 Hulton Getty/Liaison Agency; **676** Giraudon/Art Resource, NY; **679** Mary Evans Picture Library; **682** e.t. archive; **683** Jean Loup Charmet; **684** Mary Evans Picture Library; **685** bildarchiv preussischer kulturbesitz; **687** Erich Lessing/Art Resource, NY; **691** Edimedia; **694, 699** Hulton Getty/ Liaison Agency

Chapter 26

702 Hulton Getty/Liaison Agency; **705, 706** Mary Evans Picture Library; **710** Österreichische Nationalbibliothek; **711** bildarchiv preussischer kulturbesitz; **713** Roger Viollet/Liaison Agency; **714** The Phillips Collection, Washington, DC; **722** Wellcome Institute Library, London; **723** Novosti Agency; **727** Hulton Getty/Liaison Agency; **730** Weidenfeld & Nicolson Ltd.

Chapter 27

736 Mary Evans Picture Library; **740** bildarchiv preussischer kulturbesitz; **741** Mary Evans Picture Library; **743** Corbis-Bettmann; **744** Mary Evans Picture Library; **748** Corbis-Bettmann; **753** bildarchiv preussischer kulturbesitz; **756** Popperfoto/ Archive Photos; **760, 765** bildarchiv preussischer kulturbesitz; **766** Picasso, Pablo. "Les Demoiselles d'Avignon." Paris (June–July 1907) oil on canvas, (243.9 × 233.7cm). The Museum of Modern Art, New York. Acquired through the Lillie P. Bliss Bequest. © ARS, NY

Chapter 28

771 Baldwin H. Ward/Corbis-Bettmann; **772** Archive Photos; **774** Corbis; **780** Mary Evans Picture Library; **789** L'Illustration/ Sygma; **791** UPI/Corbis-Bettmann; **792** Hulton Getty/Liaison Agency; **794** Archive Photos; **798** Brown Brothers; **799** Grosz, George. "Fit for Active Service." 1916–17. Pen and brush and ink on paper, (50.8 × 36.5cm). The Musueum of Modern Art, New York. A. Conger Goodyear Fund.; **802** Hulton Getty/Liaison Agency; **803** Archive Photos

Chapter 29

808 bildarchiv preussischer kulturbesitz; **811** e.t. archive; **813** Hulton Getty/The Liaison Agency; **814** UPI/Corbis-Bettmann; **818** Cameraphoto/Art Resource, NY, Duchamp, Marcel. (1887–1968). L.H.O.O.Q., 1930. © ARS, NY. Private Collection; **820** UPI/Corbis-Bettmann; **825** Popperfoto/Archive Photos; **830** Hulton Getty/Liaison Agency; **832** Library of Congress; **833** bildarchiv preussischer kulturbesitz; **837** David King Collection

Chapter 30

840 Baldwin H. Ward/Corbis-Bettmann; **846** David Low, London Evening Standard, 9/20/1939. John Appleton, Solo Syndication and Literary Agency, /Centre for the Study of Cartoons and Caricature, University of Kent, Canterbury; **850** Hulton Getty/Liaison Agency; **852** Novosti Press Agency; **853** UPI/Corbis-Bettmann; **855** Baldwin H. Ward/Corbis-Bettmann; **857** Corbis-Bettmann; **858** Novosti Press Agency; **860** FDR Library; **862** UPI/Corbis-Bettmann; **864** Baldwin H. Ward/Corbis-Bettmann; **865** Corbis-Bettmann

Chapter 31

868 Mary Evans Picture Library; **871** Popperfoto/Archive Photos; **873** Hulton-Getty/The Liaison Agency; **874** David King Collection; **879** (top and bottom) Mary Evans Picture Library; **881** (top), Courtesy of International Business Machines; (bottom) Cahiers du Cinema; **884** E. Boubat/Agence Top; **891**(top) Stock Montage, Inc.; (bottom) National Institute of Medicine

Chapter 32

894 Archive Photos; **898, 898** e.t. archive; **899** AKG London; **902** Corbis-Bettmann; **905** Popperfoto/Archive Photos; **908** Hulton Getty/Liaison Agency; **911** UPI/Corbis-Bettmann; **913** L'Illustration/Sygma; **919, 922** UPI/Corbis-Bettmann; **923** Archive Photos

Chapter 33

926 P. Aventurier/Gamma Liaison; **928** Sipa Press; **933, 937** UPI/Corbis-Bettmann; **939** P. Aventurier/ Gamma Liaison; **945** Regis Bossu/ Sygma; **949** (top) © 1991 Gueorgui Pinkhassov/Magnum Photos; (bottom) Tass News Agency; **952** T. Boccon-Gibod/Sipa Press; **953** © 1996 Gilles Peress/Magnum Photos, Inc.; **955** Frank Spooner/The Liaison Agency

INDEX

◆◆◆◆◆◆◆◆◆◆◆◆◆◆◆◆◆◆◆◆◆◆◆